The Real World

Third Edition

W. W. NORTON

NEW YORK   LONDON

The Real World

AN INTRODUCTION TO SOCIOLOGY

Third Edition

Kerry Ferris and Jill Stein

W. W. Norton & Company has been independent since its founding in 1923, when William Warder Norton and Mary D. Herter Norton first published lectures delivered at the People's Institute, the adult education division of New York City's Cooper Union. The Nortons soon expanded their program beyond the Institute, publishing books by celebrated academics from America and abroad. By mid-century, the two major pillars of Norton's publishing program—trade books and college texts—were firmly established. In the 1950s, the Norton family transferred control of the company to its employees, and today—with a staff of four hundred and a comparable number of trade, college, and professional titles published each year—W. W. Norton & Company stands as the largest and oldest publishing house owned wholly by its employees.

Editor: Karl Bakeman
Assistant Editor: Becky Charney
Project editor: Kate Feighery
Director of Production, College: Jane Searle
Managing editor, College: Marian Johnson
Art director: Rubina Yeh
Cover illustration and Part illustrations: Alex Eben Meyer
Information graphics: Open (www.notclosed.com)
Photo research: Trish Marx and Julie Tesser
Associate e-media editor: Laura Musich
E-media editor: Eileen Connell
Marketing manager: Natasha Zabohonski
Composition: TexTech International
Manufacturing: Courier, Kendallville

Library of Congress Cataloging-in-Publication Data

Ferris, Kerry.
The real world : an introduction to sociology / Kerry Ferris and Jill Stein. — 3rd ed.
    p. cm.
    Includes bibliographical references and index.

ISBN 978-0-393-91217-3 (pbk.)

  1. Sociology.   2. United States—Social conditions—21st century.   3. Popular culture—United States.
I. Stein, Jill.   II. Title.
HM586.F48 2012
301—dc23

                              2011035897

W. W. Norton & Company, Inc., 500 Fifth Avenue, New York, NY 10110
www.wwnorton.com

W. W. Norton & Company, Ltd., Castle House, 75/76 Wells Street, London WIT3QT

2   3   4   5   6   7   8   9   0

About the Authors

Kerry Ferris is Assistant Professor of Sociology at Northern Illinois University. She uses ethnographic methods to study fame as a system of social power. Currently, she is researching the lives of professional celebrity impersonators and analyzing the emotions communicated by celebrities in red-carpet interviews.

Jill Stein is Professor of Sociology and Chair of the Department of Sociology and Anthropology at Santa Barbara City College. In addition to teaching introduction to sociology every semester, she has studied narrative processes in twelve-step programs, the role of popular culture in higher learning, and group culture among professional rock musicians.

Contents

PART II: Framing Social Life 67

CHAPTER 3: Cultural Crossroads 71

CHAPTER 4:   The Self and Interaction 97

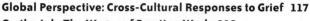

CHAPTER 5: Separate and Together: Life in Groups 123

CHAPTER 6: Deviance 153

PART III: Understanding Inequality 181

CHAPTER 7: Social Class: The Structure of Inequality 185

CHAPTER 8:   Race and Ethnicity as Lived Experience 221

CHAPTER 9: Constructing Gender and Sexuality 247

PART IV: Examining Social Institutions as Sites of Everyday Life 281

CHAPTER 12: Life at Home 357

CHAPTER 13: Recreation and Leisure in Everyday Life 383

CHAPTER 14: Health and Illness 411

PART V: Creating Social Change and Envisioning the Future 439

CHAPTER 15: City and Country: The Social World and the Natural World 443

Preface

Welcome to the new third edition of *The Real World: An Introduction to Sociology*. We hope you will appreciate what is new not only in the textbook's fresh look and updated materials, but also what is new in the innovative ways it goes about teaching sociology. That's exactly what we set out to do when we first embarked on the original project of writing this textbook, and it's what we continue to do here in the third edition.

At the beginning, we'd had years of experience in college and university classrooms, teaching Introductory Sociology to thousands of students from all backgrounds and walks of life; we had discovered a lot about what works and what doesn't when it comes to making sociology exciting and effective. As seasoned instructors, we had developed an approach to teaching and learning that reflected our passion for the subject and our concern with best practices in pedagogy. But we were having trouble finding a textbook that encompassed all the elements we had identified and that made such a difference in our own experience. We were tired of seeing the same old formulas found in almost every textbook. And we figured we were not alone. Other students and instructors were probably equally frustrated with repetitive formats, stodgy styles, and seemingly irrelevant or overly predictable materials. That is a great misfortune, for sociology, at its best, is a discipline that holds great value and is both intellectually stimulating and personally resonant. While the impetus to write this textbook began as a way of answering our own needs, our goal became to create a textbook of even greater benefit to others who might also be looking for something new.

We are gratified by the response *The Real World* has received from instructors and students alike, so we are preserving many of the features that have made the textbook a success. At the same time, we have done more than just simply revise the textbook. In this edition, you will find significant new content and added features that will further enhance the teaching and learning process, and keep us as close to the cutting-edge as possible. Many of the original elements we developed for students and instructors appear again in these pages. As a foundation, we have maintained a writing style that we hope is accessible and interesting as well as scholarly. One of the core pedagogical strengths of this textbook is its focus on everyday life, the mass media, technology, and popular culture. We know that the combination of these themes is inherently appealing to students, and that it relates to their lives. And since both new generation and more experienced sociology instructors might also be looking for something different, another of this book's strengths is an integrated emphasis on critical thinking and analytic skills. Rather than merely presenting or reviewing major concepts in sociology, which can often seem dry and remote, we seek to make the abstract more concrete through real-world examples and hands-on applications.

In this text we take a fresh and accessible theoretical approach appropriate to our contemporary world. While we emphasize the interactionist perspective, we cover a range of theoretical thought, including postmodernism. We also build innovative methodological exercises into each chapter, giving students the opportunity to put into practice what they are learning.

We present material that is familiar and relevant to students in a way that allows them to make profound analytic connections between their individual lives and the structure of their society. We provide instructors with ways to reenergize their teaching, and we give even General Education students a reason to be fascinated by and engrossed in their sociology courses. We do this by staying in touch with our students and the rapidly changing real world, and by bringing our insight, experience, and intellectual rigor to bear on a new way of teaching introductory sociology.

Whether you are a student or an instructor, you have probably seen a lot of textbooks. As authors, we have thought very carefully about how to write this textbook so as to make it more meaningful and effective for you. We think it is important to point out some newly added and unique features of this textbook and to tell you why they are included and what we hope you will get out of them.

Part Introductions

The 16 chapters in this text are grouped into five Parts, and each Part opens with its own introductory essay. Each Part Introduction highlights a piece of original sociological research that encompasses the major themes that group the chapters together. The in-depth discussion of the featured book shows what the real work of academic sociologists consists of and reveals how sociological research frequently unites topics covered in separate chapters in introductory textbooks.

Opening Vignettes

Each chapter begins with an opening vignette which gives students an idea about the topics or themes they will encounter in the chapter. The vignettes are drawn from current events and everyday life, the media, arts, and popular culture. They are designed to grab your attention and stimulate your curiosity to learn more by reading the chapter that follows.

How to Read This Chapter

After the vignette, you will find a section that provides you with some goals and strategies that we believe will be useful in reading that particular chapter. We know from our experience in teaching Introductory Sociology that it is often worthwhile to let students know what to expect in advance so that they can better make their way through the material. Not all chapters require the same approach; we want to bring to your attention what we think is the best approach to each one, so you can keep that in mind while reading and studying.

Theory in Everyday Life

Although we provide thorough coverage in Chapter 1, we find that students often benefit from additional help with understanding the mechanics of social theory and how to apply it to various real-world phenomena. These boxes in every chapter break down the major theoretical approaches and illustrate how each perspective might be used to analyze a particular real-world case study. This serves as a simple, practical model for students to then make their own applications and analyses.

Bolded In-Text Terms

As a student of sociology, you will be learning many new concepts and terms. Throughout each chapter, you will see a number of words or phrases in bold type. You may already recognize some of these from their more common vernacular use. But it is important to pay special attention to the way that they are used sociologically. For this reason you will find definitions in the margins of each page, where you can refer to them as you read. You should consider these bolded words and phrases your conceptual "tools" for doing sociology. As you progress through the chapters in this textbook, you will be collecting the contents of a toolkit that you can use to better understand yourself and the world around you. The bolded terms can also be found in the Glossary at the back of the book.

Relevance Boxes

In each chapter you will find Relevance Boxes with three different themes: "On the Job," "In Relationships," and "Changing the World." Relevance Boxes allow students to see the practical implications and personal value of sociology in their lives. "On the Job" explores the ways different people use sociological training or insights in a variety of work settings. "In Relationships" looks at how sociology can help us to better understand our friendships, intimate partnerships, and family relations. "Changing the World" focuses on the role sociology and its practitioners can play in bringing about real social change. We include these boxes to show how taking this course could bear fruit in your life (and in the lives of others) beyond just fulfilling your college requirements.

Data Workshops

Data Workshops are designed to give students the opportunity to gain hands-on experience in the practice of sociology while they are learning. We think this is one of the most fun parts of being a sociologist. Each chapter features two Data Workshops, one on "Analyzing Everyday Life" and one on "Analyzing Mass Media and Popular Culture." Students will use one of the research methods covered in Chapter 2 to deal with actual data from the real world—whether they are data they collect themselves or raw data provided from another source. The Data Workshops lead students through the process of analyzing data using the related conceptual tools they have just acquired in the chapter. There are two options for completion from which instructors can choose. The Data Workshops can serve as a homework assignment, small-group activity, or in-class discussion, or as the basis for a formal essay or research project. The Data Workshops can also be found on the Study Space website for the textbook, where students can submit completed work online.

Global Perspective Boxes

While this textbook focuses primarily on contemporary American society, we believe that in this time of increasing globalization, it is also important to look at other societies around the world. Each chapter includes a "Global Perspective" box that highlights some of the differences and similarities between the United States and other cultures. This feature will help students develop the ability to see comparative and analogous patterns across cultures, which is one of the key functions of a sociological perspective.

Images and Graphics

We think that it is crucial to include not only written information but also images and graphics in the textbook. This kind of presentation is increasingly common and students are likely to encounter complex information in graphical form in many of their textbooks. We want to help students gain in visual literacy as they are exposed to a variety of materials and learn in different ways. We also know that students share our interest in media, technology, and popular culture, and we want to show the connections between real life and sociological thinking. For these reasons, you will find many kinds of images and graphics in each chapter. These are not just decorations; they are an integral part of the text, so please study these as carefully as you would the rest of the printed page.

Closing Comments

Each chapter ends with closing comments that wrap up the discussion and give some final thoughts about the important themes that have been covered. This gives us a chance not so much to summarize or reiterate but to reflect, in a slightly different way, on what we have discussed, as well as to point to the future. We hope that the closing comments will give you something to think about, or even talk about with others, long after you've finished reading the chapter.

End-of-Chapter Materials

The end of each chapter contains additional materials that will enhance the learning process. The Questions for Review not only help you prepare for exams but also encourages you to extrapolate and apply what you have learned to other relevant examples. The Suggestions for Further Exploration provides a list of additional readings (fiction, nonfiction, and scholarly research), movies, music, websites, video games, and even field trips that are relevant to the topics of the chapter. Pursuing these suggestions will deepen your understanding of each chapter's themes and should be enjoyable too.

In our experience, the most important thing for students to take away from an introductory sociology class is a sociological perspective—not just a storehouse of facts, which will inevitably fade over time. Sociology promises a new way of looking at and thinking about the social world, which can serve students in good stead no matter what they find themselves doing in the future. We hope that this textbook delivers on that promise, making introductory sociology an intellectually stimulating and personally relevant enterprise for professors and students, in the classroom as well as outside it.

Resources for Students

The practical study aids and exciting new media that accompany *The Real World* are designed to extend the themes of the book and inspire students to connect what they learn in the classroom with the social worlds around them.

The Real World ebook
Available at NortonEbooks.com

"Same great book, one-third the price"

The Real World is also available in the Norton ebook format. An affordable and convenient alternative, the ebook retains the content of the print book and allows students to highlight and take notes with ease.

Everyday Sociology Blog
www.everydaysociologyblog.com

Designed for a general audience, this exciting and unique on-line forum encourages visitors to actively explore sociology's relevance to popular culture, mass media, and everyday life. Karen Sternheimer of the University of Southern California moderates the blog, and four other sociologist contributors write biweekly postings on topical subjects. The Everyday Sociology Blog is organized around such categories as Popular Culture and Consumption; Social Problems, Politics and Social Change; Crime and Deviance; Behind the Headlines; Relationships, Marriage, and Family; Theory; and Video: Everyday Sociology Talk.

StudySpace: Your Place for a Better Grade.
wwnorton.com/studyspace

StudySpace tells students what they know, shows them what they still need to review, and then gives them an organized study plan to master the material.

This free and easy-to-navigate website offers students an impressive range of exercises, interactive learning tools, assessment, and review materials, including:

- Quiz+ Quizzes for each chapter. Quiz+ doesn't just tell students how they did; it shows them how they can do better. Quiz+ presents students with a targeted study plan that offers specific page references and links to the ebook and other online learning tools. This allows students to instantly access the resources they need, when they need them most.
- **NEW!** Analyzing the Data Exercises, based on the new infographics, allow students to use recent data to apply general concepts.
- Data Workshop exercises (2 per chapter)
- Everyday Sociology Blog exercises (based on Everyday Sociology Blog postings)
- Sociology in Practice DVD exercises feature clips from documentary films that explore sociological concepts from various perspectives. These require a registration code—which comes free with all copies of the text—to access.
- Chapter outlines and learning objectives
- The Norton Slideshow Maker with Visual Sociology Exercises allows students to use their own photographs and captions to respond to "big" sociological questions (select chapters only)

- Vocabulary Flashcards
- Everyday Sociology Blog RSS feed
- Sociology in the News RSS feed

Resources for Instructors

Sociology DVDs: 3 DVDs including the new *Sociology in Practice: Thinking about Culture* DVD

These 3 DVDs contain over nine hours of video clips drawn from documentaries by independent filmmakers. The "Sociology in Practice" DVD series has been expanded to include a new DVD of documentary clips on culture. The DVDs are ideal for initiating classroom discussion and encouraging students to apply sociological concepts to popular and real-world issues. The clips are also offered in streaming versions on StudySpace and on the coursepack. Each streamed clip is accompanied by a DVD quiz.

Instructor's Website
wwnorton.com/instructors

The Instructor's website features instructional content for use in lecture and distance education, including coursepacks, test-item files, PowerPoint lecture slides, images, figures, and more.
    The Instructor's Website features:

- FREE, customizable Blackboard, WebCT, Angel, and D2L coursepacks
- Discussion Boards for smaller, more focused discussions about the Everyday Sociology Blog
- Lecture PowerPoints with Clicker Questions
- Art from book in PowerPoint and JPEG formats
- Glossary
- Test Bank in ExamView, WebCT, Blackboard, and RTF formats
- Website quizzes in Blackboard and WebCT formats

New! Enhanced Coursepack (available for free download at /instructors; BB/WEbCT, Angel, Desire2Learn, Moodle)

The new coursepack offers a variety of activities, and assessment and review materials for instructors who use Blackboard and other learning management systems. In addition to the chapter-based assignments, test banks and quizzes, interactive learning tools, and other content from the StudySpace website this new Coursepack includes a variety of coursepack-only premium content. Designed by an instructional technologist who understands how to make each LMS as user-friendly and attractive as possible, the Coursepack includes an optional ebook and many exclusive features, including:

- A large bank of discussion forum questions, organized by topic and/or chapter
- Additional multi-media activities that report directly to my LMS gradebook
- 16 additional Data Workshops
- 3–5 minute "How to Read this Chapter" author videos for every chapter
- Exercises that allow students to work with 2010 Census and Community Survey Data
- "Smart" review quiz feedback that directs a student to relevant resources within the coursepack
- A greater variety of question and activity types, such as drag and drop exercises, ranking questions, and "hot spot" quizzes

New! Interactive Instructor's Guide

Written by Natasha Chen Christensen of Monroe Community College. **The new Interactive Instructor's Guide** makes it easy for instructors to seamlessly integrate the "Real World Approach" into their Introduction to Sociology courses. This online database of hundreds of free resources places Norton's extensive collection of teaching resources at instructors' fingertips—from veteran professors looking for something to enliven tried and true lectures to first time instructors building lesson plans from scratch, Norton offers hundreds of activities, lecture ideas, and media for use in the classroom. With its search tools, the Interactive Instructor Guide will help instructor's search for exactly the resources they need by topic and resource type, and will alert subscribing instructor's as new resources are made available. Features include:

- One service learning project per chapter
- Everyday Sociology Blog exercises
- Handouts for Data Workshops and estimated completion times
- Suggested documentary clips from the *Sociology in Practice* DVD (divided by chapter) including a description of how to incorporate them in the classroom
- Article on teaching in the online classroom by Christina Partin of University of South Florida and Pasco-Hernandez Community College

- New YouTube video suggestions with exercises designed to be deployed in the classroom as well as in an online learning environment

Updated Test Bank

Written by Patricia Gibbs Stayte of Foothills College, Jill Stein of Santa Barbara City College, and Natasha Chen Christensen of Monroe Community College. Each chapter includes a concept map and approximately 20 True/False, 75 multiple-choice, and 10 essay questions per chapter. *New* features include figures from the text that are reproduced in the test bank and followed by a series of new questions regarding the material covered in the image. This test bank will include concept maps as well as labels for concept, question type, and difficulty for the multiple-choice questions. Available in print, Word, ExamView, and Blackboard, and WebCT formats.

DVD Library

Integrate engaging examples from television and film with the Norton DVD Library (1 per 50 new copies ordered).

Netflix Offer

Create your own video list! With orders of 100 or more new copies, Norton will provide a four-month subscription to Netflix. During the term of subscription, instructors may rent up to three DVDs at a time from Netflix's library of over 50,000 titles. The Instructor's Manual provides advice on incorporating many selections from the Netflix library into lectures.

Acknowledgments

The authors would like to thank the many people who helped make this textbook possible. To everyone at W. W. Norton, we believe you are absolutely the best publishers in the business and that we are fortunate to get to work with you. Thank you, Roby Harrington, for signing us. Our deep appreciation goes out to Steve Dunn for believing in us and playing such a critical role in shaping the original vision of this project. Thank you for showing us we could do this and for your substantial support throughout. We would like to acknowledge Melea Seward for her efforts during the early drafts of the book. Her innovative approach and enthusiasm were much appreciated. We owe much gratitude to Karl Bakeman for his tremendous talent, work, and dedication as our editor. He was instrumental in seeing this project through to completion and central to the success it has had. Thanks for your continued faith, boundless energy, and great ideas, which have made this next edition of the book all the better. We feel so lucky to be a part of your team.

We have many others to thank as well. We are especially grateful to our project editor, Kate Feighery; production director Jane Searle; and assistant editor Becky Charney, for managing the countless details involved in creating this book. Copy editor Erika Nein did a marvelous job suggesting improvements to the manuscript that have contributed in important ways to the book's final form. Julie Tesser and Trish Marx showed wonderful creativity in the photo research that they did for *The Real World*. Electronic media editor Eileen Connell and associate electronic media editor Laura Musich developed the best textbook support materials in sociology. Art director Rubina Yeh, along with Alex Meyer, Gia-Bao Tran, and the designers at Open deserve special thanks for creating the beautiful design and art for the book. And we are very appreciative of the exceptional Norton "travelers"; it is through their efforts that this book has gotten out into the world.

In the course of our creating the third edition, many instructors offered advice and comments on particular chapters, or in some cases, large sections of the text. We are deeply indebted to them.

- Evan Adelson, San Diego Mesa College
- Jeffrey Alexander, Lone Star College Kingwood
- Augustine Aryee, Fitchburg State College
- Nina Chapman, Golden West College
- Kelley Christopher, University of West Georgia
- Timothy Colyer, Seminole State College of Florida
- Linda Cornwell, Bowling Green State University
- Gayle D'Andrea, J. Sargeant Reynolds Community College
- Lynda Dodgen, Lone Star College
- Gianna Durso-Finley, Mercer County Community College
- Rebecca Ford, Florida State College, Jacksonville
- Lori B. Girshick, Chandler-Gilbert Community College
- Rosalind Gottfried, San Joaquin Delta College
- Kalynn Heald, Northwest Arkansas Community College
- Druann M. Heckert, Fayetteville State University
- Garrison Henderson, Tarrant County Community College
- Erica Hunter, SUNY Albany
- Alissa King, Kirkwood Community College
- Roger Klomegah, Fayetteville State University

- Leon Lane, Bluegrass Community and Technical College
- Ho Hon Leung, College at Oneonta
- Stephen Lilley, Sacred Heart University
- Daniel McLane, Colorado State University
- Rebecca Nees, Middle Georgia College
- Erin Niclaus, Bucks County Community College
- Kwaku Obosu-Mensah, Lorraine County Community College
- Jason Owen-Smith, University of Michigan
- Lillian Phillips, Scott Community College
- Jammie Price, Appalachian State University
- Rachel Schneider, University of Akron
- Tomecia Sobers, Fayetteville Technical Community College
- Steven Vassar, Minnesota State University, Mankato
- Timothy Wadsworth, University of Colorado at Boulder
- Stan Weeber, McNeere State University
- James Wright, Chattanooga State Community College
- Lecinda Yevchak, Bowling Green State University
- Brenda Zicha, Mott Community College

We would also like to thank the research assistants who worked with us on this project: Nathaniel Burke, Whitney Bush, Neil Dryden, Kate Grimaldi, Mary Ingram, Ja'Nean Palacios, and Karl Thulin. Very special thanks, also, to Natasha Chen Christensen, whose timely and thoughtful contributions to the text proved invaluable over all three editions.

We wish to especially thank Al Ferris for his wise and generous counsel in helping us to establish our corporate identity and at every juncture along the way. Thanks to Kevin Ebenhoch for his friendly and efficient services. We would like to thank our families and friends whose encouragement and support helped to sustain us through the length of this project and beyond. It is also with great pleasure that we thank Greg Wennerdahl and David Unger, respectively—you appreared in our lives just as we were completing the first edition, and your continued presence through this process has been a source of strength and joy. We are happy to share this (and future editions) with you. And we welcome our newest (future) reader, Eliot: may you always approach life's challenges with wonder, hope and a sense of endless possibility.

We are grateful to colleagues who have served as mentors in our intellectual development and as inspiration to a life of writing. And finally, we offer our thanks to all of the students we have had the privilege to work with over the years. Getting to share the sociological imagination with you makes it all worthwhile.

Kerry Ferris
Jill Stein

Changes in the 3rd Edition

We have **rewritten the chapter on theory** (Chapter 1), and we have created a **new chapter on Medical Sociology** (Chapter 14) in this edition.

Updated Data Workshops

- The new Data Workshop examines debt amongst 20 and 30 year olds and how access to easy credit and the pressure to consume have prevented many from getting ahead. (Chapter 7)
- This new Data Workshop discusses Jean Baudrillard's claim that the image has come to replace the real, and the term "simulacrum" he termed to describe the new artificial reality. (Chapter 10)
- A new Data Workshop analyzes student attitudes on environmentalism. (Chapter 15)
- The new Data Workshop features "Buy Nothing Day," which protests the consumerism embodied in Black Friday. (Chapter 16)

All new sports examples

- Roger Federer's sportsmanship as a type of social influence is discussed. (Chapter 5)
- A new example on steroid use among athletes shows how peer pressure can lead to deviant behavior. (Chapter 6)
- In terms of prestige, professional athletes rank higher than sociologists. Theories of Social Class are studied through major schools of thought within sociology, including classical conflict, Weberian theories, structural functionalism and postmodern and symbolic interactionist theories. (Chapter 7)
- Joining a tennis club has been added as a way to improve cultural capital. (Chapter 7)
- Historical examples of racial segregation include the U.S. military and professional sports like football, baseball and basketball. Jackie Robinson is often cited as the first person to break the color barrier in sports. (Chapter 8)
- The opening vignette features Caster Semenya, a runner who broke the world record for the 800m by 8 seconds in the 2009 World Championships. Those 8 seconds also caused others to question Semenya's gender for an entire year. (Chapter 9)
- The discussion of PACs now mentions the National Football League's "Gridiron PAC" and Major League Baseball's own PAC. The graphic on the top twenty PAC contributors to Federal Candidates has been updated to show the years 2009–2010. The money raised by the PACs has been updated to include the 2010 election as well. (Chapter 10)
- A football coach is added as an example of a job that appears on prime time TV. (Chapter 11)
- An updated example about the NFL labor dispute between players and owners is discussed. (Chapter 11)

- People who have athletic passions or people who are into fitness and sports are included as examples of homogamy. (Chapter 12)
- Michael Jordan, Tiger Woods and to a lesser degree, LeBron James are marketed as role models. However their personal lives often discredit their role as figures to emulate. (Chapter 13)
- A sports injury, like a torn ligament is used as an example of curative medicine. Celebrities and professional athletes often attribute successful recoveries from illnesses or injuries to Cam therapies. (Chapter 14)

All new infographics

- A new infographic on the research process is included. (Chapter 2)
- A new infographic compares culture, media, and technology over time and across countries. (Chapter 3)
- A new infographic features different agents of socialization. (Chapter 4)
- This infographic focuses on the "strength of weak ties," using information from Granovetter's study. (Chapter 5)
- The new infographic focuses on the differences in the prison population, both across different countries and within the United States. (Chapter 6)
- The amount of debt in both student loans and credit card debt that American students carry is the topic of the new infographic. (Chapter 7)
- This new infographic in chapter 8 shows the racial and ethnic makeup of the United States. (Chapter 8)
- The infographic features the income gap between genders based upon industry and shows what percentage of men and women work in each industry. (Chapter 9)
- The top 20 political action committees and their campaign contributions for the most recent election cycle are shown. (Chapter 10)
- The new infographic shows the world's top 40 economies, featuring both countries and companies and how their economic positions have shifted since 2008. (Chapter 11)
- This new infographic highlights the changing American family from 1960 to present day by zeroing in on how many people are married, divorced, cohabitating, or single. (Chapter 12)
- Corporate conglomerates such as TimeWarner and the Walt Disney Company and the break down of their holdings are the focus of the new infographic for chapter 13. (Chapter 13)
- The new infographic for chapter 14 breaks down the causes of death for different demographics, like race, age and gender in the U.S. (Chapter 14)

- This infographic compares major global indicators such as infant mortality rate, fertility rate and life expectancy across different countries. (Chapter 15)
- The new infographic for chapter 16 shows the stages of a social movement. (Chapter 16)

New examples from the media and popular culture

- A new chapter opener features the band, Acrassicauda, an Iraqi heavy-metal band that represents both a clash and a connection between American and Iraqi culture. (Chapter 3)
- The TV show *Brothers and Sisters* is used as an example of how television can act as an agent of socialization. (Chapter 4)
- Primary, secondary, and tertiary deviance is discussed in relation to the TV show *Celebrity Rehab*. (Chapter 6)
- A reference to Everyday Sociology Blog's post about celebrities who are no longer interested in rehab and argue that their drug use is acceptable is included. (Chapter 6)
- The film *Gran Torino* is used as an example of how racial prejudice can work both ways. It features Clint Eastwood as an old man with prejudices against his Italian barber, Irish construction workers, black street kids, and Asian neighbors and then compares his Asian neighbors' hopes that he'd move out of the neighborhood like all the other white people. (Chapter 8)
- The "Style over Substance" section now discusses Sarah Palin, including her reality show and her daughter's appearance on *Dancing with the Stars*. (Chapter 10)
- Examples are discussed, in particular *The Daily Show* and *The Colbert Report*, which are fake news shows that blur the distinction between real and fake. (Chapter 10)
- *Slum Dog Millionaire* is included in the opening vignette as a film that gave some American audiences their first taste of Bollywood. (Chapter 13)
- The section on high, low, and popular culture has been moved to chapter 13. It features the motorcycle exhibit at the Guggenheim and Andy Warhol's take of da Vinci's Last Supper as examples of mixing popular and high culture. (Chapter 13)

New research and expanded coverage

- Kathryn Edin and Maria Kefala's research on poor moms and motherhood is used as an example of ethnographic methods. (Chapter 2)
- "Sovereign Citizens" are discussed as some individuals claim the right to disregard certain laws or not pay taxes, sometimes resulting in violence. (Chapter 3)

- A new section has been added to "Primary and Secondary Groups" which focuses on how seemingly insignificant relationships with near strangers can have a powerful and positive impact on our lives. The section uses a study by Melinda Blau and Karen Fingerman that identifies "consequential strangers." There is a new section in "Social Networks," as well, which discusses six degrees of separation. There is also a new subheading under "Social Networks," titled "Winners, Losers and Influence." The "Gender and Networks" subheading has been removed because that section is combined with the previous one. There is a new paragraph in this combined section which discusses a study by Nicholas Christakis and James Fowler that explains that all social networks have a connection and that there is a contagion — that is, what flows through social ties. The section "Separate Groups: Anomie" is now "Separate Groups: Anomie or Virtual Membership?" In that section, the paragraph on Putnam's critics has been updated, and there is mention of new communications technology such as Massively Multi-person Online Role-Playing Games (MMORPGs.) (Chapter 5)
- After the Stanford Prison Experiment section, there is a new section called "Milgram Revisited." It mentions a 2006 study that attempted to replicate Stanley Milgram's experiment and found that obedience rates were only slightly lower than they had been 45 years earlier. (Chapter 5)
- A study by Melvin Pollner and Jill Stein is used to show the role of narrative storytelling in creating a sense of self and identity in an alcoholic's journey to recovery. (Chapter 6)
- Nikki Jones' ethnographic study on inner-city African American girls in Philadelphia shows how class, age, gender and race contribute to these young women's experience with violence. (Chapter 6) Research by Victor Rios is discussed through his own personal experience of how institutions like the law enforcement, judicial system, and public schools work to criminalize, stigmatize, and punish working-class youth. (Chapter 6)
- The discussion on slavery is expanded to include examples from America, where people are held as agricultural, domestic and sex slaves and American's indirect support of slavery elsewhere through the use of labor in different countries and our material appetites. (Chapter 7)
- The Middle Class is discussed in a new light due to the economic recession and housing market crash. Many members of the middle class have moved down to lower-middle class, whereas some others have moved to upper-middle class. (Chapter 7)

- A new section on structural functionalism has been added. (Chapter 7)
- In the section on Socioeconomic Status and Life Changes, statistics about people living below the poverty level indicate they are less likely to exercise than those living in a higher income level. Similarly, the 2010 census reports that income correlates highly with what level of education people attain. The 2010 census also reveals the largest income gap ever between the richest and poorest Americans. (Chapter 7)
- New studies have shown that the death penalty is sought more often if the killer is black, or if the victim was white. (Chapter 7)
- The defining poverty definition has been expanded to include absolute poverty indicators, such as hunger, malnutrition and the inability to afford medications. (Chapter 7)
- Poverty statistics for the U.S. have been updated to include new poverty threshold markers and highlight the fluctuation of the poor and homeless populations. (Chapter 7)
- Information on Oprah's wealth and power has been updated. (Chapter 7)
- A poll about the American dream explores shifting opinions of the concept between classes, education attainment and race. (Chapter 7)
- Rising credit card debt and the philosophy of "freegans" are discussed in relation to the American dream. (Chapter 7)
- Statistics about family demographics and bachelor degree holders have been updated with the 2010 Census. (Chapter 8)
- C. J. Pascoe's ethnography of high school boys, *Dude, You're a Fag* is featured as how powerful peer groups can be in enforcing gender roles and the assumptions of sexuality that underlie them. The poverty rate among custodial mothers is 27%, almost double that of custodial fathers, 12.9 percent. Updates on employment and unemployment between genders reveal the shift of more women entering the work force and the toll the recession had on men's employment rates. Statistics on rape in the military are included, showing that rape is a growing problem with nearly 3,000 women who were sexually assaulted, with 80–90 percent of military rapes unreported. (Chapter 9)
- A new section on sexuality in a political and social context is also included. (Chapter 9)
- The public high school graduation rate has been updated with 2009 and 2010 figures. (Chapter 10)
- Average annual earnings statistics have also been updated for 2008 and there is a new statistic about how

among young adults ages 25 to 29, there is a growing gap between the number of women and the number of men with bachelor's degrees. (Chapter 10)

- "No Child Left Behind" now has its own subheading and there is an update with the Obama administration's plan to implement a new method of fixing the education system. (Chapter 10)
- Online learning statistics have been updated for 2010. (Chapter 10)
- There is new information about the 18 percent of Americans who believed Obama was Muslim even well into his first term as president. (Chapter 10)
- A paragraph on unemployment is added to reflect the changes the recession has had on the unemployed demographic (college educated, white males). (Chapter 11)
- A paragraph about conservatives who accuse rivals of "socialist" tendencies are reminded that everyday items like streetlights and public schools are all part of a central system of funded and regulated services. (Chapter 11)
- The chapter opens with a discussion of Matt Wray's research on suicide in Las Vegas. (Chapter 14)
- In addition to covering classic topics like Parson's Sick Role, Ferris and Stein also discuss the intersections of race, class, gender, and health, and the impact food deserts have on the health of inner-city populations. (Chapter 14)
- In contrast to the food deserts, the growing number of locavores is discussed as a movement that focuses on the health of people, places and the planet. (Chapter 14)
- Longevity has increased dramatically, with many people around the world living past the age of 100 years old. With that and other contributing factors, the UN predicts that the world population will surpass 9 billion people by 2050 and 10 billion by the end of the century before it stabilizes. (Chapter 15)
- The BP oil spill in the Gulf of Mexico, lasting 85 days and releasing 4.9 billion barrels of oil is compared to the previously worst oil spill in U.S. history, the 1969 Union Oil Spill Santa Barbara, lasting 11 days and releasing 100,000 barrels of oil. (Chapter 15)

Revised relevance boxes

- The revised "On the Job" box features famous sociology majors, like Michelle Obama and Kal Penn. (Chapter 1)
- The "Changing the World" box has been updated with new legislation regarding marijuana. (Chapter 3)
- The relevance box on social networking sites has been renamed "Pros or Cons or Think Before You Post." The box has updated statistics on Facebook from 2010 and now explores some of the history that preceded Facebook—sites like AOL and Friendster. It also mentions cyber-bullying. (Chapter 5)

- The "Global Perspectives" box is still called "Group vs. Individual Norms" but now it focuses on honor killings, rather than the caning of Michael Fay. The box opens with the story of Lyle and Erik Menedez, who killed their parents to gain access to the family fortunes, and contrasts that with honor killings such as when a 20-year-old woman was run over by a Jeep driven by her father because he was worried she was too Westernized. (Chapter 5)
- The "On the Job" box, titled "Teamwork and Tour de France," has been updated and now mentions Lance Armstrong's struggle with cancer and his work with the Lance Armstrong Foundation. (Chapter 5)
- The "Changing the World" box has been renamed "A Paradise Built in Hell: The Extraordinary Communities that Arise in Disaster" and features the book written by Rebecca Solnit. She researched the aftermath of five disasters, the most recent being the 9/11 attacks and Hurricane Katrina, and found that people came together to help, support, and nurture each other during the crisis. (Chapter 5)
- The "In Relationships: Socioeconomic Status and Mate Selection" box adds examples of high profile politicians and celebrities who have gotten married, such as Tom Brady and Giselle Bundchen and Julie Nixon and David Eisenhower. (Chapter 7)
- Michael Moore's *Capitalism: A Love Story* is featured as the "Changing the World" box. (Chapter 7)
- The box "In Relationships" features "hooking up" amongst college students and research by Paula England, Kathleen Boge and Elizabeth Armstrong and Laura England about the sexual behaviors of college students. (Chapter 9)
- The "On the Job" box features the Dukes V. Wal-Mart Stores, Inc. case where Betty Dukes along with six other women sued Wal-Mart in a class action suit for sex discrimination. (Chapter 9)
- The "Changing the World" box includes the mural by the artist Blu, commissioned in 2010 by MOCA for the outside of their building in downtown Los Angeles. The mural was whitewashed before it could be displayed because of its powerful antiwar symbolism. (Chapter 10)
- The "On the Job" box now features Doug Lemov, who has held almost every position possible in a school and who eventually wrote a book called *Teach Like a Champion: The 49 Techniques that Put Students on the Path to College* which includes techniques such as calling on students regardless of whether they have raised their hands, and using words economically. (Chapter 10)
- The "Changing the World" box is updated to include certain states' new positions on gay marriage. (Chapter 12)

The Real World
Third Edition

PART 1

Thinking Sociologically and Doing Sociology

David came from a well-heeled Philadelphia family, attended Harvard Law School, spent his summers sailing yachts, and clerked for a Supreme Court Justice.

Pepper went to Yale when the school had just begun to admit female students, and some campus buildings didn't even have women's restrooms. She wrote the sex advice column for *Glamour* magazine for nine years.

Andrew is an outspoken Roman Catholic priest and the author of over 50 best-selling mystery novels.

Joe endured the Great Depression and violent anti-Semitism as a child. He worked as a supermarket clerk and served in the Army during World War II, but it was a series of trips to India that made the biggest impact on his life.

Jessie was a "corsetless coed," a term for young women in the 1920s who rejected the restrictive undergarments of their mothers' era and instead rolled their stockings down below their knees.

What do these people have in common? They are all prominent American sociology professors. You may not have heard of them (yet), but they have each made an exceptional impact on their profession:

David Riesman made sociology a household word with his influential study of American character and culture, *The Lonely Crowd*. He earned a JD (but never a PhD) and was a professor at the University of Chicago and Harvard. Pepper Schwartz, sociology professor at the University of Washington, is a leading researcher on sex and intimate relationships. Andrew Greeley, now at the University of Arizona, ran the National Opinion Research Center at the University of Chicago for many years and continues to research the sociology of religion as an associate there. Joseph Gusfield, a pioneering sociologist in the area of alcohol use and abuse, is Professor Emeritus in the department of sociology at the University of California–San Diego. And Jessie Bernard, the "grande dame" of American sociology, was a professor at Pennsylvania State University for most of her career, studying women, marriage, and the family. The American Sociological Association gives an annual award in her name to a scholar whose career in the study of gender is as distinguished as Bernard's.

Their stories are compiled in *Authors of Their Own Lives: Intellectual Autobiographies of Twenty American Sociologists*. Edited by University of California–Berkeley professor Bennett Berger, it's a collection of autobiographical essays by well-known contemporary sociologists in a variety of fields. Each sociologist tells the story of entering the discipline and navigating a career path in academia—the obstacles he encountered, the triumphs he experienced, and the relationships between his personal life and his professional career.

TWENTY CENTS   SEPTEMBER 27, 1954

TIME

WEEKLY NEWSMAGAZINE

SOCIAL SCIENTIST DAVID RIESMAN
What is the American character?

$6.00 A YEAR   VOL. LXIV NO. 13

Their paths to sociology were very different, and they each taught and researched different topics. But despite these differences, they share a way of looking at the world. Sociologists have a unique perspective called the "sociological imagination." In fact, we hope that you will acquire your own version of the sociological imagination over the course of this term. Then you will share something in common with the professors who tell their stories in Berger's book.

David Riesman, Andrew Greeley, Pepper Schwartz, and the others also hold in common their commitment to sociological theories and concepts. This means that their ideas, and the questions they ask and answer, are guided by the established traditions of sociological thought. They may build on those traditions or criticize them, but every sociologist engages in a theoretical dialogue that links centuries and generations. You

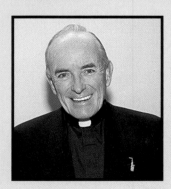

Andrew Greeley

will become part of this dialogue as you learn more about sociological theory.

Finally, Riesman, Greeley, Schwartz, and the rest conduct their research using specific sociological methods. Whether quantitative or qualitative, these means of gathering and analyzing data are distinctive to sociology, and every sociologist develops research projects using the methods best suited to the questions she wants to answer.

Pepper Schwartz

In the introduction to *Authors of Their Own Lives*, Berger states that he wants to reveal "the presence of the person in the work, the author in the authored" (p. xv)—in other words, he wants to show how a sociologist's personal journey affects her professional legacy. Berger also believes that knowing something about an author's life helps students understand her work—and we agree with him. A person's values, experiences, and family context all shape her interests and objectives—and this is as true of eminent sociologists like Jessie Bernard as it will be for you.

In the following section, we will introduce you to the discipline of sociology and its theoretical traditions (Chapter 1), and to the work of sociology and its research methodologies (Chapter 2). This section is your first opportunity to get to know sociology—its perspectives, theories, and research practices.

Perhaps someday your intellectual autobiography will be added to those of Riesman, Greeley, Schwartz, and the rest—and your story will start by opening this book . . .

CHAPTER 1

Sociology and the Real World

Agroup of housemates in their twenties who lived together last summer in the beach town of Seaside Heights, New Jersey, have moved to Miami to escape the cold Northeast. The four women (Angelina, "Snooki," Sammi, and "JWoww") and four men ("The Situation," Pauly D, Vinny, and Ronnie)—most of them Italian American—refer to each other by what some say are derogatory terms: "guidos" and "guidettes." By day they pursue the "GTL" lifestyle (gym, tanning, and laundry), while at night they flirt, fight, and fist pump in the clubs, returning home to hook up in the hot tub or the communal "smush" room. Although Sammi and Ronnie are a couple, the other girls know that he has been "creeping" behind her back. This puts them in an awkward position, so they decide to leave Sammi an anonymous note—which ignites a profanity-laden shouting match between the women once Sammi finds out how long they've known. Meanwhile, the men continue with their schemes to meet as many local hotties as possible. . . .

Eleven two-person teams—including married ministers, dating goths, best friends, a grandfather and grandson, and two sets of siblings—race 30,000 miles through ten countries on four continents in just twenty-one days, competing for various prizes along the way, until the winners ultimately claim $1 million. The teams are required to overcome "roadblocks" or "detours"—tasks they must perform before reaching their next destination: milk a camel and drink the product, perform a traditional dance before a crowd of locals, run through a barrage of fireworks, or jump into the hold of a boat and sort through 500 live crabs to find the one painted with bright racing colors. . . .

On the day that Renee and Paul Giunta's third child is born, Paul is in a devastating car accident that requires months of arduous rehabilitation. More than two years later he still has not returned home because their house cannot accommodate his wheelchair. But the family is about to receive a miracle of sorts: while they are on a weeklong vacation at Disney World, a team of hundreds of workers tears down and rebuilds their home—a project that would ordinarily take months to complete. The Giuntas return to a cheering crowd of neighbors and tour their newly remodeled, redecorated, and landscaped home, where they can finally live together under one roof. . . .

Is any of this real? Yes . . . kind of. It's "reality television"—specifically MTV's *Jersey Shore*, CBS's *The Amazing Race*, and ABC's *Extreme Makeover: Home Edition*. And there's a lot more where that came from. In the fall 2010 television lineup, there were literally hundreds of reality shows on the major networks and cable stations, with an unknown number of programs undoubtedly in the works. *The Biggest Loser*, *So You Think You Can Dance*, *Dirty Jobs*, *Keeping Up With the Kardashians*, *Top Chef*, *America's Next Top*

Model, Celebrity Rehab With Dr. Drew, and the *Real Housewives* franchise were just a few of the more popular programs from that season, and of course MTV's *The Real World* is the show that started it all.

Some of the shows claim to follow real people through their everyday lives or on the job, while others impose bizarre conditions on participants, subject them to stylized competitions and gross-out stunts, or make their dreams come true. Millions tune in every week to see real people eat bugs, get fired, suffer romantic rejection, reveal their poor parenting, get branded as fat or ugly, cry over their misfortunes, or get voted out of the house or off the island—mortifying themselves on camera for the possibility of success, money, or fame.

Why are we so interested in these people? Because people are interesting! Because we are people too—no matter how different we are from the folks on reality TV, we are part of the same society, and for that reason we are curious about how they live. We compare their lives with ours, wonder how common or unusual they or we are, and marvel that we are all part of the same, real world. We too may want to win competitions, date an attractive guy or girl, find a high-profile job, feel pretty or handsome, be part of an exclusive group, have a lovely home and family. We may even want to get on a reality show ourselves.

Reality television is interesting because of the social dynamics it reveals. However contrived or formulaic the setups, the issues—interpersonal disputes, family and work issues, racial and regional identities, class, wealth, and poverty, sexuality and gender conflicts, disabilities, body images and standards of beauty, the role of the individual in a larger group—are all sociological. Sociology as an academic discipline can help us explain the things that happen on-screen in reality television and the things that happen offscreen in real life.

Sociology allows us to peer into the lives and worlds of many different kinds of people, in many different settings, without the help of TV producers. Sociology offers us insights into our own lives as well as the lives of others, and presents systematic, scientific ways of understanding those lives. Sociology gives us tools to navigate our everyday social worlds, and it shows us ways of understanding the forces that shape and constrain those worlds. Sociology helps us understand both *The Real World* and the real world.

HOW TO READ THIS CHAPTER

You are embarking on a fascinating journey as you learn to see, think, and analyze yourself and the world around you from a sociological perspective. The tools presented here will help you build a foundation for new knowledge and insights into social life.

We will also share the story of the historical and intellectual development of the discipline of sociology. We want to show you how the ideas that shape sociology are linked, and to introduce you to the interesting men and women who came up with those ideas. Too often, theorists seem to be talking heads, icons of social analysis who experience neither life-altering calamities nor shifting professional fortunes. We want to overcome that perception. We believe that individual experiences and historical contexts shape our thoughts and the professional worlds we choose to join. This is as true for

Karl Marx as it is for Kerry Ferris, as true for Jane Addams as it is for Jill Stein—it's true for all of us; your own experiences and cultural and historical contexts will shape your ideas and work. In fact, someday, someone may write a chapter about you!

As authors and teachers, we encourage you to develop some basic study techniques that will assist you in your success as a new student to sociology (and perhaps beyond). You may want to highlight portions of the text or take notes while you are reading. Mark passages you don't understand, or keep a list of questions about any aspect of the chapter. Don't hesitate to discuss those questions with your instructor or fellow students; those dialogues can be one of the most gratifying parts of the learning process. Finally, we recommend that you attend class regularly—whether you're in a face-to-face classroom or online—as there is really no substitute for the shared experience of learning sociology with others.

We are excited to join you on this journey of discovery. Though you may know a lot about social life already, we hope to introduce you to even more—about yourself and the world around you—and to provide valuable tools for the future. We wouldn't want you to miss a thing. So here is where we start. . . .

Practical versus Scientific Knowledge

You already possess many of the skills of an astute analyst of social life, but you take your knowledge for granted because you gained it as an everyday actor. In this course, you will build a new identity: social analyst. These are two very different ways of experiencing the same social world.

The everyday actor approaches his social world with what is referred to as "reciped," or practical, knowledge (Schutz 1962), which allows him to get along in his everyday life. However, practical knowledge is not necessarily as coherent, clear, and consistent as it could be. For example, you are probably very skilled at using a cell phone. It brings you into daily contact with friends and family, puts you in touch with the pizza delivery guy, and allows you to register for classes and pick up your grades at the end of the term. But you probably can't explain how it works in a technical way; you know only how it works for you in a practical, everyday way. This is the important feature of the everyday actor's knowledge: it is practical, not scientific.

To acquire knowledge about the social world that is systematic, comprehensive, coherent, clear, and consistent, you'll need to take a different approach. The social analyst has to "place in question everything that seems unquestionable" to the everyday actor (Schutz 1962, p. 96). In other words, the social analyst takes the perspective of a stranger in the social world; she tries to verify what the everyday actor might just accept as truth. For instance, people tend to believe that women are more talkative than men. This might seem so evident, in fact, as not to be worth investigating. The social analyst, however, *would* investigate, and deliver a more complex conclusion than you might think.

There are strengths and weaknesses in both approaches: the analyst sees with clarity what the actor glosses over, but the actor understands implicitly what the analyst labors to grasp. Once you've learned more about the theories and methods that come next, you'll be able to combine the virtues of both analyst and actor. The result will be a more profound and comprehensive understanding of the social world in which we all live.

What Is Sociology?

Even among those working in the field, there is some debate about defining **sociology**. A look at the term's Latin and Greek roots, *socius* and *logos*, suggests that sociology means the study of **society**, which is a good place to start. A slightly more elaborate definition might be the systematic or scientific study of human society and social behavior. This could include almost any level within the structure of society, from large-scale institutions and mass culture to small groups and relationships between individuals.

Another definition comes from Howard Becker, who suggests that sociology can best be understood as the study of people "doing things together" (1986). This version reminds us that neither society nor the individual exists in isolation and that humans are essentially social beings. Not only is our survival contingent upon the fact that we live in various groups (families, neighborhoods, dorms), but our sense of self derives from our membership in society. In turn, the accumulated activities

> **sociology** the systematic or scientific study of human society and social behavior, from large-scale institutions and mass culture to small groups and individual interactions
>
> **society** a group of people who shape their lives in aggregated and patterned ways that distinguish their group from other groups

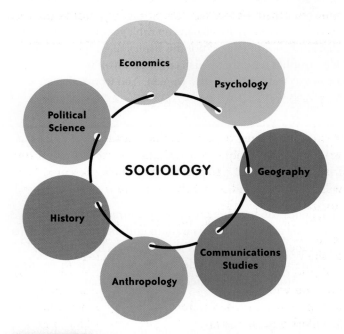

FIGURE 1.1 Sociology and the Social Sciences

Sociology overlaps with other social sciences, but much of the territory it covers is unique.

In Relationships

It's Official: Men Talk More Than Women

The practice of sociology may look pretty simple or natural at the outset. It doesn't seem to require much special training to figure out other people and to know something about how the world works. All it takes is membership in society and some life experience to count yourself an expert on the topic. Look at how successful you are already just to have arrived at the point of being a college student. So what more can sociology deliver? The practice of sociology may also seem to be about just a bunch of common sense. But this is true only part of the time. Some of what you learn may indeed seem familiar from what you already know about people and the world around you, and may confirm some of the conclusions you've made about it. Drawing upon the personal knowledge we have accumulated in life will be a valuable asset as a starting place, but it can also be a stumbling block to deeper understanding. There are times that the things that "everyone knows" turn out not to be true, or at least not as sure and simple as we might have thought.

Take for instance the widely held belief that women talk more than men. Experience seems to confirm that this is true, obviously! Women are chatty, you can't get them to stop talking. And a lot of men, if not the strong silent type, definitely have trouble getting a word in edgewise if you're talking about having a conversation with a woman. And women have a hard

time getting men to talk when they want them to; sometimes it's like having to drag it out of them to get a man to tell you what he's thinking. These statements make pretty good sense to anyone who's ever had a relationship with the opposite sex. While you may recognize this description of the different genders, and may be able to relate with your own anecdote of such an encounter (or perhaps many encounters), your casual assumptions about who talks most may need some revising. Numerous sociological studies that dismantle conversational dynamics show that, despite stereotypes to the contrary, it's actually the men who are slightly more talkative (Leaper and Ayres 2007). How could that be?

Actually, there are some nuances. It's true that researchers have found that men are more talkative overall, but especially in certain contexts. Men are more talkative with their wives and with strangers. Women are more talkative with their children and with college classmates. With close friends and families, men and women are equally talkative. Studies also showed other, perhaps more easily predictable, gender differences, that men use more assertive speech (they want to persuade others), while women use speech that is more affiliative (they are more focused on connecting with others). These findings even seem to defy what had been considered a biological fact, that the female brain is wired to be more verbal. Because who

that people do together create the patterns and structures we call society. So sociologists want to understand how humans affect society, as well as how society affects humans.

One way to better understand sociology is to contrast it with other **social sciences** (disciplines that examine the human or social world, much as the natural sciences examine the natural or physical world)—anthropology, psychology, economics, political science, and sometimes history, geography, and commu-

social sciences the disciplines that use the scientific method to examine the social world, in contrast to the natural sciences, which examine the physical world

nication studies. Each has its own particular focus on the social world. In some ways, sociology's territory overlaps with other social sciences, even while maintaining its own approach.

Like history, sociology compares the past and the present in order to understand both; unlike history, sociology is more likely to focus on contemporary society. Sociology is interested in societies at all levels of development, while anthropology is more likely to concentrate on traditional or primitive cultures. Sociology looks at a range of social institutions, unlike economics or political science, which focus on a single institution. Like

talks more varies by situation, the evidence seems to point to language and conversational differences as influenced more by social than biological forces. So despite how it might feel from your own personal experience, sociology has debunked a very common myth about women and men, requiring that we rethink simplistic gender stereotypes.

Think about that the next time you converse with a member of the opposite sex. If it's your spouse, your child, a classmate, or complete stranger, you may see an example emerge right before your eyes of what sociologists have already known about who talks more in what kinds of social settings. And, if so, it just might challenge some of your beliefs about the world that you could have sworn were true.

This is why doing sociology is in some regards a radical undertaking. It requires of us a willingness to suspend our own preconceptions, assumptions, and beliefs about the way things are. As sociologists, we need to learn to question everything, especially our own taken-for-granted notions about others and ourselves. Once these have been set aside, even temporarily, we gain a fresh perspective with which to uncover and discover aspects of social life we hadn't noticed before. We are then able to reinterpret our previous understanding of the world, perhaps challenging, or possibly confirming, what we thought we already knew.

Kanye West takes the microphone from Taylor Swift to make a speech at the MTV Video Music Awards.

geography, sociology considers the relationship of people to places, though geography is more concerned with the places themselves. And like communication studies, sociology examines human communication—at both the social and the interpersonal levels, rather than one or the other. Finally, sociology looks at the individual in relationship to external social forces, whereas psychology specializes in internal states of mind. As you can begin to see, sociology covers a huge intellectual territory, making it exceptional among the social sciences in taking a comprehensive, integrative approach to understanding human life (Figure 1.1, page 7).

The Sociological Perspective

How do sociologists go about understanding human life in society? The first step is to develop what we call the **sociological perspective**, which is also referred to as taking a sociological approach or thinking sociologically. In any case, it means looking at the world in a unique way and seeing it in a whole new light. You may be naturally inclined to think sociologically, but, for many, the following practices are helpful.

> **sociological perspective** a way of looking at the world through a sociological lens

On the Job

Famous Sociology Majors

Sociology continues to be a popular major at colleges and universities in the United States and in countries such as Canada, the United Kingdom, and Australia. According to the American Sociological Association, over a half million Bachelor of Arts degrees in sociology were awarded in the United States between 1990 and 2010. Clearly, there are many reasons why students are enthusiastic about the subject. What may be less clear is how to turn this passion into a paycheck. Students considering majoring in the subject often ask, "What can I do with a degree in sociology?" Their parents may be asking the same question. Students interested in academic careers can pursue graduate degrees and become professors and researchers—real, practicing sociologists. But the vast majority of sociology majors will not necessarily become sociologists with a capital S. Their studies have prepared them to be valuable, accomplished participants in a variety of different fields, including law and government, business administration, social welfare, public health, education, counseling and human resources, advertising and marketing, public relations and the media, and work in nonprofit organizations.

A major in sociology, in other words, can lead almost anywhere. And while the roster of former sociology majors contains names both well known and unsung, from president Ronald Reagan and civil rights leader Martin Luther King Jr. to the public defender giving legal aid to low-income clients and the health care professional bringing wellness programs into large corporations, we will focus here on three important Americans you may not have associated with sociology.

The first individual may be the least likely to be identified as a sociology major, since his career was centered in the arts. Saul Bellow (1915–2005) was one of the most acclaimed American novelists of the twentieth century; his numerous literary awards included the National Book Award (three times), the Pulitzer Prize, and the Nobel Prize in Literature. He was also a successful playwright and journalist, and taught at several universities. Bellow was born in Montreal to Jewish parents, Russian émigrés who later settled in the slums of Chicago while he was still a child. He began his undergraduate studies in English at the University of Chicago, but left within two years after being told by the department chair that no Jew could really grasp English literature. He then enrolled at Northwestern University, graduating in 1937 with honors in sociology. Literary critics have noted that Bellow's background in sociology, as well as his own personal history, may have influenced both the style and subject of his work. Many of the great themes of American social life appear in his novels: culture, power, wealth and poverty, war, religion, urban life, gender relations, and, above all, the social contract that keeps us together in the face of forces that threaten to tear us apart.

Our next profile is of Michelle Robinson Obama (b. 1964), the first African American first lady of the United States. Michelle Obama has quickly become one of the most recognizable and widely admired sociology majors in the world, using her role as first lady to fight against childhood obesity, help working mothers, and encourage public service. Born and raised in working-class Chicago, she can trace her ancestry to slaves on both sides of her family tree. Her father worked for the city's water department, but saw both of his children graduate from Princeton University and go on to successful professional careers. After obtaining her bachelor's in sociology—her senior thesis dealt with alien-

Beginner's Mind

One technique for gaining a sociological perspective comes from Bernard McGrane, who promotes a shift in thinking that's borrowed from the Zen Buddhist tradition. McGrane suggests that we practice what is called **beginner's mind**—the opposite of expert's mind, which is so filled with facts, projections, assumptions, opinions, and explanations that it can't learn anything new (McGrane 1994). If we would like to better understand the world around us, then we must unlearn what we already know. Beginner's mind approaches the world without knowing in advance what it will find; it is open and receptive to experience.

ation experienced by African American students in an Ivy League institution—she earned her law degree at Harvard, worked at a prestigious law firm in Chicago, and then served in the mayor's office. Although she turned to law and politics, her choice of majors has always been more than just a temporary stopover on the way to the White House.

Our last sociology major is Kalpen Modi (b. 1977), who has served as an associate director with the White House

Saul Bellow   **Michelle Obama**   **Kal Penn**

Office of Public Engagement (OPE) since 2009. This may have come as a surprise to those who know him as the actor Kal Penn, most famous for his role as the wisecracking, easy-going stoner Kumar in the *Harold and Kumar* film series, or perhaps as Dr. Lawrence Kutner on the television show *House*. Joining the OPE meant that Penn had to temporarily leave acting (some would say at the peak of his career) to become the liaison to young Americans, the arts, and Asian American and Pacific Islander communities. As much as Penn wanted success as an actor, he also has been critical of the racial and ethnic stereotypes often associated with playing a person of South Asian descent. At one point, he nearly turned down a recurring role as a terrorist on the TV drama *24* because he didn't want to reinforce the negative "connection between media images and people's thought processes" (Yuan 2007). While it might be easy to make similar claims against *Harold and Kumar Go to White Castle,* one of his costars defended the film, arguing that it "approached the level of sociology, albeit scatological, sexually obsessed sociology,"

as "it probed questions of ethnic identity, conformism and family expectations vs. personal satisfaction" (Garvin 2008, p. M1). Penn's career change reflects his deep commitment to sociological ideals and a desire to use his influence to help build more positive media portrayals of minorities. In addition to his activities on behalf of the White House, Penn has taught courses in Asian American studies at the University of Pennsylvania and is currently pursuing a graduate certificate in international security at Stanford. In 2010, he returned briefly to acting, playing Kumar in another movie sequel. Some fans might also find it ironic that in real life Penn is a vegetarian who says that smoking pot is not for him.

Regardless of whether you go any further in this discipline, the most important thing to take away from an introductory sociology class is a sociological perspective. Sociology promises a new way of looking at, thinking about, and taking action in the world around us, all of which can serve you in good stead no matter where you find yourself in the future.

Perhaps our greatest obstacle to making new discoveries is our habitual ways of thinking. "Discovery," McGrane says, "is not the seeing of a new thing—but rather a new way of seeing things" (1994, p. 3). One way to achieve this kind of awareness is to practice being present in the moment. We are all too often preoccupied with thoughts and feelings that prevent us from fully participating in reality. If we can find

some inner stillness, stop our normal mental chatter, then McGrane says there is a possibility for true learning to occur. It is in this quiet space that a personal "paradigm shift" (a new model for understanding self and society) can take place.

beginner's mind approaching the world without preconceptions in order to see things in a new way

DATA WORKSHOP

ANALYZING EVERYDAY LIFE

Doing Nothing

Bernard McGrane suggests that we actually "do" sociology, rather than just study it. His book *The Un-TV and the 10 MPH Car* (1994) features exercises designed to help students experience the mundane, routine, and everyday level of society in a new way. This Data Workshop is an adaptation of one of his experiments.

Step 1: Conducting the Experiment
This exercise requires that you go to a relatively busy public space (a mall, street corner, park, or campus quad) and literally do nothing for ten minutes. That means just stand there and be unoccupied. Don't wait for someone, take a break, sightsee, or otherwise engage in a normal kind of activity. Also don't daydream or think about the past or the future; don't entertain yourself with plans or internal dialogues. Don't whistle, hum, fidget, look in your purse, play with your keys, take notes, or anything else that might distract you from just being there and doing nothing. Do, however, observe the reactions of others to you, and pay attention to your own thoughts and feelings during these ten minutes.

Step 2: Thinking and Writing about the Experience
After conducting the experiment, write a journal entry (casual in tone and written in the first person) describing

Doing Nothing How does standing in a crowded place and doing nothing change how you experience the ordinary world?

the experience and its meaning to you. Describe other people's reactions and your own thoughts in as much detail as possible.

The purpose of this exercise is to get you to see that changing your perspective (from "doing something" to "doing nothing") makes everything different. It helps turn the ordinary world into a strange place. It makes you more aware of your own sense (or lack) of self and how identity is constructed in society. You can't take for granted that you "just know" what other people are doing or thinking, or how the meaning of a situation is being defined or interpreted. Divested of your perspective as an everyday actor, you'll learn how the most mundane activities (like just standing around) can become major objects of critical inquiry.

There are two options for completing this Data Workshop.

- *Option 1 (informal)*: Complete the exercise and bring your journal entry to class. Discuss your findings with other students in small groups.

- *Option 2 (formal)*: Complete the exercise and write a two-to-three-page essay describing your findings. You may want to include snippets of your journal entry to illustrate your points.

Culture Shock

Peter Berger describes what kind of person becomes a sociologist: someone with a passionate interest in the world of human affairs, someone who is intense, curious, and daring in the pursuit of knowledge. "People who like to avoid shocking discoveries . . . should stay away from sociology," he warns (Berger 1963, p. 24). The sociologist will care about the issues of ultimate importance to humanity, as well as the most mundane occurrences of everyday existence.

Another way to gain a sociological perspective is to attempt to create in ourselves a sense of **culture shock**. Anthropologists use the term to describe the experience of visiting an exotic foreign culture. The first encounters with the local natives and their way of life can seem so strange to us that they produce a kind of disorientation and doubt about our ability to make sense of things. Putting all judgment aside for the moment, this state of mind can be very useful. For it is at this point, when we so completely lack an understanding of our surroundings, that we are truly able to perceive what is right in front of our eyes.

As sociologists, we try to create this effect without necessarily displacing ourselves geographically: we become curious and eager visitors to our own lives. We often find that what is familiar to us, if seen as if from an outsider's perspective, is just as exotic as some foreign culture, only we've forgotten this is true because it's our own and we know it so well. To better understand this state of mind, you might imagine what it would be like to return home from a desert island.

Consider the real-life case of Roger Lextrait, who worked for eight years as the caretaker of Palmyra, a small, remote island in the South Pacific. During that time, Lextrait had limited radio contact with Honolulu and Tahiti, and lived mostly in the company of his three dogs. He arrived with a boat full of canned food, 500 pounds of flour, thirty gallons of olive oil, and plenty of red wine. His provisions lasted for two years; after that, he managed to live off the land. He fished, hunted, sang, and played guitar to try to keep loneliness and boredom at bay. In 1992, when Lextrait moved to Palmyra, the internet only transmitted text, no images, and was used only by people in technology and higher education. By 2000, technology had changed exponentially, and over 350 million people were using the world wide web (users now number in the billions). When Lextrait finally reentered civilization, he experienced immense culture shock. "I had no idea that the cellular phone existed, I was so lost," he said. "I came back with different eyes—I was a different person (Maslin 2010)." You don't have to live on a deserted island to experience culture shock. Perhaps it's something you've also experienced, but didn't know what to call, if you've traveled or moved away to attend college.

The Sociological Imagination

One of the classic statements about the sociological perspective comes from C. Wright Mills (1916–1962), who describes a quality of mind that all great social analysts seem to possess: the **sociological imagination**. By this, he means the ability to understand "the intersection between biography and history," or the interplay of self and the world; this is sociology's task and its "promise" (Mills 1959).

We normally think of our own problems as being a private matter of character, chance, or circumstance, and we overlook the fact that these may be caused in part by, or are at least occurring within, a specific cultural and historical context. For example, if you can't find a job, you may feel that this is because you don't have the right skills,

C. Wright Mills

educational background, or experience. But it may also be the result of problems in the larger economy like outsourcing, downsizing, restrictive policies, changing technologies, or migration patterns. In other words, your individual unemployment may be part of a larger social and historical phenomenon.

> **culture shock** a sense of disorientation that occurs when you enter a radically new social or cultural environment
>
> **sociological imagination** a quality of the mind that allows us to understand the relationship between our individual circumstances and larger social forces

Most of the time we use psychological rather than sociological arguments to explain the way things are. For instance, if someone is carrying a lot of credit card debt, psychological reasoning might focus on his lack of self-control or inability to delay gratification. Sociological reasoning, however, might focus on the impact of cultural norms that promote a lifestyle beyond most people's means, or on economic changes that require more Americans to rely on credit cards because their wages have not kept up with inflation.

The sociological imagination searches for the link between micro and macro levels of analysis. We must look for how larger social forces, such as race, class, gender, religion, economics, or politics, are involved in creating the context of a person's life. Mills's characterization of sociology as the intersection between biography and history reminds us that the process works in both directions: while larger social forces influence individual lives, individual lives can affect society as well.

One of the most important benefits of using the sociological imagination is access to a world beyond our own immediate sphere, where we can discover radically different ways of experiencing life and interpreting reality. It can help us appreciate alternative viewpoints and understand how they may have come about. This, in turn, helps us to understand better how we developed our own values, beliefs, and attitudes.

Sociology asks us to see our familiar world in a new way, and doing so means we may need to abandon, or at least reevaluate, our opinions about that world and our place in it. It is tempting to believe that our opinions are widely held, that our worldview is the best or, at least, most common. Taking a sociological perspective forces us to see fallacies in our way of thinking. Because other individuals are different from us—belonging to different social groups, participating in different social institutions, living in different cities or countries, listening to different songs, watching different TV programs, engaging in different religious practices—they may look at the world very differently than we do. But a sociological perspective also allows us to see the other side of this equation: in cases where we assume that others are different from us, we may be surprised to find that their approach to their everyday world is quite similar to ours.

Levels of Analysis: Micro- and Macrosociology

Consider a photographer with state-of-the-art equipment. She could view her subject through either a zoom lens or a wide-angle lens. Through the zoom lens, she sees intricate details about the subject's appearance; through the wide-angle lens, she gets the "big picture" and a sense of the broader context in which the subject is located. Both views are valuable in understanding the subject, and both result in photographs of the same thing.

Sociological perspectives are like the photographer's lenses, allowing us different ways of looking at a common subject (Newman 2000). Sociologists can take a microsociological (zoom lens) perspective, a macrosociological (wide-angle lens) perspective, or any number of perspectives located on the continuum between the two (Figure 1.2).

microsociology the level of analysis that studies face-to-face and small-group interactions in order to understand how they affect the larger patterns and institutions of society

Microsociology concentrates on the interactions between individuals and the ways in which those interactions construct the larger patterns, processes, and institutions of society. As the word indicates ("micro" means small), microsociology looks at the smallest building blocks of society in order to understand its large-scale structure. A classic example of research that takes a micro approach is Pam Fishman's article "Interaction: The Work Women Do" (1978). Like many scholars who had observed the feminist movements of the 1960s and '70s, Fishman was concerned with issues of power and domination in male-female relationships: are men more powerful than women in our society? If so, how is this power created and maintained in everyday interactions? In her research, Fishman recorded and analyzed heterosexual couples' everyday conversations in their homes. She found some real differences in the conversational strategies of men and women, as the transcript in Figure 1.3 illustrates (page 16).

As you can see, the woman is having a difficult time getting her husband to join her in a discussion about the history of education. He frequently interrupts, changes the subject, fails to respond for long stretches, and even flips on the garbage disposal while she is speaking. She perseveres, trying to gain control of the conversation. Fishman recorded many such conversations and found a variety of patterns. One of her findings was that women ask nearly three times as many questions as men do. While other researchers have proposed that women's psychological insecurities are the reason for

Microsociology and Macrosociology Two views of the New York Public Library. Sociologists bring different levels of analysis to the study of people and groups. Microsociology zooms in to focus on individuals and their interactions in order to understand larger social structures. In contrast, macrosociology pulls back to study large-scale social processes and their effects on individuals and groups.

this finding, Fishman noted that women are in fact following a firmly held rule of conversational structure: when the speaker cannot guarantee that she will get a response, she is more likely to ask a question. Questions provoke answers, which makes them a useful conversational tool for those who may have less power in interpersonal relationships and in society at large. And women are more likely to be in this position than men. Thus, in her micro-level analysis of conversation, Fishman was able to see how macro-level ("macro" means large) phenomena like gender and power are manifested in everyday interactions.

Macrosociology approaches the study of society from the opposite direction, by looking at large-scale social structure in order to determine how it affects the lives of groups and individuals. If we wanted to stick to the same topic of gender inequality, we could find plenty of examples of research projects that take a macro approach; many deal with the workplace. Despite the gains made in recent years, the U.S. labor market is still predominantly sex segregated—that is, men and women are concentrated in different occupations. For example, in 2009, 98.2 percent of auto mechanics were male, whereas 96.8 percent of secretaries and administrative assistants were female (U.S. Department of Labor 2010a). This feature of social structure, some argue, has a direct effect on the experiences of individual workers, male and female.

A related example comes from the work of Christine Williams. She found that while women in male-dominated fields experience limits on their advancement, dubbed the

Glass Escalators Christine Williams's study of the occupational status of men in a female-dominated industry, such as teaching, is a good example of macrosociology.

"glass ceiling" effect, men in female-dominated occupations experience unusually rapid rates of upward mobility, the "glass escalator" (Williams 1995). Here, then, we see a macro approach to the topic of gender and power: large-scale features of social structure (patterns of occupational sex segregation) create the constraints within which individuals and groups (women and men in the workplace) experience successes or failures in their everyday lives.

As you can see, these two perspectives make different assumptions about how society works: the micro perspective assumes that society's larger structures are shaped through individual interactions, while the macro perspective assumes that society's larger structures shape those individual interactions. It is useful to think of these perspectives as being on a continuum with each other; while some sociologists adhere to radically micro or exclusively macro perspectives, most are somewhere in between. The next part of this chapter explores some specific theoretical traditions within sociology, and shows you where each falls along this continuum.

Sociology's Family Tree

Great thinkers have been trying to understand the world and our place in it since the beginning of time. Some have done this by developing **theories**: abstract propositions about how things are as well as how they should be. Sometimes we also refer to theories as *approaches*,

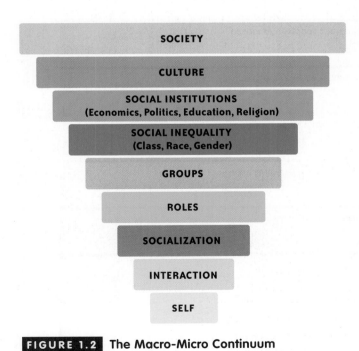

| SOCIETY |
| CULTURE |
| SOCIAL INSTITUTIONS (Economics, Politics, Education, Religion) |
| SOCIAL INEQUALITY (Class, Race, Gender) |
| GROUPS |
| ROLES |
| SOCIALIZATION |
| INTERACTION |
| SELF |

FIGURE 1.2 **The Macro-Micro Continuum**

Sociology covers a wide range of topics at different levels of analysis.

macrosociology the level of analysis that studies large-scale social structures in order to determine how they affect the lives of groups and individuals

theories in sociology, abstract propositions that explain the social world and make predictions about the future

TRANSCRIPT

1	F: I didn't know that. (=) Um you know that ((garbage disposal on)) that organizational	
	M: Hmmm? (=)	
2	F: stuff about Frederick Taylor and Bishopsgate and all that stuff? (=) ⌐ in the early	
	M: UmHm ((yes)) ⌐	
3	F: 1900's people were trying to fight favoritism to the schools (4)	
	M: That's what we needed. (18)		
4	F:	
	M: never did get my smoked oysters, I'm going to look for ((inaudible)) (14) Should we try the	
5	F: OK. That's a change. (72) Hmm. That's very interesting. Did	
	M: Riviera French Dressing? (=)	
6	F: you know that teachers used to be men until about the 1840's when it became a female occupa-	
	M:	
7	F: tion? (2) Because they needed more teachers because of the increased enroll-	
	M: Nhhmm ((no)) (=)	
8	F: ment. (5) Yeah relatively and the status (7)	
	M: And the the salaries started going down probably. (=)	
9	F: ⌐ There's two bottles I think ⌐	
	M: Um, it's weird. We're out of oil again. ⌐ Now we have to buy that. ⌐ ((whistling)) (8) Dressing	
10	F: It does yeah. (76) That's really interesting. They didn't start	
	M: looks good. See? (2) See babe? (1)	
11	F: using the test to measure and find the you know categorize and track people in American	
	M:	
12	F: schools until like the early 1900's after the army y'know introduced their array alpha things	
	M:	
13	F: to the draftees (?) And then it caught on with the schools and there was a lot of opposition right	
	M:	
14	F: at the beginning to that, which was as sophisticated as today's arguments. The same argu-	
	M:	
15	F: ments y'know (=) But it didn't work and they came (4) ⌐ heh	
	M: Yeah (=) Leslie White is probably right. ⌐	

FIGURE 1.3 **Gender and Conversational Patterns**

Conversation analysis allows us to see patterns like who interrupts more (men) and who asks more questions (women).

schools of thought, **paradigms**, or *perspectives*. Social theories, then, are guiding principles or abstract models that attempt to explain and predict the social world.

As we embark on the discussion of theory, it may be useful to think of sociology as having a "family tree" made up of real people who were living in a particular time and place, and who were related along various intertwining lines to other members of the same larger family tree. First, we will examine sociology's early historical roots. Then, as we follow the growth of the discipline, we will identify its major branches and trace the relationships between their offshoots and the other "limbs" that make up the entire family tree. Finally, we will examine some of the newest theoretical approaches and members of the family tree (Figure 1.4), and consider the possible future of sociological theory.

Sociology's Roots

The earliest Western social theorists focused on establishing society as an appropriate object of scientific scrutiny, which was itself a revolutionary concept. None of these early theorists were themselves sociologists (since the discipline didn't yet exist) but rather people from a variety of backgrounds—philosophers, theologians, economists, historians, or journalists—who were trying to look at society in a new way. In doing so, they laid the groundwork not only for the discipline as a whole but also for the different schools of thought that are still shaping sociology today.

AUGUSTE COMTE (1798–1857) was the first to provide a program for the scientific study of society, or a "social physics," as he labeled it. Comte, a French scientist, developed a theory of the progress of human thinking from its early theological and metaphysical stages toward a final "positive," or scientific, stage. **Positivism** seeks to identify laws that describe the behavior of a particular reality, like the laws of mathematics and physics, where you can gain knowledge of the world directly through your senses. Having grown up in the aftermath of the French Revolution and its lingering political instability, Comte felt that society needed positivist guidance toward both social progress and social order. After studying at an elite science and technology college, where he was introduced to the

Auguste Comte

newly discovered **scientific method** (see Chapter 2), he began to imagine a way of applying the methodology to social affairs. His ideas, featured in *Introduction to Positive Philosophy* (1842), became the foundation of a scientific discipline that would describe the laws of social phenomena and help control social life: he called it "sociology."

Although Comte is remembered today mainly for coining the term, he played a significant role in the development of the discipline. His efforts to distinguish appropriate methods and topics for sociologists provided the kernel of a discipline. Other social thinkers advanced his work: Harriet Martineau and Herbert Spencer in England and Emile Durkheim in France.

HARRIET MARTINEAU (1802–76) was born in England to progressive parents who made sure their daughter was well educated. She became a journalist and political economist, proclaiming views that were radical for her time: endorsing labor unions, the abolition of slavery, and women's suffrage. Though Martineau never married, she preferred to be addressed as "Mrs."—not because she wished for a husband (indeed, she strongly rejected marriage as a tool for the subjugation of women) but because she recognized that the title conveyed respect and status in her culture. She felt that respect was denied to her as a single woman.

In 1835 "Mrs." Martineau traveled to the United States to judge the new democracy on its own terms rather than by European standards. But she was disappointed: by condoning slavery and denying full citizenship rights to women and blacks, the American experiment was, in her eyes, flawed and hypocritical. She wrote two books describing her observations, *Society in America* (1837) and *Retrospect of Western Travel* (1838), both critical of American leadership and culture. By holding the United States to its own publicly stated democratic standards, rather than seeing the country from an ethnocentric British perspective, she was a precursor to the naturalistic sociologists who

Harriet Martineau

> **paradigm** a set of assumptions, theories, and perspectives that make up a way of understanding social reality
>
> **positivism** the theory, developed by Auguste Comte, that sense perceptions are the only valid source of knowledge
>
> **scientific method** a procedure for acquiring knowledge that emphasizes collecting concrete data through observation and experiment

would establish the discipline in America. In 1853, Martineau made perhaps her most important contribution to sociology: she translated Comte's *Introduction to Positive Philosophy* into English, thus making his ideas accessible in England and America.

Herbert Spencer

HERBERT SPENCER (1820–1903) was primarily responsible for the establishment of sociology in Britain and America. Although Spencer did not receive academic training, he grew up in a highly individualistic family and was encouraged to think and learn on his own. His interests leaned heavily toward physical science, and, instead of attending college, Spencer chose to become a railway engineer. When railway work dried up, he turned to journalism and eventually worked for a major periodical in London. There Spencer became acquainted with leading English academics and began to publish his own thoughts in book form.

In 1862, Spencer drew up a list of what he called "first principles" (in a book by that name), and near the top of the list was the notion of evolution driven by natural selection. (Charles Darwin is the best-known proponent of the theory, but the idea of evolution was in wide circulation before Darwin made it famous.) Spencer proposed that societies, like biological organisms, evolve through time by adapting to changing conditions, with less successful adaptations falling by the wayside. He coined the phrase "survival of the fittest," and his social philosophy is sometimes known as **social Darwinism**. In the late 1800s, Spencer's work, including *The Study of Sociology* (1873) and *The Principles of Sociology* (1897), was virtually synonymous with sociology in the English-speaking world. The scope and volume of his writing served to announce sociology as a serious discipline and laid the groundwork for the next generation of theorists, whose observations of large-scale social change would bring a new viewpoint to social theory.

social Darwinism the application of the theory of evolution and the notion of "survival of the fittest" to the study of society

structural functionalism a paradigm that begins with the assumption that society is a unified whole that functions because of the contributions of its separate structures

mechanical solidarity term developed by Emile Durkheim to describe the type of social bonds present in premodern, agrarian societies, in which shared traditions and beliefs created a sense of social cohesion

Macrosociological Theory

Theorists in late-nineteenth-century Europe were living during extraordinary times. They were attempting to explain social order, social change, and social inequality—especially as they watched their world changing around them in the rapid transformation of the Industrial Revolution and witnessed the changes wrought by the French and American Revolutions, each of which had overthrown monarchist rule to establish a democracy in its place. These were changes on the grandest of scale in the macro order of society. Frequently referred to as classical sociology, the theories that arose during this period reflect the broad subject matter of a sweeping era.

Structural Functionalism

Structural functionalism, or functionalist theory, was the dominant theoretical perspective within sociology well into the mid-twentieth century. New (or neo-) functionalists continue to apply their own vision of the theory to study a wide variety of social phenomena today.

FOUNDER AND KEY CONTRIBUTIONS Emile Durkheim (1858–1917) is the central figure in functionalist theory. He was born into a close-knit and deeply religious Jewish family who instilled in him a strong sense of morality (not just as an abstract concept but as a concrete influence on social relations) and a strong work ethic. After witnessing the ravages of the Franco-Prussian War (1870–71), he hoped that applied science could stabilize and revitalize France in the aftermath of its devastating defeat. He did not believe that traditional, abstract moral philosophy was effective in increasing understanding and bringing about social change, so he turned instead to the concrete science of sociology as represented in Comte's work.

In his first major study, *The Division of Labor in Society* (1893), Durkheim stated that social bonds were present in all types of societies but that different types of societies created different types of bonds. He suggested that the **mechanical solidarity** experienced by people in a simple, agricultural society bound them together on the basis of shared traditions, beliefs, and experiences. In industrial societies, where factory work was becoming increasingly

Emile Durkheim

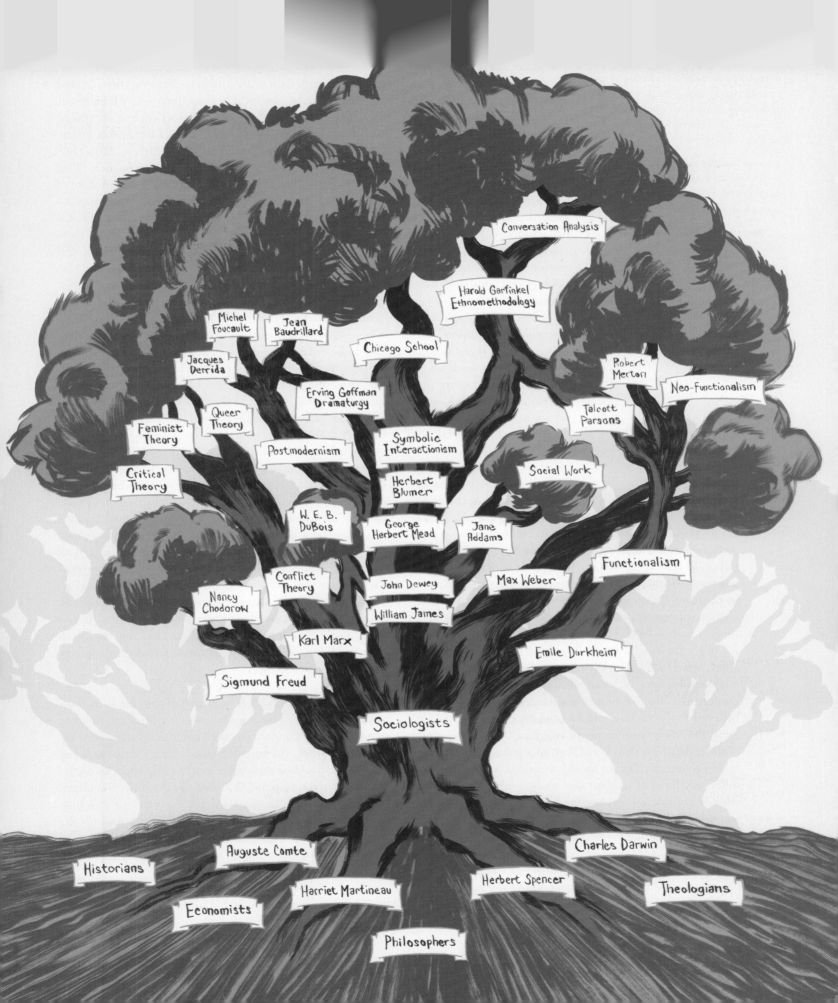

organic solidarity term developed by Emile Durkheim to describe the type of social bonds present in modern societies, based on difference, interdependence, and individual rights

anomie "normlessness"; term used to describe the alienation and loss of purpose that result from weaker social bonds and an increased pace of change

solidarity the degree of integration or unity within a particular society; the extent to which individuals feel connected to other members of their group

sacred The holy, divine, or supernatural

profane The ordinary, mundane, or everyday

collective effervescence an intense energy in shared events where people feel swept up in something larger than themselves

collective conscience the shared morals and beliefs that are common to a group and which foster social solidarity

empirical based on scientific experimentation or observation

specialized, **organic solidarity** prevailed: people's bonds were based on the tasks they performed, interdependence, and individual rights. Both types of solidarity have interpersonal bonds—just with different qualities.

Durkheim believed that even the most individualistic actions had sociological explanations and set out to establish a scientific methodology for studying these actions. He chose for his case study the most individualistic of actions, suicide, and used statistical data to show that suicides were related to social factors such as religious affiliation, marital status, and employment. Explaining a particular suicide by focusing exclusively on the victim's psychological makeup neglected the impact of social bonds. According to Durkheim in his now-classic study *Suicide* (1897), even the darkest depression has its roots in an individual's connections to the social world, or rather his lack of connection. He theorized that suicide was one result of **anomie**, a sense of disconnection brought about by the changing conditions of modern life. The more firmly anchored a person was to family, religion, and the workplace, the less anomie he was likely to experience.

In his final major study, *The Elementary Forms of Religious Life* (1912), Durkheim suggested that religion was a powerful source of social **solidarity**, or unity, because it reinforced collective bonds and shared moral values. He believed that society could be understood through examining the most basic forms of religion. Durkheim's study of the indigenous peoples of Australia led him to a universal definition of religion: though religious traditions might differ, any form of religion was unified in its definition of what is considered to be **sacred** and **profane**. Every person who follows a particular set of beliefs and practices will "unite into one single moral community" (Durkheim 1912/1995, p. 44).

Durkheim also noted that rituals or ceremonies that brought people together into community were created and practiced to enhance the feeling of emotional unity that reaf-

firmed solidarity and social order. When people gathered for religious events, their individual acts, taken together, created a feeling of being swept up in something larger than themselves. It made them feel as if they had entered a "special world inhabited by exceptionally intense forces that invade and transform" them (Durkheim 1912/1995, p. 220). Durkheim referred to this as **collective effervescence**. This sense of participants being transported by a shared wave of energy can happen during a Catholic mass, for instance, as much as it can by attending a live concert or sporting event at a sold-out arena.

A distinction between the sacred and the profane, and the creation and participation in shared ritual activity creates a **collective conscience** (or collective consciousness) that contains the morality, the cosmology, and the beliefs "common to the group" (Durkheim 1912/1995, p. 379). The shared beliefs and values that make up the collective conscience of the group are what make social solidarity possible, but they must be frequently renewed through the ritual, through which a group "revitalizes the sense it has of itself and its unity" (Durkheim 1912/1995, p. 379). Durkheim believed that this process happens in all societies, whether those united through a common religious tradition or through shared secular beliefs and practices.

Durkheim's attempt to establish sociology as an important, independent academic discipline was enormously successful. He not only made significant contributions to the existing literature, but he also demonstrated the effectiveness of using scientific, **empirical** methods to study "social reality," essentially validating Comte's proposal from half a century earlier. Durkheim became the first professor of social science in France at the University of Bordeaux in 1887 and later won a similar appointment at the Sorbonne in Paris, the very heart of French academic life. Today, Durkheim's eminence in the social sciences is as strong as ever, and his ideas are still applied and extended by contemporary theorists.

ORIGINAL PRINCIPLES The origins of structural functionalism can be traced back to the roots of sociology. Auguste Comte proposed that society itself could and should be studied. Herbert Spencer added the idea that societies are living organisms that grow and evolve, just like other species on the planet. As the discipline of biology might study the physical organism of the human body, the discipline of sociology could study social organisms in the world of human development. Durkheim integrated and advanced these insights into a comprehensive theory for understanding the nature of society.

There are two main principles of functionalism. First, society is conceived as a stable, ordered system made up of interrelated parts, or **structures**. Second, each structure has a function that contributes to the continued stability or equilibrium of the unified whole. Structures are identified as social institutions like the family, the educational system, politics, the economy, and religion. They meet society's needs by performing different functions, and every function is necessary to maintain social order and stability. Any disorganization or **dysfunction** in a structure leads to change and a new equilibrium—if one structure is transformed, the others must also adjust. For example, if families fail to discipline children, schools, churches, and the courts must take up the slack.

It may seem contradictory that a theory concerned with order and stability would emerge in a discipline that arose in a period of rapid social change. But it is important to remember that change had previously occurred much more slowly, and that one response to rapid social change is to try to understand what had come before—stability, order, and equilibrium.

OFFSHOOTS Structural functionalism was the dominant theoretical perspective in Europe for much of the early twentieth century. It was exported and updated by American functionalists, who increased its popularity and helped spread its reach well into the 1960s. Talcott Parsons (1902–1979), for example, elaborated on the theory and applied it to modern society, specifying some of the functions that social structures might fulfill in contemporary life. A healthy society must provide a means for people to adapt to their environment; for example, families, schools, and religious institutions working together to socialize children. A functional society includes opportunities for success; for example, promoting education to help its members pursue and realize their goals. For society to survive, there must be social cohesion; for example, shared religious and moral values.

Another modern American functionalist, Robert Merton (1910–2003), delineated the theory even further, identifying manifest and latent functions for different social structures.

Manifest functions are the obvious, intended functions of a social structure, while **latent functions** are the less obvious, perhaps unintended functions. For example, the manifest functions of education are to prepare future members of society by teaching them how to read and write, and by instructing them on society's system of norms, values, and laws. However, education has a latent function as well, which is to keep kids busy and out of trouble eight hours a day, five days a week, for twelve years (or longer). Do not doubt that this is also an important contribution to social order!

Functionalism's influence waned in the late twentieth century, but did not die out. A "neofunctionalist" movement, begun in the 1980s and 1990s, attempts to reconstruct functionalist theories so that they remain relevant in a rapidly changing world. Theorists such as Neil Smelser and Jeffrey Alexander have attempted to modify functionalist theory to better incorporate problems like racial and ethnic identity in a diverse society (Alexander 1988; Alexander and Smelser 1998; Smelser 1985).

ADVANTAGES AND CRITIQUES One of the great advantages of functionalism is its inclusion of all social institutions. Functionalism attempts to provide a universal social theory, a way of explaining society in one comprehensive model. Part of functionalism's appeal may also lie in its ability to bring order to a potentially disorderly world. Were it not for some of the volcanic social upheavals of recent history—the civil rights, antiwar, and women's liberation movements are not easily explained using this model—functionalist theory might still reign supreme in American sociology. Functionalism, generally preoccupied with stability, takes the position that only dysfunction can create social change. This conservative bias is part of a larger problem with the theory: Functionalism provides little insight into social processes because its model of society is static rather than dynamic. Its focus on the macro level also means that functionalism has less interest in explaining independent human action; there is no apparent approach to the lives of individuals except as part of social institutions.

Functionalism's explanations of social inequality are especially unsatisfying: if poverty, racism, and sexism exist, they must serve a function for society; they must be necessary

> **structure** a social institution that is relatively stable over time and that meets the needs of society by performing functions necessary to maintain social order and stability
>
> **dysfunction** a disturbance to or undesirable consequence of some aspect of the social system
>
> **manifest functions** the obvious, intended functions of a social structure for the social system
>
> **latent functions** the less obvious, perhaps unintended functions of a social structure

Talcott Parsons   **Robert Merton**

conflict theory a paradigm that sees social conflict as the basis of society and social change, and emphasizes a materialist view of society, a critical view of the status quo, and a dynamic model of historical change

social inequality the unequal distribution of wealth, power, or prestige among members of a society

communism a political system based on the collective ownership of the means of production; opposed to capitalism

conflict generated by the competition between different class groups for scarce resources and the source of all social change, according to Karl Marx

capitalism an economic system based on private ownership of the means of production and characterized by competition, the profit motive, and wage labor

means of production anything that can create wealth: money, property, factories, and other types of businesses, and the infrastructure necessary to run them

and inevitable. This view is problematic for many. Sociologist Herbert Gans, in a critical essay (1971), reviews the functions of poverty for society. The poor, for example, do our "dirty work," filling the menial, low-wage jobs that are necessary to keep society running smoothly but that others refuse to do. The poor provide a market for used and off-price goods, and keep thrift stores and social welfare agencies in business. They have symbolic value as well, allowing those higher in the social hierarchy to feel compassion toward the "deserving" poor as well as feeling threatened by the "undeserving" poor, who are often seen as dangerous social deviants. Ultimately, the circular reasoning that characterizes functionalist thought turns out to be its biggest problem: the mere persistence of an institution should not be seen as an adequate explanation for its existence.

Conflict Theory

Conflict theory is the second major school of thought in sociology. Like structural functionalism, it's a macro-level approach to understanding social life that dates to mid-nineteenth-century Europe. As conflict theory developed, however, its emphasis on **social inequality** as the basic characteristic of society helped to answer some of the critiques of structural functionalism.

FOUNDER AND KEY CONTRIBUTIONS The work of Karl Marx (1818–1883), a German social philosopher, cultural commentator, and political activist, was the inspiration for conflict theory, so sometimes the terms "conflict theory" and "Marxism" are used interchangeably in the social sciences. Marx's ideas have become more well known to the world as the basis for **communism**, the political system adopted by numerous countries (such as China, North Korea, and Cuba) that have often been viewed as enemies of democracy and the United States. This association has led many to a narrow belief that Marx was nothing more than a misguided agitator

Karl Marx

who helped cause more than a century of political turmoil. It is important to separate Marx himself from the current, political application of communism, and to consider the possibility that he might not have supported the ways political leaders used his ideas decades later. Sociologists have found that Marx's theory continues to provide a powerful tool for understanding social phenomena. The idea that **conflict** between social groups is central to the workings of society and serves as the engine of social change is one of the most vital perspectives in sociology today.

Marx grew up in a modernizing, industrializing yet politically and religiously conservative monarchy; this, plus the fact that his was a restless, argumentative personality, accounts in great part for his social theory. Marx studied law and philosophy in Bonn and Berlin, receiving a Ph.D. in 1841. His personal ties with radicals effectively barred him from entering academia, so he turned to journalism, writing stories that often antagonized government censors and officials.

For most of his life, Marx led an economically fragile existence. He managed to maintain a tenuous middle-class lifestyle, but only with financial support from his close friend and chief intellectual collaborator Friedrich Engels, who studied the conditions of the English working class. Marx's own circumstances may have sparked his interest in social inequality, or the uneven and often unfair distribution of resources (in this case, wealth) in society, but he never experienced firsthand the particular burdens and difficulties of the working class.

The Industrial Revolution was a time of rapid social change, when large numbers of people were moving from an agricultural life in rural areas to manufacturing jobs in urban areas. Technological advances and a wage-based economy promised an age of prosperity and abundance, but they created new kinds of poverty, crime, and disease. Marx believed that most of those problems were a result of **capitalism**, the emerging economic system based on the private for-profit operation of industry. He proposed a radical alternative to the inherent inequalities of this system in the *Manifesto of the Communist Party* (1848), perhaps his most famous book.

In industrial society, the forces of capitalism were creating distinct social and economic classes, exacerbating the disparities between the wealthy and the poor. Marx felt that this would inevitably lead to class struggle between those who owned the **means of production** (anything that could create more wealth: money, property, factories, other types of businesses) and those who worked for them. He argued that the most important factor in social life was a person's relationship to the means of production; in other words, whether someone was a worker, and thus a member of the **proletariat**, or an owner, and thus a member of the **bourgeoisie**. Everything of value in society resulted from human labor, which was the proletariat's most valuable asset. Yet, they suffered from what Marx called **alienation** because they were unable to directly benefit from the fruits of their own labor. Workers were paid wages, but it was the factory owners who grew rich as a result of their toil.

The powerful few in the bourgeoisie were not only wealthy but also enjoyed social privilege and power. They were able to protect their interests, preserve their positions, and pass along their advantages to their heirs. The proletariat were often so absorbed in making a living that they were less apt to protest the conditions that led to their oppression. But eventually, Marx believed, the oppression would become unbearable, and the proletariat would rise up against the bourgeoisie, abolishing capitalism for good. He envisioned in its place a classless society—**socialism**—in which each person contributed to and benefited from the public good. Freed from oppressive conditions, individuals would then be able to pursue higher interests such as art and education and eventually live in a more egalitarian, utopian society. But in order to achieve such a state, the oppressed must first recognize how the current system worked against them.

In 1849, Marx withdrew from political activity in order to concentrate on writing *Das Kapital* (edited by Engels and published in 1890). The multivolume book provided a thorough exposition of his program for social change, which later became the foundation of political systems such as communism and socialism. Marx intended it to be his main contribution to sociology, but developments in the social sciences have placed more emphasis on his earlier writings. Because Marx held such radical ideas, his thought was not immediately embraced by sociologists in general. It was not until the 1960s when conflict theory became a dominant perspective, that Marx was truly received as a giant of sociology.

ORIGINAL PRINCIPLES Conflict theory proposes that conflict and tension are basic facts of social life, and suggests that people have disagreements over goals and values and are involved in struggles over both resources and power. The theory thus focuses on the processes of dominance, competition, upheaval, and social change.

Conflict theory takes a materialist view of society (focused on labor practices and economic reality) and extends it to other social inequalities. Marx maintained that economic productivity was related to other processes in society, including political and intellectual life. The wealthy and powerful bourgeoisie controlled major social institutions, reinforcing the class structure so that the state, education, religion, and even the family were organized to represent their interests. Conflict theory takes a critical stance toward existing social arrangements and attempts to expose their inner workings.

Because the **ideology**, or belief system, that permeated society arose from the values of the ruling class, beliefs that seemed to be widely held were actually a kind of justification that helped to rationalize and explain the status quo. Most people readily accepted the prevailing ideology, despite its failure to represent the reality of their lives. Marx referred to this acceptance as **false consciousness**, a denial of the truth that allowed for the perpetuation of the inequalities inherent in the class structure. For example, he is often quoted as saying, "Religion is the opiate of the masses." This is not a criticism of religion as much as it is a criticism of the use of religion to create false consciousness in the working class. Encouraged in their piety, the proletariat focus on the happiness promised in the afterlife rather than on deprivations suffered in this world. Indeed, heaven is seen as a reward for patiently suffering those deprivations. How does this serve the interests of the ruling class? By keeping the working class from demanding better conditions in this life.

Conflict theory sees the transformation of society over time as inevitable. Marx argued that the only way to change the status quo was for the masses to attain **class consciousness**, or revolutionary consciousness. This can happen only when people recognize how society works and challenge those in power. He believed that social change would occur when there was enough tension and conflict. Marx proposed a **dialectical model** of historical or social change, whereby

proletariat workers; those who have no means of production of their own and so are reduced to selling their labor power in order to live

bourgeoisie owners; the class of modern capitalists who own the means of production and employ wage laborers

alienation the sense of dissatisfaction the modern worker feels as a result of producing goods that are owned and controlled by someone else, according to Marx

socialism a political system based on state ownership or control of principal elements of the economy in order to reduce levels of social inequality

ideology a system of beliefs, attitudes, and values that directs a society and reproduces the status quo of the bourgeoisie

false consciousness a denial of the truth on the part of the oppressed when they fail to recognize the interests of the ruling class in their ideology

class consciousness the recognition of social inequality on the part of the oppressed, leading to revolutionary action

dialectical model Marx's model of historical change, whereby two extreme positions come into conflict and create some new third thing between them

thesis the existing social arrangements in a dialectical model

antithesis the opposition to the existing arrangements in a dialectical model

synthesis the new social system created out of the conflict between thesis and antithesis in a dialectical model

critical theory a contemporary form of conflict theory that criticizes many different systems and ideologies of domination and oppression

feminist theory a theoretical approach that looks at gender inequities in society and the way that gender structures the social world

queer theory a paradigm that proposes that categories of sexual identity are social constructs and that no sexual category is fundamentally either deviant or normal

two extreme positions would eventually necessitate some kind of compromise between them: the resulting "middle ground" would mean that society had actually moved forward. Any existing social arrangement, called the **thesis**, would inevitably generate its opposite, or **antithesis**, and the contradictions and conflicts between the two would lead to an altogether new social arrangement, or **synthesis**.

OFFSHOOTS Marx's work has been reinterpreted and applied in various ways, and conflict theory has evolved within the greater intellectual community. Despite Marx's single-minded focus on economic exploitation and transformation, his ideas have helped inspire theorists interested in power and inequality.

One of the most widely adopted forms of modern Marxism is called **critical theory** (also sometimes referred to as the Frankfurt School or neo-Marxism). From the 1930s to the 1960s, critical theory was arguably at the cutting edge of social theory. Critical theorists were among the first to see the importance of mass communications and popular culture as powerful ideological tools in capitalist societies. They coined the term "culture industries" to refer to these increasingly important social institutions, which came to dominate and permeate social life (Adorno and Horkheimer 1979). They also criticized the growing consumerism associated with the spread of capitalism, believing that this could ultimately lead to a decline in personal freedom and the decay of democracy (Marcuse 1964/1991). Critical theory influenced several generations of radical thinkers throughout Europe and the United States, inspiring the cultural studies movement and the postmodernists, who were considered the cutting edge of social theory in the 1980s and '90s (Habermas 1984, 1987).

Other modern perspectives have taken conflict theory's insights on economic inequality and adapted them to the study of contemporary inequalities of race, gender, and sexuality (Crenshaw et al. 1996; Matsuda et al. 1993). Beginning with the pioneering work of W.E.B. DuBois, sociology started to focus on inequalities of race and ethnicity,

inspiring important studies about the causes and consequences of prejudice and discrimination, and helping to propel momentous social changes resulting from the Civil Rights Movement of the 1960s.

Feminist theory developed alongside the twentieth-century women's rights movement. By applying assumptions about gender inequality to various social institutions—the family, education, the economy, or mass media—feminist theory allows for a new way of understanding those institutions and the changing role of gender in contemporary society. Theorists such as Judith Butler (1999), bell hooks (2003), and Catharine MacKinnon (2005) link gender with inequality in other social hierarchies—race and ethnicity, class, and sexual orientation—and argue that gender and power are inextricably intertwined in our society.

The gay and lesbian rights movement that gained momentum in the 1970s and 80s inspired a new set of theoretical and conceptual tools for social scientists: **queer theory**. Queer theory proposes that categories of sexuality—homo, hetero, bi, trans—should be viewed as "social constructs" (Seidman 2003). It asserts that no sexual category is fundamentally deviant or normal; we create such definitions, so we can change them as well. Indeed, some theorists, such as Marjorie Garber (1997), argue that strict categories themselves are no longer relevant and that more

The Frankfurt School Critical theorist Theodore Adorno with his colleagues in Frankfurt.

bell hooks

fluid notions of identity should replace conventional dichotomies like gay/straight. In this way, queer theory is related to another theoretical perspective we'll be examining later: postmodernism.

ADVANTAGES AND CRITIQUES One of Karl Marx's great contributions to the social sciences is the principle of **praxis**, or practical action: intellectuals should act on what they believe. Marx wished not only to describe the world but also to change it. Indeed, Marxist ideas have been important in achieving change through many twentieth-century social movements, including civil rights, antiwar, women's rights, gay rights, animal rights, environmentalism, and multiculturalism. If these groups had not protested the status quo, we might never have addressed some of the century's social problems. Conflict theory is useful in understanding not only macro-level social issues (like systematic discrimination against minority groups), but also micro-level personal interactions (like those between bosses and employees).

Conflict theory stands in sharp contrast to structural functionalism. Conflict theory argues that a social arrangement's existence does not mean that it's beneficial; it may merely represent the interests of those in power. The theory challenges the status quo and emphasizes the need for social upheaval. In focusing on tension and conflict, however, conflict theory can often ignore those parts of society that are truly orderly, stable, and enduring. Although society certainly has its share of disagreements, there are also shared values and common beliefs that hold it together. Conflict theory can be criticized for overlooking these less-controversial dimensions of social reality.

Weberian Theory

Max Weber (1864–1920) was another important European macrosociological theorist during the Industrial Revolution. His work forms another large branch of sociology's family tree, and his ideas continue to inspire in their current application, yet he is not always included among the three *major* branches of the discipline. Weberian theory is neither a minor branch of sociology, nor is it considered merely an offshoot of one or the other major branches of the tree. It draws from a background shared by the other macro theorists but forms its own independent limb.

Weber grew up in the German city of Berlin. His father was a successful entrepreneur and member of a traditional and authoritarian aristocracy. Both his parents were Protestants and descendants of victims of religious persecution. Weber, though not religious himself, exhibited the relentless work ethic held in high regard by devout Protestants. Although he was sickly and withdrawn as a young man, work served as a way for him to rebel against his father and the leisure classes in general. He studied law and history and worked as a lawyer while establishing his credentials for a university teaching position.

While pursuing his studies, Weber remained at home and financially dependent on his father, a situation he came to resent. Eventually he broke away, marrying his second cousin in 1893 and beginning a career teaching economics at the University of Freiburg and later the University of Heidelberg. Weber rapidly established himself as a prominent member of the German intellectual scene. He might have continued in this manner had it not been for a disastrous visit from his parents in 1897, during which Weber fought bitterly with his father and threw him out of the house. When his father died a month later, Weber suffered a nervous breakdown that left him unable to work for several years. The strain of these events and years of incessant labor had apparently caught up with him. He eventually recovered and resumed his intense scholarship, but the breakdown left Weber disillusioned with the strict academic regimen.

Weber subsequently expressed a pessimistic view of social forces, such as the work ethic, that shaped modern life. Like other social theorists of his time, Weber was interested in the shift from a more traditional society to a modern industrial one. Perhaps his most overriding concern was with the process of **rationalization**, or the application of economic logic to all spheres of human activity. In *Economy and Society* (1921), Weber proposed that modern industrialized societies were characterized by efficient, goal-oriented, rule-governed **bureaucracies**. He believed that individual behavior was increasingly driven by such bureaucratic goals, which had become more important motivational factors than

Max Weber

Changing the World

Racism and Sexism in Sociology's Family Tree

The sociology of the early twentieth century would seem markedly Eurocentric, racist, and sexist by today's standards, but so was the society in which sociologists then worked and lived. From its European roots in the early 1800s until the establishment of the American branch in the 1920s and 30s, the Western field of sociology had but one nonwhite man among its membership, and very few women.

William Edward Burghardt (W.E.B.) DuBois was a notable pioneer in the study of race relations as a professor of sociology at the University of Chicago and one of the most influential African American leaders of his time. After becoming the first African American to earn a Ph.D. from

W.E.B. DuBois (1868–1963)
DuBois called the United States a country of "magnificent possibilities" but one that was "selling its birthright." He praised America for its noble souls and generous people and was grateful for the education the country provided him, but he also pointed out its ongoing history of injustices, crimes, and mistakes.

Harvard University, DuBois did groundbreaking research on the history of the slave trade, post–Civil War reconstruction, the problems of urban ghetto life, and the nature of black American society. DuBois was so brilliant and prolific that it is often said that all subsequent studies of race and racial inequality in America depend to some degree on his work. Throughout his life, DuBois was involved in various forms of social activism. He was an indispensable forerunner in the Civil Rights Movement; among his many civic and political achievements, DuBois was a founding member, in 1909, of the National Association for the Advancement of Colored People (NAACP), an organization committed to the cause of ending racism and injustice.

While it is unlikely that any of us will have the same broad, enduring impact on our society as DuBois, many of us will follow in his footsteps in some way. If you study race or social inequality as part of your college work, or participate in a group working to end discrimination against the disabled, or stop hate crimes against gays and lesbians, or join your university's chapter of MEChA (Movimiento Estudiantil Chicano de Aztlan), the Black Student Union, the Feminist Society, or the Diversity Club, you are doing what DuBois hoped we all would: use our academic knowledge to enact social change.

---

traditions, values, or emotions. Weber's classic sociological discussion of the origins of the capitalist system, *The Protestant Ethic and the Spirit of Capitalism* (1904), concluded with the image of people trapped by their industrious way of life in what he called an **iron cage** of bureaucratic rules. He believed that contemporary life was filled with **disenchantment** (similar to Durkheim's concept of anomie and Marx's of alienation) as the inevitable

iron cage Max Weber's pessimistic description of modern life, in which we are caught in bureaucratic structures that control our lives through rigid rules and rationalization

disenchantment the rationalization of modern society.

result of the dehumanizing features of the bureaucracies that dominated the modern social landscape.

Weber provided invaluable insights into the nature of society that continue to inspire sociologists today. The key concepts we have touched on here will be expanded as we apply Weberian theory to a variety of topics in upcoming chapters of the text. In addition to making some of the most important contributions to theory within the discipline, Weber was also influential in improving research methods by suggesting that researchers should avoid imposing their own opinions on their scientific analysis; we'll examine these ideas more closely in Chapter 2.

Weber's work served as a bridge between early social theory, which focused primarily on the macro level of

Jane Addams was another pioneer in the field of sociology whose numerous accomplishments range from the halls of academia to the forefront of social activism. As a member of the sociology department at the University of Chicago, Addams was among a small handful of women faculty in America. She was one of the first proponents of applied sociology—addressing the most pressing problems of her day through hands-on work with the people and places that were the subject of her research. This hands-on approach is perhaps best demonstrated by Hull House, the Chicago community center she established in 1889 to offer shelter, medical care, legal advice, training, and education to new immigrants, single mothers, and the poor. As a result of her commitment to delivering support and services where they were most needed, Addams is often considered the founder of what is now a separate field outside the discipline: social work.

Addams is recognized for other significant achievements in her career as an academic and activist. She was a founder of two important organizations that continue to fight for freedom and equality today: the American Civil Liberties Union (ACLU) and, along with W.E.B. DuBois, the NAACP. She served as the president of the Women's International League for Peace and Freedom, and in 1931 became the first American woman to receive the Nobel Peace Prize.

When it comes to making sociological insights work toward social change, Jane Addams set high standards for us to follow. She is an inspiration for sociology and social work students alike, many of whom will find themselves drawn to the areas of social welfare, education, counseling, community organizing, the judicial system, and other "helping" professions, where they can feel a part of the effort toward creating a different and better society.

Jane Addams (1860–1935)
"I do not believe that women are better than men. We have not wrecked railroads, nor corrupted legislature, nor done many unholy things that men have done; but then we must remember that we have not had the chance."

society, and subsequent theories that focused more intently on the micro level. He was interested in how individual motivation led to certain social actions, and how those actions helped shape society as a whole. Unlike Marx and Durkheim, Weber was cautious about attributing any reality to social institutions or forces independent of individual action and meaningful thought. He invoked the German term *verstehen* ("empathic understanding") to describe how a social scientist should study human action: with a kind of scientific empathy for actors' experiences, intentions, and actions. In this way, Weber helped lay the groundwork for the third major school of thought.

Microsociological Theory

As the twentieth century dawned and the careers of the macro theorists like Durkheim, Marx, and Weber matured, political, cultural, and academic power began to shift from Europe. As manifested by the waves of emigrants leaving the Old World for the New, America was seen as the land of opportunity, both material and intellectual. So it was in

verstehen "empathic understanding"; Weber's term to describe good social research, which tries to understand the meanings that individual social actors attach to various actions and events

Eurocentrism and Sociological Theory

You might get the impression from this chapter that the major sociological theorists were all either European or American. In fact, some ideas central to sociological theory were proposed in Asia, Africa, and the Middle East centuries before Marx, Weber, and Durkheim were even born, but we give these Western thinkers all the credit. Why?

Both the social world and social theory are often **Eurocentric**: they tend to privilege Europe and the West over other cultures. This means that hierarchies of global power, in which superpowers like the United States and former colonial rulers like Britain and France dominate, are replicated in academic disciplines like sociology. Scholars who work against inequality and exploitation should note this distressing irony.

One influential non-Western thinker was Ibn Khaldun (1332–1406), an Arab Muslim philosopher and politician

Ibn Khaldun

who lived in fourteenth-century North Africa. His coining of the term *as sabi-yah*, or "social cohesion," precedes Durkheim's work on the same subject by more than 500 years, and his argument that larger social and historical forces shape individual lives predates Mills's insight about sociology as "the intersection of biography and history" by almost

600 years! Yet, Khaldun is rarely credited for proposing sociology as a discipline—*ilm alumran*, he called it, or "the science of civilization." This honor is reserved for French scholar Auguste Comte, working centuries later in the West.

Also overlooked in conventional histories of sociology are Indian scholar Benoy Sarkar (1887–1949), Filipino activist and poet José Rizal (1861–1896), and Japanese folklorist Kunio Yanagita (1875–1962)—all of whom applied sociological insights to the problems of their nations. Sarkar explored India's religious divisions, Rizal analyzed the Philippines' fight for independence from Spain, and Yanagita used qualitative methods to explore Japan's culture and its longstanding isolationism. They have received virtually no notice for their achievements outside their own countries (Alatas and Sinha 2001).

Filipino sociologist Clarence Batan (2004) argues that Western theorists like Marx, Weber, and Durkheim may inspire non-Western scholars but that their theories arose in response to specific social problems that were particular to Western societies. Non-Western societies face different issues, including the legacy of colonialism imposed by the Western countries from which those classical sociological theories sprang. Batan calls for sociologists in non-Western countries to respond to the needs of their societies by developing new theoretical frameworks that take postcolonial realities into account. Batan himself, along with other contemporary non-Western sociologists, works toward this goal every day in his research and teaching. Shouldn't your sociology professors do the same?

---

the twentieth century, and increasingly in the United States, that the discipline of sociology continued to develop and the ideas of its third major school of thought began to coalesce.

Eurocentric the tendency to favor European or Western histories, cultures, and values over other non-Western societies

symbolic interactionism a paradigm that sees interaction and meaning as central to society and assumes that meanings are not inherent but are created through interaction

Symbolic Interactionism

Sociology's third major school of thought, **symbolic interactionism** (or interactionist theory), proved its greatest influence through much of the 1900s. It is America's

unique contribution to the discipline and an answer to many of the criticisms of other paradigms. Symbolic interactionism helps us explain both our individual personalities and the ways in which we are all linked together; it allows us to understand the processes by which social order and social change are constructed. As a theoretical perspective, it is vital, versatile, and still evolving.

FOUNDER AND KEY CONTRIBUTIONS Symbolic interactionism is derived largely from the teachings of George Herbert Mead (1863–1931). But there were many others involved in the development of this particular school of thought, and it is worthwhile to examine the social context in which they lived and worked.

George Herbert Mead

At the start of the twentieth century, sociology was still something of an import from the European intellectual scene, and American practitioners had just begun developing their own ideas regarding the nature and workings of society. The University of Chicago of the 1920s provided a stimulating intellectual setting for a handful of academics who built on each other's work and advanced what became known as the first new major branch within the discipline. Since there were so few social theorists in the country, the head of the department, Albion Small, a philosopher by training, recruited professors from various eastern colleges who had often studied other disciplines such as theology and psychology as well. The fledgling sociology department grew to include such influential members as Robert Park, W. I. Thomas, Charles Horton Cooley, and later Mead and Herbert Blumer. The department was also profoundly shaped by the inclusion of Jane Addams, one of the few women sociologists at the time, and by black sociologist W.E.B. DuBois, both of whom took conflict-inspired ideas about the problem of social inequality and used symbolic interactionist–inspired approaches to solving it. This group, the theory they developed together, and the way they went about studying the social world are frequently referred to (either individually or collectively) as **the Chicago School** of sociology.

Chicago was in many ways a frontier city in the early twentieth century. Rapidly transformed by industrialization, immigration, and ethnic diversity, Chicago became a unique laboratory in which to practice a new type of sociology that differed both theoretically and methodologically from the European models. Instead of doing comparative and historical work as had the macro theorists before them, the members of the Chicago School went out and into the city to conduct interviews and collect observational data. Their studies were particularly inspired by Max Weber's concept of *verstehen* as the proper attitude to adopt in the field. Their focus was on the micro level of everyday interactions (such as race relations in urban neighborhoods) as the building blocks of larger social phenomena (such as racial inequality).

The new school of thought was strongly influenced by a philosophical perspective called **pragmatism**, developed largely by William James and John Dewey, which was gaining acceptance among American social theorists in the early 1900s. James was a Harvard professor whose interests spanned art, medicine, law, education, theology, philosophy, and psychology; he also traveled extensively and was acquainted with some of the most important scholars of the time. To James, pragmatism meant seeking the truth of an idea by evaluating its usefulness in everyday life; in other words, if it works, it's true! He thought that living in the world involved making practical adaptations to whatever we encountered; if those adaptations made our lives run more smoothly, then the ideas behind them must be both useful and true. James's ideas inspired educational psychologist and philosopher John Dewey, who also grappled with pragmatism's main questions: How do we adapt to our environments? How do we acquire the knowledge that allows us to act in our everyday lives? Unlike the social Darwinists, pragmatists implied that the process of adaptation was essentially immediate and that it involved conscious thought. George Herbert Mead would be the one who eventually pulled these ideas (and others, too) together into a theory meant to address questions about the relationship between thought and action, the individual and society.

Mead came from a progressive family and grew up along the eastern seaboard in the late 1800s, where his father, a professor of theology at Oberlin College, died when he was a teenager, and his widowed mother eventually became president of Mount Holyoke College. Mead attended college at Oberlin and Harvard, and did his graduate studies in psychology at the universities of Leipzig and Berlin in Germany. Before he became a full-time professor of psychology at the University of Michigan and later the University of Chicago, Mead waited tables, and did railroad surveying and construction work. He was also a tutor to William James's family in Cambridge, Massachusetts; since his later theories were influenced by James, we can only wonder exactly who was tutoring whom in this arrangement! Mead's background and training uniquely positioned him to bridge the gap between sociology and psychology, and to address the links between the individual and society.

Mead proposed that both human development and the meanings we assign to everyday objects and events are fundamentally social processes—they require the interaction of multiple individuals. And what is crucial to the development of self and society is language, the means by which we communicate with one another. For Mead, there is no mind without language, and language itself is a product of social interactions (1934, pp. 191–92). According to

dramaturgy a theoretical paradigm that uses the metaphor of the theater to understand how individuals present themselves to others

Mead, the most important human behaviors consist of linguistic "gestures," such as words and facial expressions. People develop the ability to engage in conversation using these gestures; further, both society and individual selves are constructed through this kind of symbolic communication. Mead argued that we use language to "name ourselves, think about ourselves, talk to ourselves, and feel proud or ashamed of ourselves" and that "we can act toward ourselves in all the ways we can act toward others" (Hewitt 2000, p. 10). He was curious about how the mind developed but did not believe that it developed separately from its social environment. For Mead, then, society and self were created through communicative acts like speech and gestures; the individual personality was shaped by society, and vice versa.

Herbert Blumer, a graduate student and later a professor at the University of Chicago, was closely associated with Mead and was largely credited with continuing his life's work. While completing his master's degree, Blumer played football for the University of Missouri Tigers, and during the 1920s and '30s he maintained dual careers as a sociology professor and a professional football player for the former Chicago Cardinals. On Mondays, he would often come to class wrapped in bandages after a tough Sunday game. What he did off the gridiron, however, was of critical importance to the discipline. Blumer appealed for researchers to get "down and dirty" with the dynamics of social life. He also published a clear and compelling series of works based on Mead's fundamental ideas. After his death in 1931, Blumer gave Mead's theory the name it now goes by: symbolic interactionism. Thus, Mead and Blumer became the somewhat-unwitting founders of a much larger theoretical perspective. Blumer's long career at the University of Chicago and later at University of California, Berkeley ensured the training of many future scholars and secured the inclusion of symbolic interactionism as one of the major schools of thought within the discipline.

ORIGINAL PRINCIPLES For symbolic interactionists, society is produced and reproduced through our interactions with each other by means of language and our interpretations of that language. Symbolic interactionism sees face-to-face interaction as the building block of everything else in society, because it is through interaction that we create a meaningful social reality.

Here are the three basic tenets of symbolic interactionism, as laid out by Blumer (1969, p. 2). First, *we act toward things on the basis of their meanings.* For example, a tree can provide a shady place to rest, or it can be an obstacle to building a

Herbert Blumer Blumer in his Missouri Tigers football uniform.

road or home; each of these meanings suggests a different set of actions. This is as true for physical objects like trees as it is for people (like mothers or cops), institutions (church or school), beliefs (honesty or equality), or any social activity. Second, *meanings are not inherent; rather, they are negotiated through interaction with others.* That is, whether the tree is an obstacle or an oasis is not an intrinsic quality of the tree itself but rather something that people must figure out themselves. The same tree can mean one thing to one person and something else to another. And third, *meanings can change or be modified through interaction.* For example, the contractor who sees the tree as an obstacle might be persuaded to spare it by the neighbor. Now the tree means the same thing to both of them: it is something to protect and build around rather than to condemn and bulldoze.

Symbolic interactionism proposes that social facts exist only because we create and re-create them through our interactions; this gives the theory wide explanatory power and a versatility that allows it to address any sociological issue. Although symbolic interactionism is focused on how self and society develop through interaction with others, it is useful in explaining and analyzing a wide variety of specific social issues, from inequalities of race and gender to the group dynamics of families or co-workers.

OFFSHOOTS Symbolic interactionism opened the door for innovative sociologists who focused on social acts (like face-to-face interaction) rather than social facts (like vast bureaucratic institutions). They were able to extend the field in a variety of ways, allowing new perspectives to come under the umbrella of symbolic interactionism.

Erving Goffman (1922–1982) furthered symbolic interactionist–conceptions of the self in a seemingly radical way, indicating that the self is essentially "on loan" to us from society; it is created through interaction with others and hence ever-changing within various social contexts. For example, you may want to make a different kind of impression on a first date than you do on a job interview or when you face an opponent in a game of poker. Goffman used the theatrical metaphor of **dramaturgy** to describe the ways in which we engage in a strategic presentation of ourselves to others. In this way, he elaborated on Mead's ideas in a specific fashion, utilizing a wide range of data to help support his arguments.

Erving Goffman

Harold Garfinkel, the founder of **ethnomethodology** (the study of "folk methods," or everyday analysis of interaction), maintains that as members of society we must acquire the necessary knowledge and skills to act practically in our everyday lives. He argues that much of this knowledge remains in the background, "seen but unnoticed," and that we assume that others have the same knowledge we do when we interact with them. These assumptions allow us to make meaning out of even seemingly troublesome or ambiguous events; but such shared understanding can also be quite precarious, and there is a good deal of work required to sustain them, even as we are unaware that we are doing so.

Conversation analysis, pioneered by sociologists at University of California, Los Angeles, is also related to symbolic interactionism. It is based on the ethnomethodological idea that as everyday actors we are constantly analyzing and giving meaning to our social world (Schegloff 1986, 1999; Clayman 2002). Conversation analysts are convinced that the best place to look for the social processes of meaning-production is in naturally occurring conversation, and that the best way to get at the meanings an everyday actor gives to the things others say and do is to look closely at how he responds. Conversation analysts therefore use highly technical methods to scrutinize each conversational turn closely, operating on the assumption that any larger social phenomenon is constructed step-by-step through interaction.

ADVANTAGES AND CRITIQUES As society changes, so must the discipline that studies it, and symbolic interactionism has invigorated sociology in ways that are linked to the past and looking toward the future. The founding of symbolic interactionism provided a new and different way of looking at the world. It is "the only perspective that assumes an active, expressive model of the human actor and that treats the individual and the social at the same level of analysis" (O'Brien and Kollock 1997, p. 39). Therein lies much of its power and its appeal.

As a new school of thought focusing on the micro level of society, symbolic interactionism was not always met with immediate approval by the academy. Over time, symbolic interactionism has been integrated relatively seamlessly into sociology, and its fundamental precepts have become widely accepted. During the second half of the twentieth century,

the scope of symbolic interactionism has widened, its topics multiplied, and its theoretical linkages became more varied. In fact, there was some concern that symbolic interactionism was expanding so much that it may risk erupting into something else entirely (Fine 1993). One of symbolic interactionism's most enduring contributions is in the area of research methods. Practices such as ethnography and conversation analysis are data-rich, technically complex, and empirically well grounded (Schegloff 1999; J. Katz 1997), giving us new insights into perennial questions about social life.

As a relative newcomer to the field of social theory, symbolic interactionism was dubbed "the loyal opposition" (Mullins 1973) by those who saw it solely as a reaction or as merely a supplement to the more dominant macrosociological theories that preceded it. Gary Fine sums up the critiques in this way: symbolic interactionism is "apolitical (and hence, supportive of the status quo), unscientific (hence, little more than tenured journalism), hostile to the classical questions of macrosociology (hence, limited to social psychology), and astructural (hence, fundamentally nonsociological)" (1993, p. 65). These critiques argue that the scope of symbolic interactionism is limited, that it cannot properly address the most important sociological issues, and that its authority is restricted to the study of face-to-face interaction.

Each of these critiques has been answered over the years. Ultimately, some critics have seen the usefulness of an interactionist perspective and have even begun incorporating it into more macro work. Even in the hotly contested micro-versus-macro debate, a kind of détente has been established, recognizing that all levels of analysis are necessary for sociological understanding and that interactionist theories and methods are critical for a full picture of social life.

> **ethnomethodology** the study of "folk methods" and background knowledge that sustains a shared sense of reality in everyday interactions
>
> **conversation analysis** a sociological approach that looks at how we create meaning in naturally occurring conversation, often by taping conversations and examining them

DATA WORKSHOP

ANALYZING MASS MEDIA AND POPULAR CULTURE

Theories of Celebrity Gossip

Perezhilton.com is consistently rated as one of the most frequently visited web sites among college students. Written and operated by blogger Mario Lavandeira (who goes

Blogger Mario Lavandeira, a.k.a. Perez Hilton

by Perez Hilton, a play on the heiress Paris Hilton's name), Perezhilton.com has been exposing the real and rumored doings of celebrities since 2005, posting several blurbs each day that chronicle celebrity activities. These entries are accompanied by paparazzi photos and typically snide commentary by both Lavandeira and the throngs of readers who post their own observations and criticisms, humorous and serious.

Lavandeira's web site is part of a new breed of celebrity gossip outlets, including TMZ.com and WWTDD.com, among others. These sites can almost instantly consolidate and present information that used to take at least a week to appear in printed gossip magazines like *People*, *In Touch*, or *Us*. They can also provide more explicit editorial commentary than the print magazines or mainstream television programs like *Entertainment Tonight* or *E! News* can. For example, consider the coverage of Kim Kardashian in early 2011. *People* showed a picture of her leaving a restaurant, with the headline "Kim: She's So Hip" and copy that said "Kardashian flaunts her curves." WWTDD.com showed a picture of her at a gas station with the headline "Kim Kardashian has ass for days" and continued with the comments "Kim Kardashian normally does a pretty good job at hiding how big her ass is, but she's fashion savvy, not magic, so she can't hide it all the time. Like this weekend. From the waist down it looks like a horse."

It gets worse. Sometimes the commentary is so racy we wouldn't want to include it in a "family" textbook! Finally, these sites allow for almost immediate feedback from and discussion among far-flung readers, something not possible in the pre-internet gossip magazine days.

Other staples of celebrity gossip sites are photos of celebrities with evaluative commentary about their bodies, outfits, mates, children, and other aspects of their beings and behaviors. While many criticize such information as mean, stupid, and shallow, you don't have to enjoy celebrity gossip to see its sociological relevance. And sometimes, items from celebrity gossip blogs can end up in the mainstream news: in 2007, Lavandeira "broke a story" on the death of Cuban president Fidel Castro that was picked up by the conventional media and broadcast widely. The story turned out to be untrue, but the incident speaks to the influence of such blogs on our understanding of what constitutes news.

In 2010, Lavandeira experienced what could be called a change of heart about his style of celebrity reporting, which prompted him to reconsider the critical tone that was typical of his blog. This occurred in the aftermath of several highly publicized cases in which young victims of online gay bashing had committed suicide. He felt that the celebrity figures he targets might be equally pained by what was essentially bullying on his part. Lavandeira no longer wanted to be a role model for justifying or condoning behavior that hurt others. Whether this amounts to a significant lasting change to Perezhilton.com remains to be seen. But regardless of tone or veracity, just about every social phenomenon, including celebrity gossip blogs, is worthy of sociological analysis.

For this Data Workshop, we'd like you to immerse yourself in the celebrity gossip blog of your choice. Pick five entries—scrutinize the pictures, read the headlines and text carefully, and review the reader comments. Now ask yourself the following questions based on each of sociology's three major schools of thought:

1. Structural Functionalism
What is the function (or functions) of celebrity gossip blogs for society? What purpose(s) do they serve, and how do they help society maintain stability and order? Discuss how notions of the sacred and profane are characterized. Are there manifest and latent functions of celebrity gossip blogs? And are there any dysfunctions built into such publications?

2. Conflict Theory
What forms of inequality are revealed in celebrity gossip blogs? In particular, what do these blogs have to say about class, race, gender, or sexuality inequalities? Whose interests are being served and who gets exploited? Who suffers and who benefits from the publication of celebrity gossip blogs?

3. Symbolic Interactionism
What do celebrity gossip blogs mean to society as a whole? What do they mean to individual members of society? Can

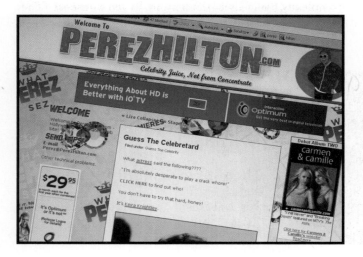

they have different meanings for different individuals or groups of individuals? How do those meanings get constructed in interaction? And how do these blogs shape and influence our everyday lives?

Make sure you can explain your answers to each of these questions, and complete one of the following two options, as directed by your instructor.

- *Option 1 (informal)*: Answer each of the three sets of questions above, and prepare some notes that you can refer to in class. Discuss your answers with other students in small groups.

- *Option 2 (formal)*: Answer each of the three sets of questions above in a three-page essay explaining your positions. You may want to include snippets from your chosen blog to illustrate your points.

New Theoretical Approaches

Because the three major schools of thought and their offshoots all have weaknesses as well as strengths, they will probably never fully explain the totality of social phenomena, even when taken together. And because society itself is always changing, there are always new phenomena to explain. So new perspectives will, and indeed must, continue to arise. In this section, we will consider two more contemporary approaches: postmodernism and midrange theory. Both grew out of the deep groundwork established by the other major schools of thought within sociology, and by looking beyond the confines of the discipline for inspiration. Each is a response to conditions both in the fast-changing social world around us and within the ongoing intellectual dialogues taking place among those continuing to study our times and selves.

Postmodern Theory

In the late twentieth century, some social thinkers looked at the proliferation of theories and data and began to question whether we could ever know society or ourselves with any certainty. What is truth, and who has the right to claim it? Or, for that matter, what is reality, and how can it be known? In an era of increasing doubt and cynicism, has meaning become meaningless? **Postmodernism**, a theory that encompasses a wide range of areas—from art and architecture, music and film, to communications and technology—addresses these and other questions.

The postmodern perspective developed primarily out of the French intellectual scene in the second half of the twentieth century and is still associated with three of its most important proponents. It's probably worth noting that postmodernists themselves don't really like that label, but nonetheless Jacques Derrida (1930–2004), Jean Baudrillard (1929–2007), and Michel Foucault (1926–1984) are the major figures most often included in the group.

In order to understand postmodernism, we first need to juxtapose it with **modernism**, the movement against which it reacted. Modernism is both a historical period and an ideological stance that began with the eighteenth-century Enlightenment, or Age of Reason. Modernist thought values scientific knowledge, a linear (or timeline-like) view of history, and a belief in the universality of human nature. In postmodernism, on the other hand, there are no absolutes—no claims to truth, reason, right, order, or stability. Everything is therefore relative—fragmented, temporary, and contingent. Postmodernists believe that certainty is illusory and prefer to play with the possibilities created by fluidity, complexity, multidimensionality, and even nonsense. They propose that there are no universal human truths from which

> **postmodernism** a paradigm that suggests that social reality is diverse, pluralistic, and constantly in flux

> **modernism** a paradigm that places trust in the power of science and technology to create progress, solve problems, and improve life

Jacques Derrida, Michel Foucault, and Jean Baudrillard
While many commentators and critics identify these French intellectuals as "postmodernists," each one distanced himself from the label.

deconstruction a type of critical post-modern analysis that involves taking apart or disassembling old ways of thinking

midrange theory an approach that integrates empiricism and grand theory

we can interpret the meaning of existence. On one hand, postmodernism can be celebrated as a liberating influence that rescues us from the stifling effects of rationality and tradition. On the other, it can be condemned as a detrimental influence that imprisons us in a world of relativity, nihilism, and chaos.

Postmodernists are also critical of what they call "grand narratives," overarching stories and theories that justify dominant beliefs and give a (false) sense of order and coherence to the world. Postmodernists are interested in **deconstruction**, or taking apart and examining these stories and theories. For example, they claim that "factual" accounts of history are no more accurate than those that might be found in fiction. They prefer the notion of mini-narratives, or small-scale stories, which describe individual or group practices rather than narratives that attempt to be universal or global. These mini-narratives can then be combined in a variety of ways, creating a collage of meaning.

One way of understanding what postmodernism looks like is to examine how it has crept into our popular culture. Hip-hop is an example of a postmodern art form. It is a hybrid that borrows from other established genres, from rhythm and blues to rock and reggae. Hip-hop also takes samples from existing songs, mixes these with new musical tracks, and overlays it all with rap lyrics, resulting in a unique new sound. Mash-ups are another postmodern twist in music. Take for instance the "Grey Album" by DJ Danger Mouse, which uses tracks from the Beatles' classic rock album called the "White Album" and combines them with Jay-Z's "Black Album" to create something wholly new yet borrowed.

Many resist the postmodern position against essential meaning or truth; the rise in religious fundamentalism may be a reaction to the postmodern view, an expression of the desire to return to absolute truths and steadfast traditions. Sociologists are quick to criticize postmodernism for discarding the scientific method and the knowledge they believe it has generated. Social leaders with a conservative agenda have been suspicious of the postmodern impulse to dismiss moral standards. While it is clear that many people criticize postmodernism, a much larger number are probably oblivious to it, which in itself may be more damning than any other response.

Nevertheless, although it is not a widely practiced perspective, postmodernism *has* gained supporters. Those who challenge the status quo, whether in the arts, politics, or the academy, find attractive postmodernism's ability to embrace a multiplicity of powerful and promising alternatives. At the very least, postmodernism allows us to question scientific ideals about clarity and coherence, revealing inherent short-comings and weaknesses in our current arguments, and

providing a way toward a deeper, more nuanced understanding of social life. As one of the most contemporary of the theoretical perspectives, postmodernism corresponds to the information age and feels natural and intuitive for students whose lives are immersed in this world. By focusing on individuals and small-scale activities in which change happens on a local, limited basis, postmodernism offers an alternative to such cultural trends as consumerism and globalization. However unwelcome the theory might be to some critics, it is likely that the postmodern shifts we have seen in society (in music and films, for example) will continue.

Midrange Theory

The second new theoretical approach is **midrange theory**. It shares some views with postmodernism, especially in its preference for mini-narratives over sweeping statements or "grand theories" made by the classical social theorists—a period dominated by what Robert Merton calls "total sociological systems" (1996, p. 46), which provided an overarching, comprehensive explanation of society as a whole.

Merton feared that an uncritical reverence for classical theory and an excessive attachment to tradition could impede the flow of new ideas, and was just as likely to hold sociology back as to advance it. Because classical theories sought to develop large-scale theoretical systems that applied to the most macro level of society, they were often extremely difficult to test or research in any practical way. As one critic lamented, too "many sociological products can—effectively and unfortunately—be considered both bad science and bad literature" (Boudon 1991, p. 522).

To counter this tendency, Merton proposed sociologists focus more on "theories of the middle range." Midrange (or middle range) theory is not a theory of something in particular, but rather a *style* of theorizing. It is not so much an attempt to make the elusive macro-micro link, but to strike a balance somewhere between those polarities, shifting both the sights and the process of doing sociology. Work in this vein concentrates on incorporating research questions and empirical data into smaller-scale theories that eventually build into a more comprehensive body of sociological theory. Midrange theories are those "that lie between the minor but necessary working hypotheses that evolve in abundance during day-to-day research and the all-inclusive systematic efforts to develop a unified theory that will explain" the whole social world (Merton 1996, p. 41).

Since the 1990s and 2000s, a host of sociologists have taken up the call to midrange theory, from Sharon Hays's study of the contradictions within modern motherhood (1996), to Dalton Conley's work on racial identity (2000), or our shifting notions of the workplace and what constitutes leisure in the digital age (2009). Midrange theory connects

		TABLE 1.1	Theory in Everyday Life

TABLE 1.1 Theory in Everyday Life

PERSPECTIVE	APPROACH TO SOCIETY	CASE STUDY: COLLEGE ADMISSIONS IN THE UNITED STATES
STRUCTURAL-FUNCTIONALISM	Assumes that society is a unified whole that functions because of the contributions of its separate structures.	Those who are admitted are worthy and well-qualified, while those who are not admitted do not deserve to be. There are other places in society for them besides the university.
CONFLICT THEORY	Sees social conflict as the basis of society and social change and emphasizes a materialist view of society, a critical view of the status quo, and a dynamic model of historical change.	Admissions decisions may be made on the basis of criteria other than grades and scores. For example, some applicants may get in because their fathers are major university donors, while others may get in because of their talents in sports or music. Some may be denied admission based on criteria like race, gender, or sexuality.
SYMBOLIC INTERACTIONISM	Asserts that interaction and meaning are central to society and assumes that meanings are not inherent but are created through interaction.	University admissions processes are all about self-presentation and meaning-making in interaction. How does an applicant present himself or herself to impress the admissions committee? How does the admissions committee develop an understanding of the kind of applicant it's looking for? How do applicants interpret their acceptances and rejections?
POSTMODERNISM	Suggests that social reality is diverse, pluralistic, and constantly in flux.	An acceptance doesn't mean you're smart, and a rejection doesn't mean you're stupid; be careful of any "facts" you may be presented with, as they are illusory and contingent.

specific research projects that generate empirical data with larger-scale theories about social structure. It aims to build knowledge cumulatively while offering a way to make sociology more effective as a science rather than just a way of thinking. With more sociologists appreciating such a stance, midrange theory is helping to push the discipline forward into the sociology of the future.

Closing Comments

We hope that this chapter has given you a thorough and compelling introduction to the study of sociology, and perhaps you too will find it an appealing pursuit. Many of you will have already started a sociological journey, although likely a casual or personal one . . . until now. The popularity of reality TV speaks to our fascination with the everyday lives of other people, whether *Hoarders* or *Ice Road Truckers* or *The Real Housewives of* _____ (fill in the blank). As students of sociology, we are interested in everyday life because we are excited to understand more about how its patterns and processes create our larger social reality. As we become better social analysts, using strategies to set aside any blinding preconceptions or distracting conclusions, we can become better acquainted with some of the fundamental tools that can turn our natural curiosity into scientific inquiry. A sociological perspective allows us to grasp the connection between our individual experiences and the forces and structures of society. As Bernard McGrane says, "Sociology is both dangerous and liberating" (1994, p. 10), as much because of what we can learn about ourselves as because of what we can learn about the world around us.

As a discipline, sociology possesses some of the qualities of the society it seeks to understand: it is broad, complex, and ever-changing. This can make mastering sociology a rather unwieldy business, as much for the students and teachers who grapple with it in the classroom as for the experts out working in the field. We want you to become familiar with the members of sociology's family tree from its varied historical roots to the tips of its offshoots that might one day become important future branches. Because we have no single acknowledged universal sociological theory that satisfactorily explains all social phenomena (despite claims otherwise by some theorists), new theories can be developed all the time. Social theory tries to explain what is happening in, to, and around us. For any and every possible new, different, or important phenomena—from the most mundane personal experience to questions of ultimate global significance—sociologists will attempt to explain it, understand it, analyze it, and predict its future. By looking at the development of the discipline, we can remember that the contemporary grows out of the classical, and that older theories inspire and provoke newer ones. Theorists past and present remain engaged in a continual and evolving dialogue through their ideas and their work, and until such time as society is completely explained, the branches of sociology's family tree will continue to grow in remarkable ways.

QUESTIONS FOR REVIEW

1. As an everyday actor, you possess a wealth of practical (but inconsistent) knowledge about your particular social world. Are there any areas of life in which you possess scientific knowledge that is completely coherent and excruciatingly clear? If so, how does this knowledge change the way you approach things?

2. What do anthropologists mean by "culture shock"? How could culture shock help you be a better sociologist? Think about the last time you returned home from a long trip. Did ordinary, everyday things seem strange or unfamiliar?

3. What does it mean to possess a sociological imagination? Think of your favorite food. What historical events had to happen and what institutions have to function in order for this food to be available? What sort of meanings does it have?

4. How does the level of analysis you adopt affect your assumptions about how society works? Could Pam Fishman have done her research on gender and power in conversations from a macro perspective? Perhaps with a survey? Could Christine Williams have done her research on gender and power in occupations from a micro perspective? Perhaps with interviews? How might this change their conclusions?

5. Think back to the biographical information about Marx, Durkheim, and Weber. Are there particular events that may have influenced their theories?

6. Pick a social structure other than education, and describe it in terms of its manifest and latent functions. For example, what is the manifest function of religion in your community? Can you think of any latent functions, ones that were not intended by the people in charge?

7. Marx argued that the proletariat suffer from alienation as a result of losing control over the products of their labor. Make a list of all the jobs you can think of where you would have control over your own work. Do you think this control would make a difference in your own happiness?

8. Weber saw the proliferation of bureaucracies as one of the key features of the modern age. Think about the bureaucracies that are relevant to you. Do they allow you to make decisions based on your own personal desires? For example, what criteria does your university or college use to determine what classes you will take?

9. The sociological theorists in this chapter are almost all white males from Europe or the United States, evidence of a Eurocentric, racist, and sexist bias in sociology. Do your classes in other disciplines admit to the same deficiencies?

10. Symbolic interactionism argues that meanings are not inherent in things themselves but are socially derived and negotiated through interaction with others. Think of some recent fashion trend. Can you describe this trend in terms of what it means to those who embrace it? What sorts of interactions produce and maintain this meaning?

11. Because society is always changing, there are always new social phenomena that need a theory to make sense of them. If postmodernism rejects the belief that experience is structured or linear, what sort of changes in society do you think necessitated this insight?

SUGGESTIONS FOR FURTHER EXPLORATION

Berman, Marshall. 2001. *Adventures in Marxism*. New York: Verso. Describes the changes in Marxism that followed the publication of *The Economic and Philosophical Manuscripts of 1844*, which revealed a Marx full of "sensual warmth and spiritual depth."

Cast Away. 2000. Dir. Robert Zemeckis. 20th Century Fox. Film starring Tom Hanks as a FedEx executive who gets plane wrecked on a desert island for four years. After escaping the island, he experiences radical culture shock when returning to his old life.

Dialectics for Kids (dialectics4kids.com). This web site was created by Jack Fleck, the father of movie director Ryan Fleck, and uses examples, songs, and essays to explain how social change happens.

Douglas, Mary. 2002. *Purity and Danger*. London: Routledge. Extends Durkheim's insights into the way that religion creates social solidarity and "religious ritual makes manifest to men their social selves."

Half Nelson. 2006. Dir. Ryan Fleck. THINKFilm. An idealistic young teacher teaches his eighth graders dialectics, illustrated with arm wrestling.

Harvey, David. 1989. *The Condition of Postmodernity: An Enquiry into the Origins of Cultural Change*. Cambridge, MA: Blackwell. Explores the way that changes in information and communication technology have made the world a smaller place and created connections between America and the rest of the world.

Hofstadter, Richard. 1992. *Social Darwinism in American Thought*. Boston: Beacon Press. Discusses the way early sociologists approached the insights of Charles Darwin and the very different conclusions drawn by pragmatist philosophers like William James.

The Magnetic Fields. 1999. "The Death of Ferdinand de Saussure." *69 Love Songs*. Merge. A tongue-in-cheek pop song about the indeterminacy associated with postmodernism.

The Magnetic Fields performing

The Namesake. 2006. Dir. Mira Nair. Fox Searchlight Pictures. A film adaptation of the book by Jhumpa Lahiri. The story of an Indian couple, who immigrate to the United States, and their American-born children struggling to bridge cultural and generational differences. The film stars Kal Penn as a modern man seeking to understand his heritage.

Theory.org.uk. Web site for fans of popular culture, and popular culture for fans of social theories. Includes items such as "theory action figures" and original trading cards featuring favorite theorists and concepts.

What the #$! Do We Know?*! 2005. Dir. Betsy Chasse, William Arntz, and Mark Vicente. 20th Century Fox. This movie—part documentary, part drama—asks some very postmodern questions about reality and how we know it.

Žižek. 2006. Dir. Astra Taylor. Zeitgeist Films. A documentary film on the Slovenian cultural theorist Slavoj Žižek, whose postmodern synthesis of Marx and Freud has made him as famous as a rock star in Europe.

CHAPTER 2

Studying Social Life: Sociological Research Methods

Humorist Dave Barry, the Pulitzer Prize–winning columnist and author, has written many entertaining articles as a reporter and social commentator. Some of his thoughts on college, however, seem particularly appropriate for this chapter. In one of his most popular essays, Barry advises students not to choose a major that involves "known facts" and "right answers" but rather a subject in which "nobody really understands what anybody else is talking about, and which involves virtually no actual facts" (Barry 1994). For example, sociology:

> For sheer lack of intelligibility, sociology is far and away the number-one subject. I sat through hundreds of hours of sociology courses, and read gobs of sociology writing, and I never once heard or read a coherent statement. This is because sociologists want to be considered scientists, so they spend most of their time translating simple, obvious observations into scientific-sounding code. If you plan to major in sociology, you'll have to learn to do the same thing. For example, suppose you have observed that children cry when they fall down. You should write: "Methodological observation of the sociometrical behavior tendencies of prematurated isolates indicates that a causal relationship exists between groundward tropism and lachrimatory, or 'crying' behavior forms." If you can keep this up for fifty or sixty pages, you will get a large government grant.

Although Barry exaggerates a bit, if there weren't some truth to what he is saying, his joke would be meaningless. While sociologists draw much of their inspiration from the natural (or "hard") sciences (such as chemistry and biology) and try to study society in a scientific way, many people still think of sociology as "unscientific" or a "soft" science. In response, some sociologists may try too hard to sound scientific and incorporate complicated terminology in their writing.

It is possible, of course, to conduct research and write about it in a clear, straightforward, and even elegant way, as the best sociologists have demonstrated. Contrary to Barry's humorous claims, sociology can be both scientific and comprehensible. So let's turn now to a discussion of how sociologists conduct their research, which includes the methods of gathering information and conveying that information to others. For the record, Dave Barry went to Haverford College near Philadelphia, where he majored in English.

HOW TO READ THIS CHAPTER

In Chapter 1 we introduced you to a set of tools that will help you develop a sociological imagination and apply particular theoretical perspectives to the social world. In this chapter you will acquire methodological tools that will help you to further understand social life. The tools will also help you in the Data Workshops throughout the book, which are designed to give you the experience of conducting the same type of research that professional sociologists do. For this reason, we recommend that you look at this chapter as a sort of "how-to" guide: read through all the "directions" first, recognizing that you will soon be putting each method into practice. Then remember that you have this chapter as a resource for future reference. These methods are your tools for real-world research—it's important that you understand them, but even more important that you get a chance to use them.

An Overview of Research Methods

While theories make hypothetical claims, methods produce data that will support, disprove, or modify those claims. Sociologists who do **quantitative research** work with numerical data; that is, they translate the social world into numbers that can then be manipulated mathematically. Any type of social statistic is an example of quantitative data: you may have read in the newspaper, for instance, that in 2009 some 40 percent of male drivers involved in fatal motor vehicle crashes had alcohol in their blood, compared with 22 percent of female drivers (Insurance Institute for Highway Safety 2009). Quantitative methodologies distill large amounts of information into numbers that are more easily communicated to others, often in the form of rates and percentages or charts and graphs.

Sociologists who do **qualitative research** work with non-numerical data such as texts, written field notes, interview transcripts, photographs, and tape recordings. Rather than condensing lived experience into numbers, qualitative researchers try to describe the cases they study in great detail. They may engage in participant observation, in which they enter the social world they wish to study, they may do in-depth interviews, analyze transcripts of conversations, glean data from historical books, letters, or diaries, or even use photos or videos in their investigations. Sociologist Gary Fine, for example, has observed a variety of different social worlds, including those of fantasy game players (1983), professional restaurant chefs (1996), and people who harvest wild mushrooms in the woods (1998)! Fine was able to discover important sociological insights through immersion in each of the social worlds he studied. Qualitative researchers like Fine find patterns in their data by using interpretive rather than statistical analysis.

The Scientific Approach

The **scientific method** is the standard procedure for acquiring and verifying empirical (concrete, scientific) knowledge. The scientific method provides researchers with a series of basic steps to follow; over the years, sociologists have updated and modified this model so that it better fits the study of human behaviors. While not every sociologist adheres to each of the steps in order, the scientific method provides a general plan for conducting research in a systematic way.

quantitative research research that translates the social world into numbers that can be treated mathematically; this type of research often tries to find cause-and-effect relationships

qualitative research research that works with nonnumerical data such as texts, fieldnotes, interview transcripts, photographs, and tape recordings; this type of research more often tries to understand how people make sense of their world

scientific method a procedure for acquiring knowledge that emphasizes collecting concrete data through observation and experiment

Sociological Methods Take Many Forms. They can be quantitative, but they can also include interviews, surveys, and participant observation.

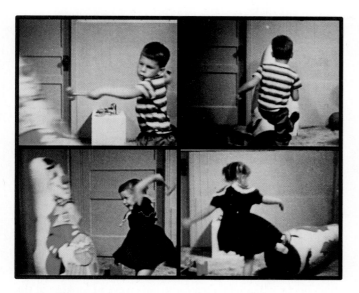

Does Watching Violence on Television Cause Children to Behave Violently? In his famous 1965 study, Albert Bandura supported his hypothesis by observing children who had watched a video of an adult beating a doll behaving similarly toward the doll afterward.

4. In this step, the researcher chooses a research design or method. A classic example is to perform an experiment meant to isolate the variables in order to best examine their relationship to one another. Other methods are also available and will be discussed later in the chapter.

5. The researcher then collects the data. In this case, the researcher would conduct the experiment by first exposing kids to TV violence, then observing their behavior toward the clown doll. Data might be collected by using video equipment as well as by taking notes.

6. Next, the researcher must analyze the data, evaluating the accuracy or inaccuracy of the hypothesis in predicting the outcome. In the real-life experiment this example is based on, the children were more likely to hit the clown doll themselves if they saw the TV actors being rewarded for their violent behavior; if the actors were punished for their behavior, the children were less likely to hit the doll (Bandura 1965).

7. Finally, the researcher then disseminates the findings of the experiment in the scientific community (often through presentations at professional meetings and/or publications) as well as among the general public, thus completing the last step in the research process.

1. In the first step, the researcher identifies a problem or asks a general question, like "Does violent TV lead to violent behavior?", and begins to think about a specific research plan designed to answer that question.

2. Before proceeding, however, a researcher usually does a **literature review** to become thoroughly familiar with all other research done previously on a given topic. This will prevent a researcher from duplicating work that has already been done and may also provide the background upon which to conduct new research.

3. Next, the researcher forms a **hypothesis**, a theoretical statement that she thinks will explain the relationship between two phenomena, which are known as **variables**. In the hypothesis "Watching violence on TV causes children to act violently in real life," the two variables are "watching violence on TV" and "acting violently." In short, the researcher is saying one variable causes the other. The researcher can use the hypothesis to predict possible outcomes: "If watching violence on TV causes children to act violently in real life, then exposing five-year-olds to violent TV shows will make them more likely to hit the inflatable clown doll placed in the room with them." The researcher must clearly give an **operational definition** to the variables so that she can observe and measure them accurately. For example, there is a wide range of violence on television and in real life. Does "violence" include words as well as actions, a slap as well as murder?

One limit of the scientific method is that it can't always distinguish between **correlation** and **causation**. If two variables change in conjunction with each other, or if a change in one seems to lead to a change in the other, they are correlated. Even if they are correlated, though, the change in one variable may not be caused by the change in the other variable. Instead, there may be some **intervening variable** that causes the changes in both. The classic example of this is the correlation between ice cream sales and rates of violent crime. As ice cream sales increase, so do rates of violent crime like murder and rape. Does ice cream consumption cause people to act violently? Or do violent actions cause people

literature review a thorough search through previously published studies relevant to a particular topic

hypothesis a theoretical statement explaining the relationship between two or more phenomena

variables one of two or more phenomena that a researcher believes are related and hopes to prove are related through research

operational definition a clear and precise definition of a variable that facilitates its measurement

correlation a relationship between variables in which they change together; may or may not be causal

causation a relationship between variables in which a change in one directly produces a change in the other

intervening variable a third variable, sometimes overlooked, that explains the relationship between two other variables

to buy ice cream? Turns out, it's neither—this is what is known as a **spurious correlation**. Both ice cream sales and violent crime rates are influenced by a third variable: weather. As the temperature climbs, so do people's rates of ice cream purchase and the likelihood that they'll be involved in a violent crime (probably because they are outside for more hours of the day and hence available to each other in a way that makes violent crime possible). Knowing that correlation does not equal causation is important, as it can help us all be more critical consumers of scientific findings.

We are constantly gathering data in order to understand what is true. Philosopher of science Thomas Kuhn, in fact, argues that truth is relative and dependent on the paradigm through which one sees the world (1962/1970). Paradigms are broad theoretical models about how things work in the social and natural worlds. For example, humans believed for centuries that the universe revolved around the earth. It's easy to understand why. The available data, after all, seemed to support such a theory: we don't feel the earth moving beneath us, and it appears from our vantage point that the stars, sun, and moon rise and set on our horizon. This earth-centered, or geocentric, view of the universe was the basis for all scientific theory until 1543, when the Polish astronomer Nicholas Copernicus proposed that the earth revolved around the sun (Armitage 1951). Using mathematical methods, Copernicus arrived at a new theory, heliocentrism, in which the earth rotates around the sun and on its own axis—thereby accounting for the twenty-four-hour days as well as the four seasons of the year. This caused what Kuhn calls a **paradigm shift**, a major break from the assumptions made by the previous model. Paradigm shifts occur when new data force new ways of looking at the world. And methods are what generate data.

What Was It Really Like at Woodstock? You could use many different methodologies to investigate this question, including ethnography, interviews, a survey, existing sources, or an experiment.

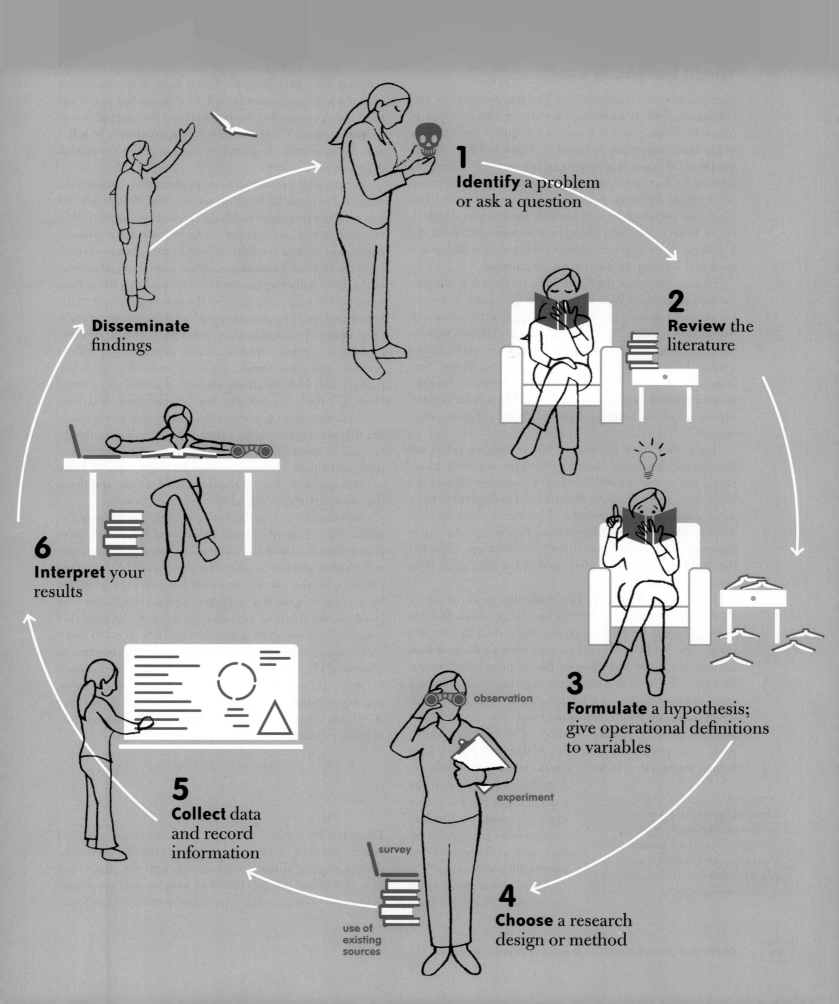

1 Identify a problem or ask a question

2 Review the literature

3 Formulate a hypothesis; give operational definitions to variables

4 Choose a research design or method

observation

experiment

survey

use of existing sources

5 Collect data and record information

6 Interpret your results

Disseminate findings

Which Method to Use?

Since each sociological method has specific benefits and limitations, each is more appropriate for certain types of research. Thus, when a researcher begins a project, one of her most important decisions is which methods to use. Suppose, for example, a sociologist is interested in studying Woodstock, one of the major musical and cultural milestones of the 1960s. Although there are many ways to approach this event, our sociologist wants to study the attendees' experiences. What was it really like to be at Woodstock? What did it mean to those who were there? What are their interpretations of this iconic moment in hippie culture?

During the event itself, the ideal method for studying the festival-goers at Woodstock might have been to assemble a team of researchers trained in participant observation: that is, they would actually be in the thick of things, observing and participating at the same time. They could gather firsthand data on the music, clothes, dancing, drugs, "free love," and so forth. However, the opportunity to conduct an ethnography (written record) of that particular cultural phenomenon has long since passed. What are some other options?

Interviews are a possibility. The researcher could ask Woodstock attendees to recount their experiences. But how would she recruit them? Woodstock-goers live all over the world now, and it might be difficult (and expensive) to track down enough of them to make an interview study feasible. Another problem with interviewing this group: the three-day concert happened more than forty years ago. How did the drugs that were so widely used at the time affect their memories of the experience?

How about a survey? The researcher could certainly send a questionnaire through the mail or by e-mail, and this method would be much less expensive than face-to-face interviews. But here she runs into the same problem as with an interview study: how does she find all these folks? A standard tactic for recruiting survey participants involves placing an ad in a local newspaper. But an ad in the *New York Times*, for example, or even a community web site like Craigslist would draw only a limited number of Woodstock alumni. Also, some people may want to put that part of their lives behind them; if they received this questionnaire in the mail, it might go straight into the trash. Finally, the researcher might encounter the problem of impostors—people who say they were at Woodstock but were really nowhere near it.

What about using existing sources? Plenty has been written about Woodstock over the years. Many firsthand accounts have been published, and there is an abundance of film and photography as well. Our researcher could use these articles to analyze the concert from the perspectives of the participants. These accounts would necessarily be selective, focusing only on particular aspects of the Woodstock experience.

Is it possible to conduct an experiment that replicates the original Woodstock? Some would say that Woodstock '99 was such an experiment and that it failed miserably, with fires, violence, arrests, and acres of mud. However, systematic scientific experiments are different from blatant attempts to cash in on the Woodstock mystique. While the unique conditions of the 1969 gathering cannot be re-created in a lab setting, it is possible to identify some of the defining features of the Woodstock experience and to explore those experimentally. Over a three-day period, tens of thousands of strangers came together in a mass gathering, mostly devoid of any official presence (no cops, fences, roads, ticket booths, or porta-potties) and had an almost entirely peaceful experience. How did this happen? Altruism, cooperation, and trust between strangers are some of the measurable group qualities that seem to have been present. An experimenter might be able to create laboratory environments in which subjects participate in activities that highlight one or more of these qualities—even without the mud, music, and drugs that were part of the original Woodstock experience.

No matter what methodological choice our researcher makes, she will sacrifice some types of information in order to acquire others, and she will trade in one set of advantages and disadvantages for another. Her choices will be guided not only by what she wants to accomplish sociologically but also by the methods she is a competent practitioner of, the time in which she wants to complete the project, the resources available from any funding agencies, and her access to cooperative, qualified people, both as respondents and as research assistants. The rest of this chapter will discuss five methods in detail: ethnography, interviews, surveys, existing sources, and experiments. We will see how various sociologists have used these methods to conduct research on the general topic of "family dynamics."

Ethnographic Methods

Ethnography means "writing [from the Greek *graphos*] culture [*ethnos*]." Ethnographers collect data by producing written records of their observations, with the goal of not only describing the activities they observe and participate in but also understanding what those activities mean to the

ethnography a naturalistic method based on studying people in their own environment in order to understand the meanings they attribute to their activities; also the written work that results from the study

On the Job

Commercial Ethnography

Recently, advertisers have become interested in the complex relationships between people and products and are looking to ethnographic methods to help them understand these relationships. Companies are hiring commercial ethnographers to learn how ordinary citizens bathe, dress, make breakfast, drive to work, do laundry, or flip hamburgers on their backyard grill—all in order to understand how consumers relate to various products. While Nissan Motors was developing the Infiniti line, for example, the company used ethnographic market research to help them understand the differences between Japanese and American perceptions of luxury. That's right—they drove around with people and talked to them about their cars! Nissan found that to Americans, high-end goods are more valuable if their lavish features are visible. This is in contrast to the Japanese concept of luxury, which values simplicity and hidden charm. Understanding these differences allowed Nissan to successfully redesign the Infiniti line to be more attractive to American buyers; other automakers realized the benefits of ethnographic market research and followed in Nissan's footsteps (Osborne 2002).

Some commercial ethnographers, known as "cool hunters," search for the newest, hippest trends in popular culture. Look-Look, a Hollywood trend-forecasting firm, recruited "youth correspondents" and amateur photographers in cities around the world as part of its "living research" strategy. Founded by Dee Dee Gordon and Sharon Lee, Look-Look (now known as "The-Collaboratory") counted on these correspondents to provide information on the latest trends in music, fashion, technology, and hip activities and hangouts. Says Gordon, "We look for kids who are ahead of the pack, because they'll influence what all the other kids do" (PBS 2001). Look-Look is somewhat secretive about its client list, which includes Universal Pictures, Disney Films, and Skyy Vodka. Other market research firms report that companies such as Xerox, Colgate-Palmolive, Kraft Foods, Duracell, Playtex, Honda, Pioneer Stereo, and Anheuser-Busch have all utilized qualitative market research to direct their production, distribution, and marketing strategies. Sociology students who become proficient in ethnographic methods may well be the hottest new hires in the field of commercial ethnography.

Cool Hunter Loic Bizel, a French "cool hunter" in Japan, picks up a pair of hand-painted sneakers in Tokyo's Harajuku shopping district. His job is to observe and report on the fast-changing street fads of Japan.

participant observation a methodology associated with ethnography whereby the researcher both observes and becomes a member in a social setting

rapport a positive relationship often characterized by mutual trust or sympathy

access the process by which an ethnographer gains entry to a field setting

members of the group they are studying.

One example of ethnography is Kathryn Edin and Maria Kefalas's study of poor moms, in their work, *Promises I Can Keep: Why Poor Women Put Motherhood Before Marriage* (2005). Edin and Kefalas wanted to examine a group that faces harsh judgments from the mainstream—urban single moms. For years, policy makers and mainstream Americans have focused on single motherhood as a source of a variety of social problems. Edin and Kefalas wanted to see the issue from the perspective and lives of the women being stigmatized in order to uncover the realities of single motherhood from the perspective of the mothers themselves. Their goal was to give poor single mothers the ability to per-

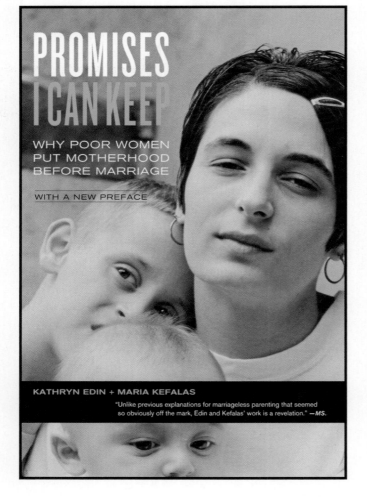

sonally answer the question that wealthier Americans ask of them: why don't they get married? And why have babies if they have to struggle so hard to support them?

Because Edin and Kefalas knew they needed to access a group that was notorious for being hard to study, their **participant observation** required full immersion in the community. Edin moved her entire family into an apartment that she rented in East Camden, New Jersey. They lived there for a total of 2.5 years while she did her research. In order to become more integrated into the community, she joined the local church, volunteered at after-school and summer programs, ate at local restaurants, shopped at local stores, taught Sunday school, and went to community events. She made herself part of the community in order to help the young women she was interested in understanding become more comfortable with her presence. Kefalas volunteered at the local GED tutoring program for teen mothers. Once she gained the confidence of a small group of mothers, she was invited into their homes to hang out with them.

Edin and Kefalas were able to interview 162 teen moms with an even distribution between black, white, and Puerto Rican. All of them were single parents who earned less than $16,000 a year. The women's ages ranged from fifteen to fifty-six with the average age being twenty-five years old. What Edin and Kefalas discovered was that motherhood, from the perspective of many of the women they interviewed, was a stabilizing agent in their lives. Rather than the middle-class expectations that single motherhood would disrupt a path to success, many of the moms they interviewed viewed their babies as the only positive factor in their lives. Numerous stories detailed the troubled directions the women's lives were heading before they had their children. The conclusions Edin and Kefalas were able to draw from their ethnographic research were contrary to widespread opinion about the consequences of single motherhood: for many women in poverty, the (perceived) low cost of early child-rearing and the high value and worth of mothering is enough to combat the difficulties of single motherhood.

The fact that the researchers were women and mothers themselves played a role in their ability to create **rapport** and gain **access** as they lived and worked in East Camden. The fact that Edin had children who accompanied her everywhere she went in the community helped to secure her position as a trustworthy fellow member. Kefalas became pregnant during the study, and found that her pregnancy allowed her even further access; in fact, the girls that she tutored were eager to talk to her about pregnancy and child-rearing since she now shared those experiences with them. Ethnographic researchers must pay attention to how their own social statuses—including gender, age, race, and parenthood—shape the kind

Richard Mitchell's *Dancing at Armageddon* In order to learn about militant groups' ideologies, Richard Mitchell had to conceal his identity and use covert methods.

of access they can have, and hence the kind of knowledge they can obtain as part of their research.

Once access is negotiated, research can begin in earnest. Like Kathryn Edin and Maria Kefalas, most ethnographers are "overt" about their research roles; that is, they are open about their sociological intentions. Overt research is generally preferred, because it eliminates the potential ethical problems of deceit. Sometimes, however, circumstances dictate that researchers take a "covert" role and observe members without letting them know that they are doing research. One researcher who kept his identity secret is Richard Mitchell, who studied militant survivalist groups for many years (2001). In order to be a participant-observer in such groups, Mitchell sometimes had to present himself as an eager apostle, a true believer in the survivalists' paranoid, racist ideologies. Often, this meant being surrounded by men who were heavily armed and deeply suspicious of outsiders (Mitchell and Charmaz 1996). However, he also felt that the value of the research was worth the risk, that it was more important than his own personal peril and the ethical objections of those who disapprove of covert research, because it provided insight into a secretive group whose actions could pose a danger to the larger society.

Participant-observers collect data by writing detailed **fieldnotes** every day. These notes describe the activities and interactions of the researcher and the members in as much detail as possible; they become the basis of the data analysis the researcher does later on. Sometimes, ethnographers take brief, sketchy notes in the field, writing key words or short quotations in small notebooks, on cocktail napkins, or in text messages. These jottings can help jog their memories when they sit down at a computer at the end of the day to elaborate on the details. Sometimes, however, ethnographers must rely on "head notes"—memory alone.

Anthropologist Clifford Geertz, well known for his work on Indonesian culture and society, coined the term "thick description" to convey the qualities of well-written fieldnotes (Geertz 1973). It takes more than mere photographic detail to make fieldnotes "thick"; sensitivity to the context and to interactional details such as facial expressions and tone of voice enrich what might otherwise be just a list of events. In order to truly understand members' meanings, one has to be immersed in the setting, usually for a sustained period of time (some ethnographers spend years in the field).

Another issue that participant-observers must consider is that their own presence probably affects the interactions

> **fieldnotes** detailed notes taken by an ethnographer describing her activities and interactions, which later become the basis of the ethnographic analysis

reflexivity how the identity and activities of the researcher influence what is going on in the field setting

grounded theory an inductive method of generating theory from data by creating categories in which to place data and then looking for relationships between categories

replicability research that can be repeated, and thus verified, by other researchers later

representativeness the degree to which a particular studied group is similar to, or represents, any part of the larger society

bias an opinion held by the researcher that might affect the research or analysis

and relationships in the group they are observing, an idea known as **reflexivity**. For example, the gender of the researcher may be important in particular settings, as it was for Edin in negotiating access. A researcher's personal feelings about the members of a group also come into play. Ethnographers may feel respect, contempt, curiosity, boredom, and other emotions during their time in the field, and these feelings may influence their observations. It is true that other kinds of researchers also have to take their feelings into account. But because ethnographers have such close personal ties to the people they study, the issue of reflexivity is especially important to them.

Analyzing the Data

Ethnographers look for patterns and processes that are revealed in their fieldnotes. In other words, they use an inductive approach: they start by immersing themselves in their fieldnote data and fitting the data into categories, such as "episodes of conflict" or "common vocabulary shared by members." Identifying relationships between these categories then allows ethnographers to build theoretical propositions, a form of analysis known as **grounded theory**.

Advantages and Disadvantages

ADVANTAGES

1. Ethnographies offer a means of studying groups that are often overlooked by other methods (Katz 1997). These include deviant groups such as fight clubs (Jackson-Jacobs 2004) and exceptional groups such as elite college athletes (Adler and Adler 1991). Ethnographic methods excel at telling stories that otherwise might not have been told.

2. Ethnographies can challenge our taken-for-granted notions about groups we thought we knew. For instance, from Edin and Kefalas's work on single mothers, we learn that these young women aren't the irresponsible, unstable individuals we may have thought they were. They desire and seek out the best for their children, just like mothers in other groups and communities.

3. The detailed nature of ethnographies can help to reshape the stereotypes we hold about others and on which social policy is often based. A study like Edin and Kefalas's can have policy consequences because it sheds light on the motivations and needs of single urban mothers, as well as giving us a clear picture of the resources available to them.

4. Much of the pioneering methodological innovation of the last half-century has come from within the field of ethnography, especially on the issue of reflexivity and researcher roles in the field.

DISADVANTAGES

1. Ethnographies suffer from a lack of **replicability**, the ability of another researcher to repeat or replicate the study. Repeating a study in order to test the validity of its results is an important element of the scientific method, but because of the unique combinations of people, timing, setting, and researcher role, no one can ever undertake the same study twice.

2. A major critique has to do with ethnographies' degree of **representativeness**, whether they apply to anything larger than themselves. What is the value of studying relatively small groups of people if one cannot then say that these groups represent parts of the society at large? Though Edin and Kefalas's work focused on East Camden, their conclusions are supposed to apply to single mothers in other cities as well.

3. Ethnographers must also be wary of **bias**. There is always a possibility that prejudice or favor can slip into the research process. Not all researchers are transparent about their own agendas. We need to keep in mind how a researcher's own values and opinions might affect his research and analysis.

DATA WORKSHOP

ANALYZING EVERYDAY LIFE

Observing and Describing Verbal and Nonverbal Communication

While producing fieldnotes may sound fairly easy (don't we all know how to describe the things we've observed?), it turns out to be one of the most grueling forms of data collection in the social sciences. Why? Because thick description is a much more demanding accomplishment than the description you're used to providing in everyday conversation. It requires a rigorous consciousness of what is going on around you while it is happening and a strenuous effort to recall those goings-on after leaving the field and returning to your computer.

This Data Workshop is a practicum in thick description. To make things a little easier for you, we have separated the verbal and the visual so that you can concentrate on one kind of description at a time. But in your future ethnographic work, you'll be writing fieldnotes that describe both verbal and non-verbal behavior at once.

Observation: First, for ten to fifteen minutes, listen to (eavesdrop on) a conversation whose participants you can't see. They might be sitting behind you on a bus or in a restaurant—you're close enough to hear them but positioned so that you can't see them. Then, for ten to fifteen minutes, observe a conversation you can't hear—one taking place, for example, on the other side of the campus quad. Even though you can't hear what's being said, you can see the interaction as it takes place.

Written Description: Write an extremely detailed description of each conversation. Describe the participants and the setting, and include your ideas about what you think is going on and what you think you know about the participants. Try to describe everything you heard or saw to support any conclusions you draw. For each ten- to fifteen-minute observation period, your written description should be two- to three-typed pages.

There are two options for completing this Data Workshop.

- *Option 1 (informal)*: Choose a partner from your class and exchange your written descriptions with your partner. As you read through your partner's descriptions, mark with a star (*) the passages where you can see and hear clearly the things your partner describes. Circle the passages that contain evaluative words (like "angry" or "sweet") or summaries of action or conversation rather than detailed description (like "They argued about who would pay the bill"). And place a question mark next to the passages where you are left feeling like you would like to know more. Your partner will do this with your description as well, and you can discuss your responses to each other's work. Finally, as a class, use your discussions to develop a group consensus about what constitutes good descriptive detail. This is the kind of detail ethnographers strive to produce in their fieldnotes every day.

- *Option 2 (formal)*: Turn in your written descriptions to your instructor for individual feedback.

Interviews

Sociologists use **interviews**—face-to-face, information-seeking conversations—to gather information directly from research subjects, or **respondents**. When researchers conduct interviews, they try to do so systematically and with a more scientific approach than is typically seen in more casual television or newspaper interviews.

Sometimes, interviews are the only method used in a research project, but sociologists may also combine interviews with other methods, such as participant observation or analysis of existing sources. Closely related to interviews are surveys, which we will consider in the next section. Interviews, however, are always conducted by the researcher, whereas surveys may be taken independently by the respondent.

When using interviews to collect data about a particular question or project, sociologists must identify a **target population**, the larger group they wish to generalize about, and then select a **sample**, or smaller group who are representative of the larger group. The number of possible respondents depends on the type of study, the nature of the questions, and the amount of time and staff available. In most research studies, interviews can be administered to a limited number of people, so the scope of such projects is usually smaller than for other methods, such as surveys. The researcher must get **informed consent** from those participating; in other words, respondents must know what they are getting into and explicitly agree to participate. This is particularly important because most interviews are recorded, audio or video.

Arlie Hochschild (Hochschild and Machung 1989) used interviews to conduct her landmark study on parents in two-career families, *The Second Shift*. In this book Hochschild looks at how couples handle the pressures of working at a job and then coming home to what she calls "the second shift"—doing housework and taking care of children. Hochschild, who was herself in a two-career family, wanted to find out how couples were dealing with changing family roles in light of the fact that more women had entered the workforce. Were women able to juggle all their responsibilities, and to what extent were men helping their wives in running the household? Hochschild and her assistants

interviews face-to-face, information-seeking conversation, sometimes defined as a conversation with a purpose

respondent someone from whom a researcher solicits information

target population the entire group about which a researcher would like to be able to generalize

sample the part of the population that will actually be studied

informed consent a safeguard through which the researcher makes sure that respondents are freely participating and understand the nature of the research

interviewed fifty couples in two-career marriages (many were interviewed more than once) and forty-five other people who were also a part of the respondents' social arrangements, such as babysitters, day-care providers, and teachers.

When conducting an interview, how do you know what to ask? Composing good questions is one of the most difficult parts of interviewing. Most interviewers use many different questions, covering a range of issues related to the project. Questions may be closed- or open-ended. A **closed-ended question** imposes a limit on the possible response: for example, "Are you for or against couples living together before they are married?" An **open-ended question**, on the other hand, allows for a wide variety of responses: "What do you think about couples living together before they are married?"

Researchers must be careful to avoid biased or **leading questions**, those that predispose a respondent to answer in a certain way. Overly complex questions are a problem, as are **double-barreled questions**, those that involve too many different issues at one time. It is also important to be aware of any ambiguous or emotional language that might confuse or spark an emotional reaction on the part of the respondent. Asking a single parent how difficult her life is will elicit data about the difficulties, but not about the joys, of parenthood. More neutral language ("Tell me about the pluses and minuses of single parenthood") is preferable.

The Second Shift In her groundbreaking book, Arlie Hochschild interviewed working women and their partners to learn about the time-binds that they face as they balance work, family, and running a household.

Analyzing the Data

Once the interviews have been conducted, they are usually transcribed so that researchers can analyze them in textual form; they can sort through the material looking for patterns of similarities and differences among the answers. Some researchers may use computer programs designed to help analyze such data; others do it "by hand." For her analysis Hochschild categorized the types of household chores done by men and women and quantified the amount of time spent daily and weekly on those chores. She then categorized couples as "traditional," "transitional," or "egalitarian," depending on how their household labor was divided.

closed-ended question a question asked of a respondent that imposes a limit on the possible responses

open-ended question a question asked of a respondent that allows the answer to take whatever form the respondent chooses

leading questions questions that predispose a respondent to answer in a certain way

double-barreled questions questions that attempt to get at multiple issues at once, and so tend to receive incomplete or confusing answers

Advantages and Disadvantages

ADVANTAGES

1. Interviews allow respondents to speak in their own words; they can reveal their own thoughts, feelings, and beliefs, internal states that would not necessarily be accessible by any other means. In so many other instances, it is the researcher who tells the story. A book like *The Second Shift*, which features direct quotations from interview transcripts, provides the reader with an authentic and intimate portrait of the lives of married couples. Hochschild was able to get at the different subjective experiences of the women and men in her study and to see how each of them perceived the reality of his or her situation.

2. Interviews may help the researcher dispel certain preconceptions and discover issues that might have otherwise been overlooked. For example, before Hochschild began her project, many other studies had already been conducted on families with two working parents, but few seemed to examine in depth the real-life dilemma of the two-career family that Hochschild herself was experiencing.

DISADVANTAGES

1. Respondents are not always forthcoming or truthful. Sometimes they are difficult to talk to, and at other times they may try too hard to be helpful. Although an adept interviewer will be able to encourage meaningful responses, she can never take at face value what any respondent might say. To counteract this problem, Hochschild observed a few of the families she had interviewed. She saw that what these couples said about themselves in interviews was sometimes at odds with how they acted at home.

2. Another problem is representativeness: whether the conclusions of interview research can be applied to larger groups. Because face-to-face interviewing is time consuming, interviews are rarely used with large numbers of people. Can findings from a small sample be generalized to a larger population? In regard to Hochschild's research, can we say that interviews with fifty couples, although carefully selected by the researcher, give a true picture of the lives of all two-career families? Hochschild answered this question by comparing selected information about her fifty couples with data from a huge national survey.

Surveys

How many times have you filled out a survey? Probably more times than you realize. If you responded to the last U.S. government census, if you have ever been solicited by a polling agency to give your opinion about a public issue, or if you have ever been asked to evaluate your college classes and instructors at the end of a semester, you were part of somebody's survey research.

Surveys are questionnaires that are administered to a sample of respondents selected from a target population. One of the earliest sociologists to use informal surveys was Karl Marx. In the 1880s, Marx sent questionnaires to more than 25,000 French workers in an effort to determine the extent to which they were exploited by employers. Although we don't know how many surveys were returned to him or what the individual responses were, the project clearly influenced his writing, which focused heavily on workers' rights.

Today, many universities have research centers devoted to conducting survey research. One such center is the National Marriage Project at Rutgers University in New Jersey, where sociologists have been engaged in studying what they call "The State of Our Unions: The Social Health of Marriage in America" over the past several years. Researchers have asked young adults in their twenties about their attitudes toward dating, cohabitation, marriage, and parenthood.

Survey research tends to be macro and quantitative in nature: it looks at large-scale social patterns and employs statistics and other mathematical means of analysis. Social scientists who use surveys must follow specific procedures in order to produce valid results. They need a good questionnaire and wise sample selection. Most surveys are composed of closed-ended questions, or those for which all possible answers are provided. Answers may be as simple as a "yes" or "no," or more complex. A common type of questionnaire is based on the **Likert scale**, a format in which respondents can choose along a continuum—from "strongly agree" to "strongly disagree," for example. Some questionnaires also offer such options as "don't know" or "doesn't apply." Surveys may include open-ended questions, or those to which the respondents provide their own answers. These are often formatted as write-in questions and can provide researchers with more qualitative data.

Both questions and possible (given) answers on a survey must be written in such a way as to avoid confusion or ambiguity. While this is also true for interviews, it is even more important for surveys because the researcher is not generally present to clarify any misunderstandings. Common pitfalls are leading questions; **negative questions**, which ask respondents what they don't think instead of what they do; and double-barreled questions. Bias can also be a problem if questions or answers are worded in a slanted fashion.

The format of a questionnaire is also important. Something as simple as the order in which the different items are presented can influence responses. Mentioning an issue like divorce or infidelity in earlier questions can mean that respondents are thinking about it when they answer later questions, and as a result their answers might be different than they would otherwise have been. Questionnaires should be clear and easy to follow. Once a questionnaire is constructed, it is a good idea to have a small group pretest it to help eliminate flaws and make sure it is clear and comprehensible.

Another important element in survey research is sampling techniques. As with interviews, the researcher must identify the specific population she wishes to study: for example, "all married couples with children living at home" or "all young adults between the ages of twenty and twenty-nine." By using correct sampling techniques, researchers can survey a smaller number of respondents and then make accurate inferences about the larger population. For example, in the National Marriage Project

survey a method based on questionnaires that are administered to a sample of respondents selected from a target population

Likert scale a way of organizing categories on a survey question so that the respondent can choose an answer along a continuum

negative questions survey questions that ask respondents what they don't think instead of what they do

representative sample a sample taken so that findings from members of the sample group can be generalized to the whole population

probability sampling any sampling scheme in which any given unit has the same probability of being chosen

simple random sample a particular type of probability sample in which every member of the population has an equal chance of being selected

weighting techniques for manipulating the sampling procedure so that the sample more closely resembles the larger population

response rate the number or percentage of surveys completed by respondents and returned to researchers

reliability the consistency of a question or measurement tool; the degree to which the same questions will produce similar answers

confidentiality the assurance that no one other than the researcher will know the identity of a respondent

validity the accuracy of a question or measurement tool; the degree to which a researcher is measuring what he thinks he is measuring

study, researchers surveyed a statistically **representative sample** of 1,003 young adults. In quantitative research, social scientists use **probability sampling**, in which the sample group mathematically represents the larger population. Researchers might generate a **simple random sample**, where each member of the larger population has an equal chance of being included in the sample. Or they might use more sophisticated manipulating or **weighting** techniques, in which the proportion of certain variables such as race, class, gender, or age in the sample group is more closely representative of the larger population.

An increasing number of researchers have recently turned to utilizing the internet to help conduct surveys (Best and Krueger 2004; Sue and Ritter 2007). The internet has opened up new possibilities for reaching respondents as more and more people have online access. While online surveys promise a certain amount of ease and cost effectiveness, they also present researchers with significant challenges, especially in terms of scientific sampling.

Analyzing the Data

In order for a survey to be considered valid, there must be a sufficiently high **response rate**. Even if only half of the group actually returned the completed surveys, that would be considered a very good result. General claims can be made about a larger population from a lower response rate of twenty or thirty percent. Once the surveys are returned, the researchers begin the process of tabulating and analyzing the data. Responses are usually coded or turned into numerical figures so that they can be more easily analyzed on a computer. Researchers often want to understand the relationship between certain variables; for instance, what is the effect of "infidelity" on "divorce"? There are many computer programs, such as SPSS (Statistical Package for the Social Sciences), that can help research-

ers perform complicated calculations and reach conclusions about relationships. This is where advanced statistical skills become an important part of social analysis.

Advantages and Disadvantages

ADVANTAGES

1. Survey research is one of the best methods to use for gathering original data on a population that is too large to study by other means, such as by direct observation or interviewing. Surveys can be widely distributed, reaching a large number of people. Researchers can then generalize their findings to an even larger population.

2. It is also relatively quick and economical and can provide a vast amount of data. Online surveys now promise a way to gain access to even greater numbers of people at even lower cost.

3. In general, survey research is comparatively strong on **reliability**. This means that we can be sure that the same kind of data is collected each time the same question is asked.

4. There is less concern about interviewer or observer bias entering into the research process. Respondents may feel more comfortable giving candid answers to sensitive questions because they answer the questions in private and are usually assured of the **confidentiality** of their responses.

DISADVANTAGES

1. Survey research generally lacks qualitative data that might better capture the social reality the researcher wishes to examine. Because most survey questions don't allow the respondent to qualify his answer, they don't allow for a full range of expression and may not accurately reflect the true meaning of the respondent's thoughts. For example, asking a respondent to choose one reason from a list of reasons for divorce might not provide a full explanation for the failure of that person's marriage. The reasons may have been both financial and emotional, but the survey may not provide the respondent with the ability to convey this. Adding write-in questions is one way to minimize this disadvantage.

2. In general, since not all respondents are honest in self-reports, survey research is comparatively weak on **validity**. For example, a respondent may be ashamed about his divorce and may not want to reveal the true reasons behind it to a stranger on a questionnaire.

3. Often, there are problems with the sampling process, especially when respondents self-select to participate, that make generalizability more difficult. Gathering data online only exacerbates this problem. If a survey seeking to know the true incidence of domestic violence in the population is administered only to the members of a domestic violence support group, then the incidence of domestic violence will be 100 percent—misrepresenting the incidence in the larger population.

4. It's possible that survey research will be used to support a point of view rather than for pure scientific discovery; for example, a manufacturer of SUVs may report that 90 percent of all American families wish they had a larger car. We will consider this limitation later, in the section on nonacademic uses of research methods.

DATA WORKSHOP
ANALYZING MASS MEDIA AND POPULAR CULTURE
Comparative Media Usage Patterns

Recent studies have shown that the average American spends more than nine hours a day using some type of media—computers, TV, iPods, and so on (Council for Research Excellence 2009). That's more than half of our waking hours each day. With the media playing such an increasingly important role in society, researchers continue to study their impact across a wide range of issues. In this Data Workshop, you will be conducting your own research about media usage in everyday life. Your task is twofold. First, you will get some practice constructing and administering surveys as a method of data collection. Second, you will do a preliminary analysis of your data and discover something for yourself about the patterns of media usage among those who participate in your **pilot study**.

There is much more to the picture than just the number of hours Americans spend using media; we want to understand more about the role the media play in these people's lives. What do you consider an interesting or important aspect of media usage to study? Here are some suggestions.

What kind of media are people using—books, television, radio, iPods, CDs, DVDs, the internet, video games, cell phones, or hand-held devices? Do different groups prefer different types of media? How many different kinds of devices do people have access to or own? How much money do individuals spend on media-related activities? How does age, education, gender, ethnicity, or religion influence media usage? What else do people do while using media—do they work, eat, clean, drive, exercise, study, or even sleep?

Now come up with more of your own questions!

Because there are a variety of ways of doing such a project, you should choose just how you would like to customize your research. Since this is only a preliminary effort at survey research, the project will have to be somewhat limited. Nonetheless, try to follow the necessary steps in the research process in order to be as scientific as possible.

1. Decide what aspects of media use you want to study.

2. Select a sample of the population you wish to study (teenagers, minority groups, people with a college degree, and so on).

3. Write and format your survey questionnaire.

4. Administer the questionnaire to the individuals in your sample.

5. Analyze the data collected in the survey.

6. Present your findings.

There are two options for completing this Data Workshop.

- *Option 1 (informal)*: Working in small groups of three to four students, begin designing a survey project by discussing steps 1 and 2 above. Members of the group can then collaborate on step 3. If time allows, they can play the role of a pilot group and test the questionnaire by taking the survey themselves as in step 4. Finally, the group should discuss what needs to be changed or what else needs to be accomplished to complete an actual survey.

- *Option 2 (formal)*: Design your own survey research project, completing all of the above steps. Choose at least five to eight people to be included in your sample. After administering the questionnaire, write a three- to four-page essay discussing the research process and your preliminary findings.

Existing Sources

Nearly all sociologists use **existing sources** when they approach a particular research question. For instance, social demography uses statistical data to study the size, composition, growth, and distribution of human populations (Fox

pilot study a small study carried out to test the feasibility of a larger on

existing sources materials that have been produced for some other reason, but that can be used as data for social research

Alice Miller's *For Your Own Good* By analyzing historical sources and child-rearing guides, Miller argued that some of the methods we use to raise children, which we accept as normal and ordinary, can create seriously aberrant individuals as well as regular folks.

and the Roots of Violence (1990) in order to investigate the childhood experiences of several notorious German historical figures, including Adolf Hitler. Miller found that Hitler was the product of a fairly traditional child-rearing, with traditional gender-role socialization and disciplinary practices. Her findings force us to acknowledge that seemingly "normal" child-rearing practices have the potential to create someone like Hitler—that it is not always the exceptions but the rules themselves that can make a monster. Miller's use of existing records allowed her to gain insight into not only the development of an individual personality but also the structure of an entire society and the role that society played in creating one of the twentieth century's most malevolent individuals.

Consulting existing data can be somewhat less involved than collecting original data (and it can be especially helpful to students, who usually don't have the resources to collect original data themselves). Researchers can generally find survey, census, or other historical information on the internet or obtain it from the social scientists or government bureaus that conducted the original studies. New technology is also making more material more readily available to researchers. We now have unprecedented access to digital media (books, magazines, articles, e-mail, web pages, music, photos, TV programs, videos, and films) that are regularly retrievable through the internet. While all of these materials may have been created for another purpose, they can constitute valuable data to be used in social research.

Analyzing the Data

After obtaining their data, researchers must decide which analytic tools will be best suited to their research questions. Survey and census data are generally subjected to statistical analysis: researchers posit a particular relationship between variables and then employ mathematical manipulations to test it (Fox 1997). For instance, a researcher might want to look at the relationship between a woman's age and her likely marital status. In 2006, *Newsweek* magazine revisited a controversial article written twenty years earlier, "The Marriage Crunch," that reported that college-educated women over the age of forty had less than a 3 percent chance of getting married. After reviewing new census data, *Newsweek* had to revise that number to more than 40 percent (McGinn 2006).

Content analysis is a method in which researchers count the number of times specific variables—such as particular words—appear in a text, image, or media message. They then analyze the variables and relationships between them. For example, content analysis shows that the roles women play on television are of lower status than men's, with women more likely to be portrayed as housewives, mothers,

1997). The original data used in such research are often collected by social scientists other than the researcher and by government agencies, such as census bureaus and public health departments. In fact, the U.S. Census Bureau makes some of its data available to the public on its web site, census. gov, to help you analyze family size, income levels, or other relevant questions.

Other sociologists use what are called **comparative and historical methods**, which seek to understand relationships between elements of society in various regions and time periods. These sociologists often analyze cultural artifacts, such as literature, paintings, newspapers, and photography (Bauer and Gaskell 2000). As an example, Alice Miller consulted child-rearing manuals and family records for her book *For Your Own Good: Hidden Cruelty in Child-Rearing*

comparative and historical methods methods that use existing sources to study relationships between elements of society in various regions and time periods

content analysis a method in which researchers identify and study specific variables—such as words—in a text, image, or media message

In Relationships

Social Networking Sites as Sources of Data

While sociologists interested in studying interpersonal relationships use a wide variety of archival materials, the internet has created whole new ways of conducting research. Letters, journals, and diaries have always been a rich source of data, but ones that have usually been unavailable until many years after they were produced. On the other hand, social networking web sites like Facebook and MySpace create a treasure-trove of data that can be accessed unobtrusively in real time. Given that Facebook is the second most-visited site on the internet and, unlike most web sites, is full of sociologically fascinating phenomena, it's not surprising to find that numerous researchers are using Facebook as a source of data to study such issues as relationships, identity, self-esteem, and popularity.

One of the most ambitious projects has been launched by Nicholas Christakis and Jason Kaufman of Harvard and Andreas Wimmer of UCLA. Their data consist of all the publicly available Facebook profiles of an entire class at an anonymous East Coast university from their freshman to senior years. These data will allow the researchers to examine the relationship "between patterns of social affiliation and aesthetic proclivities" (Kaufman 2008). In other words, they will be able to look at the relationship between the number and type of friends someone has and the type of books, music, and movies they like.

Preliminary results have both good and bad news. The bad news is that online social networks seem to look a lot like social networks established through traditional, real-life, face-to-face contact (or "meatspace," as it is called). Specifically, people's networks on Facebook tend to exhibit "homophily"; that is, people tend to be Facebook friends with other people like them, especially in terms of race and gender. The good news is, this might indicate that online relationships are quite real and therefore confer the same benefits as traditional social networks. In some ways, this isn't surprising. Increasingly, an individual's internet profile is simply an extension of her everyday life.

For researchers, Facebook is especially exciting because it offers a data set rich enough to test ideas that up to now have only been theorized about. As Harvard sociologist Christakis points out, concepts about how social networks function were "first described by Simmel 100 years ago. . . . He just theorizes about it 100 years ago, but he didn't have the data. Now we can engage that data" (Rosenbloom 2007).

But social networking web sites do more than just provide researchers with new data to answer old questions; they also connect friends and family in new ways. Young people use the "relationship status" feature of Facebook or MySpace as the new standard for evaluating dating; they aren't really a couple until they change their status to "in a relationship." And Facebook has also changed the ways that families interact. The extended family, which is often now separated geographically, is more easily reunited online. Ever since Facebook became available to users in the general community (it says "Everyone Can Join" right on the home page), college students have increasingly seen their parents, and even their grandparents, signing up to stay in touch.

How Might Facebook Be a Source for Sociological Data? Nicholas Christakis uses Facebook to study how people form social relationships.

secretaries, and nurses, while men are doctors, judges, celebrities, and athletes in addition to being husbands and fathers (Kolbe and Langefeld 1993).

Advantages and Disadvantages

ADVANTAGES

1. Researchers are able to work with information they could not possibly obtain for themselves. Census bureaus, for example, collect information about entire national populations (family size, income, and occupational and residential patterns), something an individual researcher has neither the time nor funds to do. In addition, existing data analysis can be a convenient way for sociologists to pool their resources; one researcher can take data collected by another for his own project, increasing what we can learn from those data.

2. Using sources such as newspapers, political speeches, and cultural artifacts, sociologists are able to learn about many social worlds, in different time periods, that they would never be able to enter themselves; for example, preserved letters and diaries from the early 1800s have allowed researchers to analyze the experiences of wives and mothers on the American frontier (Peavy and Smith 1998).

3. Researchers can use the same data to replicate projects that have been conducted before, which is a good way to test findings for reliability or to see changes across time.

experiments formal tests of specific variables and effects, performed in a controlled setting where all aspects of the situation can be controlled

control in an experiment, the process of regulating all factors except for the independent variable

experimental group the part of a test group that receives the experimental treatment

control group the part of a test group that is allowed to continue without intervention so that it can be compared with the experimental group

independent variable factor that is predicted to cause change

dependent variable factor that is changed (or not) by the independent variable

DISADVANTAGES

1. Researchers drawing on existing sources often seek to answer questions that the original authors did not have in mind. If you were interested in the sex lives of those frontier women in the early 1800s, for example, you would be unlikely to find any clear references in their letters or diaries.

2. Similarly, content analysis, although it can describe the messages inherent in the media, does not illuminate how such messages are interpreted. So we can say

that women's roles on television have lower status than men's, but additional research would be required to identify the effects of these images on viewers.

Experimental Methods

Unlike ethnographies, interviews, surveys, or existing sources, **experiments** actually closely resemble the scientific method with which we began this chapter. You might associate experiments with laboratory scientists in white coats, but experimental research methods are also used by social scientists, especially those who are interested in such issues as group power dynamics, racial discrimination, and gender socialization. Experiments take place not only in laboratories but also in corporate boardrooms and even on street corners.

When sociologists conduct experiments, they start with two basic goals. First, they strive to develop precise tools with which to observe, record, and measure their data. Second, they attempt to **control** for all possible variables except the one under investigation: they regulate everything except the variable they're interested in so that they can draw clearer conclusions about what caused that variable to change (if it did).

For instance, a researcher interested in divorce may want to investigate whether marriage counseling actually helps couples stay together. He would recruit couples for the experiment and divide them into two groups, making sure that members of each group were similar in terms of age, income, education, and religion as well as length of time married. One group, the **experimental group**, would receive marriage counseling, while the other, the **control group**, would not. The **independent variable** (factor that is predicted to cause change) is marriage counseling. The **dependent variable** (factor that is changed by the independent variable) is the chance of staying married or getting divorced. In such an experiment, the researcher could compare the two groups and then make conclusions about whether marriage counseling leads to more couples staying together, or more couples getting divorced, or has no impact at all.

Another area in which sociological experiments have been conducted is gender-role socialization in families. Research has shown that a child's earliest exposure to what it means to be a boy or girl comes from parents and other caregivers. Boy and girl infants are treated differently by adults—from the way they're dressed to the toys they're given to play with—and are expected to act differently (Thorne 1993). In one experiment adult subjects were asked to play with a small baby, who was dressed in either pink or blue. The

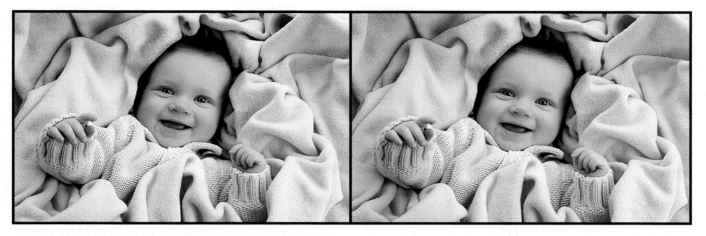

What Does It Mean to Be a Boy or a Girl? In Barrie Thorne's experiment, she asked adults to play with babies dressed in either blue or pink. Thorne found that people treated the baby differently depending on whether they thought it was a girl or a boy.

subjects assumed the gender of the infant by the color of its clothes and acted accordingly. When they thought it was a boy (blue), they handled the baby less gently and talked in a louder voice, saying things like, "Aren't you a big, strong boy?" When they thought it was a girl (pink), they held the baby closer to themselves and spoke more softly: "What a sweet little girl!" From this experiment, we can see how gender influences the way that we perceive and interact with others from a very early age.

Sociologists sometimes also use quasi-experimental methods when they study ethnic and gender discrimination in housing, employment, or policing (McIntyre et al. 1980; Brief et al. 1995; Charles 2001). In such studies, individuals who were similar in all respects except for ethnicity or gender were asked to interview for the same jobs, apply for the same mortgage loans, or engage in some other activity. As in the pink-and-blue baby experiment, people who had exactly the same qualifications were treated differently based on their race and gender, with whites and men given better jobs or mortgage rates, and women and minorities given inferior jobs or rates, or none at all. Through such studies, researchers are able to observe behaviors that may indicate discrimination or unequal treatment.

Analyzing the Data

On the whole, data analysis for experimental sociology tends to be quantitative rather than qualitative because the main goal of an experiment is to isolate a variable and explore the degree to which this variable affects a particular social situation (Smith 1990). The quantitative techniques for analyzing data range from straightforward statistical analyses to complex mathematical modeling.

Advantages and Disadvantages

ADVANTAGES

1. Experiments give sociologists a way to manipulate and control the social environment they seek to understand. They can be designed so that there is a minimal amount of outside interference. Researchers can also select participants who have exactly the characteristics they want to explore, such as the babies and adults in the gender-socialization experiment.

2. Experimental methods are especially appropriate for researchers who are developing theories about the way the social world operates: a researcher can construct a model of the social situation she is interested in and watch as it unfolds before her, without any of the unpredictable intrusions of the real world. For instance, if she wants to study what makes bystanders want to intervene, this might be easier to measure in a laboratory setting than among strangers on a busy public street.

3. Much like physics experiments, highly controlled sociological experiments can theoretically be repeated—they have replicability—so that findings can be tested more than once. An experiment such as the pink-and-blue baby study could easily be performed again and again to gauge historical and cultural changes in gender socialization. Ethnographies and surveys, on the other hand, are almost impossible to repeat in any reliable way.

DISADVANTAGES

Achieving distance from the messy realities of the social world is also the major weakness with sociological experiments. Although experiments can be useful for the development of theory and for explaining the impact of isolated variables, they are generally not very effective for describing more complex processes and interactions. By definition, experiments seek to eliminate elements that will have an unforeseen effect, and that's just not the way the real world works.

Issues in Sociological Research

As sociologists, we don't conduct our research in a cultural vacuum. In our professional as well as personal lives, all our actions have consequences, and we must be aware of how the things we do affect others. For this reason, any introduction to sociological methods is incomplete without a discussion of three topics: the nonacademic uses of sociological research; values, objectivity, and reactivity in the research process; and the importance of ethics in conducting social research.

Nonacademic Uses of Research Methods

The research methods discussed in this chapter are frequently applied outside the field of sociology. The U.S. Census Bureau, for example, has been taking a survey of the total population once every ten years since 1790. The census attempts to reach every person residing in the country and makes reports available on a wide range of social, demographic, and economic features. Many government decisions, from where to build a new school or hospital to where to install a new stoplight, are made using demographic data from the census and other major surveys.

Sociological research methods are also used by private organizations, such as political campaign offices and news agencies. You are probably familiar with polls (another form of survey research) conducted by organizations like Gallup, Zogby, and Roper. And you have certainly seen the results of election polls, which indicate the candidates or issues voters are likely to support. Polls, however, do not just reflect public opinion; they can also be used to shape it. Not all of them are conducted under strict scientific protocols. Whenever you hear poll results, try to learn who commissioned the poll and determine whether they are promoting (or opposing) any particular agenda.

Businesses and corporations have turned to sociological research in order to better understand the human dynamics within their companies. Some ethnographers, for instance, have studied organizational culture and reported their findings to executives. Edgar Schein (1997)

is often referred to as an industrial ethnographer because he conducts fieldwork in business settings in order to help management identify and deal with dilemmas in the workplace, such as how to motivate workers. Many of the experimental "games" developed by sociological researchers can be put to use in the business world to build teams, train employees, or even conduct job interviews. During a corporate retreat, for example, employees might be asked to participate in an obstacle or ropes course, in which they have to work together in order to succeed. By observing the strategies participants use, an employer might learn how task-oriented networks are formed, how leaders are chosen, or how cooperation emerges under pressure. Similarly, experimental games that require subjects to budget imaginary money or communicate an idea in a round of charades may offer insight into how social groups operate or may identify the most effective communicators from a pool of applicants. These experiments clearly benefit the corporation; do they help workers as well?

Market research is perhaps the most common of all nonacademic uses of sociological methods. In order to be successful, most companies will engage in some sort of study of the marketplace, either through their own internal sales and marketing departments or by hiring an outside consultant. The efforts of all these companies to understand the buying public have created a multibillion-dollar marketing and advertising industry. If you've ever filled out a product warranty card after making a purchase, clicked "yes" on a pop-up dialog box from a web site, or cast a vote for your favorite contestants on *Dancing with the Stars*, then someone has gathered data about your tastes and habits. It is important to note, however, that not all market studies, in fact probably very few, meet the rigorous standards that are otherwise applied to "scientific" research. Remember, too, that the bottom line for any company that uses market research is the desire to sell you their products or services. Just how well do these marketers know you already?

Values, Objectivity, and Reactivity

It's important to recognize that scientific research is done by human beings, not robots. Humans have flaws, prejudices, and blind spots, and all of these things can affect the way we conduct research.

VALUES Like biological or physical scientists, most sociologists believe that they should not allow their personal beliefs to influence their research. The classic sociological statement on neutrality comes from Max Weber (1925/1946), who, in his essay "Science as a Vocation," coined the phrase

value-free sociology to convey the idea that in doing research sociologists need to separate facts from their own individual values. Although most sociologists have agreed with this ideal, some have challenged the notion of value-free sociology. For instance, some Marxist researchers believe it is appropriate to combine social research and social action. For them, the study of society is intimately linked to a commitment to actively solve social problems. On the other hand, some symbolic interactionists, like David Matza (1969), believe that the very intention of changing the world prohibits a researcher from understanding that world. The question of whether sociologists should engage only in **basic research**, which is justified as the search for knowledge for its own sake, or rather engage in **applied research**, which requires putting into action what is learned, continues to be debated within the discipline.

Despite the safeguards built into research methodologies, there are still opportunities for bias, or personal preferences, to subtly influence how the work is done. For example a researcher with strong pro-life beliefs might refuse to ask survey questions on topics such as abortion—or might try to influence respondents into changing their opinions on the subject. Bias can infiltrate every part of the research process—from identifying a project to selecting a sample, from the wording of questions to the analysis and write-up of the data. The effects of bias are very difficult to avoid.

OBJECTIVITY The notion of **objectivity**, or impartiality, plays a fundamental role in scientific practice. As far back as Auguste Comte, sociologists have maintained that they could study society rationally and objectively. If a researcher is rational and objective, then he should be able to observe reality, distinguish actual facts from mental concepts, and separate truth from feeling or opinion. This ideal may be desirable and reasonable, but can "facts" really speak for themselves? And if so, can we discover those facts without somehow involving ourselves in them?

Some "facts" that sociologists once took to be objective reality have since been invalidated. Racist, sexist, and ethnocentric perspectives long dominated the field and passed for "truth." For many years, scientific reality consisted only of the experience of white European males, and the realities of women, ethnic minorities, and others outside the mainstream were categorically ignored or dismissed. For example, until recently, heart problems in women were likely to go undiagnosed, which meant that women were more likely than men to die from heart attacks. Why? Because medical research on heart attacks used mostly male subjects and so had not discovered that women's symptoms are different from men's (Rabin 2008). It is easy now, through hindsight, to see that our "knowledge" was severely distorted. We must, therefore,

be willing to recognize that what presently passes for fact may some day be challenged.

Another obstacle to achieving objectivity is our subjective nature as human beings. Our own experience of the world, and therefore sense of reality, is inevitably personal and idiosyncratic. Although we recognize our innate subjectivity, we still long for and actively pursue what we call absolute truth. But some social scientists question this ideal; they propose that subjectivity is not only unavoidable, it may be preferable when it comes to the study of human beings. This is especially true of sociologists who do "auto-ethnographic" research, in which they themselves—and their own thoughts, feelings, and experiences—are the focus of their research (Ellis 1997). On the other hand, some postmodern thinkers have gone so far as to reject the notion that there is any objective reality out there in the first place. Their arguments parallel certain trends in the physical sciences as well, where developments such as chaos theory and fuzzy logic suggest the need to reconsider the assumption of an orderly universe.

REACTIVITY In addition to maintaining their objectivity, social scientists must also be concerned with **reactivity**, the ways that people and events respond to being studied. One classic example of reactivity comes from studies that were conducted from 1927 to 1932 at the Hawthorne plant of Western Electric in Chicago. Elton Mayo, a Harvard business school professor, sought to examine the effect of varying work conditions on motivation and productivity in the factory. When he changed certain conditions—such as lighting levels, rest breaks, and even rates of pay—he found that each change resulted in a rise in productivity both in the individual worker and in the group. What was more surprising, however, was that returning to the original conditions also resulted in a rise in productivity. Mayo concluded, then, that the variables he had manipulated were not the causes of productivity; rather, *it was the effect of being studied*, or what is now referred to as the **Hawthorne effect**. In other words, the workers had responded to the researchers' taking interest in their performance, and it was this attention that had caused the improvement.

---

value-free sociology an ideal whereby researchers identify facts without allowing their own personal beliefs or biases to interfere

basic research the search for knowledge without any agenda or desire to use that knowledge to effect change

applied research research designed to gather knowledge that can be used learned to create some sort of change

objectivity impartiality, the ability to allow the facts to speak for themselves

reactivity the tendency of people and events to react to the process of being studied

Hawthorne effect a specific example of reactivity, in which the desired effect is the result not of the independent variable but of the research itself

Changing the World

Brown vs. Board of Education

Earl Babbie (2002) claims that research biases have come into play in the area of U.S. racial relations and documents several cases in the country's history to illustrate the point.

In 1896, the Supreme Court established the doctrine of "separate but equal" as a means of "guaranteeing equal protection" for African Americans while still allowing racial segregation. Although no social research was directly cited in the Court's ruling, it is widely believed that the justices were influenced by the writing of William Graham Sumner (1906), a leading social scientist of his time. Sumner believed that the customs of a society were relatively impervious to outside influence and that therefore the legal system should not be used to enforce social change. The saying "You can't legislate morality" is a reflection of such thinking. So instead of allowing blacks the same rights and access to resources, the Court continued to uphold segregation.

The doctrine of "separate but equal" persisted until it was finally overturned in 1954 in the landmark civil rights case *Brown vs. Board of Education of Topeka*, which outlawed racial segregation in schools. This time, the Supreme Court justices based their unanimous decision on several other, more contemporary sociological and psychological studies (Blaunstein and Zangrando 1970). Apparently, the Court was now of the belief that morality *could* be legislated. It is no surprise, then, that controversy erupted again when in 1966 a noted sociologist, James Coleman, published his findings about a national study on race and education. Coleman claimed that the academic performance of African American students attending integrated schools was no better than that of those attending segregated schools; that such things as libraries, laboratories, or expenditures per student had less influence on academic performance than neighborhoods or family. While some criticized Coleman on methodological grounds, others were more concerned that his findings might be used to support a return to segregation. This has not happened, but neither has complete integration. Much more work needs to be done toward creating an educational system that serves all students, and social research will continue to be part of that process. Most social scientists, and the American public in general, support civil rights and racial equality. These beliefs inspire research at the same time that research inspires continued social change. Even though we aim for value-free sociology, there are some topics on which it is hard to remain neutral.

Researchers must always be aware that their subjects, whether in an experiment or in a natural observation, are active and intelligent participants. The subjects may be able to sense what the researchers are trying to understand or prove and in effect "give them what they want" by responding to even the unspoken goals of the research. Our presence as researchers always has some effect on those we study, whether noticeable to us or not.

Research Ethics

Doing research that involves other human beings means that we must address moral issues (questions about right and wrong conduct) as we make decisions that will affect them. For this reason, various academic disciplines have developed ethical guidelines—professional standards for honest and honorable dealings with others—meant to help direct the decision making of such researchers. When we use other people as means to an end, we must protect them as ends in themselves.

It's easy to understand the risks of participating in, say, a pharmaceutical drug trial or a study of the effects of radiation treatment on certain types of cancers. The risks of participating in social research are different and more subtle. It is often the case, for example, that social researchers don't fully explain the details of their research project to the participating subjects. Sometimes this is necessary: survey respondents, for example, must be able to answer questions without interference from the researcher and the potential for bias. Also, ethnographic fieldworkers operate on various levels of secrecy or **deception**: even when an ethnographer has openly declared herself a researcher, it is often impossible for her to remind every person she speaks with that she is a scientific observer as well as a participant. And if she engages in "covert" research and deliberately presents an inauthentic self to the group, then that makes all her interactions inauthentic as well. This can affect the fieldworker's ability to discover the members' real, grounded meanings. What, then, has she really been able to learn about the setting and its members?

Codes of ethics in the social sciences do not provide strict rules for researchers to abide by in these cases; rather, they set out principles to guide the researcher's decision making. Secrecy and deceit are thus never strictly prohibited; instead, researchers are cautioned to acquire the informed consent of their subjects and to conduct themselves in a way that protects the subjects from harm.

What other kinds of harm can come to participants? They're not likely to get diseases, and there is usually little physical risk in sitting down to complete a survey questionnaire! But harm *can* result, mostly as a result of the breaching of confidentiality. Research subjects are entitled to "rights of biographical anonymity": researchers are required to protect their privacy. This protection is essential to gathering valid data, especially when dealing with controversial topics or vulnerable populations. Respondents must be guaranteed that no one will be able to identify them from reading the research findings. But while most researchers take steps to disguise the identities of individuals and locations, it is sometimes difficult to keep others from uncovering them. For example a classic sociological pseudonym, "Middletown" (Lynd and Lynd 1929/1959, 1937), was long ago revealed to be Muncie, Indiana—and since the Middletown studies were seen as an example of the shallowness and triviality of American culture, this was not such a good thing for Muncie's reputation!

Sometimes worse than having others recognize a place or person is having subjects themselves find out what was written about them. Carolyn Ellis (1995) had an unsettling experience when she returned to the small mid-Atlantic fishing village in which she had spent years living and doing fieldwork. In the time she had been gone, she had published a book about the village, and excerpts had made their way back to the villagers, who were upset at the way that Ellis had depicted them. These villagers, who had considered Ellis to be their friend, felt deeply betrayed; they felt that she had abused their hospitality and misrepresented them as uncouth, uneducated hicks. Despite her protests that she was simply doing her job as a sociologist, many villagers refused to speak with her again, and she was shut out of a social world of which she had once been an integral part.

Researchers may undertake other kinds of risks as well. Particularly in ethnographic research, and especially if researching a dangerous subculture, researchers may be at risk of life and limb. Sociologist Martin Sanchez-Jankowski (1991) became a member of a street gang in order to conduct his research. Ethnographer John Van Maanen (1973, 1983, 1988) found himself at risk of a prison term and in what he called a "moral fix" when he witnessed a controversial beating during the course of his fieldwork at an urban police department. A subpoena was issued requiring him to testify in the case. If he did, it would incriminate the police officers whose trust he had gained over months of fieldwork; if he didn't, it would doom the beating victim, a drifter whose only crime was being in the wrong place at the wrong time. Van Maanen felt a strong moral obligation to protect the confidentiality of his subjects and was ultimately successful in keeping his fieldnotes out of court (Adler and Adler 2000).

In order to encourage the protection of research subjects, each academic discipline has adopted its own **code of ethics** to provide guidelines for researchers. The American Sociological Association Code of Ethics, for example, sets out recommendations for how to avoid bias, adhere to professional standards, and protect respondents from harm. In addition, universities where research is conducted have a body known as an **institutional review board**, or IRB, a group of scholars who meet regularly to review the research proposals of their colleagues. If an IRB has reservations about the safety of the subjects in a given research project, it may act to stop that project from going forward. In extreme cases, funding may be revoked if the subjects are being put at undue risk; entire university power structures have been undermined as a result of pervasive research ethics problems.

The power invested in IRBs is seen as controversial by some. The boards are often made up entirely of scholars

deception the extent to which the participants in a research project are unaware of the project or its goals

code of ethics ethical guidelines for researchers to consult as they design a project

institutional review board a group of scholars within a university who meet regularly to review and approve the research proposals of their colleagues and make recommendations for how to protect human subjects

The Nuremberg Code and Research Ethics

The origins of contemporary research ethics can be traced back to the Nuremberg Military Tribunals of the late 1940s, in which a group of Nazi doctors were tried for the horrific "experiments" they had performed during World War II. These experiments involved the torture and death of thousands of concentration camp inmates. Of the twenty-three Nazi doctors tried at Nuremberg, sixteen were convicted of war crimes. Besides a kind of justice for the deaths of so many, the other enduring result of the trials was the Nuremberg Code, a set of moral and ethical guidelines for performing research on human beings. According to these guidelines, developed by two doctors, Andrew Ivy and Leo Alexander, scientists must accept certain responsibilities: to perform only research that can "yield fruitful results for the good of society, unprocurable by other methods"; to protect their human subjects from "all unnecessary physical and mental suffering and injury"; and to perform research only on subjects who give their informed, noncoerced consent.

In America, there was strong support for the Nuremberg Code. But at the same time that it was being developed, the U.S. government was involved in its own medical atrocity, though it would not be revealed to the public until decades later: the Tuskegee Syphilis Study. In 1932, the U.S. Public Health Service began a forty-year-long study of "untreated syphilis in the male negro": 399 African American men from Tuskegee, an impoverished region of Alabama, who were infected with syphilis were left untreated so that doctors could observe the natural progression of the disease. The symptoms include painful sores, hair loss, sterility, blindness, paralysis, and insanity, and finally lead to death; the disease can be transmitted by men to their sexual partners, and infected women can pass it on to their infants. By 1947, penicillin was widely accepted as the preferred treatment for syphilis, but government doctors decided to leave the Tuskegee men untreated to avoid interfering with the study's results.

While these doctors had not intentionally inflicted the disease upon subjects, neither had they offered a cure when it became available. The full story of the Tuskegee experiment was not revealed until 1972, and it was not until 1997 that President Bill Clinton issued an official apology from the U.S. government to the victims and their families. Clearly, Americans were as guilty of violating moral and ethical codes as Germany had been at a similar time in history.

What is important to take away from this lesson is the need for all scientific research to adhere to ethical standards—this includes the social as well as medical sciences. In either case, researchers must consider the potential harm that they can cause to human subjects. You may not think of sociologists as dealing with life-and-death issues; yet, as researchers, we often find ourselves in positions where certain kinds of studies can't be undertaken because of concerns for the well-being of the potential subjects.

The Nuremberg Code In the wake of the Nuremberg Military Tribunals after World War II (pictured left), science organizations adopted a set of guidelines to regulate researchers' ethical conduct. Whether studying biology, psychiatry, or sociology, researchers must consider the potential harm they could cause to research participants.

in medicine, biology, chemistry, and physics; social scientists have questioned their ability to make judgments about social research. Because IRBs have the power to shut down research projects, perhaps they should be discipline specific, with biologists judging biologists, psychologists judging psychologists, and sociologists judging sociologists.

Closing Comments

In this chapter, you have learned the different methods used by sociologists to investigate the social world. Each method has its strengths and limitations, and each can be fruitfully applied to a variety of research questions. In fact, this is exactly what you will be doing in future chapters.

Each chapter from this point on will feature two Data Workshops in which you will be asked to apply one of the methods from this chapter to an actual sociological research project. You will get a chance to practice doing the work of sociological research, and analyzing (and sometimes gathering) your own data. You may find yourself referring back to this chapter to remind yourself of the specifics of each methodology. This is exactly what you should be doing; it's okay if two months from now you don't remember the details. Just because you're moving on to Chapter 3, don't forget that Chapter 2 can continue to be useful to you throughout the term. And maybe even beyond that.

Ⓢ Need Help Studying?

wwnorton.com/studyspace

Visit StudySpace to access free review materials such as:
- **Vocabulary Flashcards**
- **Diagnostic Review Quizzes**
- **Study Outlines**

QUESTIONS FOR REVIEW

1. Kathryn Edin and Maria Kefalas carried out their ethnography of single mothers by means of participant observation, often acting as full participants within the setting. How do you think this affected what they learned? How would their conclusions have been different if they had simply done interviews?

2. Under what circumstances do you think that covert research is justified? How did Richard Mitchell, who studied militant survivalists, justify hiding his intentions from his subjects? How would you feel if you found out someone was secretly studying you?

3. According to Clifford Geertz, ethnographers should try to write "thick description." Imagine you are in the field, and you see one of your subjects quickly close his right eyelid. What sort of details would you have to record for your readers to know if this action was a wink or a twitch?

4. Does reflexivity sound like a good or bad thing to you? How did it play out for Kathryn Edin her ethnographic work? Can you imagine a field setting where you would be at a disadvantage by the way your presence affected the group? How about a field setting where you would have an advantage?

5. Try to write a survey or interview question that asks about a respondent's political affiliation without being biased or using language that might spark an emotional response.

6. "Did you understand everything in this chapter, and what was your favorite part?" If this was an interview question, what would be wrong with it?

7. Imagine that your teacher asks you to do a simple random sample of your class. How would you select your sample so that you could be sure each member had an equal chance of being included?

8. Researchers are now using social networking web sites like Facebook and MySpace to gather a wide variety of data. If researchers read your profile (or those of your friends or family), do you think they would have a valid understanding of who you (or they) are? Is there a weakness of research that relies on existing sources?

9. Do you think you would react differently to an ethnographer from a market research firm than you would to one from a university?

SUGGESTIONS FOR FURTHER EXPLORATION

Becker, Howard. 1998. *Tricks of the Trade: How to Think about Your Research While You're Doing It*. Chicago: University of Chicago Press. Describes a multitude of tricks to make research more successful; includes discussions of qualitative and quantitative research, reactivity, and sampling.

Clifford, James, and George E. Marcus, eds. 1986. *Writing Culture: The Poetics and Politics of Ethnography*. Berkeley, CA: University of California Press. Deals with the problem of treating ethnography as if it were an objective science.

Emerson, Robert M., Rachel I. Fretz, and Linda L. Shaw. 1995. *Writing Ethnographic Fieldnotes*. Chicago: University of Chicago Press. An excellent and hands-on introduction to the oft-neglected art of taking fieldnotes.

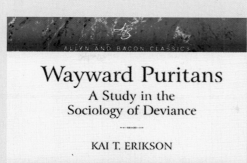

Number Our Days. 1978. Dir. Lynne Littman. Direct Cinema Limited. This wonderful short film, a record of Barbara Myerhoff's ethnographic work with an elderly Jewish population in Venice Beach, California, won an Oscar for best documentary short.

SurveyMonkey. This web site enables anyone to create online surveys quickly and easily. Learn more about writing and administering questionnaires. Of course, such surveys are not necessarily scientific. Available at: http://www.surveymonkey.com/

The *Up* series: *Seven Up* (1964), *7 Plus Seven* (1970), *21 Up* (1977), *28 Up* (1984), *35 Up* (1991), *42 Up* (1998), *49 Up* (2005), and *56 Up* (expected in 2012). Dir. Michael Apted and Paul Almond. First Run Features. Director Apted began in 1963 by interviewing fourteen English seven-year-olds from diverse class backgrounds, and he returned to interview them again every seven years.

Erickson, Kai T. *Wayward Puritans: A Study in the Sociology of Deviance.* New York: Wiley. This study of deviance in seventeenth-century Massachusetts relies on existing data (mainly court records) to present a surprising picture of crime, alcoholism, and premarital sex.

Huff, Darrell. 1993. *How to Lie with Statistics.* New York: Norton. Although not specifically about the statistical analysis of survey data, the insights expressed will still help any reader become a more skeptical consumer of survey research.

Myerhoff, Barbara. 1976. *Number Our Days.* New York: Touchstone Press. An excellent and moving example of what ethnography can be, providing insight into the process of gaining access.

Three participants in Apted's *Up* series

PART II Framing Social Life

How does culture shape our social worlds? How are our personal identities produced by our cultural contexts and social interactions? How does participation in group life shape both individual experience and social structure? How are what is normal and what is deviant defined, and what are the consequences for people who are labeled accordingly? Part II of this text addresses these questions in the next four chapters on culture (Chapter 3), the self and interaction (Chapter 4), groups (Chapter 5), and deviance (Chapter 6). The ability to examine, describe, analyze, and explain the points of intersection between the individual world and the social world is sociology's special contribution to the larger scholarly endeavor. Within the next four chapters, you will encounter many works by sociologists that illustrate the links between the individual and society. Verta Taylor and Leila Rupp's book *Drag Queens at the 801 Cabaret* (2003) is perfect for highlighting these themes.

Drag Queens at the 801 Cabaret is an ethnographic portrait of a Key West drag club, where gay male performers don sexy dresses, lavish wigs, and theatrical makeup, and sing and dance for a diverse audience: tourists and locals, men and women, gays and straights. Rupp and Taylor get to know the "801 Girls," their friends, family, and audience members, and the authors even try out their own sort of drag. (That's right—women dressed as men dressed as women!)

Rupp and Taylor recognize that the particular culture of the 801 Cabaret is nestled within multiple contemporary American subcultures. For example, Key West is an island subculture that offers a year-round, touristy, carnivalesque atmosphere as part of its charm. It "remains a flamboyant mix of cultures. . . . [I]t shelters not only vibrant Cuban and Bahamian enclaves, but also artistic, hippie, and gay communities. . . . The city, [says journalist Charles Kuralt,] is 'full of dreamers, drifters, and dropouts, spongers and idlers and barflies, writers and fishermen, islanders from the Caribbean and gays from the big cities, painters and pensioners, treasure hunters, real estate speculators, smugglers, runaways, old Conchs and young lovers . . . all elaborately tolerant of one another'" (Rupp and Taylor 2003, pp. 50–51). For the 801 girls, this means that the subcultures associated with both gay masculinity and drag performance are supported and sustained on the island in ways they might not be on the mainland. Because of the island's unique mix of subcultures, one of the performers asserts that "Key West is the true home of accepted diversity" (p. 55).

In Key West's culture, many kinds of people feel free to be themselves. But what does that really mean? For the drag queens at the 801 Cabaret, their performances are about putting on a different identity than the one they present in their everyday lives. These are men with flashy female alter-egos—Kevin becomes "Kylie"; Roger becomes "Inga"; Dean becomes "Milla." And their process of becoming is elaborate and grueling:

> Some of the girls shave all over their bodies, some their faces, chests, legs, and arms, some just their faces. . . . They powder their faces, necks, and chests, using a thick base to hide their beards. . . . Eyeliner, eye shadow, mascara, false eyelashes, lip liner, and lipstick are painstakingly applied. (pp. 12–13)

So far, this doesn't sound all that different than the rituals many women perform every morning in front of the mirror. After the makeup, however, things get a little more intricate, as the "girls"

> tuck their penises and testicles between their legs, using a gaff [a special panty], or several, to make sure everything stays out of sight . . . panty hose, sometimes several layers . . . corsets and waist cinchers . . . they all, of course, wear bras . . . [filled with] water balloons (the tied end makes an amazingly realistic nipple), half a Nerf football, lentil beans in a pair of nylons, foam or silicone prostheses. (pp. 20–21)

All this work to look like women—and that's not taking into account the exhausting work of acting the part, onstage and off. While drag queens do not seek to convince their audiences that they are "real" women, they do move, speak, sing, and dance in stereotypically feminine style as part of their performances. And that's the insight that drag queens provide about our own identities: it's *all* performance! Our male and female selves are the products of interactional accom-

Sociologists Verta Taylor and Leila Rupp

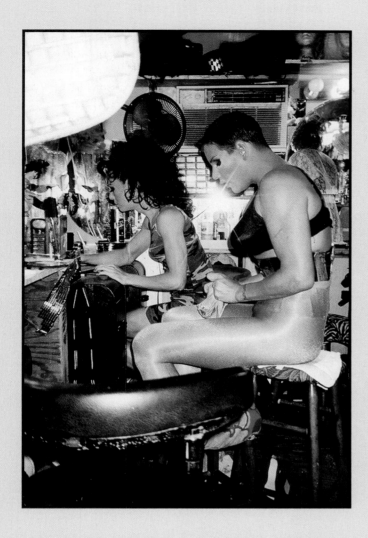

in which gender boundaries are fluid and homosexuality is normal:

> As one of the few ways that straight people encounter gay culture—where, in fact, straight people live for an hour or two in an environment where gay is normal and straight is other—drag shows . . . play an important role for the gay/lesbian movement. Precisely because drag shows are entertaining, they attract people who might never otherwise be exposed to gay politics. As one female audience member put it, they "take something difficult and make it light." (pp. 207–208)

Finally, drag shows also challenge our notions about what is normal and what is deviant, when performers embrace what would otherwise be considered a stigmatized identity and turn it into something to be proud of. Drag queens can be seen as voluntary outsiders, unconcerned about fitting into mainstream society. Rupp and Taylor make the argument that drag is a form of social protest—against a society in which gender and sexual orientation are crammed into limiting, two-category systems; against a society in which identities are seen as immutable; and against a society in which certain forms of cultural expression are marginalized. Their analysis of the social world of one Key West drag club offers sociological insights into the lives of the individual performers who work against social stigma and limitations to provide new ways of looking at culture, self, and society.

plishments, and "real" women do many of the same things that drag queens do in order to express femininity.

Because the drag queens perform different identities onstage and off, the 801 Cabaret calls into question some of our most important and taken-for-granted boundaries between social groups: males and females, and gays and straights. In fact, drag queens are living examples of the intersections between these groups. One of the performers says:

> Last night—though this happens almost every night—[this woman] goes, "I'm straight, I'm a woman, I'm not a lesbian, but you're so beautiful, I find you so attractive" . . . [and] a straight guy, has been straight for like fifty years or something like that . . . goes, "You know, I've been straight all my life, and I know you're a man, but you're so beautiful . . . I can't keep my eyes off you." (p. 201)

Drag queens and drag shows allow others to cross between groups, to see what life might be like in a world

CHAPTER 3 Cultural Crossroads

Heavy metal music has long been associated with young, white, alienated, angry, blue collar men in America. With extremely loud, pounding music accompanied by lyrics dealing with the themes of death, sex, and alienation, heavy metal has many critics among mainstream conservative Americans. *Acrassicauda* (the word is Arabic for "black scorpion") is an Iraqi heavy metal band that represents both a clash and a connection between American and Iraqi culture. Heavy metal music became popular in Iraq in the early 1990s, as middle class Iraqi teenagers discovered bands like Metallica, Slayer, and the Scorpions through black market CDs. The themes of anger, death, rebellion, and violence were all too familiar for Iraqi teens.

In 2001, four Iraqi nationals formed the band Acrassicauda, which gained fame through the 2007 documentary *Heavy Metal in Baghdad*. During Saddam Hussein's regime, the band was able to perform, but were forced to write a song glorifying Hussein with lyrics like "Following our leader Saddam Hussein, we'll make them fall, we'll drive them insane!" They were also subject to restrictions on the heavy metal custom of headbanging because of the dance's similarity to a Jewish prayer ritual called *davening*. After Hussein was overthrown, the group's lyrics became increasingly political and reflected on the horrors of a country torn apart by war. In *Vice*, a youth culture magazine, writer Gideon Yago asserts that Acrassicauda's version of metal was intensified through the terror and violence that Iraqis had to encounter on a daily basis.

Because any gathering of people in Iraq becomes a target for terrorists, Acrassicauda was only able to play six live concerts in a span of five years. Islamic militants equated heavy metal music with Satan-worshipping, much like Christian conservatives in the United States did. However, in the United States, opponents attempted to use legislation to rid the culture of heavy metal. In Iraq, the perception of heavy metal as Satan-worshipping was exacerbated by the American origins of the music. Acrassicauda received death threats that read, "You are Americanized, playing Western music. You either quit or you will be dead." These death threats escalated to the point where the members of Acrassicauda feared for their lives.

Acrassicauda did not quit playing, but instead used strategies like having random band practices rather than playing at regular times. They would hold concerts while mortar shells dropped around the venues. At the same time, they realized the danger of continuing to live in Iraq while spreading their message through heavy metal.

After watching the band's story in *Heavy Metal in Baghdad*, Alex Skolnick, from the metal band Testament, met the band and helped them record an EP, *Only the Dead See the End of the War*. The EP gathered more publicity for the group, and *Vice* magazine set up a Paypal account for donations to help members of Acrassicauda emigrate to the United States. Metal fans throughout the world donated a total of $40,000, the United States granted the band refugee status, and now Acrassicauda is living and performing in the United States.

It's interesting how an alienated U.S. subculture like heavy metal can come to represent mainstream Western culture to militant Islamic fundamentalists. It's also enlightening to see how music enjoyed by disenfranchised, rebellious American youth can be fascinating to those living in the real-life horrors of a war-torn nation. The study of culture provides an endless number of fascinating possibilities for understanding ourselves and others.

HOW TO READ THIS CHAPTER

Culture is one of the fundamental elements of social life and thus a very important topic in sociology. Many of the concepts presented here will come up again in almost every subsequent chapter. You will need to keep these concepts in mind as you learn about other substantive areas. You will also want to think about how culture is relevant to the things you already know from your own life experience. Try to come up with some of your own examples as you read along. The subject of culture is probably inherently interesting to most people. But although culture is familiar to all of us, you should be seeing it in a new and different way by the time you finish this chapter.

What Is Culture?

Culture encompasses practically all of human civilization and touches on almost every aspect of social life. It is so much a part of the world around us that we may not recognize the extent to which it shapes and defines who we are. In the broadest sense, we can say that **culture** is the entire way of life of a group of people. It can include everything from language and gestures to style of dress and standards of beauty, from customs and rituals to tools and artifacts, from music and child-rearing practices to the proper way for customers to line up in a grocery store. It forms basic beliefs and assumptions about the world and the way things work, and defines the moral parameters of what is right and wrong, good and bad.

Although culture varies from group to group, all societies develop some form of culture. It is the human equivalent of instinct in animals:

> **culture** the entire way of life of a group of people (including both material and symbolic elements) that acts as a lens through which one views the world and is passed from one generation to the next

although we humans do have some basic instincts, culture actually accounts for our great success as a species. We are totally dependent on it to deal with the demands of life in society. As culture develops, it is shared among members of a group, handed down from generation to generation, and passed along from one group or individual to another.

Although culture may seem to us to be "second nature," it is actually something that is learned, rather than innate. Because we learn it so slowly and incrementally, we are often unaware of the process. For instance, few of us would be conscious of having *learned* all the slang words we currently use or the distance we typically maintain from someone while talking with him. We may not remember exactly when we first felt patriotic or how we formed our opinions about people from the upper class. We all carry culture inside ourselves; it becomes ingrained and internalized into our way of thinking and acting. Culture guides the way we make sense of the world around us and the way we make decisions about what to do and how to do it. We can talk about the culture of a given country, state, or community, of people belonging to an ethnic or religious group, or of those working in the same profession. We can even say that sports enthusiasts, schoolmates, or a clique of friends share in a common culture. We'll discuss some of these cultural variations later in the chapter.

How Has Culture Been Studied?

People study culture in a variety of ways. Theologians and philosophers, for example, might debate the morals and values of an ideal culture. Anthropologists often investigate smaller societies outside the United States. They travel around the world and engage in empirical fieldwork, collecting stories and artifacts that document the realities of the cultures they study (Margaret Mead and Gregory Bateson are two of the most well known). In many cases, though, these cultures are often seen as "other"—interesting because of their distinctive differences from the anthropologist's home culture, which often goes unexamined.

In contrast, sociologists mainly focus on culture closer to home, usually the same societies to which they belong. They do this by using the different theories discussed in Chapter 1—functionalism, conflict theory, symbolic interactionism, and postmodernism—as well as the research methods discussed in Chapter 2. At the same time, however, sociologists may also engage in the process of "othering" by studying the unusual, extraordinary, or deviant in cultural groups. In so doing, they may fail to consider some aspects of the culture that is right in front of them. This is where the sociology of everyday life offers certain benefits. By studying the mundane as well as the exceptional, we can learn about culture in all its interesting permutations. We can learn not only about the differences between cultural groups—"us" and "them"—but also the similarities.

Ethnocentrism and Cultural Relativism

Culture acts as a lens through which we view the world. That lens, however, can either elucidate or obscure what we are looking at. Often, we can't clearly see our own culture, precisely because we are so familiar with it. Yet, when exposed to another culture, through travel, television, or other means, we can readily see what is different or exotic. Rarely does our perspective allow us to recognize the strangeness in our own culture.

One of the best examples of the challenges in observing culture is presented in a famous article by Horace Miner called "Body Ritual among the Nacirema" (1956). The article focuses on the beliefs and practices of this North American people concerning the care of their bodies. Miner observes that their fundamental belief appears to be that the human body is ugly and is susceptible to decay and disease, and the only way to counter these conditions is to engage in elaborate ceremonies and rituals. All members of the Nacirema culture conform to a greater or lesser degree to these practices and then pass them along to their children. One passage describes the household shrine where many of the body rituals take place:

> While each family has at least one shrine, the rituals associated with it are not family ceremonies but are private and secret. . . . The focal point of the shrine is a box or chest which is built into a wall. In this chest are kept the many charms and magical potions without which no native believes he could live. . . . Beneath the charm-box is a small font. Each day every member of the family, in succession, enters the shrine room, bows his head before

the charm-box, mingles different sorts of holy water in the font, and proceeds with a brief rite of ablution.

The Nacirema regularly visit medicine men, "holy-mouth men," and other specialized practitioners from whom they procure magical potions.

The Nacirema have an almost pathological horror of and fascination with the mouth, the condition of which is believed to have a supernatural influence on all social relationships. Were it not for the rituals of the mouth, they believe that their teeth would fall out, their gums bleed, their jaws shrink, their friends desert them, and their lovers reject them. The daily body ritual performed by everyone includes a mouth-rite. It was reported to me that the ritual consists of inserting a small bundle of hog hairs into the mouth, along with certain magical powders, and then moving the bundle in a highly formalized series of gestures.

Do the Nacirema seem like a strange group of people, or are they somehow familiar? Miner writes as though he were an anthropologist studying some exotic tribe of primitive people. In actuality, the passages above describe the bathroom and personal health-care habits of the average American. (Note that "Nacirema" is "American" spelled backward.) He doesn't embellish or make up anything; he merely approaches the topic as if he knew nothing about its meaning. So the "charm-box" is the standard medicine cabinet, the "holy water" font is a sink, the medicine men and "holy-mouth men" are doctors and dentists, and the exotic "mouth-rite" is the practice of brushing teeth.

"Body Ritual among the Nacirema" Horace Miner reminds us how easy it is to overlook aspects of our own culture, precisely because it seems so normal to us.

ethnocentrism the principle of using one's own culture as a means or standard by which to evaluate another group or individual, leading to the view that cultures other than one's own are abnormal or inferior

cultural relativism the principle of understanding other cultures on their own terms, rather than judging or evaluating according to one's own culture

One of the reasons that Miner's article has become so popular is that it demonstrates how easy it is to fail to see our own culture, precisely because we take it for granted. The article reminds students who are becoming social analysts how useful culture shock is in helping to see even what is most familiar to us as bizarre or strange. Throughout this chapter, keep in mind that your powers of observation must be applied to looking at both "them" and "us."

Another, related problem arises when trying to understand cultures other than our own. Generally, we think of our own culture as being the "normal" one, a belief known as **ethnocentrism**. We don't realize that culture is something learned and that there is nothing inherently better about ours. Ethnocentrism means that we use our own culture as a kind of measuring stick with which to judge other individuals or societies; anyone outside our group seems "off-center" or abnormal.

As sociologists, we want to have as clear a view of any society as possible; this requires that we suspend, at least temporarily, our ethnocentrism. There are several ways to do this. In Chapter 1, we learned about the sociological imagination, culture shock, and beginner's mind—all ways to see the world anew. We can add to that list **cultural relativism**, which means seeing each different culture as simply that—different. Not better or worse, not right or wrong, but on its own terms. This helps us place different values, beliefs, norms, and practices within their own cultural context. By practicing cultural relativism, or being culturally sensitive, we begin to see others more clearly, and without judgment, and therefore to appreciate their way of life. We can discover viewpoints and interpretations of reality different from our own. Cultural relativism becomes all the more important in our increasingly diverse society. The Data Workshop below will help you see how.

DATA WORKSHOP

ANALYZING EVERYDAY LIFE

A Comparison of Religious Services

Some people argue that religions are cultures within themselves. This is easiest to see in the case of groups such as the FLDS (a fundamentalist Mormon sect whose members practice polygamy and tend to live in isolated rural compounds)

and the white-supremacist World Church of the Creator (whose leader, Matt Hale, is currently in prison for conspiring to kill a federal judge), but even your friendly neighborhood congregation has a specific set of beliefs that are particular to itself. This Data Workshop will help you uncover some characteristics of two specific religious cultures and compare them in nonjudgmental ways. This is an ethnographic exercise and is meant to help you identify ethnocentrism and practice cultural relativism. (Refer back to Chapter 2 if you need a refresher on ethnographic methods.)

Step 1: Observing Services
Select two different houses of worship—church, synagogue, temple, mosque, or other place of worship—and attend one service at each. You may want to compare two different denominations within the same broad religious category (a Catholic mass and a Protestant service, for example, both Christian denominations) or two different religions (a Catholic mass and an Islamic prayer service). Any choice is fine (including one you are familiar with, if any) as long as it is open to the public. You may want to call their offices first, to find out if there are certain dress code requirements or other things you need to know about before you arrive. Remember, when you visit your chosen houses of worship, you must behave in a respectful manner. If you suspect that you can't maintain a quiet (if that's called for) and respectful demeanor, then choose a different service to attend.

Observe closely all that you encounter. Since it is probably not appropriate for you to jot down notes during a religious service, you should write your fieldnotes as soon as you can afterward. Record in as much detail as possible what was said, done, or sung during your period of observation.

- When do people act in unison?

- When do they act individually?

- What types of different roles do people take on in the ceremony—leaders, helpers, participants?

- Are they all deeply involved at all times?

- Who is staring at the ceiling or whispering to their neighbor?

- How do others respond to such behavior?

Observe the architecture, any decorations, the clothing worn by different participants, and the objects—books, scrolls, musical instruments, statues, paintings, vessels, collection plates—that are part of the service. Pay as much attention as possible to the interactions that are a central part of the ritual, as well as those that occur on the margins (either just before or just after the ceremony).

Comparing Religious Cultures Every religion has a culture—its own set of norms, values, beliefs, and practices that differ from those of other congregations, even within the same denomination. As an ethnographic exercise, visit two houses of worship and compare your experiences.

Step 2: Identifying Similarities and Differences
Read through your fieldnotes and reflect on each experience. Then answer the following questions.

- What similarities and differences did you notice in the material aspects of the two ceremonies; that is, in the arrangement of the space, the use of furniture, statues, or other objects that were part of the service?

- What about the "text" and "script"; the types of words that were uttered (and by whom, and when); their sources (sacred books, hymnals, photocopied programs); the music that was played or sung; the periods of prayer or meditation; the ways in which participants were invited to speak (or to remain silent) or otherwise take part? In addition to noting their differences, consider whether there were any similarities in either form or content.

- What similarities and differences did you notice in the behavior of the participants? Were both children and adults present? Did both men and women participate in the same ways? Did participants engage in similar actions and interactions?

- Can you identify any differences in actual beliefs as a result of your observations? What about similarities? Beliefs may be similar in form, if not exactly in content. For example, most religions feature beliefs about what happens after we die, but while some believe our souls dwell permanently in either heaven or hell, others believe our souls are reincarnated in new bodies in an unending cycle.

- What did you observe in either service that seemed especially unfamiliar to you? What did you observe that seemed the most familiar, even if it was in an unfamiliar setting?

The key here is to focus on both the differences and the similarities. It often happens when we step into a new cultural milieu that we see only the differences and remain blind to the similarities. But identifying fundamental commonalities can make even the most bizarre practices seem less threatening. For example, according to Emile Durkheim (1912/1995), all religions have a set of beliefs about the relationship between the sacred (holy, godlike, supernatural) and the profane (the ordinary, of this world). Can you identify these beliefs in the communities you observed? In addition, every religion has a set of practices that are designed to connect the holy and the worldly in some way. Think about the different rituals you observed: taking communion, for example, or simply praying or singing in a specially designated space. These rituals each create a sense of collective effervescence and serve to connect the sacred and profane.

There are two options for completing this Data Workshop.

- *Option 1 (informal)*: Consider the bulleted questions above, and prepare some written notes that you can refer to during in-class discussions. Compare your notes and experiences with other students in small-group discussions. Take this opportunity to learn more about culture and different religious traditions.

- *Option 2 (formal)*: Write a three- to four-page essay analyzing your field experiences and taking into consideration the bulleted questions above. Make sure to refer to your fieldnotes in the essay, and include them as an attachment to your paper.

Components of Culture

Since culture is such a broad concept, it is more easily grasped if we break it down into its constituent parts. Sociologists conceive of culture as consisting of two major categories: material culture and symbolic culture.

Material Culture

Material culture is any physical object to which we give social meaning: art and artifacts, tools and utensils, machines and weapons, clothing and furniture, buildings and toys—the list is immense. Any physical thing that people create, use, or appreciate might be considered material culture.

Examining material culture can tell us a great deal about a particular group or society. Just look around you, whether in your dorm room, a library, a coffee house, or a park—there should be many items that you can identify as belonging to material culture. Start with your own clothes

and accessories and then extend your observations to your surroundings—the room, building, landscaping, street, neighborhood, community, and further outward. For instance, the designer label on a woman's purse might convey that she follows the current fashion trends, or the athletic logo on a man's T-shirt might tell us that he is into skateboarding. Likewise, the carpeting, light fixtures, furniture, and artwork in a building can tell us something about the people who live or work there. And the sports arenas, modes of transportation, historical monuments, and city dumps reveal the characteristics of a community. Perhaps the proliferation of drive-thru fast-food restaurants in practically every corner of the United States says something about American tastes and lifestyle: we spend more time on the road, cook fewer meals at home, and prefer the ease and predictability of knowing what we'll get each time we pull up to our favorite chain. If you were visiting another country, then you might see some very different items of material culture.

Studying the significance of material culture is like going on an archeological dig, but learning about the present rather than the distant past. Let's take as an example a sociological "dig" in Santa Barbara, California, where one of the authors of this book lives. Local leaders there have been active in preserving the image of the city, particularly in its downtown historical area. The original mission, presidio (military post), courthouse, and other landmarks built by early Spanish settlers are all still intact. Although the town has grown up

> **material culture** the objects associated with a cultural group, such as tools, machines, utensils, buildings, and artwork; any physical object to which we give social meaning

How Is the Architecture of Santa Barbara an Example of Material Culture? Local leaders in Santa Barbara have preserved the city's history and resisted the pressures of encroaching urban development by insisting on maintaining the look of "old California."

Gestures and Body Language If you travel to a foreign culture, pay special attention to how others interpret your body language. Common friendly gestures in one culture can be offensive or confusing in another.

around these buildings, zoning regulations require that new construction fit with the distinctive Mediterranean architecture of the "red tile roof" district. The size and design are restricted as are the use of signs, lighting, paint, and landscaping. Thus, the newly built grocery store with its textured stucco walls, tile murals, and arched porticos may be difficult to distinguish from the century-old post office a few blocks away. By studying its material culture, we can see how Santa Barbara manages to preserve its history and heritage and successfully resist the pressures of encroaching urban development. The distinctive "old California" look and feel of the city is perhaps its greatest charm, something that appeals to locals and a steady flock of tourists alike.

Symbolic Culture

Nonmaterial or **symbolic culture** reflects the ideas and beliefs of a group of people. It can be something as specific as a certain rule or custom, like driving on the right side of the road in the United States and on the left side in the United Kingdom. It can also be a broad social system, such as democracy, or a large-scale social pattern, such as marriage. Because symbolic culture is so important to social life, let's look further at some of its main aspects.

symbolic culture the ideas associated with a cultural group, including ways of thinking (beliefs, values, and assumptions) and ways of behaving (norms, interactions, and communication)

sign a symbol that stands for or conveys an idea

FORMS OF COMMUNICATION: SIGNS, GESTURES, AND LANGUAGE One of the most important functions of symbolic culture is to allow us to communicate—through signs, gestures, and language. These form the basis of social interaction, a subject so central to sociology that the entire next chapter is devoted to it.

Signs (or symbols) such as a traffic signal, price tag, sheet of music, or product logo are something designed to meaningfully represent something else. They all convey

gestures the ways in which people use their bodies to communicate without words; actions that have symbolic meaning

language a system of communication using vocal sounds, gestures, or written symbols; the basis of symbolic culture and the primary means through which we communicate with one another and perpetuate our culture

Sapir-Whorf hypothesis the idea that language structures thought and that ways of looking at the world are embedded in language

information. Numbers and letters are the most common signs, but you are probably familiar with other graphic symbols indicating, for instance, which is the men's or women's bathroom, where the elevator is going, how to eject a DVD from the disk drive, or in what lane you should be driving.

While we can easily take for granted the meaning of most symbols, others we may have to learn—like emoticons, those cute (or devious) little expressions that we can now create on our computers. Some symbols may be nearly universal, while others may be particular to a given culture. It may take some interpretive work to understand what a sign means if you are unfamiliar with the context in which it is displayed.

Gestures are signs that we make with our body—clapping our hands, nodding our head, or smiling. Sometimes, these acts are referred to as "body language" or "nonverbal communication," since they don't require any words. Gestures can be as subtle as a knowing glance or as obvious as a raised fist.

Most of the time, we can assume that other people will get what we are trying to say with our gestures. But, while gestures might seem natural and universal, just a matter of common sense, few of them besides those that represent basic emotions are innate; most have to be learned. For instance, the "thumbs up" sign, which is associated with praise or approval in the United States, might be interpreted as an obscene or insulting gesture in parts of Asia or South America. Every culture has its own way of expressing praise and insulting others. So before leaving for a country whose culture is unfamiliar, it might be worth finding out whether shaking hands or waving good-bye are appropriate ways to communicate.

Language, probably the most significant component of culture, is what has allowed us to fully develop and express ourselves as human beings, and is what distinguishes us from all other species on the planet. Although language varies from culture to culture, it is a human universal and present in all societies. It is one of the most complex, fluid, and creative symbol systems: letters or pictograms are combined to form words, and words combined to form sentences, in an almost infinite number of possible ways.

Language is the basis of symbolic culture and the primary means through which we communicate with one another. It allows us to convey complicated abstract concepts and to pass along a culture from one generation to the next. Language helps us to conceive of the past and to plan for the future; to categorize the people, places, and things around us; and to share our perspectives on reality. In this way, the cumulative experience of a group of people—their culture—can be contained in and presented through language.

Language is so important that many have argued that it shapes not only our communication but our perception—the way that we see things—as well. In the 1930s, two anthropologists, Edward Sapir and Benjamin Lee Whorf, conducted research on the impact of language on the mind. In working with the Hopi in the American Southwest, the anthropologists claimed to have discovered that the Hopi had no words to distinguish the past, present, or future, and that, therefore, they did not "see" or experience time in the same way as those whose language provided such words. The result of this research was what is known as the **Sapir-Whorf hypothesis** (sometimes referred to as the principle of linguistic relativity), which, breaking with traditional understandings about language, asserts that language actually structures thought, that perception not only suggests the need for words with which to express what is perceived but also that the words themselves help create those same perceptions (Sapir 1949; Whorf 1956).

The studies by Sapir and Whorf were not published until the 1950s, when they were met with competing linguistic theories. In particular, the idea that Eskimos (or Inuits, as they are now called) had many more words for snow than people of Western cultures was sharply challenged, as was the notion that the Hopi had no words for future or past tense (Martin 1986; Pullum 1991). Although there is still some disagreement about how strongly language influences thought (Edgerton 1992), the ideas behind the Sapir-Whorf hypothesis continue to influence numerous social thinkers. Language does play a significant role in how people construct a sense of reality and how they categorize the people, places, and things around them. For instance, the work of sociologist Eviatar Zerubavel (2003) looks at how different groups (like Jews and Arabs, or Serbs and Croats) use language to construct an understanding of their heritage—through what he calls "social memory." In a country like the United States, where there are approximately 50 million foreign-born people who speak well over 100 different languages, there are bound to be differences in perceptual realities as a result.

Does the Sapir-Whorf hypothesis hold true for your world? Let's take an example closer to home. Perhaps you have seen the 2004 movie *Mean Girls*, loosely based on a pop sociology book by Rosalind Wiseman, *Queen Bees and Wannabes*, about the culture of high school girls (2002). Both book and film present a social map of the cafeteria and school grounds, identifying where different groups of students—the "jocks," "cheerleaders," "goths," "preppies," "skaters,"

Mean Girls and the Cafeteria Classification System This map from the film *Mean Girls* is an example of how we use different classification schemes to identify and categorize the world around us. Do these classification systems influence the way that you see other people?

"nerds," "hacky-sack kids," "easy girls," and "partiers"—hang out. The book also includes the "populars" (referred to in the movie as the "plastics") and the popular "wannabes."

You were probably aware of similar categories for distinguishing groups at your school. Do such classification systems influence the way you see other people? Do they lead you to identify people by type and place them into those categories? If no such labels existed (or if your school had different labels), would you still perceive your former classmates the same way? Probably not. These kinds of questions highlight how important language is to the meanings we give to our everyday world.

Values, Norms, and Sanctions

Values and norms are symbolic culture in action. When we know the values and norms of a group (and see how they are controlled by sanctions), then we can understand their beliefs and ideals and see the evidence of these throughout their everyday lives.

VALUES Values are the set of shared beliefs that a group of people consider to be worthwhile or desirable in life—what is good or bad, right or wrong, beautiful or ugly. They articulate the essence of everything that a cultural group cherishes in its society. For instance, most Americans value the equality and individual freedoms of democracy. Structural functionalists, like Durkheim, stress the strength of shared values and their role in regulating the behavior of society's members. However, there is not always widespread agreement about which values should represent a society, and values may change or new values may emerge over time. For

example, workers' loyalty to their company was once much more important than it is currently. In today's economy, workers realize that they may be "downsized" in times of financial trouble or that they may change careers over the course of their lifetime and hence feel less obligation to an employer.

NORMS Norms are the rules and guidelines regarding what kinds of behavior are acceptable; they develop directly out of a culture's value system. Whether legal regulations or just social expectations, norms are largely agreed upon by most members of a group. Some norms are *formal*, or officially codified. These include **laws** (such as those making it illegal to speed in a school zone or drink before you turn age twenty-one), rules for playing basketball or for membership at your local gym, the Amendments to the U.S. Constitution, and the behavioral prescriptions conveyed in the Ten Commandments. Despite the relative authority of formal norms, they are not *always* followed.

Other norms are *informal*, meaning that they are implicit and unspoken. For instance, when we wait in line to buy tickets for a movie, we expect that no one will cut in front of us. Informal norms are so much a part of our assumptions about life that they are embedded in our consciousness; they cover almost every aspect of our social lives,

values ideas about what is desirable or contemptible and right or wrong in a particular group. They articulate the essence of everything that a cultural group cherishes and honors.

norm a rule or guideline regarding what kinds of behavior are acceptable and appropriate within a culture

law a common type of formally defined norm providing an explicit statement about what is permissible and what is illegal in a given society

folkway a loosely enforced norm involving common customs, practices, or procedures that ensure smooth social interaction and acceptance

more a norm that carries great moral significance, is closely related to the core values of a cultural group, and often involves severe repercussions for violators

taboo a norm ingrained so deeply that even thinking about violating it evokes strong feelings of disgust, horror, or revulsion

sanction positive or negative reactions to the ways that people follow or disobey norms, including rewards for conformity and punishments for violations

social control the formal and informal mechanisms used to elicit conformity to values and norms and thus increase social cohesion

from what we say and do to even how we think and feel. Though we might have difficulty listing all the norms that are a part of everyday life, most of us have learned them quite well. They are simply "the way things are done." Often, it is only when norms are broken (as when someone cuts in line) that we recognize they exist. You learned this firsthand in the "doing nothing" experiment in Chapter 1's Data Workshop.

Norms can be broken down further in three ways. **Folkways** are the ordinary conventions of everyday life and are not strictly enforced. Examples are standards of dress and rules of etiquette: in most places, wearing flip-flops with a tuxedo is just not done! When people do not conform to folkways, they are thought of as peculiar or eccentric but not really dangerous. **Mores** are norms that carry a greater moral significance and are more closely related to the core values of a cultural group. Unlike folkways, mores are norms to which we all are expected to conform. Breaches are treated seriously and often bring severe repercussions. Such mores as the prohibition of theft, rape, and murder are also formalized, so that there is not only public condemnation for such acts but also strict laws against them. **Taboos**, a type of more, are the most powerful of all norms. We sometimes use

the word in a casual way to indicate, say, a forbidden subject. But as a sociological term it holds even greater meaning. Taboos are extremely serious. Sociologists say that our sense of what is taboo is so deeply ingrained that the very thought of committing a taboo act, such as cannibalism or incest, evokes strong feelings of disgust or horror.

Norms are specific to a culture, time period, and situation. What would be a folkway to one group might be a more to another. For instance, public nudity is acceptable in many cultures, whereas it is not only frowned upon in American culture but also illegal in most instances. At the same time, Americans do permit nudity in such situations as strip clubs and nudist resorts, allowing for a kind of moral holiday from the strictures of imposed norms. At certain times like Mardi Gras and spring break, mild norm violations are tolerated. Certain places may also lend themselves to the suspension of norms—think Las Vegas (and the slogan "What happens in Vegas, stays in Vegas").

Similarly, what would be considered murder on the city streets might be regarded as valor on the battlefield. And we are probably all aware of how the folkways around proper etiquette and attire can vary greatly from one generation to the next; fifty years ago, girls would never wear jeans to school, for example.

SANCTIONS Sanctions are a means of enforcing norms. They include rewards for conformity and punishments for violations. *Positive sanctions* express approval and may come in the form of a handshake or a smile, praise, or perhaps an award. *Negative sanctions* express disapproval and may come in the form of a frown, harsh words, or perhaps a fine or incarceration.

From a functionalist perspective, we can see how sanctions help to establish **social control**, ensuring that people

Norms Are Specific to a Situation, Culture, and Time Period For example, at Mardi Gras or during spring break trips, mild norm violations are tolerated.

In Relationships

Institutional Values and College Life

As a college student, you may live on campus or make use of the student health services. In doing either of these things, you are in a situation in which someone else's values (in this case, those of the college) can influence your individual choices. For example, even if you get to choose your own roommate, the university has adopted a set of values that narrows your choice for you before you even make it. And if your student health service is operated by an outside contractor (for example, the local Catholic hospital), there may be constraints placed on the type of reproductive health services you can receive there.

Rules like these come from a tradition in which the university acts *in loco parentis*—in place of the parents—to protect and provide moral guidance for its students. The Bradley University Student Handbook for 1952–53, for example, forbids women from entering men's residences at any time and places severe constraints on when and under what conditions men may enter women's residences. This same handbook lists a complicated procedure for female students to follow in order to attend off-campus events in the evenings, and there are even lists of appropriate attire for the classroom, athletic events, and other university functions.

While most universities have abandoned the strict behavior codes that were once widespread, they still act *in loco parentis* in a variety of ways. One of them is the restrictions they place on different-sex roommates, even in coed dorms. The university has taken on the job of protecting students from the apparently undesirable consequences of living with a romantic partner. And if the student health service limits your access to certain means of birth control, then choices about whom to live with, how to conduct your sex life, and how to include your romantic partner in your domestic life have already been made for you by the university. If you want to live in university housing and use student health services, you must accept the constraints imposed by university values, even if you do not share those values. If you want to live without those constraints then you must choose to live in a private, off-campus setting.

behave to some degree in acceptable ways and thus promoting social cohesion. There are many forms of authority in our culture—from the government and police to school administrators, work supervisors, and even parents. Each has a certain amount of power that they can exercise to get others to follow their rules. So when someone is caught violating a norm, there is usually some prescribed sanction that will then be administered, serving as a deterrent to that behavior.

But equally important in maintaining social order is the process of socialization by which people internalize norms. For instance, in 1983, the U.S. Department of Transportation pioneered the slogan "Friends Don't Let Friends Drive Drunk"; over the years, the slogan has helped change the way we think about our personal responsibility for others, with nearly 80 percent of Americans now claiming that they have taken action to prevent someone from driving while intoxicated. What began as an external statement of a social more quickly became our own personal sense of morality. We are often unaware of the extent to which our own conscience keeps us from violating social norms in the first place. If

we have internalized norms, then outside sanctions are no longer needed to make us do the right thing. Social control, then, frequently looks like self control.

Variations in Culture

We know there are differences between cultures, but there can also be variations within cultures. For instance, sociologists who have tried to identify the core values that make up American society (Williams 1965; Bellah et al. 1985) have found that while there do seem to be certain beliefs that most Americans share, such as freedom and democracy, there are also inconsistencies between such beliefs as individualism (in which we do what is best for ourselves) and humanitarianism (in which we do what is best for others), and between equality and group superiority. New values such as self-fulfillment and environmentalism could also be added to the list, having gained popularity in recent years.

Culture Wars Often Play Out on Early-Morning or Late-Night Television George Stephanopoulos (second from left) spends every Sunday morning interviewing politicians on *This Week with George Stephanopoulos*. On Saturday nights, comic actors on *Saturday Night Live* satirize politicians, media pundits, and other participants in the latest cultural clash.

It is even difficult to speak of an "American culture." *Cultural diversity* and *multiculturalism* have both become buzzwords in the past few decades, precisely because people are aware of the increasing variety of cultural groups within American society. **Multiculturalism** generally describes a policy that involves honoring the diverse racial, ethnic, national, and linguistic backgrounds of various individuals and groups. In the following chapters, we will explore some of these differences in greater depth.

Dominant Culture

Although "culture" is a term we usually apply to an entire group of people, what we find in reality is that there are often many subgroups within a larger culture, each with its own particular makeup. These subgroups, however, are not all equal. Some, by virtue of size, wealth, or historical happenstance, are able to lay claim to greater power and influence in society than others. The values, norms, and practices of the most powerful groups are referred to as the mainstream or **dominant culture**, while others are seen as "alternative" or minority views. The power

of the dominant culture may mean that other ways of seeing and doing things are relegated to second-class status—in this way, dominant culture can produce cultural **hegemony**, or dominance (Gramsci 1985, 1988).

Let's take popular music as an example. Commercial radio stations often have very limited playlists. No matter what the genre (country, pop, hip-hop, metal), the songs played are determined by station and record company business interests, not your artistic preferences. Truly new artists and alternative sounds can be heard only on public, college, or pirate radio stations or online—and these outlets have significantly fewer financial resources and reach far fewer listeners. The dominant status of commercial radio and the corporate interests of the music industry dictate that musicians outside the mainstream like Lower Dens, Warpaint, or The Divine Comedy will never be as big as Lady Gaga or Justin Bieber.

Subcultures

If sociologists focus only on the dominant culture in American society, we risk overlooking the inequalities that structure our society—as well as the influences that even nondominant cultural groups can exert. The United States is filled with thousands of nondominant groups, any of which could be called a **subculture**—a culture within a culture. A subculture is a particular social world that has a distinctive way of life, including its own set of values and norms, practices, and beliefs, but that exists harmoniously within the larger mainstream culture. A subculture can be based on ethnicity, age, interests, or anything else that draws individuals together. Any of the following groups could be considered

multiculturalism a policy that values diverse racial, ethnic, national, and linguistic backgrounds and so encourages the retention of cultural differences within society rather than assimilation

dominant culture the values, norms, and practices of the group within society that is most powerful (in terms of wealth, prestige, status, influence, etc.)

hegemony term developed by Antonio Gramsci to describe the cultural aspects of social control, whereby the ideas of the dominant social group are accepted by all of society

subculture a group within society that is differentiated by its distinctive values, norms, and lifestyle

Old and New Countercultures The Black Panther Party, which was founded by Huey Newton, is an example of a social movement from the 1960s counterculture. New countercultures can include polygamist families like Tom Green and his five wives.

subcultures within American society: Korean Americans, senior citizens, snowboarders, White Sox fans, greyhound owners, firefighters, Trekkers.

Countercultures

A **counterculture**, another kind of subgroup, differs from a subculture in that its norms and values are often incompatible with or in direct opposition to the mainstream (Zellner 1995). Some countercultures are political or activist groups attempting to bring about social change; others resist mainstream values by living outside society or practicing an alternative lifestyle. In the 1960s, hippies, antiwar protesters, feminists, and others in the so-called political left were collectively known as "the counterculture." But radicals come in many stripes. Any group that opposes the dominant culture, whether they are eco-terrorists, computer hackers, or modern-day polygamists, can be considered a counterculture.

In the mid-1990s, American countercultures of the far right gained prominence with the revelation that the main perpetrator of the April 1995 bombing of the Alfred R. Murrah Federal Building in Oklahoma City, Timothy McVeigh, had ties to "militia" or "patriot" groups. And he wasn't the only one. In 1996, the Southern Poverty Law Center, which tracks such groups, counted 858 active groups in the United States belonging to the "militia movement" (the number was at 512 in 2009). Members of this movement, who trace their heritage to the Minutemen of the American Revolution (an elite fighting force, the first to arrive at a battle), see themselves as the last line of defense for the liberties provided in the U.S. Constitution. They believe, moreover, that the federal government has become the enemy of those liberties. They hold that gun control, environmental protection laws, and other legislation violates individual and states' rights and that events like the FBI's 1993 siege of the Branch Davidian compound in Waco, Texas (resulting in 82 deaths), call for armed grassroots organization.

Since the Oklahoma City bombing, some militia groups have courted recognition as legitimate American institutions rather than radical organizations. Others have remained openly countercultural. While members of such groups consider themselves "patriots" and "true Americans," they believe that the institutions and values of contemporary American society need drastic revision.

At the furthest extreme are militia groups who hold that the present American government is entirely illegitimate and that they are not its subjects but rather "sovereign citizens," "common-law citizens," or "freemen." Members refuse to carry such documents as driver's licenses and social security cards, and refuse to pay taxes or observe any government restrictions on their property. They have gone so far as to establish "common-law courts" that oppose local and federal government regulations and seek to prosecute government officials (Diamond 1995). In May 2010, West Memphis, Arkansas, police officers Brandon Paudert and Bill Evans were gunned down during a traffic stop by Jerry and Joe Kane, a father and son on their way from Las Vegas to Florida. The Kanes, who were later killed as they attempted to escape, were "sovereign citizens." Their complicated conspiracy theories framed all official authority figures (such as law enforcement officers) as enemies in their attempt to access secret Treasury Department accounts that they believed were set up by the federal government to control their identities.

> **counterculture** a group within society that openly rejects and/or actively opposes society's values and norms

Principles and Practices—Values, Norms, and Laws in Flux

1770: George Washington and Thomas Jefferson grow hemp (*cannabis sativa*, the botanical classification for marijuana) on their Virginia plantations. Hemp was used to make fabric, rope, and paper, including the paper on which Jefferson drafted the Declaration of Independence.

1937: In schools across the United States, students watch a scholastic film called *Reefer Madness*, an antimarijuana propaganda piece that uses images of insanity, rape, and murder to paint a picture of pot as a catastrophic scourge on society. Every state in the country outlaws the use of marijuana as an intoxicant, and hemp farming is effectively eliminated at the federal level by the passage of the prohibitive Marijuana Tax Act.

1992: Arkansas governor and presidential candidate Bill Clinton admits on MTV's *Rock the Vote/Choose or Lose* that he smoked marijuana in college but "didn't inhale" (Schlosser 2003).

He "Didn't Inhale" Bill Clinton appears on MTV with young voters during his first presidential campaign in 1992.

2002: A number of states, including California, Colorado, Illinois, New York, and Ohio, decriminalize marijuana use and possession to varying degrees, including allowing the medical use of marijuana for cancer and AIDS patients. However, other states such as Oklahoma and Indiana punish mere possession of marijuana with long prison sentences, up to and including life without parole. In some cases, selling marijuana can be punished more harshly than rape or murder (Schlosser 2003).

Reefer Madness This cautionary film from 1937 was shown to students to warn them about the dangers of marijuana, including rape, insanity, and murder.

Hemp Can Be Used to Make Fabric, Rope, and Paper This farmer measures crops to see if they are ready for harvesting. Kim Roberts helps a customer at her store, All about Hemp, which sells hemp-based products including shoes, clothing, and shampoo.

2005: The Supreme Court rules that federal antidrug laws can be used to prosecute those involved in cultivating and prescribing marijuana for medical purposes, even in states that have legalized the practice.

2010: California voters reject Proposition 19, which would have legalized the use and cultivation of marijuana for all over age twenty-one.

As you can see, American values and norms surrounding the various uses of *cannabis sativa* have shifted over time and sometimes seem downright contradictory. The very first marijuana-related law *required* Virginia colonists to grow hemp in 1619 (Schlosser 2003, p. 19); by 1937, all its uses were outlawed. Today, we confront a kind of cultural schizophrenia about marijuana—our desire to benefit from its helpful properties is matched only by our fear of its harmful ones. Should we allow hemp farming to stop the clearcutting of ancient forests by the paper industry? Should we allow restricted marijuana use to relieve the suffering of cancer, AIDS, epilepsy, and glaucoma patients, as medical research suggests? Or should we treat pot as we treat other illegal drugs, like crack cocaine and heroin, by severely punishing those who grow, buy, and sell it? Isn't there some middle ground?

The case of changing marijuana laws serves as an example of an important cultural principle: what was once mainstream may later be defined as deviant; what is now seen as deviant may someday be normal and acceptable. Why? Because values change over time and differ across cultures. Changing values lead to changing laws and changing practices in our everyday lives.

Are there any current counterculture values that you think might someday enter the mainstream? No matter how dangerous or threatening they may seem now, it is entirely possible that they will be taken for granted as normal in ten, twenty-five, fifty, or 100 years. And what about the mainstream values that we currently take for granted? In a decade or a century, some will be rejected as aberrant. It's hard to imagine right now, but history tells us it will most definitely happen.

Unfortunately, Officers Paudert and Evans were not the first murdered by sovereign citizens—police in Alabama, New Hampshire, and Idaho have been killed at what should have been routine traffic stops when the "sovereigns" they pulled over began arguing about their rights.

As bizarre as their beliefs seem, and as tragic as their consequences have been, some of their claims have gained traction in more mainstream circles. For example, sovereign citizens' refusal to pay taxes seems to have caught on: in a 2008 criminal tax evasion trial, actor Wesley Snipes claimed to be a sovereign tax protester in his attempt to avoid paying federal taxes. Despite the roots of the movement in extreme, violent, racist ideologies, this influential African American celebrity used sovereign citizen arguments to defend himself. He was ultimately sentenced to three years in prison, but it remains to be seen whether his sentence will have a chilling effect on the activities of the estimated 300,000 sovereigns around the country.

Culture Wars

Although a countercultural group can pose a threat to the larger society, conflict does not always come from the extreme margins of society; it can also emerge from within the mainstream. Culture in any diverse society is characterized by points of tension and division. There is not always uniform agreement about which values and norms ought to be upheld. The term **culture wars** is often used to describe the clashes that arise as a result (Bloom 1987; Garber 1998). The clashes are frequently played out in the media, where social commentators and pundits debate the issues. Culture wars are mainly waged over values and morality and the solutions to social problems, with liberals and conservatives fighting to define culture in America. One notable example of a battle in the culture wars was the scuffle over media and morality that surrounded singer Janet Jackson's breast-baring during the 2004 Super Bowl telecast; another was the rise of the ultra-conservative "Tea Party" movement during 2010. Tea Partiers favor anti-gay rhetoric and call for drastic cuts in taxes and social welfare funding. Other questions of family values, changing gender roles, frontiers in bioethics, violence in the media, and school prayer have all been recent topics for discussion. Culture wars are bound to continue as we confront the difficult realities that are a part of living in a democratic society.

culture wars clashes within mainstream society over the values and norms that should be upheld

ideal culture the norms, values, and patterns of behavior that members of a society believe should be observed in principle

real culture the norms, values, and patterns of behavior that actually exist within a society (which may or may not correspond to the society's ideals)

Ideal vs. Real Culture

Some norms and values are more aspired to than actually practiced. It is useful to draw a distinction between **ideal culture**, the norms and values that members of a society believe should be observed in principle, and **real culture**, the patterns of behavior that actually exist. Whether it is an organization that falls short of its own mission statement or a person who says one thing and does another (a devout Catholic, for example, who finds himself seeking a divorce), what we believe in and what we do may be two different things.

Let's take, as another example, corporate culture in America. The ideal culture of the workplace usually dictates that raises and promotions be given to employees who have demonstrated exemplary performance or productiveness through skill, dedication, or innovative thinking. In practice, these rewards are also given to less-deserving employees who are appreciated for other qualities, such as obedience, charisma, or their special relationship with the boss. While most people believe that hard work or initiative should be what determines success, they know that in reality it is not always these qualities that are rewarded and that, indeed, sometimes employees climb the ladder for more dubious reasons (Hagberg and Heifetz 2002).

Another example of how real and ideal culture may clash in the workplace comes from a management book called *Weird Ideas That Work*, by Stanford professor Robert Sutton (2001), who observes that while corporate executives often claim they value innovation, they usually reward conformity instead. Sutton recommends that instead of hiring comfortable, familiar types of people who know the rules and submit without argument to the authority of their superiors, corporations should hire eccentrics who ignore the rules, enjoy a good fight, and defy authority. For those who claim they value creativity, Sutton argues this is the only way to really achieve their ideals.

DATA WORKSHOP

ANALYZING MASS MEDIA AND POPULAR CULTURE

Seeing Culture in Popular Magazines

Picture a sophisticated evening out: aristocrats in gowns and tuxedos, dining on caviar and truffles served by a white-gloved staff, in a grand mansion with an expansive ocean view. Now picture a more ordinary evening: neighbors in shorts and T-shirts gnawing on juicy ribs, wiping their mouths with paper napkins, at a cook-out in the backyard of a suburban tract home. These images seem very different, but they have one thing in common: culture shapes each of them.

In this Data Workshop, you will use existing sources—in this case, popular magazines—to discover how culture gives meaning to our instinctive drives for food and shelter. You will use content analysis to study the magazines and arrive at some conclusions. You may want to refer back to Chapter 2 to re-read the section on existing sources, just for a quick review.

Pick your drive—food or shelter. Now go to your local bookstore or newsstand, and identify three magazines that are dedicated to that particular drive. For instance, *Bon Appetit*, *Food & Wine*, or *Saveur* (food); *Architectural Digest*, *Metropolitan Home*, or *This Old House* (shelter); or other magazines, such as *Martha Stewart Living*, cover both of these territories. Immerse yourself in the content of each magazine, then answer the following questions. Support your answers with data (like clippings of photos or articles) from the magazines.

- How much of what is contained in these magazines is really necessary to sustain life?

- Do any of the magazines feature articles about the bare minimum of nourishment or shelter (plain rice; a tent or shack)? If so, how do they present these topics ("High-End Camping Gear," "The Jasmine Rice of My Burmese Childhood")?

- What types of regional or national differences in food and housing are revealed?

- What types of products and services are advertised?

- What elements of material and symbolic culture are visible?

- What types of values and beliefs are embedded in the recipes, entertaining tips, home improvement plans, or decorating schemes?

- How does the content of these magazines reflect the specific cultural context in which they are produced?

- How does the content affect you and your desires? Do you find yourself craving the meals pictured or wishing you lived in the beautiful homes in the photographs?

- Who benefits when you act out these desires by purchasing the goods and services presented (a package of sun-dried tomatoes, a meal at a featured restaurant, a new shower curtain, a can of paint)—or even the magazines themselves?

Finally, which force is more important in shaping human behavior when it comes to food and shelter—instinct or culture?

There are two options for completing this Data Workshop.

- *Option 1 (informal)*: Jot down notes based on your answers to the Workshop questions, and cut out pictures and articles that help support your observations. Then get together in small groups to share your findings.

- *Option 2 (formal)*: Translate those jotted notes into a three- to four-page essay, supplemented with clippings that help support your points. Make sure you address the Workshop questions in your essay.

Cultural Change

Cultures usually change slowly and incrementally, although change can also happen in rapid and dramatic ways. We saw rapid change as a result of the social movements of the 1960s, and we may be seeing it again, albeit for different reasons, as we move through the early part of the 2000s. Change is usually thought of as "progress"—we move from what seem to be outmoded ways of doing things to more innovative practices. Earlier in the chapter, we saw how variations in culture, whether they resulted from multiculturalism, countercultures, or culture wars, could all lead to growth and change in the larger society. Now we look at several other important processes that can also contribute to cultural change.

Technological Change

One of the most significant influences on any society is its material culture. And most changes in material culture tend to be technological. We usually equate **technology**

> **technology** material artifacts and the knowledge and techniques required to use them

with new "hi-tech" electronic or digital devices. But technology can be anything from a hammer to the space shuttle, from graffiti to hypertext markup language (HTML), as well as the "know-how" it takes to use them.

New technology often provides the basis and structure through which culture is disseminated to members of a social group. For instance, we are currently living in the digital age or Information Age, a revolutionary time in history spurred by the invention of the microchip. This technology has already produced radical changes in society, much as the steam engine did during the industrial revolution of the eighteenth and nineteenth centuries.

One of the most prominent features of this Information Age is the spread of mass media. It was not until the 1950s that television became a regular part of daily life in America, and only in the 1990s that the internet became commonplace. Most of us now would have trouble remembering life before these technological advancements; that's how much we rely on them and take them for granted. This digital revolution is shaping our culture—and the rest of the world's—at an increasingly rapid pace (Figure 3.1).

Some postmodern theorists argue that the rapid proliferation of new technologies creates a disconnect between old social values (like hard work and thrift) and new cultural ideals like consumerism (Bell 1976). In fact, many social thinkers believe that technology is the single greatest influence on society today, a concept known as **technological determinism** (Veblen 1921/2004). This would mean that computers, cell phones, and other forms of mass communication, are defining who we become—how we think, feel, and act in the world. Educator Marshall McLuhan, who studied the impact of media technology on human perception, is famous for his assertion that "the medium is the message" (1964). What he meant is that it is not so much the content (for instance, the advertisement, sitcom, or song) with which we should be concerned, but rather the medium itself (radio, television, or the internet), through which the content is delivered. The medium is what actually has the greater power to change our cultural framework.

This is an important proposition to consider in our increasingly connected world. We can now be in almost constant contact with each other and with sources of information and entertainment. But media and information technology also have the potential to distort our sense of time and space, identity and reality. The Information Age has not arrived without great cultural consequence.

Shoppers at a New Gap Store in Shinjuku, Downtown Tokyo, Japan As global capitalism and large multinational corporations become more dominant, we increasingly see the same companies, brands, and products around the world. Is this cultural leveling good or bad?

Cultural Diffusion and Cultural Leveling

Cultural change can also occur when different groups share their material and nonmaterial culture with each other, a process called **cultural diffusion**. Since each culture has its own tools, beliefs, and practices, exposure to another culture may mean that certain aspects of it will then be appropriated. For example, as McDonald's-style restaurants set up shop in cultures where fast food had previously been unknown, it wasn't only hamburgers that got relocated: other aspects of fast-food culture came along as well. According to Eric Schlosser (2002), Japanese diners during the 1980s doubled their consumption of fast-food meals—and their rates of obesity. Heart disease and stroke risks also have increased. While there is no direct proof of cause and effect here, it is clear that a single

technological determinism the notion that developments in technology provide the primary driving force behind social change

cultural diffusion the dissemination of beliefs and practices from one group to another

FIGURE 3.1
CHANGES IN COMMUNICATION TECHNOLOGIES

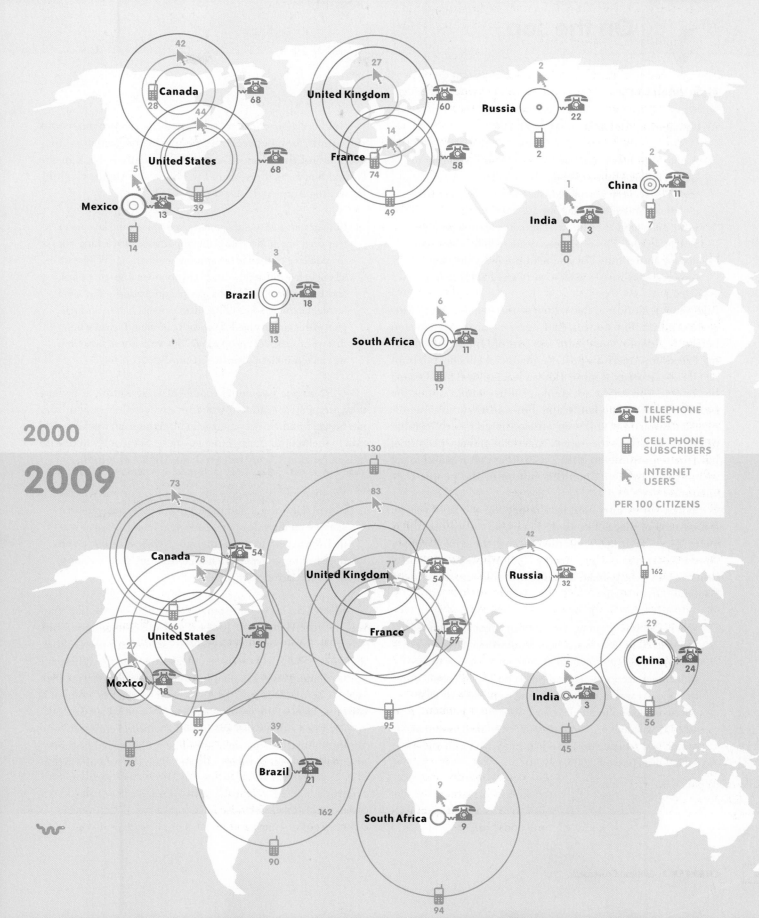

2000

2009

TELEPHONE LINES

CELL PHONE SUBSCRIBERS

INTERNET USERS

PER 100 CITIZENS

SOURCE: WORLD BANK 2011A.

On the Job

U.S. Military

An e-mail from Afghanistan, May 30, 2003:

> A couple of hours after we landed, we had a convoy to Kabul. It took about two hours, but I will never forget the trip. The scenery was incredible. I knew that there were mountains in Afghanistan, but there are so many that it is an unbelievable sight. . . . The native people are also a sight to see. These people are incredibly resourceful making shelter from clay and mud and using the minimal resources they have to work with. (Carroll 2006, p. 67)

Like most Americans, the writer of this e-mail, Army Sergeant Andrew Simkiewicz, had never been to Afghanistan before. His deployment there was part of Operation Enduring Freedom, America's post–September 11th effort to hunt Al Qaeda terrorists, depose Taliban leaders, and find Osama bin Laden. You might not think a soldier would notice the beauty of the Afghan landscape, but soldiers aren't one-dimensional warriors, and their missions aren't solely combat oriented. Wherever they serve, American military personnel have the opportunity to learn about other cultures and to act as representatives of American culture to the people they encounter.

When "in country," soldiers notice the effects of war on the citizens of places like Iraq. They also notice the differences between Iraqis' experiences and those of ordinary Americans at home. Here Army Captain James R. Sosnicky describes an Iraqi woman he knew who sold cigarettes in the Baghdad Green Zone:

> When she was a young girl, Iranian missiles pounded the street. The Americans have bombed her three times since, in 1991, 1998, and 2003. Mariam . . . knows things women her age in the United States do not. A couple of weeks ago, I was in Baghdad visiting with Mariam. There was an explosion in the distance. "What do you think," I asked, "car bomb or mortar round?" "Definitely a mortar round," she replied. Most girls in the U.S. have a tin ear for such things. (Carroll 2006, p. 130)

Soldiers also come to recognize the deep connections and similarities between the people whose territory they occupy and their friends and family members back in the United States, as does Army First Sergeant August C. Hohl, Jr., writing from Afghanistan:

> [T]heir personal and religious beliefs are not unlike ours in that everyone understands the importance of reaching out to and being charitable towards one another. . . . [W]hile we all might live differently due to environmental, geographical, and educational conditions, people are basically the same inside. Learning some of the history, social habits, and religion of this country has left me with a profound sense of hope that we can assist the people here. But we're not so smart that we can't learn from them, too. (Carroll 2006, p. 68)

U.S. service personnel represent U.S. culture anywhere they are posted—often in war zones where they may or may not be welcome. So they engage in humanitarian work in addition to their combat assignments—here, Sergeant Simkiewicz tells of breaking Army rules to help Afghan children:

> We were told not to give any of our food or water to the natives. However, I find it hard to see these cute children starving on the side of the road while I have a case of bottled water next to me in the cab. Needless to say, a half dozen of my waters were hurled from my window along the way. (Carroll 2006, p. 67)

Elsewhere in Afghanistan, soldiers like Army Chief Warrant Officer II Jared S. Jones distribute humanitarian aid, "ranging from personal hygiene to school supplies, shoes, and soccer balls. It is always a pleasure to see the difference we are making for these people, even if it is only one small village" (Carroll 2006, p. 70). As Jones reminds us, "combat is only one facet of the military, a necessary evil" (Carroll 2006, p. 71). Their other roles will include "cultural emissary" and "cultural observer" as well, roles that are just as important—and perhaps even more important—than the role of warrior.

The Voice of America: Spreading Propaganda or Democratic Values?

The Voice of America (VOA) began in 1942 as a radio news broadcast to parts of Europe and North Africa. Today, it broadcasts in forty-four languages, twenty-four hours a day, around the globe, on radio, TV, and the internet. Whether the broadcasts are in Dari, Amharic, or Macedonian, the VOA claims to provide objective news about the United States and the world, including uncensored news about the host country, whatever its internal politics may be. Some listeners, foreign and domestic, criticize VOA's claims of objectivity, saying that it is American political propaganda; others trust its world news service, even listening in secret in order to find out what is really happening in their own countries and abroad.

Daw Aung San Suu Kyi

VOA broadcasts, regardless of the actual content (which can include music, interviews, and variety shows, as well as news), also transmit core American values, such as freedom of speech and of the press, human rights, and democratic decision making. To some repressive regimes, these values are seen as dangerous and inflammatory and are held up as evidence of America's cultural imperialism. VOA frequencies are sometimes blocked by those who seek to stifle the ideas VOA communicates. And sometimes VOA listeners are punished for the very act of tuning in.

Burmese human rights activist Daw Aung San Suu Kyi spent more than fifteen years under house arrest at the hands of Myanmar's (Burma's) military dictatorship, was separated from her husband and children in London for even longer, and won the Nobel Peace Prize in 1991 for her selfless efforts on behalf of Burmese democracy. In a 2000 message to the U.N. Commission on Human Rights in Geneva, Suu Kyi told the story of a Burmese man persecuted for merely listening to VOA:

> U Than Chaun, the seventy-year-old proprietor of a coffee shop in Schwe-goo township, Kachin state, was arrested and his radio, which was tuned to the Voice of America Burmese broadcast, was seized. . . . [H]e was charged and sentenced to two years' imprisonment. U Than Chaun's wife was suffering from a heart ailment . . . and she passed away while he was in prison. He himself suffers medical problems which have now become life threatening.

She asks: "In which country of the world are people so oppressed that listening to a radio deserves two years of imprisonment?" The VOA would like the answer to that question to be "none."

cultural product cannot be exported without carrying a raft of cultural consequences with it.

Cultural diffusion usually occurs in the direction from more developed to less developed nations. In particular, "Western" culture has spread rapidly to the rest of the world—driven by capitalism and globalization and aided by new forms of transportation and communication that allow for ever-faster exchanges.

Cultural leveling occurs when cultures that were once distinct become increasingly similar to one another. If you travel, you may have already seen this phenomenon in towns across the United States and countries around the world. The Wal-Marts on the interstates, for instance, have driven independent mom-and-pop stores from town squares all over the country. Many people bemoan this development and the consequent loss of uniqueness and diversity it represents. As cultures begin to blend, new mixes emerge. This can result in an interesting hybrid, for example, of East and West, but can also mean a blander, more diluted culture of sameness. While Western culture is a dominant force in this process, cultural diffusion and cultural leveling do not necessarily have to occur in a one-way direction. Other societies have also had an influence on culture in the United States. For instance,

> **cultural leveling** the process by which cultures that were once unique and distinct become increasingly similar

TABLE 3.1	Theory in Everyday Life		
PERSPECTIVE	**APPROACH TO CULTURE**	**CASE STUDY: RELIGION**
STRUCTURAL-FUNCTIONALISM	Values and norms are widely shared and agreed upon; they contribute to social stability by reinforcing common bonds and constraining individual behavior.	Religion is an important social institution that functions as the basis for the morals and ethics that followers embrace, and that are applied to both society and the individual, thus promoting social order.
CONFLICT THEORY	Values and norms are part of the dominant culture and tend to represent and protect the interests of the most powerful groups in society.	Religion serves to control the masses by creating rules for behavior; sanctions against violators may not be equally or fairly applied. Culture wars reflect tensions between groups over which values and norms will dominate.
SYMBOLIC INTERACTIONISM	Values and norms are social constructions; meaning is created, maintained, and changed through ongoing social interaction.	Religion consists of beliefs and rituals that are part of the interaction among followers. Reciting the Lord's Prayer, bowing toward Mecca, or keeping a kosher home are meaningful displays to different religious groups. Leaders may play a role in creating social change.

Japanese anime was for many years a fringe interest in America, usually associated with computer geeks and other outsiders; now Hayao Miyazaki, Japan's leading anime filmmaker, has teamed up with Disney to sell his movies (like *Spirited Away*, *Howl's Moving Castle*, and *Ponyo*) to a mainstream American audience. Still, America, the dominant producer of global media, remains the primary exporter of cultural content throughout the world.

Cultural Imperialism

Other countries around the world are becoming inundated with America's television programs, movies, CDs, satellite radio broadcasts, magazines, and web content. You can watch MTV in India and *Jackass 3D* in Uzbekistan, surf the internet in Vietnam, or listen to Justin Timberlake in Morocco. Many see this as good news for the spread of freedom and democracy, for others to have the kind of access to information and entertainment that Americans regularly enjoy. But the media are necessarily a reflection of the culture in which they are produced. So not only are we selling entertainment, we are also implicitly promoting certain Western ideas. And it can become a problem when the images and ideas found in the media conflict with the traditional norms and values of other countries.

The proliferation of Western media amounts to what some social critics call **cultural imperialism** (Schiller 1995). These critics conceive

cultural imperialism the imposition of one culture's beliefs and practices on another culture through mass media and consumer products rather than by military force

of media as a kind of invading force that enters a country and takes it over—much like an army, but with film, television, music, soft drinks, and running shoes instead of guns. Historically, imperialism involved the conquering of other nations by monarchies for their own glory and enrichment. The British Empire, for example, was once able to use its military might to occupy and control a third of the world's total land area. But now it is possible to cross a border and to occupy a territory culturally, without setting foot on foreign soil. Because they command so many economic resources, Western media companies are powerful enough to create a form of cultural domination wherever their products go.

Of the countries that consider the messages in Western media dangerous, some forbid or restrict the flow of information, others impose various kinds of censorship, and still others try to promote their own cultural productions. Iran, for example, officially censors all non-Islamic media content on television, radio, film, and the internet (though many Iranians use hidden satellite dishes to plug into illegal Western programming). In the long run, it may be very difficult to prevent cultural imperialism from spreading.

American Culture in Perspective

Because American culture is highly visible worldwide, the country's moral and political values have equally high visibility. That means when reruns of *Friends* or *Grey's Anatomy* air in places like Egypt or Malaysia or Lebanon, American values on the topics of sex, gender, work, and family are being transmitted as well. When such military ventures as Operation Enduring Freedom (in Afghanistan) or Operation Iraqi Freedom are undertaken, part of their mission involves exporting the political values associated with democracy, capitalism, and even Christianity. Well, you may say, *Friends* is funny, and *Grey's* is a great way to kill time, and democracy is a good thing—so what's the problem here?

In some parts of the world, the premise of these shows would be unthinkable in real life: in many traditional cultures, both women and men live with their parents until they marry, sometimes to partners chosen for them by their families. A show in which young men and women live on their own, with almost no family involvement, dating and sleeping with people to whom they are not married, presents values that are distasteful in these cultures. American values, or at least the perceptions of them shaped by Hollywood and pop-culture exports, can breed negative feelings toward the United States. The value placed on individualism, sexual freedom, and material satisfaction in American life can antagonize cultures that place a higher value on familial involvement and moral and social restraint, and may result in anti-American sentiment.

Politics can generate the same anti-American feeling. For example, the United States has recently been involved in attempts to stem the development of nuclear weapons in developing countries like Iran and Pakistan while still maintaining our own nuclear arsenal at home. Other nations may question why American politicians think they should be able to withhold from other countries privileges the United States itself enjoys, such as developing a nuclear weapons program. Much of the resentment against America abroad emerges as a result of this type of phenomenon—our perceived failure to live up to our own political values and ideals, or to apply them fairly to others.

Putting American culture in perspective means recognizing that because it is pervasive, it may also be viewed with suspicion and even contempt when the values it expresses clash with those of other cultures. But the nature of anti-Americanism is complex—it's not merely a failure by other nations to understand "good" television shows or accept "superior" political systems. There are meaningful cultural differences between Americans and others, and we should keep those differences in mind as we read about or travel to other cultures. Indeed, there are cultural differences of similar magnitude within the United States as well. The question of the meaning of American culture is a complicated one.

Closing Comments

In this chapter, we have seen how seemingly simple elements of material culture (cars and comic books) and symbolic culture (norms and values) create complex links between the individual and her society, as well as between different societies around the globe. American culture in particular, sociologists often argue, is hegemonic (dominant), in that certain interests (such as creating a global market for American products) prevail, while others (such as encouraging local development and self-determination) are subordinated. Within the United States, this can mean that the cultural norms, values, beliefs, and practices of certain subcultures—such as minority ethnic or religious groups—are devalued. Elsewhere, it can mean that America is accused of cultural imperialism by nations whose values and practices are different from ours.

Whose cultural values and practices are "better" or "right"? The sociological perspective avoids these evaluative terms when examining culture, choosing instead to take a relativistic approach. In other words, different cultures should (in most cases) be evaluated not according to outside standards but according to their own sets of values and norms. But we should always recognize that this commitment to cultural relativism is a value in itself—which makes cultural relativism neither right nor wrong but rather a proper subject for intellectual examination.

ⓢ Need Help Studying?

wwnorton.com/studyspace

Visit StudySpace to access free review materials such as :

- **Vocabulary Flashcards**
- **Diagnostic Review Quizzes**
- **Study Outlines**

QUESTIONS FOR REVIEW

1. In this chapter, you read about how Horace Miner described the body rituals of the Nacirema. Choose another aspect of daily life and describe its associated artifacts, practices, and beliefs in similar detail. How might a complete stranger view the bar scene, for instance, or spectators at a sporting event? What does this tell you about ethnocentrism?

2. List five pieces of material culture you have with you right now, and explain what they indicate about the tastes, habits, and lifestyle supported by your cultural group.

3. Describe a norm that used to be a more but has transitioned to folkway status. How did you decide it was now a folkway?

4. When was the last time you violated a folkway? How were you sanctioned? What sorts of sanctions do we impose on those who go against our accepted mores?

5. Same-sex marriage has been a focal point of recent culture wars, with some states (and nations) taking steps toward legalization of such unions, some directly banning them, and others taking a middle course. What values are in conflict here? Do both sides adhere to values that may be defined as "American"? What tactics are the different sides using in this culture war?

6. In the late 1990s and the early 2000s, a series of protests against the World Trade Organization were launched worldwide. The protesters represented a multitude of organizations and causes coming together to support a loosely defined common goal. In your opinion, would these protesters be more accurately characterized as subcultures or countercultures? Why?

7. Travelers in the United States used to encounter very different customs, traditions, and foods from one region to the next. These days, one may find a McDonald's or Starbucks in almost every American town—and in many countries across the globe. Is this good or bad? Why? Does it truly lessen cultural differences?

8. Make a list of ways in which the media—including advertisements—reach you each day. How many of these media messages represent mainstream Western ideals? What kinds of media messages don't conform to these norms?

SUGGESTIONS FOR FURTHER EXPLORATION

Coupland, Douglas. 1995. *Microserfs*. New York: Harper-Collins. A darkly humorous novel about the consequences of living in a world dominated by technological change and electronic media. Although fictional, the story of overworked computer programmers' struggle to "get a life" addresses serious questions about the effects of technology.

Fadiman, Anne. 1998. *The Spirit Catches You and You Fall Down*. New York: Farrar, Straus and Giroux. A true story of clashing values, norms, and beliefs experienced by a Hmong immigrant family in the United States, it depicts the power of cross-cultural communication.

Heavy Metal in Baghdad. 2007. Dirs. Eddy Moretti and Suroosh Alvi. A documentary that follows the Iraqi heavy metal band Acrassicauda from the fall of Saddam Hussein in 2003 to the present day. Band members struggle to play music in a war-torn country, and to integrate Western and Middle Eastern influences into their art.

Hebdige, Dick. 1979. *Subculture: The Meaning of Style*. London: Methuen. The classic study of musical subcultures in Great Britain, from teddy boys to mods and rockers, to skinheads, punks, and beyond. If you've ever wondered how a subculture maintains its own distinctive identity, Hebdige has an answer.

High Times. A monthly periodical "dedicated to presenting the true independent voice of today's culture through provocative coverage of politics, arts and entertainment, news, fiction, and fashion not found in the mainstream media," with a focus on the cultivation and uses of *cannabis sativa*. Also online at www.hightimes.com.

Kincaid, James R. 1998. *Erotic Innocence: The Culture of Child Molesting*. London: Duke University Press. Examines the social functions of the fascination with one of our culture's strongest taboos. It's obvious why pedophilia is taboo but less obvious why so much attention is paid to it given its relative rarity. This book helps to explain how taboos contribute to social control.

Lewin, Ellen, and William L. Leap, eds. 1996. *Out in the Field: Reflections of Lesbian and Gay Anthropologists*. Urbana: University of Illinois Press. A collection of narratives describing the fieldwork of lesbian and gay anthropologists. Many of the entries describe how members of a culture often treated as "other" sometimes can more easily notice cultural differences and similarities.

Liberman, Mark, and Geoffrey K. Pullum. 2006. *Far from the Madding Gerund and Other Dispatches from Language Log*. Wilsonville, OR: William, James & Co. Provides an interesting assessment of the Sapir-Whorf hypothesis and summarizes, often humorously, the research on the "great Eskimo vocabulary hoax."

My Big Fat Greek Wedding. 2002. Dir. Joel Zwick. Warner Bros. A romantic comedy highlighting the differences between mainstream and subcultural groups through the story of two people who meet and fall in love, one from an immigrant Greek family and the other from a typical WASP (White Anglo-Saxon Protestant) family.

Schlosser, Eric. 2004. *Reefer Madness: Sex, Drugs, and Cheap Labor in the American Black Market*. New York: Houghton Mifflin. Discusses the contradictions between America's real and ideal culture, which harshly punishes marijuana dealers and pornographers while allowing migrant workers to toil in horrible conditions.

Žižek, Slavoj. 2002. *Welcome to the Desert of the Real*. London: Verso. A provocative discussion of the limits of multiculturalism.

CHAPTER 4

The Self and Interaction

Who are you? Well, it really depends on the situation. In the classroom, you are a student; at home, you are a child, a sibling, a parent, a spouse, and/or a partner. In your office, you are the boss or the employee; in your studio, you are an artist or a woodworker. These are all facets of who you are, grounded in the real activities of your everyday life—school, work, hobbies, relationships. Online, though, reality need not limit you to such mundane identities. Online, you can be anyone you want!

Below is a sampling of actual online usernames from a variety of internet domains. Since people generally choose their own usernames, we can assume that they are meant to express something about the user's personality—sort of like a personalized license plate. Some names might cause us to modify our opening question a bit: who do these people *think* they are? Or, perhaps, *wish* they *were*?

angelbabee3	mostwanted
bluechihuahua	motherwitch
crazyaboutjesus	nerd87
heartbreakah	rebelcutie
intensejello	superman22
ladyinpain	viciousvixen
luvsexxy	yummmiest
mauiwowee	gymrat4ever

Choosing a username is one of many ways we express ourselves in social interaction. Because our online identities are usually disembodied and removed from the context of our everyday lives, we can say anything we want about who we are (or think we are, or wish to be). Whether or not these folks are actually heartbreakers, rebel cuties, or gym rats in real life, they can be those things online. What's your username?

HOW TO READ THIS CHAPTER

In this chapter, you will learn how the self is connected to all social phenomena (such as gender and race, and the effects of mass media) and how interaction constructs them all. You will be acquiring some new analytic tools, including the concepts of socialization and impression management, which will be referenced again in the chapters to come. In addition, you will be introduced to a new way of looking at the self—indeed, a new way of looking at *your* self—that emphasizes the role of the social in creating the individual. And you will be reminded of the reverse: as your society makes you who you are, you have a role (in fact, many roles) to play in shaping your society.

What Is Human Nature?

"That's just human nature" is a phrase we often use to explain everything from violence and jealousy to love and altruism. But what is human nature, really? What is the thing about us that is unique and irreducible, that we all have in common and that separates us from other creatures? From a sociologist's perspective, it is culture and society that make us human. These things that we have created also make us who we are. We have to *learn* the meanings we give to food, housing, sex, and everything else, and society is the teacher.

You would be a very different person had you been born in fourteenth-century Japan, in an Aztec peasant family, or in the Norwegian royal court. You would have learned a different language, a different set of everyday skills, and a different set of meanings about how the world works. Also, your sense of who you are would be radically different in each case because of the particular social structures and interactions you would encounter. If you were a member of an Aztec peasant family, for example, you would expect to be married to someone of your parents' choosing in your early teens (McCaa 1994). Girls would be considered old maids if they were still single at age fifteen and might end up as prostitutes or concubines if they did not find a husband by this tender age.

nature vs. nurture debate the ongoing discussion of the respective roles of genetics and socialization in determining individual behaviors and traits

socialization the process of learning and internalizing the values, beliefs, and norms of our social group, by which we become functioning members of society

The Nature vs. Nurture Debate

If it is culture and society that make us human, what role does our genetic makeup play? Aren't we *born* with certain instincts? These are questions posed in what is often called the **nature vs. nurture debate**. Those taking the nature side, often sociobiologists, some psychologists, and others in the natural sciences, argue that behavioral traits can be explained by genetics. Those taking the nurture side, sociologists and others in the social sciences, argue that human behavior is learned and shaped through social interaction. Which of these arguments is right?

Both are right. You don't have to look far to see that genetics, or nature, plays a role in who we are. For example, research shows that high levels of testosterone contribute to stereotypically masculine traits such as aggressiveness and competitiveness (Van Goozen et al. 1994). However, it is also true that facing a competitive challenge (such as a baseball game) causes testosterone levels to rise (Booth et al. 1989). So is it the hormone that makes us competitive, or is it competition that stimulates hormone production? An additional example involves a study of moral and social development in people with brain injuries. Stephen W. Anderson and colleagues (1999) studied patients whose prefrontal cortex had been damaged. Those who had received the injury as infants struggled with moral and social reasoning, finding it difficult or impossible to puzzle out questions like "Is it acceptable for a man to steal the drug needed to save his wife's life if he can't afford to pay for it?" People who received the same injury as adults, however, were able to deal with such issues. Anderson and his research team hypothesized that there is a crucial period in brain development when people acquire the capacity for moral reasoning. In other words, nature provides a biological window through which social and moral development occurs.

The point is, there is a complex relationship between nature and nurture. Either one alone is insufficient to explain what makes us human. Certainly, heredity gives us a basic potential, but it is primarily our social environment that determines whether we will realize or fall short of that potential or develop new ones. We are subject to social influences from the moment we are born (and even before), and these influences only increase over the years. In part because the influence of social contact happens so gradually and to some extent unconsciously, we don't really notice what or how we are learning.

The Process of Socialization

We often speak of "socializing" with our friends, yet the idea of "socializing" is only part of what sociologists mean by **socialization**. Socialization is a twofold process. It includes the process by which a society, culture, or group teaches individuals to become functioning members, and the process by which individuals learn and internalize the values and norms of the group. Socialization thus works on both an individual and a social level: we learn our society's way of life and make it our own. Socialization accomplishes two main goals. First, it teaches members the skills necessary to satisfy basic human needs and to defend themselves against danger, thus ensuring that society itself will continue to exist. Second, socialization teaches individuals the norms, values, and beliefs associated with their culture and provides ways to ensure that members adhere to their shared way of life.

Social Isolation

We can appreciate how important socialization is when we see what happens to people who are deprived of social contact. When infants are born, they exhibit almost none of the learned behaviors that characterize human beings. Even their instincts for food or shelter or self-preservation are barely recognizable and almost impossible for them to act on alone. Babies do have innate capacities but can only fully develop as human beings through contact with others. There are several startling cases that demonstrate this (Newton 2004).

Perhaps you have heard myths about **feral children**, or children who have grown up in the wild. Supposedly, there are real cases of children being raised by wolves, as well as works of fiction such as *Tarzan of the Apes* and *The Jungle Book*. Such stories present images of primitive humans who have survived outside society and who are both heathen and uncivilized yet pure and uncorrupt, who lack in social graces but possess the keenest of instincts. Legend has it that as far back as the thirteenth century, experiments were conducted by German

emperor Frederick II to see whether humans could return to their natural and perfect state as depicted in the biblical Garden of Eden. Without human contact, the children who were used in these cruel experiments did not reveal any divine truths to the experimenters—they simply perished (Van Cleve 1972).

feral children in myths and rare real world cases, children who have had little human contact and may have lived in the wild from a young age

Although scientific ethics would never allow such experiments today, there are unfortunately real-life cases involving children who have lived in extreme social isolation. Sociologist Kingsley Davis (1940) studied several of these cases to better understand the relationship between human development and socialization.

One case from the 1930s involves a child named Isabelle, who was sequestered with her unmarried mother in a dark room of the family's Ohio home (Davis 1940, 1947). The mother, a deaf-mute, communicated with her using only gestures. Isabelle consequently did not learn to speak at all and communicated by making low, croaking sounds. When Isabelle was finally discovered by authorities, it was found that, in almost all ways, she had failed to develop like a normal child. Her behavior could only be described as primitive and bizarre, although there was never evidence of any congenital physical or mental disability. Isabelle did have a remarkable capacity for learning once she was exposed to regular human contact. But language skills were only part of what she later had to acquire in order to take her place as a member of society. Although she eventually overcame many of the effects of her social isolation, it was only through intensive training with medical and psychological specialists. It took two years after her rescue for her to acquire language and learn to interact with others, demonstrating that without socialization we are almost totally devoid of the qualities we normally associate with being human. Isabelle was able, with intensive remedial socialization, to "catch up" to her peers and become a normal child, something she was denied by her upbringing.

The socialization process begins in infancy and is especially productive once a child begins to understand and use language (Ochs 1986). But socialization is not complete at that point. It is a lifelong process that continues to shape us through experiences such as school, work, marriage, and parenthood, as we will see in the next few sections.

Mowgli, the "Man Cub" Fictional accounts of feral children, like Mowgli, the hero of the animated Disney film *The Jungle Book*, are quite different from real socially isolated children who struggle to learn language and interact with others.

Theories of the Self

Having a sense of one's self is perhaps the most fundamental of all human experiences. When seventeenth-century philosopher René Descartes exclaimed, "I think, therefore I am," he was expressing this basic fact—that we possess a consciousness about ourselves. More recently, some have examined whether higher mammals or primates might also have this same self-consciousness; while that has yet to be determined, we do know that consciousness is at the core of humanness.

The **self** is our experience of a distinct, real, personal identity that is separate and different from all other people. We can be "proud of ourselves," "lose control of ourselves," or want to "change ourselves," suggesting that we have the ability to think about ourselves as if we were more than one being and to see ourselves from the vantage point of an observer. Our thoughts and feelings emanate both *from* and *toward* ourselves; this is, in effect, how we come to "know" ourselves.

But just where does this sense of a self come from? How do we arrive at self-knowledge? When sociologists address these questions, they look at both the individual and society to find the answer. They believe that the self is created and modified through social interaction over the course of a lifetime. But while sociologists agree that the self is largely a social product, there are still a number of different theories about how the self develops, as we will see.

Psychoanalytic Theory: Sigmund Freud

The psychoanalytic perspective on the self, which is usually associated with Sigmund Freud, emphasizes childhood and sexual development as indelible influences on an individual's identity. While Freud's ideas have generated a great deal of controversy, they remain compelling for sociologists.

Perhaps his greatest contribution to understanding the self is his idea of the unconscious mind, as featured in *The Interpretation of Dreams* (1900/1955). Freud believed that the conscious level of awareness was but the tip of the iceberg and that just below the surface was a far greater area of the mind, the subconscious and the unconscious. He proposed that this unconscious energy was the source of our conscious thoughts and behavior. For example, the unconscious urge to slay our rivals may manifest itself in a conscious decision to work harder at the office in order to outshine a competitive co-worker.

According to Freud, the mind consists of three inter-related systems: the id, the ego, and the superego. The **id**, which is composed of biological drives, is the source of instinctive, psychic energy. Its main goal is to achieve pleasure and to avoid pain in all situations, which makes the id a selfish and unrealistic part of the mind. For example, despite all your hard work, sometimes that competitive co-worker is the one who gets the raise—not exactly what the pleasure-seeking id desired. The **ego**, by contrast, is the part that deals with the real world. It operates on the basis of reason and helps to mediate and integrate the demands of both the id and the superego. So the ego is the part of the self that says, "Okay, this time the other guy won, but if I keep trying, I'm bound to get that raise eventually."

The **superego** is composed of two components: the conscience and the ego-ideal. The conscience serves to keep us from engaging in socially undesirable behavior, and the ego-ideal upholds our vision of who we believe we should

self the individual's conscious, reflexive experience of a personal identity separate and distinct from other individuals

id, **ego**, and **superego** according to Freud, the three interrelated parts that make up the mind. The id consists of basic inborn drives that are the source of instinctive psychic energy. The ego is the realistic aspect of the mind that balances the forces of the id and the superego. The superego has two components (the conscience and the ego-ideal) and represents the internalized demands of society.

Dreams and the Subconscious In his book *The Interpretation of Dreams*, psychoanalyst Sigmund Freud outlined three psychological systems—the id, the ego, and the superego—that regulate subconscious drives and help keep an individual mentally balanced.

ideally be. The superego develops as a result of parental guidance, particularly in the form of the rewards and punishments we receive as children. It inhibits the urges of the id and encourages the ego to find morally acceptable forms of behavior. So the superego helps suppress the urge to kill your competitor and keeps you working toward getting that raise in socially acceptable ways. Each of these systems serves a different mental or emotional function, yet they all work together to keep the individual in a more or less healthy state of balance.

Freud also proposed that between infancy and adulthood, the personality passes through four distinct **psychosexual stages of development** (1905). This theory emerged from his therapy work with adult patients who were asked to try to recall earlier periods from their lives. According to the theory, a child passes through the first three stages of development between the ages of one and five. Most people have little or no memory whatsoever of this period. Yet, according to psychoanalytic theory, it is supposed to set the stage for the rest of one's adult life. The last stage of development begins around the age of twelve, but few people successfully complete this final transition to maturity. In some cases, the transitions through the first three stages are not completely successful either, so that people may find themselves stuck, or "fixated," at an earlier stage. Perhaps you've known someone who is considered to have an "oral fixation"—this person, thought to be partially stuck in the first stage of development, might smoke, overeat, or be verbally aggressive. Someone who is "anal retentive"—a neatnik, tightwad, or control freak—is thought to be partially stuck in the second stage. These kinds of personality traits, rooted in early childhood (according to Freud), appear as "hang-ups" in the adult.

Other sociologists have extended Freud's work in this area, focusing especially on gender identity—our selves as feminine or masculine. Nancy Chodorow, a feminist and psychoanalytic sociologist, has written widely on human behavior and internal psychic structures, and how patterns of gendered parenting and early childhood development can lead to the reproduction of traditional sex roles in society (1978, 1994).

The Looking-Glass Self: Charles Cooley

Around the same time Freud was developing his theories (early 1900s), other social theorists interested in the self were working on the other side of the Atlantic. Charles Cooley, an early member of the Chicago School of sociology, devised a simple but elegant way to conceptualize how individuals gain a sense of self. His idea is captured in the following short poem, which summarizes a profound and complex process.

Each to each a looking-glass,
Reflects the other that doth pass.

Cooley referred to this concept as the **looking-glass self** (1909). He believed that we all act like mirrors to each other, reflecting back to one another an image of ourselves. We do this in three steps.

1. *We imagine how we look to others*—not just in a physical sense, but in how we present ourselves. For example, we may imagine that others find us friendly, funny, or hardworking. The idea we have of ourselves is particularly important in regard to significant others. Whether they are parents, bosses, friends, or partners, we care about how we look to these people.

2. *We imagine other people's judgment of us.* We try to picture others' reactions and to interpret what they must be feeling. What is their opinion of me? Do they think I am smart enough? Lazy? Boring? Too tall? Not talkative enough?

3. *We experience some kind of feeling about ourselves based on our perception of other people's judgments.* If we imagine, for instance, that they think of us as competent, we may feel pride; conversely, if we think they consider us inadequate, then we may feel shame or embarrassment. The important point here is that we respond to the judgments that we *believe* others make about us, without really knowing for sure what they think. And we're not always right. We may draw wildly unrealistic conclusions. But according to Cooley, it is these perceptions, not reality, that determine the feelings we ultimately have about ourselves.

The social looking-glass, the way we see ourselves reflected back from others together with the feelings we develop as a result of what we imagine they see in us, forms our concept of self. For Cooley, there could be no sense of self without society, for there is no individual self without a corresponding "other" to provide us with our looking-glass self-image.

The suggestion that we are dependent on what others think of us—or rather what we think they think—for our own self-concept might seem appalling: are we really that hung up on what other people think? But while some of us may be influenced to a greater or lesser degree, *all* of us come to know ourselves through relationships, either real or imagined, with others.

psychosexual stages of development four distinct stages of the development of the self between birth and adulthood, according to Freud. Each stage is associated with a different erogenous zone.

looking-glass self the notion that the self develops through our perception of others' evaluations and appraisals of us

Mind, Self, and Society: George Herbert Mead

Another member of the Chicago School, George Herbert Mead, expanded upon Cooley's ideas about the development of the self and laid the essential groundwork that became the theory of symbolic interactionism. Mead also believed that self was created through social interaction. He believed that this process started in childhood—that children began to develop a sense of self at about the same time that they began to learn language. The acquisition of language skills coincides with the growth of mental capacities, including the ability to think of ourselves as separate and distinct and to see ourselves in relationship to others (Mead 1934).

According to Mead, the development of the self unfolds in several stages as we move through childhood. First is the **preparatory stage**. Children under the age of three lack a completely developed sense of self, and so they have difficulty distinguishing themselves from others. Such children begin the development process by simply imitating or mimicking others around them (making faces, playing patty-cake) without fully understanding the meaning of their behavior. After age three, children enter the **play stage** of development when they start to pretend or play at being "mommy," "firefighter," "princess," or "doctor." This is referred to as taking the role of the **particular or significant other**. As children learn the behavior associated with being a mother or doctor, they internalize the expectations of those particular others and begin to gain new perspectives in addition to their own. Such play also serves the purpose of anticipatory socialization for the real-life roles a child might play in the future.

In the final or **game stage** of development, children's self-awareness increases through a process Mead described using the example of games. By the early school years, children begin to take part in organized games. Each child must follow the rules of the game, which means that he or she must simultaneously take into account the roles of all the other players. Mead calls this overview the perspective of the **generalized other**. Thus children begin to understand the set of standards common to a social group—their playmates—and to see themselves from others' viewpoints. By taking the perspective of the generalized other, children are able to see themselves as objects. They gradually learn to internalize the expectations of the generalized other for themselves and to evaluate their own behavior. This is the beginning of understanding the attitudes and expectations of society as a whole.

Mead also recognized the dialectical or **dual nature of the self**; that is, the self as both subject and object. What we refer to as "I" is the subject component—the experience of a spontaneous, active, and creative part of ourselves, somewhat less socialized. What we refer to as "me" is the object component—the experience of a norm-abiding, conforming part of ourselves, more socialized and therefore reliant on others. The two components are inseparable and are united to form a single self in each of us. It is this process of recognizing the dual nature of the self, taking the role of the particular other, and seeing the perspective of the generalized other that Mead suggests leads to the development of the self.

The Particular Other According to Mead, once children learn about the self, they begin imitating others and playing roles. They begin to learn about perspectives other than their own.

preparatory stage the first stage in Mead's theory of the development of self wherein children mimic or imitate others

play stage the second stage in Mead's theory of the development of self wherein children pretend to play the role of the particular or significant other

particular or significant other the perspectives and expectations of a particular role that a child learns and internalizes

game stage the third stage in Mead's theory of the development of self wherein children play organized games and take on the perspective of the generalized other

generalized other the perspectives and expectations of a network of others (or of society in general) that a child learns and then takes into account when shaping his or her own behavior

dual nature of the self the belief that we experience the self as both subject and object, the "I" and the "me"

Dramaturgy: Erving Goffman

Erving Goffman is another among the group of symbolic interactionists who see micro-level, face-to-face interaction as the building block of every other aspect of society. Goffman believes that all meaning, as well as our individual selves, is constructed through interaction. Many of his key ideas are expressed in *The Presentation of Self in Everyday Life* (1956).

To understand Goffman's work, we first need to briefly consider another of the early Chicago School sociologists,

W. I. Thomas. What is now called the **Thomas theorem** states that "if people define situations as real, they are real in their consequences" (Thomas and Thomas 1928, p. 572). In other words, because we encounter ambiguous situations every day, many meanings are possible. The way we define each situation, then, becomes its reality.

For example, suppose you're walking down the street and you witness a woman slapping a man in public. What are the possible meanings of that situation? It could be a fight or spousal abuse; it could be a joke or a friendly greeting, depending on how hard the slap is; it could be that he has just passed out and she is hoping to revive him; or the participants could be actors shooting a scene from a film. Each of these definitions leads to a different set of potential consequences—you might intervene, call the police, stand by and laugh, ignore them, summon paramedics, or ask for an autograph, depending on which meaning you act upon. Each **definition of the situation** lends itself to a different approach, and the consequences are real.

Goffman looks at how we define situations interactionally—not just cognitively within our own heads, but in interaction with others. Think about it: how do you get your definition of the situation across to others? If you think a classroom lecture is boring, you may look over at your best friend and roll your eyes . . . she nods, indicating that she knows what you mean. The eye roll and the nod are **expressions of behavior**, tools we use to project our definitions of the situation to others.

What Goffman calls **expressions given** are typically verbal and intended—most of our speech falls into this category. Almost all of what we say, we *mean* to say, at least at that moment. Only in situations of extreme emotional response—such as fear, pain, or ecstasy—might we make unintended utterances. **Expressions given off**, like the eye roll and the nod, are typically nonverbal but observable in various ways and may be intended or unintended. Things like facial expressions, mannerisms, body language, or styles of dress are important indicators to others about the definition of the situation.

IMPRESSION MANAGEMENT Reading meaning in others' expressions of behavior requires a bit of caution. We know that people may deliberately say things to hide what they really feel, so we tend to think we get more real insight from expressions given off because we believe them to be unintended. But expressions given off can be manipulated as well. In a sense, Goffman is saying that it's not just what you say but how you say it that creates meaning. And he is a cynic, although he believes that everyday actors can be sincere. Goffman sees social life as a sort of con game, in which we work at controlling the impressions others have of us. He calls this process **impression management**. Like actors on a stage, we play our parts and use all of our communicative resources (verbal and nonverbal) to present a particular impression to others. We say and do what we think is necessary to communicate who we are and what we think, and we refrain from saying and doing things that might damage the impression we want others to have of us.

It is this focus on the performance strategies of impression management that has led scholars to refer to Goffman's central ideas as **dramaturgy**—and the theatrical allusion is entirely intended. As in the theater, we use certain tools to aid in our impression management. The **front**, for example, is the setting that helps establish a particular meaning (like a classroom for teaching or a bar for drinking). Our **personal front**—appearance, manner, and style of dress (or "costume"), as well as gender, race, and age—helps establish the definition of the situation as well.

For example, Dr. Ferris is told quite often that she "doesn't look like a professor." This illustrates how we use elements of personal front to make judgments about people: if our images of professors involve gruff, grizzled, older men in unfashionable clothes, then someone who is younger, friendlier, and female and who wears edgy, hipper styles must work harder at convincing others that she is in fact a professor. Similarly, when a student happens to see Dr. Ferris at a restaurant, movie theater, or department store, the student's response is almost always the same: "what are you doing here?"

The social setting, or **region** (which includes the

Thomas theorem classic formulation of the way individuals define situations, whereby "if people define situations as real, they are real in their consequences"

definition of the situation an agreement with others about "what is going on" in a given circumstance. This consensus allows us to coordinate our actions with those of others and realize goals.

expressions of behavior small actions such as an eye roll or head nod that serve as an interactional tool to help project our definition of the situation to others

expressions given expressions that are intentional and usually verbal, such as utterances

expressions given off observable expressions that can be either intended or unintended and are usually nonverbal

impression management the effort to control the impressions we make on others so that they form a desired view of us and the situation; the use of self-presentation and performance tactics

dramaturgy an approach pioneered by Erving Goffman in which social life is analyzed in terms of its similarities to theatrical performance

front in the dramaturgical perspective, the setting or scene of performances that helps establish the definition of the situation

personal front the expressive equipment we consciously or unconsciously use as we present ourselves to others, including appearance and manner, to help establish the definition of the situation

region in the dramaturgical perspective, the context or setting in which the performance takes place

Front and Back Regions Most of us maintain multiple selves and show a different face to different people. However, when the boundaries between front and back regions break down, as they did when news leaked about Arnold Schwarzenegger fathering a child with a member of his staff, the results can be scandalous.

location, scenery, and props), makes a big difference in how we perceive and interact with the people we encounter there. Students and professors recognize one another and know how to interact when on campus or in the classroom. But in other venues, we are out of context, and this can confuse us. We seldom think of our professors as people who have off-campus lives—it's hard to see them as people who dine out, see movies, or buy underwear (for that matter, professors rarely think of their students this way either!). So when we encounter one another in unfamiliar regions, we often don't know how to behave because the old classroom scripts don't work.

In addition, there are places known as back regions, or **backstage**, where we prepare for our performances—which take place in front regions, or **frontstage**. We behave differently—and present different selves—frontstage than we do backstage; your professor behaved differently this morning while he showered, shaved, dressed, and made breakfast for his kids than he is behaving now, lecturing and answering questions in his sociology classroom. For Goffman, the key to understanding these nuances in impression management is to recognize that we present different selves in different situations, and the responses of others to those selves continually shape and mold our definitions of situation *and* self. Thus we can say that the self is a **social construction** (Berger and Luckmann 1966). The self is something that is created or invented in interaction with others who also participate in agreeing to the reality or meaning of that self as it is being presented in the situation.

We also make claims about who we are in our interactions. These claims can be either accepted or contradicted by others, which can make things either easier or harder for our self-image. Most of the time, others support the selves we project. For example, when your professor starts lecturing and you begin to take notes, you are supporting the version of self that he is presenting: he is "doing professor," and in response, you are "doing student." Another way that we support the selves that people present is to allow them to save face—to prevent them from realizing that they've done something embarrassing. Goffman calls this **cooling the mark out**, a phrase borrowed from con games, but it can be used as a tool of civility and tact as well. When the professor mixes up two related concepts in a lecture, for example, you let it pass because you know what she really meant to say. Or, even worse, you overlook the spinach between your professor's teeth until it can be called to his attention privately!

There are also situations in which the selves we project are contested or even destroyed. For example, if you raised your hand in a 200-person lecture hall and told the professor that he had spinach between his teeth, you would be undermining the self he is trying to present. His identity as an expert, an authority figure, and a senior mentor would be publicly damaged once you called attention to his dental gaffe (unless he was able to deflect the situation gracefully).

backstage in the dramaturgical perspective, places in which we rehearse and prepare for our performances

frontstage in the dramaturgical perspective, the region in which we deliver our public performances

social construction the process by which a concept or practice is created and maintained by participants who collectively agree that it exists

cooling the mark out behaviors that help others to save face or avoid embarrassment, often referred to as civility or tact

TABLE 4.1 Theory in Everyday Life

PERSPECTIVE	APPROACH TO THE SELF AND INTERACTION	CASE STUDY: IDENTITY IN CHILDHOOD
PSYCHOANALYSIS	Freud's theory of the unconscious mind as composed of an interrelated system (id, ego, superego) that underlies human behavior; personality develops through psychosexual stages.	Parents instill a conscience (superego) in children through rules that govern their instinctual behavior (id) until children mature and are self-governing (ego).
LOOKING-GLASS SELF	Cooley's theory of the self concept as derived from how we imagine others see us, and the feelings about ourselves based on the perceived judgments of others.	Parents and significant others serve as a reflection to children, who develop a sense of self based on their appraisals, real or imagined.
MIND, SELF, AND SOCIETY	Mead's theory of the self that develops through three stages (preparatory, play, and game); in role taking the particular or generalized other, we learn to see ourselves as others do.	Children gain a sense of self through imitation, play, and games, in which they learn various roles and take on the perspectives of others.
DRAMATURGY	Goffman's theory of the presentation of self; we are like actors on a stage whose performance strategies aid in impression management.	Children learn the arts of impression management and may present a different self to their parents than to other children or teachers.

In Goffman's view, then, the presentation of self and impression management are about power as well as about self. If you embarrass your professor in front of an auditorium full of students, he no longer possesses quite as much power as he did a few moments before.

Goffman's view of our interactions can be disturbing to some people, for it suggests that we are always acting, that we are never being honest about who we really are. But Goffman would challenge this interpretation of his work. Yes, some people deliberately deceive others in their presentation of self, but we must all present *some* type of self in social situations. Why wouldn't those selves be presented sincerely? As Goffman-inspired sociologist Josh Meyrowitz says, "While a dishonest judge may pretend to be an honest judge, even an honest judge must play the role of 'honest judge' " (1985, p. 30).

ANALYZING EVERYDAY LIFE

Impression Management in Action

This exercise in ethnography is designed to help make your own impression management visible—and to help you see how integral it is to your everyday life. You will observe yourself acting and interacting in two different social situations and will then do a comparative analysis of your presentation of self in each setting. Observing one's own behavior is a variant of the ethnographic method you read about in Chapter 2 known as **autoethnography**.

> **autoethnography** ethnographic description that focuses on the feelings and reactions of the ethnographer

Step 1: Observation

Choose two different situations that you will encounter this week in everyday life, and commit to observing yourself for thirty minutes as you participate in each. For example, you may observe yourself at work, at a family birthday celebration, at lunch with friends, in your math class, riding on the bus or train, or watching an athletic match. The two situations you choose don't need to be extraordinary in any way; in fact, the more mundane, the better. But they should be markedly different from one another.

Step 2: Analysis

After observing yourself in the two situations, consider the following questions.

- What type of "front" do you encounter when you enter each situation?

- How does the "region" or setting (location, scenery, and props) affect your presentation of self there?

- Can you identify "backstage" and "frontstage" regions for each situation? Which of your activities are preparation and which are performance?

- What type of "personal front" (appearance, manner, dress) do you bring to each situation?

- How are your facial expressions, body language, and so forth ("expressions given off") different in each situation?

- What kinds of things do you say ("expressions given") in each situation?

- How do you modify what you do and say in each situation? Are there things you say or do in one that would be inappropriate, strange, or even absurd in the other?

- Who are you in each situation? Do you present a slightly different version of yourself in each? Why?

As you observe the most minute aspects of your interactions, you will probably discover that you perform somewhat different versions of yourself in the two situations. "Doing student," for instance, might be very different from "doing boyfriend."

A final Goffman-inspired question to ask is this: does engaging in impression management mean that we have no basic, unchanging self? If we bring different selves to different situations, what does that say about the idea of a "true self"? This issue is an important one, and we hope you use your Data Workshop findings to pursue it in greater depth.

There are two options for completing the Data Workshop.

- *Option 1 (informal)*: Take some informal notes about your observations in step 1, and jot down some of your responses to the questions asked in step 2. Compare your notes and experiences with other students in small-group discussions. Use this as a way to learn more about yourself and others in the group.

- *Option 2 (formal)*: For step 1, use ethnographic methods of data gathering. Create written fieldnotes to record your actions, interactions, and thoughts during each thirty-minute observation period. Be as detailed as possible. Then write a three- to four-page essay analyzing your experiences by addressing the questions in step 2. Refer to your fieldnotes in the essay, and include them as an attachment to your paper.

agents of socialization social groups, institutions, and individuals (especially the family, schools, peers, and the mass media) that provide structured situations in which socialization takes place

Agents of Socialization

Since our sense of self is shaped by social interaction, we should now turn our attention to the socializing forces that have the most significant impact on our lives. These forces, called **agents of socialization**, provide structured situations in which socialization takes place. While there are a variety of such influences in American society, notably religion, as well as our political and economic systems, we will focus here on what may be the four most predominant agents of socialization: the family, schools, peers, and the mass media (Figure 4.1).

The Family

The family is the single most significant agent of socialization in all societies. It's easy to see why. The family is the original group to which we belong. It is where early emotional and social bonds are created, where language is learned, and where we first begin to internalize the norms and values of our society. Most of our primary socialization, which teaches us to become mature, responsible members of society, takes place within the family. It is not surprising, then, that the family has perhaps the longest-lasting influence on the individual.

Most research has focused on the role of mothers in child-rearing practices (Goode 1982), although attention has recently turned to the significance of fathers, as well as siblings and other relatives. For example, Scott Coltrane's book *Family Man* (1997) looks at historical changes in the roles of men as active parents, and how men feel about their involvement in their children's lives. The family has such a powerful impact on us partly because as children we have little or no outside contact (until we start school) and therefore no basis for comparison. The family is our world.

The family is also *in* the world. Where a family is located, both geographically and socially—its ethnic, class, religious, educational, and political background—will affect family members (Lareau 2003). For example, one of the most important lessons we learn in families is about gender roles: we see what moms and dads, sisters and brothers are expected to do (like mow the lawn or fold the laundry) and convert these observations into general rules about gender in society (Chodorow 1978).

Socialization differs from family to family because each family has its own particular set of values and beliefs. A single family can also change over time. As years pass, children may not be raised in the same way as their older siblings, for the simple reason that parents have no experience with

SCHOOL

School helps individuals to become less dependent on the family, and is often the first experience with socialization away from the home. It also provides a large percentage of the pool from which one chooses their peers.

The socialization children receive at school overlaps with what they learn at home.

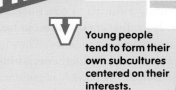

PEER GROUPS

By adolescence, young people spend more time with their peer groups than with their parents. The peer group's influence increases as a child gets older and usually replaces the family as the most influential factor.

However, peer influence is intense and immediate, while parental influence is formative and longer-lasting.

Young people tend to form their own subcultures centered on their interests.

MASS MEDIA

The mass media has recently risen to become one of the most significant sources of socialization, and many sociologists wonder if the media may be usurping many of the normal functions of the family in teaching us basic norms. By the time most children graduate, they will have spent more time with the mass media than in the classroom.

TV, radio, CDs, iPods, movies, video games, PCs, and text messaging take up to 7 hours of the average teenager's time.

FAMILY

As the original group to which each person belongs, the family forms the foundation for all other socializing agents. Most of our primary socialization takes place within in the family, which makes it the longest-lasting influence on the individual.

Where a family is located, both geographically and socially, sets the stage for the other agents of socialization.

Family Has the Longest-Lasting Influence The family is the original group to which each person belongs, and it is the most important socializing agent.

babies when their first child is born but plenty of experience by the time the youngest comes along. Nor are all aspects of socialization deliberate; some in fact are quite unintentional (as when a father's violent temper or a mother's depression is passed down to the next generation).

Schools

Many people remember their school years with fondness, dread, or perhaps relief that they're over! No wonder school makes such a great subject for bad dreams and movie scripts. Public elementary and secondary schools were first established in the United States in the 1800s. While attendance was uneven at first, education advocates believed that schooling played a critical role in maintaining a democracy (though blacks and women still lacked the right to vote) and in shaping future generations of citizens. Over the years, schools have gradually taken on greater responsibilities than merely teaching a prescribed curriculum. Schools now provide physical education, meals, discipline, and child care, all formerly the provinces of other social institutions.

When children begin attending school (including pre-school and day care), it may be their first significant experience away from home. School helps them to become less dependent on the family,

hidden curriculum values or behaviors that students learn indirectly over the course of their schooling because of the structure of the educational system and the teaching methods used

providing a bridge to other social groups. In school, children learn that they will be judged on their behavior and on academic performance. They learn not only formal subjects but also a **hidden curriculum** (Jackson 1968), a set of behavioral traits such as punctuality, neatness, discipline, hard work, competition, and obedience (to be discussed in greater detail in Chapter 10). The socialization children receive from teachers, staff members, and other students occurs simultaneously and overlaps with what they learn in the family.

Recently, there has been increasing scrutiny regarding the role of teachers, especially in public schools. Because teachers are such potent role models for students, parents are concerned about the moral standing of those who are in charge of teaching their children, as well as their training and competence. There is increasing pressure for schools to take on even more responsibilities, including dealing with issues that used to be taught at home or in church—such as sex, violence, drugs and alcohol, and general morality and citizenship.

Peers

Peer groups are groups of people who are about the same age and have similar social characteristics. Peers may be friends at school or from the neighborhood, members of a sports team, or cabin mates at summer camp. As children get older, peers often become more important than parents as agents of socialization. As the influence of peers increases, the influence of parents decreases. While the family still has the most long-lasting influence on an individual, it is peers who have the most intense and immediate effect on each other.

By adolescence, young people spend more time with their peers than with their parents or anyone else (Larson and Richards 1991). Membership in a peer group provides young people with a way of exercising independence from, and possibly reacting against, adult control. Young people tend to form peer subcultures that are almost entirely centered on their own interests, such as video gaming or disc golf or garage bands, with distinct values and norms related to those interests.

The need to "fit in" with a peer group may seem overwhelming to some young people. Some will do almost anything to belong, even betray their own values: Bradley and Wildman (2002) found that peer pressure was a predictor of adolescent participation in risky behaviors such as dangerous driving, unsafe sex, and drug and alcohol use. Peer groups, while providing important and enjoyable social bonds, can also be the source of painful self-doubt, ridicule, or rejection for many young people.

The Mass Media

The mass media's role as one of the most significant sources of socialization is a somewhat recent phenomenon. Television began appearing in American homes a little more than fifty years ago, and usage of the internet has become wide-spread only in the past two decades. Yet, for many of us, it would be almost impossible to imagine life without the mass media—whether print, broadcast, or digital. This huge explosion, the dawning of the Information Age, is something we already take for granted, but we don't always see the ways in which it is changing our lives.

Many sociologists question whether the media may have even usurped some of the functions of the family in teaching us basic norms and values and giving advice on common problems. As an example, take the people of Fiji, a South Pacific island that lacked widespread access to television until 1995. A group of Harvard Medical School researchers took this unique opportunity to study the effects of television on the native population. Specifically, they were interested in the ways in which Western programs influenced eating habits and body image among adolescent girls in a culture that "traditionally supported robust appetites and body shapes" (Becker et al. 2002).

Through surveys and interviews with the young women (the mean age was around 17) in 1995, just months after television was introduced, and again in 1998, the researchers ascertained that Western television was in fact affecting body image and corresponding behaviors among the girls. In those three years, the percentage of subjects whose survey responses indicated an eating disorder jumped from 12.5 to 29.2, and the percentage who reported self-induced vomiting as a form of weight control rose from none to 11.3. Dieting and dissatisfaction with weight were prevalent—and 83 percent of the girls who were interviewed reported that

Are television shows a socializing agent? Arguing that its deptictions of sexuality and drug use were bad influences on teens, parents protested *Skins*, a U.S. spin-off of a British series that briefly aired on MTV.

they felt television "had specifically influenced their friends and/or themselves to feel differently about or change their body shape or weight" (Becker et al. 2002).

The women of Fiji only recently encountered mass media. How do we measure the cumulative effect of the ubiquitous exposure to the mass media that pervade American society, day in and day out? Whose messages are we listening to, and what are we being told about ourselves and each other? On average, Americans watch between two and seven hours of television per day and spend more hours listening to the radio, CDs or iPods, reading, watching movies, playing video games, surfing the web, or sending instant messages and e-mail. By the time young people graduate from high school, they will have spent far more time with mass media than in the classroom. While some worry that this means kids are lost in a fantasy world, Hodge and Tripp (1986) have argued that watching TV actually helps kids learn to distinguish between reality and fantasy, an important developmental milestone. In addition to their ability to entertain, the media also have great potential to inform and educate. It is clear that we internalize many of the values, beliefs, and norms presented in the media and that their powerful influence in our lives only stands to increase as we proceed deeper into the Information Age.

DATA WORKSHOP

ANALYZING MASS MEDIA AND POPULAR CULTURE

Television as an Agent of Socialization

Television is a powerful and surreptitious agent of socialization. It is everywhere, and we devour it—so it seems important to ask what kinds of messages we are getting about our society from our viewing. How does TV socialize us? This Data Workshop will use content analysis (see the discussion of using existing sources in Chapter 2) to help you answer this question.

Choose one of the most popular TV series currently on the air—at the time of this writing, your choices might include *30 Rock*, *House*, *CSI*, or *The Office*. Choose a regular drama or comedy series rather than a newsmagazine, talk show, game show, or reality show.

Now choose some aspect of social status and individual identity that you want to focus on; for example, gender (how women or men are portrayed), race/ethnicity (how a particular ethnic group, such as African Americans or Latinos, is portrayed), sexuality (heterosexuals, gay men, or lesbians),

or class (poor people, wealthy people, or the middle class). For instance, you might look at the depiction of women in *Gossip Girl* or men in *Two and a Half Men*, the role of Latinos in *Law & Order* or African Americans in *Grey's Anatomy*, or the portrayal of the middle class in *Weeds* or the wealthy in *One Life To Live*, *Days of Our Lives*, or any other daytime soap opera.

Watch an episode of your chosen program in its entirety (you might want to record the program or look for an episode on DVD or online so that you can review it if you need to). Take notes as you watch; note the program's content with reference to your particular topic choice. To give you an example of how to do this workshop, we use depictions of women (in brackets below) as our topic and the program *Brothers and Sisters* (which ended in 2011 after five seasons). You should substitute your own current program and choice of topic for each of the following questions:

1. In the program, how many [female] characters are there? How does the number of [female] characters compare with the number of other characters? Are the [female] roles major characters or minor characters? How can you tell?

2. What types of roles do the [female] characters have? What are their activities, attitudes, and interactions like on the show? What kinds of things do they do and say that tell you who they are and what they are like?

3. Are the portrayals of [females] positive or negative? Humorous or serious? One-dimensional or multidimensional? How can you tell?

4. What image(s) of [women] does this program portray? In other words, what messages do the words, pictures, plot lines, and characters convey to viewers about [women] in general?

In the case of *Brothers and Sisters*, there were some interesting portrayals of women to analyze. For example, the central character is a woman: we first meet Nora Walker at a family party where her husband suffers a heart attack and dies. As a new widow, Nora must step up to head her large family, as well as their struggling family business. These leadership roles are new to her and uncomfortable for the family. In addition, she must face such family secrets as her late husband's long-term infidelity. Other female characters include Nora's daughters, Kitty and Sarah, both career women and mothers with messy love lives, and Holly, the former mistress of Nora's husband. These women relate to each other, as well as the men in their lives, in ways that provided powerful messages about gender roles and femininity to both female and male viewers.

Total Institutions The military, prisons, and cults are examples of total institutions where individuals' identities are stripped away and re-formed.

Now come the really important questions:

5. How does the content of this program contribute to our socialization process? What do we learn about [women] in society from watching the program? After finishing your analysis, what do you think about TV's powers of socialization?

There are two options for completing the assigned work.

- *Option 1 (informal)*: Prepare written notes that you can refer to during in-class discussions. Discuss your reactions and conclusions with other students in small groups. Listen for any differences or variations in each other's insights.

- *Option 2 (formal)*: Write a three- to four-page essay answering the Data Workshop questions. Make sure to refer to specific segments of the TV show that support your analysis.

Adult Socialization

Being an "adult" somehow signifies that we've learned well enough how to conduct ourselves as autonomous members of society. But adults are by no means completely socialized. Life is continually presenting us with new situations and new roles with unfamiliar norms and values. We are constantly learning and adjusting to new conditions over the life course and thereby participating in secondary socialization.

For example, your college training will teach you a great deal about the behaviors that will be expected of you in your chosen profession, such as responsibility and punctuality. But after graduating and obtaining a job, you will likely find further, unanticipated expectations. At the very least, you will be socialized to the local culture of a specific workplace, where new rules and customs (like "Always be closing!" in a real estate office) are observed. As your career unfolds, such episodes of socialization will recur as you take on different responsibilities or switch jobs.

Other examples of altered life circumstances include marrying, being divorced or widowed, raising a family, moving to a new community, losing a job or retiring—all of which require modifying attitudes and behaviors. For example, being divorced or widowed after many years of marriage means jumping into a dating pool that may look quite different from the last time you were in it— "safe sex," "splitting the check," and other new norms may be hard for older daters to assimilate. Adult socialization often requires the replacement of previously learned norms and values with different ones, what is known as **resocialization**. Facing a serious illness or growing old also often involves

> **resocialization** the process of replacing previously learned norms and values with new ones as a part of a transition in life

Changing the World

Sister Pauline Quinn and Training Dogs in Prison

Can adopting a puppy change the world? According to Sister Pauline Quinn, a Dominican nun, it can when the dogs are adopted by prison inmates and trained to help the disabled! Sister Pauline knew something firsthand about life in a total institution, and not just the convent. Born Kathy Quinn, she was once a chronic runaway because of a dysfunctional family life and was eventually institutionalized for lack of another place for her to go. For several years afterward, she was homeless, staying in abandoned buildings and trying to avoid getting picked up by the police as a vagrant. Kathy Quinn could well have died on the streets of Los Angeles, but instead her life was turned around when she found Joni, a German Shepherd.

Quinn felt that the dog was the beginning of the process of resocialization that helped return her to being a functioning member of society. It was the first time she had a true friend, one whose unconditional love was restoring her badly damaged self-esteem. Her time in institutions had left her "depersonalized," stripped of any positive identity with which to tackle the demands of life on the "outside." The understanding and affection she received from Joni began to heal Quinn of the traumas she had sustained in her youth. The work that Quinn did in training Joni transformed not only the dog but the person as well, eventually leading her to a happier and more productive life devoted to helping others.

Quinn was particularly drawn to the plight of women prisoners and believed that they too could find similar benefits through contact with dogs. She knew that life in prison could be extremely depersonalizing, especially for women,

and that rehabilitation, if it was offered at all, was too often unsuccessful, returning convicts to the streets without having rebuilt their lives. In 1981, with the assistance of Dr. Leo Bustad, a professor of veterinary science at the University of Washington, she approached the Washington State Correctional Center for Women and proposed that inmates volunteer to train puppies adopted from local shelters and rescue organizations to become service and therapy dogs. The result was the Prison Pet Partnership Program.

The women selected to participate in the program get more than just dogs to train; they get the opportunity for substantial resocialization, which helps them to develop new, positive identities and learn valuable social skills that can translate to the outside world. The labor-intensive process of training a dog is perfectly suited to the needs and abilities of inmates, who have a great surplus of time and a desperate need to find constructive ways to occupy it. The rigors of dog training, which place an emphasis on achieving discipline and obedience through repetition and positive reinforcement, is a lesson not lost on the trainers. During the months of training, the animals even sleep with the inmates, providing added psychological benefits. Prisons report significant improvements in morale and behavior once dog-training programs are in place. Allowing prisoners access to the dogs' unconditional love and giving the prisoners a chance to contribute to society in a meaningful way increase the likelihood that the prisoners will reenter mainstream society successfully.

While the program was originally motivated by Sister Quinn's desire to change the lives of prisoners, she was

---

total institution an institution in which individuals are cut off from the rest of society so that their lives can be controlled and regulated for the purpose of systematically stripping away previous roles and identities in order to create new ones

intensive resocialization. In order to cope with a new view of what their aging body will permit them to do, people must discard previous behaviors in favor of others (not working out every day, for example).

Another dramatic example of resocialization is found in **total institutions** (Goffman 1961), such as prisons, cults, and mental hospitals, and, in some cases, even boarding schools, nursing homes, monasteries, and the military.

In total institutions, residents are severed from their previous relations with society, and their former identities are systematically stripped away and re-formed. There may be different ends toward which total institutions are geared,

Sister Pauline Quinn, pictured on the left, has started dog training programs in prisons in 19 states. Participants include the inmates pictured on the right.

thinking of more than just the inmates, arguing that "things like this are part of a chain reaction of good." It begins with the rescue of an unwanted animal that would otherwise be put down, gives emotional support and job training to prisoners, and finally provides handicapped and disabled people service animals that improve their lives.

Service animals trained to work with disabled people cost as much as $10,000 to train, so making more of them available can transform the lives of the people they're placed with. The original program, in the Washington penal system, has now placed more than 700 dogs as service, seizure, or therapy dogs, as well as pets. Only about one out of every fifteen dogs has what it takes to work as a service or therapy dog, but the others are released into the community as "paroled pets," whose intensive training now makes them much more adoptable than they were before.

Prisons in at least nineteen states have established similar dog-training programs. The vast majority of the programs are funded without any state money, using only donations, and sometimes become nearly self-supporting by running grooming and kennel businesses. Military prisons have begun comparable programs to train service dogs for disabled veterans. Regardless of the specific mission each program pursues, prison pet-training programs provide proof that changing the world always transforms those who give as much as it does those who receive. In 2001, the story of Sister Pauline Quinn and the prison dog-training program was made into the original Lifetime TV movie *Within These Walls.*

such as creating good soldiers, punishing criminals, or managing mental illness, but the process of resocialization is similar: all previous identities are suppressed, and an entirely new, disciplined self is created.

Relatively few adults experience resocialization to the degree of the total institution. All, however, continue to learn and synthesize norms and values throughout their lives as they move into different roles and social settings that present them once again with the challenges and opportunities of continued socialization.

Statuses and Roles

While agents of socialization play an important role in developing our individual identities, so does the larger scaffolding of society. This happens as we take on (or have imposed upon us) different statuses and roles.

A **status** is a position in a social hierarchy that comes with a set of expectations. Sometimes these positions are formalized: "professor," "president," or even "parent." Parental obligations, for example, are written into laws that prohibit the neglect and abuse of children. Other statuses are more informal: you may be the "class clown," for instance, or the "conscience" of your group of friends. The contours of these informal statuses are less explicit but still widely recognizable. We all occupy a number of statuses, as we hold positions in multiple social hierarchies at once. Some statuses change over the course of a lifetime (e.g., marital or parental status), while others usually do not (e.g., gender).

There are different kinds of statuses. An **ascribed status** is one we are born with that is unlikely to change (such as our gender or race). An **embodied status** is located in our physical selves (such as beauty or disability). Finally, an **achieved status** is one we have earned through our own efforts (such as an occupation, hobby, or skill) or that has been acquired in some other way (such as a criminal identity, mental illness, or drug addiction). All statuses influence how others see and respond to us. However, some ascribed, embodied, or achieved statuses take on the power of what sociologists call a **master status**—a status that seems to override all others in our identities.

Master statuses carry with them expectations that may blind people to other facets of our personalities. People quickly make assumptions about what women, Asians, doctors, or alcoholics are like and may judge us according to those expectations rather than our actual attributes. This kind of judgment, often referred to as **stereotyping**, is looked upon as negative or destructive. However, it is important to realize that we all use these expectations in our everyday lives; stereotyping, as problematic as it is, is all but unavoidable.

A **role** is the set of behaviors expected from a particular status position. Sociologists such as Erving Goffman (1956) and Ralph Turner (1978) deliberately use the theatrical analogy to describe how roles provide a kind of script, outlining what we are expected to say and do as a result of our position in the social structure. Professors, then, are expected to be responsible teachers and researchers. Employment contracts and faculty handbooks may specify the role even further: professors must hold a certain number of office hours per week, for example, and must obtain permission from the university in order to skip classes or take a leave of absence. Class clowns don't sign a contract, nor are they issued a handbook, but they have role expectations nonetheless: they are expected to turn a classroom event into a joke whenever possible and to sacrifice their own success in order to provide laughs for others.

Multiple Roles and Role Conflict

In setting out general expectations for behavior, roles help shape our actions in ways that may come to define us to ourselves and others. For example, we often describe ourselves according to personality traits: "I am a responsible person," "a nurturer," "competitive," or "always cheerful." These traits are often the same as the role expectations attached to our various statuses as professionals, parents, athletes, or friends.

Sometimes our multiple roles clash in our everyday lives, a situation known as **role conflict**. Perhaps the most common examples of role conflict involve tensions between professional and familial roles. While preparing for an important meeting at work, you get a call from the school nurse saying your son is ill. Do you leave work to pick him up, thereby missing the meeting? Or do you attend the meeting, all the while distracted by thoughts of your ailing child? **Role strain** occurs when there are contradictory expectations within the same role; for example, many mothers and fathers feel torn between their parental duties to nurture and to discipline, and may be able to do one or the other but not both. Sometimes our life takes a turn that means we leave a role we had once occupied, a process known as **role exit**. After a divorce, for example, one is no longer a "husband" or "wife."

Statuses and roles help shape our identities by providing guidelines (sometimes formal, sometimes informal) for our own behavior and by providing the patterns that others use to interact with us. They are part of the construction of our social selves.

status a position in a social hierarchy that carries a particular set of expectations

ascribed status an inborn status; usually difficult or impossible to change

embodied status a status generated by physical characteristics

achieved status a status earned through individual effort or imposed by others

master status a status that is always relevant and affects all other statuses we possess

stereotyping judging others based on preconceived generalizations about groups or categories of people

role the set of behaviors expected of someone because of his or her status

role conflict experienced when we occupy two or more roles with contradictory expectations

role strain the tension experienced when there are contradictory expectations within one role

role exit the process of leaving a role that we will no longer occupy

NFL vs. Family: Chris and Stefanie Spielman

In 1998, Chris Spielman, a linebacker for the Buffalo (New York) Bills, was getting ready to return to the field after recovering from a major injury. He and his wife, Stefanie, and their two small children were moving from their home state of Ohio to New York, and he'd get back into the game he loved. Stefanie had been Chris's cheerleader—literally and figuratively—for ten years, supporting him as he pursued his football career. "Captain Crunch" was the nickname of this four-time Pro-Bowler, and opponents on the field had no problem understanding why: Spielman was a big, tough guy, and football was his life. Then Stefanie was diagnosed with breast cancer, and their lives changed dramatically. Stefanie needed to remain in Ohio for chemotherapy treatments, and Chris faced a crisis of decision making: go to New York to play football, or stay home with his wife and kids?

Chris Spielman was experiencing role conflict. His occupational role—professional athlete—required actions that were seemingly incompatible with his familial role, husband and father. The expectations attached to his occupational role included a willingness to move about the country to training camp and away-games and even to be traded to a team in another city. The expectations attached to his famil-ial role included being able to provide hands-on care and nurturing for a sick wife and two small children (the couple eventually had four kids). These expectations were not only incompatible, they may have created a certain amount of role strain related to his gender: it's still easier to see a big, strong man as a hard-hitting linebacker than as a nurturing husband and father. But Chris said, "I wanted to be the one to hold her hand when she vomited. I wanted to be there when they shaved her head. I wanted to take her to her chemo treatments" (Cabot 1999). None of this would have been possible if he was in Dallas one week and Tampa the next. Role conflict was forcing him into a difficult choice: his job or his family?

Chris chose his family. As he said in a 1999 interview, "I wouldn't give my life for football, but I'd give my life for my family. There's no comparison. They're not even in the same stratosphere."

You may not become a professional athlete with a critically ill spouse, but it is absolutely certain that you will find yourself in situations where the demands of your occupational role clash with those of your familial role. Perhaps you already have. How will you resolve those role conflicts? Chris Spielman, now a commentator for ESPN, sums it up this way: "My kids can look back and say, 'When Dad had a tough decision to make, he did the right thing.' I wanted to set a good example for them" (Cabot 1999). Sadly, Stefanie died in 2008, but Chris continues to care for his family, work for ESPN, and raise funds for breast cancer research.

Chris Spielman, his wife Stefanie, and their four children.

Emotions and Personality

As the Spielmans' experience (see this chapter's In Relationships box) demonstrates, role conflicts can be very emotional events. Our emotions are intensely personal responses to the unique situations of our lives. We react with happiness, anger, fear, desire, or sorrow to our own experiences, as well as things that happen to others, even events in movies and novels. Individuals sometimes react very differently—what makes one person laugh may make another cry. It would seem, then, that our emotions are the one thing about our lives that aren't dictated by society, that can't be explained with reference to sociological concepts or theories.

Well, our emotions aren't fully determined by society, but they are indeed social. We respond individually, but there also are social patterns in our emotional responses. For example, some emotional responses differ according to the culture—even an emotion as personal as grief, as noted in the Global Perspective box.

The Social Construction of Emotions

Sometimes our interaction with others affects our emotional responses: we may yell angrily at a political rally along with everyone else, realizing only later that we don't really feel that strongly about the issue at all; we may stifle our tears in front of the coach but shed them freely after the game. **Role-taking emotions**, such as sympathy, embarrassment, and shame, require that we be able to see things from someone else's point of view. When a friend is injured in an accident, you know she is feeling pain, so you feel sympathy for her. **Feeling rules** (Hochschild 1975) are socially constructed norms regarding the appropriate feelings and displays of emotion. We are aware of the pressure to conform to feeling rules even when they are unspoken or we don't agree with them (for example, "Boys don't cry," "No laughing at funerals"). Emotions are thus sociological phenomena, and our individual reactions are influenced (if not determined) by our social and cultural surroundings.

Finally, emotions can also be influenced by social institutions, such as workplaces or religious groups. Arlie Hochschild's (1983) study of flight attendants revealed that when airlines required their employees to be cheerful on the job, the employees' authentic emotions were displaced (they weren't necessarily always cheerful). Flight attendants were required to manage their own feelings as a requirement of their job—what Hochschild calls **emotion work**—maintaining a bright, perky, happy demeanor inflight, no matter what they actually felt. Because of the structural pressures of emotion work, they became alienated from their own real feelings.

New Interactional Contexts

As we learned in earlier chapters, sociological theories and approaches can change over time—indeed, they must. As the society around them changes, sociologists can't always hold on to their tried-and-true ways of looking at the world. New and innovative approaches take the place of traditional paradigms.

Most sociological perspectives on interaction, for example, focus on interactions that occur in **copresence**—that is, when individuals are in one another's physical company. More and more, however, we find ourselves in situations outside physical copresence, aided by rapidly developing technologies.

Businesspeople can hold video conferences with colleagues in other cities. The lovelorn can seek relationship advice and learn the dos and don'ts of sex and dating through late-night radio. Students can text message their friends at faraway colleges and carry on real-time conversations using webcams. Doctors on the mainland can perform remote surgery on shipboard patients in the middle of the ocean. Do

Mediating Interaction Using new technologies like webcams, we can interact with each other outside of physical copresence. How will these new technologies affect our interactions and identities?

---

role-taking emotions emotions like sympathy, embarrassment, or shame that require that we assume the perspective of another person or many other people and respond from that person or group's point of view

feeling rules socially constructed norms regarding the expression and display of emotions; expectations about the acceptable or desirable feelings in a given situation

emotion work (emotional labor) the process of evoking, suppressing, or otherwise managing feelings to create a publicly observable display of emotion

copresence face-to-face interaction or being in the presence of others

---

Cross-Cultural Responses to Grief

When it comes to emotions, grief seems one of the strongest. No matter what we believe about the afterlife (or lack thereof), we mourn the passing of our loved ones. In many different societies, the cultural practices surrounding grief and mourning are directed toward giving the deceased a proper send-off and comforting those left behind. But you might be surprised at what other cultures consider comforting in times of grief!

For example, Maoris (the native people of New Zealand) believe that death is not final until all funeral rites are complete—which takes an entire year. Though the body is buried after three days, the relatives and friends of the deceased speak of and to her as if she were alive until the year of mourning is complete.

The Roma (often incorrectly referred to as "Gypsies") mourn in particularly intense and public ways: both men and women refuse to wash, shave, or comb their hair, neglect to eat for three days, and absorb themselves totally in the process of mourning, sometimes to the point of harming themselves. In addition to this passionate grieving, Roma mourners provide the dead with clothes, money, and other useful objects for their journey to the afterlife. In contrast to Western societies, where black is the prevailing color of grief, Roma mourners traditionally wear white clothes and the favored color for funeral decorations is red.

Red is also the color of grief for the Ashanti of Ghana, who wear red clothing, smear red clay on their arms and foreheads, and wear headbands festooned with red peppers. Proper Ashanti expressions of grief are distinguished by gender: women must wail, and men must fire guns into the air. In fact, the amount of gunpowder used in a funeral is considered a mark of the grieving family's status in the community.

When mourning their dead, many cultures, including the Irish, hold "wakes": long-lasting, heavily attended parties honoring and celebrating the lives of the dead. At a wake, while tears may fall, there is also likely to be singing, dancing, drinking, laughing, and all manner of seemingly celebratory emotional outbursts. So despite the fact that all cultures mourn and all individuals feel grief, we can express those emotions in different ways depending on the society of which we are a part.

How Different Cultures Grieve Ashanti women practice a traditional funeral dance (top), mourning Roma women weep over a coffin (center), and Maori warriors row a coffin to their burial ground (bottom).

conventional theories have the explanatory power to encompass these new ways of interacting? And since interaction is vital to the development of the self, how do these new ways of interacting create new types of social identities?

Researchers like Josh Meyrowitz (1985), Marc Smith and Peter Kollock (1998), Steve Jones (1997), Philip Howard (Jones and Howard 2003), and Barry Wellman (2004) are among the pioneers in the sociology of technologically

On the Job

The Wages of Emotion Work

According to executives at Nordstrom department stores, keeping the customer happy is what it's all about. Nordstrom, along with a host of other stores, takes a great interest in developing a corporate culture based on customer service (Zemke and Schaaf 1990; Spector and McCarthy 1996). After all, loyal, satisfied customers are the key to profit making. Nordstrom has become so successful at customer service that it ranks as the national standard. The secret to the company's success lies partly in what Hochschild (1983) calls "the commercialization of feeling," or emotion work.

Nordstrom became a leader in this area through a variety of training techniques. Through staff meetings and workshops, managers coached employees in customer service. Using videotapes and role-playing scenarios, workers learned how to act out various emotions convincingly. But their acting techniques went beyond such displays as smiling and showing friendliness. Salespeople were also supposed to take an in-depth interest in their customers by keeping a "client book" with detailed information about customers' likes and dislikes, favorite brands, style preferences, color choices, and anything else that might help salespeople to better anticipate their clients' needs. Some Nordstrom managers even required their salespeople to perform extra duties

while off the clock, like writing thank-you notes to customers and delivering items to their homes.

While these practices were good for Nordstrom's bottom line, the consequences for the workers themselves were a different story. The work of producing emotions takes its toll. Though displays of feeling are actually "sold" to the customer as a kind of commodity, the worker is not necessarily compensated. What was once a private resource has now become a company asset, a new source of labor—emotional labor. But because it is impossible for anyone to be that upbeat all the time, workers must find ways to display or evoke the required emotions. They may do so through surface acting, displaying the emotion by wearing a smile, for example. In contrast, a very dedicated employee may do deep acting by trying to actually feel the emotion that he or she must display. There are consequences for faking or conjuring emotional responses: workers may experience "emotional exhaustion and burnout" (Grandey 2003) or become estranged from their real feelings (as did Hochschild's flight attendants)—a situation that Marx would refer to as alienation.

Despite a number of employee protests—and a 1991 class-action suit involving off-the-clock work—many of

---

mediated interaction. They look at how we interact with each other in virtual space and via electronic media—and how we interact with the machines themselves. Sherry Turkle, for example, directs the Initiative on Technology and the Self at the Massachusetts Institute of Technology (MIT), where she and others study different ways that technology and identity intersect—through our use of computers, robots, technologically sophisticated toys, and so on (1997, 2005). danah boyd examines how the rapid adoption of social networking sites, such as MySpace and Facebook, by teenagers is affecting their sense of self and their relationships with others (2007). These and other researchers seek answers to the following question: who will we become as we increasingly interact with and through machines? Their work is helping sociol-

saturated self a postmodern idea that the self is now developed by multiple influences chosen from a wide range of media sources

ogy enter the age of interactive media and giving us new ways of looking at interactions and identities.

Postmodern theorists claim that the role of technology in interaction is one of the primary features of postmodern life. They believe that in the Information Age, social thinkers must arrive at new ways to explain the development of the self in light of the digital media that inundate our social world (Holstein and Gubrium 2000). We are now exposed to more sources and multiple points of view that may shape our sense of self and socialize us in different ways than ever before (Gottschalk 1993). Kenneth Gergen has coined the term the "**saturated self**" to refer to this phenomenon and further claims that the postmodern individual tends to have a "pastiche personality," one that "borrow[s] bits and pieces of identity from whatever sources are available" (Gergen 1991, p. 150). What this means is that the self is being constructed in new ways that were unforeseen by early symbolic interac-

Emotion Work In many sales and service jobs, employees must engage in surface or deep acting to display the emotions that their jobs require.

the problems relating to emotion work remain unresolved (Nogaki 1993). Employees at Nordstrom and elsewhere are still trying to figure out how to preserve some sense of authenticity while making the necessary emotional adjustments to perform their job. The risk remains that employees may become burned out, cynical, or numb from the demands of their occupational roles.

Many of you will be dealing with these same issues in your careers. How will you factor in the cost to yourself of emotional labor? Do you think employees should be compensated financially for emotion work, or do you consider it part of being a good employee? What other kind of compensation—extra days off, more frequent breaks—might be appropriate, especially for salespeople?

tionists, who could not have imagined that interaction would one day include so many possible influences from both the real world and the world of virtual reality. In Chapter 13, we'll investigate in greater depth how new technologies are affecting social life.

Closing Comments

By now you may be wondering, are we all just prisoners of socialization? How much freedom do we really have if we are all shaped and influenced to such an extent by others and by society? Are our ideas of ourselves as individuals—unique and independent—just a sorry illusion?

It is true that the process of socialization can be rather homogenizing. And it tends to be conservative, pushing people toward some sort of lowest common denominator,

toward the mainstream. But still, not everybody ends up the same. In fact, no two people are ever really alike. Despite all the social forces at play in creating the individual, the process by which we gain a sense of self, or become socialized members of society, is never wholly finished.

We are not just passive recipients of all the influences around us. We are active participants. We possess what is called **agency**, meaning that we are spontaneous, intelligent, and creative. We exercise free will. Symbolic interactionism tells us that we are always doing the work of interpreting, defining, making sense of, and responding to our social environment. That gives us a great deal of personal power in every social situation. The process is not unilateral; rather it is reciprocal and multidirectional. Remember that you are shaping society as much as it is shaping you.

agency the ability of the individual to act freely and independently

⑤ Need Help Studying?

wwnorton.com/studyspace

Visit StudySpace to access free review materials such as:
- **Vocabulary Flashcards**
- **Diagnostic Review Quizzes**
- **Study Outlines**

QUESTIONS FOR REVIEW

1. Think about a social issue about which you hold a very different opinion from your grandparents or people their age, like drug legalization, sexual mores, or even fashion. How might this difference of opinion be the result of different socialization?

2. What are some of the reasons symbolic interactionism is useful for explaining the development of the self?

3. According to Erving Goffman, we all engage in impression management to control what others think of us. Choose one interaction and list every aspect of the personal front you use to manage the impression you create.

4. In a con game the criminals usually allow the victim or "mark" to win a little, then take him for everything, leaving the victim angry and embarrassed. In order to prevent retaliation, accomplices help the victim redefine the situation to make it bearable, or "cool the mark out." Erving Goffman pointed out that life abounds with situations that people redefine this way. Can you think of a situation where you helped to "cool the mark out"?

5. How do the theories on the development of the self in this chapter differ? Which theory best explains your experience? Why?

6. Are the basic principles your family taught you supported or undermined by your peers? Can you name two or more of your roles that sometimes conflict?

7. Describe a situation in which you were resocialized. Perhaps you met someone from a different culture and abandoned some cultural stereotypes, or you learned to fit into a new work environment. Do you think that your resocialization is permanent, or will you revert to your old ways?

8. Describe yourself in terms of your statuses and roles. Which are master statuses? Which roles are less important? Which statuses have changed over the course of your lifetime? Which roles do you anticipate occupying in the future?

9. What feeling rules do you find yourself obeying? Do you expect the same of others? Have you ever done emotion work? What were the circumstances?

10. Do you agree with Gergen's claim that the postmodern person has a pastiche personality? Why? Do you think that a well-read person of your grandparents' generation could have a saturated self or is that something that can only happen with access to the internet?

SUGGESTIONS FOR FURTHER EXPLORATION

FeralChildren.com A web site with extensive information and links about feral children through the ages, both real and fictional.

Goffman, Erving. 1967. *Asylums: Essays on the Social Situation of Mental Patients and Other Inmates*. Chicago: University of Chicago Press. One of the finest discussions of the effects of total institutions like asylums.

Hochschild, Arlie. 2003. *The Managed Heart: Commercialization of Human Feeling*. Berkeley: University of California Press. A classic study of the consequences of emotion work.

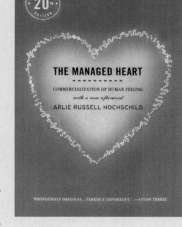

Mead, George Herbert. 1934/1967. *Mind, Self, and Society: From the Standpoint of a Social Behaviorist*. Chicago: University of Chicago Press. The foundation for the theory of symbolic interactionism. Mead gives a detailed explanation of how individuals internalize aspects of society.

Nell. 2004. Dir. Michael Apted. Fox Home Entertainment. Jodie Foster portrays a woman who has lived for years without human contact after her speech-impaired mother died. She is discovered by a doctor, played by Liam Neeson, who tries to understand her.

Six Degrees of Separation. 2000. Dir. Fred Schepis. MGM. The film, starring Will Smith, is based on a true story about a young man who deftly uses impression management to convince upper-class New Yorkers that he is one of them.

Spigel, Lynn. 1992. *Make Room for TV: Television and the Family Ideal in Postwar America*. Chicago: University of Chicago Press. A social history of the impact of television on

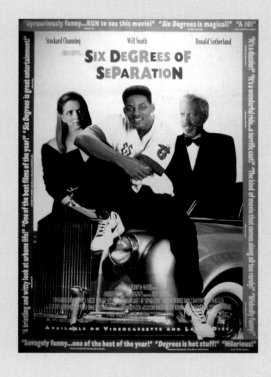

U.S. popular culture and how mass media became a significant agent of socialization.

Swofford, Anthony. 2003. *Jarhead*. New York: Scribner. A fascinating memoir about life in the U.S. Marine Corps during the First Gulf War that illustrates the effect of a total institution. Also, the 2005 film of the same name, starring Jake Gyllenhaal and directed by Sam Mendes.

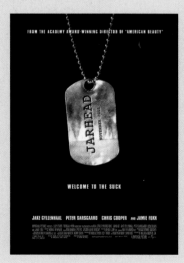

The Wild Child. 2001. Dir. Francois Truffaut. MGM. This film is based on a real-life, eighteenth-century behavioral scientist's efforts to civilize a feral boy, who was found living like an animal in the woods. Victor, the Wild Boy of Aveyron, is perhaps the best-known case of a feral child.

CHAPTER 5

Separate and Together: Life in Groups

On November 4, 2000, Robert Burgess woke up in a Los Angeles emergency room with no memory of what had happened to him the night before. How had he broken his collarbone and wrist, and why was there bleeding in his kidney? Burgess couldn't remember because his blood alcohol level had been measured at .19 percent—two and a half times the legal limit in California.

Eventually, he was able to recall the previous evening. He had attended a party at the Sigma Pi fraternity house at UCLA, where, as a pledge, he was being evaluated by the Sigma Pi brothers for full membership. He was told that he could either drink alcohol or a nonalcoholic beverage of unknown origin stirred up by the brothers; if he refused, he would relinquish his bid for membership. Burgess chose the alcohol and handed over his car keys for safety. He was then led, blindfolded, through the frat house and forced to have a drink in each room. Members of the Chi Omega sorority who were at the party scribbled on his drunken body in permanent marker. At some point during the evening, he passed out, but he later apparently woke up, retrieved his car keys, and drove away—only to crash into a wall and end up in the ER.

No doubt you've heard stories like this before. Generally referred to as "hazing," this process is meant to test newcomers and transform them into group members; if you can endure the abuse, you can be part of the group. Although hazing is usually associated with college fraternities, it has been known to occur in high school clubs, athletic teams, sororities, and even police and fire departments and the military. In fact, according to a study in the medical journal *Contemporary Pediatrics* (2000), 24 percent of high school church group members reported being hazed. Although hazing is against the law in almost every state and is usually prohibited by group charters, it is still a popular—though risky—way of initiating new members. Every year, it results in at least one student death and countless injuries, and alcohol plays a major role in most of these incidents (Nuwer 1999).

A year later, with his injuries healed, Robert Burgess filed a civil suit against both the fraternity and the sorority, alleging that he was forced to overindulge in alcohol and that the party hosts had returned his car keys while he was obviously too drunk to drive. Burgess's lawsuit highlights a key question in all hazing cases: who is responsible when the consequences of hazing include illegality, injury, or even death—the host group or the individual who submits to hazing?

The relationship between the individual and the group is a complex one. We sometimes do things in groups, both good and bad, that we might never do as individuals. Exploring group dynamics from a sociological perspective can help us understand and even eliminate problems like hazing and maximize the benefits of group life as well.

HOW TO READ THIS CHAPTER

This chapter explores some of the different ways we organize our lives in groups. Here you will gain some of the analytic tools you can use to understand the specific groups we'll be investigating in later chapters. Concepts such as peer pressure, teamwork, bureaucratization, and anomie can be fruitfully applied to analyses of families, work and volunteer organizations, political groups, and religious communities. Consider this chapter an introduction to group dynamics in general—a springboard from which to begin our sociological analysis of particular types of groups. As you read, think about the groups you belong to and how they affect your values and behavior. What is your influence on such groups? Have you ever "gone along" with group rules but later wished you hadn't?

What Is a Group?

We often use the term "group" to refer to any collection of two or more people who have something in common, whether it's their appearance, culture, occupation, or just a physical proximity. When sociologists speak of a **group** or social group, however, they mean a collection of people who not only share some attribute but also identify with one another and have ongoing social relations—like a family, a *Star Trek* fan club, a soccer team, a sorority, or the guys you play poker with every month.

> **group** a collection of people who share some attribute, identify with one another, and interact with each other
>
> **crowd** a temporary gathering of people in a public place; members might interact but do not identify with each other and will not remain in contact
>
> **aggregate** a collection of people who share a physical location but do not have lasting social relations
>
> **category** people who share one or more attributes but who lack a sense of common identity or belonging
>
> **primary groups** the people who are most important to our sense of self; members' relationships are typically characterized by face-to-face interaction, high levels of cooperation, and intense feelings of belonging
>
> **secondary groups** larger and less intimate than primary groups; members' relationships are usually organized around a specific goal and are often temporary

A **crowd**, such as the throngs of sightseers at a tourist attraction or people who gather to watch a fire, would not usually be considered a group in the sociological sense. While crowd members do interact (Goffman 1971), they don't necessarily have a sense of common identity, and they rarely assemble again once they disperse. Collections of people such as crowds, audiences, and queues are known as **aggregates**—people who happen to find themselves together in a particular physical location. People in aggregates don't form lasting social relations, but people in groups do. Similarly, people belonging in the same **category**—everyone 18 years of age or all owners of Chevy trucks, for example—don't regularly interact with one another or have any common sense of connection other than their status in the category.

Primary and Secondary Groups

Groups in which we are intimately associated with the other members, such as families and close friends, are known as **primary groups**. Primary groups typically involve more face-to-face interaction, greater cooperation, and deeper feelings of belonging. Members often associate with each other for no other reason than to spend time together.

Charles Horton Cooley (1909) introduced the term *primary* for this type of group because such groups have the most profound effects on us as individuals. Primary groups provide most of our emotional satisfaction through interaction with other members, are responsible for much of our socialization, and remain central to our identities throughout our lives. We measure who we are, and perhaps how we've changed, by the way we interact with primary group members. To Cooley (as we saw in Chapter 4), primary groups represent the most important "looking glasses" in the formation of our social selves—they constitute our "significant others."

Larger, less intimate groups are known as **secondary groups**: these include co-workers, college classes, athletic organizations, labor unions, and political parties. Interaction here is more formal and impersonal. Secondary groups are usually organized around a specific activity or the accomplishment of a task. Membership is often temporary and usually does not carry the same potential for emotional satisfaction that primary group membership does. Nonetheless, a great deal of what we do involves secondary groups.

Because secondary groups can include larger numbers of people and be geographically diffuse, membership can be almost completely anonymous. At the same time, however, secondary group membership often generates primary group ties as well. Close personal relationships can begin with the more impersonal ties of secondary groups (the friends you make at work, for example) and are sometimes a direct outgrowth of our attempts to counteract the depersonalizing nature of secondary groups. For this reason, it is sometimes difficult to classify a particular group. Your soccer team may indeed be goal oriented, but you've probably also developed personal ties to at least some of your teammates. So is your team a primary or secondary group? It features elements of both, proving that real life can be even more complex than the models sociologists devise to explain it.

There are other ways that seemingly insignificant relationships with near strangers can have a powerful and positive impact on our own lives. Many social researchers are interested in examining the ways in which people are making up for the loss of intimate contact that is commonly shared among those who belong to primary groups. Melinda Blau and Karen Fingerman (2009) have identified what they call "consequential strangers," people we might not think of as mattering much to our sense of happiness or well-being, but who nonetheless play an important role in our otherwise fragmented postmodern lives. These people are not total strangers, but are more likely to be acquaintances from the places we work, shop, play, or conduct business—from the local barista at the coffeehouse or our favorite manicurist, to the checkout clerk at the grocery store or that guy at the gym—these are people who become familiar and essential parts of our everyday lives. These people serve as social anchors, just as our close friends or family members do. Blau and Fingerman suggest that we need a new framework or perspective with which to look at the people in our world and perhaps to expand the number and range, as well as the value we ascribe to them, when we include them in our larger social circle. It seems that we need both primary and secondary relationships, as well as those along the continuum between the two.

Social Networks

You and your family, your friends, peers, colleagues, teachers, and co-workers constitute a **social network**. Sociologists who study networks call the connections between individuals **social ties**. Social ties can be direct, such as the tie between you and your friend, or indirect, such as the tie between you and your friend's cousin, whom you've never met.

Primary Groups Are Typically Families or Close Friends Deborah Daniels (front left, in pink) opened her home to four generations of her family after Hurricane Katrina destroyed their New Orleans homes in 2005.

To understand how a social network works, think of yourself at the center with lines connecting you to all your friends, family, peers, and so on. These lines represent direct ties. Now think about all the family, friends, and peers who belong to each of *these* people. The lines connecting you to this second group must pass through the people in your first network; this second set of lines represents indirect ties. Indirect ties can include business transactions—flows of goods, services, materials, or monies—between organizations or nations. They can even represent flows of ideas. For instance, when you read ancient Greek philosophy, you become part of a network that spans centuries of writing, thinking, and educating.

You've probably already heard about the principle of "six degrees of separation," which suggests that everyone in the world is connected to everyone else within six steps: "If you know 100 people, and each of them knows 100 more, then you have 10,000 friends of friends. Take that a step further to three degrees and you are connected to one million people. At six degrees, the number increases to nine billion" (Schofield 2004). This means, theoretically,

social network the web of direct and indirect ties connecting an individual to other people who may also affect the individual

social ties connections between individuals

that you're connected to every human on the planet. It might be the case that somebody you know, knows someone who knows somebody else who knows the president of the United States or a yak herdsman in the Himalayas; in other words, you might be only separated from either of these others by just four degrees.

Sociologists who study networks are concerned not only with how networks are constructed but also how influence moves along a network, and thus which persons or organizations have more influence than others within the network. In his book *Six Degrees: The Science of a Connected Age* (2003), sociologist Duncan Watts examined not only the connections individuals have to one another but also how those connections shape our actions. He found, for example, that we may change our minds about whom to vote for if enough of our friends are voting for the other candidate. Social networks can help us understand everything from the spread of fads and fashions to the way people hear about job openings or how sexually transmitted diseases are transmitted among various segments of the population.

WINNERS, LOSERS, AND INFLUENCE How does the flow of influence work at the level of an international organization? We could take the World Trade Organization (WTO) as an example. Comprising 148 member nations, the WTO monitors the trade rules between countries and resolves international disputes over trade. While all member nations are part of the network, they hold different positions of power within it. We might hypothesize that nations that win the most disputes have the most influence within the network. But Joseph Conti (2003, 2005) finds that while the United States, one of the most powerful members of the WTO, is involved in the vast majority of disputes, it usually loses. The question that remains for the network theorist is whether or not "winning" or "losing" is an effective way to measure influence. What Conti concludes is that America's centrality, a network analysis term that means an actor with the most ties in a given network, is what gives it powerful influence and not the actual outcomes of the disputes.

JOBS, GENDER, AND NETWORKS How does the flow of influence work at the level of interactions between individuals? Sociologists look at how personal ties, both direct and indirect, can influence a person's life.

In the pathbreaking work "The Strength of Weak Ties" (1973), Mark Granovetter measures how a person's distant relatives and acquaintances, attached to different social networks, pass along information about job opportunities (see Figure 5.1). An individual with high socioeconomic status, or SES (taking into account income, education, and occupation), for example, usually has relatives and acquaintances with similarly high SES. Because those relatives and acquaintances belong to different social networks, all with high SES, the job seeker now has indirect connections with a vast array of high-SES contacts who can provide job leads. In other words, if your father, mother, and sister are all actors, you would likely "inherit" a network of acting contacts. The implications of Granovetter's findings are that people tend to form homogeneous social networks—to have direct ties to those who are like themselves, whether through race, class background, national origin, or religion. Further, individuals with low SES are likely to form direct ties to others with low SES and thus indirect ties as well. Information about job opportunities is less likely to travel along those networks.

More recent findings about the strength of weak ties, from Matt Hoffman and Lisa Torres (2002), indicate that women who are part of networks that include more men than women are more likely to hear about good job leads. But if their networks include more women than men, then those same women are less likely to hear about quality jobs. The number of men or women within a man's network doesn't seem to matter; men are just as likely to get quality information about job opportunities from both men and women in their social networks. Hoffman and Torres offer two rationales to explain their findings. First, women are simply less likely than men to hear about job leads. Second, women who do hear about them are more likely to pass along that information to men; they may feel threatened by the idea of more women in their places of employment and fear loss of their own jobs.

SEXUAL HEALTH AND NETWORKS Nicholas Christakis and James Fowler (2009) provide another example of how transmission happens between individuals belonging to similar social networks. They explain two principles: first, all social networks have a *connection*, and second, that there is *contagion*, which refers to what flows through social ties. While you may have complete control of who you are connected to directly, we exert little control over our indirect connections. Contagion not only influences an individual's health, but can spread everything from obesity to smoking and substance abuse. For example, sexually transmitted diseases are more likely among people who have had four or more partners in the past year. Whites with many partners tend to have sex with other whites with many partners, and whites with few partners have sex with whites with few partners. STDs, then, are kept in "core" groups of active white partners, and are found less often in less active groups. This spread of STDs can be seen as a literal consequence of the *contagion* principle of social networks.

SOURCE: GRANOVETTER 1973.

HIGH STATUS

In the upper class there is a stress on the importance of strong ties and forming elite clubs.

ADMINISTRATIVE

Administrators are most likely to be cosmopolitans and involved in an organization to branch out and form new ties.

PROFESSIONAL

Professionals, technical, and managerial workers will most likely hear about new jobs through weak ties.

OFFICE WORKER

The office worker may have mixed connections in both higher and lower classes.

SEMI-PROFESSIONAL

Semi-professionals frequently use weak ties to land or hear about a new job.

BLUE COLLAR

The majority of people of a lower status will find a job through a relative or close friends.

LOW STATUS

For those of a lower status, weak ties of a similar status are not especially useful or far reaching.

KEY IDEAS

JOB NETWORKING

The kinds of people you know can determine your next job. "Ties" or contacts become a key method to network and reach a higher status.

STRONG OR WEAK?

Strong Ties are people you are close with, such as a relatives, good friends, and mentors.

Weak Ties are acquaintances.

EXAMPLE:

PART TIME TEACHER

4 Strong Ties
6 Weak Ties

Through both types of ties he knows people in the class above and below his own.

LOCAL BRIDGE:

A person who can connect two people who don't know each other. Bridges can connect people outside their circle and help them reach different jobs.

TIGHT CIRCLES

When everyone in a circle primarily have strong ties with each other, it becomes difficult to reach beyond that circle.

When we think of someone as being "well connected," we imagine that they not only have lots of close friends, but might have relationships and acquaintances in a large and diverse social circle. As the old adage goes, it's not *what* you know, it's *who* you know. And who they know, and who *they* know—and now you have a social network.

Separate from Groups: Anomie or Virtual Membership?

According to Durkheim, all the social groups with which we are connected (families, peers, co-workers, and so on) have this particular feature: the norms of the group place certain limits on our individual actions. For example, you may have wanted to backpack through Europe after you graduated from high school, but your parents demanded that you stay home, work, and save money for college. Durkheim argues that we need these limits—otherwise, we would want many things we could never have, and the lengths to which we would go in search of our unattainable desires would be boundless. Think about it: if you were always searching for but never getting the things you wanted, you would be very unhappy and over time might even become suicidal. Durkheim (1893/1964) called such a state of normlessness

anomie "normlessness"; term used to describe the alienation and loss of purpose that result from weaker social bonds and an increased pace of change

anomie and believed that group membership keeps us from feeling it. So group membership not only anchors us to the social world—it's what keeps us alive.

Durkheim was worried that in our increasingly fragmented modern society, anomie would become more and more common. Other scholars share Durkheim's position, noting that Americans today are less likely than ever to belong to the types of civic organizations and community groups that can combat anomie and keep us connected to one another. Harvard professor Robert Putnam, in his book *Bowling Alone: The Collapse and Revival of American Community* (2000), argues that we no longer practice the type of "civic engagement" that builds democratic community and keeps anomie at bay: fewer people bowl in leagues than ever before, and people are less likely to participate in organizations like the League of Women Voters, PTA, or Kiwanis or engage in regular activities like monthly bridge games or Sunday picnics. He even offers statistics on how many angry drivers "flip the bird" at other drivers every year—all part of his argument about our disintegrating collective bonds.

Putnam's critics argue that he longs for the "good old days" that will never be again (and perhaps never were). It may be true that we don't belong to bridge clubs anymore—but we have a new set of resources to help us connect with others and avoid anomie.

In the decade since Putnam's influential work first appeared, there has been an explosion of new communications technology. Some were concerned that the internet would only serve to exacerbate our condition of isolation and separation from one another, as individuals became fur-

The Good Old Days? In *Bowling Alone*, Robert Putnam argues that the decline of group activities, like bingo nights or league bowling, represents a decline in civic engagement. However, technologies like the internet and social networking sites have allowed large numbers of people to gather, connect, and avoid anomie.

ther distanced from face-to-face contact and more immersed in living online. Yet, the internet has made it possible for people who might not otherwise have met, to come together—albeit in cyberspace—and to belong to a variety of different online groups. From participants involved in Massively Multiperson Online Role-Playing Games (MMORPGs), such as World of Warcraft or Second Life, to support groups who "meet" regularly to deal with personal issues or medical conditions, or simply for fans of different authors, bands, artists, or filmmakers to swap comments, technology is offering us new opportunities to connect by making us members of **virtual communities**.

If both types of groups, the ones based on face-to-face contact and those that facilitate online interaction, can each serve as social anchors, then is one necessarily better for us (and for society) than the other?

DATA WORKSHOP

ANALYZING MASS MEDIA AND POPULAR CULTURE

Virtual Communities and "Netiquette"

The idea of what constitutes a group has necessarily changed as modern society has evolved through the Industrial Revolution to the current Digital Age. Sociologists have had to broaden the definition of the term. Just what do you call a bunch of people who gather together to share interests, offer advice, provide support, or exchange ideas, but who almost never meet in person and may not even know each other's real names? Such groups have come to be known as online or virtual communities.

In the 2010s, we are more familiar with the many ways people can be members of online communities. It's likely that you belong to one, if not many, such groups, and that you have some sense of how to behave within the group context and toward its other members. We may take a lot of this for granted, but online communities do not merely import the same rules for face-to-face interaction and then apply them to the online environment. In fact, when the internet was first introduced to the public in the early 1990s and its use was becoming more widespread, there were few rules about how people should communicate through the new technology. In addition, early virtual communities lacked the sense of organization that we often associate with other kinds of groups. Soon, though, sociologists who were studying the internet (Jones 1997; Smith and Kollock 1998) began to see group culture emerging where roles, language, and norms were being developed and

new members were socialized into belonging.

There were certainly technical skills that users needed to acquire, but social rules were equally important for the success of any new online community. Among the social rules that govern a specific virtual community, we are likely to find that members follow what can be called netiquette, or etiquette for how to behave on the internet. For example, on eBay, where strangers can buy and sell everything from old T-shirts to Old Masters paintings in an environment of mutual trust, participants feel confident that their payments will be received and their merchandise shipped, because everyone has agreed to a particular set of shared rules and expectations regarding how their online interactions should take place.

> **virtual communities** social groups whose interactions are mediated through information technologies, particularly the internet

This Data Workshop asks you to conduct a sort of "cyberethnography" to examine the group culture of a particular virtual community (thus drawing on material from Chapters 3 and 5). In addition to doing some participant observation in the group, you will also be gathering material from existing sources and doing a content analysis of what you find (see Chapter 2 for a review of these research methods).

Choose an online community that allows users to interact with each other. We recommend that you focus on a small group rather than, say, all Facebook users (there are more than a half billion of them!). Search for a group based on your own interests or concerns, which could include hobbies (like playing sports or video games), membership in an ethnic, religious, or geographic group (like being Jewish, Irish, or a Texan), or other aspects of your life (like being a cancer survivor or having a pet bulldog). You might be amazed at how many different groups you can find out in cyberspace.

You can begin by searching for groups on web sites such as Google or Yahoo. For example, if you search Yahoo groups for home brewers, you will find not only 193 devoted to beer, but 87 groups for winemakers, 59 groups for coffee drinkers, and 13 groups for people who really love green tea! Some of these groups have hundreds or thousands of registered members, although it's likely that only some fraction of that number will have been recently active on the site. Immerse yourself until you feel you have a sense of the life of this particular group. Try to identify the subtle ways that the culture of the group can shape members and the relationships between them. Here are some suggestions for how to conduct your research.

Roles
Describe the particular group you are studying and identify the roles for various participants in the community. You'll probably want to join the group you are studying,

In Relationships

Social Networking Sites: Pros and Cons or Think Before You Post

Who's reading about your life online? Perhaps more people than you might think.

In just a few short years, there has been astounding growth in the number of people participating in social networking sites. By the end of 2010, Facebook became the largest network, boasting more than 500,000,000 members—a number that is expected to climb to more than a billion in 2012. Facebook eclipsed Google, Yahoo, and YouTube (along with every other massively popular destination on the web) as the most-visited site on the internet, garnering almost 10 percent of all U.S. web-surfing minutes (Tsukayama 2010).

There were a number of social networking sites that preceded Facebook. In the 1990s, internet service providers like CompuServe and America Online (AOL) allowed registered users to form communities and interact with each other in chat rooms. As more and more people logged on to the internet in the 2000s, social networking sites flourished. Users flocked to such sites as Friendster, launched in 2002, and then MySpace, introduced in 2006. That same year brought Twitter, another service that allows users to interact through writing or following other people's "tweets," or short messages.

Facebook was created in 2004 when founder Mark Zuckerberg was a student at Harvard University, though its membership initially was limited to certain colleges. The site soon opened to all users and by 2008 had overtaken MySpace on its continued ascent to the top. Other companies, like Apple, Amazon, and Google, are keen on developing competing services, so we are likely to see social networking continue to grow into the 2010s and beyond.

The rise of social networking has been so rapid that social scientists can barely keep pace with studying what this new technology means, not just for our personal relationships and everyday lives but also for the nature of social interaction in groups and for the kind of influence it is exerting in other spheres as a powerful new social institution. For everybody who participates in social networking, its rewards and benefits are easily appreciated. At the same time, we should be aware of some of the less positive and more threatening aspects of this ubiquitous presence.

In sociological terms, we can see how such sites as Facebook can help us to make the most of our primary and secondary group connections. It is easier than ever to stay in touch with the important people in our lives (even if they are not in close physical proximity), and also to reconnect with lost or faded acquaintances, or to meet and interact with new people. It has brought people together who might not have otherwise been able to find each other in the past when it was not possible to search for others based on their interests, backgrounds, and demographic details. On Facebook, "Every 60 seconds is packed with a lifetime's worth of social interactions" (Grossman 2010). That includes 79,364 wall posts, 82,557 status updates, 98,604 friends approved, 135,849 photos added, 231,605 messages sent, 382,861 posts liked and 510,404 comments made—every single minute!

All that, and we are still in the infancy of social networking and how it will become an increasingly important part of our everyday lives and the interactions that we have with the world beyond just our own family and friends. The web of connections that are being built on these sites promises to weave us ever more closely into contacts with a variety of social groups, products, businesses, and to seamlessly integrate into the rest of our online lives. Many people who are on social networking sites are frequent and enthusiastic users who may log on daily and perhaps throughout that day. Some 200 million people access Facebook on mobile devices like smart phones, which can keep them in touch on a regular if not constant basis. In many ways, we accept and embrace the emergence of this new way to live online. Yet, of all the various interactions that are carried out through social networking (again with a total of 1,789,736 actions performed every minute on Facebook alone), we should not neglect the number of those that can have negative consequences for individuals and society.

In the past several years, the news has been full of stories detailing problems that have emerged in the context of such social networking sites as MySpace and Facebook. Although these sites have privacy setting options that can scan posted information and protect certain personal content from general viewing, not all users know how to set such limits, and many are naive or unaware of the possible ramifications of what they write, upload, and respond to online. What happens online, doesn't always stay online, and not everyone is using social networking with the best of intentions.

Social networking facilitates interactions between members, but participation in a virtual community can also leave you open to a variety of new types of interpersonal threats and challenges that sometimes result in real and detrimental consequences. There are numerous examples in the context of high school and college students, and incidents when students have been suspended or expelled from their institutions because of what they have posted in their profiles, including pictures of underage drinking or taking illegal drugs, and explicit threats of violence towards others. Social networking sites have also been at the center of some tragic cases of cyberbullying in recent years: in multiple cases, young people have committed suicide after being humiliated, harassed, or bullied (often about their sexuality) in the context of a community such as Facebook. In addition to school officials, law enforcement agencies have used social networking sites to target illegal activity (everything from conspiracy to commit murder to sexual crimes, assault, and theft) to make arrests and prosecute suspects.

There's a strong chance that if you're reading this, then you probably have some kind of profile somewhere in cyberspace. Students are finding out that what they post about themselves online may have other consequences. Some recognize the concern that putting too much information, or the wrong kind, online might jeopardize their academic or professional futures. One commonly reported practice is the use of Facebook to screen prospective employees' lifestyles. Increasingly, individuals are being denied jobs due to the pictures and information that they have posted on their personal profiles. Usually cited are pictures of drinking, illegal drug use, and smoking as "red flags" about personal integrity and interpersonal skills and character (Tahmincioglu 2008). The same could potentially happen in academia, with a student applying to a school being evaluated, in part, based on their online profiles.

This brings up some important issues about privacy and group affiliation with which we will continue to grapple as social media play an increasing part in our interactions with each other and the world. There will be new benefits and rewards, along with challenges, as the coming changes unfold in our lives around this rapidly changing new technology. As social networking sites grow more sophisticated, they may play an even greater role in our primary and secondary groups. They also have the potential to affect us in both positive and negative ways. So even casual users of social media should remember to think twice before they post.

group dynamics the patterns of interaction between groups and individuals

dyad a two-person social group

triad a three-person social group

in-group a group that one identifies with and feels loyalty toward

although it might be possible to observe interactions on the site without registering. So you may become a member of the group, but there could be many other roles to play. Sometimes there are "admins" or "officers" who are leaders of the group. Is there a "moderator" who manages interactions on the site, or a "webmaster" who plays a role in socializing the "newbies" (those who are new to the group) or sanctions those members who violate any group norms? See if you can identify other kinds of members; for instance, can you tell if there are any "lurkers" (those who visit the site but who may not be actively participating yet)?

Language

What kind of special language is used by the members? Make a list of commonly used terms and their definitions. Has online language evolved to include new words or phrases? For instance, a discussion topic can be called a "thread" and writing a comment on the site can be called "posting" to a "wall." Are acronyms also common, such as g2g (got to go) and LOL (laugh out loud), or IMHO (in my humble opinion) and ^5 (high five)? Do members use "emoticons" or other symbols to express feelings (like <3 to make a heart)?

Norms

Gather examples of netiquette, either formal or informal, that govern this particular community. What are some of the social rules, guidelines, and expectations that apply to members? One place to look is in the FAQ (Frequently Asked Questions) section of the web site, but the normative elements of cyber-group life are present in all online interactions in one form or another. What happens if someone is "yelling" (writing in all capital letters), engaging in a "flame war" (virulent attacks or arguments), or sending "spam" (such as solicitations or advertisements) to other members? Are there other types of inappropriate language or behavior on the group's site? Document how members sanction each other or how group leaders deal with behavioral violations.

There are two options for completing this Data Workshop.

- *Option 1 (informal)*: Prepare written notes that you can refer to in class. Share your observations and responses to the above questions with other students in small-group discussions. Listen for any differences in each other's insights.

- *Option 2 (formal)*: Write a three- to four-page essay describing your observations and answering the Workshop questions. Make sure to refer to specific features of your online group to support your analysis.

By taking part in this cyber-ethnography, you have begun to identify the ways that group life is created, maintained, and changed online by group members who might share many things, except perhaps actual physical copresence.

Group Dynamics

Sociologists have always been interested in how groups form, change, disintegrate, achieve great goals, or commit horrendous wrongs—add all these phenomena together, and they constitute **group dynamics**. How do groups affect an individual's sense of self? What forces bind members to a group? How do groups influence their members? When do groups excel at the tasks they undertake? What are the qualities of group leaders? When are groups destructive to the individual? How can relations between groups be improved? We will attempt to answer some of these questions in the next sections.

Dyads, Triads, and More

The size of a group affects how it operates and the types of individual relationships that can occur within it (Figure 5.2). A **dyad**, the smallest possible social group, consists of only two members—a married couple, two best friends, or two siblings, for example (Simmel 1950). Although relationships in a dyad are usually intense, dyads are also fundamentally unstable, because if one person wants out of the group, it's over. A **triad** is slightly more stable because the addition of a third person means that conflicts between two members can be refereed by the third. As additional people are added to a group, it may no longer be possible for everyone to know or interact with everyone else personally (think of all the residents of a large apartment building), and so policies may have to be established to help with communication and resolve conflicts. The features of dyads and triads point out an important axiom of group dynamics in general: the smaller a group is, the more likely it is to be based on personal ties; larger groups are more likely to be based on rules and regulations (as we'll see later when we examine bureaucracies).

In-Groups and Out-Groups

An **in-group** is a group a member identifies with and feels loyalty toward. Members usually feel a certain distinctness from or even hostility toward other groups, known as

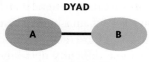

DYAD

One Relationship

TRIAD

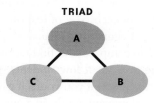

Three Relationships

GROUP OF FOUR

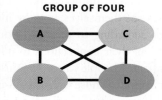

Six Relationships

GROUP OF FIVE

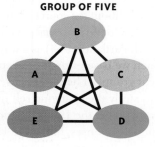

Ten Relationships

FIGURE 5.2 **The Effects of Group Size on Relationships**

Smaller groups feature fewer and more intimate personal ties; larger groups feature more relationships, but they are also likely to be more impersonal.

out-groups. Most of us are associated with a number of in- and out-groups, stemming from our ethnic, familial, professional, athletic, and educational backgrounds, for example. Group loyalty and cohesion intensify when differences are strongly defined between the "us" of an in-group and the "them" of an out-group; we may also feel a sense of superiority toward those who are excluded from our in-group. School sports rivalries make clear in-group and out-group distinctions, as evident in this popular slogan seen on T-shirts and bumper stickers all over Los Angeles: "My favorite teams are UCLA and whoever's playing USC!"

As we might expect, in-group membership can be a source of prejudice and discrimination based on class, race, gender, sexual orientation, religion, or political opinion.

The differences attributed to an out-group often become exaggerated, if not entirely fabricated to begin with— "All Irishmen are drunks," or "All Mexicans are lazy," for example. Robert Merton (1968) noted the phenomenon that the same qualities or behaviors are viewed positively when they are "ours" and negatively when they are "theirs": the out-group is "lazy," whereas the in-group is "laid-back"; they are "snobbish," we are "classy"; they are "zealots," we are "devout." At their worst, in-group/out-group dynamics create the backdrop for such social tragedies as slavery and genocide.

> **out-group** any group an individual feels opposition, rivalry, or hostility toward
>
> **reference group** a group that provides a standard of comparison against which we evaluate ourselves

Reference Groups

Our perception of a group and what it takes to be a bona fide member can be crucial to our sense of self. When a group provides standards by which a person evaluates his own personal attributes, it is known as a **reference group**. A common reference group is one's family. We often try to "live up to" the standards of our parents, siblings, and extended family members. If we don't see ourselves as having the qualities of a "true" family member, we may adopt a negative self-image. A reference group may also be one to which we aspire to belong but of which we are not yet members; we saw one example at the beginning of this chapter, the pledge who wanted to belong to the fraternity so much that he was willing to risk his own health and safety.

DATA WORKSHOP

ANALYZING EVERYDAY LIFE

The Twenty Statements Test: Who Am I?

This Data Workshop, combining material from Chapters 4 and 5, asks you to look at how social affiliations with groups help shape our self-concept. You will be using a method that is similar to survey research to complete this Data Workshop (see Chapter 2 for a review). Start your work, however, by completing Step 1 below, without reading any farther than the line of stars!

Step 1: The Twenty Statements Test (TST)
In the spaces provided below, write down twenty different responses to the question "Who am I?" Don't worry about evaluating the logic or importance of your responses—just

write the answers in the order they occur to you. Give yourself five minutes to complete this task.

1. I am _____.

2. I am _____.

3. I am _____.

4. I am _____.

5. I am _____.

6. I am _____.

7. I am _____.

8. I am _____.

9. I am _____.

10. I am _____.

11. I am _____.

12. I am _____.

13. I am _____.

14. I am _____.

15. I am _____.

16. I am _____.

17. I am _____.

18. I am _____.

19. I am _____.

20. I am _____.

* *

Step 2: Analysis

Now it's time to analyze your responses. Rate each one according to the four categories listed below. Evaluate, to the best of your ability, which responses fall into the A-mode, B-mode, C-mode, and D-mode categories.

A-mode responses are the type of physical characteristics found on your driver's license: "I am a blonde"; "I am short"; "I am a Wisconsin resident."

B-mode responses describe socially defined statuses usually associated with group membership of some sort: "I am a college student"; "I am a Catholic"; "I am an African American"; "I am a quarterback."

C-mode responses describe styles of behavior or emotional states: "I am a happy person"; "I am a country music fan"; "I am a fashionable dresser."

D-mode responses are more general than individual: "I am part of the universe"; "I am a human being."

You may have some difficulty deciding how to categorize some of your responses—for example, where does "I am an American" go—in A, B, or D? Use your best judgment. Count the number of each type of response. Now compare the totals—which category got the most responses?

You may want to compare your findings with those of your classmates; where do your fellow students get their sense of self? We predict that, even if you yourself gave more B-mode responses, the predominant mode in your classroom is C. Those with more B-mode responses base their self-concept on group membership and institutional roles. Those with more C-mode responses see themselves as more independent and define themselves according to their individual actions and emotions rather than their connections to others. It is likely that there are few (if any) people whose responses fall predominantly in the A or D mode. Those with more A-mode responses may feel that they have a "skin deep" self-concept, based more on their appearance to others than on their internal qualities. Those with more D-mode responses are harder to categorize and may feel uncertain about the source of their sense of self.

The TST was developed by social psychologist Manfred Kuhn (Kuhn and McPartland 1954) as a way of determining the degree to which we base our self-concepts on our membership in different groups. The test was used later by Louis Zurcher (1977) to study the changing self-images of Americans. Zurcher found that in the 1960s individuals were more likely to give B-mode responses, but in the 1970s and 1980s people were more likely to give C-mode responses. While you might think it better to be an independent actor than to be defined by your group membership, Zurcher and his colleague Ralph Turner became concerned about this trend away from group identification and toward a more radically individualistic sense of self. Why were they so concerned?

The primary characteristics of the C-mode, or "impulsive," self (Turner 1976) are the pursuit of individual satisfaction, an orientation toward the present, and a sense that the individual should not be linked to others and that group obligations inhibit individual expression. The primary characteristics of the B-mode, or "institutional," self are a willingness to adhere to group standards and to accept group obligations as well as an orientation toward the future and a sense that the individual is linked to others. Zurcher and Turner worried that a society full of self-interested (and even selfish), impulsive individuals might no longer care about the common good and would only work to satisfy their own needs.

Do you do things for your own benefit or for the benefit of the group? What do you think are the consequences for a society overwhelmingly populated by one personality type

Group Cohesion "People easily form clubs, fraternal societies, and the like, based on congeniality, which may give rise to real intimacy . . . Where there is a little common interest and activity, kindness grows like weeds by the roadside." —Charles Horton Cooley, 1909

or the other? Are these two orientations mutually exclusive, or can you combine the best parts of both? If the latter, what can you do in order to bring that about?

There are two options for completing this Data Workshop.

- *Option 1 (informal)*: Make some notes on your findings to share with other students in small-group discussions. How many "institutional" or "impulsive" selves are part of your discussion group? Do Zurcher and Turner's categories satisfactorily describe the way we consider our selves now, in the twenty-first century? Perhaps you can come up with a new category of self that better describes the individuals in your group.

- *Option 2 (formal)*: Find a small sample population of three to five other people and administer the TST to each of them. Collect, compare, and analyze your findings from the group. Answer the following questions in a three-page essay: If the majority of your fellow Ameri-

cans fell into the same category, what would this mean for society? How would schools, families, workplaces, sports teams, governments, and charitable organizations operate if almost everyone fell into the same category? Make sure to refer to your TST data in the essay, and include it as an attachment to your paper.

Group Cohesion

A basic concept in the study of group dynamics is **group cohesion**, the sense of solidarity or team spirit that members feel toward their group. Put another way, group cohesion is the force that binds them together. A group is said to be more cohesive when individuals feel strongly tied to membership, so it is likely that

> **group cohesion** the sense of solidarity or loyalty that individuals feel toward a group to which they belong

Group vs. Individual Norms: Honor Killings

In American culture, when reports of family members murdering each other emerge, the reasons generally include abuse, crimes of passion, and monetary gain. The murder of Jose and Kitty Menendez by their sons, Lyle and Erik, is among the notorious cases of murder within a family. The Menendez brothers killed their parents with a shotgun in order to gain access to the family fortune, spending more than a million dollars in their first six months as orphans. Both brothers are now spending life in prison. Scott Peterson murdered his pregnant wife, Laci, in order to reduce their increasing debt and to date other women. Peterson is now living on death row in San Quentin State Prison. In these two cases, public opinion has painted the Menendez brothers and Peterson as dishonorable traitors to their families, men who were more concerned with their own personal gain than their loyalty to family.

What if the reason for a murder of a family member is to uphold the reputation of the family as a whole? **Honor killing** is the murder of a family member based on the belief that the victim is bringing dishonor to the family or the community. Primarily a custom in Middle Eastern and South Asian cultures, the victim of the murder is usually a woman in the family who has not lived up to the moral codes set by the religion or community. Reasons for honor killings may include refusing to enter into an arranged marriage, being a rape victim, being immodest, or having sex outside marriage. The United Nations estimates that as many as 5,000 women a year are murdered in honor killings. The methods of killing range from being shot, to being set on fire or stoned to death. In each case of honor killing, the person who commits the murder is seen as the norm enforcer and not the norm violator as he is doing it in order to seek vindication and to right the wrong committed by the wife, daughter, or sister. In this cultural context, the murdered woman is viewed as someone who deserved to die for betraying and dishonoring her family.

Honor killings are either sanctioned by law in countries like Jordan and Syria or not prosecuted in countries like Turkey, Pakistan, and Egypt. Richard Wilkinson maintains that in countries with less access to basic resources, health care, and human capital, there is a correlating lack of social power and equality for women (2005). Gender inequality is exacerbated in places where there are fewer social resources. Clashes occur when the cultural practice of honor killing is brought to Western countries like France, Canada, and the United States, where a woman's sexual freedom may face informal sanctions, but is widely accepted as the norm.

In October 2009, in a suburb of Phoenix, Arizona, 20-year-old Noor Al-maleki was run over by a Jeep driven by her father, Faleh Al-maleki, formerly from Iraq, because he feared she was becoming too Westernized. Banned from wearing jeans, social networking on the internet, and interacting with boys, Noor had sought to live life as an American. Growing up in the United States since the age of four, Noor was immersed in American cultural norms. Defying her father's rules, Noor refused an arranged marriage at age seventeen, and eventually moved into her boyfriend's parents' home earlier in 2009 before being killed. Faleh Al-maleki faces up to fifty years in prison if convicted for his daughter's murder.

The cultural norm promoting strong family values that causes such disgust toward the Menendez brothers and Scott Peterson is the same norm behind honor killings. However, in honor killings, the family is seen as more important than each family member, therefore an individual member should suffer severe punishment for bringing shame to the family. Al-maleki's actions toward his daughter, while to most Americans' individualist notions of justice seem as betrayal to the family, are justified in his cultural understandings of family honor.

honor killing the murder of a family member—usually female—who is believed to have brought dishonor to her family

a group of fraternity brothers is more cohesive than a random group of classmates. The life of a group depends on at least a minimum level of cohesion. If members begin to lose their strong sense of commitment, the group will gradually disintegrate (Friedkin 2004).

Cohesion is enhanced in a number of ways. It tends to rely heavily on interpersonal factors such as shared values and shared demographic traits like race, age, gender, or class (Cota et al. 1995). We can see this kind of cohesion, for example, in

Social Influence (Peer Pressure)

Groupthink According to sociologist Diane Vaughan, the *Challenger* shuttle disaster may have been caused by scientists failing to take seriously weaknesses in the shuttle's design.

a clique of junior high school girls or members of a church congregation. Cohesion also tends to rely on an attraction to the group as a whole or members' abilities to cooperate in achieving goals (Thye and Lawler 2002). This might help explain cohesion among fans of the Green Bay Packers or members of a local Elks lodge.

GROUPTHINK Whereas a high degree of cohesion might seem desirable, it can also lead to the kind of poor decision making seen in fraternity hazings. In a process Irving Janus (1971, 1982) called **groupthink**, highly cohesive groups may demand absolute conformity and punish those who threaten to undermine the consensus. Although groupthink does help maintain solidarity, it can also short-circuit the decision-making process, letting a desire for unanimity prevail over critical reasoning. When this happens, groups may begin to feel invulnerable and morally superior (White 1989). Members who would otherwise wish to dissent may instead cave in to peer pressure (see the next section).

The problem of groupthink can reach the highest level of industry or government, sometimes with disastrous results. For instance, there are those who believe that the explosion of the space shuttle *Challenger* in 1986 may have been a result of NASA scientists' failing to take seriously those who suspected weaknesses in the shuttle's launch design (Vaughan 1996). More recently, groupthink may have been to blame for the failure of the CIA and the White House to accurately assess the state of Saddam Hussein's programs for weapons of mass destruction; the perceived existence of such weapons was a primary rationale for waging the Iraq War in 2003. A Senate Intelligence Committee report claims that a groupthink dynamic caused those involved to lose objectivity and to embellish or exaggerate findings that justified the U.S. invasion (Ehrenreich 2004; Isikoff 2004).

While you may not have had any personal experience with groupthink, you are certain to find the next set of sociological concepts all too familiar. When individuals are part of groups, they are necessarily influenced by other members. Sociologists refer to this as **social influence**, or **peer pressure**. Knowing how social influence works can help you when you need to convince others to act in a certain way (like agreeing on a specific restaurant or movie). In turn, it can also help you to recognize when others are trying to influence you (to drink too much or drive too fast, for example).

The idea of social influence is not new: the ancient Greek philosopher Aristotle considered persuasion in his *Rhetoric*. But the more modern studies on social influence date back to World War II, when social scientists were trying to help in the war effort by using motivational films to boost morale among servicemen. Since then, the study of social influence has become an expanding part of the field devoted to discovering the principles that determine our beliefs, create our attitudes, and move us to action (Friedkin and Cook 1990; Cialdini and Trost 1998; Friedkin and Granovetter 1998). Recent research on social influence has revealed that everything from our performance in school (Altermatt and Pomerantz 2005) to the likelihood that we will commit rape (Bohner et al. 2006) can be subject to the influence of others. We will focus here on how social influence functions in everyday situations.

Almost all members of society are susceptible to what is either real or imagined social pressure to conform. In general, we conform because we want to gain acceptance and approval (positive sanctions) and avoid rejection and disapproval (negative sanctions). We follow **prescriptions**, doing the things we're supposed to do, as well as **proscriptions**, avoiding the things we're not supposed to do.

Social psychologists have determined that social influence results in one of three kinds of conformity: compliance, identification, or internalization. **Compliance**, the mildest kind of conformity, means going along with something because you expect to gain rewards or avoid punishments (for example, shaking

groupthink in very cohesive groups, the tendency to enforce a high degree of conformity among members, creating a demand for unanimous agreement

social influence (peer pressure) the influence of one's fellow group members on individual attitudes and behaviors

prescriptions behaviors approved of by a particular social group

proscriptions behaviors a particular social group wants its members to avoid

compliance the mildest type of conformity, undertaken to gain rewards or avoid punishments

identification a type of conformity stronger than compliance and weaker than internalization, caused by a desire to establish or maintain a relationship with a person or a group

internalization the strongest type of conformity, occurring when an individual adopts the beliefs or actions of a group and makes them her own

hands with your opponent after a tennis match even if you wish you didn't have to). When people comply, however, they don't actually change their own ideas or beliefs. **Identification**, a somewhat stronger kind of conformity, is induced by a person's desire to establish or maintain a relationship with a person or group (for example, emulating the sportsmanship of someone like Roger Federer in order to impress other tennis players). A person who identifies with a group conforms to their wishes and follows their behavior. **Internalization**, the strongest kind of conformity, occurs when an individual adopts the beliefs of a leader or group. An example of internalization would involve being a good sport, win or lose, because you believe it to be morally right. When internalization occurs, people believe in what they are doing.

Experiments in Conformity

Three rather famous social psychological studies were conducted in the 1950s, '60s, and '70s, with the related goal of trying to understand more about the dynamics of social pressure and, in particular, about group conformity and obedience to authority.

THE ASCH EXPERIMENT The first of these experiments was a study on compliance conducted in 1951 by Solomon Asch (1958), who gathered groups of seven or eight students to participate in what he called an experiment on visual perception. In fact, only one of the students in each group was a real research subject; the others knew ahead of time how

they were supposed to "act." During the experiment, the participants were asked to look at a set of three straight lines and to match the length of a fourth line to one of the other three (see Figure 5.3). In each case, the real research subjects would be last to give an answer. At first, all participants gave the same correct answer. After a few rounds, however, the confederates began to give the same consistently wrong answer. They were completely unanimous in perceiving the line lengths incorrectly. How would the real subjects react when it came to their turn?

Most subjects felt considerable pressure to comply with the rest of the group. A third (33 percent) were "yielders" who gave in at least half of the time to what they knew were the wrong answers. Another 40 percent yielded less frequently but still gave some wrong answers. Only 25 percent were "independents," refusing to give in to the majority. In a debriefing period after the experiment, some subjects reported that they had assumed the rest of the participants were right and they were wrong. Other subjects knew they were not wrong but did not want to appear different from the rest of the group. Almost all of them were greatly distressed by the discrepancy between their own perceptions and those of the other participants. Clearly, it can be difficult to resist peer pressure and to maintain independence in a group situation. What would you have done?

THE MILGRAM EXPERIMENT Stanley Milgram's experience as a graduate student of Solomon Asch's led him to further work on conformity. His first experiments were conducted in 1961, just after the trial of Nazi war criminal Adolf Eichmann had begun in Israel. Many of those who were prosecuted in the years after World War II offered the defense that they were "only following orders." But it was not just soldiers who sent millions of innocents to concentration camps—ordinary citizens turned in their neighbors. Milgram wanted to know whether something particular about the German national psyche led so many to act as accomplices to the mass executions, why they complied with authority figures even when orders conflicted with their own consciences. While we usually think that following orders is a good thing, in the case of the Holocaust, it amounted to a "crime of obedience."

The Milgram experiment (1963, 1974) used a laboratory setting to test the lengths to which ordinary people would follow orders from a legitimate authority. The experiment included three roles: the "experimenter" (a scientist in a white lab coat), a "teacher," and a "learner." The teachers were the only real research subjects in the experiment: although the teachers were led to believe otherwise, the learners were actually confederates of the experimenters. When roles were assigned at the outset of the experiment,

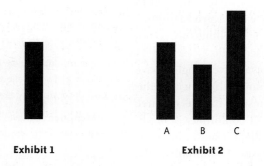

Exhibit 1   Exhibit 2

A   B   C

FIGURE 5.3 Which Line in Exhibit 2 Matches Exhibit 1?
Solomon Asch's studies showed that some people will go against the evidence of their own senses if others around them seem to have different perceptions.

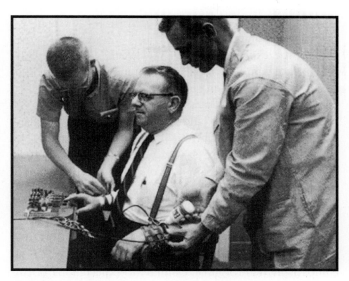

The Milgram Experiment How did Stanley Milgram test participants' obedience to authority? Do you think he would get the same results today?

the research subjects were always picked to play the teacher, despite a seemingly random assignment of roles.

The stated goal of the experiment was to measure the effect of punishment on memory and learning. The teacher was instructed to read aloud a set of word pairs for the learner to memorize. The teacher would then repeat the first word in the pair, and for each incorrect answer, administer a shock of increasing voltage to the learner. The teacher watched while the experimenter strapped the learner to a chair and applied electrodes to his arms. The teacher was then directed to an adjoining room where he could communicate with, but not see, the learner. This room contained a machine with a series of levers indicating the increasing levels of voltage that would be administered for each successive incorrect answer. (In actuality, the machine was not connected to the learner, and he received no shocks.)

The experiment began. As the teacher amplified the voltage for each incorrect answer, the learner responded in increasingly vocal ways. In reality, the teacher was hearing a prerecorded tape that included exclamations, banging on the wall, complaints by the learner about a heart condition, and finally, silence. Many subjects grew uncomfortable at around 135 volts, often pausing and expressing a desire to check on the learner or discontinue the experiment. At that point, the experimenter would give a succession of orders, prodding the teacher to continue. After being assured that they would not be held responsible, most subjects continued, many reaching the maximum of 450 volts.

Milgram and his colleagues were stunned by the results. They had believed that only a few of the subjects would be willing to inflict the maximum voltage. In the first set of experiments, 65 percent of the participants administered the maximum voltage, though many were very uncomfortable doing so and all paused at some point. Only one participant outright refused to administer even low-voltage shocks. Milgram's results highlight the dynamics of conformity revealed in the Asch experiment. A subject will often rely on the expertise of an individual or group, in this case the experimenter, when faced with a difficult decision. We also see how thoroughly socialized most people are to obey authority and carry out orders, especially when they no longer consider themselves responsible for their actions. Clearly, few people have the personal resources to resist authority, even when it goes against their conscience.

THE STANFORD PRISON EXPERIMENT The Stanford Prison Experiment, conducted by Milgram's high school classmate Philip Zimbardo (1971), also examined the power of authority. Twenty-four undergraduates deemed psychologically healthy and stable were recruited to participate in a two-week mock prison simulation. Role assignment as prisoner or guard was based on a coin toss. Guards were given batons, khaki clothing, and mirrored sunglasses, and were told they could not physically harm the prisoners but could otherwise create feelings of boredom, fear, or powerlessness. Prisoners were "arrested" and taken to a mock "jail" set up in the basement of a university building, where they were strip-searched, dressed in smocks and stocking caps (to simulate shaven heads), and assigned identity numbers. A research assistant played the role of warden, while Zimbardo himself was the superintendent.

The students quickly inhabited their roles, but soon exceeded the experimenters' expectations, resulting in an abusive and potentially dangerous situation. Rioting began by the second day; the guards quelled it harshly, harassing the prisoners and depriving them of food, sleep, and basic sanitation. Several guards became increasingly sadistic as the experiment went on, degrading and punishing any prisoner who challenged their authority, and several prisoners showed signs of psychological trauma. After only six days, Zimbardo was compelled to shut down the experiment after a graduate student researcher (whom he later married) became appalled by the conditions.

The Stanford Prison Experiment provided another example of the way situational dynamics, rather than individuals' personal attributes, can determine behavior.

MILGRAM REVISITED Some researchers have claimed that the Asch experiment was a "child of its time," that students in the 1950s were more obedient in their roles, and the culture placed greater emphasis on the value of conformity (Perrin and Spencer 1980, 1981). Researchers in recent decades

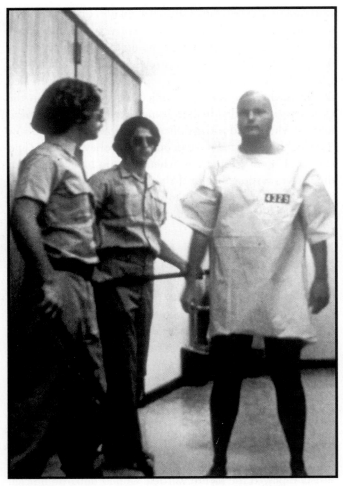

The Stanford Prison Experiment Why do you think the students in Zimbardo's experiment inhabited their roles so completely? What does it reveal about group behavior?

who have replicated the Asch experiment have in fact seen significantly lower rates of compliance, suggesting that the historical and cultural context in which the experiment was conducted seemed to have an effect on how subjects performed (Bond and Sussex 1996). This conclusion echoes some of Ralph Turner's findings about the institutional or impulsive self, discussed in an earlier Data Workshop: namely, he found that patterns of behavior can change over time and that separate generations may respond differently to social pressures.

The power of the group continues to interest sociologists, psychologists, and others who want to understand what drives our powerful impulse to comply (Cialdini 1998). Both the Milgram and the Stanford Prison experiments would be considered unethical by today's professional standards. Although each of the experiments revealed important truths about obedience to authority, some of the participants involved suffered real, and in some cases long-standing,

psychological pain beyond what is considered an acceptable threshold of minimal harm.

Yet, the experiments remain relevant because real-life examples of crimes of obedience continue to occur—whether in the case of the prison guards at Abu Ghraib or in a serial telephone hoax perpetrated on fast-food workers in which a caller posing as a police officer instructed assistant managers to abuse fellow workers (Wolfson 2005).

Nearly half a century elapsed before researchers at Santa Clara University found a means of replicating the Milgram experiment that would pass the Institutional Review Board process for research on human subjects. After a careful screening process, Jerry Burger (2009) conducted a modified version of the famous experiment that protected the well-being of the participants while still providing a valid comparison to the original. Contrary to expectations, obedience rates were only slightly lower in the 2006 replication than they had been in Milgram's lab more than forty-five years earlier.

Although we might like to imagine ourselves as being more able to resist the same forces of conformity that trip up research participants who consistently cave in to social pressure, it's likely that if we found ourselves in situations similar to those created in the laboratory, we might go along and obey authority too.

Teamwork

Are two heads better than one? Or do too many cooks spoil the broth? Early research on groups (Homans 1951) typically assumed that it was always more productive to work in a team rather than alone. However, researchers soon recognized that both the nature of the task and the characteristics of the group have a lot to do with the comparative advantage or disadvantage of working in a group (Goodacre 1953). When we measure productivity, groups almost always outperform single individuals. Things get a bit more complicated, however, when groups are compared with the same number of people working by themselves.

In one of the earliest attempts to systematically study group productivity, experimental social psychologist Ivan Steiner (1972) compared the potential productivity of a group (what they should be able to do) with their actual productivity (what they in fact got done). According to Steiner, actual group productivity can never equal potential productivity because there will always be losses in the team process. Two major sources of inefficiency in particular come with the group process, and both get worse as group size increases. One source is organization: coordinating activities and delegating tasks. For example, if four friends are going to help you move to a new apartment, some time will be lost while you figure out who should pack what, how the furniture will be arranged in the truck, where the boxes should go in the new apartment, and so forth.

Another source of inefficiency is the phenomenon known as **social loafing**, which means that as more individuals are added to a task, each one takes it a little easier (Karau and Williams 1993). Furthermore, as more people become involved, the harder it will be to discern individual effort. If it is impossible for any single person to receive credit or blame, motivation usually suffers. Have you ever asked too many people to help you move to a new apartment? If so, chances are a few did most of the work, some showed up late and helped out a bit, and others did very little but had a good time talking and eating pizza. Having too many "helpers" may contribute to social loafing.

Solutions to the problem of social loafing include recognizing individual effort and finding ways to make a task more interesting or personally rewarding, but such solutions are not always possible. It might be difficult, for instance, to make "moving day" more rewarding. Another solution, however, is suggested by **social identity theory**. Having a social identity, as opposed to a personal one, involves thinking and feeling like a representative of a group (Turner and Killian 1987); you have a real desire to belong to, not simply keep company with, the group. According to this model, the most efficient teams are characterized by the greatest social identity among their members; such social identity increases motivation and places the needs of the group above purely personal concerns.

Qualities of Leadership: Power, Authority, and Style

Effective group leaders possess a variety of qualities, some of which are particular to the kind of group they lead. The leader of a therapeutic support group, for example, needs the proper credentials as well as experience and compassion for his patients. The captain of a sports team must display expertise at her game as well as the ability to inspire her teammates. An office manager must be well-organized and good at dealing with different kinds of people. A police commander must be in good physical shape, skilled in law enforcement tactics, and quick-thinking in a crisis.

One thing almost all leaders have in common, though, is **power**—the ability to control the actions of others. Whether it is **coercive power** (backed by the threat of force) or merely

Qualities of Leadership Nelson Mandela, pictured here with the South African rugby team, The Springboks, is an example of a leader with both legal-rational and charismatic authority. Mandela used his charismatic leadership to unite post-apartheid South Africa through rugby, culminating in a narrow victory in the 1995 Rugby World Cup final.

influential power (supported by persuasion), leadership involves getting people to do things they may or may not want to do. For example, a football coach might wield both coercive and influential power over his players. Although the athletes would definitely want to win games, they might not want to run their training drills every day. During a workout, team members might respond to either the threat of being kicked off the team or the encouragement they receive from the coach. Power, in whatever form it takes, is both a privilege and a requirement of leadership.

Since leadership requires the exercise of power, most formal organizations have institutionalized it in some officially recognized form of **authority**. Max Weber (1913/1962) identified three different types of authority that may be found in social organizations. **Traditional authority**, based in custom,

social loafing the phenomenon in which as more individuals are added to a task, each individual contributes a little less; a source of inefficiency when working in teams

social identity theory a theory of group formation and maintenance that stresses the need of individual members to feel a sense of belonging

power the ability to control the actions of others

coercive power power that is backed by the threat of force

influential power power that is supported by persuasion

authority the legitimate right to wield power

traditional authority authority based in custom, birthright, or divine right

On the Job

Teamwork and the Tour de France

Lance Armstrong, the American cyclist and seven-time winner of the Tour de France, is one of the world's most recognizable and admired athletes, even among those who are not particularly fans of bike racing. Armstrong has gained a hero's reputation for his preeminence in the race, with the most victories ever in consecutive years from 1999 to 2005, after which he "retired," only to return to the Tour again in 2009, 2010, and 2011 as one of the oldest riders to compete, at forty years of age. His athletic accomplishments would be enough to distinguish him as perhaps the best professional cyclist in the history of the sport. But Armstrong is known for more than that, and his personal story is another reason for his massive popularity.

Armstrong gained his breathtaking record of wins after having survived advanced testicular cancer, which had spread to other parts of his body, requiring extensive medical treatment. He might not have been expected to live, much less to go on to become one of the most celebrated athletes of his time. Clearly, Armstrong is a striking example of pushing the limits of human achievement, and a man of unusual perseverance, courage, and physical endurance. Because of this, he serves as an inspiration for many others. He also is a bestselling author from writing about his struggles to overcome cancer, and is the founder of the nonprofit Lance Armstrong Foundation—one of the top ten organizations to raise money for cancer research, in part through sales of the yellow rubber Livestrong bracelets. He has more than 2.5 million followers on Twitter.

We can see how many extraordinary personal qualities Lance Armstrong embodies, but what might be easier to overlook is that as a professional cyclist he could not have become so successful were it not for belonging to a team of riders who compete together in their effort to win the Tour de France. We may know individual cyclists like Armstrong, or more recent three-time winner Alberto Contador, but some might not realize that these riders are supported by eight other premier athletes who must coordinate complex teamwork relations to prevail over the other twenty or so teams in competition. Yet, with Armstrong's many appearances in the Tour de France, which is, after all, a team sport, his all-important teammates include names you have probably never heard of.

In the Tour de France, a race lasting more than three weeks and covering more than 2,000 miles, each team member has a particular specialty, and each stage of the race requires a different strategy. Sprinters may be needed to make a "breakaway" early in the race; "super-climbers" are necessary in the mountainous regions; and sometimes the entire team has to protect the team leader, "blocking" and "drafting" in order to save energy. Teamwork is required to

---

birthright, or divine right, is usually associated with monarchies and dynasties. Kings and queens inherit the throne, not only through lineage but also by divine appointment, meaning by higher authority. Their personal qualities don't really matter, and they can't be replaced by legal proceedings. **Legal-rational authority**, on the other hand, is based in laws and rules, not in the lineage of any individual leader. Modern presidencies and parliaments are built on this kind of authority. The third type, **charismatic authority**, is based in the remarkable personal qualities of the leader her- or himself. Neither rules nor traditions are necessary for the establishment of a charismatic leader—indeed, the leader can be a revolutionary, breaking rules and defying traditions. This is perhaps the only place we will ever find Jesus Christ and Adolf Hitler in the same category: both were extremely charismatic leaders.

The three types of authority are not necessarily mutually exclusive—they can coexist within the same leader. Bill Clinton and Ronald Reagan were appealing and charismatic leaders within the context of the legal-rational authority of the presidency; the Kennedy family is considered an Ameri-

> **legal-rational authority** authority based in laws, rules, and procedures, not in the heredity or personality of any individual leader
>
> **charismatic authority** authority based in the perception of remarkable personal qualities in a leader

organize bathroom and food breaks, as the race stops for no man. Extremely consistent riders (*rouleurs*) are prized, as are those who ride with aggressiveness and bravery (*combativité*). When the individual winner crosses the finish line on the Champs-Elysées in Paris, it is the sacrifices of his altruistic teammates that have made his win possible.

Which position will you find yourself in when you enter the workplace? Will you be the team leader, whose individ-

ual successes depend on the contributions of others? Or will you be the team member, whose special skills support the achievements of the group? It is likely that you will find yourself in both situations over the course of your working life. So remember, when you don the *maillot jaune* (the yellow jersey worn by the Tour de France leader), that in most cases it takes a team effort to get you to the winner's circle.

can political dynasty of sorts, following a tradition of leadership within the structure of electoral politics. The late King Hussein of Jordan was revered for his extraordinary charisma and statesmanship despite his traumatic ascent to the throne: as a teenager, he witnessed his grandfather's assassination and, as his heir, was crowned less than a year later. For people like Bill Clinton (a legal-rational ruler) and King Hussein (a traditional ruler), their charisma was not necessarily the root of their authority, but it did play a part in their ability to rule.

In addition to different types of power and authority, group leaders may exhibit different personal leadership styles as well. Some are more **instrumental**—that is, they are task

or goal oriented—while others are more **expressive**, or concerned with maintaining harmony within the group (Parsons and Bales 1955). An instrumental leader is less concerned with people's feelings than with getting the job done, whereas an expressive leader conveys interest in group members' emotions as well as their achievements. We often consider leadership styles through the lens of gender, expecting men to be more instrumental and women to be more expressive. In fact, we sometimes feel surprised or upset when these gendered expectations

instrumental leadership leadership that is task or goal oriented

expressive leadership leadership concerned with maintaining emotional and relational harmony within the group

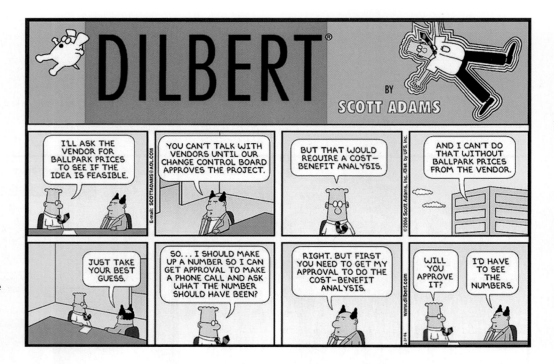

Bureaucracies Are Everywhere Bureaucratic regulations are supposed to make organizations run smoothly; however, bureaucracy can also be impersonal, inflexible, and hyperrational.

aren't met: a male leader with a more expressive style (like California governor Jerry Brown, nicknamed "Moonbeam" for his emotive, touchy-feely style) is sometimes seen as weak, while a female leader with a more instrumental style (such as U.S. secretary of state Hillary Rodham Clinton, whose ambition and drive earned her criticism both while her husband was in the White House and while she was campaigning herself in 2008) is sometimes seen as pushy.

Bureaucracy

Examples of **bureaucracies**, a specific type of secondary group, are everywhere in your life—your university, employer, internet service provider, fast-food restaurant, and even church are likely to be organized bureaucratically. Bureaucracies are designed to perform tasks efficiently, and they approach their tasks, whatever they are, with calculations designed deliberately to meet their goals.

Bureaucracies have certain organizational traits, which help them operate efficiently. Max Weber (1921/1968) identified these characteristics as follows.

1. Specialization: All members of a bureaucracy are assigned specialized roles and tasks.

2. Technical competence: Bureaucratic members are specially trained for their specific roles.

3. Hierarchy: Bureaucracies always feature the supervision of subordinates by higher-ranking managers and bosses.

4. Rules and regulations: These are meant to make all operations as predictable as possible.

5. Impersonality: In a bureaucracy, rules come before people; no individual receives special treatment.

6. Formal written communication: Documents such as memos (or e-mails) are the heart of the organization and the most effective way to communicate.

You can see these traits in action at your own college or university. Take specialization and technical competence, for instance. Virtually none of your professors could teach another's classes: your sociology professor would likely be completely useless in a chemistry lab, a math classroom, or even an English seminar. The groundskeepers, campus police officers, soccer coaches, and librarians are all specially qualified to do their own jobs and no one else's. In addition, there are layers of hierarchy at a university, from the trustees and president to the vice chancellors, provosts, deans, and department chairs. Professors are, in some ways, at the bottom of the academic hierarchy (except for you, the students)! And every other campus unit (athletics, residence life, food service, facilities maintenance) has its own hierarchy as well.

Regulations keep a university running smoothly—or at least that's what they are meant to do. Undoubtedly, though, you have run up against a regulation that kept you from doing

bureaucracy a type of secondary group designed to perform tasks efficiently, characterized by specialization, technical competence, hierarchy, rules and regulations, impersonality, and formal written communication

something you really wanted to do—add a class after a deadline, move into a campus apartment. This is where the feature of impersonality also comes into play: the rules of the bureaucracy trumped your individual needs, no matter how deserving you thought you were. This is especially true at larger universities; at small schools, special treatment is still sometimes possible. But big bureaucracies often treat you "like a number"—and in fact, you *are* a number to your college, as your student ID number is the first thing you are issued on arrival.

The McDonaldization of Society

Weber's model of bureaucracy seems cold and heartless, alienating and impersonal, rule-bound, inflexible, and undemocratic. Indeed, many bureaucracies *are* like this—they are highly efficient secondary groups that operate on the principle of **rationalization**, where the focus is on logical procedures, rules and regulations are paramount, and an individual's unique personal qualities are unimportant. Worse yet, some of the hyperrationalized features of successful bureaucracies are trickling down into other areas of our everyday lives.

Sociologist George Ritzer (1996) called this trickle-down rationalization process **McDonaldization**. We touch-tone our way through telephone calls at work, never speaking to a real person; at lunch, we construct our own salads at the salad bar and bus our own tables afterward; at the bank, we no longer interact with human tellers but rather drive through the ATM on the way home, where we microwave our dinners and watch increasingly predictable sitcoms or movie sequels on TV. Ritzer is critical of the dehumanizing aspects of McDonaldization and hopes that increased awareness of the process will help us avoid the "iron cage" of bureaucracy (a term coined by Weber to illustrate the way bureaucracies can trap individuals).

Sociologist Robin Leidner delves further into the McDonaldization phenomenon in her book *Fast Food, Fast Talk* (1993). Through fieldwork in actual McDonald's franchises, Leidner developed a model for understanding the increasing routinization of service industries, in this case the ubiquitous fast-food restaurant. In particular, she looks at how standardized "scripts" for interaction help to shape customers' experiences. The physical atmosphere of a McDonald's is not conducive to hanging out (unlike, say, a café); customers don't expect

rationalization the application of economic logic to human activity; the use of formal rules and regulations in order to maximize efficiency without consideration of subjective or individual concerns

McDonaldization George Ritzer's term describing the spread of bureaucratic rationalization and the accompanying increases in efficiency and dehumanization

McDonaldization In her ethnography *Fast Food, Fast Talk*, Robin Leidner studied how the routinization of services and physical atmosphere at McDonald's restaurants standardized the types of interactions occurring there.

Changing the World

A Paradise Built in Hell: The Extraordinary Communities that Arise in Disaster

When natural disasters happen, we generally assume that the aid offered will be primarily from the government and humanitarian organizations such as the Red Cross, or even by celebrities. As Americans, we trust that the U.S. government will rush to the aid of its citizens. As individuals, we donate to organizations like the Red Cross because we trust that they will efficiently provide supplies, medical care, and housing to those in need. We can also look to celebrities who will publicize the disaster and lend themselves to fundraising events while donating millions of their own dollars.

As individuals, we may not know how to make much of a difference in the face of a disaster in some distant locale, and our own actions may seem insignificant. News reports may give us the impression that individuals are largely helpless to respond to the damage from a massive and unexpected event like an earthquake or flood. But it is exactly on this small-scale level that some of the most profound aid can be rendered from one person to another. That is especially true for those who by luck, chance, or choice find themselves in the middle of such a situation.

Rebecca Solnit's book *A Paradise Built in Hell: The Extraordinary Communities that Arise in Disaster* documents precisely how crises such as natural disasters elicit collective action from individuals who might not otherwise have had the occasion to interact with each other in normal everyday life. "[D]isaster doesn't sort us out by preferences; it drags us into emergencies that require we act altruistically, bravely, and with initiative in order to survive or save the neighbors, no matter how we vote or what we do for a

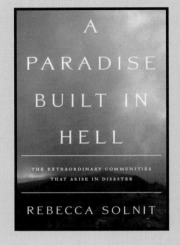

living" (Solnit 2009, p. 8). In our capitalist social structure, we often take the cynical view that the actions of most individuals are motivated by selfishness or personal gain. Disasters defy this assumption because the disruption and failure of social systems caused by crisis create opportunities where social ties, altruism, and personal sacrifice emerge and thrive. It is in the midst of disaster, Solnit argues, that humans are often at their best.

Solnit did extensive research on the aftermath of five disasters: the 1906 San Francisco earthquake, the 1917 Halifax explosion, the 1985 Mexico earthquake, the 9/11 attacks in New York City in 2001, and Hurricane Katrina in New Orleans. In each of these cases, despite the fear of mob action amidst the chaos, people came together to help, support, and nurture each other during the crisis and ensuing loss of their way of life. The most recent of these disasters was Hurricane Katrina which hit New Orleans on August 25, 2005. The storm caused the levees to break and flood 80 percent of the city. Access to basic resources like food, drinkable water, clothing, medicine, and power was obstructed or halted for weeks and even months.

to sit down and be waited on. Rather, they respond to expectations that they will enter, order food from a predetermined menu and pay for it, eat quickly, deposit trash in the receptacles, and then leave. Leidner exposes these processes of routinization by looking at what happens when breakdowns occur in these expectations.

For example, Leidner notes that McDonald's trains workers to refer to customers as "guests," reinforcing the obligation to serve them respectfully even if that respect is not reciprocated. Leidner observed that if customers were angry or uncooperative, workers tried even harder to serve them

swiftly so that they would leave faster and have less time to make trouble in the restaurant. Workers developed a mindset that allowed them to handle problem customers in a way that minimized trouble and facilitated their routinized work.

Responding to Bureaucratic Constraints

Not everything about bureaucracies is bad. In fact, in contemporary, postindustrial society, just about everything you need or want is created, produced, distributed, and serviced

Media coverage of the aftermath of Hurricane Katrina focused first on the supposed violence and looting occurring in New Orleans and later on the abysmal failure of the government and nonprofit agencies to provide adequate aid to the victims. Solnit, instead, focused on the social networks and community ties that developed informally to support the victims of Katrina. Immediately after the hurricane struck, "[a]n armada of volunteers went out in small craft that week and ferried uncounted thousands, tens of thousands, to dry ground" (Solnit 2009, p. 8). Little attention was devoted by the media to these victims who immediately began devoting their efforts to rescue others in the same situation. People on site at the disaster did whatever they could to lend a hand.

Communities in New Orleans emerged out of necessity post-Katrina. People who lost their homes sought refuge in deserted schools and churches. Solnit interviewed one of the survivors, Keith Bernard Sr., who had to dive back into his house and swim through a broken window to escape the flooding after he had been trapped in the attic. Bernard and his dog eventually found a home in an elementary school.

> It turned into a community effort. Everybody cooked. They fed one another. They scavenged the food that they had from stores that had been vandalized, whatever, but they were really, really nice. I saw people being compassionate about people that they never met, people that they never saw, people that they never knew reaching out to them, feeding them, giving them clothes. You know, we didn't have no use of money, so the basic was the clothes

and the food. This was New Orleans everywhere. This was everywhere in New Orleans (Solnit 2009, p. 274–275).

When crises emerge, popular sentiment is that the actions that follow will be motivated by greed, personal gain, and selfishness. Solnit demonstrates that individuals are willing to make great personal sacrifices to provide aid to those who are suffering. In addition, those who are suffering are willing to make great personal sacrifices to help others who are in the same position. It's during these disasters that people come to the rescue of one another and form community, and wherein the best of human nature is allowed to flourish.

A neighborhood in New Orleans, LA, completely submerged in water after Hurricane Katrina.

by a bureaucracy. The water in the tap, the lights, the streets, the car and its insurance, the food on the table, the table itself, the clothes on your back, the movies, songs, and books you enjoy—all are the products of bureaucratic organizations. As problematic as they are, we can't live without them. So how can we benefit from our contact with bureaucracies without being controlled by them?

For one thing, even the most overrationalized, McDonaldized bureaucracy is populated by people who are capable of forming primary group relationships as well, who might celebrate birthdays, throw parties, and go out for drinks after work. Indeed, interpersonal interactions help humanize bureaucracies. Further, in forward-thinking organizations, new management strategies meant to address alienation and disenchantment are being implemented. Yes, bureaucracies still seek to be as efficient and predictable as possible in their daily operations. But some, like Starbucks, UPS, and Apple, are trying to play up their human side as well—becoming "enlightened" bureaucracies by being inclusive, sharing responsibility, and providing opportunities for all to advance.

Businesses have also begun organizing corporate retreats to teach managers how to understand individual strengths and weaknesses, support individual skills and talents, and encourage teamwork, trust, and leadership. Some, like Fidelity Financial, Toyota, and Pella Windows, have adopted the Japanese management technique called *kaizen*, in which lower-level workers are encouraged to suggest new, innovative ways to improve the organization and upper-level managers are required to actually put these ideas into practice, rewarding individual creativity and benefiting the company at the same time (Pollack 1999; Hakim 2001). Make no mistake—corporations are not sacrificing the bottom line for the good of an individual. But often they are finding that the needs of the individual and those of the organization are not mutually exclusive.

BURNING MAN In the barren Black Rock Desert of Nevada, some people actively seek out an escape from their bureaucratically regimented life, at least for one week every summer, at a festival called Burning Man (Sonner 2002; Chen 2004). The festival, begun in 1990 on a beach near San Francisco with just 20 participants, drew more than 50,000 people in 2010. Burning Man is hard to describe for those who have never attended. It is a freewheeling experiment in temporary community, where there are no rules except to protect the well-being of participants ("burners") and where everyone gathers together to celebrate various forms of self-expression and self-reliance not normally encountered in everyday life.

Burning Man attracts a wide variety of individuals from different backgrounds (though it may be difficult to tell beneath the body paint, mud, or costumes that many wear), most of them in their 20s and 30s. Unlike many places in the real world, participants are encouraged to interact with each other; there are no strangers at "the Burn." Each year is characterized by a different theme—like "Hope and Fear" in 2006. "American Dream" in 2008 or "Rites of Passage" in 2011—and participants are invited to contribute in some meaningful way to its realization, most often artistically.

Much of what is appealing about Burning Man is that it challenges many of the norms and values of mainstream society, especially those that are associated with conformity, bureaucracy, and capitalism. Black Rock resembles a city when the thousands of participants converge there, but one comprised of tents and RVs gathered into neighborhoods with names like "Tic Toc Town" and "Capitalist Pig Camp" (Doherty 2000, 2004). The city has its own informal economy as well. Once an admission fee is paid, money is no longer used. Participants must bring enough supplies to support themselves or use alternate forms of currency, such as barter, trade, gifts, or services. Corporate sponsorship is strictly avoided, and logos of any kind are banned. Despite its stated

Burning Man Finale Each year thousands of "burners" gather in the Black Rock Desert to celebrate the rejection of values like conformity, bureaucracy, and capitalism.

ideals, there is not total freedom at Burning Man. Over the years, various government and local law-enforcement agencies have imposed some restrictions on the event such as bans on fireworks, guns, and dogs.

On the last night of the festival, the giant wooden structure known as the Burning Man is lit on fire, and the celebrants discover their own personal epiphanies as they watch it burn. When the festival is over, participants are committed to leaving no trace behind; the desert is returned to its pristine condition. One burner called the festival "authentic life" with the other days of the year "a tasteless mirage, a pacific struggle against the backwardness of middle America—consumer culture, bad politics, *Fear Factor*, and fear thy neighbor" (Babiak 2004). So while Burning Man participants don't abandon permanently the web of contemporary bureaucracies that shape their lives, they gain some relief by ditching it all once a year, just for a few days.

TABLE 5.1	Theory in Everyday Life	
PERSPECTIVE	**APPROACH TO GROUPS**	**CASE STUDY: FRATERNITIES**
STRUCTURAL-FUNCTIONALISM	Life in groups helps to regulate and give meaning to individual experience, contributing to social cohesion and stability.	Affiliation groups like fraternities help create social cohesion in the context of a larger, possibly alienating, university system by bringing young men with shared values together.
CONFLICT THEORY	Group membership is often the basis for the distribution of rewards, privileges, and opportunities in our society. An individual may be treated preferentially or prejudicially based on his or her group membership.	In-group and out-group dynamics can contribute to stereotyping and conflict as fraternity brothers develop an "us vs. them" perspective regarding other frats and non-Greeks.
SYMBOLIC INTERACTIONISM	Group norms, values, and dynamics are generated situationally, in interaction with other members.	The pressure to conform to group culture (as in the cases of peer pressure and groupthink) can lead individuals to do things they might never do alone, and can have negative consequences, as in the case of fraternity hazing and binge drinking. It can also lead to positive actions, such as when fraternity members volunteer or raise money for charity.

Closing Comments

Groups make our lives possible by providing us with the necessities of our existence—food, clothes, cars, homes, and all the other things we use on a daily basis. Groups make our lives enjoyable by providing us with companionship and recreation—from our friends and families to the entertainment conglomerates that produce our favorite music and films. Groups also make our lives problematic—bureaucracies can squelch our individuality, major manufacturers can create social and environmental problems, and some organizations can engender conflict and prejudice between groups. We are at our best in groups, and our worst. We can do great things together, and horrible things. Sociology helps us understand group life at both extremes and everywhere in between.

⑤ Need Help Studying?

wwnorton.com/studyspace

Visit StudySpace to access free review materials such as:

- **Vocabulary Flashcards**
- **Diagnostic Review Quizzes**
- **Study Outlines**

QUESTIONS FOR REVIEW

1. Think of at least three groups to which you belong. Are these primary or secondary groups? Which out-groups are associated with your group membership?

2. Which groups serve as your reference groups? Are you a member of all your reference groups? How do these reference groups affect your self-image?

3. Sociologists have found that even indirect ties within our social networks can be very helpful, especially economically. Describe a time when you've gained some material benefit from your social network. Job hunting is the obvious example, but there are many other ways that you might have used indirect ties to your advantage.

4. Many sociologists worry about the anomie that may result from declining membership in groups. Are you a member of any formal organizations, or do you take part in any regular group activities? Alternatively, do you belong to any electronic communities like MySpace, Facebook, or others? Which type of group influences you more?

5. The text identifies three different types of conformity: compliance, identification, and internalization. Describe some moments when you've exhibited each type of conformity.

6. One way to decrease the incidence of social loafing is to recruit members with a strong sense of group identity. Do any of your group memberships involve a particularly strong or weak social identity?

7. Legal-rational authority is by far the most common type of authority in modern society, but older forms still exist. Can you think of a contemporary authority figure whose power was granted on the basis of tradition or custom? How about a charismatic authority figure?

8. What are some institutions that you encounter in your everyday life that don't fit Max Weber's description of a bureaucracy?

9. Theorist George Ritzer believes that McDonaldization, the spread of the organizational principles of bureaucracies to all areas of life, is a growing concern. Thinking about Weber's six characteristics of bureaucracies, can you identify areas of your life that have been McDonaldized?

SUGGESTIONS FOR FURTHER EXPLORATION

Cuomo, Chris. January 3, 2007. "ABC News Primetime Basic Instincts 5: The Milgram Experiment Re-Visited." This episode of the newsmagazine program features the new experiment conducted at Santa Clara University along with clips from the classic videos of the original Milgram and Stanford Prison experiments. Includes new real-world cases of "crimes of obedience."

Doherty, Brian. 2004. *This Is Burning Man.* New York: Little, Brown and Company. A portrait of this annual desert festival from an insider's viewpoint. Into what sort of group would you classify Burning Man participants?

FitzGerald, Frances. 1986. *Cities on a Hill.* New York: Simon & Schuster. A journalistic account of four

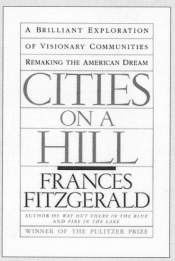

A BRILLIANT EXPLORATION OF VISIONARY COMMUNITIES

REMAKING THE AMERICAN DREAM

CITIES ON A HILL

FRANCES FITZGERALD

AUTHOR OF *WAY OUT THERE IN THE BLUE* AND *FIRE IN THE LAKE*

WINNER OF THE PULITZER PRIZE

groups with radically different ideologies and lifestyles: San Francisco's mainly gay Castro neighborhood, Jerry Falwell's Liberty Baptist Church, a Florida retirement community, and an Oregon commune. FitzGerald presents them as quintessentially American examples of the power of group life to stimulate individual and social change.

Groupthink. 1992. CRM Learning. Examines the Space Shuttle *Challenger* prelaunch conference and other historical events in which decisions based on groupthink led to disaster. See www.groupthinkfilm.com for more information.

Hausbeck, Kathryn, and Barbara Brent. 2006. "McDonaldization of the Sex Industries: The Business of Sex" in *McDonaldization: The Reader*. Ed. George Ritzer. Thousand Oaks, CA: Pine Forge Press. This essay shows just how pervasive the process of rationalization has become.

Heller, Joseph. 1955. *Catch-22*. New York: Simon & Schuster. The term "catch-22" has come to mean a no-win situation, especially one in which a bureaucracy has created rules and regulations so complicated that they create self-contradictory situations. Pay attention to how bureaucracies work (or fail) in this satirical novel.

Kreuter, Holly. 2002. *Drama in the Desert: The Sights and Sounds of Burning Man*. San Francisco: Raised Barn Press. Captures the spirit of this vibrant community through color photographs and contributions from group members.

Obedience (1962). A documentary film of Milgram's classic experiment on authority, shot at Yale University.

Quadrophenia. 1979. Dir. Franc Roddam. The Who Films. This rock opera was composed, performed, recorded, and translated onto film by The Who. Set in London in 1964,

it addresses the role of group subcultures in the lives of working-class youth by examining the clashes between Mods and Rockers. These groups give the young protagonists a sense of belonging and identity; however, group boundaries also drive individuals apart and lead to violence.

Quiet Rage: The Stanford Prison Experiment (1991). A documentary film featuring the college students who participated in the now-famous (and unethical) experiment conducted in the basement of the Stanford psychology building.

"We Do What We're Told (Milgram's 37)." This song, written by Peter Gabriel, was inspired by the Milgram experiment.

Wilson, James Q. 2000. *Bureaucracy: What Government Agencies Do and Why They Do It*. New York: Basic Books. A helpful explanation of bureaucratic behavior, especially the relationship between a government organization's structure and its specific goals.

Whenever you get the opportunity, even if it's long after you take this class, visit any of the following museums dedicated to different cultural groups in American life—or visit a similar museum in your home town.

National Museum of the American Indian
Washington, DC
www.nmai.si.edu

Simon Weisenthal Center Museum of Tolerance
Los Angeles, CA
www.museumoftolerance.com

The African American Museum
Philadelphia, PA
www.aampmuseum.org

Arab American National Museum
Dearborn, MI
www.arabamerican
museum.org

American Swedish Institute
Minneapolis, MN
www.americanswedishinst
.org

Museo de las Americas
Denver, CO
www.museo.org

Chinese Historical Society of America
San Francisco, CA
www.chsa.org

National Museum of the American Indian

CHAPTER 6 Deviance

Despite a great deal of confusion on the morning of September 11, 2001, the facts were fairly quickly established. Nineteen men armed with box cutters hijacked four planes, crashing them into both towers of the World Trade Center in New York, the Pentagon in Washington, D.C., and a field in Pennsylvania. The men were part of an organization known as Al Qaeda, headed by exiled Saudi billionaire Osama bin Laden. Despite this quick consensus, the squabble over what *really* had happened was just beginning.

In the United States, among other places, the attack was considered an act of terrorism. In his State of the Union address the following January, President Bush spoke of "truths that we will never question" and declared that "evil is real, and it must be opposed." The rhetoric of good and evil dominated the discussion of these events in the United States: the "evil" of terrorism was perpetrated by "evildoers" who belonged to a "cult of evil which seeks to harm the innocent and thrives on human suffering." As journalist Michael Kinsley (2002) put it, "There has never in our entire history been a proposition from which fewer Americans dissent than 'Osama Bin Laden is evil.'"

However, in other parts of the world, the interpretation was radically different. Although official messages of sympathy and condolence were received from every world government except Iraq, in parts of the Middle East this official attitude did not always reflect the popular mood. Pro–bin Laden demonstrations erupted in many spots around the Islamic world immediately after the attacks. In Sudan and Pakistan, Osama bin Laden T-shirts were selling briskly. Protesters in Egypt chanted, "There is no God but God, and Bush is the enemy of God" (Macfarquhar 2001). To these people, the September 11 hijackers were not "evildoers" but martyrs. An Afghani cleric who had known one of the hijackers described him as "one of the pious men in the [Al Qaeda] organization," who "became a martyr, Allah bless his soul." Bin Laden himself (in a videotaped lecture) explicitly argued that it was the United States and its troops stationed in Saudi Arabia that were evil: "Every Muslim must rise to defend his religion. The wind of faith is blowing and the wind of change is blowing to remove evil from the Peninsula of Mohammed." From this point of view, it was a religious obligation to make war on the West, and the hijackers fulfilled their duties with great success, at the expense of their own lives.

How is it possible that people who are basically in agreement about what happened on September 11 can be in such extreme disagreement over the meaning of these events? To almost all Americans, the hijackers were deviants—terrorists and murderers. However, to the supporters of Al Qaeda, the hijackers were heroes and martyrs. How can this disagreement be explained? The sociological answer is that no behavior, not even one that is intended to kill great numbers of people, is inherently deviant. It is the cultural context, the values and norms of a particular society, that makes it so.

HOW TO READ THIS CHAPTER

Have you ever driven faster than the posted speed limit? Have you ever gotten caught picking your nose in public? Did you have your first taste of beer, wine, or hard liquor before you reached the legal drinking age? Did you pierce something (your lip, eyebrow, or belly button) that your grandmother wouldn't have wanted you to pierce? If you work in an office, did you ever take home a pen, pencil, or packet of Post-it notes?

If you answered yes to any of these questions, you are the embodiment of what we seek to understand in this chapter: you are deviant. Remember this as you read the chapter.

Defining Deviance

Deviance is a behavior, trait, or belief that departs from a norm and generates a negative reaction in a particular group. The norms and the group reactions are necessary for a behavior or characteristic to be defined as deviant (Goode 1997). The importance of norms becomes clear when we remember that what is deviant in one culture might be normal in another (see Chapter 3); even within the same culture, what was deviant a century ago might be perfectly acceptable now (and vice versa). The importance of group reactions is clear when we look at the varied reactions that norm violations generate: some violations are seen as only mildly deviant (like chewing with your mouth open), but others are so strongly taboo that they are almost unthinkable (like cannibalism).

Deviant behavior must be sufficiently serious or unusual to spark a negative sanction or punishment. For example, if you were having dinner with friends and used the wrong fork for your salad, you would be violating a minor norm but your friends probably wouldn't react in a negative fashion; they might not even notice. On the other hand, if you ate an entire steak dinner—meat, mashed potatoes, and salad—with your hands, your friends probably *would* react. They might criticize your behavior strongly ("That's totally disgusting!") and even refuse to

> **deviance** a behavior, trait, belief, or other characteristic that violates a norm and causes a negative reaction

eat with you again. This latter example, then, would be considered deviant behavior among your group of friends—and among most groups in American society.

Because definitions of deviance are constructed from cultural, historical, and situational norms, sociologists are interested in a number of topics under the rubric of deviance. First, how are norms and rules created, and how do certain norms and rules become especially important? Second, who is subject to the rules, and how is rule breaking identified? Third, what types of sanctions (punishments or rewards) are dispensed to society's violators? Fourth, how do people who break the rules see themselves, and how do others see them? And finally, how have sociologists attempted to explain rule making, rule breaking, and responses to rule breaking?

Deviance across Cultures

It is important to remember that when sociologists use the term "deviant," they are making a social judgment, never a moral one. If a particular behavior is considered deviant, this means that it violates the values and norms of a *particular* group, not that it is inherently wrong or that other groups will make the same judgment.

Much of the literature on deviance focuses on crime, but not only do different cultures define strikingly different behaviors as criminal, they also differ in how those crimes are punished. Most serious crime in the United States today is punished by imprisonment. This method of punishment was rare until the nineteenth century, however, as maintaining a prison requires considerable resources. Buildings must be constructed and maintained, guards and other staff must be paid, and prisoners must be fed and clothed. For groups without these resources, incarceration is not a possibility, even assuming it would be a desirable option. Instead, there are a whole host of other techniques of punishment.

For example, the Amish, a religious community whose members do without modern devices like electricity, cars, and telephones, practice *meidung*, which means shunning those who violate the strict norms of the group (Kephart 2000). A biblical rule instructs them "not to associate with any one who bears the name of brother if he is guilty of immorality or greed, or is an idolater, reviler, drunkard, or robber—not even to eat with such a one" (1 Corinthians 5:11). In other words, the Amish believe they should not associate with lawbreakers even when they come from within their own family. No one does business with, eats with, or even talks to the guilty party. The shunning is temporary, however: after a short period, the violator is expected to publicly apologize and make amends, and is then welcomed back into the community.

A much more permanent method of punishment is total banishment from the community. For many Native American people, the social group was so important that banishment was considered a fate worse than death (Champagne 1994). It was one of a variety of practices that were used to maintain social control (along with shaming songs, contests, and challenges of strength) and something of a rarity because it completely severed ties between the group and the individual. Banishment has a long history of use in all parts of the world, from the British prisoners who were "transported" to Australia to Russian dissidents exiled to Siberia, and has been one of the most cost-effective methods of punishment ever discovered.

Just as methods of punishment vary between societies and groups, so they also change over time. In Colonial America, for example, corporal punishment was the rule for the majority of crimes (Walker 1997). These days, the phrase "corporal punishment" conjures up images of elementary school teachers spanking students, probably because spanking was the last vestige of what was once a vast repertoire of penal techniques. Thieves, pickpockets, and others who would today be considered petty criminals were flogged, had their ears cropped, had their noses slit, had their fingers and hands cut off, or were branded. These punishments were designed not only to deliver pain but also to mark the offender. As such, the particular punishment was often designed to fit the crime. A pickpocket might have a hand cut off; a forger might have an "F" branded on his forehead. Brands were also used to mark African American slaves as property during the 1800s.

Body Modification

Branding has long since died out as a method of punishment, but in a perfect illustration of the mutability of deviance, it is making a comeback as a form of body decoration (Parker 1998). What used to be an involuntary mark of shame has been reclaimed as a voluntary mark of pride. Small branding irons of stainless steel are heated with a blowtorch until white hot and held on the skin for a second or two. Some who undergo the procedure burn incense to cover the smell of their own flesh burning. Many African American fraternities have a long tradition of branding, usually in the shape of one of the fraternity's Greek letters. The practice has received a public boost in recent years as several popular athletes have

Branding Spenser Evans displays his fraternity Omega Psi Phi's brand on his chest. Branding of one's Greek Letter Organization by black men has a history dating back to the 1900s to symbolize unity and commitment among members.

prominently displayed their fraternity brands. Basketball star Michael Jordan sports such a brand, as does the Atlanta Falcons' Christopher Owens. Branding is spreading to other youth subcultures, where it is just another extension of tattoos, Mohawks, and body piercings as an outward manifestation of youthful rebellion.

When it comes to body modification, what Americans might label deviant might be identified as desirable or normal in other cultures and vice versa. Among the Suri of southwest Ethiopia, progressively larger plates are inserted into the lower lip so that it gradually becomes enlarged. The Padaung women of Burma stretch their necks with brass rings. Young girls begin by encircling their necks with just a few rings, then add more as they grow; by the time of maturity, their necks are considerably elongated. Breast augmentation surgery is commonplace in the United States, while butt augmentation is popular in Brazil.

Body modification does not always need to be dramatic. In reality, there are a great number of subtle methods of body modification practiced by most Americans that may not seem so obvious if we concentrate on nose rings and biker tattoos. First of all, there have always been body modifications for the middle and upper classes. Corsets, worn by women through the ages until the early twentieth century, are an obvious example. Stomachs were flattened with "stays," long strips of some rigid material like whalebone. A tightly laced corset could achieve a dramatically narrow waistline, but often at a serious cost to the wearer's health. Women sometimes even had ribs removed in order to accommodate them.

One Culture's Deviant Behavior Might Be Desirable or Normal in Another Padaung women use brass rings to stretch their necks, a Suri woman uses plates to modify her lip, an American man has split and pierced his tongue, and Al Harrington of the Denver Nuggets sports extensive body tattoos.

Delicious or Disgusting? Food, Culture, and Deviance

Although as Americans we enjoy a great number of ethnic foods, there are some food boundaries we will not cross. One is the ancient practice of *entomophagy*, the eating of insects. Even though the 1,462 known species of edible insects are very environmentally friendly to raise and have a better feed-to-meat ratio and better protein-to-fat ratio than any other animal, there are few taboos as indestructible in America as that against eating bugs.

People in Algeria traditionally eat desert locusts, aborigines in Australia snack on certain moths and grubs, some Africans sauté termites, and the Japanese sometimes eat fried grasshoppers.

Probably the most notorious of culinary insects is the agave worm found in bottles of the Mexican liquor *mezcal*, usually eaten (if at all) in America as the result of a drunken dare rather than for its nutritional value.

One thing Americans *do* love is bacon cheeseburgers. For billions of people throughout the world, though, this is an abomination. It violates the dietary laws of three major world religions (Judaism, Hinduism, and Islam), and members of those groups may look on you with horror, disgust, or even pity as they watch you eat one. Jewish dietary laws called *kashrut* prohibit eating meat and dairy products at the same meal. The Hindu religion prohibits eating beef, the Islamic religion regards pork as *haraam*, or forbidden food, and Jewish laws also prohibit eating pork. Sociologists maintain that what is deviant is always socially learned, relative to a particular culture. Certainly with food, standards of deviance vary widely across cultures.

How to Eat Fried Worms A cook at the upscale restaurant Hostería Santo Domingo in Mexico City adds a dollop of guacamole to a plate of deep-fried worms.

These days, we have a rich array of techniques to bring our bodies into line with contemporary standards. Recently, the Food and Drug Administration approved the use of injections of Botox, a strain of botulism toxin that works by freezing facial nerves, for removing fine lines and wrinkles on the forehead. The hair salon is another great unacknowledged center for body modification. If you get a perm, you are breaking the disulfide bonds in your hair and reshaping them to straighten them or make them curly. Even a simple haircut is a type of body modification—luckily, for those of us who have gotten bad haircuts, they're temporary! Some body modifications seem so "normal" that we practice them as routines without considering how they may seem deviant elsewhere. Other cultures may view Americans' obsession with hair removal—shaving, plucking, tweezing, and waxing— as bizarre. As you can see, whether it's corsets, branding, or shaving your legs, the boundaries between beauty and deviance are fluid across time and place.

Theories of Deviance

In this section, we will learn how three sociological theories we considered in Chapter 1—functionalism, conflict theory, and symbolic interactionism—can be applied to deviance. We will also learn about other, related theories that have been developed specifically to explain particular aspects of deviance.

Functionalism

As you may recall, adherents of functionalism argue that each element of social structure helps maintain the stability of society. What, then, is the function of deviance for society? Emile Durkheim came up with a couple of functions. First, deviance can help a society clarify its moral boundaries. We are reminded about our shared notions of what is right

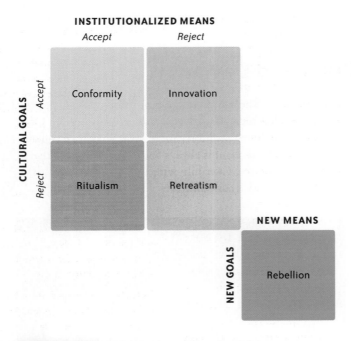

INSTITUTIONALIZED MEANS

	Accept	Reject
CULTURAL GOALS Accept	Conformity	Innovation
Reject	Ritualism	Retreatism

NEW MEANS

NEW GOALS — Rebellion

FIGURE 6.1 Merton's Typology of Deviance

Different orientations toward society's goals and differential access to the means to achieve those goals combine to create different categories of deviance.

when we have to address wrongdoings of various sorts. In 2005, Terri Schiavo, a hospital patient from St. Petersburg, Florida, received national attention when a legal battle was fought over her life. Schiavo had been in a persistent vegetative state since 1990 and kept alive through a gastric feeding tube. Her husband, Michael, petitioned the courts in 1998 to end life support—he thought it was the right thing to do and was what Terri would have wanted. Her parents, Mary and Robert Schindler, took legal action against Michael's decision—they thought it was wrong. While most people might have had a vague idea of how they felt about artificially prolonging life, the Schiavo case forced them to think concretely about how such choices affect actual people. After a seven-year process, the courts sided with Michael Schiavo, and on March 18, 2005, his wife's feeding tube was removed. She died thirteen days later.

Another function of deviance is to promote social cohesion (one of functionalism's valued ideals); people can be brought together as a community in the face of crime or other violations. For example, while the country was divided over the decision in the Schiavo case, an opinion poll by ABC News on March 21, 2005, reported that 70 percent of Americans believed that Michael Schiavo had the authority to make decisions on behalf of his wife and that the case should not have been a federal matter. In the same

poll, 63 percent maintained that the federal government was involved solely for political advantage. Whatever they believed about prolonging life, the majority of Americans thus agreed that the choice was best made by family and not the government.

STRUCTURAL STRAIN THEORY Robert Merton's **structural strain theory** (1938/1976) provides a bridge between functionalist and conflict theories of deviance. Like Durkheim, Merton acknowledges that some deviance is inevitable in society. But like conflict theorists, he argues that an individual's position in the social structure will affect his experience of deviance and conformity. Social inequality can create situations in which people experience tension (or strain) between the goals society says they should be working toward (like financial success) and the means they have available to meet those goals (not everyone is able to work hard at a legitimate job). The rewards of conformity, therefore, are available only to those who can pursue approved goals through approved means. Any other combination of means and goals is deviant in one way or another. **Innovators**, for example, might seek financial success via unconventional means (such as drug dealing or embezzlement). **Ritualists** go through the conventional motions while abandoning all hope of success, and **retreatists** (like dropouts or hermits) renounce the culture's goals and means entirely and live outside conventional norms altogether. At the far end of the continuum, **rebels** reject the cultural definitions of success and the normative means of achieving it and advocate radical alternatives to the existing social order.

For example, consider the characters in the 1999 film *Office Space*, a comedy that satirizes a large, bureaucracy-

Structural Strain Characters in the comedy *Office Space* exemplify Merton's categories of deviants. Peter Gibbons (right) is an innovator who plans to rob the company and thwart his conformist manager, Bill Lumbergh (left).

laden business. In the film, conformity is represented by Bill Lumbergh, a high-ranking boss who has apparently attained his position by following the rules of the organization. The protagonist, Peter Gibbons, is an innovator who spends most of the movie attempting to find meaning and fulfillment in a job that increasingly makes little sense. Rather than adhering to the bizarre and elaborate rules within his organization, Peter comes up with a scheme to rob the company. One of the most humorous characters in the movie, Milton, is a ritualist. Milton shows up to work every day and puts up with a lot of abuse from his superiors even though, as we soon learn, he was fired five years ago and never removed from the payroll. Peter's neighbor Lawrence provides an example of a retreatist: he doesn't work in an office at all. By the end of the movie, Peter realizes that he won't be happy working in a bureaucratized organization. He rebels by taking a lower-paying job as a construction worker and finds fulfillment in his personal relationships instead.

Conflict Theory

Conflict theorists, who study inequalities of wealth and power, note that inequalities are present in our definitions of deviance as well. In other words, they believe that rules are applied unequally and that punishments for rule violators are unequally distributed: those at the top are subject to different rules and sanctions than those nearer the bottom, and the behaviors of less powerful groups and individuals are more likely to be criminalized than the behaviors of the powerful. Norms, rules, and laws are used to regulate the behavior of individuals and groups. This process is known as **social control**, and can be either informal, as in the exercise of control through customs, norms, and expectations, or formal, as in the exercise of control through laws or other official regulations. Both formal social control and informal social control can be exercised unequally in a hierarchical society, and this is what conflict theory is concerned with when it comes to the topic of deviance.

Sociologist William Chambliss looked at the history of vagrancy laws to demonstrate the relationship between power and deviance. According to Chambliss (1973), vagrancy laws have always been used to target different groups—the homeless, the unemployed,

Social Control The HBO series *The Wire* is set in Baltimore and focuses on topics such as drug dealing, government corruption, and failed school systems. How might a conflict theorist analyze this scene?

differential association theory Edwin Sutherland's hypothesis that we learn to be deviant through our associations with deviant peers

racial minorities—depending on who seemed most threatening to the elites at the time. When preparing for big events like political conventions or televised sports tournaments, for instance, local police officers may sweep "undesirables" from downtown areas so that a city appears to be free from panhandlers, drug users, hookers, or the homeless (at least until the cameras are turned off).

As recently as 2003, some U.S. states still imposed heterosexuality on their citizens through antisodomy laws, which prohibited any sexual acts that did not lead to procreation. While in theory antisodomy laws could include acts like masturbation and heterosexual oral sex, in practice these laws are generally imposed against same-sex partners. Before the Supreme Court repealed all state antisodomy laws in *Lawrence vs. Texas* (2003), sexual acts done in the privacy of your own home could be penalized with fines and jail time in states like Virginia, Michigan, and Texas. From a conflict theorist perspective, antisodomy laws are a way for the heterosexual majority to control homosexuals.

As a final example, in 2006, Rochester, New York, had the highest murder rate per capita in the entire state, including New York City. The mayor, Robert Duffy, proposed a new law that would require all young people age sixteen and under living within city limits to be off the streets from 11:00 P.M. to 6:00 A.M. during the summer break from school.

Because statistics have shown that more crime occurs during the summer among youth living in the city, Duffy believed that the curfew would reduce violence. Not only does the curfew demonstrate ageism, in that control is wielded by adults over relatively powerless youth, but also classism, as the curfew applies only to kids who live in the city, leaving wealthier teens in the suburbs free to do what they like. Unfortunately, there is a good deal of evidence to support the conflict theorists' argument that rules are applied unequally in our hierarchical society.

Symbolic Interactionism

While conflict theorists and functionalists focus on inequalities and the social functions of deviance, interactionists consider the way that interpersonal relationships and everyday interactions shape definitions of deviance.

DIFFERENTIAL ASSOCIATION THEORY One such approach is Edwin Sutherland's **differential association theory** (Sutherland 1939; Sutherland et al. 1992), which asserts that we learn to be deviant through our interactions with others who break the rules. This is the theory of deviance that your parents subscribed to when you were a teenager: don't hang out with the bad kids! Simple peer pressure by those you associate with can lead to deviant behavior. For instance an athlete who uses steroids to help build strength might

TABLE 6.1	Theory in Everyday Life	
PERSPECTIVE	**APPROACH TO DEVIANCE**	**CASE STUDY: PLAGIARISM**
STRUCTURAL-FUNCTIONALISM	Deviance clarifies moral boundaries and promotes social cohesion.	Punishing those who plagiarize separates those who should be in college from those who aren't responsible enough.
Structural Strain Theory	An individual's position in society determines whether she has the means to achieve goals or must otherwise turn to deviance.	A student's attitude about plagiarizing depends on whether she has the means to write the paper.
CONFLICT THEORY	Definitions and rules of deviance are applied unequally based on power.	Students with fewer resources are punished more harshly and have fewer options afterward; students with more money or connections can either transfer to another school or rely on parents for help.
SYMBOLIC INTERACTIONISM	The definition of deviance is relative and depends on the culture, time period, and situation	Plagiarism may be labeled as deviant in U.S. courses but not in Russia or India.
Differential Association Theory	Deviance is learned through interactions with others who break the rules.	Students learn to cheat because they hang out with other students who plagiarize.
Labeling Theory	Deviance is determined by the reactions of others; applying deviant labels to an individual may lead them to further deviance.	A student who is caught plagiarizing may come to believe she is unable to write without cheating.

also influence his teammate to start "doping" although this practice is banned in most sports. Have you ever been influenced to do something deviant that you would have never tried on your own?

This theory of deviance seems at first glance to be pretty sensible—interacting often with those who break the rules would seem to socialize an individual into their rule-breaking culture. But, as it turns out, not all who hang out with deviants become deviant themselves, and plenty of people who engage in deviant acts have never consorted with other rule-breakers. Also, in cases where deviance is not the result of a willful act (mental illness, for example), a learning theory such as this one is not a useful explanation. While differential association theory seeks to explain "why they do it," it cannot fully explain every case of deviant behavior—nor can any theory of deviance.

LABELING THEORY Howard Becker's **labeling theory** (1963) proposes that deviance is not inherent in any act, belief, or condition; instead, it is determined by the social context. A man who kills an intruder who is attacking his child may be labeled a hero, while a man who kills a cashier in the process of robbing a store may be labeled a villain. Even though the act of homicide is the same, the way the person is treated differs greatly depending on the label.

Labeling theory recognizes that labels will vary depending on the culture, time period, and situation. David Rosenhan's study "On Being Sane in Insane Places" (1973) provides a striking demonstration of the power of labeling and the importance of context. Rosenhan and seven other researchers gained admission to psychiatric hospitals as patients. Other than falsifying their names and occupations, the eight subjects gave honest answers to all but one of the questions in the entrance examination; they all complained of hearing voices, a symptom often linked to schizophrenia. Nevertheless, the subjects felt certain that once they were hospitalized, they would be quickly exposed as "pseudo-patients," not really mentally ill.

In fact, the opposite turned out to be true. Once admitted, the pseudopatients turned immediately to the task of getting themselves discharged—and failed miserably. Although they behaved as normally and pleasantly as possible, doctors and nurses continued to treat them as mentally ill patients in need of treatment. No amount of explanation on the part of the pseudopatients could convince the hospital staff of their sanity (though, in an interesting twist, it was usually obvious to the other patients). When they were finally discharged (after one to seven weeks!), it was not because the staff had finally seen through the deception; they were all released with their schizophrenia "in remission." As Rosenhan concludes, "Once labeled schizophrenic, the pseudopatient

was stuck with that label" (1973, p. 253). The effects of this "sticky" deviant label on actual patients can follow them through their lives, even after they leave the hospital.

Labeling theory is also concerned with how individuals think of themselves once a deviant label has been applied. Recall Cooley's concept of the "looking-glass self": how we perceive ourselves depends in part on how others see us, so if others react to us as deviant, we are likely to internalize that label (even if we object to it). Applying deviant labels can also lead to further deviance, as a person moves from **primary deviance** (the thing that gets her labeled in the first place) to **secondary deviance** (a deviant identity or career) (Lemert 1951). **Tertiary deviance** occurs when the person labeled deviant rejects the notion of deviance entirely and redefines her "deviant" attributes or behavior as normal.

If you've watched an episode of VH1's *Celebrity Rehab with Dr. Drew*, you've seen examples of all three types of deviance. In the show, washed-up celebrities who suffer from addiction check themselves into a fancy rehab center, and we follow the ups and downs of their treatment over the course

labeling theory Howard Becker's idea that deviance is a consequence of external judgments, or labels, that modify the individual's self-concept and change the way others respond to the labeled person

primary deviance in labeling theory, the initial act or attitude that causes one to be labeled deviant

secondary deviance in labeling theory, the subsequent deviant identity or career that develops as a result of being labeled deviant

tertiary deviance redefining the stigma associated with a deviant label as a positive phenomenon

Labeling Theory VH1's reality show *Celebrity Rehab with Dr. Drew* centers on celebrities struggling with addiction and shows how their illness influences their identity and how others perceive them.

Changing the World

Tuy Sobil and the Tiny Toones of Phnom Penh

All around the world, from Latin America to Southeast Asia and beyond, there is an unusual problem brewing. American-style gang activity is appearing in new areas, complete with turf wars, drug dealing, graffiti, and violent crime, just like in troubled American cities. What's really unusual about this new gang problem is its source. As you might expect, it came from the United States, but instead of local teenagers imitating gangsters they see in the American media, places like Cambodia and El Salvador are getting an influx of actual gang members, unwilling immigrants deported from the United States.

In 1996, following the first attack on the World Trade Center and with an election to think about, Congress passed the Illegal Immigration Reform and Immigrant Responsibility Act, which dramatically increased the number of offenses for which noncitizens could be deported, sending many into permanent exile for nonviolent misdemeanor offenses, even if they served their sentence and had a perfect record of good conduct (Human Rights Watch 2007). The law was especially hard on families, as it was made retroactive, so legal immigrants who had committed crimes years ago were suddenly eligible to be deported, with no grounds for appeal.

Although they may seem less sympathetic, some of the most poignant cases involve troubled young people or gang members who have been deported back to countries of which they had little or no memory. El Salvador and Cambodia in particular have produced many troublesome cases, because those countries produced a great many refugees who differ from traditional immigrants in a number of ways. While immigrants purposefully seek out a new home, refugees are driven by violence and starvation. They often arrive in a new country with physical and psychological scars and little or no support, and find themselves living in bewildering new cit-ies. The children of such refugees are often at-risk as youth and sometimes end up involved in gangs, which now can lead them to be deported back to their "native" countries.

The effort to fight gangs like Mara Salvatrucha, which was "founded by Central Americans who fled wars at home in the 1980s and landed in U.S. ghettos without work or protection from existing gangs," or the Tiny Little Rascals gang, the main Asian gang on the West Coast, has led to a vast increase in the number of deportations for criminal behavior, including many legal residents who had never applied for citizenship (Lakshmanan 2006). Many of the young men who have been deported this way have only the haziest memories of their "homelands" and had never thought of themselves as anything but American. Most are not fluent in any language but English. Many had moved to the United States as infants, and in the case of some, had been born in refugee camps, and had never before lived in the country to which they were "re"-patriated.

This was the situation that Tuy Sobil faced following a conviction for armed robbery at age eighteen. After spending ten years in various jails and immigration facilities, Sobil was repatriated to Cambodia, a country he had never set foot in before, having been born in a refugee camp in Thailand after his parents fled the Khmer Rouge. He has not seen any of his family since then, including his son, and deportees are legally barred from ever reentering the United States. His nickname is K.K., gang-style initials for "Crazy Crip," after the gang he had belonged to when he lived in Long Beach, California. But since arriving in Cambodia he has reinvented himself, leaving his gang persona behind. Like many other deportees, he arrived in Phnom Penh with few resources, but he has persevered and even triumphed in his new home. After working as a drug coun-selor, he founded the Tiny Toones, a break-dancing troupe

Tiny Toones Break-Dancing School Tuy Sobil, aka K.K. (far right), started the break-dancing school in Cambodia after being deported from Long Beach, California.

he hopes can "help save Cambodian street kids from the sort of dead-end detour he took" (Krausz 2007). With little more than a boom box and the skills he learned as a teenage "b-boy" (slang for break dancer) he found a way to organize and teach hundreds of street kids who had nowhere else to turn. Having grown up in a harsh environment, with few hopes for success, Sobil understands the needs of the street children of Cambodia. And he hopes that break dancing can help kids stay out of trouble and build a sense of community based on positive achievements. Learning head spins, one-hand hops, elbow tracks, flairs, halos, air tracks and windmills brings a little slice of old-school hip hop flair to the streets of Cambodia and helps provide the

hundreds of members of the troupe with a place to go and a positive focus for their energy.

Sobil has been supported in his efforts by a variety of international nonprofit groups, and at least one group of American students has journeyed to Cambodia to make a film about him and the Tiny Toones. The Tiny Toones performed at a Christmas party for the American embassy in 2007 and were then invited to visit the United States, a trip that Sobil can't make with them, as he is legally barred from ever entering the United States again. But ultimately he has succeeded, and despite the desperate poverty and hardships faced by the children he mentors, he continues to work at changing the world, one b-boy at a time.

of the season. Their drug use, which is illegal, is an example of primary deviance, and their recognition that they are addicts is an example of secondary deviance.

Although deviant labels are sticky—they are hard to shake—it is sometimes possible for an individual to turn what could have been a negative identity into a positive one. John Kitsuse (1980) calls this tertiary deviance, and The Celebrity Rehab cast demonstrates this level of deviance as well. Every once in awhile, one of the celebrities decides that they're no longer interested in undergoing rehab, often arguing that there's really nothing wrong with their drug use, and that they should be able to indulge in it as they see fit.

Some of the most exciting, but also disturbing, research on labeling theory has focused on **self-fulfilling prophecy**, a term coined by Robert Merton in his 1948 article of the same name. Merton's concept was derived from the so-called Thomas theorem, formulated by sociologist W. I. Thomas in 1928, which held that "if men define situations as real, they are real in their consequences." From this theorem, Merton developed his notion of the self-fulfilling prophecy, which is basically a prediction that causes itself to come true merely by being stated. He offers the example of a bank in the Depression-era 1930s that collapsed through "a rumor of insolvency," when enough investors became convinced that the bank was out of money (1948, p. 194).

Merton argues that the self-fulfilling prophecy can be used to explain racial and ethnic conflict in the United States, and subsequent research has borne him out. For example, Elijah Anderson's *Streetwise* (1990) details how the police and community perceive black male inner-city teenagers as a criminal element, with the result that they are more likely to be arrested than other teenagers, and citizens are also more likely to report black males for crimes. This cloud of suspicion that surrounds black urban teens requires them to defend their innocence in situations that other teens can negotiate with little or no difficulty. Young black males are also more likely to be incarcerated, which only feeds the public image of criminality. The racial discrimination and profiling by police and the community thus lead to a negative cycle that is difficult to break.

Labels alone are not 100 percent deterministic, and prophecies are not always self-fulfilling. But in our society, deviant labels can override other aspects of individual identity and exert powerful effects on self-image, treatment by others, and even social and institutional policies.

Stigma and Deviant Identity

In ancient Greece, criminals and slaves were branded with hot irons, making a mark called a **stigma**, from the Greek word for tattoo. The stigma was meant to serve as an outward indication that there was something shameful about the bearer, and to this day we continue to use the term to signify some disgrace or failing. Although we no longer live in a society where we are forced to wear our rule violations branded onto our bodies, stigmatized identities still carry serious social consequences.

Stigma, a central concept in the sociology of deviance, was analyzed and elaborated by Erving Goffman in his book of the same name (1962). Once an individual has been labeled as deviant, he is stigmatized and acquires what Goffman calls a "spoiled identity." There are three main types of stigma: physical (including physical or mental impairments), moral (signs of a flawed character), and tribal (membership in a discredited or oppressed group). Almost any departure from the norm can have a stigmatizing effect, including a physical disability, a past battle with alcohol or mental illness, time served in jail, or sexual transgressions. Goffman recognizes that what may once have been a stigmatized identity may change over time or may vary according to culture or social context. Being black or Jewish is a stigma only if one lives in a racist or anti-Semitic society. In a community entirely populated by African Americans, it is white people who may be stigmatized; an all-Jewish enclave may see non-Jews as outside the norm. Goffman is careful to note that not all stigmatized identities are just or deserved—only that

Imitation of Life In this 1959 film, Juanita Moore (right) plays a widow whose daughter, played by Susan Kohner (left), tries to pass as white and shuns her mother.

they are specific to the norms and prejudices of a particular group, time period, or context.

Goffman was particularly interested in the effects of stigmatization on individual identity and interactions with others. At the macro level, society does not treat the stigmatized very well; if you suffer from depression, for example, you may find that your health insurance does not cover your treatment. At the micro level, you may also find that your friends don't fully understand your depression-related problems. In fact, you may find yourself working to keep others from finding out that you are depressed or receiving treatment for depression precisely in order to avoid such situations. Having a stigmatized identity—of any sort—makes navigating the social world difficult.

Passing

How can stigmatized individuals negotiate the perils of everyday interaction? One strategy analyzed by Goffman is called **passing**, or concealing stigmatizing information. The allusion to racial passing is entirely intended—Goffman means to call to mind the experiences of light-skinned African Americans who, for more than 300 years and particularly in the decades before the Civil Rights Movement of the 1960s, sought access to the privileges of whiteness (and relief from discrimination) by concealing their racial heritage and passing as white. The case of racial passing is instructive in developing an understanding of all types of passing—such as the passing a depressed person might engage in to hide his condition.

In-Group Orientation

Not everyone can pass, though, because not all stigma is concealable. While it may be possible to conceal your status as an ex-convict or victim of rape, it is more difficult to conceal extreme shortness or obesity. And while some people cannot pass, others refuse to do so as a matter of principle. These people don't believe that their identities should be seen as deviant, and they certainly don't believe that they should have to change or conceal those identities just to make "normals" feel more comfortable. They have what Goffman calls an **in-group orientation**—they reject the standards that mark them as deviant and may even actively propose new standards in which their special identities are well within the normal range. For example, such groups as ACT UP (the AIDS Coalition to Unleash Power) and NAAFA (the National Association to Advance Fat Acceptance) have allowed members of stigmatized groups to feel greater self-esteem and to unite in fighting against prejudice and discrimination. Activism might also take a more indi-

vidual form of merely being "out," open and unapologetic about one's identity. This in itself can be difficult and exhausting (as passing is); however, those with an in-group orientation see it as a more responsible, genuine, and powerful way to address society's changing definitions of deviance.

passing presenting yourself as a member of a different group than the stigmatized group you belong to

in-group orientation among stigmatized individuals, the rejection of prevailing judgments or prejudice and the development of new standards that value their group identity

outsiders according to Howard Becker, those labeled deviant and subsequently segregated from "normal" society

Deviance Avowal and Voluntary Outsiders

Under most circumstances, people reject the deviant label and what it seems to imply about their personal identity. However, there are some who *choose* to be called a deviant. Those who belong to a particular subculture, for example— whether outlaw biker, rock musician, or eco-warrior—may celebrate their membership in a deviant group. Howard Becker (1963) refers to such individuals as **outsiders**, people living in one way or another outside mainstream society. They may pass among "normals," continuing to work and participate in everyday life. Or their deviant identity may have become a master status, thus preventing them from interacting along conventional lines; when this happens, a person's deviance may be thought to reveal

United Against Prejudice Groups like the National Association to Advance Fat Acceptance embrace an in-group orientation and reject the standards that mark them as deviant.

deviance avowal process by which an individual self-identifies as deviant and initiates her own labeling process

his underlying nature. For instance, members of the punk subculture, easily identified by their distinctive look, are generally assumed to be loud troublemakers, whatever their individual personality traits may be.

Some potential deviants may actually initiate the labeling process against themselves or provoke others to do so, a condition Ralph Turner (1972) calls **deviance avowal**. Turner suggests that it may be useful to conceive of deviance as a role rather than as an isolated behavior that violates a single norm. And in some cases, it may be beneficial for an individual to identify with the deviant role. In the Alcoholics Anonymous program, for example, the first step in recovery is for a member to admit that she is an alcoholic. Since total abstinence from drinking is the goal, only those who believe they have a drinking problem and willingly accept the label of alcoholic can take the suggested steps toward recovery.

Deviance avowal can also help a person avoid the pressures of having to adopt certain conventional norms, or what Turner calls the "neutralization of commitment." For instance, a recovering alcoholic might resist taking a typical nine-to-five job, claiming that the stress of corporate work had always made him drink before. Another recovering alcoholic who refuses to attend family gatherings might offer as an excuse that she can't be around family because they drink at every occasion. In such ways, people become voluntary outsiders, finding it preferable to be a deviant in spite of the prevailing norms of mainstream society.

features accounts of thousands of recovered alcoholics as well as AA's basic twelve-step program. The first 164 pages have remained virtually the same since the first printing in 1939, but in each subsequent edition, the personal stories of additional members have been added. These stories are intended to help newcomers to the program to identify with and relate to the lives of other recovering alcoholics.

For this workshop, you will focus on "Women Suffer Too," one of the first stories published in the Big Book. The title refers to the fact that years ago many people believed that only men were alcoholics. The story is told from the perspective of a sober alcoholic looking back on her life and understanding that through the process of deviance avowal (by accepting her alcoholism) she was able to transform a negative past into a positive life.

The text of the story can be found in the Big Book or accessed online at silkworth.net/bbstories/2nd/222_229 .html. Read it in its entirety, keeping in mind how the study of life histories or oral histories can reveal important features of societal norms and everyday life. Pay close attention to how the story describes both deviant behavior and the process of deviance avowal, and consider the following questions.

- Identify the instances of deviance described in the writer's story. Why do we consider these behaviors deviant?

- In what ways was she in denial, or actively trying to disavow the deviant behavior?

- At what point did she engage in deviance avowal?

- How did deviance avowal affect her self-concept?

- In what ways did deviance avowal allow her to consider her past in a different light?

- How has her deviant identity become a positive part of her life?

There are two options for completing this Data Workshop.

- *Option 1 (informal)*: Prepare some written notes based on your answers to the questions above that you can refer to during in-class discussions. Share your reactions and conclusions with other students in small-groups. Listen for any differences in each other's insights.

- *Option 2 (formal)*: Write a three- to four-page essay answering the questions above. Include your own reactions to the story. Make sure to refer to specific passages that support your analysis.

DATA WORKSHOP

ANALYZING EVERYDAY LIFE

Personal Stories of AA Members

In this Data Workshop, you will examine the life history of selected members of Alcoholics Anonymous in order to analyze the process of deviance avowal. Research by Melvin Pollner and Jill Stein has focused on the role of narrative storytelling as a key feature of reconstructing the alcoholic's sense of self and turning a stigmatized identity into a valued asset in the process of recovery (Pollner and Stein 1996, 2001). You will be doing a content analysis of an existing source (see Chapter 2 for a review of this research method). The stories appear in *Alcoholics Anonymous* (1939/2001), often referred to by members as the "Big Book," which

In Relationships

Forming Friendships in the Face of Stigma

In her book *Autobiography of a Face* (1994), poet Lucy Grealy tells the story of her struggle with childhood cancer and the disfiguring surgery that resulted. Because of a series of operations that removed one-third of her jaw, she survived Ewing's sarcoma but grew to adulthood looking—and feeling—very different from her peers.

When other kids reacted negatively to her scars, Grealy tried to cover them with turtlenecks, scarves, and hats but couldn't completely conceal her disfigurement. Boys at school yelled at her to "take off that monster mask!" Ironically, the only time she felt perfectly comfortable was on Halloween, when she could wear a mask and feel just like part of the crowd. Her high school years were lonely—she had a hard time making friends and worried that she would never have a boyfriend or be in love. She felt as though she fit in only when she was with her family—or on the children's ward in a hospital.

At Sarah Lawrence College, a private school just outside New York City, Grealy finally found a group of friends with whom she felt comfortable, who were themselves outsiders:

> To be on the fringe at a school as fringy as Sarah Lawrence was itself an accomplishment, but it was this very quality that I loved most about my friends. They wore their mantles as "outsiders" with pride, whether because of their politics, their sexuality, or anything else that makes a person feel outside of the norm. Their self-definition was the very thing that put me at ease with them. I didn't feel judged. (p. 196)

Grealy finally experienced real friendship when she was able to feel accepted by others, and she felt this only with those who were similarly stigmatized. While they didn't share her specific facial disfigurement, they each felt marginalized or abnormal in some way. They were, in Goffman's terms, "the own"—those who share the experience of being stigmatized and thus find comfort and safety in each other's presence.

Lucy Grealy

Grealy suffered through several more grueling reconstructive surgeries on her face, which left her in chronic pain. After college, she enrolled in the Iowa Writer's Workshop, where her roommate was another student she had known from Sarah Lawrence, Ann Patchett. The two women became best friends and, as they moved from the Midwest to New York in pursuit of their careers, embarked on a relationship that helped define their lives and work over the next twenty years. Grealy went on to win awards for her poetry and essays and wrote her critically acclaimed and hugely successful memoir. Patchett, too, became successful as an award-winning novelist (Patchett 2001).

Unfortunately, Lucy Grealy's story does not have a happy ending. Ultimately, fame, fortune, and friendship were not enough to save her from her own demons. Ann Patchett's book *Truth & Beauty: A Friendship* (2004) details Grealy's decline into depression, drug addiction, and repeated attempts to commit suicide. She died in December 2002 from what was ruled an "accidental" overdose of heroin.

It would be too simplistic to conclude that Grealy killed herself because of the years of suffering she had endured as a result of her stigmatized identity. There are too many factors involved in her complex life story to assign blame with any assurance. Perhaps she would have become depressed or addicted even if she hadn't been disfigured. Perhaps it was the physical pain rather than the psychic pain that became too much for her. Whatever the reasons, these two books about Lucy Grealy's life and death reveal in gritty and compelling details the desperate desire to fit in and the lengths to which this woman went in order to pass as "normal" in society.

Studying Deviance

When studying deviance, sociologists have often focused on the most obvious forms of deviant behavior—crime, mental illness, and sexual deviance. This "nuts and sluts" approach (Liazos 1972) tends to focus on the deviance of the poor and powerless, while accepting the values and norms of the powerful in an unacknowledged way. Social scientists tended to apply definitions of deviance uncritically in their research and failed to question the ways in which the definitions themselves may have perpetuated inequalities and untruths.

One sociologist at the University of California, Berkeley, David Matza (1969), set out to remedy this situation. Matza urged social scientists to set aside their preconceived notions in order to understand deviant phenomena on their own terms—a perspective he called "naturalism." Verta Taylor and Leila Rupp, for example, spent three years with a dozen drag queens in order to gain perspective for their research in *Drag Queens at the 801 Cabaret*—at one point, they even performed onstage. Matza's fundamental admonition to those studying deviance is that they must appreciate the diversity and complexity of a particular social world—the world of street gangs, drug addicts, strippers, fight clubs, outlaw bikers, homeless people, or the transgendered. If such a world is approached as a simple social pathology that needs correcting, the researcher will never fully understand it. A sociological perspective requires that we seek insight without applying judgment—a difficult task indeed.

The Foreground of Deviance: The Emotional Attraction of Doing Bad Deeds

Most sociological perspectives on deviance focus on aspects of a person's background that would influence him to act in deviant ways. This is the case with both functionalist and conflict perspectives: for example, many sociological studies of crime make the case that youth with limited access to education may be more likely to turn to dealing drugs or theft. Labeling theory also suggests that a person's social location is a crucial determinant: it shapes how others see the person, as well as his or her own self-view, and these perceptions can lead a person from primary to secondary deviance and into a deviant career. One of the main problems with such theories, however, is that they can't explain why some people with backgrounds that should incline them to deviance never actually violate any rules, while others with no defining background factors do become deviant.

The Seduction of Crime Jack Katz's research on the emotional rush produced by crime might help explain why celebrities like Lindsey Lohan would steal a necklace from a jewelry store.

Approaches that focus exclusively on background factors neglect one very important element—the deviant's own in-the-moment experience of committing a deviant act, what sociologist Jack Katz refers to as the "foreground" of deviance. In *The Seductions of Crime* (1988), Katz looks at how emotionally seductive crime can be, how shoplifting or even committing murder might produce a particular kind of rush that becomes the very reason for carrying out the act. For example, what shoplifters often seek is not the DVD or perfume as much as the "sneaky thrill" of stealing it. Initially drawn to stealing by the thought of just how easy it might be, the shoplifter tests her ability to be secretly deviant—in public—while appearing to be perfectly normal. This perspective explains why the vast majority of shoplifters are not from underprivileged backgrounds but are people who could easily afford the stolen items. How else might we explain why a wealthy and famous actress such as Lindsey Lohan would try to steal a necklace from a jewelry store?

Similarly, muggers' and robbers' actions reveal that they get more satisfaction from their crimes than from the things they steal. They are excited by the sense of superiority they gain by setting up and playing tricks on their victims. In fact, they can come to feel morally superior, thinking that their victims deserve their fate because they are less observant and savvy. Even murderous rages can be seen as seductive ways to overcome an overwhelming sense of humiliation. A victim of adultery, for example, may kill instead of simply ending the relationship because murder, or "righteous slaughter," feels like the most appropriate response. In effect, he is seduced by the possibility of becoming a powerful avenger rather than remaining a wounded and impotent victim.

Katz's foreground model of deviance deepens our appreciation for the complexity of deviant behavior and reminds us that social actors are not mere products of their environment but active participants in creating meaningful experiences for themselves even if harmful to others.

Deviance in a New Interactional Context: Cyberbullying

Although parents and schools have been worried about cyberbullying ever since children and teenagers started using the internet, the phenomenon moved to the forefront of national consciousness after the suicide of thirteen-year-old Megan Meier in October of 2006. Megan had received a MySpace message from a boy named Josh, who said that he lived nearby but that his family didn't have a phone. During the next several weeks, they sent messages back and forth and seemed to have become close very quickly. Then, without warning, Josh started taunting and abusing her. Megan was devastated and hung herself in her closet. Several weeks later the Meiers learned that "Josh" was not a real person and that the MySpace account had been created by their neighbor, Lori Drew, in order to get back at Megan for snubbing her daughter. But regardless of who was sending the messages, Megan was a victim of **cyberbullying**, the use of electronic media (web pages, social networking sites, e-mail, instant messengers, and cell phones) to tease, harass, threaten, or humiliate someone.

The one thing that seems beyond doubt is that cyberbullying is on the rise, with girls and older teens more likely to be at risk. A report from the Centers for Disease Control found 50 percent more teens reported being the victims of electronic harassment in 2005 compared to 2000. In 2009, somewhere between 9 and 35 percent of all young people said they had been the victim of cyberbullying (Hertz and David-Ferdon 2009). As more schools require laptops, and computers and cell phones become a more important part of the daily life of children and teenagers, this trend will surely continue.

Although cyberbullying is still less common than its off-line equivalent, in several ways it's more frightening. Like

Cyberbullying Tina Meier holds two pictures of her daughter Megan, who committed suicide after receiving cruel messages on MySpace.

every phenomenon created by the Information Revolution, cyberbullying (sometimes called "electronic aggression") is faster and connects more people than off-line activity. Traditional bullying usually happens at school, while cyberbullying can happen anytime and in the privacy of your own home. Likewise, the effects are longer lasting. One of the most common forms of cyberbullying involves spreading rumors about someone. Traditional bullying relied on word of mouth or the proverbial graffiti on the bathroom wall to do this. But word of mouth is limited, and only so many people can read nasty comments scrawled on the stall in the bathroom before the janitor washes it off. Online, there is almost no limit to how many people might see a nasty comment, even if it is later taken down.

So far, most research has focused on cyberbullying that is perpetrated by someone who knows the victim in real life, but there have always been internet bullies

cyberbullying the use of electronic media (web pages, social networking sites, e-mail, instant messengers, and cell phones) to tease, harass, threaten, or humiliate someone

(or "trolls") who seek to abuse people they've never met or only have encountered online. For example, after Megan Meier's suicide, a blog was created called "Megan Had It Coming" and contained posts from a cast of characters who purported to know Megan, all expressing a distinct lack of remorse. Later it was established that the entire blog was really the work of a 32-year-old computer programmer from Seattle with no connection to anyone involved in the case. As more and more of people's lives play out online, this sort of cyberbullying will only become more common.

DATA WORKSHOP

ANALYZING MASS MEDIA AND POPULAR CULTURE
Norm Breaking on Television

It's clear that deviance is a fascinating subject not only for sociologists but for television viewers as well. In recent years, shows have begun to feature people breaking every kind of social norm from folkways to taboos. Some obvious exam-ples might include MTV's reality series *16 and Pregnant*, which shows what happens when high schoolers deal with pregnancy and parenthood, or A&E's reality series *Dog the Bounty Hunter*, whose criminals are attempting to evade justice. But it's not just documentaries and reality shows that feature deviance. Various other types of programs like crime dramas *Law and Order* or *Criminal Minds*, newsmagazine programs *Dateline NBC* or *48 Hours*, and even comedies such as *Glee* or *South Park* regularly deal with the pathological or dysfunctional.

Why is there so much deviance on television? Are these shows merely entertainment, or is something more going on here? When we watch them, do we feel morally superior or get some kind of vicarious thrill? Does the experience re-inforce our social norms or serve to break them down?

This Data Workshop asks you to do a content analysis of an existing source, in this case a particular TV show (see Chapter 2 for a review of the research method). You will be documenting the ways in which deviant behavior is portrayed in the show you choose. Choose a show that is on DVD or online, or simply record an episode off TV so that you can watch it multiple times.

Why Is There So Much Deviance on Television? *Glee* portrays high school students who don't always fit into their school's social norms. How does this show serve to reinforce or challenge prevailing social norms?

On the Job

Is "Cash Register Honesty" Good Enough?

While we might like to think that most employees wouldn't take money from the cash register or merchandise from the showroom floor, wouldn't walk away with a laptop computer, drive away with the company car, or filter sales receipts to their own bank account, employee theft is still a major problem. The U.S. Chamber of Commerce estimates that employee theft costs businesses somewhere between $20 billion and $40 billion a year and accounts for about 30 percent of business failures (INC.com 1999). According to research by Michael Cunningham, a professor of psychology at the University of Louisville and a consultant to the security industry, only one in every three potential employees will be completely trustworthy. Of the other two, one may be tempted to steal given the opportunity, while the other will be more or less constantly looking for a chance to get away with taking company property.

Although we may consider ourselves the trustworthy ones, we may not recognize that our own behavior could still be contributing to the billions of dollars lost each year. How? Well, have you ever taken home paper clips, Post-it notes, a pen, or a pad of paper from the office? Made personal copies on the Xerox machine? Used the company computer to surf the net, download MP3s, play solitaire, or send an e-mail message to a friend? Eaten or drunk company products? How about taking a little more time than you're supposed to on your lunch break or leaving work a little early?

It's called **pilfering**, and it happens on the job tens of thousands of times a day. And it all adds up. Most companies consider these kinds of losses as just another factor in the cost of doing business. But how is it that so many people think nothing of these small infractions in spite of prevailing social norms that discourage stealing and while otherwise being upstanding or even exemplary employees?

You could say that these people are practicing "cash register honesty." That is, they draw the line at actually stealing money (or its equivalent) out of the till but don't hesitate to make off with other odds and ends that might have a less easily calculable value. They might be appalled at the suggestion that they are less than honest, especially since everyone else seems to take something (if only internet time) now and then. But is this kind of honesty really enough? Perhaps more employees should strive to adhere to a higher standard. Not because they are necessarily going to be caught by the boss or that they individually are costing the company a lot, but because of the inherent satisfaction of knowing that they are doing the right thing.

What kind of honesty do you practice in the workplace?

Consider the following:

- Who is the intended audience for this program? Why did you choose it?

- What kind of deviance is featured? Give specific examples of situations, scenes, dialogue, or characters, and explain why they are examples of deviance.

- Is the deviance celebrated or condemned?

- How does it make you feel to watch the program?

- What effect do you think the show has on other viewers?

- Do you think the program serves to reinforce or challenge prevailing social norms?

There are two options for completing this Data Workshop.

- *Option 1 (informal)*: Prepare some written notes that you can refer to in small-group discussions. Compare and contrast the analyses of the different programs in your group. What are the similarities and differences between programs?

- *Option 2 (formal)*: Write a three- to four-page essay answering the Workshop questions and reflecting on your own experience in conducting this content analysis. What do you think these shows tell us about contemporary American society and our attitudes toward deviance?

Crime and Punishment

Crime is a particular type of deviance: it is the violation of a norm that has been codified into law for which you could be arrested and imprisoned. Official, state-backed sanctions, such as laws, exert more power over the individual than do non-legal norms. For example, if you risked arrest for gossiping about your roommate, you might think twice about doing it. "Might," however, is the key word here, for the risk of arrest and jail time does not always deter people from breaking laws. In fact, ordinary people break laws every day without really thinking about it (driving faster than the speed limit, drinking while underage, taking pens or pencils home from work). As we saw earlier, being bad can feel good, and even murder can feel "righteous" at the time, depending on the circumstances (Katz 1988).

In the United States, crime is officially measured by the **Uniform Crime Report (UCR)**, the FBI's tabulation of every crime reported by more than 17,000 law enforcement agencies in the country. In particular, the UCR is used to track the "crime index," or the eight offenses considered especially reprehensible in our society. Murder, rape, aggravated assault, and robbery are categorized as **violent crime**. Burglary (theft inside the home), larceny-theft (of personal property), motor vehicle theft, and arson are considered **property crime**. Even though the UCR has been shown to be a flawed system, it is useful in helping to track trends in overall crime as well as particular patterns; it also records the number of arrests made compared with the number of crimes committed, which is the most traditional measure of police effectiveness.

Through the UCR, criminologists are able to make comparisons in crime rates using such variables as year and region. One notable finding is that rates of violent crime declined significantly in the last decade of the twentieth century. The year 1991 saw the highest number of homicides in U.S. history, 24,000. But between 1991 and 2000, there was a dramatic drop of 44 percent in homicide rates, and that number has continued to decline since then. Other findings include the observation that murder rates peak in the months of July and August. Perhaps related to the influence of heat, they are also higher in the southern states. However, southern states also have the lowest median family incomes in the United States, which suggests that class may play a role as well. Murder is committed most frequently by a friend or relative of the victim, seldom by a stranger. Robbery occurs most frequently in urban areas among youth.

Other trends are visible in the UCR as well. Property crimes occur more frequently than violent crime. The most common crime is larceny-theft, with burglary and motor vehicle theft trailing far behind. Although there has also been a decline in rates of property crime in the last decade, it is not as extreme as the drop in violent crime.

Crime and Demographics

When criminologists look at quantitative crime data, which provide information on who is more likely to commit or be a victim of crime, they may learn more about the cause of crime. We should, however, question the assumptions and biases of the data. For example, Robert Merton's theory of the self-fulfilling prophecy prompts us to ask, if society has a tendency to cast certain categories of people as criminal types, will this assumption ensure that they will indeed be labeled and treated like criminals? And, as David Matza warns, will our preconceived notions about a category of people influence our interpretations of numerical data? In this section, we will look at the relationship between crime and demographics like class, age, gender, and race and examine alternate explanations for what may seem like clear numerical fact.

CLASS Statistics consistently tell us that crime rates are higher in poor urban areas than in wealthier suburbs, but these higher crime rates may not actually be the result of increased criminal behavior. Rather, police tend to concentrate their efforts in urban areas, which they assume are more prone to crime, and thus make more arrests there. It appears that social class is more directly related to how citizens are officially treated by the police, courts, and prisons than to which individuals are likely to commit crime. And even if we do accept these statistics as an accurate representation of crime rates, such theorists as Robert Sampson and William Julius Wilson (2005) argue that the same factors that cause an area to become economically and socially disadvantaged also encourage criminal activity. Lack of jobs, lack of after-school child care, and lack of good schools, for example, are all factors that can lead to economic strain and criminal activity.

On the other end of the social class spectrum, **white collar crime** has been defined by sociologist Edwin Sutherland

---

crime a violation of a norm that has been codified into law

Uniform Crime Report (UCR) an official measure of crime in the United States, produced by the FBI's official tabulation of every crime reported by more than 17,000 law enforcement agencies

violent crime crimes in which violence is either the objective or the means to an end, including murder, rape, aggravated assault, and robbery

property crime crimes that did not involve violence, including burglary, larceny-theft, motor vehicle theft, and arson

white collar crime crime committed by a high-status individual in the course of his occupation

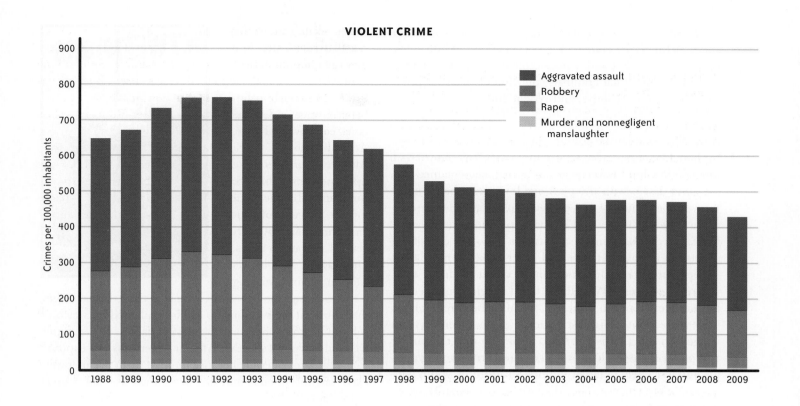

VIOLENT CRIME

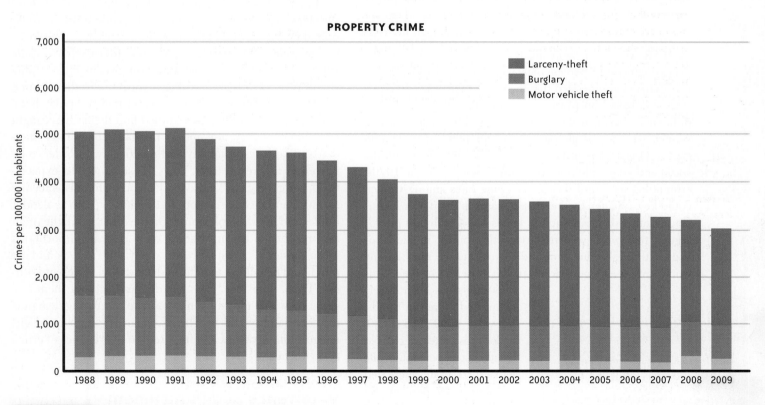

PROPERTY CRIME

FIGURE 6.2 Crime in the United States, 1988–2009

SOURCE: FBI 2010a.

as "a crime committed by a person of respectability and high social status in the course of his occupation." White collar crime can include fraud, embezzlement, or insider trading, and most white collar criminals come from a relatively privileged background (Shover and Wright 2001).

AGE The younger the population, the more likely its members are to commit crimes. Criminologists have shown that this relationship between age and crime has remained stable since 1935, with the peak age for arrests being nineteen. In the United States, thirteen- to seventeen-year-olds make up about 6 percent of the population, yet account for 13 percent of criminal arrests. On the other end of the spectrum, people sixty-five and older make up more than 12 percent of the population and account for fewer than 1 percent of arrests. We call this trend of aging out of crime **desistance**. Here too, however, we must be careful about what we read into official statistics. Since our stereotypical image of a criminal is youthful, it may be that the public and police are more likely to accuse and arrest young people and less likely to target seniors. In addition, youth may commit more visible crimes (like robbery or assault), while older people may commit crimes that are more difficult to detect, like embezzlement or fraud.

GENDER Males are more likely to commit crime. In fact, males comprise 81 percent of all violent crime arrests. Earlier researchers hypothesized that the gender difference in crime rates was based on physical, emotional, and psychological differences between men and women. The logic was that women were too weak, passive, or unintelligent to commit crime. This argument has been replaced by a focus on the social and economic roles of women. Starting in the 1970s, criminologists found that lower crime rates among women could be explained by their lower status in the power hierarchy. Conflict theorists such as James Messerschmidt (1993) argued that once women start gaining power in the labor market through education and income, crime rates among women will rise to more closely match those among men. This hypothesis has been largely supported by recent trends. Between 2000 and 2009, male arrest rates decreased by almost 5 percent, while female arrest rates increased by almost 23 percent. So while at first glance it may seem logical to argue that women's crime rates are lower because of biology, on

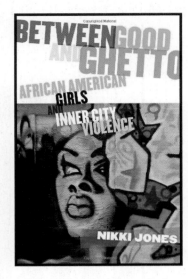

closer examination, we see that social structure plays an important role.

RACE The relationship between race and crime is a controversial one. According to the UCR, African Americans make up 12 percent of the U.S. population but account for 39 percent of violent crimes and 30 percent of property crimes. Once again, sociologists caution against making a link between biology and criminal activity. Instead, they maintain that the relationship can be explained by Merton's self-fulfilling prophecy and by class variables. For example, we could hypothesize that African Americans are exposed to higher rates of crime because more of them live in lower-class neighborhoods—and that here, it is class that matters more than race.

Finally, it is important to recognize that none of these variables—class, age, gender, race—affect crime rates in isolation; they work together to shape the experiences of individuals as well as the larger society. Nikki Jones' ethnographic study on inner-city African American girls in Philadelphia shows how all of these variables contribute to these young women's experiences with violence in their everyday lives. For example, the girls Jones studied find themselves caught in a bind as they attempt to navigate community standards of both respectability and practicality. In order to be perceived as "respectable," they must adhere to expectations, be "good girls," and avoid violence, while also meeting feminine and race-based appearance norms (such as slender bodies and light complexions). On the other hand, the practical realities of life in what are often risky neighborhoods mean these girls must be ready at any time to look and act tough and be willing to fight to defend themselves and others. Thus, their race, class, gender, and age put them in a situation where they must navigate the competing demands of respectability and toughness, balancing their good girl image while always being prepared for the realities of crime and violence.

Deterrence and Punishment

The question of **deterrence** is part of an ongoing debate about our criminal laws. Theorists who maintain that offenders carefully calculate the cost and benefits of each crime

desistance the tendency of individuals to age out of crime over the life course

pilfering stealing minor items in small amounts, often again and again

deterrence an approach to punishment that relies on the threat of harsh penalties to discourage people from committing crimes

SOURCE: INTERNATIONAL CENTRE FOR PRISON STUDIES 2011;
BUREAU OF JUSTICE STATISTICS 2010A.

COUNTRY — PRISONERS PER 10,000 RESIDENTS

BRAZIL 25.3
FEMALE: **7.4%** UNDER 18: **0%**

CANADA 11.7
FEMALE: **4.7%** UNDER 18: **5%**

CHINA 12.2
FEMALE: **5.1%** UNDER 18: **1.4%**

FRANCE 10.2
FEMALE: **3.4%** UNDER 18: **1.1%**

UNITED KINGDOM 15.2
FEMALE: **4.9%** UNDER 18: **1.8%**

INDIA 3.2
FEMALE: **4.1%** UNDER 18: **.03%**

MEXICO 20.0
FEMALE: **4.5%** UNDER 18: **14%**

RUSSIA 56.8
FEMALE: **8.2%** UNDER 18: **.9%**

SOUTH AFRICA 31.6
FEMALE: **2.4%** UNDER 18: **.5%**

USA 74.3
FEMALE: **8.8%** UNDER 18: **.4%**

% OF PRISON POPULATION

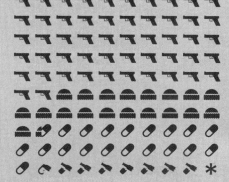

WHO
GOES TO JAIL
IN THE

USA

AND WHAT
ARE THEY
IN FOR?

34.2% 38.2% 20.7%
PRISON POPULATION

64.9% 12.1% 15.8% 7.1%
TOTAL U.S. POPULATION

WHITE, non-hispanic — HISPANIC
BLACK — OTHER

VIOLENT OFFENSE — PROPERTY OFFENSES
DRUG OFFENSES — PUBLIC ORDER
OTHER

argue that punishment has a deterrent effect—that if the punishment seems too severe, people won't commit the crime. That's the logic behind California's controversial "three strikes" law: the punishment for three felonies is an automatic life sentence. While deterrence theory seems practical enough, it is important to note that in matters of sociology, seldom is there such a direct and causal link between two factors; in this case, the cost of punishment vs. the benefit of the crime.

Other justifications for punishment include **retribution**—the notion that society has the right to "get even"—and **incapacitation**, the notion that criminals should be confined or even executed to protect society from further injury. Some argue, though, that society should focus not on punishment but on **rehabilitation**: the prison system should try to reform the criminal so that once released, he will not commit the same crimes again. Each approach to punishment invokes different ideas about who the criminal is and what his relationship is to the larger society: Is he someone who can plan ahead and curb his illegal behavior so as not to face a possible negative outcome? Is she someone who can work toward personal transformation? Is he someone who must be punished quid pro quo? Or should she just be removed from society permanently?

In the United States, the local, state, and federal government bureaucracies responsible for making laws together with the police, courts, and prison systems make up the **criminal justice system**—a system that, like any other social institution, reflects the society in which it operates. This means that the American criminal justice system, while it provides important benefits, such as social control and even employment for its workers, also replicates some of the inequalities of power in our society. The research of Victor Rios focuses on this issue. Rios, a professor of sociology at University of California, Santa Barbara, went from gang member to Ph.D. partly because a teacher intervened and put him in touch with a mentoring program at a local university. Otherwise, Rios believes, he would have become another victim of the "youth control complex," his term for the way a variety of institutions, including law enforcement, the judicial system, and public schools, work together to "criminalize, stigmatize, and punish" working-class youth. Rios believes that the educational system has adopted a self-defeating strategy by adopting the attitudes and tactics of law enforcement, even as law enforcement and the judicial system have turned to increasingly draconian measures. Increasingly, our society attempts to control gang violence and drug use with brute force, but this sort of indiscriminate policing often creates the very crime it is designed to eliminate as "enhanced policing, surveillance, and punitive treatment of youth of color" helps to create a "school-to-prison pipeline" (Rios 2009, p. 151).

In another example, in 2003 seventeen inmates on Illinois's death row were found to be innocent of the crimes for which they had been sentenced to die; some cases involved errors made by overworked or underqualified defense attorneys. Further, more than two-thirds of the inmates were African American, many of them convicted by all-white juries (Ryan 2003). As a result, then-governor George Ryan became convinced that **capital punishment** was unfairly and even wrongly applied in some cases, and he suspended the death penalty altogether. When inequities and errors such as these exist in the criminal justice system, we must question the true meaning of the word "justice" in our society.

"Positive" Deviance?

Are there instances in which a rule violation is actually a principled act that should generate a positive rather than negative reaction? The next two examples are cases of what we might call **positive deviance**. Both individuals broke laws; in hindsight, they are now considered heroes.

The first example is the simple act of civil disobedience by Rosa Parks on December 1, 1955, in Montgomery, Alabama, an act often considered pivotal in launching the Civil Rights Movement. In those days, a Montgomery city ordinance required buses to be segregated: whites sat in front and blacks in the back. Rosa Parks defied the law by refusing to give up her front seat to a white man and move to the back. Her arrest galvanized the black community and triggered a bus boycott and subsequent protests that eventually ended segregation in the South. It is worth recognizing that Parks was not an accidental symbol; she was an experienced activist. In her one small, courageous act of defiance, she served as a catalyst that eventually helped advance the fight against racial discrimination all across America. More than 50 years after the day she had taken her seat on the bus, Parks was awarded the Presidential Medal of Freedom. When she died in 2005, it was front-page news. Her funeral was attended

retribution an approach to punishment that emphasizes retaliation or revenge for the crime as the appropriate goal

incapacitation an approach to punishment that seeks to protect society from criminals by imprisoning or executing them

rehabilitation an approach to punishment that attempts to reform criminals as part of their penalty

criminal justice system a collection of social institutions, such as legislatures, police, courts, and prisons, that create and enforce laws

capital punishment the death penalty

positive deviance actions considered deviant within a given context but are later reinterpreted as appropriate or even heroic by luminaries of all types and races: mayors, members of Congress, presidents, CEOs, clergy, celebrities, and as many others as could fit into the packed church and spill outside its doors.

The second example is the story of three soldiers who put a stop to a massacre during the Vietnam War. On March 16, 1968, the men of Charlie Company, a U.S. battalion under the command of Lieutenant William Calley, stormed into the village of My Lai in South Vietnam on a "search and destroy" mission and opened fire on its civilian inhabitants. The boys and men of the village had gone to tend the fields, leaving only unarmed women, children, and the elderly. Hundreds were killed on that terrible day, in direct violation of military law. Although the soldiers should have ceased fire when they saw that the enemy (members of the Viet Cong) was not present, they obeyed the commands of their leaders and continued ravaging the village. Calley was later convicted in a court-martial; his men, claiming that they were only "following orders," were not held responsible.

The massacre would have continued unchecked had it not been for three other American soldiers—Hugh Thompson, Lawrence Colburn, and Glenn Andreota—who flew their helicopter into the middle of the carnage at My Lai, against the orders of their superiors, and called for back-up help to airlift dozens of survivors to safety. They then turned their guns on their fellow Americans, threatening to shoot if they tried to harm any more villagers. For years, the army tried to cover up the three men's heroism in order to keep the whole ugly truth of My Lai a secret. But finally, in 1998, the men were recognized for their bravery with medals and citations—for having had the courage and skill to perform a perilous rescue and the moral conviction necessary to defy authority as well.

Closing Comments

The sociological study of crime and deviance raises complicated issues of morality and ethics. When we study sensitive topics like rape and alcoholism or vulnerable populations like juvenile delinquents and the mentally ill, we have a responsibility as scholars to recognize the effects our attention may have on the people we study. As David Matza noted, we must try to eschew moral judgments in our work, no matter how difficult that may be. And as our professional code of ethics demonstrates, we must protect the people we study from any negative outcomes. Groups lodged under the rubric of deviance can be disempowered by this label, and policy decisions made on the basis of social science research may further injure an already marginal group. On the other hand, a sociological perspective on deviance and crime provides for the possibility that groups previously labeled and marginalized may someday receive assistance and legitimacy from the larger society as well. The sociological perspective is a powerful tool.

⑤ Need Help Studying?

wwnorton.com/studyspace

Visit StudySpace to access free review materials such as:

- **Vocabulary Flashcards**
- **Diagnostic Review Quizzes**
- **Study Outlines**

QUESTIONS FOR REVIEW

1. Years ago, it was considered deviant in the United States for women to wear pants and for men to wear jewelry like earrings. Today, both are common. What did these notions of deviance say about American norms? What does the fact that these "deviant" behaviors are now normal say about the nature of deviance?

2. There are many ways to be mildly deviant without breaking any laws. How do we sanction minor deviant acts?

3. Think of the last act of deviance you committed and describe how the different sociological theories of deviance would explain it. Which theory fits best, and why?

4. Every cultural group maintains different standards for body modification, and in our society these change rapidly. What kinds of body modification that seem normal to you would appear deviant to your parents or grandparents?

5. Symbolic interactionist theories of deviance focus on the way that interpersonal relationships and everyday interactions shape definitions of deviance. Did you ever find yourself doing deviant things because of your friends? What theory describes this pathway to deviance?

6. Howard Becker's labeling theory focuses on how judgments of deviance are made and the consequences of labeling an individual deviant. Have you witnessed people being labeled as deviant? If so, did the label stick?

7. What are some of the advantages and disadvantages of passing? Are there ways in which you pass? What effect do you think passing has on those who disguise their stigmatized identities?

8. Have you ever known someone to reject the "deviant" label and turn his negative identity into a positive one? What was the deviant identity? What term describes this sort of deviance? Do you know anyone who has embraced a stigmatized role through deviance avowal? How might these strategies be useful to individuals?

9. The United States has the dubious distinction of leading every other nation in both the largest total number and largest percentage of its population incarcerated. Why do you think America has more prisoners than any other country?

10. Provide a real-life example of positive deviance (other than the ones described in the chapter). What norms were violated? What was the outcome? Does your belief system affect whether you perceive this deviance as positive? (How might someone else have viewed it as negative?)

SUGGESTIONS FOR FURTHER EXPLORATION

Barthelme, Frederick, and Steven Barthelme. 2001. *Double Down: Reflections on Gambling and Loss*. San Diego, CA: Harvest/HBJ Books. A remarkable memoir of a gambling problem that cost the two brothers $250,000 in just a few years. The book explores the personal appeal of gambling and explains the social changes that allowed riverboat gambling to return to Mississippi.

Becker, Howard S. 1953. "Becoming a Marihuana User." *American Journal of Sociology*, vol. 59 (November): 235–243.

Describes the way that deviant behaviors are learned, in terms of both practical technique and learned enjoyment. Becker argues that deviance should not be explained away through preexisting psychological traits but rather should be understood as learned though experience.

Cohen, Rob, and David Wollock. 2001. *Etiquette for Outlaws*. New York: Harper Paperbacks. This book and the web site www .etiquetteforoutlaws.com provide a rather racy field guide to contemporary deviance, detailing the unspoken rules and proper manners for engaging in numerous deviant behaviors, including gambling, smoking, drinking, stripping, fighting, and other vices.

Foucault, Michel. 1995. *Discipline and Punish: The Birth of the Prison*. New York: Vintage. Analyzes the ways that changing social structures lead to changes in the nature of punishment, which has tended away from public torture and toward private imprisonment. Be warned, though, the first chapter describes an execution in France in 1775 that would be considered horribly deviant today!

Grand Theft Auto. Rockstar Games. A video game series in which the player controls a character in the employ of organized crime. Throughout the game, the player is rewarded for committing deviant and criminal acts. (Warning: Some of these are rated Mature.) What does this game say about societal norms and deviance? How do video games affect players?

Hegi, Ursula. 1995. *Stones from the River*. New York: Simon & Schuster. The story of Trudi Montag, a dwarf living in Germany in the 1930s and 40s. Trudi's village is home to many unusual characters, including her mentally ill mother, her cross-dressing friend, and her Jewish neighbors—but the Nazis see only some of these people as "undesirable." The story addresses views of "deviance" and "normalcy" during a horrific time in German history.

The Human Stain. 2004. Dir. Robert Benton. Miramax. This film is based on Philip Roth's best-selling book of the same title. Anthony Hopkins plays a classics professor who is hiding a deep secret about his racial background and is forced to retire under false charges of racism.

Larsen, Nella, and Thadious M. Davis. 1997. *Passing*. New York: Penguin. A story about a black woman passing for white and living the high life in Chicago and New York in the 1930s, this book shows the perils of losing one's carefully constructed false identity.

Menzel, Peter, and Faith D'Aluisio. 1998. *Man Eating Bugs: The Art and Science of Eating Insects*. Berkeley, CA: Ten Speed Press. A humorous take on the eating habits of diverse cultures that describes such tasty dishes as fried tarantula and Simple Scorpion Soup.

Pileggi, Nicholas. 1985. *Wiseguy*. New York: Pocket Books. An account of the criminal career of Henry Hill, whose life in the mob ended when he entered the witness protection program. This book includes lots of interviews with Hill and helps explain the appeal of criminal acts, as distinct from the appeal of their reward. It later became the basis for the movie *GoodFellas*.

Twitch and Shout. 1995. Dir. Laurel Chiten. Fanlight Productions/New Day Films. A compassionate, disturbing, and even humorous documentary about Tourette's syndrome. Chiten's film examines how Tourette's sufferers deal with a neurological disorder that causes physical and vocal tics: they may jerk, blink, moan, or shout words uncontrollably. In a society that values self-control, Tourette's sufferers are often stigmatized because of these disruptive, involuntary behaviors.

Connect with sociologists and other students who use

THE REAL WORLD

You Tube™

Subscribe to our channel
NortonSoc

Follow us on Twitter
WWNsoc

Find us on Facebook
**Norton
Sociology**

PART III Understanding Inequality

All societies have systems for grouping, ranking, and categorizing people, and within any social structure, some people occupy superior positions and others hold inferior positions. While such distinctions may appear to be natural, emanating from real differences between people, they are actually social constructions. Society has created and given meaning to such concepts as class, race, and gender, and as such, those concepts have taken on great social significance. The social analyst's job is to understand how these categories are established in the first place, how they are maintained or changed, and ways they affect society and the lives of individuals.

For instance, sociologist Mitchell Duneier's book *Sidewalk* (1999) includes the story of a marginalized group of New York City street vendors whose lives and social identities are much more complex than the casual passerby might imagine. The story considers the convergence of class (Chapter 7), race (Chapter 8), and gender (Chapter 9) in the social structure of the city and its inhabitants' everyday interactions. In many ways, *Sidewalk* brings together the themes of these next three chapters.

Duneier studied men and women who live on the streets of New York's Greenwich Village, selling used goods—mostly books and magazines—to passersby. Duneier befriended the vendors and became part of their curbside culture for five years, during which he conducted his ethnographic research. By examining the intersecting lives of people who frequent the Village, Duneier shows what social inequality looks like and feels like and what it means to those who live with it every day. On Sixth Avenue, the class differences between the vendors and their customers are obvious. The vendors

live from day to day in a cash-based, informal economy; they are poor and often "unhoused"; most are African American males; some are educated, others are not; and all have stories of how they became part of the sidewalk culture. The passersby, on the other hand, are of all ages, races, and occupations, and they are likely to be both employed and housed. They are often well-educated; some are wealthy. Interactions between these vendors and customers cut across boundaries of both class and race, and sometimes gender—all interrelated forms of social inequality.

A key insight in Duneier's work is that the street vendors are not necessarily what they seem at first glance. It would be easy to characterize these people as lacking any social aspirations, given that so many are homeless and don't fit into conventional social roles. Though they might offend some by their appearance, few are drug addicts, alcoholics, or criminals—and they are pursuing the same kinds of goals as many of the passersby. In this liberal neighborhood, sales of written material are allowed on the streets without permits or fees, thus providing these marginalized citizens an opportunity for entrepreneurial activity and a chance to earn an honest living. Most vendors say they are trying "to live 'better' lives within the framework of their own and society's weaknesses" (p. 172). Most work hard to construct a sense of decency and reputability in their dealings with customers. Although some of them violate social norms, in most ways the vendors adhere to a code of conduct that minimizes any negative impact they might have on the surrounding community.

Many vendors develop friendly, ongoing relations with regular buyers despite their different positions in social status hierarchies. Sometimes, however, the chasm between the

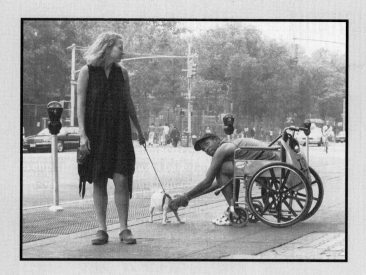

vendors and their customers is difficult to bridge. For example, the male vendors in Duneier's study regularly engaged in flirtatious banter with female passersby. Their efforts at engaging the women in interactions brought a fleeting sense of entitlement and power to men who otherwise have few resources. Typically, the vendors were ignored or rebuffed by the women. When asked why this was the case, one of the vendors said, "She wants room and board, clothing, makeup, hairdos, fabulous dinners, and rent" (Duneier 1999, p. 196). In other words, because he is poor, he cannot provide these upper-middle class amenities. The women, however, may perceive this behavior as sexual harassment, and accordingly may use standard streetwise avoidance techniques. Here, social class becomes the great divide in everyday gender relations.

Some people oppose the street vendors' presence in the neighborhood, and they are frequently the target of anti-peddling campaigns by the mayor's office, police, and local businesses. Yet, Duneier believes that expelling these street vendors in an effort to "improve" the neighborhood would actually be counterproductive. Without the unconventional form of employment that street vending provides to these otherwise destitute people, there would likely be more crime, panhandling, and deviance. Moreover, as law-abiding citizens with a strong desire to conform to social norms, the vendors often serve as mentors to other homeless people, easing them back into mainstream society. Duneier contends that street vendors are an asset to the area and that they contribute to the vibrancy and health of the Village.

While the study is particularly focused on New York's Sixth Avenue vendors, it provides insights into the structure of difference and social inequality in the United States, showing that interactionist perspectives can also be relevant to the study of class, race, and gender, which are more often examined through macrosociological theories. What we come to learn is that the world of sidewalk vending is highly complex and organized, with its own rules and social order.

CHAPTER 7

Social Class: The Structure of Inequality

The photographs on the next page show average families from six different countries—the United States, Kuwait, Mali, Bhutan, Argentina, and Albania. They are each pictured outside the family home, with all their worldly goods displayed around them. These pictures, from Peter Menzel's book *Material World: A Global Family Portrait*, clearly illustrate some of the inequalities of wealth and power between societies worldwide.

Compare, for example, the U.S. and Albanian families, the Skeens and the Cakonis. What are the differences between these families as evidenced by their possessions? The two Skeen children have their own bedrooms; the four Cakoni kids sleep together on a couch in the kitchen. The Cakonis own a number of working animals: a donkey for transportation, and goats, cows, and chickens to provide milk, meat, and eggs. In contrast, the Skeens have a pet dog and several stuffed deer heads hanging on the wall, trophies of Mr. Skeen's favorite pastime, hunting. Every two weeks, the Cakonis hike seven miles to the nearest town to shop for groceries; Mrs. Skeen drives her minivan to a suburban supermarket to stock up whenever she wants. The Skeens have three radios, three stereos, five telephones, two televisions, a VCR, a computer, and three different vehicles; the Cakonis own one radio and a television that the family considers its most valued possession.

Similar comparisons may be made between the Natoma family in Mali, the Namgay family in Bhutan, the Carballo family in Argentina, and the Abdulla family in Kuwait. The younger Mrs. Natoma carries water from the village well in a bucket balanced on her head; the Abdullas have a private indoor swimming pool. The Carballos have been robbed several times, and Mr. Carballo loads his gun every night at dusk to protect his family; the Namgays own little and live near a Buddhist monastery where monks chant daily for peace. These photographs reveal stark contrasts between the world's wealthiest citizens in places like the United States and Kuwait and its poorest people in countries like Albania and Bhutan. What are the real meanings of terms like "rich" and "poor," and how do sociologists define them?

Family Portraits From the top left: the Skeens (Pearland, Texas), the Cakonis (Bei Burrel, Albania), the Natomas (Kouakourou, Mali), the Namgays (Shingkhey, Bhutan), the Carballos (Salta, Argentina), and the Abdullas (Kuwait City, Kuwait).

HOW TO READ THIS CHAPTER

In this chapter, we will examine, from a sociological perspective, the stratification that occurs in all human societies. Despite rhetorical claims about equality of opportunity for all, America is a profoundly hierarchical society, with the benefits and opportunities of living here unequally distributed among its citizens. A sociological perspective on stratification will increase your understanding in several important ways. First, it will help you to see inequities in places you may have overlooked, such as your own town, neighborhood, and school. Second, it will help you consider how positions in social hierarchies tend to shape the lives of individuals: access to health care, the justice system, employment, and housing are all governed by structures of inequality. Third, it should enable you to identify your own place in these social arrangements and to see how some of your own life chances have been shaped by your position (or your family's position) in certain hierarchies. Finally, a knowledge of stratification may help you play a role in changing systems of inequality. Look for ways that you can alleviate some of the problems that social inequality causes—if you can have an impact, even a small one, then this chapter will not have been in vain!

Social Stratification and Social Inequality

Social stratification in one form or another is present in all societies. This means that members of a given society are categorized and divided into groups, which are then placed in a social hierarchy. Members may be grouped according to their gender, race, class, age, or other characteristics, depending on whatever criteria are important to that society. Some groups will be ranked higher in the social strata (levels), while others will fall into the lower ranks. The higher-level groups enjoy more access to the rewards and resources within that society, leaving lower-level groups with less.

This unequal distribution of wealth, power, and prestige results in what is called **social inequality**. We find several different systems of stratification operating in the United States, where it is not hard to demonstrate that being wealthy, white, or male typically confers a higher status (and all that goes along with it) on a person than does being poor, non-white, or female. Because social inequality affects a person's

life experience so profoundly, it is worthwhile to examine how stratification works.

There are four basic principles of social stratification. First, it is a characteristic of a society, rather than a reflection of individual differences. For instance, if we say that in Japan men rank higher in the social hierarchy than women, this doesn't mean that a particular woman, such as actress Ryoko Hirosue, couldn't attain a higher status than a particular man; it means only that in Japan as a whole, men rank higher. Second, social stratification persists over generations. In Great Britain, a child inherits not only physical characteristics such as race but also other indicators of class standing such as regional accent. It is because of this principle of stratification that wealthy families remain so through many generations.

Third, while all societies stratify their members, different societies use different criteria for ranking them. For instance, the criterion in industrialized nations is material wealth (social class), but in hunter-gatherer societies, such as the Khoisan Bushmen of southern Africa, it is gender. Fourth, social stratification is maintained through beliefs that are widely shared by members of society. In the United States, it is still common to think that people are poor not only because of the existing class structure but also because they have somehow failed to "pull themselves up by their bootstraps."

Systems of Stratification

In order to better understand social stratification, it is useful to examine different historical periods and to make global comparisons across cultures. So here we look at three major systems of stratification: slavery, caste, and social class.

Slavery

Slavery, the most extreme system of social stratification, relegates people to the status of property, mainly for the purpose of providing labor for the slave owner. Slaves can thus be bought and sold like any other commodity. They aren't paid for their labor and in fact are forced to work under mental

> **social stratification** the division of society into groups arranged in a social hierarchy
>
> **social inequality** the unequal distribution of wealth, power, or prestige among members of a society
>
> **slavery** the most extreme form of social stratification, based on the legal ownership of people

or physical threat. Occupying the lowest rank in the social hierarchy, slaves have none of the rights common to free members of the same societies in which they live.

Slavery has been practiced since the earliest times (the Bible features stories of the Israelites as slaves) and has continued for millennia in South America, Europe, and the United States. Sometimes the race, nationality, or religion of the slave owners was the same as the slaves', as was the case in ancient Greece and Rome. Historically, a person could become enslaved in one of several ways. One way was through debt; a person who couldn't repay what he owed might be taken into slavery by his creditor. Another way was through warfare: groups of vanquished soldiers might become slaves to the victors, and the women and children of the losing side could also be taken into slavery. A person who was caught committing a crime could become a slave as a kind of punishment and as a means of compensating the victim. And some slaves were captured and kidnapped, as was the case of the transatlantic slave trade from Africa to the Americas.

Slavery as an economic system was profitable for the slave owner. In most systems of slavery, people were slaves for life, doing work in agriculture, construction, mining, or domestic service, and sometimes in the military, industry, or commerce. Their children would become slaves too, thus making the owner a greater profit. In some systems, however, slavery was temporary, and some slaves could buy their own freedom.

Slavery is now prohibited by every nation in the world, as declared in the Universal Declaration of Human Rights. Not only is it illegal, it is considered immoral as well. Nevertheless, the shocking fact is that it continues to exist today in such places as India, South Asia, and West Africa in the form of child slavery, serfdom, forced and bonded laborers, human trafficking, and sex slaves.

America is not exempt from these same shocking practices either, where people are held as agricultural, domestic, and sex slaves as well. And Americans may also play an indirect role in supporting slavery elsewhere in the world, by means of our material appetites and the type of labor utilized in certain countries to satisfy our varied consumer demands (Bales and Soodalter 2009). Using a somewhat broader definition of slavery that includes all of the above plus other conditions such as forced marriage or child soldiers, researchers believe there may be approximately 25 million people in slavery, more in terms of total numbers (not proportion) than at any other time in human history (Bales 2000). By the latest estimates, that number would have reached almost 30 million by 2010 (Kara 2008).

caste system a form of social stratification in which status is determined by one's family history and background and cannot be changed

Slavery Actress Demi Moore and Anuradha Koirala, chairperson of the organization Maiti Nepal that works to protect girls and women in Nepal from human trafficking and violence, stand with children at a rehabilitation center in Kathmandu.

Caste

Caste represents another type of social stratification found in various parts of the world. The traditional **caste system** is based on heredity, whereby whole groups of people are born into a certain stratum. Castes may be differentiated along religious, economic, or political lines, as well as by skin color or other physical characteristics. The caste system creates a highly stratified society where there is little or no chance of a person changing her position within the hierarchy, no matter what she may achieve individually. Members must marry within their own group, and their caste ranking is passed on to their children. In general, members of higher-ranking castes tend to be more prosperous, whereas members of lower-ranking castes tend to have fewer material resources, live in abject poverty, and suffer discrimination.

India is the country most closely associated with the caste system, based there in the Hindu (majority) religion. The caste system ranks individuals into one of five categories: Brahman (scholars and priests), ksatriya or chhetri (rulers and warriors), vaisya (merchants and traders), sudra (farmers, artisans, and laborers), and the untouchables (social outcasts). The caste system is a reflection of what Hindus call *karma*, the complex moral law of cause and effect that governs the universe (Cohen 2001). According to this belief, membership in a particular caste is seen as a well-deserved reward or punishment for virtuous or sinful behavior in a past life. Caste is thus considered a spiritual rather than material status. Caste-related segregation and discrimination were prohibited in 1949 by India's constitution, but they are still prevalent. Resistance to social change remains, and thus far the social ramifications of the caste system have not been completely dismantled.

THE CASE OF SOUTH AFRICA An interesting example of the caste system was the **apartheid** system, a legal separation of racial and ethnic groups that was enforced between 1948 and 1991 in South Africa. The term itself literally means "apartness" in Afrikaans and Dutch. The consequence of apartheid was to create great disparity among those in the different strata of society.

South Africans were legally classified into four main racial groups: white (English and Dutch heritage), Indian (from India), "colored" (mixed race), and black. Blacks formed a large majority, at 60 percent of the population. These groups were geographically and socially separated from one another. Blacks were forcibly removed from almost 80 percent of the country, which was reserved for the three minority groups, and relocated to independent "homelands" similar to the Indian reservations in the United States. They could not enter other parts of the country without a pass— usually in order to work as "guest laborers" in white areas. Ironically, African Americans visiting South Africa were given "honorary white" status and could move freely within white and nonwhite areas. Social services for whites and nonwhites were separate as well: schools, hospitals, buses, trains, parks, beaches, libraries, theaters, public restrooms, and even graveyards were segregated. Indians and "coloreds" were also discriminated against, though they usually led slightly more privileged lives than blacks. Despite claims of "separate but equal," the standard of living among whites far exceeded that of any other group.

In South Africa under the apartheid system, whites held all the political, economic, and social power, despite being a numerical minority. It was not long before civil unrest and resistance to the system began developing within South Africa and among the international community. Blacks and even some whites began to organize to wage strikes and demonstrations, and sanctions were imposed by Western nations. The plights of high-profile anti-apartheid leaders such as Steve Biko and Nelson Mandela became known worldwide. Pressure on the white government continued to grow, until the country was in an almost constant state of emergency. In 1991, apartheid as a legal institution was finally abolished.

Its legacy, however, has been much more difficult to dismantle. Although nonwhites now share the same rights and privileges as whites, social inequality and discrimination between the races have decreased little (Nattras and Seekings 2001; Seekings and Nattras 2005). South Africa remains a country with one of the most unequal distributions of income in the world. In 2004, 60 percent earned less than US$7,000 a year, whereas just over 2 percent earned more than US$50,000 per year. Blacks made up 90 percent of the poor. The income gap in South Africa has continued to grow, with the rich, and especially the already rich whites, getting richer (Boyle 2009). The restoration of land seized during apartheid is only slowly being accomplished and at a price to those making claims. In some ways, new patterns of class stratification are replacing rather than erasing old patterns of racial stratification.

> **apartheid** the system of segregation of racial and ethnic groups that was legal in South Africa between 1948 and 1991
>
> **social class** a system of stratification based on access to such resources as wealth, property, power, and prestige
>
> **socioeconomic status (SES)** a measure of an individual's place within a social class system; often used interchangeably with "class"

Social Class

Social class, a system of stratification practiced primarily in capitalist societies, ranks groups of people according to their wealth, property, power, and prestige. It is also referred to by sociologists as **socioeconomic status (SES)**. The social class system is much less rigid than the caste system. Although children tend to "inherit" the social class of their parents, during the course of a lifetime they can move up or down levels in the strata. Strictly speaking, social class is not based on race, ethnicity, gender, or age, although, as we will learn later, there is often an overlap between class and those other variables.

Sociologists are not always in agreement about what determines class standing or where the boundaries are between different social classes. We will consider some of these disagreements after first taking a look at the United States and its system.

Social Classes in the United States

It is difficult to draw exact lines between the social classes in the United States; in fact, it may be useful to imagine them along a continuum rather than strictly divided. The most commonly identified categories are upper class, middle class, and lower class. If we want to make even finer distinctions, the middle class can be divided into upper, middle, and lower (Wright et al. 1982). You probably have some idea of which class you belong to even if you don't know the exact definition for each category. Interestingly, most Americans claim that they belong somewhere in the middle class even when their life experiences and backgrounds would suggest otherwise. While keeping in mind that the borders between the classes can be blurry, let's examine a typical model of the five different social classes.

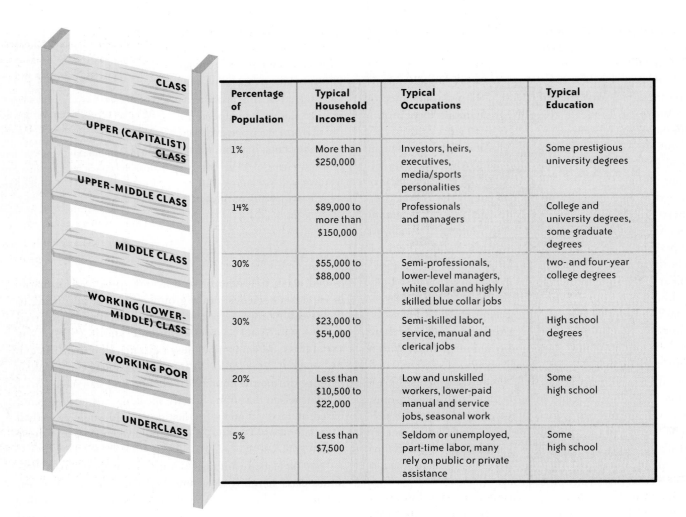

	Percentage of Population	Typical Household Incomes	Typical Occupations	Typical Education
CLASS				
UPPER (CAPITALIST) CLASS	1%	More than $250,000	Investors, heirs, executives, media/sports personalities	Some prestigious university degrees
UPPER-MIDDLE CLASS	14%	$89,000 to more than $150,000	Professionals and managers	College and university degrees, some graduate degrees
MIDDLE CLASS	30%	$55,000 to $88,000	Semi-professionals, lower-level managers, white collar and highly skilled blue collar jobs	two- and four-year college degrees
WORKING (LOWER-MIDDLE) CLASS	30%	$23,000 to $54,000	Semi-skilled labor, service, manual and clerical jobs	High school degrees
WORKING POOR	20%	Less than $10,500 to $22,000	Low and unskilled workers, lower-paid manual and service jobs, seasonal work	Some high school
UNDERCLASS	5%	Less than $7,500	Seldom or unemployed, part-time labor, many rely on public or private assistance	Some high school

FIGURE 7.1 The U.S. Social Class Ladder

The Upper Class

The **upper class** makes up just 1 percent of the U.S. population, and its total net worth is greater than that of the entire other 99 percent (Beeghley 2008). The upper class consists of elites who have gained membership in various ways. Some, like the Rockefellers and Carnegies, come into "old money" through family fortunes; others, like Bill Gates and Oprah Winfrey, generate "new money" through individual achievements. Members of this class earn in excess of $250,000 per year and are often highly educated, cultured, and influential. They tend to attend private schools and prestigious universities and display a distinctive lifestyle; some seek positions of power in government or philanthropy. The upper class is largely self-sustaining, with most members remaining stable and few new ones able to gain its ranks.

The Upper-Middle Class

The **upper-middle class** comprises about 14 percent of the population. This group tends to be well educated (with college or postgraduate degrees) and highly skilled. Members work primarily in executive, managerial, and professional jobs. They may enjoy modest support from investments but generally depend on income from salaried work, making upward of $89,000 to $150,000 per year. As a result, the upper-middle class is most likely to feel some financial stability. They usually own their homes and may own a second one as well.

upper class a largely self-sustaining group of the wealthiest people in a class system; in the United States, they constitute about 1 percent of the population and possess most of the wealth of the country

upper-middle class mostly professionals and managers who enjoy considerable financial stability, they constitute about 14 percent of the U.S. population

The Middle Class

The **middle class** makes up about 30 percent of the population, though some social analysts believe that the middle class is shrinking as a result of a variety of phenomena, including economic recession and the housing market crash, along with high unemployment, corporate downsizing, and outsourcing of work to foreign countries. Many people who would have once been considered middle class may have moved down to the lower-middle class, while some others have moved up to the upper-middle class. The middle class comprises primarily **white collar** workers, skilled laborers in technical and lower-management jobs, small entrepreneurs and others earning a range from $55,000 to $88,000. Most members have a high school education and a two- or four-year college degree. While members of the middle class have traditionally been homeowners (a sign of having achieved the American Dream), this trend changed during the recent recession and the associated banking and mortgage crises. Along with issues like the cost of housing, and given other debts carried by many Americans, not all middle class people can afford their own homes anymore.

The Working (Lower-Middle) Class

The **working class**, or **lower-middle class**, makes up about 30 percent of the population. Members typically have a high school education and generally work in manual labor, or **blue collar**, jobs, as well as in the service industry (retail, restaurant, tourism, etc.)—jobs that are often more routine, where employees have little control in the workplace. Members of the working class typically earn between $23,000 and $54,000 per year. A small portion, especially those who belong to a union, may earn above-average incomes for this class. Working class people typically have a low net worth and live in rental housing or in a modest home they have inherited or long saved for.

The Working Poor and Underclass

The **working poor** comprise approximately 20 percent of the population. Members are generally not well educated; most have not completed high school and experience lower levels of literacy than the other classes. They may also lack other work skills valuable in the job market. Typical occupations include unskilled, temporary, and seasonal jobs—including minimum-wage jobs, housekeeping, day labor, and migrant agricultural work. The average income ranges from less than $10,500 to

$22,000. This group suffers from higher rates of unemployment and underemployment, with some members receiving welfare subsidies.

In addition, another 5 percent of the population, the **underclass**, could be categorized as truly disadvantaged. These very poorest of Americans typically earn less than $7,500 per year and may have chronic difficulty getting enough money to support their basic needs. They may hold few steady jobs and depend on public benefits or charity to survive. They are most often found in inner cities, where they live in substandard housing or are homeless. They are part of a group that is considered officially impoverished by federal government standards. A separate section later in this chapter will be devoted to discussing poverty and the poor.

middle class composed primarily of "white collar" workers with a broad range of incomes; they constitute about 30 percent of the U.S. population

white collar a description characterizing workers and skilled laborers in technical and lower-management jobs

working class or **lower-middle class** mostly "blue collar" or service industry workers who are less likely to have a college degree; they constitute about 30 percent of the U.S. population

blue collar a description characterizing workers who perform manual labor

working poor poorly educated workers who work full-time but remain below the poverty line; they constitute about 20 percent of the U.S. population

underclass the poorest Americans who are chronically unemployed and may depend on public or private assistance; they constitute about 5 percent of the U.S. population

status inconsistency a situation in which there are serious differences between the different elements of an individual's socioeconomic status

Problematic Categories

Because SES is based on a collection of complex variables (including income, wealth, education, and occupation, as well as power or prestige), it is difficult to say exactly where, for example, middle class ends and upper class begins. In addition, individuals may embody a variety of characteristics that make precise SES classification difficult. Someone may be highly educated, for example, but make very little money while working on her novel. Also, as we learned during the financial crisis that began in 2008, people of all social classes, including the very wealthy, can find themselves unable to pay their mortgages when real estate "bubbles" burst.

And how do we categorize a person such as the late Sam Walton, founder of Wal-Mart, billionaire businessman, Oklahoma farm boy, and state college graduate? The product of a nonelite educational institution and a struggling "Okie" farm family, he nevertheless made tons of money and achieved great occupational success. What sociologists would say is that Walton was an example of **status inconsistency**,

Systems of Stratification Around the World

Although stratification systems in other countries may appear different from those in the United States, they share many features. For one thing, most such systems result in patterns of inequality.

Brazil

Race is a powerful influence on social stratification in Brazil, where the situation is even more complex than in the United States. By any standards, Brazil is a remarkably diverse nation. The early settlers to the area were mainly European, and with

their arrival the number of native inhabitants declined sharply as a result of violence and disease, although they remained a factor in the local population. Through the mid-1800s, slaves from Africa were imported, and in the twentieth century, a new wave of immigrants arrived from Asia and the Middle East.

For much of Brazilian history, the European whites enjoyed a privileged status. However, as people from different races married and raised children, new racial categories emerged. Sociologist Gilberto Freyre claimed in 1970 that this new mixture of races and cultures was a unique strength that led to something like a "racial democracy." Although the idea was appealing, it was subsequently challenged by other social scientists who argued that Brazil was still highly stratified by race, if only in a less obvious way (Telles 2004). Intermarriage may have eliminated clearly defined racial groups, but skin color still largely defines an individual's place in society, with light-skinned

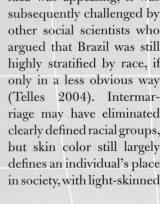

Polite Racism As different ethnic groups in Brazil intermarried and had children, new racial categories emerged. Many have argued that this has led to a new "racial democracy"; however, critics say stratification still exists. They refer to it as "polite racism."

or stark contrasts in the level of different statuses he occupied. Two-time Oscar-winner Hilary Swank is another example: she never went to college, lived in her car for a while in Los Angeles, and earned only $3,000 for the role in *Boys Don't Cry* for which she won her first Academy Award for Best Actress. She remarked on her own status inconsistency when she accepted her second Oscar (for *Million Dollar Baby*): "I'm just a girl from a trailer park who had a dream."

Status inconsistencies are especially prevalent in the United States because of our "open" class system. Class mobility (which will be discussed in more detail later) is more easily attainable here than in many other countries—here, a girl from a trailer park *can* win an Oscar (or two). So while we seem to be able to recognize class distinctions implicitly, there are no systematic ways of delineating each category. Still, sociologists have made an effort to understand and define class, and we turn now to the theories that result from those efforts.

Brazilians enjoying privileges of wealth and power that their dark-skinned countrymen don't have access to. Contemporary critics have referred to this inequality as *racismo cordial*, or "polite racism."

Iran

The basis for social stratification in Iran has undergone radical changes since the Islamic Revolution in 1979, which transformed the country from a constitutional monarchy to a theocracy. Before the revolution, political and economic power was concentrated in the upper class, made up of landowners, industrialists, and business executives; the middle class consisted of entrepreneurs, small-business owners, merchants, and members of the civil service. Economic mobility was an option largely for those with secular values and a Western education; that is, those who had gone to college in the United States or Europe and who believed in the separation of church and state. After the revolution, however, religion became a primary influence on stratification. Many members of the civil service with Western university degrees were forced into exile; those who remained were required to attend special classes on Islamic law in order to keep their positions. Strict observance of Islamic law and custom has become a new prerequisite for maintaining one's social position, and many of the new political elites are religious leaders.

Sweden

Sweden has deliberately attempted to craft a system that lessens social inequality, a policy made somewhat easier, perhaps, by the country's relative homogeneity of race,

Inequality in Sweden? The Swedish have crafted social policies to promote access to child care, public libraries, education, and unemployment benefits in order to lessen social stratification.

ethnicity, and religion. Sweden has provided its citizens with a far greater number of social services than the United States has: the government guarantees its citizens a high level of access to health care, education, child and elderly care, unemployment benefits, and public facilities like libraries and parks. In order to furnish such programs, taxes are high, with a top taxation rate of 60 percent for the wealthiest Swedes. Although the Swedish system certainly has its problems (high taxation rates among them), there are demonstrated benefits, including increased life expectancy and literacy, and decreased infant mortality, homelessness, poverty, and crime.

Theories of Social Class

In this section, we will look at social stratification from the perspectives of each of the major schools of thought within sociology. We start with classical conflict and Weberian theories and structural functionalism, and will also consider postmodern and symbolic interactionist theories. Each perspective offers different ideas about what determines social class, with the macro theorists focusing on larger-scale social structures and the postmodern and micro theorists focusing more on meaning and interpretation of face-to-face interactions in everyday life.

Conflict Theory

Karl Marx formed his so-cial theories at a time when monumental changes were occurring in the stratification systems

Status Inconsistencies Sam Walton, the "Okie" billionaire, and Hilary Swank, the two-time Academy Award-winner who lived out of her car, are two examples that complicate SES classifications.

that characterized nineteenth-century Europe. The **feudal system**, which consisted of a hierarchy of privileged nobles who were responsible for and served by a lower stratum of serfs (forced laborers), was breaking down. Cities were growing larger as more people moved from rural areas to take part in the new forms of industry that were emerging there. With these changes, what had traditionally determined a person's social standing (whether they were born a noble or a serf) was no longer as relevant. Marx was concerned about a new kind of social inequality that he saw emerging—between the capitalists (bourgeoisie), who owned the means of production, and the workers (proletariat), who owned only their own labor.

Marx argued that economic relationships were quickly becoming the only social relationships that mattered: the impersonal forces of the market were creating a new, rigid system of social stratification in which capitalists had every economic advantage and workers had none. He believed that the classes would remain divided and social inequality would grow; that wealth and privilege would be concentrated among a small group of capitalists and workers would continue to be exploited. Contemporary conflict theorists continue to understand social class in a similar way. Erik Olin Wright (1997), for example, describes an animated film he made as a student in which the pawns on a chessboard attempt to overthrow the aristocracy (kings, queens, knights, and bishops) but realize that the "rules of the game" doom them to relive the same unequal roles—a metaphor for the way social structure shapes and sustains inequality.

feudal system a system of social stratification based on a hereditary nobility who were responsible for and served by a lower stratum of forced laborers called serfs

wealth A measure of net worth that includes income, property, and other assets.

prestige the social honor people are given because of their membership in well-regarded social groups

Weberian Theory

Max Weber noted that owning the means of production was not the only way of achieving upper-class status; a person could also accumulate **wealth** consisting of income and property. As a contemporary example, Microsoft is a publicly traded company (which means that thousands of shareholders own it), but its CEO Steve Ballmer is one of the world's top 20 richest individuals—and its chairman, Bill Gates, is the richest. Thus, Weber suggests that power (the ability to impose one's will on others) should be considered as part of the equation when measuring a person's class standing. Although they may not own their corporations, executives do exercise power over employees and are able to control their access to salaries, benefits, and job security.

Weber believed that another important element in social class has to do with **prestige**, the social honor granted to people because of their membership in certain groups. A person's occupation is a common source of prestige: in a typical ranking, you might find doctors near the top and janitors near the bottom (and note that professional athletes rank higher than sociologists on Table 7.1). People's relative

TABLE 7.1
The Relative Social Prestige of Selected Occupations in the United States

WHITE COLLAR OCCUPATIONS	PRESTIGE SCORE	BLUE COLLAR OCCUPATIONS	WHITE COLLAR OCCUPATIONS	PRESTIGE SCORE	BLUE COLLAR OCCUPATIONS
Physician	86		Realtor	49	
Lawyer	75		Bookkeeper	47	
College/University Professor	74			47	Machinist
Architect	73			47	Mail Carrier
Chemist	73		Musician/Composer	47	
Physicist/Astronomer	73			46	Secretary
Aerospace Engineer	72		Photographer	45	
Dentist	72		Bank Teller	43	
Member of the Clergy	69			42	Tailor
Psychologist	69			42	Welder
Pharmacist	68			40	Farmer
Optometrist	67			40	Telephone Operator
Registered Nurse	66			39	Carpenter
Secondary-School Teacher	64			36	Brick/Stone Mason
Accountant	65			36	Child-Care Worker
Athlete	65		File Clerk	36	
Electrical Engineer	64			36	Hairdresser
Elementary-School Teacher	64			35	Baker
Economist	63			34	Bulldozer Operator
Veterinarian	62			31	Auto Body Repairperson
Airplane Pilot	61		Retail Apparel Salesperson	30	
Computer Programmer	61			30	Truck Driver
Sociologist	61		Cashier	29	
Editor/Reporter	60			28	Elevator Operator
	60	Police Officer		28	Garbage Collector
Actor	58			28	Taxi Driver
Radio/TV Announcer	55			28	Waiter/Waitress
Librarian	54			27	Bellhop
	53	Aircraft Mechanic		25	Bartender
	53	Fire Fighter		23	Farm Laborer
Social Worker	52			23	Household Laborer
	51	Electrician		22	Door-to-Door Salesperson
Computer Operator	50			22	Janitor
Funeral Director	49			9	Shoe Shiner

SOURCE: Data from National Opinion Research Center 2009.

The Rules of the Game As a student, Marxist sociologist Erik Olin Wright made a film using chess pieces as a metaphor for the ways that social structure sustains inequality.

prestige can affect not only their wealth or power but also how they are perceived in social situations. Wealth by itself can also be a source of prestige, though not always. In some social circles, especially those that are more traditional or have a history of aristocracy, a distinction is made between "old money" and "new money." In the United States it is more prestigious to come from a family heritage of wealth than to have recently made a fortune.

For Weber, wealth, power, and prestige are interrelated because they often come together, but it is also possible to convert one to the other. Paris Hilton, for example, a socialite from a wealthy, hotel-owning family, turned that aspect of her status into a certain type of contemporary prestige—celebrity. Still, it is important to distinguish these three elements: property and wealth can be inherited or earned, power usually comes from occupying certain roles within organizations, and prestige is based on a person's social identity and bestowed by others.

Structural Functionalism

Functionalism emphasizes social order and solidarity based on commonly shared values about what is good and worthwhile. The system of stratification that has emerged over time, though not egalitarian, is still functional for society in a number of ways. Because there are a variety of roles to perform for the maintenance and good of the whole, there must be incentives to ensure that individuals will occupy those roles that are most necessary or important. Kingsley Davis

social reproduction the tendency of social classes to remain relatively stable as social class status is passed down from one generation to the next

and Wilbert Moore (1948) discuss some of the principles of stratification that result in a system of rewards that is unequally distributed among various roles. The assumption is that some roles are more desirable than others and may require greater talent or training. In addition, certain roles may be more critical than others to the functioning of society, as well as difficult to fill, so there must be a mechanism for attracting and securing the best individuals to those positions. This would mean that there is widespread consensus about which positions are most important—either in terms of their special qualifications or the potential scarcity of qualified individuals to occupy those positions—and that society accepts the need to bestow rewards upon people who are considered of greater importance.

Take, for instance, the role of a physician, which has the highest ranking of occupational prestige in American society. Doctors play an important role in providing highly prized services to other members of society. Think of the steps it takes to become a doctor. A person must have an extensive education and graduate training, and complete a long and intensive internship before being certified to practice medicine. This individual also devotes a great deal of their personal resources of time and money to this process. It is further assumed that there are only so many people who might have the talent and determination to become doctors, and so it follows that there must be incentives or rewards for them to enter the field of medicine.

The functionalist perspective helps to explain the existing system of social stratification and its persistence, but it still leaves us with questions about the structured inequalities that it continues to reproduce. Is it really functional for social rewards (such as wealth, power, and prestige) to be so unequally divided among members of society? And while we might agree that doctors are very important to society, are they more so than teachers and carpenters? Our heroes of popular culture (famous actors, athletes, musicians) can rise to the highest ranks while our everyday heroes (day-care providers, firefighters, mechanics) may struggle to make a living. Whose values are structuring the system and, after closer scrutiny, is it clear that compensating stockbrokers more than bricklayers is really functional to society as a whole? Despite these questions, Americans largely agree with functionalist principles on social class. We will revisit some of these questions in later sections of the chapter.

Postmodernism

Sociologist Pierre Bourdieu studied French schools to examine a phenomenon referred to as **social reproduction**, which means that social class is passed down from one generation to the next and thus remains relatively stable (1973, 1984). According to Bourdieu, this happens as a result of

Social Reproduction Paris Hilton, pictured at left, is heiress to the Hilton Hotel & Resort chain. How did Hilton's family influence her career path, as opposed to someone who may have grown up in a working-class family, like the firefighter pictured at right?

each generation's acquisition of what he called **cultural capital**: children inherit tastes, habits, and expectations from their parents, and this cultural capital either helps or hinders them as they become adults. For example, having highly educated parents who can help with homework and enforce useful study habits makes it more likely a child will succeed in school. Just the parents' expectation that their children will earn similar credentials can be a powerful incentive. Since better-educated parents tend to come from the middle and upper classes, their children will also have better chances to attain that same status.

According to Bourdieu, cultural capital also shapes the perceptions that others form about a person. For instance, in job interviews, the candidates who can best impress a potential employer with their social skills may be chosen over others who are less adept. Since cultural capital has such profound effects, people often try to acquire it—to "better" themselves. They may take adult education classes,

attend lectures and concerts, join a tennis club or travel to Europe—all in an attempt to improve their cultural capital. Often, however, the effects of early childhood are too powerful to overcome. It can be difficult for someone who grew up in a less privileged environment to project a different class background; their accent, for example, may give them away ("He talks like a hillbilly," "She just sounds too 'street'"). There is evidence that around half of all children will wind up with the same SES as their parents, despite any efforts to climb the social class ladder (Krueger 2002).

Symbolic Interactionism

If macrosociologists believe that there is little an individual can do to change systems of structured inequality, interactionists believe that all

> **cultural capital** the tastes, habits, expectations, skills, knowledge, and other cultural dispositions that help us gain advantages in society

Everyday Class Consciousness Clothes, cars, homes, and vacation plans are all indicators of socioeconomic status. What kind of impression does this living room give of who might live here?

social structures—including systems of inequality—are constructed from the building blocks of everyday interaction. For instance, sociologist David Sudnow (1972) argues that we make split-second judgments about who people are and which social status they occupy based on appearance. We take action based on what we observe "at a glance." Along the same lines, Aaron Cicourel (1972) suggests that we make inferences about the status of others when we encounter them in different social situations. For example, you may assume that the passengers sitting in the first-class section of an airplane are wealthier than those in coach, whether or not this is true. Maybe one of those first-class passengers is a "starving student" whose seat was upgraded because coach was overbooked—by thrifty millionaires. "Wealthy," "poor," and "middle class" are statuses that, rather than existing in and of themselves, are continuously being negotiated in interaction.

Erving Goffman (1956) noted that we "read" different aspects of identity by interpreting the behavior of others and that we become accustomed to others "reading" our behavior in the same way. This means that our clothing, our speech, our gestures, the cars we drive, the homes we live in, the people we hang out

everyday class consciousness
awareness of one's own social status and that of others

with, and the things we do on vacation are all part of our presentation of self and provide information that others use to make judgments about our SES. In turn, we look for these same clues in the behavior of others. This type of **everyday class consciousness**, or awareness of our own and others' social status, is important for us to understand but difficult to identify empirically.

As a humorous answer to this dilemma, University of Pennsylvania English professor Paul Fussell (1983) created the "living room scale," which lists items that we may find in someone's living room and attaches point values to them. For example, if you have a copy of the *New York Review of Books* on your coffee table, add five points. A copy of *Popular Mechanics*? Subtract five. A working fireplace? Add four. A wall unit with built-in television and stereo? Subtract four. Add three points for each black-and-white family photograph in a sterling silver frame; subtract three points for any work of art depicting cowboys. When we total the final score, higher numbers indicate higher SES, and vice versa.

While Fussell's living room scale may seem like a joke, we really do make snap judgments about the status of others based on just this sort of information. (Here it should be noted that in Dr. Stein's living room, the fireplace and TV wall unit are side by side, while Dr. Ferris's living room features a silver-framed black-and-white photograph of her father as a child—dressed like a cowboy, on horseback! As we've said before, real life sometimes defies easy categorization.) The Data Workshop on the next page will help you see how swiftly and automatically you employ class categories in your interactions with others.

While we have considered the theories of macrosociologists and symbolic interactionists separately here, there are actually some intersections between interaction and structure. Our identities as "working class" or "privileged" individuals may be structured by preexisting categories, yet those identities are also performed every day in our interactions with others. The structural perspective and the interactionist perspective are not mutually exclusive when it comes to a discussion of class: they are complementary. Status inequality is structured, categorical, and external; it is also interactionally created and sustained. Structure shapes interaction, and interaction generates structure (Table 7.2). Contemporary sociologists have conducted studies that make this connection clear. For example, Geoffrey Hunt and Saundra Satterlee, who studied drinking habits in village pubs (1986), found that pub interactions tended to reinforce class divisions in the larger society: the village men chose drinking and billiards companions based on the class divisions already in place outside the pub.

TABLE 7.2 Theory in Everyday Life

PERSPECTIVE	APPROACH TO SOCIAL INEQUALITY	CASE STUDY: POVERTY
STRUCTURAL FUNCTIONALISM	Social inequality is a necessary part of society. Different reward structures are necessary as an incentive for the best qualified people to occupy the most important positions. Even poverty has functions that help maintain social order.	The functions of poverty for society include the facts that the poor take otherwise undesirable jobs and housing, purchase discount and secondhand goods, and provide work for thousands, including social service caseworkers and others who work with the poor.
CONFLICT THEORY	Social inequality creates intergroup conflict—poor and rich groups have different interests and may find themselves at odds as they attempt to secure and protect these interests.	Social welfare programs that assist the poor are funded by tax dollars, which some wealthy citizens may be reluctant to provide because taxes reduce their net income. This can create conflict between rich and poor groups in society.
SYMBOLIC INTERACTIONISM	Social inequality is part of our presentation of self. We develop everyday class consciousness as a way to distinguish the status of others.	Poor and wealthy persons have differential access to the "props" used to project particular versions of self. In particular, professional clothing such as business suits can be too expensive for poor individuals to purchase, which can put them at a disadvantage in job interviews, where a professional image is necessary. Organizations like Dress for Success provide professional clothing for those who can't afford it, leveling the playing field a bit in terms of impression management.

DATA WORKSHOP

ANALYZING EVERYDAY LIFE

Everyday Class Consciousness

How do you determine the class status of others? How do you deal with the fact that others will be assessing *your* class status? How do these assessments influence your actions?

This Data Workshop asks you to do some participant observation research (see Chapter 2 for a refresher, if needed) to understand more about how we size up others in terms of their SES. Next time you're in a public place—for example, waiting for someone at the airport, sitting in the food court at the mall, or standing in line at the post office—select the seventh person to walk by you, and spend several seconds looking closely at him or her. Ask yourself quickly: what class status do you think this person holds? Don't think too long, just register your guess. Then consider the following.

What did you look at to make the evaluation—height, weight, race, gender, hairstyle, tattoos, piercings, clothes, makeup? Perhaps dress style, colors, fabrics, writing on T-shirt, hat, purse, shoes, jewelry? Did you notice anything else, such as posture, voice, or mannerisms? If you observed someone outdoors, did you see the car he or she was driving? What was its make, age, or condition? Did you notice other

status clues—books, a laptop, a baby stroller, shopping bags? How did the setting itself (mall, post office, airport) influence your guess?

There are two options for completing this Data Workshop.

- *Option 1 (informal)*: Prepare written notes that you can refer to in class. Share your evaluations with other students in small-group discussions. Note similarities and differences in the criteria used by group members.

- *Option 2 (formal)*: Select two to three people in a public setting to evaluate. Write a three- to four-page essay describing your observations and answering the questions in the preceding paragraphs. You may also want to refer to the section on symbolic interactionism (page 197) as a framework for your essay.

All the information that we gather at a glance is used to make evaluations of others' wealth, income, occupation, education, and other categories that indicate status and prestige. In some ways, it doesn't matter whether we're right or not—especially in anonymous public places like airports. You should be aware, however, that you do use these cues to evaluate the status of others in split seconds and that you act on those evaluations every day. Maybe you chose to stand on the bus or subway rather than sit next to someone who didn't look quite "right"—whatever that means to you. Often, we end up falling back on stereotypes that may lead us to false conclusions about a person's status or character. When it comes to everyday class consciousness, appearances are sometimes deceiving, but they are always consequential.

Socioeconomic Status and Life Chances

Belonging to a certain social class brings such profound consequences that it's possible to make general predictions about a person's life chances in regard to education, work, crime, family, and health just by knowing his SES. The following discussion may help you appreciate the respective privileges and hardships associated with different levels of the social hierarchy.

Family

Sociologists know that people are likely to marry or have long-term relationships with persons whose social and cultural backgrounds are similar to their own—not because they are looking for such similarities, but simply because they have more access to people like themselves. When you develop ties to classmates, fellow workers, neighbors, and members of clubs, these people may share your cultural background as well as your social class. It is from such groups that marriage and domestic partners come.

Social class also plays a role in the age at which people marry: the average age of first marriage for women with high school diplomas is twenty-five, while for women with graduate degrees it is thirty. The age at which people start a family and the number of children they have are also related to social class. The U.S. census found that women with only high school diplomas had twice the birthrate of women with graduate degrees. Further, of the women with less than a high school education who gave birth to a first child, almost 64 percent were unmarried (U.S. Census Bureau 2000a). That's more than twice the figure of premarital births for women who have at least some college.

Health

Those at the bottom of the social class ladder are the least likely to obtain adequate nutrition, shelter, clothing, and health care and are thus more prone to illness. They often cannot afford to see a doctor, fill a prescription, or go to a hospital. Instead of preventing an illness from becoming worse, they must wait until a health crisis occurs, and then they have no option but expensive emergency room care.

Sociologists have found that people who occupy a higher SES are more likely to simply *feel* healthier. In one study of Americans older than twenty-five, researchers found that regardless of age, race, or gender, people with more education were more likely to report being in excellent health: fewer than 40 percent of those with less than a high school education reported being in good health, compared with nearly 80 percent of those with a college degree (Baum and Payea 2004). Another study found that not only do people of higher SES feel healthier, they in fact live longer—almost five years longer than people of low SES (Singh and Siahpush 2006).

One factor that contributes to disparities in health is exercise. As education and income increase, so does the likelihood of a person engaging in some exercise, as reported in 2010 by the CDC's National Center for Health Statistics. For instance, nearly 57.5 percent of respondents living below the poverty level (an annual income of $10,590 or less) reported not exercising at all, compared with only 27.8 percent of those living at four times above the poverty level (an annual income of approximately $42,360). Only 20 percent of individuals living below the poverty level reported exercising regularly, compared with almost 40 percent of those at the higher income level. Education may have something to do with these contrasts, as more knowledge about the health benefits of exercise may lead to more active participation. But we can also see exercise as rather a luxury for those in higher social classes, who are not struggling with the day-to-day efforts to survive that characterize the lives of the poor.

Education

How children perform in school usually determines whether and where they go to college, what professions they enter, and how much they are paid. And generally, those with more education make more money. According to a 2010 Census Bureau report, the average annual income for those with advanced (master's and doctorate) or professional (medical and law) degrees was $83,144, followed by $58,613 for those with bachelor's degrees, and $31,283 for those with high school diplomas (U.S. Census 2010c). On the surface, these earnings may seem fair; after all, shouldn't people with more education make more money? However, as sociologists, we must probe further and ask some fundamental questions; for example, who has access to education, and how good is that education?

One of the main goals of education is to make sure students get a chance to succeed both in school and in life. But to meet this goal, schools would have to serve all students equally, and they aren't always able to do so. Schools with low-income students often receive fewer resources, have

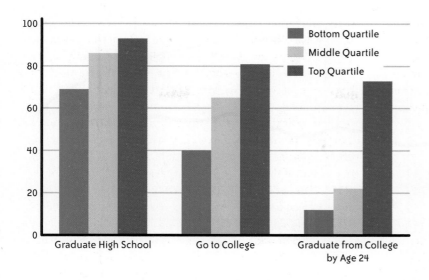

FIGURE 7.2 **Rate that High School Students Go on to Earn Advanced Degrees**

The higher the family's SES, the higher the student's expectation of educational achievement. Increasing numbers of students now expect to attend graduate or professional school.

SOURCE: Mortenson 2007.

greater difficulty in attracting qualified teachers, and experience less support from parents (Fischer and Kmec 2004). A student's social class background will also influence her attitude toward education. The higher the family's SES, the higher the student's expectations (see Figure 7.2). Students from higher social classes are also expected to complete more years of school and are more likely to attend college than those from lower social classes (Berends 1995; Goyette and Xie 1999; Bozick et al. 2010).

According to a U.S. Census Bureau report (2010d), approximately 31 percent of adults aged twenty-five and over had a high school education, 17 percent had some college, 19 percent had a bachelor's degree, and 10 percent had advanced degrees. But although educational attainment is at an all-time high in the United States, a high school education doesn't mean what it once did. College and advanced degrees are becoming more important. If the trends continue, fewer and fewer jobs will be available to those without college degrees, and of those jobs, fewer will support middle-class lifestyles. Yet, not all students are equally prepared for or able to afford a college education, and this creates a risk that children from lower socioeconomic backgrounds will slip farther down the social class ladder.

Work and Income

In the past couple of decades, we have seen a widening income gap between those at the top, middle, and bottom of the scale (Bernstein et al. 2000; Wolff 2002). The 2010 census reported the largest income gap ever between the richest and poorest Americans (U.S. Census Bureau 2010e). Income is the product of work, and members of different social classes, with unequal educational opportunities, tend to work in different types of jobs (Figure 7.3).

At the bottom of the scale, members of the lower class generally experience difficulties in the job market and may endure periods of unemployment or underemployment (working in a job that doesn't pay enough to support a person's needs, or that doesn't make full use of his skills). Among the lower class are people receiving such government aid as Temporary Assistance for Needy Families (3.9 million in 2007; U.S. Census Bureau 2010f) or food stamps (36 million in 2009; DeParle and Gebeloff 2009) and the three million migrant farm workers who earn low wages picking strawberries, tomatoes, and other produce in places like California, Texas, and Kansas (González 2007).

Members of the working, or lower-middle, class work for wages in a variety of blue collar jobs. They can generally earn a dependable income through skilled or semiskilled occupations, but they may also experience periods of unemployment tied to fluctuations in the economy, layoffs, and plant closings. For example, in 2008 alone the United States lost more than 600,000 jobs as a result of factory shutdowns and other problems associated with the economic downturn (Garr 2008).

While factory work and other types of skilled labor were once enough to support a middle-class lifestyle, most middle-class jobs today are found in the service, information, and technology sectors. Most households here require two incomes to maintain a comfortable lifestyle, and many middle-class jobs require some sort of college degree.

The upper-middle class tends to work in executive and professional fields. Some members are business owners; a small portion own large farms or ranches. Others, known as the "creative class" (Florida 2002)—architects, writers, scientists, artists, professors, and engineers—tend to cluster in "creative" cities, such as Austin, San Francisco, and Seattle.

Through exceptional success in any profession or art, or sometimes through inheritance, one can join the upper class.

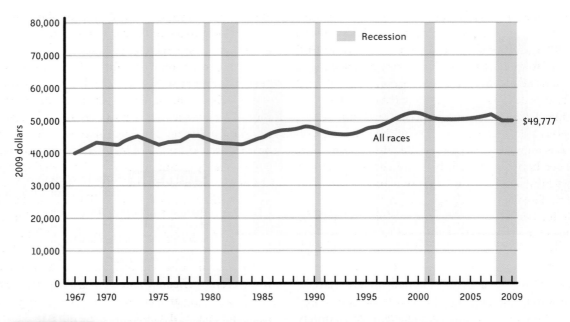

FIGURE 7.3 Real Median Income for Working-Age Households, 1967–2009

NOTE: Median household income data are not available prior to 1967.

SOURCE: U.S. Census Bureau 2010e.

In the United States, the upper class is influential in politics, business, and culture, largely because of their economic privilege: in our highly stratified society, the top 1 percent consistently control more than 33 percent of the national wealth (Wolff 2004; Kennickell 2009).

As a result of the recent recession, more workers are at risk of layoffs because of outsourcing. Corporations seeking to cut costs have been relocating their operations overseas, in countries where labor costs are lower. Both manufacturing and service jobs are subject to outsourcing, meaning that blue collar and white collar workers—and even some higher-ranking executives—are now vulnerable.

Criminal Justice

In general, people of lower SES are more likely to encounter the criminal justice system, whether as a perpetrator or victim of a crime, than those of higher SES. But the statistics are not as straightforward as they might seem. One influential study (Blau and Blau 1982) showed that while poverty is associated with higher rates of violent crime, variables such as dense population and anomie (a sense of alienation or lack of social connections) have an even greater impact on crime rates.

As we saw in Chapter 6, people in lower classes are often more visible, less powerful, and thus more likely to be apprehended and labeled as criminals than those from higher social classes. There are also differences in how crimes are prosecuted. White collar criminals are less likely to be arrested, or convicted than ordinary "street" criminals (Schwellenbach 2008). White collar criminals (such as Enron heads Jeffrey Skilling and the late Kenneth Lay, or Bernie Madoff whose Ponzi scheme bilked wealthy clients of billions of dollars) can also afford the best legal representation and hence enjoy distinct advantages in the courtroom. Studies have claimed that 90 percent of inmates on death row could not afford to hire a lawyer when they were tried (Lane and Tabak 1991) and that the quality of representation, rather than the actual facts presented in a trial, determines whether someone is sentenced to death (ACLU 2003). If they are convicted, white collar criminals' sentences are likely to be lighter. Still, while Enron's Ken Lay avoided prison time by dying of a massive heart attack several months before his October 2006 sentencing date, Jeffrey Skilling was sentenced to twenty-four years in prison and Madoff received 150 years for his crimes. Perhaps their punishments will serve as a deterrent for other high-status criminals.

Studies have shown that race and SES influence whether the death penalty is sought. Prosecutors are more likely to seek the death penalty if the killer is black, or if the victim was white. SES influences the likelihood of a death sentence, as those who are able to hire legal counsel are less likely to be sentenced to death. Therefore, the intersection of race and SES can dramatically affect the outcome of criminal sentencing (Phillips 2009).

Lower-class people are also more likely to be the victims of violent crime. Statistics consistently show that poor people are more than one and a half times more likely to be victims of violent crime than those in higher social class brackets (Levinson 2002). At the same time, people with lower SES are also more likely to feel at risk of harassment by police. As both education and income decreased, respondents reported feeling more threatened by police; as education and income increased, they felt less threatened (Levinson 2002).

Social class affects more than just our financial or material state—it is intricately woven into the fabric of our lives. You may once have concluded that differences in people's education, work, family, or health were simply a matter of individual preference or effort, or that each individual is responsible for her own circumstances. While this may be true to some extent, research shows that social class background has a profound impact on one's life chances, leading those with different statuses into very different life courses. This means that we can't take for granted whatever advantages or disadvantages we might experience but should acknowledge how hierarchies of inequality have helped to create our particular social realities.

Social Mobility

How do people move from one social class to another? In other words, how do they achieve **social mobility**? Sociologists use the concept of social mobility to measure movement within the stratification system of a particular society, whether it's a small town, a state or nation, or the entire world. In some societies, social mobility is highly restricted by formal or informal rules. India's caste system is an example of what sociologists refer to as a **closed system**: there is very little opportunity for social mobility between classes. The United States, where social mobility is possible, is perceived to be an **open system**. It was not always so, however: in the period of history preceding the Civil War, slavery was widespread, keeping African Americans from climbing the social class ladder.

The movement of people between social classes can happen in three different ways: through intergenerational mobility, intragenerational mobility, or structural mobility. **Intergenerational mobility** refers to the movement that occurs from one generation to the next, when a child eventually moves into a different social class from that of her parents. Research shows that baby boomers (children born immediately after World War II) have, for the most part, achieved upward intergenerational mobility: they have generally amassed more wealth during the course of their lives and consequently moved up the social class ladder. Some social scientists, however, claim that the distribution of income across generations has grown more static and that there are fewer opportunities for advancement than before (Krueger

2002), as tax laws and social policies allow the wealthy to protect their assets and make it more difficult for the middle and lower classes to increase theirs.

Intragenerational mobility refers to the movement that occurs during the course of an individual's lifetime. In other words, it is the measure between a person's ascribed status, the social class she is born into, and the social class status she achieves during her lifetime. Intragenerational mobility can be measured in two directions. **Horizontal social mobility**, which is fairly common, refers to the changing of jobs within a class: a therapist who shifts careers so that he can teach college experiences horizontal mobility. **Vertical social mobility** is movement up or down the social ladder, and thus is often called upward or downward mobility. If this same therapist marries a president of a large corporation, he might experience upward mobility. On the other hand, if he or his wife becomes unemployed, he might experience downward mobility. People are far more likely to experience horizontal than vertical social mobility.

Although we usually think of social mobility as the result of individual effort (or lack thereof), other factors can contribute to a change in one's social class. **Structural mobility** occurs when large numbers of people move up or down the social ladder because of structural changes in society as a whole, particularly when the economic sector is affected by large-scale events. For instance, during the Great Depression of the early 1930s, precipitated by the stock market crash of 1929, huge numbers of upper- and middle-class people suddenly found themselves among the poor. Conversely, during the dot-com boom of the late 1990s, developing and investing in new technologies made many people into overnight millionaires. Both of these extreme periods eventually leveled out. Still, many people in the Depression era remained in their new class, never able to climb up the social ladder again.

social mobility the movement of individuals or groups within the hierarchal system of social classes

closed system a social system with very little opportunity to move from one class to another

open system a social system with ample opportunities to move from one class to another

intergenerational mobility movement between social classes that occurs from one generation to the next

intragenerational mobility the movement between social classes that occurs during the course of an individual's lifetime

horizontal social mobility the occupational movement of individuals or groups within a social class

vertical social mobility the movement between different class statuses, often called either upward mobility or downward mobility

structural mobility changes in the social status of large numbers of people due to structural changes in society

In Relationships

Socioeconomic Status and Mate Selection

You say you don't judge a book by its cover? You say it's the person who matters, and not the social categories he or she belongs to? We may believe these things, but sociological studies strongly suggest that we don't act on them. When it comes to dating, courtship, and marriage ("mate selection" activities, as defined by social scientists), we tend to make homogamous choices. **Homogamy** ("like marries like") means that we choose romantic partners based on our similarities in background and group membership. Despite the old adage that "opposites attract," decades of sociological research show that we make choices based on similarities in race, ethnicity, religion, class, education, age—even height and levels of physical attractiveness (Kalmijn 1998). Homogamy based on socioeconomic status is especially clear: we tend to marry those who share the same economic and educational backgrounds as we do. This holds true even if we practice **heterogamy** (marrying someone who is different from us) in other areas, such as race or religion. Why is class-based homogamy so prevalent?

As it turns out, we have relatively few opportunities to meet people of different socioeconomic backgrounds during the course of our everyday lives. At home, at school, on the job, at the coffee shop or gym, we are likely to be surrounded by those who are like us, classwise. Homogamy is more strictly enforced in upper-class families than in other

social classes. Those who enjoy the privileges of wealth often want to make sure those privileges continue into the next generation and may monitor their children's activities by sending them to prestigious schools and posh summer camps so that they don't get the opportunity to meet anyone but other privileged kids. This helps ensure that wealth and power remain consolidated within a relatively small community. If you spend all your free time at the country club pool instead of getting a summer job working at Starbucks or McDonald's, your opportunities to meet the *hoi polloi* are limited.

If we focus only on those in the public eye, it is easy to see how limits on opportunity result in marriages between affluent and powerful families. This happens in political families. For example, Julie Nixon, daughter of the former president, married David Eisenhower, grandson of another former president. Kerry Kennedy, daughter of former attorney general Robert Kennedy, married (and later divorced) Andrew Cuomo, son of former New York governor Mario Cuomo. And it happens among celebrities, whether movie stars Brad Pitt and Angelina Jolie, singers Beyonce Knowles and Jay-Z, or NFL quarterback Tom Brady and supermodel Gisele Bündchen, all practiced a form of status homogamy by partnering with people from the same social circles—other

Defining Poverty

Social mobility is most difficult—and most essential—for those who live at the bottom of the socioeconomic ladder. In this section, we look at what it means to be poor in America.

relative deprivation a relative measure of poverty based on the standard of living in a particular society

absolute deprivation an objective measure of poverty, defined by the inability to meet minimal standards for food, shelter, clothing, or health care

Poverty can be defined in relative or absolute terms. **Relative deprivation** is a comparative measure, whereby people are considered poor if their standard of living is less

than that of other members of society—for example, a Wal-Mart clerk who works part-time for minimum wage is poor compared with a neurosurgeon whose salary is $500,000. **Absolute deprivation**, on the other hand, is a measure whereby people are unable to meet minimal standards for food, shelter, clothing, and health care. In Burundi, for example, between 60 percent and 70 percent of the population experience chronic malnutrition (U.N. Millennium Project 2001). In Swaziland, more than 25 percent of adults are living with HIV. Poverty has resulted in a lack of access to health care, exacerbating the HIV epidemic and making this the country with the lowest life expectancy in the world at 32 years. Hunger, malnutrition, and/or the inability

famous and wealthy celebrities. Whether they met on the set, at the yacht club, or at an awards show, they met in a status-restricted setting to which not everyone is eligible for entry.

Questions have arisen recently about how internet technologies may facilitate—or impede—our tendency toward homogamy. Dating sites such as eHarmony, Match.com, and others allow people who occupy vastly different social circles to meet online—and perhaps fall in love. In this way, it would seem that internet dating has the potential to inhibit our off-line predilection for people who belong to the same social groups as we do. On the other hand, internet dating can also assist us in choosing people who are like us, in that certain sites cater to particular social groups. J-Date (for Jewish singles), The Right Stuff (for Ivy Leaguers) and other specialty sites select for social group membership and may actually strengthen homogamous effects in our online mate selection processes.

Vast differences in class standing between marital partners are usually the stuff of fairy tales and fantasy. The "Cinderella story," in which a low-status woman is romantically "rescued" by a high-status man, is familiar to us all—yet we likely have seen it happen only in storybooks and movie theaters. *Pretty Woman*, in which Julia Roberts plays a prostitute who is romanced by Richard Gere's wealthy businessman, is a perfect example of this type of heterogamous fantasy, as is

Jay-Z and Beyonce Knowles

Maid in Manhattan, in which Jennifer Lopez plays a hotel housekeeper who is wooed by Ralph Fiennes's character, a rich political candidate. The only touch of sociological reality in these tales is the portrayal of women's **hypergamy** and men's **hypogamy**; that is, when class boundaries are crossed, women usually marry up while men marry down. Take a look at the role of SES in your own mate selection activities: are you homogamous or heterogamous?

to afford medications are some of the basic indicators of absolute poverty.

In the United States, the federal poverty line—an absolute measure, calculated annually—indicates the total annual income below which a family would be considered poor. These figures are derived from either the poverty thresholds established by the Census Bureau or the guidelines established by the Department of Health and Human Services. In 2009, the Census Bureau defined the poverty threshold as $21,954 for a family of four, $17,098 for a family of three, $13,991 for a family of two, and $10,956 for an individual (U.S. Census 2009a). In fact, families making much more than these amounts, although not officially qualifying as

poor, might still be unable to afford some basic necessities.

How many people fall below the poverty line? The numbers are startling, given that we usually think of the United States as a wealthy nation. In 2009, 15.7 percent of the population, or 47.8 million people, were considered poor, a rise in both numbers and percentage over the 2008 rate (U.S. Census 2010g).

homogamy choosing romantic partners who are similar to us in terms of class, race, education, religion, and other social group membership

heterogamy choosing romantic partners who are dissimilar to us in terms of class, race, education, religion, and other social group membership

hypergamy marrying "up" in the social class hierarchy

hypogamy marrying "down" in the social class hierarchy

On the Job

Digital Divide

In a postindustrial economy, most of us will have to demonstrate a certain level of computer proficiency in order to secure a job. One way or another, the majority of jobs in contemporary society involve computers, so you'll have to know how to program one or use certain programs to do your work, whatever it may be—editing and publishing, say, or accounting or graphic design, fine woodworking or auto repair, teaching or engineering or nursing. Because you are attending college, you'll probably be lucky enough to acquire some of these skills in the course of your education. But not everyone has the opportunities you have, and many in the United States and around the world lack the basic computer skills, experience, and access necessary to secure a decent job. This inequality in access to and use of digital technology is known as the **digital divide**.

Actually, in the words of PBS media and technology reporter Mark Glaser, "there are many digital divides." The hierarchies of inequality in the larger society—such as race, class, and educational attainment—all shape one's access to technology (Glaser 2007). For example, while 79 percent of all adults in the United States use the internet regularly, only 71 percent of African Americans, 63 percent of those with a household income under $30,000, and 52 percent of those with less than a high school education do so (Pew Internet and American Life Project 2010).

These disparities mirror the contours of other sorts of social inequality, especially because computer and internet technology access requires resources—funds to purchase computers and subscribe to broadband, or to feed the meter at the internet café, or even to support public libraries that sometimes provide free access. The wealthy and privileged tend to have more of these resources than do the poor or underprivileged.

The digital divide is really about the benefits of technology access rather than merely the access itself. This is because access to computers and the internet offers additional related opportunities and privileges, especially in education and the job market. Sure, everyone deserves the opportunity to play video games, but think of the other things you do with your digital access: you take online classes, utilize job search and resume-posting services, and develop skills that facilitate recruitment into your chosen career. Without these

benefits, certain educational and employment opportunities would be closed to you, no matter how smart or ambitious you might be.

Just as there are digitally disadvantaged groups and individuals domestically, there are digitally disadvantaged countries—the digital divide is global. In underdeveloped and developing nations, real poverty leads to "information poverty" as well (Norris 2001) and creates further obstacles to development—a kind of self-sealing loop. The organization One Laptop Per Child (OLPC) has developed a small, sturdy, low-power portable computer with the goal of distributing the green and yellow machines to children in developing countries such as Uruguay, Cambodia, Peru, and Rwanda. As of early 2011, they had distributed nearly two million units to children in more than a dozen nations. OLPC corporate sponsors such as Intel, Google, and eBay recognize the benefits of trying to help the organization bridge the digital divide; indeed, they may be helping to put computers in the hands of kids who will someday grow up to work for them!

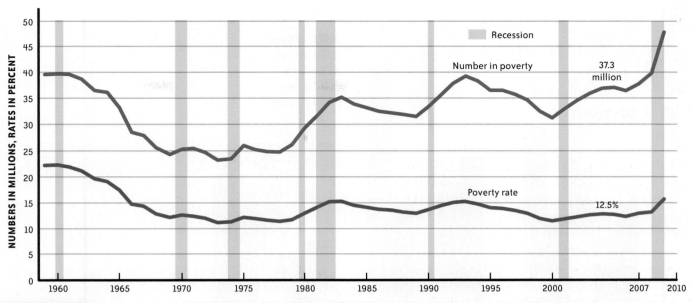

FIGURE 7.4 Number in Poverty and Poverty Rate, 1959–2009

Although poverty rates declined sharply during the "war on poverty" of the early 1960s, they have remained relatively stable in the decades since.

SOURCE: U.S. Census Bureau 2010g.

During the past forty years, the percentage of poor people has fluctuated, but it has never dipped below 10 percent. In fact, the number has occasionally risen to more than 15 percent, as it did recently in 2009, while in the late 1950s it rose as high as 22 percent (see Figure 7.4). And contrary to popular myth, most poor people are not unemployed; they are known as the working poor. The annual earnings of a full-time worker making $7.25 an hour (the 2010 federal minimum wage) still puts him below the poverty line if he is trying to support a family. According to researchers, more than 80 percent of low-income minimum-wage workers, even if they are working full-time, are not earning enough to guarantee a decent living standard, and many cannot afford some of the basic necessities (Wicks-Lim and Thompson 2010).

The poverty line has often been criticized because of the way it is uniformly applied without regard to regional or other differences. For instance, a family living in Washington, D.C., might need twice or three times as much income as a family in Des Moines for expenses like rent, transportation, health insurance, and child care (exceptions are made for Alaska and Hawaii, both states with extremely high costs of living). In addition, some families may be eligible for some form of government assistance, such as food stamps or the Earned Income Tax Credit (EITC), which makes a difference in the total amount of their household money. Many

working families thus live close to the edge and struggle to make ends meet but are not included as part of the official poverty statistics (Waldron et al. 2004).

Poverty is also more prominent among certain population groups (Figure 7.5). For instance, poverty rates are higher among blacks and Hispanics than Asians or whites. They are higher for the elderly, disabled, and for those who are foreign born, as well as for women, children, and single-parent households. And they are higher in the South, inner cities, and rural areas.

Social Welfare and Welfare Reform

Some of the most heated debates about the nature of poverty involve how or even whether society should help the poor. Some argue that government assistance helps poor people become self-supporting; others say that it just fosters a dependence on aid and causes further problems.

The idea behind the current American welfare state, which consists of such programs as Social Security, unemployment insurance, and Temporary Assistance for Needy Families (TANF), was first proposed by President Franklin D. Roosevelt during the Great Depression of the

> **digital divide** the experience of unequal access to computer and internet technology, both globally and within the United States

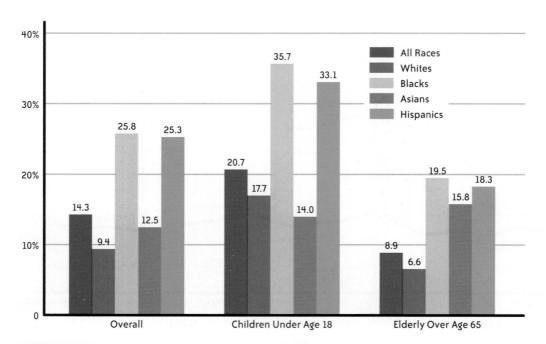

FIGURE 7.5 Poverty in the United States by Selected Characteristics, 2009

SOURCE: U.S. Census Bureau 2010g.

1930s. These programs, collectively called the New Deal, were a response to a national crisis and were meant to serve as a safety net for citizens, helping them in times of adversity or old age, poverty, or joblessness. A second wave of programs, such as Medicaid and Head Start, intended to solve a variety of social and economic problems, were proposed by President John F. Kennedy and instituted by President Lyndon B. Johnson as part of his Great Society program in 1964.

The welfare system attempted to be fair by providing uniform, standard benefits to all the nation's needy without regard to their personal circumstances and with no time limit. Social Security and Medicaid lifted seniors out of poverty, and programs like Head Start and Upward Bound offered educational support for poor children. Food stamps improved nutrition for those with limited incomes, and job-training programs helped the poor gain marketable skills. By 1970, the poverty rate had declined from 22.2 percent to 12.6 percent (Califano 1999), the fastest it has ever dropped.

In the 1980s, political opinion turned against social welfare programs despite their successes. Critics claimed that these programs were responsible for creating a permanent underclass of people living off government checks—some receiving benefits they didn't deserve—and essentially discouraging them from seeking work. These critics are still voicing their disapproval today.

Americans in general have felt a deep ambivalence toward welfare (Mayer 1997). Polls show that a majority (55 percent) think poverty is a "big problem," yet addressing the issue is not among their highest priorities. They are divided too as to how to solve the problem. Few (18 percent) feel that there is too much being spent on assistance to the poor, but the remainder are split into those who feel that the country spends too little (38 percent) and those who feel that it spends about the right amount (36 percent). This may be because Americans are ambivalent about the causes of poverty: in 2001, 48 percent thought that the cause of poverty was "poor people not doing enough," while 45 percent attributed poverty to "circumstances beyond their control" (NPR/Kaiser/Kennedy poll 2001).

Most of the rhetoric surrounding welfare programs stems from concerns about federal spending. People commonly assume that welfare constitutes a large portion of the federal budget, when in fact welfare and unemployment together represented just over 13 percent of government spending in 2011, or $324 billion (Figure 7.6). Compare that with Social Security (about 21 percent of spending, or $608 billion) or defense and the war on terror (about 20 percent of spending, or $626 billion). But given these misconceptions, it makes sense that welfare abuse and reform have received so much press in the past twenty years.

In response to criticism of welfare programs, reform arrived in the 1990s. Under President Bill Clinton, the Personal

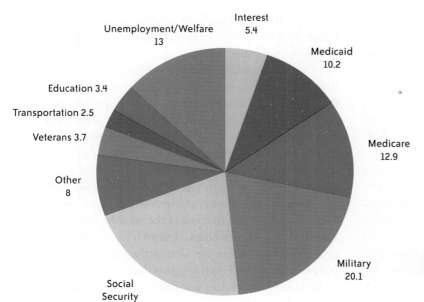

FIGURE 7.6 Federal Spending, 2011

Spending on welfare and unemployment combined represented just over 13 percent of the 2011 federal budget.

SOURCE: GPO Access 2011.

Interest 5.4

Unemployment/Welfare 13

Medicaid 10.2

Education 3.4

Transportation 2.5

Veterans 3.7

Medicare 12.9

Other 8

Military 20.1

Social Security 20.8

Responsibility and Work Opportunity Reconciliation Act was passed into law in 1996. Often referred to as the Welfare Reform Act, it ended the concept of "entitlements" by requiring recipients to find work within two years of receiving assistance and imposing a limit of five years as the total amount of time in which families could receive assistance. The act also decentralized the federal system of public assistance, allowing individual states to design their own programs, some of which would deny or reduce certain benefits, and impose their own criteria for eligibility. The rationale was to encourage people on welfare to take responsibility for working themselves out of poverty. In 2003, Congress approved changes to the act, requiring an even larger percentage of recipients to take jobs and work longer hours.

While welfare reform has been an economic success in terms of reducing the number of people on welfare, there is still a great deal to be learned about its success or failure in transforming the lives of the poor. Evidence suggests that moving from welfare to work does not increase income levels—in other words, federal assistance is merely replaced with an equally low-paying job, which has the effect of keeping families beneath the poverty line once they're off welfare. The reasons for this—the increased costs of child care, health insurance, and transportation—make it difficult for former welfare recipients to succeed outside the system (Hays 2003).

Studies are now being conducted to evaluate the consequences of welfare policy changes. One of the largest, "Welfare, Children, and Families: A Three-City Study," is a longitudinal study (one that follows the children of welfare over time) done in Boston, Chicago, and San Antonio. A team of researchers from three different universities, including sociologists, anthropologists, psychologists, and economists, using methods as diverse as survey research, interviews, and in-depth ethnographies, sought to discover whether welfare reform was really helping to eradicate poverty and what kind of an impact welfare reform had on the lives of struggling families. They found that for families leaving welfare, their income rose only incrementally (less than 20 percent), and the impact on the lives of children (school achievement, mental health, etc.) was also only mildly positive (Hao and Cherlin 2004; Slack et al. 2006). So getting off welfare does bring positive results, but often those results aren't strong enough to serve as much of an incentive. It is likely that new policy recommendations will emerge in the future as a result of such research.

The "Culture of Poverty" Theory and Its Critics

Some argue that what keeps people poor is not public policy but rather the result of entrenched cultural attitudes. Oscar Lewis (1959) first promoted the idea of a **culture of poverty** after he studied poor Hispanics in Mexico and the United States. Lewis suggested that the poor, because they were excluded from the mainstream, developed a way of life that was qualitatively different from that of middle-class societies and allowed them to cope with the dire circumstance of poverty.

culture of poverty entrenched attitudes that can develop among poor communities and lead the poor to accept their fate rather than attempt to improve their lot

This way of life includes attitudes of resignation and fatalism, which lead the poor to accept their fate rather than trying to improve their lot. It also emphasizes immediate gratification, making it difficult for the poor to plan or save for the future or to join trade unions or community groups that might help them improve their situation. Once such a culture is formed, Lewis argued, it takes on a life of its own and is passed on from parents to children, leaving them ill-equipped to change.

The culture of poverty theory was later adopted by other social scientists (Banfield 1970) and applied to the American poor, particularly those in inner cities. Not surprisingly, though, the theory has been met with considerable controversy, in part because it suggests that there is little point in trying to eradicate poverty because it's more a problem of culture (attitudes, lifestyle, and behavior) than of economics. By focusing on individual character and personality, the theory tends to blame the victims of poverty for their own misfortunes while overlooking the force of their social conditions.

The tendency to see victims of social injustice as deserving of their fates is explained by what social psychologists call the **just-world hypothesis**. According to this argument, we have a strong need to believe that the world is orderly, predictable, and fair in order to achieve our goals in life. When we encounter situations that contradict this belief, we either act quickly to restore justice and order or persuade ourselves that no injustice has occurred. This can result in assuming that the victim has "asked for it" or deserves whatever has befallen her. This attitude is continually reinforced through the morality tales that are a ubiquitous part of our news and entertainment, which tell us that good is rewarded and evil punished (say, in a news story about a homeless man who returns a lost wallet full of cash to its owner, who then shares the money with him).

The just-world hypothesis, developed by Melvin Lerner (1965, 1980), was tested through a series of experiments that documented how people can convince themselves that others deserve what they get. In these experiments, cash prizes were randomly distributed to students completing the exact same tasks in the exact same way. Observers, however, judged the cash recipients as the more deserving, harder workers. Other researchers (Rubin and Peplau 1975) have found that people with strong beliefs in a just world tend to "feel less of a need to engage in activities to change society or to alleviate the plight of social victims." In the face of poverty, many simply become apathetic. It is important to be aware of our own tendencies to follow such thinking, so that we might avoid becoming blind to others' misfortunes.

Another problem with the culture of poverty theory is that it lacks a certain sociological imagination. It fails to take into account the structural factors that shape culture and are part of the preexisting problem in which poor individuals find themselves. Dalton Conley, a sociologist at New York University, argues that to solve the problem of poverty, we must examine wealth as well (2002). A social system that allows extremes of both wealth and poverty (as ours does) reveals structural reasons why poverty persists, such as laws that protect the inheritances of the wealthy but provide few breaks for working families. Research like Conley's helps us understand that there are alternative explanations for why people are poor and even suggests that extreme wealth ought to be conceptualized as a social problem similar to that of extreme poverty.

The Invisibility of Poverty

Although we are used to seeing televised images of abject poverty from overseas—crying children with bloated bellies and spindly limbs in Asia, Africa, or Latin America—we rarely see similar images from the United States. While it may be true that few Americans are as poor as the starving Somalis or Bangladeshis, some 47.8 million Americans lived below the poverty line in 2009 (U.S. Census Bureau 2010g). That's almost 16 percent of the population of the wealthiest nation in the world. How can such large numbers of people remain hidden to their fellow Americans? What makes poverty invisible?

RESIDENTIAL SEGREGATION One factor is **residential segregation**—the geographical isolation of the poor from the rest of the city (or in the case of the rural poor, from any neighbors at all). Such segregation often occurs along racial as well as socioeconomic lines, further exacerbating class divisions (Massey and Denton 1993). In the phrase "wrong side of the tracks," used to describe poverty-stricken neighborhoods, there is usually a racial connotation as well, since railroad tracks traditionally served as boundaries that kept black neighborhoods separated from white ones in the nineteenth century (Ananat 2005).

Residential segregation is accomplished most notably through public housing projects, which are typically high-density apartment complexes in urban areas, funded and managed by the Department of Housing and Urban Development (HUD). Living in these apartment complexes, many of which are in low-income, high-crime neighborhoods and are poorly maintained, can be dangerous as well as unpleasant.

just-world hypothesis argues that people have a deep need to see the world as orderly, predictable, and fair, which creates a tendency to view victims of social injustice as deserving of their fates

residential segregation the geographical separation of the poor from the rest of the population

Residential Segregation
High-density housing projects frequently isolate the poor from the rest of the city.

Residential segregation is also exacerbated by the practice of "redlining," in which banks and mortgage lenders identify high-risk areas (usually poor or minority neighborhoods) and either refuse mortgages to applicants from those neighborhoods or offer loans at prohibitively high rates. Redlining keeps the poor from acquiring assets (like real estate) that might allow them to rise out of poverty and move to a more affluent neighborhood. Though redlining is technically illegal, the practice is still in evidence today in banking, insurance, and other industries, disproportionately affecting the poor and minorities (Wilson 2009). In one instance, a major mortgage company, MidAmerica Bank, settled a redlining case in Chicago by agreeing to open more branches in poor and minority neighborhoods and to include poor and minority consumers in their advertising campaigns, which had previously targeted only buyers at higher income levels.

POLITICAL DISENFRANCHISEMENT The poor may remain invisible to the larger society because of their lack of political power as well. **Disenfranchisement** is a correlate of poverty: the poor are less likely to vote or otherwise participate in political life (Kerbo and Gonzalez 2003). When everyday life is a struggle to make ends meet, it is difficult to muster the extra energy necessary to work for political change. The poor may also feel that the system has not served them; if the government ignores their interests, why bother to become involved? Because of their lack of involvement, the poor lack political clout and the resources to make their plight a high-profile political priority. Politicians at the local and national levels have little motivation to address their needs, because as a constituency the poor wield less power than such groups as senior citizens, "soccer moms," and small-business owners. When the poor do organize politically, even their successes may not be well known. One group, Mothers of East Los Angeles (whose motto includes the phrase "not economically rich, but culturally wealthy"), has been successfully protecting their neighborhood from environmental degradation and exploitation for twenty years. They have rebuffed plans to build a prison, toxic waste plants, and an oil pipeline near homes and schools in their community. But have you ever heard of them?

HOMELESSNESS In certain situations, the very poor are deliberately removed from public view. Police are sometimes ordered to scour the streets, rousting the homeless and herding them out of sight, as they did in 1988 in New York City's Tompkins Square Park (an infamous riot ensued). High-profile occasions, such as political conventions and major sporting events, put a media spotlight on city streets. In the summer of 2000, for example, on the eve of the Republican National Convention, the city of Philadelphia denied a permit to a group of welfare rights protesters who wanted to demonstrate against government poverty policies. The hope was that in denying the permit, the group would not make an appearance on streets already crawling with politicians, demonstrators,

disenfranchisement the removal of the rights of citizenship through economic, political, or legal means

Homelessness Two volunteers speak with a homeless man on a subway for the all-night Homeless Outreach Population Estimate (HOPE), run by the Department of Homeless Services in New York City. HOPE is the first population survey to obtain a city-wide estimate of homeless individuals living on the street and helps the government to provide better services and resources for the homeless population.

journalists, and photographers. But the protesters marched anyway—with a police escort—and were able to make their voice heard despite the lack of official permission to do so.

Mostly, though, the poor and homeless remain invisible. We don't know exactly how many homeless live in the United States. The Census Bureau focuses its population counts on households, so the homeless living in long-term shelters may get counted, but not those on the streets. One recent estimate is that more than 3.5 million people (approximately 1 percent of the U.S. population) will experience homelessness at least once during a given year (National Law Center on Homelessness and Poverty 2010). The recession that started in 2008 and has continued during the past several years, has left many people unemployed and their finances drained, creating a surge in homelessness that includes many who were formerly among the middle classes. "Nationally, homelessness has now reached crisis proportions not seen since the Great Depression," says Maria Foscarinis, executive director of the National Law Center on Homelessness and Poverty (Goodman 2010).

Each year, the city of New York attempts to measure the number of homeless men and women. Volunteers comb the streets in the overnight hours, making note of all those they find sleeping on park benches or in building stairwells. They do not, however, enter abandoned buildings or subway tunnels, where many of New York's homeless seek shelter. The 2010 count of homeless found a 34 percent increase in people living on the city's streets vs. the previous year (3,111 in 2009 compared with 2,328 in 2008), along with another 38,000 living in shelters (Bosman 2010). Although this is sometimes

a difficult population to locate and there may be questions about the accuracy of reports, such counts help the city estimate its needs for homeless services in the coming year.

The homeless also remain invisible to most of us because of our own feelings of discomfort and guilt. John Coleman, a former college president and business executive, discovered this when he lived in poverty, if only temporarily, on the streets of Manhattan. Coleman went "undercover" as a homeless man for ten days and found that the minute he shed his privileged identity, people looked at him differently—or not at all. During his days on the streets, Coleman passed by and made eye contact with his accountant, his landlord, and a co-worker—each looked right through him, without recognition. But he was not invisible to everyone. Police officers often shook him awake to get him moving from whatever meager shelter he had found for the night. A waiter at a diner took one look at him and forced him to pay up front for his 99-cent breakfast special. Other homeless men, though, showed him kindness and generosity (Coleman 1983).

To whom are the poor visible? Those who work with them: caseworkers, social service providers, government bureaucrats, volunteers and charity workers, clergy, cops, business owners (including those who may not want to deal with the poor, as well as those who may exploit them). And now, you.

With a sociological perspective, you can now see the effects of social stratification everywhere you turn. And when you recognize the multiple, complex causes of poverty— such as limited educational and job opportunities, stagnating wages, economic downturns, racism, mental illness, and substance abuse—it will no longer be as simple to consider each individual responsible for his or her own plight. Finally, the sociological perspective will give you the ability to imagine possible solutions to the problems associated with poverty—solutions that focus on large-scale social changes as well as individual actions, including your own. Don't let poverty remain invisible.

Inequality and the Ideology of the American Dream

Ask almost anyone about the American Dream and they are likely to mention some of the following: owning your own home; having a good marriage and great kids; finding a good job that you enjoy; being able to afford nice vacations; having a big-screen TV, nice clothes, or season tickets to your team's home games. For most Americans, the dream also means that all people, no matter how humble their beginnings, can succeed in whatever they set out to do if they work hard enough. In other words, a poor boy or girl could grow up to become president of the United States, an astronaut, a professional basketball player, a captain of industry, or a movie star.

One problem with the American Dream, however, is that it doesn't always match reality. It's more of an ideology: a belief system that explains and justifies some sort of social arrangement, in this case America's social class hierarchy. The ideology of the American Dream legitimizes stratification by reinforcing the idea that everyone has the same chance to get ahead and that success or failure depends on the person (Hochschild 1996). Inequality is presented as a system of incentives and rewards for achievement. If we can credit anyone who does succeed, then logically we must also blame anyone who fails. The well-socialized American buys into this belief system, without recognizing its structural flaws. We are caught in what Marx would call "false consciousness," the inability to see the ways in which we may be oppressed.

Nevertheless, it's not easy to dismiss the idea of the American Dream, especially when there are so many high-profile examples. Take, for instance, Oprah Winfrey. Born in Mississippi in 1954, Winfrey endured a childhood of abject poverty. In 2010, *Forbes* magazine listed her as number 138 of the 400 richest Americans, a ranking she has continued to climb during the past several years, with a likewise increasing personal wealth of $2.7 billion. Not only is Winfrey the highest-paid black female, but she is also one of the highest-paid entertainers of all time. *Forbes* further honored her as the most powerful celebrity (of 100), based on a composite that included earnings and dominance across various media. Also in 2010, Oprah Winfrey launched her own independent cable network—the Oprah Winfrey Network or OWN.

The American Dream Oprah Winfrey's meteoric rise from a childhood of poverty to her position as one of the most powerful celebrities in America is often cited as a prime example of the American Dream. How does Oprah's success represent the exception rather than the rule?

The accolades and awards span many categories. Not only is she extremely successful as a media mogul and personality, but Winfrey is also widely praised for her philanthropic efforts and is admired as a symbol of what can be achieved in pursuit of the American Dream. The problem is, we tend to think of her as representing the rule rather than the exception. For most Americans, the rags-to-riches upward mobility she has achieved is very unrealistic.

Though popular opinion and rhetoric espouse the American Dream ideology or that the United States is a **meritocracy** (a system in which rewards are distributed based on merit), sociologists find contrary evidence. In fact, no matter how hard they work or seek a good education, most people will make little movement at all. And the degree of mobility they do achieve can depend on a person's ethnicity, class status, or gender rather than merit. For example, whites are more likely to experience upward mobility than persons of color (Davis 1995), and married women are more likely to experience upward mobility than nonmarried women (Li and Singelmann 1998). Immigrant persons of color are the most likely to experience downward social mobility (McCall 2001). A poll conducted in 2010, which defined the American Dream as "if you work hard, you will get ahead," found that 50 percent of Americans believe

meritocracy a system in which rewards are distributed based on merit

Michael Moore's *Capitalism: A Love Story*

Twenty years after his film-making debut with *Roger & Me*, Michael Moore brought us his seventh and latest theatrical release, *Capitalism: A Love Story*, in 2009. Moore has come a long way in those twenty years. In terms of *making* the movie, things couldn't have been more different. When he made *Roger & Me*, he was an unemployed journalist with no experience in film and no financial backing. Ralph Nader donated some money and office space, but to finance the rest of the film's eventual $160,000 budget Moore sold his house and held weekly bingo games. Then, miraculously, despite being a grim portrayal of the economic meltdown of his hometown, Flint, Michigan, following the closing of the General Motors plant there, the movie became a surprise hit.

This success allowed Moore to launch a career as a professional gadfly, making a series of documentaries about various social and political problems in the United States, from gun violence (*Bowling for Columbine*) and the war in Iraq (*Fahrenheit 9/11*) to the health care crisis (*Sicko*). These films were all enormously popular. *Bowling for Columbine* won the 2002 Academy Award for Best Documentary. *Fahrenheit 9/11* earned $222 million and is the highest-grossing documentary of all time. Given this success, the process of making *Capitalism* must have been very different from his earlier films, but the topics are remarkably familiar to those

A scene from *Capitalism: A Love Story*.

who remember *Roger & Me*. Twenty years of making movies has provided Moore with the means for a larger soapbox. The high profile he has achieved can be viewed, in some ways, as enabling him to remake his first film on a larger scale.

Like *Roger & Me*, *Capitalism: A Love Story* is grounded in Moore's life. He reminisces about growing up in Michigan, as well as his uncle's participation in the landmark sit-down strike at the GM plant in Flint that helped establish the United Auto Workers union. He also spends some time talking to his own father, who worked for General Motors

---

the American Dream still exists, while 43 percent said it "once held true"; just 4 percent believe it has never existed (Bailey 2010). The numbers shift when broken down by such background factors as income, education, and race of the respondent. People with household incomes above $75,000 were more likely to believe in the dream (57 percent) than those making less than $25,000 (46 percent). More college graduates (58 percent) believe in the American Dream than those with just a high school education (48 percent). More nonwhites believe in it (57 percent) than whites (48 percent).

Although the American Dream tends to promote consumerism as a way to achieve "the good life," the fact is that

chasing after it has left us feeling less secure and satisfied—not to mention less wealthy—than previous generations (De Graaf et al. 2002). Some pundits suggest that we have lost focus on the original meaning of the American Dream, that our increasing obsession with the idea of "more (or newer or bigger) is better" is leading to more debt, less free time, and greater discontent. Americans now carry twice as much credit card debt than they did in 1990 (Walker 2004); in 2010, credit card holders had an average balance owed of $5,100 (Copeland 2010). An Ohio State University study recently reported that Americans have less free time and feel more rushed than they did thirty years ago (Sayer and Mattingly 2006).

making spark plugs for thirty-three years. And like *Roger & Me*, *Capitalism* features chilling scenes of sheriff's deputies evicting homeowners who could no longer make their mortgage payments. But the real link between the two movies comes about halfway through, when Moore is interviewing a family being evicted from their home. When the Hacker family showed Moore the eviction papers, he noticed that the foreclosure statement from Citibank was printed and mailed from Flint, Michigan. It turns out that more than 60 percent of all foreclosure notices are mailed from Michael Moore's hometown. As he put it, "in what seems to be some sort of cruel joke," they were "helping to turn the rest of America into Flint."

If *Roger & Me* was the story of what happened to a single town when an industry imploded, *Capitalism: A Love Story* is the story of what happened to the entire country when the banking industry melted down. The main focus of the film was the financial crisis that began in 2007 with the collapse of the housing industry, but the narrative ranges as far back as the Roosevelt administration and lays the blame for the subsequent recession on the process of deregulation that began with the Reagan administration. Like the demise of Flint when the GM plant laid off 30,000 workers, Moore makes it clear that this is not a crisis that affected everyone equally. GM posted $5 billion in profits the year they laid off those workers, and so while many Americans lost their homes or their jobs at the end of the first decade of the twenty-first century, a small number of the very wealthy made out like bandits—perhaps literally, as he reports that as early as 2004 the FBI was charting an "epidemic of mortgage fraud."

The story that Moore tells is not just about the recent recession that resulted from these events, but to say something about how capitalism works in America today. He believes that we are in love with capitalism, but that it is an unhealthy love, based on greed. Much of the movie is devoted to examining the linkages between Wall Street and Washington, and the revolving cast of characters who move from lucrative multimillion-dollar jobs in finance and banking to government work and back again. Moore believes that the slim chance of getting rich in the "casino" that is the American economy is the "carrot" that capitalism uses to disguise the systematic and structural ways in which the very wealthy enrich themselves at the expense of the rest of the country. The film opens with scenes from a security camera showing a bank robbery, and spends the better part of two hours arguing that what has been typically called a financial crisis was in fact "the greatest wave of white collar crime in the nation's history—in fact, in the world's history."

A countervailing trend in American life, however, sometimes referred to as the **simplicity movement**, rejects rampant consumerism and seeks to reverse some of its consequences for the individual, for society, and for the planet. This movement, a backlash against the traditional American Dream, encourages people to "downshift" by working less, earning less, and spending less in order to put their lifestyles in sync with their (nonmaterialistic) values (Schor 1999). What does this mean in practice? Growing your own vegetables, perhaps, or riding your bike to work, recycling and composting, and spending more time with friends and family and less time commuting, spending money, or watching TV.

One of the most radical extensions of this philosophy is embraced by "freegans"—a term that merges "free" with "vegan" (a person who eats no animal products). Freegans are people who avoid consumerism and who engage in strategies to support themselves without participating in a conventional economic system. This can mean scavenging for usable food, clothing, and other goods, sometimes called "urban foraging" or "dumpster diving," along with sharing housing and transportation with others in order to work less and minimize their impact on the planet.

> **simplicity movement** a loosely knit movement that opposes consumerism and encourages people to work less, earn less, and spend less, in accordance with nonmaterialistic values

DATA WORKSHOP

ANALYZING MASS MEDIA AND POPULAR CULTURE

Advertising and the American Dream

We are surrounded by advertising, which aims not only to give us information about products but also to create and stimulate a buying public with demands for an ever-increasing array of goods and services. Advertising shapes our consciousness and tells us what to dream and how to pursue those dreams. It provides us with a concept of the good life and tells us that it's available to everyone. Advertising equates shopping and acquisition with emotional fulfillment, freedom, fun, happiness, security, and self-satisfaction.

And the sales pitch seems to be working. Like no other generation, today's eighteen- to thirty-four-year olds have grown up in a consumer culture with all its varied enticements, but they are having a harder time reaching financial stability in adulthood than did their parents. Tamara Draut (2006) describes their predicament in her book *Strapped: Why America's 20- and 30-Somethings Can't Get Ahead*. Many young people are finding themselves caught in a difficult job market where wages have declined at the same time they are carrying larger college loans and mounting credit card debt (Figure 7.7). Draut is critical of the credit card industry, which she claims is designed to keep people in debt. Many young people have embraced easy credit only to discover that late payment fees and high interest rates can keep them from paying down their balances. While some may be spending on luxuries like fancy clothes or restaurant meals, high-tech toys, and new cars that they really can't afford, many young people are using credit cards for basic household needs and expenses, such as prescription medications and car repairs. Almost two-thirds of young people are in debt: on average, their college loan debt is $23,200, revolving (credit card) debt is $3,173, and installment (car loans) debt is $17,208 (Fetterman and Hansen 2006; TICAS 2010; Credit.com 2011). Some are slipping into a troubling downward financial spiral. About 15 percent to 20 percent of all young adults are in debt hardship, where monthly debt payments reach 40 percent or more of household income, and they have the second-highest rates of bankruptcy of any age group (Draut and Silva 2004). So let's examine where some of this pressure to spend comes from—advertising.

In this Data Workshop, you will evaluate some advertisements in terms of the ideology of the American Dream. You will use existing sources to do a content analysis of the ads (see Chapter 2 for a review of the research method). To start your research, find three or more ads from magazines, news-papers, web sites, or other sources. Look for ads that are of interest to your particular age group or that are selling the idea of the "good life."

Consider the following questions for each ad.

- For whom is the message intended?

- What product or service is being advertised?

- In addition to a product or service, what else are the advertisers trying to sell?

- How does the message make you feel? Does it play on your emotions or sense of self-worth? If so, in what ways?

- Does the ad "work"? Would you like to buy the product? Why or why not?

More generally:

- How does advertising affect your life and buying habits?

- What ads have a strong effect on you? Why?

- What is the lure of shopping and material possessions?

- What kinds of pressures do you feel to keep up with the material possessions of your friends, neighbors, or co-workers?

There are two options for completing this Data Workshop.

- *Option 1 (informal)*: Bring your ads to class, and discuss your answers to the questions with other students in small groups. Compare and contrast each other's contributions.

- *Option 2 (formal)*: Write a three- to four-page essay discussing your general thoughts on consumption and the American Dream. Apply these thoughts to your conclusions about the specific ads you chose.

Closing Comments

Social stratification is all about power. Stratification systems, like SES, allocate different types of social power, such as wealth, political influence, and occupational prestige, and do so in fundamentally unequal ways. These inequalities are part of both the larger social structure and our everyday interactions. In the following chapters, we will examine other systems of stratification, namely race and ethnicity, and sex, gender, and sexual orientation. While we separate these topics for organizational purposes, they are not experienced as separate in our everyday lives. We are women or men, working class or upper class, black or white, gay or straight simultaneously. Our experiences of these social categories are intertwined, as we will see.

FIGURE 7.7
STUDENT DEBT IN AMERICA

STUDENT LOAN DEBT

67%

OF STUDENTS GRADUATED WITH STUDENT LOAN DEBT IN 2008, A 27% INCREASE FROM 2004

THAT TOTALS **1.4** MILLION STUDENTS

SENIORS GRADUATING WITH STUDENT LOAN DEBT BY TYPE OF INSTITUTION
62% PUBLIC
72% PRIVATE NONPROFIT
96% PRIVATE FOR-PROFIT

1 IN 10 STUDENTS GRADUATE WITH $40,000+ IN STUDENT LOANS

$23,200

AVERAGE DEBT LEVEL FOR GRADUATING SENIORS A 24% INCREASE FROM 2004

CREDIT CARD DEBT

84%

OF UNDERGRADUATES HAVE AT LEAST ONE CREDIT CARD

4.6 AVERAGE NUMBER OF CREDIT CARDS

1/2 OF STUDENTS HAVE 4 OR MORE CARDS

19% OF SENIORS CARRY A BALANCE GREATER THAN $7,000, WHILE ONLY 11% CARRY A ZERO BALANCE

1 IN 3 STUDENTS SAID THEY RARELY OR NEVER DISCUSSED CREDIT CARD USE WITH THEIR PARENTS

$3,173

AVERAGE BALANCE CARRIED BY UNDERGRADUATES

TAKING **10 YEARS** TO REPAY AN AVERAGE LOAN COSTS
$8,838
IN INTERESTS PAYMENTS ALONE
(WITH THE STAFFORD LOAN INTEREST RATE OF 6.8%)

WITH AN AVERAGE MONTHLY PAYMENT OF
$267

PEOPLE IN THE 18–24 AGE BRACKET SPEND
30%
OF THEIR MONTHLY INCOME ON DEBT REPAYMENT

IT WOULD TAKE **12 YEARS** TO PAY BACK THAT CREDIT CARD BALANCE, WITH A STUDENT INTEREST RATE OF
13.71%
MAKING THE MINIMUM MONTHLY PAYMENT
(MAKING NO NEW CHARGES AND PAYING ON TIME EVERY MONTH)

SOURCE: TICAS 2010; CREDIT.COM 2011; SALLIE MAE 2009.

⑤ Need Help Studying?

wwnorton.com/studyspace

Visit StudySpace to access free review materials such as:
- **Vocabulary Flashcards**
- **Diagnostic Review Quizzes**
- **Study Outlines**

QUESTIONS FOR REVIEW

1. Think about your own class status. Is it consistent across the criteria that make up socioeconomic status (income, wealth, education, occupation, and power)? Or are you an example of status inconsistency?

2. Max Weber theorized that there is more to class than wealth and advocated classifying socioeconomic status according to power and prestige. Why do we need these additional elements? Can you think of a job that brings more wealth than power? How about one that brings little wealth but lots of prestige?

3. According to Pierre Bourdieu, the cultural tools we inherit from our parents can be very important in trying to gain economic assets. What sort of cultural capital did you inherit? Has it ever helped you materially? Have you ever done something to acquire more cultural capital?

4. Erving Goffman says we "read" other people through social interaction to get a sense of their class status. What sort of clues can tell you about a person's social class within thirty seconds of meeting her?

5. People of lower socioeconomic status are more likely to encounter the criminal justice system, both as perpetrators and as victims of crime. Many people believe this is because the poor are more criminally minded. What are some other explanations?

6. Sociologists know that people are more likely to marry someone with a social and cultural background similar to their own, largely because those are the people we tend to encounter. Add up the people you know on a first-name basis who come from a different class than you according to the six-part definition of U.S. social class.

7. The United States considers itself a meritocracy with an open class system. What kinds of structural factors in American society make vertical social mobility more difficult? Do these factors apply to everyone in society or just certain groups?

8. Are you aware of anyone within your community who suffers from absolute deprivation? If not, do you think you just live in a lucky community, or are there other factors that make the poor invisible?

9. When you picture the good life, what do you see? If you had a choice between making more money or having more free time, which would you pick? How much of your leisure time involves spending money or consuming? What does this tell you about the ideology of the American Dream?

SUGGESTIONS FOR FURTHER EXPLORATION

The Global Rich List (www.globalrichlist.com). Find out how your income compares to earnings worldwide. From the site's authors: "[W]e gauge how rich we are by looking upwards at those who have more than us. This makes us feel poor. We wanted to do something which would help people understand, in real terms, where they stand globally."

Hardt, Michael, and Antonio Negri. 2000. *Empire*. Cambridge, MA: Harvard University Press. A neo-Marxist explanation for the way that inequality is structured globally and how this changes the functioning of power. Interestingly, while Michael Hardt is a professor of literature at Duke University, Antonio Negri is an inmate at Rebibbia Prison in Rome,

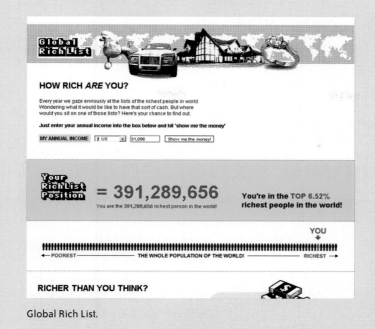

HOW RICH *ARE* YOU?

Every year we gaze enviously at the lists of the richest people in world. Wondering what it would be like to have that sort of cash. But where would you sit on one of those lists? Here's your chance to find out.

Just enter your annual income into the box below and hit 'show me the money'

MY ANNUAL INCOME $ US   ▾   31,096   Show me the money!

Your RichList Position = **391,289,656**
You are the 391,289,656 richest person in the world!

You're in the TOP 6.52% richest people in the world!

YOU
↓

◄— POOREST ——————— THE WHOLE POPULATION OF THE WORLD! ——————— RICHEST —►

RICHER THAN YOU THINK?

Global Rich List.

convicted in the 1970s of trying to overthrow the Italian state, a charge he has always denied.

Harrison, Bennett, and Barry Bluestone. 1988. *The Great U-Turn: Corporate Restructuring and the Polarization of America*. New York: Basic Books. A compelling analysis of the increasing polarization of the American economy and the specific ways that the wealthy protect their assets while the middle class and the poor are increasingly hard-pressed.

The House of Yes. 1997. Dir. Mark Waters. Miramax. A darkly comic peek at cultural capital in a wealthy, dysfunctional family. When Marty Pascal attempts to get married, his jealously possessive twin sister mocks his fiancée for lacking refinement and for being from Pennsylvania, "a state that's in your way when you want to go someplace else."

Katz, Michael B. 1986. *In the Shadow of the Poorhouse: A Social History of Welfare in America*. New York: Basic Books. Explores the ways in which the welfare system has remained in place, despite being consistently unpopular throughout American history.

Krog, Antjie. 1999. *Country of My Skull: Guilt, Sorrow, and the Limits of Forgiveness in the New South Africa*. New York: Times Books. The story of South Africa's Truth and Reconciliation Commission, established to deal with the crimes committed under apartheid. The commission powerfully gives voice to those who suffered in a racially segregated South Africa, while the author, an Afrikaner, also tries to find an honorable way to live in a country still deeply divided along racial lines.

People Like Us: Social Class in America (www.pbs.org/peoplelikeus). 2001. Dirs. Louis Alvarez and Andrew Kolker. A documentary that uses many individuals' life experiences to explore the American class system, which most of us have trouble talking about.

Pollin, Robert, and Stephanie Luce. 1998. *The Living Wage: Building a Fair Economy*. New York: New Press. As part of the ongoing effort to document the struggles of the working poor, Pollin and Luce document a nationwide movement for economic justice that argues that paying a living wage is good for employers, cities, and employees.

Schor, Juliet B. 1999. *The Overspent American: Why We Want What We Don't Need*. New York: HarperCollins. A breezily written indictment of America's obsession with designer clothes, athletic shoes, luxury cars, and other high-status consumer goods.

Twine, France Winddance. 1998. *Racism in a Racial Democracy: The Maintenance of White Supremacy in Brazil*. New Brunswick, NJ: Rutgers University Press. An ethnographic study of the way that racial segregation in Brazil is disguised by a class-based ideology.

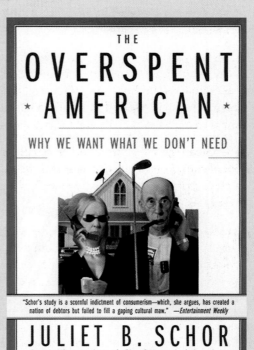

THE **OVERSPENT AMERICAN**

WHY WE WANT WHAT WE DON'T NEED

"Schor's study is a scornful indictment of consumerism—which, she argues, has created a nation of debtors but failed to fill a gaping cultural maw." —*Entertainment Weekly*

JULIET B. SCHOR
Bestselling author of *The Overworked American*

CHAPTER 8

Race and Ethnicity as Lived Experience

Despite the recent scandal, Tiger Woods is often hailed as the person who opened up the field of professional golf to African Americans. But Woods doesn't describe himself as black: he's "Cablinasian," a term he coined to describe his multiracial background (which includes Caucasian, black, American Indian, and Asian American ancestries). In 2002, Halle Berry became the first African American ever to win the Academy Award for Best Actress. As she tearfully accepted the statuette on stage, the camera cut to her mother sitting in the audience, beaming with pride at her daughter's accomplishment—and unmistakably white. Blonde actress Heather Locklear is a descendant of a group known as the Lumbees: an isolated triracial community in North Carolina that is part Caucasian, part African American, and part Tuscarora Indian. And former American Idol judge Paula Abdul, commonly thought to be African American, is actually of Syrian, Jewish, Brazilian, and French-Canadian descent.

Despite America's record of racial discrimination and segregation, there have always been multiracial people in its history, beginning with the European settlers who mixed with Native Americans and black slaves alike (Clinton and Gillespie 1997; Brooks 2002). More and more, we are recognizing and celebrating our multiracial heritage. In 2000, the Census Bureau gave Americans the opportunity for the first time to check multiple boxes to identify their race, thus creating 63 different racial categories. Approximately seven million, or 2.4 percent of the population, took advantage of the new option. Ten years later, the 2010 Census reported that approximately nine million Americans, or 2.9 percent of the population, identified themselves as belonging to more than one racial category, a 32 percent increase from 2000. The number identifying themselves as multiracial will only continue to grow, according to the bureau: by 2050, the population of multiracial identities will double to about 16 million. As the United States is a nation of immigrants (some involuntary), it is only logical that the separate lineages of the American population would eventually meld. We might, therefore, wonder: will race continue to be as important in the future as it has been in the past? In this chapter, we will examine the sociological understandings of race, which will provide us with the insights we need to answer this question.

HOW TO READ THIS CHAPTER

Our goal in this chapter is for you to acquire a fundamental understanding of race and ethnicity as socially constructed categories. While each is based on traits we may see as biological, such as skin color or facial features, the meanings attached to race and ethnicity are created, maintained, and modified over time through social processes in which we all take part.

When a society categorizes people based on their race and ethnicity (and all societies do), it creates a system of stratification that leads to inequality. Society's resources—wealth, power, privilege, opportunity—are distributed according to these categories, and this perpetuates inequalities that are all too familiar here in the United States. We also hope you will come to understand the importance of race and ethnicity in forming individual identity. Our racial and ethnic identities have profound effects on our sense of self, and our bonds to other people may be based on shared identities—or may transcend those categories entirely.

Defining Race and Ethnicity

"Race" and "ethnicity" are words we use so often in everyday speech that we might not think we need a definition of either. But people tend to use the words interchangeably, as if they mean essentially the same thing. There is, however, a significant difference between common sense notions of race and ethnicity and what social scientists have to say about them.

The idea of different races as belonging to distinguishable categories has existed for hundreds of years. In the nineteenth century, biologists came up with a schema that grouped humans into three races: Negroid, Mongoloid, and Caucasoid (corresponding roughly to black, Asian, and white). It was believed that each race was characterized by its own biological makeup, separate and distinct from the others. Modern scientists, however, possess advanced tools for examining race in a much more sophisticated way. What they have found, ironically, is that there are no "pure" races, that the lines between races are blurry rather than fixed. A person who looks white will inevitably have biological material from other races, as will someone who looks black. There is also no such thing as a

> **race** a socially defined category based on real or perceived biological differences between groups of people
>
> **ethnicity** a socially defined category based on common language, religion, nationality, history, or another cultural factor

"superior" race, as race itself is not the reason that different groups might display positive or negative characteristics (such as intelligence, athleticism, or artistic ability). Furthermore, there is greater genetic diversity *within* racial populations than between them. So within the Asian population, members differ more from each other (Koreans from Chinese, for example) than they do from whites. From a biological standpoint, the difference between someone with type O blood and someone with type A blood is much more significant than the differences between a dark-skinned and a light-skinned person. And yet, blood types have no correlation to race at all.

New genetic testing technologies seem to hold out the prospect of accurately identifying biological differences between racial groups—some "ancestry testing" services purport to be able to identify clients' genetic and geographic origins down to the region, village, or tribe. However precise or imprecise such conclusions may be, they overlook the fact that all humans, whatever racial categories they seem to inhabit, are 99.9 percent genetically identical. And of that remaining 0.1 percent of our genetic material, only 15 percent of its variation occurs between geographically distinct groups. In other words, there's not enough "wiggle room" in the human genome for race to be a genetic trait (*Harvard Magazine* 2008).

Sociologists, then, have come to understand **race** as a social category, based on real or perceived biological differences between groups of people. Race is more meaningful to us on a social level than it is on a biological level (Montagu 1998). Actress Heather Locklear certainly "looks white," and you have probably perceived her in that way, but in some Southern states in 1925, she could just as easily have been considered black or Native American. Does knowing Locklear's racial background now make you think of her in a different way?

Ethnicity is another social category that is applied to a group with a shared ancestry or cultural heritage. The Amish, for instance, are a distinct ethnic group in American society, linked by a common heritage that includes language, religion, and history; the Amish people, with few exceptions, are also white. The Jewish people, on the other hand, contrary to what the Nazis and other white supremacists may believe, are an ethnic group but not a race. The stereotypical image is challenged when we see a blonde, blue-eyed Jew from Scandinavia or a black Ethiopian Jew.

As an example of the social construction of race and ethnicity, let's look at the evidence documenting the historical changes in the boundaries of the category "white." In the early 1900s, native-born Americans, who were frequently Protestant, did not consider recent Irish, Italian, or Jewish immigrants to be white and restricted where these groups could live and work (Ignatiev 1996; Brodkin 1999). Such housing discrimination forced new immigrants to cluster in urban neighborhoods or "ghettos." After World War II, however, as the second generation of Irish, Italian, and Jewish immigrants reached adulthood, the importance of ethnic identity declined and skin color became the main way to differentiate between who was white and who was not. Today, the question is whether people of Middle Eastern descent are white. In the post–9/11 climate, Arabs and Muslims have been identified as racially and ethnically distinct in significant and even harmful ways. While these groups possess a range of skin colors and facial features, it may be their symbolic labeling in these difficult times that makes them "nonwhite."

"Ethnic Options": Symbolic and Situational Ethnicity

How do we display our racial and ethnic group membership? We may do so in a number of ways: through dress, language, food, religious practices, preferences in music, art, or literature, even the projects we find interesting and the topics we pursue at school. Sometimes, these practices make our group membership obvious to others; sometimes, they don't. White ethnics like Irish Americans and Italian Americans, for example, can actually choose when and how they display their ethnic group membership.

One way group membership is displayed is through **symbolic ethnicity**, enactments of ethnic identity that occur only on special occasions. For example, most Irish Americans have been so fully assimilated for several generations that their Irish ancestry may not matter much to them on a daily basis. But on St. Patrick's Day (especially in cities like Boston and New York), displays of Irish identity can be pretty overwhelming! Parades, hats, "Kiss me, I'm Irish" buttons, green clothing, green beer (and in Chicago, a green river!), corned beef and cabbage—all are elements of symbolic ethnicity. Similar ethnic displays occur on such holidays as Passover, Cinco de Mayo, and Nouruz.

Another way we can show group membership is through **situational ethnicity**, when we deliberately assert our ethnicity in some situations while downplaying it in others. Situational ethnicity involves a kind of cost-benefit analysis that symbolic ethnicity does not: we need to appraise each situation to determine whether or not it favors our ethnicity. For example, Dr. Ferris's Lebanese ancestry never mattered much, outside her own family, when she lived in Southern California. In fact, it was often something she felt she should downplay, given a political climate in which people of Arabic background were sometimes viewed with suspicion. But when she moved to Peoria, Illinois, she discovered that

> **symbolic ethnicity** an ethnic identity that is only relevant on specific occasions and does not significantly impact everyday life
>
> **situational ethnicity** an ethnic identity that can be either displayed or concealed depending on its usefulness in a given situation

Mulberry Street at the Turn of the Century In the early 1900s, Irish, Italian, and Jewish immigrants were not considered "whites." Because of residential segregation, new immigrants poured into densely populated neighborhoods like this one on New York's Lower East Side where they had little choice but to live in squalid tenements and work in sweatshops.

Heritage Tourism: Getting in Touch with Our Roots

As global travel becomes easier, faster, and more affordable, a phenomenon called "heritage tourism" has been on the rise. Heritage tourism is related to the idea of the pilgrimage—a journey to a geographical location of significance to one's religion. Examples of traditional pilgrimages include the *hajj*, an excursion to Mecca in Saudi Arabia, which is required of all Muslims once in their lifetime. Catholics may travel to the Vatican or to other important sites, such as the grotto and sanctuary at Lourdes in France or the Cathedral of Santiago de Compostela in Spain. But heritage tourism is less about religion and more about the cultural legacies of different racial and ethnic groups. Members of racial and ethnic groups who now live outside the countries of their ancestors (such as African Americans or Irish Americans) are sometimes attracted by the possibility of traveling to the "old country," and tourism ministries worldwide market their countries and cultures as must-see places for members of the diaspora—displaced peoples who may have emigrated generations ago. Here are a few examples of heritage tourism campaigns from around the world:

Ireland

The U.S. Census reports that 10 percent of the American population—or 30 million people—claimed Irish heritage in 2000. That's a lot of potential tourists, and the official Irish tourist bureau caters specifically to those who wish to investigate their Irish ancestry. The tourism industry in Ireland encourages people of Irish descent to take tours that trace their family's heritage. The tourism office, in association with the Irish Genealogical Project, entices travelers to visit Irish Family History Foundation Centres around the country and promises "a personal and emotional journey . . . of discovery" as travelers discover the roots of their family tree.

Israel

For many contemporary Jews, their Jewish identity is as much ethnic as it is religious, and the existence of a Jewish state may have an impact on their travel plans. For example, Israel's Ministry of Tourism encourages American Jewish families to consider traveling to Israel for their children's Bar or Bat Mitzvah celebrations. Ceremonies can be held at any of a number of well-known historical locations, such as the Western Wall or the Masada, and Bar or Bat Mitzvah visitors may also tour the important religious, cultural, and political sites of Jerusalem as part of their holiday. Parents and politicians alike hope that vacations such as these will strengthen the children's connection to their Jewish heritage and begin a process of attachment to Israel itself that may ultimately lead to "making *aliyah*," or moving there permanently.

Ghana

Because of the historical brutalities of slavery, it is often difficult for African Americans to pinpoint their cities or countries of ancestral origin—but since most African slaves were taken from West Africa, some countries in that region have begun exploring the touristic implications of slavery's tragic legacy. Ghanaian tourism officials, for example, want the far-flung "diasporan" descendants of American, European, and Caribbean slaves to think of Africa as home and to consider making a pilgrimage to the land of their ancestors. They offer tours that focus on slave-trade sites, like the forts in which newly enslaved Africans were imprisoned before being shipped to the New World (which most visitors find both deeply moving and disturbing). But they also entertain visitors and educate them about Ghanaian culture and customs with colorful festivals, dancing, and feasting. Ghanaian officials hope that some visitors will choose to make Ghana their permanent home, offering special visas for diasporans to make it easy to travel to and from the homeland.

---

this small city had a relatively large population of Lebanese descent and that the mayor, a city councilman, the state senator, the congressman, local business, arts, and religious leaders, and prominent families were all Lebanese. This suddenly made Dr. Ferris's ethnicity a valuable asset in a way that it had never been before. She received a good deal of social support and made new friends based on shared revelations of ethnic group membership. In the case of situational ethnicity, we see how larger social forces can govern the identities we choose—if we have a choice.

Neither situational nor symbolic ethnicity is available to those who are visibly nonmainstream, whatever that may

Ethnic options We can display group membership by embracing ethnic identity on special occasions like St. Patrick's Day or Cinco de Mayo (symbolic ethnicity) or in special situations (situational ethnicity).

look like in a given society. In the United States, this generally means that nonwhites find themselves in fewer situations where they have a choice about whether to display their group membership (although this may eventually change as we become a "majority minority" nation). As sociologist Mary Waters says, "The social and political consequences of being Asian or Hispanic or black are not, for the most part, symbolic, nor are they voluntary. They are real, unavoidable, and sometimes hurtful" (1990, p. 156).

DATA WORKSHOP

ANALYZING EVERYDAY LIFE

Doing Symbolic Ethnicity

Choose a setting where you can watch people "doing" ethnicity. For instance, you can go to a St. Patrick's Day parade, if your city hosts one, or attend an ethnic festival of some sort (such as St. Anthony's Feast Day in Boston's Italian North End or Los Angeles's annual African Marketplace). Or just visit one of your city's ethnic neighborhoods: stroll through an Italian market in South Philadelphia, or shop the streets of Chicago's Ukrainian Village, Greektown, or Pilsen (a Mexican American neighborhood). If you think your town is too tiny to have any ethnic diversity, think again: even minuscule Postville, Iowa (population 1,500), includes a large Hasidic Jewish population, with significant clusters of Mexican, Guatemalan, Ukrainian, Nigerian, Bosnian, and Czech immigrants. You may even find an appropriate setting on your college campus or at one of your own family gatherings.

For this Data Workshop you will be using ethnographic methods and doing participant observation (see Chapter 2 for a review). Once you have chosen a setting, join in the activities around you while at the same time carefully observing how the other participants display their ethnic membership. As part of your observation, consider the following.

- What are participants wearing: traditional ethnic costumes, contemporary T-shirts, other symbols displaying their ethnic identity?

- What kind of music is being played, and what types of foods or crafts are available?

- Are different languages being spoken? If so, by whom, and in what situations?

- What are the differences in the activities of adults and children, men and women, members and visitors?

- Listen for snatches of conversation in which members explain such traditions as buying a goldfish on the first day of spring (Iranian), wrapping and tying a tamale (Mexican), or wearing the claddagh ring (Irish).

Record your observations, and bring them back into the classroom for discussion and analysis. There are two options for completing this Data Workshop.

- Option 1 (informal): Prepare written notes that you can refer to in class. Discuss your experience with other students in a small group. Consider all the questions and points above.

- Option 2 (formal): Write a three- to four-page essay describing your observations and answering the questions in this workshop. Ask yourself the same questions about your own ethnic identity as you did about the people you observed. Do you have the option to display your ethnicity in some situations and withhold it in others? Why or why not? How do you decide whether/when/how to do this? What kind of cost-benefit analysis do you use? What role do ethnic and racial stereotypes play in this process? And how are these displays received by others?

What Is a Minority?

A minority is commonly thought of as a group that's smaller in numbers than the dominant group. Thus, most Americans would say that in the United States, whites are a majority while African Americans, Asians, Hispanics/Latinos, and Native Americans are minorities, because whites outnumber each of these other groups. In South Africa, however, blacks dramatically outnumber whites by a ratio of seven to one, yet before the 1994 election of President Nelson Mandela, whites controlled the country while blacks occupied the lowest status in that society. California provides us with a different kind of example. In 2005, the Census Bureau reported that whites made up less than 45 percent of the state's population, whereas other ethnic groups (Hispanics, African Americans, Asian Americans, Native Americans) when added together constituted a majority of 56 percent (Longley 2005). California, then, is technically a "majority minority" state: whites are less than half the population but still remain the dominant group in terms of power, resources, and representation in social institutions (Texas and New Mexico are also "majority minority" states). Hispanics/Latinos continue to be underrepresented in the University of California system (as both students and faculty) as well as in the state government and as business owners. They are, however, overrepresented in prisons, in poverty counts, and as victims of violent crimes.

As sociologists, then, we must recognize that minority status is not just about numbers—it's about social inequalities. Sociologists define a **minority group** as people who are recognized as belonging to a social category (here either a racial or an ethnic group) and who suffer from unequal treatment as a result of that status. A minority group is denied the access to power and resources generally accorded to others in the dominant groups. Members of a minority group are likely to perceive themselves as targets of collective discrimination (Wirth 1945).

Membership in a minority group may serve as a kind of "master status," overriding any other status, such as gender or age. Members may be subjected to racist beliefs about the group as a whole and thus suffer from a range of social disadvantages. Unequal and unfair treatment, as well as lack of access to power and resources, typically generates a strong sense of common identity and solidarity among members of minority groups. Perhaps because of this sense of identification, minorities also tend to practice high rates of in-group marriage (endogamy), although the percentage of mixed-race couples in America continues to grow.

Racism, Prejudice, and Discrimination

In order for social inequality to persist, the unequal treatment that minority groups suffer must be supported by the dominant groups. **Racism**, an ideology or set of beliefs about the superiority of one racial or ethnic group over another, provides this support; it is used to justify social arrangements between the dominant and minority groups. Racist beliefs are often rooted in the assumption that differences between groups are innate, or biologically based. They can

minority group members of a social group that is systematically denied the same access to power and resources available to society's dominant groups but who are not necessarily fewer in number than the dominant groups

racism a set of beliefs about the superiority of one racial or ethnic group; used to justify inequality and often rooted in the assumption that differences between groups are genetic

WHITE NON-HISPANIC
199,325,978

64.9%

**HISPANIC
OR LATINO**
48,356,760

15.8%

**AFRICAN
AMERICAN**
37,144,760

12.1%

ASIAN
13,627,633

4.4%

**TWO OR MORE
RACES**
199,325,978

1.8%

**AMERICAN INDIAN
AND ALASKAN NATIVE**
.6% 1,975,193

**NATIVE HAWAIIAN
AND PACIFIC ISLANDER**
.1% 426,897

OTHER RACE
.2% 676,733

Gran Torino

also arise from a negative view of a group's cultural characteristics. In both cases, racism presumes that one group is better than another.

Prejudice and discrimination are closely related to racism, and though the terms are often used interchangeably, there are important distinctions between them. **Prejudice**, literally a "prejudgment," is an inflexible attitude (usually negative, although it can work in the reverse) about a particular group of people and is rooted in generalizations or stereotypes. Examples of prejudice include opinions like "All Irish are drunks" or "All Mexicans are lazy." Prejudice often, though not always, leads to **discrimination**: an action or behavior that results in the unequal treatment of individuals because of their membership in a certain racial or ethnic group. A person might be said to suffer discrimination if she is turned down for a job promotion or a home loan because she's black or Hispanic.

It is possible, though unlikely, that a person can be prejudiced and still not discriminate against others. For example, a teacher can believe that Asian American students are better at math and science, yet deliberately not let this belief influence his grading of Asian American students. Conversely, a person may not be prejudiced at all but still unknowingly participate in discrimination. For instance, a small child can innocently use the racist terminology she learns from her parents even though she herself holds no racist views. And prejudice and discrimination don't always flow from the dominant group toward minorities. The 2008 film *Gran Torino* features Clint Eastwood as a crotchety old man with prejudices against his Italian barber, Irish construction workers, black street kids, and Asian neighbors. But in an interesting turn of storytelling, the prejudice goes both ways: for example, while Eastwood's character complains about the Hmong families moving into his neighborhood, his Hmong neighbors wish that he would move out of the neighborhood like all the other white people. And even given this mutual dislike based on ethnic backgrounds, Eastwood's character comes to know and love his Hmong neighbors, protecting them with a tremendous act of self-sacrifice in the end.

Discrimination can also take different forms. **Individual discrimination** occurs when one person treats others unfairly because of their race or ethnicity. A racist teacher might discriminate against a Hispanic student by assigning him a lower grade than he deserves. **Institutional discrimination**, in contrast, usually more systematic and widespread, occurs when institutions (such as governments, schools, or banks) practice discriminatory policies that affect whole groups of individuals.

prejudice an idea about the characteristics of a group that is applied to all members of that group and is unlikely to change regardless of the evidence against it

discrimination unequal treatment of individuals based on their membership in a social group; usually motivated by prejudice

individual discrimination discrimination carried out by one person against another

institutional discrimination discrimination carried out systematically by institutions (political, economic, educational, and others) that affect all members of a group who come into contact with it

A rather startling example of institutional discrimination comes from Ira Katznelson (2005) in his book *When Affirmative Action Was White: An Untold History of Racial Inequality in Twentieth Century America*. We usually associate affirmative action with the advances of the Civil Rights Movement of the 1960s and with benefiting blacks and other minorities. Katznelson, however, examines one instance of special government policies benefiting whites. In 1944, Congress passed the G.I. Bill of Rights, which provided funding for college or vocational education and home loans to returning World War II veterans. While this should have supported black and white veterans alike, in practice blacks were largely impeded from taking advantage of the new benefits, while whites more easily climbed into the rapidly expanding American middle class. Typically, loans were granted only to those buying homes in all-white neighborhoods. And blacks were effectively barred from buying homes in those neighborhoods, either through legal restrictions or from hostile actions on the part of loan officers, realtors, and homeowners who were prejudiced against having blacks live next door. To make matters worse, loans were even denied to blacks who wished to buy homes in black neighborhoods; these were seen as risky investments. Later affirmative action programs were actually modeled after those of the postwar era that ironically benefited whites and created an even greater economic disparity between racial groups.

Another example comes from Lawrence Otis Graham, a Princeton- and Harvard-trained African American lawyer who investigated firsthand institutionalized racism in the upper-crust world of the East Coast elite. He found that, for example, he was not able to join a particular Connecticut country club as a member; however, he was welcome to serve in the capacity of busboy to the club's all-white membership and wait staff (1996). This shocked Graham; he believed his Ivy League credentials would have opened any door but discovered that in a racially stratified society, a black man with privileged socioeconomic status is still a black man in the end.

Some students have difficulty in recognizing just how persistent and pervasive racism is in contemporary American society, while others experience it on a daily basis. We hear claims that it has been erased. But although there have been tremendous strides, especially in the wake of the Civil Rights Movement, racism is not yet a thing of the past. There is still deep skepticism among minorities that negative racial attitudes are changing in America (Bobo, Kluegel, and Smith 1997; Bobo and Smith 1998). A survey conducted by Gallup in 2003 showed that 59 percent of whites believe that race relations in the United States are good and 24 percent believe they are bad, while 48 percent of blacks believe that race relations are good and 37 percent believe

they are bad. Another striking result of the survey revealed that more than half of both whites and blacks believe that relations between the two will always be a problem in the United States.

Racism today may not be as blatant as it once was—blacks and whites don't use separate bathrooms or drinking fountains—but it has taken other, more subtle forms (such as the high concentration of liquor stores in predominantly black urban areas). If we are to have a truly egalitarian society, it will take much more education and change in the social conditions that perpetuate inequality.

Theoretical Approaches to Understanding Race in the United States

Sociologists reject the notion that race has an objective or scientific meaning, and instead seek to understand why race continues to play such a critical role in society. They have produced a number of different theories about the connections between race, discrimination, and social inequality.

For example, functionalist theory has provided a useful lens for analyzing how certain ethnic groups, mainly European immigrants (like the Irish and Italians) arriving in the early 1900s, eventually became assimilated into the larger society. Functionalism, however, has proven less successful in explaining the persistence of racial divisions and why other races and ethnicities, such as African Americans and Hispanics, have continued to maintain their distinct identities alongside the white majority culture today.

Perhaps what functionalism can best offer is an explanation of how prejudice and discrimination develop, by focusing on social solidarity and group cohesion. Groups have a tendency toward ethnocentrism, or the belief that one's own culture and way of life are right and normal. Functionalists contend that positive feelings about one's group are strong ties that bind people together. At the same time, however, this cohesiveness can lead members to see others, especially those of other races or ethnicities, in an unfavorable light. According to functionalists, these cultural differences and the lack of integration into the larger society on the part of minorities tend to feed fear and hostility.

Conflict theory focuses on the struggle for power and control. Classic Marxist analyses of race, developed by sociologists in the 1960s, looked for the source of racism in capitalist hierarchies. Edna Bonacich, for instance, argues that racism is partly driven by economic competition and the struggle over scarce resources. A "split labor market,"

TABLE 8.1	Theory in Everyday Life	
PERSPECTIVE	**APPROACH TO RACE AND ETHNICITY**	**CASE STUDY: RACIAL INEQUALITY**
STRUCTURAL FUNCTIONALISM	Racial and ethnic differences are a necessary part of society. Even racial inequality has functions that help maintain social order.	The functions of racial inequality and conflict for society could include the creation of social cohesion within both the dominant and minority groups.
CONFLICT THEORY	Racial and ethnic differences create inter-group conflict—minority and majority groups have different interests and may find themselves at odds as they attempt to secure and protect their interests.	Some members of majority groups (whites and men in particular) object to affirmative action programs that assist underrepresented groups. This can create conflict between racial groups in society.
SYMBOLIC INTERACTIONISM	Race and ethnicity are part of our identity as displayed through our presentation of self.	Some individuals (white ethnics and light-skinned nonwhites in particular) have the option to conceal their race or ethnicity in situations where it might be advantageous to do so. This may allow them as individuals to escape the effects of racial inequality but does not erase it from society at large.

in which one group of workers (usually defined by race, ethnicity, or gender) is routinely paid less than other groups, keeps wages low for racial and ethnic minorities, compounding the effects of racism with those of poverty (1980). William Julius Wilson believes that openly racist government policies and individual racist attitudes were the driving forces behind the creation of a black underclass, but that the underclass is now perpetuated by economic factors, not racial ones (1980). While this link between race and class is useful and important, it doesn't provide a satisfactory explanation for all forms of racial and ethnic stratification.

In recent years, conflict theorists have developed new approaches to understanding race. In his book *Racial Fault Lines: The Historical Origins of White Supremacy in California* (2008), for example, Tomas Almaguer looks at the history of race relations in California during the late nineteenth century. He describes a racial hierarchy that placed whites at the top, followed by Mexicans, blacks, Asians, and Native Americans at the bottom. Rather than focusing exclusively on class, he examines how white supremacist ideology became institutionalized. Racist beliefs became a part of political and economic life during that period. Ideas like "manifest destiny" (the belief that the United States had a mission to expand its territories) helped justify the taking of lands, and the notion that Native Americans were "uncivilized heathens" helped justify killing them. Sociologists like Michael Omi and Howard Winant also argue that race isn't just a secondary phenomenon that results from the class system: it permeates both lived experience and larger-scale activity, such as the economy and the government (1989).

Still others have sought to understand the meaning of race from the individual's point of view and have begun to analyze the ways that race, class, and gender inequalities intersect. For instance, writers like Patricia Hill Collins (2006), bell hooks (1990), and Gloria Anzaldúa (1987) argue that race must be explained in the terms in which it is experienced, not as overarching general theories. Though some of these writers have been sharply critical of the symbolic interactionist tradition, which they believe does not take into account macro social forces that shape the realities of stratification, they share with interactionism a conviction that race, like all other aspects of social life, is created symbolically in everyday interactions. It is this idea to which we now turn.

Race as an Interactional Accomplishment

Remember Erving Goffman's ideas about how we project our identities in interaction with others? This process is constant and ongoing—there is no "time out." We "read" others through a myriad of cues, and we in turn make ourselves readable to others by our own self-presentations. Our identity is constructed in the negotiation between what we project and what others recognize. Even master statuses like race, gender, and age are negotiated in this way. So how *do* we project our racial or ethnic identities and read the racial or ethnic identities of others? We

The Sweeter the Juice Shirlee Taylor Haizlip's grandfather, who abandoned his family to live as a white man, is an example of racial passing.

might think immediately of stereotypes like hip-hoppers with baggy pants, skateboard dudes, sorority girls, "welfare moms," and so on. But in fact there are more subtle ways in which we project and receive our racial and ethnic identities.

Passing

Racial **passing**, or living as if one is a member of a different racial category, has a long history in the United States. Both during and after slavery, some light-skinned African Americans would attempt to live as whites in order to avoid the dire consequences of being black in a racist society. And people of different racial and ethnic backgrounds still pass, intentionally or unintentionally, every day in the United States. Passing involves manufacturing or maintaining a new identity that is more beneficial than one's real identity. W. E. B. DuBois's concept of "double-consciousness" (see Chapter 1) seems relevant to a discussion of passing—DuBois asks whether one can be black and at the same time claim one's rights as an American. Given the history of oppression and enslavement of African Americans, DuBois is not the only person to wonder if this is possible. There are many social forces that disenfranchise and exclude African Americans, and the phenomenon of passing suggests that, in some places and times, it has been more advantageous to play down the "African" part of "African American" if at all possible.

But whatever its perceived benefits, living as if one is a member of a different racial category takes its toll. Passing is stressful, hard work, and almost entirely interactional: light-skinned blacks can "do white" only if they are skillful at behaving and talking like a white person and keeping their past racial identity a secret from people in their white present.

Shirlee Taylor Haizlip, a Los Angeles journalist, chronicled the passing stories of one half of her family in her book *The Sweeter the Juice* (1994). Haizlip grew up the daughter of a prominent black Baptist minister, attended Wellesley College, and lived a life of privilege and comfort as a member of a small East Coast African American elite in the 1950s. She always knew that she had white relatives (75 percent of all African Americans do) and that these relatives had something to do with her mother's story of being abandoned as a child by her own father. Haizlip decided to use her journalistic skills to find out who these relatives were and how they had disappeared into the white world. She tracked down an aunt (her mother's sister) and learned that her grandfather, who was very light skinned, had apparently not been able to resist the desire to escape the constraints of blackness for the privileges of whiteness. So he fled with his lightest-skinned child (Haizlip's aunt), leaving his other, darker children behind—and lived the rest of his life as a white man, cut off from his black ancestry.

In this story of passing, situational context is important: merely by surrounding himself with white people, Haizlip's grandfather accomplished whiteness rather effectively. In a socially segregated world, who you hang out with goes a long way toward defining who you are, whether you are passing or not. But there are other requirements as well. Haizlip's aunt, for example, made sure her face was always well powdered, married a white man, and had no children, lest genes give her secret away. Indeed, while some of the white relatives Haizlip contacted knew about the black-white schism in the family, others did not—some were so surprised when Haizlip revealed that they had a former slave as a common great-grandfather, they blurted out, "Do you mean a *black* slave?" Their pasts had been so successfully erased through passing that after only one generation they were completely unaware of their black heritage.

Embodied and Disembodied Identities

When we interact with others online, we're usually not able to see what they look like. This has been touted as one of the democratizing traits of the internet—that aspects of **embodied identity** (the way we are perceived in the physical world), historically used as the basis for discrimination, are not available to those interacting online. But in online communities

In Relationships

"Jungle Fever": Interracial Romance, Dating, and Marriage

Forty-one out of the fifty American states prohibited **miscegenation**—romantic, sexual, or marital relationships between people of different races—at some point in history. In 1958, for example, Mildred and Richard Loving, an African American woman and a white man, married and settled in their native state of Virginia. In July of that year, they were arrested for violating the state's "Act to Preserve Racial Purity" and convicted. The judge sentenced them to a year in prison but suspended the sentence on the condition that the couple leave the state. The Lovings moved to Washington, D.C., where in 1967 the Supreme Court overturned all such laws, ruling that the state of Virginia had denied the Lovings their constitutional rights. While the Loving decision technically cleared the way for interracial marriages nationwide, states were slow to change their laws; Alabama finally overturned its antimiscegenation statute in 2000.

Society at large does seem more accepting of interracial relationships now than it was in 1967. By 2002, almost 20 percent of eighteen- and nineteen-year-olds reported being in an interracial relationship (Kao and Joyner 2005). At the same time, though, about 27 percent of Americans still expressed disapproval. Despite all the steps we have taken toward racial equality and integration, American society is not ideally structured to promote interracial contact, let alone romance. Cultural stereotypes and media images, for example, provide serious obstacles to interracial relationships. Several researchers point out that minorities

Mildred and Richard Loving

tend to be exoticized or stereotyped by the general population. Thus, Asian women are seen as subservient, mysterious, seductive, and/or sex objects; conversely, Asian men are portrayed as nonsexual geeks or martial arts pros (Le 2001).

that are *based* on racial identity, race must still be "done" interactionally (in this case, textually), as sociologist Byron Burkhalter found in his study of an internet community based on African American culture (1999). To sound authentically African American online, for instance, you have to include what Burk-

miscegenation romantic, sexual, or marital relationships between people of different races

halter calls "racially relevant" content and language—for example, "sister" to refer to other African American women. Responses also help establish racial identity: it's not just what you say, but how others receive it.

In some discussions, the African American identity of participants is accepted, but in other cases, that status is contested, in what Burkhalter calls "identity challenges." Identity challenges are usually accusations that one is not "really" black or

The Complexities of Interracial Dating The network drama *Parenthood* features several storylines on interracial relationships, such as the high school romance of Hattie and Alex (pictured above).

Black men are mythologized as having especially strong sex drives, and black women are assumed to be unable to control their sexual urges (Foeman and Nance 1999); white women are thought to be accommodating in bed (Shipler 1997). These stereotypes, though they are not borne out in reality, still have the power to influence our attitudes and behavior.

Movies sometimes provide a warning. In both Spike Lee's 1991 movie *Jungle Fever* and the 2001 Julia Stiles movie *Save the Last Dance*, white women in interracial rela-

tionships are criticized by people in the African American community for taking available black men away from black women, a problem that is exacerbated by the higher levels of incarceration and death among young black men. A young African American woman is quoted in an *Ebony* magazine article as saying, "Every time I turn around and I see a fine Brother dating outside his race, I just feel disgusted. I feel like, what's wrong with us? Why do you choose her over me?" (Hughes 2003).

People who date interracially must deal with in-group pressures to date—and especially marry—someone of their own race. This phenomenon is most commented on in the African American community (though by no means exclusive to it). In fact, although blacks are as likely to date interracially as members of any other group, they are less likely to out-marry than any other nonwhite group. Anita Allen, a professor of law and philosophy at the University of Pennsylvania, has observed that many African Americans view marrying a nonblack as being disloyal to the community (NPR 2003). Commentary on this subject can be found in scores of magazine articles, movies, and even comic strips (see Aaron McGruder's "Boondocks" or Darrin Bell's "Candorville").

How do you feel about interracial relationships? This topic is not just a hot-button issue for you to discuss with friends and family; it provides an opportunity for you to apply your sociological perspective to understand an important area of debate in everyday social life.

not black enough, or that one is a "Tom"[1] or a racist. These challenges are usually made when postings reveal opinions that don't fit into a certain set of socially approved boundaries, such as opinions about the use of "proper" English versus slang.

[1] "Tom" is a derogatory reference to the main character (a black slave) in Harriet Beecher Stowe's 1852 novel *Uncle Tom's Cabin*, whose servile devotion to his white masters earned him the reputation (some argue, undeserved) of being a traitor to his race.

Burkhalter argues that race is not irrefutably identifiable even in face-to-face interactions (as evidenced by the familiar, if irritating, question "What are you?") and that we must establish it interactionally both on- and offline. Stereotypes come into play in both arenas but in different directions: in face-to-face interaction, seeing racial characteristics leads to stereotyping; online, applying stereotypical templates leads to assumptions about race. The

Racial Identity: "More Than the Sum of Our Parts" President Barack Obama, left, listens to the inauguration ceremony at the U.S. Capitol on January 20, 2009. Behind Obama is his family, including wife Michelle, daughters Malia and Sasha, his sister Maya Soetoro-Ng and her husband Konrad Ng, and Obama's mother-in-law Marian Robinson.

internet is thus not a place where all the problematic distinctions disappear—they just manifest themselves in different ways.

DATA WORKSHOP

ANALYZING MASS MEDIA AND POPULAR CULTURE

The Politics and Poetics of Racial Identity

I am the son of a black man from Kenya and a white woman from Kansas. I was raised with the help of a white grandfather who survived a Depression to serve in Patton's Army during World War II and a white grandmother who worked on a bomber assembly line at Fort Leavenworth while he was overseas. I've gone to some of the best schools in America and lived in one of the world's poorest nations. I am married to a black American who carries within her the blood of slaves and slaveowners—an inheritance we pass on to our two precious daughters. I have brothers, sisters, nieces, nephews, uncles and cousins, of every race and every hue, scattered across three continents, and for as long as I live, I will never forget that in no other country on Earth is my story even possible.

It's a story that hasn't made me the most conventional candidate. But it is a story that has seared into my genetic makeup the idea that this nation is more than the sum of its parts—that out of many, we are truly one.

—from Barack Obama's speech to the nation,
March 18, 2008, Philadelphia, Pennsylvania

Barack Obama, the forty-fourth president of the United States, is the first black man to be elected to the office. Issues of race featured prominently in his 2008 campaign, and during a campaign stop in Philadelphia Obama gave one particularly famous speech on race that was discussed, analyzed, scrutinized, and evaluated by pundits and ordinary citizens alike for months afterward. In the speech, Obama ostensibly addressed some controversial comments about race delivered by the pastor of the church his family attended in Chicago. But he also spoke to bigger issues that everyone, regardless of race, has had to grapple with simply as part of being an American. Indeed, he presented the issue of racial prejudice as one of America's defining social problems and challenged all Americans to work toward solving it.

This Data Workshop asks you to do a content analysis of an existing source such as a speech, song, poem, or performance that deals with racial and ethnic identity (see Chapter 2 for a review of this research method). Check out text and audio of Obama's speech at http://www.nytimes.com/2008/03/18/us/politics/18text–obama.html. You can also look up other important political speeches at the Library of Congress's "American Memory" web site, dedicated to providing the public with electronic access to "written and spoken words, sound recordings, still and moving images, prints, maps and sheet music that document the American experience": http://memory.loc.gov/ammem/index.html.

You may also choose a poem from your favorite writer and consider how racial and ethnic identity are socially constructed in poetry. Or you might rent or record an episode of the HBO series *Def Poetry Jam*, which features artists such as Mos Def, Jay-Z, Caroline Kennedy, Rakim, Erykah Badu, Mutaburuka, and Jill Scott. Or analyze the lyrics from your favorite musical artist (in the case of rap or hip-hop artists, some are also Def Jam poets). Consider other kinds of sources as well, such as the stand-up routines of Korean American comic Margaret Cho, the Chicano comedy troupe Culture Clash, the Middle Eastern comics in "Axis of Evil," or the African American Queens of Comedy. Finally, you could also write an original speech or poem about your own racial or ethnic identity experience, then discuss it using the principles of content analysis. Whichever option you choose, remember to focus on how the text expresses ideas about race, ethnicity, identity, inequality, and solidarity.

There are two options for completing this Data Workshop.

- Option 1 (informal): Prepare written notes on your chosen text that you can refer to in class. Compare your notes and experiences with other students in small-group discussions.

- Option 2 (formal): Write a three- to four-page essay analyzing your chosen text.

Race, Ethnicity, and Life Chances

A law professor decides that it is time to buy a house. After careful research into neighborhoods and land values, she picks one. With her excellent credit history and prestigious job, she easily obtains a mortgage over the phone. When the mortgage forms arrive in the mail, she sees to her surprise that the phone representative has identified her race as "white." Smiling, she checks another box, "African American," and mails back the form. Suddenly, everything changes. The lending bank wants a bigger down payment and higher interest rates. When she threatens to sue, the bank backs down. She learns that the bank's motivation is falling property values in the proposed neighborhood. She doesn't understand this because those property values were completely stable when she was researching the area. Then she realizes that *she* is the reason for the plummeting values.

As Patricia Williams's (1997) experience illustrates, membership in socially constructed categories of race and ethnicity can often carry a high price. We now look at other ways this price might be paid, in the areas of health, education, work, family, and criminal justice.

Family

Race, ethnicity, and their correlates (like SES) shape family life in a variety of ways. Data from the Census Bureau (2010b) showed that of the white population over eighteen years

of age, 58.1 percent were married, 10.9 percent divorced, 6.8 percent widowed, and 22.6 percent never married. Of the African American population over age eighteen, 34.4 percent were married, 11.7 percent divorced, 6.7 percent widowed, and 42.8 percent never married. The Hispanic population was more similar to the white population with 49.4 percent over age eighteen married, 8.2 percent divorced, 3.8 percent widowed, and 34.2 percent never married. Thus, African Americans are more likely than whites and Hispanics to never marry, to be divorced, or to be widowed.

Kathryn Edin (2000) argues that low-income women of all ethnicities see marriage as having few benefits. They feel that the men they are likely to encounter as possible husbands will not offer the advantages (financial stability, respectability, trust) that make the rewards of marriage worth the risks. This doesn't mean, of course, that most low-income women don't love their male companions; it only means that they believe a legal bond would not substantially improve their lot in life.

In 2008, the birth rates for American teenage mothers (ages fifteen to nineteen) varied significantly by race. The birth rate for white teenage moms was twenty-six per 1,000 births, while the birth rate for African Americans was fifty-nine per 1,000; for Hispanics it was seventy per 1,000 (Hamilton 2010). Social thinkers such as Angela Y. Davis argue that African American teenage girls in particular see fewer opportunities for education and work, and choose motherhood instead (2001). Davis believes that social aimed at punishing teenage mothers of color will be ineffective; only by attacking the racism inherent in the educational system and the workforce will these teens be at less risk of becoming mothers.

Health

Health care is an area in which we find widespread disparity between racial and ethnic groups. Because there is no universal health care in the United States, consumers must rely on insurance benefits provided through their employer or buy individual policies in order to meet their medical needs. This may change when new health insurance "exchanges" are created in 2014. In the meantime, however, many Americans cannot afford basic health-care coverage. In 2009, some 12 percent of whites were without health insurance, along with 17.2 percent of Asian Americans, 21 percent of blacks, and 32.4 percent of Hispanics (Figure 8.2).

Disparities in access to health care may help explain the life expectancy rates for men and women of different races. White male children born in 2009 can expect to live to be 76.2 years old, while white females can expect to live to age 80.9. However, African American males' life expectancy is only 70.9 years, and African American females' is 77.4. Hispanic males' life expectancy, on the other hand, is 77.9 years,

On the Job

Race in College Admissions

Affirmative action policies were first put in place in the 1960s to make sure that racial and ethnic minorities and women had equal access to opportunities that had historically been available only to whites and men. While in principle these policies were lauded as a way to create a "level playing field" for all Americans, problems began to surface in practice. In 1978, a white student named Alan Bakke sued the University of California for "reverse discrimination": Bakke claimed that his application to UC Davis's medical school had been rejected in favor of lesser-qualified minority applicants because the school had set aside 16 percent of its medical school slots for minority applicants. The case went to the Supreme Court, and while the Court upheld the idea of affirmative action in general, it outlawed the "quota system" that had contributed to Bakke's rejection.

Since then, colleges and universities, private employers, and governments at all levels have struggled with the principles of affirmative action. Influential state university systems in California, Washington, Texas, and Michigan have faced additional legal challenges to their admissions criteria and have attempted to craft race-blind policies that produce the same effects as affirmative action. While seeking to avoid "quotas" and "preferential treatment," these schools also wish to increase diversity and create opportunities for historically underrepresented groups. How can these goals be accomplished simultaneously? Not without difficulty, it seems. California's public university system saw a substantial decrease in the number of minority applicants immediately following the policy changes made in 1996 that prohibited using race, sex, or ethnicity as a basis for admission or financial aid (Weiss 2001). Although the admission rates in the University of California system for non-Asian minority students rose in fall 1999 (almost to the levels of 1997, the last year of race-based admissions), they have continued to decline in the years since.

College admissions staff grapple with questions about race every day when they arrive at work. Rachel Toor, a former admissions officer at Duke University, maintains that "Duke was firmly committed to affirmative action," but evidently there was much confusion over what its affirmative action policies actually were. In her position on the admissions committee, Toor says, "I tried to discuss larger social and cultural issues relating to race . . . I rolled my eyes when [colleagues] made racist comments." But decisions taking

Alan Bakke

race into account remained difficult and contentious. Toor herself supports affirmative action policies because, she says, "if left in the hands of admissions officers, the way Duke's rating system is set up, there would be very few students of color" (2001).

The problems facing Toor and her committee are not unique to Duke. Until 2003, the University of Michigan had affirmative action programs for both its undergraduate and law school students. The undergraduate admissions procedure was based on a rigid point system, which led white students who had been denied admission to complain that additional points given to minority students solely on the basis of race gave them an unfair advantage. The law school admissions procedure used race as one of several factors to be considered. In 2003, the Supreme Court upheld the law school policy and revised the undergraduate policy. Supporters at the University of Michigan argued that the Court had firmly endorsed the principle of diversity articulated by Justice Powell in the *Bakke* decision. Outgoing Dean Jeffrey Lehman said, "By upholding the University of Michigan Law School's admissions policy, the court has approved a model for how to enroll a student body that is both academically excellent and racially integrated." Further, "The question is no longer whether affirmative action is legal; it is how to hasten the day when affirmative action is no longer needed" (J. Peterson 2003).

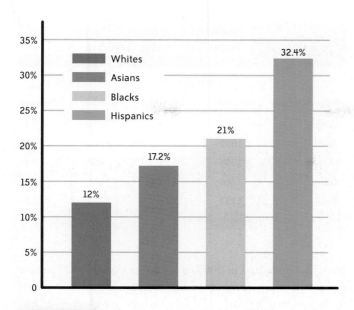

FIGURE 8.2 Americans without Health Insurance by Race, 2009

Disparities in access to health care adversely affect different groups.

SOURCE: DeNavas-Walt, Proctor & Smith 2010.

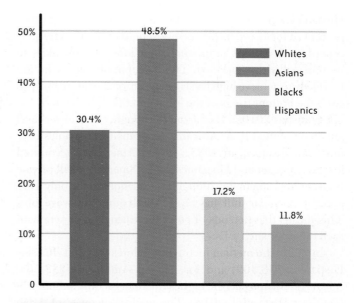

FIGURE 8.3 U.S. Bachelor's Degree Holders by Race, 2009

SOURCE: U.S. Census Bureau 2009b.

and Hispanic females' is 83.1. Minorities are also often disproportionately exposed to other factors that impact lifespan, such as dangers in the workplace, toxins in the environment, or personal behaviors like drinking and poor diet (Kochanek 2011). While life expectancy statistics are only crude indicators of general health, they do reveal continuing race-based discrepancies, including the ongoing mystery of why Hispanics live longer, a question researchers are still trying to answer.

Education

One of America's cultural myths is that everyone has equal access to education, the key to a secure, well-paying job. However, by looking at those who actually receive degrees, we can see that the playing field is not that level. According to the Census Bureau (2009b), in 2009, 90.8 percent of white students earned a high school diploma, while 82.7 percent of African American students and 63 percent of Hispanic students did so. The reasons for dropping out are complex, but the highest rates are associated with those from economically disadvantaged and non–English-speaking backgrounds.

In higher education, the numbers are similar. In 2009, 48.5 percent of Asian Americans, 30.4 percent of whites, 17.2 percent of blacks, and 11.8 percent of Hispanics earned a bachelor's degree (Figure 8.3). Further, 18.7 percent of Asian Americans, 10.6 percent of whites, 5.6 percent of African Americans, and 3.0 percent of Hispanics earned advanced degrees (master's, professional degrees, and doc-

torates). Thus, Asian Americans and whites enjoy more success overall in the U.S. educational system than African Americans and Hispanics. The reasons for the disparity are again complex, involving both economic and cultural factors. Earning an education is extremely important in American society. Not only does it translate to greater success in the workforce, it also confers social status and cultural capital that can prove valuable in other arenas.

Work and Income

African Americans make up 10.7 percent and Hispanics 14 percent of the total workforce. If jobs were truly given to people regardless of racial or ethnic identity, we would expect to see these same distributions across occupations. However, that is not the case. For example, in 2009, African Americans constituted 8.4 percent and Hispanics 7.3 percent of all executive and managerial professions (U.S. Bureau of Labor Statistics 2010a). That means that these positions, usually requiring advanced degrees, are primarily held by whites.

In contrast, persons of color carry the burden of some of society's most difficult jobs. In 2009, 25.3 percent of all nurses and home health aides and 28.3 percent of all postal clerks were black, while

affirmative action programs or policies that seek to rectify the effects of past discrimination by increasing representation and ensuring equal opportunity for any previously disadvantaged group

Hispanics were more likely to be employed in farming (40.7 percent of total) and as private household cleaners (41.7 percent of total). Except for nursing, these jobs are more likely to be semiskilled or unskilled. Thus, people of color, who are less likely to achieve high levels of education, are more likely to swell the bottom rungs of the job market (U.S. Bureau of Labor Statistics 2010a). Interestingly enough, some lower-level jobs have shifted from African Americans to Hispanics over time. For instance, in 1983, African Americans accounted for 42.4 percent and Hispanics for 11.8 percent of all private household cleaners; by 2009, blacks accounted for only 16.1 percent. A similar shift may be seen with other low-wage jobs. This means that persons of color increasingly compete with each other for such jobs.

In 2009, the median income for whites was $54,461, for Hispanics $38,309, and for African Americans $32,584. Asian Americans had the highest median income at $65,469 (DeNavas-Walt, et al. 2010). The median incomes of Asian Americans and whites thus place them in the middle class, while those of blacks and Hispanics place them in the lower-middle (working) class. African Americans and Hispanics are more disproportionately represented than whites in the income brackets between $0 and $49,999, while whites are more disproportionately represented in income brackets above $50,000. In 2009, 12.3 percent of whites lived below the poverty line, compared with 25.8 percent of African Americans and 25.3 percent of Hispanics (DeNavas-Walt, et al. 2010). These numbers make it easy to see how race and class intersect to influence life outcomes.

Criminal Justice

Although the majority of the U.S. population is white—about 69 percent, as opposed to about 13 percent black and 13 percent Hispanic—we don't find these same proportions in the prison population. Of all state and federal male prisoners in 2009, 40 percent were African American, while 33 percent were white and 21 percent Hispanic (West 2010). Why are larger proportions of African American and Hispanic men in prison?

Some laws that don't seem race based still create racially differentiated outcomes (Table 8.2). For example, federal law until 2007 handed out tougher sentences to crack users (who are more likely to be black) than to users of powdered cocaine (who are more likely to be white): if you possessed a small amount of crack (for personal use), you'd get the same stringent sentence that you would if you possessed a huge amount of cocaine (enough for hundreds of uses). While this discrep-

genocide the deliberate and systematic extermination of a racial, ethnic, national, or cultural group

TABLE 8.2	Federal Cocaine Offenders by Race/Ethnicity, 2006			
	POWDER		**CRACK**	
Race/Ethnicity	**Number**	**Percent**	**Number**	**Percent**
White	821	14.3	474	8.8
Black	1550	27.0	4411	81.8
Hispanic	3296	57.5	452	8.4
Other	66	1.2	56	1.0
Total	5733	100.0	5393	100.0

SOURCE: U.S. Sentencing Commission 2007.

ancy was remedied in 2007, it left more than 17,000 people convicted of crack possession awaiting official reductions in their sentences—over 15,000 of whom are black (US Sentencing Commission 2010). Unemployment rates are higher among minority groups, as are dropout rates, and these may affect incarceration rates. There is also some evidence that there are connections to declining marriage rates and incarceration (Pettit and Western 2004).

It is also clear that African Americans are far more likely than whites to be murdered: In 2009, while both whites and blacks accounted for approximately 48 percent of murder victims nationwide, these percentages don't reflect the racial distribution of the U.S. population as a whole (FBI 2009a). Finally, more than half of the reported hate crimes in 2009 were attributed to racial discrimination, with nearly three-quarters of those targeting blacks (U.S. Department of Justice 2009).

Race Relations: Conflict or Cooperation

The relationships between racial and ethnic groups in a society can take different forms. In some instances, groups may be tolerant and respectful of one another, while in other cases there is unending hostility. In this section, we will examine five basic patterns of intergroup relationships, from the most violent to the most tolerant. Keep in mind that some ethnic groups, such as Native Americans, may suffer several different patterns of hardship over a period of time.

Genocide

The first pattern represents the worst possible outcome between a dominant and a subordinate group. Not only has **genocide**, the deliberate and systematic extermination of a racial, ethnic, national, or cultural group, taken place in the past, it continues today in certain parts of the globe. One of the most horrific and wide-scale examples was the Holocaust of World War II, when more than six million European Jews and several million more non-Jewish "undesirables" (including Gypsies, Poles, Slavs, political enemies, Jehovah's Witnesses, Catholic clergy, homosexuals, and people with disabilities) were moved to concentration camps and executed by the German Nazis (Friedman 1995). Since then, genocide, or "ethnic cleansing," has destroyed many more millions of lives in Eastern Europe, Southeast Asia, and Africa. It is also possible to consider the violence perpetuated by the early Americans against the Native American tribes who occupied North America as a form of genocide. While Native Americans died from diseases introduced by the settlers, they were also systematically killed by the European colonists. In the few hundred years that it took for the United States to be settled from coast to coast, the Native American population was almost completely decimated. Estimates for the total number killed range anywhere from 15 million up to 100 million (Stannard 1993; Cook 1998).

Population Transfer

The treatment of Native Americans leads us to the next pattern of group relations—**population transfer**, or the forcible removal of a group of people from the territory they have occupied. In the early nineteenth century, Native Americans who had not perished in battles with U.S. soldiers were forced by the U.S. government to move onto Indian reservations (also referred to as tribal lands or American Indian nations) west of the Mississippi River. They were often moved far away from the lands where they had lived for generations (mostly Southern states), as these were desirable territories that the whites wished to acquire for themselves. Between 1838 and 1839, in one of the most well-known examples, the state of Georgia and the federal government forcibly marched 17,000 Cherokees westward over 800 miles, a grueling journey known as the "Trail of Tears." Along the way, more than 4,000 people died of hunger, exposure, or disease.

The separate territories established for the Native Americans are an example of a kind of partitioning that we can see happening today in Israel between the Israelis and Palestinians in the West Bank and Gaza Strip. There, the Israeli government restricts the movement of Palestinians and has even built miles of barriers designed to wall them in and keep them separate from the Israeli population. Sometimes, population transfer takes a more indirect form. For instance, it is possible to make life so miserable in a region

that a group of people will choose to leave "voluntarily." This was the case with early Mormons, whose religious persecution in the East and Midwest between 1846 and 1869 drove 70,000 to cross the country (taking what is called the Mormon Pioneer Trail) and settle in the Great Salt Lake Valley region of Utah.

Internal Colonialism and Segregation

The term "colonialism" refers to a policy whereby a stronger nation takes control of a weaker foreign nation (the "colony") in order to extend its territory or to exploit the colony's resources for its own enrichment. The British Empire, which once included such distant countries as India, Burma (now Myanmar), the West Indies, South Africa, and Australia, as well as America before its independence, is an example of colonialism. **Internal colonialism** describes the exploitation of a minority group within the dominant group's own borders.

Internal colonialism often takes the form of economic exploitation and includes some sort of physical **segregation** of groups by race or ethnicity. For example, in the U.S. South up to the 1960s, not only did blacks live in separate neighborhoods, but they also were restricted to "coloreds"-only sections of buses, parks, restaurants, and even drinking fountains. If members of the minority group live close by yet in their own part of town (for instance, on the "other side of the tracks"), they are separate, and hence unequal, but still near enough to serve as workers for the dominant group. Segregation was not just confined to the South; it permeated other areas of society. Separation by races could be found in divisions serving in the U.S. military and among teams playing in professional sports like baseball, football, and basketball. Efforts to desegregate American society accelerated through the mid-twentieth century.

Assimilation

With **assimilation**, a minority group is absorbed into the dominant group: this process is the central idea behind America's "melting pot." On the surface, assimilation seems like a reasonable solution to the potential conflicts

population transfer the forcible removal of a group of people from the territory they have occupied

internal colonialism the economic and political domination and subjugation of the minority group by the controlling group within a nation

segregation the formal and legal separation of groups by race or ethnicity

assimilation a pattern of relations between ethnic or racial groups in which the minority group is absorbed into the mainstream or dominant group, making society more homogenous

Changing the World

Stories of Genocide

The twentieth century witnessed numerous incidents of genocide. From 1915 to 1923, during and after World War I, the Turkish government massacred 1.5 million Armenians in what is often referred to as the "forgotten genocide." Nazi Germany under Adolf Hitler's rule killed two-thirds of the Jews of Europe. Few paid attention to the Armenian tragedy, and many refused to believe the initial reports of Hitler's death camps as well (Hitler himself recognized this, and is alleged to have asked, "Who remembers the Armenians?" when he embarked on his own genocidal project). In the latter half of the century, such events became all too common. From the atrocities of Darfur to Slobodan Milošević's ethnic cleansing in the Balkans and the Hutu slaughter of Tutsis in Rwanda, genocide has become a familiar feature of the modern landscape.

Faced with such overwhelming horror, it would be easy to give up and assume that there's nothing one person can do to stop it. However, this has not been the attitude of those who lived through these events, some of whom have begun recording their life histories. The documentarians who collect these stories hope to change the world in two different ways. First, they hope the histories will serve as a permanent reminder so that future generations might avert such tragedies. Second, they hope to provide some relief to the survivors, who are often traumatized and guilt ridden.

Around the world, for example, wherever Holocaust survivors have settled, archives have sprung up to record their testimony. The most ambitious of these programs may also be the most recent. In 1994, after filming *Schindler's List*, director Steven Spielberg founded the Survivors of the Shoah Visual History Foundation to document the experiences of Holocaust survivors. Spielberg believed the foundation's mission was particularly pressing because of the advanced age of most of the survivors. To capture their experiences, the foundation videotaped more than 51,000 testimonies in thirty-two languages by people living in fifty-seven countries. These interviews are available to anyone, not just researchers, and are especially valuable to the communities where they were recorded.

Another project comes from Donald and Lorna Miller, who present a written record of the Armenian tragedy in their book *Survivors: An Oral History of the Armenian Genocide* (1999). After interviewing 100 survivors, the authors chronicled their experiences of brutality, despair, strength, and hope for future generations. And the photography exhibit "I Witness," which toured the United States in 2002, features portraits of aging Armenian survivors taken by photographers and activists Ara Oshagan and Levon Parian.

Telling these stories is immensely painful but also very important to survivors. This is why, even fifty years later, so many come forward to be interviewed. As Miriam Fridman, president of the Holocaust Survivors of South Florida, put it: "Telling our story rips us apart . . . but they will see us, know that we existed and what happened. Then we leave a legacy that history should not repeat" (quoted in Adams 1994). The Armenian ethnographer Verjine Svazlian offered her collection of life histories "as evidence of the past and a warning for the future" (Svazlian 2000).

This sort of large-scale enterprise is not necessarily available for victims of more recent crises. Atrocities in the Balkans, Sudan, Rwanda, and elsewhere have created a large new refugee population that does not yet have the

between different groups. If everyone belongs to the same group, if the society is largely homogenous, then conflict will decrease.

During much of the twentieth century, immigrants to the United States were eager to adopt an American way of life, become citizens, learn English, and lose any trace of their "foreign-ness." The Irish, Italians, and Eastern Europeans were all once considered "ethnics" but eventually assimilated into the larger category of white Americans. Today, they are practically unrecognizable as distinct ethnic groups, unless they choose to emphasize characteristics that would so distinguish them. It is likely that this process will con-

Survivors of Genocide Holocaust survivor Ehud Valter, 79, displays the card documenting his transfer between the Auschwitz and Buchenwald concentration camps. Anna Karakian, 101, survived the mass killings of Armenians in 1915 in what was then the Ottoman Empire.

organization or the resources to create something like the Shoah Foundation (though see the creative nonfiction book *What Is the What* [Eggers 2006]). They do, however, have a desperate need to document their experiences.

Does the telling of stories of genocide actually help to prevent such events? Earlier life histories don't seem to have prevented racism and intolerance: after all, ethnic violence and genocide seem to be alive and well in the world today. However, we might argue that changing the world for the better is a process to engage in, not a goal that can be easily reached. In each generation, atrocities will be committed, and each generation must reach out to the survivors and look for the seeds of social change. Telling and preserving stories can change the world—even if only one person at a time.

tinue with the newer wave of immigrants; for instance, some census-type forms no longer distinguish Hispanic or Middle Eastern as separate categories from white.

But although there is something to be gained by assimilation, namely membership in the dominant population, there is also something to be sacrificed. Minority group members may lose their previous ethnic or racial identity, either through **racial assimilation** (having children with the dominant group until the different races are completely

> **racial assimilation** the process by which racial minority groups are absorbed into the dominant group through intermarriage

Jackie Robinson is most often cited as the first athlete to break the "color barrier" in professional sports when he made his debut in major league baseball in 1947.

mixed) or through **cultural assimilation**, in which members learn the cultural practices of the dominant group. In some cases, both types of assimilation take place at the same time.

In addition, the process of assimilation is not always entered into voluntarily. Sometimes a minority group may be forced to acquire new behaviors and forbidden to practice their own religion or speak their own language, until these are all but forgotten. For some, assimilation results in the tragic loss of a distinctive racial or ethnic identity. This is true for many Native Americans, for instance, who in just a few generations have lost the ability to speak their tribal languages or have forgotten cultural practices of their not-so-distant ancestors.

cultural assimilation the process by which racial or ethnic groups are absorbed into the dominant group by adopting the dominant group's culture

pluralism a cultural pattern of intergroup relations that encourages racial and ethnic variation within a society

Pluralism

Pluralism not only permits racial and ethnic variation within one society, it actually encourages people to embrace diversity—to exchange the traditional melting pot image

for a "salad bowl." In the last few decades, the United States has seen more and more groups celebrating their racial or ethnic roots, developing a strong common consciousness, and expressing pride in their unique identity.

At the core of multiculturalism is tolerance of racial and ethnic differences. A country like Switzerland provides an interesting example. Although the Swiss are largely homogenous in terms of race, the country is made up of several major ethnic and linguistic groups, including Protestants and Catholics as well as speakers of French, German, and Italian, who live in relative harmony and equality. There is little of the prejudice and discrimination that characterize other, diverse European countries. But the Swiss were not always so tolerant of diversity; their history is rife with ethnic conflict and the threat of civil war. It was not until 1848 that a new constitution established a legal system designed to share power among different groups, making sure that each had proportional representation at all levels of government. There is also no one "official" language; rather, all three are considered the national languages. Although some have called Switzerland an exception when it comes to multiculturalism, others claim that its success is due precisely to a political system that legislates democratic pluralism and depends on minorities being continually accommodated so that none become disenfranchised (Schmid 1981).

Another example of successful multiculturalism is Canada. This country's population is even more diverse than Switzerland's, composed of not only two official linguistic groups (English and French) but also ethnic and racial minorities that include European, Chinese, and Indian immigrants as well as members of "First Nations," or Canadian native peoples. The Canadian government is committed to the ideals of multiculturalism, with a great deal of funding directed to programs aimed at improving race relations and encouraging multicultural harmony. As a sign of that commitment, the 1988 Canadian Multiculturalism Act declares that the role of government is to bring about "equal access for all Canadians in the economic, social, cultural, and political realms" (Mitchell 1993).

The United States is still moving toward becoming a more multicultural and egalitarian society, although in recent years there has been a backlash against the idea of pluralism. Some critics blame the educational system for allowing what they consider marginal academic areas, such as ethnic studies, women's studies, gay and lesbian studies, and the like, to be featured alongside the classic curriculum. Others question the need for bilingual education and English as a Second Language (ESL) programs, despite research showing benefits to nonnative speakers (Krashen 1996). And groups such as U.S. English and English First advocate for legislation making English the national language and setting limits on the use of other languages. Nevertheless, since the future seems sure to bring an ever greater racial and ethnic mix to the country, Americans may yet be able to incorporate multiculturalism into our sense of national identity.

Closing Comments

Constructing categories of race and ethnicity seems inevitably to lead to stratification and inequality and such destructive social processes as stereotyping, segregation, prejudice, and discrimination. Are there any positive consequences, either for society or for individuals? As it turns out, there are.

Racial and ethnic categories help create a sense of identity for members of these groups, which can lead to feelings of unity and solidarity—a sense of belonging to something that is larger than oneself, of cultural connection, and of shared history. We see this in action during ethnic festivals and holidays. When we share our own group unity with others in this way, we contribute to the diversity of our community and society. The more we understand and appreciate the diverse population of our nation, the less likely we may be to contribute to the destructive consequences of racial and ethnic categorization.

The important sociological insight here is that since categories of race and ethnicity are socially constructed, their meanings are socially constructed as well. Historically, we have constructed meanings that favor some and exploit and oppress others. Is it possible to construct meanings for racial and ethnic categories that value and celebrate them all? Over time, and with your newly acquired sociological insights, we hope you will be part of that transformation.

ⓢ Need Help Studying?

wwnorton.com/studyspace

Visit StudySpace to access free review materials such as:

- **Vocabulary Flashcards**
- **Diagnostic Review Quizzes**
- **Study Outlines**

QUESTIONS FOR REVIEW

1. How do you identify yourself in terms of race or ethnicity? Are there special occasions or situations in which you are more likely to display your ethnicity or race? Do you identify with more than one racial or ethnic group or know anyone who does? What does this tell you about the origin of these categories?

2. Do you ever find yourself buying into prejudices? Can you think of examples of prejudices based on positive attitudes? What do you think is the long-term effect of such "positive" prejudices?

3. Many sociologists believe that institutional discrimination causes more harm than individual discrimination in the long run. Can you think of a social, political, or economic institution whose policies systematically benefit one racial group more than another?

4. This chapter argued that racial and ethnic identities are accomplished in interaction. Do you notice anything about the way you talk, the type of clothes you wear, your body movements, or facial expressions that project your racial identity? Have you ever changed something about yourself because you weren't comfortable with the identity it projected?

5. Robert Park, a functionalist theorist, believed that communication and exchange between racial and ethnic groups would inevitably lead to integration and the elimination of racial diversity, though it has become apparent that this theory is more applicable to some groups than to others. For whom is this kind of integration effective, and why?

6. Affirmative action in college admissions is one of the most controversial topics in America today. Why would a college want to consider race or ethnicity when making admissions decisions? What factors do you think admissions boards should consider?

7. Two metaphors are often used to describe racial and ethnic relations in the United States: the "melting pot" and the "salad bowl." What are the differences between these two phrases, and which one do you think best describes the United States? What are the advantages and disadvantages of each model?

8. Although the Supreme Court ruled against antimiscegenation laws in 1967, homogamy, or assortive mating, is reinforced by social conventions. Would you date someone of a different race? Does your answer change depending on which racial or ethnic group you're thinking about?

9. This chapter described five different types of intergroup relations, ranging from genocide to multiculturalism. Choose three of these patterns and provide real-world examples not mentioned in the chapter. Do you think modern societies are trending one way or another?

SUGGESTIONS FOR FURTHER EXPLORATION

Ararat. 2002. Dir. Atom Egoyan. Miramax Films. Examines the Armenian genocide that took place in Turkey in 1915 as well as the contemporary cultural memory of the event and its lasting impact on the Turkish and Armenian peoples.

Bamboozled. 2000. Dir. Spike Lee. New Line Cinema. In this dark, biting satire of the television industry, a new minstrel show, complete with actors in blackface, becomes a surprise hit. Lee makes parallels between minstrel and contemporary hip-hop, pointing out the ways that blacks are involved in perpetuating racism.

Crash. 2005. Dir. Paul Haggis. Lion's Gate Films. This movie follows the interlocking lives of two dozen Los Angeles residents over the course of two days. In this socially and racially diverse group, people collide with one another in shocking and sometimes unsettling ways.

Darfur Is Dying (www.darfurisdying.com). 2006. This free, web-based video game about the atrocities in the Darfur region of Sudan aims to inspire social activism by connecting players to the lives of those suffering in the genocide. In the game, the player's character must try to provide for the needs of his fellow refugees without being captured by militiamen.

Eggers, Dave. 2006. *What Is the What: The Autobiography of Valentino Achak Deng.* New York: Vintage. Creative nonfiction based on the real-life story of one of the Lost Boys of Sudan.

Gourevitch, Philip. 1998. *We Wish to Inform You that Tomorrow We Will Be Killed with Our Families: Stories from Rwanda.* New York: Picador. Details the modern genocide between the Tutsi and Hutu people in Rwanda. Although the book is an excellent illustration of the way that racial categories are socially constructed, Gourevitch writes for many of the same reasons that museums record the testimony of Holocaust survivors. As he puts it, "the best reason I have come up with for looking more closely into Rwanda's horror stories is that ignoring them makes me more uncomfortable about existence and my place in it."

Gran Torino. 2008. Dir. Clint Eastwood. Warner Bros. An angry and alienated Korean war vet slowly overcomes his prejudices against his Hmong neighbors, including the teenage boy who tried to steal his car.

Kingston, Maxine Hong. 1989. *The Woman Warrior: Memoirs of a Girlhood among Ghosts.* New York: Vintage. A memoir of growing up Chinese American in California, the child of immigrant parents. Like many social theorists, Kingston

focuses on race as it is experienced by the individual and the ways that the meaning of race changes depending on one's social position.

Massey, Douglas S., and Nancy A. Denton. 1993. *American Apartheid: Segregation and the Making of the Underclass.* Cambridge, MA: Harvard University Press. A sociological analysis of the way that segregation continues in America and its important consequences for race relations.

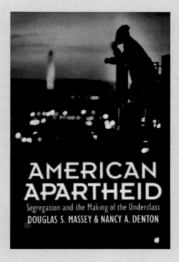

Oliver, Melvin, and Thomas Shapiro. 1997. *Black Wealth, White Wealth: A New Perspective on Racial Inequality.* London: Routledge. A contemporary, class-based account of racial inequality; the authors argue that differences in wealth, not income, hold the key to understanding racial inequality.

Project Implicit (implicit.harvard.edu). An intriguing research project at Harvard University that is finding new ways to measure racial attitudes, assuming that any traditional survey of attitudes about race and ethnicity will be hampered because on these issues, "people don't always 'speak their minds,' and it is suspected that people don't always 'know their minds.'"

Senna, Danzy. 1998. *Caucasia.* New York: Riverhead Trade. A moving novel about one young girl's experience of "passing." Birdie, the narrator, is the child of a racially mixed couple in Boston in the 1970s. When her parents split up, she stays with her mother and passes as white. The novel takes an unflinching look at the cost of being the child of a mixed-race couple in a racially intolerant society and the equally demanding pressures of passing as white.

CHAPTER 9

Constructing Gender and Sexuality

Eight seconds is an infinitesimally small amount of time to most people. In fact, there are very few tasks that you can accomplish in eight seconds. For Caster Semenya, eight seconds was enough time to cause the world to question her gender for an entire year. Semenya was born in 1991 and raised in the small village of Ga-Masehlong in South Africa. She lived her life as a girl without any question until her outstanding performance at the 2009 African Junior Championships, where she broke previous records with a time of 1:56.72 in the 800-meter race. One month later, she broke the world record at the 2009 World Championships. She drew the attention of the International Association of Athletics Federation (IAAF) because her race time in the 2009 African Junior Championships beat her performance in the 2008 competition by eight seconds. Eight seconds was all it took for Semenya to be cast into the world spotlight by the fall of 2009.

Female athletes frequently have to face the stigma of not being seen as "feminine" due to the physicality required to be a superior athlete. The low body fat percentages and accentuated muscles that occur through sports training may even cause women to stop having menstrual periods. As our notions of gender are strongly linked to the body, female athletes often find themselves in the difficult position of defending themselves against the sanctions associated with being perceived as lesbian or "masculine." In fact, sex-determination testing has been a recurring theme for female athletes since the 1968 Olympics when many Soviet female athletes were accused of being male. Sex-determination testing is generally performed by a team of physicians, including gynecologists and endocrinologists. Critics claim that these tests are humiliating, inaccurate, and insensitive. The Olympic committee ceased sex-determination testing in 1996.

In 2009, the IAAF required Semenya to undergo sex-determination testing to confirm eligibility to compete as a woman after her eight-second improvement in the 800-meter race. The public announcement of her testing coincided with her win at the World Championships. In the media storm that followed, the public at large speculated that Semenya may be intersexed and possess undescended testicles that produced extra testosterone that enhanced her performance. Bloggers, tabloids, and talk shows all made Semenya a household name around the world. It seemed like everyone had a diagnosis for Caster Semenya, and few of them involved her being female. In the eleven months that it took the IAAF to complete the testing, Semenya was banned from competing. If the testing revealed that she was not biologically female, her gold medals would be taken from her and she would relinquish her title as World Champion in the 800-meter.

On July 6, 2010, the IAAF publicly announced that Semenya could keep her title and medal, and that she was eligible to compete in future races as a woman. The results of the sex-determination test were never released to the public. Unfortunately for Semenya, the stigma of having her sex questioned has already done its damage. While she won the first 800-meter race that she was allowed to compete in after the IAAF made its decision, her competitors still view her with suspicion and question her legitimacy on the racetrack. Even though Semenya has been "officially" declared a woman, there will always be those who question her "real" sex.

Sports will continue to have to address the issue of gender as the awareness of intersexed, transgendered, and transsexual individuals increases. How will eligibility be determined for athletes in these categories? Does gender identity even still matter in athletic competition? Should having higher levels of testosterone disqualify an individual from competing as a woman? Should any female athlete have to face the public humiliation that Semenya did? It will be fascinating to see how future cases of sex-determination testing will be handled after the trauma that Semenya had to endure for almost an entire year. For Semenya, eight seconds changed her life as she knew it, and raised everyone's awareness of how important and complicated issues of gender are for society.

HOW TO READ THIS CHAPTER

We often think of gender and sexuality as part of our biological inheritance, unchanging and unchangeable. We hope that after reading this chapter you will understand the ways in which our gender and sexual identities are about *what we do* in addition to being about *who we are*. Gender and sexuality may be based in physiology, but their meanings are constructed in social contexts. As you read, pay attention to the processes involved in how the meaning of gender is constructed, as well as to the real consequences of gender inequality. As you become aware of these problems, perhaps you'll begin to think about solutions as well.

What Is Sex? What Is Gender?

Although people often use the terms "sex" and "gender" interchangeably, sociologists differentiate between the two:

most view "sex" as biological but "gender" as social or cultural. Even though a person is usually the same sex and gender, this is not always the case, as we will see.

Sex

Sex refers to an individual's membership in one of two categories—male or female. The distinctions between male and female are based on such biological factors as chromosomes, hormones, and reproductive organs, all of which make up the primary sex characteristics. Males and females also possess different secondary sex characteristics, such as facial and body hair and musculature (Table 9.1).

Most people assume that everyone is either male or female. However, about seventeen babies in 1,000 are born **intersexed** (what used to be called "hermaphroditic"), having a variant chromosomal makeup and mixed or indeterminate male and female sex characteristics (Fausto-Sterling 2000). For these infants, since nature hasn't clearly indicated their sex, parents and doctors choose one and take the appropriate medical steps (in most cases, female is the most viable and expedient choice). In modern Western society, the prospect of an ambiguously sexed person seems so threatening and unacceptable that surgical and other procedures are quickly sought to remedy the situation.

sex an individual's membership in one of two biologically distinct categories—male or female

intersexed term to describe a person whose chromosomes or sex characteristics are neither exclusively male nor exclusively female

TABLE 9.1	Human Sex Characteristics	
	FEMALES	**MALES**
Chromosomes	XX	XY
Dominant Hormone	Estrogen	Testosterone
Primary Sex Characteristics	Reproductive organs: vagina, cervix, uterus, ovaries, fallopian tubes, other glands	Reproductive organs: penis, testicles, scrotum, prostate, other glands
Secondary Sex Characteristics	Shorter than males; larger breasts; wider hips than shoulders; less facial hair; more subcutaneous fat; fat deposits around buttocks, thighs, and hips; smoother skin texture	Abdominal, chest, body, and facial hair; larger hands and feet; broader shoulders and chest; heavier skull and bone structure; greater muscle mass and strength; Adam's apple and deeper voice; fat deposits around abdominals and waist; coarser skin texture

Gender

Gender refers to the physical, behavioral, and personality traits that a group considers to be normal, natural, right, and good for its male and female members. In other words, gender reflects our notions about what is appropriately "masculine" or "feminine." Some societies, for example, expect men to be more aggressive and competitive and women to be more emotional and nurturing. We often think of such characteristics as biologically determined or "natural," but no society leaves it completely up to nature to dictate the behavior of its male and female members. Gender, then, is something that is culturally transmitted or learned.

Nature and Nurture

Despite the social scientific evidence to the contrary, some people argue that gender differences between men and women are innate. To some extent, it is true that men and women really are built differently. We have different brain structures and different types of chemicals running through our bodies, which lead to somewhat different experiences and perceptions. But biology alone can't tell us everything about how sex and gender work. **Human sexual dimorphism**, the belief that anatomy defines men and women, is now highly contested owing to the media's attention to crossdressers, transsexuals, and the transgendered, who broaden our definitions of sex and gender (Eller 2003). Biology may be neither the sole nor the primary factor in determining masculinity and femininity.

Here, it bears revisiting the "nature vs. nurture" debate we considered in Chapter 4. Too often, scientists fail to consider the interrelationship between these two forces. While nature may play some role in determining male or female traits, we must also consider the role of nurture—the social, cultural, and environmental context. In fact, Lepowsky (1993) suggests that in some cases, biological differences may be the result of culturally prescribed masculine and feminine behavior rather than the cause of it. For example, for both men and women, engaging in aggressive behavior increases the production of testosterone, a male hormone; it is thus possible that behavior influences biology, just as biology influences behavior (Sapolsky 1997).

gender the physical, behavioral, and personality traits that a group considers normal for its male and female members

human sexual dimorphism the extent, much debated in recent years, to which inherent physical differences define the distinctions between the two sexes

essentialists those who believe gender roles have a genetic or biological origin and therefore cannot be changed

gender identity an individual's self-definition or sense of gender

Essentialist and Constructionist Approaches to Gender Identity

Depending on their field of study, sociologists look at gender from different perspectives. **Essentialists** see gender as immutable and biological, and **gender identity**—an individual's self-definition or sense of gender—as an unambiguous, two-category system. According to this view, you're either male or female from birth to death, and you have no other option. Chromosomes, hormones, and genitalia determine your identity—the way you see yourself, the way you interact with others, and the activities you engage in every day. Culture plays no role. Essentialists are generally found outside sociology in such fields as medicine, theology, and biology,

Different Societies, Different Genders

In modern Western societies, we don't have a voice in what our gender will be. Someone looks us over at birth and declares, "It's a boy!" or "It's a girl!" Even though some infants are born with indeterminate genitals, they are always assigned to one gender or the other as soon as possible, even if surgery is required. We have no words for someone who identifies as neither male nor female, nor do we find such an identity acceptable. Even those who undergo sex-reassignment surgery do so in order to move from one category to the other—very few individuals remain in gender limbo. But consider two societies that acknowledge a "third gender."

Berdaches

When nineteenth-century explorers and missionaries wrote about the native tribes they encountered in America, they also described individuals within those tribes who were neither male nor female, but somehow both. These people—called berdaches by nonnatives and "two-spirit" by natives—were usually biological males who dressed as women and took on types of work we think of as feminine, such as cooking and domestic labor. They could also be biological females who took on traditionally male pursuits, such as hunting, trapping, and warfare. Male berdaches have been documented in nearly 150 Native American cultures, and female berdaches in almost half that number. Some researchers believe that people who became berdaches were assigned to such a role from a very young age, if not from birth, for reasons

of "demographic necessity" (Trexler 2002). In the northern reaches of Canada, for example, couples who had given birth to all girls may have decided that their next child would be raised as a boy (and therefore a hunter who could provide food for the family)—no matter what. In more southern regions, a family who needed a female child may have deliberately raised a boy as a girl; male berdaches were valued for their height and strength.

Research on berdaches seems contradictory. Some believe that, based on the records of the early Europeans, they were looked down on by their own tribes. Others point out that some berdaches were respected and played important roles in the religious life of their communities. What we do know is that berdaches were acknowledged as a third gender. Indian creation myths include such references as "When the spirit people made men and women, they also made berdaches" (Roscoe 2000, p. 4)—allowing these people a recognized place in the order of things.

Hijras

The hijras of India are a modern example of third-gender individuals. Like the berdaches, the hijras are recognized by their society as an acceptable variation on gender—neither male nor female, but something else entirely. They are usually biological males who have all or part of their genitals removed, and most become hijras voluntarily in their teens or twenties. They dress and live as females and are referred to as daughter, sister, grandmother, or aunt.

and within sociology in the field of sociobiology. Some sociobiologists reduce male-female relationships to the biological function of procreation.

Most mainstream sociologists, however, use a **constructionist** approach to gender: they see gender as a social construction and acknowledge the possibility that the male-female categories aren't the only way of classifying individuals. Nor are the systems of gender inequality that result from these labels necessary or natural. Constructionists

constructionists those who believe that notions of gender are socially determined, such that a dichotomous system is just one possibility among many

patriarchy literally meaning "rule of the father"; a male-dominated society

believe that the meaning of masculinity and femininity may differ drastically in different societies and historical periods. We'll use a variety of sociological perspectives in this inquiry but will find ourselves returning again and again to constructionism as a helpful way to comprehend both the phenomenon of gender inequality and the theories that attempt to explain it.

Gender Inequality

Gender inequality can be found in all past and present societies. It invariably takes the form of **patriarchy**, or male domination. There is little evidence that a matriarchal

"Two-spirit" people Berdaches (left), a term used by anthropologists and sociologists but considered insulting by many Native Americans, provide an example of a third gender that is neither male nor female. Hijras (right) occupy a similar place in the society of India. It is considered good luck to have a hijra at a wedding or at the birth of a male child.

Like the berdache, hijras take part in the religious life of their people; they are specifically mentioned (and thus validated) in the epic Indian Hindu texts as having been recognized by the deity Rama. Today, the presence of hijras at weddings and at the births of male children is thought to be auspicious.

The berdache and hijra may sound similar to cross-dressers and transsexuals in Western society, but the analogy isn't entirely appropriate. For one thing, because of our two-gender system, we would still refer to someone who appeared to be a male but who felt like a female as "he"; if that same person decided to undergo sex-reassignment surgery, afterward we would call that individual "she." There is no room in our language for anything else. A berdache or hijra, on the other hand, is always referred to by that term, not "he" or "she." Keep in mind, then, that characteristics we think of as definitive, such as sexuality, dress, and biological gender, may be viewed differently in other cultures and time periods.

(female-dominated) society has ever existed, although some societies have been more pro-feminine than others. The Vanatinai, for example, are a small society in New Guinea in which women share equal access to positions of prestige, power, and control over the means of production (Lepowsky 1993).

From the patriarchal point of view, gender inequality can be traced back to biological differences in early societies, when activities like hunting and warfare were more essential to the livelihood of human groups. Women could not participate as effectively as men in these activities because of their lesser physical strength and because of the demands of bearing and nursing children. Therefore, a division of labor arose, with women handling activities within the secured, "home" territory. Men delivered the scarcest and most prized resources to the group, such as game from hunting or territory from warfare, and thus became powerful by controlling the distribution of these resources.

But this account of the origins of gender inequality does not explain its persistence in contemporary societies. Physical strength is no longer required in the vast majority of jobs. Nor are large numbers of children required for the continuation of society, and women are not necessarily restricted in their activities because of the demands of caring for them. Theories of modern gender stratification must therefore look beyond biological sex differences.

The Function of Gender Inequality In the 1950s, Talcott Parsons argued that gendered role expectations upheld the traditional family. Male "breadwinners" fulfilled an instrumental role by being task oriented and authoritative, while female "homemakers" embodied an expressive role by providing support and nurturing. *The Adventures of Ozzie and Harriet* featured the prototypical family of that era.

Macro Theoretical Perspectives

There are two major macrosociological theories of gender inequality. Functionalists generally believe that there are still social roles better suited to one gender than the other, and societies are more stable when norms are fulfilled by the appropriate sex. In particular, they emphasize how a particular "female" role may work in tandem with a particular "male" role within the family. Talcott Parsons, for example, identified two complementary roles (Parsons and Bales 1955). One is an **instrumental role**: being task oriented, a "breadwinner,"

instrumental role the position of the family member who provides the family's material support and is often an authority figure

expressive role the position of the family member who provides emotional support and nurturing

and an authority figure. The other is an **expressive role**: providing emotional support and nurturing. The expressive role is crucial not only to the care of children but also for stabilizing the personality of the instrumental partner against the stresses of the competitive world. In this view, since women are considered better suited to the expressive role and men to the instrumental role, gender segregation serves to uphold the traditional family and its social functions.

Expressive and instrumental roles may be complementary, but the social rewards for filling them are far from equal. The functionalist view does not explain very well why gender relations are characterized by such inequality. While the work of raising children and maintaining a household is intensive and difficult, there is a tendency to dismiss it as being unskilled and instinctive, which results in the devaluation of traditionally feminine work. Those who support a patriarchal society argue that this is again because resources provided by men in their instrumental roles are ultimately more valuable. This value, however, is being questioned in light of evidence indicating that juvenile delinquency and crime rates are higher when there is no adult supervision in the home and that expressive roles are thus important. The functionalist view also fails to acknowledge that families are often sources of social instability, with violence within families all too common.

Conflict theorists take a different approach. According to this perspective, men have historically had access to most of society's material resources and privileges, and consequently they generally seek to maintain their dominant status. Thus, conflict theorists see gender inequality in much the same way as they see race and class—as manifestations of exploitation.

Some conflict theorists argue that gender inequality is just a derivative of class inequality and that it therefore originates with private property. This theory was introduced by Friedrich Engels in 1884. Engels noted that capitalists (the owners of property) benefited from maintaining patriarchal families, with women in the private sphere and men in the public workplace, in at least two ways. Women do the work of reproducing the labor force (on which the capitalists depend) without receiving any direct compensation, and they serve as an inexpensive "reserve army" of labor when the need arises. Engels suggested that if private property were abolished, the material inequalities producing social classes would disappear, and there would no longer be powerful interests forcing women into domestic roles.

Conflict theorists point out that whether or not gender inequality is a product of class conflict, all men benefit from it in the short term. Zillah Eisenstein (1979) notes that men stand to lose a good deal if gender segregation disappears: they would have to do more unpaid work, or pay to have their homes kept up and children cared for; they would have to find jobs in a larger and more competitive market; and they would lose some power and prestige if they were no longer the most viable breadwinners.

TABLE 9.2	Theory in Everyday Life	
PERSPECTIVE	**APPROACH TO GENDER INEQUALITY**	**CASE STUDY: MALE- AND FEMALE-DOMINATED OCCUPATIONS**
FUNCTIONALISM	Sex determines which roles men and women are best suited to; it is more appropriate for men to play instrumental roles and for women to play expressive roles.	Women are naturally more nurturing and thus make better nurses and teachers of young children; men are naturally more logical and thus make better lawyers and computer programmers.
CONFLICT THEORY	Because of the traditional division of labor in families, males have had more access to resources and privileges and have sought to maintain their dominance.	Male-dominated occupations generally hold more prestige and are better paid; women may encounter difficulties entering male-dominated occupations, whereas men may more easily succeed in female-dominated occupations.
SYMBOLIC INTERACTIONISM	Gender is learned through the process of socialization; gender inequalities are reproduced through interactions with family, peers, schools, and the media.	Girls and boys are socialized differently and may be encouraged to seek out gender-appropriate training, college majors, and career goals, leading them to enter male- and female-dominated occupations.

Interactionist Perspectives

While conflict theorists and functionalists focus on gender from a macrosociological perspective, interactionists emphasize how gender is socially constructed and maintained in our everyday lives. According to interactionists, gender identity is so important to our social selves that we can barely interact with anyone without first determining that person's gender. We need to categorize, and we need to be categorizable as well. For some people, this is no easy matter.

For example, **transgendered** (or TG) individuals' sense of self and gender identity may differ from their physical sex. A TG person may have female genitalia, for instance, but identify as a man. The TG category may also include others who transgress binary gender categories, such as cross-dressers, bi-gendered, ungendered, and intersexed people. The challenge for TG people is to present a social gender identity that differs from the expectations others may have of them.

In the 1960s, Harold Garfinkel (1967/1984), in one of the first studies to show how gender is based on interaction, conducted intensive interviews with "Agnes," a **transsexual** person born with male genitalia and raised as a boy, who was undergoing sex-reassignment treatment (including surgery and counseling) at the UCLA medical center. While Agnes had always known that she was a "120 percent natural normal woman," it was only when she was seventeen that she began to learn how to "do being female"—to look, behave, and talk like a woman. Agnes got a job and a roommate—even a boyfriend—and set about learning what would be expected of her as a woman. She carefully adopted her roommate's style of dress, makeup, and body language; she listened to what her friends said and how they spoke. She learned how to maintain proper deference to her male boss at work, and she listened to

her boyfriend and his female family members as they expressed their expectations for her as a future wife and mother. Unlike other women, though, Agnes had to take extra precautions, such as avoiding sexual intercourse with her boyfriend (not too unusual in the early 1960s), wearing skirts and other clothing that would disguise her male anatomy, and avoiding activities (such as swimming at the beach) that would make her differences obvious until after she had gotten surgery. "Passing" as a female was a good deal of work for Agnes, and she constantly dealt with the fear that her secret would be discovered. But even Garfinkel, who knew her secret already, found her enactment of femininity quite convincing. Indeed, he was utterly charmed by her.

Even though you may think you have nothing in common with Agnes or other TG people, you actually enact gender in much the same way Agnes did. It is this process of observing and learning the feminine and masculine behaviors of others to which we now turn.

Gender Role Socialization

Gender role socialization—the subtle, pervasive process of becoming masculine or feminine—begins early and continues throughout our lives. It is accomplished primarily by the four major agents of socialization: families, schools, peers,

transgendered term describing an individual whose sense of gender identity transgresses expected gender categories

transsexuals individuals who identify with the other sex and have surgery to alter their own sex so it fits their self-image

gender role socialization the lifelong process of learning to be masculine or feminine, primarily through four agents of socialization: families, schools, peers, and the media

and the media, though other social institutions, such as religion, may also play a part in the process.

Family

Families are usually the primary source of socialization. Indeed, Kara Smith (2005) argues that gender role socialization begins even before birth. Because the sex of the fetus now can be determined in utero, families may begin relating to the new baby as either a girl or a boy far in advance of the baby's arrival. Smith's research demonstrates how knowing the baby's sex affects how the mother talks to her fetus—the choice of words as well as tone of voice. Once babies are born, female and male clothes, rooms, and toys will differ, as will the stories the children are told.

Most telling, however, is the way in which significant others—parents, siblings, extended family, and caregivers—interact with the baby. Through **social learning**, the process of learning behavior and meanings through social interaction, babies respond to and internalize the expectations of others around them. For example, a baby girl who is treated gently may observe the roughhousing of baby boys with alarm. Sometimes there is a conscious effort to instill certain behaviors in children—by reprimanding a young boy, for example, for crying. At other times, social learning happens in a more subtle way, as the baby learns through observation, imitation, and play. Children rather quickly begin to exhibit gender-stereotyped behaviors. By the age of two, they are aware of their own and others' gender, and by age three, they begin to identify specific traits associated with each gender.

Gender pervades every aspect of family life. It may be implicit in the chores or privileges girls and boys are given (washing the dishes vs. mowing the lawn), the way they are disciplined or punished, where they go or don't go, what they are encouraged or forbidden to do. Lessons such as "that's not very ladylike" and "big boys don't cry" are echoed in children's literature, in toys made specifically for girls or boys, and in the games they play. And as we grow up, we are always watching our other family members, using them as role models for our own beliefs and behaviors. In adulthood, our families may still influence what kind of career or mate we choose, how we run our household, and how we raise our own children.

Schools

Differences in the educational experiences of girls and boys also begin to appear early, both in the classroom and on the playground. By the fifth grade, gender norms are firmly estab-lished, as can be seen in the segregation that takes place even in co-ed schools. Girls and boys are frequently put in same-sex groups and assigned gender-stereotyped tasks, such as playing with dolls or playing with trucks. Same-sex groups also form on the playground, with girls and boys engaging in different kinds of social and athletic activities (Thorne 1993).

One of the key areas of difference is in the way that teachers, both women and men, typically interact with students. Whether or not they realize it, teachers tend to favor boys in several ways. Boys receive more attention and instructional time and are more likely to be called on in class. And boys are posed with more challenging questions or tasks, and are given more praise for the quality of their work. Boys are also, however, more likely to make teachers angry by misbehaving and therefore to receive some form of punishment more often (Smith 1999).

Despite boys' favorable treatment, girls in elementary school tend to earn higher grades. But their academic achievements are often discounted. In fact, the media often paint this gender discrepancy as a crisis for boys. When they do perform well, girls are typically credited for hard work

Gender Role Socialization Our families are among the primary agents of gender socialization. From a very young age, we learn and internalize gendered behaviors from our parents and siblings.

rather than intellectual ability. They are encouraged to focus on social skills or appearance rather than brain power. By the time they reach middle or junior high school, girls begin to slip behind and to lose their sense of academic self-esteem. These troubles are compounded in adolescent girls, who begin to feel uneasy about competing with boys, embarrassed by their own success, or uncomfortable engaging in male-dominated subjects like math or science.

Gender role socialization in schools can take other forms as well. Textbooks often still contain sexist language and gender stereotypes. Women and minorities are underrepresented, both as subjects and as authors (Robson 2001). In the social structure of the school itself, women tend to be concentrated at the lower levels, as teachers and aides, while men tend to occupy upper management and administrative positions. In such ways, schooling as a whole reinforces gender stereotypes.

Peers

In Western societies, peer groups are an increasingly important agent of socialization. By the age of three, children develop a preference for same-sex playmates, a tendency that increases markedly as childhood progresses. Children in preschool are three times more likely to play with same-sex playmates—eleven times more likely in kindergarten—and it is not until well after puberty that this pattern changes even a little (Maccoby and Jacklin 1987). While some have argued that such gender segregation is the *result* of inherent differences between men and women, there is evidence to support

the notion that same-sex peer groups can help *create* gendered behavior. Researchers have found, for example, that when children play with same-sex peers, their activities are more likely to be gender typed (girls have pretend tea parties, for example) than when boys and girls play together (Fabes, Martin, and Hanish 2003). In addition, children (especially boys) are punished (mocked) by their peers for crossing over these gendered borders (Thorne 1993).

C. J. Pascoe's ethnography of high school boys, "Dude, You're a Fag," shows just how powerful peer groups can be in enforcing gender roles and the assumptions about sexuality that underlie them. Not only do boys police each others' performance of masculinity by criticizing non-normative (and, in their minds, effeminate) behavior, dress, and other practices, they "lay claim to masculine identities by lobbing homophobic epithets at one another" (Pascoe 2007, p. 5). Calling someone a "fag" inflates the offender's own sense of masculinity, while demonstrating to others the consequences of deviating from masculine norms.

The need to impress others and to feel popular with peers increases in the teenage years. Boys tend to gain prestige through athletic ability, a well-developed sense of humor, or taking risks and defying norms. Girls tend to gain prestige through social position and physical attractiveness. It's easy to imagine what kind of behaviors result from such peer pressure and the consequences of falling short in any way. In the extreme, it can lead to bullying and rebellious behavior on the part of boys and to eating disorders with girls. Similar pressures in regard to dating and mating continue through the early adult years as well.

The Changing Culture of Gaming How are young women challenging stereotypes about video game fans?

The Media

From a variety of media sources, such as movies, comic books, or popular music, we learn "how to behave, how to be accepted, what to value, and what is normal" as well as "how gender fits into society" (Barner 1999). When it comes to television, there is no question that "sex-role behavior is portrayed in highly stereotypic fashion in virtually every aspect" of the programming (McGhee and Frueh 1980). Boys and girls learn that certain activities and attitudes are more appropriate for one gender than for the other. Girls should be beautiful, caring, sensitive, and reserved, while boys should be assertive, strong, and analytic. This starts at a particularly young age; chillingly, "by the time a child reaches kindergarten, she will 'know' more television characters than real people" (Barner 1999). In addition to TV, magazines like *Seventeen*, *Teen*, and *Young Miss* are aimed mostly at adolescents. Some have even speculated that increases in anorexia and bulimia among teenage girls can be linked to the images of women they see in the media (Kilbourne 1999). Teenage girls may consider actresses and models the standard of beauty to aspire to, even though such women "often are far below the normal weight recommendations" (Schiller et al. 1998).

The case of video games presents some contradictions regarding media and gender role socialization. What was once thought of as a male bastion is becoming increasingly more gender balanced. It used to be that the stereotype of a video game enthusiast was a male player who preferred first-person shooter-style video games, with such popular titles as *Mortal Kombat*, *Halo*, and *Grand Theft Auto*. While males still make up some 60 percent of video game players, some interesting changes are happening to the market. Females are beginning to represent a greater portion of game players, particularly when it comes to online games played on computers (as opposed to video games played on consoles). And the games that they are interested in most are such multiplayer games as *World of Warcraft* or the top-selling *The Sims* series, both of which focus on building relationships. An even greater number of females play arcade-style, or what are referred to as casual, games, where they represent 74 percent of all players. Gaming is no longer dominated by males, but the games that boys and girls choose to play may still be guided by gender differences.

For many centuries of human history, children have learned how to act appropriately from family, peers, and school. As the influence of the media becomes more pervasive in our society, we can see how it may compete with or even contradict that of other agents of socialization. At the same time, the media also serve to socialize families, peers and educators, giving them an even more overarching power in society.

DATA WORKSHOP

ANALYZING MASS MEDIA AND POPULAR CULTURE

The Fashion Police: Gender and the Rules of Beauty

This workshop will help you identify the messages about gender that permeate our lives through the media. You will be using existing sources as a research method and engaging in a content analysis (please see Chapter 2 for a review). Look through *two* magazines from *each* of the following lists of women's and men's magazines (there may be other comparable titles that you might also include). Keep in mind that

Rules of Beauty What do magazines like these tell us about the "rules" governing male and female appearance in our society?

you will need to photocopy or cut pages from these magazines at a later point.

- List A: *Cosmopolitan, Elle, Essence, In Style, Glamour, Latina, Seventeen*
- List B: *Details, Esquire, GQ, Maxim, Men's Health, Men's Journal*

Immerse yourself in the *visual images* and the accompanying text in these magazines—in both articles and advertisements. As you look at the photos, cartoons, drawings, headlines, captions, and other features, ask yourself what they say about what is attractive for both males and females. Choose some pages from each magazine that stand out to you, and jot down answers to the following questions:

- What types of bodies are displayed? What shapes, sizes, colors?
- What kinds of activities are shown?
- What does the text say about the images?
- How do these images reflect the "rules" about male and female beauty in our society?

Next, compare and contrast the "rules of beauty" in the magazines from list A with those from list B. What are the similarities and differences, and how do you explain them? Besides gender, how do other factors—race, class, age, sexual orientation—seem to affect the rules of beauty in these magazines?

Finally, and just for fun, use some of the images and text you've found in the magazines to construct the "perfect" man or woman. Take "officially beautiful" parts from selected images and put them together to form a whole person. What does this person look like? Something more like Frankenstein's monster than a supermodel? What kinds of words are used to describe the feminine or masculine ideal? What does that say about expectations for women and men? Perhaps when such words and images are broken down into their component parts, they are not so attractive after all.

There are two options for completing this Data Workshop.

- *Option 1 (informal)*: From your answers to the questions above, prepare some written notes that you can refer to in class. Make sure to bring examples you've chosen from the magazines. Compare your notes and experiences with those of other students in small-group discussions.
- *Option 2 (formal)*: Write a three- to four-page essay analyzing your data and addressing the specific standards of beauty presented in the magazines. Attach pages from the magazine you refer to in your essay.

Sex, Gender, and Life Chances

If two infants, one girl and one boy, are born at the same time in the same location from parents of similar racial and socioeconomic background, sociologists can predict answers to questions like the following: Who is more likely to live longer, go to college, or go to prison? Who might make a good living or live in poverty? Who is more likely to be married, divorced, or widowed, be a single parent or the victim of a violent crime, or join the military?

In this section, we will analyze how gender affects our lives. We will look specifically at how gender expectations shape our experiences with family, health, education, work and income, and criminal justice. For instance, women traditionally are caretakers of their families and more likely than men to go to college. Men make more money than women and are more likely to head religious institutions. These conditions are the result of values and norms that encourage certain behaviors in women and men.

It is important to remember, however, that gender is intertwined with other factors, such as race and class. Therefore, it is difficult to separate out the effects of gender on categories like marriage, education, and work. Single women with children are probably more likely to live in poverty, less likely to have a college education, and more likely to work in service-sector jobs. However, a person is not automatically poor or destined to be divorced because she is female. The categories all work together to construct the complexity of a person's life.

Family

When it comes to family, men are more likely than women to report never having been married, perhaps reflecting the stronger societal pressure for women to marry at some point in their lives. Men are also slightly more likely than women to report being married. About 9.1 percent of women are widowed (only 2.5 percent of men are), and 11.1 percent of women (8.5 percent of men) are currently divorced (U.S. Census Bureau 2010b). Some of these differences may be accounted for by the longer lifespans of women.

Divorce seems to be much more difficult for women with children than for men. Women are more likely to retain the primary caregiving role after divorce and to suffer financially because of it. In 2006, about five of every six custodial parents were mothers (or 82.6 percent). Less than half of all custodial parents receive the full amount of child support due, and nearly 24 percent received none. In 2007, about one-quarter (24.6 percent) of custodial parents and their children had incomes below the poverty level, a rate twice as high as the total population. The poverty rate of custodial mothers (27 percent) is more than double that of custodial fathers (12.9 percent).

The legacy of a woman's traditional role as caretaker of her family can be seen in a variety of statistical data. First, women are more likely than men to be single parents. Single women head more than 16.7 million households, and single men only 2.3 million.

And while women are contributing to household income by working outside the home, they are finding that they are still responsible for being the family's primary caretaker. In the workplace, this creates problems. Time taken out of work in order to care for sick children is seen as nonproductive time, and women who do take such time off may face discrimination (Wharton and Blair-Loy 2002). And most women, when they leave work, still face household chores at home—the "second shift" (see the Data Workshop on pp. 264–65).

Health

Of the almost 300 million Americans, more than half are female. Why are there more women? One reason is that women live longer; females born in 2010 are expected to live for an average of 81.4 years, whereas males are expected to live 75.6 years (U.S. Census Bureau 2008a). Research by Thomas Perls and Ruth Fretts at Harvard Medical School suggests that the sex hormones estrogen and testosterone may be a possible cause. For example, young men aged fifteen to twenty-four are four or five times likelier than young women to die from car accidents, homicides, and drownings. After age twenty-four, the gap narrows again until middle age. Then, starting at age fifty-five, death rates for men increase again, this time from heart disease, stroke, suicide, car accidents, and illness related to smoking and alcohol consumption. Perls and Fretts note that testosterone is linked to aggressive and violent behavior, as well as heart disease and harmful cholesterol in the blood. On the other hand, estrogen lowers harmful cholesterol and reduces the likelihood of heart disease and stroke. These days, however, more women are engaged in stress-related behavior—such as working outside the home, smoking, and drinking—so the gap may be closing. For example, female deaths from lung cancer have tripled in the past twenty years, leading Perls and Fretts to label smoking as "the great equalizer" (Perls and Fretts 1998).

While both women and men suffer from heart disease and cancer in fairly equal numbers, other health disorders are gender related. One example is depression, which women are twice as likely to suffer from men (Kessler 2003). Historically, the medical profession has diagnosed women far more than men with depression, "hysteria," and other mental conditions. Thus, women have been denied equal rights and equitable working conditions and pay because they were thought, as a category, to be mentally unfit. This issue, however, is controversial. Some maintain that the larger percentage of depressed women may be due to reporting rather than the actual numbers of cases. In other words, women may be more likely to report such symptoms, whereas men may ignore them or may feel a greater sense of stigma in reporting them (Byrne 1981).

Education

Women are more likely than men to finish high school and attend college. Of the estimated 16.6 million students in college in 2007, approximately 9.5 million were women and 7.1 million were men (*Christian Science Monitor* 2007). In fact, since 1980, women have increasingly outnumbered men in college, especially in the traditional eighteen-to-twenty-two age group (U.S. Bureau of Labor Statistics 2010c). However, men have been more likely to attain four-year and advanced degrees. In 2009, 30.1 percent of men twenty-five

TABLE 9.3	Hourly Earnings for Men and Women by Education Level, 1973–2005					
EDUCATIONAL ATTAINMENT	**HOURLY EARNINGS, 1973 (2005 DOLLARS)**		**HOURLY EARNINGS, 2005**		**PERCENT CHANGE IN REAL EARNINGS, 1973–2005 (2005 DOLLARS)**	
	Men	Women	Men	Women	Men	Women
Less than high school	$14.68	$8.85	$11.48	$8.88	−24%	0%
High school diploma	$17.41	$10.96	$15.65	$12.34	−11%	9%
Some college	$17.79	$11.84	$17.76	$14.18	0%	17%
College graduate	$24.01	$16.40	$28.06	$21.30	15%	27%
Advanced degree	$26.67	$21.72	$35.67	$27.08	27%	21%
SOURCE: Mishel, Bernstein, and Alegretto 2007.						

years and over had a bachelor's degree or higher compared with 29.1 percent of women. (Even though women numerically earn more bachelor's and master's degrees, men proportionately earn more.) Men are also more likely to earn more money per degree granted (U.S. Census Bureau 2011a).

In fact, men out-earn women at every level of education, from incomplete high school to advanced degrees. These wage discrepancies make gender inequality very difficult to ignore. Women with four-year and professional degrees earn significantly less than their male counterparts, as shown in Table 9.3.

Work and Income

In whatever aspect of work we analyze—the rates of participation in the labor force, the kinds of jobs, the levels of pay, the balance between work and family—gender inequality is highly visible. For example, in 2009, 72 percent of men were in the labor force, but only 59.2 percent of women (though women's participation rates have been increasing over time). Interestingly, while men and women have historically had relatively similar rates of unemployment, in 2009 significantly more men (10.3 percent) were unemployed than women (8.1 percent). But because traditional family dynamics still endure, women are more likely than men to be found outside the labor force altogether (U.S. Census Bureau 2011b).

Marriage seems to have opposite effects on women and men's participation rates. Single women are more likely to work than married women, while married men are more likely to work than single men. In 2009, 64.2 percent of single women (as opposed to 61.4 percent of married women) worked, while 76.3 percent of married men (compared with nearly 68.3 percent of single men) did. This discrepancy could possibly be explained by the assumption that men are head of the household, and single women are considered responsible for their own finances.

TABLE 9.4	Selected Occupations by Gender, 2007	
OCCUPATION	**PERCENT MEN**	**PERCENT WOMEN**
Preschool and kindergarten teachers	2.2	97.8
Secretaries and administrative assistants	3.2	96.8
Dental hygienists	3.4	96.6
Registered nurses	8.0	92.0
Maids and housekeepers	10.2	89.8
Paralegals and legal assistants	14.1	85.9
Librarians	18.2	81.8
Travel agents	20.3	79.7
Waiters and waitresses	28.5	71.5
Psychologists	31.2	68.8
Customer service representatives	32.1	67.9
Medical scientists	43.1	56.9
Retail salespersons	48.2	51.8
News reporters and correspondents	57.2	42.8
Lawyers	67.6	32.4
Physicians and surgeons	67.8	32.2
Chief executives	75.0	25.0
Computer programmers	79.8	20.2
Clergy	83.0	17.0
Firefighters	96.6	3.4
Automotive service technicians and mechanics	98.2	1.8
Carpenters	98.4	1.6
Aircraft pilots and flight engineers	98.7	1.3

SOURCE: U.S. Bureau of Labor Statistics 2010b.

Since 1970, the number of mothers in the labor force has been on the rise. Only 53 percent of single mothers and 40.8 percent of married mothers in 1970 participated in the labor force. In 2009, this rose to 63.7 percent for single mothers and 61.7 percent for married mothers. These numbers are slightly less than the peak of 68.6 percent for single mothers and 62 percent for married mothers in 2000 (U.S. Census Bureau 2011b).

Many jobs are gendered; they traditionally have been and continue to be performed by women or men. As Table 9.4 shows, nurses, kindergarten teachers, dental hygienists, secretaries, paralegals, and housekeepers are female-dominated professions, whereas airplane pilots, auto mechanics, firefighters, carpenters, mechanical engineers, and the clergy are male-dominated professions. In 2009, 97.8 percent of all teachers of young children and 96.8 percent of secretaries were women. Only 1.3 percent of all aircraft pilots and 1.6 percent of all carpenters were women. Gendered jobs have far-reaching consequences. For example, physicians often earn four or more times as much as do nurses. So, when women constitute 92 percent of all nurses but only 32.2 percent of all physicians, the monetary stakes are striking.

Why are some jobs considered best performed by women and others by men? Why are women vastly underrepresented as pilots and auto mechanics and men nearly absent as nurses, secretaries, and child-care workers? Socially constructed categories of occupations are extremely resilient. Despite advances in workplace technologies that would enable both women and men to perform similarly in jobs, men still vastly outnumber women in certain professions, especially those with high salaries and prestige. It is also interesting to note that jobs that are traditionally female are consistently undervalued and underpaid (Figure 9.2). "Pink-collar" jobs—nurses, secretaries, librarians—are considered less desirable in a patriarchal society (England 1992).

Income levels and poverty rates also show inequality between women and men. In 2009, men earned an average of $47,127, while the average for women was $36,278. The earnings ratio (sometimes called the earnings gap) has improved since the 1960s and 70s; however, the 2009 earnings ratio of 77:100 still translates to 77 cents earned by women for each dollar earned by men (Figure 9.1).

In 2009, the median income for married-couple households was $71,830. For male-headed households with no female present, the median income was $48,084—dramatically higher than the $32,597 for female-headed households with no male present. The median household income for women living alone was $25,269, while for single men it was $36,611. Finally, women are more likely to live

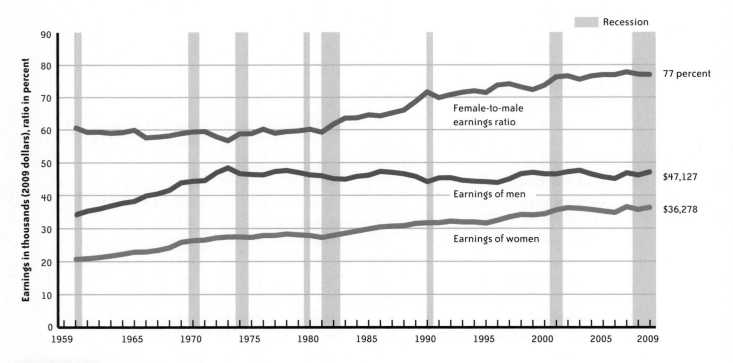

FIGURE 9.1 Female-to-Male Earnings Ratio, 1960–2007

The earnings gap between men and women has narrowed somewhat, but it has yet to close.
SOURCE: DeNavas-Walt et al. 2010.

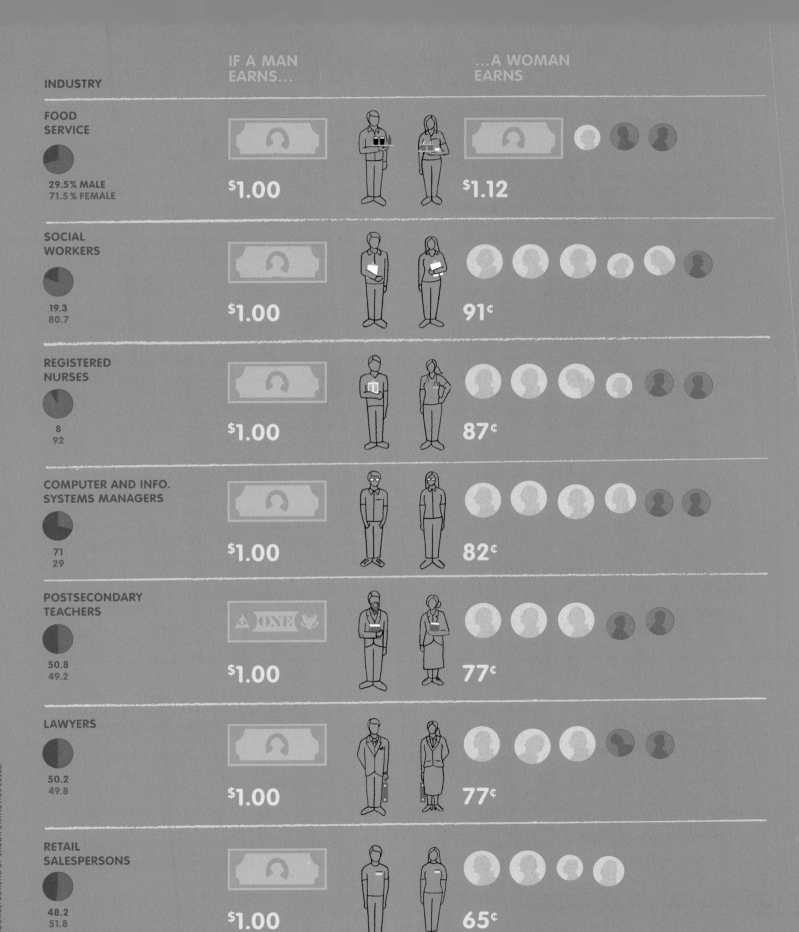

SOURCE: BUREAU OF LABOR STATISTICS 2010B.

INDUSTRY	IF A MAN EARNS…			...A WOMAN EARNS
FOOD SERVICE 29.5% MALE 71.5% FEMALE	$1.00			$1.12
SOCIAL WORKERS 19.3 80.7	$1.00			91¢
REGISTERED NURSES 8 92	$1.00			87¢
COMPUTER AND INFO. SYSTEMS MANAGERS 71 29	$1.00			82¢
POSTSECONDARY TEACHERS 50.8 49.2	$1.00			77¢
LAWYERS 50.2 49.8	$1.00			77¢
RETAIL SALESPERSONS 48.2 51.8	$1.00			65¢

On the Job

Dukes v. Wal-Mart Stores, Inc.

Back in 1994, Betty Dukes began working at Wal-Mart in Pittsburg, California. She was attracted to the job because she liked working with customers and because she hoped that the entry-level cashier's job would lead to better and better jobs inside the retail giant. After a year on the job, she was given a raise and a full-time position and promoted to customer service manager shortly after that. However, despite the word "manager" in the title, this was still an hourly position, and Dukes was eager to move up the corporate ladder. But despite her best efforts, she complains, she was denied the training needed to advance and was not allowed to work in traditionally male departments of the store. She says that complaints to her managers caused them to reprimand her for minor offenses that were routinely overlooked in other employees. After she complained to her district manager, she was demoted back down to cashier, which made her ineligible for promotion and meant a pay cut and fewer hours. At this point, she sought legal counsel, and eventually came to be represented by Brad Seligman, who asked Dukes to serve as the lead plaintiff in Dukes v. Wal-Mart Stores in 2001.

In 2004, along with six other women who had joined her as plaintiffs, Betty Dukes's case was certified as a class action lawsuit, meaning that these seven women were now filing suit on behalf of all the female employees at Wal-Mart who could have suffered from systematic sex discrimination in promotions, training, and pay. With as many as 1.6 million current and former workers represented, this was easily the largest class action suit in history. The basis of the suit is

Title VII of the 1964 Civil Rights Act, which made it illegal for an employer to discriminate in terms of "compensation, terms, conditions, or privileges of employment" based on race, nationality, religion, or sex. It is depressingly easy to argue that female employees don't fare as well at Wal-Mart as male ones do. Activists who mobilized to support the case they call "Betty versus Goliath" assembled a damning set of statistics documenting the way sex and gender matter when working at Wal-Mart. In 2001, the year Betty Dukes filed her suit, 65 percent of the company's hourly workers were female compared to around 33 percent of managers. Only 38 percent of assistant managers were women, only 16 percent of store managers were female, and women took significantly longer to reach management positions compared to their male counterparts. While these trends exist in almost every part of the American economy, Wal-Mart's own internal studies found that women were considerably less represented in management positions, even compared to other large retail organizations.

Demonstrating that Wal-Mart was at fault required more than just the raw numbers, especially since women are paid less and promoted slower in almost every occupational category in the United States. The claim in Dukes v. Wal-Mart rested on two further points. First, it argued that Wal-Mart's lack of an objective and uniform policy regarding raises and promotions allowed sex discrimination. Managers have wide latitude to offer raises and promotions based on their own personal preferences, often without even advertising new job

---

feminization of poverty the economic trend showing that women are more likely than men to live in poverty, caused in part by the gendered gap in wages, the higher proportion of single mothers compared to single fathers, and the increasing costs of child care

in poverty than men. This situation, often referred to as the **feminization of poverty**, results from a combination of social forces, including the gendered gap in wages, the higher proportion of single women taking on the financial responsibility of children, and increasing costs of child care. Of the 43.6 million Americans living below the poverty

line in 2009, females constituted the largest group, whether living alone or in female-headed households (DeNavas-Walt et al. 2010).

The Military

The military provides a particular case study when it comes to issues of work and gender. The huge institution that is the military is composed mostly of men. As such, it presents a relatively hostile environment for women. In 2006,

openings. Second, the plaintiffs argue that, as District Judge Martin Jenkins put it in his judgment, Wal-Mart maintains "a strong corporate culture that includes gender stereotyping."

Why are sex discrimination cases still being filed in the twenty-first century, four decades after the Civil Rights Act of 1964 made unequal pay for equal work illegal? One of the most difficult challenges facing claims of sex discrimination is making the link between things like "corporate culture" and specific decisions about pay and promotion. This is where sociologists have played a part arguing these cases. William Bielby, a professor of sociology at the University of Illinois at Chicago, was called by the plaintiffs as an expert witness in this case to help demonstrate a link between Wal-Mart's corporate policy and discrimination against its female employees. In order to make this connection, Bielby examined a wide range of corporate memos and documents, as well as Wal-Mart managers' deposition testimony and the history of the company. He testified that Wal-Mart was particularly vulnerable to sex discrimination because it allowed managers to give raises and promotions based on little more than their own personal opinions, which "tends to allow people to 'seek out and retain stereotyping-confirming information and ignore or minimize information that defies stereotypes." From this analysis Dr. Bielby testified that "Wal-Mart's personnel policies and practices make pay and promotion decisions vulnerable to gender bias," and it was this conclusion that lead the judge to certify the suit as a class action lawsuit.

Dukes v. Wal-Mart From right, Betty Dukes, Patricia Surgenson, Stephanie Odle, and Christine Kwapnoski sued Wal-Mart for sex discrimination.

Wal-Mart has been appealing the suit ever since, primarily by arguing that it should not be a class action lawsuit, but rather each woman who feels she has a legitimate claim should have to make her own claim, and in June of 2011 the United States Supreme Court agreed with Wal-Mart's argument. In a 5-4 decision, the court left the plaintiffs "Betty Dukes, Patricia Surgeson, Edith Arana, Karen Williamson, Deborah Gunter, Christine Kwapnoski, and Cleo Page, on behalf of themselves and all others similarly situated" to struggle individually against the corporate giant. Interestingly, all three female justices were in the minority.

only 14.6 percent of enlisted personnel were female. Of the reserves, only 17 percent were women. At the end of 2006, 85.4 percent of the five branches of the military, including the Coast Guard, were male. In 2008, Lieutenant General Ann E. Dunwoody became the first woman promoted to the rank of four-star general in the U.S. armed forces.

Slightly more women than men in the military report being the object of unwanted sexual attention. However, women are far more likely than men to report gender harassment. Laura Miller (1997) makes the distinction that gender harassment,

rather than being sexual in nature, instead is used to enforce traditional gender norms, such as aggression in males and nurturing in females, as well as to punish violations of these norms. Interestingly, men in Miller's study were more likely to report being harassed by their drill sergeants, while women were more likely to be harassed by their fellow trainees. Rape is a growing problem in the military as well. A 2009 Pentagon report states that nearly 3,000 women were sexually assaulted in 2008—up almost 10 percent from the prior year—but that same report also acknowledges that 80 percent–90 percent of military rapes go unreported due to fears of ostracism, retaliation, and lack of institutional response. Indeed, 80 percent of male service members convicted in sexual assault cases still receive honorable discharges (Gibbs 2010). Despite the progress made by women in ascending the ranks, the military can still be an inhospitable place for women.

Criminal Justice

The experience of men and women differs with regard to almost every social institution, and the criminal justice system is no exception. The social construction of masculinity as aggressive, dominant, and physical translates directly into statistics regarding gender and crime. Men are more likely to die violent deaths and to be victims of assault. Women are slightly more likely to be victims of personal theft and much more likely to be victims of rape. Also, women are far more likely to be victimized by their intimate partners (spouses or current or former boyfriends). Between 1998 and 2002, almost 85 percent of spouse abuse victims were female and a little more than 85 percent of dating partner abuse victims were female (U.S. Department of Justice 2005).

In analyzing arrest rates for 2009, we find that men are overwhelmingly represented in nearly all categories, including murder, rape, sex offenses, theft, assault, and drug charges. In only two categories do women and girls outnumber men and boys: prostitution and runaways (a juvenile offense). In 2009, there were 27,709 arrests of women for prostitution and 13,105 arrests of men for the same charge; 35,653 girls were arrested as runaways compared with 29,503 boys. It is important for us as sociologists to recognize this discrepancy as an example of how crime is influenced by the social construction of gender. Because of the tendency to think of girls as weak and needing protection, female runaways are more likely to be reported as missing by parents as well as intercepted by the police. On the other hand, because males are perceived as being more likely to be involved in violent and property crime, they are generally kept under more scrutiny by the police than are females. Of the nearly two million people in correctional institutions, the vast majority (around 90 percent) are men (U.S. Department of Justice 2007a).

By analyzing such visible indicators as labor participation rates, income levels, arrest rates, and experiences related to the family, work, education, and the military, we can easily see the real consequences of gender inequality: women and men experience life differently. So what can we say about the life outcomes of our two infants? The female is more likely to live longer. Though they are both likely to marry, she is more likely to be divorced or widowed. She is more likely to graduate from high school and to attend college. However, if the male also attends college, he is more likely to graduate. If they earn the same degree, he will probably earn more money. Each has a good chance of ending up in certain professions over others (the military for him, nursing for her). He is more likely to die a violent death, while she is more likely to experience rape or some other crime perpetrated by someone with whom she's intimate. While their gender categories surely do not guarantee these experiences, we as sociologists can safely make such predictions in the aggregate.

DATA WORKSHOP

ANALYZING EVERYDAY LIFE

The Second Shift: Gendered Norms and Household Labor

The **second shift**, a term coined by sociologist Arlie Hochschild, refers to the unpaid work—cooking, cleaning, laundry, child care, home repair, yard work—that must be done at home after the day's paid labor is complete. For this Data Workshop, you will investigate second shift work by using interviews as a research method (see Chapter 2 for further discussion) and asking a working parent about how he or she juggles family and work. Here are some guidelines to follow:

- Ask your working parent to be candid and to answer your questions as fully as possible. Prepare to take detailed notes, and ask if you can tape-record the interview for later transcription.

- Come up with a list of questions before you start the interview. Include some open-ended as well as closed-ended questions.

- For starters, ask the person to describe *everything* he or she does in a typical day, perhaps using the previous day as an example. Be sure nothing is overlooked. For example, if the description starts with the parent's arrival at the office, remind him or her of earlier morning activities, such as making breakfast or getting children ready for school.

- Try to identify all the types of work that your respondent does in a typical day, including paid work, unpaid work, interaction work, emotion work, and so on.

- Find out how tasks are divided between members of the household (spouse/partner, children, others). Also

second shift the unpaid housework and child care often expected of women after they complete their day's paid labor

try to determine how completing all these tasks (or not completing them) affects her relationships with other members of the household.

As you conduct the interview, you'll notice that some tasks must be done every day, or even several times each day—cooking meals, for example. Other tasks (such as laundry) are done less often but on a regular basis. Still others are irregular or seasonal: raking leaves or taking the car in for a tune-up. You'll also find that some tasks are focused on people (like planning birthday parties), whereas others (cleaning out the gutters) are focused on objects. And some tasks are paid labor, while some are not.

After completing the interview, look at all the tasks your respondents have mentioned. Then ask *yourself* these questions:

- Does there appear to be a gendered division of labor at home?

- How are the tasks divided?

- Who does most of the daily tasks?

Chances are, you'll find that there are gendered patterns in terms of who does what at home. Studies show that men tend to participate in more instrumental tasks, such as car repair and yard work, jobs that are more irregular and seasonal, while women tend to the daily needs of their family by doing the endless tasks of cooking and cleaning and by engaging in expressive work, such as mediating arguments and calming upset children. This is how women rack up an extra month of housework a year (that's a month of twenty-four-hour days)! What effects might these inequities have on marriages and live-in relationships? Does one person always seem to be doing more work than the other person? What are some possible solutions to this problem?

There are two options for completing this Data Workshop.

- *Option 1 (informal)*: Prepare some written notes, and compare your notes and experiences with those of other students in small-group discussions. Take this opportunity to learn more about how families do the everyday work required to keep a household running and about the different hierarchies of inequalities that shape this work.

- *Option 2 (formal)*: Write a three- to four-page essay analyzing your interview data. Make sure to use specific quotations from your respondent, and include a transcript of the interview (or your notes) as an attachment.

Gender and Language

- What is the difference between a stud and a slut?

- What do the following have in common: bitch, cow, heifer, angel, baby, doll, sweetie pie, cupcake, sugar?

- What do the following have in common: man-made, mankind, manpower, manslaughter?

To answer these questions, we need to think about how language reflects culture. Some sociologists argue that language shapes culture, while others say the opposite. In any case, by looking at our language, we can see how certain words reflect cultural values and norms, particularly sexism.

For instance, positions of power and authority often directly emphasize the male gender in their very names. Examples are "congressman," "chairman," "policeman," "fireman," and "mailman." Such words imply that one gender is more suited for a particular job than the other. Other words, like "nurse/doctor," "flight attendant/pilot," and "secretary/executive," have been gendered without the use of explicit male or female markers. In this case, markers are usually attached if the job holder is of "the other" gender: "woman doctor," "woman pilot," "woman astronaut," "male nurse," and "male secretary." Again, these examples reinforce stereotypes of gendered jobs.

The English language also seems to assume that the default category for all human experience is male. We have traditionally referred to the human race as "mankind" and noted that "all men are created equal." The root of words like "man-made," "manslaughter," and "manpower," "man," means "human." If something is man-made, it is made by humans. But clearly, not everyone experiences the world from a male perspective.

Our language is also a good site for analyzing double standards, which have long been researched by sociologists (Carns 1973; Sprecher, McKinney, and Orbuch 1987). For instance, in the workplace, aggressive men are called "go-getters," while aggressive women may be called "bitches." Men who frequently have sex are called "players," while women are called "sluts." To be called a player is a different experience than to be called a slut. The behaviors are similar, but the labels have very different connotations. A 2001 study of sex education films that were aimed at adolescents found the player/slut double standard embedded in the actual film scripts (Hartley and Drew 2001). These films legitimized male sexual desire while minimizing female desire, implying that males should engage in sexual pursuit while females should wait to be pursued. Women are often referred to as "cows," "heifers," "babies," or

feminism belief in the social, political, and economic equality of the sexes; also the social movements organized around that belief

"cupcakes." Boyfriends aren't usually called "baby dolls," and males don't call their male friends "heifers." Food must be consumed, babies must be coddled, animals must be controlled. Sociologists understand that these nicknames for women function as mechanisms of social control.

Along with words, speech patterns also reflect our sexist culture (Tannen 2001). Conversation analysts, sociologists who study verbal and nonverbal language patterns, find that men dominate women in conversation. They are more likely to interrupt women than they are to interrupt men (Smith-Lovin and Brody 1989) and more likely to control the subject matter of conversations. Women tend to be more concerned with keeping a conversation going rather than with controlling its direction. However, some research suggests that authority rather than gender dictates conversation patterns (Kollock, Blumstein, and Schwartz 1985; C. Johnson 1994). Thus, women may control the conversation when they are in positions of legitimate authority, as a manager is when talking with her employee. Since men are more likely to occupy authoritative positions, however, they are still more likely to dominate in conversation.

It is worth noting that language can also reflect social change. It is now fairly common to see and hear "Will every-one please open his or her book" or "their book" in place of "his book." Also, increasingly, we hear such gender-neutral references as "mail carriers," "firefighters," "servers," "chairpersons," and "humankind." These efforts at gender neutrality are efforts to reform sexist language. For if language shapes culture, then using gender-neutral language should facilitate social change. On the other hand, if language is shaped by culture, then the use of nonsexist words is a signal of positive social change.

The Women's Movement

Feminism is the belief in the social, political, and economic equality of the sexes *and* the social movements organized around that belief. Thus, feminism is both a theoretical perspective and a social movement. It is important to keep in mind that feminist concepts and goals are not static but are always focused on bringing about greater gender equality in a particular time and place. Rebecca West, an early twentieth-century feminist, put it this way in 1913: "I myself have never been able to find out precisely what feminism is. I only know that people call me a feminist whenever I express sentiments that differentiate me from a doormat or a prostitute" (Shiach 1999).

The Suffrage Movement Of the 100 women and men who signed the Declaration of Sentiments in Seneca Falls in 1848 only one, a young worker named Charlotte Woodward, lived to cast a ballot in 1920.

First Wave

In the United States, the history of the women's movement can be divided into three historical waves. The **first wave** began with a convention held in Seneca Falls, New York, in 1848, organized by Elizabeth Cady Stanton and Lucretia Mott. The convention, numbering about three hundred people, issued a Declaration of Sentiments stating generally that "all men and women are created equal" and demanded specifically that women be given the right to vote. Stanton believed that in a democracy the right to vote was the fundamental right on which all others depended. Not surprisingly, then, the campaign to win the vote (known as the **suffrage movement**) became the cause most identified with the first wave of the women's movement, even though that goal would not be achieved until 1920. Neither Stanton nor Mott nor the well-known suffragist Susan B. Anthony would live to see victory. Of the one hundred women and men who signed the Declaration of Sentiments, only one, a young worker named Charlotte Woodward, lived to cast a ballot.

Second Wave

Just as the first wave of feminism is most closely associated with the right to vote, the **second wave**, which took place during the 1960s and 70s, is associated with equal access to education and employment. The publication of Betty Friedan's *The Feminine Mystique* in 1963, the establishment of the National Organization for Women (NOW) in 1966, and the emergence of women's consciousness-raising groups were key events in second-wave feminism. In those decades, young activists felt that the women's movement had lost its momentum after the vote was won and that other issues needed to be addressed. In the opening pages of *The Feminine Mystique*, Friedan spoke of "the problem that had no name," a problem that "lay buried, unspoken, for many years in the minds of American women" (1963/2001, p. 55): the sense of limitation and dissatisfaction that many women felt with their lives.

During one of the most prosperous periods in American history, Friedan was discovering that countless women were unhappy with the traditional roles they had been assigned, that the "mystique of feminine fulfillment" was no longer so fulfilling (1963/2001, p. 18). Women were restricted from pursuing activities outside these traditional roles, whether by cultural norms or by actual laws that barred them from schools, workplaces, and professional organizations. Women who tried to breach these barriers were seen as "unfeminine."

> **first wave** the earliest period of feminist activism in the United States, including the period from the mid-nineteenth century until American women won the right to vote in 1920
>
> **suffrage movement** the movement organized around gaining voting rights for women
>
> **second wave** the period of feminist activity during the 1960s and 1970s often associated with the issues of women's equal access to employment and education

The Problem That Had No Name In *The Feminine Mystique*, Betty Friedan (center) articulated a sense of limitation and dissatisfaction that many women felt with their lives.

third wave the most recent period of feminist activity, focusing on issues of diversity and the variety of identities women can possess

male liberationism a movement that originated in the 1970s to discuss the challenges of masculinity

men's rights movement an offshoot of male liberationism whose members believe that feminism promotes discrimination against men

pro-feminist men's movement an offshoot of male liberationism whose members support feminism and believe that sexism harms both men and women

sexuality the character or quality of being sexual

sexual orientation or **sexual identity** the inclination to feel sexual desire toward people of a particular gender or toward both genders

Some were even told, as former North Carolina Senator Elizabeth Dole was when she entered Harvard Law School in 1962, that they were taking an opportunity away from a more deserving man.

So the second wave of the women's movement pushed for and achieved such reforms as equal opportunity laws, legislation against sexual harassment and marital rape, and a general increase in public awareness about gender discrimination in our society. Some of the public, however, reacted with hostility to women's demands for legal and cultural "liberation," and there continues to be a certain amount of backlash against feminist causes as a result.

Third Wave

Beginning in the 1980s and 90s, the **third wave** of feminism focused primarily on diversity. These feminists criticize the first two waves for concentrating on "women" as one category (mainly white and middle class) and marginalizing the concerns of women of color, lesbians, and working-class women. Third-wave feminism is also concerned with the rights of women in all countries and with environmental and animal rights. The movement includes many if not most college students—even if you don't call yourself a feminist, you likely believe in feminist values, such as equality, diversity, and global interconnectedness. You are the third wave, and you will help make a difference.

The Men's Movement

The men's movement emerged from the same cultural climate in the late twentieth century that had ushered in the second and third waves of feminism. The women's movement had asked us to rethink gender roles and the place of women in society, and men have responded in a variety of ways. Some have countered feminists' arguments, some have agreed with and supported feminism, and some have taken positions somewhere in between. And just as feminism called womanhood into question, so too did men begin reexamining what it means to be man.

In the mid-1970s the notion of **male liberationism** (or the need to free men from oppressive gender roles) became more widespread. Influential studies pointed to evidence that men suffer from greater stress, poorer health, and a shorter life expectancy, and argued that these were due to pressures to achieve success combined with an inability to express themselves (Farrell 1975; Goldberg 1976). American men had become confused about what it means to be a "real man" (Kimmel 1987). They were facing new discomfort and anxiety about their masculinity. These ideas became fairly popular, largely among middle-class heterosexual men, and some sought counseling or formed discussion groups about "the male role" (Segal 1990). Men were coming together and organizing in an attempt to address their own concerns, and what was called a "crisis of masculinity" (Bly 1990; Connell 1995; Faludi 1999).

As the men's movement grew, it also splintered into two primary factions. The **men's rights movement** (which also includes the father's rights movement) argues that because of feminism, men are actually discriminated against and even oppressed in both the legal arena and in everyday life. These men (and some women too) suggest that feminism has created a new kind of sexism by privileging women, or by attempting to erase differences altogether. The **pro-feminist men's movement**, on the other hand, is based in the belief that men should support feminism in the interest of fairness to women and because men's lives are also constrained by gender and sexism—and are enriched by feminist social change. Pro-feminists suggest that the idea that men are superior is a burden and that, in the long term, men will be happier if society becomes less sexist. They argue that men need to share more of the responsibilities of child care, contest economic disparities and violence against women, and generally respect women's lives. However much society has changed because of these movements, serious questions remain about men's and women's roles and the future of their relations with each other.

Sexuality

What is **sexuality**? And what is it doing in a sociology textbook? The term sexuality is used in a variety of ways; for example, it is used to describe sexual behavior, desires, and fantasies (the things people actually do as well as the things we think or dream about doing). It is also used to describe **sexual orientation** or **sexual identity**, which is the inclination to feel sexual desire toward and engage in sexual behavior with persons of a particular gender. For the purposes of this text, we will be using sexuality to describe sexual identity or orientation.

Our society recognizes a number of different sexual identities or orientations, and they are each related to our two-category gender system. **Heterosexuality**, or sexual desire for the other gender, is the normative and dominant category, which may be why the slang term for it is "straight." Most people identify themselves as heterosexual, and there are privileges attached to membership in this category. **Homosexuality**, or sexual desire for the same gender, is a minority category—the National Survey of Sexual Health and Behavior found that about 4 percent of adults self-identify as gay or lesbian (Reece et al. 2010), and as with other minority statuses, there are a variety of difficulties and disadvantages attached to membership in this category. **Bisexuality**—sexual attraction to both genders—is also a minority category, with about 3 percent of men and 4 percent of women identifying as bisexual (Reece et al. 2010). **Asexuality** involves the lack of sexual attraction of any kind: asexual people are basically nonsexual and are a very small minority group, with only about 1 percent of adults identifying as asexual (Bogaert 2004).

Where does our sexual identity originate? Is it genetic, or is it a result of cultural or environmental factors? This question has long been debated. In the late 1800s, Karl Heinrich Ulrichs, a German lawyer who was perhaps the first gay activist, contended that sexuality was linked to gender and that gender was a product of hereditary factors, probably related to hormones (Ulrichs 1994). This line of thinking has persisted, but it was only with the arrival of genetic research in the 1990s that it gained added awareness. Is there in fact a "gay gene," or is homosexuality the product of socialization? Or might it be a combination of both?

One of the first studies to gain widespread attention was conducted in the early 1990s by J. M. Bailey and R. C. Pillard, researchers who hypothesized that homosexuality was at least in part congenital, or present at birth (1991). They tested this hypothesis by examining the sexual orientation of different sets of twins, and their results suggested that they were right. Bailey and Pillard found that 52 percent of the identical twins of gay men were also gay and that 48 percent of the identical twins of lesbian women were also lesbian. Another study, conducted in 1992 by Allen and Gorski, found that a segment of the fibers connecting the hemispheres of the brain was up to one-third larger in gay men, again suggesting a biological basis.

One of the most consequential studies was done by neurobiologist Simon LeVay, who performed autopsies on gay

> **heterosexuality** sexual desire for other genders
>
> **homosexuality** the tendency to feel sexual desire toward members of one's own gender
>
> **bisexuality** sexual attraction to both genders; bisexuals are sexually attracted to both males and females
>
> **asexuality** involves the lack of sexual attraction of any kind; asexual people have no interest in or desire for sex

Civil Unions Legal recognition of same-sex couples' committed relationships grants them many of the benefits that are given to married heterosexual couples, such as insurance and Social Security benefits, the right to make medical decisions for one's partner, and federal income tax breaks.

"Hooking Up"

Something happened to dating in 2001, when the longtime practice among college students of "hooking up" gained national attention. The American Values Institute (AVI) released its report to the great dismay of parents, educators, cultural critics, and policy makers. The study, by a team of sociologists at the University of Texas, entitled "Hooking Up, Hanging Out and Hoping for Mr. Right: College Women on Mating and Dating," looked at how young people meet and mate and examined their experiences with sexuality, courtship, and marriage. The findings shocked the nation and generated a firestorm of media coverage that has barely died down. While knowledge of this practice worried many, to students themselves, the notion of hooking up was commonplace and largely accepted, hardly a matter for such alarm.

Much of the concern centered around the meaning of "hooking up" and what exactly young people were up to. The public perception was that hooking up meant casual sex without commitment, typically between people who were but brief acquaintances beforehand. Other terms were also used to refer to the behavior, including "booty call" and "friends with benefits." Some suggested that hooking up was connected to a variety of other social problems, such as binge drinking, drug abuse, and sexually transmitted diseases. The media featured numerous stories told in moralistic terms about how the culture of the hook up was leading young women, especially, to their own demise with respect to any hope of having decent relationships and the possibility of marriage. At the same time, others were celebrating the phenomenon, and books with such titles as *The Happy Hook-Up: A Single Girl's Guide to Casual Sex* and *Hooking Up: A Girl's All-Out Guide to Sex and Sexuality* appeared on the scene.

When asked to define hooking up themselves, the majority of college students responded that it was "when a girl and a guy get together for a physical encounter and don't necessarily expect anything further." The physical encoun-

ter, however, could mean anything from kissing to oral sex or intercourse. The ambiguity of the term might, in part, account for its popularity—it allows young people to remain vague about the nature or extent of an interaction when they say they hooked up with someone.

Paula England has done widescale research on the sexual behaviors of college students. Her Online College Social Life Survey (OCSLS) asked more than 14,000 students from nineteen different colleges and universities to report their participation in hook ups using "whatever definition of a hook up you and your friends use." Seventy-two percent of both men and women participating in the OCSLS reported at least one hook up by their senior year in college. Of these, roughly 40 percent engaged in three or fewer hook ups, 40 percent between four and nine hook ups, and 20 percent ten or more hook ups. Only about one-third engaged in intercourse in their most recent hook ups, although—among the 80 percent of students who had intercourse by the end of college—67 percent had done so outside of a relationship.

The AVI report warned that parents and other older adults were woefully unaware of how extraordinarily different today's behavior was from the "dating" of previous generations. Women reported that it was rare for men to ask them out on a date, that they would more often just "hang out," a loosely organized and undefined term for spending time together. Furthermore, after hanging out or hooking up, the women still did not know whether that constituted them as a couple. There was widespread confusion among women about how to navigate these encounters, and about the rules and expectations for hook ups as well as relationships. The report concluded that although women aspire to be married and believe that college is a good place to meet a husband, the current practices of hooking up and hanging out were not leading to that goal.

Laura Hamilton and Elizabeth Armstrong did an in-depth longitudinal ethnographic and interview study of a group of women who started college in 2004 at a university in the Midwest to uncover female college students' attitudes about hooking up. Although the sample was homogeneous—all the females were white, eighteen to twenty years of age, heterosexual except for two subjects, and overwhelmingly wealthy—Hamilton and Armstrong were able to present an alternative to the AVI's assumption that hooking up was problematic behavior for women. For many of the privileged females, college was seen as a time that they were allowed to be independent, as they expected to marry and have children shortly after they graduated. The ability to hook up rather than have relationships allowed them to be sexual without demanding the time, energy, and emotional labor that a relationship requires. Rather than simply being framed as women accommodating men's desires, the women in Hamilton and Armstrong's study expressed genuine interest in hooking up, with many claiming that the ability to experiment with sexual behavior was empowering to them. For at least some proportion of young women, hooking up is seen as a way to express sexual freedom.

Kathleen Bogle presents yet another alternative based on extensive interviews with college students. Bogle proposed that hooking up was not synonymous with the "one night stand" but rather, like dating, was a system of socializing with the opposite sex for the purpose of finding romantic partners. The big difference, however, was that in dating people would get to know one another en route to sexual intimacy, while the sex comes first in hooking up. Bogle claims that for the students involved, hooking up is about more than sex; it is a way for students to find a relationship. Although there are no strings attached in hooking up, and more often than not it does not evolve into anything else, it can still lead some couples to become exclusive.

So, how worried should we be about the phenomenon of hooking up on college campuses? Have the social and sexual mores of students become too lax? Are young people doomed to superficial and fleeting encounters that leave them empty and confused? Or are they simply celebrating sexual freedom and finding new ways of relating to one another? Whatever your opinion on the matter, it is clear that the dating and mating game has changed and will continue to change in the future. And with the dominance of hooking up within the culture of the college social scene, young people may believe that they have few alternatives on the route to romance and marriage.

queer theory social theory about gender identity and sexuality that emphasizes the importance of difference and rejects as restrictive the idea of innate sexual identity

LGBTQ lesbian, gay, bisexual, transgender, and queer; sometimes "A" is added to include "allies"

men who had died of AIDS. LeVay examined the anterior hypothalamus, a part of the brain long thought to relate to sexual behavior, and discovered that gay men have a smaller hypothalamus than heterosexual men. The hypothalamus of the small sample of gay men he studied was actually closer in size to that of heterosexual women, and LeVay thought this was possibly due to prenatal differences in hormone levels (1991, 1993). In another widely publicized study, Dean Hamer examined a specific strand of DNA and the X chromosome in order to determine whether gay men shared a similar genetic trait and concluded that there was a possibility that homosexuality is genetic through the paternal side (Hamer et al. 1993).

Despite the considerable evidence pointing to a genetic origin of homosexuality, some believe that scientists, the media, and gay activists have overestimated its significance. One problem with the studies is that they may neglect the fact that genes interact in complicated ways—the same gene, or combination of genes, may produce different results in different environments. In other words, possessing a particular gene doesn't guarantee that a person will have a particular sexual orientation. Along these same lines, sociologists have criticized the idea of a gay gene for its narrow understanding of sexual orientation. For instance, it doesn't explain bisexuality or how biology and social environments interact to produce various sexual behaviors.

It may be some time before science can resolve these issues, but it's easy to see what's at stake in favoring one side over the other. Gays and lesbians have embraced the genetic model because it is seen as a weapon in the fight for gay rights. After all, if sexual orientation is something a person is born with, then discrimination based on sexual orientation is as unacceptable as discrimination based on gender, race, or disability. The biological view also offers a way to bypass some of the moral and religious debates about homosexuality. In addition, straight Americans often become more tolerant when they assume that sexual orientation is something people are born with rather than a lifestyle choice.

A Sexual Continuum?

As early as the late 1940s, the pioneering sex researcher Alfred Kinsey was suggesting that human sexuality was far more diverse than was commonly assumed. His own studies led him to believe that people were not exclusively heterosexual or homosexual but could fall along a wide spectrum

(Kinsey et al. 1948/1998, 1953/1998). Kinsey and his associates developed a scale to measure this spectrum based on the degree of sexual responsiveness people had to members of the same and opposite sex. They took into account not only measurements but also an individual's fantasies, dreams, and feelings, and the frequency of particular sexual activities. Kinsey and others who have followed him have suggested that we can best understand sexual orientation not through simplistic categories but rather as a fluid continuum that can change over the course of a person's lifetime.

More recently, researchers have argued that Kinsey's theory reduces orientations such as bisexuality and asexuality to a point on a single continuum. Thus, bisexuals have had a hard time achieving recognition for their sexuality; often they are accused of being either timid homosexuals or adventurous heterosexuals. And those who are asexual don't appear at all. Those who are associated with such sexualities deny that their orientation can be reduced to such a model, and seek other ways of understanding sexuality.

For most of the twentieth century, "queer" was a pejorative term for homosexuals, mainly gay men. But in the 1990s, with the emergence of "queer theory," the term underwent a remarkable transformation as both activists and academics began using it. Why did this change occur? For one thing, the term includes many different sexualities and is thus more manageable. **Queer theory** rejects the idea of a single gay, lesbian, bisexual, or transgender identity, emphasizing instead the importance of difference (Butler 1993). It asserts that being queer is about "possibilities, gaps, overlaps, dissonances and resonances" (Sedgwick 1993, p. 8). Thus, queer theory goes against the arguments made by mainstream gay rights advocates who focus on the biological basis of homosexuality and the equal treatment of gays and lesbians; it holds that innate, inborn sexual identity is too limiting. In this spirit, "queers" are sometimes called a "third sex," emphasizing the claim that people don't have to be restricted to either heterosexuality or homosexuality.

Sexuality and Social Issues

In a society in which heterosexuality is the dominant category of sexuality, those with other types of sexual identities, often referred to as the **LGBTQ** community, are likely to experience certain disadvantages and be the objects of particular types of prejudices. Sexuality becomes a form of social stratification based on individual traits and identities, just like stratification systems based on race, class, or gender. Unfortunately, in our society, this means that there is a hierarchy of sexualities in which privileges, opportunities, prejudices, and discrimination are distributed based on category membership. Many believe that sexual minorities should not

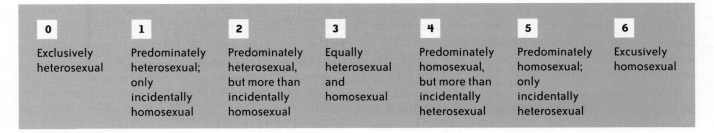

KINSEY SCALE OF SEXUALITY

0	1	2	3	4	5	6
Exclusively heterosexual	Predominately heterosexual; only incidentally homosexual	Predominately heterosexual, but more than incidentally homosexual	Equally heterosexual and homosexual	Predominately homosexual, but more than incidentally heterosexual	Predominately homosexual; only incidentally heterosexual	Excusively homosexual

FIGURE 9.3 The Kinsey Scale

The Kinsey Scale shows the spectrum of human sexuality.

be granted the same rights as heterosexuals. The debates over same-sex marriage and the Don't Ask, Don't Tell laws help illustrate this problem.

While six of the fifty states, plus the District of Columbia, perform same-sex marriages, legal debates continue in each, and victories for gay rights can be short-lived and tenuous. In May 2008, the California Supreme Court overturned the state's previous ban, holding that statutes limiting marriage to heterosexual couples violated the state constitution, creating the opportunity for same-sex couples to begin marrying. Opponents to same-sex marriage immediately placed Proposition 8 on the November 2008 ballot to define marriage as solely "between a man and a woman." The ballot initiative passed, creating two legally distinct categories of California same-sex couples: those who no longer had the right to marry, and those who had married between May and November. Subsequent appeals to the California Supreme Court have ruled the proposition unconstitutional, though the debate over Proposition 8 continues in federal court. While similar debates over same-sex marriage have occurred in other states, each is overshadowed by the Defense of Marriage Act (DOMA), a federal law which declares that no state is required to acknowledge same-sex marriages performed in other states, nor is the federal government required to do so.

Opponents of same-sex marriage have used the rhetoric of "protecting marriage" or "protecting family," implying that gay marriage would harm or destroy those institutions. This largely ignores prolific research that shows that the psychological and physical well-being of children benefit from being raised by two parents whose union is legally recognized by social institutions. While polls of public opinion have shown an increase in favor of recognizing same-sex marriage, many believe that same-sex couples should only be granted **civil unions** and not "marriages." The term "marriage," for many, has religious meaning, which raises concern for many religions that do not support or condone same-sex relations: should gay marriage be legal-

ized, they worry that clergy would be required to perform such unions.

It is worth noting that while civil unions afford many of the same rights as marriages, they do not confer the right to federal benefits (per DOMA) and do not offer "portability," since civil unions performed in one state are not recognized by all states. This has financial ramifications for these families, as many couples who depend on social security, veteran's, or disability benefits cannot inherit those benefits upon their partner's passing. Furthermore, if a state's health insurance plans are governed by federal law, employers are not required to provide health insurance benefits to same-sex partners. As we can see, there is much at stake in the gay marriage debate. It is a political, social, civil rights, moral, and religious issue. If same-sex marriage is legally recognized, gay families will be afforded the same legal standing as heterosexual families.

While not often discussed, gay marriage is also an economic issue. A study conducted at UCLA (Sears and Badgett 2008) estimated that if same-sex marriage were legalized in California, it would provide $63.8 million in state and local government revenue over three years; a factor largely ignored but worth considering given California's ongoing budget crisis. Other states, as well as the federal government, might also consider these benefits.

Finally, it is important to note that amid these debates, generalizations run rampant. Opponents to gay marriage are largely portrayed as members of religious institutions and the conservative right, but there are many institutions and members within those groups that support same-sex marriage. Conversely, there are many within the LGBTQ community who do not support same-sex marriage as it is viewed as assimilationist,

> **civil unions** proposed as an alternative to gay marriage; a form of legally recognized commitment that provides gay couples some of the benefits and protections of marriage

and accepts heteronormative structures, such as binary gender roles and monogamy, rather than critiquing them. Lisa Duggan (2003) and Cathy Cohen (2005) contend that arguing for same-sex marriage creates "hierarchies of worthiness," in that benefits are afforded to the most "socially acceptable" within the LGBTQ community—those who most closely mimic heterosexual unions.

Despite the erratic progress in same-sex marriage laws, the gay rights movement won a large victory in 2010 with the repeal of Don't Ask, Don't Tell (DADT). Signed into law in 1993, DADT arose amidst existing military policies that required the discharge of gay military service members, built on a rhetoric of difference, undesirability, and incompatibility with military practice. DADT was an attempt to curb those discharges by requiring that military administration not "ask" about a service member's sexual activity or orientation, and that service members not "tell" about it either. Initially offering promise that gay service members would be allowed to serve, DADT brought about an environment of secrecy in which gay military personnel had to keep silent or lie about their orientation and lives, as well as accept or engage in anti-gay activities and discourse or face discharge. This environment spurred witch hunts that brought the involuntary discharge of more than 14,000 service members. Its repeal, as with most social change, did not come easily or quickly. With his 2008 election, President Barack Obama promised to repeal DADT, but it took nearly two years, several filibusters in the U.S. Senate led by Obama's presidential competitor Senator John McCain, and a revised bill before that promise became a reality. With the repeal of Don't Ask, Don't Tell, gay service members are now legally permitted to serve openly without recrimination and cannot be discharged because of their sexual identity.

While the military was one of the last federal employers actively supported by law to discriminate based on sexuality, there are countless businesses that are still allowed to do so in states that do not have laws that prohibit such discrimination. A study conducted by William Rubenstein (2001), a law professor at UCLA, found that reports of discrimination based on sexual orientation are roughly equal in number to those based on race or gender. Considered in the context of the number of gay people in the workforce, this is a concerning statistic given that at the lowest estimate of gay people in the workforce, the rate of discrimination filings is several times higher than those based upon gender. The Employment Non-Discrimination Act (ENDA), a bill placed before Congress in 2010, would seek to correct this by placing sexual orientation within a protected class with race and gender, so that employers could not legally discriminate based upon the sexual orientation of their employees. But while legal discrimination against gay and lesbians may slowly be ending, other forms of prejudice can be harder to overcome.

homophobia fear of or discrimination toward homosexuals or toward individuals who display purportedly gender-inappropriate behavior

Homophobia

In 1968, police raided a gay bar in New York City called the Stonewall Inn. At the time, patrons of gay bars were frequently singled out for harassment from the police. The pent-up resentment and frustration this caused erupted into violence during the raid. The Stonewall riots began a new era of campaigning for civil rights for gays, lesbians, bisexuals, and transgendered individuals. Although many homosexuals still remain "in the closet," not revealing their sexual orientation even to friends or family members, others are open and vocal: "We're here, we're queer, get used to it!" goes one motto. Sociologist Dana Rosenfeld, who studies gay and lesbian identity, asserts that there are at least two distinct cohorts, those who lived before the gay liberation movement of the 1960s and those who lived during and after it. The earlier generation would have felt discredited if their sexual orientation had become public knowledge, whereas the later generation believed that making their orientation public was celebrating an essential aspect of the self that should not be denied (Rosenfeld 2003).

One reason gays and lesbians hide their identity is the extent of **homophobia**, "the dread of being in close quarters with homosexuals," in society (Weinberg 1972). A sociological perspective on homophobia shifts the burden from gays and lesbians to those who have a negative reaction to them. In other words, instead of asking why gays and lesbians act the way they do, sociologists ask why people have a problem with homosexuality.

Some have pointed out that homophobia is not a true "phobia," like agoraphobia or claustrophobia, which are psychological phenomena. Rather, it is a prejudice, like racism or anti-Semitism, which are cultural norms that are learned and transmitted socially. Homophobia as a concept is problematic because it suggests that the problems faced by gays and lesbians are the result of a few maladjusted individuals rather than the product of deeply institutionalized cultural values and norms (Kitzinger 1987). Indeed, some have suggested that "heterosexism" would be a more useful term in that it is analogous to sexism and racism and describes an ideological system that stigmatizes any non-heterosexual behavior (Herek 1990; Rothblum 1996).

Queer Youth

For many queer youth, the most difficult period in dealing with their sexual and gender identities in a homophobic culture occurs during their adolescent years. Research shows that LGBTQ youth are up to four times more likely to attempt suicide and up to 8.4 times more likely among adolescents to be rejected by their families for being LGBTQ (Ryan et al. 2009). The middle school and high school years are challenging for any young person, but this is especially true for those with a hidden ("closeted") or open LGBTQ identity. The 2009 National School Climate Survey (Kosciw et al. 2010) showed that nearly nine out of ten LGBTQ students experience harassment in school. Nearly 85 percent of LGBTQ students reported being verbally harassed, while 40.1 percent reported being physically harassed, and 18.8 reported physical assault in the past year because of their sexual orientation.

School administration and faculty can have a positive impact on these developmental years, as schools with supportive staff reported fewer incidents of their LGBTQ students being absent and/or feeling unsafe, and contributed to the greater academic achievement and higher educational aspirations of LGBTQ youth. Those schools that enact anti-bullying policies not only have lower instances of harassment, but also higher rates of staff intervention in such instances—an important factor specifically for transgender youth who face even higher rates of harassment and abuse in school than their lesbian, gay, and bisexual peers.

A supportive peer environment can also help LGBTQ students to be open about their sexual orientation and/or gender identity. School programs can heighten all students' awareness of stigma and its consequences (Rabow, Stein, and Conley 1999), and clubs such as Gay-Straight Alliances can enhance feelings of belonging, healthy development, and positive well-being.

The Mass Media and Sexual Stereotypes

As with other prejudices, there are both institutional and individual forms of homophobia. Individual homophobia is expressed through derogatory comments, discriminatory actions, and physical attacks. It is sometimes legitimized by institutional homophobia, which occurs when a government, business, church, or other organization discriminates against people on the basis of sexual orientation. One social institution that has played a particularly interesting role in creating and sometimes challenging sexual stereotypes is the mass media. While homosexuality is more visible now than it has ever been, many people still have no firsthand knowledge of homosexuality and turn to the media as their exclusive source for understanding it.

Before the 1960s, homosexuality was altogether absent from television. When it did appear, it was usually treated in a negative manner: in the 1967 CBS documentary *The Homosexuals*, one psychiatrist claims that "the fact that somebody's homosexual . . . automatically rules out the possibility that

"Acting Out" In 2000, the comedy *Will & Grace* featured the first gay kiss on network television.

Changing the World

ACT-UP and AIDS Activism

ACT-UP stands for AIDS Coalition to Unleash Power, a worldwide social movement whose motto is "Silence = Death." Since 1987, ACT-UP has used demonstrations to noisily challenge doctors, researchers, and politicians to address the AIDS crisis. Members seek funding for AIDS research and affordable drug treatments in the United States and abroad, and the commitment of powerful policy makers to fight the disease. ACT-UP originated at Manhattan's Lesbian and Gay Community Services Center, but its membership now includes thousands of committed activists worldwide.

At ACT-UP demonstrations called "die-ins," thousands of protesters lie down on the steps of government buildings or drug company headquarters in order to illustrate the real outcome of ineffective AIDS policies and corporate greed. Members have scattered the ashes of AIDS victims on the White House lawn and delivered condoms to prison officials. ACT-UP activists have also used clever, well-designed stickers such as "Condoms, not coffins. AIDS won't wait!" to get their message across, plastering them on all available surfaces. Their marches and demonstrations sometimes feature the ceaseless, deafening blast of dog whistles, guaranteed to get the attention of passersby.

ACT-UP has played a role in reversing the discriminatory health-insurance practices of certain employers; pressuring the Centers for Disease Control to include illnesses suffered by women, children, and people of color in its definition of AIDS; increasing government funding for AIDS research; lowering prices of generic AIDS drugs in Africa; raising awareness about the spread of AIDS in prisons; protecting clean-needle programs for intravenous drug users; and encouraging celebrities like comedian Eddie Murphy to apologize publicly for making jokes about people with AIDS.

Over the past two decades, ACT-UP has had an important impact on other social movements. Animal rights activists, antiwar protesters, opponents of globalization, and environmentalists have all tailored ACT-UP "direct-action" strategies (such as "die-ins" and scattering ashes) to their own particular movements. ACT-UP has even developed an offshoot program that provides civil-disobedience training for demonstrators. During the Persian Gulf War of 1991, for instance, Dr. Ferris was part of a group of student antiwar protesters who learned "how to get arrested" from an ACT-UP volunteer; his advice included pointers on how to cross your wrists properly while being handcuffed in order to avoid pain.

ACT-UP is an example of a social movement that started in a small way, in a local gay and lesbian community, but has now achieved worldwide recognition. It knows how to make itself heard and, in so doing, it has helped to change the world.

---

he will remain happy for long." In recent years, however, increasing levels of tolerance toward homosexuality have been reflected in increasingly positive representations of gays and lesbians on television, although these gains have not been without controversy. In 1997, the ABC sitcom *Ellen* introduced the first lesbian lead character in a prime-time series; two years later, the NBC sitcom *Will & Grace* featured two gay male characters. Other shows followed, with a variety of minor gay and lesbian characters: *Dawson's Creek*, *Party of Five*, *NYPD Blue*, *Spin City*, *Friends*, and *Buffy the Vampire Slayer*, and later *Grey's Anatomy*, *Brothers & Sisters*, *Ugly Betty*, *Modern Family*, and *Glee*. Cable networks also developed gay- and lesbian-themed shows, such as *Queer as Folk*, *Queer Eye for the Straight Guy*, and *The L Word*.

Just because gay and lesbian characters are included on television, however, doesn't mean that they have achieved equal status. Clearly, there is not the same kind of acceptance of same-sex relations as of heterosexual relations, as evidenced by how romantic couples are treated on TV. Until 2000, there had never been a gay male kiss on a network program (although there had been two lesbian kisses). This issue was brought up in an episode of *Will & Grace* called "Acting Out," which featured a clever show-within-a-show format. Will and his best friend, Jack, both gay, are watching their favorite TV show, also about gay characters, which is supposed to feature the first prime-time gay kiss ever. However, right before the much-anticipated kiss the cameras cut away and instead focus on the fireplace, a mere metaphor. Jack is upset but has trouble convincing Will that the incident really matters:

> Jack: I am outraged by this. Why aren't you?
> Will: Because I'm realistic. Clearly, nobody wants to see two men kissing on television, not the network, not the viewers, not the advertisers . . .
> Jack: That's right, Will. They wanna pretend we're invisible.

Later, a group of gays, including Will and Jack, gather outside the NBC studios to protest. There, the *Today Show* meteorologist, Al Roker, is giving the weather report in front of the usual early-morning crowd of fans. Jack calls out to him, and as the camera focuses on Jack, he grabs Will and kisses him, on live TV. And there it is, finally, the first-ever gay kiss on network television. However, the fact that this is done in a humorous and backhanded way may actually undermine to some extent the political message the writers of the show were trying to convey.

What we can say as social scientists is that the more personal contact between members of different social groups, the less prejudice and discrimination may occur between them. If the mass media provide some people's only exposure to gays and lesbians, then it is all the more important that their portrayals represent those communities in realistic ways.

Closing Comments

Sex, gender, and sexuality are status categories that structure social inequality and shape individual identities. They are different but interrelated, and we all experience their overlap in our everyday lives: we categorize ourselves and others and make assumptions about one another based on these perceived categories. A sociological perspective allows us to see the cultural and environmental influences on what may be considered biologically based identities, and lets us identify and critique the stratification systems that have resulted from these influences. Most important, a sociological perspective allows us to see how destructive sexism is for men and women and how crippling homophobia can be for the straight majority as well as the gay minority. Stereotypes are socially constructed: they can therefore be socially deconstructed and socially reconstructed as well.

⑤ Need Help Studying?

wwnorton.com/studyspace

Visit StudySpace to access free review materials such as:
- **Vocabulary Flashcards**
- **Diagnostic Review Quizzes**
- **Study Outlines**

QUESTIONS FOR REVIEW

1. Are women and men truly "opposite" sexes? What assumptions are involved in talking about males and females as opposites? Do you think that sex and gender are each composed of two discrete categories? Why or why not?

2. This chapter uses a constructionist approach to explain gender inequality. Can you imagine any behaviors or activities that you think could be better explained from an essentialist point of view? Which approach makes more sense to you? What sort of data or test could help you determine if a particular behavior or activity is innate?

3. How are berdaches and hijras different from the cross-dressers or transsexuals in our society? Given that this chapter is primarily about the sociology of gender in the United States, why are we interested in these cross-cultural examples? What can they tell us about our own society?

4. Our society upholds expectations about which gender more appropriately fills the instrumental and the expressive roles. In your family, were the nurturing and emotional support primarily provided by women? How do these gendered expectations reinforce the traditional family structure? How do they perpetuate gender inequality?

5. From an interactional perspective, gender is not an internal essence, but something we achieve through interaction. This implies that throughout everyday life we are "doing gender." Picture the gendered differences in behaviors like sitting, walking, or conversing. Can you think of a time when you did gender "wrong" and other people reacted negatively? Why did they react this way?

6. Consider the ways you were socialized by your family. In what ways was your socialization gendered? What toys did you play with as a child? What extracurricular activities were you encouraged to pursue? What household chores did you perform?

7. The second shift refers to the housework that must be done after the day's paid labor is complete; women do a disproportionate amount of this work. Why do you think this is? What types of tasks does our society expect women to do? How do the tasks expected of men differ?

8. Do you believe that there is a "gay gene"? Why do you think so many people have strong opinions on the possibility of a genetic component of sexual orientation, even though research in this area is just beginning? What is at stake in this debate?

9. Television has played an important role in perpetuating stereotypes about gays and lesbians. For years, portrayals of gays and lesbians on television were quite rare—and typically negative. In recent years, this has started to change, with more shows offering positive representations of homosexual characters. How have such changes affected social attitudes about gays and lesbians?

SUGGESTIONS FOR FURTHER EXPLORATION

The Aggressives. 2005. Dir. Daniel Peddle. Image Entertainment. A documentary that follows women who feel more comfortable dressing and acting as men. The film documents the women's efforts at passing—even those who interact with them closely don't always know they are women—and as the name suggests, this involves changes in demeanor as much as in clothing and hair cuts.

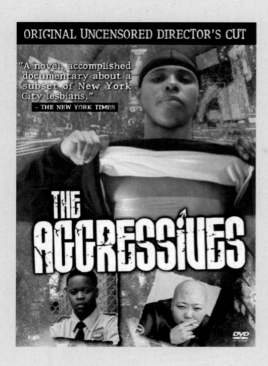

Eugenides, Jeffrey. 2003. *MiddleSex*. New York: Picador. A novel about Cal Stephanides, born Calliope Stephanides, who discovers at age fourteen that genetically and chromosomally—even if not anatomically—he is male. The novel incorporates fantastical elements to explore issues surrounding the scientific study and the lived experience of gender.

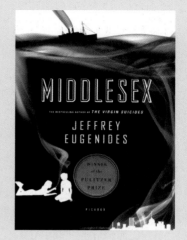

It Gets Better Project. www .itgetsbetter.org. Begun in 2010 by columnist Dan Savage, this ever-expanding collection of YouTube videos shows both celebrities and ordinary folks who tell their stories of coming out, and the trials and rewards they experienced. The messages are meant to help LGBTQ teens get through their own tribulations and make it to a happier, healthier adulthood.

Amnesty International's *Stop Violence Against Women* campaign (web.amnesty.org/actforwomen/index-eng). This site provides information and resources to help fight violence against women around the world.

Bly, Robert. 2004. *Iron John*. Cambridge, MA: DaCapo Press. A touchstone of the branch of the men's movement that remains allied with feminist goals. Bly argues that men need to find ways to become more introspective about aggression and responsibility.

Butler, Judith. 2000. *Gender Trouble: Feminism and the Subversion of Identity*, 10th ed. New York: Routledge. A demanding read and one of the most influential studies of the social and political origins of the sex/gender system.

Naylor, Gloria. 1985. *The Women of Brewster Place*. New York: Penguin. This novel follows a group of seven African American women living in the same apartment building who must rely on each other to survive in a world where they are disadvantaged by their race, class, and gender.

Paragraph 175. 2000. Dirs. Rob Epstein and Jeffrey Friedman. Telling Pictures. A documentary about the persecution of homosexuals in Nazi Germany, named after the section of the German penal code that criminalized homosexuality. This law, written long before the Nazis came to power, stayed on the books until 1973.

Sedgewick, Eve Kosofsky. 1991. *The Epistemology of the Closet*. Berkeley: University of California Press. This highly influential work of queer theory closely examines the ways that our categories for sexual identities shape contemporary society.

Russo, Vito. 1987. *The Celluloid Closet: Homosexuality in the Movies*. New York: HarperCollins. Like the 1995 documentary of the same name, this book offers a sharp, insightful analysis of the ways that institutional homophobia has played out in the movies, in everything from *Spartacus* to *Philadelphia*.

Trembling Before G-d. 2001. Dir. Sandi Simcha Dubowski. New Yorker Films. This film documents the lives of gays and lesbians in the Orthodox Jewish community, paying close attention to the tensions that result from the strict prohibition of homosexuality within their religion.

Dan Savage (right) and his partner.

everydaysociologyblog.com

HOW DOES SOCIOLOGY RELATE TO YOUR LIFE?

EVERYDAY SOCIOLOGY BLOG

everydaysociologyblog.com

 Visit the Everyday Sociology blog to explore sociology's relevance to:

- **Popular** culture
- **Mass** media
- **Everyday** life

PART IV

Examining Social Institutions as Sites of Everyday Life

Our everyday lives take place within the contexts of many overlapping and interdependent social institutions. A social institution is a collection of patterned social practices that are repeated continuously and regularly over time and supported by social norms. Politics, the economy, family, religion, health care, and education are all social institutions, and you have contact with many of these (and others) on a daily basis. The patterns and structures of social institutions shape your individual experiences; at the same time, it's important to remember that social institutions are created, maintained, and changed by individual actions.

In the next four chapters, we will look at specific social institutions, such as politics, education, and religion (Chapter 10), the economy (Chapter 11), the family (Chapter 12), media and leisure (Chapter 13), and the health care system (Chapter 14), their role in structuring your everyday life. You will be introduced to a variety of sociological research that focuses on how these social institutions and others work; here, we highlight a sociological researcher whose work integrates many of them. In his book *Heat Wave: A Social Autopsy of Disaster in Chicago* (2002), Eric Klinenberg examines the circumstances surrounding Chicago's catastrophic heat wave in 1995, which killed more than 700 people. Klinenberg analyzes the week-long heat wave as more than a meteorological phenomenon. People died, he argues, because of a combination of disturbing demographic trends and dangerous institutional policies present at all times in all major urban areas.

For one week in mid-July of 1995, the city of Chicago suffered the worst heat wave in its history: temperatures exceeded 100 degrees for four days in a row, and heat indices (the "real feel" air temperature) hit a high of 126 degrees. Historic buildings baked like ovens, but fear of crime left many people feeling trapped inside their apartments. Children passed out in overheated school buses. City residents blasted their air conditioning (if they had it), mobbed the tiny beaches on Lake Michigan, and broke open fire hydrants to stay cool. As a result, power outages peppered the area and water pressure dropped dangerously. Roads buckled, train tracks warped, and people suffered from heat-related illnesses in large numbers. The city's 911 emergency system overloaded, and some callers waited two hours for ambulances to arrive; more than twenty hospitals closed their emergency rooms, overwhelmed with patients. The death toll mounted, with the elderly and the poor especially vulnerable. In this single week, 739 Chicagoans died as a result of the heat. According to Klinenberg, the individual "isolation, deprivation, and vulnerability" that led to these deaths resulted from a variety of institutional structures, including poverty, racial segregation, family dislocation, and city politics. These institutional arrangements must be examined and changed in order to avoid future tragedies.

Many of those who died during the heat wave were elderly people who lived alone: sick or fragile, their mobility compromised, their neighborhoods changing around them, their families far away or neglectful, and their social networks dissolving. In many cases, the elderly victims of the heat wave were so isolated that no one ever claimed their bodies (p. 15). The story of Pauline Jankowitz, 85, who survived the heat wave, illustrates these demographic trends (pp. 50–54). Pauline lived alone on the third floor of an apartment building with no elevator. She suffered from incontinence and walked with a crutch. She recognized her vulnerability and left her apartment only once every two months. Her two children lived in other states and rarely visited, so a volunteer from a charitable organization did Pauline's weekly grocery shopping. However, Pauline no longer had any connections with her immigrant neighbors and spent most of her time in her apartment listening to radio talk shows. Pauline's isolation is hardly unique. Her circumstances illustrate the ways that

the geographic mobility of the contemporary family, the changing populations of urban neighborhoods, the financial limitations of retirement incomes, and the lack of supportive social services all contribute to situations in which elderly individuals may live, face crises, and die alone.

Klinenberg argues that race and class inequality also contributed to the death toll in the Chicago heat wave. He shows that the death tolls were highest in the city's "black belt," a group of predominantly African American neighborhoods on the south and west sides of the city. (These neighborhoods also have relatively high levels of poverty and crime and relatively large populations of elderly residents.) Social ties in these neighborhoods are hard to maintain: poverty contributes to residential transiency, so neighbors may not get to know one another before they must move to different housing elsewhere. Gang activity and crime make residents afraid to walk down the street or sit on their own front porches. And although some of the neighborhoods in question have powerful religious organizations in their midst, even the most proactive church needs significant financial resources to reach out to its members—and such resources may be hard to come by in poor neighborhoods. So, a person's risk of heat-related death during July of 1995 was partly place-based. In Chicago, as in most major cities, place, race, and class are closely connected.

In July 1995, Chicago's government services also failed in a number of ways when the city's residents needed them most. However, Klinenberg argues that the city's bureaucracies were no more ill-prepared to deal with catastrophe during that week than during any other. Long-term, macro-level changes in city politics mean that both the political will and the material resources to provide assistance to the poor were fatally absent. For example, overextended paramedics and firefighters had no centralized office with which to register their observations or complaints. As a result, many problems went unheeded by the city until emergency services were too swamped to provide timely assistance. There was little coordination between the local, state, and federal agencies that dealt with social welfare and emergency services. Finally, Klinenberg indicts city officials for "governing by public relations" (p. 143); that is, for using the mass media to deflect attention from the city's problems, including minimizing both the scope of the heat wave and the city's accountability.

Klinenberg's "social autopsy" reveals the failure of social institutions on a massive scale—and the disturbing prospect that this disaster could happen again, anywhere, if we do not take steps to change flawed social systems. Structural and institutional arrangements—including city government, health care providers, families, schools, religious organizations, and the media—must change in order to avoid individual tragedies. But individual actions help bring about institutional change, and *Heat Wave* reveals important ways in which all our fates intertwine, as they are shaped by the social institutions we encounter every day. How can we better manage this interdependence, for the good of all?

ou probably know the Pledge of Allegiance by heart and have said it countless times in elementary and high school, but you may not have thought much about its words or why you were required to say them.

> *I pledge allegiance to the Flag*
> *of the United States of America,*
> *and to the Republic for which it stands:*
> *one Nation, under God, indivisible,*
> *with Liberty and Justice for all.*

Reciting the pledge was just a routine part of being a student in the United States. Could it possibly be controversial? A lot of people think so. The Pledge of Allegiance brings together questions about three important social institutions in American life: politics, education, and religion, as you will see.

Dr. Michael Newdow, an emergency room physician and self-described atheist in California, is committed to preserving the separation of church and state. When his daughter's second-grade class began reciting the Pledge of Allegiance, Newdow became disturbed because it contained the phrase "one Nation, *under God*." Acting as his own attorney, Newdow filed a lawsuit, and in February 2003 the 9th Circuit Court held the pledge to be in violation of the Constitution because the reference to God violated the separation of church and state.

Many civic and political leaders—liberals as well as conservatives—denounced the decision. The Senate passed a resolution condemning it, and the attorney general announced that the Justice Department would "spare no effort to preserve the rights of all our citizens to pledge allegiance to the American flag" (Weinstein 2003). Almost universally lawmakers came out in defense of the pledge, agreeing with Judge Ferdinand Fernandez, who in his dissenting opinion argued that the phrase "under God" had "no tendency to establish a religion in this country or to suppress anyone's exercise, or non-exercise, of religion, except in the fevered eye of persons who most fervently would like to drive all tincture of religion out of the public life of our polity" (Egelko 2002). Ultimately, the case went all the way to the Supreme Court, which overturned the lower court's ruling on a technicality but did not address whether the language in the pledge violates the First Amendment.

The Pledge of Allegiance was originally written in 1892 and did not contain the phrase "under God"; that was added in 1954, when President Eisenhower signed a bill making the change official. The added words generated no controversy at the time. The president declared that their addition would affirm "the dedication of our nation and our people to the Almighty," and Senator Joseph McCarthy said "it was a clear indication that the United States was committed to ending the threat of 'godless' Communism" (Brinkley-Rogers 2002).

Since as early as 1943, the Supreme Court has ruled that children cannot be forced to recite the pledge. In 1943, the issue addressed was the patriotic nature of the pledge. However, a 2002 ruling by Judge Alfred Goodwin states that reciting the pledge in public schools "places students in the untenable position of choosing between participating in an exercise with religious content or protesting," an especially damaging scenario because "the coercive effect of the policy here is particularly pronounced in the school setting, given the age and impressionability of schoolchildren" (Weinstein 2003). After all, how many second graders will be willing to stand out from their peers in so dramatic a fashion?

Although there is a great deal of disagreement over what should be done in this case, all the participants agree, even if only implicitly, that social institutions play an important role in the lives of Americans. **Social institutions** (systems and structures that organize our group life, such as school, religion, and the government) shape and constrain our everyday lives. For example, if school starts at 8:00 A.M. and ends at 3:00 P.M., this structures the life of an entire household—it dictates what time children should go to bed and get up in the morning; when breakfast and dinner are prepared, served, and eaten; and what types of arrangements must be made for transportation, after-school activities, and child care. In turn, these same institutions are created and sustained through our everyday interactions. For example, a school exists only because of the actions of the teachers, students, parents, and administrators who are part of the surrounding community.

Social institutions represent a bit of a sociological paradox. They function at the macro level to shape our everyday interactions, but at the micro level those same everyday interactions construct social institutions. Because they are at the center of both micro- and macrosociology, social institutions give us the opportunity to examine the connection between interaction and structure, between the individual and society. In this chapter, we will focus on the social institutions of politics, education, and religion as places where the micro and the macro come together, and we will show how the intersections between social institutions shape everyday life.

HOW TO READ THIS CHAPTER

We have devoted entire chapters to other social institutions such as health care, work, and family, but here we have grouped politics, education, and religion together for a reason. These institutions intersect in distinctive and often unexamined ways in our everyday lives—the daily recitation of the Pledge of Allegiance is just one example. Local and national controversies over

social institutions systems and structures within society that shape the activities of groups and individuals

school vouchers or sex education are other examples of the ways in which political, educational, and religious concerns overlap. Every day we make decisions or engage in debates that address moral values, political practicalities, and educational expectations all bundled together.

When you read this chapter, we want you to be able to see the relationships among these three social institutions as well as to make the connection between micro- and macrosociology. This is a key opportunity to use the sociological theories and methods you have learned in previous chapters to find the intersections between individual experience and social structure, and the overlaps between various social institutions in everyday life. After reading this chapter, you should have a deeper understanding of how social institutions shape your individual experience and how you as an individual contribute to shaping those institutions.

What Is Politics?

Politics has concerned social thinkers since at least the time of the philosophers in ancient Greece. The word *politics* comes from the Greek *politikos*, meaning of or relating to citizens. As a sociological term, **politics** pertains especially to the methods and tactics of managing a political entity, such as a nation or state, as well as the administration and control of its internal and external affairs. But it can also mean the attitudes and activities of groups and individuals. To understand the relationship between citizens and their particular political environment, we must first look at the variety of different political systems and study the American system of democracy. Then we will examine elections and voting, lobbies and special interest groups, and the role of the media in the political process.

Political Systems: Government

Government is the formal, organized agency that exercises power and control in modern society. Governments are vested with the power and authority to make laws and enforce them. As you probably remember from Chapter 1, Max Weber defined **power** as the ability to get others to do one's bidding. When sociologists talk about **authority**, they refer to the legitimate, noncoercive exercise of power. Throughout the world and throughout history, governments have taken a variety of forms. When evaluating types of governance as sociologists, we ask certain questions about the relationship between leaders and followers: who has power and who does not, what kind of power is exerted, and how far does that power extend?

TOTAL POWER AND AUTHORITY Authoritarianism is a political system that denies ordinary citizens representation by and control over their own government. Thus, citizens have no say in who rules them, what laws are made, or how those laws are enforced. Generally, political power is concentrated in the hands of a few elites who control military and economic resources. A *dictatorship* is one form of authoritarian system. In most instances, a dictator does not gain power by being elected or through succession but seizes power and becomes an absolute ruler. Dictators may gain control through a military coup, as occurred when General Augusto Pinochet came to power in Chile in 1973. In other cases, leaders may be legally elected or appointed but then become dictators once in power, abolishing any constitutional limits on their authority—such as President Charles Taylor of Liberia, who was deposed in 2003 and is still in custody and facing international war crime charges in The Hague. Dictators are most often individuals but can also be associated with political parties or groups, such as the Taliban in Afghanistan.

politics methods and tactics intended to influence government policy, policy-related attitudes, and activities

government the formal, organized agency that exercises power and control in modern society, especially through the creation and enforcement of laws

power the ability to impose one's will on others

authority the legitimate, noncoercive exercise of power

authoritarianism system of government by and for a small number of elites that does not include representation of ordinary citizens

Dictators Try to Control All Aspects of Citizens' Lives Leaders such as Kim Jong Il of North Korea, Augusto Pinochet of Chile, and Charles Taylor of Liberia are among the world's most notorious dictators.

Totalitarianism is the most extreme and modern version of authoritarianism. The government seeks to control every aspect, public and private, of citizens' lives. Unlike older forms of authoritarianism, a totalitarian government can utilize all the contrivances of surveillance technology, systems of mass communication, and modern weapons to control its citizens (Arendt 1958). Totalitarian governments are usually headed by a dictator, whether a ruler or a single political party. Through propaganda, totalitarian regimes can further control the population by disseminating ideology aimed at shaping their thoughts, values, and attitudes. An example of a modern totalitarian ruler is Kim Jong Il of North Korea, whose nation has one of the worst human rights records in the world, restricts the basic freedoms of its people, and has a stagnant, internationally isolated economy.

MONARCHIES AND THE STATE Monarchies are governments ruled by a king or queen. In a **monarchy**, sovereignty is vested in a successive line of rulers, usually within a family, such as the Tudors of England, the Ming Dynasty of China, and the Romanovs of Russia. Nobility is handed down through family lines and can include numerous family members who hold royal titles. Monarchs are not popularly elected and not usually accountable to the general citizenry, and some may rule by "divine right," the idea that they are leaders chosen by God.

Monarchies can be divided into two categories: absolute and constitutional. Absolute monarchs typically have complete authority over their subjects, much like a dictator. Constitutional monarchs are royal figures whose powers are defined by a political charter and limited by a parliament or other governing body. Most monarchies were weakened, overthrown, or otherwise made obsolete during the many social revolutions of the eighteenth, nineteenth, and twentieth centuries, such as the French Revolution (1789) and the Russian Revolution (1917). In contemporary times, some Asian and European nations, such as Japan, Thailand, Great Britain, and Sweden, still enjoy their royal families as national figureheads and celebrities, though their kings, queens, princes, and princesses don't have any real power in these constitutional monarchies. There are, however, a few remaining modern examples of more absolute monarchies in the world, among them Saudi Arabia, Brunei, and Morocco.

monarchy a government ruled by a king or queen, with succession of rulers kept within the family

democracy a political system in which all citizens have the right to participate

CITIZENS AND DEMOCRACY Democracy originated in ancient Greece and represented a radical new political system. In a **democracy**, citizens share in directing the activities of their government rather than being ruled by an autocratic individual or authoritarian group. The idea is that educated citizens should participate in the election of officials who then represent their interests in law making, law enforcement, resource allocation, and international affairs. Democracy is not only a political system but also a philosophy that emphasizes the right and capacity of individuals, acting either directly or through representatives, to control through majority rule the institutions that govern them. Democracy is associated with the values of basic human rights, civil liberties, freedom, and equality.

Democracy may seem like the ideal system of government, but remember that not all citizens are equally represented even by a democratic government. In many democratic nations, women, ethnic or racial minorities, members of certain religions, and immigrants have been excluded from citizenship or from equal participation in the political process. In the United States, women did not have the right to vote until 1920. And while the Fifteenth Amendment to the U.S. Constitution technically gave adult males of all races voting rights in 1870, barriers such as poll taxes, literacy tests, and "grandfather clauses" kept African Americans from exercising those rights for almost 100 years, until the 1965 Voting Rights Act was passed. Native Americans were legally excluded from voting in federal elections until 1924, and residents of the District of Columbia were not allowed to vote in presidential elections until 1961. As you can see, even the world's leading democracy has not always seen all citizens as equal.

The American Political System

When American colonists rebelled against British authority in 1776, they created the first modern democracy. American democracy, however, is much more complicated than "rule by the people." In the following sections, we focus on voting, theories about who governs, the power of interest groups, and the influence of the mass media on the political system.

VOTING IN THE UNITED STATES The American political system prides itself on being a democracy, a government that confers power to the people. In this form of government, power is formally exercised through the election process, which provides each person with a vote. Sociologists have long been interested in the social factors—such as age, education, religion, or ethnic background—that influence whether and how individuals vote.

By the end of the twentieth century, many had become concerned about a steady, decades-long decline in American voter turnout. For example, in the 1960 presidential election, 63 percent of the electorate cast ballots, but by 1996, that number fell to below 50 percent for the first time since 1924.

Voter turnout began improving in the 2004 presidential election, but it is important to consider how voter turnout has been measured. Prior to the 2004 election, the voter turnout rate was typically calculated by dividing the total number of votes by the "voting-age population"—*everyone* aged eighteen and older residing in the United States. This figure included people who were ineligible to vote—mainly noncitizens and felons—and excluded eligible overseas voters. Since the 2004 election, voting rates have been based on the "voting-eligible population," which changes the overall voting picture and challenges the notion of decline in voter turnout. In the 2004 election, voter turnout was 55 percent for the "voting-age population" and 60 percent for the "voting-eligible population." And among eligible voters under age twenty-five, turnout rose by almost 6 percent over the 2000 election, with some 10.5 million of them going to the polls.

Voter turnout improved again in the presidential election of 2008 in which Barack Obama, the first African American president, was elected. An estimated 61.4 percent of the voting-eligible population, or 130.9 million Americans, cast their ballots. That represents an increase of 1.3 percentage points over 2004 but falls short of the record turnout of 62.5 percent in 1968. Among young voters aged eighteen to twenty-nine, the 2008 election represented the second highest turnout in history, with approximately 22 million–24 million, or 49 percent–54 percent of eligible voters, casting their ballots. The record youth voter turnout belongs to the election in 1972, the first year that eighteen-year-olds had the right to vote.

Barack Obama Joined by his wife Michelle, Obama takes the oath of office to become the 44th president of the United States.

Even so, why are voter participation rates so much lower in the United States than in some comparable democratic nations? Is it simply voter apathy or cynicism? A number of social factors affect the likelihood that someone will or will not vote. Age, race, gender, sexual orientation, religion, geographic location, social class, and education are all demographic variables that influence voter participation as well as how people vote. For example, Minnesota had the highest voter turnout of any state in the 2008 presidential

TABLE 10.1	Theory in Everyday Life	
PERSPECTIVE	**APPROACH TO SOCIAL INSTITUTIONS**	**CASE STUDY: UNDERSTANDING POLITICAL POWER IN AMERICA**
STRUCTURAL FUNCTIONALISM	Social institutions such as politics, education, and religion provide critical functions for the needs of society and help to maintain order and unity.	The theory of pluralism suggests that in a democracy, power is held in a variety of hands; each group is assumed to have equal access to power and can thus serve as a system of checks and balances.
CONFLICT THEORY	Social institutions such as politics, education, and religion represent the interests of those in power and thus create and maintain inequalities in society.	The theory of the power elite suggests that power in the United States is concentrated in the hands of a small group of decision makers and that the masses have little power in the democratic process.
SYMBOLIC INTERACTIONISM	Social institutions such as politics, education, and religion are created through individual participation; they give meaning to and are part of the everyday experience of members.	The theory of the social construction of presidential candidates suggests that the messages we receive from the media help to shape our perceptions and influence public opinion and voting behavior.

Changing the World

Patriotism and Protest

In the United States, the Constitution guarantees freedom of the press and freedom of speech. Anyone—an individual, a newspaper's editorial staff, a group, or an organization—can criticize the system, call for change, and openly express disapproval of the president, other leaders, and government policies. In some political systems, this kind of speech could get you censured, imprisoned, "disappeared," or even executed. For instance, during Argentina's "Dirty War" in the late 1970s and early 80s, the military dictatorship killed or "disappeared" 10,000–30,000 citizens.

Even though freedom of speech is a legal right in the United States, when we criticize some policy or some action of the government, we may, ironically, be called unpatriotic by those who support it. This is especially true in times of war or national crisis, when many citizens believe we should pull together as a country and present a united front to the world. During the 1960s, for example, at the height of U.S. involvement in Vietnam, many Americans considered antiwar protesters "un-American" because of their vocal criticism of American intervention in Southeast Asia. After September 11, 2001, those who questioned the competence of U.S. intelligence agencies (such as journalists, elected representatives, and survivors of those killed in the attacks) were effectively silenced until more than a year later, when Congress impaneled a commission to investigate intelligence agencies' preparation for and response to the attacks. The commission's report confirmed problems within the intel-

ligence community that contributed to the inability to foresee and forestall the attacks—corroborating the criticisms of "unpatriotic" protesters.

Numerous protests have occurred during the course of the Iraq War, attracting both proponents and critics. For example, when the war began in 2003, the country music group The Dixie Chicks expressed their antiwar sentiments by saying that, as Texans, they were ashamed that President George W. Bush was also from their home state. This comment caused a storm of controversy, and many radio stations all over the country refused to play The Dixie Chicks' songs. The protests at the 2004 Democratic and Republican national conventions in Boston and New York City were notable for their size, their creativity, and the intense response they provoked from law enforcement. Both protesters and police used the internet and mobile phones to coordinate their actions, and in one demonstration 5,000 bicyclists clogged the streets of Manhattan for a protest ride. Using a different strategy, peace activist Cindy Sheehan, whose son was killed in Iraq, set up camp outside George W. Bush's Texas ranch in August 2005, vowing to stay there until the president came outside and spoke with her. He never did, and in July 2006 Sheehan purchased several acres of land near the Bush ranch to create a more permanent memorial to her son. In 2010, the Museum of Contemporary Art (MOCA) commissioned noted street artist Blu to paint a mural on the outside wall of their Geffen building in downtown Los Angeles.

election—almost 78 percent of its citizens voted, whereas only 51 percent of the eligible voters from Hawaii and 50 percent from Utah turned out. What explains this difference? Turnout may be affected by factors ranging from the number of other races on the ballot to the weather. Senior citizens are much more likely to vote than young adults—compare a 72 percent turnout for those over age fifty-five with a 47 percent turnout among eighteen- to twenty-four-year-olds. But the top reason people give for not voting, according to surveys, is that they are simply too busy (Holder 2006).

In some instances, however, people do not vote because they are **disenfranchised**—barred from voting. All states except Maine and Vermont disenfranchise convicted felons while they are incarcerated. Thirty-five states disenfranchise felons on parole, thirty-one do so for felons on probation, and seven others permanently disenfranchise them (Weedon 2004). Human rights groups have long protested this policy, arguing that it is not a legitimate function of the penal system. In addition, individuals may be mistakenly identified as

> **disenfranchised** stripped of voting rights, either temporarily or permanently

Blu's mural on the Geffen Building.

Building and a nearby Japanese American war memorial (Vankin 2010).

Is it unpatriotic to criticize your government or to call for change in times of national crisis? Those who do so argue that such criticism is the most patriotic act of all: that uncritical acceptance of government is not the same as patriotism and that citizens should make every effort to correct its flaws. Those on the opposite side may say, "My country, right or wrong" and believe that the decisions of our elected leaders, once made, are beyond criticism. Regardless of your views, keep in mind that those who criticize government policies are doing exactly what our democratic system calls for and protects. Dissent and its tolerance are crucial elements of an open society, and you have a constitutionally protected right to oppose, criticize, and protest. And to boycott The Dixie Chicks, organize a bicycle flash mob, stage a camp out, and to make or destroy offensive art work (if it belongs to you).

Before the painting could be viewed by the public, MOCA's director ordered it to be whitewashed. The museum had been unaware that Blu's mural would feature powerful anti-war symbolism in the form of coffins draped in dollar bills. While some, including the artist, called MOCA's action censorship, others were equally upset about the insensitivity of displaying the art so close to the Veteran's Administration

former felons and improperly stricken from the rolls, which occurred in Florida in the 2000 presidential election (Hull 2002; Uggen and Manza 2002). Consequently, many eligible voters were turned away from the polls.

Another obstacle to potential voters lies with registration, which must be done well in advance of an election. In the United States, even individuals with the legal right to vote cannot do so unless they are registered. Recent legislation, such as the 2000 Motor-Voter Act, allows voters to register when renewing a driver's license and has made registration easier. Another problem for many working Americans is

that elections are held on a Tuesday rather than a weekend or a national holiday (something done in other democratic countries).

Even when voters do appear at the polls, there may be other troubles. During the 2000 presidential election, irregularities in ballots and vote counts in Florida delayed the state's ability to declare a winner for several weeks. In some of Florida's poor and minority districts, faulty voting equipment, poorly trained poll workers, and scarce resources kept almost 200,000 votes from being counted—votes that were likely predominantly Democratic. The National Association

Power Elites Many of the most powerful men in the United States spend two weeks of every summer in a campground north of San Francisco called Bohemian Grove. Founded as a place for the nations' leaders to gather and escape from outside concerns like business, politics, and power, the men's club's members include every Republican president since 1923, many CEOs, and other prominent businessmen. In this photo, Ronald Reagan and Richard Nixon sit on either side of Harvey Hancock (standing).

for the Advancement of Colored People (NAACP) brought a voting discrimination suit against the state of Florida that was settled with a donation to the organization's efforts toward voter education and mobilization. Much media attention has focused on the invisible disenfranchisement of poor and minority voters, and some states have enacted more progressive laws to deal with these problems by providing greater access to the disabled, making absentee balloting easier, or keeping the polls open longer. This election controversy is an example of how structural issues (unequal state voting resources) can affect individual experience (the ability to make one's vote count) and how those individual experiences in turn affect the larger society (electing Bush rather than Gore).

Who Rules America?

Ideally, in a democracy, elected officials represent the interests of the people in doing the business of government. But how much do we really know about what legislators do or how government business is conducted? What about the interests of other groups besides "the people"? To what extent do other groups influence how government is run? Who has the most power in directing the course of the nation? The president and Congress? Judges? Big business and the military? What happens behind the scenes? Who really rules America?

pluralist model a system of political power in which a wide variety of individuals and groups have equal access to resources and the mechanisms of power

power elite a relatively small group of people in the top ranks of economic, political, and military institutions who make many of the important decisions in American society

PLURALISM Sociologists have devised two answers to the question of who rules America—the *pluralist* theory of power and the idea of a *power elite*. According to the **pluralist model**, power is held by a variety of organizations and institutions (such as corporations, political parties, professional organizations, and ethnic and religious groups), each with its own resources and interests. Each organization is assumed to have equal access to the power structure, and a system of checks and balances in the form of laws, policies, and the courts keeps any one group from having too much power over the others (Dahl 1961). Conflict theorists, however, argue that power is held by a small but extremely influential group of individuals who form an elite social class.

THE POWER ELITE C. Wright Mills (1956/1970) was one of the first to propose a theory of the **power elite**, a relatively small number of influential individuals who occupy the top positions within the major economic, political, and military institutions of the country. This insular and self-perpetuating group controls much of the key decision-making processes in the United States. Members of the power elite have the full power and weight of their respective institutions at their disposal. Their close association allows them to collaborate in ways that best serve their particular interests, which may not coincide with those of the people. Thus, their actions have tremendous implications for the rest of the population. For instance, military leaders may persuade the president to declare war, senators may pass legislation that cuts billions of dollars from social welfare programs, and corporate executives may post record gains for stockholders or downsize companies and lay off thousands of workers.

G. William Domhoff has studied the power elite extensively, looking at how the economic, political, and military institutions overlap and form a network of influence (1983, 1987, 1990, 2002). The relationships among the individuals heading these different institutions is fascinating. The power elite not only know each other personally and professionally, but they also recognize their status as part of the ultimate "members only" club. Many of them were born into powerful families who still control huge U.S. corporations. Many of the power elite attended the same prep schools and Ivy League colleges. They may live in the same neighborhoods or belong to the same country clubs. They may go to the same churches or give to the same charities. More important, they often serve on each other's boards of directors and do business directly with other members.

Drawing on the same theoretical background, Thomas Dye also studied power elites in his book *Who's Running America? The Bush Restoration*. Dye systematically investigated the actual formal positions in "major corporate, governmental, legal, educational, civic, and cultural institutions in the nation" (2002, p. 8). In so doing, he identified only 5,778 individuals in elite positions, meaning that fewer than 0.0026 percent of the entire U.S. population are among the power elite. These individuals also tend to be white males, although a few powerful women and ethnic or racial minorities also hold elite positions.

What are the implications of this class dominance theory of power? For one, it debunks the original American rags-to-riches mythology that says anyone who works hard can get to the top. If power is concentrated in such a small fraction of a percentage of the population, chances are that the average person will never wield any real power, regardless of his or her work ethic or life choices. Furthermore, the United States continues to be controlled by white, upper-class men. Finally, those who have the power to create social change by economic, political, or military reforms may choose to do so only when it is to their own advantage. So who runs America after all?

SPECIAL INTEREST GROUPS The American political system is organized so that individuals, groups, and organizations can contribute to candidates' campaigns. **Special interest groups** (sometimes called pressure groups) play an important role in the political process. These are organizations formed expressly to raise and spend money in order to influence elected officials and public opinion. Special interest groups can include corporate organizations, lobbies, political action committees (PACs), and, more recently, 527 committees. Despite strict regulations and recent reforms on campaign finance spending, these groups' contributions

to candidates can reach into the hundreds of millions of dollars.

The average citizen may have little idea of the influence of wealthy donor organizations in the political process. There is almost always a positive correlation between a candidate's campaign spending and his success: money wins elections. During the 2008 election, for instance, in 93 percent of House of Representatives races and 94 percent of Senate races, the candidate who spent the most money won. And in the presidential race, Barack Obama, the victor, raised more than $639 million to John McCain's $360 million (Center for Responsive Politics 2008a, 2008b; Figure 10.2). As in the presidential race, incumbents (those already occupying the electoral seat) are usually in the best position to raise money because of their high-profile position, and incumbency, therefore, is the most important advantage a candidate can have because it tends to lead to fund-raising success and victory at the polls.

Political action committees (PACs) are organizations designed to raise money to support the interests of a select group or organization. For instance, BAMPAC, or Black America Political Action Committee, represents the special interests of African Americans, while AAPAC, the Arab American PAC, lobbies for political interests of Arab Americans. NOW PAC, the National Organization for Women PAC, advocates feminist issues. The National Football League is represented by the "Gridiron PAC," and Major League Baseball has its own PAC as well. Even the interests of extraterrestrials are represented through X-PPAC, the Extraterrestrial Phenomena PAC. By 2010, there were more than 4,618 registered PACs in the United States (Federal Election Commission 2010). PACs direct their efforts to local, state, and/or national governmental levels. They might focus on individuals, parties, or branches of government, such as the Federal Drug Administration. They might endorse candidates most likely to win or those who would best represent their specific interests (Sorauf 1988; Clawson, Neustadtl, and Scott 1992).

Political action committees have emerged as a primary source of campaign contributions, rivaling political parties and extremely wealthy individual donors. PAC spending has increased dramatically in the past few decades, with 2009 reaching peak sums: PACs raised approximately $555 million, spent $465 million on ads and mailings, and contributed $175 million to federal candidates (Federal Election Commission 2010). Figure 10.1 shows the top 20 PAC donors to federal candidates in the 2009–2010 election

special interest groups organizations that raise and spend money to influence elected officials and/or public opinion

political action committee (PAC) an organization that raises money to support the interests of a select group or organization

cycle. Note the range of interests represented, from unions to corporate groups. Perhaps not surprisingly, most unions tend to fund Democrats, while most corporate groups support Republicans.

Another type of special interest group, **527 committees**, also became particularly important in the 2004 presidential election. Their name comes from section 527 of the tax code, which was originally designed to help political parties avoid taxation. However, it is now being used by supporters of politicians and special interests to get around campaign finance laws, especially limits on individual contributions and the spending caps imposed on political candidates. Although not officially or formally connected to a candidate, 527s do all the same things that any campaign does: conduct polls and surveys, buy advertisements, and try to influence voters. Examples of high-profile 527s from the 2004 election were the Swift Boat Veterans for Truth and MoveOn.org, unofficially affiliated with the Republican and Democratic parties, respectively.

These 527 committees became much more important after passage of the bipartisan Campaign Reform Act of 2002, more commonly known as the McCain-Feingold Act. There have long been limits on how much money individuals may donate to a particular candidate, but before McCain-Feingold was passed, individuals and interest groups could funnel much larger amounts of "soft money" directly to a political party, essentially a sneaky way to give more. The McCain-Feingold Act attempted to eliminate this practice. Under the new law, hard money contribution limits were raised to $2,000 per person and soft money contribution limits were set at $25,000. However, there are still no limits on the contributions donors can make to 527 committees. Consequently, more money than ever is being spent on political campaigns. In particular, 527s spent close to $600 million on the 2004 election. Although 527s remained important to political fund-raising, the amount of money they raised in the 2008 and 2010 elections declined to just $517 million and $527 million, respectively (Center for Responsive Politics 2010b).

Scholars, activists, and politicians often disagree about the extent of special interest influence on the decision-making processes of elected officials (Magleby 2000; Green 2004). Those who support PACs claim that more minority candidates are elected to office with their funding and that PACs ensure the representation of a diversity of interests (Berry 1993). Opponents argue that PACs are responsible for increased overall campaign spending and that they can thus exert influence over legislation, usually representing corporate interests to the exclusion of public interests (*Common Cause* 1996). They also argue that PACs increase the odds that incumbents will be reelected. Though it has been difficult to make definitive conclusions about the relationships between special interest groups and legislators, the staggering amounts of money these groups generate cannot be ignored. As sociologists, we seek to uncover the mechanisms of influence in our political system. Monitoring the actions of top donors, PACs, 527s, and other special interest groups brings insight into how our political system works.

The Media and the Political Process

THE MEDIA AS THE FOURTH ESTATE In addition to the executive, legislative, and judicial branches of government, the media play a key role in the political process. This has been true since the founding of the country and has taken on even more significant proportions in the Information Age. Often referred to as the **Fourth Estate** of government, the media render checks and balances on power much like the three government branches. Although the media can also serve to entertain, they were originally intended to inform and educate the populace and to serve as a watchdog on government. In fact, the framers of the U.S. Constitution probably envisioned the watchdog role as the media's primary function. After all, they believed that a free press was essential to the health of the new democracy. Thus, the First Amendment guarantees freedom of expression and freedom of the press (along with other rights).

Still, it's hard to imagine that our founding fathers could have envisioned what "the press" would become. To them, it literally meant printing presses. There were no broadcast media or digital media back then—no mass media as we know them. So, contemporary lawmakers have had to interpret the Constitution in light of modern concerns and developments. They must try to balance the rights of a free press while protecting the country from abuses of power by the media or by the individuals who own the media. And we must all consider the media's tremendous potential to sway and manipulate our thoughts and feelings and to impact the political process.

The media have always played a role in American politics, informing the public about the important issues of the day. But their role has increased dramatically during the past fifty years, coinciding with the spread of television in the 1950s and '60s and the internet in the 1990s and 2000s. Many of the social movements and landmark political events of the past several decades have unfolded before us on the TV or computer screen. It's unlikely that the Civil Rights

WHICH PARTY DID THE MONEY GO TO?

DEMOCRATIC

REPUBLICAN

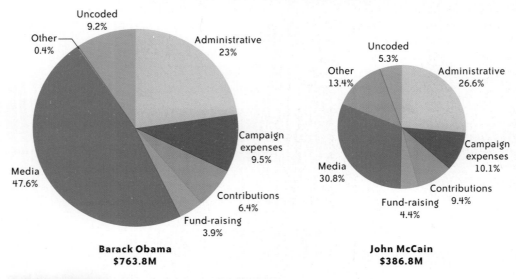

2008 PRESIDENTIAL CAMPAIGN: MAJOR EXPENSES

Barack Obama
$763.8M

- Uncoded 9.2%
- Other 0.4%
- Administrative 23%
- Campaign expenses 9.5%
- Contributions 6.4%
- Fund-raising 3.9%
- Media 47.6%

John McCain
$386.8M

- Uncoded 5.3%
- Other 13.4%
- Administrative 26.6%
- Campaign expenses 10.1%
- Contributions 9.4%
- Fund-raising 4.4%
- Media 30.8%

FIGURE 10.2 **Spending on the Campaign Trail**

Compare the proportion of each candidate's budget spent on media to the proportions devoted to all other campaign expenses. The size of each pie chart reflects the total expenditures of each candidate.

SOURCE: Center for Responsive Politics 2008b.

Movement, the Vietnam War, Watergate, the impeachment of President Clinton, the attacks of 9/11, or the tragedy of Hurricane Katrina would have emerged, developed, and resolved the way they did without the media to bring those issues and images into our living rooms. And for a little while, Americans talked about those issues. The media can make momentous events a part of the national dialogue and involve voters, citizens, and even global attention, influencing public opinion and promoting political activism and change.

MEDIA INFLUENCE ON POLITICS Some of the most significant changes in the political process have occurred in the realm of campaigns and elections. Political actors have adapted to a media-saturated society, and their strategies for success must include great media savvy (Skarzynska 2004). Any group or individual wishing to influence the voters must court the media, either through attempting to gain coverage of a particular issue or candidate or by directly buying space or time through advertisements. Fund-raising, gathering money to spend on media exposure, has become the first order of political business (Ulbrich 2004).

At one time, the voting public was informed of the issues through local political party representatives, town hall meetings, church groups, speeches made by politicians

opinion leaders high-profile individuals whose interpretation of events influences the public

or activists out on the stump, or exhaustive coverage in newspapers or on radio. Nowadays, media coverage of politics is more likely to emphasize human interest stories, personalities, high-profile spectacles, and planned events—and less likely to explain the background and implications of issues and policy debates (Kellner 2005). And not all news programs offer strictly objective reporting. We hear a lot about politics through pundits, those who offer political media commentary.

The public is also influenced by **opinion leaders**, high-profile people who interpret political information for us (Katz and Lazarsfeld 1955). Instead of getting information about the issues directly, we allow our views to be shaped by these opinion leaders whom we trust to tell us what to believe. Someone like Oprah Winfrey, for instance, can influence not only what we read but perhaps our political values as well. Even within your group of friends, there may be someone who, while not as famous as Oprah, is more politically savvy than the rest of the group and can communicate information to you in ways that may influence your opinions.

One of the first and most dramatic examples of the media's impact on politics occurred during the presidential campaign of 1960. The debates between John F. Kennedy, the Democrat, and Richard Nixon, the Republican, were the first to be broadcast live on television. Kennedy, the younger candidate, recognized the power of television and understood the importance of presenting a "telegenic" image. He allowed media

The Media's Role in the Political Process The power of television to bring political news from around the world has transformed the political process. For example, the Civil Rights Movement, the attacks on September 11, 2001, or the disaster surrounding Hurricane Katrina would not have had such widespread impact without mass media.

handlers to advise him on makeup, hairstyle, clothes, and the appropriate demeanor for the TV cameras. Conversely, Nixon refused to make any special preparation for the event. As a seasoned politician, he planned to rely on his command of the issues and his considerable debating skills.

Those who watched the debates on television saw dramatic differences between the two candidates. Kennedy looked fresh, young, and energetic; Nixon looked sweaty, old, and tired. Those who listened to the debates on the radio, as previous generations had for years, judged the two candidates not by looks or mannerisms but by the content of their speech. When polled after the debates, audiences who watched on TV thought that Kennedy won the debate; audiences who listened on radio thought Nixon was the winner. As history shows, Kennedy won the election and helped to change the relationship between the media and political campaigns. Although Kennedy's performance during the debate was only one factor in the election, it was significant. Other presidential candidates became so nervous about the effects of televised debates that none agreed to participate in them until 1976.

STYLE OVER SUBSTANCE? Another feature of modern politics is "sound bytes"—those short audio or visual snippets taken from press releases, press conferences, photo opportunities, or sometimes protests. In our postmodern era, the news has been condensed into just a few seconds' worth of information. What politicians say to the press is often scripted by "spin doctors" who manipulate rhetoric to give it a positive appearance designed to be catchy and compelling while not necessarily delivering much substance; many people form their views of candidates from these processed bits of information. It is no wonder that celebrity politicians are becoming more common and popular. After all, who knows better how to use the media, how to stand before the cameras and speak in interviews, than those who have been professionally trained as actors? President Ronald Reagan, formerly a Hollywood actor and commercial

Celebrity Politics How do politicians such as Sarah Palin carefully craft their image to make them more relatable to the public?

spokesperson, is perhaps the greatest example of this. He knew how to hit his marks and deliver his lines. He was even called "The Great Communicator" despite his inability to speak extemporaneously.

Any form of celebrity seems to make an individual more visible and popular. Others have followed in Reagan's path, from basketball star Bill Bradley, astronaut John Glenn, and comedian Al Franken, who became senators, to wrestler Jesse Ventura and actor Arnold Schwarzenegger, who both became governors, singer Sonny Bono, who became a congressman, and actor Clint Eastwood, who became a mayor.

Sarah Palin is another kind of celebrity politician. The Republican vice presidential candidate and former Alaska governor became a high-profile political figure and is an example of what some call "style over substance." Her image as a Washington outsider and folksy hockey mom was carefully promoted; she was coached and groomed for public appearances. Critics cited her lack of knowledge and experience, but it was her personal life, or at least the part of it that was portrayed in the media, that people were relating to. She has continued to be popular among supporters, even after losing the election. She is the author of two best-selling books, star of the reality-TV series *Sarah Palin's Alaska,* and a regular contributor to Fox News. Her daughter, Bristol Palin, has also been in the spotlight as a memoirist, a spokesperson about teen pregnancy, and a finalist on the show *Dancing with the Stars.* Sarah Palin remains a galvanizing and controversial figure.

Does the increased focus on a politician's style and personality, rather than on the politician's platform and policies, mean that we are getting less of real substance in what we consume? This Data Workshop may help you answer this question.

simulacrum an image or media representation that does not reflect reality in any meaningful way but is treated as real

DATA WORKSHOP

ANALYZING MASS MEDIA AND POPULAR CULTURE

Real and Fake News

Postmodern sociologist Jean Baudrillard claimed that "the image has come to replace the real" (1981/1994). By this, he meant that we have lost the ability to distinguish between what is real and what is fake, especially where media representations are involved, and that we also have come to accept the fake as sufficient—thereby no longer needing the real. He called this new artificially constructed "reality" the **simulacrum**, or a simulation that becomes as good as the original. Some would warn that we need to be more aware of how this plays out in the political arena, even beyond its role in style over substance.

A key example of Baudrillard's simulacrum can be found in the growing popularity of "fake news" programs. These include such comedy TV shows as *The Daily Show, The Colbert Report, Saturday Night Live*'s Weekend Update segment, and, new in 2011, the Onion News Network. Although these shows get their humor from parodying or satirizing real news, there are many instances where they generate and deliver real news, thus blurring the line between fake and real, and making it harder to tell the difference. Some young people may have little other regular exposure to news. In a recent survey, more than 40 percent of young people between eighteen and twenty-nine years of age cited Comedy Central's Jon Stewart and *The Daily Show* and Stephen Colbert of *The Colbert Report* as primary sources of political news (Pew Research Center for the People and the Press 2008a). Jon Stewart has only half-jokingly been called "the most trusted name in fake news." These shows are consistently ranked among the most popular of any kind for the age group (Gross 2010). Although the primary intent of these programs is to be funny and entertaining, it doesn't prevent them from also taking on serious subjects and disseminating messages with a viewpoint and the potential to influence their audiences. Fake news has become an important voice in humor and in American political culture.

Stewart and Colbert play news anchors who cover the latest current events, talk with reporters in the field, and conduct live in-studio interviews with newsmakers. Although Stewart and Colbert play the role of journalist, their performances blur the distinction between real and fake, and they often exhibit the same qualities and characteristics of "real" journalists. Guests on their shows have ranged from celebrities and journalists to newsmakers and politicians, including an appearance on *The Daily Show* by President Obama in October 2010 in which Jon Stewart asked him hard questions about such issues as health care reform and unemployment. Stewart and Colbert have each won numerous awards (Peabody, Emmy) and have both written best-selling books about American politics that have as much substantive social commentary as they do funny lines. They make guest appearances on real news shows on other networks, further blurring their roles as mere comedians.

Stewart and Colbert are also ideally placed to make meta criticism about the state of journalism and news in this postmodern era. In late October 2010, just a week preceding the midterm elections, Stewart and Colbert organized a huge rally on the Mall in Washington, a place usually reserved for serious political activity, to protest against the increasingly caustic tone and divisive partisanship that is dominant among the major news organizations. The event was billed as the "Rally to Restore Sanity and/or Fear" (to represent their two respective viewpoints) and featured the two hosts and a variety of speakers and musical acts, including Kid Rock, Sheryl Crow, and Jeff Tweedy. A crowd of more than 200,000 was estimated to be in attendance (Montopoli 2010).

This Data Workshop asks you to analyze the new phenomenon of fake news, its real popularity and possible influence on young people and politics. Choose a recent episode of either *The Daily Show* or *The Colbert Report* that you can watch and refer to. You will be gathering data from an existing source (recorded or online) and making a content analysis of the program. (See Chapter 2 for more on these research methods.) Consider the following questions after viewing, or add your own commentary.

- In what ways does the show resemble a traditional network news program? Examine the format of the show, the cast and correspondents, the regular program segments (news reporting, interviews), the structure of the stage set, the design of the graphics, and other aspects of the production.

- Make a list of the topics that are covered on the show. Compare the stories presented on the fake news show with stories presented in the real news during the same time period. How much of the news is completely fake, and how much is actually about real world events?

- A fake news show, even when it covers real issues, is not held to the same journalistic standards as traditional news outlets. How does an audience member know what to believe about the truth of any particular statement or story?

- Despite being satirical, fake news shows also make serious commentary about important issues in American life. What are some of the underlying messages of the humorous material on the show?

- Are you among the audience members who get political news from fake news shows? To what extent do you believe these shows might influence people's political ideas? Do you think that they serve to increase young people's awareness of issues, or are they a confounding distraction?

Real and Fake News *The Colbert Report* and *The Daily Show* blur the lines between real and fake news. At left, Stephen Colbert takes a more journalistic approach to interviewing Ray Odinero, Commanding General of U.S. forces in Iraq. At right, Colbert and Jon Stewart poke fun at the divisive partisanship dominating major news organization in their Rally to Restore Sanity and/or Fear.

TABLE 10.2 **Generational Divide in Sources of Campaign News**

REGULARLY LEARN SOMETHING FROM . . .	AGE			AGE GAP
	18–29	30–49	50+	
Local news	25%	39%	50%	−25
Sunday political TV	4	12	21	−17
Nightly network news	24	28	40	−16
Daily newspaper	25	26	38	−13
Morning TV shows	18	21	25	−7
Religious radio	5	8	12	−7
Cable news networks	35	36	41	−6
National Public Radio	13	19	19	−6
Newsmagazines	8	9	13	−5
Talk radio	12	16	17	−5
TV magazine programs	21	19	25	−4
C-SPAN	6	9	9	−3
Comedy TV shows	12	7	6	+6
Internet	42	26	15	+27

SOURCE: Pew Research Center for the People and the Press 2008b.

• If we consider what postmodernists say about the increasing power of the image or simulacrum in our everyday lives, how can we tell the difference between what is real and what is fake?

There are two options for completing this Data Workshop.

• *Option 1 (informal):* Choose a recent episode of *The Daily Show* or *The Colbert Report* and take notes while watching. Keep in mind the Data Workshop questions and prepare to discuss your thoughts with other students in small groups.

• *Option 2 (formal):* Choose a recent episode of *The Daily Show* or *The Colbert Report* and take notes while watching. Write a two- to three-page paper answering the Workshop questions and making your own reflections about the role of journalism—real and fake—in the American political process.

NEW MEDIA AND POLITICS As much as the mass media changed the political process in the twentieth century, it seems likely that the so-called new media will transform it all the more. Sometimes called "Web 2.0," the new media that have developed on the internet all move beyond simply providing information, and stress interaction, networking, and user-generated content.

The internet has now become a leading source of campaign news for young people, and social networking sites play an important part in the story. In the 2008 election, 42 percent of eighteen- to twenty-nine-year-olds said that they regularly learned about the campaign from the internet, the highest percentage for any news source (Table 10.2). In the 2010 midterm elections that percentage had increased to 65 percent of young adults. That represents a big jump since the 2004 election, when just 20 percent of young people said they got their campaign news from the internet (Pew Research Center for the People and the Press 2008b, 2011).

But the power and potential of the new media in the political process cuts both ways. It used to be that politicians only had to really watch what they said when reporters were around, and even then they could go off the record if they needed to. But today, all it takes is one person with a camera phone or her own blog to turn an off-hand comment into big news.

That is exactly what happened to Republican Senator George Allen of Virginia in 2006 during a very tight race against Democrat Jim Webb. The Webb campaign had begun sending a video "tracker" to cover Allen's public appearances, a practice that has become common. For many of these events, the videographer was Shekar Ramanuja Sidarth, a campaign volunteer whose parents had immigrated to the United States from India before he was born. Although he reported that the campaign staff had been quite courteous to him up to that point, on August 11 Allen was giving a speech at a state park when he noticed Sidarth filming him. Ironically, Allen began by saying he was going to "run this campaign on positive, constructive ideas" but then proceeded to point out Sidarth, referring to him as "macaca, or whatever his name is," and asking the crowd to welcome him to America.

When asked about the incident later, Sidarth said "I could feel his hostility. I just did my best to keep filming. As soon as I was finished I called the Webb campaign. They were shocked and they posted it on YouTube pretty quickly" (Baldwin 2007). The video swiftly went "viral," garnering hundreds of thousands of hits and showing up in blogs to underscore allegations of racism against Allen. The story, of course, was also picked up by the mainstream media. Allen tried to defend himself by claiming that "macaca" was just a made-up word, while his critics argued that it was a racist slur and that he had used it as such. Allen was defeated as much by his opponent Webb as by a shameful moment captured and disseminated through the new media.

Clearly, the media play an important role in informing and educating the voting public. Despite our "free press," however, we must also be aware of how the media can be used to achieve the purposes of powerful interest groups and individuals. The democratic system stands to suffer if only those with the most money or celebrity can influence public opinion by buying their way into the hearts and minds of Americans.

Politics: Linking Micro- and Macrosociology

Political institutions and their products (such as laws or bureaucratic systems) shape our everyday lives. A law such as Title VII of the Civil Rights Act of 1964 ensures your right to apply for and hold a job without being discriminated against because of race, gender, or religion. No matter who you are or what kind of work you do, you are protected by this law. And even if you have never experienced discrimination in the workplace, this law is probably one of the reasons why. Huge government bureaucracies like the Department of Education shape your everyday life as well. Even if you attend a private university, you had to fill out a FAFSA (Free Application for Federal Student Aid) in order to determine your eligibility for any type of financial aid—federal and state grants and loans and aid programs administered by your campus. All these student aid sources require the FAFSA, and your ability to attend the college of your choice may therefore depend on the decisions made by this government bureaucracy.

In addition to seeing how political institutions shape our everyday lives, it is important to remember that we have built these institutions ourselves, through our participation in the democratic process. When we vote, sign petitions, or participate in demonstrations, we bring our individual influence to bear on the larger social structure—even if, ultimately, the cause or candidate we support doesn't prevail. So remember, micro-macro connections are made every day as you participate with others in political processes and live in a culture shaped by its political institutions.

Democratic processes require a free press and an educated polity; to make decisions and cast votes, you must have the tools to gather information and comprehend the issues your vote will influence. This is only one of the many links between political institutions and educational institutions in our society. As we move into the segment of this chapter that deals with education, try to think of all the ways that politics and education are connected—and remember to look for micro-macro connections as you learn about educational institutions as well.

What Is Education?

Most modern political systems recognize the importance of universal education. The framers of the U.S. Constitution realized that an informed public was essential to the survival of democracy. Education, therefore, was seen as critical to the founding of the new republic. In the United States, public education has traditionally been under state and local control, although the federal government began playing a larger role in the latter half of the twentieth century. However, private schools and religious schools are also involved in education. About 10 percent of K–12 students attend private schools (either religious or secular); 88 percent attend public schools, and 2 percent are homeschooled (U.S. Department of Education 2009).

Education is the central means by which a society transmits its knowledge, values, and expectations to its members. The general goal of education is to give students the necessary understanding for effective social functioning. Education often includes the transmission of principles and values, the regulation of personal character, and discipline of the mind. It can provide information and convey knowledge to individuals. Education can be either formal or informal and can occur in a variety of settings, although we commonly think of it as tied to school systems.

> **education** the process by which a society transmits its knowledge, values, and expectations to its members so they can function effectively

A Brief History of Modern Education

Formal, institutionalized, secular education in Western civilization began in ancient Greece around the eighth century B.C.E., when students studied philosophy, mathematics, music, and gymnastics. Higher education was carried out by philosophers before the rise of schools as an institution. In the Middle Ages, the church was the main educator, with schools in monasteries and cathedrals, and until about 1200, the schools focused mainly on training students to be priests. During the thirteenth century, lay education emerged. It consisted of apprentice training for a small group of the common people or education in chivalry for the more privileged. During the Middle Ages, universities offered courses in three subjects—law, theology, and medicine—and these courses were available only to the most privileged members of the society: royals, aristocrats, and those from families with ties to the monarchy and the church.

While systems of education have evolved a great deal since the Middle Ages, the roots of what we would recognize as modern mass education can be traced back to the idealism of the European Enlightenment of the eighteenth and nineteenth centuries. During this period, the value of education greatly increased. The leading thinkers of the day, such as Voltaire, Locke, and Franklin, emphasized knowledge—reason, logic, and science—over religious tradition. They were convinced that the well-being and future of modern society depended upon enlightened self-knowledge, which could be achieved only through learning.

Education in the United States grew rapidly during this same period. The founders' belief that the government has the responsibility to provide basic education to all its citizens—and that fulfilling this obligation is beneficial for both society and the individual—helped to create the U.S. public education system. Schooling came to be seen as a necessity rather than a luxury and became legally mandatory for all children ages sixteen and younger; Massachusetts was the first state to enact such a law in 1852. As larger proportions of the population began attending schools, curricula became more varied and included both academic and vocational education to prepare students for a diversifying set of future occupations (not just farming or housewifery). Elementary, junior high, and high schools had spread to every state and territory in the nation, including Alaska, by 1929, and opportunities for higher education also expanded, especially in the land-grant colleges of the western United States.

Higher education is now available to everyone in the United States. Before 1900, fewer than 2 percent of Americans finished high school, and even fewer went on to college. The current high school graduation rate has been hovering around 75 percent nationwide, up from 72 percent in 2001 but lower than the record high of 77 percent in 1969 (Dillon 2010, Khadaroo 2010). If you count adults up to twenty-five years of age, then 84.6 percent of Americans hold a high school degree or equivalency (U.S. Census Bureau 2009b). There are variations according to state and school district (Nevada had the lowest high school graduation rate of 51.3 percent, and Wisconsin had the highest, at 89.6 percent). Different race and ethnic groups have varying rates (Blacks with

The Rise of Mass Education Beginning in the nineteenth century, schooling began to be considered a necessity for preparing children to enter modern industrial occupations.

61.5 percent, Hispanics 63.5, American Indians 64.5, Whites 81, and Asian/Pacific Islanders at 91.4 percent). Another 27.5 percent of Americans hold a bachelor's or higher college degree (Rampell 2010).

Education and the Reproduction of Society

Schooling serves a number of important functions in our society. The transmission of knowledge is a clear function of education, but in addition, we learn to follow society's rules and to respect authority, and we are socialized to develop other qualities that will eventually make us efficient and obedient workers. In school, we also learn our places in the larger society—practices such as **tracking**, in which students are identified as gifted or placed into remedial education, teach us about success and achievement and our chances for both. When placed in a lower ability or remedial track, for instance, students lose access to courses such as calculus and advanced placement classes (Useem 1990), which effectively locks them out of certain colleges, certain majors, and even certain future careers, all by the time they're 16.

EDUCATION AND INEQUALITY While we firmly believe, as a society, that education is the key to achievement and success, it is also true that educational institutions can replicate systems of inequality. Educational achievements do improve our life chances—U.S. Census data consistently indicate that those with higher educational attainment also have higher median incomes. In 2008, the average earnings for someone with an advanced degree totaled $83,144, compared with $58,613 for those with a bachelor's degree, or $31,283 for those with only a high school diploma. Women with the same educational achievement, however, made considerably less than their male counterparts (U.S. Census Bureau 2009b). It is also worth noting, however, some of the complexity of gender inequality in higher education, as we find that among young adults ages twenty-five to twenty-nine there is a growing gap between the percent of women (35 percent) to men (27 percent) with a bachelor's degree or more (U.S. Census Bureau 2009b). Thus, the data indicate that the benefit of a higher education does not operate in equal measure for all Americans. Stratification within schools often mirrors stratification systems in the larger society, wherein women and girls, minority group students, poor or working-class students, or students with disabilities are discriminated against both by individuals and institutional systems (Oakes 1985; Orfield 2001). So, education benefits everyone, but it does not benefit everyone equally, and inequality in educational benefits mirrors inequality in the larger society.

How do these patterns manifest themselves? What do these educational inequalities look and feel like for students in the classroom? Female students may notice, for instance, that their teachers pay more attention to male students, and they may learn to think that boys are smarter than girls. Caucasian or Asian students may notice that there are fewer African American and Latino students in the gifted classroom than in the remedial classroom, and they may learn to think that whites and Asians are smarter than blacks and Latinos. Children without disabilities may see disabled kids left out of activities or sent to the special education center and learn to think that these students are less worthy than nondisabled kids. These micro-inequities are common in American classrooms. They are experienced by individuals but are the result of structural forces external to those individuals—in other words, micro-inequities result from macro-level inequalities in the larger educational and social systems. And these micro-inequities teach us as much as our more explicit lessons in math, literature, or history. Acquiring a sociological perspective on educational institutions and processes will help us "unlearn" these lessons and understand that educational attainment is often as much about social stratification as it is about individual ability.

THE HIDDEN CURRICULUM Sociologists have long been interested in the **hidden curriculum**, the lessons that students learn indirectly but that are an implicit part of their socialization in the school environment (Jackson 1968). Many sociologists have analyzed the hidden curriculum to explain the nonacademic roles filled by mass education.

One such role is the training of future workers, which was examined by Bowles and Gintis (1977) in their study *Schooling in Capitalist America*. They argue that schools train a labor force with the appropriate skills, personalities, and attitudes for a corporate economy. Although the official curriculum is supposed to promote personal improvement and social mobility, the hidden curriculum of "rules, routines, and regulations" actually produces a submissive and obedient workforce that is prepared to take orders and perform repetitive tasks. According to this analysis, schools look a lot like factories. Students have no control over their curriculum, must obey instructions, and gain little intrinsic satisfaction from their schoolwork. Because students learn these norms and values in school, they are willing to accept similar conditions when they become workers.

tracking the placement of students in educational "tracks," or programs of study (e.g., college prep, remedial), that determine the types of classes students take

hidden curriculum values or behaviors that students learn indirectly over the course of their schooling because of the structure of the educational system and the teaching methods used

A similar analysis can explain how the hidden curriculum reinforces and reproduces conditions of social inequality by presenting and reinforcing an image of what is considered "normal," "right," or "good." While the official curriculum has come a long way toward recognizing the racial, ethnic, and gender diversity of the nation, there are still major gaps and exclusions (FitzGerald 1980, Thornton 2003). Schools cannot always rectify these oversights because the hidden curriculum can work through much more subtle mechanisms as well. How the curriculum is presented and the way the school is organized can be powerful messengers of the hidden curriculum. For instance, even schools that attempt to implement multicultural education may undermine their own efforts if the staff and administration do not mirror the lessons they teach. If teachers and administrators are mostly white, mostly heterosexual, or mostly male (or mostly female, as is the case in lower grades), they may belie the very lessons they try to teach—what students hear and what they see just don't add up. When schools attempt to alter only what is taught and not the way it is taught, they may change the curriculum but they won't affect what students are learning (Falconer and Byrnes 2003; Christakis 1995).

Classic Studies of Education

Sociologists and other researchers have studied education from a variety of perspectives. In this section, we review three classic studies of education, each offering a different approach and distinctive insights into its significance, both as a social institution and in the lives of individuals.

A SYMBOLIC INTERACTIONIST STUDY The first study looks at education from the symbolic-interactionist perspec-tive, which maintains that the social world is constructed through the interactions of individuals. Robert Rosenthal, a Harvard psychologist, and Leonore Jacobson, an elementary school principal, worked together on *Pygmalion in the Classroom: Teacher Expectation and Pupils' Intellectual Development* (1968). The researchers began the experiment by administering a basic IQ test to students in the first through sixth grades, although they told teachers the test was designed to predict which students would "bloom" academically in the next year. They then randomly selected an experimental group of students and falsely told their teachers that these students were predicted to develop rapidly in the coming school year. At the end of the year, the researchers administered the same IQ test and found that students in the experimental group had increased their IQ scores by a significantly greater margin than their peers in the control group. They concluded that the teachers' attitudes about their students unintentionally influenced their academic performance. In other words, when teachers expected students to succeed, the students indeed tended to improve (and it was assumed that the opposite would be true as well).

The results of *Pygmalion in the Classroom* have been critiqued by other researchers, on both theoretical and methodological grounds, especially because the researchers used standardized IQ tests and small subject samples (Baker and Crist 1971). Nonetheless, this study and others support the proposition that teacher expectations affect students' behavior and achievement in measurable ways. Some studies indicate that student labeling is often arbitrary and biased, with the result that teachers—whether consciously or unconsciously—may be reinforcing existing class, ethnic, ability, and gender inequalities (Fairbanks 1992; Sadker and Sadker 1995). This also means that changes in classroom interac-

Hidden Curriculum Bowles and Gintis argue that schools train students to be ideal workers by promoting a curriculum of "rules, routines, and regulations." These honor students at Philadelphia High School for Girls (left) and soldiers at the U.S. Central Command's "Deployable Headquarters" (right) apply their training.

tion could lead to an improvement in academic performance among students from underprivileged backgrounds.

A CONFLICT STUDY The next study, which also looks at inequalities in schools, is consistent with a conflict perspective, which sees society as a system characterized by inequality and competition. Former teacher Jonathan Kozol wrote *Savage Inequalities* (1991), which describes his ethnographic study of public schools in Chicago and its suburbs. Kozol contends that because schools are funded by local property taxes, children in poor neighborhoods are trapped in poor schools, which reinforces inequality. He documents the significant differences among America's schools: "the highest spending districts have twice as many art, music, and foreign language teachers . . . 75 percent more physical education teachers . . . 50 percent more nurses, school librarians, guidance counselors, and psychologists . . . and 60 percent more personnel in school administration than the low-spending districts" (Kozol 1991, p. 167).

When Kozol interviewed the parents and students in wealthy school districts, he discovered that many of them believe educational inequalities are a thing of the past, "something dating maybe back to slavery or maybe to the era of official segregation" but not to anything "recent or contemporary or ongoing" (Kozol 1991, p. 179). In stark contrast to this view, Kozol describes underfunded schools he visited—the hundreds of classrooms without teachers in Chicago, the thousands of children without classrooms in schools throughout New Jersey. His overall impression was that these urban schools were, by and large, extraordinarily unhappy places. How, he asks, could the children in these schools have an equal chance at success? A structural functionalist might respond that schools are not intended to provide equal chances.

A STRUCTURAL FUNCTIONAL STUDY According to the structural functionalist perspective, educational inequality is merely preparation for occupational inequalities later in life. (Remember, functionalists believe that every social phenomenon has a role to play in keeping society at equilibrium.) In the third study, *The Credential Society*, sociologist Randall Collins (1979) argues that class inequalities are reproduced in educational settings and that there is very little schools can do to increase learning. Although many people assume that better teachers, better facilities, and better funding could increase test scores, he points out that when class background factors are held constant, none of these other factors seem to have any effect. Collins believes that reproducing the existing class structure is the true function of education. Schools, for example, provide the credentials to assure that the children of the middle class will continue to receive

middle-class jobs. To protect their own job security, members of lucrative occupations, such as accountants, lawyers, and financial analysts, have set up a complicated credential system (education) to keep the number of job applicants down and to ensure that there is a large population forced to work at unpleasant jobs for low wages. Collins makes the radical recommendation that we consider "abolishing compulsory school requirements and making formal credential requirements for employment illegal" (Collins 1979, p. 198). This would make it illegal for employers to ask how much education a job applicant has, much as it is currently illegal to ask about race or gender.

The Crisis in Education

During the past several decades, many educators, parents, and legislators have come to believe that America's educational system is in crisis, that public schools are failing to provide adequate training for students. Critics list a variety of problems, including low rates of literacy and poor standardized test scores, lack of sufficient funding and crumbling infrastructure, low pay for teachers, overcrowded classrooms, and high rates of crime on campus.

A number of studies point to the problems. In 1983, the National Commission on Excellence in Education released a report on the state of American public schools. *A Nation At Risk* concluded, in apocalyptic terms, that the American educational system was in a crisis so serious that "if an unfriendly foreign power" had created it, "we might well have viewed it as an act of war." Largely on the basis of declining standardized test scores, the report argued that the United States was "committing an act of unthinking, unilateral educational disarmament." Since then, the conclusions of the commission have been affirmed. A 1999 study showed that while 40 percent of white students passed a history exam required for public high school graduation in Virginia, only 23 percent of Hispanic students and 13 percent of black students scored passing grades (Fairfax County Public Schools 1999). This type of "achievement gap" was visible in other states' educational data as well. And in 1998, an international survey showed U.S. twelfth graders ranked sixteenth and seventeenth in the world in science and math, respectively (U.S. Department of Education 1998). Data like these seemed to point to a decline in American educational standards and competitiveness, and politicians began to respond.

NO CHILD LEFT BEHIND To address some of these crises, Congress passed the "No Child Left Behind" (NCLB) act in 2002. According to this policy, each state is responsible for testing every student in its public education system at specific grade intervals to determine levels of success.

Low-performing schools are identified with "school report cards" and are required to improve both student and teacher performance. Parents also have the option of removing their children from consistently low-performing schools and placing them in other schools within the district.

In theory, No Child Left Behind seems to promote equal education. It holds schools and teachers accountable for student performance, and it gives parents some autonomy in school choice. On the surface, these aims are ideal, but is NCLB really achieving equality of education? Critics believe it is not.

One concern is that NCLB relies on standardized test scores (in reading comprehension, writing, and math) to determine educational success. Standardized tests rest on the assumption that one level of aptitude is appropriate for all students, regardless of race, nationality, or intellectual capabilities and desires. Researchers have long noted that standardized test scores are ambiguous predictors of success for women and students of color (Epps 2001). Girls tend to get better grades than boys, but they score lower on standardized tests like the SAT and ACT. Thus, if standardized tests are increasingly used to evaluate students' progress, designate grades, and award diplomas and/or scholarship funds, women and students of color may lose out. An alternate approach for NCLB might be to use other measures, such as the schools' retention rates of minorities and/or low-income students, volunteerism and other social activism, or even depression levels of students. While most people agree that standardized testing of basic skills does have some validity as a measure of students' aptitude, such tests cannot evaluate the entire experience of a student in the public schools.

A related concern about NCLB is that the test scores are also being used to measure teacher and school performance. Teachers, now under pressure to ensure that their students perform satisfactorily on standardized tests, often are "teaching to the test." As a result, other learning experiences—music, art, sports, field trips, and so on—may be dropped from the curriculum. Schools that perform well will be rewarded with a variety of incentives, possibly including financial rewards. Schools that do not perform well will be sanctioned with withdrawal of funds because of departing students and possible school closure or "restructuring." Thus, some schools, like suburban schools with homogenous racial, ethnic, and socioeconomic populations, will continue to do well while others, such as inner-city schools with more diverse populations, will suffer.

For many of these reasons, in 2010 the Obama administration proposed dismantling the law and replacing it with a new blueprint for change

charter schools public schools run by private entities to give parents greater control over their children's education

that moves away from punishing schools that don't meet certain benchmarks and toward rewarding those schools that improve, particularly in the performance of poor and minority students (Associated Press 2010). The primary focus of NCLB had been on the attainment of grade-level proficiency on test score results while the new mandate proposes instead to focus on preparing students for either college or a career. Another feature would be a swifter and more aggressive response to the worst performing 5 percent of schools, which would include takeovers, firings, and possible closures. The new law would go by another name, as "No Child Left Behind" has become synonymous with the failings and frustrations of that law.

But will the proposed overhaul to education, whatever it is eventually called, present a more effective means of addressing the crisis in education? As sociologists, we must ask: what are the other options for fixing the American system of education? We look at some of the answers in the next section.

The Present and Future of Education

What will American education look like in the future? A number of educational trends are already in place and may play an important role in the years ahead: charter schools, early college high schools, homeschooling, school vouchers, community colleges, and distance learning.

CHARTER SCHOOLS **Charter schools** are public schools, but they are run by private entities, such as a parents' group or an educational corporation. Also, they operate with relative freedom from many of the bureaucratic regulations that apply to traditional public schools. Charter schools represent a compromise position between public and private schools and provide a way for parents to exercise control over their students' educational experiences without completely abandoning the public school system. By 2010, 41 states and the District of Columbia had established charter school programs and more than 5,400 charter schools were serving a total of more than 1.7 million students (Center for Education Reform 2010). State laws regarding charter schools governed sponsorship, number of schools, regulatory waivers, degree of fiscal or legal autonomy, and performance expectations.

The "charter" establishing such schools is a contract detailing the school's mission, program, goals, students served, methods of assessment, and ways to measure success. Charter schools are designed to support educational innovation; some have special emphases like arts or science; others offer special services like health clinics or community-based internships for students. A high school in

St. Louis called the Construction Careers Center instructs students in the skills needed to work in the building trades while also teaching the traditional high school curriculum. In Madison, Wisconsin, educators started Nuestro Mundo Community School, a Spanish immersion program. By fifth grade, all the students are equally fluent in Spanish and English. The Madison school district created the school to help close the gap between the test scores of Hispanic students and their non-Hispanic peers. Ideally, charter schools can make changes and implement decisions faster than ordinary public schools because of their freedom from district governance. They can monitor their successes (and failures) more closely and are more responsive to the needs of students, parents, and communities.

In reality, charter schools face many challenges. They are difficult and sometimes expensive to launch and run. Many struggle to raise funds and meet endless lists of state and local regulations. There are also questions about whether charter schools are any better than ordinary public schools. They have met with only mixed success. A report on charter school students in California found great variation in how well the schools and their students performed (RAND Education 2003). Although achievement varies by school and by subject matter, charter school students generally have comparable or slightly lower test scores than those in conventional schools. These schools did not necessarily serve more minority students. Nonetheless, charter schools continue to be popular and more will probably open in the coming years, looking to benefit from both the experience of earlier charter schools and the findings of social scientific research.

EARLY COLLEGE HIGH SCHOOLS Early college high schools are new institutions that blend high school and college into a coherent educational program in which students earn both a high school diploma and two years of college credit toward a bachelor's degree. In addition to local efforts to create these schools, the Bill & Melinda Gates Foundation, in partnership with the Carnegie Corporation of New York, the Ford Foundation, and the W. K. Kellogg Foundation, has contributed over $120 million to launch early college high schools. In 2010, more than 208 schools in twenty-four states were serving over 47,000 students; through continued efforts, some 250 schools are planned that would serve more than 100,000 students. Each early college high school is a collaborative endeavor between a public school district and an accredited higher education partner. In Phoenix, Arizona, high school students can join the Gateway High School program and simultaneously get a high school diploma and an associate's degree from Gateway Community College. Antioch University in Seattle, Washington, offers a similar

Homeschooling The Wilson family in Myrtle Point, Oregon, study together at the kitchen table as part of their homeschooling program.

program for Native American youth, who have the highest college dropout rate and the lowest graduation rate of any ethnic group in the United States. The goal for these programs is to develop new high schools that engage low-income and underrepresented students by offering them challenging academic work while simultaneously providing the necessary guidance and support structures. Early college high schools are small (with no more than 75–100 students per grade) and thus can provide the benefits of a close community, an intimate learning environment, and personalized academic attention.

For many students the path to postsecondary education is difficult. Large, impersonal middle and high school programs, limited financial resources, and the daunting processes of applying to and entering higher education may hinder academic achievement. By changing the structure of the high school and compressing the number of years required for an undergraduate degree, early college high schools are designed to reduce obstacles to student success. These schools are already having a significant impact on underserved youth, who are demonstrating high levels of attendance, improved promotion rates, and success in college-level courses.

HOMESCHOOLING Homeschooling or home-based education is the education of school-aged children under

> **early college high schools** institutions in which students earn a high school diploma and two years of credit toward a bachelor's degree

> **homeschooling** the education of children by their parents, at home

On the Job

Teach Like a Champion

A decade after the passage of No Child Left Behind, there is still widespread belief that the public school system in the United States continues to fail in its mission to educate generations of children. One of the problems of the law is that it didn't propose any new methods or techniques for improving schools beyond harsh sanctions for those that couldn't bring their scores up. At the same time, an increasing amount of evidence seemed to suggest that "excellence in teaching is the single most powerful influence" on student achievement (Hattie 2003). Even in poor schools with relatively overcrowded classrooms, students with excellent teachers learn more, test better, and achieve more academically.

Doug Lemov has held almost every position possible in a school, starting as a teacher, then working as dean of students and principal at a charter school he helped found, and finally working as a consultant for other schools. It was in this last capacity that he was confronted by a simple fact: he didn't know how to solve the most important and intractable problems facing schools. If the most important factor in a school's success is good teaching, the obvious answer is to hire better teachers. Unfortunately, none of the criteria schools use to hire teachers, like test scores, educational credentials, or teaching certificates, seem to help predict who will be a good teacher. Another solution would be to fire the bad teachers, but aside from the practical problems with this solution, it would just demand that schools hire even more new teachers. So Lemov took the last available option—figure out what the best teachers are doing right, and find ways to teach it to everyone else.

Unlike other educational reformers, Lemov is an advocate of standardized tests, but he sees them as a tool to evaluate the effectiveness of individual teachers rather than schools. This approach, sometimes called "value added" education reform, assumes that the change in a student's test scores from the beginning of the year to the end of it is one measure (but not the only measure) of how good a job their teacher has done, or how much "value" they have added to the student. In this way, Lemov is following a growing group of researchers who use the data generated by standardized testing to investigate the effectiveness of teachers and schools regardless of the powerful effects of such non-educational factors like poverty and family background.

Frustrated by the "dispiriting exercise in good people failing" that he saw in so many schools, Lemov decided to try and find out what the good teachers were doing differently (Green 2010). A self-described "data geek," he started with reams of information about student performance and began visiting the classrooms of the teachers who were getting above-average test scores out of schools in low-income neighborhoods (Green 2010). While Lemov is quick to emphasize that test scores are only one way to evaluate a teacher's effectiveness, those scores provided him with an effective map of high-performing teachers, whom he could then visit. Videotaping their classrooms helped him figure out how they taught and then later provided the raw materials for developing a book designed to demystify the teaching process and to teach other teachers. Lemov worried that too many people assume that great teachers are born, rather than

their parents' supervision outside a regular school campus. Many parents homeschool their children not only to control their academic education but also to limit their exposure to the socializing effects of peer culture in public schools. Some homeschooled children enroll in regular schools part time or share instruction with other families, but most of their education takes place at home. Many families homeschool their children for their entire K–12 years, but many others try it for only a short time.

Homeschooling in the United States has been growing steadily since the 1980s, with current growth rates of 5 percent to 12 percent a year. There were estimated to be more than 2 million homeschooled students in the United States in 2007–2008. This represents approximately 35 percent of the over 6 million privately schooled student population. Clearly, homeschooling is a significant phenomenon in education, but how is it working? One of the largest studies of homeschooling arrived at rather startling results. The academic achieve-

made. Since America's schools employ millions of teachers, this attitude amounts to giving up on the notion of improving education. Instead, Lemov looked at good teaching as a matter of deliberate technique, just like riding a bicycle—complicated at first, but easily learn-able if properly taught. His book, *Teach Like a Champion: The 49 Techniques That Put Students on the Path to College* (2010), was eagerly circulated among teachers as "Lemov's Taxonomy" long before it was published, for simple instructions like these:

- **The cold call**: "To make engaged participation the expectation, call on students regardless of whether they have raised their hands."

- **Strong voice**: Use words economically, don't talk over students who aren't listening, don't engage in conversation outside the topic, stand upright and still, and use silence. "Drop your voice, and make students strain to listen. Exude poise and calm."

- **Vegas**: "The Vegas is the sparkle, the moment during class when you might observe some production values: music, lights, rhythm, dancing."

- **Everybody writes**: "Set your students up for rigorous engagement by giving them the opportunity to reflect first in writing before discussing. As author Joan Didion says, 'I write to know what I think.'"

None of these, or the other forty-five techniques detailed and illustrated in his book, are original; Lemov simply collected them as a way to fill a void in the way teachers are

Teach Like a Champion Doug Lemov observes a teacher to evaluate her teaching strategy and effectiveness.

trained. As he points out, education departments spend a lot of time teaching theory, and even teaching workshops designed to be more practical tend to focus on "inspiring messages, such as 'have high expectations' and 'teach kids not content'" which leave new teachers "excited and in touch with all the reasons" they want "to be a teacher" (Tucker 2010). But when they go to actually run a classroom, slogans aren't much help, and what they need are simple, practical steps. Only time will tell how much value-added reforms can change teaching, but Doug Lemov is convinced that one way or another, by paying close attention, carefully gathering data, and trying to see the world from the student's point of view, teaching—and learning—can change for the better.

ment of homeschooled students, on average, was significantly above that of public school students (Ray 1997, 2008). In addition, homeschooled students did well even if their parents were not certified teachers and the state did not highly regulate homeschooling. One advantage of homeschooling seems to be the flexibility in customizing curriculum and pedagogy to the needs of each child. Yet, questions remain about the possible academic and social disadvantages to students removed from typical school environments.

SCHOOL VOUCHERS First proposed in the 1990s, **school vouchers** allow parents in neighborhoods where the public schools are inadequate to send their children to the private school of their choice. In other words, taxpayers receive a voucher for some of the money that a public school would have received to educate their child, and

school vouchers payments from the government to parents whose children attend failing public schools; the money helps parents pay private school tuition

they apply that money to private school tuition. Most school-voucher programs fund 75 percent to 90 percent of the cost of a private school, with parents making up the rest. Proponents of school vouchers—most notably Bush administration Secretary of Education Margaret Spellings (2006)—argue that they give parents more choice and control over their children's education and pressure public schools to improve or risk the loss of their voucher-eligible student body. Opponents—such as Congresswoman Eleanor Holmes Norton (2006)—argue that vouchers do not improve public education but do the opposite: they drain funds from vulnerable public schools and cause them to deteriorate further. Opponents also say that if parents use vouchers for parochial schools, public monies are funding religious education, thus threatening the separation of church and state. In the 2008–2009 school year, there were twenty-four voucher programs operating in fourteen states plus the District of Columbia and serving over 160,000 students. While the Supreme Court has ruled the voucher system to be constitutional and numerous experimental voucher programs are already in place, the privatization of public education remains controversial in any form.

COMMUNITY COLLEGES You know what a community college is—you may even attend one right now. A **community college** is a two-year school that provides general education classes for students who want to save money while preparing to transfer to a four-year university, right? While this definition of a community college is technically true, community colleges have become much more than just a springboard to a four-year degree. They provide vocational and technical training for people planning practical careers, retrain "downsized" workers seeking new career paths, offer enrichment classes for retirees, and currently provide opportunities of all sorts. In 1901, six students enrolled at the first "junior college" in Joliet, Illinois; just over 100 years later, there are 1,202 community colleges across the country (Merrow 2007). Community colleges account for almost half of all higher education enrollments, with over 6.8 million students taking degree, certificate, or transferable courses in 2007–2008. Another 5 million or more community college students take various noncredit courses, such as English as a Second Language or job force training. The contemporary community college typically offers more than just basic general education and college preparatory courses. Honors pro-

community college two-year institution that provides students with general education and facilitates transfer to a four-year university

online education any educational course or program in which the teacher and the student meet via the internet, rather than meeting physically in a classroom

grams, study abroad options, intercollegiate sports, music programs, on-campus residence halls, and internships may now be part of the two-year experience. Community colleges help students prepare for careers that give back to the community—the two "hottest" community college programs of study are law enforcement and nursing, with 80 percent of firefighters, police officers, and EMTs and more than half of all new nurses and health-care workers trained at community colleges (American Association of Community Colleges 2011). Community colleges also struggle with such issues as declining public funding sources and the changing needs of a growing, diverse student body. Despite these hurdles, though, community colleges continue to provide a wealth of opportunities.

DISTANCE LEARNING **Online education** is not really a new concept—"correspondence courses" have been available for hundreds of years and served as a way for people in remote locations (like farmers and their families) or people who were homebound or physically disabled to benefit from the same educational opportunities available to others. In previous years, distance learning courses relied on the postal service and more recently on audiotapes and videos to help students learn independently. With the advent of the internet and real-time electronic communication, distance learning was transformed forever. Universities and private businesses use these technologies to offer courses to anyone with an internet connection. Certificates and degrees of all kinds are within the reach of students who, because of time, geography, or other constraints, cannot come to campus.

The Rise of Online Colleges Suzanne Lee, who lives in New Jersey, takes an online class in economic crime investigation at New York's Syracuse University.

According to a frequently cited report by the Sloan Consortium (2010) on the state of online learning, in fall 2008 more than 4.6 million, or 25 percent of all college students, were taking at least one class online, a nearly 17 percent increase over the previous year. The growth rate in online enrollments far exceeds the 1.5 percent overall growth of the college student population. Furthermore, the growth rate is especially concentrated at two-year institutions, which account for more than one-half of all online enrollments for the past five years (Sloan Consortium 2010).

Indeed, some of you may be reading this or another textbook as part of an online course. While you may never be in the physical presence of your professor or fellow students, you can interact with them online, use electronic bulletin boards or chat rooms for class discussions, and get feedback on your work by e-mail. As with any application of technology to education, there may be both pros and cons. Like the old-fashioned correspondence courses, online technologies provide educational access for those who might otherwise not be able to pursue a degree. However, distance learning sometimes lacks the personal touch and dynamic interaction of standard classroom instruction. For this reason, students may feel that there is something important (if intangible) missing from their educational experience. Since you will probably experience both traditional and online learning in your college career, ultimately you'll be the judge.

Education: Linking Micro- and Macrosociology

As societies change, so do educational institutions, and so does the individual's experience of education. For example, you likely enroll in your courses online, but before the advent of the internet, you might have had to enroll by phone or even stand in line at the registrar's office and sign up for classes in person. This is one of the many ways that macro-level change (in this case, the development of internet technology) affects your everyday life through your participation in the social institution of education. What you learn about the world in school on an everyday basis—as well as how you learn it—is shaped by larger social forces, such as politics and religion.

Education is not the only social institution concerned with teaching members of society important information, values, and norms. Religion is another social institution from which we learn a great deal about being members of society. Even if we rebel against our religious upbringing or have no religious affiliation, our lives are touched in important ways by religion because it is a dominant social institution. As you read the following section, think about the intersection of the micro and the macro in the study of religion and about the intersection of religion with other social institutions, including politics and education.

What Is Religion?

No doubt we each have our own definition of religion based on personal experience. But a sociological definition must be broad enough to encompass all kinds of religious experiences. For sociologists, **religion** includes any institutionalized system of shared **beliefs** (propositions and ideas held on the basis of faith) and **rituals** (practices based on those beliefs) that identify a relationship between the **sacred** (holy, divine, or supernatural) and the **profane** (ordinary, mundane, or everyday). Those who study religion recognize that there are different types of religious groups: denominations (major subgroups of larger religions, such as Protestantism within Christianity or Shia within Islam), sects (smaller subgroups, such as the Amish or Mennonites), and cults (usually very small, intense, close-knit groups focused on individual leaders—like David Koresh and the Branch Davidians—or specific issues like the UFO cult Heaven's Gate). Sociologists do not evaluate the truth of any system of beliefs; they study the ways that religions shape and are shaped by cultural institutions and processes, as well as the ways that religions influence and are influenced by the behavior of individuals.

Functions and Dysfunctions of Religion

For members of any religion, beliefs and rituals serve a number of functions. First, religion shapes everyday behavior by providing morals, values, rules, and norms for its participants. From the Judeo-Christian commandment "Thou shall not kill" to the Buddhist commitment to reconcile strife to the Qur'anic requirement to eschew alcohol and impure foods, religious rules govern both the largest and smallest events and actions of followers' daily lives. Religious practices usually include some type of penance or rehabilitation for those who break the rules: Catholics can confess their sins to a priest and be assigned prayer or good works to redeem themselves; Muslims spend the month of Ramadan fasting during daylight hours

religion any institutionalized system of shared beliefs and rituals that identify a relationship between the sacred and the profane

belief a proposition or idea held on the basis of faith

ritual a practice based on religious beliefs

sacred the holy, divine, or supernatural

profane the ordinary, mundane, or everyday

monotheistic a term describing religions that worship a single divine figure

liberation theology a movement within the Catholic Church to understand Christianity from the perspective of the poor and oppressed, with a focus on fighting injustice

to purify their bodies and souls; Yom Kippur is the Jewish Day of Atonement and also involves fasting, as well as appeals for wrongs to be forgiven.

Another function of religion is to give meaning to our lives. Religious beliefs can help us understand just about everything we encounter because every religion has a system of beliefs that explains the fundamental questions like: How did we get here? What is our purpose in life? Why do bad things happen to good people? All religious traditions address these questions, helping their followers explain the inexplicable, making the terrible more tolerable, and assuring believers that there is a larger plan. Finally, religion provides the opportunity to come together with others—to share in group activity and identity, to form cohesive social organizations, and to be part of a congregation of like-minded others.

These are the (mostly unifying) functions of religion for individuals and for society, but there are also ways in which religion can promote inequality, conflict, and change. From a conflict perspective, the doctrines of the three major **monotheistic** religions—religions that worship one divine figure (Judaism, Christianity, and Islam)—are quite sexist. Orthodox Judaism mandates the separation of men and women in

worship and in everyday life; Catholicism and many Protestant sects prohibit women from becoming priests or pastors; traditional, observant Muslim women must keep their bodies completely covered at all times. There are very few nonsexist religions, and those with strongly nonsexist values and practices (such as Wicca) are usually marginalized. Some religions have antihomosexual or racist doctrines as well: some Protestant sects refuse to ordain gay clergy, and until 1978 the Church of Jesus Christ of Latter Day Saints (Mormons) believed that people with dark skin were cursed by God and forbade African Americans from marrying in the temple.

Religious organizations have also been agents of social justice and political change. For example, religion has been closely linked to movements for African American rights. The movement for the abolition of slavery was entwined with Christian reformers like the Methodists and Baptists. The Civil Rights Movement in the twentieth century began in southern Protestant churches and was led by a team of Christian ministers, including the Reverend Martin Luther King, Jr. In Africa and Latin America, **liberation theology** has been instrumental in fighting exploitation, oppression, and poverty—Archbishop Óscar Romero of El Salvador used this distinctive combination of Marxism and Christianity to argue against the country's repressive military dictatorship. Though Romero was assassinated while saying mass in 1980, his legacy lives on in human rights movements all over the world. The Polish labor movement Solidarność, led by Catholic shipyard workers in Gdansk and supported by

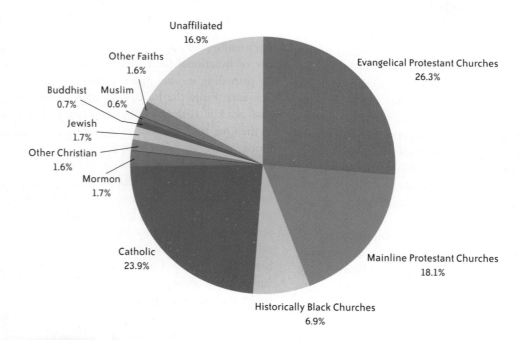

FIGURE 10.3 Religious Composition of the United States

SOURCE: Pew Forum on Religion and Public Life 2008.

Religion and Social Justice Óscar Romero, archbishop of El Salvador (left), and Lech Walesa (right, speaking into a bullhorn) of Poland both led movements against repressive political regimes.

the late Pope John Paul II, was the crucible for democratic change in the Eastern bloc in the 1980s. Communist regimes throughout Eastern Europe had restricted religious freedom and labor union organizing for decades—Solidarność helped break down both of those barriers.

From a conflict perspective, then, religion is complex: it can subjugate and oppress at the same time it can liberate. This may help explain Americans' seemingly contradictory approach to religion. While quasi-religious principles are at the core of many of our closely held national ideologies, many Americans also believe that religion should be kept separate from our collective political life.

Religion in America

How religious is the American public? That depends on the measures used (Hill and Wood 1999). Sociologists usually define **religiosity** as the consistent and regular practice of religious beliefs, and gauge religiosity in terms of frequency of attendance at worship services and the importance of religious beliefs to an individual (see the next Data Workshop for more detailed measures of religiosity). One study found that 56 percent of Americans say religion is very important to them and that on average, 39 percent of Americans say they go to religious services at least once a week (Pew Forum on Religion and Public Life 2008). These numbers are somewhat misleading, however, because there are big differences in religious affiliation and participation across demographic groups. Gender, age, race, geographic region, political party, and education are all variables that influence religiosity.

DATA WORKSHOP

ANALYZING EVERYDAY LIFE

Measures of Religiosity

From what the majority of Americans report in polls, we can conclude that they are significantly more religious than people of other industrialized nations. Some researchers suspect, however, that these results may be due to the discrepancy between what people say and what they actually do (Vedantam 2010).

The term "religiosity" refers to the extent of a person's commitment to a religion. Researchers have identified two broad categories of religiosity: extrinsic and intrinsic (Allport and Ross 1967). **Extrinsic religiosity** refers to a person's public display of commitment, such as attendance at religious services or activities at other related functions. **Intrinsic religiosity** refers to a person's inner religious life or personal relationship to the divine.

This Data Workshop asks you to examine the role of religion in everyday life by measuring religiosity in a sample of research participants. The data can be collected using

religiosity the regular practice of religious beliefs, often measured in terms of frequency of attendance at worship services and the importance of religious beliefs to an individual

extrinsic religiosity a person's public display of commitment to a religious faith

intrinsic religiosity a person's inner religious life or personal relationship to the divine

either interview or survey methods. (See Chapter 2 on these research methods.)

In each case, choose a population for the research, construct a good questionnaire or instrument, administer it to your sample respondents, and analyze the findings. In choosing a population, consider such variables as race and ethnicity, class, national background, gender, and/or age for your sample. Researchers have documented variations of religiosity across different social groups. There are many possibilities for comparing and contrasting within or across categories.

With an interview, decide whether the questions will be closed- or open-ended and how many questions you must have to gather sufficient data. This will help you determine how many people you will need to interview (for the formal option, we suggest at least three to five respondents). With a survey, the number of respondents will also depend on the length of the questionnaire (for the formal option, we suggest at least six to eight respondents). Remember that your questions will need to be structured according to the principles of survey research, by providing a set of possible answers for the respondents.

Questions about religious affiliation, membership, and attendance at services can tell you something about an individual's level of commitment, but there are many other ways you can measure religiosity, both extrinsic and intrinsic. You can create questions that measure people's concrete practice of religion and their abstract sense of what religion means to them. Regardless of whether you do an interview or survey, you can choose from the following list of questions (adapted from Lewis et al. 2001). You will need to modify the wording of these questions or add questions for either an interview guide or a survey questionnaire.

- Are you affiliated with any religion?
- Are you affiliated with any particular sect or denomination?
- Do you belong to a church, synagogue, temple, or other place of worship?
- How often do you attend religious services?
- Do you participate in other church-related activities?
- How often do you read or study sacred texts or scripture?
- How often do you pray or meditate or engage in some other religious practice?
- How important is your relationship with God [or another religious figure]?
- To what extent is your religious faith important to you?

- To what extent do you consider your religious faith to be an important part of who you are as a person?
- Do you look to your faith as a source of comfort?
- Do you look to your faith as a source of inspiration?
- Do you look to your faith as providing meaning, direction, or purpose in your life?
- Does your faith impact your relationships with other people?
- Does your faith impact your decisions in regard to family, friends, work, school, or other aspects of your life?
- How has your commitment to your religion changed over time?

After gathering data through interviews or surveys, describe and analyze your findings. See what kinds of patterns you can find—similarities, differences, comparisons, and contradictions. How do your findings confirm or refute any hypotheses you might have had before beginning the study? What do you think these data reveal about the role of religion in your subjects' lives? About the role of religion in society?

There are two options for completing this Data Workshop.

- *Option 1 (informal)*: Conduct interviews or administer surveys with a small sample of your population. Prepare written notes that you can refer to in class. Discuss your findings with other students in small-group discussions. Note the similarities and differences in your findings and those of your group members. Write a statement that identifies and incorporates the patterns found in the data gathered by the entire group.

- *Option 2 (formal)*: Conduct interviews or administer surveys to your sample following the suggested questions above. Write a two- to three-page essay describing and analyzing your findings, attaching any notes or transcripts to your paper.

Religious Affiliation Trends

A slim majority of Americans maintain the same religious affiliation throughout their lifetimes (56 percent according to a 2008 survey by the Pew Forum on Religion and Public Life), but there have been shifts in religious preferences in the past few decades. One of those trends is toward fundamentalism, which is not a religion in itself but a traditionalist approach that can be applied to any religion. Another trend is away from organized churches, toward an "unchurched" spirituality that borrows elements from many traditions but is affiliated with none.

In Relationships

Can We Have a Relationship with God?

Sociologists usually don't address questions like "Is there a God?" as these are not questions to which empirical, scientific methods can be applied. It is impossible to prove that God exists (at least by the rules of the scientific method)—and it is equally impossible to prove that God doesn't exist.

Social scientists don't have to answer the question of any god's existence to study the relationships people have with their particular deity. Those who believe in God may talk about that belief in terms usually used to describe interpersonal relationships. For instance, they may talk about speaking with God or having a conversation with God. Since sociology is, at one level, the study of various types of relationships, sociologists are interested in people's perceptions of their bonds with the divine.

John Caughey, a professor of American Studies, specializes in studying these relationships and argues that relationships with a god or gods (or, depending on the culture, spirits, saints, or dead ancestors) are necessary to participate in many cultures. In other words, in most cultures we are actually required to be able to carry on such relationships in order to seem normal (Caughey 1984, 1999).

Practices such as prayer, in which individuals speak directly to God, saints, or spirits, are ways of establishing relationships with these entities. Only in very unusual cases do individuals claim that a god or saint has spoken directly to them in anything resembling face-to-face interaction. Instead, we tend to look for the entity's response to our prayers in various sorts of signs. If we have appealed to God to intervene in a particular situation (to help us do well on an exam or to improve the health of a sick relative), we often see God's "reply" in seemingly unrelated places; for example, the parting of the clouds to reveal a sunny sky just as we set off to the lecture hall or hospital. The number of times that the image of Jesus, Mary, or some other Christian figure has been seen in a rock formation, a pane of window glass, or even a malformed tortilla should indicate how hungry we are for tangible, concrete reciprocity in these faith-based relationships.

So, can you have a relationship with God? Of course you can—if you believe. Sociologists will never be able to confirm or deny the existence of any deity; what we are interested in, ultimately, is the role that these faith-based relationships play in our everyday social lives.

FUNDAMENTALISM Fundamentalist approaches to religious belief and practice are on the rise both worldwide and in the United States. **Fundamentalism** is a way of understanding and interpreting sacred texts that can be part of any denomination or sect. Fundamentalist Christianity, for example, centers on a strict, sometimes literal, interpretation of the Bible and advocates a return to the historic founding principles of Christianity, arguing that modern approaches to Christianity are corrupt and inauthentic. Other religions have fundamentalist strains as well. Orthodox Judaism, for example, promotes a literal reading of the Torah and other Jewish spiritual and legal tracts. Fundamentalist Islam parallels Jewish and Christian fundamentalisms in that it also requires strict, literal, and traditional interpretations of the Qur'an and other sacred texts. Fundamentalist approaches to all three of these major religions gained popularity in response to the complex social changes of the 1960s and 1970s in the United States and around the world (Patterson 2004) because fundamentalism provides a return to tradition and to simple, unambiguous values and ideologies. Declaring one's loyalty to a traditional religious group that promises certainty in the face of change may be comforting to individuals—but it has broader social and political consequences as well.

Between 1990 and 2001, the number of Americans who described themselves as "Fundamentalist Christians" tripled, and the number describing themselves as "Evangelical Christians" (a variant of fundamentalist groups) more than quadrupled (Kosmin, Mayer, and

> **fundamentalism** the practice of emphasizing literal interpretation of texts and a "return" to a time of greater religious purity; represented by the most conservative group within any religion

Megachurches Rick Warren, the senior pastor of Saddleback Church and author of *The Purpose Driven Life*, preaches to his congregation. Because his church attracts 20,000 parishioners on an average Sunday, Warren shows his sermons on video screens inside the church.

Keysar 2001). With the rapidly increasing popularity of these groups, their beliefs have also spilled over into other areas of social life. Fundamentalists who take an **evangelical** approach attempt to convert individuals to their way of worshipping. Evangelicals see their conversion work as a service to others—an attempt to save souls—and have adapted many modern technologies (including television and the internet) to their cause.

UNCHURCHED SPIRITUALITY About 17 percent of Americans claim no religious affiliation (Pew Forum on Religion and Public Life 2008)—interestingly, this group is more likely to be younger and to live in western states, such as California, Colorado, Nevada, and New Mexico (Kosmin, Mayer, and Keysar 2001). Having no religious affiliation, however, does not necessarily mean they are "unbelievers." In fact, fewer than 2 percent describe themselves as atheists, and agnostics are another 2 percent. As yet another indicator of our paradoxical attitudes about religion, Americans are increasingly seeking guid-

evangelical a term describing conservative Christians who emphasize converting others to their faith

unchurched a term describing those who consider themselves spiritual but not religious and who often adopt aspects of various religious traditions

secular nonreligious; a secular society separates church and state and does not endorse any religion

ance and fulfillment through nontraditional means, with many labeling themselves "spiritual but not religious." This trend involves new definitions of belief and practice, often expressed privately and individually rather than in organized group settings. As noted earlier, some organized religions still include elements of sexism, racial prejudice, homophobia, anti-Semitism, and conformity that turn people off, and so spiritual seekers may utilize a kind of "cafeteria" strategy, choosing elements from various traditions and weaving them together into something unique. This type of **unchurched** spirituality (Fuller 2002), frowned upon by some religious organizations, is becoming increasingly popular, as spiritual seekers mix bits of astrology, alternative healing, twelve-step programs, and even witchcraft with elements of more traditional doctrines.

A Secular Society?

The separation of church and state is a time-honored (and controversial) American principle, established by the founders to preserve freedom of religion—one of the main reasons Europeans came to North America. As important and central as this principle is to American politics, we haven't always been able to maintain it in practice. Consider the dollar bill with the motto "In God We Trust." Witness the 2003 controversy about displaying the Ten Commandments in public buildings in Alabama, or President George W. Bush's allocation of federal monies to "faith-based" charitable organizations. Even the school voucher debate centers around this issue: should public education funds be used to send children to private schools, many of which are religious? And, of course, specifically Christian values and practices shape the everyday life of all Americans—Christian or not. Whether we are a **secular** society, one that separates church and state, is a complicated issue.

In both government and private industry, schedules are organized around Christian holidays with little or no attention paid to religious holidays of other groups. Schools, banks, and government employers are all closed on Christmas Day, even though this holiday is not observed by more than 15 percent of Americans. Your university's system of vacation periods is likely organized around both Christmas and Easter—important Christian holidays. Universities rarely give days off for Yom Kippur or Passover, two very important Jewish holidays. This means that Jewish students and staff who observe these holidays must go through the hassle of making special arrangements to compensate for classes or meetings missed. They may have to use valuable vacation or sick time or even forfeit credit for exams given on that day. Eid al Fitr, the last day of the Muslim holy month of Ramadan, calls for a variety of special celebrations that schools and employers rarely

Thou Shall Not Kill: Religion, Violence, and Terrorism

The history of religious conflict is extensive and convoluted, having been around for as long as humans have worshipped gods. No faith is exempt, and religion has played a significant role in conflicts from the ancient Israelites and Canaanites around 1200 B.C.E. to Al-Qaeda's destruction of New York City's World Trade Center in 2001 to Sri Lanka's civil war between the Hindu Tamil Tigers and the Buddhist Sinhalese in which more than 50,000 lives were lost.

Mark Juergensmeyer's book *Terror in the Mind of God* (2003) analyzes the history and meaning of religious violence in general and terrorism in particular. He notes that groups using terror have historically had diverse agendas and motivations, but only within the past thirty years has religion come to play a prominent role in terrorist violence:

> In 1980, the U.S. State Department roster of international terrorist groups listed scarcely a single religious organization. In 1998, U.S. Secretary of State Madeleine Albright listed thirty of the world's most dangerous groups; over half were religious. They were Jewish, Muslim, and Buddhist. If one added to this list other violent religious groups around the world, including the many Christian militia and other paramilitary organizations found domestically in the United States, the number of religious terrorist groups would be considerable. (Juergensmeyer 2003, p. 6)

Juergensmeyer uses several examples to illustrate the cross-cultural similarities of religious violence. Within the Christian tradition, he discusses a wide range of examples, from the Irish Republican Army (IRA) in Northern Ireland to the killing of doctors who perform abortions in the United States. Within Judaism, he examined the case of Baruch Goldstein, who killed 28 Muslims in 1994 when he opened fire in the Ibrahim Mosque in the Cave of the Patriarchs, a shrine holy to both Jews and Muslims. Juergensmeyer also investigated Islamic terrorism, such as the first attempt to bomb the World Trade Center in 1993, and the activities of the Palestinian group Hamas, which pioneered the use of suicide bombings in the Middle East. Sikh terrorists were responsible for the assassinations of Indira Gandhi and Beant Singh, and a Buddhist Japanese cult, Aum Shinrikyo, launched the notorious sarin nerve gas attack on the Tokyo subway.

Juergensmeyer argues that the common thread linking religious violence in such disparate traditions and far-flung corners of the world is a reliance on a particular kind of religious perspective. "The social tensions of this moment of history . . . cry out for absolute solutions," he says, and in a world that seems increasingly beyond individual control, religious violence offers a way to reassert some kind of power.

The list of wars, conflicts, and terrorist acts inspired or justified by religion is tragically long, extending throughout history and reaching across continents. Religious conflict is not a thing of the past, nor is your country (or your religion, whatever it may be) untouched by it.

Terror in the Mind of God Shoko Asahara (left) was the leader of a Japanese Buddhist cult, Aum Shinrikyo, whose 1995 nerve gas attack on the Tokyo subway killed 27 people and injured thousands. The Provisional IRA (right), which emerged in 1969, sees itself as a continuation of the Irish Republican Army, which fought in the Irish War of Independence. Through bombings and other attacks, the IRA has tried to unite Northern Ireland with the Republic of Ireland.

Separation of Church and State? This portrait of Jesus has hung in the main hallway of Bridgeport High School, a public school in Bridgeport, West Virginia, for more than three decades. In 2006, the American Civil Liberties Union filed a lawsuit to have the portrait removed.

recognize; those who wish to observe this holiday must make their own arrangements as well.

RELIGION IN THE WHITE HOUSE The only official eligibility requirements for the job of U.S. president are that the person be 35 years old, a natural-born U.S. citizen, and a resident in the United States for at least fourteen years. There is no requirement that the president be a man, though all of them have been, or a Christian, but all of them have been. It seems that an unspoken requirement for the presidency includes being a man of Christian faith, with Protestant Christianity being preferred. The only Catholic to hold the office, John F. Kennedy, endured a storm of controversy during his 1960 campaign, when critics feared that America would be ruled by the Pope if Kennedy was elected.

As late as the month of October during the 2008 presidential campaign, a persistent 12 percent of Americans continued to believe that Barack Obama was a Muslim, a rumor that may have derived from his middle name "Hussein," despite his clear affiliation as a Christian (Pew Research Center for the People and the Press 2008c). Indeed, Obama's Christianity took center stage at one point during the campaign when he had to address the controversial comments of his pastor, Reverend Jeremiah Wright. The Obamas eventually left Chicago's Trinity United Church of Christ in order to distance themselves from Reverend Wright, but not until after Wright's divisive sermons began to interfere publicly with the candidate's campaign. Even well into his first term as president, the number of Americans who believed that

Obama is Muslim actually rose to 18 percent. Only 34 percent of adults thought he was Christian, while more than 43 percent said they didn't know his religion. The view that Obama is Muslim is more widespread among his political opponents than it is among supporters (Pew Forum on Religion and Public Life 2010).

Given America's explicit constitutional commitment to the separation of church and state, it seems we shouldn't be concerned about a president's religious affiliation (or lack thereof). But it matters.

The administration of George W. Bush was particularly notable for the controversy it stirred over the influence of religion on the leader of the free world. President Bush was famously quoted by former aide David Frum as saying that "I had a drinking problem . . . [and] there is only one reason I am in the Oval Office and not in a bar. I found faith. I found God" (Goodstein 2004). Bush managed, to some degree, to placate opponents concerned with the separation between church and state. His public comments on the subject were consistently conciliatory and inclusive. In his first press conference after winning reelection in 2004, Bush was asked by a reporter, "What do you say to those who are concerned about the role of a faith they do not share in public life and in your policies?" (Noah 2004). The president answered:

> I will be your president regardless of your faith, and I don't expect you to agree with me necessarily on religion. As a matter of fact, no president should ever try to impose religion on our society. A great—the great—tradition of America is one where people can worship the way they want to

Religion and the White House President Barack Obama prays alongside churchgoers during a Sunday-morning service at the Harvest Cathedral Chapel in Macon, Georgia.

worship. And if they choose not to worship, they're just as patriotic as your neighbor. That is an essential part of why we are a great nation. (Noah 2004)

Bush is one of many presidents who were advised by the unofficial White House chaplain, the Reverend Billy Graham. Graham advised every president since Dwight D. Eisenhower up through George W. Bush on matters of state and personal spirituality. With a man of the cloth as such a high-profile presidential advisor, and with Christianity as an unstated requirement for holding presidential office, are we really a secular society? Are church and state truly separate? Is every person equally free to practice his or her faith in American society?

Religion: Linking Micro- and Macrosociology

Religion is the source of conflict and misunderstanding, but also a wellspring of comfort and meaning, for many. Whether you are Catholic or Methodist, Orthodox or Reform Jewish, Muslim or Buddhist, Mormon or Wiccan or Scientologist, you share common experiences with others in the practice of your religion, no matter how different your belief systems and rituals may be. A sense of meaning, a set of rules and guidelines by which to live your life, a way of explaining the world around you, a feeling of belonging and group identity—sociologists recognize these patterns across religious traditions.

Religion is yet another social institution that helps us see the link between macro-level social structure and micro-level everyday experience. Religious beliefs, practices, and prejudices can inflame global conflicts and resolve them, and can shape national political life in observable and unexamined ways. At the same time, religion is integral in the everyday lives of many Americans who find comfort and kinship in their religious beliefs and practices. "In God We Trust" is the motto for both our nation and many of its people, no matter what their faith.

Closing Comments

All three of the social institutions examined in this chapter—politics, education, and religion—are part of the structure of our society, and they are linked in a variety of ways. For example, state and federal policy decisions about school vouchers affect individual students and neighborhood public schools, and they benefit parochial schools and the religious institutions that run them. Politics, education, religion, and other social institutions influence your everyday lives in ways you may not have realized. We hope you have gained greater awareness of how these social institutions shape your life as a member of society—and how you can influence them as well. Your vote changes the political landscape; your role as a student influences the culture of your college and university; your membership in a religious congregation affects the lives of your fellow worshippers. Institutions impact individuals, but individuals can influence institutions as well—this is the essence of the sociological imagination and the macro-micro link.

⑤ Need Help Studying?

wwnorton.com/studyspace

Visit StudySpace to access free review materials such as:

- **Vocabulary Flashcards**
- **Diagnostic Review Quizzes**
- **Study Outlines**

QUESTIONS FOR REVIEW

1. Were you eligible to vote in the last election? If so, did you? If you didn't vote, why not? The voting rates for voting-eligible U.S. citizens ages eighteen to twenty-four are much lower than those for senior citizens; why do you think that is?

2. If America really is ruled by a tiny power elite, what does this mean for the American rags-to-riches mythology that says anyone who works hard can get to the top? Whose interests are served by such a mythology?

3. Many sociologists believe that public opinion is shaped by opinion leaders, high-profile people who interpret political information for us. Are you aware of any celebrities who have taken a stand on political or social issues? Do such people affect your opinions?

4. This chapter opened with a discussion of the Pledge of Allegiance. Given what you learned about the hidden curriculum, what sort of implicit lessons do you think are being taught when students say the pledge?

5. Much of this chapter's discussion of education focused on elementary and high schools. Do you think the same theories apply to college classrooms? Have you experienced a hidden curriculum since you left high school?

6. What does Randall Collins say about the true function of education? If you want to stop the class system from automatically reproducing itself, what steps could you take?

7. Is religion really just beliefs and rituals about the sacred and the profane? What does the religious tradition you're most familiar with consider sacred and profane?

8. There is some debate over how to measure religiosity: Should it be based on how spiritual you feel or how often you attend religious services? Which way do you think is more valid? Why? Can you think of a better way than either of these?

9. Mark Juergensmeyer believes that the common thread linking religious violence in radically different religious traditions is a particular kind of religious perspective: a need for absolutes. Why does he think this need is being expressed in our time? Do you agree?

SUGGESTIONS FOR FURTHER EXPLORATION

Bellah, Robert, Richard Madsen, William Sullivan, Ann Swidler, and Steven Tipton. 1985. *Habits of the Heart: Individualism and Commitment in American Life*. Berkeley: University of California Press. The authors explore the social significance of religiosity in America.

Berger, Peter L. 1970. *A Rumor of Angels: Modern Society and the Rediscovery of the Supernatural*. Garden City, NJ: Anchor. One of the principal figures within symbolic interactionism gives his views about religion in an increasingly secular world.

Covington, Dennis. 1995. *Salvation on Sand Mountain: Snake-Handling and Redemption in Southern Appalachia*. Reading, MA: Addison Wesley. Covington provides a close look at a particularly conservative form of Christianity, whose members handle snakes, speak in tongues, and remain profoundly alienated from the secular world.

High School. 1968. Dir. Frederick Wiseman. Osti Productions. This documentary was shot in Philadelphia's Northeast High School in the late 1960s when teachers and administrators seemed to value discipline above all other virtues. The National Film Preservation Board selected it for inclusion in the National Film Registry.

Jesus Camp. 2006. An Academy Award–nominated documentary that focuses on three devoutly religious kids who attend a charismatic Christian summer camp. Most of the campers are also homeschooled because of their parents' concerns about what is taught in a public curriculum. Follows the children at camp as well as in their local churches and homes.

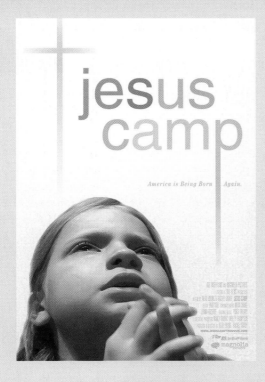

Kapuscinski, Ryszard. 1989. *The Emperor.* New York: Vintage. An account of the fall of Haile Selassie, His Most Puissant Majesty and Distinguished Highness the Emperor of Ethiopia, who ruled from 1930 until he was overthrown by the army in 1974. The author interviews many of the emperor's servants and associates to describe a living, twentieth-century monarch and his final days in power.

Moore, Barrington. 1993. *Social Origins of Dictatorship and Democracy: Lord and Peasant in the Making of the Modern World.* Boston: Beacon Press. An examination of the social and economic factors that influence the development of particular political modes.

Orenstein, Peggy. 1994. *Schoolgirls: Young Women, Self Esteem, and the Confidence Gap.* New York: Doubleday. Orenstein's engaging overview of the research on gender bias in education puts a human face on the quantitative research in this area.

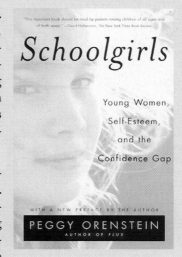

School, the Story of American Public Education. 2001. Dir. Sarah Mondale. A four-part PBS series chronicling the history of American public education from the late 1770s to the present, this film explains the deeply rooted connections between American education and democracy. Also check the web site: www.pbs.org/kcet/publicschool.

The War Room. 1993. Dirs. D. A. Pennebaker and Chris Hegedus. McEttinger Films. An excellent primer on how media forces interact with politics. This documentary about Bill Clinton's 1992 campaign combines behind-the-scenes footage with news clips to show the connections between political gamesmanship and media coverage.

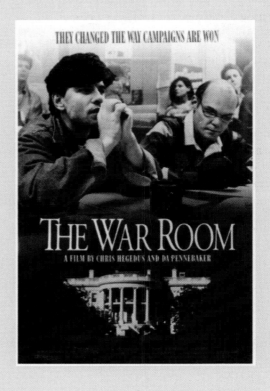

CHAPTER 11

The Economy, Work, and Working

The history of one family's jobs and careers can provide some insight into the sociological development of work and the economy over time. For example, Dr. Ferris's great-grandfathers included a military man in Missouri, a tailor in Texas, and a stonemason and a butcher, both in a tiny mountain village in Lebanon. Despite their geographical and cultural distance from one another, they all were involved in occupations that have existed since ancient times and were still common in the late nineteenth century. Their various jobs represent much of the range of possible jobs in agricultural societies. Some people were skilled craftsmen, some were soldiers, and most others farmed. While women sometimes helped with the farming or other types of work, their primary task was homemaking and child-rearing—and this was what all of Ferris's great-grandmothers did, serving as helpmates to their husbands and caregivers to their children.

Moving up a generation in the family tree, you can see that in the first half of the twentieth century, Ferris's grandparents were involved in military and service work, with some industrial labor experience as well. One grandfather emigrated from Lebanon to Massachusetts, where he worked in the local brass foundry. This kind of hard physical labor in a stiflingly hot factory setting was the norm during the industrial era. While he worked at the foundry, his wife secretly worked at a local laundry, hiding her earnings from him. When he discovered her deception, he was angry, as he felt that women shouldn't work outside the home. However, these secret earnings later helped them afford to take a step up in the occupational hierarchy: they bought a restaurant and ran it successfully. Ferris's other grandfather was an Army doctor who was stationed all over the United States and the world. His wife followed, making a home with the children wherever they were stationed. She served as a hostess and provided crucial support for her husband's career, which was customary in the early twentieth century.

By the time Ferris's parents started working in the second half of the twentieth century, her mother was part of a new generation of women who were far more likely than their own mothers had been to pursue a college education and a career outside the home, even while raising children. Both of Ferris's parents earned advanced degrees (mom an MA and dad a JD); as a writer and an attorney, respectively, they both engage in service- and knowledge-based work. These areas experienced tremendous growth as the country moved into a postindustrial, Information Age economy. Dr. Ferris, as a professor with a Ph.D., is also a knowledge-worker—still just two generations away from great-grandparents without formal educations. Because of historical changes in gendered career expectations, she has enjoyed opportunities her grandmothers and great-grandmothers could never have imagined. And as we move into the twenty-first century, developments in the economic and occupational landscape are likely to create a world in which Dr. Ferris's son, E. J., may hold a job that has not even been invented yet—perhaps in an entirely new, currently unimagined field.

Your own occupational family tree probably holds similar insights into the development of both world and U.S. economic systems over time. And this is no accident—as different as our families and their experiences may be, the patterns and trends in the kinds of work our relatives did can be a rich topic for sociological analysis. Our individual occupational choices are always made within the context of larger economic and social structures, both local and global. In this chapter, we will examine those structures and the experiences of individuals within them.

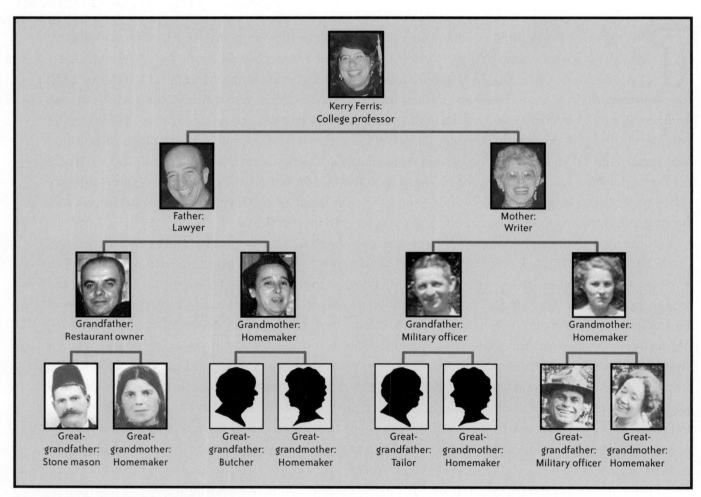

Kerry Ferris's Occupational Family Tree

HOW TO READ THIS CHAPTER

After reading this chapter, you should understand why work is a classic topic of sociological inquiry: it is a fulcrum point between the micro and the macro and a link between the individual and the social. You will see the connection between the everyday conditions of your life on the job and the larger structural changes related to history, technology, and the economic system in which you work. We want you to become familiar with the classic and more recent sociological studies in this area and how they have shaped our ways of thinking about the social world of economy and work. You will know something about the past and perhaps have more insight about the future and your place in it.

An economy deals not only with money but also with the production, distribution, and consumption of goods and services within a society. In this chapter, we look at issues regarding the economy, focusing specifically on work, because the economy shapes the types of work available as well as our patterns of working.

Historical and Economic Changes

We start with the history of U.S. economies, paying special attention to the agricultural, industrial, and postindustrial periods—and how new technologies have changed the nature of work in each of these periods.

Pre-Colonial United States: Hunting and Gathering and Horticultural Societies

Perhaps the earliest form of economy in the Americas was in pre-sixteenth-century Native American societies. An estimated 2 million to 10 million tribal people inhabited the continent prior to colonization by Europeans. Some were hunting and gathering societies, which had to be highly mobile, relocating for food and weather conditions. The division of labor revolved around survival, with the men hunting animals or foraging for plant sources of food. The women, children, and elderly cooked, sewed, and did other tasks at the campsite. Horticultural societies were different in that they were based on the domestication of animals, farming, and generating a surplus of resources. They had more

Slaves at Work in the Field The southern agricultural economy depended on slavery to grow cotton and tobacco.

permanent settlements and a greater diversification of labor because different types of workers, such as farmers, craftspeople, and traders, were all necessary to the economy.

The Agricultural Revolution

The **Agricultural Revolution** continued some of the social and economic changes that began with horticultural societies. Better farming and ranching techniques allowed larger groups to thrive and remain in one location for longer periods of time. The Agricultural Revolution lasted for many centuries, but in the eighteenth century food production was greatly increased by new innovations in farming and animal husbandry: the invention of new types of plows and mechanized seed spreaders and new techniques of crop rotation, irrigation, and selective breeding.

The agricultural economy that flourished in the early United States encouraged a stratified labor force. For large plantation owners to accumulate wealth from cotton or sugar-cane crops, they depended on cheap, plentiful labor. The division of labor fell largely along race, gender, and class lines (Amott and Matthaei 1996). In the pre–Civil War era, many of the plantations of the South that were owned by whites were farmed by black slaves brought from Africa (Davis 2001). Poorer white people sometimes owned small farms or worked as tenant farmers or sharecroppers. White men were usually owners of land and small businesses, while white women were usually household managers.

> **Agricultural Revolution** the social and economic changes, including population increases, that followed from the domestication of plants and animals and the gradually increasing efficiency of food production

The Industrial Revolution

The **Industrial Revolution** was a time of rapid technological, social, and economic change that almost completely transformed life in modern times—a radical break from the past, disrupting social patterns that had been relatively stable for centuries. When we discuss the Industrial Revolution in this section, we will look at the technological innovations of the era and how they changed American society and culture, the economy, and the lives of workers.

The Industrial Revolution began in England with the invention of the steam engine in 1769, which was first used to power machinery, starting with the manufacture of textiles. By the end of the eighteenth century, Britain's steam-powered factories had spread to the United States and other nations (Hughes and Cain 1994). With more mechanized machinery such as the cotton gin, the American economy moved from manual labor to machine manufacturing. Even farming would change with the introduction of mechanical plows and reapers. The nineteenth century brought steam-powered ships and railways, the internal combustion engine, electrical power generation, and new tools and appliances. By the end of the 1800s, the modern corporation had emerged—a business that could manage a range of activities across geographic regions. A successful corporation not only manufactured products but also managed all aspects of marketing and distribution.

With the shift to a manufacturing economy, vast numbers of people migrated into cities from rural areas in search of work. There was a great influx of immigrants, primarily from Europe, who provided a steady source of cheap, easily exploitable labor. By 1910, more than 13 million people living in the United States were foreign born (Gibson and Lennon 2001). Densely populated neighborhoods sprang up to accommodate the masses, housing was often substandard, and many families lived in poverty. Employment in manufacturing meant that people no longer worked in or around their homes as artisans or craftsmen, as many had in the past, but that they went off into the industrial districts of large cities to work in factories. Wage labor replaced the household subsistence model of the agricultural society.

The industrial economy increased stratification of the workforce along class, race, and gender lines (Amott and Matthaei 1996). Wealthy white families owned the means of production, such as factories, energy sources, or land, and the financial institutions that supported the accumulation of wealth; the men were in the workplace while the women ran the household. A middle class of educated, skilled workers emerged, often in managerial professions. Working-class white men now earned a "family wage" at the factory, while women worked in the household. But for families that needed more than one income, women and even children joined the workforce. Poor women, immigrant women, and women of color increasingly performed domestic labor in white women's households (Amott and Matthaei 1996). But they also worked at factory jobs that were reserved for women, such as millwork and sewing in textile factories, for meager wages and under dangerous conditions.

The industrial economy revolved around the mass production of goods, aided by use of the assembly line in the manufacturing process, in which parts were added to a product in sequential order. The moving assembly line is attributed to Henry Ford, who in 1913 used it to manufacture automobiles in Detroit, Michigan. With assembly line production, the process of manufacturing became not only more mechanized but also more routine driven. In contrast to the artisan mode, in which one worker or a team of workers would produce an item in its entirety from start to finish, on an assembly line each worker would do one or two specific tasks over and over again. Many workers disliked the assembly line because they never had the satisfaction of seeing the finished product, and they were also frustrated with the unsafe, exhausting working conditions.

The Industrial Revolution changed not only working conditions but also the lives of workers. The United States and most other industrializing nations experienced great population booms not only because of immigration but also because of discoveries in science and medicine that led to increased life expectancy and decreased infant mortality. Also, many more people had access to dependable food and water sources and some form of health care. Laws giving

Women Working in a Shoe Factory Many factory jobs that were reserved for women paid meager wages and required working under dangerous conditions.

> **Industrial Revolution** the rapid transformation of social life resulting from the technological and economic developments that began with the assembly line, steam power, and urbanization

some protections to workers, such as child labor reforms, also emerged as an important aspect of the overall health of working populations. Although many factory workers were unskilled, the American workforce of the early twentieth century was becoming better trained and more educated than that of any other previous generation.

The growing population of the United States became a market for the mass-produced goods it was manufacturing. Because industrial workers no longer worked on farms and in the home producing their own food and clothes, they had to purchase those items with the wages they earned for their labor. They also had to buy services, such as health care and child care, from other providers. Other changes in everyday life were also part of the Industrial Revolution: Americans were introduced to new forms of communication with the Morse telegraph in 1837 and the invention of the telephone in 1876, and they traveled more easily across the country with the completion of the transcontinental railroad in 1869.

The Information Revolution

The **Information Revolution** is the most recent of the historical and technological changes that have led to new economic and working conditions in the United States and around the world. Also referred to as the Digital Revolution, Digital Age, or Postindustrial Age, it is expected to bring about as dramatic a transformation of society as the revolutions that preceded it (Castells 2000). We may not recognize how truly radical this change is, partly because we are at the edge of a revolution that will continue to evolve over our lifetimes.

The Information Revolution began in the 1970s with the development of the microchip or microprocessor used in computers and other electronic devices. The performance capacity of microprocessors has continued to increase according to Moore's Law (doubling about every eighteen months). When computers were coupled with the introduction of the internet in the early 1990s and became more affordable, they were soon widely used. Other technologies associated with the Information Revolution include computer networking and all types of digital media, satellite and cable broadcasting, and telecommunications. The Information Revolution had become a ubiquitous part of everyday life in the twenty-first century.

The Information Revolution brought a profound shift from an economy based on the production of goods to one based on the production of knowledge and services (Castells 2000). Of course, the United States is still involved in agriculture and manufacturing, but these are shrinking parts of our economy. As American companies compete on the global market, they may find it more profitable to move production overseas to exploit cheaper materials and labor in developing countries. According to the Department of Labor, the U.S. economy currently consists of some 11 "supersectors," or areas in which people work. Fully two-thirds of these are in the knowledge or service sectors.

11 Supersectors of the U.S. Economy:

Construction

Education and Health Services

Financial Activities

Government

Information

Leisure and Hospitality

Manufacturing

Natural Resources and Mining

Other Services

Professional and Business Services

Trade, Transportation, and Utilities

A **knowledge worker** is anyone who works primarily with information or who develops and uses knowledge in the workplace (Drucker 1959, 2003). For these workers, information and knowledge are both the raw material and the product of their labor. Knowledge workers produce with their heads rather than with their hands. They create value in the economy through their ideas, judgments, analyses, designs, and innovations. Some examples of knowledge work include advertising, engineering, marketing, product development, research, science, urban planning, and web design. Microsoft, a major software development company, further broadens this category to include anyone who works with the flow of information within businesses.

The service sector, or service industry, also experienced tremendous growth in the postindustrial economy and employs a large number of American workers. **Service workers** provide a service to businesses or individual

Information Revolution the recent social revolution made possible by the development of the microchip in the 1970s, which brought about vast improvements in the ability to manage information

knowledge workers those who work primarily with information and who create value in the economy through their ideas, judgments, analyses, designs, or innovations

service workers those whose work involves providing a service to businesses or individual clients, customers, or consumers rather than manufacturing goods

Knowledge Workers The Information Revolution has shifted the economy away from manufacturing toward jobs that produce knowledge and provide services. Knowledge workers, like these employees at Google, create value through their ideas, judgments, and analyses.

of workers accustomed to seeing themselves as immune to layoffs—older workers, the college-educated, men, and whites saw higher rates of unemployment compared with other groups (Anderson 2009).

The postindustrial economy presents a very different social reality from the economy in other periods in history. The Information Revolution has changed almost every aspect of our lives and has become a part of many of our social institutions, including the economy and work. And with those changes have come new vulnerabilities, as the recent recession has demonstrated. In the next sections, we look at current world economic systems and the features of work in industrial and postindustrial settings. But first, let's see what kinds of jobs the characters on prime time television hold by doing the content analysis assigned in this Data Workshop.

clients. Services may entail the distribution or sale of goods from producer to consumer (wholesaling and retailing) or transformation in the process of delivering goods (the restaurant business) or no goods at all (massage therapy). All service work has a focus on serving and interacting with people. Service work can be found in such industries as banking, consulting, education, entertainment, health care, insurance, investment, legal services, leisure, news media, restaurants (including fast-food), retailing, tourism, and transportation.

Some service work pays well, particularly at the management and executive levels, and in certain fields, such as banking, entertainment, and law; but much service sector employment is unstable, part-time or temporary, low paying, and often without such benefits as health care or retirement. Women, persons of color, and the poor are likely to be found in the service sector, thus perpetuating a lower-class status among those holding such positions (Amott and Matthaei 1996). Finally, unemployment rates for service sector workers are substantially higher than for knowledge workers (U.S. Census Bureau 2002a).

Since 2008, when the recent recession began, all sectors of the contemporary global economy have experienced slowdown, but some have been hit harder than others. The United States saw its highest unemployment rates since the Great Depression—close to 10 percent overall, with much higher rates in certain regions and industries. States like California and Nevada, previously the sites of seemingly nonstop growth, topped the unemployment numbers along with more traditional "rust-belt" states like Ohio and Michigan. This is because of the crash in the real estate and finance sectors, in addition to the drop in the construction and manufacturing trades. The recession also affected groups

DATA WORKSHOP

ANALYZING MASS MEDIA AND POPULAR CULTURE

The Work World of Prime Time Television

FBI agent, salesperson, newscaster, football coach, presidential press secretary, firefighter, private investigator, district attorney, forensics expert, massage therapist, plastic surgeon, police officer, interior designer, school principal, military officer . . . these are just some of the jobs of characters in different prime time network television shows. How do these jobs compare with those of your family, friends, or acquaintances? What kinds of work-related issues do characters on television experience compared to those of real people in those same job titles or industries?

Sociologists who are interested in the media often ask such questions when comparing media content to the real world. This Data Workshop asks you to look at how prime time television shows represent jobs and the realities of working life. Your instructor might want you to do all the exercises, or she may ask you to choose just one or two.

Exercise One: What Are the Jobs in Prime Time?
Do a simple count of the jobs in prime time television. Look at the lineup of current shows between 8:00 P.M. and 11:00 P.M. (depending on your time zone) on the major networks (CBS, NBC, ABC, FOX, and CW) and choose at least two shows each night for a total of fourteen or more nights to analyze. Review the key characters and see if you can determine what kinds of jobs they have. While some shows are

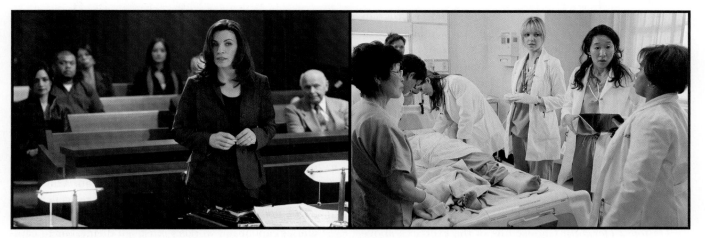

Working in Prime Time How do television shows like *The Good Wife* (left) and *Grey's Anatomy* (right) represent working life?

based almost entirely in the workplace, others may rarely refer to work. There may be some characters whose job status is unclear or absent. Once you have compiled a list of jobs and the number of characters working in each job category, compare these to workers in the real world. What is the actual percentage of people who hold these types of positions? (Sources for this information include the U.S. Census Bureau [www.census.gov] and Bureau of Labor Statistics [www.bls.gov] among other web sites.) See if you can find out whether certain jobs are under- or overrepresented on television or whether there are other kinds of disparities between the statistics of the TV world and the real world. If you present your findings in essay form, use charts or graphs where necessary.

Exercise Two: Working Conditions and TV Jobs
Examine the workplace as depicted on prime time television. You may choose one or more programs (depending on the context) to gather enough data to do a content analysis. Look at the way characters perform their jobs in television shows. Often workers are shown socializing or engaging in other kinds of personal activities while on the job. How much real work gets done? And when characters are actually working, what aspects of that work are featured during the program? Often we see only the most unusual or glamorous aspects of work while the day-to-day routine or behind-the-scenes aspects rarely appear. Another dimension is how characters relate to their jobs and to their co-workers. Are they happy and fulfilled by the work they do? Do they complain about work, or experience other kinds of troubles with their jobs? How are power and resistance exercised in the workplace? Discuss your findings and assess the extent to which you believe the programs accurately reflect these professions in real life.

Exercise Three: Real Working Professionals and Representations on TV
For this exercise you will need to identify a particular job or profession portrayed on a prime time television program and find someone you know who works in that job or profession to interview. Watch the television show with this person (you might consider recording episodes in advance to prescreen for relevance). After you have viewed the program, discuss with the interviewee the similarities and differences between real work and the same work done by the characters on television. How closely does the show reflect the actual job or profession? In what ways does TV distort or otherwise misrepresent the job or profession? If your analysis of the interview is in essay form, include a transcript of your questions and answers.

Exercise Four: Making a Living on TV
As one of the most powerful sources of socialization in the lives of young people, television may contribute to our attitudes and ideas about the working world. What kinds of lessons do we learn about work and money from what we see on TV? How do television characters influence our career goals and aspirations? Some jobs are totally absent, some are shown as merely the butt of jokes, while others are made to seem hip, glamorous, or exciting. We rarely get much information about how characters have gotten their jobs or what kind of training or experience got them to their positions. We also know very little about how hard they work or what they get paid. TV characters often seem to live extravagant lifestyles with little relationship between actual salaries and what they can afford to buy. Take examples from one or more television shows and discuss the characters' standard of living. Could real people working comparable jobs afford the same lifestyle that the television characters seem to enjoy? Do a content

analysis, recording at least one episode of a chosen program and describing as many of the details of work and lifestyle of the characters as possible to answer these questions.

There are two options for completing this Data Workshop.

- *Option 1 (informal)*: Choose one of the exercises above and follow the instructions as outlined. Bring notes to class to discuss with others in small groups. Your instructor may organize groups so that all members have done the same exercise or all members have done a different exercise. In either case, compare your findings with those of other members of the group.

- *Option 2 (formal)*: Choose one of the exercises above (or your instructor may assign a specific exercise) and follow the instructions as outlined. Write a three- to four-page essay analyzing your findings.

Economic Systems: Comparing Capitalism and Socialism

Capitalism and socialism are political-economic systems found around the world, often in overlapping forms. Capitalism and socialism are ideal types, but most nations have a mix of both. For example, the United States, a capitalist nation, has some degree of socialism in government subsidies to businesses, regulation of markets, and support for public education and social welfare.

Capitalism

Capitalism is an economic system based on the laws of free market competition, privatization of the means of production, and production for profit. In its purest form, values for goods and services are derived solely by the market relationship between supply and demand. The resources necessary for production of goods and services are all privately owned. Owners, or capitalists, must employ workers to make products and perform services to generate a profit. Workers sell their labor to capitalists for a wage. The difference between the cost of production of a product or service and its price is profit to which the capitalist is entitled.

Capitalism tends to encourage class stratification. Because owners, or capitalists, make profits, they can accumulate wealth. Workers are not in a structural position to get ahead financially. The ideologies of the free market, private property, and profit-seeking motives that define capitalism also shape institutions other than the economy. In capitalist nations, we see increasing privatization of such basic human services as health care, housing, and education. Thus, hospitals, public school systems, and even welfare agencies are increasingly taken over by private for-profit firms.

Under capitalism, workers must sell their labor to capitalists for a wage. They are encouraged to be productive and efficient or they will suffer reduced wages, decreased social welfare services such as health insurance and retirement, downsizing, and layoffs. Until recently, under the capitalist system in the United States, disgruntled workers could withhold their labor by striking. Now, under a transnational capitalist system, firms experiencing strikes may decide to move their operations overseas to countries where few workers have the right to strike.

A capitalist economy encourages efficiency through technological innovation, expansion of markets, and reduction of production costs. Thus, owners or capitalists, in their efforts to seek efficiency, often replace workers with new technologies, reduce social welfare spending, and cut labor costs. Therefore, workers are responsible for maintaining their own competitiveness. They must seek an education and/or skills to compete for jobs and maintain their competency over their working lifetimes. However, firms must also increase their competitiveness. They may move production operations to overseas sites where they can take advantage of deregulated environments and cheap labor costs.

Socialism

Socialism is an economic system based on collective ownership of the means of production, collective distribution of goods and services, and government regulation of the economy. Under socialism, there are no private for-profit transactions. In its purest form, socialism seeks to meet the basic needs of all citizens rather than encouraging profits for some individuals over others.

In a socialist system, the government rather than individuals owns or at least regulates the ownership of all businesses, farms, and factories, and profits are redistributed to the collective citizenry. This encourages a collectivist work ethic with workers theoretically working for the common good of all citizens. Citizens have access to such resources as

capitalism an economic system based on the laws of free market competition, privatization of the means of production, and production for profit, with an emphasis on supply and demand as a means to set prices

socialism an economic system based on the collective ownership of the means of production, collective distribution of goods and services, and government regulation of the economy

health care, food, housing, and other social services to meet their basic needs. This is different from capitalism, as these services are an entitlement of all people, not just those who can afford them.

In socialism, a central and usually highly bureaucratic government regulates all aspects of the economy—ownership of resources and means of production, regulation of lending policies, interest rates, and currency values—as well as setting labor policies regarding such issues as maternity/paternity leave, retirement, and the right to strike. Such intense regulation of the economy should effectively reduce class inequalities and extreme poverty. In **communism**, the most extreme form of socialism, the government owns everything and all citizens work for the government and are considered equal, with no class distinctions. Socialism and communism, like capitalism, are theoretical or ideal types. Thus, no nations are purely socialist or communist. Even communist countries like Cuba or the People's Republic of China are increasingly incorporating capitalist ideologies into their regimes.

Under socialism, workers are not at risk of extreme poverty and class division as some might be within a capitalist society. They are not as vulnerable as capitalist workers to new technological innovations or the movement of transnational capital. However, they also do not enjoy the same consumption patterns that capitalist economies encourage. Socialism cannot provide capitalism's middle-class luxuries. Though class division is reduced, it is still present. Many socialist nations have political elites who enjoy a higher class of living than workers, and urban workers often benefit from having closer access to resources than rural workers. Further, reduction of class inequalities cannot guarantee a reduction in other types of inequalities, such as racism, sexism, and ageism.

> **communism** a system of government that eliminates private property; the most extreme form of socialism, because all citizens work for the government and there are no class distinctions

The United States: A Capitalist System with Some Socialist Attributes

To understand the political economy of various nations, think of capitalism and socialism as opposite sides of a continuum and nations placed along its span as being more capitalist or more socialist. The United States would undoubtedly lie closer to the capitalist side than would Sweden, but even U.S. capitalism is not a pure form.

While the United States is a capitalist nation, it also has socialist elements. Although capitalist businesses are privately owned, many benefit from government subsidies—grants, tax incentives, and special contracts. This is often referred to as "corporate welfare." In pure capitalism, such support would not exist. Government intervenes in the economy in other ways as well. Agencies such as the Federal Reserve Board often manipulate interest rates to stimulate the economy and control inflation. The Emergency Economic Stabilization Act of 2008 (also referred to as "the Bailout Bill") funneled more than $700 billion in government funds into banks, insurance companies, and other struggling private corporations in order to prop up the U.S. economy. Such government interventions constitute forms of socialism.

Social Welfare in the United States Hit hard by the recession, many unemployed Americans rely on government aid, such as the extension of unemployment benefits.

If the United States were purely capitalist, such institutions as education and health care would all be privately owned. However, most schools and many universities are publicly owned and operated. Even private universities usually get government subsidies. Health care is a trickier example. Many individuals and their employers buy health insurance from for-profit insurers, and hospitals are often run for profit. But Medicare and Medicaid are federal programs that provide subsidized health care for the elderly and the poor. The health care reform act of 2010 ushered in more federally-mandated health care coverage for millions more Americans.

The government also spends millions of dollars annually for other general assistance or public aid programs for low-income families, including Food Stamps and Temporary Assistance to Needy Families, often referred to as "entitlements." Thus, the poor, the elderly, current and former armed forces personnel, and expectant mothers, infants, and children have some public services to meet their health care needs. Even our Social Security system, though partially funded through payroll taxes, is a public system providing retirement, survivorship, and disability benefits to eligible Americans. Debates continue about whether these populations' needs are satisfactorily met and whether it's the government's responsibility to provide these services. Conservative politicians who periodically accuse their rivals of "socialist" tendencies may need to be reminded that things they enjoy every day—like streetlights, police protection, and public schools—are all part of a system of centrally funded and regulated services they likely would not want to do without.

In their purest forms, capitalism and socialism are opposites. In reality, capitalism and socialism can be characterized as lying along a continuum, with nations having some features of both economic systems. Each system represents a different political ideology and economic reality for the people and workers in its economy. Economic systems evolve and change over time, and with them, the institution of work.

The Nature of Industrial and Postindustrial Work

Historical and technological changes leading to the Agricultural, Industrial, and Information Revolutions fundamentally changed societies across several centuries. Societies have also adopted economic systems—capitalist or socialist, or a combination of both—and these economic systems influence the types of work that are available as well as our patterns of working.

Industrial Work

The spread of industrialism in the eighteenth and nineteenth centuries created "work" in the modern sense. Before the Industrial Revolution, most of the population engaged in agriculture, and the production of goods was organized around the household or small craft shops. In the industrial world, progress meant making machines produce more goods, more efficiently.

According to Karl Marx, the powerful have always exploited workers. As he said in the *Communist Manifesto*, "oppressor and oppressed stood in constant opposition to one another" in a perpetual struggle for economic resources, as all history "is the history of class struggles" (Marx 2001, p. 245). Though Marx studied ancient Rome and medieval Europe to help form his theories, they are most often associated with the Industrial Revolution, the capitalist economies that it produced, and the workers who toiled in its factories. However, much of what Marx asserted about class conflict and the circumstances of his time can apply with slight modification to capitalists and workers in the current industrial workplace.

Economic exploitation is still present in a modern industrial economy, which allows for the accumulation of what Marx called "surplus value." The proletariat or workers in an industrial economy possess only one thing of economic value, and that is their time, which they sell to capitalists who own the means of production. Workers are paid for their time and labor, but their wages do not represent the full profit from the sale of the goods they produce. The sale of the goods not only covers the workers' wages and the expenses of running the factory but also generates additional revenue or surplus value, which then belongs to the owner.

Marx believed that workers in capitalist societies experienced alienation as a result of this system of production, because they are paid for their labor but do not own the things they produce. He believed workers were alienated in four ways: from the product of their labor, from their own productive activity, from their fellow workers, and finally from human nature. First, the products of the worker's labor are the property of the capitalists to do with as they see fit. Unlike the farmers and craft workers of prior eras, the industrial worker is "robbed of . . . the objects of his work" and "the worker relates to the product of his labor as an alien object" (Marx 2001, p. 87). Workers feel no sense of personal satisfaction in producing goods that are owned and controlled by someone else.

Second, workers in a capitalist society are alienated from the process of work, their own productive activity. Marx argues that labor is "not the satisfaction of a need but only the means to satisfy needs" outside work (Marx 2001,

Twenty-First-Century Industrial Work Many workers still toil in the conditions that Marx criticized in the nineteenth century. For example, compare this photo of workers at Emyco Shoe Factory in Guanajuato, Mexico, to the workers in the shoe factory in 1910 on page 326.

p. 88), such as earning enough money to live on. In precapitalist societies, many found joy and fulfillment in the process of production. But the worker under capitalism cannot feel that kind of satisfaction.

Third, the worker is alienated from other people, "the alienation of man from man," as Marx calls it. Capitalism forces individuals into competition with each other, as "each man measures his relationship to other men by the relationship in which he finds himself placed as a worker" (Marx 2001, p. 91). Instead of cooperating, workers are forced to compete for scarce jobs and resources, making other workers an alien and hostile presence. Workers are also alienated from the owners, as they recognize work as "an activity that is under the domination, oppression, and yoke of another man" (Marx 2001, p. 92).

Fourth, workers are alienated from human nature, what Marx tends to refer to as "human essence." He believes that work should not be an unhappy burden taken up only out of the need to preserve physical existence. Instead, he assumes that it is in our nature to seek out "work, vital activity, and productive life" (Marx 2001, p. 90). The essence of what it means to be human is to engage in free conscious activity, but capitalism degrades human labor to a mere means of survival. Marx acknowledges that all species must work to satisfy immediate physical needs, but only human beings "fashion things according to the laws of beauty" and find satisfaction in their work (Marx 2001, p. 90). However, in a capitalist economy, this capacity is largely lost, as workers are alienated from their own human qualities.

Marx was describing work in the industrial era of the nineteenth century, but his analyses can apply to today's workers as well. Many workers are still toiling in the same conditions of exploitation, alienation, and class struggle that Marx thought needed to change.

Postindustrial Service Work

Social theorists of the Industrial Age, like Karl Marx and his contemporaries, were unable to predict how technological innovation would transform work and the economy in the twentieth century and beyond. They could not foresee the transition to a postindustrial, service-oriented economy. Nor could they foresee the advent of easily available consumer credit, which has meant that workers can now buy things they can't currently afford, materially improving their everyday lives without the hassle of starting a class revolution (even if it means they may never pay off their debts).

So, are service workers exploited? Alienated? Ready to revolt? A look at the nature of service work in the Postindustrial Age and a case study seem to suggest that these old problems have taken on new forms in our current times.

Service work, as the dominant form of employment in the postindustrial economy, often involves direct contact with clients, customers, patients, or students by those rendering the service, whether they are waiters, cashiers, nurses, doctors, teachers, or receptionists. In service work, situations arise when the worker's concerns, standards, and expectations conflict with those of clients. For example, an emergency for a client may be routine for a worker, as when your TV cable service goes out during the Packers' game and the customer service representative just keeps telling you they're working on it! As another example, you have a toothache, but the dentist doesn't have an open appointment until tomorrow. It's not the dentist who has to give you the bad news but the receptionist who must try to convince you to wait until then.

At the same time, service workers are also subject to the scrutiny and critique of a manager or supervisor—so in addition to the potential clash between workers and clients, there are also issues of autonomy and control over their work. This can create distinctive tensions in service work interactions, and power relationships both subtle and more obvious are clearly present in this type of work.

Barbara Ehrenreich explored some of these power issues in her book *Nickel and Dimed: On (Not) Getting By in America* (2001). As research for the book, Ehrenreich took minimum-wage service jobs in three different cities—as a waitress in Florida, a hotel maid in Maine, and a Wal-Mart employee in Minnesota—and experienced the difficulties of

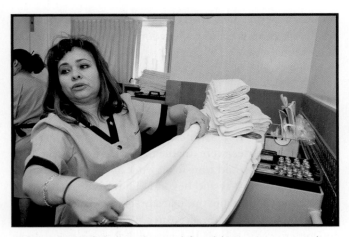

Nickel and Dimed Barbara Ehrenreich found that many service workers barely scrape by working long hours for minimum wage and no benefits. Because many service workers live paycheck to paycheck, they may have trouble asserting their rights or taking time off for illnesses for fear of losing their jobs.

trying to make ends meet and maintain her self-respect in low-wage service positions.

Ehrenreich found that service workers in these types of jobs are likely to be exploited in a number of ways. First, the low wages, lack of benefits, and grueling hours make it difficult to pay even the most basic bills. She discovered this herself when she couldn't scrape up enough money for a deposit on an apartment and ended up living in a sleazy hotel and getting her dinner from the local charity's food pantry. Her co-workers lived in flophouses, their cars, or small apartments crowded with family, friends, and strangers, and one ate nothing but a small bag of Doritos every day for lunch. They got fired for asserting their rights or for getting ill or injured, and they developed chronic health problems because of the stress and poor conditions under which they labored. And yet, they couldn't stop—they were all reliant on the next paycheck to get by (or not get by, as Ehrenreich argues), and so they had to endure abuse, exploitation, and all sorts of risks for the tenuous security of serving, scrubbing, and selling.

You encounter these people every day—when you eat at a restaurant, shop at a "big box" retailer, or stay at a hotel—and you may even be one yourself. Ehrenreich argues that there's no way to "make it" under these circumstances, and her experiences illustrate this argument with chilling clarity.

Inequalities of power in service work have many sources—gender, race, age, and immigration status—and those with greater power (cli-

telecommuting working from home while staying connected to the office through communications technology

ents, managers) may take advantage without even realizing it. Ehrenreich reminds us that even in "respectable" forms of service work, exploitation is common. What about jobs that are illegal—such as prostitution or the work of undocumented farm laborers? These workers lack the legal protections that even Wal-Mart workers or chain restaurant waitstaff have access to, and they may be subject to prosecution and punishment merely for doing their jobs.

Postindustrial Knowledge Work

In the new millennium, intellectual or information work is increasingly common while manual labor is increasingly rare (Tapscott 1997). The massive changes wrought by information technologies—often referred to as the "new economy"—have again transformed the nature of work in ways that are not yet fully understood (Kellner 2001).

The majority of the workforce in the United States now hold jobs that involve working with information, and most new jobs created are primarily within this sector. While many of these technologies purport to increase productivity and save time, the average worker is also working more hours in a week than her predecessor in the pre–Information Age workplace.

Another important feature of the Information Age workplace is greatly diminished importance of place. This phenomenon has been called the "death of distance" (Caincross 1995). Work that can be done on a computer can be done from any location, as networking through computers, satellite, cell phones, and other technologies makes workers' location almost irrelevant to their ability to get the work done and to work with others (Poster 2002).

More and more workers are **telecommuting**. They stay at home rather than commute to the office, and they are connected to their workplace through communications technology. According to a 2009 survey, more than 33 million Americans telecommute at least part-time, and this number is projected to increase significantly in the coming years (World at Work Telework Trendlines 2009).

Supporters claim that telecommuting has many benefits for the worker, the business, and society at large. Employees get flexible work schedules. Traffic delays, parking problems, and time wasted commuting don't exist for the telecommuter. Businesses get increased productivity and fewer sick days when they allow employees to telecommute. Although many employers worry that allowing employees to work from home would reduce accountability, some believe that the opposite is true. In traditional office environments, the only measure of employee value is the number of hours present in the office, regardless of what gets done, whereas telecommuters must demonstrate their accomplishments more concretely. Telecommuting and similar uses of information technology have also made it easier for single parents or workers with disabilities to stay employed full-time.

There is much debate around the positive and negative aspects of telecommuting and other technologies that physically and geographically separate workers. Some suggest that new information technologies will actually increase the need for face-to-face contact and tightly knit workplaces. For example, workers who write codes for computer software can do it anywhere they have a computer and instantly send the results to those who will package and market the software, but software companies are still the most geographically concentrated of any industry. Microsoft, the world's largest software company, refers to its home office as "the campus" and has gone to great lengths to make it an appealing place for employees precisely because the company still needs them at the same location in order to work. In the Information Age, more and more work requires the creative manipulation of knowledge, and for this workers need to brainstorm and share ideas in more interactive ways than the technology allows even now. The computer industry suggests that even when work can be done anywhere there will still be a real need to bring people together, at least some of the time.

The rise of new technologies may roll back many of the original effects of the Industrial Revolution. Manufacturing made it necessary for many people to work at the same location, causing the growth of cities and the decline of rural and small-town populations. However, with new technologies that let people work from anywhere, perhaps telecommuting will cause cities to shrink again as more people will be able to live without reference to the company that employs them. Small towns are now offering an attractive alternative to outsourcing. High-tech jobs are beginning to relocate to rural areas, where companies are finding it cheaper to do business and more attractive for their employees (Pinto 2005). It's possible that information technology may one day reunite the worlds of work and home that the Industrial Revolution tore asunder.

Last, it's not just knowledge workers who rely on this new information technology. The Digital Age has also changed the way industrial and service work is conducted. Even jobs traditionally considered to be in manufacturing now have a knowledge component. For example, the big three automakers in the United States have in the past hired college graduates for the assembly line because they needed employees able to identify and suggest quality improvements (Brandon 1996). In the service sector, retail outlets and grocery stores use computer databases to predict exactly how much of a product they need to keep on hand and to order new merchandise in a timely fashion, a system called "just in time inventory," drastically reducing overhead and waste. Insurance companies use instant messaging (IM) technology to connect workers in different offices or in the field, "finding IM not only improves accuracy and provides timely customer response but adds dollars to their bottom line" (Chordas 2003).

The Postindustrial Office?
To attract the best knowledge workers and to motivate them to work long hours, information and technology companies like Google and Microsoft go to great lengths to make the workplace appealing.

In Relationships

Disembodied Colleagues

Ironically, all the communication technologies that increase connections between people may ultimately make them feel more alienated from other human beings. This is a common complaint of workers in the software industry. In the novel *Microserfs* by Douglas Coupland, a neurotic Microsoft employee describes the joys of e-mail:

> I'm an e-mail addict. Everybody at Microsoft is an addict. The future of e-mail usage is being pioneered right here. The cool thing with e-mail is that when you send it, there's no possibility of connecting with the person on the other end. It's better than phone answering machines, because with them, the person on the other line might actually pick up the phone and you might have to talk. (Coupland 1995)

Coupland was probably exaggerating somewhat, but there is no doubt that the business practices first adopted by cutting-edge technology companies have influenced almost every part of the economy.

Even a seemingly minor change, like the adoption of e-mail, can profoundly affect the way people experience their workplace. In his article "Workers as Cyborgs: Labor and Networked Computers," Mark Poster details the increase in alienation that can come when a workplace switches to electronic communications. For instance, "a hospital in the Midwest that introduced a software program for ordering supplies from the Internet" saw increases in efficiency but also found that the technology "furthers the alienation of the worker" (Poster 2002). Using the new software may have gotten supplies ordered more quickly and with fewer errors, but "electronic communications are void of personal nuances characteristic of face-to-face communications" (Poster 2002). In short, it gets lonely when the only person you talk to is your computer.

Telecommuters who live alone may experience alienation and loneliness because the traditional workplace is often a major source of shared experience. Even worse, many of those who had hoped telecommuting would give them more quality time with their families are finding that working from home can actually intensify the conflict between work and family. As one study of telecommuters explains, "work can take over our personal lives. . . . If you're working from the family computer in the middle of the family room, your kids see you at work and don't understand why you're physically there, but mentally you're someplace else" (AHENS 2003).

All these situations stress increased alienation as the result of the Information Age. Will your work involve you with others in face-to-face interaction, or will you "know" your co-workers, colleagues, customers, and clients only through disembodied relationships?

Individual and Collective Resistance Strategies: How Workers Cope

Individuals and groups cope with their working conditions in a variety of ways called **resistance strategies**. These are tactics that let workers take back a degree of control over the conditions of their labor and feel that they have some sense of autonomy even in the face of dehumanizing,

resistance strategies ways that workers express discontent with their working conditions and try to reclaim control of the conditions of their labor

alienating constraints imposed by the terms and demands of their employment.

Individual resistance can range from the fairly benign, like using work time to surf the web, to the truly dangerous, like sabotaging the assembly line. More often, individual resistance may be simply personalizing the workspace with photos or daydreaming on the job as a type of escape (Roy 1960). Collective forms of resistance that seek solutions to shared workplace problems include union organizing and membership, strikes, walkouts, and work stoppages.

This discussion begins with an examination of individual resistance strategies within service work. We bring Max Weber's theory on bureaucracy into the present to see how workers today are coping with the constraints of those organizations. Last, we look at collective resistance strategies—union organization, both past and present.

Individual Resistance Strategies: Handling Bureaucratic Constraints

Bureaucratic organizations are found in almost every sector of the economy. In Weber's theory of bureaucracies, he highlighted the rational, impersonal, and coldly efficient nature of this form of social organization (refer to Chapter 5 for a review). Workers in highly bureaucratic organizations often feel the lack of autonomy in their everyday work lives. Autonomy is the ability to direct one's individual destiny—to have the power to control the conditions of one's labor—and this is generally lacking for people who work in highly structured, rule-bound, and depersonalized environments. Their daily tasks are structured by external forces; for example, the pace of the assembly line is decided for them and they cannot slow it down or speed it up if they need to take a break or want to finish work early.

In many corporate settings, employees at all levels are under various types of surveillance: electronic key cards monitor their comings and goings, cameras record their activities, computer transactions are screened, and phone calls are recorded. In retail sales, workers' interactions with customers are often scripted, so that even what they say to others is outside their control. Not only is there a lack of autonomy, but there is also a lack of individuality in the workplace. Workers are treated more like robots than people. Unlike a robot, however, human workers can resist and undermine the bureaucratic constraints that limit their autonomy in the workplace—and they do so in a wide variety of ways.

Robin Leidner's study *Fast Food, Fast Talk* provides an in-depth look at individual resistance strategies in the workplace (Leidner 1993). The study focuses on McDonald's employees and the routinized nature of their interactions with customers. Under the golden arches, every contact between the counter staff and the hungry consumer is strictly scripted, seemingly with no room for improvisation or creativity. Or is there?

McDonald's workers are trained to interact with customers using "The Six Steps": greeting, taking orders, assembling food, presenting it, receiving payment, and thanking them for their business. As monotonous as these steps are, workers don't necessarily resent routinization—it helps them do their jobs effectively. And some workers, like this woman, improvise on the steps, personalizing them in tiny but still noticeable ways:

Fast Food, Fast Talk In her study of restaurant employees, Robin Leidner looks at the ways that workers subvert the scripts that McDonald's requires them to follow when interacting with customers.

Just do the Six Steps, but do it in your own way. It's not like you have to say "Hi, welcome to McDonald's." You can say, "Hi, how are you doing?" or "Good morning," "Good afternoon," "Good evening," things like that. (Leidner 1993, p. 138)

Leidner observed that there were limits within which workers could

use the script as a starting point and inject [their] own personality into the interactions. Thus, some window workers joked or chatted with customers and tried to make the exchanges enjoyable for both parties. This stance implied an assertion of equality with customers and a refusal to suppress the self completely. (Leidner 1993, p. 190)

Leidner proposes that submitting to scripted interactions all day long suppresses the real self and that this sort of tightly controlled work environment can actually be damaging to the individual.

One of the functions of McDonald's service script is to regulate the power relationship between customer and worker: customers' demands can be delivered with all types of attitude, but workers must always serve customers with a smile. The script constrains workers' responses—if they have rude or even abusive customers, they must still stick to the script:

You have to take their crap. [Laughs.] I'm not the type of person to say, "OK, have it your way." I mean, I have to admit, I'm tempted to backtalk a lot. That gets me in a lot of trouble. So I mean, when a customer's rude to me I just have to walk away and say, "Could you take this order please, before I say something I'm not supposed to say?" (Leidner 1993, p. 133)

union an association of workers who bargain collectively for increased wages and benefits and better working conditions

If they do pervert the script or talk back to a rude customer, workers may be inviting a reprimand from their supervisor. But they are also engaging in resistance, asserting their own identities in the face of the depersonalizing routine. They are being active rather than passive, controlling the interaction rather than being controlled by it. They are asserting their own autonomy on the job, and it is apparently worth the risk.

It is difficult to think of a form of employment that would allow us to avoid these bureaucratic constraints altogether. What types of resistance strategies have you used to regain a bit of independence and power in the workplace?

Collective Resistance Strategies: Unions in the Past and Present

Although individual resistance strategies may provide a small measure of autonomy for some workers, they don't fundamentally change the working conditions or make permanent improvements to the terms of employment for all workers. That is why workers sometimes seek more lasting solutions to their problems by organizing to instigate collective resistance strategies—by forming unions.

A **union** benefits workers in various ways and serves to counterbalance the power of employers. A labor union is an association of workers who come together to improve their economic status and working conditions. The two main types of unions are craft unions, in which all the members are skilled in a certain craft (e.g., the International Brother-

hood of Carpenters and Joiners), and industrial unions, in which all the members work in the same industry regardless of their particular skill (e.g., the Service Employees International Union). Some unions are local with small memberships; others are large, national organizations representing millions of workers. Unions have legal status to represent workers in contract negotiations with employers.

When disagreements arise between management and employees, unionized workers may threaten to or actually stage a temporary "walkout," "work stoppage," or "strike" to express their grievance and force corporate managers and owners to negotiate. Often the striking workers will try to discourage the public from patronizing the businesses implicated in the labor dispute and try to prevent other, outside replacement workers (sometimes called "scab labor") from taking their jobs while they are out on strike. Union negotiations with employers about the terms of employment and working conditions are coordinated through collective bargaining in which contract decisions between management and union representatives must be mutually agreed upon rather than imposed unilaterally.

Unions have a long history in the United States. At various times, they have existed on the margins of society and been vigorously opposed by capitalists and other free-market supporters. Unions in the nineteenth and early twentieth centuries were brutally suppressed by capitalists, and union organizers were frequently arrested and jailed. Often they were charged with conspiracy because attempts to form unions were illegal for much of American history. The Typographical Union (representing print typesetters), which formed in 1852, is usually considered the "first durable national organization of workers" in the United States. By 1881, a number of smaller labor groups had banded together

Lawrence, Massachusetts, 1912 During the 1912 textile mill strike, workers demanded "bread and roses," eloquently capturing their desire for something more than the wages needed to survive.

to form the American Federation of Labor (AFL), which eventually became the AFL-CIO (by adding the groups in the Congress of Industrial Organizations).

Unions of this era fought for a variety of workplace reforms. During the 1912 textile mill strikes in Lawrence, Massachusetts, the workers' slogan was "bread and roses," emphasizing their desire for something more than wages sufficient to survive. Unions also led campaigns to end child labor, establish an eight-hour workday and a five-day work week, and to increase workplace safety. For this reason, unions are still sometimes referred to as "the people who brought you the weekend." Before the eight-hour workday was instituted, many workers literally didn't see the sun because they went to work before daybreak and left after dark. It is not surprising that many were willing to fight for unionization even in the face of extreme opposition.

In 2010, approximately 14.7 million American workers belonged to a union organization (U.S. Bureau of Labor Statistics 2011a). However, union membership has been in steep decline since its peak in the 1950s. In 1955, approximately 35 percent of the labor force was unionized; by 2010, fewer than 12 percent of the workforce belonged to a union (U.S. Bureau of Labor Statistics 2011a). In the 1950s, an average of 352 major strikes occurred each year; by the early 2000s, that number had fallen to fewer than 30 (Commission for Labor Cooperation 2003).

Perhaps the first major blow to union strength came with the Taft-Hartley Act of 1947, which instituted limitations on secondary strikes and boycotts, established restrictions on picketing, and allowed the federal government to force strikers back to work during "cooling-off periods" that not only gave workers time to reconsider but also gave businesses time to gather resources to counteract a strike. After Taft-Hartley, various states passed so-called right-to-work laws that prohibited "closed shops," workplaces where all employees had to be members of the union. Supporters say that workers should be free to decide whether to join a union; opponents argue that all employees who benefit from collective bargaining should help to support the union that represents the workers.

The laws regarding union activity were one part of larger social changes that have occurred during the past fifty years and have diminished the power of unions in the United States. Between 1945 and 1973, the economy grew rapidly, and as long as wages and benefits continued to rise, the perceived need for unions waned. However, in the 1970s the economy entered a serious decline, and American corporations found it was cheaper to move production overseas to countries whose working conditions were more like those of nineteenth-century than twentieth-century America. As a result, unions have largely changed focus from fighting for better wages and working conditions to keeping jobs in this country.

Industries that leave the United States, referred to as "runaway shops," are mostly in manufacturing, where firms take advantage of cheap labor and lax environmental laws in other countries. But even Hollywood has out-of-country production sites. Many movies purporting to depict American cities like Chicago and New York are actually filmed in Toronto, where labor costs are on average 20 percent lower than in the United States (Cooper 2003). In 1998, when this practice was really taking off, 27 percent of U.S. film and television productions were runaway productions (285 out of 1,075)—almost triple the number from just a decade before (Monitor Report 1999). Some 81 percent of these were made in Canada with its cheaper labor and weaker unions. The direct production expenditures lost from the United States were estimated at $2.8 billion for 1998 alone.

With a shift in the U.S. economy from manufacturing to the service sector, the only unions to grow since the early 1970s have been public employees' unions. In some instances, service jobs are being moved overseas. But even when jobs remain in the United States, other problems emerge among workers.

When Wal-Mart began opening Supercenters in the late 1990s that included full grocery stores, many industry watchers became fearful that the retail behemoth's wage policies and antiunion stance would force local grocers "to push for drastically lower wages to stay competitive with the new mega-warehouse on the block" (Green 2002). As a consequence, union organizers made concerted efforts to organize Wal-Mart employees, only to be met with substantial opposition. Union leaders reported that Wal-Mart maintained a "hit list" of employees to be fired because they favor unionization and that in some instances they instructed employees to call the police if organizers tried to contact them. In those rare instances when Wal-Mart employees have voted to unionize, the company has resorted to even more drastic measures. In 2002, after the butchers at the Wal-Mart Supercenter in Jacksonville, Texas, voted to join the United Food and Commercial Workers (UFCW), the company decided to eliminate the meat cutters in their Texas stores and buy precut meat from their suppliers.

The 1997 strike by UPS drivers was widely hailed as the beginning of a comeback for organized labor. It was the biggest strike in more than a decade, with 185,000 workers walking picket lines for fifteen days before a new contract was signed. Shortly after the settlement, Ron Carey, then president of the Teamsters labor union, declared, "this is not just a Teamster victory, this is a victory for all working people" (Roberts and

Millionaires versus Billionaires Labor disputes between the National Football League Player's Association union and NFL team owners threatened to disrupt the 2011 season. Players including Tom Brady, Drew Breese, Peyton Manning, and others entered into an anti-trust lawsuit against the owners after collective bargaining negotiations broke down.

Bernstein 2000). The Teamsters emphasized that their first concern was the increasing number of part-time jobs without benefits, a concern that large numbers of Americans shared. However, the UPS strike was relatively unique and unlikely to be repeated by other unions. Not only does UPS offer a service that can't be moved outside the country, but its workers also have good rapport with the customers, which may help to explain why public support for the union was so high. UPS has traditionally been a labor-friendly, worker-owned corporation, with a number of top executives who started out as drivers. Additionally, UPS is the overwhelming market leader in the parcel delivery business, which decreases the pressure for top executives to cut costs. Competitors like Federal Express aren't unionized, emphasizing the extent to which the service sector has succeeded in resisting unionization.

The successful UPS strike may still encourage other workers to pursue unionization. Despite several decades of decline in union power, the recognition of workers' rights, including the right to organize, continues to be a feature of the American economic system. Shortly after the UPS strike ended, Nelson Lichtenstein, a professor of history specializing in labor issues, predicted, "Right now, discussions are going on in executive offices in Wal-Mart, Kmart, Federal Express, all these labor-intensive service firms, about how to rethink their labor strategy" (Greenhouse 1997). Whether such collective resistance strategies become more prevalent again in the future remains to be seen.

The Best of Corporate America

From a Weberian perspective, we can see that large bureaucracies laden with rules and procedures can deprive employees of a sense of autonomy, individuality, and control. From a Marxist perspective, we can see how large capitalist corporations sometimes exploit their workers and cause alienation and that their power hierarchies often exclude women and minorities. These criticisms are true in the aggregate—money, power, and influence converge in corporate America, and with these forms of power come opportunities for exploitation and abuse. But not all corporations are evil, and sometimes we see major corporate players transcend self-interest and act with great altruism.

Compared to the big firms like Morgan Stanley and Goldman Sachs, Sandler O'Neill and Partners is a tiny investment brokerage firm. It was located on the 104th floor of the World Trade Center in New York, and on September 11, 2001, it was devastated in the terrorist attacks. Sixty-six of its 171 employees died in the towers, all of their equipment and business information was destroyed, and only one of the senior partners survived. That partner, Jimmy Dunne, immediately began what seemed like an impossible task: address overwhelming grief, rebuild the company, and take care of the families of all 66 lost employees.

Jimmy Dunne In the September 11, 2001, attacks on the World Trade Center, Sandler O'Neill & Partners lost 66 of its 171 employees, including two of its three founders. Jimmy Dunne, the surviving founder, consoled the company's other survivors and inspired them to rebuild the company.

Within a matter of days, Dunne had set up shop in temporary offices (donated by Bank of America). Sandler O'Neill began trading again, but without the knowledge or experience of the employees it had lost. And in what constitutes a miracle in corporate America, its competitors began to help out. Stockbrokers from other companies started calling in market information to Sandler O'Neill's inexperienced traders. A retired vice president from Goldman Sachs just showed up one day and started volunteering at the equity desk. Major investment brokerages like Merrill Lynch and J. P. Morgan Chase cut Sandler O'Neill in on their deals, just so the crippled company could earn a portion of the commission. And Sandler O'Neill needed every penny it could get its hands on: Dunne had paid out the full year's salary and benefits to the families of all the dead employees and had guaranteed year-end bonuses as well.

These powerhouse investment brokerages—ordinarily in a position to squash a tiny firm like Sandler O'Neill—suspended their rivalries to get another corporation and its devastated employees back in the game. They shared office space, information, workers, deals, and commissions with a competitor. They subverted their own bureaucratic rules and the imperatives of capitalist competition to help a struggling company survive. And it did: Sandler O'Neill was profitable again before the end of 2001 and had the necessary funds to continue supporting the families of its lost staff members. Granted, September 11 created extraordinary circumstances, and many people and organizations rose to the challenge of this national tragedy. But the case of Sandler

O'Neill shows that corporate competitors can become collaborators and provide support. Corporate America is, after all, populated by human beings.

Globalization, Economics, and Work

Globalization describes the cultural and economic changes that have occurred as a result of dramatically increased international trade and exchange in the late twentieth and early twenty-first centuries. Although there has always been some global economic trade—East Asia's ancient spice and silk trade routes and the sixteenth-century English and Dutch shipping empires are early examples of this—the effects of globalization have become more highly visible since the 1970s. Globalization has been fostered through the development of international economic institutions; innovations in technology; the movement of money, information, and people; and infrastructure that supports such expansion. Today, it is possible to view the world as having one global economy, with huge corporations whose production processes span national borders, international regulatory bodies such as the World Trade Organization (WTO), and transnational trade agreements such as the North American Free Trade Agreement (NAFTA) redefining economic relationships between and among nations.

Supporters of globalization believe that "free trade" can lead to more efficient allocation of resources, lower prices, more employment, and higher output, with all countries involved in the trade benefiting. Critics believe that free trade promotes a self-interested corporate agenda and that powerful and autonomous multinational corporations can exploit workers and increasingly shape the politics of nation-states. And the recent global recession shows us that all world economies are connected, for better or for worse.

International Trade: Shallow and Deep Integration

To explain economic globalization, social scientists have used the terms "shallow integration" and "deep integration" (Dicken 1998). Shallow integration refers to the flow of goods and services that characterized international trade until several decades ago. In a shallow integration model, a national company

> **globalization** the cultural and economic changes resulting from dramatically increased international trade and exchange in the late twentieth and early twenty-first centuries

would arrange with a foreign company to either import or export products but exclusively within that single nation's economy. For example, not even thirty years ago, a Japanese car would have been made almost entirely in Japan, and a pair of American jeans would have been made in the United States. Thus, Japan would export cars to the United States, which would import Japanese cars. And the United States would export jeans to Japan, which would import American jeans. To protect their interests, nations would impose taxes on imports, sometimes making those imports more expensive to buy than similar products made at home.

Deep integration refers to the global flow of goods and services in today's economy. While companies still make arrangements with other companies for imports and exports, their relationships are far more complex. Most significantly, companies are no longer national; they are multinational, with major decision-making, production, and/or distribution branches of a particular company spread all over the world. When we look at the labels on our clothing, the global nature of their origin is often concealed. The label may say "Made in . . . ," but the raw materials or other parts may have originated somewhere else.

When nations make laws to protect national economic interests, they must often do so with a host of other nations in mind. NAFTA is an excellent example of this complex web of global relationships. Many major apparel companies, such as Nike or the Gap, have marketing and design headquarters in the United States but their garment factories are in Mexico, another country in NAFTA. Under NAFTA, American companies can avoid paying taxes when they export raw materials to Mexico and then import the finished products. These global trade agreements often benefit private industry much more than they do nations.

Transnational Corporations

Transnational corporations (TNCs) are another part of the global economy. These firms purposefully transcend national borders so that their products can be manufactured, distributed, marketed, and sold from many bases all over the world. We may think of companies like Coca-Cola or General Electric as quintessentially American, but they are more accurately understood as global or transnational corporations. What is distinctive about today's TNCs is the way they shape the global economy. In the past fifty years, they have experienced unprecedented growth in both numbers of firms and amount of economic impact.

The United Nations 2006 list of "The World's Top 100

sweatshop a workplace where workers are subject to extreme exploitation, including below-standard wages, long hours, and poor working conditions that may pose health or safety hazards

Non-Financial TNCs" assigns firms a "transnationality index" by assessing the ratios between foreign employment and total employment, foreign investments and total investments, and foreign sales and total sales (UNCTAD 2007). In their 2006 listing, the top five "transnational" firms included four U.S. firms: General Electric (1), Exxon Mobil (5), Ford Motor Co. (6), and Wal-Mart (10). Just over half the workforce is foreign at both General Electric and Ford—with Exxon coming in at almost two-thirds and Wal-Mart at just over one-quarter. All of these firms are marketed strongly as "American" brands, yet they are clearly global institutions.

Figure 11.1 shows how much economic influence TNCs exert in the global economy. Among the top forty global economies, ranked by either Gross Domestic Product (GDP) or total sales, there are three TNCs. Firms such as Wal-Mart and Royal Dutch Shell actually rank higher than the nations of Egypt, Pakistan, and Colombia. When we consider that firms have the economic weight of nations, we can understand just how much political clout TNCs wield in terms of global governance. For instance, an American TNC can exercise powerful influence by donating huge amounts of money to lobbyists and political campaigns. Further, in international regulatory bodies, such as the WTO, TNCs are often able to influence trade law at a global level.

Another manifestation of the ever-increasing economic power of TNCs is competition in the global market. Because TNCs can take advantage of cheap pools of labor by either relocating their own factories or outsourcing, nations compete with each other for these contracts by undercutting their citizens' wages and offering incentives, such as tax-free zones. Scholars, politicians, activists, and commentators have called this the "race to the bottom." These kinds of policies hurt the local populations, often depriving workers of decent wages and the potential benefits, such as schools and hospitals, that would have been derived from taxes.

Global Sweatshop Labor

One way the race to the bottom hurts workers in their own countries is by creating an environment where sweatshop labor can exist. A **sweatshop** is a workplace where workers are subjected to extreme exploitation, including below-standard wages, long hours, and poor working conditions that may pose health or safety hazards. Sweatshop workers are often intimidated with threats of physical discipline and are prevented from forming unions or other workers' rights groups. Historically, sweatshops originated during the Industrial Revolution as a system where middlemen earned profits from the difference between what they received for delivering on a contract and the amount they paid to the workers who produced the contracted goods. The profit was said to

Top 40

RANK	ENTITY		GDP / REVENUES $ BILLIONS PPP
1	— United States	⚑	$14,119
2	— Japan	⚑	$5,069
3	— China	⚑	$4,985
4	— Germany	⚑	$3,330
5	— France	⚑	$2,649
6	— United Kingdom	⚑	$2,174
7	— Italy	⚑	$2,112
8	— Brazil	⚑	$2,594
9	— Spain	⚑	$1,460
10	— India	⚑	$1377
11	— Canada	⚑	$1,336
12	— Russian Federation	⚑	$1,231
13	— Australia	⚑	$924
14	— Mexico	⚑	$874
15	— Republic of Korea	⚑	$832
16	— Netherlands	⚑	$792
17	— Turkey	⚑	$614
18	— Indonesia	⚑	$540
19	▲21 Switzerland	⚑	$491
20	— Belgium	⚑	$471

RANK	ENTITY		GDP / REVENUES $ BILLIONS PPP
⬆ 21 ▲28	Royal Dutch Shell	🏭	$458
⬆ 22 ▲27	Exxon Mobil	🏭	$442
⬇ 23 ▼19	Poland	⚑	$430
24 ▼22	Sweden	⚑	$406
25 ▲26	Wal-Mart Stores	🏭	$405
⬇ 26 ▼23	Norway	⚑	$381
27 ▼25	Austria	⚑	$381
⬇ 28 ▼24	Saudi Arabia	⚑	$375
⬆ 29 ▲34	BP	🏭	$367
30 ▼29	Iran, Islamic Republic	⚑	$331
31 ▼30	Greece	⚑	$329
32 ▲33	Venezuela, RB	⚑	$326
33 ▼31	Denmark	⚑	$309
34 ▼32	Argentina	⚑	$307
35 —	South Africa	⚑	$285
36 —	Thailand	⚑	$263
☀ 37	Chevron	🏭	$263
38 ▼37	Finland	⚑	$237
☀ 39	Total	🏭	$234
40 ▼39	Colombia	⚑	$234

— held position   ▲# up / 2008 position   ▼# down / 2008 position   ⚑ country   🏭 company   ⬇ fell more than 3 places from 2008   ⬆ rose more than 3 places   ☀ new to chart

Are Sweatshops Good or Bad? While workers sew at *maquilas*, or sweatshops, such as this one in Guatemala City, Guatemala, students like Christine Hoffmann, left, and Bradley Heinz, right, at Stanford University are calling on universities to ensure that apparel bearing their school's logo is made in factories where workers are paid a living wage.

be "sweated" from the workers, because they received minimal wages and worked excessive hours under unsanitary and dangerous conditions.

Sweatshops, however, are not a thing of the past. Unfortunately, there are many in the world today making large numbers of the goods that we unknowingly consume. Though perhaps more prevalent overseas, sweatshops exist in the United States as well. The General Accounting Office defines a sweatshop as "an employer that violates more than one federal or state labor law governing minimum wage and overtime, child labor, industrial homework, occupational safety and health, workers compensation, or industrial regulation" (Ross 1997, p.12). The Department of Labor estimated that in 2001 there were more than 7,000 sweatshops in U.S. cities such as New York, Los Angeles, New Orleans, Chicago, Philadelphia, and El Paso. American companies may also manufacture goods overseas using foreign sweatshop labor. Nike, the Gap, and clothing lines associated with Mary-Kate and Ashley Olsen and Sean "Diddy" Combs have all

been charged with using sweatshop labor in Southeast Asia, Central America, and elsewhere and have been pressured to reform their practices.

Many universities purchase their logo apparel from manufacturers that use sweatshop labor. In 1999, students at the University of Michigan, University of North Carolina, University of Wisconsin, Madison, Duke University, and Georgetown University staged sit-ins to pressure their respective administrators into agreeing to fully disclose factory conditions and wages paid to workers who produce university apparel. Other similar campaigns were launched at Seattle Community College in 2004 and systemwide at the University of California in 2005 to change university purchasing policy to allow for preferences for union-made and verifiably sweatshop-free products (Greenhouse 1999). We encourage you to do your own research on whether sweatshop products have reached the stores where you shop—or even your own closet—in completing the next Data Workshop.

DATA WORKSHOP

ANALYZING EVERYDAY LIFE

Are Your Clothes Part of the Global Commodity Chain?

You probably own and consume a large number of products that originated in faraway countries, including your car, clothing, or shoes. These items have traveled widely during the process from production to consumption. Food, pharmaceuticals, and electronics are other examples of globally made products. Social scientists call these international movements of goods "global commodity chains" (Gereffi and Korzeniewicz 1994).

Global commodity chains are networks of corporations, product designers and engineers, manufacturing firms, distribution channels (such as ocean freightliners, railroads, and trucking firms), and consumer outlets (such as Wal-Mart). Global commodity chains start with a product design and brand name and end with the consumer making a purchase. But between start and finish is often a complex global process with many different people, in many different nations, all contributing to the final product.

The manufacturing of goods, from garments to electronics to automobiles, used to happen in the United States and other Western nations; today's manufacturing centers are primarily located in poorer nations, such as the Philippines, China, Indonesia, and many Latin American countries. American corporations such as Nike, the Gap, and Levi-

Strauss have closed all their U.S. manufacturing plants and hired contractors and subcontractors from East Asia and Latin America to make their products at substantially lower prices. Now these companies focus large amounts of financial resources on "branding" their products (Klein 2000). Branding is the process, usually accomplished through advertising, by which companies gain consumers' attention and loyalty. Much of the money you pay for some products goes toward financing these branding campaigns, while a much smaller sum pays the workers who actually make the products.

The following three exercises will help you to understand where the things that you buy come from and the increasing disparity between product values and workers' wages.

Exercise One: The Global Closet

Pick out five to ten items of clothing from your closet. Now check the labels. Where were your clothes made? Make a list of the nations represented in your closet. How many nations are from East Asia or Latin America? Is there a difference between where an item is made and where it is assembled? Does the label indicate where the fabric originated?

Exercise Two: No Longer "Made in the U.S.A."

Ask your parents, aunts or uncles, or grandparents if you can look at the labels of their older clothes. Or go to a thrift store and look for older or vintage clothes there. Again pick out five to ten items of clothing. How many of those items were made in the United States? Compare your answers in Exercise 1 and Exercise 2. What does this tell you about the globalization of the garment manufacturing industry over the past fifty years?

Exercise Three: Are Your Favorite Brands "Sweat Free"?

List your favorite brands of clothing, shoes, or other fashion accessories. What is your brand's stance on sweatshop labor? Do workers who make your favorite products earn a living wage? You can check many corporations' ethics regarding labor conditions by doing some research on the internet. See how your brands score at the following web sites:

CorpWatch: www.corpwatch.org

Interfaith Center on Corporate Responsibility: www.iccr .org

National Labor Committee for Workers' and Human Rights: www.nlcnet.org

There are two options for completing this Data Workshop.

- *Option 1 (informal)*: Choose one of the exercises above and follow the instructions as outlined. Bring notes to class to discuss with others in small groups. Your instructor may organize groups so that all members have done the same exercise or all members have done a different exercise. In either case, compare your findings with those of other members of the group.

- *Option 2 (formal)*: Choose one or more of the exercises above (or your instructor may assign specific exercises) and follow the instructions as outlined. Write a three- to four-page essay analyzing your findings.

Outsourcing

The U.S. economy is increasingly affected by globalization, and as a result, American companies have sought out new business models to reduce costs and remain competitive. One increasingly popular approach is outsourcing or offshoring. **Outsourcing** involves "contracting out" or transferring to another country the labor that a company might otherwise have employed its own staff to perform. Typically, a company's decision to outsource is made for financial reasons and is usually achieved by transferring employment to locations where labor is cheap. In 1992, U.S. firms employed 7 million workers in other countries (O'Reilly 1992); but with technological advances, particularly the internet, over the past decade or more, businesses have been able to increase their foreign employment pool significantly at a minimum cost.

Information technology–producing industries, such as data entry, communication services, communication equipment, and computer hardware, software, and services, are the main jobs involved in outsourcing. Although countries such as China, the Philippines, and those in Eastern Europe are also key sites, India has been the primary location for outsourcing because of the shared English language and cheap employment. A company can hire an engineer in India for $10,000 a year compared with $60,000–$90,000 in the United States. In 2005, India controlled some 44 percent of the global offshore outsourcing market for software and back-office services, with revenues worth more than $17 billion (Associated Press 2005).

The economic benefits of outsourcing are gained by businesses, but the drawbacks are felt by the labor pool. Between 2001 and 2004, some 403,300 information technology jobs

> **outsourcing** "contracting out" or transferring to another country the labor that a company might otherwise have employed its own staff to perform; typically done for financial reasons

Sweatshop Labor and "Gold Farming" in China

Many people are familiar with the concept of sweatshops, where cheap labor is exploited to make clothing and goods for people in industrialized nations. While individuals are able to understand easily how labor can be exploited for the production of material goods, a more difficult concept to grasp is how labor can be exploited in the market for virtual goods. Rather than working long hours under inhuman conditions for little pay in order to produce luxury items such as Nikes and Levi's, "gold farmers" are exploited in order to create the ultimate luxury product—status in an online computer game.

The Real World is the title of your textbook and a long-running MTV reality show. Online, the term "real world" is also used to differentiate life outside the "virtual world." Some of the most popular forms of virtual worlds are Massively Multiplayer Online Role Playing Games (MMORPGs) such as *World of Warcraft*, *Ultima Online*, and *Everquest*. *World of Warcraft* (*WoW*) is the most popular of these games, with approximately 10.9 million monthly subscribers as of 2008. As with many MMORPGs, players make an initial investment to purchase the software for the game, and they are also charged a monthly subscription fee in order to play. In *WoW*, players use a character avatar through which they explore the virtual world, complete quests, and interact with other players or nonplayer characters (NPCs). Quests are assignments given by an NPC (who is programmed into the game) that usually involve killing a monster, gathering resources, transporting an item from one location to another, or finding a difficult-to-locate object. Successful quests are rewarded with in-game money and experience points that a character can spend to buy new skills and equipment. As with most MMORPGs, there is an emphasis on character improvement. Because of the interactive nature of *WoW*, advancing in the game isn't just a matter of personal achievement but also a matter of reputation and status in the community.

"Gold farms" profit from the importance of advancement in an MMORPG. According to estimates, around 100,000 people in China are employed as "gold farmers," making $120 to $250 (U.S.) per month playing *WoW* for 12- to 18-hour shifts. These Chinese gold farmers carry out in-game actions so that they can earn virtual money to buy equipment, skills, and status. These virtual assets are sold to real (recreational) players for real world money, creating a unique intersection of virtual and real world economies. Literally, a player can spend real world money to buy status and reputation in an online game. Since many of the beginning levels of *WoW* involve spending long hours doing repetitive and dull virtual tasks, the idea of being able to bypass this tedium to start at more advanced levels appeals to many players. Creating characters requires time and effort that players who use the services of gold farmers are unable or unwilling to devote to the game. So they buy the labor of gold farmers to advance their gaming strategies.

Many of the critiques of manufacturing sweatshops can be applied to the gold farming phenomenon. Gold farmers labor for the benefit of middle-class gamers in industrialized nations. Ge Jin, a Ph.D. student at the University of California in San Diego, documents working conditions in the gold farming "sweatshops," where he has filmed workers crowded into an airport hangar, bleary eyed, chain-smoking, and sleeping two to a single mat on the floor (Jin 2006). Are bad jobs better than no jobs? Certainly it is easier to live in most of modern society with money than without. Though most people in developed nations would view $3 a day as extremely low pay, in impoverished communities "$1 or $2 a day can be a life-transforming wage" (Kristof and WuDunn 2000). While there are those who argue that playing a computer game takes less of a physical toll than subsistence farming or factory work, it is evident that there is an imbalance between the amount of money that workers are paid to pro-

were lost in the United States due to outsourcing (Associated Press 2004). Some companies required their employees to train their offshore replacements, after which the American employees were fired. A 2003 study conducted by the University of California, Berkeley warned that as many as 14 million Americans held jobs at risk of being outsourced

(Bardhan and Kroll 2003). This affects not only those already in the workforce but those who are about to enter. Many new college graduates with high-tech degrees are faced with large-scale lack of employment in the United States.

While outsourcing is practiced by the majority of U.S. businesses, they are often reluctant to fully disclose details.

Chinese Gold Farmers How has the popularity of online games such as *World of Warcraft* led to new forms of sweatshops?

the services of gold farmers affect the virtual economy by driving up the prices of the rarest items. Traditional players then become resentful, as these price increases require them to work longer to acquire items that players with real world cash can purchase with little effort. On the other hand, does playing a game qualify as work? After all, it is "only a game."

Strategies for retaliation against players identified as gold farmers include verbal harassment inside the game. Rather than taking out their anger and frustrations on the gold farm brokers who benefit from the process, some traditional players will

duce these virtual resources and the prices that gamers pay to buy them. The sum of $200 can buy 500 pieces of online gold in *WoW*, which would take an estimated 100 hours of playing to earn.

The gaming world is up in arms about the gold farming phenomenon. While some gamers find that the opportunity to buy gold augments their playing experience, other gamers hold that buying from gold farmers confers an unfair advantage to those with expendable income. Purists argue that MMORPGs should be free of the corruption of the real world and that escapism is not possible with people buying status and reputation in the virtual world. Players who use

follow suspected gold farmers within the game and bombard them with racist comments. Gamers have put together racist videos to post on YouTube, venting their anger over the gold farming phenomenon. Gold farming then becomes a matter not just of class and economics, but also of race and racism.

Are gold farms good or bad? Are bad jobs better than no jobs at all? Should the virtual world be free of the corruption of the real world? Are gamers just too invested in their games? These are all questions to ask when pondering the intersections of the virtual world and real world that collide in the gold farming sweatshops.

International Business Machines (IBM) is a major information technology company that manufactures and sells computer hardware, software, and services. IBM would not say exactly how many workers it had hired under outsourcing agreements, how many it laid off, nor how many jobs were moved offshore, but in 2004 the vice president of human resources stated that 3,500 to 4,500 IBM jobs would be relocated from developed nations to emerging countries (Bulkeley 2004). Financial considerations are typically the reason a company decides to outsource, leaving anxious workers with a lack of job security, especially in troubled economic times.

Alternative Ways of Working

There are alternative ways of working, not all of which fit into typical categories of work. First we look at professional socialization, the process by which new members learn and internalize the norms and values of their group, examining case studies of workers in three unusual fields. Then we examine the contingent workforce—those who work in positions that are temporary or freelance or who work as independent contractors. Finally, there are the nonprofit corporations—private organizations whose missions go beyond the bottom-line—and volunteerism, the work of people who seek no compensation for their investment of time and energy.

Professional Socialization in Unusual Fields

Every new job requires some sort of training for the prospective employee. Anyone in a new position confronts an unfamiliar set of expectations and workplace norms that must be learned so the new person can fit into the environment. This process, called professional socialization (see Chapter 4 for a review), involves learning not only the social role but also the various details about how to do the job. Several sociological studies have explored the process of professional socialization focusing on medical students (Fox 1957; Becker et al. 1961; Haas and Shaffir 1977, 1982), teachers (Lortie 1968), clergy (Kleinman 1984), nurses (Stimson 1967), social workers (Loseke and Cahill 1986), and lawyers (Granfield 1992).

Spencer Cahill's study of students preparing to become funeral directors focused on the practical skills developed by mortuary science students and the emotional labor (see Hochschild 1983) involved in this occupation. Most social interaction within the mortuary science program revolved around death; as a result, students learned how to engage in the practice of "normalizing talk." "Mortuary science education requires students to adopt an occupational rhetoric and esoteric language that communicate professional authority and a calm composure towards matters that most of the lay public finds emotionally upsetting" (Cahill 1999, p. 106). In addition, students were required to control their own emotional responses to the work. "Some students told me that they found 'cases' of young children emotionally disturbing. . . . Yet, these students reportedly did 'get used to it,' 'keep it down,' and deal with emotionally distressing 'cases'" (Cahill 1999, pp. 108–9). Cahill found that successful mortuary science students were those who could best deal with the emotional component of the work.

Loren Bourassa and Blake Ashforth studied how inexperienced newcomers are socialized into the work life onboard an Alaskan fishing boat. The occupation of a fisherman differs greatly from other occupations because it requires no previous experience or even a high school education, as physical strength and stamina are the primary prerequisites. Work on a fishing boat pays well for a relatively short amount of time, and this often lures a large number of workers. However, their romantic notions about life on a fishing boat are quickly dispelled. "New workers were indoctrinated collectively by their more experienced co-workers and underwent a process of divestiture. . . . Specifically, newcomers were called 'new guys,' rather than by name, were subjected to constant taunts and verbal abuse, were constantly made to perform the least desirable jobs and other odd tasks, were required to obey incessant and often arbitrary instructions, and were routinely denied the privileges given to more experienced members" (Bourassa and Ashforth 1998, p. 181). This intense socialization proved effective as newcomers worked hard and came to understand the culture of the fishing boat workplace. "It became a badge of honor to survive the initiation phase" (Bourassa and Ashforth 1998, p. 189). Yet, the fleeting moment of self-satisfaction and positive feelings gave way to the continuous physical demands. Even the promise of economic rewards failed to sustain them. "The money was generally held in bank accounts until the completion of a contract. Workers could not use their money or even hold their paycheck in their hands. Thus, onboard the ship, money remained an abstract and distant notion" (Bourassa and Ashforth 1998, p. 189).

Jacqueline Lewis examined the socialization of exotic dancers and what goes into learning their job. "For exotic dancers, achieving job competence involves getting accustomed to working in a sex-related occupation and the practice of taking their clothes off in public for money" (Lewis 1998, p. 1). On-the-job socialization was essential for the women who entered this line of work. "Similar to the socialization experiences of individuals in other occupations, novice dancers learn through interaction and observation while on the job. . . . Since there is no formal certification structure, peers play an important role in this transformation process" (Lewis 1998, p. 5). Lewis found that several women felt the socialization process "inadequately prepared them for some of the realities of the life of an exotic dancer" (Lewis 1998, p. 12)—mainly the negative impact it would have on their private lives and the difficulties of having long-term heterosexual relationships with men outside the industry.

While professional socialization occurs on the job, anticipatory socialization is the process of learning the behaviors, expectations, and standards of a role or group to which one aspires but does not yet belong. One way to acquire anticipatory or early professional socialization is to do an internship while you're in college. This chapter's On the Job box describes how internships work and why they are such a valuable learning experience before entering the job market.

On the Job

Internships and Experiential Learning

Someone mentions an internship, and you think . . . what? Bored college students making coffee for the boss? Good-looking medical students on *Grey's Anatomy*? Monica Lewinsky? In fact, internships are an increasingly important part of the college experience. According to the *New York Times* (Altschuler 2002), more than half of the graduating seniors of 2001 had participated in some sort of experiential learning program during their college careers. At worst, the hapless intern may get really good at adding toner to the copier; at best, an internship can benefit both the intern and the company and may be useful in the long run for everyone involved.

Although some internships come with some compensation, others are unpaid; in either case, you gain valuable work experience. You may arrange an academic internship through your college or university and receive academic credit, or you may set up a nonacademic internship that leaves out the school altogether. Firms of all kinds look for college students to fill some of their employment needs. Of course, there's always the possibility that the work you're assigned as an intern will be mind numbing or pointless, so why bother with an internship?

First and most important, an internship may help you decide what you want to be—or don't want to be—when you graduate. After interning in a state's attorney's office, you may decide that being a lawyer isn't everything you thought it would be but that you would like to work with crime victims in a social service capacity. Even if you are sure about your future career path, you may want to consider branching out in the internships you apply for. You'll gain diverse skills and experience and be exposed to careers you might like just as much. Most Americans don't remain in the same job for their entire working lives, so keeping your options open during college doesn't seem like such a bad idea.

An internship on your résumé is also likely to make you an attractive job candidate. Even if your experience doesn't deal directly with the job you're applying for, having completed an internship demonstrates to potential employers your ability to work hard and manage your time. Almost two-thirds of the students from the class of 2004 who were hired after graduation had participated in an internship (McWilliams 2005). One study of recent graduates showed that those who had held internships during college were paid an average of almost 10 percent more than those without internship experience. In addition, many corporations turn first to their own interns when hiring. Results from a 2010 survey showed that employers offered full-time jobs to 83 percent of students who interned for them (NACE 2010). The entire internship can, in some respects, be viewed as an extended job interview.

There will always be competition for the most prestigious positions, though interning for a big name company doesn't necessarily guarantee a good experience. But even if you decide you'd prefer not to work for that corporation or in that field, the contacts you develop may help you find another position. These are people who are already established in the profession, and a good reference is always valuable when you're in the job market.

Internships work out well for employers too. At the very least, they're getting cheap labor, but more than that, interns can be very beneficial for companies that need a highly educated or highly trained workforce. Taking on young workers can also help a company stay connected to younger consumers and may provide them with some new perspectives and ideas. Corporations also realize that providing internships can create goodwill—from the students who intern with them, from the universities through which the internships are organized, or from the general public.

The Contingent Workforce: Temps, Freelancers, and Independent Contractors

Traditionally, most Americans have hoped to find a job they would keep their whole lives, one that would provide forty-hour work weeks along with vacations and health and retire-ment benefits. Increasingly, this sort of job is becoming rare. A growing percentage of Americans have less steady work arrangements that could be defined as "work that does not involve explicit or implicit contracts for long-term employment" (Bendapudi et al. 2003). These workers are referred to as the contingent workforce. It is made up of four categories: independent contractors, on-call workers, temporary help

Changing the World

Millions of Volunteers

Have you ever donated time or money to a cause that you support? In addition to working in internships and participating in other forms of experiential learning (see On the Job: Internships and Experiential Learning, p. 349) as a part of their academic careers, students often do community service and volunteer in a wide variety of charitable organizations and nonprofit settings. National Volunteer Week, the third week of April each year, celebrates such people and their efforts to help others.

The Bureau of Labor Statistics (2011) reports that in 2010 an estimated 62.8 million Americans, or more than 20 percent of the total population, engaged in some form of volunteer work. Volunteers each spent a median of fifty-two hours on volunteer activities during the given year. Women

tend to volunteer in larger numbers, such that more than 22 percent of all U.S. women and 17 percent of men volunteered in 2010. Men, however, spent more hours in volunteering than women, a median of fifty-two to fifty hours, respectively. Volunteers are represented fairly evenly from all age groups, though persons forty-five to fifty-four years old were the most likely to volunteer. Volunteer rates were lowest among those in their early twenties. Volunteers come from every socioeconomic level, but members of the middle and upper-middle classes are most likely to volunteer. All races and ethnicities are represented as well.

Many Americans volunteer at religious organizations to which they belong. Lawyers do "pro bono" work for those who can't afford representation. Veterinarians offer free

TABLE 11.1	Volunteers by Type of Organization for Which Volunteer Activities Were Performed and Selected Characteristics, 2010			
		TOTAL VOLUNTEERS (THOUSANDS)	CIVIC, POLITICAL, PROFESSIONAL, OR INTERNATIONAL	EDUCATIONAL OR YOUTH SERVICE	ENVIRONMENTAL OR ANIMAL CARE
	All	62790	5.3%	26.5%	2.4%
Gender	Men	26787	6.4	25.4	2.4
	Women	36004	4.5	27.2	2.5
Age	16 to 24 years	8297	4.2	30.3	3.3
	25 years and over	54493	5.5	25.9	2.3
Race	White	53556	5.5	26.8	2.7
	African American	5580	4.6	23.0	0.5
	Asian	2207	2.3	27.0	1.3
	Hispanic	4982	3.1	35.7	1.4
Education	Less than High School Diploma	2231	3.3	23.9	0.4
	High School Graduates	10887	5.1	23.7	1.5
	Some College	15505	5.5	25.2	2.4
	College Graduates	25870	5.7	27.3	2.7
Marital Status	Single	14145	5.7	28.4	3.5
	Married	38765	5.9	27.5	1.9

SOURCE: U.S Bureau of Labor Statistics 2010c.

clinics for homeless persons' animal companions. "Candy-stripers" help patients and their visitors in hospitals. Families serve in soup kitchens during holiday times such as Thanksgiving and Christmas. Every Election Day, neighborhood volunteers organize and staff local voting booths. And college students volunteer in a wide variety of organizations, from tutoring elementary school students and answering rape crisis hotlines to coaching sports teams, caring for animals at local shelters, and helping out at the Red Cross. Table 11.1 shows the types of organizations for which Americans most often volunteered in 2010.

People do volunteer work for many reasons—for social justice, social change, religious values, work experience, participation in clubs and social groups, and even out of boredom. Not only does volunteering satisfy our most altruistic ideals; it can also be a way to enhance our careers, strengthen our relationships with others, and even let us live out fantasies or dreams that are not part of our normal, everyday lives. And in so doing, volunteers help create a different world for themselves and others.

HOSPITAL OR OTHER HEALTH	PUBLIC SAFETY	RELIGIOUS	SOCIAL OR COMMUNITY SERVICE	SPORT, HOBBY, CUTURAL, OR ARTS	OTHER
7.9%	1.3%	33.8%	13.6%	3.3%	3.7%
6.5	2.2	32.9	14.2	3.9	4.0
9.0	0.6	34.5	13.1	2.8	3.5
9.0	1.8	28.2	13.5	3.4	3.5
7.8	1.2	34.7	13.6	3.3	3.8
8.1	1.4	32.6	13.6	3.5	3.8
5.9	0.3	45.4	13.7	1.6	2.8
8.3	0.3	38.9	10.9	3.3	4.1
5.3	1.2	35.9	10.9	2.2	2.7
4.7	1.0	49.7	11.1	1.2	3.6
8.1	1.8	39.0	12.9	2.5	3.8
8.4	1.7	34.3	13.2	3.1	4.2
7.6	0.7	31.9	14.3	3.9	3.5
9.4	1.4	25.1	15.2	4.1	4.2
6.8	1.3	37.5	12.2	3.0	3.1

agency workers, and contract company workers—sometimes called "temps" or "freelancers." During the past couple of decades, contingent work has provided an alternative to long-term, full-time employment and has grown three times faster than traditional jobs. The Bureau of Labor Statistics reports that approximately 10 percent of the total American workforce in 2005 fell into this category and predicted that by 2010 up to 25 percent would be contingent or part-time (Whitehead 2005).

Many see this situation as a potential disaster, as inferior jobs are created by corporations seeking to slash overhead, especially those costs associated with health benefits, which are almost never available to contingent workers. Employers have a number of financial and legal responsibilities to their regular workers—overtime pay, health insurance, Social Security, disability and worker's compensation benefits—that don't apply to temps or independent contractors. Many fear businesses will increasingly turn to alternative employment arrangements solely to cut costs to the distinct disadvantage of their employees.

Sometimes, businesses will classify workers as "independent contractors" even though they do the same work in the same place as regular workers. In an infamous example in the late 1990s, Microsoft was forced to pay $97 million to settle a lawsuit alleging it had wrongly classified a group of employees as independent contractors, making them ineligible for benefits. These workers had been hired as freelancers to work on specific projects, but "the workers were fully integrated into Microsoft's workforce, working under nearly identical circumstances as Microsoft's regular employees . . . the same core hours at the same location and the same supervisors as regular employees" (Muhl 2002).

A different, though equally exploitative, tactic was used by the contractors hired to clean Wal-Mart stores. In October 2003, federal agents arrested 245 undocumented workers in sixty different Wal-Mart stores around the country. The workers came from eighteen nations but very few of them actually worked for Wal-Mart. Instead, they were employed by independent contractors hired by Wal-Mart to do its nightly cleaning (Bartels 2003). Although companies are not responsible for the actions of subcontractors they hire, they can be held responsible if it is proven they knew something illegal was going on. This is especially important when the jobs offered to the illegal aliens are abusive. When contractors hire employees who work seven days a week and receive no overtime pay or benefits, then those contractors are in violation of overtime, Social Security, and workers' compensation laws (Greenhouse 1997). Furthermore, it is much harder for legitimate contractors to win bids for contracts when their competition can offer lower prices by illegally underpaying their workers.

It is not surprising to discover a lack of job satisfaction among temporary workers, mainly clerical and manufacturing workers, and on-call workers, like construction workers, nurses, substitute teachers, and truck drivers (Cohany 1996). Many temporary workers hope they will be able to use their temp job as a springboard to a permanent one, but often this does not happen. However, the flexibility and freedom of alternative work arrangements appeal to a substantial number of workers, such as students, parents with children at home, and retirees. Though the increase in nontraditional employment has many potential negative effects, "there is as much diversity in the characteristics of jobs and workers within each type of employment arrangement, whether traditional or otherwise, as there is between different types of arrangements" (Cohany 1996).

While there is clearly a downside to being a temp or independent contractor, research indicates that there can also be great satisfaction among these freelance workers. Of the four categories tracked by the Bureau of Labor Statistics, independent contractors make up the largest group—almost two-thirds of the total. In contrast to the traditional worker, the occupational profile of the independent contractor is skewed toward several high-skilled fields, including writers and artists, insurance and real estate agents, construction trade employees, and other technical and computer-related professions. They tend to be better paid than the average worker and prefer their employment situation for the flexibility and freedom it offers (Cohany 1996). However, even in this category, a significant minority, especially women,

"Always Low Prices," at What Cost? In October of 2003, federal agents arrested 245 illegal immigrant workers in sixty different Wal-Mart stores who were employed by the independent contractors that Wal-Mart hired to do its nightly cleaning. The subcontracted employees worked seven days a week and received no overtime pay or benefits from the contractors, who had thus violated overtime, Social Security, and workers' compensation laws.

TABLE 11.2	Theory in Everyday Life	
PERSPECTIVE	**APPROACH TO WORK AND THE ECONOMY**	**CASE STUDY: OUTSOURCING OF WORK**
STRUCTURAL FUNCTIONALISM	Different types of work (high prestige and pay to low prestige and pay) are necessary to the economy and have functions that help maintain social order.	Outsourcing is necessary to keep both national and global economies stable in the current market.
CONFLICT THEORY	A stratified labor market creates intergroup conflict—wealthier capitalists may exploit less-powerful workers.	Outsourcing exploits poor and developing nations and laid-off local workers, all while enriching corporations.
SYMBOLIC INTERACTIONISM	Work is central to our self-concept—we are intensely identified with our work, both by ourselves and by others.	Workers whose jobs are outsourced may come to see themselves as worthless and expendable because it seems that others see them that way too.

make less money and are less satisfied with their situation. Some also suffer from alienation, disenchantment, and burnout.

The Third Sector and Volunteerism

Not all corporations seek a profit, nor do all workers get paid a wage for their labor. Numerous organizations engage in social welfare, social justice, and/or environmental services. Typically, these are churches, schools, hospitals, philanthropic foundations, art institutions, scientific research centers, and a multitude of other organizations, both permanent and temporary. They are private, rather than government, organizations and devoted to serving the general welfare, not their own financial interests. They are nonprofit organizations, designed to run as cost-effectively as possible and to direct any gains or earnings, above basic operating expenses, back into the causes they support. Together, these organizations and the workers who staff them constitute what social scientists call the **Independent** (or **Third**) **Sector** of the economy.

In 2009, more than 1.5 million nonprofit organizations were registered with the U.S. Treasury Department and accorded tax privileges. In addition, there may be 2 million to 3 million other private nonprofit groups and associations less formal in nature. The Third Sector helps society in a number of ways. First, these organizations play a significant part in the American system of pluralism, operating alongside the first two sectors of government and business while helping to strengthen and make them work better. Although we think of nonprofits, business, and government as separate, they are really interconnected through their impact on public policy. Second, nonprofit organizations deliver a wide range of vital services to millions of people in almost every social category. Last, they are a humanizing force in American society, allowing an important avenue of expression for altruism.

The Third Sector represents one of the most distinctive and commendable features of our society. While most nonprofits have some paid employees, they also rely on volunteers to deliver their services to the public.

Independent (or **Third**) **Sector** the part of the economy composed of nonprofit organizations; their workers are mission driven, rather than profit driven, and such organizations direct surplus funds to the causes they support

Volunteerism reflects a profound and important American value, that citizens in a democracy have a personal responsibility to serve those in need. Millions of Americans give their time as volunteers every year. The average value of an hour of volunteering in 2009 was estimated to be worth $20.85 (Independent Sector 2010), and the estimated total value of donated hours in 2009 was more than $169 billion.

There are many ways of working—some conventional, some alternative. Not all workers have jobs in traditional fields; not all workers have permanent or full-time jobs; and not all workers do it for a paycheck.

Closing Comments

You may never have imagined that work was such a big part of life. You might have had a job of some kind, but now you probably have a better idea of just how important work is on both a collective and an individual level. It is so important that sociologists have devoted much of their work to studying work. We can be fairly certain that work will remain a major reality in the human experience into the distant future. We hope that you have gained some insight into the structure and meaning of work in your own lives and the lives of others in society.

QUESTIONS FOR REVIEW

1. Think about the jobs you would like to get after you finish college. Do any of them involve directly participating in the production of physical goods?

2. Think about the objects you use every day. How many of them use microchips? How many of them didn't even exist twenty-five years ago?

3. Thinking of the United States as a capitalist nation with some socialist elements, are there any ways you directly benefit from government intervention in the economy?

4. Marx described four ways that modern wage labor is alienating. Do you think these apply to you and to the job you have or would like to have? If you have a job, would you choose to keep it even if you became independently wealthy?

5. Information technology has changed the workplace in many ways, including increasing numbers of people who telecommute. Have you experienced anything like telecommuting? How about at school? What are the advantages and disadvantages of distance learning?

6. Resistance strategies are ways that workers can assert some degree of autonomy in a workplace that increasingly exerts control and keeps workers under surveillance. What sorts of actions qualify as individual resistance strategies? Have you ever done anything like this?

7. The U.S. General Accounting Office defines a sweatshop as "an employer that violates more than one federal or state labor law governing minimum wage and overtime, child labor, industrial homework, occupational safety and health, workers' compensation, or industrial regulation." How do you think we should define sweatshops in other countries? What sort of working conditions would lead you to stop buying a product as a way to protest the treatment of the people who produced it?

8. Outsourcing involves the "contracting out" or transferring to another country tasks that used to be taken care of in-house. Have you ever noticed this sort of outsourcing? What sorts of jobs get outsourced? How does this practice affect the economy?

9. Almost every job requires some degree of professional socialization. Have you ever experienced anything like this? Did you engage in any anticipatory socialization first?

SUGGESTIONS FOR FURTHER EXPLORATION

Clerks. 1994. Dir. Kevin Smith. Miramax Films. A darkly humorous (though R-rated) take on what it means to be a service worker on the bottom rungs of the American economy and the unique challenges of dealing with customers.

The Corporation. 2003. Dir. Mark Achbar and Jennifer Abbott. Big Picture Media Corporation. A documentary arguing that because the law treats corporations as "persons," we should analyze them the same way we do real people. The film concludes that if viewed

this way, corporations are psychopaths, unable to act with a conscience.

Ford, Richard (editor). 2011. *Blue Collar, White Collar, No Collar: Stories of Work*. New York: Harper Collins. A collection of short fiction by notable writers focusing on the theme of work lives and the workplace across a variety of occupations.

Gibson, William. 2003. *Pattern Recognition*. New York: Putnam. This novel uses a plot about a mysterious film being released little by little on the internet as a way of examining the effects of the Information Revolution. The *Economist* called it "not, strictly speaking, a business book—but probably the best exploration yet of the function and power of product branding and advertising in the age of globalization and the internet."

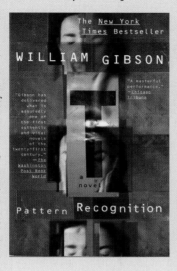

In Good Company. 2005. Dir. Paul Weitz. Universal Pictures. A feel-good corporate movie that gives a humorous, emotional picture of the consequences of a corporate take-over and the real human faculties that come out when the workplace lets people down.

Norma Rae. 1979. Dir. Martin Ritt. 20th Century Fox. Sally Field won an Oscar for her performance as a single mother who struggles to unionize a textile factory. Based on a true story, the movie dramatizes the challenges in convincing individuals that collective resistance can be effective and improve their lives.

Polanyi, Karl. 1944. *The Great Transformation*. Boston: Beacon Hill. In this classic account of the social changes wrought by the Industrial Revolution, Polanyi argues that the Great Depression and both world wars can be viewed as a result of unchecked market capitalism.

Protzman, Ferdinand. 2006. *Work: The World in Photographs*. Washington, DC: National Geographic. This coffee table book celebrates the diverse ways that people in all parts of the world earn a living. The pictures, which span the past 150 years, convey wealth and poverty, pain and violence, joy and triumph, all in the workplace.

Smith, Patti. "Piss Factory." *Land (1975–2002)*. Arista Records. Inspired by her experience as a teenager working in a factory in New Jersey, Smith details in explicit terms the anger and alienation she felt toward the conditions of factory work and her desire to make a living without sacrificing her autonomy.

Up In the Air. 2009. Dir. Jason Reitman. Paramount Pictures. A dark comedy about a corporate downsizer who travels to various companies around the country to break the news to large groups of employees that they have been laid off. His slick presentations are meant to placate the newly unemployed, but he starts to question himself and his line of work.

Up In the Air

Von Drehle, David. 2003. *Triangle: The Fire That Changed America*. New York: Atlantic Monthly Press. A chilling description of the fire that was New York City's worst disaster until 9/11, as well as an analysis of the social, political, and economic context that gave rise to such dangerous conditions.

CHAPTER 12 Life at Home

Tom, a single doctor in his sixties, lived in the same home for thirty years with three much-loved dogs: two boxers named Blaze and Pepe, and a Boston terrier named Brownie. They were his devoted companions. When one of the dogs died, Tom would get a new dog of the same breed and keep the dog's name. Thus, if Blaze died, the new boxer would be named Blaze; if Brownie died, the new Boston terrier would also be Brownie. Tom's relationship with his dogs went on for thirty years. Are Tom and the dogs a family?

Stacie and Eric met in graduate school and married the year they received their degrees. Their job hunts, however, led them in different directions: Stacie took a job with an international policy agency in Washington, DC, and Eric went to work for a major corporation in Miami, Florida. Living in their respective cities, they ran up huge phone bills and spent lots of money on weekend plane tickets. After about five years, Stacie became pregnant, and the baby is due in a few months. Are Stacie and Eric a family?

Jeannie and Tammy also met in graduate school—almost twenty years ago. They are both professors in Minneapolis, and together they bought and fixed up an old house. They would like to formalize their commitment to one another, but they cannot do so legally because Minnesota does not allow same-sex partners to marry. Nevertheless, they've adopted a little boy named Conor and are looking forward to celebrating his first Christmas. Are Jeannie, Tammy, and Conor a family?

For some of you, the answers may come easily, but others of you may find yourself wondering—are these groups really families? Tom loves Brownie, Blaze, and Pepe, but can you really be a family if most of your members aren't human? And is Tom's replacement policy similar to or different from the practice of remarrying when a spouse dies? What about Stacie and Eric—they're married and are having a biological child, which seems to make them easily definable as a family. Yet, they don't live under the same roof. What does that make them? Even Tom and the dogs live together. And so do Jeannie and Tammy; they can own property together and designate each other as heirs in their wills—though they can't legally marry. They're raising their son Conor together, even though Tammy had to adopt Conor on her own first, and then Jeannie legally became his second parent later, since they could not adopt together like a married heterosexual couple can. Do these complications mean that they aren't a real family?

It all depends on how you define family. If emotional bonds and mutual support are the only criteria, then all of these groups are families. But if a marital bond is required, then only Stacie and Eric are a family. If other legal ties are included, then Tammy, Jeannie, and Conor can be a family too. If you have to be heterosexual, then Jeannie and Tammy are out, and we really don't know about Tom, do we? If the longevity of the relationships is the key, then Tom and the dogs win over both of these other potential families. But if you have to be human and irreplaceable, then all those Brownies, Blazes, and Pepes don't qualify. And if a shared residence must be part of the equation, then Tom and the dogs are in but Stacie and Eric are out. So, how do you define family?

HOW TO READ THIS CHAPTER

In this chapter, we examine society's most basic social group—the family. Yet, what makes a family is subject to debate. Sociology doesn't define a family by who its members are but by what they do, how they relate to one another, and what their relationship is to the larger society. We'll look at the dynamic diversity of family forms in the contemporary United States, the functions of family for society, the hierarchies of inequality that shape family life, the work that gets done by and in families, the kinds of troubles families experience, and the political and cultural controversies that affect family life. You will learn that when it comes to family life, change is the only constant.

What Is the Family?

The U.S. Census Bureau defines family as two or more individuals related by blood, marriage, or adoption living in the same household. This definition is a good starting point, but it's too limited to encompass even the family arrangements described in the opening vignette. Contemporary sociologists use the word **family** to mean a social group whose members are bound by some type of tie—legal, biological, emotional, or a combination of all three. They may or may not share a household, but family members are interdependent and have a sense of mutual responsibility for one

another's care. We don't define family by specific types of people (parents or children) or specific types of ties (marriage) because we believe the definition should be broad enough to encompass a variety of forms. However, this very variety is the source of controversy both within and outside academia. Regardless of the definition, most people recognize family as an integral social institution found in every society.

The family as an institution has always changed in response to its social, cultural, political, and economic milieu. Before the Industrial Revolution, "family" tended to mean **extended family**—a large group of **kin**, or relatives, which could include grandparents, uncles, aunts, and cousins living in one household. After the Industrial Revolution, this configuration was largely superseded by the **nuclear family**—a heterosexual couple in their own household raising children. Along the way, the family moved from a more public social institution to a private one, as many functions formerly associated with the family were transferred to other institutions. For example, work and production moved from the family to the factory, education moved from the family to the school, and government took over a variety of social welfare and medical functions formerly taken care of by the extended family.

Subsequent waves of social change, such as the women's liberation movement and the move toward individual independence and self-fulfillment, have begun to erode the dominance of the nuclear family, as increased divorce rates, working mothers, single parents, gay and lesbian families, and other alternative family arrangements become more common. Many sociologists speak of the sociology not of *the* family but rather of *families*. "Family situations in contemporary society are so varied and diverse that it simply makes no sociological sense to speak of a single ideal-type model of 'the family' at all" (Bernardes 1985, p. 209).

Even though a two-parent household with a stay-at-home mother is no longer the norm, this type of family remains the model by which new forms of family are judged. However, there are exceptions, as common sense definitions of fam-

family a social group whose members are bound by legal, biological, or emotional ties, or a combination of all three

extended family a large group of relatives, usually including at least three generations living either in one household or in close proximity

kin relatives or relations, usually those related by common descent

nuclear family a heterosexual couple with one or more children living in a single household

ily reflect the changes occurring in the larger society at any given moment. Children seem to be important in our common sense definitions, as one study found that unmarried couples, both gay and heterosexual, are more likely to be considered a family if children are present (Powell 2003). Unrelated roommates who are not romantically involved are significantly more likely to be considered family by those over the age of sixty-five:

> I call this the *Golden Girls* effect. . . . People at retirement, on one hand, tend to be very traditional about issues of sexuality, but in terms of what they count as family, they are more likely to accept housemates as a sort of family unit. Their views may be affected by major changes in life, such as a move to a retirement home or a loss of a spouse. (Powell 2003)

As you will see as you read this chapter, what constitutes the model or hypothetical family may be very different from how families define themselves "on the ground."

Diversity in Families

Artistic representations of the traditional family generally show a mother, a father, and their two children all with the same skin tone and hair color. These pictures reflect a practice called **endogamy** that refers to marrying someone from within the same social group. **Exogamy** refers to marrying someone from a different social group.

As an example of how family forms and definitions change over time, marriage between people of different racial, ethnic, or national backgrounds has actually been prohibited for most of the history of the United States. From the time of slavery through the 1960s, mixed-race relationships were considered criminal and were also punished outside the law. Fears of interracial relationships led to the lynching of African American men and the creation of **antimiscegenation** laws in several U.S. states that prohibited the mixing of racial groups through marriage, cohabitation, or sexual interaction (Messerschmidt 1998). The most significant of these laws fell after the 1967 Supreme Court declared that Virginia's law banning marriage between persons of different races was unconstitutional under the Fourteenth Amendment (*Loving v. Virginia* 1967).

Though mixed-race unions are now legal, they are still uncommon but increasing. In 1960, only 0.4 percent of all couples were interracial, increasing to 2.2 percent by 1992 (U.S. Census Bureau 1994), 5.7 percent in 2000 (U.S. Census Bureau 2003), and 8 percent in 2008 (Pew Research Center 2010a). Mixed-race couples still face discrimination; in their analysis of a white supremacist internet chat room, Glaser,

Dixit, and Green (2002) found that respondents were far more threatened by interracial marriage than by persons of color moving into white neighborhoods or competing for jobs.

Monogamy, or marrying only one individual at a time, is still considered the only legal form of marriage in modern Western culture. **Polygamy**, or having multiple spouses, may be practiced among some subcultures around the world, but is not widely acknowledged as a legitimate form of marriage. The more commonly known form of polygamy is **polygyny**, where a man is married to multiple wives. **Polyandry**, where a woman has multiple husbands, has been documented in Tibet but is the rarer form of polygamy. **Polyamory** is a type of multiple-person partnership in which each individual, regardless of gender or sexual orientation, is in a relationship with each other individual.

Sociological Perspectives on the Family

Among the sociological perspectives on the family, those with the structural functionalist view see it as a cultural universal and try to identify its functions for society. Conflict theorists argue that there are inherent inequalities both within and between families. Symbolic interactionists focus on the family as the product of interactional processes. Each of these theories offers useful insights into our understanding of this unit.

Structural Functionalism

In *Suicide*, Emile Durkheim (1897/1951) argued that the Industrial Revolution and the division of labor had undermined the older social institutions that formerly regulated society, leaving some people suffering from anomie, or normlessness, that sometimes resulted in suicide. He found that marriage and family, at least for men, decreased their chances of suicide because these provide the structure and regulation that Durkheim believed people require to be happy.

endogamy marriage to someone within one's social group

exogamy marriage to someone from a different social group

antimiscegenation the prohibition of interracial marriage, cohabitation, or sexual interaction

monogamy the practice of marrying (or being in a relationship with) one person at a time

polygamy a system of marriage that allows people to have more than one spouse at a time

polygyny a system of marriage that allows men to have multiple wives

polyandry a system of marriage that allows women to have multiple husbands

polyamory a system of multiple-person partnership

Changing the World

Who Can Marry?

Many people think of marriage as a natural right for everyone. In the United States, though, marriage is a privilege that is generally reserved for two consenting adults of opposite sexes. Historically, marriage in the United States has been restricted at times to citizens, whites, and couples of the same race. Though mixed-race unions are no longer illegal, same-sex marriages are outlawed in most states. In this box, we explore the question: who can marry?

In the United States, marriage is a contract between two people and the government. Thus, married couples enjoy legal privileges, such as tax benefits, insurance protections, hospital visitation and decision making, and other legal rights denied to nonmarried couples. Even "common law" marriage (an option in some states in which a period of cohabitation is substituted for legal marriage) is recognized for heterosexual couples only.

In only ten nations in the world—the Netherlands (as of 2001), Belgium (as of 2003), Spain and Canada (as of 2004), South Africa (as of 2006), Sweden and Norway (2009), Portugal, Iceland, and Argentina (2010)—do same-sex couples enjoy all the rights of full legal marriage. Several other nations—including Finland, France, Hungary, Denmark, Israel, Colombia, the Czech Republic, Germany, the United Kingdom, and New Zealand—and the states of New Jersey, California, Colorado, Hawaii, Maine, Nevada, Oregon, Wisconsin, and Washington, offer some range of legal recognition

and protection of same-sex or civil unions (Legal Marriage Alliance of Washington 2007). However, these fall short of the full rights reserved for heterosexual married couples. By 2011, only six states had legally recognized same-sex marriage: Connecticut, Iowa, Massachusetts, New Hampshire, New York, and Vermont, as well as Washington, D.C. Gay rights activists believe that the momentum is in their favor, as at least eight other states were then poised to consider legislation that would allow gay couples to marry (Goodnough 2009). Opponents, however, have been successful in defeating some same-sex measures, and continue to launch legal and constitutional challenges to the practice.

In February 2004, San Francisco Mayor Gavin Newsom began issuing marriage licenses to gay and lesbian couples, and more than 3,000 couples came from around the country and the world to avail themselves of what proved to be a narrow legal window. On August 12, 2004, the California Supreme Court nullified all those marriages and declared them to be in violation of state law. Later, in June 2008, another state Supreme Court decision legalized gay marriage again in California, but in November of that year voters narrowly approved a state constitutional amendment banning marriage between same-sex individuals.

The legal battles over this issue continue in California and other states. In October of 2008, the Connecticut

---

The structural functionalists who followed Durkheim argued that society's survival requires institutions that can serve its essential functions: economic production, the socialization of children, instrumental and emotional support, and sexual control. Although the family is no longer directly involved in economic production, it performs the functions that allow production to happen. Talcott Parsons (1955) argued that "the modern nuclear family was especially complementary to the requirements of an industrial economy" because it freed individuals from onerous obligations to extended family members and made possible the geographic and social mobility demanded by the modern economy (Mann et al. 1997). In the most basic sense, the family is responsible for the reproduction of

society as it produces and socializes children. This is what Parsons referred to as "pattern maintenance," whereby the values and norms of a society are passed on to the next generation. Family also, ideally, provides emotional support for its members and regulates sexuality by helping define with whom we can and cannot mate. These patterns, according to functionalists, help society run smoothly and maintain stability and order.

Conflict Theory

Conflict theorists realize that the family produces and socializes children to function efficiently in a capitalist economy, but they see this function as problematic. The nuclear

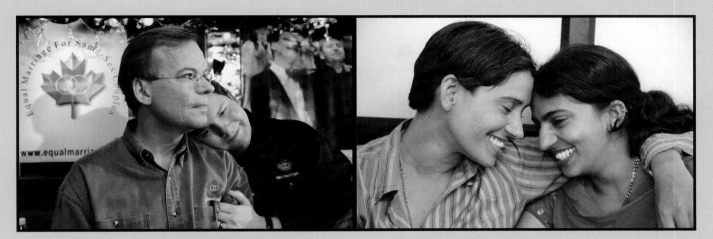

Who Gets to Marry? Kevin Bourassa and Joe Varnell (left) from Toronto are the first North American gay couple to be married. They embrace after the Supreme Court of Canada affirmed the legality of same-sex marriage in December 2004. Baljit Kaur and Raljwinder Kaur (right) from Amritsar, India, embrace after their wedding in India. Gay and lesbian couples throughout India are increasingly open about their sexuality and same-sex marriages are becoming increasingly common there.

Supreme Court ruled that to prohibit gay marriage was unconstitutional. Hawaii, Alaska, Nevada, Nebraska, and Missouri have passed constitutional amendments explicitly limiting marriage to heterosexual couples. The 1996 U.S. congressional Defense of Marriage Act was also designed to reserve marriage for heterosexual couples only, and President George W. Bush was reelected in 2004 partly on his promise to amend the Constitution to prohibit gay marriage (a promise he was unable to keep). Though some public attitudes seem to be shifting toward growing acceptance of gay marriage, not everyone is welcoming the change—including many public officials.

family, a relatively recent historical invention, acts as the primary economic unit in modern capitalist society, and since conflict theorists see capitalism as oppressive, they claim that this form of family contributes to that oppression—and is often understood as an oppressive institution in itself. Conflict theorists believe that society revolves around conflict over scarce resources and that conflict within the family is also about the competition for resources: time, energy, and the leisure to pursue more interesting recreational activities.

In this analysis, the family can allow exploitation through a sexual rather than a class-based division of labor. Conflict perspectives overlap with feminist perspectives on the family as feminists assume that the family is a gendered social institution and that men and women experience family differently. In patriarchal societies, men wield greater power than women, both within and outside the family, and women's contributions to family and society are devalued (Thorne 1992).

Symbolic Interactionism

As Jim Holstein and Jay Gubrium point out in their book *What Is Family* (1990), the *family* does not exist, only *families*. These symbolic interactionists consider it more effective to look at how family relations are created and maintained in interaction than how they are structured. Even though the legal bond of marriage has the same technical meaning

Talking About Kin

In P. D. Eastman's children's book *Are You My Mother?*, a newly hatched bird wanders about asking everyone—and everything—she encounters, "Are you my mother?" Sadly for the newborn, neither the construction crane, the cow, nor the cat is the parent she is searching for. On the last page of the book, however, the tiny bird is serendipitously returned to her nest and reunited with a maternal-looking chickadee.

When reading something like *Are You My Mother?*, most people in the Western world would assume that the word "mother" means "female parent." However, in the Hawaiian language, *makuahine* means both "mother" and "aunt" and refers to any female relative in the generation of that person's parents (*makuakane* is the equivalent term for men) (Stanton 1995; Schwimmer 2001). In Hawaiian, then, "are you my mother?" could just as easily mean "are you my father's brother's wife?" In China, though, kinship terms are very precise. There are particular terms for a "father's brother's wife" that vary depending on whether the wife is married to the older brother or a younger one (Levi-Strauss 1949/1969)!

One reason we name our kin is to delineate the relationships and obligations we share. In some cases, we use the term **fictive kin** to refer to people who are not related to us through blood or through marriage. Such kin are created through closely knit friendships to the family. You may have a family friend you call Auntie So-and-So. In other societies, fictive kin may be culturally prescribed. In Jordan, it is perfectly normal for adult strangers to address one another with the Arabic equivalents of brother/sister, maternal aunt/uncle, and paternal aunt/uncle. In addition, an older Jordanian woman may affectionately refer to a child (of either gender) as "mother" (Farghal and Shakir 1994).

In China, labeling an older individual as an uncle or an older brother is a required sign of respect (Baker 1979). Sometimes fictive kinship ties are formalized through cer-

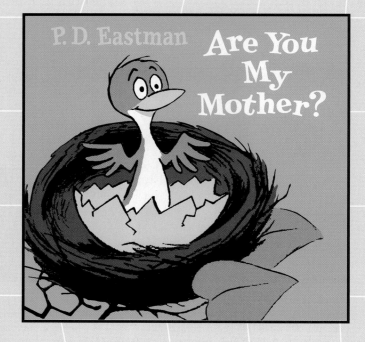

emony, as when a female in India ties a sacred thread around the wrist of an unrelated close male friend to indicate that she considers him a brother. In Latin America, godparents (*compadrazgo*, a word that can be translated as "co-parent" rather than "godparent") are considered permanent members of their godchildren's family. Not surprisingly, the Spanish words for "daughter" and "son" are very close to the words for "goddaughter" and "godson" (Davila 1971; van den Berghe 1979).

Examining kinship terms is one way to understand the diversity of families and how kin fulfill their social roles. As you can see, aunts, elder brothers, godparents, and family friends can all be important family members.

---

for every couple, individual marriages may have very different expectations and rules for behavior. One couple may require sexual monogamy within their marriage, while their neighbors may not; one couple may pool their finances while another husband and wife may keep separate bank accounts. This approach conceives of family as a fluid, adaptable set of concepts

> **fictive kin** close relations with people we consider "like family" but who are not related to us by blood or marriage

and practices that people use "for constructing the meaning of social bonds" (Holstein and Gubrium 1995a), a set of vocabularies to describe particular relationships.

Consider the number of relatives, defined by blood or marriage, most people have who play no meaningful role in their lives, who "aren't really family." When we describe people in terms of family, we are making claims about the "rights, obligations, and sentiments" that exist within their relationships (Gubrium and Buckholdt 1982). Consequently, we

TABLE 12.1 Theory in Everyday Life

PERSPECTIVE	APPROACH TO FAMILY	CASE STUDY: MARRIAGE
STRUCTURAL FUNCTIONALISM	Family performs necessary functions, such as the socialization of children, that help society run smoothly and maintain social order.	Marriage regulates sexuality and forms the basis for family, with all its other functions.
CONFLICT THEORY	Family is a site of various forms of stratification and can produce and reproduce inequalities based on these statuses.	Marriage as a civil right is extended only to heterosexual couples in most states and nations. This is both a cause and a consequence of homophobia in society.
SYMBOLIC INTERACTIONISM	Family is a social construction; it is created, changed, and maintained in interaction.	Marriage is not made solely by completing a legal contract but is also constructed through the accretion of everyday interactions between partners over the years.

are constantly evaluating and reevaluating the attitudes and behaviors of those around us, assigning family status to new people and dismissing others from our circle of meaningful family relations. In *All Our Kin*, an ethnography of kinship relations in an urban African American community, Carol Stack found this dynamic at work in the way people talked about family—including this woman, who says,

> Most people kin to me are in this neighborhood . . . but I got people in the South, in Chicago, and in Ohio too. I couldn't tell most of their names and most of them aren't really kinfolk to me. . . . [T]ake my father, he's no father to me. I ain't got but one daddy and that's Jason. The one who raised me. My kids' daddies, that's something else, all their daddies' people really take to them—they always doing things and making a fuss about them. We help each other out and that's what kinfolks are all about. (Stack 1974)

A symbolic interactionist might say that "family members do not merely passively conform to others' expectations" but rather "actively and creatively construct and modify their roles through interactions" (Dupuis and Smale 2000)—that is, the people who help each other out, who care for each other, and who express that care are family, whether they are legally related or not.

Forming Relationships, Selecting Mates

You may think that you are attracted to certain people because of their unique individual characteristics or something intangible called "chemistry." In reality, however, Cupid's arrow is largely aimed by society. Two time-tested concepts in social science—homogamy and propinquity—tell us a lot about how the mate-selection process works. **Homogamy** literally means "like marries like": we tend to

choose mates who are similar to us in class, race, ethnicity, age, religion, education, and even levels of attractiveness. You can certainly find examples of people whose romantic relationships cross these category lines—interracial or interreligious couples, or May/December romances—but these relationships are often viewed with disapproval by others in the couples' social circles. There are considerable social pressures to adhere to homogamy.

Propinquity refers to geographical proximity: we tend to choose people who live nearby. This is logical; we are likely to find possible mates among the people in our neighborhood, at work, or at school. The internet makes courtship and romance possible across much greater geographical areas, as we can now meet and converse with people in all parts of the world, so our pool of potential mates moves beyond local bounds. But even this technology may intensify homogamy by bringing together people with very specific interests and identities. Examples include internet services such as J-Date, for Jewish singles; Prime Singles, for people over age fifty; Athletic Passions, for people into fitness and sports; and EbonyConnect, for African American singles.

Courtship, romance, and intimacy are all influenced by the larger culture—and are also historically specific. While we experience courtship at an individual, interactional level, it will always be shaped by macro-structural forces in the larger society, such as racial, ethnic, or religious prejudices, and gendered role expectations. But courtship changes as other aspects of the surrounding culture change. As our society becomes less racist, sexist, and heterosexist, romantic options will expand as well. The development of intimate romantic relationships is not something "natural"; it is socially constructed to *appear* natural.

homogamy the tendency to choose romantic partners who are similar to us in terms of class, race, religion, education, or other social group membership

propinquity the tendency to marry or have relationships with people in close geographic proximity

Doing the Work of Family

When we think of work, we usually think of activities done for a paycheck. But paid labor is not the only type of work that sociologists are interested in—especially in the study of the family. Many types of work—both paid and unpaid—are necessary to keep a family operating: child care, housecleaning, car maintenance, cooking, bill-paying, vacation planning, and doing laundry—the list seems endless, especially when you are the one doing the work!

These tasks can be instrumental or expressive. **Instrumental tasks** generally achieve a tangible goal (washing the dishes, fixing the gutters), whereas **expressive tasks** generally achieve emotional or relational goals (remembering relatives' birthdays, playing Chutes and Ladders with the kids). In a real family, however, much of the work has both instrumental and expressive elements. The expressive work of remembering and celebrating birthdays, for example, includes all sorts of instrumental tasks, such as buying presents, writing cards, and baking cakes (Di Leonardo 1987; Pleck 2000).

As a social scientist committed to making the invisible labor of family visible, Marjorie DeVault (1991/1994) excavates all the knowledge, skills, and practices—both instrumental and expressive—we take for granted when, for example, we feed our families. Not only is the knowledge of cooking needed, but there must be appropriate shopping to keep a stocked kitchen; to make meals that account for family members' likes, dislikes, and allergies; and to create a varied and balanced menu. Producing meals that please, satisfy, and bring individuals together is just one of the ways that family is created and sustained through interactional work. We constitute family in and through meals and every other mundane activity of everyday life.

DATA WORKSHOP

ANALYZING EVERYDAY LIFE

Comparative Mealtime

Some of us carry a strong and positive image of our family gathered around the dining room table for dinner each evening. While we were growing up, dinner may have been the one time in the day when the whole family was together and shared food, stories, lessons, and news. For many of us, a great deal of socialization took place around the dinner table; we learned about manners ("sit up straight," "don't speak with your mouth full") as well as morality, politics, or anything else that seemed important to the adults raising us. Some of us, on the other hand, may have different memories of family mealtimes. Perhaps they were a time of tension and arguments, or perhaps the family rarely ate a meal together.

In this Data Workshop, you will be using participant observation as a research method (see Chapter 2 for a review) and doing ethnographic research on mealtime activity. You will compare two or more different mealtime settings and situations. You can choose from among a range of different possibilities, including the following:

- Which meal you study—breakfast, lunch, or dinner

- Where the meal takes place—in your family home; at a friend's or a relative's house; at your own apartment or dormitory dining hall; or at a workplace lunch room, picnic in the park, or restaurant

- Who is eating—family members, roommates, friends, co-workers, or strangers

After you participate in and observe two mealtimes, write down answers to the following questions:

- What are the prevailing rules, rituals, norms, and values associated with the setting and situation? For example, does everyone sit down to eat at the same time? Do people leave after they finish even if others are still eating?

- What kinds of complementary roles are the various participants engaged in? Who cooks the food, sets the table, clears the table, does the dishes, and so forth?

- What other types of activities (besides eating) are taking place at mealtime? Are people watching TV, listening to music or a ball game, reading the newspaper?

- What social purposes does the setting or situation serve other than providing a mealtime environment for the participants? For example, what do the participants talk about? If children are involved, do they talk about school or their friends? Are family activities or problems discussed?

In addition to taking detailed notes, you may also wish to interview some of the participants.

There are two options for completing the assigned work in the Data Workshop.

- *Option 1 (informal)*: Make the observations prescribed and conduct any formal or informal interviews you wish. Prepare some written notes that you can refer to during in-class discussions. Compare and contrast the analyses

instrumental tasks the practical physical tasks necessary to maintain family life

expressive tasks the emotional work necessary to support family members

What's for Dinner? Compare these two family meals. What do our mealtime practices tell us about contemporary American families?

of the different family meals observed by participants in your group. What are the similarities and differences in your observations?

- *Option 2 (formal)*: Make the observations prescribed, and conduct any formal or informal interviews you wish. Write a three- to four-page essay answering the questions listed above and reflecting on your own experience in conducting this study. What do you think your observations tell us about contemporary American families and the practices of family mealtimes? Don't forget to attach your fieldnotes and interview transcripts.

Gender and Family Labor

Imagine working a labor-intensive forty to sixty hours waiting tables, making automobile parts, doing data entry, or teaching second graders. You arrive home feeling tired, hungry, and worn out, but you cannot sit down to relax. You still need to cook a meal, do some laundry and cleaning, and take care of your children or perhaps your elderly parents.

Who is more likely to come home to this scenario? Among heterosexual couples, women are more likely to have the dual workload of paid labor outside the home and unpaid labor inside the home. In this section, we will discuss the division of labor within the household.

Men and women have always performed different roles to ensure the survival of their families, but these roles were not considered unequal until after the Industrial Revolution. At that time, men began to leave their homes to earn wages working in factories. Women remained at home taking care of children and carrying out other domestic responsibilities. As men's earned wages replaced subsistence farming—in which women had always participated—these wages became the primary mechanism for providing food, clothing, and shelter for families, thus giving men economic power over women. Feminist sociologists contend that women's "second shift" is the legacy of this historic economic change.

Despite women's increasing participation in the paid workforce, they are still more likely to perform the bulk of household and caregiving labor. In a few cases, men share household chores (Coltrane 1997) but women bear the brunt of unpaid household labor. Arlie Hochschild and Anne Machung's 1989 study of working couples and parents found that women were indeed working two jobs: paid labor outside the home, or the first shift, and unpaid labor inside the home, or the **second shift**. Hochschild and Machung found that these women tried numerous strategies to achieve balance between work and home: hiring other women to clean their houses and care for their children; relying on friends or family members for help; refusing to

second shift the unpaid hours of childcare often expected of women when they return home from doing work in the workforce

ermutations of Family Living: From Boomerang Kids to he Sandwich Generation

Vhen people talk about the disappearance of the nuclear amily, they usually are referring to the divorce rate, but, specially for the baby boom generation, families are chang-ng in other ways as well. Traditionally, becoming middle-ged was associated with the "mid-life crisis" but also with naturity, wisdom, and increased professional skills. While his might seem like a contradiction, changes in the nature f the family make it seem more like a necessity! Increasing umbers of middle-aged people are becoming members of "sandwich generation," adults who provide material and motional support for both "young children and older liv-ng parents" (Lachman 2004, p. 322). This effect is magni-ed by the increasing number of so-called boomerang kids, ho leave home at eighteen to attend college but often return ome for at least a short period of time afterward.

Both of these dynamics are being driven less by choice han by demographic and economic necessity. In 1970, the verage age at first marriage was less than twenty-one for omen and a little over twenty-three for men. Today, the nedian age at first marriage for women is twenty-five, and for nen it's almost twenty-seven. As a result, people are having hildren later, increasing the chances that child rearing and lder care will overlap. Advances in life expectancy also con-ibute to the sandwich effect, even as many of the medical dvances that allow people to live longer also increase their eed for material support. While there have always been dults caring for their elderly parents, never before have there een this many elderly. According to the U.S. Census Bureau, ne number of the "oldest old," those eighty-five and older, ncreased 274 percent between 1960 and 1994, while "the derly population in general rose 100 percent and the entire

U.S. population grew only 45 percent" (U.S. Census Bureau 1995). Meanwhile, between tuition increases, student loans, and the high price of real estate, students are leaving college more likely to need help from their parents than ever before. In 1980, fewer than 9 percent of all individuals between twenty-five and thirty-four lived with their parents. By the year 2007, this number had increased to almost 12 percent, still a small group, but one that has increased 34 percent dur-ing the past three decades, and the recent recession is likely to increase the size of this group even further.

Members of the sandwich generation have found them-selves with more responsibilities than ever before. Not only are their parents living longer than before, but medical costs associated with old age are growing rapidly, and often they have children, of all ages, still dependent on them as well. Never before has there been a substantial cohort of Ameri-cans so directly burdened with such a wide range of family responsibilities. However, in some ways, the more the sand-wich generation adults and the boomerang kids change the family, the more they stay the same, especially in the way that gender roles manifest themselves. Even among eighteen- to twenty-four-year-olds, boys are more likely to live at home than girls, and 60 percent of the boomerang kids between ages twenty-five and thirty-four are male. While men and women might be driven by the same financial troubles, mov-ing back in with her parents has different consequences for a woman. She is likely to be asked to take on more domes-tic responsibilities, and typically she feels a greater loss of independence. Gender functions in similar ways for the sandwich generation, as it is still mostly women who are called on to provide the emotional and instrumental support

o certain chores, especially those considered to be generally men's work"; lowering their expectations for cleanliness or uality of child care; or reducing the number of hours they orked outside the home. But some women accept their dual orkloads without any help to avoid conflicts with spouses

and children. Hochschild and Machung called these women "Supermoms" but also found that these "Supermoms" often felt unhappy or emotionally numb.

Although Hochschild and Machung's observations were groundbreaking in their analysis of post-feminist families,

Sandwich Generation Julie Winokur (far left) juggles taking care of her father, who is suffering from Parkinson's disease, and raising her daughter (on the far right). How typical is the Winokur family today?

for elderly parents, even when those women also work. In fact, "working women who do take on caregiving tasks may reduce their work hours" (Velkoff and Lawson 1998, p. 2), finding themselves having to prioritize family over career in ways men often don't.

Despite the many costs associated with being a member of the sandwich generation, there is good news as well. Although there are challenges associated with "dual respon-

sibilities," these are mostly experienced as "a 'squeeze' but not stress," and these relationships are also a source of happiness and well-being (Lachman 2004, p. 322). And while there is still a certain stigma associated with moving back in with your parents, the fact that so many are willing to do so suggests that today's boomerang kids may enjoy closer relationships with their parents than kids of previous generations did.

their concept of the "Supermom" has been applicable to working-class mothers all along. The stay-at-home parent is possible only when one salary can support the entire family. Before college-educated women were encouraged to work in the paid labor force, working-class women were there out

of necessity. The strategies that middle-class women use to negotiate their second shift are available only to wealthier families. After all, a woman who cleans another family's house and takes care of their children rarely has the financial resources to hire someone to do the same for her.

Supermom For many American women, "work" doesn't end when they leave the workplace. On returning home, many begin what Arlie Hochschild calls "the second shift," doing the unpaid work of running a household, including doing the laundry, feeding the children, and helping with homework.

Family and the Life Course

As an agent of socialization and the most basic of primary groups, the family molds everyone—young children, teenagers, adults, and senior citizens—and its influences continue throughout the life course.

When we are children, our families provide us with our first lessons in how to be members of society (see Chapter 4 on socialization). Children's experiences are shaped by family size, birth order, presence or absence of parents, socioeconomic status, and other sociological variables. Dalton Conley's 2004 work *The Pecking Order* maintains that inequality between siblings and things outside the family's control, such as the economy, war, illness, and death, as well as marital discord create effects that impact each child at different stages in his or her life, resulting in different experiences for each child. Conley argues that family proves not to be the consistent influence many people view it to be.

In addition, the presence of children shapes the lives of parents. Marital satisfaction tends to decline when there are small children in the house, and couples' gendered division of labor becomes more traditional when children are born, even if it has been nontraditional up to that point. As children get older, they may exert other types of influence on their parents—for example, children can pressure their parents into quitting smoking or eating healthier food. And of course, later in life, they may be called on to care for their elderly parents as well as their own offspring—a phenomenon known as "the sandwich generation" effect.

Aging in the Family

The American population is aging—the number of Americans sixty-five or older is growing twice as fast as the population as a whole (Baca Zinn and Eitzen 2002). This is because of the baby boom generation (the large number of Americans born in the post–World War II era) moving into middle age and beyond, concurrent with advances in medical technology. Current average life expectancy in the United States is approximately seventy-eight years (with women living an average of almost six years longer than men). More people are living longer, and that has an impact on families and society.

Planning for an aging population means taking into account both the basic and special needs of older individuals. Retirement income is an important part of this planning—Social Security benefits are the major source of income for about 80 percent of the elderly in the United States and the only source of income for 54 percent of America's retired population. Without other sources of income, retired citizens may find themselves with limited resources; currently, about 10 percent of the elderly live below the poverty line. Some seniors solve the problems by living with their adult children or with nonfamily members; even so, about 50 percent of women and about 20 percent of men over age sixty-five live alone. Like other traditional functions of the family (such as educating children), the care of the elderly is no longer a primary duty of family and has been taken over by other institutions: more than 40 percent of senior citizens will spend time in a nursing home, being housed and cared for by people other than their family members (Baca Zinn and Eitzen 2002).

Coping with the transitions of retirement, widowhood, declining health, and death are central tasks for seniors. However, as the average life span extends, the elderly are also taking on new roles in society. Many live healthy, vibrant, active lives and are engaged with their families and communities in ways that are productive for both the individual and the person's groups.

Marie Wilcox-Little, Age 73, Swimmer   **Donald Goo, Age 73, Surfer**

Trouble in Families

While families are often a place of comfort, support, and unconditional love, some are not a "haven in a heartless world" (Lasch 1977). The family may be where we are at the greatest risk—emotionally, socially, and physically. "People are more likely to be killed, physically assaulted, sexually victimized . . . in their own homes by other family members than anywhere else, or by anyone else, in our society" (Gelles 1995, p. 450).

Because family is the site of unequal power relations and intense feelings, and because of current social norms about the privacy of family life, the circumstances for trouble and violence are ripe. The concept of private nuclear families did not occur in the United States until the early 1900s. In colonial times, child raising was a community activity in which community leaders and neighbors often overruled parental decisions about children. In the late 1800s, mothers looked to other mothers for advice about their children (Coontz 2000). Mothers' journals at the time show that the opinions of other women were often more important than the husband's in family decisions. Not until the 1900s did the isolated nuclear family become the ideal in the minds of Americans.

Domestic Violence and Abuse

Imagine that tomorrow's newspapers ran front-page headlines about a newly discovered disease epidemic that could potentially kill one-third of all American women. Between 1 million and 4 million women would be afflicted in the next year alone. What kind of public reaction would there be?

Let's reframe the scenario: in the United States, one out of every three women suffers physical violence at the hands of an intimate partner at some point in her adult life (National Domestic Violence Hotline 2003). In addition, millions of women suffer verbal, financial, and psychological abuse from those who are supposed to love them. Despite these statistics, such abuse is a silent epidemic, seldom reported.

Domestic violence is an umbrella term for the behaviors abusers use to gain and maintain control over their victims. These behaviors fall into five main categories: physical (slapping, punching, kicking, choking, shoving, restraining), verbal (insults, taunts, threats, degrading statements), financial (insisting on complete control of all household finances, including making decisions about who will work and when), sexual (rape, molestation), and psychological or emotional abuse (mind games, threats, stalking, intimidation). Although not all abusers are physically violent toward their partners, any one type of abuse increases the likelihood of the others. In an abusive relationship, it is extremely rare to find only one form of abuse.

Rates of domestic violence are about equal across racial and ethnic groups, sexual orientations, and religions (Bachman and Saltzman 1995). Women are certainly not the only demographic group to suffer from domestic abuse, but statistically, they are five to eight times more likely than men to be victimized by an intimate partner (Greenfeld et al. 1998; National Domestic Violence Hotline 2003). According to the U.S. Department of Justice, women between the ages of sixteen and twenty-four are victims of abuse at the hands of an intimate partner more frequently than women in any other age group (Rennison 2001). Poor women

domestic violence any physical, verbal, financial, sexual, or psychological behaviors abusers use to gain and maintain power over their victims

On the Job

Juggling Work and Family

Since we now understand that being "on the job" can mean doing the work of family *or* the work of an employer, let's take a look at a typical day—in this case, election day—in the Brown family home in suburban Bellwood, Illinois. Deborah Brown is assistant chief of patient administration and financial services at a major hospital in Chicago, and her husband, Alvin, is a data-solutions consultant for a telecommunications firm. They have two sons: Jeffery, nine, and Jalen, six.

5:00 A.M.: Deborah's alarm goes off. She showers and takes her daily supplements: a multivitamin for the body and fifteen minutes of daily meditations for the soul.

5:30 A.M.: She packs a salad for lunch.

6:00 A.M.: Time to awaken Jeffery and nudge him toward the new day.

6:05 A.M.: She wakes up Alvin to help with the daily child-readiness project.

6:15 A.M.: Alvin awakens Jalen and helps get him dressed. "It's not easy," Alvin says. "He's a sleepyhead."

6:20 A.M.: As the rest of the family pulls together books and backpacks, Deborah makes all the beds and finishes getting dressed.

6:30 A.M.: Alvin heads out to the garage to get Deborah's car out and pull it around to the front of the house.

6:40 A.M.: Deborah and the kids head out. Alvin, who will be working from his home office, sees them off and heads back into the house to do a little cleaning.

6:55 A.M.: Arriving at school, Deborah signs the boys in and they scamper off to the dining area. Jeffery chooses sausage and biscuits, while Jalen goes for his favorite: French toast sticks with syrup.

7:00 A.M.: Back in the car, Deborah heads to work.

7:10 A.M.: At home, Alvin tosses a load of laundry into the washer and prepares for a conference call with his sales team.

7:20 A.M.: Deborah arrives at the medical center.

7:30 A.M.: At her desk, she settles in with a bagel, milk, and her e-mail. Meanwhile, back home, Alvin starts his conference call, and at school Jeffery is reading a Harry Potter book while Jalen plays during before-school care.

7:50 A.M.: Employees from the midnight shift start briefing Deborah, in preparation for a staff meeting.

8:15 A.M.: She meets with senior staff members, while at school the first bell rings and the boys head for class. At home, Alvin grabs a bagel and shower, irons his clothes, and gets dressed for the day.

8:30 A.M.: At school, the students begin their daily devotional, then say the Pledge of Allegiance. Afterward, they fill in their prayer journal. Jalen later will explain that he prayed for his broken Power Rangers toy.

9:00 A.M.: Deborah begins her daily conference call with managers at remote sites, while at home, Alvin puts in another load of laundry and sits to read the newspaper. He has had the TV next to his office tuned to MSNBC since he first went downstairs. He cannot stop listening to coverage of the presidential election.

9:10 A.M.: Alvin's mother, Maryann, calls to say hello. "She's my best friend," Alvin says. "We talk two or three times a day."

9:20 A.M.: A co-worker calls Alvin to work on quotes for a sales offer.

9:30 A.M.: Deborah starts returning calls and starts on paperwork that will carry her to lunch.

10:00 A.M.: Alvin looks through papers the boys brought home from school before the holidays.

10:40 A.M.: Still expecting a slow day of work, Alvin grabs a load of laundry from the dryer and starts folding and sorting. "I do the wash," he says. "Deborah puts it away." All the while, MSNBC still can't tell him who his next president will be.

10:55 A.M.: Now the work phone won't leave Alvin alone. He has finished folding one load of laundry, but the dryer will spit out another load shortly. He is holed up in his office, in front of his computer. Though he can't watch it, the TV news remains audible.

11:15 A.M.: Alvin leaves the office for a minute to sit in front of the TV. Still no president.

11:45 A.M.: Alvin is back in his office, going through e-mail.

12:00 P.M.: At school, the boys are having meatloaf, carrots, and potatoes.

12:10 P.M.: Deborah calls Alvin to say hello, then finishes some correspondence to get to her lunch.

1:10 P.M.: Alvin grabs the last load of laundry from the dryer and starts folding, while at the hospital, Deborah is grinding out correspondence, and at school, the boys are back to their studies.

2:00 P.M.: The work phone has recaptured Alvin.

2:40 P.M.: Alvin runs upstairs to grab the mail, then heads back to his office, where he is reviewing faxes that have been trickling in all day.

3:00 P.M.: Deborah starts answering e-mails that have been mounting up. At school, class is over and the boys have gone to the after-school care program. At home, Alvin's work phone has been getting busier and busier. So much for the easy day.

4:30 P.M.: The taxi is back in business as Deborah leaves work and heads for the school.

4:40 P.M.: Alvin escapes his office and heads up to the kitchen to start getting dinner ready. He prepares potatoes for boiling and retrieves a slab of salmon from the refrigerator for broiling. He flips on the under-the-counter TV. Still no president.

5:00 P.M.: Back in his office, Alvin is on a conference call with his boss. They have a problem and need to talk with some technicians. Upstairs, the potatoes are starting to boil.

5:05 P.M.: He runs upstairs to check the potatoes and put the fish in the broiler.

5:13 P.M.: Still waiting for someone to answer their call, Alvin races upstairs to check the food again. In a flash, he's back to his phone.

5:20 P.M.: The Brown family has arrived. Alvin is still on the phone, trying to resolve the problem while Deborah rescues the salmon from the broiler and turns down the heat on the potatoes. Jeffery starts unloading his book bag, including his letter to Santa.

5:45 P.M.: Dinner is served with a prayer.

6:05 P.M.: Dinner over, Alvin and Deborah clear the table and start washing dishes.

6:45 P.M.: Jalen heads up to his room to start homework. Jeffery starts practicing on the electronic keyboard, preparing for a piano lesson the next day. Alvin returns to his office and work.

7:45 P.M.: Jalen is in the tub for a bath, and Jeffery is reading Harry Potter again but will hop into the tub once Jalen finishes.

8:00 P.M.: The boys get ready for prayers and sleep. Deborah tucks them in and gets good-night hugs.

8:15 P.M.: "Now it's time for Round Two," Deborah says. She starts gathering books and book bags and clothes for the morning routine.

8:30 P.M.: The boys are asleep, and Deborah irons the boys' clothes for tomorrow, then her own.

9:00 P.M.: Deborah packs her lunch for the next day and starts going through family mail.

9:30 P.M.: Alvin brings up a basket of the laundry he folded earlier for Deborah to put away. Then she starts getting ready for bed.

9:58 P.M.: Alvin pulls Deborah's car around and puts it in the garage, then runs to a gas station to fill his tank because he will be up early to go to work.

10:30 P.M.: Alvin is back, catches Jay Leno's monologue and starts watching the rest of the video he started the night before.

10:35 P.M.: Deborah finishes reviewing work. "It's been a long day," she says, "and it's only Tuesday!"

12:15 A.M.: Alvin decides to go to bed. He still hasn't been able to finish the video. And still no president. (Werland 2000)

The Browns experience the "spillover" of work and family in a number of areas: Deborah is "on the job" at home even when she's at the office, and Alvin is "on the job" from his home office even when he's folding laundry and cooking dinner. The boys' needs are attended to by both parents and are incorporated into their schedules beginning early in the morning and ending late in the evening. And the needs of extended family members (like Alvin's mother) are part of the Browns' routine, even if they don't live in the same household. This ordinary day is uncomplicated by any of the little glitches that families routinely experience—a sick child or a broken-down car or a trip to the polls (they could have voted by absentee ballots)—and it is still long, tiring, and complex. Spouses and parents are always "on the job" when it comes to family.

are also more likely to be abused than women with higher incomes (Bachman and Saltzman 1995). Age and economic security, however, do not make someone immune to abuse.

Contrary to popular opinion, most abusive partners are not "out of control," nor do they have "anger management problems" in the traditional sense. They often seem charming and calm to co-workers, friends, and police officers; they deliberately decide to be violent with those least likely to report the crime and over whom they maintain the most control: their family members. Domestic violence results from the abuser's desire for power over the victim, and abusers often blame their victims: I wouldn't have beaten you if dinner had been on time, or if you hadn't been "flirting" with the sales associate at the mall. One abuser is reported to have said to police officers, "Yes, I hit her five or six times but it was only to calm her down" ("Even in the Best of Homes" 2003).

A four-stage **cycle of violence** seems to occur in almost every abusive relationship. In the first stage, the abusive partner is charming, attentive, and thoughtful; disagreements are glossed over and the relationship looks stable and healthy. However, tension is building to the second stage, often described as "walking on eggshells." Here, both parties sense that something will happen no matter what the victim may do to try to avoid it. During the third stage, acute battering and violence occur, lasting for seconds, hours, or even days. Whatever happens, the abuser will invariably blame the victim for the incident. The fourth stage, often referred to as "loving contrition," is the "honeymoon" phase and is one of the reasons victims remain in violent relationships. After the violence, the abuser will apologize profusely and promise that it will never happen again. The abuser may buy the victim gifts, beg forgiveness, and talk about getting help or making a change. Most abusers, however, have no interest in changing because they don't want to give up their control over their victims. Soon the cycle starts again, with flowers and gifts giving way to tension, uneasiness, and another battering.

Victims of domestic violence stay with their abusers for many reasons. After years of abuse, victims often believe what their abusers tell them: that they can't make it on their own and are somehow responsible for the abuse. If they have not been allowed to attend school or to work, they may not have employment skills. Often, children are involved, or abusers threaten to harm other family members. Many victims have been isolated from friends and family and are afraid to speak of the abuse to anyone, and they see no options but to remain where they are.

Child and Elder Abuse

Adult partners are not the only victims of domestic violence. Children and the elderly also suffer at the hands of abusive family members—and can suffer in distinctive ways that are linked to their special status in the family. Child abuse and elder abuse are likely to be underreported, partly because of the relative powerlessness of their victims and the private settings of the abuse. The best official estimates are that about forty-seven of every 1,000 children in the United States are abused in some way (Weise and Daro 1995) and that about 5 percent of all seniors in this country have been subject to elder abuse in some form (Wolf 2000).

In addition to physical violence and verbal, emotional, and sexual abuse, children may experience a distinctive type of abuse known as **neglect**—inadequate nutrition, insufficient clothing or shelter, and unhygienic or unsafe living conditions. Because children depend on adults for their care and well-being, they suffer when those adults abandon or pervert that responsibility. **Incest** is another form of child abuse that exploits the trust that children must place in their caregivers. Inappropriate sexual relationships between parents and children have devastating lifelong consequences for child victims, which may include self-destructive behavior (including eating disorders and substance abuse) and the inability to form trusting relationships later in life. In addition, those who were physically or sexually abused as children have a much higher likelihood of becoming abusers themselves.

Elder abuse can also take distinctive forms. As well as physical, verbal, emotional, and sexual abuse, there is financial exploitation or theft—relatives or other caregivers may steal or misuse the elder's property or financial resources. Another form is neglect and abandonment. Some elders are dependent on others to care for them. Refusal to provide food, shelter, health care, or protection can be as devastating to an elder as it is to a child. Both elder and child abuse exploit the special powerlessness of victims and are difficult to monitor and control.

cycle of violence a common behavior pattern in abusive relationships; the cycle begins happily, then the relationship grows tense, and the tension explodes in abuse, followed by a period of contrition that allows the cycle to repeat

neglect a form of child abuse in which the caregiver fails to provide adequate nutrition, sufficient clothing or shelter, or hygienic and safe living conditions

incest proscribed sexual contact between family members; a form of child abuse when it occurs between a child and a caregiver

ANALYZING MASS MEDIA AND POPULAR CULTURE

Family Troubles in Film

Family relations have long been the basis of good comedic, tragic, and dramatic films. This Data Workshop asks you to use existing sources as a research method (see Chapter 2 for a review) and to do a content analysis of a film concerning family dynamics. Choose a film to watch and then analyze its relevance to some of the family issues discussed in this chapter. Although many films feature families, this assignment asks you to focus on one or more family problems.

The following films depict a variety of family troubles, such as marital problems, divorce, domestic abuse, parental neglect, disabilities and illnesses, sex and dating, pregnancy, death, delinquency, and financial difficulties. Other movies could certainly be added to this list, as long as your instructor approves the film you would like to choose. Whatever movie you choose must be available on video or DVD so that you can view it carefully. Please be aware of the MPAA ratings for these or other movies, and watch only those titles that are appropriate for your age group and that you would feel comfortable viewing.

The Kids Are Alright	*The Ice Storm*
Amreeka	*In America*
Affliction	*In the Bedroom*
American Beauty	*The Joy Luck Club*
Baby Boy	*Kramer vs. Kramer*
How to Deal	*Mi Familia (My Family)*

Mrs. Doubtfire	*Stepmom*
My Big Fat Greek Wedding	*Terms of Endearment*
Ordinary People	*Thirteen*
Pieces of April	*We Don't Live Here Anymore*
Rachel Getting Married	*What's Eating Gilbert Grape?*
The Royal Tennenbaums	*You Can Count on Me*
Saving Face	

Select a movie that is primarily about contemporary family relations and problems. Once you have chosen a movie, read through the rest of the workshop points and guidelines. Then watch the film closely and pay attention to the plotlines, scenes, characters, and dialogues in which family troubles are depicted. Take notes as you watch the movie; you may have to review it several times before you can do a thorough content analysis. This assignment has several parts, and you may also wish to add your own questions or comments.

Consider the following points and answer these questions:

- Give some background information on the film and why you chose it.

- Using sociological terms, describe the family troubles that are the focus of the film. How are these problems manifested in the lives of the family members? How do the various characters deal with their problems? What solutions do they propose through their actions? How effective are these solutions in addressing the family's troubles?

- Put the family's problems in a broader sociological perspective. Do you believe the family's troubles are more psychological or sociological in nature? In what ways are the individual troubles of family members linked to larger social patterns and problems? Compare the

Family Troubles? What do films like *The Kids Are Alright* and *Amreeka* tell us about contemporary American families?

problems in the movie with their counterparts in the real world. Gather recent data relating to the family problems featured in the film, using sources such as the U.S. Census Bureau, other government or private agencies, or various news sources. How widespread are these problems? How are they being discussed and dealt with at a public level? How accurately do you think the family's troubles, and their possible solutions, were depicted in the film? What kind of a role, if any, do you think the media can play in helping to reduce family troubles or associated social problems?

There are two options for completing this Data Workshop.

- *Option 1 (informal)*: Make the observations described above and answer the preceding questions. Then prepare some written notes that you can refer to during in-class discussions. Compare and contrast the analyses of the films observed by participants in your discussion group.

- *Option 2 (formal)*: Make the observations described above and answer the preceding questions. Then write a three- to four-page essay talking about your answers and reflecting on your observations of the film. What do you think your observations tell us about contemporary American families and the ways in which family troubles are portrayed on film?

Divorce and Breakups

Although many people stay in bad relationships, many couples also break up every day. In this section, we consider the changing patterns of divorce and remarriage as they affect children and adults. We also look at the resulting social problems of custody, visitation, and child support.

Changing Patterns

As of March 2002, the U.S. Census Bureau reported that more than 123 million persons were married while about 21 million were divorced. Thus, in 2002 about 55 percent of the entire U.S. population were married while just fewer than 10 percent were divorced. Figure 12.1 shows that the numbers of those who have married and the rates of divorce have increased over time. The percentage of married people who have divorced has increased more than five and a half times since 1950, indicating that about 50 percent of all first marriages now end in divorce (Kreider and Fields 2001).

Most who divorce eventually marry other people. Among parents of young children, the remarriage rate is very high. According to Cherlin and Furstenberg (1994), 75 percent of divorced men and 67 percent of divorced women ultimately remarry, and between 75 percent and 80 percent of divorced parents remarry (Weissbourd 1994). But remarriage rates in the United States are actually lower now than they were before the 1960s, a fact attributable to the increase in

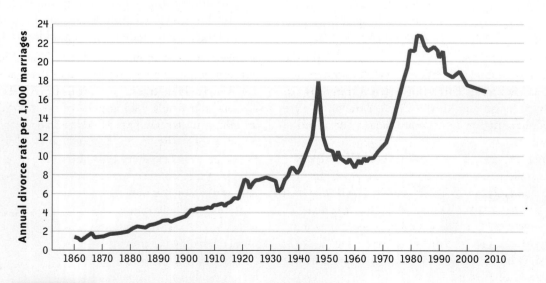

FIGURE 12.1 U.S. Divorce Rate Over the Past Century

SOURCE: Cherlin 2010.

cohabitation, or living together, among unmarried couples. Census data reveal that about 5 percent of all households are occupied by unmarried heterosexual couples, which may reflect a certain caution about marriage as a result of rising rates of divorce.

In the early 1970s, the children of divorced parents were more than three times more likely to divorce than their peers from intact families. But by the mid-1990s, this figure had dropped to about one and a half times (Wolfinger 1999, 2000). According to Wolfinger (2003), the decline of intergenerational divorce and marriage rates probably has three sources. One is the growing acceptance of divorce. Children of divorced parents no longer suffer the social stigma that was once the byproduct of divorce and are less likely to develop psychological problems as a result—which may have contributed to their divorces in the past. Second, the age of marriage has changed. Children of divorce are still more likely to marry as teenagers, but those not married by age twenty are more likely not to marry at all than their peers from intact families. Third, children of divorced parents are more likely to cohabit with their partners and are less likely to marry them than children of nondivorced parents. Therefore, the decline in marriage rates among children of divorced parents can be explained by both increased rates of cohabitation and an increased propensity not to marry at all.

Custody, Visitation, and Child Support

Reviewing the legal policies that address the consequences of divorce for children, sociologists are concerned with whether custody, visitation, and child support effectively replace the resources, both emotional and financial, of an intact household. Do they help children?

Custody is the physical and legal responsibility for the everyday life and routines of children. While mothers still disproportionately receive custody, there is a trend toward joint custody (Cancian and Meyer 1998). Parents who are well educated, have high socioeconomic status, live in cities, and are nonwhite are more likely than others to have joint custody of their children (Donnelly and Finkelhor 1993). A father is more likely to be awarded sole custody when his income is substantially more than the mother's (Cancian and Meyer 1998), when his children are older, or when the oldest child is male (Fox and Kelly 1995). A mother is more likely to receive sole custody when she has a high level of education, her children are younger, and the father is unemployed (Fox and Kelly 1995).

Courts award visitation to noncustodial parents to protect parent-child relationships. Generally, parents with regular visitation patterns are better able to meet the psychological and financial needs of their children. Fathers who visit regularly are more likely to maintain strong relationships with their children and to pay child support (Seltzer, Schaeffer, and Charng 1989). Despite increased vigilance of courts and lawmakers regarding mandated child support policies, noncustodial parents often fail to make regular payments to the custodial parent. Sociologists have found that many parents make informal arrangements, or decisions without the mediation of the legal system, about child support schedules soon after the divorce (Peters et al. 1993) and the stability of payments varies substantially, even among the most reliable payers (Meyer and Bartfeld 1998).

As children are more likely to live in poverty after their parents' divorce, child support policies are important. Women are more likely to suffer downward economic mobility after divorce, especially if they retain custody of their children. Furstenberg, Hoffman, and Shrestha (1995) found that women experience on average a 25 percent decline in their economic well-being after a divorce. Accompanying this post-divorce decline in financial resources are often scholastic failure, disruptive conduct, and troubled relationships in children of divorced families (Keith and Finlay 1988; Morrison and Cherlin 1995). Further, divorce seems to negatively affect male children more than female children as boys are more likely to act out than girls.

Stepparents and Blended Families

Most divorced people will eventually marry someone else, which means that one in three Americans is a member of a stepfamily (Baca Zinn and Eitzen 2002). However, statistics about stepfamilies are inconsistent and often contradictory because quantifying and defining the intricate relationships involved in a stepfamily are difficult. The U.S. Census has not routinely accounted for them in its data gathering. There are historically no traditional norms or models for stepfamilies, and our firmly held notions of the "traditional" family lead many in stepfamilies to find the transition to a new family situation difficult. Stepfamilies face special challenges, for example, when there are children in different stages of the life cycle. The needs and concerns of teenagers may be vastly different from those of their infant half-sibling, and it may take more work to adjust to the new living situation. With the added challenges of blending in-laws, finances, and households, remarriages are even more likely to end in

---

cohabitation living together as a romantically involved, unmarried couple

custody the physical and legal responsibility of caring for children; assigned by a court for divorced or unmarried parents

The Brady Bunch America's best-known blended family.

divorce than first marriages. However, in successful remarriages, partners are usually older and have learned important lessons about compatibility and relationship maintenance from the failure of their first marriages.

Trends in American Families

"There's this pervasive idea in America that puts marriage and family at the center of everyone's lives," says Bella M. DePaulo, visiting professor of psychology at the University of California at Santa Barbara, "when in fact it's becoming less and less so" (personal communication 2003). Many people live outside such arrangements. In fact, the average American now spends the majority of his or her life unmarried because people live longer, delay marriage, or choose a single lifestyle (Kreider and Fields 2002).

Being Single

The term "single" often implies a young adult who is actively seeking a partner for a relationship or marriage. But singles also include gays and lesbians who may not have the option to marry, people living alone who are in long-distance relationships, people living in communes, widows and widowers, minors in group homes, and some clergy members as well as those who are single due to divorce or deliberate choice.

Married couples were the dominant model through the 1950s, but their numbers have slipped from nearly 80 percent of households to just above 50 percent now. Married couples with children—the traditional model of family—total just 25 percent of households, and that number is projected to drop (National Opinion Research Center 1999). The remaining households are single parents, cohabiting partners, or others. A stunning 27 percent of all households are made up of people who live alone, and, in 2005, unmarrieds became the new majority (U.S. Census Bureau 2010b).

Among the growing movement of activists promoting the rights of unmarried people in the United States is the nonprofit Alternatives to Marriage Project and its associated advocacy group Unmarried America (Solot and Miller 2002). They engage in research, education, and advocacy for unmarried and single adults of all types and are concerned about discrimination that is built into the American social system, especially at an economic and political level, but also in terms of culture and values. One of their efforts is to increase recognition of unmarrieds and singles as a constituency of voters, workers, taxpayers, and consumers worthy of equal rights and protection (Warner, Ihara, and Hertz 2001).

Cohabitation

Between 1960 and 2000, the number of unmarried cohabiting couples in the United States increased 1,000 percent. More than 11 million people are living with an unmarried partner, including both same-sex and different-sex couples. In addition, marriage is no longer the prerequisite for childbearing. More than one in three unmarried-couple households have children (U.S. Census Bureau 2000a), and one-third of all first births are to unmarried parents (National Center for Health Statistics 2001). Most couples that choose to cohabit rather than marry are twenty-five to thirty-four years of age. A possible reason may be the growing economic independence of individuals today, resulting in less financial motivation for a marriage contract. Also, changing attitudes about religion have made sexual relationships outside marriage more socially acceptable.

Single Parenting

Although some people become single parents through divorce or death, others choose to have children without the support of a committed partner—through adoption,

1960

Percentage of Americans ages eighteen and older in 1960

15% NEVER MARRIED   **NO DATA**   **72% MARRIED**   **5% DIVORCED/ SEPARATED**

1970

Percentage of Americans ages eighteen and older in 1970

17% NEVER MARRIED   **NO DATA**   **69% MARRIED**   **6% DIVORCED/ SEPARATED**

1980

Percentage of Americans ages eighteen and older in 1980

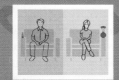  

20% NEVER MARRIED   **NO DATA**   **62% MARRIED**   **9% DIVORCED/ SEPARATED**

1990

Percentage of Americans ages eighteen and older in 1990

23% NEVER MARRIED   **3% COHABITATING**   **58% MARRIED**   **11% DIVORCED/ SEPARATED**

2000

Percentage of Americans ages eighteen and older in 2000

23% NEVER MARRIED   **6% COHABITATING**   **57% MARRIED**   **13% DIVORCED/ SEPARATED**

2010

Percentage of Americans ages eighteen and older in 2010

27% NEVER MARRIED   **8% COHABITATING**   **54% MARRIED**   **13% DIVORCED/ SEPARATED**

SOURCE: PEW RESEARCH CENTER 2010A; U.S. CENSUS BUREAU 2010B.

Intentional Communities
Members and former members of the Twin Oaks commune in Yanceyville, Virginia, celebrate the fortieth anniversary of the founding of the community.

artificial insemination, or surrogacy. In the United States, only 10 percent of single parents are single fathers. Attitudes about single mothers vary greatly and are often dependent on the mother's age, education level, occupation, and income, and the family's support network from friends and extended family members.

A prevailing middle-class assumption about poor single mothers is that young women in the inner city become mothers to access welfare benefits. Kathryn Edin and Maria Kefalas (2005) spent five years doing in-depth research with 162 low-income single mothers to understand their attitudes about parenthood and marriage. They dispelled the myth that these women become mothers to cash in on welfare benefits and instead found that for these young women, having a baby is a symbol of belonging and being valued. Being a good mother is an accessible role that can generate respect and admiration in the community.

Regardless of the circumstances of single parenting, raising children without the help of a partner is challenging and difficult. Financially, physically, and emotionally, single parents must perform a task that was traditionally shared by a community rather than an individual.

Intentional Communities

> **intentional community** any of a variety of groups who form communal living arrangements outside marriage

As an increasing number of people choose to remain or become single, cohabit with others, or choose something else altogether, they are creating alternative models to organize their lives. Some join an **intentional community**, an inclusive term for a variety of different groups who form communal living arrangements that include ecovillages, cohousing, residential land trusts, communes, monasteries and ashrams, farming collectives, student co-ops, or urban housing cooperatives.

Members of an intentional community have chosen to live together with a common purpose, working cooperatively to create a lifestyle that reflects their shared core values. They may live on rural land, in a suburban home, or in an urban neighborhood, and they may share a single residence or live in a cluster of dwellings. Although quite diverse in philosophy and lifestyle, each of these groups places a high priority on fostering a sense of community—a feeling of belonging and mutual support that is increasingly hard to find in mainstream Western society (Kozeny 1995).

The Postmodern Family

Families adapting to the challenges of a postmodern society may create family structures that look very different from the "traditional" family. Sociologist Judith Stacey explored some of these adaptations for her book *Brave New Families* (1990). The families and households she studied expanded and contracted over time and included members who were never part of the traditional *Leave It to Beaver* model of the nuclear family. Ex-spouses and their new partners and children, adult children and other kin, and even nonkin—friends and co-workers—populated the working-class Silicon Valley households she studied. Multiple earners and a diversity of generations, genders, and relational connections were the rule rather than the exception in her study:

> No longer is there a single culturally dominant family pattern, like the modern one, to which a majority of Americans conform and most of the rest aspire. Instead, Americans today have crafted a multiplicity of family and household arrangements that we inhabit uneasily and reconstitute frequently in response to changing personal and occupational circumstances. (Stacey 1990, p. 19)

We have entered an era of improvisation or do-it-yourself family forms; household members respond to social-structural changes in ways that fit their family's needs. These improvisational forms are not new; they are merely new to mainstream working- and middle-class families. Minorities, the poor, and gays and lesbians have always had to improvise to fit into a society that ignored or devalued their needs and activities (Stack 1974; Weston 1991; Edin and Lein 1997; Stacey 1998). These improvisational, post-modern family forms will become more and more familiar to the rest of society as we all cope with the social and cultural changes of the twenty-first century.

Closing Comments

When sociologists study the dynamics of family, they must define the subject of their interest. What exactly is family? This process sometimes leads to definitions that lie outside the traditional notions of biological or legal relations that have historically defined family. Certainly, this is true if one looks outside the United States at the astonishing variety of customs and practices that define family around the world. In the early twenty-first century, the nature of the nuclear family is changing, as divorced and blended families are altering the structure and function of all families, with a tendency to decrease the amount of contact and assistance between generations. The emergence of these "brave new families" has led to a sea change in the study of families, with an increasing recognition of the diversity and plurality that characterize family arrangements.

ⓢ Need Help Studying?

wwnorton.com/studyspace

Visit StudySpace to access free review materials such as:

- **Vocabulary Flashcards**
- **Diagnostic Review Quizzes**
- **Study Outlines**

QUESTIONS FOR REVIEW

1. How does this chapter's definition of family differ from the one used by the U.S. Census Bureau? Make a list of everyone you consider a family member. Is there anyone on this list who wouldn't qualify according to the Census Bureau's definition?

2. What do sociologists mean when they argue that instead of the sociology of the *family* we should have a sociology of *families*? Why do we think of particular people as family members?

3. Same-sex marriage is prohibited in most of the United States. At different points in American history, couples of mixed race, ethnic background, or nationality were not legally allowed to marry. What do these three groups have in common with same-sex couples? What are the advantages of a legally recognized marriage?

4. Conflict theorists believe that strife within the family is fueled by competition for resources. What is the basis for inequality within the family? In families, who tends to receive fewer resources?

5. Homogamy helps explain a lot about mate selection in contemporary society: we tend to date and marry people who are similar to us in culturally meaningful ways. What cultural factors influence your relationship choices?

6. Another important factor that helps explain mate selection is propinquity, the tendency to choose mates who live in close geographic proximity to us. Some sociologists believe that technological changes are making propinquity less important. What sorts of changes make geographic location less relevant to mate selection?

7. Throughout history, there has almost always been a division of labor by gender, but, before the Industrial Revolution, men's and women's labor were more equally valued. What changes led to the devaluation of tasks traditionally done by women?

8. Arlie Hochschild and Anne Machung found that women who work outside the home often face a "second shift" of housework when they get home. How do men avoid doing their share of this work? Have you ever noticed someone—perhaps even yourself—adopting these tactics?

9. A popular stereotype holds that poor women have more children in order to gain welfare benefits, though researchers who have studied the issue tend to reject this idea. Why else might poor single women have children?

SUGGESTIONS FOR FURTHER EXPLORATION

Big Love. 2006–2011. HBO. Created by Mark V. Olsen and Will Scheffer. Fictional television series about a polygamous Mormon family in Utah. Artfully addresses such family

Big Love

issues as commitment and fidelity, secrecy and openness, parent-child relations, religion and public-private dichotomies.

Stephanie Coontz

Coontz, Stephanie. 2005. *Marriage, a History: From Obedience to Intimacy, or How Love Conquered Marriage*. New York: Penguin Books. An analysis of the "traditional" marriage associated with the nuclear family. Coontz argues that this relatively new type of marriage is in crisis today.

Gilbert, Elizabeth. 2010. *Committed: A Skeptic Makes Peace with Marriage*. New York: Viking. Part memoir, part expose on the practice of marriage, this book examines different historical periods and cultural contexts in an effort to understand more about the author's own romantic journey and the choices she's made.

Cinema Verite. 2011. HBO. A dramatic film about the making of *An American Family* a 1973 PBS documentary series on the private lives of the Loud Family of Santa Barbara, who were the unwitting stars of what would be the first reality TV program, causing great scandal and controversy at the time. The original series was released again for the first time in 2011.

Hua, Cai. 2001. *A Society Without Fathers or Husbands: The Na of China*. Cambridge, MA: Zone Books. A startling counterpoint to some of our assumptions about the family, this ethnography describes the Na people of southern China who live without marriage. In Na culture, children are raised by their mother's family, without the participation of their biological father.

Krakauer, Jon. 2003. *Under the Banner of Heaven: A Story of Violent Faith*. London: Pan Books. A compelling look at Mormon fundamentalist groups in the United States who espouse and practice polygyny. Although his book is primarily an account of a murder, Krakauer provides a wealth of background on both the history of the Mormon Church and the splinter groups who maintain some of the early church's most controversial beliefs and practices.

Number Our Days. 1976. Dir. Lynne Littman. Community Television of Southern California. This short documentary film based on the ethnographic study of elderly Jews in Venice, California, won an Oscar for its moving depiction of aging and the life course.

The OYEZ Project's site about *Loving vs. Virginia* (www .oyez.org/cases/1960-1969/1966/1966_395). A comprehensive account of the landmark case that effectively ended race-based marriage restrictions in the United States. The site includes sound files of the oral arguments and full text of the unanimous opinion written by Chief Justice Earl Warren striking down Virginia's antimiscegenation laws.

Rufus, Anneli. 2002. *Party of One: The Loners' Manifesto*. Washington, DC: Marlowe and Company. A polemic defense of the introvert and the loner, as well as a popular history of the prejudice against being alone. Rufus argues that people should be able to be single without feeling imperfect.

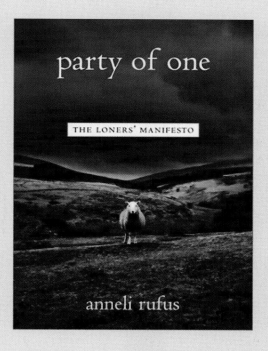

Three of Hearts. 2004. Dir. Susan Kaplan. Hibiscus Films. A documentary about two men in a romantic relationship who add a female partner to their home and develop a polyamorous relationship that redefines the limits of family.

Weston, Kath. 1997. *Families We Choose*. New York: Columbia University Press. A discussion of the way that members of the gay and lesbian community have reinterpreted the idea of family as a more inclusive, less kin-based institution, especially as many of them were rejected by and cut off from their birth families.

CHAPTER 13

Recreation and Leisure in Everyday Life

Y ou're sitting in a darkened theater watching a movie unfold on the big screen. Two young lo ers meet, woo, and marry. They honeymoon at a mountain resort—where, unfortunately, the are kidnapped by political rebels who break into song, swinging their rifles in unison as the dance in camouflage fatigues. After the ransom is paid, the couple return to the city, where they sho for housewares—at a store where clerks croon and shoppers dance in the aisles. But before they a allowed to live happily ever after, their baby is switched at birth with another infant, and they mu track down their child with the help of a singing police detective/spiritual adviser. The film lasts mo than three hours; during that time, audience members (men in one section, women and children i another) come and go, fetching delicious snacks that extend far beyond prosaic popcorn and sod They yell, groan, sing, talk back, and even throw things at the screen—but nobody shushes ther Where are you? You're in "Bollywood."

Unless you are South Asian, have traveled to India, or are a *very* dedicated film buff, you've prob ably never seen a Bollywood film. This term, an obvious take-off on the American film capital, is use to describe a particular class of movies produced in Mumbai or Bombay. The Indian film industry is th most prolific in the world, and the movies it produces are very different from those Americans are use to. A typical film usually includes romance, political intrigue, and dramatic events such as kidnapping military battles, or natural disasters—and there is always lots of singing and dancing! In other word Indian films are a mixture of what American audiences understand to be separate genres: romance, mus cal, action, thriller, and so on. As a result, Americans react to Indian films as strange, exhausting, and di; organized, while Indians find American movies boring, unemotional, and too short (Srinivas 1998).

Some American audiences got their first taste of Bollywood from British director Danny Boyle "Slumdog Millionaire," a film that borrowed some of the same stylistic elements and won the best pi ture Academy Award in 2009. The film was a "sleeper hit" that gradually grew in popularity by goo word of mouth, much of it about how different the movie looked and felt. Still, it's unlikely that th theater-going experience for U.S. audiences was anything close to what is typical in India. In India theaters, silence is not the norm; audience members respond to what's on-screen in ways that see startling or even wrong to Americans. The only American film experience that resembles the Bolly wood model is the midnight showings of *The Rocky Horror Picture Show*, where enthusiastic fan dress up, sing along, talk back, throw toast, and shoot squirt guns at the screen. In Bollywood, thoug this type of behavior is the rule.

ready know, different cultures may hold very differ-
ns and values when it comes to work, family, edu-
nd politics. This is just as true of the things we do
In this chapter, we will examine the different types
ies that fall under the heading of recreation and lei-
consider how culture shapes and is shaped by these
. Recreation and leisure activities actually form the
numerous subcultures, and we will examine some
as well. Experiences with the mass media, sports,
and nature and the wilderness are all subject to
from various theoretical perspectives, and all can be
ively examined through the lenses of race, gender,
. In short, we will apply our sociological tools to the
e do for fun.

lying Leisure
Recreation

ns "recreation" and "leisure" are both defined pri-
y their difference from paid labor or other obligatory
. **Leisure** is time that can be spent doing whatever
t, or just relaxing. **Recreation** is any activity that is
g or amusing, experienced as refreshing for body and
his means that just about any activity could fall under
ding, depending on individual preference, and that
an spend their leisure time engaged in all sorts of rec-
activities (or not). The sociology of recreation and
broad enough, then, to encompass all sorts of pas-
aying volleyball, traveling to Italy, gardening, wood-
, needlepoint, listening to music, watching television,
shopping, writing poetry, hiking, baking cookies—
ibilities are endless. It's important to note that what
mething a recreational activity is not its appearance
r any other list, but rather the experience of the activ-
. Does it feel enjoyable, liberating, even transforma-
tive? Then it's recreational.
So what might be one per-
son's job could be another
person's recreational activity.
If you bake cookies all day at
work, for example, it's unlikely
that you'll feel like doing so in
your free time; those who do
feel this way about their paid
labor are extremely lucky!

ime that can be
ging in recreation,
ing in freely chosen

sfying, amusing, and
that is experienced
newing for body,

Recreation and leisure have changed dramatically in
recent history. In the premodern world, the line between
work and play was not nearly as clearly defined as it is
today—in part because there was an awful lot of work to be
done and there were fewer recreational options. Activities
we now engage in almost exclusively as recreation (like gardening, hunting and fishing, or knitting) were necessities in
the past, and common pastimes like going to the movies and
watching television didn't even exist. Even in the late nineteenth century, low wages and long hours meant that only the
wealthy had the time and resources to pursue recreational
activities with any consistency. This situation began to
change between 1890 and 1940, as the amount of time that
the middle class could devote to leisure activities grew rapidly (Fischer 1994). The increase in leisure time was largely
fueled by technological progress that increased industrial
productivity and inventions such as the washing machine,
dishwasher, and air-conditioning. Technological changes
also fundamentally altered the nature of leisure activities.

Three Developments

Most discussions of modern leisure-time activities emphasize three related developments that have changed the ways
in which we engage in them. We now look at each of these
developments in turn.

THE DECLINE OF PUBLIC LIFE Sociologist Richard Sennett argues that modernity has seen the "fall of public man,"
as people more and more seek refuge in "ties of family or
intimate association" (Sennett 1977, p. 3). This decline in
public life has affected leisure in far-reaching ways. After
World War II, the mass migration to the suburbs and the
development of television encouraged people to stay home
and even displaced public activities such as moviegoing
(Fischer 1994). Television may have begun this process, but
more recent developments have only intensified it. Video
games, DVD players, personal computers, and the internet have all made the private home an even more attractive
site for leisure. The internet in particular has begun to isolate individuals even within the home. While it can facilitate
contact between people who live in different corners of the
world, the internet can just as easily cut off individuals from
family, friends, and spouses (Jackson 1999).

One large-scale longitudinal study sponsored by the
National Endowment for the Arts found that "Americans are
increasingly less likely to go out for a dose of the arts, and
more likely to stay home and enjoy performances in front
of their home entertainment centers" (Yin 2003). The effect

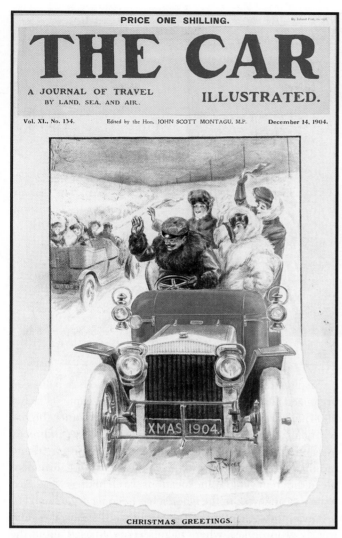

PRICE ONE SHILLING.

THE CAR
A JOURNAL OF TRAVEL
BY LAND, SEA, AND AIR.
ILLUSTRATED.

Vol. XI., No. 134.   Edited by the Hon. JOHN SCOTT MONTAGU, M.P.   December 14, 1904.

XMAS 1904.

CHRISTMAS GREETINGS.

Rise of the Leisure Class Around the turn of the twentieth century, industrial productivity and new technologies created new opportunities for leisure among the middle and upper classes.

has been most obvious in music and theater, but even the visual arts are starting to see a change. People still visit museums and galleries, but a growing proportion are also looking at pictures online, in magazines, and in books. Here, as in many other ways, technology is moving our recreation inside the home, away from public spaces.

COMMERCIALIZING LEISURE AND RECREATION The second development, and this one has made a greater mark on our leisure time than any other, is the massive increase in the **commodification** of recreational activities: where people formerly made their own fun, they now purchase it as goods and services. What Americans spend on entertainment per year will surpass $700 billion (Cohen 2005), most of it on mass media products (movies, CDs, DVDs, and so

on). Television in particular is referred to as "the 800-pound gorilla of leisure time" (Putnam 1995). More than 98 percent of all American households have television. In fact, the average household has two or more TVs in it. In 2007 alone, Americans spent more than $26 billion to purchase digital TV sets. And in 2008, Americans spent an average of well over four and a half hours per day in front of those TVs watching a record number (118) of available channels (U.S. Census Bureau 2008b, 2008c).

Simple, inexpensive outdoor activities like hiking are still popular, but they increasingly compete with "technologically innovative forms of play such as scuba diving, parasailing, skydiving, and hang-gliding, snowmobiling, and other kinds of off-road travel [that] have opened up new environments for the play experience" (Kraus 1995).

Even those activities that were once necessities, like hunting and fishing, now come with a dizzying array of commodities. Sport fishing relies on expensive boats, lures, rods, and sonar to help locate the fish. Hunting seems to demand special clothing, scent blockers, calls and decoys, infrared vision enhancement, and even special hearing aids that allow hunters to tune in to specific frequencies while stalking particular animals. Instead of visiting the local swimming hole, we pay to visit water parks. Instead of playing softball or soccer, many simply watch sports on TV, played by professionals. In almost every case, our recreation is mediated by goods and services that we seem to "require" in order to have fun.

The ultimate example of the commercialization of leisure, however, is shopping: where the purchase of commodities becomes an end in itself. Recreational shopping is a recent historical development. Until the mid-twentieth century, people shopped mainly to acquire food, clothing, fuel, and other essential goods. But now, in addition, we shop to live out daydreams, to experience a "sensual and emotional high" (Zukin 2004, p. 220). Shopping is no longer just about "bread"—it has also become its own "circus," with more than 45,000 malls and shopping centers nationwide to support our habit.

Leisure, money, and business intersect in other ways as well. When you go to a professional baseball or basketball game, chances are that you're there to root for your favorite team, eat hot dogs and drink soda or beer, and generally have a good time with family or friends. Work is probably the last thing on your mind. But what about the people who help provide that experience for you—the parking attendants, ticket-takers, security officers, ushers, food and souvenir vendors, janitors, and maintenance workers? What about the team owners, talent scouts, agents, managers, coaches, trainers, and players

commodification the process by which it becomes possible to buy and sell a particular good or service

Commercialized Leisure Today, many of our forms of leisure and recreation are mediated by commodities, goods, and services that we seem to "require" in order to have fun.

themselves? If the game is covered by the media, then you can add announcers, reporters, sportscasters, photographers, camera crews, producers, editors, publishers, advertisers, and more.

Clearly, the business of recreation and leisure is a big business. To take baseball as an example, in 2008 more than 4.3 million people attended the New York Yankees' eighty-one home games, with an average of about 53,000 per game (ESPN 2008). Millions more tuned in to the televised games. Overall, the businesses that could be broadly classified as providing recreation or entertainment are easily worth trillions of dollars. As such, these industries account for a major part of the U.S. and global economies.

Like a baseball game, almost any kind of activity we enjoy must be supported in some way by others. From hiking in the local foothills (consider how the Parks and Recreation Department might be involved in maintaining trails) to eating an ice cream cone (consider the manufacturing, delivery, and service involved in getting the cone to your hand), many people work to make these activities possible. By some estimates, there are more than 25 million leisure and recreation jobs that are staffed in the United States alone.

FORMALIZING RECREATION: ORGANIZATION OVER SPONTANEITY In addition to moving from the public to the private sphere and becoming increasingly commodified, many forms of leisure and recreation seem to have shifted from spontaneous or informal activities to organized and formal. This "development of organization over spontane-

ity" is illustrated by the rise of Little League baseball as an organized alternative to after-school sand-lot games (Fischer 1994). There is a great deal of debate as to whether the rise of organization is good or bad. Technology has indirectly assisted this process: cell phones, e-mail, the internet, and radio and TV advertising all make it easier to organize people in different geographic locations. Even hiking, what used to be a casual walk in the woods, has become organized. For instance, local chapters of the Sierra Club sponsor regular weekly group hikes, where members are advised about the proper gear to bring and encouraged to carpool.

Leisure: The Opposite of Work?

Work has typically been understood as serious and consequential, while leisure activities are seen as minor and unimportant. Leisure and recreation, though, absorb so much time, energy, and resources that they must represent "important developmental goals and meet other personal needs of both children and adults" (Kraus 1995). In many ways, it is leisure that provides the most "meaningful experiences" and allows people "opportunities to reveal their true selves" (Havitz and Dimanche 1999).

Many people think of their nonwork time as free time, or leisure time (using the terms interchangeably). Therefore, leisure must be the opposite of work, right? Consider the following scenario. With final exams looming around the corner, Amber, Zack, and Juan—all taking the same sociology class—plan an evening study session at a local café. Amber arrives late from her waitressing job. Zack and Juan have already outlined a few chapters and drunk a few cups of coffee. The three chat for a while before continuing to study. The café is bustling with other students studying, too. At the end of the night, they plan to meet again the following day.

When does work end and leisure begin? In our scenario, it is difficult to decide which is which. Meeting at a café to study seems more like a leisure activity than waitressing at a restaurant. However, studying at a café seems more like work than merely meeting friends to chat.

Rather than understanding leisure as the opposite of work, sociologists see the two as complementary activities within a capitalist economic system—two activities linked by **consumption** (Rojek 1985, 1995). Thus, we work for wages to consume a variety of goods and services, including leisure. As we consume more leisure, we must earn more wages to pay for it. As we have seen, leisure is itself a booming industry, with millions of workers servicing our leisure desires. We choose leisure time to supplement our working lives, and the connection between the two is more than merely oppositional.

So, what is free time? Sociologist Chris Rojek warns us not to equate free time (or nonworking time) with leisure time (1985, 1995, 2000). Consider the following example. When Cheryl finishes work for the day, picks up her children from school, cooks her family an evening meal, helps her children with their schoolwork, and then puts them to bed, has she had any free time? Is free time only the time not spent working for wages? What about an office worker who realizes that he is already prepared for a meeting and thus has a few minutes with nothing to do; are those few minutes free time? Is time spent driving to class or to work or volunteering at a local homeless shelter free time? Or is free time when we have "nothing" to do? If so, what constitutes "nothing"?

Free time is as ambiguous as it is difficult to measure. Arguably, Cheryl continues to work after she leaves her job at 5:00 P.M. and thus has no free time. She, however, may think of spending time with her family as her free time. Rojek argues that leisure, by its very definition, constitutes some kind of choice about how to spend one's time (1985). People make choices to *do* something with their time, whether it's honing their tennis skills or studying a new language. Therefore, free time is not necessarily leisure time.

Leisure and Inequality

Leisure activities can range from sleeping in to building houses for Habitat for Humanity. For some people, watching TV is a leisure activity. For others, leisure means such activities as skydiving or snowboarding. For many, it's both.

Sociologists have long associated types of leisure activities with social class.

Thus, working-class people do different things with their leisure than wealthy elites do. Interestingly, the wealthy do not necessarily have more leisure time; rather, their work sometimes closely resembles play (Rojek 1997, 2000). Networking on the golf course, for example, is still a kind of work but vastly divergent from teaching school. Also, professional athletes' work would not be considered in the same way by people who play football with their neighbors on the weekends; nor would professional musicians' work by people who play in a local amateur band. Famous actors and actresses work by managing what they eat, "working" out, attending lavish parties, and just looking beautiful for the cameras. In this way, many people strive for leisure activities that resemble the work of elites, celebrities, athletes, and musicians.

DATA WORKSHOP

ANALYZING MASS MEDIA AND POPULAR CULTURE
"Unsports*man*like" Conduct

Since the late 1980s and early 1990s, sociologists have noted a dramatic disparity in the reporting of men's and women's sporting events. For instance, Lumpkin and Williams (1991) observed that more than 90 percent of almost 4,000 articles in *Sports Illustrated* focused on men's lives and achievements, and those articles about women athletes were shorter than the ones about men. A comparative study of CNN and ESPN sports shows found a similar gap of reporting on men's and women's sports (Billings and Eastman 2000). More than 90 percent of the coverage on television news and sports highlights programs were devoted to men's sports (Messner, Duncan, and Wilms 2005). Not only were women's sports less likely to be broadcast than men's, but they were also presented differently from men's (Messner 2007). Commentators were more likely to infantilize and sexualize female athletes by referring to them as "girls" and calling them by their first names only. Male athletes, in contrast, were almost always referred to as "men" or even "young men" and were usually called by their first and last names. Men's successes were reported with enthusiasm, while women's were more likely to be reported with ambivalence. Women's losses were attributed to a stereotypical weakness or ineptness resulting from their physical

TYPE OF NEWS PROGRAM	WOMEN'S SPORTS	MEN'S SPORTS	FEMALE ATHLETES	MALE ATHLETES	TOTAL NUMBER OF SECONDS
Network News					
Local News					
Sports Channel News					

inferiority, while men's losses were more likely chalked up to "bad luck."

Does this inequality still exist? The following exercises asks you to use existing sources as a research method (refer back to Chapter 2 if you need a review) and to do a content analysis of sports programs in order to answer this question.

1. *Comparing news sources*: Record a regular network (national) news program, a local news program, and a sports channel (Fox, ESPN) news program. Count the amount of broadcast time in seconds given to men's and women's sports and to male and female athletes in each program. Fill in this information in the table at the top of the page.

Which type of show demonstrates the most equality in reporting on women's and men's sports?

2. *Comparing sports presentations*: Pick two equivalent televised sporting events, one women's game and one men's game (examples include golf, beach volleyball, tennis, snowboarding, and collegiate basketball). Watch each game, and make a list for each. The list should include notes on the gender of the commentators and how they refer to the players, individually and collectively. Are the athletes referred to as "girls" and "boys," or "women" and "men"? Are they called by their first names only, or first and last names? Do the commentators mention such characteristics as confidence, natural strength, intelligence, tenacity, or aggressiveness? Note also how athletes' successes and losses are presented by the announcers.

Now compare your two lists. How are women and men framed? How is the reporting similar and different for women and men?

There are two options for completing the assigned work.

- *Option 1 (informal)*: Prepare your data tables and bring them to class for discussion. Discuss your reactions and conclusions with other students in small-group discussions. Listen for any differences or variations in each other's findings.

- *Option 2 (formal)*: Write a three- to four-page essay answering the questions posed in this Data Workshop.

Make sure to refer to specific data and observations that support your analysis and include your data tables in the appendix.

Spectatorship

As spectators, we have many choices of how to watch a sports or other event. We can attend a live soccer match in our own country or watch it beamed from another country on TV or the internet. We can also choose when to watch it, if we record the game. Via the internet, we can participate in chat rooms, gambling rings, and role-playing games associated with our favorite sport. In such ways, spectatorship has become a huge and complex leisure activity.

The Structure of Media Industries

As we have seen, people spend their leisure time engaged in a wide variety of activities. For many Americans, consuming mass media—reading the newspaper, watching TV, listening to the radio, or surfing the internet—accounts for a large portion of this time. Clearly, the media are a major social institution and one with increasing power and importance in the Information Age. At first glance, we might conclude that its purpose is simply to supply information, educate, or entertain. While this is not incorrect, it is a somewhat naïve view of a complex and sophisticated social institution.

The Media and Democracy

One of the first things to remember about the media is their intimate relationship to a democratic system of government. The media have always been seen as both an instrument of the state and a tool for social change. Some of the original struggles during the fight for American independence were waged around these very issues. Early American leaders recognized the importance of news in educating and mobilizing the new citizenry. They were opposed to European

On the Job

Musicians "Playing" Music

Who wouldn't want to be a rock star? Lear-jetting from city to city, mobbed by adoring fans, staying in four-star hotel suites, partying backstage with models and celebrities. And getting paid tons of money to play, and the operative word is "play," music.

This stereotype of the rock and roll lifestyle is widespread, and one of the most underappreciated aspects of the work that professional musicians do is that it *is* work. Certainly no musician could deny the perks and privileges that come with success. But they would also say that there is no such thing as an overnight success, that practically everyone has had to pay his dues, and that few ever become rich and famous. Many professional musicians work in relative obscurity as band members, session players, songwriters, or producers. Their careers can be tenuous and short-lived.

Musicians recognize that their work is not manual labor, that they're not out sweating in the fields or laying bricks, nor are they stuck in an office from 9:00 to 5:00. But neither is what they do as fun and easy as it might appear. In order to achieve and maintain success over the years, it is necessary for any musician, regardless of how talented, to work consistently and hard. Professionals typically devote endless hours to learning and practicing their craft. The work conditions can be difficult and the days long and grueling. Writing, recording, rehearsing, and touring require sustained concentration, teamwork, and stamina. The work is often characterized by drudgery and repetition rather than spontaneity and creativity. After years in the business, some musicians suffer from the same kind of disenchantment with their careers that workers in other fields experience, despite whatever notions of romance might have attracted them to music in the first place (Stein 1997).

The rewards of working in any glamorous profession, whether it's music, show business, or sports, probably seem worth any of these difficulties. As social observers, however, we need to consider what goes on behind the scenes and to remember that what looks like play to one person might feel a lot more like work to another.

Playing and Working The band Sonic Youth performing on stage and working in the recording studio. Longevity in the music business is the exception, and remaining successful requires a strong work ethic on the part of the musicians.

governments' control over the media (which consisted at that time of books and newspapers) and sought instead to free the press so that it could be used as a voice of the people. That is precisely why the framers of the U.S. Constitution included guarantees to freedom of expression and freedom of the press in the First Amendment:

> Congress shall make no law respecting an establishment of religion, or prohibiting the free exercise thereof; or abridging the freedom of speech, or of the press; or the right of the people peaceably to assemble, and to petition the Government for a redress of grievances.

These are among our most precious and fiercely defended rights as Americans. Furthermore, the press was also to serve as a kind of "**Fourth Estate**," which could independently examine political leaders and give the people another means of checks and balances against the three branches of government.

While the principle of a free press still stands today, it is worth considering just who is free to own what we currently refer to as "the press"; in other words, a media outlet. Who has access to the media, who controls media products, whose voice is reaching a mass audience, and what kind of message is being sent by this powerful instrument of "free speech"?

Fourth Estate the media is considered like a fourth branch of government (after the executive, legislative, and judiciary) and thus serves as another of the checks and balances on power

conglomeration the process by which a single corporation acquires ownership of a variety of otherwise unrelated businesses

synergy a mutually beneficial interaction between parts of an organization that allows it to create something greater than the sum of its individual outputs

merger the legal combination of two companies, usually in order to maximize efficiency and profits by eliminating redundant infrastructure and personnel

concentration the process by which the number of companies producing and distributing a particular commodity decreases, often through mergers and conglomeration

Concentration of Media Power

Media companies are among the many big businesses that drive the American economy, and their profits and losses are closely followed by investors in the stock market. Media products are among the country's biggest exports, and there are almost too many publishers, TV networks, film studios, radio stations, and record companies to name. What is not readily evident from this seeming proliferation is that the businesses are often owned by the same large parent companies. There is currently a trend toward **conglomeration** (McChesney 2000), with huge corporations acquiring media companies as part of their larger holdings. This is how a company like Seagram's, which manufactured alcoholic beverages, came to own Universal (then MCA), which produces film, television, and music in the 1990s. Or how General Electric, which makes everything from washing machines to warheads, came to own the NBC television network.

A typical media conglomerate might comprise many divisions: book and magazine publishing, radio and TV broadcasting, a cable network, a movie studio and theaters, a record company, video distribution, web sites, a theme park, even a sports franchise. This allows the company to take advantage of its own organizational structure and market its products across a wide range of different media. Media companies favor products they can "cross-promote" along their various divisions, thus creating what is referred to as **synergy**. For example, a company might produce a movie that is adapted from a book it published, distribute the film to theaters it owns, advertise and review it in company newspapers and magazines, put the soundtrack on its record label, create recognizable characters that appear in commercials or at its theme park, release the movie on its DVD label, and later broadcast it on the company's cable channel and television network.

The cornucopia of media choices is thus somewhat deceiving. If you look at Figure 13.1, you'll see that many different brands and labels are all really just different company identities within its larger structure. There are actually very few "independent" media producers that can remain viable in such a marketplace. Often, once an independent becomes successful, it is quickly bought out by a larger conglomerate, which is searching for ways to increase revenues. Another trend consists of a **merger** between two or more companies to create an even bigger media giant. The model for this trend, and at the time the largest media company ever, took place in 2000 with the merger between a new media company, AOL (America Online), and an older one, Time Warner (Disney has since surpassed it in size).

Mergers and acquisitions associated with conglomeration result in yet another major trend: **concentration**. The ownership of media companies of all kinds is now concentrated in the hands of fewer and fewer large conglomerates. Communication researchers who follow media ownership have seen a consistent trend through the 1980s and 1990s characterized by mergers and buyouts and resulting in fewer but larger media companies in the 2000s (McChesney 1997, 2004; Bagdikian 2004). Researchers often refer to the "Big 6" global media conglomerates, down from more than 25 such companies just a decade or two ago, that now dominate the media industries (Klinenberg 2007, Shah 2007, FreePress .net 2011). While few in number, these media giants keep

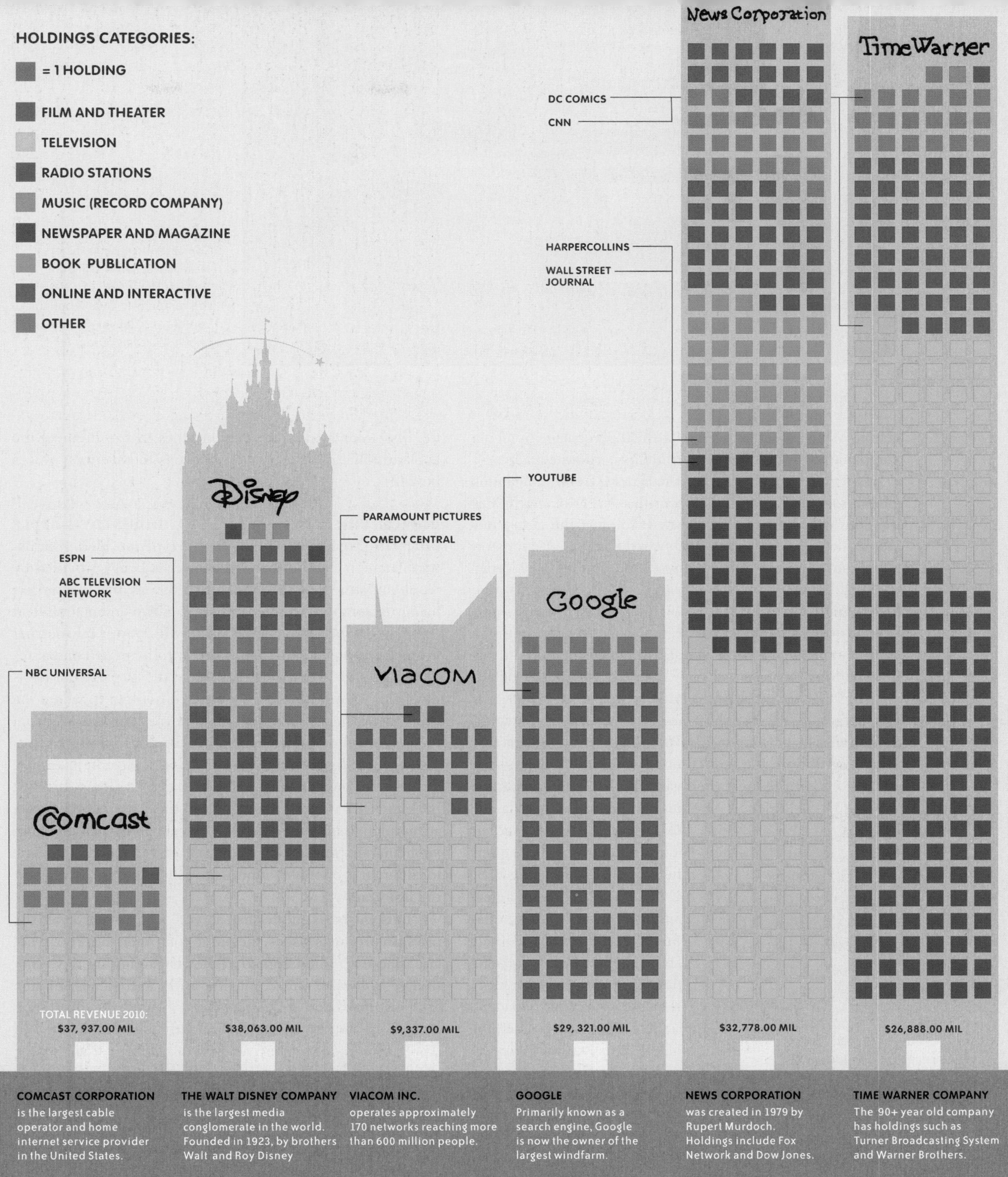

SOURCE: COLUMBIA JOURNALISM REVIEW 2010; GOOGLE.COM 2011.

HOLDINGS CATEGORIES:

■ = 1 HOLDING

■ FILM AND THEATER
■ TELEVISION
■ RADIO STATIONS
■ MUSIC (RECORD COMPANY)
■ NEWSPAPER AND MAGAZINE
■ BOOK PUBLICATION
■ ONLINE AND INTERACTIVE
■ OTHER

News Corporation

TimeWarner

DC COMICS
CNN

HARPERCOLLINS

WALL STREET
JOURNAL

Disney

YOUTUBE

PARAMOUNT PICTURES
COMEDY CENTRAL

ESPN

ABC TELEVISION
NETWORK

Google

VIACOM

NBC UNIVERSAL

Comcast

TOTAL REVENUE 2010:
$37, 937.00 MIL

$38,063.00 MIL

$9,337.00 MIL

$29, 321.00 MIL

$32,778.00 MIL

$26,888.00 MIL

COMCAST CORPORATION
is the largest cable
operator and home
internet service provider
in the United States.

THE WALT DISNEY COMPANY
is the largest media
conglomerate in the world.
Founded in 1923, by brothers
Walt and Roy Disney

VIACOM INC.
operates approximately
170 networks reaching more
than 600 million people.

GOOGLE
Primarily known as a
search engine, Google
is now the owner of the
largest windfarm.

NEWS CORPORATION
was created in 1979 by
Rupert Murdoch.
Holdings include Fox
Network and Dow Jones.

TIME WARNER COMPANY
The 90+ year old company
has holdings such as
Turner Broadcasting System
and Warner Brothers.

Cable television company Comcast purchased a majority stake in NBC-Universal from General Electric in 2011, allowing the company to control both the content *and* delivery of television shows like *Law & Order* to audiences.

getting bigger. That leaves only a small percentage of media companies truly independent from this corporate reality.

Two government agencies, the Federal Communications Commission (FCC) and the Securities and Exchange Commission (SEC), are charged with regulating the large conglomerates. The FCC has established some restrictions on media-outlet ownership by any single company in order to avoid a **monopoly** in any one market. Otherwise, one media giant might be able to own all the newspapers and TV and radio stations in a region, effectively stifling any competition and potentially providing a single voice for information where several voices serve a democracy better. And the SEC is involved in **antitrust legislation**, governing mergers between companies and further discouraging monopolies from forming. However, in recent years increasing **deregulation**, the reduction or removal of government restrictions on the media industry, has allowed companies to gain control of ever-larger chunks of the media market. These decisions are often fiercely debated by the U.S. Congress, media companies, and media watchdog groups. Social critics are concerned about the increasing concentration and its possible consequences for a democratic society that values freedom of the press and a plurality of voices. If the largest companies are allowed to control

> **monopoly** a situation in which there is only one individual or organization, without competitors, providing a particular good or service
>
> **antitrust legislation** laws designed to maintain competition in the marketplace by prohibiting monopolies, price fixing, or other forms of collusion among businesses
>
> **deregulation** reduction or removal of government controls from an industry to allow for a free and efficient marketplace

the dissemination of information, does that undermine the constitutional rights of average citizens to have their voices heard?

POWER SHIFTS IN THE MEDIA INDUSTRY—APPLE EDITION So how will the structure of the media industry change in the future? One answer is being provided by Apple and the iPods, iPads, and iPhones that Apple has made ubiquitous. Apple represents a fundamental shift in the way that media industries work, with power transferring from the companies that produce products to companies that distribute them. In this way, Apple is part of a postmodern economy, as David Harvey described it, where the need to sell more products faster will lead to "a shift from the consumption of goods and into the consumption of services," including "entertainments, spectacles, happenings, and distractions" (1989, p. 285). Harvey predicted this shift back in 1989 when he noticed that there are "limits to the accumulation and turnover of physical goods" making more "ephemeral" products like an mp3 or a downloaded movie ideal for an economy that needs to sell more this year than it did last year.

This business model has served Apple well. Even the physical products it sells, the i-Mac computer, the iPod, iPad, and iPhone, are all designed to allow customers to buy other things—software, music, movies, apps, and games. In fact, it's even possible to buy a song from iTunes without involving anyone but the record company that owns the song and Apple, which owns "the Web browser software (Safari), the computer media player (iTunes), the portable digital music player (iPod), the streaming technology to play music videos

(Quicktime), the software that creates the service (Web-Objects), the computer itself (Macintosh) and the operating system (MacOS)" (Strauss 2003). What is becoming clear is that in a digital age, the companies that provide access to entertainment and media will be at least as important as the companies that actually make the entertainment.

New Voices in Media

Even in today's heavily concentrated media market, there are still opportunities for alternative voices to be heard. These voices, though, are often confined to small, marginal outlets. Bloggers and podcasters are able to circumvent the constraints of commercial radio and print journalism to transmit their opinions and musical sensibilities to an (admittedly small) audience. Online and print "zines" (underground self-publications) are created by individuals who feel that a topic close to their hearts (such as a favorite band or comic book or an important political issue) is not getting proper treatment from the mainstream press. Punk rock bands like the 1970s' Sex Pistols and New York Dolls, as well as their more contemporary descendants like Fugazi, Bikini Kill, and Sleater-Kinney, produced and promoted their music outside the major record-label system, as part of a "D.I.Y." (do it yourself) movement (Shippers 2002). Even afternoon talk shows like *Dr. Phil* or the *Tyra Banks Show*, as bizarre as they may sometimes seem, have provided an opportunity for disenfranchised, nonmainstream individuals (like transsexuals or recovering addicts) to be heard by the masses (Gamson 1999).

Self-Regulation and Censorship

Another area of intense debate about media industries revolves around the content they produce and government censorship. The FCC imposes regulations on what the media may produce, once again qualifying the notion of absolute freedom of expression. As you may be aware, certain types of speech are not protected under the Constitution. Material considered to be obscene, for example, is illegal. The criteria used to define obscenity are based on a momentous 1959 Supreme Court decision, *Roth vs. United States*. According to the ruling, child pornography and other "material which deals with sex in a manner appealing to prurient interest" are considered obscene. However, the line between "indecent" material, which is restricted but not forbidden, and obscene material is sometimes hard to draw.

Over the past several decades, various media industries have turned to self-regulation of the materials they produce, often in the face of threats of censorship and in an effort to

Are Video Game Ratings Effective? The Entertainment Software Rating Board created ratings such as "T" for teen and "M" for mature for video games in the 1990s.

avoid outside regulation by government agencies. These efforts first began in 1968 when the Motion Picture Association of America established the movie ratings with which you are likely familiar. Those ratings are G, PG, R, and more recently PG-13 and NC-17, the latter to distinguish material unfit for anyone under seventeen from adult or pornographic material carrying an X rating. Next was the music business in 1985, when the Recording Industry Association of America agreed to place warning stickers on certain albums containing songs about drugs, sex, violence, and other potentially objectionable subjects. These labels ("Parental Advisory: Explicit Lyrics") were the recording industry's response to pressure from U.S. Senate hearings and lobbying from the Parents' Music Resource Center, headed by Tipper Gore (former wife of then Senator and future Vice President Al Gore).

The 1990s ushered in self-regulation for other media industries. The Entertainment Software Rating Board established a rating system for video games in 1993 based on age-appropriateness. In 1997, television programs began featuring a ratings system that not only suggests the appropriate age for viewers but also warns of violence (real-life or cartoon), sex (including dialogue with sexual innuendo), and offensive language. The "V-chip" in TVs allows parents to block reception of violent programs altogether.

These voluntary measures at regulating content, self-imposed by media industries, acknowledge the concern that some material is unsuitable, especially for children. Some studies of the effectiveness of these measures indicate that children are still being exposed to objectionable material and that parents may be misled if they believe ratings systems are preventing their children from having access to those materials (Garry and Spurlin 2007).

Debates about the content and power of the media rage on. Some claim that media content, especially when it is violent or sexual in nature, has a negative effect on society and should therefore be restricted; others support a media free-market or believe that the right to free speech or artistic freedom should in no way be infringed. These issues are frequently in the spotlight, usually in the wake of some controversial event such as the Super Bowl 2004 half-time show, during which singer Janet Jackson's breast was exposed as the result of a "wardrobe malfunction." These types of controversies expose some of the conflicts between different types of culture, media, and audiences.

High, Low, and Popular Culture

"Culture wars" can be fought just about anywhere. In the summer of 1998, an exhibit opened at the Guggenheim Museum in New York City that was uniformly panned by the critics. The *New Republic* called the exhibit "a pop nostalgia orgy masquerading as a major artistic statement," and *Salon*'s art critic accused the Guggenheim of "wear[ing] its cultural pants around its ankles" and "sucking down to our lowest impulses." What were they so upset about?

The exhibit was entitled "The Art of the Motorcycle," and the critics were upset because motorcycles weren't, in their opinion, art. The public, on the other hand, loved it—the exhibit broke all previous museum attendance records. People who might never otherwise have set foot in the museum came to view this colorful collection of motorcycles dating from 1868 to 1998.

The motorcycles at the Guggenheim stirred up a long-standing debate that questioned the very definitions of art and culture. The critics' objections were based on their perception that **popular culture**, or mass culture (motorcycles), had invaded a **high culture** venue (the Guggenheim Museum). In this case, popular culture was seen as unsavory and even dangerous—the implication being that pop culture is a mass phenomenon that somehow threatens the position of the elites by challenging their preferences. As with so many sociological concepts, these terms come originally from the German; in this case, *kultur* (the culture of the elite classes) and *massenkultur* (the culture of the masses). But are these two categories really that separate?

First, there are multiple high cultures and multiple pop cultures, based on differences in taste and aesthetics. Also, each category has its own set of hierarchies. For example, rap and hip-hop music are definitely pop culture phenomena. Produced by mostly minority artists for whom "street credibility" is one of the most important qualifica-

Is This Art? The 1998 show "The Art of the Motorcycle" at the Guggenheim Museum in New York broke attendance records but attracted negative reviews from art critics for "sucking down to our lowest impulses."

tions, these musical forms have widespread popular appeal, especially among teenagers and young adults. But rap and hip-hop have their own elites, artists who are at the top of the charts and who have a great deal of influence within and outside their pop culture domain. Examples such as Kanye West, Queen Latifah, Beyonce, and Jay-Z, the elites of the rap and hip-hop worlds, show that the distinction between mass and elite is a fuzzy one.

There is another way in which this distinction is problematic. In the real world, most cultural products contain elements of both mass and high culture. Why do you think we call certain TV programs soap "operas"? The storylines and intense emotions of *The Young and the Restless* parallel and sometimes rival those of Giacomo Puccini's *Madama But-*terfly and Wolfgang Amadeus Mozart's *Don Giovanni*. Led Zeppelin and Van Halen songs, when written out in standard musical notation, show a recognizable symphonic structure. Rap and hip-hop overtly draw on other types of music in the practice of sampling, and Ludwig von Beethoven, Georges Bizet, and Béla Bartók have all been sampled by R&B artists. These examples, and many others, indicate that high and pop culture are not mutually exclusive and can coexist within the same product.

The distinctions between high and popular culture are based on the characteristics of their audiences. Differences of class, education, race, and even religion help create these categories. Sociologist Herbert Gans (1999) calls the groups of people who share similar artistic, recreational,

High Art and Pop Art Are Not Mutually Exclusive Even though Warhol's work is now exhibited in high culture venues like esteemed modern art museums, he was perceived as a threat to the "real" art world when he began his work in the 1960s. At the bottom is Warhol's subversion of a high art masterpiece, Leonardo da Vinci's *Last Supper* (above).

taste publics groups of people who share similar artistic, literary, media, recreational, and intellectual interests

taste cultures areas of culture that share similar aesthetics and standards of taste

polysemy having many possible meanings or interpretations

hypodermic needle theory (magic bullet theory) a theory that explains the effects of media as if their contents simply entered directly into the consumer, who is powerless to resist their influence

and intellectual interests **taste publics**. Taste publics aren't necessarily organized groups, but they do inhabit the same aesthetic worlds, which Gans calls **taste cultures**; that is, people who share the same tastes will also usually move in the same cultural circles as well. For example, sociologist David Halle (1993) found that members of the upper class are more likely to have abstract paintings hanging in their homes, while members of the working class are more likely to display family photographs in their homes.

The music, movies, clothes, foods, art, books, magazines, cars, sports, and television programs you enjoy are influenced at least in part by your position in society. Unknowingly, you belong to a number of taste publics and inhabit a number of taste cultures, in that you share your interests with others who are similar to you sociologically. What you think of as your own unique individual preferences are in some ways predetermined by your age, race, class and education levels, and regional location.

Polysemy, Audiences, and Fans

The saga of the motorcycles at the Guggenheim should help us understand an important concept in the study of media and culture: polysemy. Sociologists use the term **polysemy** to describe how any cultural product is subject to multiple interpretations and hence has many possible meanings (Hall 1980; Fiske 1989). For instance, a cartoon like *The Simpsons* can be enjoyed on a variety of levels, by children and adults, for its humor alone, and for its political commentary. Polysemy helps us understand how one person can absolutely love the same movie (or song, painting, cartoon, necklace, car, meal, or tattoo) that another person absolutely hates. Meaning is not a given, nor is it entirely open—we make meaning individually and together, as audiences and consumers of culture.

Some researchers have been concerned with whether popular culture can cause certain types of behavior (Gerbner and Gross 1976; Gerbner et al. 1980; Malamuth and Donnerstein 1984; Weinstein 1991, 2000). Do TV crime shows increase our propensity to violence? Do pornographic magazines lead to the abuse of women? Does heavy metal music make teenagers suicidal? Such questions suggest that cultural products impose their intrinsic meanings on their

audiences in a simplistic, stimulus-and-response fashion. But while it is true that mass media products are potentially powerful transmitters of cultural values and norms, the process is neither immediate nor uncomplicated. As we know, audiences come from different backgrounds, which help define experiences and interpret the cultural products we consume. This makes it more likely, then, that polysemy will come into play: that audience members will interpret the same texts in different ways.

We may acknowledge that things like watching soap operas, reading comic books, and playing video games are trivial in the larger scheme of things, but if these forms of pop culture give us pleasure and connect us with others, they may not be so trivial after all. Serious sociological insights can be gained from studying what appear to be superficial pursuits (Postman 1987; Schudson 2003). Recreation, leisure, culture, and media are actually serious business and are empirically analyzable from a sociological perspective.

Mass Media Consumption: Passive vs. Active Audiences

The influence or effects of the media have been studied by scholars in a range of disciplines including psychology, communications, and sociology. The theories they have generated run along a spectrum, from the media having great power and influence over audiences, to their having little or none, to audiences themselves being central in the creation of meaning. It is worth examining what each of these theories has to say about the effects of media on society and the individual and to consider the applicability of any theory to the postmodern, digital world in which we now live.

The Hypodermic Needle (or Magic Bullet) Theory

In the early years of mass media, it was thought that audience members of all sorts (including readers) were passive recipients of content and that whatever meaning was in the "texts" they consumed was transmitted, unaltered, and absorbed straight into their consciousness. (The term "text" is a general one that can include sound and image as well as print.) This notion was contained in the model known as the **hypodermic needle theory** (or **magic bullet theory**). The assumption was that, like an injection, media content was shot directly into the audience members, who responded instantaneously to its stimulus (Lazarsfeld and Katz 1955). One of the key examples often cited to support this theory was the 1938 radio broadcast of H. G. Wells's short story "War of the Worlds" narrated by Orson Welles. The radio show used a mock news-bulletin format and was played uninterrupted by commercial breaks. Listeners who tuned in after the beginning of the show did not realize it was merely a dramatization of a Martian invasion. It was reported that audience members numbering in the millions actually believed the "news" was true and were so frightened as to have sparked widespread panic.

Minimal Effects Theories

Media scholars quickly realized that the hypodermic needle theory was not accurate or applicable for the most part—that audience members were not as passive or easily persuaded as first believed and that the various forms of media themselves were not as all-powerful in their influence over individuals. A number of related theories were developed during the 1960s and '70s that proposed the media had limited or minimal effects.

Instead of asking, "What do media do to people?" scholars began to ask, "What do people do with media?" (Severin and Tankard 1997). The **uses and gratifications paradigm** contains several theories that focus on a more actively engaged audience member (Katz 1959). Blumler and Katz (1974) highlighted five areas in which audiences sought gratification and fulfilled needs through their use of the media. First, audiences could achieve some sense of escape from reality; second, audiences could use media for social interaction, forming relationships to characters, or conversing with others about products and programs; third, they could gain some aspect of personal identity by incorporating elements found in the media into their everyday lives; fourth, the media could serve to inform and educate audiences; and fifth, audience members could consume media purely for the sake of entertainment.

Many media scholars have been interested in the persuasive powers of the media, whether they were used in advertising to get consumers to buy products or used in the political arena to sway public opinion or to garner votes. Two related theories suggest that the influence of the media is more limited than marketing executives or campaign managers might otherwise wish. **Reinforcement theory** argues that individuals tend to seek out and listen to only those messages that are in alignment with their existing attitudes and beliefs. Thus audience members typically tune out anything that might seem too challenging and instead prefer only those messages that support what they already believe (Atkin 1973, 1985; Klapper 1960). The **agenda-setting theory** focuses on how the mass media can influence the public by the way stories are presented in the news (McCombs and Shaw 1972, 1977).

Depending upon which stories are chosen as newsworthy and how much time and space are devoted to their coverage, the public then gets a sense of the value or importance of any given event. The media may not be able to tell audiences what to think, but they do set the agenda for what (stories) to think about. Finally, the **two-step flow model** of communication suggests that audiences get much of the information from "opinion leaders" who can convey and explain important news rather than from more direct or firsthand sources (Lazarsfeld and Katz 1955). Certainly someone like Oprah Winfrey is known for her influence and can introduce millions of her audience members to whatever is her latest concern.

Active Audiences and Cultural Studies

Media research since the 1980s and '90s has focused largely on **active audiences**, suggesting that media consumers bring to the experience different **interpretive strategies**. This approach argues that different individuals, because of their different experiences, perspectives, and personalities, may respond to media content in unique ways. This means that whatever meanings may be inherent in texts, consumers may read them in the intended ways but can also modify and even invert the meanings of texts depending upon their own backgrounds and purposes.

Working within the cultural studies perspective, Stuart Hall's **encoding/decoding model** (1980) combines elements of the hypodermic needle/magic bullet and active audience theories. This model assumes on the one hand that specific ideological messages are loaded into cultural

uses and gratifications paradigm approaches to understanding media effects that focus on individuals' psychological or social needs that consumption of various media fulfills

reinforcement theory theory that suggests that audiences seek messages in the media that reinforce their existing attitudes and beliefs and are thus not influenced by challenging or contradictory information

agenda-setting theory theory that the mass media can set the public agenda by selecting certain news stories and excluding others, thus influencing what audiences think about

two-step flow model theory on media effects that suggests audiences get information through opinion leaders who influence their attitudes and beliefs, rather than through direct firsthand sources

active audiences a term used to characterize audience members as active participants in "reading" or constructing the meaning of the media they consume

interpretive strategies the ideas and frameworks that audience members bring to bear on a particular media text to understand its meaning

encoding/decoding model a theory on media that combines models that privilege the media producer and models that view the audience as the primary source of meaning; this theory recognizes that media texts are created to deliver specific messages and that individuals actively interpret them

In Relationships

Fan-Celebrity Relations

Interacting with a god or gods, spirits, or ancestors is compulsory in many cultures—but what about our own? In his book *Imaginary Social Worlds*, John Caughey (1984) argues that the contemporary American equivalents are relationships between fans and celebrities (including politicians and athletes). These are people with whom few of us have actual, face-to-face interaction but whom many of us feel we know—sometimes intimately. "It is simply taken for granted," Caughey observes, "that an American will know about a huge swarming throng of unmet figures through his consumption of the various media" (p. 32). Celebrities can be important in the lives of ordinary people—as role models, objects of desire, or just friendly figures encountered daily on the TV screen. Just because these relationships are one-sided doesn't mean that they aren't relationships.

If there was ever an athlete, actor, musician, or politician whom you admired but never met, then you have engaged in some version of the asymmetrical relationships Caughey outlines in his book. Maybe you read a magazine article or watched a TV show to learn more about this person; maybe you bought a ticket to a performance with the hopes of seeing him or her after the show. Most of us put very little energy into developing these relationships—frankly, we don't have to, as we are bombarded with information about celebrities all the time. We can't help but acquire information about their professional and personal lives (Ehrenreich 1990).

In addition to reading *People* and *Us* magazines or watching *Entertainment Tonight* and *Access Hollywood*, some fans attend organized activities such as book signings or store openings in which face-to-face contact with a celebrity is available and highly regulated (Ferris 2001). At these prestaged events, buying a ticket and standing in line will yield a brief, formulaic encounter with the celebrity in which a few words are exchanged, an autograph is signed, and the line moves on. Unstaged encounters ("celebrity sightings")—at the supermarket, say, or in line at the post office—are exciting, but by definition uncertain (Ferris 2004a).

Fan-staged encounters help solve this problem: here the fan seeks out and uses information about the celebrity in ways that put the fan in control. For example, one avid fan sneaked onto a television studio lot and came away with a celebrity address list: "We couldn't get onto the set, but I took a bunch

A Prestaged Event Fans meet actor Johnny Depp on the red carpet at a movie premiere.

of stuff, papers, from the bike messenger's basket when it was parked. I figure that's not stealing, they can just make more Xeroxes. Anyway, the addresses were on it. . . . they live in the Hills, mostly, and I can go by their houses" (Ferris 2001, p. 39). Fan-staged encounters avoid the restrictions of prestaged events and the unpredictability of celebrity sightings. They partially solve the problem of asymmetry that characterizes fan-celebrity relations—fans can ensure that they will be able to see and maybe speak with their favorite celebrity, as though the relationship were an ordinary personal one. It should be noted, however, that fan-staged encounters usually occur without the consent of the celebrity herself, which means that the fan can feel unwelcome and even dangerous to the celebrity, even if the fan may mean no harm.

Recently the internet has opened up new means for fans wishing to encounter celebrities and improved the odds of having an actual celebrity sighting. Gawker.com, TMZ.com, and PerezHilton.com are a few of a proliferation of web sites that are making big business out of celebrity watching. They all carry the latest gossip and prized candid photos of the stars that generate millions of web traffic visitors every month. Gawker, which is based in New York City, distinguished itself by introducing Gawker Stalker, a feature that tries to visually pinpoint celebrities as soon as they are spotted. In order to help readers in their "celebrity-hunting adventures," Gawker encourages fans to send the whereabouts of any celebrity they might see, whether at a restaurant, dry cleaners, or market, and Gawker will immediately post the exact location using Google Maps. With more and more people accessing the internet via handheld devices like the iPhone and Blackberry, news about celebrities travels fast, as do those wishing to chase them.

Which brings us to the phenomenon of real celebrity stalking. Stalking is usually defined as any unwanted pursuit or threat and can be practiced by ex-spouses, business rivals, or total strangers. But the most familiar type is celebrity stalking. Security experts usually try to keep the details under wraps, but it is safe to say that most public figures have a number of potentially dangerous fans whose activities are monitored by both public law enforcement and private security firms. Several celebrities have been killed (ex-Beatle John Lennon, actress Rebecca Shaeffer, Tejano star Selena) or seriously wounded (actress Theresa Saldana) by obsessed fans. Others have endured repeated home break-ins (singer Madonna, director Steven Spielberg, talk-show host David Letterman, actor Brad Pitt), and many are plagued by "popup" visits from fans who have followed them surreptitiously and then revealed themselves in airports, restaurants, or public restrooms. Threatening letters are sometimes sent to the stars' management offices and even delivered to their home addresses—a danger signal, say stalking experts. In order to protect Hollywood celebrities and other public figures from dangerous fans, the Los Angeles Police Department has created a division called the Threat Management Unit, and California further led the nation in passing antistalking laws in 1990 that have served as models for those in other states. Unfortunately, legislation doesn't deter all stalkers.

For some people, celebrity stalking is a professional obligation. These people include members of the press, and especially the paparazzi, freelance photographers who pursue celebrities in order to get candid shots. Paparazzi may charter helicopters, hack through forests, or scale castle walls in such daring stunts as the two photographers dressed in camouflage who attempted to photograph the new twin babies of actors Brad Pitt and Angelina Jolie. Their intrusiveness can even provoke violence from a celebrity, as witnessed in singer Britney Spears beating the car of a member of the paparazzi with the wooden handle of an umbrella, or rapper Kanye West smashing the expensive camera equipment belonging to another. In some instances, it is actually the photographer who is assaulted, as in the case of one who took a punch in the jaw from actor Alec Baldwin.

While paparazzi can be annoying to celebrities, we consume their products every day. When we read supermarket tabloids, watch TV entertainment shows, or surf the web for photos of our favorite actors, we support the paparazzi's activities—because they support ours. They feed our imaginations, provide us with information about celebrities, and help us envision the worlds of those who are part of our everyday lives yet not personally known to us.

products and that they therefore have the potential to influence individuals, especially with regard to promoting the interests of capitalist elites. On the other hand, individuals may respond to messages embedded in the media in a variety of ways. In fact, when faced with ideologically encoded cultural products like movies or music, for example, we can engage in "cultural resistance" or choose "oppositional" or "against the grain" readings of products, subverting their meaning. For example, Madonna's classic video "Like a Virgin" was seen by many cultural critics as sexually exploitative and demeaning, while teen fans exercising interpretive resistance subverted the dominant meaning, embracing the video as empowering to them as young women.

Henry Jenkins extends the model to something he calls **textual poaching** (1992), wherein audience members take the original product and manipulate it themselves—often to tell stories or express ideologies very different from the original. For example, fans of the TV show *Star Trek* have used videotaped programs and home-editing equipment to create stories (called "K/S," or "Slash") in which Captain Kirk and Mr. Spock are not just best friends and co-workers, but passionate gay lovers. This oppositional restructuring indicates that viewers can read different meanings into the text than were intended by the producers—indeed, can reproduce the text in order to make those meanings central.

K/S or "Slash" In these examples of textual poaching, *Star Trek* fans manipulate old footage in order to create new stories that suggest a very different interpretation of Kirk and Spock's relationship than the one portrayed on the show.

Interpretive Communities and Shared Meanings

Responding to cultural texts is thus an exercise in the distribution of power. The more active the audience is in interpreting the text, the less control the producers have over the messages that are communicated. While you may not go so far as one of Jenkins's "textual poachers," neither are you a passive recipient of predigested pop-culture pabulum. Your consumption of media (film, television, music, books) and live performance (concerts, theater, sports) is active in the sense that you contribute your own interpretive resources—context, experience, and perspective. And to the extent that you share these experiences with others, you may find that you are part of an **interpretive community**—a group of like-minded people who enjoy cultural products in the same way. The concept of the interpretive community is usually attributed to literary theorist Stanley Fish (1980), who believed that although an author might have intended a certain meaning in a text, it is individual readers who inevitably interpret the text in their own ways, thus creating the potential for an almost infinite number of meanings of the same text. The fact that we usually end up interpreting the same books in the same ways has to do with shared culture and frameworks that members of the same interpretive communities have in common. Janice Radway (1991), in her ethnography of romance-novel readers, argued that cultural context is the reason that readers share similar sets of reading strategies and interpretive codes. Whether visiting a museum exhibit, going to a concert, or watching a TV show, members of interpretive communities bring with them shared sensibilities about understanding cultural products through their own particular lens.

Recreation, Leisure, and Relationships

Our recreational choices can lead us to form unique bonds with others. Some of those bonds take the form of **role model** relationships, in which more prominent members of a leisure or recreational subculture serve as examples for us to strive toward. In the 1990s, for example, kids chanted "I wanna be like Mike" to communicate their admiration for Chicago Bulls player Michael Jordan. Tiger Woods, who in 1997 became the youngest golfer and first person of color ever to win the Masters Tournament, generated the same type of hero worship among youngsters, who intoned "I am Tiger Woods" as they stepped up to the tee in record numbers. Role models like Woods and Jordan may inspire us to

LeBron James

excel in sports and in other areas as well—since his retirement from basketball, Jordan has become a savvy businessman and is involved in such charitable organizations as the Boys and Girls Clubs of America. But their personal failures (both men admitted to marital infidelity) make us wonder what kinds of role models they really are.

Some would argue that sports figures are not appropriate role models: even though they must work hard in order to excel, they still possess unique skills and talents that the rest of us don't. Another basketball player, Charles Barkley of the Houston Rockets, in fact, asserted "I am not a role model," arguing that parents and teachers were more appropriate examples for children to follow. And interestingly, each of the above quotes ("I wanna be like Mike," "I am Tiger Woods," *and* "I am not a role model") was used in Nike commercials—to inspire consumers to buy expensive sporting goods. In an even more recent Nike commercial, Miami Heat star LeBron James plays on the "I am not a role model" theme by asking "What should I do?" of his audience. "Should I be who you want me to be?" or should he just be himself and not worry about what fans think of him? Can any celebrity afford to be that cavalier?

Aside from celebrity role models, we also build relationships with people who share our interests—our soccer teammates, fellow collectors of *Star Wars* memorabilia, bluegrass aficionados, or backgammon players. These are important members of our social world.

Leisure and Community

Your friendship with the people you play pick-up basketball with every Thursday evening, the members of your gardening club, or the folks you watch *Survivor* with is unlikely to be confined solely to basketball, gardening, and television; your bonds probably extend into other areas of your lives as well. But it is your shared interests that have brought you together, and these activities speak to the heart of Emile Durkheim's pioneering sociological questions about community and social cohesion, first asked more than 100 years ago and still central today.

Some scholars argue that in contemporary society, in important social groups, such as family, church, and labor union, group values are eclipsed by the rhetoric of radical individual rights. For instance, dinner with the family might be passed up in favor of a mother's Pilates lesson or a brother's going to a friend's house to watch the fight on TV. Or the Catholic requirement of attending mass each week might be fulfilled only on Christmas and Easter. Sociologist Amitai Etzioni is the leading proponent of a movement that seeks to remedy this problem: **communitarianism** argues that individual rights do not cancel out collective responsibility. The movement is an attempt to rebuild a sense of group values that benefit all rather than merely the individual. Etzioni's version of communitarianism (1996) is specific in its proposals about how to balance individual rights with social responsibilities. But the question for us here is this: Are bonds based on shared leisure interests enough to constitute a sense of group responsibility compatible with communitarian aims? Or are basketball, gardening, television, and the like just too flimsy a basis for real group identity?

Robert Bellah, whose work has been referred to in earlier chapters, has a potential answer for us. He argues that bonds based on shared interests like those mentioned above don't create real community. Rather, such groups constitute **lifestyle enclaves**, which are different from real communities in that they are likely to remain private and segmented, focused on their own shared interests rather than involved in the larger group life (Bellah, Sullivan,

communitarianism a political and moral philosophy focused on strengthening civil society and communal bonds

lifestyle enclaves groups of people drawn together by shared interests, especially those relating to hobbies, sports, and media

The Other Football

Do you know the rules for cricket? What's up with the Canadians and curling? And why can't anyone get Americans to care about football? No, not *that* football—the other one. What Americans call soccer but everyone else calls football is wildly popular internationally, but it has not yet taken off in the United States, especially at the professional level.

In the United States, soccer is primarily a youth sport; of the country's 18 million soccer players, only about 5 million are adults, and many of these are part of a recent influx of foreign-born players. American interest in soccer spikes every four years when the World Cup games roll around; otherwise, major league soccer is not even as popular as ice hockey and lags well behind the professional sports behemoths of football, baseball, and basketball. The rest of the world, however, thinks Americans are crazy. In almost every other country, football (soccer) is a major sport—there are local and national competitions between teams and international competition between national teams. Salaries for top players often surpass deals made with top American athletes, with tens of millions of dollars going to players like Didier Drogba, Lionel Messi, and Iker Casillas. Perhaps another season of watching former England captain David Beckham, who in 2007 signed a very lucrative five-year deal to play with the Los Angeles Galaxy team, will draw more attention to soccer in the United States.

It's not just the money and the competition that make international soccer unique, it's the fans—more specifically, the rowdy and violent fans often referred to as "hooligans." Violence in American sports is certainly not unheard of (ever been to an Oakland Raiders game?), but the scale of soccer hooliganism overseas is in another league entirely. The British, especially, are infamous for the mobs of "yobs" (slang for hooligans) who cause damage both in Great Britain and elsewhere in the soccer-playing world. Soccer actually has a violent history: in the medieval period, entire towns would participate in soccer matches to resolve disputes, and kings and queens at times had the game banned because of violence. In those days, it was the players who had to be concerned for their safety; since the rise of contemporary hooliganism, spectators must also be wary.

Since the 1960s, there have been hundreds of deaths caused by upheaval at soccer matches. Although most soccer-playing countries endure some form of hooliganism, the English yobs are infamous and were, until recently, the only fans who traveled abroad with their teams and brought their violence with them (Taylor 2000). One of the most notorious riots took place in Brussels, in 1985, at a match between the English team from Liverpool and the

Italian team Juventus. The Liverpool yobs, later revealed by videotape to have come to the match with ski masks and weapons, instigated attacks on the rival fans, which resulted in a crush of people trying to flee. In the end, 39 Italian spectators were killed, and British teams were banned from European competition for five years (Haley and Johnston 1998).

Some theorists speculate that the fanaticism of hooligans is only an excuse to be violent. Skinheads and other racists, for example, sometimes use soccer matches to broadcast their beliefs. Others speculate that fandom can develop into a nationalistic fervor that increases the likelihood of violence.

For example, for British fans who feel united against a foreign team while in a foreign country, it may be easy to feel both isolated and compelled to defend the honor of their team and country—especially when emotions are already heightened with the fury of athletic competition (King 1995).

Why is true mob violence rare in the United States? Is it because U.S. teams are seldom involved in truly international competition? Or because there are so many professional sports and teams to follow? Or is it simply because hooliganism is endemic to a sport with a long history of violence—the real football—which is not yet widely popular in this country?

Yobs English football fans are particularly famous for their fanaticism. Here, English hooligans (rear) chase a French supporter (front) in Charleroi, Belgium. At the Euro 2000 championships, English fans attacked celebrating French supporters who drove in a convoy through the city center.

and Tipton et al. 1985). So you and your fellow ball players, gardeners, or TV fans may find your connections to each other to be personally rewarding, but you aren't necessarily contributing to the common good. Or are you?

In Dr. Ferris's research on *Star Trek* and soap opera fan clubs, she found that while people in these clubs did initially bond solely because of their dedication to particular TV shows, these bonds developed over time in ways that Bellah might not have predicted. Eventually, the groups branched out from their narrow focus and began to pursue things like charitable fund-raising and community service projects that expanded the boundaries of their lifestyle enclave. One *Star Trek* fan club, for example, raised money to help an animal welfare organization that was sponsored by *Trek* actor William Shatner; while their contributions were guided by their specific interests (how many other people even know what Shatner's favorite charity is?), their community spirit was obvious. So perhaps a sense of shared mission within a small group of TV viewers or tulip enthusiasts is not incompatible with a larger sense of social responsibility after all. You can indulge your individual sense of play and work for the common good as well.

Collectors and Hobbyists

Sports are not the only recreational pursuits that draw people together. Many collectors' groups organize annual conventions so that members with shared interests can hobnob with one another for one intensive weekend. Collectors of Dolly Parton memorabilia, for example, meet once a year in Pigeon Forge, Tennessee, to buy, sell, and trade Dolly-related items and share their love of the country music diva. Fans of a different kind of dolly, Barbie, also meet annually to connect with others who collect Barbie, her friends, and all their accessories (in 2001, this convention was hijacked by fans of the Ken doll, with the goal of making Barbie's long-suffering boyfriend the star of the show!). And at yet another weekend convention, collectors gather together to "keep history alive" and honor real military heroes both past and present, by buying, selling, and trading twelve-inch action figures die cast in the image of notable members of the armed forces.

But collectors and hobbyists no longer need to meet face-to-face at a convention or weekend workshop. The internet has helped spawn a myriad of virtual communities where enthusiasts can interact online. Do-it-yourselfers and garage woodworkers who might normally work alone have found compatriot crafters with whom they can converse. Connecting with others who share the same interests

third place any informal public place where people come together regularly for conversation and camaraderie when not at work or at home

is facilitated by blogs, chat rooms, wikis, Facebook, Twitter, and auction sites like eBay where collectors and hobbyists can meet, organize activities, swap tips, and search for the perfect purchases (Rubel and Rosman 2001).

Hangouts: The Third Place

Away from work or school, where else do you spend your time? Researcher Robert Putnam (2000) laments that, in the United States at least, you will probably be watching television at home rather than gathering in a public place to talk with others. But if you lived in France, you might head to the corner café; in Germany, the neighborhood Bierstube; in Greece, the local taverna. Establishments such as these bear the label **third place** (after home and work, which are first and second). They are informal public places where people come together regularly for conversation and camaraderie. Roy Oldenburg (1999) worries that there are few such places left in the United States—and that we might be suffering as a society because of it.

Where's Your Third Place? Whether it's a coffeehouse, a barbershop, or a neighborhood pub, third places are informal public places where people come together regularly for conversation and camaraderie.

TABLE 13.1   Theory in Everyday Life

PERSPECTIVE	APPROACH TO RECREATION AND LEISURE	CASE STUDY: SPECTATOR SPORTS IN AMERICA
STRUCTURAL FUNCTIONALISM	Social institutions such as recreation and leisure provide for the needs of society and its members and help to maintain social cohesion and unity.	Participation in spectator sports helps to reaffirm social bonds; rooting for a team underscores the value of performance and competition.
CONFLICT THEORY	Social institutions such as recreation and leisure reflect the existing power structures in society and thus create and maintain social inequalities.	Participation in spectator sports legitimizes conflict between groups in society and the belief in winners and losers.
SYMBOLIC INTERACTIONISM	Social institutions such as recreation and leisure are produced when people act together; they play a meaningful role in the everyday lives of members.	Participation in spectator sports provides members with a sense of group affiliation and personal identification.

You know the place—the local diner with a counter that's always full of old men, talking about fishing for bluegill, complaining about the cost of prescription medications, or bemoaning the irresponsibility of youth. You might have thought such talk trivial or silly, but the interactions and relationships that develop in third places are important far beyond any specific conversational content.

Coffeehouse, bar, or barbershop—third places are more than just hangouts. Oldenburg argues that they are core settings for informal but essential aspects of public and community life. They provide opportunities to connect with others in ways that relieve alienation and anomie, problems Durkheim attributed to modern society. And there are more generalized benefits to society as well—the feeling of public spirit generated in third places can strengthen **civil society**, increase political awareness and participation, and sustain democracy from the ground up. So that local diner—or barbershop or bar—is more important than it appears to be. It helps maintain social cohesion and links the individual to the community. Where's your third place?

ANALYZING EVERYDAY LIFE
Observing a Hangout

This Data Workshop asks you to investigate the phenomenon of the local hangout using participant observation (see Chapter 2 for a review). It doesn't matter which kind of hangout you choose; it could be a bar, restaurant, gym, park,

student union, or bookstore. What's important is to make sure that it's a real hangout, someplace where people linger, that they return to regularly to socialize. Part of your work will be to determine just what constitutes a good hangout. So think a bit about your own habits and those of your friends, and choose what you think is a good hangout to study using participant observation.

Once you've chosen one, make some ethnographic fieldnotes describing both the physical and social setting. What makes this place a good hangout for the people there? You'll also need to distinguish who are the "regulars" and who are not. How do you tell a one-time visitor from a regular? How do people establish themselves as regulars? What kinds of interactions take place at the hangout? Interview a few people you think are regulars. What does the hangout mean to them? How does it function in their everyday life? In what respect is being a regular a part of their identity? In writing up your analysis, include some examples of the particular **idioculture** you find—the customs and values expressed in the place and in the interactions of the people who hang out there.

There are two options for completing the assigned work.

- *Option 1 (informal):* Prepare written fieldnotes that you can refer to during in-class discussions. Discuss your reactions and conclusions with other students in small-group discussions. Listen for any differences or variations in each other's insights.

civil society those organizations, institutions, and interactions outside government, family, and work that promote social bonds and the smooth functioning of society

idioculture the customs, practices, and values expressed in a particular place by the people who interact there

Ecotourism

Two sociology professors fly into Costa Rica for their spring break vacation. From the capital of San Jose, they hire a local pilot to fly them to the coast. When they reach the coastal airport, an open-air set of wooden benches with a simple covering, they take an old bus to their hotel. Their "hotel room" turns out to be a treehouse with screens rather than walls. It's March and thus extremely hot and humid. There is no air conditioning, electricity, or running water in their treehouse. They must climb down to use an outhouse. During the hottest parts of the day, they nap in the shade. In the early mornings and evenings, they visit the rain forests and nearby beaches. They are careful to stay on trails, leave no trash, and respect the rain forest.

The professors have planned their trip to be as **eco-friendly** as possible. Thus, they chose primitive lodging over a resort with modern conveniences and hiking into the rain forests rather than diving into the coastal reefs. They use mass transportation rather than renting a car. They researched various means of visiting the rain forests and beaches to avoid using companies that exploit workers or harm the environment. Does this type of travel lessen the negative impacts of tourism?

Ecotourism is characterized by the efforts of tourists and the travel industry to lessen the negative consequences of tourism on the environment as well as local cultures. Thus, ecotourism generally promotes consciousness about environmentally and culturally sensitive travel options. Tourists are often from highly industrialized nations in North America, Europe, and Australia, and they usually visit less developed nations in Central and South America as well as in Africa. Sociologists who study the tourism and travel industries have mixed views about the effectiveness of ecotourism. Some argue that ecotourism is merely consumerism with a "green" wrapping, while others argue that it offers tourists less invasive travel options for enjoying precious natural resources as well as foreign cultures.

Every year, for example, many tourists want to visit tropical rain forests, even though they may be aware of the conservation efforts to protect them. The question arises: should ecotourists avoid environmentally sensitive locations such as rain forests or the habitats of endangered species? Some sociologists say no, because ecotourism educates travelers about environmentalism and foreign cultures, as well as brings in revenue to

Finca Esperanza Verde Ecolodge in Nicaragua

economically depressed areas. Stamou and Paraskevopoulos's (2003) study of visitors to a national park where endangered species of condors live found that visitors were more likely to be motivated by enjoyment of the park rather than environmentalism; however, they still gained an appreciation for the condors and the efforts to maintain their habitats.

Other sociologists argue that the "eco" part of the label is a marketing technique to lure tourists seeking "guilt-free" travel. The idea behind this view is that most travelers understand the relationship between consumption and the depletion of natural resources. Therefore, travel companies make claims that ecotourism alleviates some of the environmental and economic damage wrought by industrialized nations. The problem, as argued by some sociologists, is that ecotourism does not usually live up to these claims (Bandy 1996; Weinberg, Bellows, and Ekster 2002).

Nevertheless, some sociologists claim that ecotourism, if effectively managed, *can* make positive contributions to both the environment and local communities (Bandy 1996; Wearing and Wearing 1999; Scheyvens 2000; Weinberg, Bellows, and Ekster 2002; Wood 2002). Effective management means that tourists and travel companies must actively attempt to balance recreational activities with sensitivity to the environment as well as the values of local communities. Further, ecotourism must place environmental and cultural concerns before profits. For example, tourists can enjoy special habitats but also maintain certain distances from endangered wildlife as well as flora and fauna. Also, travel companies can offer classes that help tourists understand how their presence influences local communities.

- *Option 2 (formal)*: Write a three- to four-page essay answering the questions posed above. Use specific excerpts from your fieldnotes to support your analysis and attach them to your paper.

Travel and Tourism

While some people find respite in hangouts close to home, others relax and rejuvenate by seeing the world. The travel and tourism industries (which include airlines, hotels, car-rental agencies, restaurants, theme parks, resorts, and other attractions) are multibillion-dollar businesses and play an important part in the U.S. economy. In 2007, the industries employed 17 million workers and generated $740 billion in expenditures and nearly $104 billion in tax revenues (Forbes Businesswire 2008). Americans spent more than $80 billion traveling abroad and within the United States; domestic travelers spent $490 billion. More than 56 million international visitors spent a record-breaking $122 billion on travel- and tourism-related activities in the United States (Reuters 2008).

The impact of tourism is both economic and cultural. We may travel in order to learn to appreciate different cultures, but we may also exoticize or even mistreat other groups as we fit them into our own recreational needs, rather than learning about them on their own terms (Urry 1990, 1992, 2002). Travel and tourism shape not just our individual relations with others but also political and economic relations between nations on a global scale. This chapter's Changing the World box addresses these issues as they pertain to what is known as "ecotourism."

eco-friendly a term describing any activity or product that attempts to minimize its environmental impact

ecotourism foreign travel with the goal of minimizing the environmental consequences of tourism as well as its possible negative effects on local cultures and economies, typically involves people from highly industrialized nations traveling to less developed countries

Closing Comments

Who would have thought that the things you do for fun might actually be important? The many activities considered part of leisure—travel, entertainment, sports, hobbies—while prevalent features of our everyday lives, play an increasingly significant role in the shape of society. We hope we haven't spoiled their pleasure by asking you to examine their various structures and meanings—you can still enjoy your recreational activities even after you've learned to take a critical, sociological perspective on them!

⑤ Need Help Studying?

wwnorton.com/studyspace

Visit StudySpace to access free review materials such as:
- **Vocabulary Flashcards**
- **Diagnostic Review Quizzes**
- **Study Outlines**

QUESTIONS FOR REVIEW

1. What does "commercialization of leisure" mean? Think of one of your favorite leisure activities and make a list of every aspect of this activity that costs money, either directly or indirectly.

2. Sociologist Richard Sennett argues that modernity has seen a decline in the importance of public life. Technological developments, especially information and media technology, have helped shift recreation and leisure from the public to the private sphere. Which technologies make you more likely to pursue leisure activities alone? Are there technologies that make you more likely to pursue social leisure activities? Which kind of leisure is more common?

3. Sociologists have long associated types of leisure activities with different social classes. Which leisure activities are associated with wealthy elites or with the working class? Which leisure activities, if any, have no class associations?

4. Many sociologists worry that conglomeration and the resulting concentration of media power might adversely affect democracy. How could this happen? What are the consequences for the media consumer when there are fewer sources of information?

5. How powerful are the media in persuading us to buy certain products or hold particular beliefs? Discuss reinforcement theory, agenda setting, and/or the two-step flow model. Which of these theories best explains the influence of the media?

6. Stuart Hall's encoding/decoding model assumes that particular ideological messages are loaded into cultural products and that individuals respond to those messages in a variety of ways. Can you think of a cultural product that is decoded in a way that clearly runs counter to the way it was encoded?

7. Describe an example of textual poaching, in which audience members take the original cultural product and manipulate it themselves. This could be something as simple as a T-shirt or as complicated as a short movie. Which theories of media consumption does your example support? Why did someone take the time to create this media product?

8. Celebrities can be very important in our lives even though our "relationships" with celebrities are asymmetrical and media-facilitated. Does this mean they aren't relationships? Are any particular celebrities important to you? What have you done to learn more about them?

9. Are bonds based on shared leisure interests sufficient to constitute a sense of group responsibility? Or are recreational activities too inconsequential to create true group identity? Think about people you know through shared recreational and leisure pursuits. Are they part of your primary group, or more like members of your "lifestyle enclave"?

10. Some people worry that American society has too few hangouts, or "third place" locations, where people come together regularly for conversation and camaraderie outside work and home. If you regularly visit any location like this, what sorts of things go on there? Have the bonds you formed there been important to other parts of your life?

11. Ecotourism seeks to make tourism as ecofriendly as possible. What other products or services claim environmental friendliness to increase sales?

SUGGESTIONS FOR FURTHER EXPLORATION

Bride and Prejudice. 2005. Dir. Gurinder Chadha. Miramax Films. A Bollywood adaptation of the classic Jane Austen novel *Pride and Prejudice*. Some elements translate easily from the book, but the story is also infused with the distinctive cultural traditions of Bollywood.

Columbia Journalism Review (www.cjr.org/tools/owners). This site's guide to major media companies' holdings offers a hands-on understanding of the concentration of media power.

Fine, Gary Alan. 1998. *Morel Tales: The Culture of Mushrooming*. Cambridge, MA: Harvard University Press. A humorous, in-depth description of three years spent hunting mushrooms with dedicated amateurs and trained professionals. Fine describes and analyzes the subculture of mushroom hunting, revealing the ways that a shared recreational interest can create community.

Joshua Gamson

Gamson, Joshua. 1998. *Freaks Talk Back: Tabloid Talk Shows and Sexual Nonconformity*. Chicago: University of Chicago Press. A discussion of the way that "tabloid television" helps increase the exposure of groups whose sexual orientation or gender identity makes them outsiders in American culture.

Guralnick, Peter. 1999. *Feel Like Going Home: Portraits in Blues and Rock 'n' Roll*. Boston: Back Bay Books. Describes the history of the commercialization of music in the United States and the effect this change in the industry had on musicians, as they were forced to go out on the road and play for strangers.

Jenkins, Henry, and Justine Cassell. 2000. *From Barbie to Mortal Kombat*. Cambridge, MA: MIT Press. An exploration of the role of gender in computer games—particularly the development of video games for girls. The authors raise the concern that marketing computer games primarily to boys widens the technology gap between the genders. However, attempts to make video games "for girls" risk reinforcing gender stereotypes.

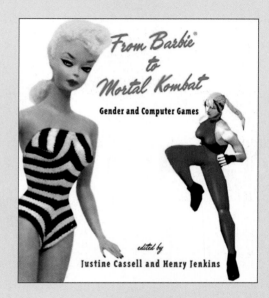

Johnson, Steven. 2005. *Everything Bad Is Good for You*. New York: Riverhead Books. An examination of pop culture arguing that contemporary TV shows, video games, and other electronic media give the mind a better workout than critics typically acknowledge and that the most criticized elements of today's media are actually more complex—and better for us—than the sitcoms and movies of the past.

The Merchants of Cool. 2001. Dir. Barak Goodman. PBS. A documentary that examines the ways products are marketed to teenagers and investigates the impact of conglomeration and cross-marketing. The whole documentary is available online (www.pbs.org/wgbh/pages/frontline/shows/cool).

Metallica: Some Kind of Monster. 2005. Dir. Joe Berlinger and Bruce Sinofsky. Paramount Pictures. A behind-the-scenes look at the real work that underlies the art and the business of rock and roll, and the repetitive daily grind of life on tour.

Miller, Mark Crispin. January 7, 2002. "What's Wrong with This Picture?" *The Nation* (www.thenation.com/special/bigten.html). Miller profiles the ten conglomerations that control the vast majority of media in the United States and outlines the consequences of this state of affairs. Pay special attention to the chart he provides, showing the synergistic links between elements of each corporation.

Visit the place where Elvis Presley lived: Graceland. Elvis Presley's estate in suburban Memphis, Tennessee, is perhaps the ultimate location for observing fan culture and celebrity worship.

CHAPTER 14 Health and Illness

On the 1995 film *Leaving Las Vegas*, Nicolas Cage plays Ben, a down-and-out screenwriter who heads to Vegas intending to drink himself to death. His plan is delayed when he meets and befriends a local prostitute, Sera (played by Elisabeth Shue). Ben and Sera connect for a short while and come to an agreement: he won't ask her to quit her job, and she won't ask him to quit drinking. They provide each other with acceptance, companionship, and a temporary respite from their isolated lives. But not even their connection can stop Ben from fulfilling his self-destructive goal. He dies in Sera's arms, leaving Las Vegas the way he always planned. Cage won a Best Actor Oscar and Golden Globe Award for his performance (while Shue received corresponding Best Actress nominations), and the film has taken its place among top Hollywood portrayals of the desperation and destruction of alcoholism.

But there's more to this story than the suicide of a fictional alcoholic in a seedy hotel. Las Vegas itself can be seen as another main character as well—a real American city with an unfortunate connection to self-destruction. According to sociologist Matt Wray and his colleagues (2008), merely being in Las Vegas, as either a resident or a tourist, increases one's suicide risk. Vegas residents' odds of suicide are 50 percent greater than people who live elsewhere, and visitors' risk of suicide doubles while there, compared with those who stay home or travel elsewhere. Indeed, if you are a resident of the city, getting out of town is good for you—leaving Las Vegas results in a reduction in suicide risk of more than 20 percent. Should Las Vegas, which consistently has the highest urban suicide rate in the nation, also be referred to as "Suicide City" in addition to its nickname of "Sin City"? What explains these disturbing statistics?

Wray and his colleagues (2008) offer three possible explanations: ecological, selection, and contagion theories of suicide. The ecological argument is place-based: there is something about the city itself that makes people suicidal. For example, Vegas has long been one of the fastest-growing cities in the nation, although growth has slowed dramatically since the recession. This kind of rapid social change can lead to social isolation and dislocation and a weakening of community bonds (Trudeau 2008), all factors classically correlated with suicide by Emile Durkheim (1897/1951). Additionally, some research suggests that gambling or the large number of hotel rooms (where chances of rescuing someone mid-attempt are slim) make Vegas conducive to suicide (Phillips, Welty, and Smith 1997; Gemar, Zarkowski, and Avery 2008). The selection argument is somewhat more psychological: Vegas residents and tourists might be disproportionately prone to impulsiveness or other risky behaviors (Wray et al. 2008), and, indeed, may be choosing Vegas as a site for making a new start or having a "last hurrah," a gamble that more frequently ends in their suicide because the city beckons people with these and other relevant personality traits, such as depression. The contagion argument combines ecological and selection concerns: the high suicide rate inspires a kind of "copycat" effect (Cosgrove-Mather 2004) and through processes of social imitation the rate remains high.

So, is it the place, the people, or a combination of the two that makes Las Vegas the suicide capital of the country? Wray and his colleagues cannot provide us with a definitive answer just yet. But their research recognizes what we will be exploring in this chapter: that although health, illness, and mortality are physiological phenomena, they are also unquestionably shaped by social factors. Narrow biomedical models can miss the important social and cultural elements behind disease and injury—because individuals live and die in the context of groups and communities, the social aspects of health and medicine cannot be ignored.

HOW TO READ THIS CHAPTER

Health and illness are constants of human existence, a natural part of having a physical body that is subject to injury, disease, aging, and death. Health and illness are not just physical states—they also include aspects of our mental well-being and are influenced by shifting cultural beliefs about what is ideal and desirable. As a society, we have established the social institution of medicine to address the challenges of our physical existence. Sociologists ask you to consider how larger social forces help to shape this institution and your own experience of health or illness.

The Sociology of Medicine, Health, and Illness

Why is sociology interested in topics that might seem more at home in a medical school textbook? Well, for one thing, our bodies (where health and illness are ostensibly located) are social objects. Our physical selves have socially constructed meanings and are also affected by social forces. This means that the very definition of health is social; it also means that our individual health is subject not just to cross-cultural or historically specific interpretive differences, but to different

Health in a Cultural Context The Senegalese women pictured to the left live in a society that values fuller body types that might be classified as overweight in other cultures. The United States puts such a strong emphasis on straight, white teeth that many people spend thousands of dollars on cosmetic dental procedures.

influences depending on where and when we live, as well as what statuses we hold in our society.

Let's look at a couple of examples where the nature of health is defined by its social rather than biological context. Think about what having a healthy body means in a developed country like the United States. We value slim, athletic bodies and consider people with these body types to be healthier than people with fleshy builds. But in Dakar, Senegal, people tend to value body types that in the United States would be considered clinically overweight. Senegalese women in particular associate these body types with health (and by extension with wealth enough to eat well): slimmer women actually want to gain weight in order to attain the "desirable," "healthy" build (Holdsworth et al. 2004). Another example: in the United States, "healthy" teeth are not just free of cavities, but also straight and white. So in addition to brushing teeth daily and visiting the dentist regularly, Americans spend big money on orthodontic and whitening procedures. Meanwhile, in many other parts of the world, irregularly shaped or unevenly colored teeth are not necessarily seen as "bad" or "unhealthy," and cosmetic dentistry is far less common. These examples indicate that our definitions of health (and beauty as a sign of health) are determined at least in part by our cultural context, and not always by a biological bottom line.

Another important aspect of health as a social phenomenon involves the spread of disease. Think about it: you've caught a good number of illnesses from other people. Someone behind you in the movie theater coughed, and you got a cold (if you were lucky) or tuberculosis (if you were unlucky). Someone flipping burgers at the fast-food restaurant forgot to wash their hands, and you got an upset stomach (if you were lucky) or hepatitis A (if you were unlucky). If you have young children in school or day care, you know that kids are like family disease vectors—they catch bugs from other kids, bring them home, and spread them around to family members.

As an example of how social milieu affects risk of disease, take the recent whooping cough epidemic in California. The disease, which can easily be fatal in small children, is highly contagious but has an effective vaccine. In 2010, California saw an unprecedented increase in whooping cough cases, with five infants dead by the end of July (McKinley 2010). The areas with the most cases included Fresno County, a largely agricultural area with a high population of vaccination-averse immigrants, and Marin County, a wealthy suburb of San Francisco that has the highest rate of voluntary vaccine refusal in the state (DeNoon 2010). So, some parents (like those in Fresno) may not have access to vaccines, may come from countries that don't vaccinate, or may fear contact with the medical establishment because of their immigration status. Other parents (like those in Marin) believe that vaccines increase their child's risk of such conditions as autism,

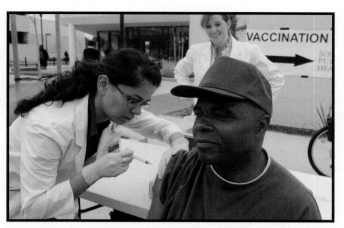

Whooping Cough Epidemic A doctor administers a Tdap vaccination to a man in Vallejo, California, to protect him against the outbreak of whooping cough.

and opt out. Either way, failing to vaccinate puts everyone in their communities at risk of contracting disease.

Our bodies are social objects, and our social experiences and social location shape our prospects for health and risks of disease. These are only some of the reasons that health and illness are social phenomena. As you read this chapter, you'll find that there are social, cultural, and subcultural factors affecting just about everything having to do with health and illness. How we categorize illnesses, how we treat them, and who gets to treat them are all sociological questions.

Definitions of Health and Illness

Terms such as "healthy" or "sick" may seem straightforward, but their meanings are not absolute or universal. The World Health Organization (a division of the United Nations charged with overseeing global health issues) defines health as "a state of complete physical, mental, and social well-being and not merely the absence of disease or infirmity" (WHO 1946). Let's look further at how illnesses are defined and treated in the United States.

Types of Illnesses

Diseases and illnesses are commonly categorized as either acute or chronic. **Acute diseases** have a sudden onset, may be briefly incapacitating, and are either curable or

acute diseases diseases that have a sudden onset, may be briefly incapacitating, and are either curable or fatal

chronic diseases diseases that develop over a longer period of time and may not be detected until symptoms occur later in their progression

curative or crisis medicine type of health care that treats the disease or condition once it has manifested

preventive medicine type of health care that aims to avoid or forestall the onset of disease by taking preventive measures, often including lifestyle changes

palliative care type of health care that focuses on symptom and pain relief and providing a supportive environment for critically ill or dying patients, rather than fighting the illness or disease

fatal. These illnesses are often caused by an organism such as a germ, virus, or parasite that infects the body and disrupts the normal functioning of one or more areas. Many acute illnesses are contagious and can spread from one person to many people. The common cold, pneumonia, and measles could all be considered acute illnesses. **Chronic diseases** develop over a longer period of time and may not be detected until later in their progression. They can sometimes be related to environment, lifestyle, and personal choices. Many chronic diseases are manageable, but others progress and eventually become fatal. Cancer, cerebrovascular disease, and some forms of diabetes can all be considered chronic diseases.

The kinds of diseases that affect us can vary over time and by place. For most of history, humans worried about becoming afflicted with acute diseases. Indeed, prior to 1900, the leading causes of death in the United States were influenza, pneumonia, tuberculosis, and gastroenteritis. Over the past century, there have been drastic changes in medicine and public health that have all but wiped out certain acute diseases (such as polio), while chronic ones (such as diabetes)

have grown vastly in proportion (CDC 1998). Chronic diseases have become among the most important factors governing health and illness today. The top three causes of death in the United States are currently cerebrovascular disease, cancer, and heart disease (CDC 2011a). However, acute diseases continue to pose significant threats to people living in the developing world, where the top killers still include respiratory infections, diarrheal diseases, tuberculosis, and malaria (WHO 2008).

Approaches to Medical Treatment

The health-care system in the United States is characterized by three approaches: curative or crisis, preventive, and palliative. **Curative** or **crisis medicine** treats the disease once it has become apparent. Sometimes this works well, especially in the case of acute illnesses, like food poisoning, or sports injuries, like a torn ligament, that have no early treatment option. But in the case of chronic illnesses, a delay in recognizing causes or symptoms before the disease advances may mean the difference between recovery and death. **Preventive medicine** aims to avoid or forestall the onset of disease by making lifestyle changes: regular exercise, proper diet and nutrition, smoking cessation, stress reduction, and other measures to maintain or improve one's health. Lifestyle changes are often the most effective and least costly ways to prevent a range of chronic conditions (McKinlay 1997). **Palliative care** focuses on symptom and pain relief and on providing a nurturing and supportive environment to those suffering from a serious illness or at the end of life, either in addition to or in place of fighting the illness or disease.

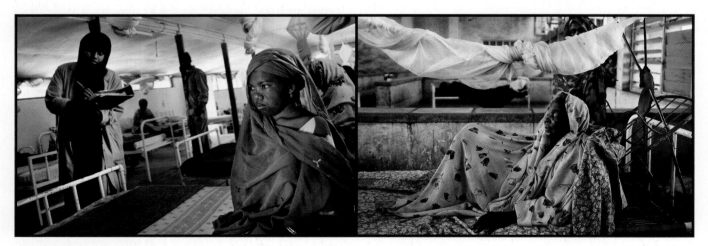

Acute Diseases Above, patients in Sudan wait for treatment in the TB ward of a hospital. Diseases such as tuberculosis, diarrheal diseases, and malaria are the top causes of death in the developing world.

ANALYZING EVERYDAY LIFE
Health Practices Survey

For many young people, moving away from home and going to college marks the beginning of their independent lives as adults. While there is much to celebrate at this milestone, it can also be a time full of new demands and challenges. Perhaps you or someone you know is dealing with homesickness, an abusive relationship, or stress and anxiety. As a college student, you can learn to become more responsible and disciplined, and more conscientious about taking care of yourself. But you can also be threatened by alcohol or substance abuse, eating disorders, or depression. The college years are an important phase of development and one in which many young people struggle to some degree with their newfound adult lives.

The American College Health Association (ACHA) is an organization that helps colleges and universities conduct large-scale surveys on the habits, behaviors, and perceptions affecting the health and well-being of their student populations. In 2008, the ACHA surveyed almost 35,000 students; the results have helped colleges and universities offer education and support services regarding a variety of issues (2009).

This Data Workshop asks you to conduct your own small-scale study on health and wellness issues. There are a number of ways that you can structure your survey questionnaire (see Chapter 2 for a review of survey research methods). You might want to ask a handful of students about a wide range of issues, or you might want to ask a greater number of students more in-depth questions about one or two specific areas. Here is a list of possible topics—feel free to add your own:

anger
depression
drugs and alcohol
eating disorders
exercise
gambling
grief and loss
homesickness
relationships
sexual assault
sleep difficulties
stress and anxiety
suicide
tobacco

You might ask students about their lifestyles—what they eat, how much they sleep, whether they exercise, drink or smoke,

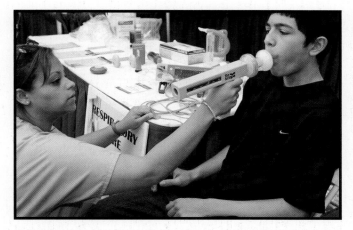

College Health A student at Miami-Dade College in Florida attends a community health fair.

or practice safe sex. Do they play a musical instrument, are they on a sports team, or do they belong to any campus clubs? You might ask about their physical health—how often they get sick, or what they do to stay healthy. Or you might ask about their mental health—whether they experience stress and anxiety, what causes them to feel it, and what they do to alleviate it. Typically, survey questions are close-ended and provide quantitative results, but you may also include open-ended questions or write-in answers. There's no right way to structure the survey, but do keep the questionnaires as clear and simple as possible.

You might also ask about your respondents' demographic backgrounds, such as age or gender. Remember that you're dealing with human subjects and you'll need to get informed consent from anyone who participates. Because of ethical concerns, it may not be possible to ask about certain personal or sensitive issues. However interesting the data, you will need to respect the privacy and confidentiality of your respondents.

There are two options for completing this Data Workshop:

• *Option 1 (informal):* Prepare a set of questions in survey format to administer to students. Conduct your survey with a small pilot group (three to five students). Discuss your findings with other students in small-group discussions.

• *Option 2 (formal):* Conduct your survey on a small pilot group (five to eight students). Write a three- to four-page essay describing your preliminary findings. Be sure to attach your survey questionnaire to the paper.

Your instructor will let you know which of these options you should complete.

Medicalization and the Social Construction of Health and Illness

Since what constitutes illness can be socially constructed, it's interesting to look at how some problems that were once not considered medical conditions have been transformed into illnesses over time. This process is known as **medicalization**, and it has affected our perspective on a variety of forms of deviance. A century ago, we thought of alcoholism and addiction as the result of weak will or bad character, but we now see them as hereditary diseases that respond to medical and therapeutic treatment. Kids who might have been written off as "unruly" or "inattentive" in the 1950s are now diagnosed with attention-deficit/hyperactivity disorder, or ADHD, and given drugs to keep them calm and focused (Conrad 2006). Obesity, once seen as a failure of willpower, can now be treated with surgery and drugs.

Even birth and death have been medicalized. In the early years of the twentieth century, more than half of American women gave birth at home, attended only by family, friends, or midwives, without drugs or surgeries (Cassidy 2006). By 1955, that number had declined steeply, to about 1 percent of American women, and it continues at about that rate to this day (Cassidy 2006). We now see pregnancy as a "medical condition" for which a hospital birth—and, often, a doctor's intervention in the form of an episiotomy or caesarean section—is the "treatment." Death has undergone the same transformation: once a natural (though sad) part of family life, it is now something that we will go to great medical lengths to delay (though we can never stave it off forever). Death also used to occur at home, but today at least 75 percent of patients die in hospitals or nursing homes (Cassel and Demel 2001), despite the fact that studies show it is less stressful for terminally ill patients to die at home (Searing 2010). For many people living great distances away from relatives, dying at home is no longer even an option.

Medicalization changes both the meaning of a condition and the meaning of the individual who suffers from it. In the case of birth and death, it turns a natural part of the human life cycle into something unfamiliar that we fear we can't handle on our own. We therefore turn to medical experts who may or may not intervene in ways that actually help and may in fact further traumatize patients and their families. In other cases, such as with forms of deviance like addiction, obesity, or mental or emotional problems, medicalization takes the pressure off the person. The fact that they drink too much, eat too much, can't concentrate, or are sad all the time is no longer their fault as individuals—it is the fault of the disease. We would never advise someone to "just get over" pneumonia or a broken leg—and as the process of medicalization continues, we are less likely to think of addiction, obesity, or depression as conditions people should "just get over" on their own.

> **medicalization** the process by which some behaviors or conditions that were once seen as personal problems are redefined as medical issues

Living with HIV Greg Louganis, the five-time Olympic medal winner for diving, is pictured here coaching in California. Louganis was diagnosed with HIV in 1988, when HIV was largely misunderstood and often a death sentence. Through modern treatment, Louganis and others affected maintain healthy, fulfilling lives.

The Changing Meaning of HIV/AIDS

Understanding that disease can be socially constructed allows us to see how its meanings can change over time. For example, the social meaning of AIDS (acquired immunodeficiency syndrome, caused by the human immunodeficiency virus, or HIV) has shifted significantly since it was identified in the early 1980s. At that time, AIDS was poorly understood and largely associated with stigmatized or outsider social groups, such as gay men, intravenous drug users, and Haitians. There was no effective treatment, and the average length of survival after diagnosis hovered around six months (Rowniak 2009). Prevention through safer sex and drug practices was the only real defense against the disease, and propaganda campaigns were everywhere. But by the mid-1990s, treatment strategies utilizing a "cocktail" of multiple drugs extended patients' lifespans significantly, and allowed HIV to be treated as a chronic disease.

Effective treatment for HIV is a momentous development, bringing hope to the approximately 33 million people living with the virus worldwide (UNAIDS 2010). But the social consequences of this transformation—from certain killer to manageable chronic illness—have not been entirely positive. The notion that one might *live with* HIV rather than *die from* it has resulted in what some researchers call "safe-sex fatigue"—a growing disinclination toward condom use and other safer-sex practices. This relaxed attitude has led to a renewed increase in HIV infection rates for some populations (Rowniak 2009). It is a disturbing example of how changing socially constructed meanings of illnesses affect the behavior of individuals—and hence the development and epidemiology of those diseases.

millions around the world. What future illnesses might threaten humanity next, and can we identify them before widespread devastation occurs? Epidemiologists combine data and methods from the biological and social sciences with a public health orientation to answer important questions about the origins and spread of disease.

Epidemiologists swing into action whenever a new disease emerges or an unexpected outbreak of a previously eradicated disease resurfaces. For example, in the H1N1 influenza (or "swine flu") **epidemic** of 2009, epidemiological researchers established the connection between hundreds of seemingly unrelated patients, analyzed the genetic makeup of the virus that infected them, and confirmed that they were suffering from a strain of influenza virus that had not previously infected humans—all in a matter of weeks (Novel Swine-Origin Influenza A [H1N1] Virus Investigation Team 2009). As a result of this research, a vaccine was developed and a widespread public health awareness campaign was put in place to educate people about the transmission, prevention, and treatment of the disease.

The H1N1 outbreak of 2009 began as an epidemic, but eventually became what is known as a **pandemic**. What are the differences between those two terms? An epidemic occurs

> **epidemiology** the study of disease patterns to understand the cause of illnesses, how they are spread, and what interventions to take
>
> **epidemic** occurs when a significantly higher number of cases of a particular disease occur during a particular time period than might otherwise be expected
>
> **pandemic** occurs when a significantly higher number of cases of a disease also spreads through an especially large geographical region spanning many countries or even continents

Disease Patterns as Social Epidemiology

As we have noted, sociologists are interested in the social aspect of disease patterns. The study of these patterns is known as **epidemiology**. Epidemiologists collect and analyze data in order to understand the causes of a particular illness, how it is communicated, the factors affecting its development and distribution in a population, where it is likely to spread, and what the most effective interventions might be. Over many centuries of human history, major illnesses such as cholera, typhus, yellow fever, and smallpox swept across vast stretches of the globe and decimated populations from practically every continent. More recently, such illnesses as tuberculosis, malaria, and measles continue to kill

Climate Change and Health A woman hands out hand sanitizer in Times Square to help prevent the spread of H1N1. As the climate changes, vector organisms carry and spread pathogens outside of their normal habitat to contribute to the spread of illnesses like H1N1.

HIV and AIDS Around the World

For a long time, the story of the human immunodeficiency virus (HIV) and the disease it causes, acquired immunodeficiency syndrome (AIDS), had a single narrative. Genetic analysis has led researchers to believe that the simian immunodeficiency virus (SIV) was present in primates in Africa for at least 32,000 years (Worobey et al. 2010). Researchers still disagree as to why, but at some point in the late nineteenth or early twentieth century a strain of this virus mutated into a form that infected humans. Analysis of blood samples taken at different points in time suggests that HIV moved from the Congo to Haiti, and then migrated to the United States through Haitian immigrants. The disease continued its spread throughout the world.

Today, at least 25 million people have died since AIDS appeared in the early 1980s, and approximately 33 million people are currently infected with HIV (UNAIDS 2009, 2010). AIDS is now a pandemic—a global event made possible by the increasing connections that come with a global economy—but it has also become a series of epidemics. AIDS is always the same disease, but it is a very different epidemic depending on where it is.

One of the most important ways in which medical researchers study AIDS is by determining the different ways in which it is transmitted, and which parts of the population are most affected. In many places, AIDS is a concentrated epidemic, with the majority of cases transmitted by a particular method and concentrated in a particular subpopulation within a given country. In Central Europe and Central Asia, intravenous drug use is responsible for

the majority of cases (O'Neill 2007). In Latin America, the routes by which HIV is transmitted are much more diverse, but homosexual intercourse is a more common route to infection. In Southeast Asia, commercial sex workers make up a much larger percentage of the HIV-positive population. In sub-Saharan Africa, AIDS is a generalized epidemic, spread through the entire population, such that in some countries more than 30 percent of adults are infected.

Understanding the ways in which HIV spreads is vital for those who seek to treat those who are infected and prevent future infections, but these differences are not the most important ways in which AIDS is experienced differently around the world. For one thing, AIDS is distributed disproportionately: only about 4 percent of all cases are in the developed world, places like the United States, Western Europe, Japan, and other wealthy, industrialized nations. This is important because in the developed world the vast majority of AIDS sufferers have access to antiretroviral drugs, which transform the disease into something much closer to a chronic condition, and significantly improve the physical, emotional, and mental life of those who receive them. In the developing world, however, these drugs are prohibitively expensive for the vast majority of AIDS patients (Beard, Feeley, and Rosen 2009).

The expense of antiretroviral drugs has led to important discussions about how the international community should respond to AIDS in the developing world. Some advocate a pragmatic approach, focusing on education and other pre-

when a significantly higher number of cases of a particular disease occur during a particular time period than might otherwise be expected, while the term pandemic is used when those cases also cover an especially large geographical region (say, a continent, or the entire globe). What constitutes an epidemic is usually determined by national public health organizations—in the United States, that would be the Centers for Disease Control (CDC) in Atlanta (Koerner 2003). The World Health Organization (WHO), in Geneva, Switzerland, monitors and defines pandemics.

Epidemiologists are now identifying the role of global climate change in spreading some of the most important diseases afflicting the world, and they are tracking how this process occurs (Associated Press 2006). Because climate affects things like the availability of fresh water and "arable" (or farmable) land, it also affects where people live and their patterns of migration. As people leave places where climate change has made food, water, and other resources scarce, they crowd into other areas that may then experience overpopulation. When people live in very close quarters, the risks

ventive strategies, rather than treating the disease. Those who hold this position assume that antiretroviral drugs are both too expensive to supply and too complicated to administer. For example, new treatment regimens for both mother and baby can entirely eliminate the transmission of AIDS from mother to child. However, this care has not been comprehensively extended to pregnant women with AIDS in the less-developed world. Not only are the drugs very expensive, but the regimen requires pregnant women to undergo a lengthy course of oral and injected treatments and to refrain from breastfeeding. The baby also undergoes six weeks of drug treatments, and both mother and infant must be carefully monitored for side effects (Varmus and Satcher 1997). Following the pragmatic approach means that millions of people are being condemned to suffering and an early death even though proven medical treatments exist.

This approach has also led to intense controversy in the research world. In 1997, the Public Citizen Health Research Group wrote an editorial for the *New England Journal of Medicine* (Lurie and Wolfe 1997) condemning a number of clinical trials for new AIDS treatments, many of which were funded by the U.S. government. The trials in question compared the performance of new AIDS treatments and drugs against a placebo group that received no treatment, rather than comparing the new therapies to antiretrovirals, which were recognized as the most effective treatment. The editorial compared the research to the infamous Tuskegee Syphilis Experiment (see the Global Per-

Seeking Treatment Patients wait at the HIV/AIDS clinic in Arua Regional Hospital in northern Uganda where Doctors without Borders provides medical care and access to antiretroviral drugs.

spective box in Chapter 2), and pointed out that the World Medical Association's ethical guidelines would prohibit this research: the WMA's Helsinki Declaration says that medical research must always ensure that "every patient—including those of a control group, if any—should be assured of the best proven diagnostic and therapeutic methods" (1964). When researchers test only newer, cheaper treatments and compare them against each other rather than against the best available treatment, they are accepting that the treatment afforded AIDS patients in the developed world cannot be extended to the many millions of people suffering in the developing world.

rise for malnutrition, water-borne illnesses such as cholera, and other infectious diseases to spread (Khasnis and Nettleman 2005).

Global climate change can also affect animal populations that spread diseases among humans. Even small increases in temperature can multiply the numbers of **vector organisms** that carry and spread pathogens (germs or other infectious agents) in a given area. Mosquitoes carrying malaria, for example, used to be limited to sub-Saharan Africa and other hot or tropical regions. But in Kenya, malaria has recently penetrated mountainous regions that were once too chilly for mosquitoes to survive, and similar reports have come from parts of Europe and as far north as Moscow, Russia (Associated Press 2006). Other illnesses such as Lyme disease (carried by ticks), yellow and dengue fevers and West Nile virus (carried by mosquitoes), avian influenza (carried by birds), and even plague (carried by fleas on

> **vector organisms** animals like mosquitoes, ticks, and birds that carry and spread pathogens (germs or other infectious agents) in a given area

rodents) may skyrocket as climate change drives these vector animals out of their customary territories and into new ecosystems (Dell'Amore 2008).

Foreseeing this serious threat to human health and the possibility of it resulting in greater epidemics in the future, networks of scientists have called for action by all nations to mandate caps on greenhouse gas emissions, as well as to begin preparing for what appear to be the unavoidable public health consequences of the global climate change that has already occurred.

Social Inequality, Health, and Illness

As you already know from reading Chapters 7, 8, and 9, our experiences of health and illness are also shaped by our race, gender, and socioeconomic statuses. Answers to such questions as "Who gets sick?" "What kinds of diseases do they get?" "Who gets treatment?" and "What kind of treatment do they get?" are all influenced by social hierarchies and structures of inequality. Since we gave you a fairly comprehensive picture of the relationships between different forms of inequality and different health outcomes in the prior chapters, we'll just summarize some of the main findings first, and then go into more depth here about a specific problem that is linked to a variety of illnesses and is caused largely by social inequalities.

Health and Intersections of Class, Race, and Gender

It's easy to see how one's social class might have an effect on their health. People of higher socioeconomic status (SES) can afford not only more and better health-care services (insurance plans, doctor visits, diagnostic tests and treatments, prescription medications), but may also have greater access to other resources (better nutrition, cleaner neighborhoods, more preventive practices like exercise) that positively impact their health. People of higher SES can expect to live longer lives, and they generally enjoy feeling more physical well-being than those in lower groups. Being on the lower end of the social class ladder brings many problems that are the inverse of the advantages above. People with lower SES have substantially higher rates of various diseases along with higher death rates and shorter life expectancy (Lynch et al. 1998). They may have little regular access to health-care providers and may lack the ability to participate in preventive practices or have trouble affording prescription medi-

cations and other recommended procedures (Lynch et al. 1997). The effects of poverty consistently correlate with higher incidences of depression and other mental health problems (Groh 2007).

Inequalities of race and gender are often connected to lower socioeconomic status. When we add race or gender to the health equation, we find significant differences between groups who are higher or lower in the social hierarchy. Many problems that affect people of lower SES are further exacerbated in minority groups. African Americans have long been discriminated against and still suffer disproportionately from the stresses of poverty. They have higher rates of death and disease, and shorter life expectancy than whites (Bennett et al. 2002). African Americans and Hispanics are less likely to be able to afford health insurance and, consequently, to engage in regular health practices. Researchers have shown that minorities are more often exposed to unhealthful surroundings, whether in the workplace or in residential neighborhoods. For example, Emily Rosenbaum (2008) found that Hispanics and blacks in New York City tended to live in poorer quality housing in lower-income neighborhoods, and to suffer much higher incidents of asthma than their Asian, white, and higher-SES counterparts.

Gender is another source of inequality that also complicates the health picture for men and women. Health is one place where gender inequality benefits women over men, as they are generally healthier and enjoy a longer life expectancy in spite of having a lower SES than men. Traditional male gender role expectations may result in men who work in more dangerous occupations and engage in more risky life-

Socioeconomic Status and Health A man visits the Family Van in Boston, Massachusetts, to get his blood pressure checked. Many residents from low-income neighborhoods in Boston visit the Family Van, a non-profit clinic, to get free health screenings they wouldn't normally have access to.

FIGURE 14.1
HOW ARE WE LIKELY TO DIE?

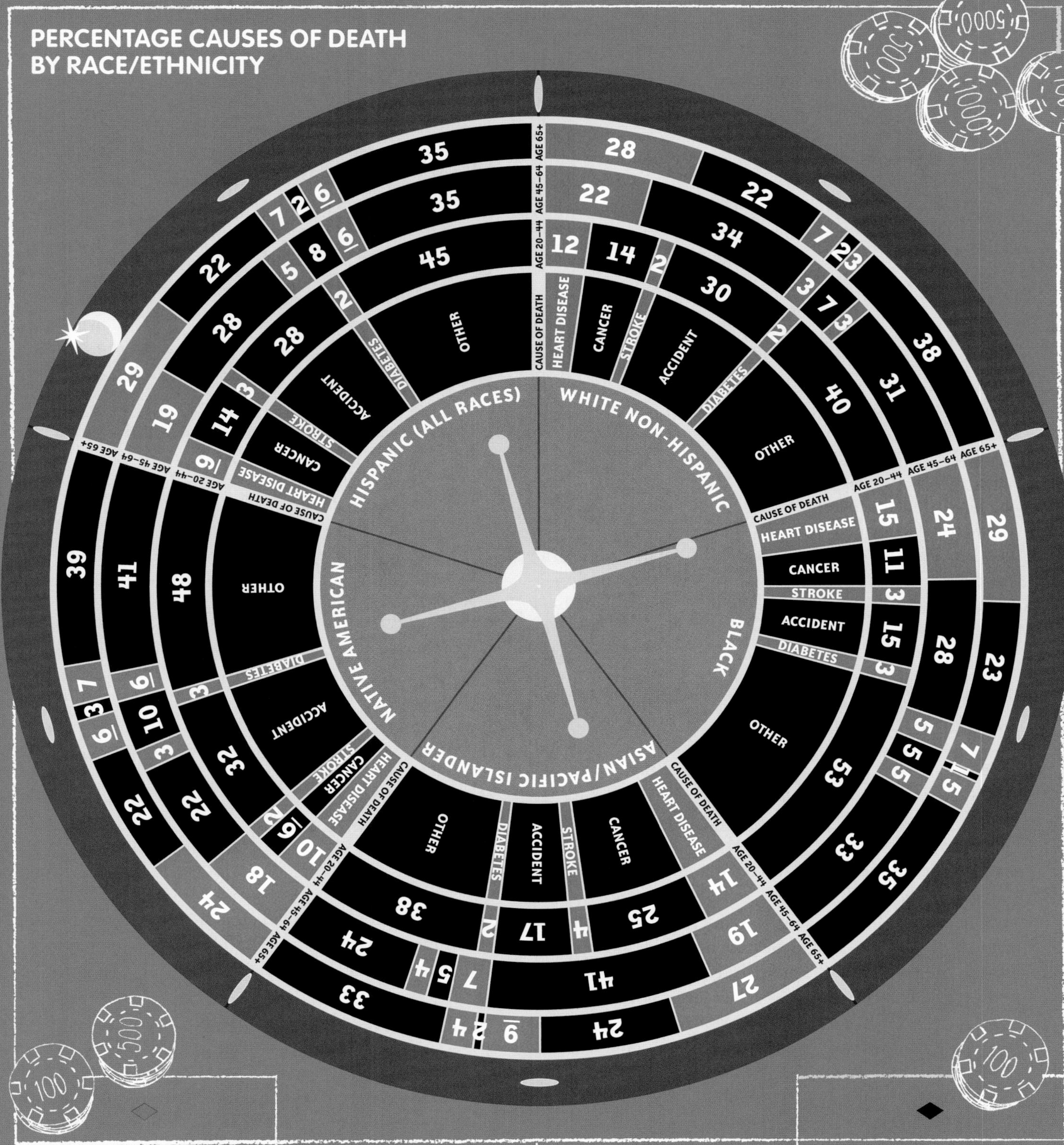

PERCENTAGE CAUSES OF DEATH BY RACE/ETHNICITY

HISPANIC (ALL RACES)

WHITE NON-HISPANIC

BLACK

ASIAN/PACIFIC ISLANDER

NATIVE AMERICAN

CAUSE OF DEATH — HEART DISEASE — CANCER — STROKE — ACCIDENT — DIABETES — OTHER

AGE 20–44 — AGE 45–64 — AGE 65+

WHITE NON-HISPANIC
28, 22, 34, 30, 22, 7, 2, 3, 38, 3, 7, 3, 40, 31, 12, 14, 2, 35, 35, 45

BLACK
HEART DISEASE 15, 24, 29 / CANCER 11, 3, 23 / STROKE 3, 15 / ACCIDENT 15, 28 / DIABETES 3 / OTHER 53, 5, 5, 5, 7, 5, 35, 33, 19, 14

HISPANIC (ALL RACES)
35, 35, 22, 7, 2, 6, 5, 8, 6, 28, 28, 2, 29, 19, 3, 14, 3, 9, 45, OTHER, DIABETES, ACCIDENT, STROKE, CANCER, HEART DISEASE

NATIVE AMERICAN
OTHER 39, 41, 48, 32, 22, 22, 18, 24, 33, 24, 7, 3, 9, 6, 3, 10, 3, 6, 9, 2, DIABETES, ACCIDENT, STROKE, CANCER, HEART DISEASE

ASIAN/PACIFIC ISLANDER
OTHER 38, 25, 17, 41, 7, 5, 24, 2, 6, 14, 19, 27, 9, 2, CANCER, STROKE, ACCIDENT, DIABETES, HEART DISEASE

HOMICIDE
20.2% of 20–44 year old black male deaths occurred by homicide.

SUICIDE
14.9% of 20–44 year old white male deaths were by suicide.

LIVER DISEASE
10% of 45–64 year old Native American male deaths were by liver disease.

PREGNANCY COMPLICATIONS
3% of 25–44 year old Asian/Pac. Islander female deaths were from pregnancy.

ALZHEIMER'S DISEASE
5.7% of 65+ year old white female deaths were from Alzheimer's Disease.

H.I.V.
11.2% of 20–44 year old black female deaths were caused by H.I.V.

CHRONIC LOWER RESPIRATORY DIS.
4.6% of 65+ year old Asian/Pac. Islander male deaths were from chronic lower resp. dis.

KIDNEY DISEASE
2.2% of 45–64 year old hispanic female deaths were from kidney disease.

NOTE: CENTERS FOR DISEASE CONTROL 2011A.

In Relationships

Concierge Medicine: Paying For Your Own Private Doctor?

You break out in an itchy rash on your leg . . . or you pull a muscle in your back . . . or you've got another splitting sinus headache and it's not getting any better. You should probably go see the doctor. But that process may end up being a bigger pain than the physical hurt in your leg, back, or head. Why? First of all, it may be weeks before you can get into the doctor's office in the first place: nationally, it takes an average of about three weeks to get an appointment (Merritt Hawkins 2009). Once you arrive, you may sit for quite a long time in the waiting room—an average of more than twenty minutes, according to the AMA (Arnst 2010). Once you get into the exam room, you may wait some more (this time in a flimsy paper gown). And when the doctor finally arrives, it may not be the same doctor you saw last time, so you may have to spend extra time bringing her up to speed. That time is precious—studies indicate that you will only have ten minutes with your doctor once she arrives in the exam room (Ohtaki et al. 2003)—ten minutes to give your history, describe your symptoms, receive your diagnosis, and discuss your treatment. And let's not even talk about the process of paying for this visit: insurance company paperwork and bureaucracy may be the biggest pain of all.

Is there a solution to this tedious, impersonal approach to health care? Maybe. You could have a very different relationship with your doctor—no waiting, no insurance forms,

Royal Pains

and maybe even house calls—if you've got enough cash. We're talking about a phenomenon known as concierge medicine, where doctors provide direct care to patients who have paid an annual fee ($1,500 or more in addition to the costs of their actual care) so that they can retain the services of a personal physician who is always available to address their health-care needs. It's a growing niche—the American Academy of Private Physicians estimates that there are now 5,000 doctors practicing this type of

---

style behaviors (like smoking, drinking, drugging, and driving fast). The more strongly men identify with the "macho" aspects of masculinity, the more likely they are to avoid preventive health care, regardless of their level of SES (Springer and Mouzon 2011). Men and women suffer some diseases, such as cancer and diabetes, in about equal numbers. However, men still have a higher incidence of heart dis-

ease and strokes, while women more often report that they suffer mental health disorders like anxiety or depression (WomensHealth.gov 2010).

Health and the Problem of Food Deserts

A **food desert** is a community in which the residents have little or no access to fresh, affordable, healthy foods. Most food deserts are located in densely populated, urban areas that

food desert a community in which the residents have little or no access to fresh, affordable, healthy foods, usually located in densely populated, urban areas

medicine, only fifteen years after such "boutique" medical practices began to appear (Wahlgren 2010). And in 2009, concierge medicine even broke into the world of popular culture, with USA Network's television series *Royal Pains*, about a doctor-for-hire in the Hamptons and his wealthy, demanding patients.

There are obvious advantages for both the patients who get twenty-four-hour care with no waiting, and for the doctors who get to avoid many of the bureaucratic nightmares of belonging to health management organizations (HMOs). Concierge doctors tend to have far fewer patients and can spend far more time with each patient as a result—one doctor predicted that his daily consultations would drop from twenty-five to six if he made the switch from conventional to concierge care (Sonn 2004). Concierge medicine allows doctors to forge more substantial relationships with their patients, which is what may have inspired them to practice medicine in the first place. James Benoit, an M.D. from Colorado, started a concierge practice and says that "it's changed my life . . . [and] given me my profession back" (Sonn 2004). Patients feel similarly: "I'm so grateful to know that truly he's at my beck and call," says Marilyn Morris about her concierge physician (Archer 2010). And Joan Holzman says of her concierge doctor's practice: "I adore it. . . . Before, wherever you went, you felt like cattle. But everyone here is top-notch—the doctors, the secretaries, the nurses. They're warm, like family. It's a wonderful feeling of security" (Zuger 2005).

But the fact that patients must pay a steep price for this kind of personal connection with their health-care providers means that questions of inequality arise. Because of the additional fees, concierge services will only be obtainable by those in higher income brackets. What about the patients who can't come up with the required fees? Where will they go for medical care if their doctor decides to switch to a smaller practice with fewer, more affluent patients? Does concierge medicine stratify the health-care system even more than it already is? Harvard Medical School professor John Goodson uses the term "country club medicine" to describe concierge practices (Williams 2006), and worries that those not in the "club" will no longer be able to find the health care they deserve. While all patients may want a more personal, more committed connection with their doctor, is it fair if only those with the deepest pockets can get it? Medical ethicists caution doctors that this type of practice may violate their professional obligations and be at odds with their philosophical codes (Zuger 2005).

Should our relationships with those who hold our health—and even our lives—in their hands depend on the size of our bank accounts? Use your sociological perspective to consider this issue, and then decide: what do you think about "concierge medicine"?

may have convenience stores and fast-food restaurants, but no grocery stores or other outlet for fresh fruits, vegetables, meats, and other healthy foods. (Sparsely populated rural areas, where stores are far away and hard to access are also considered food deserts.) For example, more than 20 percent of Chicago's 3 million residents live in neighborhoods without supermarkets (Gray 2009), which means that they may have to shop at drug stores, liquor stores, or corner mini-marts for food items, or subsist on the chicken nuggets, burritos, or burgers and fries from the takeout chain on the corner. People who live in food deserts may have few meal choices that aren't highly processed and loaded with fat, sugar, and chemicals.

Food deserts are often in neighborhoods that are predominantly low-income or nonwhite in population. This means that the effects of food deserts are experienced disproportionately by the poor, African Americans, Hispanics, and other minority groups. The health effects of living in a food desert are significant: the risk of obesity, diabetes, and heart disease for African Americans increases by half, and

Food Deserts The absence of grocery stores contributes to the lack of healthy food options available in urban and poor neighborhoods.

for Hispanics by two-thirds (Whitacre et al. 2009; Powell et al. 2007). So, while any given individual may be at risk for obesity, diabetes, or heart disease, living in a food desert increases those risks.

Why do food deserts exist? They are not a new phenomenon. Grocery chains began leaving urban areas for the suburbs in the 1960s and 1970s due to perceived problems with security, profitability, real estate costs, and parking (Ferguson and Abell 1998). In their place, bodegas, liquor stores and fast-food chains popped up, leaving central urban populations with far fewer healthy food options. Some city and state governments are trying to entice supermarkets back to these neighborhoods with programs like tax incentives, grants, or loans for big food retailers and subsidies for farmers' markets. Similar programs are being proposed at the federal level (Haber 2010).

As we have seen, our individual health is shaped by our neighborhood context, which is itself shaped by race and class inequality, the actions of big corporations, and the responses of governmental bodies at all levels. This phenomenon is known as **deprivation amplification**, meaning that our individual disease risks (based on our heredity and physiology) may be amplified by social factors (Macintyre, Macdonald, and Ellaway 2008). The solutions to these health problems are not going to be found merely at

deprivation amplification when our individual disease risks (based on our heredity and physiology) are amplified by social factors

the individual level—they must incorporate social action as well. Yes, you need to eat more healthily in order to control your diabetes . . . but you must be able to find healthy foods close by and at affordable prices in order to do so, and you are more likely to do that in some neighborhoods than in others.

Medicine as a Social Institution

For proof that medicine is a social institution, take a look at the American Medical Association (AMA). The AMA is usually thought of as an organization that makes health recommendations on such topics as childhood obesity and cancer prevention to benefit the general public. But physicians and other medical professionals know the AMA as a trade union that creates the rules and regulations governing medical licensure (AMA 2010). Almost all issues concerning medicine in both public health and professional regulation are governed by the AMA.

Milton Friedman, the winner of the 1976 Nobel Prize in Economics, was a vocal critic of the AMA. Friedman argued that the AMA limits admissions to medical schools and restricts medical licensing to advance the interests of physicians. He viewed the AMA as a monopolizing organization that reduced the quantity and quality of medical care by forcing the public to pay more for medical services due to the lack of qualified physicians (Friedman 1994).

For example, the AMA does not allow physicians who are trained in foreign countries to practice in the United States without passing the United States Medical Licensing Exam (USMLE). For many of these physicians, fulfilling the requirements of the USMLE is a lengthy and arduous process that often necessitates repeating medical residency before they are allowed to practice medicine—even though they were fully licensed and practicing physicians in their country of origin. The AMA and the American College of Obstetricians and Gynecologists also restrict such practices as home births. Even though trained midwives and doulas (who provide emotional support) can safely assist at home births, pregnant women have their options limited by the pressure that the AMA places on women to have labor and delivery at a hospital attended by physicians. As a result, these professionals are forced to operate on the margins of the industry, while physicians and hospitals are able to make more profit from hospital births.

The AMA serves a number of purposes: it establishes and transmits the norms and values of medicine and medical knowledge; it regulates, licenses, and legitimizes the practitioners of medicine; and it polices various forms of encroachment on its own powers. In these ways, medicine itself can be seen as a social institution, with the AMA playing a primary role in creating and maintaining social order, legitimacy, and control.

The Power of the Institution to Define the Situation

The institutional context can have a powerful effect on the interactions that occur within it. You might remember David Rosenhan's study, "On Being Sane in Insane Places" (1973) from Chapter 6, in which "pseudo-patients" who were admitted to a mental hospital were unable to convince hospital staffers of their sanity. In this case, the place itself overrode the individuals' claims to normalcy: once they were defined by and situated within the institution, they could no longer exert any power over their own status, and every interaction they had served as "proof" of their presumed mental illness. Erving Goffman found something very similar in his study of hospitalized mental patients, *Asylums* (1961): psychiatric patients frequently offered explanations for being there that highlighted their normalcy and attempted to reframe their selves as sane and healthy. They inevitably failed to change anyone's mind, however, since the power of their institutionally inflicted diagnoses was indisputable.

Sociologist Elaine Feder-Alford's ethnomethodological analysis of her own hospitalization (for streptococcal pneumonia) shows that these social processes are still at work in medical institutions. She describes being treated like a "piece of meat," an object, or an "incompetent child" by hospital staff during her illness (2006). She felt dehumanized and powerless, as if they saw her as a diagnosis, rather than as a human being. Medical professionals plunged long syringes into her

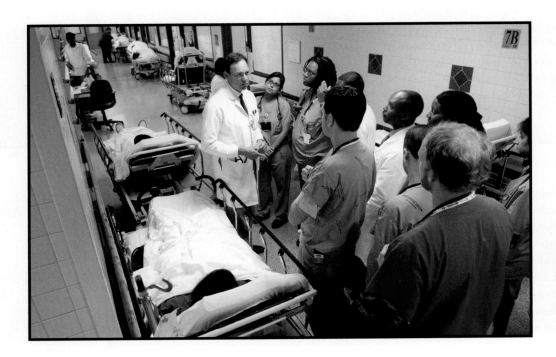

Medicine as a Social Institution Medical students shadow a doctor in an emergency room. The path to becoming a doctor is often regimented and only more rules and regulations apply once becoming a doctor.

Locavores

In an effort to reduce their impact on the planet, and to avoid the negative health consequences of eating products full of preservatives and chemicals, a growing number of people are becoming "locavores," or local eaters. Why eat locally? Most supermarket food has traveled hundreds or even thousands of miles before arriving at your neighborhood store. It takes an inordinate amount of resources to process, package, refrigerate, and ship that food and that long-distance delivery may leave behind an equal trail of waste. Even organic companies can be part of large-scale agribusiness firms and lack environmental consciousness. Does it make sense to send farm-raised eggs from Massachusetts all the way to California? So locavores seek out food sources that are much closer to home. They are willing to give up a certain amount of convenience (like the convenience of the corner store) in order to support local, independent, sustainable farmers and food producers. Many even grow and process their own foods in order to eat fresh, seasonal foods that they believe are better for our health, the health of our communities, and the environment.

One dedicated locavore is Lenae Weichel, who embarked on a year-long campaign to feed her family from sources available within a 100-mile radius of her home in Rockford, Illinois. During the summer, she shopped at farmers' markets and tended her own massive vegetable garden, canning and "putting up" produce for winter storage. She sought out local meat sources (mostly goats from a nearby herd) and visited regional chicken farmers for eggs. She milled her own oat flour, since virtually no wheat is grown in Illinois,

Rooftop Honey Locavores in Brooklyn raise bees on the roof of their apartment.

and she even took up beekeeping so that her family could enjoy the sweetness of honey (no sugar is produced within their local area). Weichel's family had to give up some regular favorites, such as oranges and bananas, and she did allow some products that were technically in violation of their 100-mile rule, such as chocolate and cooking oil, as well as coffee, tea, and spices. Locavore experiments like Weichel's require a lot of work and can seem inconvenient depending on where one lives (and what one has to give up). But many, including Weichel, feel it's worthwhile to eat fresh, healthy, tasty seasonal food, support community farms, and stand up to the "big food" corporations that bring us overprocessed frozen foods and rock-hard pink tomatoes in the middle of winter.

stomach without explaining why and accused her of being an alcoholic because she contracted a liver infection. The institution she inhabited as a patient defined her very differently than she defined herself, creating conflict at just the point in time when she was most ill, and hence least able to defend her definition of herself and the situation. As her condition improved, so did her ability to assert her humanity and negotiate for better treatment within the institutional setting. But her experience left her dismayed at the power of the hospi-

tal to reduce the patient to an object, and led her to promote "proposals that acknowledge patients in a hospital setting as human beings with individual needs and feelings" (p. 618).

Doctor Patient Relations

The institutional context of medicine shapes the interactions between individuals within it. But those interactions also contribute to the shape of the institution itself. Since

Locavores are part of a movement that focuses on food but that is really about the health of people, places, and the planet. Their proposal—that knowing where your food comes from makes a difference in all of these areas—is backed by research and has some vocal advocates in policy circles. One supporter, well-known journalist and University of California, Berkeley professor Michael Pollan, notes that the current corporate food system in the United States is built to "produce cheap calories in great abundance" (Pollan 2008), which may sound like a worthy goal but has in fact been very bad for us over time. It has led to a profusion of fast-food restaurants, heavily processed and chemical-filled food-stuffs, overfarming of corn and soy, and profound dependence on fossil fuels to transport all of this junk around the country. What if, Pollan asks, we "re-regionalize" the food system? What if we make it part of our national food policy to support diversified regional farming operations, sponsor year-round local farmers' markets, and subsidize real, unprocessed, fresh, local food in school lunch, Women, Infants and Children (WIC), and food-stamp programs? How would things be different if you were personally acquainted with the farmer who provided your steak, and if you grew your own salad to go with it?

Locavores like Weichel—and their supporters like Pollan—believe that shortening the food chain will have consequences that will both directly and indirectly improve the health of the nation. The direct consequences would include diets that rely more on fresh fruits and vegetables (often organic) rather than meats, processed products, or fast foods. This, they argue, will lead to a reduction in such health problems as obesity, diabetes, and heart disease. Local farm economies will also benefit from crop diversification and direct connections with local buyers. And since local food has a much shorter trip from farm to table, the indirect consequences would include less reliance on fossil fuels to transport food, and hence a reduction in the health problems associated with global warming (see page 418).

You may be thinking, "Can I really do this? I live in an apartment—I really don't think I can care for my own honeybees!" This is a movement in which we can all participate, even if we can't commit to serious backyard farming or eating local foods 100 percent of the time. For example, learning to cook is a big step toward the individual and global health benefits that locavores tout: improving your cooking skills will help reduce your reliance on processed food and fast food, which is good for your health. And when you eat less processed and fast foods, you are also reducing your carbon footprint, since these foods require enormous amounts of energy to produce and transport, which means that cooking from scratch is also better for the health of the planet (and the other people on it). From there, you can make other small changes: reading labels to find out where your food is from, growing herbs on your kitchen windowsill or tomatoes in pots on your porch, going to farmers' markets in the summer (or year-round, if you're lucky), and steering clear of things like South American strawberries in January. According to locavores, these are attainable steps that can improve your own individual health and the public health as well.

the 1970s, ethnographers, conversation analysts, and other observational sociologists (see Chapters 1 and 2 for a review of these methods) have studied interactions in health-care settings. Studies of doctor-patient interactions have shown that, while we may think that doctors automatically have more status (and hence more power) than patients, this actually has to be established in the interaction—it is not an inevitable feature of medical settings (Pilnick, Hindmarsh, and Teas Gill 2009). Other findings are equally counterintuitive: while you might think that what constitutes good or bad medical news is pretty obvious (say, a benign tumor versus a malignant one), doctors and patients do not always agree on whether a particular diagnosis is pleasant or unpleasant, trivial or serious (Heritage and Stivers 1999; Maynard and Frankel 2006). So the institutional setting does not always exert the type of power we might think it does over the interactions that occur within it. Instead, the people involved in interactions must establish who has power or status, as they must also distinguish good news from bad. It is through such subtle interactional processes that social institutions are constituted, maintained, or changed.

Additional research on medical interaction has moved beyond focusing merely on doctor-patient interaction, acknowledging that there are other important dyads (and triads and groups) in medical institutions that are worth examining. Interactions between patients and speech therapists, pharmacists, or dentists are structured differently and address different issues than those between patients and physicians. And interactions between health-care practitioners (such as doctor-nurse, surgeon-anesthetist, or trainee-teacher), either within or outside of patients' presence, are equally important. So are interactions facilitated by medical technologies, such as ultrasound or x-ray screenings (Pilnick, Hindmarsh, and Teas Gill 2009). One powerful analysis of an emergency services call shows what happens "when words fail," as the dispatcher becomes irritated with the panic-stricken caller, and their clash about what constitutes an appropriate call for help results in the victim's death (Whalen, Zimmerman, and Whalen 1988). Studies such as this one indicate that rules, roles, and other elements of institutional order are emergent and situational. They are not necessarily written down somewhere for the rest of us to follow, but instead are created and maintained (and sometimes distorted) in interaction.

Sick Role and Genetic Risk How might people with a genetic risk of certain diseases, but who show no symptoms, exist in a space between the healthy and the sick?

The Sick Role

Of course, in addition to being shaped in interaction, rules and roles in medical institutions are influenced by external social structures as well. One example of this is the **sick role**. This concept, advanced by functionalist Talcott Parsons, was a way of encapsulating the actions and attitudes that society expects from someone who is ill, as well as the actions and attitudes that a person might expect from other members of society (1951). Being ill is, from a functionalist perspective, a form of deviance. So, as part of the sick role, a patient is exempted from his or her regular responsibilities (such as work, child care, or other, less tangible obligations), and is not held responsible for his or her illness. However, he or she also has a new set of duties as well, which include seeking medical help as part of an earnest effort to recuperate and get back to normal. If the sick person abides by these requirements, he or she will not be treated as deviant by society; but if he or she languishes for too long, doesn't do much to improve his or her condition or seems too interested in staying sick, he or she is likely to experience negative sanctions from society. In this case, it is society's definition of deviance that shapes patients' experiences and their contact with medical institutions.

As you might imagine, the concept of the sick role has changed over the many decades since Parsons first proposed it, in part because of advances in diagnostic technology. For example, with genetic testing, we can now identify people who are at risk of certain diseases before they ever become ill (and indeed, not everyone who is at risk becomes ill). What does this new diagnostic label—"at risk"—mean for the performance of the sick role? Those people with genetic risk factors but no symptoms of disease exist in a liminal space between the healthy and the sick. They inhabit a "potential sick role," with a different set of expectations than in Parson's traditional model. One particularly interesting finding is that those who are in the lowest risk category sometimes try to get themselves recategorized as high risk. This may be because it is easier to determine the expectations for a high-risk patient (regular screenings, warning family members that they might be at risk, etc.) than for a low-risk patient. Research such as this suggests a more dynamic, nuanced definition of the "sick role," and provides for the possibility that the experience of health and illness is not as straightforward as Parsons originally hypothesized.

sick role the actions and attitudes that society expects from someone who is ill

ANALYZING MASS MEDIA AND POPULAR CULTURE

Medicine on Television

From *M*A*S*H* to *St. Elsewhere*, from *Dr. Kildare* to *Doogie Howser* and *House*, Americans have been captivated by television shows about hospitals. Medical dramas and comedies have been some of the most critically acclaimed and highest-rated primetime television shows over the years. Many medical shows have multiple fan sites for discussing every detail of every episode. And because these dramas are so prevalent and popular, they impact America's perception of different diseases and treatments, the roles of patients and medical staff, and the nature and function of the medical institution.

In conventional American television, the medical problems faced by the protagonists are easily solved. There is generally a patient or multiple patients with medical conditions that are triaged, diagnosed, treated, and healed within a single episode. Anyone who has dealt with a serious illness or accident knows that the reality of health care in America is a prolonged process that involves long waits, multiple visits to multiple doctors and different facilities for testing, and complicated interactions with insurance providers. The anger, sadness, and frustration of the patient's experience is generally glossed over in favor of the viewpoint of the medical professionals involved in the process.

For this Data Workshop, you will be using existing sources to do a content analysis comparing the world of TV with the real world (refer to Chapter 2 for a reminder about this research method). Select a scripted medical drama or comedy (not a reality or documentary show), using the examples above or the following list as inspiration:

> *Chicago Hope*
> *ER*
> *Grey's Anatomy*
> *HawthoRNe*
> *House, M.D.*
> *Nurse Jackie*
> *Private Practice*
> *Royal Pains*
> *Scrubs*
> *St. Elsewhere*

Select an episode or scene that deals with a specific disease or condition. Next, look up the epidemiology of that disease or condition. You may start with the internet, but make sure that you are consulting a medical journal site or an organization such as the Mayo Clinic or Centers for Disease Control rather than Wikipedia or WebMD. For example, articles from the *New England Journal of Medicine*, the American Medical Association, or American Association of Family Physicians will yield more thorough and accurate data for the purposes of this exercise.

You may want to consider the following questions when looking at the disease's epidemiology:

- How common is the disease or condition?

- What are the causes of and contributing factors to the disease or condition?

Medicine on Television *Nurse Jackie* and *House* are both medical dramas on TV that portray hospitals in ways that don't often resonate with real life.

- Does it affect different groups (for example, men and women, or patients of different races or ethnicities) in different ways?

- Which groups are more likely to contract the disease or condition? Why?

- Who is involved in the diagnosis and treatment of the disease or condition?

- How expensive, rare, dangerous, and/or available are the treatments, and are there any side effects?

- How rich, lucky, or well-insured would a patient have to be to undergo treatments?

Compare and contrast the show's treatment of the disease or condition to the statistics your research has revealed. How accurate was the portrayal? How does the television show's treatment of illness reflect the average experience of an American patient with the same illness? And most importantly, what kind of effects would any discrepancies have on audiences', patients', or even physicians' perceptions of the disease or condition and its treatment? How does this affect America's understanding of the health-care system?

There are two options for completing this Data Workshop:

- *Option 1 (informal)*: Prepare written notes for in-class discussions. Go over your response to the above questions with other students in small group discussions. Compare and contrast your findings.

- *Option 2 (formal)*: Write a three- to four-page essay detailing your content analysis and comparative work.

Your instructor will let you know which of these options you should complete.

Issues in Medicine and Health Care

The fields of medicine and health care have continued to evolve and advance, often affecting individual lives in profound ways and addressing some of the most pressing problems facing humanity. While much of the progress over the last decades has been tremendously positive, there are still unfulfilled promises and new questions to resolve. In this last section, we examine some of the current trends and future challenges in medicine and health care.

Health Care Reform in the United States

In 1974, when Richard Nixon gave his final State of the Union address before a joint session of Congress, he called for "a new system that makes high-quality health care available to every American in a dignified manner and at a price he can afford" (1974). Nixon had previously described comprehensive health-care reform as the highest priority goal on his unfinished agenda for America (1972). It would remain a national priority that eluded many other politicians for many more decades until March 2010, when the Patient Protection and Affordable Care Act was signed into law. Commonly known as health-care reform (and also somewhat derisively as "Obama Care"), the United States had finally passed legislation that would bring something like universal health-care coverage to all citizens. Yet, the act was not met with universal approval. The bill simultaneously frustrated many longtime advocates of health-care reform by not going far enough, while infuriating others by going too far.

Almost as soon as the legislation was passed, opponents began organizing to repeal the law. Some believe that it will cost too much, raise taxes, hurt businesses, and lead to a government takeover of health care, among other complaints. The midterm elections in November 2010 brought many new members into the U.S. House of Representatives, effectively changing it to a Republican majority that vowed to dismantle the new reforms. A vote in February 2011 to defund the law was largely symbolic, but it reflected some of the controversy and dissension over how to provide health care to Americans (Condon 2011). Opponents have also challenged the constitutionality of the new law, taking their cause to state and federal courts.

Health Care Reform What will be the impact of the health care legislation passed in 2010?

TABLE 14.1	Theory Box: Explanations of Addiction	
	APPROACH TO MEDICINE AND HEALTH	**CASE STUDY: EXPLAINING DRUG AND ALCOHOL ADDICTION**
STRUCTURAL FUNCTIONALISM	Disease is a threat to social order, and sick people cannot fulfill their roles and contribute to society; the health-care system should return patients to health and normal functioning as members of society.	People who become addicted to drugs or alcohol may be responding to strains in the social system and their own lives; they may adapt by retreating or escaping through drugs or alcohol.
CONFLICT THEORY	Health and the health-care system are seen as valuable resources that are unequally shared in society; conflict may arise between different groups seeking access to and control over these resources.	Those in power can define social policy and create laws regarding medicine and health care; people of lower social status are more likely to be scrutinized as problem drinkers or drug addicts, and may be unduly punished.
SYMBOLIC INTERACTIONISM	The meaning of health and illness are dependent upon historical, cultural, and situational contexts. Stigma may be attached to certain disease states and those who suffer from them.	People learn to use alcohol and drugs in social interaction and are influenced by peers and other groups; they may attach different meanings and values to substances and behaviors.

Health-care reform is likely to remain a battleground, and new legislation may alter some aspects of the recent reforms. In the meantime, the legislation will be phased in slowly over ten years, with many important changes coming into effect in 2014.

Two major elements of the bill took effect shortly after it was signed into law in 2010. The first focused on increasing coverage for children and young adults: insurance companies must now allow children to remain on their parents' insurance plan through age twenty-six, rather than the previous limits of age twenty-one or after college graduation. Also, insurance companies are no longer allowed to deny coverage to children with pre-existing conditions (starting in 2014, no one will be denied coverage for this reason). The second element of the bill closed loopholes that allowed insurance companies to deny or limit coverage to people who became ill. Insurers are no longer allowed to impose lifetime spending caps—allotting a certain amount of money for a given patient over that patient's lifetime—a limit surpassed by many who have serious illnesses. Additionally, the new law bans **rescission**—canceling coverage only after a person gets sick. The new law allows an insurance company to act in the case of fraud, but not simply to look for technicalities that would allow them to cancel a policyholder's coverage when they need it most.

In the long term, the bill is designed to cover 32 million currently uninsured people. Part of this extended coverage will be achieved through insurance reforms (like the ones described above), but one of the most important new provisions will be the creation of state-run insurance exchange systems to cover the unemployed, self-employed, and any-

one else without insurance. Other mandates will require more people to buy into coverage plans. There will be some exceptions for the poor, and subsidies for other low-income individuals and families to help in purchasing insurance. Companies that employ more than fifty people will also have to provide health insurance or suffer fines, but new small-business exchanges will be created to help companies to comply. The bill will also provide changes in Medicare for seniors (closing the "donut-hole" for prescription drug coverage) and expand Medicaid by opening it up to all adults of working age, not just the disabled or pregnant (The White House 2011).

Despite these changes, even the most optimistic estimates suggest that these reforms will cover only 95 percent of all American citizens. The nonpartisan Congressional Budget Office estimates that the bill will cost $940 billion over ten years, but that it will cut the federal budget deficit by $130 billion over that same time period (Condon 2010). The plan has a number of funding sources, including increases in taxes on investment income for households making more than $250,000 a year, a tax on high-end insurance plans (sometimes referred to as "Cadillac plans"), and a 10 percent tax on indoor tanning (Johnson and Nolen 2010).

Until 2010, the United States was the last wealthy, industrialized nation in the world without some form of universal health coverage for its citizens. Although there may be challenges in the future that change some aspects of the new law, it undeniably constitutes a sweeping overhaul of America's health-care system.

> **rescission** the practice by insurance companies of canceling coverage only after a person gets sick

On the Job

Cultural Competence in Health Professions

Lia Lee was a baby when her epileptic seizures began. In 1985, when she was three years old, she had an especially serious attack, and her parents, Hmong immigrants living in California's Central Valley, brought her to the Merced County Medical Center for treatment. What happened to Lia, her family, and her doctors during the next two years is the subject of journalist Anne Fadiman's 1998 book *The Spirit Catches You and You Fall Down*.

The book's title refers to the way the Hmong, a Southeast Asian ethnic group, see Lia's affliction. Indeed, their understanding of all health problems involves malevolent attempts by evil spirits, known as *dabs*, to meddle with human souls. The differences between Hmong understandings of epilepsy and its treatment and those of the Western medical establishment created the conflict in which Lia Lee was trapped.

The details of Lia's case are heart-wrenching: both her parents and her doctors tried their best to heal her. But because of cultural and language differences, they were unable to understand each other's perspective. They became suspicious and mistrustful of each other, which made collaboration even harder. The doctors firmly believed in Western biomedical approaches to epilepsy—they thought that if the Lees gave Lia the right medicines at the right times, she would be fine. Meanwhile, the Lees firmly believed that the *dab* had Lia's soul in its grip, and that traditional Hmong procedures (such as shamanic healing ceremonies) should be part of her treatment.

Both parties saw the other side's actions as counterproductive; they resisted cooperating because they each believed the other's approach would make Lia's condition worse. Caught in this standoff between Western medicine and Hmong tradition, Lia did get worse, eventually suffering "The Big One," a seizure that left her with severe and permanent brain damage. Today, Lia lingers in a vegetative state, tended by her family and representing failure to the team of medical professionals who treated her.

Lia Lee's case has been the touchstone for a number of recent attempts to increase the cultural awareness of healthcare professionals, with the hopes of avoiding future cases like hers. This movement has coined the term **cultural competence** to describe the concept of acknowledging and incorporating a patient's cultural background as part of the treatment process. The recognition that patients' beliefs shape their approach to health care may not seem like news to sociology majors, but the cultural competence movement for health professionals (including doctors, nurses, medical social workers, pharmacists, and physical therapists) is less than fifteen years old.

For example, the Association of American Medical Colleges is among the many organizations that have instituted cultural competence initiatives. The AAMC has produced a set of curriculum recommendations for medical schools, and provides evaluation tools for assessing the impact of cultural

Complementary and Alternative Medicine

In all likelihood, you or someone you know has participated in some form of alternative medicine. If you've ever tried deep-breathing for relaxation or a nutritional supplement to gain or lose weight, or an herbal remedy for a cold, if you've gone to a chiropractor, had a massage, or taken a yoga class, then you've made use of alternative medicine. Complementary or alternative medicine (CAM) is a group of medical treatments, practices, and products that includes acupuncture, homeopathy, hypnosis, and meditation, as well as traditional healers like shamans and movement therapies like Pilates. **Complementary medicine** can be used in conjunction with conventional Western medicine, whereas **alternative medicine** is used instead of it. Some of these practices or products are ancient (like acupuncture or herbs), while others are only new to the Western world—or arose in the past few decades (like biofeedback and "super food" formulas).

Complementary and alternative medicine has generated both enthusiasts and critics. Some skeptics call this type of medicine "quackery," nothing more than modern-day "snake

cultural competence to describe the concept of acknowledging and incorporating a patient's cultural background as part of the treatment process; the recognition that patients' beliefs shape their approach to health care

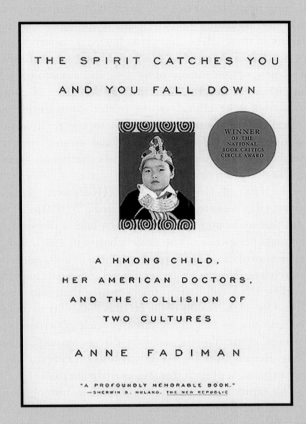

THE SPIRIT CATCHES YOU

AND YOU FALL DOWN

WINNER
OF THE
NATIONAL
BOOK CRITICS
CIRCLE AWARD

A HMONG CHILD,

HER AMERICAN DOCTORS,

AND THE COLLISION OF

TWO CULTURES

ANNE FADIMAN

"A PROFOUNDLY MEMORABLE BOOK."
—SHERWIN B. NULAND, THE NEW REPUBLIC

of cultural knowledge and beliefs—their patients' and their own—in health-care encounters, and to provide them with strategies for effective diagnosis, treatment, and interaction in cross-cultural encounters.

As part of the AAMC's plan, students are encouraged to examine their own cultural backgrounds, assumptions, and biases, and to exercise nonjudgment when asking questions and listening to patients discuss their own health beliefs. They are trained to respect patients' diverse ideas about health and illness, to recognize when to use interpreters, and even to collaborate with traditional healers from their patients' cultures. They are also urged to appreciate the power imbalances between doctors and patients, and to work to eliminate racism and stereotyping from health-care practices.

Students often assume that they should major in a "hard" science if they want to go into a health profession, particularly a life science such as biology. But given the rising importance of cultural competence in health professions, this may not be the ideal foundation. A student with a social science major, like sociology, may be even better prepared for working in the medical field than a biologist. An understanding of such issues as ethnocentrism, inequality, and the importance of culture in the lives of individuals means that students of sociology are already ahead of bio majors when it comes to issues of cultural competence in the practice of medicine.

competency initiatives once they are in place (2005). The goal is to train new physicians to recognize the importance

oil" that promotes false hopes to a vulnerable public. Others who may have found few satisfactory answers within the medical establishment become staunch believers in the benefits of various CAM treatments. Indeed, some CAM practices and practitioners are slowly gaining legitimacy (and popularity), and **integrative medicine** is a burgeoning part of the field that combines conventional medicine with particular CAM practices that have proven most safe and effective. Scientific studies of CAM practices lag behind those done on conventional medicine, and more evidence is needed about whether and how the great variety of CAM practices work and on which patients with what conditions. It's possible that some forms of alternative medicine may one day

prove better at treating some conditions than conventional medicine. But it is still rare for insurers to cover alternative medicine, so patients currently seeking those treatments typically have to pay out of pocket.

The increasing number of people who have turned to CAM practices is remarkable. In the United States, over 38 percent of adults

complementary medicine a group of medical treatments, practices, and products that can be used in conjunction with conventional Western medicine

alternative medicine a group of medical treatments, practices, and products that are used instead of conventional Western medicine

integrative medicine the combination of conventional medicine with complementary practices and treatments that have proven to be safe and effective

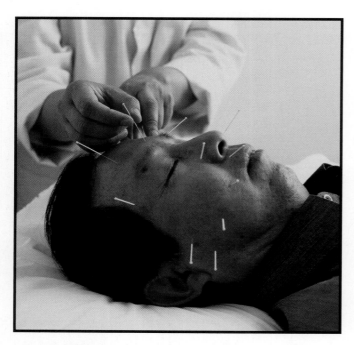

Alternative Medicine A man receives acupuncture treatment, an ancient medical practice that is sometimes used instead of conventional Western medicine.

and nearly 12 percent of children used one or more forms of CAM within the past year (Barnes, Bloom, and Nahin 2008). Celebrities and professional athletes often attribute successful recoveries from illnesses or injuries to CAM therapies. Both the New York Yankees and the San Francisco Giants employ a "staff acupuncturist" (Healthcmi .com 2010), and NBA star Grant Hill said in a recent interview, "Chiropractors, massage therapists, acupuncture, if it makes me feel good and it's legal, then I'm gonna do it. All of that stuff aids and helps with recovery, so I've been willing to incorporate it into my preparation." (Blinebury 2010).

The largest category of CAM users is women with higher levels of education and income. Natural supplements (nonvitamin products such as fish oil/omega 3, glucosamine, echinacea, flaxseed, and ginseng), deep breathing, meditation, chiropractic, yoga, and massage are some of the most frequently used forms of CAM. Americans are most likely to seek these treatments for neck, back, joint, and headache pain, but may also use them for anxiety, high cholesterol, head and chest colds, and insomnia. In 2007, American adults spent close to $34 billion on CAM treatments: two-thirds on self-care CAM products, classes, and materials; and one-third on visits to CAM practitioners. That amounts to just more than 11 percent of the total out-of-pocket U.S. spending on all forms of health care (Nahin et al. 2009).

bioethics the study of controversial moral or ethical issues related to scientific and medical advancements

eugenics an attempt to selectively manipulate the gene pool in order to produce and "improve" human beings through medical science

Medical Technology and Bioethics

Medical science continues to progress at a rapid pace, bringing new discoveries and producing innovations that are bound to change human health in the future. We tend to think of these advancements as having a uniformly positive impact on society, but this is not always true. In many cases, new advancements bring new and sometimes troubling issues to the fore. **Bioethics** is the study of controversial moral or ethical issues related to scientific and medical advancements. Among hot topics are questions about extending life through artificial means, stem cell research, the use of animals in medical experiments, or even the idea of human cloning.

The Human Genome Project (HGP) is a scientific endeavor that seeks to identify and map the 20,000 to 25,000 genes that make up human DNA from both a physical and functional perspective. The project began in 1990, and the first version of the genome was completed in 2003, although research based on the project continues. Scientists hope that decoding DNA will help to uncover how the human body works. One of the results of the HGP is the ability to identify predisposition to hereditary diseases such as certain types of cancer, cystic fibrosis, and liver disease through genetic testing. Results from the HGP may also provide the key to the management of such diseases as Alzheimer's.

The rapid advancement of medical technologies like the HGP also brings numerous ethical issues to the table. One of the more controversial aspects of these advances is genetic testing in utero and at birth. For example, preimplantation genetic diagnosis allows doctors to test DNA samples from embryos that are grown in vitro. These tests can tell whether or not a baby will be born with certain disorders and allow for the selection of only certain embryos for implantation. Genetic testing in utero can inform parents of possible genetic mutations in the embryo, potentially allowing parents to choose whether or not to have a disabled child. There are ethical concerns about genetic testing becoming a modern-day form of **eugenics**, in which the human gene pool is "improved" through science.

In cases where genetic testing reveals future susceptibility to disease for otherwise healthy individuals, there are ethical issues about the use of the genetic profiles. Can a person be stigmatized because of their genetic profile? Will insurance companies be able to deny coverage or even treatment of pre-existing conditions that can now be revealed through genetic testing? Certainly, medical technology is advancing rapidly enough to cause a cultural lag in the legal, ethical, and social issues surrounding its use.

Closing Comments

Concerns about health and illness are a constant part of human existence. As individuals we will each face the pleasures and difficulties of living in a physical body that is further affected by our lifestyles and life chances. A sociological approach is especially helpful in allowing us to understand the links between social structures and processes and health outcomes. We recognize that health is not merely a biological state, but another important area of human life affected by social institutions and social inequalities. Medicine and health care are rapidly advancing, and as a result we may someday live longer and healthier lives, but we will always be shaped by the social contexts in which our lives take place. Science may soon discover new treatments for old diseases, but it is just as likely that we will have to continue dealing with current and as yet unknown challenges to our health in the future. It is certain that there will be cultural changes in our values and beliefs that bring about new understandings and practices regarding the relationship between society and the health of people and the planet.

ⓈNeed Help Studying?

wwnorton.com/studyspace

Visit StudySpace to access free review materials such as:

- **Vocabulary Flashcards**
- **Diagnostic Review Quizzes**
- **Study Outlines**

QUESTIONS FOR REVIEW

1. What kinds of illnesses have you observed most often in yourself or in family members or close friends? What conditions are most or least common? What approach to treatment tends to be used in different cases? Could preventive health measures alleviate some proportion of the illnesses you see?

2. What do you think about the process by which such things as hyperactivity or obesity are now seen as medical conditions as opposed to behavioral problems? Can you think of other behaviors or conditions that are becoming "medicalized"? Should we consider video game or internet addiction as a medical condition?

3. What are some of the merits or deficits of "concierge" medicine? Do you believe that health care was better back in the days when doctors knew their patients well and still made house calls? Think about the last time you saw a doctor. How long was the wait? How much time did the doctor spend in the exam room with you? Do you feel it is possible for patients to have meaningful relationships with their doctors?

4. What kind of food would be available to you if you had to shop in a neighborhood that was considered a "food desert"? Describe the kind of food items bought from a convenience or liquor store that could compose a menu. Can you have a healthy diet if you eat exclusively at fast-food chains?

5. What kinds of food might you eat as a locavore? Consider your particular geographic region. What is grown nearby that you don't eat now, but could? What would you have to give up that you currently eat, but that is produced far away? Do you think your diet would be more healthy as a locavore, or less so? What kinds of social changes might result from many more people eating from local sources?

6. Think about the last time you were ill or injured. Describe what it was like to be cast into the "sick role." What kind of special privileges or excuses from obligations could you claim during the time you were sick? What kind of sympathy or special care did you receive? What kind of expectations did others have about you taking care of yourself as well?

7. Do you believe that the U.S. health-care reforms of 2010 will be successful in bringing comprehensive medical coverage to more Americans? Do you believe that health care is a basic right that should be provided to all citizens, or is it a privilege that individuals must earn? What are some of the benefits included in universal health-care systems in such countries as France, Canada, and Britain?

8. Have you made use of any complementary or alternative medicine? For what kinds of conditions or cases do you think that CAM practices might be more or less effective than conventional medicine? Are you skeptical about the efficacy or safety of new CAM practices and treatments? Or do you think that more research should be devoted to investigating practices and treatments outside the medical mainstream?

9. As science and medicine continue to advance, what kind of ethical issues will arise in the future? Is all medical progress positive, or are there some areas of research that should be forbidden? Do you agree that bioethics should be taught to all students in the medical sciences?

SUGGESTIONS FOR FURTHER EXPLORATION

And the Band Played On. 2001. Directed by Roger Spotiswoode. HBO Pictures. Watch the film based on the book by journalist Randy Shilts who chronicled the early days of the

And the Band Played On

AIDS crisis. Shilts documents the beginning of what would later become a worldwide pandemic. Sociologists working at the CDC (among others) were critical in discovering the epidemiology of the disease. The film shows the connection between the social, medical, and political forces that shaped the response to AIDS.

The Cosby Show. Watch an episode from 1992 called the "The Price is Wrong," which is available on YouTube. The plot focuses on the problem of food deserts that were already beginning to emerge in urban, inner-city neighborhoods. This episode highlights the practice by some supermarket chains to sell inferior goods (dented cans and wilted lettuce) at an inflated price in certain stores located in poorer neighborhoods. The characters organize to protest the supermarket chain to make them change this practice. www.youtube.com/watch?v=CqW1d2URNRE

Goldberg, Robert. 2010. *Tabloid Medicine: How the Internet is Being Used to Highjack Medical Science for Fear and Profit.* Kaplan Publishing. This medical doctor questions the consequences of having easy access to medical information on the internet. While this has empowered some patients, Goldberg is alarmed by the potential for hype, misinformation, and commercial interests to persuade naïve readers into using questionable measures to treat medical problems.

Gray, Stevens. "Urban Deserts: Fresh-Food-Free Zones." Time Video. Watch this CBS News video clip about food deserts and what one grocer in Chicago is doing to bring more fresh fruits and vegetables, dairy, and meats to predominantly African American and Latino shoppers in this Southside neighborhood. www.time.com/time/video/player/0,32068,24222955001_1900870,00.html

Kingsolver, Barbara, Camille Kingsolver, and Steven L. Hopp. 2007. *Animal, Vegetable, Miracle: A Year of Food Life.* HarperCollins. Best-selling novelist and poet Barbara Kingsolver wrote this nonfiction book documenting the year in which her family procured as much of their food as possible from

neighboring farms and their own backyard. Kingsolver also provides a web site with many useful resources for others interested in becoming locavores. www.animalvegetablemiracle.com/

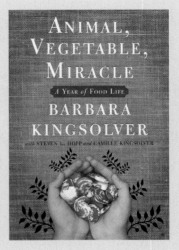

Sicko. 2007. Dir. Michael Moore. Weinstein Company. This documentary, by successful and controversial filmmaker Michael Moore, was nominated for an Academy Award. The film examines health care in the United States, and is especially critical of the health insurance and pharmaceutical industries. The film features many poignant personal (and sometimes humorous) stories, and compares the for-profit U.S. system with the universal health care in Canada, the United Kingdom, France, and Cuba.

Super Size Me. 2004. Dir. Morgan Spurlock. Sony Pictures. See this documentary film that won the Best Director Award at the Sundance Film Festival for Morgan Spurlock, who is also its star. The film documents an experiment by Spurlock to see what happens to his health if he eats nothing but fast food from McDonald's for every meal for thirty days in a row. Both funny and disturbing, the negative impacts from his diet quickly appear.

Weichel, Lenae. Read more about the story of the locavore who embarked on a year-long campaign to feed her family from sources available within a 100-mile radius of her home in Rockford, Illinois. Her blog can be found at: www.eatnearrockford.blogspot.com.

Women's Health or *Men's Health* magazines. Pick up a copy or access some of the online content from their web sites: www.womenshealthmag.com/, www.menshealth.com/.

Visit the web sites for one or more of the twenty-seven institutes, centers, and offices that make up the National Institutes for Health. For instance, learn more from the National Center for Complementary and Alternative Medicine web site at: http://nccam.nih.gov/, or check out the National Human Genome Project web site at: www.genome.gov

wwnorton.com/studyspace

WANT TO LEARN MORE?

VISIT STUDYSPACE

wwnorton.com/studyspace

Ⓢ **Visit StudySpace** to find these additional resources:

- **Video clips** from Dalton Conley's interviews with social scientists.
- **"Sociology in the News"** lets you read the latest media coverage about sociology.
- **Watch "Sociology in Practice"** video clips from indie documentaries (*by using the password on the inside front cover of your book*).

PART V

Creating Social Change and Envisioning the Future

as Vegas—Sin City, Entertainment Capital of the World, home of glitz, glitter, and gambling; fantasy mecca, international tourist destination where fortunes and marriages are made and broken; populated by showgirls, gangsters, high-rollers, and Elvis impersonators. This is the "Hollywood Vegas" according to Mark Gottdiener, Claudia C. Collins, and David R. Dickens. Their book, *Las Vegas: The Social Production of an All-American City* (1999), chronicles the development of Las Vegas from its days as a pit stop for Spanish explorers in the early 1800s to the neon marvel it has become.

Gottdiener, Collins, and Dickens analyze the Hollywood Vegas, but they argue that there is another Las Vegas as well, where regular people live, work, and go to school, the supermarket, and the movies. What is the real Las Vegas like? It's big, it's growing fast, and its demographic, economic, and cultural trends represent the social changes taking place in many cities across the country—even those without pulsating neon or posh casinos.

The 2000 Census confirmed that Las Vegas was the fastest growing metropolitan area in the United States—its population increased 83 percent during the 1990s and continued to grow into the twenty-first century, with the Clark County Metro Area (of which Las Vegas is a part) hitting the 2 million mark in 2007. Las Vegas's population boom started to taper off in 2008, the county population having reached about 2 million (Access Clark County 2009). The 2010 census showed a continued population decline in this once burgeoning locale (El Nasser 2010).

People flocked to Las Vegas because of its booming employment and housing market, and they came from all over the country and the world. A large proportion of newcomers to Las Vegas were former residents of California, seeking refuge from skyrocketing housing prices and a tight job market. Another major segment of the Las Vegas population boom was senior citizens, who now make up 25 percent of the populace. Retirees are valued consumers who spend money on new homes and other items when they arrive in the city; however, as they age, they may create a strain on local health-care resources. Another major population segment is Hispanic Americans, who make up almost 25 percent of Las Vegas's population. They are the fastest growing ethnic group in southern Nevada, and they, too, are valued consumers, courted by advertisers in both English- and Spanish-language media. In addition, the area has a growing population of undocumented Hispanic immigrants, who work at casinos, hotels, and resorts and whose labor supports the region's biggest industry, tourism.

In addition to these demographic trends, Las Vegas is also an economic trendsetter, for better or worse. Its employment rates were consistently high because of the large number of

service jobs in the casino, resort, and tourist industries, but these jobs generally offer low pay and few benefits. There is also other work to do in Las Vegas. Major industries include construction and real estate sales (though these industries have been hit hard by the recent recession), banking, and other financial services, often related to the casino industry (p. 112). As the economy diversifies, the population grows— and as the population grows, more services and other work become necessary. Cards must be dealt, meals must be cooked, hotel rooms must be cleaned, children must be taught, cars must be repaired, and houses must be built, sold, and financed. However, if a population begins to decline, the market for all those goods and services diminishes, and jobs of all sorts become harder to find.

Las Vegas's housing boom began in the 1970s with the advent of master-planned communities. These residential developments, often built around golf courses, were move-in-ready when the economy began growing and diversifying in the 1980s, and more middle-class families began moving into the city. Master-planned suburbs continue to sprout in and around Las Vegas, filling Clark County with people and all the things they use, like houses, schools, stores, roads, and cars. Recently, though, this boom has gone bust, with Las Vegas holding one of the highest real estate foreclosure rates in the country (*International Business Times* 2008). Whatever takes place in the larger U.S. real estate market happens even more spectacularly in Las Vegas.

Environmental issues are important to life in the real Las Vegas, which is located in a desert ecosystem where water is scarce and rainfall is infrequent. Hundreds of thousands of people live in this ecosystem, in sprawling suburban housing developments. Lawns, pools, and golf courses require billions of gallons of water that the immediate environment does not provide, yet growth continues. Las Vegas competes with several other arid states, including California, for water resources. Water from the Colorado River is pumped in at great expense from Lake Mead to fill pools and water lawns, as well as for household use. Lake Mead is also the destination for all of Las Vegas's out-going effluent—treated sewage and runoff full of lawn chemicals. These environmental toxins cycle back into the drinking water consumed by the area's residents.

Water isn't the only environmental issue that Las Vegas faces. Atomic test sites from the 1950s and '60s, located in the Mojave Desert, were once in the middle of nowhere—but suburban sprawl continues to draw closer to these areas. The same is true of a number of desert chemical plants in areas that are also being encroached upon by residential development. Recently, environmental activists have successfully prohibited nuclear waste transport and dumping in the Las Vegas area.

A fluctuating population; an economy dominated by service industry work; a natural environment strained to its limits by desert sprawl—this is the real Las Vegas. Add the glittery, neon-lit Hollywood fantasy town, and you have a vanguard city for the twenty-first century. Economic, environmental, and demographic trends that already appear in Las Vegas—including the booms and busts of the larger economy—will become increasingly visible in other U.S. cities.

Cultural and social changes occurring in Las Vegas may also be visible where you live—including the legalization of gambling. While Las Vegas was once the center of a gambling industry dominated by organized crime, legal casinos are now operated all over the country by groups of all sorts,

including state governments and Native American tribes. Gambling boats float on many Midwestern lakes and rivers, and resort casinos continue to spring up on Indian reservations in almost half the U.S. states.

Las Vegas is also the site of unusually powerful labor unions, which represent many of the service employees—cooks, waiters, musicians, hotel employees—whose work keeps the city running. At a time when union membership is down in the rest of the country, Las Vegas is a strong union city—ironically located in Nevada, a right-to-work state. Union laborers tend to have higher wages and benefits than nonunion workers because of the power of collective bargaining. The resurgence of union membership in Las Vegas's service industries may inspire workers in other cities with service- and tourism-dominated economies.

Gottdiener and his co-authors argue that "in many ways Las Vegas represents, though often in exaggerated form, several important trends in contemporary American society as a whole" (p. xi). In Part V, we will examine many of those trends from a sociological perspective as part of our focus on social change. In Chapter 15, we will examine a variety of demographic, economic, and environmental trends, such as suburbanization, migration, and aging. And we will consider processes of cultural and social change, such as activism by labor unions and environmentalists, in Chapter 16. As you read these chapters, think about your own city or town and the trends you have observed close to home. Also, think about the changes you would like to see in your surroundings; a sociological perspective can help you strategize to make those changes happen. In any case, keep an eye on Las Vegas for changes yet to come—because, as Gottdiener, Collins, and Dickens demonstrate, what happens in Vegas doesn't necessarily stay in Vegas!

CHAPTER 15 City and Country

The Social World and the Natural World

Chris McCandless was the picture of success. The son of upper-middle class professionals in Washington, D.C., he had just graduated from Emory University in Atlanta and was headed for law school. Nonetheless, he felt constrained and even betrayed by a society that perpetuated poverty and inequality and often seemed to care so little for its individual members. He wanted to experience the personal freedom of being untethered by obligations to family, school, and work—even though that meant letting go of the emotional and material security they provide.

In the summer of 1990, Chris headed for the wilderness, which he saw as pure and untainted while he saw society as corrupt and damaged. Chris moved in and out of the social world during the next two years; he lived in the wilderness successfully for long stretches of time but always had to come back to civilization for supplies, to earn a little money, and to make some human connections. After spending months alone in the deserts of the Southwest, he arrived in Bullhead City, Arizona, and took a job at McDonald's. He was leather-skinned and malnourished, had no money or belongings, and had lost his car in a flash flood—but he was still alive, and after a brief stint in what he considered the most sinister of all social institutions (the fast-food industry) he disappeared back into nature again, this time headed to the great unspoiled expanses of Alaska.

Chris did a lot of reading in preparation for his journey, and he seemed able to endure the physical and emotional hardships of being alone in the wilderness for months at a time. His journal entries reveal that he often felt exhilarated and truly believed that his was the superior way of life. But Chris's story did not end happily. Two years after he left Atlanta, his body was found on the Alaskan tundra many miles outside Fairbanks by a group of moose hunters. In his book *Into the Wild*, John Krakauer reconstructed Chris's journey through diaries and interviews. Krakauer determined that while living on the tundra for four months alone, Chris had inadvertently eaten something that may have poisoned him. Realizing how sick he was, he began to yearn for the saving presence of other humans—for both assistance and companionship. At the very end, Chris's journal entries reveal a desire to return to the social world and a recognition of the protection society offers from the rigors of nature. Chris did not get to reenter society with his newfound insight, but perhaps we can learn more about our own relationship to both the natural and the social worlds from his story.

HOW TO READ THIS CHAPTER

This chapter covers three big and deeply connected topics in sociology: population, urbanization, and the environment. To this point, we have focused mostly on society, on people and their effect on each other. But humans live in a natural as well as a social world, and their environment is another key factor in their lives. They are affected by and have a profound effect on the planet Earth. The number of humans who live on the planet has more than tripled in just the past fifty years, from 2 billion to 7 billion in late 2011. Population studies show that an ever greater portion of people are settling into large, sprawling cities—a trend called urbanization. Growing populations and increased urbanization create new demands and pressures on the global environment as more natural resources are consumed and more pollution and waste are produced, and this has a profound effect on the earth and its inhabitants.

Population

If we want to understand the relationship between the social world and the natural world, we must examine human population. The next sections look at how sociologists study population and its related issues. To paraphrase sociologist Samuel Preston, the study of population has something for everyone: the confrontations of nature and civilization; the dramas of sex and death, politics and war; and the tensions between self-interest and altruism.

demography study of the size, composition, distribution, and changes in human population

fertility rate a measure of population growth through reproduction; often expressed as the average number of births per 1,000 people in the total population or the average number of children a woman would be expected to have

mortality rate a measure of the decrease in population due to deaths; often expressed as the number of deaths expected per 1,000 people per year in a particular population

infant mortality average number of infant deaths per 1,000 live births in a particular population

life expectancy average age to which people in a particular population live

Demography

Demography is the study of the size, composition, distribution, and changes in human population. Sociologists and others who study population are called demographers. Demography is essentially a macro-level, quantitative approach to society, but it is more than just simply counting heads. Population dynamics are influenced not only by biological factors such as births and deaths but also by sociological factors such as cultural values, religious beliefs, and political and economic systems. People are not just animals who reproduce by instinct, but are subject to structural constraints as well as individual agency, all of which affect their behavior and ultimately the world in which they live.

The United States government has long been interested in keeping track of those residing within its geographic boundaries. The U.S. Census Bureau, a part of the Department of Commerce, conducts regular studies of the population, going back to the first such attempt in 1790. Each new decade, census takers try to contact every person living in the country. Surveys, either short or long form, are sent to every household to gather a range of demographic information from the size and age of family members to their gender, education level, income, and ethnic background. Other countries are less systematic at gathering data, so many statistics that refer to global population are necessarily based on scientific estimates.

Three basic demographic variables are crucial to understanding population dynamics. The first is **fertility rate**—the average number of births per 1,000 people in the total population. The total fertility rate is the average number of children a woman would be expected to have during her childbearing years. In 2010 the total fertility rate in the United States was approximately 2.06. Fertility rates vary across the globe, with some of the highest rates in sub-Saharan Africa, with Niger at 7.68, and some of the lowest in Southeast Asia, with Macau at 0.91.

The next demographic variable is **mortality rate** (or death rate)—the number of deaths that can be expected per 1,000 people per year. This statistic is usually modified by other factors, so the mortality rate within a particular country varies within different age, sex, ethnic, and regional groups. A related concept is **infant mortality** rate, or the average number of deaths per 1,000 live births. In 2010, the U.S. death rate was approximately 8.38 and the infant mortality rate was 6.14. Mortality and infant mortality rates vary across the globe, some of the highest being in African countries, with a death rate 23.74 in Angola and infant mortality rate of 178.13. Some of the lowest mortality rates are found in wealthier Middle Eastern countries such as the United Arab Emirates with 2.08, and some of the lowest infant mortality rates are found in Asian countries such as Singapore with 2.32.

Another related concept is **life expectancy**, or the average age to which a person can expect to live. Here, too, other

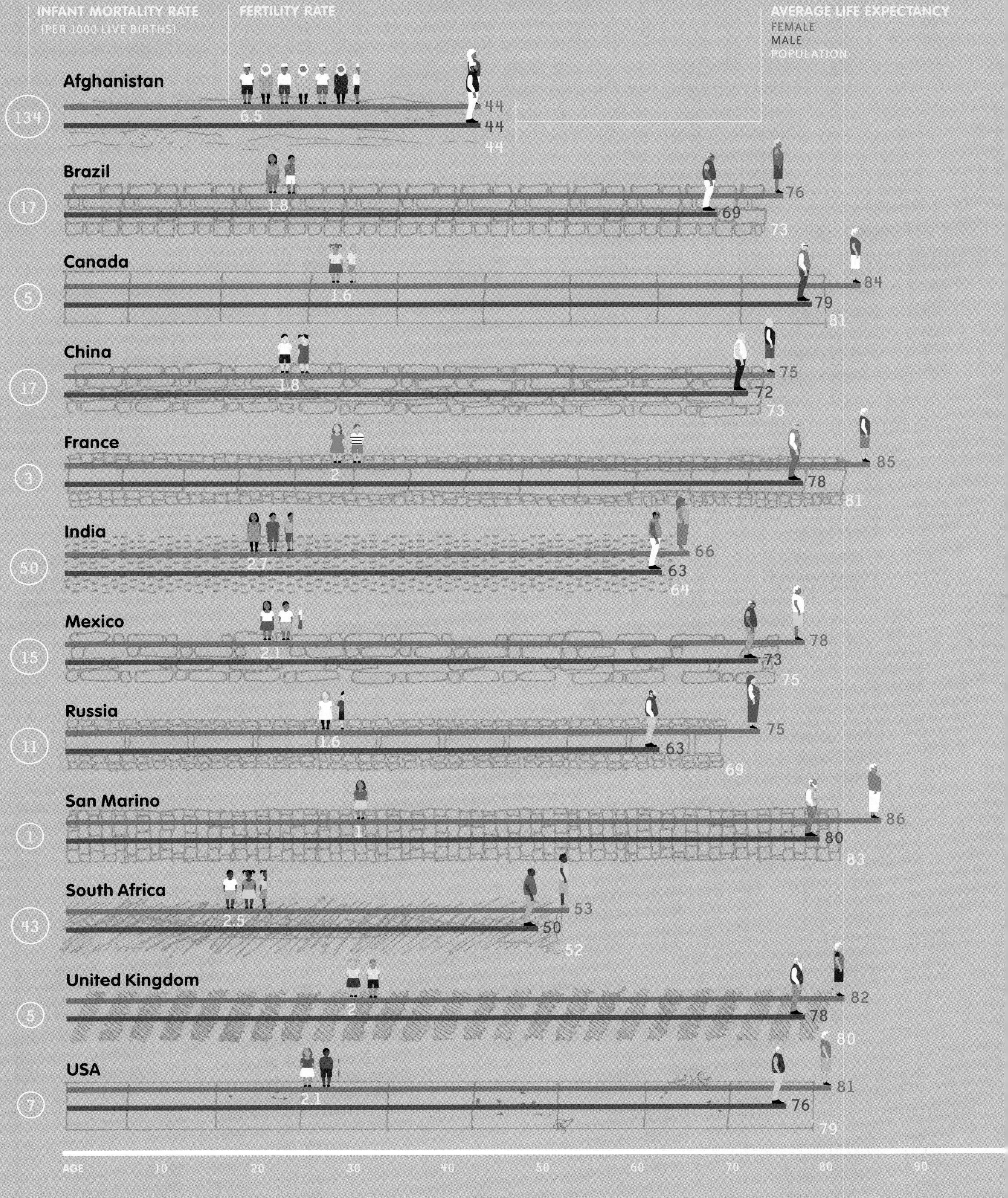

INFANT MORTALITY RATE
(PER 1000 LIVE BIRTHS)

FERTILITY RATE

AVERAGE LIFE EXPECTANCY
FEMALE
MALE
POPULATION

Afghanistan
134
6.5
44
44
44

Brazil
17
1.8
76
69
73

Canada
5
1.6
84
79
81

China
17
1.8
75
72
73

France
3
2
85
78
81

India
50
2.7
66
63
64

Mexico
15
2.1
78
73
75

Russia
11
1.6
75
63
69

San Marino
1
1
86
80
83

South Africa
43
2.5
53
50
52

United Kingdom
5
2
82
78
80

USA
7
2.1
81
76
79

AGE   10   20   30   40   50   60   70   80   90

SOURCE: WORLD BANK 2011A.

Life span or **longevity** the uppermost age to which a person can potentially live

migration movement of people from one geographic area to another for the purpose of resettling

immigration entering one country from another to take up permanent residence

emigration leaving one country to live permanently in another

internal migration movement of a population within a country

net migration net effect of immigration and emigration on an area's population in a given time period; expressed as an increase or decrease

factors are involved, so life expectancy of people within a particular country varies by sex, ethnicity, and social class. In general, life expectancy rose dramatically in the twentieth century. In 2010, life expectancy in the United States on average was approximately 78.24 years of age; the average for men was 75.78, while for women it was 80.81. Life expectancy also varies greatly across the globe, with some of the highest averages in wealthier nations like Monaco at over eighty-nine, and some of the lowest in African countries like Angola at approximately thirty-eight years—in large part because of the AIDS epidemic. **Life span**, or **longevity**, has also increased dramatically—again, depending on where you live. More people around the globe are living past 100 years of age. The current record for oldest living person at 122 years has been reached several times and may soon be surpassed.

The last demographic variable that we will consider is **migration**—the movement of people from one geographic area to another for the purposes of resettling. Migrations have occurred throughout human history and have played an important part in populating the planet. As a demographic variable, migration neither adds to nor subtracts from the total number of people on the planet; it simply refers to their relocation from place to place. Related concepts are **immigration** and **emigration**. Immigrants are those people coming into a country or region to which they are not native. Emigrants are those departing from a country or region with the intention of settling permanently elsewhere. **Internal migration** refers to patterns within a country, where the movement is generally from rural to urban areas. The **net migration** for any country is the difference between the number of persons entering and leaving a country during the year per 1,000 persons. In 2010, the net migration for the United States was 4.25, which means that after adjusting for the people who emigrated, there was a total of 4.25 persons per 1,000 who immigrated. In general, worldwide migration patterns show that people are moving from least industrialized to most industrialized countries. There are often other economic or political reasons for migration, with refugees pouring in and out of some countries. Countries with the highest net migration rates include Afghanistan and Singa-

pore, while those with the lowest rates include Greenland and American Samoa.

The study of population dynamics involves the interplay among the three sources of population change: fertility, mortality, and migration. These variables are used to construct current population models and future projections. We can apply demographic variables to the global population or to a population within a particular region or country.

If we focus on the United States, we could track several interesting population trends. The U.S. is currently the third-most populous nation after China and India, with more than 308 million people. It is also the fastest growing industrialized nation. According to the Census Bureau, between 2000 and 2030 the net population change will be most evident in three states—California, Texas, and Florida. They will account for nearly 46 percent of the nation's population growth. Projected immigration during that period will be highest in California (8.7 million), New York (3.8 million), and Florida (1.8 million). The fastest growing states will be Nevada with a 114.3 percent increase in population, followed by Arizona at 108.8 percent and Florida with 79.5 percent. A few states will even see shrinking populations; the District of Columbia will decrease by 24.2 percent, North Dakota by 5.5 percent, and West Virginia by 4.9 percent. Some of this change will be internal migration among the states, with people moving to the "sunbelt" states in the South and West from "rustbelt" states in the North and East (U.S. Census Bureau 2005a). See Figure 15.2 for reference on these trends.

Theories on Population Growth

Concerns about population growth first emerged in the eighteenth century during the Industrial Revolution. Many demographic variables at that time contributed to rapid growth in the newly burgeoning urban areas of Europe. Mechanization, which increased agricultural production, and the introduction of a hearty new staple from South America—the potato— made available enough food for people to sustain themselves and support larger families. Other technological and scientific advances helped to decrease infant mortality rates while increasing fertility and extending life expectancy. As a result, the first real population boom in human history occurred.

Thomas Malthus, a British clergy member turned political economist, was one of the first scholars to sound the alarm on overpopulation. Although he lived at a time when people believed in technology and progress, the promise of prosperity and abundance, and the perfectibility of human society, he himself was less than optimistic about the future. Based on his observation of the world around him, Malthus wrote a book in 1798 called *An Essay on the Principle*

Population Change

- 1.6% to 2.5%
- 1.0% to 1.5%
- 0 to 0.9%
- -0.1% to -0.5%

U.S. percent 0.9

FIGURE 15.2 Population Change in the United States, 2009–10

The populations of Midwest and East Coast states are holding steady or decreasing, while the populations of Inter-Mountain West, Pacific Northwest, and some Southern states are growing.

SOURCE: U.S. Census Bureau 2010e.

of Population, in which his basic premise, the **Malthusian theorem**, stated that the population would expand at a much faster rate than agriculture; inevitably at some future point, people would far outnumber the available land and food sources. If population increases surpass the ability of the earth to provide a basic level of subsistence, then massive suffering will follow. His theory has two simple principles: that population growth is exponential or geometric (1, 2, 4, 8, 16, 32 . . .), whereas food production is additive or arithmetic (1, 2, 3, 4, 5, 6 . . .).

According to his calculations, society was headed for disaster, or what is called the **Malthusian trap**. To avoid such a catastrophe, Malthus made several rather radical policy recommendations. He may have been the first to propose that humans should collectively limit their propagation to save themselves and preserve their environments. He urged "moral restraint" in sexual reproduction to curtail overpopulation. If human beings were unable to restrain themselves (by postponing marriage or practicing abstinence), nature would exert "positive checks" on population growth through famine, war, and disease (Malthus 1798/1997). Malthus also advocated state assistance to the lower classes so they could more readily achieve a middle-class lifestyle supported by decent wages and benefits and adopt the values associated with later marriage and smaller families (New School 2004).

Malthus's ideas were not always popular, though they were influential and widely read. Charles Darwin noted that Malthusian theory was an important influence on his own theory of evolution and natural selection. Malthus also influenced whole new generations of social thinkers,

Malthusian theorem the theory that exponential population growth will outpace arithmetic growth in food production and other resources

Malthusian trap Malthus's prediction that a rapidly increasing population will overuse natural resources, leading inevitably to a major public health disaster

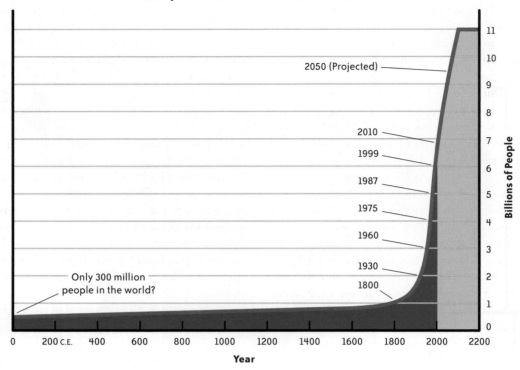

World Population Growth over 2,000 Years

FIGURE 15.3 World Population Growth over 2,000 Years

The world's population grew slowly for most of human history, then began to increase rapidly in the nineteenth century. With the world population continuing to grow it could reach 10–11 billion by 2100.

SOURCE: Population Reference Bureau 2010.

not just demographers but others as well, and their respective ideas on population growth.

More than 200 years later, some people, the **Neo-Malthusians**, or New Malthusians, essentially still agree with him. Among the notable modern voices looking at the problem of overpopulation are William Catton (1980), Paul and Ann Ehrlich (1990), and Garrett Hardin (1993). They worry about the rapid pace of population growth and believe that Malthus's basic prediction could be true. In some respects, they claim, the problem has even gotten worse. There are a lot more people on the planet in the twenty-first century, so their continued reproduction expands even more quickly than in Malthus's time. And with continued technological advancements—such as wars that use "surgical strikes," modern standards of sanitation, and the eradication of many diseases—people are living much longer than before. When Malthus was alive, there were approximately 1 billion people on the planet; it was the first time in recorded history that the population reached that

> **Neo-Malthusians** contemporary researchers who worry about the rapid pace of population growth and believe that Malthus's basic prediction could be true

number. The time required for that number to double and for each additional billion to be added has continued to shorten (Figure 15.3). Today there are 7 billion people on the planet—and counting. The United Nations predicts that world population will surpass 9 billion by 2050 and continue to grow to more than 10 billion before it stabilizes and plateaus at the end of the century (United Nations 2011).

The New Malthusians also point to several sociological factors that influence the reproductive lives of many and promote large families. Religion still plays a role in many societies, with the Old Testament commanding, "Go forth and multiply." The Catholic Church still forbids members to practice any birth control besides the rhythm method, even though 78 percent of American Catholics said the church should allow them to use some form of artificial contraception (CNN 2005). In many poorer nations, more children mean more financial support for the family. They work various jobs in their youth to help sustain the household, and for parents, children may be the only source of support they have in old age. Some governments encourage the expansion of their population base and promote the addition of new citizens who can become taxpayers or soldiers. They may even provide incentives to parents, such as tax deductions for each child. Last, cultural influences, from "family values" to "machismo," sometimes confer more prestige on those with children; women gain status in the valued role of mother, while men gain status for their perceived virility.

At the same time, contrary arguments are proposed by the **Anti-Malthusians**. Economists such as Julian Simon (1996, 2000) and demographers such as William Peterson (2003) believe that Malthus reached faulty conclusions and that he couldn't have envisioned the many modern developments that would impact population dynamics. In fact, the Anti-Malthusians worry more about the population shrinking and the possibility of a **demographic free fall** than they do about it growing indefinitely. Some countries, such as Japan, are already dealing with new problems caused by a rapidly shrinking population. They don't see that happening immediately, but they forecast a very different future when the pattern of **demographic transition**, now occurring in many industrialized nations, spreads to the rest of the developing world.

The Anti-Malthusians believe that when people have a better standard of living they also prefer smaller families, as children become more of an economic liability than an asset. Better education and easier access to health care bring more reproductive choices such as methods of **family planning**. Governments in some countries are adopting policies that discourage large families. Further, the Anti-Malthusians claim that technological advancements have enabled humans to produce much larger quantities of food than ever before, thus providing for the nutritional needs of more of the world's population.

So who is right? Will the world population eventually stabilize, or will it continue to spiral out of control? We may not know the answer to those questions for many years, so in the meantime we continue to speculate. The populations of some countries continue to grow rapidly, while others remain stable or begin to decline. The **growth rate** is the number of births minus deaths plus net migration of a population, expressed as a percentage change from the beginning of the time period measured, often resulting in what is referred to as a **natural increase**. The growth rate in the United States in 2008 was 0.89 percent. It was highest in African countries such as Liberia at 4.84 percent and Burundi at 3.59 percent and lowest in Pacific Islands such as Niue at –0.03 percent and Cook Island at –1.20 percent.

What about the other elements in Malthus's theorem? Food production has grown remarkably since Malthus's time. In particular, the "Green Revolution" that began in Mexico in 1948 and spread to India and other less developed nations in the 1960s caused an explosion in food production. This was partly because of better agricultural mechanization as well as newly engineered seeds, pesticides, and artificial fertilizers. Was this a unique increase, or can it be expected again in the future? The United Nations Food and Agriculture Organization estimates that world agriculture will grow at a slower pace, from an annual 2.1 percent over the past two decades to 1.6 percent from 2005 to 2015 and 1.3 percent from 2015 to 2030. Growth in agriculture will continue to surpass world population growth, estimated to be 1.2 percent from 2005 to 2015 and 0.8 percent from 2015 to 2030.

Nonetheless, hunger remains widespread, not only in foreign countries but also in the United States. Worldwide, an estimated 1 billion people suffer from chronic hunger and malnutrition—a lack of adequate food plus other factors such as insufficient protein and nutrients, poor feeding habits, and unsafe water and sanitation. Some 10 million people die every year from hunger or hunger-related causes; three-fourths of them are children under the age of five (United Nations World Food Programme 2007). In the United States, every day 15 percent of households—over 46 million people—experience hunger or food insecurity, that is, the limited or uncertain ability to acquire adequate and safe foods (U.S. Department of Agriculture 2010).

Other factors must also be considered in projecting the future of population impacts. Science constantly brings technological advancements that enhance health and prolong life, but new and deadly diseases such as AIDS claim an ever greater death toll in nations too poor to afford the medicines to treat these diseases. As the world's current occupants, we have to live now with the consequences of our choices. Many policy and advocacy groups concerned with population matters have been established in the past few decades, including Zero Population Growth, World Overpopulation Awareness, the Population Institute, and the Population Reference Bureau. To find out more, visit their web sites listed at the end of the chapter.

Anti-Malthusians contemporary researchers who believe the population boom Malthus witnessed was a temporary, historically specific phenomenon and worry instead that the worldwide population may shrink in the future

demographic free fall decrease in fertility rates among populations that have industrialized their economies as children become an economic liability rather than an asset

demographic transition a theory suggesting the possible transition over time from high birth and death rates to low birth and death rates, resulting in a stabilized population

family planning contraception, or any method of controlling family size and the birth of children

growth rate expression of changes in population size over time figured by subtracting the number of deaths from the number of births, then adding the net migration

natural increase change in population size that results from births and deaths; linked to a country's progress toward demographic transition

Urbanization

The dynamics of population growth (and sometimes shrinkage) throughout human history have been accompanied by the development of larger cities in which more people are now living. Cities, however, are not a modern development. They have been in existence for thousands of years. We find evidence of ancient cities in the Middle East, Africa, Asia, and South America. By comparison to today's standards, these early cities would be considered quite small. They generally had just several thousand residents and were typically agricultural centers along major trade routes. Some much larger cities, however, had hundreds of thousands of residents, such as the Mediterranean cities of Athens and Rome. One reason cities were able to thrive was the advances in agriculture that allowed surpluses of food to be readily available to support a population that was not directly involved in its production. People were thus freed to engage in other activities necessary for the functioning of the city and its residents.

Cities were not the prevalent residential areas until well into the nineteenth and twentieth centuries. Until then, the vast majority of people worldwide lived in **rural** or country areas. The wide-scale development of cities, or **urban** areas, was made possible by the significant social, economic, and political changes accompanying the Industrial Revolution, when masses of people were drawn into cities to find housing and the manufacturing jobs they needed to earn a living. Fewer families were involved in farming, as large companies, or agribusiness, began to emerge. Cities were populated not only by migrants from rural areas but also by immigrants from other countries, seeking opportunity and a better way of life. Industrialization provided the jobs and the means of communication and transportation to build the burgeoning city infrastructure that could support growing numbers of residents. This process in which growing numbers of people move from rural to urban areas is called **urbanization**.

> **rural** relating to sparsely settled areas; in the United States, any county with a population density between 10 and 59.9 people per square mile
>
> **urban** relating to cities; typically describes densely populated areas
>
> **urbanization** movement of increasing numbers of people from rural areas to cities
>
> **metropolis** an urban area with a large population, usually 500,000 to 1 million people
>
> **Metropolitan Statistical Area (MSA)** or **agglomeration** one or more adjacent counties with at least one major city of at least 50,000 inhabitants that is surrounded by an adjacent area that is socially and economically integrated with the city
>
> **megalopolis** or **megacity** a group of densely populated metropolises that grow dependent on each other and eventually combine to form a huge urban complex

In the early 1800s, only about 3 percent of the world's population lived in urban areas and only one city had a population greater than 1 million people: Peking, China (now called Beijing). In the early 1900s, almost 14 percent lived in urban areas, and another dozen or so cities around the world (including New York, London, Paris, Moscow, and Tokyo) had 1 million or more residents. In the early 2000s, more than 50 percent of the world's population were living in urban areas, and we now have to count as large cities those with 5 million people or more; there are more than sixty of these in the world (United Nations 2006).

A similar pattern can be seen in the United States. In the early 1800s, just 6 percent of the population lived in urban areas, whereas 94 percent lived in rural areas. In the early 1900s, the split was 40 percent urban and 60 percent rural. In the early 2000s, 79 percent were urban and 21 percent were rural. As of 2010, nine American cities had populations over 1 million; the largest among them, New York, has over 8 million (U.S. Census Bureau 2011c).

Features of Urbanization

The term "city" is currently used to refer to an urban settlement with a large population, usually at least 50,000 to 100,000 people. Although a few states, including North Dakota, West Virginia, and Vermont, have no cities with populations of 100,000 people or more, California has forty-six cities with more than 100,000 people, followed by Texas with nineteen and Florida with twelve. Urban demographers use the word **metropolis** to refer to an urban area with an even larger population—usually at least 500,000 people—that typically serves as the economic, political, and cultural center for a region. The U.S. Census Bureau defines the term **Metropolitan Statistical Area (MSA)**, also called an **agglomeration**, as a metropolitan area that includes a major city of at least 50,000 inhabitants that is surrounded by an adjacent area that is socially and economically integrated with the city. In 2009, the United States contained 363 MSAs; fifty of these had populations of 1 million or more (U.S. Office of Management and Budget 2006). Many of the largest American cities, such as New York, Los Angeles, Chicago, Houston, Philadelphia, Phoenix, and San Diego, have continued to grow rapidly in the past decade.

Largest of all is a **megalopolis**, also sometimes called a **megacity**—a group of densely populated metropolises (or agglomerations) that grow contiguous to each other and eventually combine to form a huge urban complex (Gottman 1961). One American megalopolis is referred to as "Chi-Pitts," a group of metropolitan areas in the Midwest, extending from Pittsburgh to Chicago (and including Detroit,

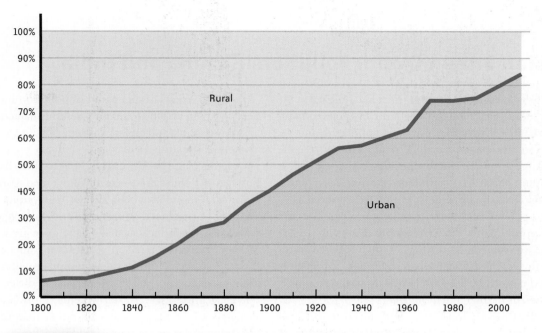

FIGURE 15.4 Rural/Urban Makeup of the U.S. Population, 1800–2010

As the U.S. population grew, so did the proportion of urban dwellers compared to rural inhabitants.

SOURCE: U.S. Census Bureau 1993 and 2000b; Yen 2011.

Cleveland, Columbus, Cincinnati, and Indianapolis), with a total population of more than 30 million. The ChiPitts metro areas are linked not only by geographic proximity but also by economics, transportation, and communications systems (Gottman and Harper 1990). An even larger megalopolis is "BosWash," extending from Boston to Washington, D.C., and including 22 other metropolises including New York and Philadelphia. BosWash has a total population of more than 44 million, or approximately 16 percent of the entire population of the country. Megalopolises are found worldwide, in countries including Brazil, Mexico, Indonesia, India, China, and Japan (Castells and Susser 2002). These are sometimes called **global cities** to emphasize their position in an increasingly globalized world as centers of economic, political, and social power (Sassen 1991).

Cities are often characterized by **urban density**, measured by the total number of people per square mile. Some of the most densely populated cities in the United States include Union City, New Jersey, with 52,972 residents per square mile; New York City with 26,401; San Francisco with 16,633; and Chicago with 12,749 (U.S. Census Bureau 2005a). By contrast, rural areas are characterized by low density. Rural counties are those with populations of 10 to 59.9 people per square mile; frontier counties are those with 0.5 to 9.9 people; and remote counties are those with 0.04 people per square mile or fewer. Alaska is the most rural state in the United States, followed by Wyoming, Nevada, Utah, New Mexico, and North Dakota.

Trends in Urbanization

Along with urbanization, an important counter-trend surfaced in the years immediately following World War II. **Suburbanization** is the shift of large segments of population away from the urban core and toward the edges of cities, where larger expanses of land were available for housing developments that provided families with a chance to buy a home of their own and avoid the overcrowding of central urban life. One of the first significant suburbs in the late 1940s was called Levittown (based on the name of the builders), a community of 17,450 tract houses for 75,000 people in Hempstead, New York. The simply designed homes were mass-produced and sold at prices affordable to returning veterans and the new growing middle class (Wattel 1958). In the 1950s, the second Levittown was built near Philadelphia and in the

global cities a term for megacities that emphasizes their global impact as centers of economic, political, and social power

urban density concentration of people in a city, measured by the total number of people per square mile

suburbanization beginning after World War II, the shift of large segments of population away from the urban core and toward the edges of cities

The Asian Brown Cloud: Pollution in China and India

China and India are the two most populated countries in the world, with more than 1 billion residents in each. In comparison, the United States, the third most populated country, has 301 million residents. According to calculations from the United Nations, no other country besides China and India will reach a population size of 1 billion. Despite the fact that the United States is the third most populated country, making up only 5 percent of the world's total population, it also consumes approximately 25 percent of its resources—in other words, we're currently the pigs of the planet. Unfortunately, though, as China and India develop into completely industrialized countries, they are following in the resource-hogging footsteps of the United States.

The "Asian Brown Cloud" is a name given to the layer of pollution that hangs over China, India, and parts of Southwest Asia. In satellite photos, the Asian Brown Cloud appears as a giant brown stain over this part of the world during the months of January through March. To the residents of China and India, the Asian Brown Cloud appears as a haze of air pollution hovering over their countries. Environmental scientists maintain that the Asian Brown Cloud consists of airborne pollutants from car and factory combustion and biomass burning that collect when there are no rains to wash it away. This atmospheric pollution has both immediate and long-term impacts on the citizens of Asia. Mumbai and Beijing report high rates of chronic respiratory problems, including cancer. Air quality in large cities such as Beijing is so poor—and even dangerous—that Chinese officials have spent more than US $17 billion in the past few years on attempts to reduce the air pollution. Despite these efforts, some Olympians refused to participate in the 2008 Summer Olympics in Beijing because of the fear that the air quality would affect their health and their performance. Projected long-term effects of this cloud of pollution include reduced crop growth leading to famine, melting glaciers creating devastating floods, and global warming affecting rainfall average, potentially leading to drought.

Much of the pollution in India and China has been a result of factory emissions, coal-burning, and garbage-burning. Now that there have been stricter regulations governing the emissions produced by factories and garbage dumps, a new culprit is emerging because of the growing wealth of these Asian countries. In recent years, both China and India have registered record-breaking economic growth rates. Personal incomes have increased, and because of the constant barrage of images from the Western media, more and more Asian citizens are buying private cars rather than relying on public transportation or more traditional forms of commuting like bicycles. In Beijing alone, 1,300 new cars are registered every day. In 2008, India's Tata motors introduced the Nano, a $2,500 car that will make car ownership accessible for millions of Indians. Environmentalists fear that the Nano will flood already gridlocked roads as well as releasing millions of tons of carbon dioxide into the already polluted air.

Even with the recent increases in prices, America is still the most disproportionate consumer of fossil fuels in the world. Not only do Americans drive more cars than citizens from almost any other country, we also use many times more gas than anyone else. At 446 gallons per capita annually, we're gallons ahead of the Canadians (311 gallons), boatloads ahead of countries like Germany and Italy (130 gallons and 114 gallons, respectively), and veritable oceans ahead of almost everyone else (United Nations Development Programme 2000). At the same time, developing countries like India and China are putting more and more cars on the roads. India consumed nearly 120 million tons of petroleum

1960s a third in New Jersey. Herbert Gans's study *The Levittowners* (1967) found that homeownership gave suburbanites a sense of pride and more privacy and space, which they valued greatly.

Suburbanization also reflected a retreat from some of the problems associated with city living—close quarters, noise, and crime. As more families were able to afford single-family homes, large yards with the proverbial white picket fence and a two-car garage became the literal image of the "American Dream" (Fava 1956; Kelly 1993). But suburban life has its own problems: long commutes, little contact between neighbors, and de facto racial segregation in housing and schools. Some observers have also criticized the monotonous uniformity of the new suburbs, claiming that they promote listless personalities, conformity, and escapism (Riesman 1957; Whyte 1956; Jackson 1985). The decades-long shift of

The Asian Brown Cloud This photo from a NASA satellite shows the layer of pollution that hangs over China, India, and parts of Southwest Asia.

Rajendra Pachauri, head of the 2007 Nobel Prize–winning Intergovernmental Panel on Climate Change (IPCC), said that investing in improving urban public transportation and enforcing restrictions on industrial waste are ways that countries such as China and India could balance the need for fighting climate change with that for economic growth. However, the burden of the problem does not lie in the hands of the Chinese and Indian governments. Ultimately, the images transmitted from the United States are inspiring the world to aspire to the same excessive lifestyle and standard of living as those of Americans. People in developing countries want

products in 2006–2007, according to the Petroleum Ministry, up from 113 million tons the previous year. China also saw a record high in terms of petroleum consumption in the first quarter of 2008, with a rise of 16.5 percent from the previous year. While the cars sold in China and India are not as gas-guzzling as American cars, the collective impact of the sheer number of cars owned in these densely populated countries is potentially devastating.

to achieve our level of economic development, and our own trade policy benefits from their consumption rates when they buy our products. Can America lead by example? If we become more environmentally conscious, will the world follow suit? These are pressing questions that we will have to address in the very near future.

populations to the suburbs has accelerated and expanded throughout the nation, with more families moving farther and farther away into what's been called the "exurbs" (Frey 2003).

A problem related to suburbanization is **urban sprawl** (sometimes also called suburban sprawl). This phenomenon has to do with how cities and suburbs grow. It is often a derogatory term applied to the peripheral expansion of

urban boundaries and is associated with irresponsible or poorly planned development. Critics say these areas are often unsightly, characterized by a homogenous landscape of housing subdivisions, office parks, and corner strip-malls lacking character or green space (Kunstler 1993; Duany,

> **urban sprawl** a derogatory term applied to the expansion of urban or suburban boundaries, associated with irresponsible or poorly planned development

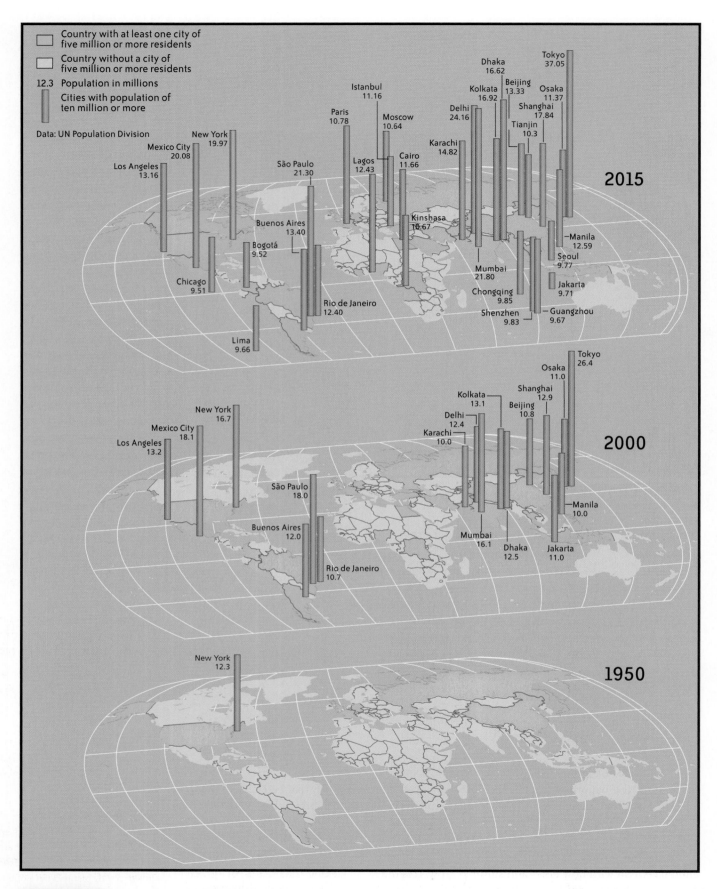

FIGURE 15.5 The Growth of Global Cities

This map shows the skyrocketing growth of the world's major cities. Asia and Africa are expected to see particularly strong urban growth in the near future.

SOURCE: Zwingle 2002.

Smart Growth vs. Suburban Sprawl Urban neighborhoods like this one in Brooklyn are examples of the trend toward revitalizing America's urban centers. Pedestrian-friendly neighborhoods with a mix of residential and commercial buildings are an alternative to suburban bedroom communities that have few sidewalks and many strip malls.

Plater-Zyberk, and Speck 2001; Gutfreund 2004) and bringing problems of traffic, pollution, crowded schools, and high taxes.

While most suburbs remain "bedroom communities" or primarily residential, others have become **edge cities** with their own centers of employment and commerce (Garreau 1992). Edge cities are usually in close proximity to intersecting highways and urban areas. "Silicon Valley" is a prime example: the once-sleepy suburb of San Jose became a center of high-tech industry during the dot-com boom of the 1990s. Edge cities are one answer to the problems associated with suburbanization. **Smart growth** advocates are also promoting alternatives to suburban growth, emphasizing redevelopment of inner cities or older suburbs to create better communities. Elements of smart growth include town centers; transit- and pedestrian-friendly streets; a greater mix of housing, commercial, and retail properties; and the preservation of open space and other environmental amenities.

Many long-established cities suffered when populations began moving to the suburbs—such as Detroit, Chicago, and Philadelphia in the North and East (the rustbelt) as well as New Orleans, St. Louis, and San Francisco in the South, Midwest, and West (U.S. Census Bureau 2005a). Since the 1950s and 60s, people have left cities not only to find more space and bigger homes in the nearby suburbs but also because they were fleeing other problems endemic to the city. Largely, those escaping the cities were upper- and middle-class whites who could afford to leave—a trend often referred to as **white flight** (or sometimes suburban flight). Those remaining in cities were predominantly minorities, seniors, immigrants, working class, or poor. White flight left urban areas abandoned by businesses and financial institu-

tions, leading to broken-down and boarded-up shops and streets and creating ghettos that further exacerbated the problems associated with inner cities (Wilson 1996).

In the 1960s and '70s, to address the problem of decaying inner cities, local city governments and private investors took advantage of **urban renewal** efforts that included renovation, selective demolition, commercial development, and tax incentives aimed at revitalizing business districts and residential neighborhoods (Frieden and Sagalyn 1992). Urban renewal has been a limited success. While it did revitalize many areas, it often came at a high cost to existing communities. In many cases, it resulted in the destruction of vibrant, if rundown, neighborhoods (Mollenkopf 1983).

Urban renewal is linked to another trend that has also changed many formerly blighted cities: **gentrification**. This is the transformation of the physical, social, economic, and cultural life of formerly working-class or poor inner-city neighborhoods into more affluent middle-class communities as wealthier people return to the cities (Glass 1964). This trend, which began in the 1990s, is evident in some of

Although urbanization (or suburbanization) is still the predominant demographic trend in the United States, an interesting reversal emerged in the 1990s, called the **rural rebound** (Johnson and Beale 1994, 1995, 1998). An increase in rural populations has resulted from a combination of fewer people leaving such areas and the in-migration of urban and suburban dwellers (Long and Nucci 1998). While most rural counties continue to decline, those near urban centers or with rich scenic or amenity values are generally experiencing an upsurge in population. Gains have been greatest in the Mountain West, Upper Great Lakes, the Ozarks, parts of the South, and rural areas of the Northeast. Rural migrants include families with young children, small-scale farmers, retirees, blue collar workers, single professionals, and disenchanted city dwellers all seeking a better way of life. They are willing to forsake the amenities of the city in exchange for a simpler, slower, more traditional rural lifestyle (Johnson 1999).

Another example of our contemporary ambivalence about city life is simulated cities—social spaces engineered to maximize the benefits of city life without the risks. A prime example is Universal CityWalk, a collection of shops, restaurants, and movie theaters in a suburb of Los Angeles. CityWalk mimics an urban shopping street, with sidewalk café seating and strolling street performers. However, it has no connection to a real urban street—CityWalk is bordered on one side by a theme park (Universal Studios) and on the other by a vast expanse of parking lots and freeway traffic. The parking fees to visit this street range from $7.50 to $17.50, which makes CityWalk a semiprivate attraction—distinctly unlike a real city street, which anyone can walk on without paying high fees for parking. The parking fees were instituted to minimize certain kinds of visitors found on real city streets, including homeless people and hustlers of various sorts.

The urban experience provided by CityWalk is sanitized, soothing, and a model of social control through architectural planning. Says Kevin McNamara of the University of Houston, "They omitted . . . the handbill-passers, bag ladies, streetcorner salesmen, and three-card-monte—because part of CityWalk's attraction rests on the certainty that distractions will remain pleasing, never truly surprising, let alone shocking" (McNamara 1999). CityWalk doesn't reject the grit of urban life entirely: when laying the sidewalks, developers embedded fake trash in the concrete. CityWalk and other artificial urban environments such as Celebration and Seaside, Florida, reveal our desire to experience the positive aspects of urban life without having to endure the problems. But this kind of engineering tends to turn cities into theme parks, erasing what is authentically urban—for better and for worse.

Building "Green" Theressa Hamilton reads the newspaper as she eats lunch on the greenroof garden at Atlanta's City Hall. Her building is one of more than a dozen buildings in Atlanta designed to be more energy efficient.

the nation's largest cities, such as Boston, New York, Philadelphia, Chicago, and San Francisco (Mele 2000). Various higher-income individuals, whether they were young professionals ("yuppies"), artists, or retirees, recognized the potential for rehabilitating downtown buildings (Castells 1984). They valued the variety and excitement of urban living more than the mini-malls of sleepy suburbia (Florida 2004). The term "gentrification" carries a distinct class connotation; while converting, renovating, remodeling, and constructing new buildings beautifies old city neighborhoods, it also increases property values and tends to displace poorer residents (Zukin 1987, 1989). Gentrification, then, does not eradicate the problems of poverty; it simply forces the poor to move elsewhere.

rural rebound population increase in rural counties that adjoin urban centers or possess rich scenic or amenity values

Real or Fake? People mingle outside Pastis restaurant in New York City's meatpacking district. Contrast this urban scene with Universal CityWalk in Los Angeles, which was designed to feel like an urban street.

DATA WORKSHOP
ANALYZING MASS MEDIA AND POPULAR CULTURE
Imagining the Cities of Tomorrow

People have always been interested in the future. Storytellers, inventors, scientists, politicians, and daydreamers have tried to imagine and, in some instances, create a vision of what will come.

Imagining the city of tomorrow is an almost constant theme in contemporary popular culture—books and comics, radio and TV, movies, and video games. Some of these represent a brighter vision of tomorrow, a **utopia** where humankind is finally freed from drudgery and disease, strife, and suffering. Some represent a darker vision of tomorrow, a **dystopia** where humankind is trapped in a ruthless, apocalyptic world of machines and nature gone mad.

Although examples of the city of the future appear in many different media, this Data Workshop asks that you focus on film. See Chapter 2 for more on how to do research using existing sources. You may have a favorite movie depicting the future, whether it's in the genre of science fiction, fantasy, thriller, horror, drama, or comedy. In deciding which movie to choose for your content analysis, consider whether the movie proposes a serious or realistic possibility of the future and avoid anything too far out in terms of monsters, aliens, or fantasy worlds.

Below is a partial list of movies that could satisfy the assignment. This list is not exhaustive, and you may prefer to use a film not in the list.*

---
* Please be aware of MPAA ratings for movies and select appropriate material for your age group.

12 Monkeys	*Independence Day*
1984	*Left Behind*
A.I. (Artificial Intelligence)	*Mad Max*
Back to the Future	*The Matrix*
District 9	*Metropolis*
V for Vendetta	*Minority Report*
Blade Runner	*Road Warrior*
Brazil	*Slaughterhouse Five*
Children of Men	*Solaris*
The Day after Tomorrow	*Strange Days*
Demolition Man	*The Terminator*
eXistenZ	*Terminator 2: Judgment Day*
Fahrenheit 451	*Total Recall*
The Fifth Element	*Tron*
Gattaca	*The Truman Show*
Idiocracy	*Videodrome*

Watch the movie while keeping in mind the concepts you have learned from this chapter, especially with regard to urbanization. Note the settings and environments in the movie. Capture key scenes or dialogue that can serve as examples of your argument. In conducting your content analysis, consider some of the following questions.

• At what point in the future does the movie take place?

• What is the major theme of the movie? What is its overall message?

• Does the movie represent a utopian or dystopian vision of the future? Does it represent positive or negative changes to society?

---

utopia literally "no place"; an ideal society in which all social ills have been overcome

dystopia opposite of a utopia; a world where social problems are magnified and the quality of life is extremely low

Operation Weed and Seed

On any given day, Ashley Enter might have consulted with a U.S. attorney or a local church leader, designed a mental health resource directory, helped set up a job training center, attended a neighborhood association meeting, or met with landlords who wanted to keep their rental properties crime- and drug-free. Ashley's job as the Weed and Seed Coordinator for the city of Peoria, Illinois, meant that she was in charge of a host of community-based initiatives meant to revitalize high-crime urban neighborhoods. Operation Weed and Seed is a community-based, multi-agency approach to law enforcement, crime prevention, and neighborhood restoration and is sponsored by the U.S. Department of Justice. The "weeding" process involves local, state, and federal law enforcement agencies and targets violent crime and gang- and drug-related activity through programs such as community policing. But the program is not merely a crackdown on crime. The "seeding" process is equally—if not more—important.

"Seeding" involves a variety of programs designed to help transform previously unsafe neighborhoods into places where individuals, families, and community spirit can thrive. The Peoria Weed and Seed program was a good example of how many different organizations and services are necessary to effectively seed a neighborhood: a "Safe Haven" located in a local hospital provided job training, mentoring, tutoring, and computer access; Safe Havens at several area churches provided after-school services and counseling for families and individuals. Other activities included neighborhood cleanup and beautification programs, mutual assistance services (such as one program in which volunteers did chores including shoveling snow or pulling weeds for elderly or handicapped neighbors), and fun events such as block parties and cookouts.

Operation Weed and Seed's multifaceted approach is admirable in that it refuses to oversimplify the complex problems of urban living by mandating reductive remedies. It's not a panacea either, for a variety of reasons. Ashley spent a good deal of her time, for example, navigating the byzantine bureaucracies of the many local, state, and federal agencies involved in the program. Organizing and attending meetings, scheduling telephone conferences, seeking committee

Operation Weed and Seed Ascher Henrikson uses a magnifying glass to see worms and other creatures in a compost pile at the Earth Day celebration in Peoria, Illinois.

approval for program decisions, writing and filing endless reports, and coordinating the demands of multiple funding sources are some of the challenges she faced in the office. Outside the office, the program runs up against a number of obstacles as well, not least of which is longstanding mutual suspicion between residents and police. But progress is being made.

Ashley graduated from Southern Illinois University with a bachelor's degree in public relations and a minor in community development. She joined the AmeriCorps VISTA program (Volunteers in Service to America) and built low-income housing with Habitat for Humanity. After her VISTA service was completed, she took a development job with the American Red Cross. Then she entered city government, specializing in neighborhood coordination and liaison work. She took the Weed and Seed job because she believed strongly in the values, goals, and strategies of the program, and despite the bureaucratic obstacles and funding uncertainties, she was optimistic about the program's potential to make a real difference in the city of Peoria and in the lives of the people living there. After Peoria "graduated" from the Weed and Seed program, Ashley moved on to other related nonprofit work.

For more information about Operation Weed and Seed, visit its web site: www.ojp.usdoj.gov/ccdo/ws/welcome.html.

City of the Future In the film *The Fifth Element*, flying cars buzz between ultra-tall skyscrapers. Could this version of the future realistically occur? Would you like to live in such a future?

- What sorts of futuristic elements are included in the movie, such as time travel, virtual reality, mind control, wars between humans and machines, apocalyptic destruction?

- How is the modern city or landscape of the future depicted? What are its structural features in both public and private realms?

- Compare the future with the present. How is the future the same or different? How is it better or worse?

- What are people like in the future? How are they affected by their environment? How does their environment impact their lives?

- Could this version of the future realistically occur? Would you like to live in such a future?

There are two options for completing this Data Workshop.

- *Option 1 (informal)*: Follow the instructions for viewing the movie and reflect on the Workshop questions. You may wish to take notes to prepare for a discussion with other students in small groups. Compare and contrast the movies you watched with others in the group. What similarities or differences are there between movies?

- *Option 2 (formal)*: Follow the instructions for viewing the movie, and write a three- to four-page essay answering the Workshop questions.

Living in the City

Who lives in cities? What about city life continues to attract droves of people? Big cities offer residents bright lights, a fast pace, excitement, and opportunity. They differ from small rural towns and suburban neighborhoods, so a certain type of person is more likely to be found living there.

Louis Wirth, a member of the Chicago School of sociology, proposed "urbanism as a way of life" that affected the outlook, mentality, and lifestyle of those who lived in the city. He believed that cities provided personal freedom, relaxed moral restraints, relative anonymity, variety, and diversity. At the same time, there was a certain social cost involved. People tended to belong to more formal organizations with more narrow goals and to engage less frequently in intimate interaction with one another. His analysis was in line with the belief that cities caused **social atomization**, that they were filled with free-floating individuals rather than members of a community (Wirth 1938).

Another sociologist, Claude Fischer, found that people create a sense of community by dividing the city into little worlds within which they feel familiar and involved. These groups allowed for informal and close relationships, giving city dwellers more intimacy and a feeling of belonging (Fischer 1976).

In 1962, Herbert Gans published a major ethnographic study, *The Urban Villagers*, in which he identified distinct categories of **urbanites**, or people who live in urban areas. The first are called "cosmopolites"—students, intellectuals, artists, entertainers, and other professionals who are drawn to the city because of its cultural benefits and convenience to their lifestyles. The next group are the "singles," unmarried people seeking jobs, entertainment, and partners with whom to settle down. Singles may include cosmopolites as well. When singles do find a marriage partner or mate, they tend to move to the suburbs, often in preparation to start a family.

Another group of city dwellers are the "ethnic villagers," often recent immigrants to the area. They tend to settle near others with whom they share a common

social atomization a social situation that emphasizes individualism over collective or group identities

urbanites people who live in cities

TABLE 15.1 | **Theory in Everyday Life**

PERSPECTIVE	APPROACH TO THE NATURAL ENVIRONMENT	CASE STUDY: URBAN SPRAWL
STRUCTURAL FUNCTIONALISM	The natural world exists in order to keep the social world running smoothly. The environment provides raw materials and space for development in order to meet society's needs.	As populations increase, cities must grow in order to accommodate the growing population, so urban sprawl is functional for society.
CONFLICT THEORY	Not all groups or individuals benefit equally from society's use of the natural environment.	Urban sprawl creates largely white, upper- and middle-class suburbs around cities whose residents are minorities, seniors, immigrants, working class, and/or poor. This means that suburban residents may have access to resources, like well-funded schools, which urban dwellers may not.
SYMBOLIC INTERACTIONISM	The meanings assigned to the natural environment will determine how society sees and uses it.	Redefining open land as a scarce resource, and redefining urban areas as valuable spaces, may lead to the reduction of urban sprawl: open land could be conserved, while urban spaces could be rehabilitated and revitalized.

racial, ethnic, national, religious, or language background; these are often distant relatives or others with whom they have a connection. This is why many major cities still have Chinatowns, Little Italys, and other ethnic neighborhoods. Once here, immigrants form tightly knit ethnic enclaves that resemble the villages of their home countries. The last group of urban dwellers is the "deprived" and the "trapped." These are the people at the bottom of the social hierarchy—the poor, homeless, disabled, elderly, and mentally ill. Without resources and means of support, they cannot afford to leave the city, even if they could find jobs, services, or housing elsewhere; they are inescapably stuck where they are. This perpetuates a cycle of poverty and despair.

Alienation and Altruism: The Case of New York City

As products of the Industrial Revolution, cities are celebrated for providing unprecedented degrees of freedom for individuals. Life in rural agricultural communities was much more restrictive, with family and neighbors placing tight constraints on behavior. However, sociology has been suspicious of cities, seeing this very freedom as a source of **alienation**. Early sociologist Georg Simmel argued

alienation decreasing importance of social ties and community and the corresponding increase in impersonal associations and instrumental logic

civil inattention an unspoken rule governing interactions in public places, whereby individuals briefly notice others before ignoring them

that while urban environments "allowed a much greater degree of individual liberty," they did so only "at the expense of treating others in objective and instrumental terms" relating to others only through a "cold and heartless calculus" (Harvey 1990). In short, except for their chosen subcultures, city dwellers fail to develop community, feel little connection with neighbors, have relationships that are largely shallow and impersonal, and fail to care about each other (Simmel 1950).

The murder of Catherine "Kitty" Genovese has come to represent all such fears about urban life. Late on March 13, 1964, she was returning home from her job as a bar manager when she was attacked by a man named Winston Moseley. He first attacked Genovese after she parked her car outside the Kew Gardens apartment building where she lived. She was stabbed several times before her attacker was frightened off when lights went on in nearby apartments. Badly wounded and bleeding, Genovese was later reported to have shouted, "Oh, my God, he stabbed me! Please help me! Please help me!" (Gansberg 1964). Somehow, she then made her way to the back of the building, apparently trying to get to the staircase that led to her apartment. However, her assailant returned and stabbed and beat her to death, before sexually assaulting her. The entire attack, although intermittent, was reported to have lasted nearly thirty minutes.

As horrible as this was, it wouldn't be remembered today if it were just a tragic murder. What has made this case memorable was the number of bystanders who must have heard the crime taking place but failed to take action. A friend of Genovese made the following comments during an interview

In Relationships

Encounters with Strangers

Cities are places where strangers come together. Before there were cities, there were also no strangers; those who were unknown were driven off, killed, or quickly assimilated into the clan, tribe, or group (Lofland 1973). With the advent of cities came the prospect of living life in close proximity to hundreds, thousands, or even millions of people we will never know and from whom we cannot be completely segregated. City life would seem to bring the prospect for all sorts of chaos and conflict—and yet every day, in contemporary cities, millions of people go about their business in relative harmony, brushing elbows with each other on the sidewalk or subway in encounters that are neither friendly nor unfriendly but merely orderly.

What are the interactional structures that order urban life? Public interactions with strangers can be treacherous, as we encounter people we do not know and whose reactions we cannot predict. For the most part, we are not talking about the danger of physical attack. More common than getting mugged is being "looked at funny," getting "goosed," or being the target of "wolf whistles." These are threats to self more than anything else—being treated as a nonperson, or as a piece of meat. How do we guard against these minor molestations when we walk down the street every day?

A specific way we deal with strangers in public is by doing what Erving Goffman calls **civil inattention**. This is a taken-for-granted rule of public place interaction, a basic public courtesy we extend to one another that helps guard against unpleasant interactions with strangers (Goffman 1971). About eight or ten feet away from one another, we tend to look at and then look away from the person we are approaching—all in one sweep of our gaze. We have looked, but not too intently or for too long. This allows us to navigate through

Sidewalk Etiquette Whether listening to an iPod, talking on a cell phone, or just averting their gaze, urbanites use civil inattention to order public place interaction.

urban spaces without bumping into strangers and to avoid the kinds of interactions that might lead to trouble. The practice of civil inattention is so commonplace that you may not realize you do it every day. Now, walk down the street and notice your own gazework and that of others—with full comprehension of how this simple act helps avoid conflict, enables smooth interactions between strangers, and basically makes city life possible.

Kitty Genovese Her murder case shocked the nation. How could so many bystanders have failed to intervene? What did this say about the harsh realities of modern big city life?

on National Public Radio in 2004, some forty years after the crime took place.

> The police later established that thirty-eight people either saw Kitty Genovese stabbed and raped or heard her scream for her life, but no one called the police; no one rushed down to the street to try to scare off her attacker. Her death was a small story in the next day's newspapers, but two weeks later, the *New York Times* ran a story on how shocked the Queens police had been that so many people heard Kitty Genovese being murdered and didn't lift a finger to help her. The story set off a national soul-searching. How could so many Americans, even New Yorkers, it was sometimes added, have turned away from cries for help? The murder of Kitty Genovese became a kind of modern morality tale. Her death seemed to symbolize an age in which people counseled, "Don't get involved." "Mind your own business." "Not in my back yard." (Simon 2004)

A. M. Rosenthal, who was the editor of the *New York Times* in 1964, later wrote a

book about the incident, which focused attention on the most disturbing aspect of the case: why didn't somebody help her? For many, this seemed to be the ultimate indictment of big cities in general, and New York City in particular, but much of the press coverage seemed to demonize the individuals involved. Regardless of individual responsibility, it's important to also look at the social factors that made the situation possible.

Especially useful in understanding the social origins of this unfortunate incident has been the work of social psychologists John Darley and Bibb Latane (1968), who conducted several experiments on **altruism** and helping behaviors. These experiments were designed to test what came to be called the **bystander effect**, or the **diffusion of responsibility**. In one experiment, different-sized groups of test subjects heard what sounded like a woman having an accident in the next room. Darley and Latane found that the higher the number of bystanders present, the lower the chances that any of them would attempt to help. Basically, they theorized that the responsibility "diffused" throughout the crowd so that no one person felt responsible enough to do anything, most assuming that someone else would help. However, when groups were small, the chances that someone would do something increased greatly.

In a similar experiment, they placed different-sized groups of subjects in a room, under the pretense of taking a test, and gradually filled the room with smoke. Again, they found that the greater the number of subjects in a room, the lower the chances that anyone would mention the smoke. Here, along with the diffusion of responsibility, they argued that **pluralistic ignorance** was at work. When large groups of people encounter an ambiguous or unusual situation, they tend to look to each other for help in defining the situation. If no member of the group decides that it is an emergency, and therefore worthy of worry, it is likely that all members will continue to ignore the situation.

On the twentieth anniversary of the Genovese murder, Fordham University held the "Catherine Genovese Memorial Conference on Bad Samaritanism," which attempted to shed some light on what sorts of situations would produce bystanders who would help. Although no single character trait correlated with being a Good Samaritan, researchers largely confirmed earlier findings—that bystanders in groups were tentative about helping, especially when they were unsure of the nature of the problem.

These conclusions can also help to explain a time when New Yorkers did come to each other's aid out of a sense of belonging and **community**: in the September 11, 2001, attacks on the World Trade Center. In the hours and days after the attacks, Americans rushed to help however they could. "Tens of thousands of patriotic Americans rolled up their sleeves and gave blood," monetary donations poured in, and ordinary New Yorkers rushed to pitch in (Stapleton 2002). Some of the most heroic rescue efforts at the World Trade Center were made by ordinary people who rushed to help as soon as they heard. Two Port Authority Police Officers, Will Jimeno and John McLoughlin, were the last people to be found alive in the collapsed remains of the World Trade Center towers. They were discovered by Charles Sereika, a former paramedic, and David Karnes, "an accountant from Connecticut" who "had changed into his Marine camouflage outfit" and driven down to Manhattan as soon as he heard the news (Dwyer 2001). The movie *World Trade Center* (2006) by Oliver Stone depicts their story. And even if things have somewhat returned to normal (meaning people are less friendly now), almost everyone agrees that New Yorkers "were wonderful during the crisis, and we were tender to each other. . . . Volunteers streamed to the site" and "after only a few days there were so many, they were turned away by the hundreds. . . . Strangers spoke to each other in the street, in stores, and on the subway" (Hustvedt 2002).

So what made the difference in the two events? Many of those who heard Kitty Genovese being murdered believed that it was a bar fight or a lover's quarrel. Not knowing what was happening, they were unsure how to respond. With September 11, there was no ambiguity. Also, on September 11, many people understood where to go and what to do to help. In 1964, the "911" emergency system didn't exist, and many people were reluctant to get personally involved with the police. This largely supports the conclusions of sociologists like Lee Clarke (2001), who has studied how people respond to various kinds of disasters. His work shows that altruism, rather than panic, tends to prevail in disasters. Clarke posits that the rules for behavior in extreme situations are essentially the same as the rules of ordinary life—that when faced with danger, people help those next to them before helping themselves. This was the case in the destruction of the World Trade Center. People survived the disaster because they did not become hysterical but instead helped to facilitate a successful evacuation of the buildings (Clarke 2001). There are many obvious reasons why the September 11 attacks would bring people together in ways that the attack on Kitty Genovese did not. September 11 was clearly and obviously a disaster; it was also an attack on the entire country, so loyalties were further cemented. Formal institutions were set up so people could easily volunteer and receive positive social sanctions in return. Kitty Genovese was just one young woman living in a building full of immigrants and elderly pensioners. However, whenever bystanders do jump in to help, it is in part because of the outrage her murder provoked. In the aftermath of the Kitty Genovese murder, the "911" emergency system was created, neighborhood watch groups were formed, Good Samaritan laws were passed to protect bystanders from liability in emergencies, and people started to get more involved.

Urban Legends

The story of Kitty Genovese's murder is true. But that cannot be said about every sensational story you hear, especially if it is passed along through informal social networks among friends or over the internet.

Did you hear the one about the missing kidneys? A businessman was attending a convention in Las Vegas, and after a hard day's work he stopped off for a drink in the hotel lounge. A prostitute approached him, and after a few drinks, she suggested they go up to his room. The next morning, the business traveler woke up in a bathtub, filled with ice, and a note telling him that if he wanted to live he should call "911" immediately. The emergency dispatcher asked him to examine his lower back, where he found two neat incisions. The traveler was then told to get back in the tub and wait for help because his kidneys had been removed by black market organ thieves.

Or maybe you're more familiar with the alligators in the New York City sewers, purchased as pets when still small but flushed down the toilet, where they grew to full size. Perhaps you've heard about apples with razor blades given to trick-or-treaters on Halloween. Or that the taco restaurant down the street has an earthworm farm that supplies their "ground beef." Or maybe you even got an e-mail from Bill Gates promising to give you $1,000 if you forwarded an e-mail often enough, because he was testing new e-mail tracking software. If you live near Southern California or in Puerto Rico, you may have even heard about the "chupacabra," a blood-sucking alien devil beast that preys on goats and the occasional stray dog.

All are examples of **urban legends**, a specific and very modern variety of folklore. The study of folklore involves "collecting, classifying, and interpreting in their full cultural context the many products of everyday human interaction that have acquired a somewhat stable underlying form" (Brunvand 1981, p. 2). Folklorists look at fairy tales, legends, folk music, jokes, and other forms of popular art because understanding the themes and ideas that commonly appear in such material can tell you a great deal about the culture that produced it. Urban legends, in particular, are defined by their believability and their contemporary setting; they are often legitimized or "authenticated" through either personal acquaintance with a supposed witness or some sort of media coverage.

An urban legend can be defined as a story that is

> **urban legend** modern folklore; a story that is believed (incorrectly) to be true and is widely spread because it expresses concerns, fears, and anxieties about the social world

Urban Legends Worried about razor blades or poison in his children's Halloween candy, Ray Orozco inspects their haul after a night of trick-or-treating in Miami, Florida.

bizarre, whimsical, 99 percent apocryphal yet believable, a story that is almost, but not quite, too good to be true (Brunvand 2001). Incredible stories exist in many forms, like ghost stories that are told around a campfire; but to work as an urban legend, people must believe that the story is true or could be true. Jan Brunvand, a noted folklorist, says that urban legends are particularly compelling because someone claims that "the story is true; it really occurred, and recently, and always to someone else who is quite close to the narrator, or at least a 'friend of a friend'" (1981, p. 4).

Urban legends are like a folk sociology, as every successful urban legend is told and retold because it expresses "in a succinct and entertaining form what narrators wish to present as a truth about contemporary life and behavior" (Boyes 1984, p. 64). Two qualities of an urban legend can contribute to its success. First, the most popular legends are repeated and spread because they speak to our concerns, fears, and anxieties about our social world. Often, there is a moral expressing the "fears and anxieties of a group and serv[ing] as warnings about potentially dangerous situations, behaviors, and

assumptions." In this way, urban legends serve a function in society "whether of education, social control, expression of attitudes and emotions, or strengthening of social bonds" (Whatley and Henken 2000, pp. 2, 6). For instance, stories about Halloween candy with razor blades warn us not to trust strangers (Best and Horiuchi 1985). Stories about condoms or intravenous needles in soft drink cans play on fears about the purity of our food. Stories about serial killers and crime often reveal our fears of being alone or of being among strangers in the darkened world outside the security of our own home or car (Brunvand 1981).

A second quality that contributes to the success of an urban legend is its affective punch. Urban legends that circulate the most tend to inspire an emotional reaction—typically anger, fear, disgust, or amusement. One study conducted at Duke University to determine what drives urban legends took a number of familiar stories and created several variations, each inspiring varying degrees of disgust. Undergraduates in the study were then asked to retell the stories. The researchers found that while transmitting basic information was important, the students preferred to tell versions that elicited the most emotion from listeners (Lockman 2002).

The most popular urban legends may be circulated for years, and though they may traverse the nation, they are often given local details in the telling, which makes them seem more believable (Best and Horiuchi 1985). In some ways, modern technology has changed the dissemination of urban legends. The internet and e-mail have vastly accelerated the speed and reach of the modern urban legend. As Brunvand recounts, "a combination of oral tradition, electronic communication, and mass media exposure have sustained a wide range of modern urban legends over broad areas of space and long stretches of time" (1981); stories that "are simply too beguiling to fade away" are now spread faster and to more people than ever before (Jensen 2000). Ironically, electronic communication may actually slow the rate of change to stories, as people may simply cut and paste or forward e-mail messages verbatim. Whether told face-to-face or through electronic media, the continued circulation of urban legends speaks to the enduring power of a few compelling themes about modern social life.

The Environment

The final section of this chapter once again considers the connection between the social and the natural worlds. Human populations have grown tremendously, as have the cities in which most of them live. Now how do those people interact with the natural environment and what impact does the environment have on how they live? Whether we go camping, go surfing, or just take a walk through Central Park, we all go to nature to escape, to recreate, to relax. It is ironic that we now seek out nature as a retreat from the demands of society because society itself originated and evolved at least in part to protect us against the demands of nature. The cooperation and interdependence that characterize most social groups allow individuals to withstand the risks of the natural environment. The products of culture—clothing, architecture, automobiles, and many others—contribute to our ability to live in what would otherwise be inhospitable surroundings. Without her insulated house and its furnace, her layers of clothing topped with a Gore-Tex parka, and her car with a remote starter and all-weather tires, Dr. Ferris would have a hard time surviving the harsh winters in northern Illinois. And all these survival tools are supplied because she is part of a society whose other members have created what she needs to be safe and warm in the elements. Society provides all of us with a buffer against nature; without it, we wouldn't last very long in the ocean, the snowdrifts, or the desert.

Social Ecology

While society buffers individuals against the rigors of nature, it also allows them to impact the natural world. Trees are cut down to build homes; furnaces and automobiles burn fuels and create air pollution; and manufacturing artificial fibers creates chemical waste—just a few of the ways the collective actions of a society impact the natural world. The study of human populations and their impact on the natural world is

Social Ecology Society affects nature even in the remotest places—including on the highest mountaintops and in outer space! Hikers leave garbage on Mount McKinley (left), and NASA illustrates the debris orbiting the Earth (right). The European Space Agency estimates that there are 8,500 objects larger than 3 inches wide currently circling the planet.

social ecology the study of human populations and their impact on the natural world

environment in sociology, the natural world, the human-made environment, and the interaction between the two

biosphere the parts of the earth that can support life

environmental sociology the study of the interaction between society and the natural environment, including the social causes and consequences of environmental problems

called **social ecology**. Under this heading, you might study how cities are organized, how populations migrate, or how technological developments influence the social order, to see how these social developments occur within a physical environment that shapes and responds to social trends.

Sociologists are interested in both the social and the natural worlds because those worlds interact with each other. Even the most remote corner of the Amazon rain forest is not immune from the effects of society, even if no human has ever set foot there. Global climate change is slowly impacting that forest's environment; jets fly above the trees, creating noise and pollution; and animals that have been squeezed out of their natural habitats elsewhere (by trends like urban sprawl) may begin moving into new territories, upsetting the balance of native creatures and plants. Society impacts nature relentlessly—and vice versa—as the rhythms, rigors, and risks of the natural world shape how society is organized.

Studying the Environment

The environment is a recent area of interest among sociologists, coinciding with the general public's concern about environmental issues (Guber 2003). When sociologists use the term **environment**, it encompasses aspects of both the natural and the human-made environment and includes everything from the most micro level of organisms to the

entire **biosphere**. Sociologists study the ways that societies are dependent on the natural world; how cultural values and beliefs shape views about and influence usage of the environment; the politics and economics of natural resources; and the social construction of conflicts, problems, and solutions that are a result of our relationship to the natural world.

Environmental sociology is a growing subfield within the larger discipline that has continued to gain scholarly interest and to impact other academics, policy makers, and society as a whole. Its emergence paralleled the modern environmental movement in the late 1970s. The contours of the subfield are still being established, as we will see in the next section.

First, we will look at the environment as a social problem. This encompasses two big areas: problems of consumption and problems of waste. Sociologists, however, must look beyond descriptions of problems and attempt to apply analytic frameworks for understanding the social complexities underlying them.

The Environment as a Social Problem

Many students first become acquainted with the subject of the environment as a social problem. Learning the "three R's" in schools has now come to mean Reduce, Reuse, Recycle. We need to help "save" the environment because it is under threat from consumption and waste.

PROBLEMS OF CONSUMPTION: RESOURCE DEPLETION
The planet Earth provides an abundance of natural resources, including air, water, land, wildlife, plants, and minerals. We have learned to exploit these resources not only for basic survival but also to build everything in material culture that

Threats to Biodiversity Rain forests, which play a key role in regulating the global climate and are home to almost 50 percent of the world's plant and animal species, are being destroyed at a rate of millions of acres each year.

is part of the modern world. Humans have long been presented with the challenge of managing their use of natural resources, but those challenges have changed in the postindustrial era.

Renewable resources are natural resources that can be regenerated; for instance, oxygen is replenished by plants and trees, water by evaporation and rain clouds, trees and plants by pollens and seeds, and animals by mating and reproduction. **Nonrenewable resources** are those that cannot be replaced (except through tens of thousands of years of geological processes); for instance, fossil fuels like oil, or minerals like coal, copper, or iron. All natural resources are susceptible to overuse or overconsumption and eventually to depletion or even exhaustion. As a result of rising demands, we have already seen rising costs or outright shortages for such commodities as seafood, timber, and gasoline.

It may be hard to imagine that we'll ever run out of some things, like air and water, but even these are threatened. We may not be aware of the connection between the things we consume in our everyday life and their sources. We're removed from the fields and the mines, the oceans, and the mountains that are the origin of our goods. But we are already confronting real problems of resource depletion, and the course of such depletion may now be irreversible.

One of the world's most pressing problems is how to meet enormous and growing demands for energy. We need energy—gas, electric, or nuclear—to help us power everything from our cars and televisions to factories and airplanes. But these forms of energy are not inexhaustible. We have relied primarily on nonrenewable sources, such as coal and fossil fuels to meet our needs. The current mix of fuel sources comes from 37 percent petroleum, 25 percent natural gas, 21 percent coal, 9 percent nuclear, and only 8 percent renewable energy sources. Some renewable sources besides wood and hydroelectric (water-generated) power, such as wind or solar power, are being developed, but they are not sufficient yet to provide us with the substantial quantities of energy we will need in the future.

Industrialized nations are the largest consumers of energy, using approximately 70 percent of the total energy produced in the world; of those nations, America uses nearly 20 percent, Russia uses more than 6 percent, and Germany 4.5 percent. Developing nations that now use the remaining 30 percent are becoming more industrialized, and their energy needs will also increase, thus closing the energy usage gap among nations during the next 25 years. In that same time, total worldwide energy consumption is projected to grow between 50 percent and 60 percent (U.S. Energy Information Administration 2004). Oil is a finite resource, and at some point the supply will be exhausted. We may have already hit a peak of production and be in decline. We know that limited amounts and rising costs of energy are likely to spur development of substitutes for oil.

Another critical area of consumption is the rain forests in South America, Central America, Australia, Africa, and Southeast Asia. Rain forests are ecosystems located in tropical and temperate regions that are home to diverse plant and animal life (as well as indigenous peoples). Although rain forests cover only about 6 percent of the earth's landmass, they contain close to 50 percent of all microorganisms and plant and animal species in the world (Mittermeier, Myers, and Mittermeier 2000). Previously unknown life forms are being discovered there every year, while at the same time thousands are being driven to extinction. Products derived from the rain forest include not only foods and woods, but importantly, pharmaceuticals; more than 7,000 medical compounds are derived from native plants. Rain forests also play a key role in global climate control, evaporation and rainfall, and clearing the air of carbon dioxide (Myers and Kent 2005).

In 1950, rain forests covered twice as much area as they do today, and they are disappearing at an alarming rate. Currently, there are approximately 3.5 billion acres of rain forest worldwide, down from more than 7 billion. More than 78 million acres of rain forest are lost every year—215,000 acres every day, or about 150 acres every minute! Destruction of the rain forests is of sociological import because it results from collective human behavior. The immediate cause of this destruction is to accommodate the logging, mining, and ranching industries. Although these industries benefit the peoples of those regions, they are primarily providing for the consumption demands of the more developed nations of the world (Myers and Kent 2004).

In addition to rain forests, worldwide **biodiversity** is in dangerous decline. According to a 2005 United Nations report prepared by 1,360 scientists from ninety-five countries, humans pose a distinct threat to thousands of other species on the planet. The report asserts that the natural rate of extinction has multiplied by as much as a thousand times within the past century. Perhaps hardest hit has been marine life, with a 90 percent decrease in the number of fish in the world's oceans. In addition, roughly 12 percent of birds, 23 percent of mammals, 25 percent of conifers, and 32 percent of amphibians are threatened with extinction. These mass dieoffs are being driven by human activities, including the destruction of habitats, pollution, the introduction of nonnative species, and overuse. "We will need to make

renewable resources resources that replenish at a rate comparable to the rate at which they are consumed

nonrenewable resources finite resources, including those that take so long to replenish as to be effectively finite

biodiversity the variety of species of plants and animals existing at any given time

sure that we don't disrupt the biological web to the point where collapse of the whole system becomes irreversible," says Anantha Duraiappah of Canada, who co-chaired the study.

PROBLEMS OF WASTE: POLLUTION Problems of consumption are linked to problems of waste, often two sides of the same coin. Consider water and air. Water is another natural resource that can be overused—we understand what happens during a drought, or when lakes, rivers, or underground aquifers are drained and then go dry. But water can also be damaged by what we put into it. And while we don't normally think of consuming air, it is an essential natural resource, and we can damage its quality and change for the worse the very atmosphere of the planet. Let's look at these examples of **pollution**.

Water is indispensable for life. Some 70 percent of the earth's surface is covered with water. Almost 97 percent of this is in oceans of saltwater, home to a vast array of sea creatures and plants. Only 1 percent of the total accounts for freshwater, found in lakes, rivers, and underground aquifers; the other 2 percent is in polar ice caps and glaciers. This is a small percentage to meet human needs—from drinking water to water for agricultural and ranching purposes. The world's water supply, both in oceans and freshwater, has been under increased threat from pollution by industrial development and population growth—mostly by allowing contaminants to enter the oceans, lakes, and rivers or to seep into underground water supplies. The sources of this pollution are many: factories dumping chemical and solid wastes, agricultural run-off of pesticides and fertilizers, human sewage and urban run-off, and toxic chemicals falling from the skies in rain.

Access to freshwater is not equal throughout the world. Most Americans can take safe drinking water for granted. Although the **Environmental Protection Agency (EPA)** claims that the United States has one of the safest supplies of drinking water, even here more than 10 percent of water systems in the nation don't meet EPA standards (U.S. EPA 2008). In developing nations, waterborne diseases are a significant cause of disease and death. There is a definite link between water scarcity and poverty; in some African countries, up to 50 percent of the population are without access to adequate water (Gleick 1998).

The atmosphere is made up of thin layers of gases surrounding the planet and making life possible. It interacts with the land, oceans, and sun to produce the earth's climate and weather. The air that we breathe is ubiquitous, so that we might not even think of it as a natural resource. But

pollution any environmental contaminant that harms living beings

Environmental Protection Agency (EPA) a government agency organized in 1969 to protect public health and the environment through policies and enforcement

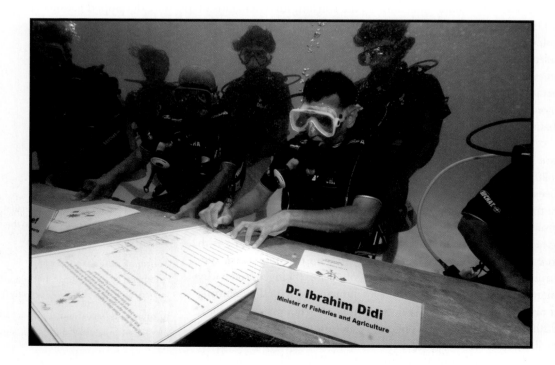

Climate Change Maldivian Minister of Fisheries and Agriculture Ibrahim Didi calls attention to the threat of global warming to low-lying countries by holding an underwater meeting to sign a document calling on all countries to cut down their carbon dioxide emissions.

Dr. Ibrahim Didi
Minister of Fisheries and Agriculture

Opening Day of the Beijing Olympics Heavy pollution practically shrouds the Olympic stadium in Beijing in 2008.

our earth's atmosphere and its ability to sustain life are at risk from pollution. Not all sources are human; for instance, volcanoes or forest fires started by lightning can emit massive clouds of smoke, ash, and debris into the atmosphere. Human activity, however, accounts for a tremendous amount of air pollution, especially emissions from factories and automobiles. The most common pollutants (carbon monoxide, lead, nitrogen dioxide, ozone, sulfur dioxide, and particulates such as soot, smoke, and dust) together are often referred to as **greenhouse gases**. These not only create ugly smog and haze but also are hazardous to the health of humans and other species.

The U.S. Congress passed the first Clean Air Act in 1963, which has been followed over the decades by numerous amendments and other legislation to help regulate industries involved in emissions. Regulations and technological advancements have helped reduce air pollution in the United States. Still, we have the highest per capita rate of any nation, emitting some 6.6 tons of greenhouse gases per person per year. It is estimated that more than 100 million people, or about 40 percent of the U.S. population, live in areas reporting higher levels of ozone than are safe by national standards (U.S. EPA 2003). Pollution problems may be even greater in developing nations that are rapidly becoming industrialized.

Greenhouse gases are also contributing to a change in the makeup of the earth's atmosphere. Scientists call this the **greenhouse effect**. The earth's climate is regulated through a process in which some of the sun's heat and energy is retained within the atmosphere. Naturally occurring gases (such as water vapor or carbon dioxide) help trap some of the earth's outgoing

greenhouse gases any gases in the earth's atmosphere that allow sunlight to pass through but trap heat, thus affecting temperature

greenhouse effect the process in which increased production of greenhouse gases, especially those arising from human activity (e.g., carbon dioxide, nitrous oxide, and methane) cause the earth's temperature to rise

global warming gradual increase in the earth's temperature, driven recently by an increase in greenhouse gases and other human activity

global (or **solar**) **dimming** a decline in the amount of light reaching the earth's surface because of increased air pollution, which reflects more light back into space

heat, which in turn maintains a stable, livable climate. An increase in greenhouse gases from air pollution results in greater retention of heat within the earth's atmosphere, leading to **global warming**, an increase in the world's average temperature.

Scientists believe that in the past 50 to 100 years, the average temperature of the earth has risen one degree Fahrenheit. They predict that greenhouse gases will continue to increase the earth's temperature another one to five degrees over the next fifty years, and two to ten degrees in the next 100 years (U.S. EPA 2000). A climate change of a few degrees can cause catastrophic consequences for the world and its inhabitants. Even slightly higher temperatures could melt polar ice caps and increase the sea level, shrink the landmasses of islands and continents, change global weather patterns, and alter ecosystems that support life on Earth.

In addition to the greenhouse effect, pollutants in the air have also caused **global dimming** (or **solar dimming**). This newly discovered phenomenon means that the earth is becoming darker than it used to be. Because of all the particles in the atmosphere, some natural and some from human activity, less light from the sun's rays reaches Earth. Climate researchers estimate that the earth's surface is receiving 15 percent less sunlight than it did just fifty years ago (Boyd 2004). The sun has remained as bright as always, but the amount of energy or solar radiation that hits the earth has been shrinking by about 3 percent per decade. In some respects, global dimming is counteracting global warming, but that only means that global warming would be worse were it not for the pollutants that are blocking the sun.

Another pollution problem is garbage. U.S. waste production is twice that of any other nation. The average American generates four pounds of trash per day—1,460 pounds per year. The country dumps about 200 million tons of garbage a year, and less than 25 percent of it is recycled, leaving the rest for landfills and incinerators. Some of our trash even gets blasted into outer space (such as satellites and other objects that have become obsolete), where more than 600,000 pieces of litter are orbiting the planet! And have you ever thought about light pollution or noise pollution? Depending on your sensitivity to these, you may be dismayed not to see stars in the night sky because of so many street lights and neon signs, or be annoyed by the almost constant sound of traffic and other noise, both of which are part of life in big cities.

DATA WORKSHOP

ANALYZING EVERYDAY LIFE

Measuring Student Attitudes on Environmentalism

"Sustainability," "Environmentalism," and "Being Green" are all terms that refer to reducing human impact on the environment. Even though environmentally based social movements have become so mainstream that there is now an entire television channel, Planet Green, devoted to the topic, there are those who believe that environmentalists are alarmists who have invented issues like global warming, resource depletion, and growing landfills.

This Data Workshop asks you to examine the attitudes of your fellow college students in order to determine the extent of their environmental beliefs and behaviors. Do they believe that climate change has human causes? Do they recycle/conserve various resources, and, if so, how? Do they worry about things like their "carbon footprints"?

For this assignment, construct a survey about environmental attitudes and actions, administer it to your fellow students, and analyze the findings. Refer to Chapter 2 for further information on survey research design. Make sure to collect such demographic data as age, gender, race/ethnicity, GPA, major, and SES so that you can determine whether there is any relationship between the demographics and attitudes.

In constructing the survey, consider using a Likert scale in order to collect data on attitudes as this will help to streamline your analysis. Survey respondents can select the degree to which they agree or disagree with statements. You can use the following statements as a starting place, and modify or add new ones when you construct your own survey questionnaire.

- Eating facilities on campus should use environmentally friendly products.

- I use environmentally friendly products at home as much as I can.

- I feel motivated to recycle.

- I use the recycling bins on campus.

- There are enough recycling bins on campus.

- If I see a piece of trash on the ground when I am outside, I will pick it up and dispose of it properly.

- Global warming is a threat to our planet.

- Humans and industry have contributed to global warming.

- I make attempts to reduce my carbon footprint in my daily life.

- Sustainability is an important issue for the entire world.

- If we don't reduce, reuse, and recycle, our world will face serious consequences.

- Environmentalism is a worthwhile cause.

Administer the survey to your fellow students. For the purposes of this exercise, you should start with a small pilot group and collect between twenty-five and thirty surveys. After gathering data, describe and analyze your findings. See what kinds of patterns you can find. Are college students concerned about the environment? Does this concern translate into action? How do your findings confirm or refute any hypotheses that you might have had before beginning this Data Workshop? What do you think your data reveals overall?

There are two options for completing this Data Workshop.

- *Option 1 (informal)*: Bring your survey questionnaires to share with the rest of your class. Discuss the findings in small groups. Note the similarities and differences in your findings and those of your group members. Write a statement that identifies and incorporates the general patterns found in the data gathered by the entire group.

- *Option 2 (formal)*: Write a three- to four-page essay describing your research project and analyzing your findings. Attach your completed surveys and any notes to your paper.

Environmental Sociology

To analyze problems of the environment, sociologists have developed "environmental sociology," a distinct subfield of sociology that describes environmental issues and examines the reciprocal interactions between the physical environment, social structure, and human behavior. Although this subfield is still developing, four major analytic frameworks within environmental sociology have emerged during the past thirty years. These concern the political economy of the environment, attitudes about the environment, environmental movements (including environmental justice), and sustainable development.

THE POLITICAL ECONOMY OF THE ENVIRONMENT

The political economy of the environment is a core area of study within environmental sociology that takes a classical or neo-Marxist and Weberian approach to understanding the environment (Schnaiberg 1975). Its focus is on how economic factors influence the way organizations (typically corporations) use the environment and how this use is often supported by political systems and policies.

> **treadmill of production** term describing the operation of modern economic systems that require constant growth, which causes increased exploitation of resources and environmental degradation

Contemporary industrial societies have been built on the premise of progress—on conquering nature and using natural resources to fuel production and expand profits (Schnaiberg and Gould 1994). Government policies and economic systems have frequently supported this belief. While progress has usually meant great wealth for some and goods and services for many, it has come at a price: environmental degradation and the accompanying social problems.

Environmental sociologists refer to this process as the **treadmill of production**. They assert that the drive for economic growth in capitalist societies persists, even at the expense of the environment and despite opposition from activists and other groups, because corporate expansion provides critical taxable wealth and the jobs essential to the economic life of a society. Although such development creates a multitude of problems, there are also serious consequences for attempts at regulating or limiting the production practices of these corporations (Schnaiberg 1975). Large corporations can typically defend themselves against calls for accountability for damages and exercise considerable influence through political lobbying and campaign contributions as well as appeals to change public opinion. Attacking the practices of these corporations can also be detrimental to the workers who need their jobs and to governments that may depend on these industries for products critical to the nation's well-being and security (Schnaiberg and Gould 1994). Even though the treadmill of production is not an environmentally friendly process, numerous societies are invested in its continued existence, and we will likely see enduring conflict between the economy and the environment at the international, national, regional, and local levels.

ENVIRONMENTAL ATTITUDES Understanding societal attitudes about the environment is an essential part of environmental sociology. Early work in this area began with a group of Chicago School sociologists including Robert Park

(1961) and Amos Hawley (1950), who helped to establish the field of human ecology. Extending on this in the 1970s, William Catton and Riley Dunlap developed the **new ecological paradigm** (Catton and Dunlap 1978, 1980).

Historically, Westerners have had a particularly **anthropocentric,** or human-centered, relationship with the environment, perceiving nature as something to master. Nature is believed to be inexhaustible and hence can be used with impunity to serve humankind. Consumption is equated with success. This is consistent with the Judeo-Christian belief in man's dominion over the earth. Western culture thus perpetuates **human exceptionalism**, an attitude that humans are exempt from natural ecological limits (Dunlap and Catton 1994). Much of our progress through industrialization supports this notion that technology will allow us to overcome any environmental challenge. In contrast, the new ecological paradigm poses humans as part of the ecosystem or biosphere, one of many species that interact with the natural environment. Nature has limits that we must respect, and this may constrain economic development. The new ecological paradigm recognizes that human activity can have both intended and unintended consequences that shape social life and life on the planet.

Scientists as well as environmental advocates and policy makers are in disagreement about the future consequences of global climate change. Some argue that global warming is part of the natural progression of the earth. Others say it has been brought about primarily by human activity and that we are headed toward catastrophe. Still others argue that though global warming exists, it is not a cause for concern. How such problems as global warming are defined and understood depends on underlying values and beliefs. You might not consider global climate change so bad if you also thought that extinction of some plant and animal life was an acceptable part of the evolutionary process of natural selection. Or you might not be so concerned by such issues if you thought that clean air, fossil fuels, or other natural resources were commodities in a free market and that nations must compete for their availability and take responsibility for their consequences. Our definitions and interpretations of evidence regarding environmental problems are also filtered through our own cultural beliefs and values.

Research on environmental attitudes has had a marked influence on studies of environmental movements (Dunlap and Catton 1979; Buttel 1987). Environmental sociologists are interested in the processes that create attitude change and the relationship between attitudes and behavior. They want to understand why certain groups have become more "biocentric" (as opposed to anthropocentric), or more environmentally sensitive, and what inspires great numbers of people to participate in environmental movements.

THE ENVIRONMENTAL MOVEMENT   People have long been concerned about the relationship between humans and nature and about the impact of society on the environment. When people organize around these concerns, their collective efforts can have profound impacts. When sociologists study the **environmental movement**, topics of interest include the origins of the groups involved, their internal organization and social network formation, their political role, and their presence at local, regional, national, and international levels. In this section, we will trace the four major eras in the history of the environmental movement in the United States while discussing major flashpoints in its development.

Most social scientists and historians date the beginning of the American environmental movement to the writings of Henry David Thoreau in the mid-1800s, especially *Walden; or, Life in the Woods*, which concerns the rejection of urban materialism and the virtues of simple living. Thoreau has inspired many generations, and his central argument, about how humans impact the natural environment and thus must actively choose to preserve it, continues to be the backbone of environmental activism in the United States. While preservation or conservation remains a key focus, the environmental movement has become increasingly interested in how to respond to or prevent ecological disasters.

The late nineteenth and early twentieth centuries are often referred to as the **conservation era**; environmentalism in that time tended to reflect Thoreau's preservation argument. In this time, state and national parks, such as Yosemite (1864), Yellowstone (1872), and the Grand Canyon (1906), were established through legislative protection and funding. Congress approved the creation of the National Park Service in 1916 and continued to pass environmental laws to protect the wilderness and to regulate industries that impinged on it, such as mining and logging. Early environmental groups such as the Audubon Society (1886) and the Sierra Club (1892) that emphasized the conservation of wildlife and nature were also established around that time and are still in existence today.

new ecological paradigm a way of understanding human life as just one part of an ecosystem that includes many species' interactions with the environment; suggests that there should be ecological limits on human activity

anthropocentric literally "human centered"; the idea that needs and desires of human beings should take priority over concerns about other species or the natural environment

human exceptionalism the attitude that humans are exempt from natural ecological limits

environmental movement a social movement organized around concerns about the relationship between humans and the environment

John Muir An early conservationist, Muir led the movement to establish national parks like Yosemite.

From the mid-twentieth century on, environmentalism changed in response to several ecological disasters. For example, in 1948, in the town of Donora, Pennsylvania, twenty people died and more than 7,000 others were hospitalized when industrial waste that formed concentrated smog was released into the atmosphere and settled over the town, severely compromising the air quality for its residents. Congress responded to that ecological disaster (albeit late) by passing some of the first environmental legislation of the modern era, the Air Pollution Control Act of 1955.

The second era, the **modern environmental movement**, began in the 1960s in part as a response to Rachel Carson's landmark book *Silent Spring*. Her book was an impassioned critique of the effects of pesticide use, specifically dichloro-diphenyl-trichloroethane, commonly known as DDT. The 1950s had witnessed an explosion of development in new chemicals such as fertilizers and pesticides, often hailed as revolutionary and miraculous in the practice of agriculture. But these same chemicals harmed or killed beneficial organisms and wildlife such as songbirds (hence the title of the book). There was even speculation that they could work their way up the food chain, becoming carcinogens in humans. Although the companies manufacturing DDT and other chemicals vigorously fought such allegations, public outcry eventually led to government hearings and an EPA ban on DDT in the United States and other countries (Bailey 2002).

While there has been considerable debate about the validity of the science behind the DDT scare, it drew unprecedented public attention to environmental issues that had never been addressed before. As former vice president

Al Gore explained in the foreword to the twenty-fifth anniversary edition of the book, *Silent Spring* "brought environmental issues to the attention not just of industry and government; it brought them to the public, and put our democracy itself on the side of saving the earth." As awareness about environmental issues grew, so did the amount of environmental legislation. As a result, environmentalism was able to find credibility in American society, and its practice has become an enduring force in public policy.

Unfortunately, many other ecological disasters occurred in the decades that followed. Some of the most notable were the oil spill in Santa Barbara in 1969 (Molotch 1970) and the Exxon Valdez spill off the coast of Alaska in 1989; the discovery of toxic waste in the Love Canal in 1978; the nuclear accident at Three Mile Island in 1979; the discovery of a thirty-year oil spill at the Guadalupe Dunes in California in 1994 (Beamish 2002) and an even much larger oil spill in the Gulf of Mexico in 2010. Each of these events elicited public outrage. Through a series of amendments and executive orders, the EPA was given broader powers that included the means to investigate ecological crises, organize cleanups, punish offenders, establish further regulations, and research environmentally friendly technologies.

The third era of the environmental movement, referred to as **mainstream environmentalism**, began in the 1980s. It emerged, in part, as a response to the Reagan administration's anti-environmental deregulation policies. National and international environmental organizations, such as the Sierra Club and Greenpeace as well as other watchdog groups, were becoming increasingly institutionalized. They began using well-crafted promotional campaigns and sophisticated political tactics to gain the attention of legislators and secure victories in their ongoing battles. Mainstream environmentalism evolved into a cluster of public interest groups, many of which had their own political action committees, or PACs, to lobby for positive legislative change. In addition to legal expertise, they developed economic and scientific expertise to support research, generate grants, and acquire land for preservation.

A link between the modern era and the mainstream era of environmentalism is

conservation era earliest stage of the environmental movement, which focused on the preservation of "wilderness" areas

modern environmental movement beginning in the 1960s, the second major stage of the environmental movement; focused on the environmental consequences of new technologies, oil exploration, chemical production, and nuclear power plants

mainstream environmentalism beginning in the 1980s, the third major stage of the environmental movement; characterized by increasing organization, well-crafted promotional campaigns, sophisticated political tactics, and an increasing reliance on economic and scientific expertise

Julia "Butterfly" Hill

On New Year's Day in 1997 a giant mudslide destroyed seven homes in Stafford, a small town in California's Humboldt County. Heavy December rains played a role, but many were convinced that the real cause was logging that had stripped nearby slopes bare of vegetation. The Pacific Lumber Corporation owned the land and had recently clear-cut the timber from the mountain, harvesting all the significant trees from an area and using fire and herbicides to clear the area of plants that would impede the growth of "merchantable timber."

Shortly after the slide, Pacific Lumber received permission to begin clear-cutting timber on the slopes immediately around the slide. At this point, Earth First!, a radical environmental group, decided to act. A reconnaissance team explored the slopes scheduled for logging and discovered that an enormous redwood known to locals as the "Stafford Giant," estimated to be between 600 and 1,000 years old, was marked to be harvested. Late one night, members of the team hiked in and built a small platform 180 feet above the ground where a volunteer protester could sit in the tree and thus prevent it from being cut down. To commemorate the moonlight by which they worked, they named the tree "Luna."

Julia Hill, in Arkansas, had worked in a restaurant until the fall of 1996, when she was seriously injured in a car accident. Ten months later, after long and intensive therapy for her injuries, she emerged with a deep-seated conviction that her life had to be about more than just a paycheck, "that our value as people is not in our stock portfolios and bank accounts but in the legacies we leave behind" (Hill 2000, p. 5). She resolved that as soon as she was well enough she wanted to find a sense of purpose, and on a visit to the California coast to see the redwoods, she found one.

She put her belongings in storage, moved to Humboldt County, and made her way to the Earth First! base camp; there she adopted her own "forest name," Butterfly, and got ready to help however she could. That chance came when organizers were looking for someone to sit in Luna for at least five days. No one could have guessed that Julia would eventually sit in Luna continuously for more than two years.

Tree sitting is a rather radical form of activism. Almost all tree sits fail, because missing one day of sitting can allow the loggers to return and cut down the tree—if activists aren't forcibly removed before then. Pacific Lumber made the process as uncomfortable for Julia as possible. Foghorns and floodlights disturbed her sleep, and the company's helicopter sprayed her with rotor wash—the dust and wind kicked up underneath the helicopter (Garlington 1998). The company even tried to starve her down by preventing her support team from delivering fresh supplies.

Julia stayed on the platform. Although the tree sit started with little fanfare, the number of requests for interviews rose rapidly as the protest continued. Julia could contact the

Earth Day a holiday conceived of by environmental activist and former senator Gaylord Nelson to encourage support for and increase awareness of environmental concerns; first celebrated on March 22, 1970

Earth Day. The original event was conceived of by environmental activist and then senator Gaylord Nelson as both a "teach-in" and a protest gathering to express concerns about environmental issues. In the first Earth Day, celebrated on March 22, 1970, 20 million people participated. Earth Day is still celebrated nationally and internationally. Typically, it includes a variety of groups—environmentally friendly businesses, nonprofit organizations, local government agencies, and others—teaching people about ways to help the environment while celebrating their relationship to it.

outside world with a solar-powered radio phone. Her supporters built an official web site and set up a media office to field local, national, and international inquiries. Musicians Bonnie Raitt and Joan Baez played at a rally for Luna, and actor Woody Harrelson even stayed in the tree overnight, joining the protest (Hill 2000).

Eventually the group's tactics and Hill's perseverance paid off. By putting a human face on the struggle to save the forests, public pressure mounted on Pacific Lumber to reach a settlement that preserved Luna. On December 18, 1999, a little more than two years after Julia began her treetop residency, a deed of covenant was signed that protected Luna and a 200-foot buffer zone around it in perpetuity. Despite a serious attack by vandals almost a year later, the tree is still standing today.

Of course, this wasn't the end of the story for Hill. She established the Circle of Life Foundation, with the stated goal of "inspiring, supporting, and networking individuals, organizations, and communities to create environmental solutions with respect for the interconnectedness of all life" (Shakara 2004). Hill's second book, *One Makes the Difference: Inspiring Actions That Change Our World* (2002), claims that any individual can and should make a difference. The book opens with a quote from Bette Reese: "If you think you're too small to be effective, you have never been in bed with a mosquito."

Julia "Butterfly" Hill The environmental activist perches near the top of Luna, a 200-foot redwood tree.

A fourth era of the environmental movement, representing grassroots efforts, emerged after criticism that although mainstream environmental organizations were serving important functions in the overall effort, they were too accommodating to industry and government. **Grassroots environmentalism** is distinguished from mainstream environmentalism by its belief in citizen participation in environmental decision making. Its focus is often regional or local, and it can include both urban and rural areas. Grassroots groups are often less formally organized than their mainstream counterparts, and,

grassroots environmentalism fourth major stage of the environmental movement; distinguished by the diversity of its members and belief in citizen participation in environmental decision making

The 1969 Union Oil Spill in Santa Barbara Workers rake hay along a Southern California beach in an effort to protect the coast from more than 200,000 gallons of oil that leaked into the sea when an off-shore oil rig broke.

in some instances, this frees members from ineffective bureaucratic structures as they fight for issues of great importance to them. Grassroots environmentalism draws on a variety of ideologies, including feminist, native, and spiritual ecologies, and cuts across ethnic, racial, and class lines.

NIMBY, which stands for "Not In My Back Yard," was originally a derogatory term applied to those who complained about any kind of undesirable activity in their neighborhoods that would threaten their own health or local environment but were not concerned if it happened to people somewhere else. Now the term "NIMBY" has been appropriated by the environmental movement for the people "somewhere else" who are fighting against environmental degradation on their home turf, often without significant resources, to protect their families and surrounding communities. Sometimes it makes sense to wage battles at the local level where the problems are readily apparent and the approaches to solving them more tangible. And, of course, if people everywhere were willing to fight in this way, then anti-environmental corporations would have to change their practices or be forced out of all possible locations.

Another expression of grassroots environmentalism is the **Green Party**. Established in 1984, the basic Green Party platform of ten principles includes a commitment to environmentalism, social justice, decentralization, community-based economics, feminism, and diversity. The environmental goal is a sustainable world in which nature and human society coexist in harmony. The Green Party seeks to be an alternative voice in political and policy debates that often challenges the mainstream Republican and Democratic parties and rejects corporate backing. Members would like to see the political process returned to the people. Candidates from the Green Party have been elected to various political seats at the local and state levels, and Ralph Nader, a longtime consumer protection advocate, was its candidate in the presidential election of 2000, garnering enough votes to have perhaps changed the outcome of that election.

Ecoterrorism is an example of radical grassroots environmentalism. Ecoterrorists (or ecoextremists) use violent and often criminal methods to achieve their goals of protecting the environment. These groups operate underground, without centralized organization or known membership. Law enforcement officials call ecoterrorist tactics—including arson, explosives, vandalism, theft, sabotage, and harassment—"direct action" campaigns to disrupt or destroy businesses and organizations the groups believe are a threat to the environment. They have so far avoided targeting people, though there may be victims in the course of ecoterrorist operations. FBI counterterrorism agents recently told a Senate committee that radical environmental and animal rights activists represented the nation's top domestic terrorist threat (Heilprin 2005).

NIMBY short for "Not In My Back Yard"; originally referred to protests that aimed at shifting undesirable activities onto those with less power; now sometimes used without negative connotations to describe local environmental activists

Green Party a U.S. political party established in 1984 to bring political attention to environmentalism, social justice, diversity, and related principles

ecoterrorism use of violence or criminal methods to protect the environment, often in high-profile, publicity-generating ways

It is unclear how many ecoterrorist groups currently exist in the United States, Canada, England, and elsewhere. One visible group calls itself the Earth Liberation Front, or ELF, and claims to have originated in 1977 near Santa Cruz, California. Although it disavows any connection to illegal activity, the ELF acknowledges that some individuals have used its name to claim responsibility for their actions. The ELF says that those individuals have acted on their own without ELF's direction or endorsement. Targets are often chosen for their symbolic nature and have included logging operations, sport utility vehicle dealerships, recreational resorts, and new home and condominium developments.

The **environmental justice** (or "ecojustice") movement represents a significant branch of the environmental movement and is also an example of grassroots organization. It emerged as a response to environmental inequities, threats to public health, and the differential enforcement and treatment of certain communities with regard to ecological concerns. Despite significant improvements in environmental protections, millions of people in the United States live in communities threatened by ecological hazards. The poor and minorities are disproportionately at risk and bear a greater portion of the nation's environmental problems. The term **environmental racism** is applied when an environmental policy or practice negatively affects individuals, groups, or communities based on race or color (Bullard 1993). Access to environmental equality, or living in a healthy environment, has been framed as a basic human right.

Research on environmental justice is one of the fastest growing areas of scholarship within environmental sociology. Sociologist Robert Bullard is among the leading researchers in this area, linking social justice to environmental movements. His book *Dumping in Dixie: Race, Class, and Environmental Quality* (Bullard 1990) examined the economic, social, and psychological impacts associated with locating noxious facilities (such as landfills, hazardous-waste dumps, and lead smelters) within lower-income African American communities where they have been less likely to meet with significant opposition.

Blacks have historically been underrepresented in the environmental movement. Often, they were already engaged in other civil rights causes that seemed more pressing. They also lacked

> **environmental justice** a movement that aims to remedy environmental inequities such as threats to public health and the unequal treatment of certain communities with regard to ecological concerns
>
> **environmental racism** any environmental policy or practice that negatively affects individuals, groups, or communities because of their race or ethnicity

Ecoterrorism   To protest logging, wild horse roundups, genetic engineering of plants, SUV sales, and the expansion of the Rocky Mountain resort town of Vail, Colorado, ecoterrorists firebombed this mountain lodge restaurant and other buildings in the Northwest.

the experience and money to fight large corporations, and many had little hope of change, even though they strongly opposed environmental destruction, especially the kinds found in their communities. However, some groups have been moved to action.

Bullard looked at five black communities in the South that challenged public policies and industrial practices threatening their neighborhoods. After years of environmental problems, these activists began to demand environmental justice and equal protection. They grew increasingly incensed at the industries and the government regulatory agencies that allowed those industries to violate codes and continue polluting. The industries, though heavy polluters, had often gained favor in the communities by promising a better tax base and much-needed jobs. Real environmental justice, however, would mean that communities could enjoy jobs and economic development but not at the expense of their health and the environment. That is just what they achieved.

Work by Bullard and others in the field of environmental justice has had profound impacts not only on academia but also on public policy, industry practices, and community organizations. Environmental justice groups are beginning to sway administrative decisions and have won several important court victories (Bullard and Wright 1990; Kaczor 1996; Bullard, Johnson, and Wright 1997). The EPA was even convinced to create an Office on Environmental Equity. There is still much work to be done in this area. Some of the most important battles in the environmental justice movement will be fought beyond the U.S. borders, in other countries suffering from similar and even worse environmental problems.

SUSTAINABLE DEVELOPMENT The study of **sustainable development** is among the most recent areas of environmental sociology, having emerged in the 1990s, and it continues to generate some controversy (McMichael 1996). The idea of sustainable development was popularized in a United Nations World Commission on Environment and Development report entitled "Our Common Future," often referred to as the Brundtland Report (1987). Sustainable development is a broad concept that tries to reconcile global economic development with environmental protection; it is based on the premise that

sustainable development economic development that aims to reconcile global economic growth with environmental protection

ecological footprint an estimation of the land and water area required to produce all the goods an individual consumes and to assimilate all the wastes she generates

the development aspirations of all countries cannot be met by following the path already taken by industrialized nations because the world's ecosystems cannot support it. Yet, since improving the conditions of the world's poor is an international goal, we must find ways of promoting economic growth that both respect social justice and protect the environment, not only in the present but for future generations (Humphrey, Lewis, and Buttel 2002; Agyeman, Bullard, and Evans 2003).

One way to grasp the magnitude of supporting humans on the planet is the **ecological footprint**, an estimation of how much land and water area is required to produce all the goods we consume and to assimilate all the wastes we generate. The current ecological footprint of the average American, approximately thirty acres, represents about three times her fair share of the earth's resources (Wackernagel and Rees 1996). Compare that to someone from the United Kingdom, whose ecological footprint is approximately fifteen acres, or someone from Burundi with a little over one acre (People and the Planet 2002). Modern industrialized countries are appropriating the carrying capacity of "land vastly larger than the areas they physically occupy" (Rees and Wackernagel 1994). Projections are that we would need four additional planet Earths to support the world's population if everyone else were to adopt the consumption habits of Americans. (You can measure your own ecological footprint by following the link listed in "Suggestions for Further Exploration" at the end of this chapter.)

Working toward sustainable development is a challenge. We have to find ways to meet the needs of a growing world population—for food, shelter, health care, education, and employment—while ensuring that we sustain nature and the environment, whether that is fresh water, clean air, natural resources, nontoxic communities, or the protection of wildlife. Often, these goals are posed as adversaries. It is even more important to work toward sustainable development as we become increasingly globalized and have to think about the rest of the world and far into the future (Holdren, Daily, and Ehrlich 1995).

Some solutions toward sustainable development are already being implemented. These include lifestyle modifications—engaging in voluntary simplicity, recycling, vegetarianism and veganism, buying organic foods, and using goods or services from environmentally friendly and fair trade companies. Others are modifications to our infrastructure, such as green building, ecological design, xeriscape (water-conserving) gardening, and land conservation. Technological changes can be made in the way we use energy—from hybrid or biodiesel cars to solar power. Some state and local governments are enforcing higher environmental standards and regulations than those imposed at the federal level. In 2005, more than 160 U.S. mayors signed on to an urban anti–global warming agreement that some call the "municipal Kyoto" in reference to the Kyoto Protocol, an international treaty on global climate change that the United States has declined to ratify (Caplan 2005). All these efforts help move us toward sustainable development, but much more must be done if we are to create that vision for the future.

Closing Comments

In this chapter, we have crossed a huge terrain—from population through urbanization to the environment. We hope that you can now see the connection among these three seemingly disparate areas of study. Human population has grown throughout history, particularly in the past 200 years. The rate at which the population increases is influenced by both biological and social factors. Where all these people live has also changed over time. As more of them locate in cities, cities play a key role in how we inhabit the world and what kind of world that becomes. The billions of people inhabiting the planet are part of an ecosystem, and they continue to have an impact on it. The natural environment both affects and is affected by human activity. So population, urbanization, and the environment are intimately related. There is a mutual effect and interdependence between them, where trends and changes in one reverberate through the others. As residents of planet Earth, we all take part in the dynamic, both enjoying or suffering current realities and creating future ones.

⑤ Need Help Studying?

wwnorton.com/studyspace

Visit StudySpace to access free review materials such as:

- **Vocabulary Flashcards**
- **Diagnostic Review Quizzes**
- **Study Outlines**

QUESTIONS FOR REVIEW

1. How many children would you like to have? The demographic predictions of the Neo-Malthusians and the Anti-Malthusians disagree sharply. According to the Anti-Malthusians, what changes in social structure might make people less interested in having lots of children?

2. This chapter described Americans as "pigs of the planet," in reference to the way we consume resources. Make a list of all the ways you use water other than for drinking. Do you believe that the planet can continue to support the kind of consumption and waste of the American standard of living? What do you think will happen when growing populations in developing nations want to live like Americans?

3. Do you prefer to live in a dense urban area, or a more lightly populated suburban one? What are the advantages and disadvantages of each? What sorts of social and/or environmental problems are created by the situation you prefer?

4. The chapter describes the social problems associated with the environment in terms of consumption and waste. How are these two types of social problems connected? Describe one thing you've consumed today in terms of the pollution that can be directly linked to it.

5. What is the difference between an anthropocentric point of view and the new ecological paradigm? How do these ways of understanding the relationship between human beings and the natural world relate to the social construction of environmental problems?

6. Today, the environmental movement is much more diverse than when it began in the latter part of the nineteenth century. Although few would object outright to national parks, what sort of criticisms might those concerned with environmental racism have for conservationists?

7. In the past, NIMBY has been used as a derogatory term, but grassroots environmental activists have reclaimed it as a positive one. When does "not in my backyard" become a worthwhile resistance strategy?

8. Mainstream environmental activism focused on influencing government. Grassroots environmentalism often stresses the importance of direct action, like that of Julia "Butterfly" Hill, who stayed in a redwood tree for two years to keep it from being cut down. Pick a contemporary environmental problem and describe how you would attempt to remedy it if you belonged to a mainstream environmental organization. How would you approach it differently as a member of a grassroots organization?

9. How and why is it helpful to consider the environment and urbanization as related issues? Specifically, think about the issues associated with internal migration. Describe how internal migration within the United States affects three of the environmental problems described in this chapter.

SUGGESTIONS FOR FURTHER EXPLORATION

Climate Challenge (www.bbc.co.uk/sn/hottopics/climate change/climate_challenge). A free online video game that puts the earth's future in your hands. As the president of the European nations, you must tackle climate change while remaining popular enough with voters to stay in office. Released in 2007, the game uses carbon dioxide emission forecasts produced by the Intergovernmental Panel on Climate Change.

Davis, Mike. 1999. *Ecology of Fear*. New York: Vintage. A case study in social ecology, examining the impact of the city of Los Angeles on the natural world and the ways that its residents have been affected by local ecology. Wildfires, mudslides, and mountain lions may seem to be purely natural, but as Davis illustrates, they are closely connected to social forces.

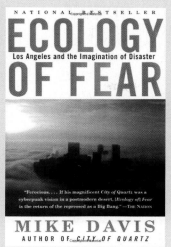

The last photo of Chris in Alaska

Ecological Footprint Quiz (www.earthday.net/footprint). This quiz allows you to estimate how much productive land and water you need to support what you use and what you discard. After answering fifteen simple questions, you can compare your ecological footprint to those of others and to the planet's available resources.

Hawken, Paul, Amory Lovins, and L. Hunter Lovins. 2000. *Natural Capitalism: Creating the Next Industrial Revolution*. Boston: Back Bay Books. A controversial look at "natural capitalism," which the authors believe can be simultaneously good for business and good for the environment, primarily through closer attention to waste and energy use.

Al Gore

An Inconvenient Truth. 2006. Dir. Davis Guggenheim. Paramount. A documentary featuring former vice president Al Gore. This is an in-depth discussion of global warming and its potential consequences on weather, biodiversity, disease, and sea level. The film echoes the concerns of those who study the political economy of the environment.

Into the Wild. 2007. Dir. Sean Penn. Paramount Vantage. A retelling of the story of Chris McCandless based on Jon Krakauer's book of the same name. This film addresses the relationship between the social world and the natural world by chronicling McCandless's travels and his shifting allegiances to nature, himself, and his society.

Kolbert, Elizabeth. 2006. *Field Notes from a Catastrophe*. New York: Bloomsbury. An accessible overview of the linkages between human action and climate change, with chapters covering specific case studies from the melting glaciers of the arctic to conservation efforts in Burlington, Vermont.

Lopez, Barry. 2004. *Of Wolves and Men*. New York: Scribner. A social history of the interaction between American society and *canis lupus*. Lopez demonstrates the importance of cultural values and beliefs in determining public reaction to wolves, from a history of extermination to an increasing belief in wolf conservation.

The Meatrix and *The Meatrix II: Revolting* (www.themeatrix.com). Using themes from the *Matrix* films, these short online animations describe the effects of factory farms, including negative impacts on animal welfare, antibiotic-resistant bacteria, pollution, and destroyed communities.

The World Clock (www.poodwaddle.com/clocks/worldclock/). Check out this web site that calculates demographic change in real time, running statistics on birth, death, energy use, environmental harm, food production, and more.

CHAPTER 16

Social Change: Looking Toward Tomorrow

Of you haven't seen one already, ask your parents (or maybe one of your professors) to show yo the scar from their smallpox vaccination. It's a dime-sized circle that was made with multipl pricks of a tiny fork-like needle that held one drop of vaccine, and it would now be almost invis ible as it sits at the top of their left arm. This little scar shows your parents and professors were pro tected from a disease that has killed billions of people and left billions more blind and disfigured, fo which there is no effective treatment. Yet, if you check your own arm, you will see that you do *not* hav a similar scar; you are not protected from smallpox. Why not?

Smallpox is one of the diseases that have been effectively eliminated by the advances of med cal technology. Scientific discoveries during the eighteenth and nineteenth centuries meant that b the middle of the twentieth century, a global campaign to stamp out the disease was well under wa The last natural case of smallpox in the world occurred in Somalia in 1977, and a lab accident killed British researcher in 1978. But since then, no one has contracted the disease. The World Health Orga nization (WHO) declared smallpox officially eradicated in 1979, and vaccinations were discontinue worldwide by 1986.

Does the WHO declaration mean that the smallpox virus no longer exists? No. Two high-securit research labs, one in the United States and one in Russia, hold samples of the virus, and anothe lab in the Netherlands houses the seed virus used to produce the vaccine. Why keep samples c a vanquished virus? If it ever reappears, if even the smallest amount somehow escapes laborator quarantine, an epidemic is almost certain: smallpox is transmitted through face-to-face contact befor individuals even know they are infected, and it can also be spread through building ventilation sys tems. It will thus be critical for us to have stores of the virus ready so that more vaccines can be mad The fact that large portions of the world's population—including you—are unprotected makes u vulnerable to the use of smallpox as a biological weapon. In the wake of the terrorist attacks of 9/1 U.S. health officials began considering reinstituting mass vaccination programs; although at this date they have not yet done so.

The story of smallpox is a story of social change—change in the incidence, experience, and mear ing of smallpox over time. The disease was a ubiquitous killer for thousands of years, up to the 1940s; some cultures, families waited to name babies until after they had contracted and survived smallpo It killed peasants and royalty alike, but through deliberate human effort a defense against the diseas

entually developed. Medicine, politics, culture, demography, individual and collective actions—
ox was conquered through the synergy of all these elements. In the late 1700s, for example, English
ian Edward Jenner observed a pattern of smallpox immunity in milkmaids who had previously
cted the less virulent cowpox, and he developed the first vaccine. Beginning in the 1950s, the WHO
political and financial support for a worldwide vaccination campaign. Your grandparents obeyed
and took your parents to be vaccinated when they were children. All of these processes contributed
ge in the meaning and incidence of smallpox. And the meaning may change yet again as a result of
ions of another group: international terrorists. So perhaps no disease can ever truly be eradicated—
lly, it is our lingering fear of smallpox that means we must keep it with us in some form.

TO READ THIS CHAPTER

re a couple of reasons why we are ending this book
chapter on social change. The first is that, to para-
an old cliché, change is the only constant. It is hap-
everywhere, all the time, in myriad variations. One of
allenges after reading this chapter will be to identify
f these social changes and to understand their pat-
auses, and consequences.

other reason is more personal: we hope that read-
chapter will motivate you to work for social change
f. The study of sociology can sometimes be a bit
tening, as we learn the many ways in which our lives
strained by social forces and institutional structures.
chapter helps us remember that C. Wright Mills's
ction of biography and history" is a two-way street:
ociety shapes the individual, the individual can shape
You have the power to bring about social change,
lly when you work together with others who share
ws, values, and visions for a better world. So we want
read this chapter with optimism; by understanding
cesses of social change, you will be better qualified to
happen yourself.

t Is Social Change?

bt you've heard your parents, grandparents, or other
mily members reflect on "the way things were" when
re children. Hard-to-imagine times such as those
ndoor plumbing or television, or during the Great
Depression or World War II,
undeniably made their lives
very different from your own.
People born even one genera-

ransformation of a

tion apart can have different overall life experiences as a result
of ongoing processes of social change. Consider how different life might be for American children growing up in the
immediate aftermath of the tragedies of September 11, 2001,
or for those who have never known a time without cell phones
and the internet. Our culture evolves over time, as do our
social institutions—the family, work, religion, education, and
political systems. Sociologists define the transformation of
culture over time as **social change**.

It's easy to identify particular historical periods where
major social transformation was unmistakable: the Renais-
sance, the French Revolution, the Civil War, the women's
rights movement. But it's important to realize that social
change is occurring at all times, not just at moments of obvious cultural or political upheaval. The rate at which it happens, however, varies over time, with some historical periods
experiencing rapid social change and others experiencing
more gradual change. For example, social scientists recognize several major "social revolutions"—periods of time during which large-scale social change took place so rapidly
that the whole of human society was dramatically redefined.
The Agricultural Revolution made it possible for previously
nomadic peoples to settle in one place, store surplus food for
future use, and sustain larger populations with the products
of their farms, herds, and flocks. The Industrial Revolution
altered the way people worked, produced, and consumed
goods and lived together in cities. And the Information
Revolution (which is ongoing in Western countries) saw the
advent of computer and internet technology and a profound
shift from economies based on manufacturing to economies
based on information technologies (Castells 2000).

In addition to the pace, other elements of social change
vary as well: some changes are deliberate or intended,
while others are unplanned or unintentional. For example,
the invention of the automobile brought about intended
changes—like the ability to travel greater distances more

efficiently—yet it also brought about unforeseen events, such as the pollution of the atmosphere and the deaths of over 50,000 people every year in car accidents. Some social changes are more controversial than others (the racial integration of public schools, for example, versus salsa's overtaking ketchup as America's top condiment) and some are more important than others. Most fashion trends have little lasting impact—remember the fingerless lace gloves of the 1980s? We thought not. But some—like pants for women, miniskirts, and the bikini—are extremely influential in their impact on gender roles in society.

So society is always changing, and the rates, intentionality, controversy, and importance of individual changes vary. But how does social change occur? One way is through a major physical event: tornadoes, earthquakes, and volcanic eruptions can radically alter the structures and cultures of the communities they strike. Demographic factors also come into play; for instance, as the baby boomers have aged, American society has had to build schools and colleges (in the 1950s and '60s), suburbs (in the 1960s, '70s, and '80s), and retirement facilities (in the 2000s) to accommodate this huge population bulge. Another source of social change lies in discoveries and innovations, such as fire or the wheel. Try to imagine what your life would be like if humans had not figured out how to generate light and heat by striking sparks into kindling.

Social change is often the result of such human action. Jonas Salk, for example, developed a cure for polio, and Helen Keller overcame her own handicaps to advocate for the rights of the disabled. But our most important contributions to social change are made through collective action: the Civil Rights Movement led by Martin Luther King Jr., for example, fundamentally reshaped American society. For this reason, we will spend a good portion of this chapter examining collective behavior in its many variations.

Collective Behavior

When we join a group, we don't disappear as individuals. But we do tend to act differently in groups than we might alone. **Collective behavior** occurs when individuals converge, thus creating a group or crowd, and embark on some sort of action. While crowds gather for different purposes and may seem disorderly, collective behavior theories suggest that such occurrences are often organized and do maintain a certain amount of order.

One of the first theories to focus on collective behavior was the **contagion theory** (Le Bon 1896), which suggested that when people come together, a unified crowd or mob mentality results. Contagion theorists likened such groups to herds of animals, where individuality and rational thought disappear and the external stimulus of the collective action takes over. So, in the case of rampaging soccer hooligans, contagion theory would argue that these fans have given their rational thought over to a mob impulse and can no longer make individual decisions about their actions. But while the theory may seem useful when looking at cases like hooliganism, it doesn't fully

collective behavior behavior that follows from the formation of a group or crowd of people who take action together toward a shared goal

contagion theory one of the earliest theories of collective action; suggested that individuals who joined a crowd could become "infected" by a mob mentality and lose the ability to reason

What Are the Sources of Social Change? Disasters such as the wildfires that swept across Australia in 2009 can radically change the structures and cultures of the communities they destroy.

explain the wide range of collective behavior beyond the "mindless mob."

A more recent idea gives us a better understanding. **Emergent norm theory** (Turner and Killian 1987) argues that collective behavior is not as uniform as Le Bon suggests, and that there are any number of factors that motivate people to participate in crowd activities. The underlying assumption here is that a group is guided by norms (shared cultural expectations for behavior) that emerge in response to a situation, and, as a result, the behavior of those in the crowd is structured to fit within the collective action. So while it may appear that a crowd is one large, indistinguishable mass, the individuals who make it up can have varying understandings of what their roles are within the crowd as well as the meaning of their actions.

Collective behavior generally takes three different forms: crowd behavior, mass behavior, and social movements. While these three types are discussed separately here, they are not mutually exclusive. In the real world, they may overlap whenever collective behavior actually occurs.

Crowd Behavior

A **crowd** is formed when a large number of people come together, either on purpose or randomly. If you have ever strolled around a large city, you may have noticed a street performer (such as a mime or break dancer) trying to entertain people as they walk by. In time, a crowd starts to develop. So, despite the fact that those who are stopping to watch had different reasons to be walking down that street at that particular time, they have now become part of a crowd whose purpose is to be an audience for a street performer. As a crowd, they must adjust their behavior somewhat: perhaps they put away their cell phones so as not to disturb the performer or those around them, and they clap at the end of the performance. Even with this conformity of behavior, however, the fact remains that the individual motivation for joining the onlookers may vary. One person may have stopped because he was struck by the performer's talent, another because her feet hurt from walking. At a certain point, others may pause simply because they see the existing crowd and are curious.

While the street performer type of crowd comes about in a somewhat random way and doesn't yield any demonstrative action, other types of crowds form in a more deliberate manner and lead to highly expressive action. Two examples took place in 1999: a concert in Woodstock, New York, and protests at the World Trade Organization (WTO) meeting in Seattle.

"Woodstock 1999" was the second rock concert (a previous one occurred in 1994) that attempted to emulate the success of the original Woodstock concert of 1969. Around 200,000 attended the three-day event. Like its 1969 predecessor, Woodstock 1999 was supposed to be both a culture-shaping event and financial success; however, it failed on both counts because of poor security, high prices ($150 for a ticket and $4 for a bottle of water), and lack of

"I Predict a Riot" While the majority of the people at the WTO protest in Seattle were peaceful, a small group started some violence and looting that led the Seattle police and National Guard to declare a state of emergency. They issued curfews and even shot rubber bullets and tear gas at innocent, nonviolent protesters.

sanitation. With such tenuous conditions, the crowd began to vent their frustration on the evening of the last day by tearing down and burning fences, breaking into ATM machines, and looting vendor booths and setting them afire. Such action was characterized as a **riot**: a group of people engaged in disorderly behavior directed toward other people and/or property that results in disturbing the peace.

The Seattle protests led to riots on a larger scale. While protests against the WTO are part of an ongoing and larger social movement against current forms of globalization, much attention has been paid to the 1999 meeting in Seattle, where crowds numbering 50,000 to 100,000 gathered to protest. Protesters came from all over the world and included human rights groups, students, environmental groups, religious leaders, and labor rights activists, all seeking fairer trade with less exploitation. While the majority were peaceful, a small group became violent and began looting, leading the Seattle police and National Guard to declare a state of emergency. This was followed by the issuing of curfews, arresting, tear-gassing, pepper spraying, and even shooting rubber bullets at nonviolent protesters. The riots that ensued were an incredibly significant moment in the history of popular protests. People from diverse constituencies that represented a wide range of interests had succeeded in coming together and disrupting the meetings of the world's most influential trade-governing bodies.

Both Woodstock 1999 and the Seattle WTO protests demonstrate how collective behavior can develop into riots. Furthermore, we can see in these two events how collective behavior can be both organized and chaotic, depending on the shared norms that emerge (McPhail 1991).

Mass Behavior

Mass behavior occurs when large groups of people not necessarily in the same geographical location engage in similar behavior. Mass behavior can range from buying a certain type of jeans or getting a tattoo to playing FarmVille on Facebook. Sociologists have focused on three areas of mass behavior in particular. Two, fads and fashions, should be familiar to you. The third too often goes unrecognized by those involved: social dilemmas.

FADS AND FASHIONS Fads are interests that are followed with great enthusiasm for a period of time. They can include products (such as Razor scooters or iPods), words or phrases ("random" or "Don't go there"), clothing styles (head bands or Ugg boots), activities (Wii Fit or text messaging), or even pets (purse-sized toy dogs or anything mixed with a poodle, e.g., a labradoodle). For fads to continue for any length of time, social networks are necessary to spread the enthusiasm (Aguirre,

Quarantelli, and Mendoza 1988). While fads tend not to result in lasting social change, they do follow certain social norms and can create a unified identity for those who practice them. Dieting is a good example. Many Americans have followed such fad diets of the past as the all-grapefruit or all-white-food diet, and in recent years many have joined the low-carbohydrate fad of the Atkins and South Beach diets. During their heyday in the mid-2000s, the low-carbohydrate diets in particular had an impact on food industries, with grocery stores and fast-food chains trying to cater to the needs of their customers. Now, those same low-carb products take up less shelf space, and it may be harder to find a "bunless" burger on the menu. Whatever comes next, it is likely that in wealthy countries like the United States, diet fads are sure to continue.

Another type of mass behavior is **fashion**: a widespread style of behavior and appearance. Fashion can mark you as belonging to a certain group: military fatigues and school uniforms are two examples. Like fads, certain fashions (such as extremely baggy clothes for boys and miniskirts for girls) can enjoy huge popularity for a time. Celebrities can also drive fashion. The hit TV show *Mad Men* became popular not only for its interesting content and great writing and acting, but also for its celebration of 1960s fashion. The men's dapper suits and the women's full skirts and cinched waists brought glamour back to the world of fashion. Similarly, *Gossip Girl* has been as closely watched for its shifting romantic relationships as for the New York designer label clothing worn by its high school stars. The real life stars of both shows are also closely followed in the tabloids and fashion magazines, where fans like to critique or emulate their styles, both onscreen and off.

SOCIAL DILEMMAS In the third category of mass behavior, called a **social dilemma**, behavior that is rational for an individual can lead to collective disaster. Let's take an example that's familiar to everyone: getting stuck in a traffic jam. You creep along slowly for what seems like forever and finally arrive at the source of the holdup. It's an accident, with two cars, a police car, and an ambulance pulled over to the shoulder. But the accident isn't even on your side of the freeway; it's on the other side, and there's nothing blocking your lanes

riot continuous disorderly behavior by a group of people that disturbs the peace and is directed toward other people and/or property

mass behavior large groups of people engaging in similar behaviors without necessarily being in the same place

fads interests or practices followed enthusiastically for a relatively short period of time

fashion the widespread custom or style of behavior and appearance at a particular time or in a particular place

social dilemma a situation in which behavior that is rational for the individual can, when practiced by many people, lead to collective disaster

Fashion The clothing styles of the 1960s, as shown here on the TV show *Mad Men*, have become popular fashion choices today.

of traffic. The holdup on your side is a result of everybody slowing down to get a good look. If they had just kept on driving at their normal speed, you wouldn't have had a traffic jam. So what do you do when you finally get up to the scene of the accident? You slow down and take a look too.

When many people make that same (seemingly) rational decision (to slow down for only a few seconds), the cumulative effect causes a kind of collective disaster (a traffic jam). As social beings, we deal with such situations almost daily, yet rarely do we see how best to handle them. According to many social thinkers, going all the way back to philosopher Thomas Hobbes (1588–1679), we live in a world governed by self-interest. How is our self-interest balanced with the interests of the collective? Social dilemmas help us understand this calculation.

There are two classes of social dilemmas. The first is known as a **tragedy of the commons**. In 1968, Garrett Hardin wrote an essay describing why this kind of dilemma emerges in society. He begins with the classic example of the "commons," which in the past served as a pasture shared by the whole community and on which anyone could graze their livestock. Because access to the commons was free and without restriction, each individual had an incentive to put as many head of livestock on the commons as possible, thereby increasing his own personal gain. But as everyone made that same decision, the commons inevitably became overgrazed. When a common resource is used beyond its carrying capacity, it eventu-

tragedy of the commons a particular type of social dilemma in which many individuals' overexploitation of a public resource depletes or degrades that common resource

ally collapses, becoming totally incapable of supporting any life at all. In a tragedy of the commons, therefore, the benefit is to the individual but the cost is shared by all.

The example of the commons applies to recent history as well. Our natural resources, such as water, air, fossil fuels, forests, plants, and animals, might all be considered similar to a commons. In the case of the U.S. fishing trade, especially, we have seen how, as Hardin put it, "freedom in a commons brings ruin to all" (1968). For example, Dr. Stein remembers living in Santa Barbara in the late 1970s, when local abalones were plentiful. Divers off the California coast and around the Channel Islands could make a good living harvesting these mollusks along rocky shorelines. Any good seafood restaurant regularly offered abalone steaks on its menu, and a casual beachgoer might find abalone shells strewn along the sand. By the 1990s, however, abalones had all but disappeared. As each diver reached the same conclusion—that catching as many abalones as possible would increase his own profits—and more divers moved into the same fishing territory, the abalones were no longer able to regenerate their stocks and were eventually depleted to near extinction.

In a variety of similar cases, like the lobster trappers off the New England coast, regulatory agencies have had to step in and place restrictions on the amount of yields allowed. Otherwise, a tragedy of the commons is likely to ensue. We might also consider social, as well as natural, resources as similar to a commons. For example, when too many people crowd the freeways at rush hour or throw litter out the window of their cars, the result is the commons in ruin.

So what can we do to solve these problems? If we could somehow increase the number of abalones in the sea or the number of lanes on the freeway, that would help solve two of them, but only temporarily. At some point, use overwhelms supply. To Hardin, social dilemmas are a "class of human problems which can be classified as having 'no technical solution'" (1968). What he means is that science or technology alone cannot solve the problems. The solutions must come from the members of society: people will have to change their behavior.

The other class of social dilemma is called a **public goods dilemma**, in which individuals must contribute to a collective resource they may or may not ever benefit from. Blood banks are a good example. Because human blood can't be stored for much longer than a month at a time, many people must volunteer to donate blood regularly in order to keep supplies steady. Blood donors can be viewed as helping to create what is referred to as a "public good," in this case a blood bank. What motivates these people, on average some 8 million a year, to contribute something vital to themselves for which they may never receive anything in return? Everyone is equally entitled to draw from the blood bank regardless of whether or not they have ever given blood. People who take advantage of a public good without having contributed to its creation are called "free riders." In a public goods dilemma, unlike a tragedy of the commons, the cost is to the individual but the benefit is shared by all.

So how do we get people to contribute to a public good if they are not required to? There are numerous examples of this social dilemma in everyday life, as you know if you've ever witnessed a membership drive on public radio or public television. These noncommercial networks must appeal to individuals to contribute money so that they can continue to produce and broadcast programs. But whether or

not anyone responds to the pledge drive, as free riders they can still tune in anytime for nothing. Public goods dilemmas are also a class of human problems for which there are no technical solutions. This is why the government requires us to make certain contributions, in the form of taxes, in order to create such public goods as roads, schools, and fire departments. But there are many other types of public goods, like blood banks, that only individuals can create through their own voluntary contributions.

By examining social dilemmas, we are presented with a dramatic example of mass behavior. We begin to see how seemingly small individual acts add up and cumulatively shape society. So the next time you are faced with a problem like where to throw your litter or whether to give blood, ask yourself what kind of collective outcome you would like your behavior to contribute to.

> **public goods dilemma** a type of social dilemma in which individuals incur the cost to contribute to a collective resource, though they may never benefit from that resource
>
> **social movement** any social groups with leadership, organization, and an ideological commitment to promote or resist social change

Social Movements

If you're like most Americans, the term **social movement** is inextricably linked in your mind to thoughts of long-haired hippies, VW buses, and the antiwar protests of the 1960s. You may not think of the 19th Amendment to the U.S. Constitution, birth control, the AFL-CIO, Protestantism, the Revolutionary War, or Nazism—and yet all of these were, at the time of their inceptions, rightly termed "social movements."

So what precisely is a social movement? Does the term as accurately describe the efforts of liberals to elect a Democrat to Congress as it does the efforts of peace activists to end war? The answer is no. According to Perry and Pugh, "Social movements are collectives with a degree of leadership, organization, and ideological commitment to promote or resist change" (1978, p. 221); Meyer adds that social movements "challenge cultural codes and transform the lives of their participants" (2000, p. 39). A political campaign cannot usually be described as a social movement, because although it may be considered an organized collective with leadership and (sometimes) ideological commitment, and although it may indeed transform the lives of its participants, its purpose is not to fundamentally alter the status quo. Antiwar protesters, on the other hand, are usually trying to change cultural support of war as an accepted means of solving disputes.

We can safely say that most of the institutions with which we are familiar began as social movements. How did they

Tragedy of the Commons Abalone divers rest after making a climb up a cliff. Since the 1990s, abalones have all but disappeared from the coast of California. As the population of the mollusks dwindled, their price increased (they can sell for $100 apiece on the black market), which led more divers to move into the same fishing areas and deplete the population to near extinction.

John Robbins and *Diet for a New America*

John Robbins, heir to the Baskin-Robbins estate, had the kind of childhood every kid dreams of: he grew up with an unlimited supply of ice cream! His uncle (Baskin) and his father (Robbins) started the highly successful chain of ice cream stores that famously features 31 flavors, and John stood to inherit a massive fortune as a result. But he turned down all this wealth and instead devoted himself to promoting the cause of sustainable living. His story makes for an interesting example of how intensely an individual can become personally committed to creating social change.

Robbins has described feeling as though he grew up in two different worlds. In one, ice cream was both a delicious thing to eat and the means for material success. In the other, ice cream was a substance loaded with saturated fat and sugar, which contributed to obesity, heart disease, and diabetes. Robbins had good reasons to be concerned about the effects of ice cream on health: he suffered from serious childhood ailments himself, and his uncle Bert Baskin had a fatal heart attack in the late 1960s. Moreover, he noticed that the same kinds of health problems were widespread in the larger society, and he began to explore the possibility that what people were eating was connected to their illnesses. As a result, Robbins developed an interest in social activism. He also adopted what is called a plant-based, or vegan, diet (and regained much of his health) and began to research how diet affects not only the individual but society as well.

In his Pulitzer Prize–nominated book *Diet for a New America: How Your Food Choices Affect Your Health, Happiness and the Future of Life on Earth* (1987), Robbins argues that while a diet heavy in animal products such as meat and dairy foods can be bad for individual health, it can also be catastrophic for the health of the planet. He links what is essentially a personal choice (for instance, whether to eat eggs and bacon for breakfast or a burger and milkshake for lunch) to a chain of events that ultimately implicates the future of the entire global ecosystem. For example, animals such as cows, pigs, and chickens must be fed large quantities of water and grain—much more than they eventually provide to humans as food.

Large-scale meat production is thus simply not an efficient way to feed people. Further, a single cow requires the grass equivalent of one acre of land to produce "58 pounds of protein, enough to sustain one person for 77 days," but "that same acre planted in soybeans produces 580 pounds of protein," enough to sustain a person for 2,200 days (Hizer 1997). As one study found, "even the *least* efficient plant food is *nearly ten times* as efficient as the *most* efficient animal food" (italics added), and when compared head to head, soybeans are 40 times more energy efficient than beef (Robbins 1987, p. 376).

Robbins wants to make people aware that "hunger is really a social disease caused by unjust, inefficient and wasteful control of food" (1987, p. 353). We may assume that famines are caused by drought or poor soil conditions, or perhaps corrupt governments. According to Robbins, though, there is more than enough food to go around; it's just that we're feeding it to cows instead of needful humans. Problems of hunger are therefore linked to the type of diet that people in Western countries have come to prefer. As more and more of the world's population adopt this type of diet, associated with the "good life" and consisting of animal products with practically every meal, the problems only grow accordingly.

There's more. Most livestock do not graze in large pastures or fields, but are raised in "factory farms" that consist of huge feed lots and containment facilities where thousands of cows do nothing but eat. Under older methods of farming, most animal waste, in the form of manure, returned to the soil and enriched it. But with factory farming, the amount of waste that makes its way into the ground is so enormous that it eventually seeps into the water supply, contaminating the flora and fauna of nearby streams and rivers. In addition, forests are cut down to create fields that can be planted with grain and then harvested to feed livestock. This practice contributes to the growing problem of global warming, with trees no longer available to help mitigate the effects of carbon monoxide in the atmosphere. Cutting trees and planting fields also exacerbates water shortages. "More water is withdrawn from the Ogallala aquifer" in the High Plains to grow grain for cattle than "is used to grow all the fruits and vegetables in the entire country" (p. 370). Furthermore, fields of grain require not only water but also pesticides, herbicides, and other highly toxic chemicals that make their way into the air and water, further polluting the planet.

With his book, John Robbins was making a sociological point: our personal, private decisions have public, collective consequences. A different diet, one consisting of more plant-based foods and fewer animal products, could produce a "new America," one that is "truly healthy, practicing a wise and compassionate stewardship of a balanced ecosystem" (p. xiii). Moreover, the choices Americans make have a global impact. By producing so many meat and dairy products, we not only injure our own health but also grossly underutilize our capacity to produce food for a world racked by hunger. What we eat for dinner might seem like the most personal decision we could make, but actually the "future of life on earth" is "rarely so much in your own hands as when you sit down to eat" (p. xvii).

In order to further the work he began with *Diet for a New America*, Robbins founded the nonprofit organization EarthSave International (www.earthsave.org). Through EarthSave, he hopes to bring together those interested in a range of social causes—from health and hunger to animal rights and the environment—to work for social change. Robbins may not have ended up with the family fortune, but as a respected and admired opinion leader, he has inspired many people to reconsider their food choices and to join him in becoming activists fighting for social change.

John Robbins

mass society theory a theory of social movements that assumes people join not because of the movements' ideals, but to satisfy a psychological need to belong to something larger than themselves

relative deprivation theory a theory of social movements that focuses on the actions of oppressed groups who seek rights or opportunities already enjoyed by others in the society

resource mobilization theory a theory of social movements that focuses on the practical constraints that help or hinder social movements' action

arise? Why do people join them? And how do today's radicals become tomorrow's establishment?

Several theories attempt to address these questions, but the assumptions behind them have evolved over time. For example, scholars working in the 1940s, '50s, and early '60s generally viewed social movements with suspicion— as "dysfunctional, irrational, and exceptionally dangerous" (Meyer 2000, p. 37). People who joined a movement were thought to be attracted not by its ideals but by the refuge it offered "from the anxieties, barrenness, and meaninglessness of an individual existence" (Eric Hoffer, quoted in Zirakzadeh 1997, p. 9). This explanation, labeled by sociologists as **mass society theory**, was not so remarkable when you consider that researchers in those decades had witnessed the impacts of Nazism, Fascism, Stalinism, and McCarthyism, all of which originated as social movements that eventually devastated millions of lives (Zirakzadeh 1997).

By the 1960s, however, a sea change had occurred, and a new generation of scholars researching the hows and whys of social movements were inclined to be more sympathetic. After all, the 1960s had seen the rise and relative success of the Civil Rights Movement. While people of color may have been alienated from the larger white society, they were certainly not isolated "joiners" who took up with social movements simply to "satisfy some kind of psychological need" (Meyer 2000, p. 37). The Civil Rights Movement and others were practical political responses to inequality and oppression and provided opportunities for the oppressed to "redistribute political and economic power democratically and fairly" (Zirakzadeh 1997, p. 15). This explanation is called **relative deprivation theory** because it focuses on the actions of deprived or oppressed groups who seek rights already enjoyed by others in society—they are deprived relative to other groups.

VOTING RIGHTS A look at the history of voting rights in America shows the power of relative deprivation theory in explaining certain types of social movements. For more than a hundred years, women and persons of color lobbied hard for the right to vote. (We could also turn this claim on its head by saying that for more than a hundred years, many white men fought hard to exclude women and persons of color from voting.) Officially, African American males were granted the right to vote with the 15th Amendment in 1870, but individual states effectively nullified this right by passing regulations requiring literacy tests, prohibitive poll taxes, and grandfather clauses (if your grandfather had voted, you could too) that specifically excluded them from voting. It wasn't until the 1965 Voting Rights Act was passed that African Americans (men *and* women) gained the ability to exercise their constitutionally protected freedom to vote.

Women, meanwhile, had won the right to vote in 1919 with passage of the 19th Amendment. To reach this point, suffragists had spent decades protesting male-only voting through parades, written propaganda, debates, sit-ins, and hunger strikes. The suffrage movement, however, was primarily a white women's battle. At a rally in 1851, Sojourner Truth gave a famous speech ("Ain't I a Woman") highlighting the exclusion of women of color from the movement. These women would have to wait until the Voting Rights Act of 1965 before they could legally vote.

But neither the Voting Rights Act nor the 19th Amendment secures voting rights for all Americans. To become a registered voter, you must be a U.S. citizen (either native born or naturalized), legally reside in the state in which you vote, and have an address of some kind. Most states do not allow ex-convicts, prisoners, or those designated mentally ill to vote. There are presently social movements under way to secure this right for some of these disenfranchised Americans, such as certain categories of prisoners and people with no stable addresses.

MOBILIZING RESOURCES The kind of society we live in has a lot to do with whether or not we are likely to join social movements, the tactics those movements will use, and whether or not they will succeed. For example, in a country like the United States, with strong free-speech protections, anyone wanting to support same-sex marriage can publish books and articles, march in the streets (with some restrictions), and write to their legislators. On the other hand, under a restrictive regime like that of the Taliban in Afghanistan, merely teaching a female to read would have been considered an act of rebellion—and marching in the streets would not even have been an option.

In addition to a tolerant society, social movements also need volunteers, funding, office space, telephone banks, computers, internet access, copy machines, and pens and pencils— as well as the know-how to put these into action. Theorists who focus on how these practical constraints help or hinder social movements operate under the assumptions of **resource mobilization theory**. However interesting or important a type of social change may be, no progress will be made unless such practical resources are available. So if we consider the plight of women in Taliban-ruled Afghanistan, for instance, we realize that some of the most basic human activities, such as reading and meeting together freely, are actually social movement resources that not everyone can take for granted.

The day after Thanksgiving is also known as Black Friday, the biggest shopping day of the year. Thought of by many as the kickoff day to the Christmas shopping season, retailers give incentives to customers by offering extended hours, tremendous discounts, and free gifts on that day. Customers sleep in parking lots waiting for the stores to open, and are so eager to buy merchandise at discounted prices that injuries and even deaths have resulted. Numerous people have been knocked over and stepped on, fights have broken out in the lines and the aisles, and in 2008 a Wal-Mart employee was trampled to death when crowds rushed through the doors. In the same incident, a woman who was eight months pregnant miscarried after being crushed by people stampeding to buy merchandise.

Protesting the rampant consumerism of Black Friday, social activists promote Buy Nothing Day. Adbusters, an anticonsumerist group founded in Vancouver in 1989 by Kalle Lasn and Bill Schmalz, promotes Buy Nothing Day "as a day for society to examine the issue of overconsumption." The basic goal of Buy Nothing Day is to actually spend no money purchasing items on Black Friday in order to raise awareness of the dangers of consumerism and overconsumption. However, Adbusters also encourages other forms of awareness. Groups have staged protests by holding credit card cut-ups in shopping malls where protesters hold up scissors and encourage customers to liberate themselves from debt. Other protesters go on Buy Nothing Hikes to connect with nature instead of shopping. The messages about Buy Nothing Day are largely spread using posters, the internet, and e-mail.

For some, the idea of Buy Nothing Day has grown into a Buy Nothing Year. The Compact is an anticonsumerist group whose members pledge to go a year without buying anything new. Members are only allowed to purchase new underwear, food, and health and safety items, such as brake fluid and toilet paper. Otherwise, they have to make do with the items that they already have in their homes (come on: how many bottles of lotion or sunscreen are lurking in your bathroom cabinet right now?), buy from secondhand stores, or make their own items. Members take The Compact pledge in order to coun-

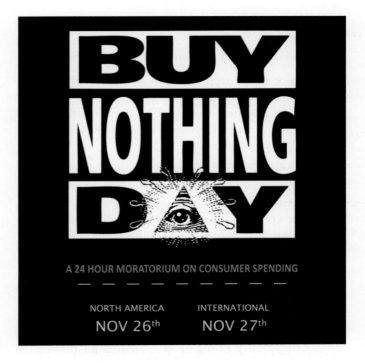

BUY NOTHING DAY

A 24 HOUR MORATORIUM ON CONSUMER SPENDING

| NORTH AMERICA | INTERNATIONAL |
| NOV 26th | NOV 27th |

teract the negative global environmental and socioeconomic effects of U.S. consumerist culture and to simplify their lives. Many of The Compact members blog about their experience participating in a Buy Nothing Year. While it might seem extreme to most Americans to go for an entire year without buying new items, many of the members of The Compact find multiple benefits to taking the pledge and, through their blogging, are able to raise other people's consciousness about consumption, waste, and carbon footprints.

This Data Workshop asks you to analyze any activist group that is working for social or political change (for a review of activism and interest group politics, see Chapter 11). You will be using existing sources to do a content analysis of various materials developed by the organization (see Chapter 2 for a review of this research method). In particular, you will be looking at how the group uses media technology to advance its agenda—the so-called new media (internet, e-mail, and texting) as well as more traditional kinds (television, newspapers, magazines, and brochures).

1. Choose an activist or interest group. Identify the group's commitment to a larger social movement or cause, and discuss its larger goals.

2. Discuss the ways in which the group is attempting each of the three aspects of resource mobilization listed below. What specifically would your group like to accomplish in each category?

a. recruiting members and organizing supporters

b. raising funds

c. transforming public opinion or achieving change

3. How does your group attempt to achieve each of the goals listed in #2? Is it through old or new media, or some combination? Do you think they would be more successful if they found ways to use new media more often? Why or why not?

4. In addition to the use of media, does the group employ any other strategies to achieve their goals? For instance, do they organize rallies or protests, or participate in community events? (These activities may be connected to larger media strategies; for example, a film screening or protest march might be advertised to attract greater support, or be covered by news agencies.)

You can complete this Workshop in one of two ways.

- *Option 1 (informal)*: Jot down your observations and the answers to the Workshop questions in informal notes. Use these notes as points of references for discussion with classmates in small groups. Compare your analyses and insights with others in your group.

- *Option 2 (formal)*: Write a three- to four-page essay in which you answer the Workshop questions.

STAGES IN A SOCIAL MOVEMENT Social movements begin with a few ideas and some people who believe in them. How do they reach the point of marching in the streets (or recruiting members online)? They develop in stages (Figure 16.1), and those stages were identified by Armand Mauss (1975), who described the first one as the "incipient" stage, when the public takes notice of a situation and defines it as a problem (Perry and Pugh 1978). People do not start organizing because they are content; rather, they "see a discrepancy, either real or perceived, between what they are getting and what they believe they should be getting" and decide to take action (Perry and Pugh 1978, p. 237).

For example, in the late nineteenth and early twentieth centuries, many laborers were frustrated over their long working hours, low wages, lack of free weekends, and unsafe working conditions. In response, they began to organize—or, in Mauss's words, to "coalesce," which is the second stage—and their movement gained momentum. Laborers, long an exploited segment of the workforce, drew on both traditionally accepted means of dissent, such as pushing for legislation that would improve working conditions, and tactics that were (at the time) "at the edges of political legitimacy," such as striking (Meyer 2000, p. 40).

Today, working conditions have greatly improved for many (though by no means all) blue collar workers, and unions, once considered marginal or radical, are now seen as part of the establishment. Mauss and others would argue that all successful social movements are eventually incorporated into institutions—that they become "bureaucratized" (stage three). Perry and Pugh assert that "in order to survive, social movements must adapt to their host society or succeed in changing it. When they are successful, they become social institutions in their own right" (1978, p. 265). To take another example, early American colonists rebelling against British rule were part of a social movement, but by the late 1700s, they had ceased to be radicals and had become part of the new nation's government themselves.

A social movement's development can sometimes look a lot like failure; that is, one way or another, the movement will eventually "decline" (stage four). If it succeeds, it is incorporated into the dominant culture; if it fails, it ceases to exist as an active movement—but may have left an indelible mark on its host society nevertheless. Prohibitionists are an excellent case in point. Although those who wished to outlaw alcohol in the United States eventually failed, after the 18th Amendment (Prohibition) was repealed in 1933, their efforts had a huge impact on American culture. There are still "dry" municipalities (where alcohol is not sold) in the country, for example, and a number of infamous gangsters like Al Capone got their start smuggling booze during Prohibition.

WHO TAKES PART What kind of individual is most likely to respond to the recruitment efforts of a particular group? Certainly, more people are asked to join a social movement than ever actually end up participating. Studies done on student protesters in the 1960s showed that they "were more likely than their less active colleagues to be politically oriented, socially engaged, and psychologically well adapted" and that "participation in non-conventional politics tend[ed] to be an addition rather than an alternative to conventional means of participation" (Meyer 2000, pp. 37, 42). In other words, despite the assumptions of theorists working in the mid-twentieth century, activists are not disaffected loners but are instead highly engaged individuals seeking to address perceived injustices on several fronts.

Interestingly, the poorest and most oppressed people tend not to participate in social movements. For these individuals, the consequences of participation may be too high, and they may not have the resources necessary to join in (Perry and Pugh 1978; Zirakzadeh 1997). After all, if someone is working three jobs to support her family, it is unlikely that she would have the time or energy to carry a sign in a street protest. There have been notable exceptions to this trend. In the American West during the 1960s and '70s, migrant farm workers organized

FIGURE 16.1
THE FOUR STAGES OF SOCIAL MOVEMENTS

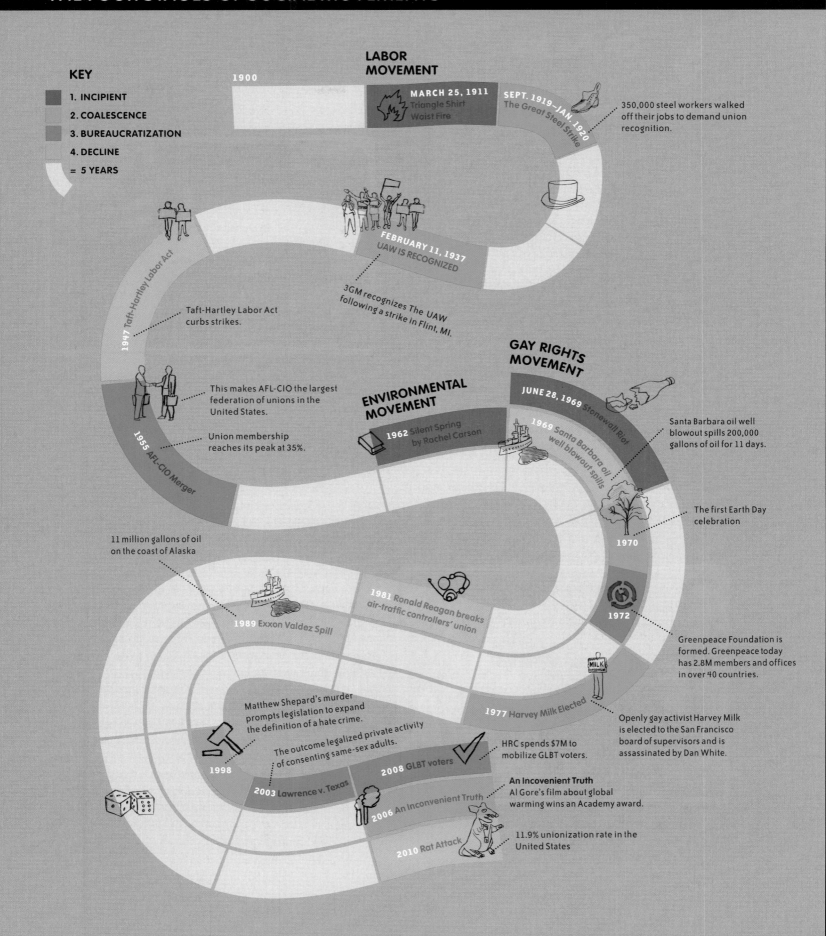

KEY

1. INCIPIENT
2. COALESCENCE
3. BUREAUCRATIZATION
4. DECLINE

= 5 YEARS

1900

LABOR MOVEMENT

MARCH 25, 1911 Triangle Shirt Waist Fire

SEPT. 1919–JAN. 1920 The Great Steel Strike

350,000 steel workers walked off their jobs to demand union recognition.

FEBRUARY 11, 1937 UAW IS RECOGNIZED

3GM recognizes The UAW following a strike in Flint, MI.

1947 Taft-Hartley Labor Act

Taft-Hartley Labor Act curbs strikes.

This makes AFL-CIO the largest federation of unions in the United States.

Union membership reaches its peak at 35%.

1955 AFL-CIO Merger

ENVIRONMENTAL MOVEMENT

1962 Silent Spring by Rachel Carson

GAY RIGHTS MOVEMENT

JUNE 28, 1969 Stonewall Riot

1969 Santa Barbara oil well blowout spills

Santa Barbara oil well blowout spills 200,000 gallons of oil for 11 days.

The first Earth Day celebration

1970

1972

Greenpeace Foundation is formed. Greenpeace today has 2.8M members and offices in over 40 countries.

1977 Harvey Milk Elected

Openly gay activist Harvey Milk is elected to the San Francisco board of supervisors and is assassinated by Dan White.

11 million gallons of oil on the coast of Alaska

1989 Exxon Valdez Spill

1981 Ronald Reagan breaks air-traffic controllers' union

Matthew Shepard's murder prompts legislation to expand the definition of a hate crime.

The outcome legalized private activity of consenting same-sex adults.

HRC spends $7M to mobilize GLBT voters.

1998

2003 Lawrence v. Texas

2008 GLBT voters

2006 An Inconvenient Truth

An Incovenient Truth
Al Gore's film about global warming wins an Academy award.

2010 Rat Attack

11.9% unionization rate in the United States

Helping Professions and Social Change

Does it sometimes seem as though there's no possible way you could ever make a contribution to changing society? You're just one person, after all, and you may not be rich, famous, or all that influential. Right now, your primary concerns probably include graduating and perhaps getting your teaching credential (or social work certification or nursing license) so you can get a job! Also on the "to do" list: find a life partner, start a family, maybe buy a house. But don't think that focusing on your personal goals means that you're totally out of the social change loop. The way you live your life can make a difference all by itself.

Many sociology majors enter what are termed helping professions—these include nursing, counseling, and teaching, and can also include careers in the social service, nonprofit, and law enforcement sectors. If you do go into this type of profession, you will find that every individual encounter you have with a client, student, patient, or offender will be an opportunity to make a tiny step toward social change.

As a first-grade teacher, for example, you will be able to introduce students to the joys of reading—a contribution to overcoming illiteracy, even if it involves only twenty kids. As a public health nurse, you urge patients with tuberculosis to finish their courses of antibiotics or you vaccinate children against polio, diphtheria, and measles—and in doing so, you

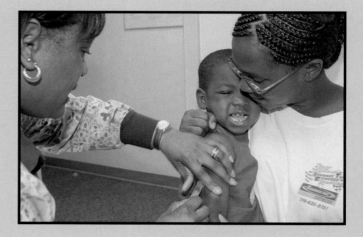

protect the community's health as well as your patients'. When, as a social worker or psychologist, you lead a therapy group for husbands who batter their wives, you have the opportunity to help change the behavior of these men—and to protect their children from continuing a generational cycle of violence. When, as a police officer, you help run your neighborhood's antigang program, you give teenagers alternatives to violent crime, and their choices affect the entire community. When, as a lawyer, you donate your services to a legal clinic that helps undocumented workers gain residency, work permits, and citizenship, you contribute to solving the problems associated with illegal immigration and help change the demographic makeup of your city, state, and country. And even when you volunteer at the adult education center, teaching a computer-training class just once a week, you give your students the opportunity to add a new set of skills to their résumés, find new jobs, and reduce your county's unemployment figures, even if minutely.

Your contributions to social change don't stop here— whom you marry, where you choose to live, and what you teach your children all contribute to the ever-present, ongoing processes of social change. So you don't have to sail away on Greenpeace's *Rainbow Warrior* to make a difference in the world—you can do so in your everyday life as a member of a helping profession, as a community volunteer, and as a parent.

Arab Spring In 2011, Egyptians gathered to overthrow the regime of President Hosni Mubarak. Protests and demonstrations continued throughout the Arab world, often coordinated through social media sites like Facebook, Twitter, and YouTube.

successfully under the leadership of Cesar Chavez. And more recently, thousands of low-income janitors across the United States have gained fairer wages and benefits by organizing unions as part of a Justice for Janitors campaign.

It is perhaps impossible to overstate the importance of social movements in any given society; life as we know it has been shaped by the rise and fall of all sorts of such movements. Imagine what the religious makeup of the world would be like if Martin Luther and his Protestants had not rebelled against the Catholic Church in the early sixteenth century, or what American culture would be like if Martin Luther King Jr. and the Civil Rights Movement hadn't successfully organized. What would world politics have been like if the Nazis hadn't come to power in the 1930s or the Soviet Union hadn't broken up in 1991? The list is endless. Take a moment to consider a few ideas and movements that, in today's culture, seem radical. Whether or not those movements succeed in the traditional sense of the word, it is a pretty safe bet that they will help to shape the world for generations to come. And while the progress made by any social movement tends to happen slowly, the possibility for change and a better society for those future generations is the driving force for those who participate.

Emergent Social Movements: Promoting and Resisting Change

Because society is constantly changing, new social movements are always on the horizon, and even long-standing ones change their goals, strategies, and organizational forms over time. For example, American feminism has taken mul-

tiple forms during the past 150 years. Contrast the focus in the early twentieth century on voting rights for women with the 1960s' broader concerns with equal opportunity and "liberation" from the constraints of sexism, and then with the 1990s' crusade to include previously excluded groups like minority women (see Chapter 9 for a review of the different "waves" of feminist activism). Feminism's self-definition, public profile, objectives, and tactics have changed in response to the movement's own successes and failures.

You may be involved yourself in social movements that didn't even exist in your grandparents' or parents' generation (or even ten years ago). Movements like Critical Mass (cyclists who ride through city streets in large groups each month to protest an automobile-centric society), Straight Edge (nonviolent, drug-free, politically aware, and sometimes even vegan punk rockers who reject promiscuous youth cultures), and PETA (People for the Ethical Treatment of Animals, which campaigns against meat, leather and furs, animal experimentation, and other forms of cruelty) have taken shape since you were born. You have different opportunities for **activism** because you live in a different world than your parents did—even if you're still in the same town.

Some emerging social movements are actually **regressive**, or reactionary; that is, they explicitly resist certain social changes, working to make sure things stay the same or even move backward to earlier forms of social order. For example, reactionary hate movements like Matt Hale's World Church of the Creator, a white supremacist group in Illinois, want to stop the ethnic and religious integration of American society and live in a homogeneous, all-white society. Other regressive movements aren't necessarily motivated by prejudice or hatred of diversity. The voluntary simplicity movement urges members to downsize in all areas of their lives—consumption, time at work, hours in front of the TV, impact on the environment—in the belief that returning to a simpler approach to life will allow them more personal freedom and will benefit society in the long run by conserving resources and reducing stress. Similarly, the Slow Food movement, founded in 1989 as a radical response to the "McDonaldization" of world cuisines, focuses on fresh, local, traditional foods, prepared with care and served in an atmosphere of calm and hospitality—the polar opposite of overprocessed, reheated hamburgers served in a paper bag and eaten in the car.

The "rural rebound" of the 1990s, in which urban residents moved to nonmetropolitan areas in unprecedented numbers, is a type of demographic change that seems, on its face, to represent

> **activism** any activity intended to bring about social change

> **regressive** term describing resistance to particular social changes, efforts to maintain the status quo, or attempts to reestablish an earlier form of social order

progressive term describing efforts to promote forward-thinking social change

technological determinism a theory of social change that assumes changes in technology drive changes in society, rather than vice versa

cultural lag the time between changes in material culture or technology and the resulting changes in the broader culture's relevant norms, values, meanings, and laws

a regressive, back-to-basics movement as well (Johnson 1999). But a rural rebound doesn't necessarily mean that people have returned to declining rural industries, such as farming or mining. The 1990s rebound occurred at least in part because of **progressive**, or forward-thinking, social changes—new technologies that made rural living less isolating and facilitated new ways of working. Fax machines and the internet allow for telecommuting from anywhere in the world, which means that high-powered stock brokers needn't necessarily live in Manhattan and work in a "pit" on Wall Street. They can move to Eagle County, Colorado, or Walworth County, Wisconsin, and enjoy cheaper real estate, less crime, and more natural beauty while still performing their jobs.

Emerging social movements, whether progressive, regressive, or some combination of both, will undoubtedly change the social landscape over time. If your activism is successful—and even if it isn't—then the social world will be a different place by the time your children are your age. What kinds of activism will they be able to engage in?

Technology and Social Change

As we have already seen, revolutionary social change is often the result of a technological development, whether that technological development is the plow, the assembly line, or the microchip. Social movements can arise as a result of technological advancements as well: labor unions multiplied in the factories of the Industrial Revolution, and today the internet can bring more people together to work for social change than ever before. As you might imagine, then, sociologists have generated theories that seek to explain the role of technology in social change (Kurzweil 1990; Pool 1997). One common characteristic of these theories is an emphasis on **technological determinism**—the idea that technology plays a defining role in shaping society. As one of the earliest proponents of this approach, William Ogburn (1964) described the process of social change as beginning with invention or discovery and proceeding when the invention is spread from one group or society to another. In the remainder of the chapter, we look at the relationship between technology and social change.

Faith in Technology: Can It Solve Social Problems?

At the beginning of this chapter, we saw how the same medical breakthrough that vanquished smallpox has now made us vulnerable to an epidemic of this virus. It seems that no social change is without its unforeseen, unintentional outcomes, some of which are positive and some of which are not.

This is often especially noticeable in the case of technological advances. We may welcome the invention of a new vaccine, the World Wide Web, in-vitro fertilization, or sport utility vehicles (SUVs) and notice only later that they bring unanticipated problems. For example, the web speeds up communication and gives us access to information, goods, services, and people we would never have been able to find otherwise. However, it has also created the opportunity for new kinds of problems: advertisers can now learn about your spending habits by infiltrating your PC with spyware; hackers use similar strategies to shut down entire networks with worms, bots, and viruses; states lose revenues to untaxed internet purchases; and travel agencies struggle to stay in business as individuals use the internet to make their own plane and hotel reservations. Similarly, in-vitro fertilization has opened up a Pandora's Box of ethical and moral questions about intervening in the natural process of conception. And SUVs, besides guzzling gasoline (a nonrenewable resource), are more likely than other cars to kill or injure people when involved in an accident.

As a society, how do we respond to technological developments that seem to solve one set of problems (such as disease, infertility, communication, and transportation) while creating new ones? Often we must play "catch-up," scrambling to fix a problem once it manifests itself, rather than being able to plan ahead and prevent it in the first place. **Cultural lag** is the term sociologists use to describe this disconnect between a changing social condition and cultural adjustment to that change. Material culture (such as the technologies discussed above) often changes faster than nonmaterial culture (like beliefs and laws), and we struggle to create new values and norms that correspond with new technologies.

DATA WORKSHOP

ANALYZING MASS MEDIA AND POPULAR CULTURE

The "Un-TV" Experiment

Zen sociologist Barney McGrane (1994) has designed a series of experiments that he has used in his classroom for many years (including the "Doing Nothing" experiment from Chapter 1). While the experiments are simple, the ideas they highlight are very sophisticated. We'd like you to try another one, this time focusing on the ways in which technology permeates our everyday lives and what happens when you resist or try to reverse technology's influence. In this Data Workshop, you will be doing participant observation research while also preparing to write an autoethnography of your experience (see Chapter 2 for a review of ethnographic methods).

For this experiment, you will be watching TV with a level of consciousness that is unusual; in McGrane's words, "I want you to watch *TV*—not a show, or a program, *just* TV" (p. 61). For each of the numbered tasks in this exercise, focus clearly on exactly what is asked of you. Don't daydream, and try not to think about anything else but what's going on around and inside you. Don't try to figure out what the goal is before you begin. Just "see what you can see."

1. For ten minutes, watch TV and count the "technical events." (A technical event is anything a camera does that a person can't do—zooming in or out; cutting to a different angle, setting, or scene; adding a voice-over or background music; playing in slow motion or fast forward; putting words or graphics on the screen.)

2. For ten minutes, watch your favorite TV program without sound.

3. For ten minutes, watch the news without sound.

4. For ten minutes, watch someone else watching TV.

5. For ten minutes, watch TV without turning it on.

After you complete each of these tasks, write down what you observe during that period of time, in as much detail as possible.

What are the insights and patterns in your findings? McGrane's students observed a number of different things that may correspond with your own observations. First, they all had a strong emotional reaction to the assignment itself; they felt anger about and resistance to "wasting" time in front of the TV, despite the fact that most of us voluntarily "waste" at least some time in front of the TV.

After completing the assignment, McGrane's students found themselves wrestling with profound issues of meaning vs. meaninglessness; passivity vs. activity; isolation vs. socialization; entertainment vs. hypnosis; and reality vs. fantasy. They made disturbing discoveries about the effect of this particular technology on their everyday lives as individuals and members of society: TV programming, they concluded, makes real life seem dull, isolates people from social interaction, and deadens feeling as effectively as any addictive substance.

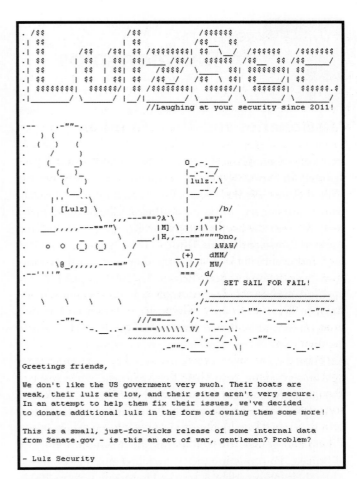

Technology The Lulz Security Hacking Group hacked the U.S. Senate website, posted this message, and released internal data. With advances in technology also comes the need for new forms of security.

How do your observations compare with those of McGrane's students? And what would happen if you modified this experiment to include other types of everyday technology—to go for a full twenty-four hours, say, without using your cell phone, text messaging, or e-mail? How would that make you feel, and what would it reveal about the role of technology in our social world? We take these technologies for granted and cannot imagine our lives without them—but maybe life would be better!

There are two options for completing this Data Workshop.

- *Option 1 (informal)*: Complete your observations, and prepare some written notes that you can refer to during in-class discussions. Compare your notes and experiences with other students in small groups.

- *Option 2 (formal)*: Complete your observations, and write a three- to four-page essay analyzing your experience. Make sure to attach your fieldnotes.

In Relationships

Missionaries and Their Families

In 1996, Evan Carl Hunzike, an American citizen, was arrested in North Korea on suspicion of spying for the United States. He was eventually revealed to be a Christian whose missionary work in northeast China accidentally took him over the border into North Korea. Two years later, Andrew Propst and Travis Tuttle were kidnapped, "roughed up," and eventually released while they were on their Mormon mission in southern Russia. In 2001, a plane carrying an American missionary family was shot down over the Amazon River when the Peruvian Air Force mistook it for a drug-running aircraft; two of the passengers died. Missionaries Gracia and Martin Burnham were vacationing at a Philippine beach resort that same year when they were kidnapped by Abu-Sayyaf rebels and held for over a year; when a rescue was attempted, Gracia was wounded and Martin was killed. A group of Tennessee-based Baptist missionary students had to be evacuated from the Ivory Coast in 2002 as rebels staged a coup and gunfire erupted around their school in the city of Bouake. Four missionaries were killed and one wounded when their motorcade was attacked in Mosul, Iraq, in 2004.

What do all these people have in common? Their willingness to endure hardship and undergo great risk to convert the world's people to their particular branch of Christianity. Their work can be controversial, but even if you object to their activities, you can recognize the radical commitments they have made to social change. They will travel around the globe, move their families to inhospitable places, and put their own safety at risk to promulgate their beliefs. Their goal is to change the world in the ways that they believe are best, even if others disagree.

Researchers estimate that there are up to half a million Christians of all denominations scattered about the world on foreign missions (Barrett and Johnson 2004). While most complete their work without incident, such a mission is still a very serious undertaking. It requires a good deal of financial, legal, and logistical planning as well as a willingness to commit one's family to an unfamiliar lifestyle. Some guidebooks and web sites specifically help missionary families prepare for their journeys.

For example, one experienced missionary doctor, Roy Dearmore, advises that families embarking on a mission execute "power of attorney" documents before they go so that a reliable person at home can make decisions about property, child welfare, finances, and medical treatments if anything were to happen to the family while abroad (1997). Passports, visas, and vaccinations must be obtained for all family members. New languages need to be learned. Some supplies—such as prescription medicines, extra glasses or contact lenses, toiletries, even peanut butter or Kool-Aid—may need to be purchased in bulk before leaving because they can be prohibitively expensive or even unavailable in certain areas. Some missionary families live in cities and can rent or buy homes; others in remote areas may have to build their own lodgings.

Dearmore's book (1997) includes an entire chapter on "wells, springs and outdoor toilets," in case the family needs

Technology in the Global Village

Over the years, social thinkers have expressed concerns about the effects of new technology. Some believed that electronic media would prove to be a dangerous, divisive, and degrading force in modern culture. Marshall McLuhan (1964), a Canadian communications researcher who also subscribed to the notion of technological determinism, expressed a degree of optimism that amounted to a utopian vision of what the various media could do for human society. McLuhan was particularly interested in television, which in the early 1960s was just then infiltrating practically every household in America. He imagined that television could re-create a sense of intimate community by linking people in disparate locations around the world through its broadcasts. Just as tribe members had

virtual community a community of people linked by their consumption of the same digital media

Missionary Families The Mortimers from the Baptist Evangelical Mission visit the community of Esperanza in the Tahuayo River region of Peru. The family built a well for this community.

Missionary kids ("MKs") may experience distinctive difficulties as American adolescents in unfamiliar environments and may have equal difficulties on returning to the United States when they realize that they have become strangers in their home country as well. Some MKs use humor to deal with their unique situations ("You know you're a missionary kid when you can't answer the question 'Where are you from?'"), but others need more organized forms of assistance. The International Society of Missionary Kids (www.ismk.org) sponsors "re-entry seminars" to help these children adjust to life in the United States after spending their childhoods abroad. For other family members, who may themselves have experienced loneliness, culture shock, or depression, there are specialized counseling agencies that provide mental health services tailored to their needs.

Though their work is difficult and sometimes dangerous, missionaries who have faith in their endeavors are willing to take the risk. Families make great sacrifices in order to disseminate their religious beliefs in foreign places, even though they might meet with resistance. Missionary work is often implicated in cultural imperialism, imposing ideas on people who already have their own perfectly suitable belief systems. You undoubtedly have your own beliefs about the types of social change you'd like to see in the world. The question raised by examining the experiences of missionary families is this: what are you willing to risk to make it happen?

to dig their own pit-privy! Some can buy food at local markets, while others have to grow their own. In the rural interior of less developed countries, there may be no cell phone relays, no internet connections, no regular mail delivery, and no cable TV. Often, ham radios are the best communication devices available. Finally, missionaries may be affected by coups, civil wars, guerrilla fighting, natural disasters, epidemics, or kidnappings. Some missionary "how-to" books address these matters along with more mundane concerns (Koteskey 2003).

once gathered to share stories around the light of a campfire, people would now sit in the glow of their TV screens, making television a kind of "virtual campfire" and those watching together members of a **virtual community**. McLuhan coined the term **global village** to capture that notion. He did not live to see the advent of the internet a few decades later, but he certainly understood the potential for media to extend the human senses and join us to one another in unprecedented ways.

CULTURAL DIFFUSION The intervening years have not totally confirmed McLuhan's utopian vision. New technologies have in fact had a profound impact on society, but in what ways and whether this has been positive or negative are still to be determined. What we do know is that media technology, through

> **global village** Marshall McLuhan's term describing the way that new communication technologies override barriers of space and time, joining together people all over the globe

cultural diffusion the dissemination of beliefs and practices from one group to another

globalization the increasing connections between economic, social, and political systems all over the globe

cultural imperialism cultural influence caused by adopting another culture's products

the process of **cultural diffusion**, has become a global reality. Social scientists use the term **globalization** to refer to social structures and institutions, like politics or commerce, that must now be conceived on a global rather than national scale. We can no longer remain isolated from social and political forces that reverberate around the world. There are now billions of people who have access to television and the internet. More than 1 billion were estimated to have watched the first walk on the moon in 1969. Since then, other events such as the funeral of Princess Diana in 1997 and the Live 8 concert in 2005, as well as footage of catastrophic events like the 9/11 attacks or the tsunamis in Indonesia or Japan, have attracted even larger audiences. These are among the most significant images burned into our collective minds.

Most of these global TV events are produced by media conglomerates in the United States and other industrialized nations. For example, the largest television networks belong to MTV and CNN, which broadcast to 166 and 137 countries, respectively. In 2009, the most popular dramatic television series in the world was *CSI*, which ranked highest on viewing surveys of 68 countries. *Desperate Housewives* was the number-one comedy in the world, and *The Bold and the Beautiful* topped the list of global soap operas (AFP 2010). Programs

like these potentially attract billions of viewers each week. Very few other countries have the infrastructure or budgets to produce similar shows with the same technical quality.

CULTURAL IMPERIALISM With this proliferation of Western media, we also find that the contents tend to reflect Western values. Communication researchers often talk about the "politics of information flow," and we can see that the message, or ideology, embedded in TV shows or films tends to disseminate from industrialized countries like the United States to the rest of the world (Schiller 1976, 1992, 1996; Tomlinson 1991). Americans brought up on the principle of a free press and living in a media-saturated society are not typically alarmed by the proliferation of our popular culture to other parts of the globe. In fact, we might assume that ours is the voice of freedom and democracy, a force for positive change in places where there have been censorship and disinformation (Rothkop 1997). But others question this flood of ideas, especially ideas about individualism and consumerism, coming from the West.

And Western ideas can cross cultural boundaries all too easily: it is almost impossible to block the reception of satellite and internet communications to audiences anywhere in the world. This sets up a new kind of tension in the struggle for power and influence. It is now possible for a country to be "occupied" by an invisible invader that arrives through airwaves and wireless networks; it can be conquered by ideas rather than by force, a phenomenon known as **cultural imperialism** (recall the example of the Voice of America radio broadcasts in Chapter 3). Some consider the Western

Cultural Diffusion *CSI*, one of the most popular TV shows in the world, acts as a medium for spreading American culture and ideas to other countries.

media's powerful influence as a kind of cultural domination. The result of this domination is often **cultural leveling**, a homogenizing process whereby societies lose their particular uniqueness as they all start to resemble one another.

As media technology makes possible a multiplicity of voices, Westerners have also been influenced by Eastern ideas (witness the popularity of yoga). Yet, Western values continue to dominate and to shape the "village" that is the global village. They sometimes conflict with the values of other nations, some of which have tried to resist the Western media stranglehold and maintain their own distinctive cultural identity (see the Global Perspective box). Challenges persist as to whether meaningful and egalitarian communication on a global level can really take place (Gozzi 1996). Perhaps as technology advances, cultural distinctions can be maintained while divisions continue to fade, thus approaching McLuhan's vision of a world united.

Implications for a Postmodern World

Today, the Digital Age is but a few decades old, and already most of you probably cannot remember a time when you did not have a remote control, mouse, or cell phone in hand. And you cannot imagine living without them. It is safe to assume that we will see many more scientific and technological advancements in the near future. In particular, media technologies are likely to become cheaper, lighter and easier to use, faster, more flexible, interactive, and capable of carrying more information. Despite what some call the "digital divide" (the uneven distribution of technology among different groups of people), technologies will play an increasingly important role in almost every aspect of our lives, and

technological literacy will be a necessary skill for anyone participating in contemporary society.

Is all progress good? Is every technological advance beneficial? These questions arise because our society is in the midst of a major transformation: we are moving from a modern society to a postmodern society. **Modernity** refers to the social conditions and attitudes characteristic of industrialized societies, which include the decline of traditional community, an increase in individual autonomy and diversity of beliefs, and a strong belief in the ability of science and technology to improve our quality of life (Berger 1977). In many ways, this last promise of modernity has in fact been fulfilled. Since the Industrial Revolution, rates of infant mortality have declined, life expectancies have increased, and a number of common diseases have been cured or controlled. However, along with these advances have come increases in income inequality, violent crime, and child poverty (Miringoff and Miringoff 1999). So while modern society has its benefits, there are also problems, which is where the postmodern critique begins.

Postmodernity refers to the social conditions and attitudes characteristic of postindustrialized societies, which include a focus on ideas and cultural debates rather than

cultural leveling the process by which societies lose their uniqueness, becoming increasingly similar

modernity a term encompassing the forms of social organization that characterize industrialized societies, including the decline of tradition, an increase in individualism, and a belief in progress, technology, and science

postmodernity a term encompassing the forms of social organization characteristic of postindustrial societies, including a focus on the production and management of information and skepticism of science and technology

TABLE 16.1	*Theory in Everyday Life*	
PERSPECTIVE	**APPROACH TO SOCIAL CHANGE**	**CASE STUDY: THE ENVIRONMENTAL MOVEMENT**
STRUCTURAL FUNCTIONALISM	Sometimes social change is necessary to maintain equilibrium and order in society.	Natural resources are necessary for the survival of society, so the growth of a social movement dedicated to the wise use and conservation of natural resources is functional for society.
CONFLICT THEORY	Social change is the inevitable result of social inequality and conflict between groups over power and resources.	Environmental privileges (such as scenic natural vistas, clean water, and unpolluted air) are unequally distributed among different groups in society. The environmentalist movement works to secure the rights of all citizens, rich and poor, to a clean, healthy, beautiful, and sustainable world.
SYMBOLIC INTERACTIONISM	Social change involves changes in the meanings of things as well as changes in laws, culture, and social behavior.	The environmental movement works to safeguard animal species by having them declared "endangered" or "threatened." Redefining groups of animals in this way allows for their protection through endangered species laws rather than their decimation through hunting or habitat reduction.

Bhutan and Gross National Happiness

While change may be inevitable, perhaps we may be able to determine the direction, elements, and pace of that change. That is exactly what the current leaders of Bhutan are attempting to do. They provide an example of how to hold on to tradition, maintain a unique cultural identity, and exercise control over the pace of social change.

Bhutan is a tiny country of fewer than a million people, precariously perched at the "roof of the world" in the Himalayan Mountains. Despite its remote location between two of the world's most powerful and populous nations—China to the north and India to the south—Bhutan has remained a sovereign, independent nation throughout its history. In this ancient land, it seems almost as if time has stood still. It is only in the past few decades that Bhutan has emerged from its almost total isolation and taken some cautious steps into the modern era.

Bhutan is a predominantly Buddhist country that until recently had been ruled by a king who had four wives (who were all sisters!) along with a cadre of mostly Western-educated officials. In 2008, at the behest of its enlightened monarch, Bhutan held its first democratic elections. Despite that political change, it may still be the only country in the world where the government's number-one concern is something it calls "Gross National Happiness": a blend of economic development and cultural richness; food, clothing, and shelter; health care and education; spiritual values; and individual contentment.

The government hopes to achieve Gross National Happiness by carefully identifying and adopting what the West is doing right while also rejecting its cynicism and consumerism. For example, the Bhutanese do not allow exploitation of their natural resources. There is no lumber industry in their millions of acres of lush forests, which instead have been designated national parks. Although Mt. Everest is nearby in Nepal, mountain climbers are forbidden to ascend the peaks of Bhutan's mountains. The Bhutanese have, however, taken advantage of one natural resource originating in the snowcap—immense, fast-flowing rivers that generate hydroelectric power, which is then exported to neighboring countries. Tourism to Bhutan could also have become a lucrative trade. But here, too, the government has limited the number of visitors who can enter the country each year, and this small group is reminded to practice cultural sensitivity when interacting with the local people.

For the most part, Bhutan has managed to avoid being overwhelmed by the forces of globalization and cultural leveling. While some Bhutanese enjoy basic modern conveniences like cell phone service and wireless internet, in the

material things and a questioning of the achievements of science and technology. According to postmodern thought, the progress promised by modernity has failed to solve important social problems (such as income inequality), and modern institutions (families, schools, workplaces, governments) are implicated in this failure. Although change is forecast in all these areas, there is no agreed-upon blueprint for what that change might look like. For example, Judith Stacey (1990) argues that traditional family arrangements (working husband, stay-at-home wife, 2.3 children) are ill-suited to the demands of life in a postmodern world and that more creative household arrangements are more conducive to life in contemporary society.

The Industrial Revolution transformed Western society from traditional to modern. The Information Revolution is transforming Western society from modern to postmodern. While we are not yet certain what this particular transformation will mean in our everyday lives, we can be sure that it will not be the final transformation our society will undergo.

Society will continue to be shaped by technology, not only at the macro level of culture and social institutions but also at the micro level of groups and individuals. Technology will change what the world looks like as well as how we perceive it. It will greatly extend our abilities to obtain information and will influence the way we use it. We will become more comfortable with multitasking; navigating through nonlinear hyperspace, dealing with symbols, image, and sound as well as text; moving at a rapid pace; coping with a fractured sense of self; socializing online; experimenting with game strategies; and accepting the unpredictable.

Should we call such developments progress? What will we gain, and what do we stand to lose? Your parents and grandparents will not understand the postmodern, digital era in the same way that you do. So it is you who will be engineering the terms of the future. Perhaps now would be a good time to ask yourself what you can do as part of this new social revolution. Can you risk just sitting back to watch what will happen? Or are you willing to take what you have learned and

Gross National Happiness Global networks like MTV and CNN that cross borders via satellite concern Bhutanese leaders who see their children emulating foreign television programs. To counterbalance Western influence, the government created a national television network, the Bhutan Broadcasting Service (BBS).

capital city of Thimphu there are still no chain stores—no Starbucks, no Gap, no Wal-Mart or Burger King. Especially remarkable is that the Bhutanese have so far been able to defend themselves against what might be the most powerful global intruder of all—television.

While networks like MTV and CNN do sneak in via satellite, the government has created its own national television network, the Bhutan Broadcasting Service (BBS), to balance Western networks. Yet, a homegrown production can barely compete with *Baywatch*; the Bhutanese are already sophisticated enough to be critical when comparing a local show with those from Hollywood. So far, the BBS has produced only limited programming, including a daily half-hour newscast in both English and the native language of Dzongkha. Still, would-be TV producers have been pitching new ideas that are responsive to audiences' taste for soap operas but include a particularly Bhutanese touch, and they still align themselves with the guiding principle of their country. They see audience members not as primarily consumers, but as citizens in need of knowledge that can help them in their pursuit of Gross National Happiness (Schell 2002).

It is important not to romanticize life in Bhutan or even the pursuit of Gross National Happiness. Although the country is now a democracy, and it endures high rates of infant mortality, poverty, and illiteracy. Life expectancies are low, and women's opportunities are limited. Certain types of social change would seem to be necessary and inevitable. However, as they prepare for change, Bhutanese leaders remain idealistic about the ability of their traditional culture to resist Western values and to avoid the social problems that are so commonplace in the other parts of the world.

go out and make a difference? We hope this chapter has given you the insight and tools you will need to take an active role in creating whatever positive social change you envision.

Closing Comments

Throughout this text, we have focused on the sociological features of everyday life, including the role of mass media and popular culture in society. The media are often the place where new developments, trends, or social changes first become visible. And our everyday lives are the places where we experience both social constraints and social change at the most fundamental level. You now have the tools necessary to understand these phenomena, because you now possess the sociological perspective.

The sociological perspective sometimes highlights distressing facts—the persistence of poverty and prejudice, for example, or the realities of crime. But it allows for optimism

as well. This is because the intersection of biography and history goes both ways: society shapes individual lives, but individuals impact their society as well. Any disconcerting realizations you may have had during the course of this semester should be tempered by your knowledge that change is possible, and that *you* are its primary source.

Ultimately, this should be the most relevant element of your education in sociology. Years from now, no one will care whether you remember the details of labeling theory or the difference between organic and mechanical solidarity. What will continue to matter is your sense of investment in your society—your commitment to your family, your workplace, your community, and your world. Your mindful involvement in all of these areas can make each of them better places—to raise children, to live, to work, to collaborate with others. Armed with the sociological perspective, you now have a new set of responsibilities: to investigate and participate in your social world, both locally and globally. We hope you do so with optimism and persistence, and in partnership with others.

⑤ Need Help Studying?

wwnorton.com/studyspace

Visit StudySpace to access free review materials such as:

- **Vocabulary Flashcards**
- **Diagnostic Review Quizzes**
- **Study Outlines**

QUESTIONS FOR REVIEW

1. People born even one generation apart can have quite different life experiences because of ongoing social and technological changes. List at least three technologies that did not exist when your parents were your age. What social changes have these technologies generated?

2. Some social changes are deliberate, while others are unplanned. Many influential technologies, like the automobile, bring both kinds of change. For example, what kinds of changes were cell phones designed to bring about? What changes did they cause unexpectedly?

3. This chapter argues that social networks are necessary for fads to continue and cites the recent popularity of low-carbohydrate diets as an example. Have you ever been on such a diet, like Atkins or South Beach, or do you know someone who has? How did you or that person hear about it? What convinced you or that person to try it? Describe the social network behind the fad.

4. Fashion can be a marker of group status and often symbolically represents group identity. Do you wear any pieces of clothing, jewelry, or other accessories that indicate your membership in a group? Describe the items and the group(s) they signify.

5. This chapter describes the tragedy of the commons, using overgrazing, overfishing, and exploitation of other natural resources as examples. What other kinds of "commons" or public goods that are provided and paid for by the community benefit you as an individual?

6. Mass society theory and relative deprivation theory offer two basic explanations for why people join social movements. Think of someone you know who belongs to a social movement. Which theory do you think more accurately characterizes this person's motivations? How can you tell?

7. "Cultural lag" is the term sociologists use for the period of time when norms, values, and laws are not yet up to date with new technology because material culture changes faster than nonmaterial culture. Describe at least one change in material culture for which there is still some degree of cultural lag. What evidence suggests that we haven't developed adequate norms yet?

8. Marshall McLuhan had a utopian vision for society based on the wonders of communications technology. Even before the advent of the internet, he thought that television would create a global village. What did he mean by the term "global village"? Which changes brought about by the internet fit McLuhan's predictions? What are the positive and negative aspects of a global village?

SUGGESTIONS FOR FURTHER EXPLORATION

Haenfler, Ross. 2006. *Straight Edge: Clean Living Youth, Hardcore Punk and Social Change*. New Brunswick, NJ: Rutgers University Press. A firsthand history of a seemingly unlikely social movement and its resistance to commercialization and drug use in the American punk music scene.

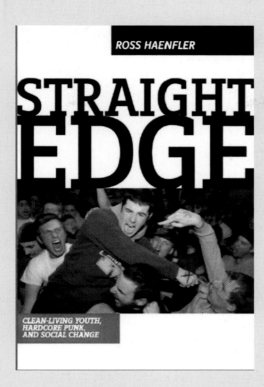

Le Bon, Gustave. 1983. *The Crowd: A Study of the Popular Mind*. Atlanta, GA: Cherokee. The earliest and most influential source of the contagion theory of collective behavior, from the author who was convinced that being part of a crowd meant losing oneself to a herd mentality.

Mackay, Charles. 2003. *Extraordinary Popular Delusions and the Madness of Crowds*. Hampshire, UK: Harriman House. A popular history of crowds and economic fads, with special attention to the Dutch tulip craze of the early seventeenth century. Some bulbs cost more by weight than gold—until the bubble burst.

Morris, Aldon. 1986. *Origins of the Civil Rights Movements*. New York: Free Press. A history of the Civil Rights Movement in the American South that draws on firsthand accounts of the major moments in the movement, many of which suggest that motivations to join civil rights groups at

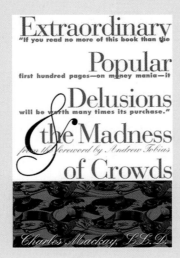

that time were often closely aligned with the explanations offered by relative deprivation theory.

Morris, Aldon, and Carol Mueller. 1992. *Frontiers in Social Movement Theory*. New Haven, CT: Yale University Press. A collection of pioneering research on the social movements of the 1960s and '70s, including the gay and lesbian movement and the women's movement.

MoveOn.org (www.moveon.org/about.html). This internet-based social movement attempts to provide the resources people need to get involved in the political process.

Tilly, Charles. 2004. *Social Movements 1768–2004*. St. Paul, MN: Paradigm. A comprehensive overview of the origin and growth of the contemporary social movement and the mechanisms by which social movements function.

Union Maids. 1976. Dir. James Klein, Miles Moguleski, and Julia Reichert. New Day Films. This documentary features interviews with three women, Kate Hyndman, Stella Nowicki, and Sylvia Woods, who recall the challenges of labor organizing and union activity in Chicago in the 1930s.

Food, Inc. 2008. Dir. Robert Kenner. Magnolia Pictures. A critical documentary that examines corporate farming in America, and its abuses of people, animals, and the environment. Not for the faint of heart.

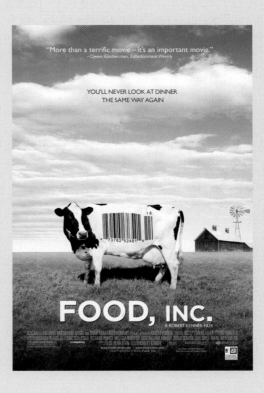

GLOSSARY

absolute deprivation An objective measure of poverty, defined by the inability to meet minimal standards for food, shelter, clothing, or health care.

access The process by which an ethnographer gains entry to a field setting.

achieved status A status earned through individual effort or imposed by others.

active audiences A term used to characterize audience members as active participants in "reading" or constructing the meaning of the media they consume.

activism Any activity intended to bring about social change.

acute diseases Diseases that have a sudden onset, may be briefly incapacitating, and are either curable or fatal.

affirmative action Programs or policies that seek to rectify the effects of past discrimination by increasing representation and ensuring equal opportunity for any previously disadvantaged group.

agency The ability of the individual to act freely and independently.

agenda-setting theory Theory that the mass media can set the public agenda by selecting certain news stories and excluding others, thus influencing what audiences think about.

agents of socialization Social groups, institutions, and individuals (especially the family, schools, peers, and the mass media) that provide structured situations in which socialization takes place.

agglomeration or MSA One or more adjacent counties with at least one major city of at least 50,000 inhabitants that is surrounded by an adjacent area that is socially and economically integrated with the city.

aggregate A collection of people who share a physical location but do not have lasting social relations.

Agricultural Revolution The social and economic changes, including population increases, that followed from the domestication of plants and animals and the gradually increasing efficiency of food production.

alienation Decreasing importance of social ties and community and the corresponding increase in impersonal associations and instrumental logic; also, according to Marx, the sense of dissatisfaction the modern worker feels as a result of producing goods that are owned and controlled by someone else.

alternative medicine A group of medical treatments, practices, and products that are used instead of conventional Western medicine.

altruism Unselfish concern for the well-being of others and helping behaviors performed without self-interested motivation.

anomie "Normlessness"; term used to describe the alienation and loss of purpose that result from weaker social bonds and an increased pace of change.

anthropocentric Literally "human centered"; the idea that needs and desires of human beings should take priority over concerns about other species or the natural environment.

Anti-Malthusians Contemporary researchers who believe the population boom Malthus witnessed was a temporary, historically specific phenomenon and worry instead that the worldwide population may shrink in the future.

antimiscegenation The prohibition of interracial marriage, cohabitation, or sexual interaction.

antithesis The opposition to the existing arrangements in a dialectical model.

antitrust legislation Laws designed to maintain competition in the marketplace by prohibiting monopolies, price fixing, or other forms of collusion among businesses.

apartheid The system of segregation of racial and ethnic groups that was legal in South Africa between 1948 and 1991.

applied research Research designed to gather knowledge that can be used learned to create some sort of change.

art world The group composed of everyone involved in the creation, distribution, and consumption of any cultural product.

ascribed status An inborn status; usually difficult or impossible to change.

asexuality Involves the lack of sexual attraction of any kind; asexual people have no interest in or desire for sex.

assimilation A pattern of relations between ethnic or racial groups in which the minority group is absorbed into the mainstream or dominant group, making society more homogenous.

authoritarianism System of government by and for a small number of elites that does not include representation of ordinary citizens.

authority The legitimate right to wield power.

autoethnography Ethnographic description that focuses on the feelings and reactions of the ethnographer.

backstage In the dramaturgical perspective, places in which we rehearse and prepare for our performances.

basic research The search for knowledge without any agenda or desire to use that knowledge to effect change.

beginner's mind Approaching the world without preconceptions in order to see things in a new way.

belief A proposition or idea held on the basis of faith.

bias An opinion held by the researcher that might affect the research or analysis.

biodiversity The variety of species of plants and animals existing at any given time.

bioethics The study of controversial moral or ethical issues related to scientific and medical advancements.

biosphere The parts of the earth that can support life.

bisexuality Sexual attraction to both genders; bisexuals are sexually attracted to both males and females.

blue collar A description characterizing workers who perform manual labor.

bourgeoisie Owners; the class of modern capitalists who own the means of production and employ wage laborers.

bureaucracy A type of secondary group designed to perform tasks efficiently, characterized by specialization, technical competence, hierarchy, written rules, impersonality, and formal written communication.

bystander effect or diffusion of responsibility The social dynamic wherein the more people there are present in a moment of crisis, the less likely any one of them is to take action.

capital punishment The death penalty.

capitalism An economic system based on the laws of free market competition, privatization of the means of production, and production for profit, with an emphasis on supply and demand as a means to set prices.

caste system A form of social stratification in which status is determined by one's family history and background and cannot be changed.

category People who share one or more attributes but who lack a sense of common identity or belonging.

causation A relationship between variables in which a change in one directly produces a change in the other.

charismatic authority Authority based in the perception of remarkable personal qualities in a leader.

charter schools Public schools run by private entities to give parents greater control over their children's education.

the Chicago School a type of sociology practiced by researchers at the University of Chicago in the 1920s and 30s which centered on urban sociology and field research methods.

chronic diseases Diseases that develop over a longer period of time and may not be detected until symptoms occur later in their progression.

civil inattention An unspoken rule governing interactions in public places, whereby individuals briefly notice others before ignoring them.

civil society Those organizations, institutions, and interactions outside government, family, and work that promote social bonds and the smooth functioning of society.

civil unions Proposed as an alternative to gay marriage; a form of legally recognized commitment that provides gay couples some of the benefits and protections of marriage.

class consciousness The recognition of social inequality on the part of the oppressed, leading to revolutionary action.

closed system A social system with very little opportunity to move from one class to another.

closed-ended question A question asked of a respondent that imposes a limit on the possible responses.

code of ethics Ethical guidelines for researchers to consult as they design a project.

coercive power Power that is backed by the threat of force.

cohabitation Living together as a romantically involved, unmarried couple.

collective behavior Behavior that follows from the formation of a group or crowd of people who take action together toward a shared goal.

collective conscience The shared morals and beliefs that are common to a group and which foster social solidarity.

collective effervescence An intense energy in shared events where people feel swept up in something larger than themselves.

commodification The process by which it becomes possible to buy and sell a particular good or service.

communism A system of government that eliminates private property; the most extreme form of socialism, because all citizens work for the government and there are no class distinctions.

communitarianism A political and moral philosophy focused on strengthening civil society and communal bonds.

community A group of people living in the same local area who share a sense of participation and fellowship.

community college Two-year institution that provides students with general education and facilitates transfer to a four-year university.

comparative and historical methods Methods that use existing sources to study relationships between elements of society in various regions and time periods.

complementary medicine A group of medical treatments, practices, and products that can be used in conjunction with conventional Western medicine.

compliance The mildest type of conformity, undertaken to gain rewards or avoid punishments.

concentration The process by which the number of companies producing and distributing a particular commodity decreases, often through mergers and conglomeration.

confidentiality The assurance that no one other than the researcher will know the identity of a respondent.

conflict Generated by the competition between different class groups for scarce resources and the source of all social change, according to Karl Marx.

conflict theory A paradigm that sees social conflict as the basis of society and social change, and emphasizes a materialist view of society, a critical view of the status quo, and a dynamic model of historical change.

conglomeration The process by which a single corporation acquires ownership of a variety of otherwise unrelated businesses.

conservation era Earliest stage of the environmental movement, which focused on the preservation of "wilderness" areas.

constructionists Those who believe that notions of gender are socially determined, such that a dichotomous system is just one possibility among many.

consumption The utilization of goods and services, either for personal use or in manufacturing.

contagion theory One of the earliest theories of collective action; suggested that individuals who joined a crowd could become "infected" by a mob mentality and lose the ability to reason.

content analysis A method in which researchers identify and study specific variables—such as words—in a text, image, or media message.

control In an experiment, the process of regulating all factors except for the independent variable.

control group The part of a test group that is allowed to continue without intervention so that it can be compared with the experimental group.

conversation analysis A sociological approach that looks at how we create meaning in naturally occurring conversation, often by taping conversations and examining them.

cooling the mark out Behaviors that help others to save face or avoid embarrassment, often referred to as civility or tact.

copresence Face-to-face interaction or being in the presence of others.

correlation A relationship between variables in which they change together; may or may not be causal.

counterculture A group within society that openly rejects and/or actively opposes society's values and norms.

crime A violation of a norm that has been codified into law.

criminal justice system A collection of social institutions, such as legislatures, police, courts, and prisons, that create and enforce laws.

critical theory A contemporary form of conflict theory that criticizes many different systems and ideologies of domination and oppression.

crowd A temporary gathering of individuals, whether spontaneous or planned, who share a common focus.

cultural assimilation The process by which racial or ethnic groups are absorbed into the dominant group by adopting the dominant group's culture.

cultural capital The tastes, habits, expectations, skills, knowledge, and other cultural dispositions that help us gain advantages in society.

cultural competence To describe the concept of acknowledging and incorporating a patient's cultural background as part of the treatment process; the recognition that patients' beliefs shape their approach to health care.

cultural diffusion The dissemination of beliefs and practices from one group to another.

cultural imperialism Cultural influence caused by adopting another country's products.

cultural lag The time between changes in material culture or technology and the resulting changes in the broader culture's relevant norms, values, meanings, and laws.

cultural leveling The process by which societies lose their uniqueness, becoming increasingly similar.

cultural relativism The principle of understanding other cultures on their own terms, rather than judging or evaluating according to one's own culture.

culture The entire way of life of a group of people (including both material and symbolic elements) that acts as a lens through which one views the world and is passed from one generation to the next.

culture of poverty Entrenched attitudes that can develop among poor communities and lead the poor to accept their fate rather than attempt to improve their lot.

culture shock A sense of disorientation that occurs when you enter a radically new social or cultural environment.

culture wars Clashes within mainstream society over the values and norms that should be upheld.

curative or crisis medicine Type of health care that treats the disease or condition once it has manifested.

custody The physical and legal responsibility of caring for children; assigned by a court for divorced or unmarried parents.

cyberbullying The use of electronic media (web pages, social networking sites, e-mail, instant messengers, and cell phones) to tease, harass, threaten, or humiliate someone.

cycle of violence A common behavior pattern in abusive relationships; the cycle begins happily, then the relationship grows tense, and the tension explodes in abuse, followed by a period of contrition that allows the cycle to repeat.

deception The extent to which the participants in a research project are unaware of the project or its goals.

deconstruction A type of critical postmodern analysis that involves taking apart or disassembling old ways of thinking.

deep acting Trying to change your mood to match the expectations associated with the part you are playing in a specific situation.

definition of the situation An agreement with others about "what is going on" in a given circumstance. This consensus allows us to coordinate our actions with those of others and realize goals.

democracy A political system in which all citizens have the right to participate.

demographic free fall Decrease in fertility rates among populations that have industrialized their economies as children become an economic liability rather than an asset.

demographic transition A theory suggesting the possible transition over time from high birth and death rates to low birth and death rates, resulting in a stabilized population.

demographics Statistical characteristics of a population, including but not limited to population size, age, race and gender representation, and rates of mortality and fertility.

demography Study of the size, composition, distribution, and changes in human population.

dependent variable Factor that is changed (or not) by the independent variable.

deprivation amplification When our individual disease risks (based on our heredity and physiology) are amplified by social factors.

deregulation Reduction or removal of government controls from an industry to allow for a free and efficient marketplace.

desistance The tendency of individuals to age out of crime over the life course.

deterrence An approach to punishment that relies on the threat of harsh penalties to discourage people from committing crimes.

deviance A behavior, trait, belief, or other characteristic that violates a norm and causes a negative reaction.

deviance avowal Process by which an individual self-identifies as deviant and initiates her own labeling process.

dialectical model Marx's model of historical change, whereby two extreme positions come into conflict and create some new third thing between them.

differential association theory Edwin Sutherland's hypothesis that we learn to be deviant through our associations with deviant peers.

diffusion of responsibility The social dynamic wherein the more people there are present in a moment of crisis, the less likely any one of them is to take action.

digital divide The experience of unequal access to computer and internet technology, both globally and within the United States.

discrimination Unequal treatment of individuals based on their membership in a social group; usually motivated by prejudice.

disenchantment The rationalization of modern society.

disenfranchised Stripped of voting rights, either temporarily or permanently.

distance learning Any educational course or program in which the teacher and the students do not meet together in the classroom; increasingly available over the internet.

domestic violence Any physical, verbal, financial, sexual, or psychological behaviors abusers use to gain and maintain power over their victims.

dominant culture The values, norms, and practices of the group within society that is most powerful (in terms of wealth, prestige, status, influence, etc.).

double-barreled questions Questions that attempt to get at multiple issues at once, and so tend to receive incomplete or confusing answers.

double consciousness W. E. B. DuBois's term for the conflict felt by and about African Americans, who were both American (and hence entitled to rights and freedoms) and African (and hence subject to prejudices and discrimination) at the same time.

dramaturgy An approach pioneered by Erving Goffman in which social life is analyzed in terms of its similarities to theatrical performance to understand how individuals present themselves to others.

dual nature of the self The belief that we experience the self as both subject and object, the "I" and the "me."

dyad A two-person social group.

dysfunction A disturbance to or undesirable consequence of some aspect of the social system.

dystopia Opposite of a utopia; a world where social problems are magnified and the quality of life is extremely low.

early college high schools Institutions in which students earn a high school diploma and two years of credit toward a bachelor's degree.

Earth Day A holiday conceived of by environmental activist and former senator Gaylord Nelson to encourage support for and increase awareness of environmental concerns; first celebrated on March 22, 1970.

eco-friendly A term describing any activity or product that attempts to minimize its environmental impact.

ecological footprint An estimation of the land and water area required to produce all the goods an individual consumes and to assimilate all the wastes she generates.

ecoterrorism Use of violence or criminal methods to protect the environment, often in high-profile, publicity-generating ways.

ecotourism Foreign travel with the goal of minimizing the environmental consequences of tourism as well as its possible negative effects on local cultures and economies; typically involves people from highly industrialized nations traveling to less developed countries.

edge cities Centers of employment and commerce that began as suburban commuter communities.

education The process by which a society transmits its knowledge, values, and expectations to its members so they can function effectively.

ego According to Freud, one of three interrelated parts that make up the mind; the ego is the realistic aspect of the mind that balances the forces of the id and the superego.

virtual communities Social groups whose interactions are mediated through information technologies, particularly the internet.

elites Those in power in a society.

embodied identity Those elements of identity that are generated through others' perceptions of our physical traits.

embodied status A status generated by physical characteristics.

emergent norm theory A theory of collective behavior that assumes individual members of a crowd make their own decisions about behavior and that norms are created through others' acceptance or rejection of these behaviors.

emigration Leaving one country to live permanently in another.

emotion work (emotional labor) The process of evoking, suppressing, or otherwise managing feelings to create a publicly observable display of emotion.

empirical Based on scientific experimentation or observation.

encoding/decoding model A theory on media that combines models that privilege the media producer and models that view the audience as the primary source of meaning; this theory recognizes that media texts are created to deliver specific messages and that individuals actively interpret them.

endogamy Marriage to someone within one's social group.

environment In sociology, the natural world, the human-made environment, and the interaction between the two.

environmental justice A movement that aims to remedy environmental inequities such as threats to public health and the unequal treatment of certain communities with regard to ecological concerns.

environmental movement A social movement organized around concerns about the relationship between humans and the environment.

Environmental Protection Agency (EPA) A government agency organized in 1969 to protect public health and the environment through policies and enforcement.

environmental racism Any environmental policy or practice that negatively affects individuals, groups, or communities because of their race or ethnicity.

environmental sociology The study of the interaction between society and the natural environment, including the social causes and consequences of environmental problems.

epidemic Occurs when a significantly higher number of cases of a particular disease occur during a particular time period than might otherwise be expected.

epidemiology The study of disease patterns to understand the cause of illnesses, how they are spread, and what interventions to take.

eros In Freudian psychology, the drive or instinct that desires productivity and construction.

essentialists Those who believe gender roles have a genetic or biological origin and therefore cannot be changed.

ethnicity A socially defined category based on common language, religion, nationality, history, or another cultural factor.

ethnocentrism The principle of using one's own culture as a means or standard by which to evaluate another group or individual, leading to the view that cultures other than one's own are abnormal or inferior.

ethnography A naturalistic method based on studying people in their own environment in order to understand the meanings they attribute to their activities; also the written work that results from the study.

ethnomethodology The study of "folk methods" and background knowledge that sustains a shared sense of reality in or everyday interactions.

eugenics An attempt to selectively manipulate the gene pool in order to produce and "improve" human beings through medical science.

Eurocentric The tendency to favor European or Western histories, cultures, and values over other non-Western societies.

evangelical A term describing conservative Christians who emphasize converting others to their faith.

everyday actor One who has the practical knowledge needed to get through daily life but not necessarily the scientific or technical knowledge of how things work.

everyday class consciousness Awareness of one's own social status and that of others.

existing sources Materials that have been produced for some other reason, but that can be used as data for social research.

exogamy Marriage to someone from a different social group.

experimental group The part of a test group that receives the experimental treatment.

experiments Formal tests of specific variables and effects, performed in a controlled setting where all aspects of the situation can be controlled.

expressions given Expressions that are intentional and usually verbal, such as utterances.

expressions given off Observable expressions that can be either intended or unintended and are usually nonverbal.

expressions of behavior Small actions such as an eye roll or head nod that serve as an interactional tool to help project our definition of the situation to others.

expressive leadership Leadership concerned with maintaining emotional and relational harmony within the group.

expressive role The position of the family member who provides emotional support and nurturing.

expressive tasks The emotional work necessary to support family members.

extended family A large group of relatives, usually including at least three generations living either in one household or in close proximity.

extrinsic religiosity A person's public display of commitment to a religious faith.

fads Interests or practices followed enthusiastically for a relatively short period of time.

false consciousness A denial of the truth on the part of the oppressed when they fail to recognize the interests of the ruling class in their ideology.

family A social group whose members are bound by legal, biological, or emotional ties, or a combination of all three.

family planning Contraception, or any method of controlling family size and the birth of children.

fashion The widespread custom or style of behavior and appearance at a particular time or in a particular place.

feeling rules Socially constructed norms regarding the expression and display of emotions; expectations about the acceptable or desirable feelings in a given situation.

feminism Belief in the social, political, and economic equality of the sexes; also the social movements organized around that belief.

feminist theory A theoretical approach that looks at gender inequities in society and the way that gender structures the social world.

feminization of poverty The economic trend showing that women are more likely than men to live in poverty, caused in part by the gendered gap in wages, the higher proportion of single mothers compared to single fathers, and the increasing costs of child care.

feral children In myths and rare real world cases, children who have had little human contact and may have lived in the wild from a young age.

fertility rate A measure of population growth through reproduction; often expressed as the average number of births per 1,000 people in the total population or the average number of children a woman would be expected to have.

feudal system A system of social stratification based on a hereditary nobility who were responsible for and served by a lower stratum of forced laborers called serfs.

fictive kin Close relations with people we consider "like family" but who are not related to us by blood or marriage.

fieldnotes Detailed notes taken by an ethnographer describing her activities and interactions, which later become the basis of the ethnographic analysis.

first wave The earliest period of feminist activism in the United States, including the period from the mid-nineteenth century until American women won the right to vote in 1920.

527 committees Organizations that have no official connection to a candidate but that raise and spend funds like a campaign does; named after the section of the tax code that authorizes their existence.

folkway A loosely enforced norm involving common customs, practices, or procedures that ensure smooth social interaction and acceptance.

food desert A community in which the residents have little or no access to fresh, affordable, healthy foods, usually located in densely populated, urban areas.

formal social control The regulation of behavior through laws and other official regulations and sanctions.

Fourth Estate The media is considered like a fourth branch of government (after the executive, legislative, and judiciary) and thus serves as another of the checks and balances on power.

front In the dramaturgical perspective, the setting or scene of performances that helps establish the definition of the situation.

frontstage In the dramaturgical perspective, the region in which we deliver our public performances.

fundamentalism The practice of emphasizing literal interpretation of texts and a "return" to a time of greater religious purity; represented by the most conservative group within any religion.

game stage The third stage in Mead's theory of the development of self wherein children play organized games and take on the perspective of the generalized other.

gender The physical, behavioral, and personality traits that a group considers normal for its male and female members.

gender identity An individual's self-definition or sense of gender.

gender role socialization The lifelong process of learning to be masculine or feminine, primarily through four agents of socialization: families, schools, peers, and the media.

generalized other The perspectives and expectations of a network of others (or of society in general) that a child learns and then takes into account when shaping his or her own behavior.

genocide The deliberate and systematic extermination of a racial, ethnic, national, or cultural group.

gentrification Transformation of the physical, social, economic, and cultural life of formerly working-class or poor inner-city neighborhoods into more affluent middle-class communities.

gestures The ways in which people use their bodies to communicate without words; actions that have symbolic meaning.

global cities A term for megacities that emphasizes their global impact as centers of economic, political, and social power.

global (or solar) dimming A decline in the amount of light reaching the earth's surface because of increased air pollution, which reflects more light back into space.

global village Marshall McLuhan's term describing the way that new communication technologies override barriers of space and time, joining together people all over the globe.

global warming Gradual increase in the earth's temperature, driven recently by an increase in greenhouse gases and other human activity.

globalization The increasing connections between economic, social, and political systems all over the globe.

government The formal, organized agency that exercises power and control in modern society, especially through the creation and enforcement of laws.

grassroots environmentalism Fourth major stage of the environmental movement; distinguished by the diversity of its members and belief in citizen participation in environmental decision making.

Green Party A U.S. political party established in 1984 to bring political attention to environmentalism, social justice, diversity, and related principles.

greenhouse effect The process in which increased production of greenhouse gases, especially those arising from human activity (e.g., carbon dioxide, nitrous oxide, and methane) cause the earth's temperature to rise.

greenhouse gases Any gases in the earth's atmosphere that allow sunlight to pass through but trap heat, thus affecting temperature.

grounded theory An inductive method of generating theory from data by creating categories in which to place data and then looking for relationships between categories.

group A collection of people who share some attribute, identify with one another, and interact with each other.

group cohesion The sense of solidarity or loyalty that individuals feel toward a group to which they belong.

group dynamics The patterns of interaction between groups and individuals.

groupthink In very cohesive groups, the tendency to enforce a high degree of conformity among members, creating a demand for unanimous agreement.

growth rate Expression of changes in population size over time figured by subtracting the number of deaths from the number of births, then adding the net migration.

Hawthorne effect A specific example of reactivity, in which the desired effect is the result not of the independent variable but of the research itself.

hegemony Term developed by Antonio Gramsci to describe the cultural aspects of social control, whereby the ideas of the dominant social group are accepted by all of society.

hermaphroditic Term to describe a person whose chromosomes or sex characteristics are neither exclusively male nor exclusively female.

heterogamy Choosing romantic partners who are dissimilar to us in terms of class, race, education, religion, and other social group membership.

heterosexuality Sexual desire for other genders.

hidden curriculum Values or behaviors that students learn indirectly over the course of their schooling because of the structure of the educational system and the teaching methods used.

high culture Those forms of cultural expression usually associated with the elite or dominant classes.

homeschooling The education of children by their parents, at home.

homogamy The tendency to marry or have relationships with people who are like us.

homophobia Fear of or discrimination toward homosexuals or toward individuals who display purportedly gender-inappropriate behavior.

homosexuality The tendency to feel sexual desire toward members of one's own gender.

honor killing The murder of a family member—usually female—who is believed to have brought dishonor to her family.

horizontal social mobility The occupational movement of individuals or groups within a social class.

human exemptionalism The attitude that humans are exempt from natural ecological limits.

human sexual dimorphism The extent, much debated in recent years, to which inherent physical differences define the distinctions between the two sexes.

hypergamy Marrying "up" in the social class hierarchy.

hypodermic needle theory (magic bullet theory) A theory that explains the effects of media as if their contents simply entered directly into the consumer, who is powerless to resist their influence.

hypogamy Marrying "down" in the social class hierarchy.

hypothesis A theoretical statement explaining the relationship between two or more phenomena.

id According to Freud, one of three interrelated parts that make up the mind; the id consists of basic inborn drives that are the source of instinctive psychic energy.

ideal culture The norms, values, and patterns of behavior that members of a society believe should be observed in principle.

identification A type of conformity stronger than compliance and weaker than internalization, caused by a desire to establish or maintain a relationship with a person or a group.

ideology A system of beliefs, attitudes, and values that directs a society and reproduces the status quo of the bourgeoisie.

idioculture The customs, practices, and values expressed in a particular place by the people who interact there.

immigration Entering one country from another to take up permanent residence.

impression management The effort to control the impressions we make on others so that they form a desired view of us and the situation; the use of self-presentation and performance tactics.

incapacitation An approach to punishment that seeks to protect society from criminals by imprisoning or executing them.

incest Proscribed sexual contact between family members; a form of child abuse when it occurs between a child and a caregiver.

Independent (or Third) Sector The part of the economy composed of nonprofit organizations; their workers are mis-sion driven, rather than profit driven, and such organizations direct surplus funds to the causes they support.

independent variable Factor that is predicted to cause change.

individual discrimination Discrimination carried out by one person against another.

Industrial Revolution The rapid transformation of social life resulting from the technological and economic developments that began with the assembly line, steam power, and urbanization.

infant mortality Average number of infant deaths per 1,000 live births in a particular population.

influential power Power that is supported by persuasion.

informal social control The regulation of behavior through unofficial customs, norms, expectations, and sanctions.

Information Revolution The recent social revolution made possible by the development of the microchip in the 1970s, which brought about vast improvements in the ability to manage information.

informed consent A safeguard through which the researcher makes sure that respondents are freely participating and understand the nature of the research.

in-group A group that one identifies with and feels loyalty toward.

in-group orientation Among stigmatized individuals, the rejection of prevailing judgments or prejudice and the development of new standards that value their group identity.

innovators Individuals who accept society's approved goals but not society's approved means to achieve them.

institutional discrimination Discrimination carried out systematically by institutions (political, economic, educational, and others) that affect all members of a group who come into contact with it.

institutional review board A group of scholars within a university who meet regularly to review and approve the research proposals of their colleagues and make recommendations for how to protect human subjects.

instrumental leadership Leadership that is task or goal oriented.

instrumental role The position of the family member who provides the family's material support and is often an authority figure.

instrumental tasks The practical physical tasks necessary to maintain family life.

integrative medicine The combination of conventional medicine with complementary practices and treatments that have proven to be safe and effective.

intentional community Any of a variety of groups who form communal living arrangements outside marriage.

intergenerational mobility Movement between social classes that occurs from one generation to the next.

internal colonialism The economic and political domination and subjugation of the minority group by the controlling group within a nation.

internal migration Movement of a population within a country.

internalization The strongest type of conformity, occurring when an individual adopts the beliefs or actions of a group and makes them her own.

interpretive community A group of people dedicated to the consumption and interpretation of a particular cultural product and who create a collective, social meaning for the product.

interpretive strategies The ideas and frameworks that audience members bring to bear on a particular media text to understand its meaning.

intersexed Term to describe a person whose chromosomes or sex characteristics are neither exclusively male nor exclusively female.

intervening variable A third variable, sometimes overlooked, that explains the relationship between two other variables.

interviews Face-to-face, information-seeking conversation, sometimes defined as a conversation with a purpose.

intragenerational mobility The movement between social classes that occurs during the course of an individual's lifetime.

intrinsic religiosity A person's inner religious life or personal relationship to the divine.

iron cage Max Weber's pessimistic description of modern life, in which we are caught in bureaucratic structures that control our lives through rigid rules and rationalization.

just-world hypothesis Argues that people have a deep need to see the world as orderly, predictable, and fair, which creates a tendency to view victims of social injustice as deserving of their fates.

kin Relatives or relations, usually those related by common descent.

knowledge workers Those who work primarily with information and who create value in the economy through their ideas, judgments, analyses, designs, or innovations.

labeling theory Howard Becker's idea that deviance is a consequence of external judgments, or labels, that modify the individual's self-concept and change the way others respond to the labeled person.

language A system of communication using vocal sounds, gestures, or written symbols; the basis of symbolic culture and the primary means through which we communicate with one another and perpetuate our culture.

latent functions The less obvious, perhaps unintended functions of a social structure.

law A common type of formally defined norm providing an explicit statement about what is permissible and what is illegal in a given society.

leading questions Questions that predispose a respondent to answer in a certain way.

legal-rational authority Authority based in laws, rules, and procedures, not in the heredity or personality of any individual leader.

leisure A period of time that can be spent relaxing, engaging in recreation, or otherwise indulging in freely chosen activities.

LGBTQ Lesbian, gay, bisexual, transgender, and queer; sometimes "A" is added to include "allies."

liberation theology A movement within the Catholic Church to understand Christianity from the perspective of the poor and oppressed, with a focus on fighting injustice.

life expectancy Average age to which people in a particular population live.

life span or longevity The uppermost age to which a person can potentially live.

lifestyle enclaves Groups of people drawn together by shared interests, especially those relating to hobbies, sports, and media.

Likert scale A way of organizing categories on a survey question so that the respondent can choose an answer along a continuum.

literature review A thorough search through previously published studies relevant to a particular topic.

looking-glass self The notion that the self develops through our perception of others' evaluations and appraisals of us.

lower-middle class Mostly "blue collar" or service industry workers who are less likely to have a college degree; they constitute about 30 percent of the U.S. population.

macrosociology The level of analysis that studies large-scale social structures in order to determine how they affect the lives of groups and individuals.

magic bullet theory (hypodermic needle theory) A theory that explains the effects of media as if their contents simply entered directly into the consumer, who is powerless to resist their influences. Also called the hypodermic needle theory.

mainstream environmentalism Beginning in the 1980s, the third major stage of the environmental movement; characterized by increasing organization, well-crafted promotional campaigns, sophisticated political tactics, and an increasing reliance on economic and scientific expertise.

Malthusian theorem The theory that exponential population growth will outpace arithmetic growth in food production and other resources.

Malthusian trap Malthus's prediction that a rapidly increasing population will overuse natural resources, leading inevitably to a major public health disaster.

manifest functions The obvious, intended functions of a social structure for the social system.

mass behavior Large groups of people engaging in similar behaviors without necessarily being in the same place.

mass society theory A theory of social movements that assumes people join social movements not because of the movements' ideals, but to satisfy a psychological need to belong to something larger than themselves.

master status A status that is always relevant and affects all other statuses we possess.

material culture The objects associated with a cultural group, such as tools, machines, utensils, buildings, and artwork; any physical object to which we give social meaning.

McDonaldization George Ritzer's term describing the spread of bureaucratic rationalization and the accompanying increases in efficiency and dehumanization.

means of production Anything that can create wealth: money, property, factories, and other types of businesses, and the infrastructure necessary to run them.

mechanical solidarity Term developed by Emile Durkheim to describe the type of social bonds present in premodern, agrarian societies, in which shared traditions and beliefs created a sense of social cohesion.

medicalization The process by which some behaviors or conditions that were once seen as personal problems are redefined as medical issues.

megalopolis or megacity A group of densely populated metropolises that grow dependent on each other and eventually combined to form a huge urban complex.

merger The legal combination of two companies, usually in order to maximize efficiency and profits by eliminating redundant infrastructure and personnel.

meritocracy A system in which rewards are distributed based on merit.

metropolis An urban area with a large population, usually 500,000 to 1 million people.

Metropolitan Statistical Area (MSA) or agglomeration One or more adjacent counties with at least one major city of at least 50,000 inhabitants that is surrounded by an adjacent area that is socially and economically integrated with the city.

microsociology The level of analysis that studies face-to-face and small-group interactions in order to understand how they affect the larger patterns and institutions of society.

middle class Composed primarily of "white collar" workers with a broad range of incomes; they constitute about 30 percent of the U.S. population.

midrange theory An approach that integrates empiricism and grand theory.

migration Movement of people from one geographic area to another for the purpose of resettling.

minority group Members of a social group that is systematically denied the same access to power and resources available to society's dominant groups but who are not necessarily fewer in number than the dominant groups.

miscegenation Romantic, sexual, or marital relationships between people of different races.

modern environmental movement Beginning in the 1960s, the second major stage of the environmental movement; focused on the environmental consequences of new technologies, oil exploration, chemical production, and nuclear power plants.

modernism A paradigm that places trust in the power of science and technology to create progress, solve problems, and improve life.

modernity A term encompassing the forms of social organization that characterize industrialized societies, including the decline of tradition, an increase in individualism, and a belief in progress, technology, and science.

monarchy A government ruled by a king or queen, with succession of rulers kept within the family.

monogamy The practice of marrying (or being in a relationship with) one person at a time.

monopoly A situation in which there is only one individual or organization, without competitors, providing a particular good or service.

monotheistic A term describing religions that worship a single divine figure.

more A norm that carries great moral significance, is closely related to the core values of a cultural group, and often involves severe repercussions for violators.

mortality rate A measure of the decrease in population due to deaths; often expressed as the number of deaths expected per 1,000 people per year in a particular population.

multiculturalism A policy that values diverse racial, ethnic, national, and linguistic backgrounds and so encourages the retention of cultural differences within society rather than assimilation.

natural increase Change in population size that results from births and deaths; linked to a country's progress toward demographic transition.

nature vs. nurture debate The ongoing discussion of the respective roles of genetics and socialization in determining individual behaviors and traits.

negative questions Survey questions that ask respondents what they don't think instead of what they do.

neglect A form of child abuse in which the caregiver fails to provide adequate nutrition, sufficient clothing or shelter, or hygienic and safe living conditions.

Neo-Malthusians Contemporary researchers who worry about the rapid pace of population growth and believe that Malthus's basic prediction could be true.

net migration Net effect of immigration and emigration on an area's population in a given time period; expressed as an increase or decrease.

new ecological paradigm A way of understanding human life as just one part of an ecosystem that includes many species' interactions with the environment; suggests that there should be ecological limits on human activity.

NIMBY Short for "Not In My Backyard"; originally referred to protests that aimed at shifting undesirable activities onto those with less power; now sometimes used without negative connotations to describe local environmental activists.

nonrenewable resources Finite resources, including those that take so long to replenish as to be effectively finite.

norm A rule or guideline regarding what kinds of behavior are acceptable and appropriate within a culture.

nuclear family A heterosexual couple with one or more children living in a single household.

objectivity Impartiality, or the ability to allow the facts to speak for themselves.

online education Any educational course or program in which the teacher and the student meet via the Internet, rather than meeting physically in a classroom.

open system A social system with ample opportunities to move from one class to another.

open-ended question A question asked of a respondent that allows the answer to take whatever form the respondent chooses.

operational definition A clear and precise definition of a variable that facilitates its measurement.

opinion leaders High-profile individuals whose interpretation of events influences the public.

organic solidarity Term developed by Emile Durkheim to describe the type of social bonds present in modern societies, based on difference, interdependence, and individual rights.

out-group Any group an individual feels opposition, rivalry, or hostility toward.

outsiders According to Howard Becker, those labeled deviant and subsequently segregated from "normal" society.

outsourcing "Contracting out" or transferring to another country the labor that a company might otherwise have employed its own staff to perform; typically done for financial reasons.

palliative care Type of health care that focuses on symptom and pain relief and providing a supportive environment for critically ill or dying patients, rather than fighting the illness or disease.

pandemic Occurs when a significantly higher number of cases of a disease also spreads through an especially large geographical region spanning many countries or even continents.

paradigm A set of assumptions, theories, and perspectives that make up a way of understanding social reality.

paradigm shift The term used to describe a change in basic assumptions of a particular scientific discipline.

participant observation A methodology associated with ethnography whereby the researcher both observes and becomes a member in a social setting.

particular or significant other The perspectives and expectations of a particular role that a child learns and internalizes.

passing Presenting yourself as a member of a different group than the stigmatized group you belong to.

patriarchy Literally meaning "rule of the father"; a male-dominated society.

personal front The expressive equipment we consciously or unconsciously use as we present ourselves to others, including appearance and manner, to help establish the definition of the situation.

pilfering Stealing minor items in small amounts, often again and again.

pilot study A small study carried out to test the feasibility of a larger one.

play stage The second stage in Mead's theory of the development of self wherein children pretend to play the role of the particular or significant other.

pluralism A cultural pattern of intergroup relations that encourages racial and ethnic variation within a society.

pluralist model A system of political power in which a wide variety of individuals and groups have equal access to resources and the mechanisms of power.

pluralistic ignorance A process in which members of a group individually conclude that there is no need to take action because of the observation that other group members have not done so.

political action committee (PAC) An organization that raises money to support the interests of a select group or organization.

politics Methods and tactics intended to influence government policy; policy-related attitudes and activities.

pollution Any environmental contaminant that harms living beings.

polyamory A system of multiple-person partnership.

polyandry A system of marriage that allows women to have multiple husbands.

polygamy A system of marriage that allows people to have more than one spouse at a time.

polygyny A system of marriage that allows men to have multiple wives.

polysemy Having many possible meanings or interpretations.

popular culture Usually contrasted with the high culture of elite groups; forms of cultural expression usually associated with the masses, consumer goods, and commercial products.

population transfer The forcible removal of a group of people from the territory they have occupied.

positive deviance Actions considered deviant within a given context but are later reinterpreted as appropriate or even heroic.

positivism The theory, developed by Auguste Comte, that sense perceptions are the only valid source of knowledge.

postmodernism A paradigm that suggests that social reality is diverse, pluralistic, and constantly in flux.

postmodernity A term encompassing the forms of social organization characteristic of postindustrial societies, including a focus on the production and management of information and skepticism of science and technology.

power The ability to impose one's will on others.

power elite A relatively small group of people in the top ranks of economic, political, and military institutions who make many of the important decisions in American society.

pragmatism A theoretical perspective that assumes organisms (including humans) make practical adaptations to their environments. Humans do this through cognition, interpretation, and interaction.

praxis Practical action that is taken on the basis of intellectual or theoretical understanding.

prejudice An idea about the characteristics of a group that is applied to all members of that group and is unlikely to change regardless of the evidence against it.

preparatory stage The first stage in Mead's theory of the development of self wherein children mimic or imitate others.

prescriptions Behaviors approved of by a particular social group.

prestige The social honor people are given because of their membership in well-regarded social groups.

preventive medicine Type of health care that aims to avoid or forestall the onset of disease by taking preventive measures, often including lifestyle changes.

primary deviance In labeling theory, the initial act or attitude that causes one to be labeled deviant.

primary groups The people who are most important to our sense of self; members' relationships are typically characterized by face-to-face interaction, high levels of cooperation, and intense feelings of belonging.

probability sampling Any sampling scheme in which any given unit has the same probability of being chosen.

profane The ordinary, mundane, or everyday.

progressive Term describing efforts to promote forward-thinking social change.

proletariat Workers; those who have no means of production of their own and so are reduced to selling their labor power in order to live.

property crime Crimes that did not involve violence, including burglary, larceny-theft, motor vehicle theft, and arson.

propinquity The tendency to marry or have relationships with people in close geographic proximity.

proscriptions Behaviors a particular social group wants its members to avoid.

psychoanalysis The therapeutic branch of psychology founded by Sigmund Freud in which free association and dream interpretation are used to explore the unconscious mind.

psychosexual stages of development Four distinct stages of the development of the self between birth and adulthood, according to Freud. Each stage is associated with a different erogenous zone.

public goods dilemma A type of social dilemma in which individuals incur the cost to contribute to a collective resource, though they may never benefit from that resource.

qualitative A type of data that can't be converted into numbers, usually because they relate to meaning.

qualitative research Research that works with nonnumerical data such as texts, fieldnotes, interview transcripts, photographs, and tape recordings; this type of research more often tries to understand how people make sense of their world.

quantitative A type of data that can be converted into numbers, usually for statistical comparison.

quantitative research Research that translates the social world into numbers that can be treated mathematically; this type of research often tries to find cause-and-effect relationships.

queer theory A paradigm that proposes that categories of sexual identity are social constructs and that no sexual category is fundamentally either deviant or normal.

race A socially defined category based on real or perceived biological differences between groups of people.

racial assimilation The process by which racial minority groups are absorbed into the dominant group through intermarriage.

racism A set of beliefs about the superiority of one racial or ethnic group; used to justify inequality and often rooted in the assumption that differences between groups are genetic.

rapport A positive relationship often characterized by mutual trust or sympathy.

rationalization The application of economic logic to human activity; the use of formal rules and regulations in order to maximize efficiency without consideration of subjective or individual concerns.

reactivity The tendency of people and events to react to the process of being studied.

real culture The norms, values, and patterns of behavior that actually exist within a society (which may or may not correspond to the society's ideals).

rebels Individuals who reject society's approved goals and means and instead create and work toward their own (sometimes revolutionary) goals using new means.

recreation Any satisfying, amusing, and stimulating activity that is experienced as refreshing and renewing for body, mind, and spirit.

reference group A group that provides a standard of comparison against which we evaluate ourselves.

reflexivity How the identity and activities of the researcher influence what is going on in the field setting.

region In the dramaturgical perspective, the context or setting in which the performance takes place.

regressive Term describing resistance to particular social changes, efforts to maintain the status quo, or attempts to reestablish an earlier form of social order.

rehabilitation An approach to punishment that attempts to reform criminals as part of their penalty.

reinforcement theory Theory that suggests that audiences seek messages in the media that reinforce their existing attitudes and beliefs and are thus not influenced by challenging or contradictory information.

relative deprivation A relative measure of poverty based on the standard of living in a particular society.

relative deprivation theory A theory of social movements that focuses on the actions of oppressed groups who seek rights or opportunities already enjoyed by others in the society.

reliability The consistency of a question or measurement tool; the degree to which the same questions will produce similar answers.

religion Any institutionalized system of shared beliefs and rituals that identify a relationship between the sacred and the profane.

religiosity The regular practice of religious beliefs, often measured in terms of frequency of attendance at worship services and the importance of religious beliefs to an individual.

renewable resources Resources that replenish at a rate comparable to the rate at which they are consumed.

replicability Research that can be repeated, and thus verified, by other researchers later.

representative sample A sample taken so that findings from members of the sample group can be generalized to the whole population.

representativeness The degree to which a particular studied group is similar to, or represents, any part of the larger society.

repression The process that causes unwanted or taboo desires to return via tics, dreams, slips of the tongue, and neuroses, according to Freud.

rescission The practice by insurance companies of canceling coverage only after a person gets sick.

residential segregation The geographical separation of the poor from the rest of the population.

resistance strategies Ways that workers express discontent with their working conditions and try to reclaim control of the conditions of their labor.

resocialization The process of replacing previously learned norms and values with new ones as a part of a transition in life.

resource mobilization theory A theory of social movements that focuses on the practical constraints that help or hinder social movements' action.

respondent Someone from whom a researcher solicits information.

response rate The number or percentage of surveys completed by respondents and returned to researchers.

retreatists Individuals who reject both society's approved goals and the means by which to achieve them.

retribution An approach to punishment that emphasizes retaliation or revenge for the crime as the appropriate goal.

riot Continuous disorderly behavior by a group of people that disturbs the peace and is directed toward other people and/or property.

ritual A practice based on religious beliefs.

ritualists Individuals who have given up hope of achieving society's approved goals but still operate according to society's approved means.

role The set of behaviors expected of someone because of his or her status.

role conflict Experienced when we occupy two or more roles with contradictory expectations.

role exit The process of leaving a role that we will no longer occupy.

role model An individual who serves as an example for others to strive toward and emulate.

role strain The tension experienced when there are contradictory expectations within one role.

role-taking emotions Emotions like sympathy, embarrassment, or shame that require that we assume the perspective of another person or many other people and respond from that person or group's point of view.

rural Relating to sparsely settled areas; in the United States, any county with a population density between 10 and 59.9 people per square mile.

rural rebound Population increase in rural counties that adjoin urban centers or possess rich scenic or amenity values.

sacred The holy, divine, or supernatural.

sample The part of the population that will actually be studied.

sanction Positive or negative reactions to the ways that people follow or disobey norms, including rewards for conformity and punishments for norm violations.

Sapir-Whorf hypothesis The idea that language structures thought and that ways of looking at the world are embedded in language.

saturated self A postmodern idea that the self is now developed by multiple influences chosen from a wide range of media sources.

school vouchers Payments from the government to parents whose children attend failing public schools; the money helps parents pay private school tuition.

scientific method A procedure for acquiring knowledge that emphasizes collecting concrete data through observation and experiment.

second shift The unpaid housework and child care often expected of women after they complete their day's paid labor.

second wave The period of feminist activity during the 1960s and 1970s often associated with the issues of women's equal access to employment and education.

secondary deviance In labeling theory, the subsequent deviant identity or career that develops as a result of being labeled deviant.

secondary groups Larger and less intimate than primary groups; members' relationships are usually organized around a specific goal and are often temporary.

secular Nonreligious; a secular society separates church and state and does not endorse any religion.

segregation The formal and legal separation of groups by race or ethnicity.

self The individual's conscious, reflexive experience of a personal identity separate and distinct from other individuals.

self-fulfilling prophecy An inaccurate statement or belief that, by altering the situation, becomes accurate; a prediction that causes itself to come true.

service workers Those whose work involves providing a service to businesses or individual clients, customers, or consumers rather than manufacturing goods.

sex An individual's membership in one of two biologically distinct categories—male or female.

sexuality The character or quality of being sexual.

sexual orientation or sexual identity The inclination to feel sexual desire toward people of a particular gender or toward both genders.

sick role The actions and attitudes that society expects from someone who is ill.

sign A symbol that stands for or conveys an idea.

simple random sample A particular type of probability sample in which every member of the population has an equal chance of being selected.

simplicity movement A loosely knit movement that opposes consumerism and encourages people to work less, earn less, and spend less, in accordance with nonmaterialistic values.

simulacrum An image or media representation that does not reflect reality in any meaningful way but is treated as real.

situational ethnicity An ethnic identity that can be either displayed or concealed depending on its usefulness in a given situation.

slavery The most extreme form of social stratification, based on the legal ownership of people.

smart growth Term for economic and urban planning policies that emphasize responsible development and renewal.

social atomization A social situation that emphasizes individualism over collective or group identities.

social change The transformation of a culture over time.

social class A system of stratification based on access to such resources as wealth, property, power, and prestige.

social construction The process by which a concept or practice is created and maintained by participants who collectively agree that it exists.

social control The formal and informal mechanisms used to increase conformity to values and norms and thus promote social cohesion.

social Darwinism The application of the theory of evolution and the notion of "survival of the fittest" to the study of society.

social dilemma A situation in which behavior that is rational for the individual can, when practiced by many people, lead to collective disaster.

social ecology The study of human populations and their impact on the natural world.

social identity theory A theory of group formation and maintenance that stresses the need of individual members to feel a sense of belonging.

social inequality The unequal distribution of wealth, power, or prestige among members of a society.

social influence (peer pressure) The influence of one's fellow group members on individual attitudes and behaviors.

social institutions Systems and structures within society that shape the activities of groups and individuals.

social learning The process of learning behaviors and meanings through social interaction.

social loafing The phenomenon in which as more individuals are added to a task, each individual contributes a little less; a source of inefficiency when working in teams.

social mobility The movement of individuals or groups within the hierarchal system of social classes.

social movement Any social groups with leadership, organization, and an ideological commitment to promote or resist social change.

social network The web of direct and indirect ties connecting an individual to other people who may also affect the individual.

social reproduction The tendency of social classes to remain relatively stable as social class status is passed down from one generation to the next.

social sciences The disciplines that use the scientific method to examine the social world, in contrast to the natural sciences, which examine the physical world.

social stratification The division of society into groups arranged in a social hierarchy.

social ties Connections between individuals.

socialism An economic system based on the collective ownership of the means of production, collective distribution of goods and services, and government regulation of the economy.

socialization The process of learning and internalizing the values, beliefs, and norms of our social group, by which we become functioning members of society.

society A group of people who shape their lives in aggregated and patterned ways that distinguish their group from other groups.

socioeconomic status (SES) A measure of an individual's place within a social class system; often used interchangeably with "class."

sociological imagination A quality of the mind that allows us to understand the relationship between our individual circumstances and larger social forces.

sociological perspective A way of looking at the world through a sociological lens.

sociology The systematic or scientific study of human society and social behavior, from large-scale institutions and mass culture to small groups and individual interactions.

solar dimming A decline in the amount of light reaching the earth's surface because of increased air pollution, which reflects more light back into space.

solidarity The degree of integration or unity within a particular society; the extent to which individuals feel connected to other members of their group.

special interest groups Organizations that raise and spend money to influence elected officials and/or public opinion.

spurious correlation The appearance of causation produced by an intervening variable.

status A position in a social hierarchy that carries a particular set of expectations.

status inconsistency A situation in which there are serious differences between the different elements of an individual's socioeconomic status.

stereotyping Judging others based on preconceived generalizations about groups or categories of people.

stigma Erving Goffman's term for any physical or social attribute that devalues a person or group's identity and that may exclude those who are devalued from normal social interaction.

structural functionalism A paradigm that begins with the assumption that society is a unified whole that functions because of the contributions of its separate structures.

structural mobility Changes in the social status of large numbers of people due to structural changes in society.

structural strain theory Robert Merton's argument that in an unequal society the tension or strain between socially approved goals and an individual's ability achieve those goals through socially approved means will lead to deviance as individuals reject either the goals or the means or both.

structure A social institution that is relatively stable over time and that meets the needs of society by performing functions necessary to maintain social order and stability.

subculture A group within society that is differentiated by its distinctive values, norms, and lifestyle.

sublimation The process in which socially unacceptable desires are healthily channeled into socially acceptable expressions, according to Freud.

suburbanization Beginning after World War II, the shift of large segments of population away from the urban core and toward the edges of cities.

suffrage movement The movement organized around gaining voting rights for women.

superego According to Freud, one of three interrelated parts that make up the mind; the superego has two components (the conscience and the ego-ideal) and represents the internalized demands of society.

surface acting Trying to "act the part" expected in a specific situation, even if that part does not match your underlying mood.

survey A method based on questionnaires that are administered to a sample of respondents selected from a target population.

sustainable development Economic development that aims to reconcile global economic growth with environmental protection.

sweatshop A workplace where workers are subject to extreme exploitation, including below-standard wages, long hours, and poor working conditions that may pose health or safety hazards.

symbolic culture The ideas associated with a cultural group, including ways of thinking (beliefs, values, and assumptions) and ways of behaving (norms, interactions, and communication).

symbolic ethnicity An ethnic identity that is only relevant on specific occasions and does not significantly impact everyday life.

symbolic interactionism A paradigm that sees interaction and meaning as central to society and assumes that meanings are not inherent but are created through interaction.

synergy A mutually beneficial interaction between parts of an organization that allows it to create something greater than the sum of its individual outputs.

synthesis The new social system created out of the conflict between thesis and antithesis in a dialectical model.

taboo A norm ingrained so deeply that even thinking about violating it evokes strong feelings of disgust, horror, or revulsion.

target population The entire group about which a researcher would like to be able to generalize.

taste cultures Areas of culture that share similar aesthetics and standards of taste.

taste publics Groups of people who share similar artistic, literary, media, recreational, and intellectual interests.

technological determinism A theory of social change that assumes changes in technology drive changes in society, rather than vice versa.

technology Material artifacts and the knowledge and techniques required to use them.

telecommuting Working from home while staying connected to the office through communications technology.

tertiary deviance Redefining the stigma associated with a deviant label as a positive phenomenon.

textual poaching Henry Jenkins's term describing the ways that audience members manipulate an original cultural product to create a new one; a common way for fans to exert some control over the media they consume.

Thanatos In Freudian psychology, the drive or instinct toward aggression or destruction.

theories In sociology, abstract propositions that explain the social world and make predictions about the future.

thesis The existing social arrangements in a dialectical model.

third place Any informal public place where people come together regularly for conversation and camaraderie when not at work or at home.

Third Sector The part of the economy composed of nonprofit organizations; their workers are mission driven, rather than profit driven, and such organizations direct surplus funds to the causes they support. Also called the Independent Sector.

third wave The most recent period of feminist activity, focusing on issues of diversity and the variety of identities women can possess.

Thomas theorem Classic formulation of the way individuals define situations, whereby "if people define situations as real, they are real in their consequences."

total institution An institution in which individuals are cut off from the rest of society so that their lives can be controlled and regulated for the purpose of systematically stripping away previous roles and identities in order to create new ones.

tracking The placement of students in educational "tracks," or programs of study (e.g., college prep, remedial), that determine the types of classes students take.

traditional authority Authority based in custom, birthright, or divine right.

tragedy of the commons A particular type of social dilemma in which many individuals' overexploitation of a public resource depletes or degrades that common resource.

transgendered Term describing an individual whose sense of gender identity transgresses expected gender categories.

transsexuals Individuals who identify with the other sex and have surgery to alter their own sex so it fits their self-image.

treadmill of production Term describing the operation of modern economic systems that require constant growth, which causes increased exploitation of resources and environmental degradation.

triad A three-person social group.

two-step flow model Theory on media effects that suggests audiences get information through opinion leaders who influence their attitudes and beliefs, rather than through direct firsthand sources.

unchurched A term describing those who consider themselves spiritual but not religious and who often adopt aspects of various religious traditions.

underclass The poorest Americans who are chronically unemployed and may depend on public or private assistance; they constitute about 5 percent of the U.S. population.

Uniform Crime Report (UCR) An official measure of crime in the United States, produced by the FBI's official tabulation of every crime reported by over 17,000 law enforcement agencies.

union An association of workers who bargain collectively for increased wages and benefits and better working conditions.

upper class A largely self-sustaining group of the wealthiest people in a class system; in the United States, they constitute about 1 percent of the population and possess most of the wealth of the country.

upper-middle class Mostly professionals and managers who enjoy considerable financial stability, they constitute about 14 percent of the U.S. population.

urban Relating to cities; typically describes densely populated areas.

urban density Concentration of people in a city, measured by the total number of people per square mile.

urban legend Modern folklore; a story that is believed (incorrectly) to be true and is widely spread because it expresses concerns, fears, and anxieties about the social world.

urban renewal Efforts to rejuvenate decaying inner cities, including renovation, selective demolition, commercial development, and tax incentives.

urban sprawl A derogatory term applied to the expansion of urban or suburban boundaries, associated with irresponsible or poorly planned development.

urbanites People who live in cities.

urbanization Movement of increasing numbers of people from rural areas to cities.

uses and gratifications paradigm Approaches to understanding media effects that focus on individuals' psychological or social needs that consumption of various media fulfills.

utopia Literally "no place"; an ideal society in which all social ills have been overcome.

validity The accuracy of a question or measurement tool; the degree to which a researcher is measuring what he thinks he is measuring.

value-free sociology An ideal whereby researchers identify facts without allowing their own personal beliefs or biases to interfere.

values Ideas about what is desirable or contemptible and right or wrong in a particular group. They articulate the essence of everything that a cultural group cherishes and honors.

variables One of two or more phenomena that a researcher believes are related and hopes to prove are related through research.

vector organisms Animals like mosquitoes, ticks, and birds that carry and spread pathogens (germs or other infectious agents) in a given area.

verstehen "Empathic understanding"; Weber's term to describe good social research, which tries to understand the meanings that individual social actors attach to various actions and events.

vertical social mobility The movement between different class statuses, often called either upward mobility or downward mobility.

violent crime Crimes in which violence is either the objective or the means to an end, including murder, rape, aggravated assault, and robbery.

virtual community A community of people linked by their consumption of the same digital media.

virtual communities Social groups whose interactions are mediated through information technologies, particularly the Internet.

wealth A measure of net worth that includes income, property, and other assets.

weighting Techniques for manipulating the sampling procedure so that the sample more closely resembles the larger population.

white flight Movement of upper- and middle-class whites who could afford to leave the cities for the suburbs, especially in the 1950s and 60s.

white collar A description characterizing workers and skilled laborers in technical and lower-management jobs.

white-collar crime Crime committed by a high-status individual in the course of his occupation.

working class Mostly "blue collar" or service industry workers who are less likely to have a college degree; they constitute about 30 percent of the U.S. population.

working poor Poorly educated workers who work full-time but remain below the poverty line; they constitute about 20 percent of the U.S. population.

REFERENCES

Access Clark County. 2009. "Clark County/Las Vegas Valley average population and growth rates, 1990–2008." www.accessclarkcounty .com/depts/comprehensive_planning/demographics/Pages/ demographics.aspx

ACLU. 2003. "Inadequate representation." American Civil Liberties Union online publication, October 8. www.aclu.org/capital/ unequal/10390pub20031008.html

Adams, Damon. 1994. "Holocaust survivors face cameras; Spielberg heading project to create videotape library." *Times-Picayune*, November 24, p. D1.

Adler, Patricia A.; and Adler, Peter. 1991. *Backboards and Blackboards: College Athletes and Role Engulfment.* New York: Columbia University Press.

_____. 2000. *Constructions of Deviance: Social Power, Context and Interaction.* Belmont, CA: Wadsworth.

Adorno, T.; and Horkheimer, M. 1979. "The culture industry: Enlightenment as mass deception." In T. Adorno and M. Horkheimer, eds., *Dialectic of Enlightenment.* London: Verso.

Aguirre, Benigno; Quarantelli, Enrico; and Mendoza, Jorge L. 1988. "The collective behavior of fads: The characteristics, effects and career of streaking." *American Sociological Review*, vol. 53: 569–589.

Agyeman, Julian; Bullard, Robert D.; and Evans, Bob; eds. 2003. *Just Sustainabilities: Development in an Unequal World.* Cambridge, MA: MIT Press.

AHENS. 2003. "Setting boundaries between work, life helps families thrive." *Ascribe Higher Education News Service*, May 8.

Alatas, Syed Farid; and Sinha, Vineeta. 2001. "Teaching classical sociological theory in Singapore: The context of Eurocentrism." *Teaching Sociology*, vol. 29, no. 3: 316–331.

Alcoholics Anonymous. 2001 (orig. 1939). *Alcoholics Anonymous: The Story of How Many Thousands of Men and Women Have Recovered from Alcoholism.* 4th ed. New York: Alcoholics Anonymous World Service.

Alexander, Jeffrey. 1988. "Parsons' 'structure' in American sociology." *Sociological Theory*, vol. 6, no. 1: 96–102.

Alexander, Jeffrey; and Smelser, Neil. 1998. *Diversity and Its Discontents: Cultural Conflict and Common Ground in Contemporary American Society.* Princeton, NJ: Princeton University Press.

Allport, G.; and Ross, M. 1967. "Personal religious orientation and prejudice." *Journal of Personality and Social Psychology*, vol. 5, no. 4: 432–443.

Almaguer, Tomas. 2008. *Racial Fault Lines: The Historical Origins of White Supremacy in California.* Berkeley, CA: University of California Press.

Altermatt, Ellen Rydell; and Pomerantz, Eva M. 2005. "The implications of having high-achieving versus low-achieving friends: A longitudinal analysis." *Social Development*, vol. 14, no. 1: 61–81.

Altschuler, Glenn C. 2002. "College prep: A tryout for the real world." *New York Times*, April 14. www.nytimes.com/2002/ 04/14/education/college-prep-a-tryout-for-the-real-world. html?scp=5&sq=2001%20internships&st=cse, accessed 4/24/09

American College Health Association (ACHA). 2009. *American College Health Association National College Health Assessment II.* Linthicum, MD: American College Health Association. www .acha-ncha.org/docs/ACHA-NCHA_Reference_Group_ ExecutiveSummary_Fall2009.pdf

American Association of Community Colleges. 2011. http://aacc.nche .edu/pages/default.aspx

American Medical Association (AMA). 2010. "Medical licensure." *Becoming a Physician.* www.ama-assn.org/ama/pub/education-careers/becoming-physician/medical-licensure.shtml

Amott, Teresa; and Matthaei, Julie. 1996. *Race, Class, Gender, and Work: A Multicultural Ethnic History of Women in the United States.* 2nd ed. Boston: South End Press.

Ananat, Elizabeth Oltmans. 2005. "The wrong side of the tracks: Estimating the causal effects of racial segregation on city outcomes." Unpublished working paper. MIT Department of Economics.

Anderson, Doug. 2009. "The Changing Face of Unemployment." Nielsenwire. March 1. blog.nielsen.com/nielsenwire/consumer/ the-changing-face-of-unemployment

Anderson, Elijah. 1990. *Streetwise: Race, Class and Change in an Urban Community.* Chicago: University of Chicago Press.

Anderson, Steven W.; Bechara, Antoine; Damasio, Hann; Tranel, Daniel; and Damasio, Antonio R. 1999. "Impairment of social and moral behavior related to early damage in human prefrontal cortex." *Nature Neuroscience*, vol. 2, no. 11 (November): 1032–1037.

Anzaldúa, Gloria. 1987. *Borderlands/La Frontera: The New Mestiza.* San Francisco: Aunt Lute Books.

Archer, Kim. 2010. " 'Concierge medicine': Patients pay extra to keep doctor." *Tulsa World*, July 6. www.tulsaworld.com/news/article.as px?subjectid=17&articleid=20100706_17_A1_DrJohn537025

Arendt, Hannah. 1958. *The Origins of Totalitarianism.* London: Allen and Unwin Press.

Armitage, Angus. 1951. *The World of Copernicus.* New York: Mentor Books.

Arnst, Catherine. 2010. "Tired of waiting for the doctor? Try one that gives same-day appointments." *Kaiser Health News–Boston Globe*, July 14. www.kaiserhealthnews.org/stories/2010/july/14/waiting-for-the-doctor.aspx?referrer=search

Asch, S. 1958. "Effects of group pressure upon the modification and distortion of judgments." In E. E. Maccoby, T. M. Newcomb, and E. L. Hartley, eds., *Readings in Social Psychology.* New York: Holt, Rinehart, & Winston.

Associated Press. 2004. "Bush warns CIA against 'groupthink' culture." www.msnbc.msn.com/id/6571310/

_____. 2005. "India controls 44 percent of outsourcing." June 12. www.enable24x7.com/MustRead_44percent.asp

_____. 2006. "Global warming causing disease to rise: Malaria, dengue fever increasing as temperature heats up, experts warn." MSNBC, November 14. www.msnbc.msn.com/id/15717706/

_____. 2010. "Obama seeks to overhaul 'No Child Left Behind.'" March 13. http://msnbc.msn.com/id/35852205/nx/us_news-education/

Atkin, C. 1973. "Instrumental utilities and information seeking." In P. Clark, ed., _New Models for Mass Communication Research_. Beverly Hills, CA: Sage.

_____. 1985. "Informational utility and selective exposure." In D. Zillmann and J. Bryant, eds., _Selective Exposure to Communication_. Hillsdale, NJ: Erlbaum.

Babbie, Earl. 2002. _The Basics of Social Research_. Belmont, CA: Wadsworth.

Babiak, T. 2004. "Everything goes at Burning Man: Counterculture fest is everything that North America isn't." _National Post_, September 6, p. B10.

Baca Zinn, Maxine; and Eitzen, D. Stanley. 2002. _Diversity in Families_. Boston: Allyn and Bacon.

Bachman, R.; and Saltzman, L. 1995. "Violence against women: Estimates from the redesigned survey." Bureau of Justice Statistics Special Report. www.ojp.usdoj.gov/bjs/pub/pdf/femvied.pdf.

Bagdikian, Ben H. 2004. _The New Media Monopoly_. Boston: Beacon Press.

Bailey, Holly. 2010. ABC News/Yahoo! News Poll: "People Are Losing Faith in the American Dream." Sept. 21. http://news.yahoo.com/s/yblog_upshot/abc-newsyahoo-news-poll-people-are-losing-faith-in-the-american-dream

Bailey, J. M.; and Pillard, R. C. 1991. "A genetic study of male sexual orientation." _Archives of General Psychiatry_, vol. 48: 1089–1096.

Bailey, Ronald. 2002. "_Silent Spring_ at 40: Rachel Carson's classic is not aging well." _Reason Online Magazine_, June 12. http://reason.com/rb/rb061202.shtml

Baker, H.D.R. 1979. _Chinese Family and Kinship_. London: Macmillan Press.

Baker, J. P.; and Crist, J. L. 1971. "Teacher expectancies: A review of the literature." In J. D. Elashoff and R. E. Snow, eds., _Pygmalion Reconsidered: A Case Study in Statistical Inference: Reconsideration of the Rosenthal-Jacobson Data on Teacher Expectancy_. Worthington, OH: Charles A. Jones.

Baldwin, Tom. 2007. "Fear and blogging on the campaign trail." _London Times_, December 29, Times Magazine: 36.

Bales, Kevin. 2000. _Disposable People: New Slavery in the Global Economy_. Berkeley, CA: University of California Press.

_____; and Soodalter, Ron. 2009. _The Slave Next Door: Human Trafficking and Slavery in America Today_. Berkeley, CA: University of California Press.

Bandura, A. 1965. "Influence of models' reinforcement contingencies on the acquisition of imitative response." _Journal of Personality and Social Psychology_, vol. 1: 589–595.

Bandy, Joe. 1996. "Managing the other of nature: Sustainability, spectacle, and global regimes of capital in ecotourism." _Public Culture_, vol. 8, no. 3: 539–566.

Banfield, Edward. 1970. _The Unheavenly City_. Boston: Little, Brown.

Bardhan, Ashok D.; and Kroll, Cynthia. 2003. "The new wave of outsourcing." Fisher Center for Real Estate and Urban Economics. Berkeley, CA: University of California Press.

Barner, Mark R. 1999. "Sex-role stereotyping in FCC-mandated children's educational television." _Journal of Broadcasting & Electronic Media_, vol. 43, no. 4 (fall): 551.

Barnes, P. M.; Bloom, B.; and Nahin, R. 2008. "Complementary and alternative medicine use among adults and children: United States, 2007." _National Health Statistics Reports_, no. 12 (December 10), 1–23.

Barnett E., C.R. Williams, L. Moore and F. Chen. "Social class and heart disease mortality among African Americans." Ethnicity and Disease. 2002 Fall; 12(4):S3-76-81.

Barrett, David B.; and Johnson, Todd M. 2004. _International Bulletin of Missionary Research_. Center for the Study of Global Christianity, Gordon-Conwell Theological Seminary, South Hamilton, Massachusetts, January.

Barry, Dave. 1994. _The World According to Dave Barry_. Illus. Jeff MacNelly. New York: Wings Books.

Bartels, Chuck. 2003. "Wal-Mart starting to look at all its 1.1 million U.S. workers." _Times-Picayune_ (New Orleans, LA), October 25, "Money," p. 1.

Batan, Clarence M. 2004. "Of strengths and tensions: A dialogue of ideas between the classics and Philippine sociology." _UNITAS_, vol. 77, no. 2: 163–186.

Baudrillard, Jean. 1994 (orig. 1981). _Simulacra and Simulation_. Trans. Sheila Glaser. Ann Arbor, MI: University of Michigan Press.

Bauer, Martin W.; and Gaskell, George; eds. 2000. _Qualitative Researching with Text, Image and Sound_. London: Thousand Oaks; New Delhi: Sage.

Baum, S.; and Payea, K. 2004. "Education pays: The benefits of higher education for individuals and society." New York: The College Board. http://eprints.ecs.org/html/Document.asp?chouseid=5664

Beamish, Thomas. 2002. _Silent Spill: The Organization of an Industrial Crisis_. Boston: MIT Press.

Beard, Jennifer; Feeley, Frank; and Rosen, Sydney. 2009. "Economic and quality of life outcomes of antiretroviral therapy for HIV/AIDS in developing countries: A systematic literature review." _AIDS Care_, vol. 21, no. 11, 1343–1356.

Becker, A.; Burwell, R.; Herzog, D.; Hamburg, P.; and Gilman, S. 2002. "Eating behaviours and attitudes following prolonged exposure to television among ethnic Fijian adolescent girls." _The British Journal of Psychiatry_ 180: 509–514

Becker, Howard S. 1963. _Outsiders: Studies in the Sociology of Deviance_. Chicago: University of Chicago Press.

_____. 1986. _Doing Things Together: Selected Papers_. Evanston, IL: Northwestern University Press.

_____; Greer, Blanche; Hughes, Everett C.; and Strauss, Anselm L. 1961. _Boys in White: Student Culture in Medical School_. Chicago: University of Chicago Press.

Beeghley, Leonard. 2008. _The Structure of Social Stratification in the United States_. Boston: Allyn and Bacon.

Bell, Daniel. 1976. _The Coming of Post-Industrial Society: A Venture in Social Forecasting_. New York: Basic Books.

Bellah, Robert; Sullivan, William; and Tipton, Steven. 1985. _Habits of the Heart: Individualism and Commitment in American Life_. Berkeley, CA: University of California Press.

Bendapudi, Venkat; Mangum, Stephen L.; Tansky, Judith W.; and Fisher, Max M. 2003. "Nonstandard employment arrangements: A proposed typology and policy planning framework." _Human Resource Planning_, vol. 26, no. 1: 3.

Berends, M. 1995. "Educational stratification and students' social bonding to school." *British Journal of Sociology of Education*, vol. 16, no. 3: 327–351.

Berger, Peter. 1963. *Invitation to Sociology*. New York: Bantam Doubleday.

_____. 1977. *Facing Up to Modernity: Excursions in Society, Politics, and Religion*. New York: Basic Books.

_____; and Luckmann, Thomas. 1966. *The Social Construction of Reality: A Treatise in the Sociology of Knowledge*. Garden City, NY: Doubleday.

Bernardes, Jon. 1985. "Do we really know what the family is?" In P. Close and R. Collins, eds., *Family and Economy in Modern Society*. New York: Macmillan.

Bernstein, Jared; McNichol, Elizabeth C.; Mishel, Lawrence; and Zahradnik, Robert. 2000. "Pulling apart: A state-by-state analysis of income trends." Economic Policy Institute Study. www.epi.org/content.cfm/studies_pullingapart

Berry, Sharon. 1993. "Will curbing PACs hurt black reps? Impact of new politication action committee financing rules on African American congressmen." *Black Enterprise*, September.

Best, Joel; and Horiuchi, Gerald. 1985. "The razor blade in the apple: The social construction of urban legends." *Social Problems*, vol. 32, no. 5: 488–499.

Best, Samuel J., and Brian S. Krueger. 2004. *Internet Data Collection*. Sage University Paper Series no. 141. Thousand Oaks, CA: Sage.

Billings, Andrew C.; and Eastman, Susan Tyler. 2000. "Sportscasting and sports reporting." *Journal of Sport and Social Issues*, vol. 24, no. 2: 192–213.

Blau, Judith R.; and Blau, Peter M. 1982. "The cost of inequality: Metropolitan structure and violent crime." *American Sociological Review*, vol. 47, no. 1 (February): 114–129.

Blau, Melinda; and Fingerman, Karen. 2009. *Consequential Strangers: The Power of People Who Don't Seem To Matter . . . But Really Do*. New York: W. W. Norton.

Blaunstein, Albert; and Zangrando, Robert; eds. 1970. *Civil Rights and the Black American*. New York: Washington Square Press.

Bloom, Allan. 1987. *The Closing of the American Mind*. New York: Simon & Schuster.

Blumer, Herbert. 1969. *Symbolic Interactionism: Perspective and Method*. Berkeley, CA: University of California Press.

Blumler, J. G.; and Katz, Elihu. 1974. *The Uses of Mass Communication: Current Perspectives on Gratifications Research*. Beverly Hills, CA: Sage.

Bly, Robert.1990. *Iron John: A Book About Men*. Upper Saddle River, NJ: Addison-Wesley.

Bobo, Lawrence; Kluegel, James R.; and Smith, Ryan A. 1997. "Laissez-faire racism: The crystallization of a 'kindler, gentler' anti-black ideology." In Jack Martin, ed., *Racial Attitudes in the 1990s: Continuity and Change*. Westport, CT: Praeger.

Bobo, Lawrence; and Smith, Ryan A. 1998. "From Jim Crow racism to laissez-faire racism: The transformation of racial attitudes in America." In Wendy Katkin, Ned Landsman, and Andrea Tyree, eds., *Beyond Pluralism: Essays on the Conception of Groups and Group Identities in America*. Urbana, IL: University of Illinois Press.

Bogaert, Anthony F. 2004. "Asexuality: Prevalence and Associated Factors in a National Probability Sample." *Journal of Sex*, vol. 41, no. 3: 279–287.

Bohner, Gerd; Siebler, Frank; and Schmelcher, Jurgen. 2006. "Social norms and the likelihood of raping: Perceived rape myth acceptance of others affects men's rape proclivity." *Personality and Social Psychology Bulletin*, vol. 32, no. 3: 286–297.

Bonacich, Edna. 1980. *The Economic Basis of Ethnic Solidarity: Small Business in the Japanese American Community*. Berkeley, CA: University of California Press.

Bond, Rod; and Sussex, Peter B. 1996. "Culture and conformity: A meta-analysis of studies using Asch's (1952b, 1956) line judgment task." *Psychological Bulletin*, vol. 119, no. 1: 111–137.

Booth, A.; Shelley, G.; Mazur, A.; Tharp, G.; and Kittock, R. 1989. "Testosterone and winning and losing in human competition." *Hormones and Behavior*, vol. 23: 556–571.

Bosman, Julie. 2010. "Number of People Living on New York Streets Soars." *New York Times*. March 19. www.nytimes.com/2010/03/20/nyregion/20homeless.html

Boudon, Raymond. 1991. "What Middle-Range Theories Are." *Contemporary Sociology*, vol. 20, no. 4: 519–22.

Bourassa, Loren; and Ahforth, Blake E. 1998. "You are about to party *Defiant* style: Socialization and identity aboard an Alaskan fishing boat." *Journal of Contemporary Ethnography*, vol. 27 (July): 171–196.

Bourdieu, Pierre. 1973. "Cultural reproduction and social reproduction." In Richard Brown, ed., *Knowledge, Education, and Social Change: Papers in the Sociology of Education*. London: Tavistock.

_____. 1984. *Distinction: A Social Critique of the Judgement of Taste*. Cambridge, MA: Harvard University Press.

Bowles, Samuel; and Gintis, Herbert. 1977. *Schooling in Capitalist America: Educational Reform and the Contradictions of Economic Life*. New York: Basic Books.

boyd, danah. 2007. "Why youth (heart) social network sites: The role of networked publics in teenage social life." In *MacArthur Foundation Series on Digital Learning—Youth, Identity and Digital Media Volume*, ed. David Buckingham. Cambridge, MA: MIT Press.

Boyd, Robert. 2004. "World may be darkening as clouds, air pollution dim the sun's rays." Knight Ridder News Service, *Santa Barbara News-Press*, May 9.

Boyes, Georgina. 1984. "Belief and disbelief: An examination of reactions to the presentation of rumour legends." In Paul Smith, ed., *Perspectives on Contemporary Legend*. Sheffield, UK: Continuum International.

Boyle, Brendan. 2009. "Income gap is growing: The rich are getting richer—and rich whites quicker than rich blacks." *South African Times*, October 8. www.timeslive.co.za/business/article143706.ece

Bozick, Robert; Alexander, Karl; and Entwisel, Doris, et al. 2010. "Framing the Future: Revisiting the Place of Educational Expectations in Status Attainment." *Social Forces*, vol. 88, no. 5: 2027–52.

Bradley, Graham; and Wildman, Karen. 2002. "Psychosocial predictors of emerging adults' risk and reckless behaviors." *Journal of Youth and Adolescence*, vol. 31, no. 4: 253–265.

Brandon, Michael C. 1996. "From need to know to need to know." *Communication World*, vol. 13, no. 8 (October–November): 18.

Brief, Arthur P.; Buttram, Robert T.; Elliott, Jodi D.; Reizenstein, Robin M.; and McCline, Richard L. 1995. "Releasing the beast: A study of compliance with orders to use race as a selection criterion." *Journal of Social Issues*, vol. 51, no. 3 (fall): 177–193.

Brinkley-Rogers, Paul. 2002. "Pledge of allegiance reflects timeline of nation's history." *Columbus Dispatch*, June 28, p. 2A.

Brodkin, Karen. 1999. *How Jews Became White Folks and What That Says about Race in America*. New Brunswick, NJ: Rutgers University Press.

Brooks, James F. 2002. *Confounding the Color Line: The Indian-Black Experience in North America*. Lincoln, NE: University of Nebraska Press.

Brunvand, Jan Harold. 1981. *The Vanishing Hitchhiker.* New York: Norton.

———. 2001. *Encyclopedia of Urban Legends.* Santa Barbara, CA: ABC-Clio.

Bulkeley, William M. 2004. "New IBM jobs can mean fewer jobs elsewhere." *Wall Street Journal*, March 8, p. B1.

Bullard, Robert. 1990. *Dumping in Dixie: Race, Class and Environmental Quality.* Boulder, CO: Westview Press.

———. 1993. *Confronting Environmental Racism: Voices from the Grassroots.* Boston: South End Press.

———; Johnson, Glenn S.; and Wright, Beverly H. 1997. "Confronting environmental injustice: It's the right thing to do." *Race, Gender & Class*, vol. 5, no. 1: 63–79.

Bullard, Robert; and Wright, Beverly H. 1990. "The quest for environmental equity: Mobilizing the African-American community for social change." *Society and Natural Resources*, vol. 3: 301–311.

Burger, Jerry M. 2009. "Replicating Milgram: Would People Still Obey Today?" *American Psychologist*, vol. 64, no. 1: xxxx.

Burkhalter, Byron. 1999. "Reading race online." In Marc Smith and Peter Kollock, eds., *Communities in Cyberspace.* London: Routledge

Butler, Judith. 1993. *Bodies That Matter: On the Discursive Limits of "Sex."* New York: Routledge.

———. 1999. *Gender Trouble.* New York: Routledge.

Buttel, Frederick H. 1987. "New directions in environmental sociology." *Annual Review of Sociology*, iss. 13: 465–488.

Byrne, D. G. 1981. "Sex differences in the reporting of symptoms of depression in the general population." *British Journal of Clinical Psychology*, vol. 20: 83–92.

Cabot, Mary Kay. 1999. "Against opponents or cancer, Stefanie and Chris Spielman prove what devotion can do." *Cleveland Plain Dealer*, May 9.

Cahill, Spencer. 1999. "Emotional capital and professional socialization: The case of mortuary science students (and me)." *Social Psychology Quarterly*, vol. 62 (June): 101–116.

Caincross, Francis. 1995. "The death of distance." Survey Telecommunications, *The Economist*, 30 September, p. 5.

Califano, Joseph A., Jr. 1999. "What was really great about the Great Society." *Washington Monthly*, October.

Cancian, Maria; and Meyer, Daniel R. 1998. "Who gets custody?" *Demography*, vol. 35, no. 2: 147–157.

Caplan, Jeremy. 2005. "How green is my town." U.S. Snapshot, *Time*, July 18.

Carns, Donald. 1973. "Talking about sex: Notes on first coitus and the double standard." *Journal of Marriage and the Family*, vol. 35, no. 4 (November): 677–688.

Carroll, Andrew, ed. 2006. *Operation Homecoming: Iraq, Afghanistan, and the Home Front, in the Words of U.S. Troops and Their Families.* New York: Random House.

Carson, Rachel. 1962. *Silent Spring.* New York: Houghton Mifflin.

Cassel, Christine K.; and Demel, Beth. 2001. "Remembering death: Public policy in the USA." *Journal of the Royal Society of Medicine*, vol. 94, no. 9: 433–436.

Cassidy, Tina. 2006. *Birth.* New York: Atlantic Monthly Press.

Castells, Manuel. 1984. "Cultural identity, sexual liberation and urban structure: The gay community in San Francisco." In *The City and the Grassroots: A Cross-Cultural Theory of Urban Social Movements.* Berkeley, CA: University of California Press.

———. 2000. *The Rise of the Network Society*, vol. 1. 2nd ed. Malden, MA: Blackwell.

———; and Susser, Ida. 2002. *The Castells Reader on Cities and Social Theory.* Malden, MA: Blackwell.

Catton, William R., Jr. 1980. *Overshoot: The Ecological Basis of Revolutionary Change.* Urbana, IL: University of Illinois Press.

———; and Dunlap, Riley E. 1978. "Environmental sociology: A new paradigm." *American Sociologist*, vol. 13: 41–49.

———. 1980. "A new ecological paradigm for post-exuberant society." *American Behavioral Scientist*, vol. 24, no. 1: 15–47.

Caughey, John L. 1984. *Imaginary Social Worlds: A Cultural Approach.* Lincoln, NE: University of Nebraska Press.

———. 1999. "Imaginary social relationships." In Joseph Harris and Jay Rosen, eds., *Media Journal: Reading and Writing about Popular Culture.* Boston: Allyn and Bacon.

Center for Education Reform. 2010. "Charter School Laws Across the States 2010–2011." Dec. 1. www.edreform.com/download/CER-Charter-Laws-2011.pdf

Center for Responsive Politics. 2008a. "Banking on becoming president." www.opensecrets.org/pres08/index.php

———. 2008b. "Money wins presidency and 9 of 10 congressional races in priciest U.S. election ever." www.opensecrets.org/news/2008/11/money-wins-white-house-and.html

———. 2010a. "Top 20 PAC Contributors to Candidates, 2009–2010." www.opensecrets.org/pacs/toppacs.php?Type=C&cycle=2010

———. 2010b. "527s: Advocacy Group Spending in the 2010 Elections." www.opensecrets.org/527s/

Centers for Disease Control and Prevention. 1998. "Leading Cause of Death, 1900–1998." www.cdc.gov/nchs/data/dvs/lead1900_98.pdf

———. 2011a. "Mortality Tables: Leading Causes of Death." www.cdc.gov/nchs/nvss/mortality_tables.htm#lcod

Chambliss, William J. 1973. "The saints and the roughnecks." *Society*, November, pp. 24–31.

Champagne, Duane. 1994. *Native America: Portrait of the People.* Canton, MI: Visible Ink Press.

Charles, Camille Zubrinsky. 2001. "Processes of racial residential segregation." In Alice O'Connor, Chris Tilly, and Lawrence Bobo, eds., *Urban Inequality: Evidence from Four Cities.* New York: Russell Sage.

Chen, Katherine K. 2004. "The Burning Man organization grows up: Blending bureaucratic and alternative structures." Doctoral Dissertation. Harvard University.

Cherlin, Andrew J. 2010. "Figure 12.1 Annual divorce rate, United States, 1860–2007." *Public and Private Families: An Introduction*, 6th ed. New York: McGraw-Hill.

———; and Furstenberg, Frank F., Jr. 1994. "Stepfamilies in the United States: A reconsideration." *Annual Review of Sociology*, vol. 20: 359–381.

Chodorow, Nancy. 1978. *The Reproduction of Mothering: Psychoanalysis and the Sociology of Gender.* Berkeley, CA: University of California Press.

———. 1994. *Femininities, Masculinities, Sexualities: Freud and Beyond.* Lexington, KY: University Press of Kentucky.

Chordas, Lori. 2003. "Instant connection: Instant messaging is taking the business world by storm, and some insurers already are finding it improves productivity and reduces costs." *Best's Review*, vol. 104, no. 3 (July): 100.

Christakis, N. A. 1995. "The similarity and frequency of proposals to reform U.S. medical education: Constant concerns." *Journal of the American Medical Association*, vol. 274: 706.

———; and Fowler, James. 2009. *Connected: The Surprising Power of Our Social Networks and How They Shape Our Lives.* New York: Little, Brown and Company.

Christian Science Monitor. 2007. "Gender bias in college admissions." July 24. www.csmonitor.com/2007/0724/p08s01-comv.html

Cialdini, Robert B. 1998. *Influence: The Psychology of Persuasion*, rev. ed. Foxboro, Canada: Perennial Currents.

_____; and Trost, M. R. 1998. "Social influence: Social norms, conformity, and compliance." In D. T. Gilbert, S. E. Fiske, and G. Lindzey, eds., *Handbook of Social Psychology*, vol. 2. 4th ed. Boston: McGraw-Hill.

Cicourel, Aaron V. 1972. "Basic and normative rules in the negotiation of status and role." In D. Sudnow, ed., *Studies in Social Interaction.* New York: Free Press.

Clarke, Lee. 2001. *Mission Improbable: Using Fantasy Documents to Tame Disaster.* Chicago: University of Chicago Press.

Clawson, Dan; Neustadtl, Alan; and Scott, Denise. 1992. *Money Talks: Corporate PACs and Political Influence.* New York: Basic Books.

Clayman, Steven E. 2002. "Sequence and Solidarity." *Advances in Group Processes*, vol. 19: 229–253.

Clinton, Catherine; and Gillespie, Michelle; eds. 1997. *The Devil's Lane: Sex and Race in the Early South.* New York: Oxford University Press.

CNN. 2005. "Poll: U.S. Catholics would support changes." April 3. http://edition.cnn.com/2005/US/04/03/pope.poll/

_____. 2008. Global 500. http://money.cnn.com/magazines/fortune/global500/2008/full_list/

_____. 2009. Global 500. http://money.cnn.com/magazines/fortune/global500/2009/full_list/

Cohany, Sharon. 1996. "Workers in alternative employment arrangements." *Monthly Labor Review*, vol. 119, no. 10 (October): 31.

Cohen, Cathy J. 2005. "Punks, Bulldaggers, and Welfare Queens: The Radical Potential of Queer Politics?" in *Black Queer Studies.* Edited by E. Patrick Johnson and Mae G. Henderson. Durham, N.C.: Duke University Press: 24.

Cohen, S. P. 2001. *India: Emerging Power.* Washington, DC: Brookings Institution Press.

Coleman, John R. 1983. "Diary of a homeless man." *New York Magazine*, February.

Collins, Patricia Hill. 2006. *From Black Power to Hip Hop: Racism, Nationalism, and Feminism.* Philadephia: Temple University Press.

Collins, Randall. 1979. *The Credential Society: An Historical Sociology of Education and Stratification.* New York: Worthington Press.

Coltrane, Scott. 1997. *Family Man: Fatherhood, Housework and Gender Equity.* New York: Oxford University Press.

Columbia Journalism Review. 2010. "Who Owns What?" www.cjr.org/resources/index.php?c=disney

Commission for Labor Cooperation. 2003. "Work stoppages in North America." Briefing Note, October. www.naalc.org/english/pdf/work_stoppage_eng.pdf

Common Cause. 1996. "CC pushes for action campaign reform bills." Spring–summer.

Comte, Auguste. 1988 (orig. 1842). *Introduction to Positive Philosophy.* Edited, with introduction and revised translation, by Frederick Ferré. Indianapolis, IN: Hackett.

Condon, Stephanie. 2010. "Dem health care bill pegged at $940B over 10 years." *Political Hotsheet*, CBS News, March 18. www.cbsnews.com/8301-503544_162-20000691-503544.html?tag=mncol;lst;1

_____. 2011. "GOP rep. calls health reforms "worst bill" ever, House votes to defund laws." *CBS News Political Hotsheet.* February 18. www.cbsnews.com/8301-503544_162-20033441-503544.html

Conley, Dalton. 2000. *Honky.* Berkeley and Los Angeles: University of California Press.

_____. 2002. *Wealth and Poverty in America: A Reader.* Malden, MA: Blackwell.

_____. 2004. *The Pecking Order: Which Siblings Succeed and Why.* New York: Pantheon.

_____. 2009. *Elsewhere, U.S.A.: How We Got from the Company Man, Family Dinners and the Affluent Society to the Home Office, BlackBerry Moms and Economic Anxiety.* New York: Pantheon Books.

Connell, R. W. 1995. *Masculinities.* Berkeley, CA: University of California Press.

Contemporary Pediatrics. 2000, vol. 17, no. 10 (October): 12.

Conrad, Peter. 2006. *Identifying Hyperactive Children: The Medicalization of Deviant Behavior.* Burlington, VT: Ashgate.

Conti, Joseph. 2003. "Trade, power, and law: Dispute settlement in the World Trade Organization, 1995–2002." Unpublished Master's Thesis. University of California, Santa Barbara.

_____. 2005. "Power through process: Determinants of dispute resolution outcomes in the World Trade Organization." Unpublished Dissertation. University of California, Santa Barbara, Department of Sociology.

Cook, Noble David. 1998. *Born to Die: Disease and New World Conquest, 1492–1650.* Cambridge, UK: Cambridge University Press.

Cooley, Charles Horton. 1909. *Social Organization: A Study of the Large Mind.* New York: Scribner.

Coontz, Stephanie. 2000. *The Way We Never Were: American Families and the Nostalgia Trap.* New York: Basic Books.

Cooper, Marc. 2003. "Runaway shops." *The Nation*, vol. 270, no. 13 (April 3): 28.

Copeland, Larry. 2010. "Americans give thumbs up to free time—mostly TV." *USA Today*, December 23. www.usatoday.com/news/americawants/2010-12-22-leisure-main_N.htm

Cosgrove-Mather, Bootie. 2004. "The suicide capital of America: They come to Las Vegas not to gamble but to kill themselves." Associated Press, *CBS News Healthwatch*, February 9. www.cbsnews.com/stories/2004/02/09/health/main599070.shtml

Cota, A. A.; Evans, C. R.; Dion, K. L.; Kilik, L. L.; and Longman, R. S. 1995. "The structure of group cohesion." *Personality and Social Psychology Bulletin*, vol. 21: 572–580.

Coupland, Douglas. 1995. *Microserfs.* New York: HarperCollins.

Credit.com. 2011. "Student Credit & Debt Statistics." www.credit.com/press/statistics/student-credit-and-debt-statistics.html

Crenshaw, Kimberle; Gotanda, Neil; Peller, Garry; and Thomas, Kendall; eds. 1996. *Critical Race Theory: The Key Writings That Formed the Movement.* New York: New Press.

Dahl, Robert A. 1961. *Who Governs?* New Haven, CT: Yale University Press.

Darley, John; and Latane, Bibb. 1968. "Bystander intervention in emergencies: Diffusion of responsibility." *Journal of Personality and Social Psychology*, vol. 8.

Davila, M. 1971. "Compadrazgo: Fictive kinship in Latin America." In N. Graburn, ed., *Readings in Kinship and Social Structure.* New York: Harper and Row.

Davis, Angela Y. 2001. "Outcast mothers and surrogates: Racism and reproductive politics." In Laurel Richardson, Verta Taylor, and Nancy Whittier, eds., *Feminist Frontiers IV.* Boston: McGraw-Hill.

Davis, Kingsley. 1940. "Extreme social isolation of a child." *American Journal of Sociology*, vol. 45 (January): 554–565.

_____.; and Moore, Wilbert. 1945. "Some Principles of Stratification." *American Sociological Review*, vol. 10, no. 2. 1944 Annual Meeting Papers (April): 242–49.

_____. 1947. "Final note on a case of extreme isolation." *American Journal of Sociology*, vol. 52, no. 5: 432–437.

Davis, T. 1995. "The occupational mobility of Black males revisited—Does race matter?" *Social Science Journal*, vol. 32, no. 2: 121–135.

Dearmore, Roy F. 1997. *Biblical Missions: History, Principles, Practice.* Garland, TX: Rodgers Baptist Church.

De Graaf, John; Waan, David; and Naylor, Thomas. 2002. *Affluenza: The All-Consuming Epidemic.* San Francisco: Berrett-Koehler.

Dell'Amore, Christine. 2008. " 'Deadly dozen' diseases could stem from global warming." *National Geographic News*, October 7. http://news.nationalgeographic.com/news/2008/10/081007-climate-diseases.html

DeNavas-Walt, Carmen; Proctor, Bernadette D.; and Smith, Jessica C. 2010. "Income, Poverty and Health Insurance Coverage in the United States: 2009." U.S. Census Bureau Report.

DeNoon, Daniel. 2010. "Whooping cough epidemic hits California." *WebMD Health News*, July 21. http://children.webmd.com/vaccines/news/20100721/whooping-cough-epidemic-hits-california

DeVault, Marjorie. 1994 (orig. 1991). *Feeding the Family: The Social Organization of Caring as Gendered Work.* Chicago: University of Chicago Press.

Di Leonardo, Micaela. 1987. "The female world of cards and holidays: Women, families, and the work of kinship." *Signs*, vol. 12, no. 3: 340–350.

Diamond, Sara. 1995. *Roads to Dominion: Right Wing Movements and Political Power in the United States.* New York: Guilford Press.

Dicken, Peter. 1998. *The Global Shift: Transforming the World Economy*, 3rd ed. New York: Guilford Press.

Dillon, Sam. 2010. "U.S. School Graduation Rate Is Rising." *New York Times*, Nov. 30. www.nytimes.com/2010/11/30/education/30graduation.html

Doherty, Brian. 2000. "Burning Man grows up." *Reason*, vol. 31: 24–33. http://reason.com/0002/fe.bd.burning.shtml

_____. 2004. *This is Burning Man.* New York: Little, Brown and Company.

Domhoff, G. William. 1983. *Who Rules America Now? A View from the Eighties.* Englewood Cliffs, NJ: Prentice Hall.

_____. 1987. *Power Elites and Organizations.* Newbury Park, CA: Sage.

_____. 1990. *The Power Elite and the State: How Policy Is Made in America.* New York: de Gruyter.

_____. 2002. *Who Rules America Now? Power and Politics in the Year 2000.* 3rd ed. Mountain View, CA: Mayfield.

Donnelly, Denise; and Finkelhor, David. 1993. "Who has joint custody? Class differences in the determination of custody arrangements." *Family Relations*, vol. 42, no. 1: 57–60.

Draut, Tamara; and Silva, Javier. 2004. "Generation broke: The growth of debt among young Americans." A Demos Group Report, October 13.

Draut, Tamara. 2006. *Strapped: Why America's 20- and 30-Somethings Can't Get Ahead.* New York: Doubleday.

Drucker, Peter. 1959. *Landmarks of Tomorrow: A Report on the New "Post-Modern" World.* New York: Harper.

_____. 2003. *The Essential Drucker: The Best of Sixty Years of Peter Drucker's Writings on Management.* New York: Collins.

Duany, Andres; Plater-Zyberk, Elizabeth; and Speck, Jeff. 2001. *Suburban Nation: The Rise of Sprawl and the Decline of the American Dream.* New York: North Point Press.

Duggan, Lisa. 2003. *The Twilight of Equality?: Neoliberalisam, Cultural Politics, and the Attack on Democracy.* Boston: Beacon Press.

Duneier, Mitchell; and Carter, Ovie. 1999. *Sidewalk.* New York: Farrar, Straus and Giroux.

Dunlap, Riley, E.; and Catton, William, Jr. 1979. "Environmental sociology." *Annual Review of Sociology*, iss. 5: 243–273.

_____. 1994. "Struggling with human exemptionalism: The rise, decline, and revitalization of environmental sociology." *American Sociologist*, vol. 25, no. 1: 5–30.

Dupuis, Sherry L.; and Smale, Bryan J. A. 2000. "Bittersweet journeys: Meanings of leisure in the institution-based caregiving context." *Journal of Leisure Research*, vol. 32, no. 3 (June): 303.

Durkheim, Emile. 1951 (orig. 1897). *Suicide: A Study in Sociology.* Trans. John A. Spaulding and George Simpson. Glencoe, IL: Free Press of Glencoe.

_____. 1964 (orig. 1893). *Suicide.* New York: Free Press.

_____. 1984 (orig. 1893). *The Division of Labor in Society.* Trans. W. D. Halls. New York: Free Press.

_____. 1995 (orig. 1912). *The Elementary Forms of Religious Life.* Trans. Karen E. Fields. New York: Free Press.

Dwyer, Jim. 2001. "A nation challenged." *New York Times*, November 6, p. A1.

Dye, Thomas R. 2002. *Who's Running America? The Bush Restoration.* 7th ed. Upper Saddle River, NJ: Prentice Hall.

Edgerton, Robert B. 1992. *Sick Societies: Challenging the Myth of Primitive Harmony.* New York: Free Press.

Edin, Kathryn. 2000. "Few good men." *American Prospect*, vol. 11, no. 4 (January 3).

_____; and Kefalas, Maria. 2005. *Promises I Can Keep: Why Poor Women Put Motherhood Before Marriage.* Berkeley, CA: University of California Press.

_____; and Lein, Laura. 1997. *Making Ends Meet.* New York: Russell Sage Foundation.

Egelko, Bob. 2002. "Pledge of allegiance ruled unconstitutional; many say ruling by S.F. court hasn't a prayer after appeals." *San Francisco Chronicle*, June 27, p. A1.

Eggers, Dave. 2006. *What Is the What.* San Francisco: McSweeny's Books.

Ehrenreich, Barbara. 1990. *The Worst Years of our Lives: Irreverent Notes from a Decade of Greed.* New York: Pantheon.

_____. 2001. *Nickel and Dimed: On (Not) Getting by in America.* New York: Metropolitan Books.

_____. 2004. "All together now." *New York Times*, July 15. www.nytimes.com/2004/07/15/opinion/

Ehrlich, Paul R.; and Ehrlich, Anne H. 1990. *The Population Explosion.* New York: Simon & Schuster.

Eisenstein, Zillah. 1979. "Capitalist patriarchy and the case for socialist feminism." *Monthly Review*, February.

El Nasser, Haye. 2010. "Downturn Douses Nevada's population Growth Streak. *USA Today*, November 8.

Eller, Cynthia. 2003. *Am I a Woman? A Skeptic's Guide to Gender.* Boston: Beacon Press.

Ellis, Carolyn. 1995. "Emotional and ethical quagmires in returning to the field." *Journal of Contemporary Ethnography*, vol. 24: 68–96.

_____. 1997. "Evocative autoethnography: Writing emotionally about our lives." In W. G. Tierney and Y. S. Lincoln, eds., *Representation and the Text: Re-framing the Narrative Voice.* Albany, NY: SUNY Press.

England, Paula. 1992. *Comparable Worth: Theories and Evidence.* Edison, NJ: Aldine Transaction.

Epps, Edgar. 2001. "Race, class, and educational opportunity: Trends in the sociology of education." In Bruce R. Hare, ed., *Race Odyssey: African Americans and Sociology: A Critical Analysis*. Syracuse, NY: Syracuse University Press.

ESPN. 2008. "Major league baseball attendance report 2008." http://sports.espn.go.com/mlb/attendance, accessed 4/15/08

Etzioni, Amitai. 1996. "The responsive community: A communitarian perspective." *American Sociological Review*, vol. 61, no. 1: 1–11.

"Even in the best of homes." 2003. www.vday.org/ contents/victory/success/0305051

Fabes, Richard A.; Martin, Carol Lynn; and Hanish, Laura D. 2003. "Young children's play qualities in same-, other-, and mixed-sex peer groups." *Child Development*, vol. 74, no. 3 (May–June): 921.

Fairbanks, C. 1992. "Labels, literacy and enabled learning: Glenn's story." *Harvard Educational Review*, vol. 62, no. 4, 475–493.

Fairfax County Public Schools, Office of Testing and Evaluation. 1999. "Assessments: State & Fairfax County public schools passing rates." Data: Virginia Standards of Learning, 11/4/99, as cited in Bracey, Gerald. 2000. "High Stakes Testing." Center for Education Research, Analysis, and Innovation, School of Education, University of Wisconsin-Milwaukee. www.asu.edu/educ/epsl/EPRU/documents/cerai-00-32.htm#_ednref22.

Falconer, Renee C.; and Byrnes, Deborah A. 2003. "When good intentions are not enough: A response to increasing diversity in an early childhood setting." *Journal of Research in Childhood Education*, vol. 17, no. 2 (spring–summer): 188.

Faludi, Susan. 1999. *Stiffed: The Betrayal of the American Man*. New York: William & Morrow.

Farghal, M.; and Shakir, A. 1994. "Kin terms and titles of address as relational social honorifics in Jordanian Arabic." *Anthropological Linguistics*, iss. 36: 240–253.

Farrell, Warren. 1975. *The Liberated Man*. New York: Bantam.

Fausto-Sterling, Anne. 2000. *Sexing the Body: Gender Politics and the Construction of Sexuality*. New York: Basic Books.

Fava, S. F. 1956. "Suburbanism as a way of life." *American Sociological Review*, vol. 21, 34–37.

Feder-Alford, Elaine. 2006. "Only a piece of meat: One patient's reflections on her eight-day hospital experience." *Qualitative Inquiry*, vol. 12, no. 3: 596–620.

Federal Election Commission. 2010. "PAC Activity Remains Stable in 2009." April 6. www.fec.gov/press/press2010/20100406PAC.shtml

Ferguson, Bruce; and Abell, Barbara. 1998. "The urban grocery store gap." *Commentary* (Winter): 6–14.

Ferris, Kerry. 2001. "Through a glass, darkly: The dynamics of fan-celebrity encounters." *Symbolic Interaction*, vol. 24, no. 1 (February).

———. 2004a. "Seeing and being seen: The moral order of celebrity sightings." *Journal of Contemporary Ethnography*, vol. 33, no. 3 (June): 236–264.

Fetterman, Mindy; and Hansen, Barbara. 2006. "Young People struggle to deal with kiss of debt." *USA Today*, November 22. www.usatoday.com/money/perfi/credit/2006-11-19-young-and-in-debt-cover_x.htm

Fine, Gary Alan. 1983. *Shared Fantasy: Role Playing Games as Social Worlds*. Chicago, IL: University of Chicago Press.

———. 1993. "The sad demise, mysterious disappearance, and glorious triumph of symbolic interactionism." *Annual Review of Sociology*, vol. 19: 61–87.

———. 1996. *Kitchens: The Culture of Restaurant Work*. Berkeley, CA: University of California Press.

———. 1998. *Morel Tales: The Culture of Mushrooming*. Cambridge, MA: Harvard University Press.

Fischer, Claude. 1976. *The Urban Experience*. New York: Harcourt Brace Jovanovich.

Fischer, Claude S. 1994. "Changes in leisure activities, 1890–1940." *Journal of Social History*, vol. 27, no. 3 (spring): 453.

Fischer, Mary J.; and Kmec, Julie A. 2004. "Neighborhood socioeconomic conditions as moderators of family resource transmission: High school completion among at-risk youth." *Sociological Perspectives*, vol. 47, no. 4 (winter): 507–527.

Fish, Stanley. 1980. *Is There a Text in This Class? The Authority of Interpretive Communities*. Cambridge, MA: Harvard University Press.

Fishman, Pamela. 1978. "Interaction: The work women do." *Social Problems*, vol. 25: 433.

Fiske, Jonathan. 1989. *Understanding Popular Culture*. London: Unwin Hyman.

FitzGerald, Frances. 1980. *America Revised: History Schoolbooks in the Twentieth Century*. New York: Vintage Books.

Florida, Richard. 2002. *The Rise of the Creative Class: And How It Is Transforming Work, Leisure, Community and Everyday Life*. New York: Basic Books.

———. 2004. *Cities and the Creative Class*. New York: Routledge.

Foeman, A. K.; and Nance, T. 1999. "From miscegenation to multiculturalism: Perceptions and stages of interracial relationship development." *Journal of Black Studies*, vol. 29: 540–557.

Forbes Businesswire. 2008. "North American hospitality and tourism sector: A company and industry analysis." June. www.forbes.com/businesswire/feeds/businesswire/2008/10/13/businesswire20081013005502r1.html

Fox, Greer Litton; and Kelly, Robert F. 1995. "Determinants of child custody arrangements at divorce." *Journal of Marriage and the Family*, vol. 57, no. 3: 693–708.

Fox, John. 1997. *Applied Regression Analysis, Linear Models, and Related Methods*. Thousand Oaks, CA: Sage.

Fox, Renee. 1957. "Training for uncertainty." In Robert Merton, ed., *The Student Physician*. Cambridge, MA: Harvard University Press.

FreePress.net. 2011. "Ownership Chart: The Big Six." www.freepress.net/ownership/chart/main

Freud, Sigmund. 1955 (orig. 1900). *The Interpretation of Dreams*. London: Hogarth.

———. 1905. *Three Essays on the Theory of Sexuality*. New York: Avon Books.

Frey, William H. 2003. "The new migration equation." *Orlando Sentinel*, November 9.

Friedan, Betty. 2001 (orig. 1963). *The Feminine Mystique*. New York: Norton.

Frieden, Bernard; and Sagalyn, Lynne B. 1992. *Downtown, Inc.: How America Rebuilds Cities*. Cambridge, MA: MIT Press.

Friedkin, Noah E. 2004. "Social cohesion." *Annual Review of Sociology*, vol. 30 (August): 409–425.

———; and Cook, Karen S. 1990. "Peer group influence." *Sociological Methods and Research*, vol. 19, no. 1: 122–143.

———; and Granovetter, Mark, eds. 1998. *A Structural Theory of Social Influence*. Structural Analysis in the Social Sciences. Cambridge, UK: Cambridge University Press.

Friedman, Ina R. 1995. *The Other Victims: First-Person Stories of Non-Jews Persecuted by the Nazis*. New York: Houghton Mifflin.

Friedman, Milton. 1994. "Medical licensure." *Freedom Daily*, January. www.fff.org/freedom/0194e.asp

Fuller, Robert C. 2002. *Spiritual but Not Religious: Understanding Unchurched America*. New York: Oxford University Press.

Furstenberg, Frank; Hoffman, Saul; and Shrestha, Laura. 1995. "The effect of divorce on intergenerational transfers: New evidence." *Demography*, vol. 32, no. 3: 319–333.

Fussell, Paul. 1983. *Class: A Guide Through the American Status System*. New York: Touchstone.

Gamson, Joshua. 1999. *Freaks Talk Back: Tabloid Talk Shows and Sexual Nonconformity*. Chicago: University of Chicago Press.

Gans, Herbert J. 1962. *The Urban Villagers: Group and Class in the Life of Italian-Americans*. New York: MacMillan.

———. 1967. *The Levittowners: Ways of Life and Politics in a New Suburban Community*. New York: Columbia University Press.

———. 1971. "The uses of poverty: The poor pay all." *Social Policy*, July–August: 20–24.

Gans, Herbert J. 1999. *Popular Culture and High Culture: An Analysis and Evaluation of Taste*. New York: Basic Books.

Gansberg, Martin. 1964. "37 who saw murder didn't call the police: Apathy at stabbing of Queens woman shocks inspector." *New York Times*, March 27.

Garber, Marjorie. 1997. *Vested Interests: Cross Dressing and Cultural Anxiety*. London: Routledge.

———. 1998. *The Symptoms of Culture*. New York: Routledge.

Garfinkel, Harold. 1984 (orig. 1967). *Studies in Ethnomethodology*. Englewood Cliffs, NJ: Prentice Hall.

Garlington, Phil. 1998. "Protester lives in Redwoods 7 months; California environmentalists take a stand." *Pittsburgh Post-Gazette*, September 13, p. A13.

Garr, Emily. 2008. "The unemployment trend by state." Economic Policy Institute Economic Snapshots. www.epi.org/content.cfm/ webfeatures_snapshots_20080924

Garreau, Joel. 1992. *Edge City: Life on the New Frontier*. New York: Anchor Books.

Garry, Patrick M.; and Spurlin, Candice J. 2007. "The effectiveness of media rating systems in preventing children's exposure to violent and sexually explicit media content: An empirical study." *Oklahoma City University Law Review*, vol. 32, no. 2. http://ssrn.com/ abstract=1139167

Garvin, Glenn. 2008. "Too Pretty? That's When It Got Ugly." *The Miami Herald*, March 23.

Geertz, Clifford. 1973. "Deep play: Notes on the Balinese cockfight." *The Interpretation of Cultures*. New York: Basic Books.

Gelles, Richard J. 1995. *Contemporary Families: A Sociological View*. Thousand Oaks, CA: Sage.

Gerbner, George; and Gross, L. 1976. "Living with television: The Violence Profile." *Journal of Communication* (spring).

———; Morgan, M.; and Signorielli, N. 1980. "The mainstreaming of America: Violence Profile No. 11." *Journal of Communication*, vol. 30: 10–29.

Gereffi, Gary; and Korzeniewicz, Miguel; eds. 1994. *Commodity Chains and Global Capitalism*. Westport, CT: Praeger.

Gergen, Kenneth. 1991. *The Saturated Self*. New York: Basic Books.

Gibbs, Nancy. 2010. "Sexual Assaults on Female Soldiers: Don't Ask, Don't Tell." *Time.com*, March 8. www.time.com/time/magazine/ article0,9171,1968110,00.html

Gibson, Campbell; and Lennon, Emily. 2001. "Historical census statistics on the foreign-born population of the United States: 1850–1990." U.S. Bureau of the Census, Population Division. www.census.gov/population/www/ documentation/twps0029.html

Glaser, Jack; Dixit, Jay; and Green, Donald P. 2002. "Studying hate crime with the Internet: What makes racists advocate racial violence?" *Journal of Social Issues*, vol. 58, no. 1: 177–193.

Glaser, Mark. 2007. MediaShift. PBS. "Your guide to the digital divide." January 17. www.pbs.org/mediashift/2007/01/digging_ deeperyour_guide_to_th.html

Glass, Ruth. 1964. "Aspects of change." In Centre for Urban Studies, ed., *London: Aspects of Change*. London: MacGibbon and Kee.

Gleick, P. H. 1998. "The world's water 1998–1999." Washington, DC: Island Press. Companion web site: www.worldwater.org/table7.html

Goffman, Erving. 1956. *Presentation of Self in Everyday Life*. Garden City, NY: Anchor Books.

———. 1961. *Asylums: Essays on the Social Situation of Mental Patients and Other Inmates*. Garden City, NY: Anchor Books.

———. 1962. *Stigma: Notes on the Management of Spoiled Identity*. Upper Saddle River, NJ: Prentice Hall.

———. 1971. *Relations in Public: Microstudies of the Public Order*. New York: Basic Books.

Goldberg, Herb. 1976. *The Hazards of Being Male*. New York: Nash.

González, Eduardo. 2007. "Migrant farm workers: Our nation's invisible population." National Extension Diversity Center. www .ediversitycenter.net/migrantfarmers.php

Goodacre, Daniel M. 1953. "Group characteristics of good and poor performing combat units." *Sociometry*, vol. 16, no. 2 (May): 168–179.

Goode, Erich. 1997. *Deviant Behavior*. 5th ed. Upper Saddle River, NJ: Prentice Hall.

Goode, William J. 1982. *The Family*. Englewood Cliffs, NJ: Prentice Hall.

Goodman, Peter. 2010. "U.S. Offers a Hand to Those on Eviction's Edge." *New York Times*, April 21. www.nytimes.com/2010/04/22/ business/economy/22prevent.html

Goodnough, Abby. 2009. "Gay rights groups celebrate victories in marriage push." *New York Times*, April 7. www.nytimes. com/2009/04/08/us/08vermont.html

Goodstein, Laurie. 2004. "Personal and political, Bush's faith blurs lines." *New York Times*, October 26, p. A21.

Google.com. 2011. Google history. www.google.com/about/corporate/ company/history.html

Gottdiener, Mark; Collins, Claudia C.; and Dickens, David R. 1999. *Las Vegas: The Social Production of an All-American City*. Malden, MA: Blackwell.

Gottman, Jean. 1961. *Megalopolis: The Urbanized Northeastern Seaboard of the United States*. New York: Twentieth Century Fund.

———; and Robert Harper. 1990. *Since Megalopolis: The Urban Writings of Jean Gottman*. Baltimore, MD: Johns Hopkins University Press.

Gottschalk, Simon. 1993. "Uncomfortably numb: Countercultural impulses in the postmodern era." *Symbolic Interaction*, vol. 16, no. 4: 357–378.

Goyette, Kimberly; and Xie, Yu. 1999. "Educational expectations of Asian-American youth: Determinants and ethnic differences." *Sociology of Education*, vol. 71: 24–38.

Gozzi, Raymond, Jr. 1996. "Will the media create a global village?" *ETC: A Review of General Semantics*, vol. 53: 65–68.

Graham, Lawrence Otis. 1996. *A Member of the Club: Reflections on Life in a Racially Polarized World*. New York: Harper Perennial.

Gramsci, Antonio. 1985. *Selections from Cultural Writings*. Cambridge, MA: Harvard University Press.

_____. 1988. *An Antonio Gramsci Reader.* Ed. David Forgacs. Boston: Schocken.

Grandey, A. 2003. "When 'the show must go on': Surface and deep acting as determinants of emotional exhaustion and peer-rated service delivery." *Academy of Management Journal*, vol. 46, no. 1: 86–96.

Granfield, Robert. 1992. *Making Elite Lawyers.* New York: Routledge.

Granovetter, Mark. 1973. "The strength of weak ties." *American Journal of Sociology*, vol. 78, no. 6: 1360–1380.

Gray, Steven. 2009. "Can America's urban food deserts bloom?" *Time*, May 26. www.time.com/time/nation/article/0,8599,1900947,00.html

Grealy, Lucy. 1994. *Autobiography of a Face.* Boston: Houghton Mifflin.

Green, Elizabeth. 2010. "Building a Better Teacher." *New York Time Magazine*, March 2. www.nytimes.com/2010/03/07/magazine/07Teachers-t.html

Green, Frank. 2002. "Food fight: County's 11,000 unionized grocery workers fear pay will plummet when Wal-Mart enters the market." *San Diego Union Tribune*, August 18, p. H1.

Green, John C. 2004. "Fourth national survey of religion and politics." In *The American Religious Landscape and Politics, 2004.* Pew Forum on Religion and Public Life, Washington, DC. www.pewforum.org/publications/surveys/green.pdf

Greenfeld, L., et al. 1998. "Violence by intimates: Analysis of data on crimes by current or former spouses, boyfriends, and girlfriends." *Bureau of Justice Statistics Factbook.* www.ojp.usdoj.gov/bjs/pub/pdf/vi.pdf

Greenhouse, Steven. 1997. "Concluding the UPS strike." *New York Times*, August 20, p. A1.

_____. 1999. "Activism surges at campuses nationwide, and labor is at issue." *New York Times*, March 29. www.sweatshopwatch.org/swatch/headlines/1999/nyt_mar.html

Groh, Carla J. 2007. "Poverty, Mental Health, and Women: Implications for Psychiatric Nurses in Primary Care Settings." *Journal of the American Psychiatric Nurses Association*, vol. 13, no. 5: 267–274.

Gross, Terry. 2010. "Jon Stewart: The Most Trusted Name in Fake News." National Public Radio. Oct. 4. www.npr.org/templates/story/story.php?storyId=130321994

Grossman, Lev. 2010. "Person of the Year: Mark Zuckerberg." *Time Magazine*, December 27.

Guber, Deborah Lynn. 2003. *The Grassroots of a Green Revolution: Polling America on the Environment.* Cambridge, MA: MIT Press.

Gubrium, Jaber; and Buckholdt, D. R. 1982. "Fictive family: Everyday usage, analytic, and human service considerations." *American Anthropologist*, vol. 84, no. 4: 878.

Gutfreund, Owen. 2004. *Twentieth Century Sprawl: Highways and the Reshaping of the American Landscape.* New York: Oxford University Press.

Haas, Jack; and Shaffir, William. 1977. "The professionalization of medical students: Development competence and a cloak of competence." *Symbolic Interaction*, vol. 1: 71–88.

_____. 1982. "Taking on the role of doctor: A dramaturgical analysis of professionalization." *Symbolic Interaction*, vol. 5: 187–203.

Haber, Gary. 2010. "Bill tries to lure grocers to Maryland's poor areas." *Baltimore Business Journal*, March 26. http://baltimore.bizjournals.com/baltimore/stories/2010/03/29/story4.html

Habermas, Jürgen. 1984. *The Theory of Communicative Action, Vol. 1: Reason and the Rationalization of Society.* Trans. Thomas McCarthy. Boston: Beacon Press.

_____. 1987. *The Theory of Communicative Action, Vol. 2: Lifeworld and System: A Critique of Functionalist Reason.* Trans. Thomas McCarthy. Boston: Beacon Press.

Hagberg, Richard; and Heifetz, Julie. 2002. "How to tell the CEO his baby is ugly." http://w3.hcgnet.com/research_uglybaby.html

Haizlip, Shirlee Taylor. 1994. *The Sweeter the Juice: A Family Memoir in Black and White.* New York: Simon & Schuster.

Hakim, Danny. 2001. "Fidelity picks a president of funds unit." *New York Times*, May 22, p. C1.

Haley, A. J.; and Johnston, B. S. 1998. "Menaces to management: A developmental view of British soccer hooligans, 1961–1986." *Sport Journal*, vol. 1. www.thesportjournal.org/1998journal/vol1-no1/menaces.asp

Hall, Stuart. 1980. "Encoding/decoding." In S. Hall, D. Hobson, A. Lowe, and P. Willis, eds., *Culture, Media, Language.* London: Hutchinson.

Halle, David. 1993. *Inside Culture: Art and Class in the American Home.* Chicago, IL: University of Chicago Press.

Hamer D. H.; Hu, S.; Magnuson, V. L.; Hu, N.; and Pattatucci, A. M. 1993. "A linkage between DNA markers on the X chromosome and male sexual orientation." *Science*, vol. 261, no. 5119: 321–327.

Hamilton, Bradley, Joyce A. Martin, and Stephanie J. Ventura. 2010. *National Vital Statistics Reports.* Births: Preliminary Data for 2009 www.cdc.gov/nchs/data/nvsr/nvsr59/nvsr59_03.pdf

Hao, Lingxin; and Cherlin, Andrew J. 2004. "Welfare reform and teenage pregnancy, childbirth, and school dropout." *Journal of Marriage and Family*, vol. 66: 179–194.

Hardin, Garrett. 1968. "The tragedy of the commons." *Science*, vol. 162: 1243–1248.

_____. 1993. *Living within Limits.* New York: Oxford University Press.

Hartley, Heather; and Drew, Tricia. 2001. "Gendered messages in sex ed films: Trends and implications for female sexual problems." *Women & Therapy*, vol. 24, nos. 1–2: 133–146.

Harvard Magazine. 2008. "Race in a genetic world." May–June: 62–65.

Harvey, David. 1990. *The Condition of Postmodernity: An Enquiry into the Origins of Cultural Change.* Cambridge, MA: Wiley-Blackwell.

Hattie, J. A. 2003. "Teachers make a difference: What is the research evidence?" Paper presented at the 2003 ACER Research Conference at the Carlton Crest Hotel in Melbourne, Australia. Oct. 19–21.

Havitz, Mark E.; and Dimanche, Frederic. 1999. "Leisure involvement revisited: Drive properties and paradoxes." *Journal of Leisure Research*, vol. 31, no. 2 (spring): 122.

Hawley, Amos H. 1950. *Human Ecology: A Theory of Community Structure.* New York: Ronald Press.

Hays, Sharon. 1996. *The Cultural Contradictions of Motherhood.* New Haven, CT: Yale University Press.

_____. 2003. *Flat Broke with Children: Women in the Age of Welfare Reform.* New York: Oxford University Press.

Heilprin, John. 2005. "FBI: Radical-activist groups are major threat." *Seattle Times*, May 19. http://seattletimes.nwsource.com/html/nationworld/2002280292_ecoterror19.html

Herek, G. M. 1990. "The context of anti-gay violence: Notes on cultural and psychological heterosexism." *Journal of Interpersonal Violence*, vol. 5: 316–333.

Heritage, J.; and Stivers, T. 1999. "Online commentary in acute medical visits: A method of shaping patient expectations." *Social Science and Medicine*, vol. 49, no. 11: 1501–1517.

Hertz, Marci Feldman, and David-Ferdon, Corrine. 2009. "Electronic media and youth violence: A CDC issue brief for educators and caregivers." Atlanta, GA: Centers for Disease Control.

Hewitt, John. P. 2000. *Self and Society: A Symbolic Interactionist Social Psychology.* Boston: Allyn and Bacon.

Hill, Julia. 2000. *The Legacy of Luna: The Story of a Tree, a Woman and the Struggle to Save the Redwoods.* San Fancisco: HarperCollins.

———. 2002. *One Makes the Difference: Inspiring Actions That Change Our World.* San Francisco: HarperCollins.

Hill, Peter; and Wood, Ralph. 1999. *Measures of Religiosity.* Birmingham, AL: Religious Education Press.

Hizer, Cynthia. 1997. "Versatile vegetarian; Diet based on plants has saving graces." *Atlanta Journal-Constitution,* June 5, p. H3.

Hochschild, Arlie Russel. 1975. "The sociology of feeling and emotion." In Marcia Millman and Rosabeth Moss Kanter, eds., *Another Voice.* Garden City, NJ: Doubleday.

———. 1983. *The Managed Heart: The Commercialization of Human Feeling.* Berkeley, CA: University of California Press.

———; and Machung, Anne. 1989. *The Second Shift: Working Parents and the Revolution at Home.* New York: Viking.

Hochschild, Jennifer L. 1996. *Facing Up to the American Dream: Race, Class, and the Soul of the Nation.* Princeton, NJ: Princeton University Press.

Hodge, Robert; and Tripp, David. 1986. *Children and Television: A Semiotic Approach.* Cambridge, UK: Polity Press.

Hoffman, Matt; and Torres, Lisa. 2002. "It's not only 'who you know' that matters: Gender, personal contacts, and job lead quality." *Gender and Society,* vol. 16, no. 6: 793–813.

Holder, Kelly. 2006. "Voting and registration in the election of November 2004." U.S. Census Bureau Report, March.

Holdren, John P.; Daily, Gretchen; and Ehrlich, Paul R. 1995. "The meaning of sustainability: Biogeophysical aspects." In M. Munasinghe and W. Shearer, eds., *Defining and Measuring Sustainability: The Biogeophysical Foundations.* Washington, DC: World Bank.

Holdsworth, M.; Gartner, A.; Landais, E.; Maire, B.; and Delpeuch, F. 2004. "Perceptions of healthy and desirable body size in urban Senegalese women." *International Journal of Obesity and Related Metabolic Disorders,* vol. 28, no. 12: 1561–1568.

Holstein, James; and Gubrium, Jaber. 1990. *What Is Family?* Mountain View, CA: Mayfield.

———. 1995a. "Deprivatization and the construction of domestic life." *Journal of Marriage and the Family,* vol. 57, no. 4 (November): 894.

———. 2000. *The Self We Live By: Narrative Identity in a Postmodern World.* New York: Oxford University Press.

Homans, George. 1951. *The Human Group.* New York: Harcourt Brace Jovanovich.

hooks, bell. 1990. *Yearning: Race, Gender and Cultural Politics.* Boston: South End Press.

———. 2003. *We Real Cool: Black Men and Masculinity.* London: Routledge.

Hughes, Jonathon; and Cain, Louis. 1994. *American Economic History.* 4th ed. New York: HarperCollins College Publishers.

Hughes, Z. 2003. "Why some brothers only date whites and 'others.'" *Ebony,* vol. 58: 70–74.

Hull, Elizabeth. 2002. "Florida's former felons: You can't vote here." *Commonwealth,* vol. 129, no. 12 (June 14): 16.

Human Rights Watch. 2007, July. *Forced Apart: Families Separated and Immigrants Harmed by United States Deportation Policy.* New York: Human Rights Watch. www. hrw.org/reports/2007/us0707/

Humphrey, Craig R.; Lewis, Tammy L.; and Buttel, Frederick H. 2002. *Environment, Energy, and Society: A New Synthesis.* Belmont, CA: Wadsworth.

Hunt, G.; and Satterlee, S. 1986. "Cohesion and division: Drinking in an English village." *Man* (New Series), vol. 21, no. 3: 521–537.

Hustvedt, Siri. 2002. "9/11 six months on." *The Observer,* March 10, Special Supplement, p. 6.

Ignatiev, Noel. 1996. *How the Irish Became White.* London: Routledge.

INC.com. 1999. "Employee theft still costing business." www.inc.com/articles/1999/05/13731.html

Independent Sector. 2010. "Value of Volunteer Time." Independent-sector.org/volunteer_time

Insurance Institute for Highway Safety. 2009. "Estimated number and percent of fatally injured passenger vehicle drivers with BAC (greater than or equal to sign) 0.08 percent, 1982-2009." www.iihs.org/research/fatality_facts_2009/gender.html

International Business Times. 2008. "Which U.S. cities rank highest in foreclosure rates?" October 23. www.ibtimes.com/articles/20081023/which-cities-rank-highest-foreclosure-rates.htm

International Centre for Prison Studies. 2011. World Prison Brief. www.prisonstudies.org/info/worldbrief/

Isikoff, Michael. 2004. "The dots never existed." *Newsweek,* July 19.

Jackson, Edgar L. 1999. "Leisure and the Internet." *Journal of Physical Education, Recreation & Dance,* vol. 70, no. 9 (November): 18.

Jackson, K. T. 1985. *Crabgrass Frontier: The Suburbanization of the United States.* New York: Oxford University Press.

Jackson, Phillip. 1968. *Life in Classrooms.* New York: Holt, Rinehart, and Winston.

Jackson-Jacobs, Curtis. 2004. "Taking a beating: The narrative gratifications of fighting as an underdog." In Hayward et al., eds., *Cultural Criminology Unleashed.* London: Glasshouse.

Janus, Irving L. 1971. "Groupthink." *Psychology Today,* November.

———. 1982. *Groupthink.* 2nd ed. Boston: Houghton-Mifflin.

Jenkins, Henry. 1992. *Textual Poachers: Television Fans and Participatory Culture.* London. Routledge.

Jensen, Joyce. 2000. "Old urban legends never die (but they don't get any truer)." *New York Times,* April 8, p. B9.

Jin, Ge. 2006. "Chinese gold farmers." www.we-make-money-not-art.com/archives/2006/03/ge-jin-a-phd-st.php.

Johnson, Cathryn. 1994. "Gender, legitimate authority, and leader-subordinate conversations." *American Sociological Review,* vol. 59, no. 1 (February): 122–135.

Johnson, Kenneth M. 1999. "The rural rebound." *Population Reference Bureau Reports on America,* vol. 1, no. 3 (August).

Johnson, Kenneth M.; and Beale, Calvin L. 1994. "The recent revival of widespread population growth in nonmetropolitan America." *Rural Sociology,* vol. 59, no. 4: 655–667.

———. 1995. "The rural rebound revisited." *American Demographics,* July.

———. 1998. "The revival of rural America." *Wilson Quarterly,* vol. 22, no. 2: 16–27.

Jones, Steve. 1997. *Virtual Culture: Identity and Communication in Cybersociety.* Thousand Oaks, CA: Sage.

———; and Philip Howard, eds. 2003. *Society Online: The Internet in Context.* Thousand Oaks, CA: Sage.

Juergensmeyer, Mark. 2003. *Terror in the Mind of God: The Global Rise of Religious Violence.* Berkeley, CA: University of California Press.

Kaczor, Bill. 1996. " Neighborhood blames years of woe on 'Mount Dioxin.'" *Charleston Gazette*, March 11.

Kalmijn M. 1998. "Intermarriages and homogamy—Causes, patterns, trends." *Annual Review of Sociology*, vol. 24: 395–421.

Kao, Grace; and Joyner, Kara. 2005. "Interracial relationships and the transition to adulthood." *American Sociological Review*, vol. 70, no. 4: 563–582.

Kara, Siddharth. 2008. *Sex Trafficking—Inside the Business of Modern Slavery*. New York: Columbia University Press.

Karau, S. J.; and Williams, K. D. 1993. "Social loafing: A meta-analytic review and theoretical integration." *Journal of Personality and Social Psychology*, vol. 65: 681–706.

Katz, Elihu. 1959. "Mass communication research and the study of popular culture." *Studies in Public Communication*, 2.

_____; and Lazarsfeld, Paul F. 1955. *Personal Influence: The Part Played by People in the Flow of Mass Communications*. New York: Macmillan Free Press.

Katz, Jack. 1988. *Seductions of Crime: Moral and Sensual Attractions of Doing Evil*. New York: Basic Books.

_____. 1997. "Ethnography's warrants." *Sociological Methods & Research*, vol. 25, no. 4: 391–423.

Katznelson, Ira. 2005. *When Affirmative Action Was White: An Untold History of Racial Inequality in Twentieth Century America*. New York: Norton.

Kaufman, Jason. 2008. Harvard University, Department of Sociology home page. www.wjh.harvard.edu/soc/faculty/kaufman/

Keith, Verna M.; and Finlay, Barbara. 1988. "The impact of parental divorce on children's educational attainment, marital timing, and likelihood of divorce." *Journal of Marriage and the Family*, vol. 50, no. 3: 797–809.

Kellner, Douglas. 2001. "Globalization, technopolitics and revolution." *Theoria*, iss. 98: 14–34.

_____. 2005. *Media Spectacle and the Crisis of Democracy: Terrorism, War and Election Battles*. Boulder, CO: Paradigm.

Kelly, Barbara. 1993. *Expanding the American Dream: Building and Rebuilding Levittown*. Albany, NY: State University of New York Press.

Kennickell, Arthur B. 2009. "Ponds and Streams: Wealth and Income in the U.S., 1989 to 2007." Federal Reserve Board Working Paper, January 7. Figure A3a: 63.

Kephart, William. 2000. *Extraordinary Groups: An Examination of Unconventional Lifestyles*. New York: W. H. Freeman.

Kerbo, Harold R.; and Gonzalez, Juan J. 2003. "Class and non-voting in comparative perspective: Possible causes and consequences in the United States." *Research in Political Sociology*, vol. 12: 175–196.

Kessler, R. C. 2003. "Epidemiology of women and depression." *Journal of Affective Disorders*, vol. 74, no. 1: 5–13.

Khadaroo, Stacy Teicher. 2010. "Graduation rate for US high-schoolers falls for second straight year." *Christian Science Monitor*, June 10. www.csmonitor.com/USA/Education/2010/0610/Graduation-rate-for-US-high-schoolers-falls-for-second-straight-year

Khasnis, Atul A.; and Nettleman, Mary D. 2005. "Global warming and infectious disease." *Archives of Medical Research*, vol. 36, no. 6: 689–696.

Kilbourne, Jean. 1999. *Killing Us Softly 3*. Dir. Sut Jhally. Center for Media Literacy.

Kimmel, Michael. 1987. *Changing Men: New Directions in Research on Men and Masculinity*. Thousand Oaks, CA: Sage.

King, A. 1995. Outline of a practical theory of football violence." *Sociology*, vol. 24: 635–652.

Kinsey, Alfred C.; Pomeroy, Wardell B.; and Martin, Clyde E. 1998 (orig. 1948). *Sexual Behavior in the Human Male*. Bloomington, IN: Indiana University Press.

_____; and Gebhard, Paul H. 1998 (orig. 1953). *Sexual Behavior in the Human Female*. Bloomington, IN: Indiana University Press.

Kinsley, Michael. 2002. "Deliver us from evil." *Slate*, September 19. www.slate.com/id/2071148

Kitsuse, John I. 1980. "Coming out all over: Deviants and the politics of social problems." *Social Problems*, vol. 28: 1–13.

Kitzinger, C. 1987. *The Social Construction of Lesbianism*. London: Sage.

Klapper, J. 1960. *The Effects of Mass Communication*. New York: Free Press.

Klein, Naomi. 2000. *No Logo: Taking Aim at the Brand Bullies*. New York: Picador.

Klinenberg, Eric. 2002. *Heat Wave: A Social Autopsy of a Disaster in Chicago*. Chicago: University of Chicago Press.

_____. 2007. "Breaking the news." *Mother Jones*, March/April. www.motherjones.com/news/feature/2007/03/breaking_the_news.html

Kleinman, Sherryl. 1984. *Equals Before God: Seminarians as Humanistic Professionals*. Chicago: University of Chicago Press.

Kenneth D. Kochanek, Jiaquan Xu, Sherry L. Murphy, Arialdi M. Miniño, and Hsiang-Ching Kung, P. 2011. Deaths: Preliminary Data for 2009. National Vital Statistics Reports. www.cdc.gov/nchs/data/nvsr/nvsr59/nvsr59_04.pdf

Koerner, Brendan I. 2003. "Outbreaks vs. epidemics: Whether it's time to freak about the flu." *Slate*, December 19. www.slate.com/id/2092969

Kolbe, Richard H.; Langefeld, Carl D. 1993. "Appraising gender role portrayals in TV commercials." *Sex Roles*, vol. 28, no. 7: 393–417.

Kollock, Peter; Blumstein, Phillip; and Schwartz, Pepper. 1985. "Sex and power in interaction: conversational privileges and duties." *American Sociological Review*, vol. 50, no. 1. (February): 34–46.

Kosciw, Joseph G.; Greytak, Emily A.; Diaz, Elizabeth M.; and Bartkiewicz, Mark J. 2010. "The 2009 National School Climate Survey." www.glsen.org/cgi-bin/iowa/all/library/record/2624.html?state=research&type=research

Kosmin, Barry A.; Mayer, Egon; and Keysar, Ariela. 2001. "American Religious Identification Survey." The Graduate Center of the City University of New York. www.gc.cuny.edu/faculty/research_briefs/aris/aris_index.htm

Koteskey, Ronald L. 2003. *What Missionaries Ought to Know: A Handbook for Life and Service*. Wilmore, KY: New Hope International Ministries.

Kozeny, Geoff. 1995. "Intentional communities: Lifestyle based on ideals." www.ic.org/pnp/cdir/1995/01kozeny.html

Kozol, J. 1991. *Savage Inequalities: Children in America's Schools*. New York: Crown Publishing.

Krashen, S. D. 1996. *Under Attack: The Case against Bilingual Education*. Culver City, CA: Language Education Associates.

Kraus, Richard G. 1995. "Play's new identity: Big business." *Journal of Physical Education, Recreation & Dance*, vol. 66, no. 8 (October): 36.

Krausz, Tibor. 2007. "In exile, a former gang member finds a reason to dance." *Christian Science Monitor*, October 23, p. 20.

Kreider, Rose M.; and Fields, Jason M. 2001. "Number, timing, and duration of marriages and divorces: Fall 1996." In U.S. Bureau of the Census, *Current Population Reports*, P70-80. Washington, DC: U.S. Government Printing Office.

__. 2002. "Number, timing, and duration of marriages and divorces: 1996," in U.S. Bureau of the Census, *Current Population Reports*. Washington, DC: U.S. Government Printing Office.

Kristof, N.; and WuDunn, S. 2000. "Two cheers for sweatshops." *New York Times Magazine*, September 24. www.nytimes.com/library/magazine/home/20000924mag-sweatshops.html

Krueger, Alan B. 2002. "The apple falls close to the tree, even in the land of opportunity." *New York Times*, November 14, p. C2.

Kuhn, Manfred; and McPartland, T. S. 1954. "An empirical investigation of self-attitude." *American Sociological Review*, vol. 19: 68–79.

Kuhn, Thomas S. 1970 (orig. 1962). *The Structure of Scientific Revolutions*. Chicago, IL: University of Chicago Press.

Kunstler, J. H. 1993. *The Geography of Nowhere: The Rise and Decline of America's Man-Made Landscape*. New York: Simon & Schuster.

Kurzweil, Ray. 1990. *The Age of Intelligent Machines*. Cambridge, MA: MIT Press.

Lachman, Margie. 2004. "Development in midlife." *Annual Review of Psychology*, vol. 55: 305–31.

Lakshmanan, Indira. 2006. "Gangs roil Central America; troubles linked to US deportees." *Boston Globe*, April 17, p. A1.

Lane, J. Mark; and Tabak, Ronald J. 1991. "Judicial activism and legislative 'reform' of federal habeas corpus: A critical analysis of recent developments and current proposals." *Albany Law Review*, vol. 55, no. 1: 1–95.

Lareau, Annette. 2003. *Unequal Childhoods: Class, Race and Family Life*. Berkeley, CA: University of California Press.

Larson, R. W.; and Richards, M. H. 1991. "Daily companionship in late childhood and early adolescence: Changing developmental contexts." *Child Development*, vol. 62: 284–300.

Lasch, Christopher. 1977. *Haven in a Heartless World: The Family Besieged*. New York: Basic Books.

Lazarsfeld, Paul; and Katz, Elihu. 1955. *Personal Influence*. New York: Free Press.

Le, C. N. 2001. "Interracial dating and marriage." *Asian-Nation: The Landscape of Asian America*. www.asian-nation.org/issues3.html

Le Bon, Gustave. 1896. *The Crowd: A Study of the Popular Mind*. New York: Viking Press.

Leaper, Campbell; and Ayers, Melanie M. 2007. "A Meta-Analytic Review of Gender Variations in Adults' Language Use: Talkativeness, Affiliative Speech, and Assertive Speech." *Personality and Social Psychology Review*. November.

Legal Marriage Alliance of Washington. 2007. "FAQs—quick answers about the freedom to marry." www.lmaw.org/faqs.htm#a5 and www.lmaw.org/faqs.htm#a6

Leidner, Robin. 1993. *Fast Food, Fast Talk*. Berkeley, CA: University of California Press.

Lemert, Edwin M. 1951. *Social Pathology: A Systematic Approach to the Theory of Sociopathic Behavior*. New York: McGraw-Hill.

Lemov, Doug. 2010. *Teach Like a Champion: 49 Techniques That Put Students on the Path to College*. San Francisco: Jossey-Bass.

Lepowsky, Maria Alexandra. 1993. *Gender and Power from Fruit of the Motherland*. New York: Columbia University Press.

Lerner, Melvin. 1965. "Evaluation of performance as a function of performer's reward and attractiveness." *Journal of Personality and Social Psychology*, vol. 1, no. 4.

__. 1980. *The Belief in a Just World: A Fundamental Delusion*. New York: Plenum Press.

LeVay, Simon. 1991. "A difference in hypothalamic structure between heterosexual and homosexual men." *Science*, vol. 253: 1034–1037.

__. 1993. *The Sexual Brain*. Cambridge, MA: MIT Press.

Levinson, David. 2002. *Encyclopedia of Crime and Punishment*. Thousand Oaks, CA: Sage.

Levi-Strauss, C. 1969 (orig. 1949). *The Elementary Structures of Kinship*. Rev. ed. Ed. R. Needham. Trans. J. Bell and J. von Sturmer. Boston: Beacon Press.

Lewis, Christopher Alan; Shelvin, Mark; McGuckin, Conor; and Navratil, Marek. 2001. "The Santa Clara Strength of Religious Faith Questionnaire: Confirmatory factor analysis." *Pastoral Psychology*, vol. 49, no. 5. www.infm.ulst.ac.uk/~chris/64.pdf

Lewis, Jacqueline. 1998. "Learning to strip: The socialization experiences of exotic dancers." *Canadian Journal of Human Sexuality*, vol. 7: 1–16.

Lewis, Oscar. 1959. *Five Families: Mexican Case Studies in the Culture of Poverty*. New York: Basic Books.

Li, J.; and Singelmann, J. 1998. "Gender differences in class mobility: A comparative study of the United States, Sweden, and West Germany." *Acta Sociologica*, vol. 41, no. 4: 315–333.

Liazos, Alexander. 1972. "The poverty of the sociology of deviance: Nuts, sluts and perverts." *Social Problems*, vol. 20: 103–120.

Lockman, Darcy. 2002. "What fuels urban legends? (emotional selection)." *Psychology Today*, vol. 35, no. 2 (March–April): 21.

Lofland, Lyn. 1973. *A World of Strangers: Order and Action in Urban Public Space*. New York: Basic Books.

Long, L.; and Nucci, A. 1998. "Accounting for two population turnarounds in nonmetropolitan America." *Research in Rural Sociology and Development*, iss. 7: 47–70.

Longley, Robert. 2005. "Number of 'majority-minority' states grows: Texas' minority population hits 50.2 percent." About.com. http://usgovinfo.about.com/od/censusandstatistics/a/minmajpop.htm.

Lortie, Dan. 1968. "Shared ordeal and induction to work." In Howard Becker, Blancher Greer, David Reisman, and Robert Weiss, eds., *Institutions and the Person*. Chicago: Aldine.

Loseke, Donileen; and Cahill, Spencer. 1986. "Actors in search of a character: Student social workers' quest for professional identity." *Symbolic Interaction*, vol. 9: 245–258.

Loving v. Virginia. 1967. 388, U.S. 1. June 12.

Lumpkin, Angela; and Williams, Linda D. 1991. "An analysis of *Sports Illustrated* feature articles, 1954–1987." *Sociology of Sport Journal*, vol. 8, no. 1: 16–32.

Lurie, P and S. Wolfe. 1997. "Unethical Trials of Interventions to Reduce Perinatal Transmission of the Human Immunodeficincy Virus in Developing Countries." *The New England Journal of Medicine*. September 18; 337(12).

Lynch, J.W.; Kaplan, G.A.; and Shema, S.J. 1997. "Cumulative impact of sustained economic hardship on physical, cognitive, psychological, and social functioning." *New England Journal of Medicine*. December 25; 337(26):1889–95.

__. 1998. "Income inequality and mortality in metropolitan areas of the United States." *American Journal of Public Health*. July; 88(7): 1074–1080.

Lynd, Robert S.; and Lynd, Helen Merrell. 1937. *Middletown in Transition: A Study in Cultural Conflicts*. New York: Harcourt Brace.

__. 1959 (orig. 1929). *Middletown: A Study in Modern American Culture*. San Diego, CA: Harvest Books/Harcourt Brace.

Maccoby, E. E.; and Jacklin, C. N. 1987. "Sex segregation in childhood." In H. W. Reese, ed., *Advances in Child Development and Behavior*. Orlando, FL: Academic Press.

Macfarquhar, Neil. 2001. "As anger smolders in the streets, Arab governments temper remarks, or say nothing." *New York Times*, October 9, p. B8.

Macintyre, S.; MacDonald, L.; and Ellaway, A. 2008. "Do poorer people have poorer access to local resources and facilities? The distribution of local resources by area deprivation in Glasgow, Scotland." *Social Sciences & Medicine*, vol. 67, no. 6: 900–14.

MacKinnon, Catharine A. 2005. *Women's Lives, Men's Laws*. Cambridge, MA: Belknap Press.

Magleby, David B., ed. 2000. *Outside Money: Soft Money and Issue Advocacy in the 1998 Congressional Elections*. Lanham, MD: Rowman & Littlefield.

Malamuth, Neil; and Donnerstein, Edward; eds. 1984. *Pornography and Sexual Aggression*. New York: Academic Press.

Malthus, Thomas. 1997 (orig. 1798). *An Essay on the Principle of Population: An Essay on the Principle of Population, as it Affects the Future Improvement of Society with Remarks on the Speculations of Mr. Godwin, M. Condorcet, and Other Writers*. London: printed for J. Johnson, St. Paul's Churchyard. Rendered into HTML format by Ed Stephan, 8/10/97. www.ac.wwu.edu/~stephan/malthus/malthus.0.html

Mann, Susan A.; Grimes, Michael D.; Kemp, Alice Abel; and Jenkins, Pamela J. 1997. "Paradigm shifts in family sociology? Evidence from three decades of family textbooks." *Journal of Family Issues*, vol. 18, no. 3 (May): 315.

Marcuse, Herbert. 1991 (orig. 1964). *One-Dimensional Man: Studies in the Ideology of Advanced Industrial Society*. Boston: Beacon Press.

Martin, Laura. 1986. "Eskimo words for snow: A case study in the genesis and decay of an anthropological example." *American Anthropologist*, vol. 88, no. 2: 418–423.

Martineau, Harriet. 1837. *Society in America*. London: Saunders and Otley.

———. 1838. *Retrospect of Western Travel*. London: Saunders and Otley.

———. 1853. *The Positive Philosophy of Auguste Comte*. London: Chapman

Marx, Karl. 1982 (orig. 1848). *The Communist Manifesto*. New York: International.

———. 2001. *Selected Writings*. Ed. David McLellan. Oxford: Oxford University Press.

———. 2006 (orig. 1890). *Das Kapital*. Miami, FL: Synergy International of the Americas, Ltd.

Maslin Nir, Sarah. 2010. "Embracing A Life of Solitude." *New York Times*, April 14. www.nytimes.cOml2010/04/15/gardenl15alone.html

Massey, D. S.; and Denton N. A. 1993. *American Apartheid: Segregation and the Making of the Underclass*. Cambridge, MA: Harvard University Press.

Matsuda, Mari J.; Lawrence, C. R.; Delgado, Richard; and Crenshaw, Kimberle. 1993. *Words That Wound: Critical Race Theory, Assaultive Speech and the First Amendment*. Boulder, CO: Westview Press.

Matza, David. 1969. *Becoming Deviant*. Englewood Cliffs, NJ: Prentice Hall.

Mauss, Armand L. 1975. *Social Problems as Social Movements*. Philadelphia, PA: J. B. Lippincott.

Mayer, Susan. 1997. *What Money Can't Buy: Family Income and Children's Life Chances*. Cambridge, MA: Harvard University Press.

Maynard, D.W.; and Frankel, R.M. 2006. "On diagnostic rationality: bad news, good news, and the symptom residue." In J. Heritage and D. Maynard, eds., *Communication in Medical Care: Interaction between Primary Care Physicians and Patients*. Cambridge: Cambridge University Press.

McCaa, Robert. 1994. "Child marriage and complex families among the Nahuas of ancient Mexico." *Latin American Population History Bulletin*, 26: 2–11.

McCall, L. 2001. "Sources of racial wage inequality in metropolitan labor markets: Racial, ethnic, and gender differences." *American Sociological Review*, vol. 66, no. 4 (August): 520–541.

McChesney, Robert. 1997. *Corporate Media and the Threat to Democracy*. Open Media Pamphlet Series. New York: Seven Stories Press.

———. 2000. *Rich Media, Poor Democracy: Communication Politics in Dubious Times*. New York: New Press.

———. 2004. *The Problem of the Media: U.S. Communication Politics in the Twenty-First Century*. New York: Monthly Review Press.

McCombs, Maxwell; and Shaw, Donald. 1972. "The agenda-setting function of mass media." *Public Opinion Quarterly*, vol. 36, no. 2 (summer): 176–187.

———. 1977. "The agenda-setting function of the press." In D. Shaw and M. McCombs, eds., *The Emergence of American Political Issues: The Agenda-Setting Function of the Press* (89–105). St. Paul, MN: West Publishing.

McGhee, Paul E.; and Frueh, Terry. 1980. "Television viewing and the learning of sex-role stereotypes." *Sex Roles*, vol. 6, no. 2: 179.

McGinn, Daniel. 2006. "Marriage by the numbers." *Newsweek*, June 5.

McGrane, Bernard. 1994. *The Un-TV and the 10 MPH Car: Experiments in Personal Freedom and Everyday Life*. New York: Small Press.

McIntyre, Shelby; Moberg, Dennis J.; and Posner, Barry Z. 1980. "Preferential treatment in preselection decisions according to sex and race." *Academy of Management Journal*, vol. 23, no. 4 (December): 738–749.

McKinlay, J.B. 1997. "A case for refocusing upstream: the political economy of health and illness." In P. Conrad, ed., *The Sociology of Health and Illness: Critical Perspectives*. New York: St. Martin's Press.

McKinley, Jesse. 2010. "Whooping cough kills 5 in California; State declares an epidemic." *New York Times*, July 23.

McLuhan, Marshall. 1964. *Understanding Media: The Extensions of Man*. New York: McGraw Hill.

McMichael, Philip. 1996. *Development and Social Change: A Global Perspective*. Thousand Oaks, CA: Pine Forge Press.

McNamara, Kevin. 1999. "CityWalk: Los(t) Angeles in the shape of a mall." In Ghent Urban Studies Team, ed., *The Urban Condition*. Rotterdam: 010 pub.

McPhail, Clark. 1991. *The Myth of the Madding Crowd*. New York: de Gruyter.

McWilliams, James. 2005. "Internships pay off in opportunity." *The State*, August 5. www.thestate.com/mld/thestate/business/12307544.htm

Mead, George Herbert. 1934. *Mind, Self and Society*. Ed. Charles Morris. Chicago: University of Chicago Press.

Mele, Christopher. 2000. *Selling the Lower East Side: Culture, Real Estate, and Resistance in New York City*. Minneapolis, MN: University of Minnesota Press.

Merrow, John. 2007. "Dream catchers." *New York Times*. Education Life special section. April 27, sec. 4A, 18–22.

Merton, Robert K. 1948. "The self-fulfilling prophecy." *Antioch Review*, vol. 8, no. 2 (June): 193–210.

———. (1938). "Social Structure and Anomie." *American Sociological Review* 3 (5): 672–682.

_____. 1968. *Social Theory and Social Structure*. 2nd rev. ed. New York: Free Press.

_____. 1976. *Sociological Ambivalence and other essays*. New York: Simon & Schuster.

_____. 1996. *On Social Structure and Science*. Chicago: University of Chicago.

Messerschmidt, James W. 1993. *Masculinities and Crime: Critique and Reconceptualization of Theory*. Totowa, NJ: Rowman and Littlefield.

_____. 1998. "Men victimizing men: The case of lynching: 1865–1900." In Lee H. Bowker, ed., *Masculinities and Violence*. Thousand Oaks, CA: Sage.

Messner, M. A. 2007. *Out of Play: Critical Essays on Gender and Sport*. Albany, New York: State University of New York Press.

_____; Duncan, M. C.; and Willms, N. 2005, July. "Gender in televised sports: News and highlights shows, 1989–2004." Amateur Athletic Foundation of Los Angeles. www.la84foundation. org/9arr/ResearchReports/tv2004.pdf

Meyer, D. 2000. "Social movements: Creating communities of change." In R. Teske and M. Tetreault, eds., *Conscious Acts and the Politics of Social Change*. Columbia, SC: University of South Carolina Press.

Meyer, Daniel R.; and Bartfeld, Judi. 1998. "Patterns of child support compliance in Wisconsin." *Journal of Marriage and the Family*, vol. 60, no. 2: 309–318.

Meyrowitz, Joshua. 1985. *No Sense of Place: The Impact of Electronic Media on Social Behavior*. New York: Oxford University Press.

Milgram, Stanley. 1963. "Behavioral Study of Obedience." *Journal of Abnormal Social Psychology*, vol. 67: 371–378.

_____. 1974. *Obedience to Authority: An Experimental View*. New York: Harper & Row.

Miller, Alice. 1990. *For Your Own Good: Hidden Cruelty in Child-Rearing and the Roots of Violence*. New York: Noonday Press.

Miller, Donald E.; and Miller, Lorna Touryan. 1999. *Survivors: An Oral History of the Armenian Genocide*. Berkeley, CA: University of California Press.

Miller, Laura. 1997. "Women in the military." *Social Psychology Quarterly*, vol. 60, no. 10 (March).

Mills, C. Wright. 1959. "The promise." *The Sociological Imagination*. New York: Oxford University Press.

_____. 1970 (orig. 1956). *The Power Elite*. New York: Oxford University Press.

Miner, Horace. 1956. "Body ritual among the Nacirema." *American Anthropologist*, vol. 58, no. 3 (June).

Miringoff, Marc; and Miringoff, Marque-Luisa. 1999. *The Social Health of the Nation: How America Is Really Doing*. New York: Oxford University Press.

Mishel, Lawrence; Bernstein, Jared; and Alegretto, Sylvia. 2007. Tables 3.18 and Table 3.19 in *The State of Working America 2006/2007*. Ithaca, NY: Cornell University Press.

Mitchell, Katharyne. 1993. "Multiculturalism, or the united colors of capitalism?" *Antipode*, vol. 25, no. 4: 263–294.

Mitchell, Richard. 2001. *Dancing at Armageddon: Survivalism and Chaos in Modern Times*. Chicago: University of Chicago Press.

Mitchell, Richard; and Charmaz, Kathy. 1996. "The myth of silent authorship: Self, substance and style in ethnographic writing." *Symbolic Interaction*, vol. 19, no. 4 (winter): 285–302.

Mittermeier, Russell A.; Myers, Norman; and Mittermeier, Cristina Goettsch. 2000. *Hotspots: Earth's Biologically Richest and Most Endangered Terrestrial Ecoregions*. Arlington, VA: Conservation International.

Mollenkopf, John. 1983. *The Contested City*. Princeton, NJ: Princeton University Press.

Molotch, Harvey. 1970. "Oil in Santa Barbara and power in America." *Sociological Inquiry*, vol. 40: 131–144.

Monitor Report. 1999. "U.S. runaway film and television production study report." www.dga.org/thedga/leg_rp_runaway.pdf

Montagu, A. 1998. *Man's Most Dangerous Myth: The Fallacy of Race*. 6th ed. Thousand Oaks, CA: Altamira Press.

Montopoli, Brian. 2010. "Jon Stewart Rally Attracts Estimated 215,000." *CBS News*, Oct. 30. www.cbsnews.com/8301-503544_162-20021284-503544.html

Morrison, Donna Ruane; and Cherlin, Andrew J. 1995. "The divorce process and young children's well-being: A prospective analysis." *Journal of Marriage and the Family*, vol. 57, no. 3: 800–812.

Mortenson, T. (2007). Bachelor's Degree Attainment by Age 24 by Family Income Quartiles, 1970 to 2005. Oskaloosa, IA: Postsecondary Education Opportunity.

Muhl, Charles J. 2002. "What is an employee? The answer depends on the federal law; in a legal context, the classification of a worker as either an employee or an independent contractor can have significant consequences." *Monthly Labor Review*, vol. 125, no. 1 (January).

Mullins, N. 1973. *Theories and Theory Groups in Contemporary American Sociology*. New York: Harper and Row.

Myers, Norman; and Kent, Jennifer. 2004. *The New Consumers: The Influence of Affluence on the Environment*. Washington, DC: Island Press.

_____, eds. 2005. *The New Atlas of Planet Management*. Berkeley, CA: University of California Press.

Nahin, Richard, et al. 2009. "Costs of complementary and alternative medicine (CAM) and frequency of visits to CAM practitioners: United States, 2007." *National Health Statistics Reports*, July 30. www.cdc.gov/NCHS/data/nhsr/nhsr018.pdf

National Center for Health Statistics. 2001. "Number and percent of office visits with corresponding standard errors, by the 20 principal reasons for visit most frequently mentioned by patients according to patient's sex: United States, 1999."

National Domestic Violence Hotline. 2003. "What is domestic violence?" www.ndvh.org/dvInfo.html

National Law Center on Homelessness and Poverty. 2010. "Homelessness and Poverty in America." http://nlchp.org/hapia.cfm

National Opinion Research Center, University of Chicago. 1999. "The emerging 21st century American family." GSS Social Change Report No. 42.

National Public Radio. 2003. "Interracial marriage." *Odyssey*. WBEZ, Chicago. February 28.

_____, Kaiser Family Foundation, and Harvard University Kennedy School of Government. 2001. National Survey on Poverty in America: Summary of Findings. www.kff.org/kaiserpolls/3118-index.cfm

Nattras, Nicoli; and Seekings, Jeremy. 2001. "Two nations? Race and economic inequality in South Africa today." *Daedalus*, vol. 139 (winter): 45–70.

New School. 2004. "Thomas Robert Malthus, 1766–1834." Economics Department, New School. The History of Economic Thought web site. http://cepa.newschool.edu/het/ profiles/malthus.htm

Newman, David M. 2000. *Sociology: Exploring the Architecture of Everyday Life*. 3rd ed. Thousand Oaks, CA: Pine Forge Press.

Newton, Michael. 2004. *Savage Girls and Wild Boys: A History of Feral Children*. New York: Picador.

Nixon, Richard. 1974. "Address on the state of the union delivered before a joint session of the Congress," January 30. *The American Presidency Project* (J. T. Wooley and G. Peters, eds.). www.presidency.ucsb.edu/ws/index.php?pid=4327

Nixon, Richard. 1972. "Special message to the Congress on health care," March 2. *The American Presidency Project* (J. T. Wooley and G. Peters, eds.). www.presidency.ucsb.edu/ws/?pid=3757

Noah, Timothy. 2004. "Something nice about Bush." *Slate*, November 4. http://slate.msn.com/id/2109228/

Nogaki, Sylvia Weiland. 1993. "Judge oks Nordstrom lawsuit settlement." *Seattle Times*, April 13.

Norris, Pippa. 2001. *Digital Divide: Civic Engagement, Information Poverty, and the Internet Worldwide*. Cambridge: Cambridge University Press.

Norton, Eleanor Holmes. 2006. "Where's school voucher 'success' in Washington, D.C.?" *USA Today*, August 23.

Novel Swine-Origin Influenza A (H1N1) Virus Investigation Team. 2009. "Emergence of a novel swine-origin influenza A (H1N1) virus in humans." *New England Journal of Medicine*, vol. 360: 2605–2615.

Oakes, Jeannie. 1985. *Keeping Track: How Schools Structure Inequality*. New Haven, CT: Yale University Press.

O'Brien, Jodi; and Kollock, Peter. 1997. *The Production of Reality: Essays and Readings on Social Interaction*. Thousand Oaks, CA: Pine Forge Press.

Ochs, Elinor. 1986. "Introduction." In Bambi B. Schieffelin and Elinor Ochs, eds., *Language and Socialization Across Cultures*. New York: Cambridge University Press.

Ogburn, William. 1964. *On Cultural and Social Change: Selected Papers*. Chicago: University of Chicago Press.

Ohtaki, Sachiko; Ohtaki, Toshio; and Fetters, Michael D. 2003. "Doctor–patient communication: a comparison of the USA and Japan" *Family Practice*, vol. 20, no. 3: 276–282.

Oldenburg, Ray. 1999. *The Great Good Place*. New York: Marlowe and Company.

Omi, Michael; and Winant, Howard. 1989. *Racial Formation in the United States: From the 1960s to the 1980s*. New York: Routledge.

O'Neill, J. 2007. "HIV/AIDS in the developing world: What can we do?" In R. Gallo, ed., *Retroviruses: Biology, Pathogenic Mechanisms and Treatment, The Biomedical & Life Sciences Collection*. London: Henry Stewart Talks.

O'Reilly, Brian. 1992. "Looking ahead: Jobs are fast moving abroad." *Fortune*, December 14, pp. 52–66.

Orfield, Gary. 2001. "Schools more separate: Consequences of a decade of resegregation." Civil Rights Project Report. Harvard University. www.civilrightsproject.harvard.edu/research/deseg/separate_schools01.php

Osborne, Lawrence. 2002. "Consuming rituals of the suburban tribe." *New York Times Magazine*, January 13.

Park, Robert Ezra. 1961. "Human ecology." Reprinted in G. A. Theodorson, ed., *Studies in Human Ecology*. New York: Row, Peterson & Company.

Parker, Lonnae O'Neal. 1998. "Brand identities." *Washington Post*, May 11.

Parsons, Talcott. 1951. *The Social System*. Glencoe, IL: The Free Press.

_____. 1955. "The American family: Its relation to personality and social structure." In Talcott Parsons and R. Bales, eds., *Family Socialization and Interaction Process*. New York: Free Press.

_____; and Bales, R.; eds. 1955. *Family, Socialization and Interaction Process*. New York: Free Press.

Pascoe, C. J. 2007. "Dude, you're a fag: masculinity and sexuality in high school." University of California Press, 5.

Patchett, Ann. 2001. *Bel Canto*. New York: Harper Perennial.

_____. 2004. *Truth & Beauty: A Friendship*. New York: HarperCollins.

Pathways to Hope Prison Dog Project. 2009. www.pathwaystohope.org/prison.htm.

Patterson, Margot. 2004. "The rise of global fundamentalism." *National Catholic Reporter*, May 7.

PBS. 2001. Frontline: Merchants of Cool. pbs.org/wgbh/pages/frontline/shows/cool/

Peavy, Linda; and Smith, Ursula. 1998. *Pioneer Women: The Lives of Women on the Frontier*. Norman, OK: University of Oklahoma Press.

People and the Planet. 2002. "Two more Earths needed by 2050." www.peopleandplanet.net/doc.php?id+ 1685&section=17

Perls T. T.; and Fretts, R. 1998. "Why women live longer than men." *Scientific American Presents: Women's Health: A Lifelong Guide*, vol. 9, no. 4: 100–104.

Perrin, S.; and Spencer, C. P. 1980. "The Asch effect: A child of its time." *Bulletin of the British Psychological Society*, vol. 32: 405–406.

_____. 1981. "Independence or conformity in the Asch experiment as a reflection of cultural and situational factors." *British Journal of Social Psychology*, vol. 20: 215–210.

Perry, J.; and Pugh, M. 1978. *Collective Behavior: Response to Social Stress*. St. Paul, MN: West Publishing Company.

Peters, H. Elizabeth; Argys, Laura M.; Maccoby, Eleanor E.; and Mnookin, Robert H. 1993. "Enforcing divorce settlements: Evidence from child support compliance and award modifications." *Demography*, vol. 30, no. 4: 719–735.

Peterson, Julie. 2003. "U.S. Supreme Court rules on University of Michigan cases." www.umich.edu/news/Releases/2003/Jun03/supremecourt.html

Peterson, William. 2003. *From Persons to People: Further Studies in the Politics of Population*. Edison, NJ: Transaction.

Pettit, Becky; and Western, Bruce. 2004. "Mass imprisonment and the life course: Race and class inequality in U.S. incarceration." *American Sociological Review*, vol. 69: 151–169.

Pew Forum on Religion and Public Life. 2008. U.S. Religious Landscape Survey. http://religions.pewforum.org

_____. 2010. "Growing Number of Americans Say Obama is a Muslim." Poll taken Aug. 18, 2010. http://pewforum.org/Politics-and-Elections/Growing-Number-of-Americans-Say-Obama-is-a-Muslim.aspx

Pew Internet and American Life Project. 2010. "Demographics of Internet Users." May. www.pewinternet.org/Static-Pages/Trend-Data/Whos-Online.aspx

Pew Research Center for the People and the Press. 2008a. "Key News Audiences Now Blend Online and Traditional Sources." Aug. 17. http://people-press.org/report/?pageid=1353

_____. 2008b. "Internet's broader role in campaign 2008." January 11. http://people-press.org/report/384/internets-broader-role-in-campaign-2008

_____. 2008c. "Growing doubts about McCain's judgment, age and campaign conduct." Section 2: Candidate Traits. Survey Report, October 21. http://people-press.org/report/462/obamas-lead-widens

_____. 2010a. Interactive: The Changing American Family. http://pewsocialtrends.org/2010/11/18/five-decades-of-marriage-trends/

_____. 2010b. "Marrying Out." www.pewsocialtrends.org/files/2010/10/755-marrying-out.pdf

_____. 2011. "Internet Gains on Television as Public's Main News Source: More Young People Cite Internet Than TV." Jan. 2. http://people-press.org/report/689

Phillips. S. 2009. "Criminology: Legal Disparities in the Capital of Capital Punishment." *Journal of Criminal Law & Criminology*, vol. 99, no. 3: 717. Retrieved from EBSCO*host*.

Pilnick, Alison; Hindmarsh, Jon; and Teas Gill, Virginia. 2009. "Beyond 'doctor and patient': developments in the study of healthcare interactions." *Sociology of Health & Illness*, vol. 31 no. 6: 787–802.

Pinto, Barbara. 2005. "Small town USA may offer solution to outsourcing: Company redeploys workers to rural towns instead of sending jobs overseas." *ABC World News Tonight*, television broadcast, August 25.

Pleck, Elizabeth H. 2000. *Celebrating the Family: Ethnicity, Consumer Culture, and Family Ritual.* Cambridge. MA: Harvard University Press.

Pollack, Andres. 1999. "Aerospace gets Japan's message: Without military largess, industry takes the lean path." *New York Times*, March 9, p. C1.

Pollan, Michael. 2008. "Farmer in Chief." *New York Times Magazine*, October 9. www.nytimes.com/2008/10/12/magazine/12policy-t.html

Pollner, Melvin; and Stein, Jill. 1996. "Narrative mapping of social worlds: The voice of experience in Alcoholics Anonymous." *Journal of Symbolic Interaction*, vol. 19, no. 3: 203–223.

_____. 2001. "Doubled-over in laughter: Humor and the construction of selves in Alcoholics Anonymous." In Jaber Gubrium and James Holstein, eds., *Institutional Selves: Personal Troubles in Organizational Context.* New York: Oxford University Press.

Pool, Robert. 1997. *Beyond Engineering: How Society Shapes Technology.* Oxford, UK: Oxford University Press.

Population Reference Bureau. 2010. "World Population Data Sheet." www.prb.org/pdf10/10wpds_eng.pdf

Poster, Mark. 2002. "Workers as cyborgs: Labor and networked computers." *Journal of Labor Research*, vol. 23, no. 3 (summer): 339.

Postman, Neil. 1987. *Amusing Ourselves to Death: Public Discourse in the Age of Show Business.* New York: Methuen.

Powell, Brian. 2003. Unpublished survey results. Indiana University, Department of Sociology, Center for Survey Research, Bloomington.

Powell, L.M.; Slater, S.; Mirtcheva, D.; Bao, Y.; and Chaloupka, F.J. 2007. "Food store availability and neighborhood characteristics in the United States." *Preventive Medicine*, vol. 44, no. 3: 189–195.

Pullum, Geoffrey K. 1991. *The Great Eskimo Vocabulary Hoax and Other Irreverent Essays on the Study of Language.* Chicago: University of Chicago Press.

Putnam, Robert D. 1995. "Tuning in, tuning out: The strange disappearance of social capital in America." *Political Science & Politics*, vol. 28, no. 4 (December): 664.

_____. 2000. *Bowling Alone: The Collapse and Revival of American Community.* New York: Simon & Schuster.

Rabin, Roni Caryn. 2008. "Severe Heart Attacks Deadlier for Women." *The New York Times*, December 8.

Rabow, Jerome; Stein, Jill; and Conley, Terri. 1999. "Teaching social justice and encountering society: The pink triangle experiment." *Youth and Society*, vol. 30, no. 4: 483–514.

Radway, A. Janice. 1991. *Reading the Romance: Women, Patriarchy, and Popular Literature.* Chapel Hill, NC: University of North Carolina Press.

Rampell, Catherine. 2010. "Graduation Rates, by State and Race." *New York Times*, June 2. http://economix.blogs.nytimes.com/2010/06/02/graduation-rates-by-state-and-race/

RAND Education. 2003. *Charter School Operation and Performance: Evidence from California.* Santa Monica, CA: The Rand Corporation. www.rand.org/pubs/monograph_reports/MR1700

Ray, Brian. 1997. "Strengths of their own—home schoolers across America: Academic achievement, family characteristics, and longitudinal traits." Salem, OR: National Home Education Research Institute.

_____. 2008. "Research facts on homeschooling." National Home Education Research Institute. www.nheri.org/Research-Facts-on-Homeschooling.html

Reece, M.; Herbenick, D.; Schick, V.; Sanders, S.; Dodge, B.; and Fortenberry, J. 2010. "Condom Use Rates in a National Probability Sample of Males and Females, Ages 14 to 94 in the United States." *Journal of Sexual Medicine* 7 (suppl. 5): 266–267.

Rees, W.; and Wackernagel, M. 1994. "Ecological footprints and appropriated carrying capacity: Measuring the natural capital requirements of the human economy." In A-M. Jansson, M. Hammer, C. Folke, and R. Costanza, eds., *Investing in Natural Capital: The Ecological Economics Approach to Sustainability.* Washington, DC: Island Press.

Rennison, Callie Marie. 2001. "Intimate partner violence and age of victim, 1993–1999." Bureau of Justice Statistics Special Report. Washington, DC: U.S. Department of Justice. NCJ #187635.

Reuters. 2008. "Visa study shows Canada and Mexico are top destinations for Americans traveling abroad." July 24. www.reuters.com/article/pressRelease/idUS135782+24-Jul-2008+BW20080724

Riesman, D. 1957. "The suburban dislocation." *Annals of the American Academy of Political and Social Science*, vol. 314: 123.

Rios, Victor. 2009. "The Consequence of the Criminal Justice Pipeline on Black and Latino Masculinity." *The Annals of the American Academy of Political and Social Science.* May: 150–162.

Ritzer, George. 1996. *The McDonaldization of Society.* Thousand Oaks, CA: Pine Forge Press.

Robbins, John. 1987. *Diet for a New America: How Your Food Choices Affect Your Health, Happiness and the Future of Life on Earth.* Walpole, NH: H. J. Kramer.

Roberts, D.; and Bernstein, A. 2000. "A life of fines and beating." *Business Week*, October 2, pp. 122–128.

Robson, D. 2001. "Women and minorities in economics textbooks: Are they being adequately represented?" *Journal of Economic Education*, vol. 32, no. 2 (spring): 186–191.

Rojek, Chris. 1985. *Capitalism and Leisure Theory.* London: Tavistock.

_____. 1995. *Decentering Leisure: Rethinking Leisure Theory.* London: Sage.

_____. 1997. "Leisure theory: Retrospect and prospect." *Loisir et Société/Society and Leisure*, vol. 20, no. 2: 383–400.

_____. 2000. "Leisure and the rich today: Veblen's thesis after a century." *Leisure Studies*, vol. 19, no. 1: 1–15.

Roscoe, W. 2000. "How to become a berdache: Toward a unified analysis of gender." In G. Herdt, ed., *Third Sex, Third Gender: Beyond Sexual Dimorphism in Culture and History.* New York: Zone Books.

Rosenbaum, Emily. 2008. "Racial/Ethnic Differences in Asthma Prevalence: The Role of Housing and Neighborhood Environments." *Journal of Health and Social Behavior.* June, vol. 49, no. 2: 131–145.

Rosenbloom, Stephanie. 2007. "On Facebook, scholars link up with data." *New York Times*, December 17. www.nytimes.com/2007/12/17/style/17facebook.html?ex=1355720400&en=33ca15953318a6f5&ei=5124&partner=permalink&exprod=permalink

Rosenfeld, Dana. 2003. *The Changing of the Guard: Lesbian and Gay Elders, Identity, and Social Change.* Philadelphia: Temple University Press.

Rosenhan, David. 1973. "On being sane in insane places." *Science*, vol. 179 (January): 250–258.

Rosenthal, R.; and Jacobson, L. 1968. *Pygmalion in the Classroom: Teacher Expectation and Pupils' Intellectual Development.* New York: Rinehart and Winston.

Ross, Andrew. 1997. "Introduction." In Andrew Ross, ed., *No Sweat: Fashion, Free Trade and the Rights of Garment Workers.* New York: Verso.

Rothblum, Esther. 1996. *Preventing Heterosexism and Homophobia.* Thousand Oaks, CA: Sage.

Rothkop, David. 1997. "In praise of cultural imperialism? Effects of globalization on culture." *Foreign Policy*, June 22.

Rowniak, Stefan. 2009. "Safe sex fatigue, treatment optimism, and serosorting: New challenges to HIV prevention among men who have sex with men." *Journal of the Association of Nurses in AIDS Care*, vol. 20, no. 1: 31–38.

Roy, Donald. 1960. "'Banana time': Job satisfaction and informal interaction." *Human Organization*, vol. 18: 158–168.

Rubel, Paula; and Rosman, Abraham. 2001. "The collecting passion in America." *Zeitschrift fur Ethnologie* (English), vol. 126, no. 2: 313–330.

Rubenstein, William B. 2001. "Do Gay Rights Laws Matter? An Empirical Assessment." *Southern California Law Review*, vol. 75, 65: 65–120. www.law.ucla.edu/williamsinstitute/programs/dogayrightslawsmatter.pdf

Rubin, Zick; and Peplau, Letitia Anne. 1975. "Who believes in a just world?" *Journal of Social Issues*, vol. 31, no. 3: 65–89.

Rupp, Leila; and Taylor, Verta. 2003. *Drag Queens of the 801 Cabaret.* Chicago: University of Chicago Press.

Ryan, Caitlin; Huebner, David; Diaz, Rafael; and Sanchez, Jorge. 2009. "Family Rejection as a Predictor of Negative Health Outcomes in White and Latino Lesbian, Gay, Bisexual Young Adults." *Pediatrics*, vol. 123, no. 1. January: 346–352. http://pediatrics.aappublications.org/cgi/content/abstract/123/1/346

Ryan, George. 2003. "The death penalty: Arbitrary and capricious." Salon.com

Sadker, Myra; and Sadker, David. 1995. *Failing at Fairness: How Our Schools Cheat Girls.* New York: Scribner.

Sampson, Robert J.; and Wilson, William Julius. 2005. "Toward a theory of race, crime and urban inequality." In Shaun L. Gabbidon and Helen Taylor Greene, eds., *Race, Crime and Justice: A Reader.* New York: Routledge.

Sanchez-Jankowski, Martin. 1991. *Islands in the Street: Gangs and American Urban Society.* Berkeley, CA: University of California Press.

Sapir, Edward. 1949. *Selected Writings in Language, Culture, and Personality.* Ed. David G. Mandelbaum. Berkeley, CA: University of California Press.

Sapolsky, Robert. 1997. *Trouble with Testosterone and Other Essays on the Biology of Human Nature.* New York: Scribner.

Sassen, Saskia. 1991. *The Global City: New York, London, Tokyo.* Princeton, NJ: Princeton University Press.

Sayer, Liana C.; and Mattingly, Maribeth. 2006. "Under pressure: Gender differences in the relationship between free time and feeling rushed." *Journal of Marriage and Family*, vol. 68, no. 1 (February): 205–221.

Schegloff, Emanuel. 1986. "The routine as achievement." *Human Studies*, vol. 9, nos. 2–3: 111–151.

_____. 1999. "What next? Language and social interaction study at the century's turn." *Research on Language and Social Interaction*, vol. 32, nos.1–2: 141–148.

Schein, Edgar H. 1997. *Organizational Culture and Leadership.* San Francisco: Jossey-Bass.

Schell, Orville. 2002. "Gross national happiness." *Red Herring*, January 15. www.pbs.org/frontlineworld/stories/bhutan/gnh.html

Scheyvens, Regina. 2000. "Promoting women's empowerment through involvement in ecotourism: Experiences from the Third World." *Journal of Sustainable Tourism*, vol. 8, no. 3: 232–249.

Schiller, Herbert I. 1976. *Communication and Cultural Domination.* White Plains, NY: International Arts and Sciences Press.

_____. 1992. *Mass Communications and American Empire.* 2nd ed. Boulder, CO: Westview Press.

_____. 1995. "The global information highway: Project for an ungovernable world." In J. Brook and I. A. Boal, eds., *Resisting the Virtual Life: The Culture and Politics of Information.* San Francisco: City Lights Books.

_____. 1996. *Information Inequality.* New York: Routledge.

_____; Schlenker, Jennifer A.; Caron, Sandra L.; and Halteman, William A. 1998. "A feminist analysis of *Seventeen* magazine: Content analysis from 1945 to 1995." *Sex Roles: A Journal of Research*, vol. 38, no. 1–2: 135.

Schlosser, Eric. 2002. *Fast Food Nation: The Dark Side of the All-American Meal.* New York: Perennial.

_____. 2003. *Reefer Madness: Sex, Drugs and Cheap Labor in the American Black Market.* Boston: Houghton Mifflin.

Schmid, C. L. 1981. *Conflict and Consensus in Switzerland.* Berkeley, CA: University of California Press.

Schnaiberg, Allan. 1975. "Social synthesis of the societal-environmental dialectic: The role of distributional impacts." *Social Science Quarterly*, vol. 56: 5–20.

_____; and Gould, Kenneth Alan. 1994. *Environment and Society: The Enduring Conflict.* New York: St. Martin's Press.

Schofield, Jack. 2004. "Social network software; software to help you network." *Computer Weekly*, March 16, p. 32.

Schor, Juliet B. 1999. *The Overspent American: Why We Want What We Don't Need.* New York: HarperCollins.

Schudson, Michael. 2003. *The Sociology of News.* New York: Norton.

Schutz, Alfred P. 1962. "The stranger: An essay in social psychology." In A. Brodersen, ed, *Collected Papers II: Studies in Social Theory.* Dordrecht, The Netherlands: Martinus Nijhoff.

Schwellenbach, Nick. 2008. "Finance: A good time to be a white-collar criminal?" Center for Public Integrity, December 18. www.publicintegrity.org/blog/entry/1096

Schwimmer, B. 2001. "Figure 43. Hawaiian kin terms (actual usage)." www.umanitoba.ca/faculties/arts/ anthropology/tutor/image_list/43.html

Searing, Linda. 2010. "Study: Dying at home may be less traumatic for patients as well as caregivers." *Washington Post*, September 27.

www.washingtonpost.com/wp-dyn/content/article/2010/09/27/AR2010092705374.html

Sears, Brad; and Badgett, M.V. Lee. 2008. "The Impact of Extending Marriage to Same-Sex Couples on the California Budget." The Williams Institute. UCLA School of Law. www.law.ucla.edu/williamsinstitute/publications/EconImpactCAMarriage.pdf

Sedgwick, Eve Kosofsky. 1993. *Tendencies.* Durham, NC: Duke University Press.

Seekings, Jeremy; and Nattras, Nicoli. 2005. *Class, Race and Inequality in South Africa.* New Haven, CT: Yale University Press.

Segal, Lynne. 1990. *Slow Motion: Changing Masculinities, Changing Men.* New Brunswick, NJ: Rutgers University Press.

Seidman, Steven. 2003. *The Social Construction of Sexuality.* New York: Norton.

Seltzer, Judith A.; Schaeffer, Nora Cate; and Charng, Hong-Wen. 1989. "Family ties after divorce: The relationship between visiting and paying child support." *Journal of Marriage and the Family,* vol. 51, no. 4: 1013–1031.

Sennett, Richard. 1977. *The Fall of Public Man.* New York: Norton.

Severin, W. J.; and Tankard, J. W. 1997. *Communication Theories: Origins, Methods, and Uses in the Mass Media.* 4th ed. New York: Longman.

Shah, Anup. 2007. "Media conglomerates, mergers, concentration of ownership." *Global Issues,* April 29. www.globalissues.org/article/159/media-conglomerates-mergers-concentration-of-ownership

Shakara, Aaron. 2004. "More than a tree sitter." *Oregon Daily Emerald,* April 29.

Shiach, Morag. 1999. *Feminism and Cultural Studies.* New York: Oxford University Press.

Shipler, D. K. 1997. *A Country of Strangers: Blacks and Whites in America.* New York: Alfred A. Knopf.

Shippers, Mimi. 2002. *Rockin' Out of the Box: Gender Maneuvering in Alternative Hard Rock.* New Brunswick, NJ: Rutgers University Press.

Shover, Neal; and Wright, John Paul. 2001. *Crimes of Privilege: Readings in White-collar Crime.* New York, NY: Oxford University Press.

Simmel, Georg. 1950. *The Sociology of George Simmel.* Ed. Kurt Wolff. New York: Free Press.

Simon, Julian. 1996. *The Ultimate Resource 2.* Princeton, NJ: Princeton University Press

———. 2000. *The Great Breakthrough and Its Cause.* Ann Arbor, MI: University of Michigan Press.

Simon, Scott. 2004. "Friend of Kitty Genovese discusses her memories of Kitty and her murder." *National Public Radio,* "Weekend Edition Saturday," March 13.

Singh, Gopal K.; and Siahpush, Mohammad. 2006. "Widening socioeconomic inequalities in U.S. life expectancy, 1980–2000." *International Journal of Epidemiology,* online journal, May 9. http://ije.oxfordjournals.org/cgi/reprint/dyl083v1.pdf

Sisario, Ben. 2009. "One Band Moves Its Metal Out of Iraq." *New York Times,* Feb. 2. www.nytimes.com/2009/02/03/arts/music/03metal.html

Skarzynska, Krystyna. 2004. "Politicians in television: The big five in impression formation." *Journal of Political Marketing,* vol. 3, no. 2: 31–45.

Slack, Kristin, et al. 2006. "Family economic well-being following the 1996 welfare reform: Trend data from five non-experimental panel studies." *Children and Youth Services Review,* vol. 29, no. 6: 698–720.

Sloan Consortium. 2010. "Learning on Demand: Online Education in the United States, 2009." http://sloanconsortium.org/publications/survey/pdf/learningondemand.pdf

Smelser, Neil. 1985. "Evaluating the model of structural differentiation in relation to educational change in the nineteenth century." In Jeffrey C. Alexander, ed., *Neofunctionalism.* Beverly Hills, CA: Sage Publications.

Smith, Dorothy. 1999. "Schooling for inequality." *Signs: Journal for Women in Culture and Society,* vol. 5, no. 4: 1147–1151.

Smith, Herbert L. 1990. "Specification problems in experimental and nonexperimental social research." *Sociological Methodology,* vol. 20: 59–91.

Smith, Kara. 2005. "Gender talk: A case study in prenatal socialization." *Women and Languages,* March 22.

Smith, Marc; and Kollock, Peter. 1998. *Communities in Cyberspace.* London: Routledge.

Smith-Lovin, Lynn; and Brody, Charles. 1989. " Interruptions in group discussions: The effects of gender and group composition." *American Sociological Review,* vol. 54, no. 3 (June): 424–435.

Solnit, Rebecca. 2009. *A Paradise Built in Hell: The Extraordinary Communities that Arise in Disaster.* New York: Penguin Books.

Solot, Dorian; and Miller, Marshall. 2002. *Unmarried to Each Other: The Essential Guide to Living Together as an Unmarried Couple.* New York: Marlowe and Co.

Sonn, Bill. 2004. "Concierge medicine: Physicians weigh financial, ethical issues." *Physician's Practice,* vol.14, no. 3. www.physicianspractice.com/display/article/1462168/1590867

Sonner, Scott. 2002. "Burning Man gives fodder for questing sociologists." Associated Press, August 28. www.religionnewsblog.com/641-Scientists_find_Burning_Man_a_research_bonanza.html

Sorauf, Frank J. 1988. *Money in American Elections.* Boston: Scott, Foresman and Company.

Spector, Robert; and McCarthy, Patrick D. 1996. *The Nordstrom Way: The Inside Story of America's #1 Customer Service Company.* Hoboken, NJ: John Wiley & Sons.

Spellings, Margaret. 2006. "Opportunity for all children." *USA Today,* August 13.

Spencer, Herbert. 1862. *First Principles.* London: Williams and Norgate.

———. 1873. *The Study of Sociology.* London: King.

———. 1897. *The Principles of Sociology.* 3 vols. New York: Appleton.

Sprecher, Susan; McKinney, Kathleen; and Orbuch, Terri. 1987. "Has the double standard disappeared? An experimental test." *Social Psychology Quarterly,* vol. 50, no. 1 (March): 24–31.

Springer, Kristen W.; and Mouzon, Dawne. 2011. "Masculinity and Health Care Seeking Among Older Men: Implications for Men in Different Social Classes." *Journal of Health and Social Behavior.*

Srinivas, Lakshmi. 1998. "Active viewing: An ethnography of the Indian film audience." *Visual Anthropology,* vol. 11, no. 4.

Stacey, Judith. 1990. *Brave New Families: Stories of Domestic Upheaval in Late Twentieth-Century America.* New York: Basic Books.

———. 1998. "Gay and lesbian families: Queer like us." In Mary Ann Mason, Arlene Skolnick, and Stephen D. Sugarman, eds., *All Our Families: New Policies for a New Century.* New York: Oxford University Press.

Stack, Carol. 1974. *All Our Kin.* New York: Harper & Row.

Stamou, Anastasia G.; and Paraskevopoulos, Stephanos. 2003. "Ecotourism experiences in visitors' books of a Greek reserve: A critical discourse analysis perspective." *Sociologia Ruralis,* vol. 43, no. 1: 34–55.

Stannard, David E. 1993. *American Holocaust: The Conquest of the New World*. New York: Oxford University Press.

Stanton, M. E. 1995. "Patterns of kinship and residence." In B. Ingoldsby and S. Smith, eds., *Families in Multicultural Perspective*. New York: Guilford Press.

Stapleton, Christine. 2002. "Donated blood sold off overseas after 9/11." *Atlanta Journal-Constitution*, September 8, p. 19A.

Stein, Jill. 1997. "Rock musician careers: The culture of the long-term professional." Unpublished doctoral dissertation. University of California, Los Angeles.

Steiner, I. D. 1972. *Group Process and Productivity*. New York: Academic Press.

Stimson, Ida H. 1967. "Patterns of socialization into professions: The case of student nurses." *Sociological Inquiry*, vol. 37: 47–54.

Strauss, Neil. 2003. "The pop life: Apple finds a route for online music sales." *New York Times*, May 29, p. E5.

Sudnow, David. 1972. "Temporal parameters of interpersonal observation." In D. Sudnow, ed., *Studies in Social Interaction*. New York: Free Press.

Sue, Valerie M., and Lois A. Ritter. 2007. *Conducting Online Surveys*. Thousand Oaks, CA: Sage.

Sumner, William Graham. 1906. *Folkways: A Study of the Sociological Importance of Usages, Manners, Customs, Mores, and Morals*. Boston: Ginn and Co.

Sutherland, Edwin. 1939. *Principles of Criminology*. 3rd ed. Philadelphia: J.B. Lipincott.

_____; Cressey, Donald R.; and Luckenbill, David F. 1992. *Principles of Criminology*. 11th ed. Dix Hills, NY: General Hall.

Sutton, Robert. 2001. *Weird Ideas That Work: 11½ Practices for Promoting, Managing and Sustaining Innovation*. New York: Free Press.

Svazlian, Verjine. 2000. *The Armenian Genocide: Testimonies of the Eye-Witness Survivors*. Yerevan, Armenia: Gitutiun Publishing House of the NAS RA. (In Armenian, with English, French, and Russian summaries.)

Tahmincioglu, Eve. 2008. "Facebook friends as job references?" MSNBC, August 18. www.msnbc.msn.com/id/26223330/

Tannen, Deborah. 2001. *You Just Don't Understand: Men and Women in Conversation*. New York: Perennial Currents.

Tapscott, Don. 1997. *Growing Up Digital: The Rise of the Net Generation*. New York: McGraw-Hill.

Taylor, R. 2000. "The empire strikes back: Soccer violence continues to be England's ugliest export." *Time International*, vol. 155 (July 19): 36.

Telles, Edward. 2004. *Race in Another America: The Significance of Color in Brazil*. Princeton, NJ: Princeton University Press.

Thomas, W. I.; and Thomas, D. S. 1928. *The Child in America*. New York: Alfred A. Knopf.

Thorne, Barrie. 1992. "Feminism and the family: Two decades of thought." In Barrie Thorne and Marilyn Yalom, eds., *Rethinking the Family: Some Feminist Questions*. Boston: Northeastern University Press.

_____. 1993. *Gender Play: Girls and Boys in School*. New Brunswick, NJ: Rutgers University Press.

Thornton, Stephen J. 2003. "Silence on gays and lesbians in social studies curriculum." *Social Education*, vol. 67, no. 4 (May–June): 226.

Thye, Shane R.; and Lawler, Edward J., eds. 2002. *Advances in Group Processes: Group Cohesion, Trust and Solidarity*, vol. 19. Oxford, UK: Elsevier Science.

Tomlinson, John. 1991. *Cultural Imperialism*. Baltimore, MD: John Hopkins University Press.

Trexler, R. C. 2002. "Making the American berdache: Choice or constraint." *Journal of Social History*, vol. 35: 613–636.

Tsukayama, Hayley. 2010. "Facebook More Popular Than Google." *Washington Post*, December 30. http://voices.washingtonpost.com/posttech/2010/12/the_circuit_facebook_more_popu.html

Tucker, Ian. 2010. "A Different Class." *The Observer Magazine*, sec. 36. Lexis-Nexis Academic. May 9.

Turkle, Sherry. 1997. *Life on the Screen: Identity in the Age of the Internet*. New York: Touchstone Books.

_____. 2005. *The Second Self: Computers and the Human Spirit* Cambridge, MA: MIT Press.

Turner, Ralph. 1972. "Deviance avowal as neutralization of commitment." *Social Problems*, vol. 19, no. 3: 308–321.

_____. 1976. "The real self: From institution to impulse." *American Journal of Sociology*, vol. 81: 989–1016.

_____. 1978. "The role and the person." *American Journal of Sociology*, vol. 84, no. 1: 1–3.

_____; and Killian, Lewis M. 1987. *Collective Behavior*. 3rd ed. Englewood Cliffs, NJ: Prentice Hall.

Uggen, Christopher; and Manza, Jeff. 2002. "Democratic contraction? Political consequences of felon disenfranchisement in the United States." *American Sociological Review*, vol. 67, iss. 6: 777–803.

Ulbrich, Chris. 2004. "Blogs pump bucks into campaigns." *Wired*, February 18.

Ulrichs, Karl H. 1994. *The Riddle of Man-Manly Love: The Pioneering Work on Male Homosexuality*. Amherst, NY: Prometheus Books.

UNAIDS. 2009. *Towards Universal Access: Scaling Up Priority HIV/AIDS Interventions in the Health Sector*. September 2009.

_____. 2010. *Global Report: UNAIDS Report on the Global AIDS Epidemic, 2010*. www.unaids.org/GlobalReport/Global_report.htm

United Nations. 2006. "World population prospects, 2006 revision." www.un.org/esa/population/publications/wpp2006/WPP2006_Highlights_rev.pdf

United Nations Development Programme. 2000. *World Resources 2000–2001*. Washington, DC: World Resources Institute.

United Nations Millennium Project. 2001. www.unmillenniumproject.org

United Nations World Commission on Environment and Development. 1987. *Our Common Future*. Oxford, UK: Oxford University Press.

United Nations World Food Programme. 2007. "World hunger series: 2007." www.wfp.org/policies/introduction/other/documents/pdf/WHS_leaflet_English_2007.pdf

UN News Centre. 2011. "Global population to pass 10 billion by 2100, UN projections indicate." May 3. www.un.org/apps/news/story.asp?NewsID=38253

Urry, John. 1990. *The Tourist Gaze*. London: Sage.

_____. 1992. "The tourist gaze and the 'environment.'" *Theory, Culture & Society*, vol. 9, no. 3: 1–26.

_____. 2002. *The Tourist Gaze*. 2nd ed. London: Sage.

U.S. Bureau of Labor Statistics. 2010a. "Employed persons detailed by occupation, sex, race and Hispanic or Latino ethnicity." www.bls.gov/cps/cpsaat11.pdf

_____. 2010b. Ratio of Women's to Men's Earnings by Occupation. www.bls.gov/spotlight/2011/women/data.htm#cps_occ_earnings_ratio

_____. 2010c. "Household Data Annual Averages." www.bls.gov/vps/cpsaatll.pdf

_____. 2011a. "Union Members Summary." January 21. www.bls.gov/news.release/union2.nr0.htm

U.S. Census Bureau. 1993. 1990 Census Tabulations, *Population and Housing Unit Counts.* "Table 4. Population: 1790 to 1990" www.census.gov/population/censusdata/table-4.pdf

_____. 1994. "Table 1. Race of wife by race of husband: 1960, 1970, 1980, 1991, and 1992." *Interracial Tables.* Washington, DC: U.S. Government Printing Office. www.census.gov

_____. 1995, May. Statistical Brief. "Sixty-five plus in the United States." www.census.gov/population/socdemo/statbriefs/agebrief.html

_____. 2000a. "Marital status of women 15 to 44 years old at first birth by selected characteristics: 1990–94." Statistical Abstract of the United States: 2000. Washington, DC: U.S. Government Printing Office.

_____. 2000b. "GCT-P1. Urban/Rural and Metropolitan/Nonmetropolitan Population: 2000." Data from Census 2000 Summary File 1. http://factfinder.census.gov

_____. 2002a. "No. 32. Annual averages: Unemployed persons by occupation, industry, and duration of unemployment." ftp://ftp.bls.gov/pub/special.requests/lf/aat32.txt www.census.gov/prod/2004pubs/p20-553.pdf

_____. 2003. "Married couple and unmarried partner households: 2000." Census 2000 Special Report. February. www.census.gov/prod/2003pubs/censr-5.pdf

_____. 2004. "Figure 1. Family groups with children by type of family group: 1970 to 2003" and "Table 4. Single parents by sex and selected characteristics: 2003." *America's Families and Living Arrangements: 2003.* Current Population Report (November).

_____. 2005a. "Interim projections: Ranking of Census 2000 and projected 2030 state population and change: 2000 to 2030." April. www.census.gov/Press-Release/www/2005/stateproj7.xls

_____. 2008a. Table 98. "Expectation of life at birth, 1970 to 2004, and projections, 2010 and 2015." www.census.gov/compendia/statab/tables/08s0098.pdf

_____. 2008b. Table 1000, *Statistical Abstract of the United States: 2008.* www.census.gov/compendia/statab/tables/08s1000.xls

_____. 2008c. Table 1099, *Statistical Abstract of the United States: 2008.* www.census.gov/compendia/statab/tables/08s1099.xls

_____. 2009a. "2005–2009 American Community Survey 5-Year Estimates Social Characteristics." *Fast Sheet.* http://factfinder.census.gov/servlet/ACSSAFFFacts?_submenuId=factsheet_0&_sse=on

_____. 2009b. "Educational Attainment in the United States: 2009." http://census.gov/hhes/socdemo/education/data/cps/2009/tables.html

_____. 2010a. "Selected social characteristics in the United States." http://factfinder.census.gov/servlet/ADPTable?_bm=y&-geo_id=01000US&-ds_name=ACS_2009_1YR_G00_&-_lang=en&-_caller=geoselect&-format=

_____. 2010b. "America's Families and Living Arrangements: 2010." http://census.gov/population/www/socdemo/hh-fam/cps/2010.html

_____. 2010c. "Census Bureau Reports Nearly 6 in 10 Advanced Degree Holders Age 25–29 Are Women." April 20. http://census.gov/newsroom/releases/archives/education/cb10-55.html

_____. 2010d. "Educational Attainment of the Population 25 Years and Over, by Selected Characteristics: 2009." http://census.gov/hhes/socdemo/education/data/cps/2009/Table2-Both.xls

_____. 2010e. "Current Population Survey, 2010 Annual Social and Economic (ASEC) Supplement." http://census.gov/apsd/techdoc/cps/cpsmar10.pdf

_____. 2010f. "Temporary Assistance for Needy Families (TANF)—Families and Recipients: 1980 to 2007." http://census.gov/compendia/statab/2010/tables/10s0553.pdf

_____. 2010g. "Income, Poverty, and Health Insurance Coverage in the United States: 2009." http://census.gov/prod/2010pubs/p60-238.pdf

_____. 2011a. "Table 225. Educational Attainment by Race and Hispanic Origin: 1970-2009." http://census.gov/compendia.statab/2011/tables/11s0226.pdf

_____. 2011b. "Labor, Force, Employment, and Earnings." http://census.gov/prod/2011pubs/11statab/labor.pdf

_____. 2011c. "Population Distribution and Change: 2000 to 2010." www.census.gov/prod/cen2010/briefs/c2010br-01.pdf

U.S. Department of Agriculture. 2010. "Food Security in the United States." www.ers.usda.gov/Briefing/FoodSecurity

U.S. Department of Education, National Center for Education Statistics. 1998. "Pursuing excellence: A study of U.S. twelfth-grade mathematics and science achievement in international context." http://nces.ed.gov/pubs98/twelfth

_____. 2009. "Numbers and types of public elementary and secondary schools from the common core of data: School year 2006-2007." http://nces.ed.gov/pubs2009/2009304.pdf

U.S. Department of Justice. 2005. NCJ 207846, *Bureau of Justice Statistics, Family Violence Statistics: Including Statistics on Strangers and Acquaintances, at 31-32 (2005).* Matthew R. Durose et al. www.ojp.usdoj.gov/bjs/pub/pdf/fvs.pdf

_____. 2007a. Crime in the United States. Table 35. "Five-year arrest trends by sex, 2003–2007." www.fbi.gov/ucr/cius2007/data/table_35.html

_____. 2009a. "Hate Crime Statistics." www2.fbi.gov/ucr/hc2009/incidents.html

_____. 2010a. Uniform Crime Report. "Crime In The United States." www2.fbi.gov/ucr/cius2009/data/table_01.html

U.S. Energy Information Administration. 2004. "International energy outlook 2004: Highlights." www.eia.doe.gov/oiaf/ieo/highlights.html

U.S. Environmental Protection Agency (EPA). 2000. "Climate—global warming." http://yosemite.epa.gov/oar/globalwarming.nsf/content/climate.html

_____. 2003. "The Ozone Report: Measuring progress through 2003." Office of Air Quality Planning and Standards Emissions, Monitoring, and Analysis Division. Triangle Park, NC. EPA Publication No. EPA 454/K-04-001. www.epa.gov/air/airtrends/pdfs/2003ozonereport.pdf#page=8

_____. 2008, November. "Factoids: Drinking water and ground water statistics for 2008." www.epa.gov/safewater/databases/pdfs/data_factoids_2008.pdf

U.S. Office of Management and Budget. 2006. "Update of statistical area definitions and guidance on their uses." OMB Bulletin No. 07-01, December 18. www.whitehouse.gov/omb/bulletins/fy2007/b07-01.pdf

U.S. Sentencing Commission. 2010. "Preliminary Crack Cocaine Retroactivity Data Report." www.ussc.gov

Useem, E. L. 1990. "You're good but you're not good enough: Tracking students out of advanced mathematics." *American Educator,* vol. 14, no. 3, 24–27: 43–46.

Van Cleve, Thomas Curtis. 1972. *The Emperor Frederick of Hohenstaufen, Immutator Mundi.* Oxford, UK: Clarendon Press.

van den Berghe, P. L. 1979. *Human Family Systems: An Evolutionary View.* New York: Elsevier/North-Holland.

Van Goozen, S.; Frijda, N.; and Van DePoll, N. 1994. "Anger and aggression in women: Influence of sports choice and testosterone administration." *Aggressive Behavior*, vol. 20: 213–222.

Van Maanen, John. 1973. "Observations on the making of policemen." *Human Organizations*, vol. 32: 407–418.

———. 1983. *Qualitative Methodology.* Thousand Oaks, CA: Sage.

———. 1988. *Tales of the Field: On Writing Ethnography.* Chicago: University of Chicago Press.

Vankin, Deborah. 2010. "Blue says MOCA's remova of his mural amounts to censorship." *Los Angeles Times*, Dec. 15. www.latimes.com/entertainment/news/la-et-moca-mural-20101215,0,6698582.story

Varmus, Harold; and Satcher, David. 1997. "Ethical complexities of conducting research in developing countries." *New England Journal of Medicine*, vol. 337: 1003–1005.

Vaughan, Diane. 1996. *The Challenger Launch Decisions: Risky Technology, Culture and Deviance at NASA.* Chicago: University of Chicago Press.

Veblen, Thorstein. 2004 (orig. 1921). *Engineers and the Price System.* Whitefish, MT: Kessinger Publishing.

Vedantam, Shankar. 2010. "Why do Americans claim to be more religious than they are?" *Slate.* Dec. 22. www.slate.com/id/2278923/

Velkoff, Victoria; and Lawson, Valerie. 1998. "Caregiving." *Gender and Aging.* December: 1–7.

Wackernagel, Mathis; and Rees, William. 1996. *Our Ecological Footprint: Reducing Human Impact on the Earth.* Philadelphia: New Society.

Wahlgren, Eric. 2010. "Concierge Medicine: Patients Pay Up for a Doctor's Undivided Attention." *Daily Finance*, February 10. www.dailyfinance.com/story/concierge-medicine-patients-pay-up-for-a-doctors-undivided-att/19349963

Waldron, T.; Roberts, B.; and Reamer, A. 2004. "Working hard, falling short: America's working families and the pursuit of economic security." A national report by the Working Poor Families Project. Baltimore, MD: Annie E. Casey Foundation.

Walker, Samuel. 1997. *Popular Justice: A History of American Criminal Justice.* New York: Oxford University Press.

Walker, Susan C. 2004. "U.S. consumer credit card debt may crash economy." FoxNews.com, December 31.

Warner, Ralph; Ihara, Toni; and Frederick Hertz. 2001. *Living Together: A Legal Guide for Unmarried Couples.* Berkeley, CA: Nolo.

Waters, Mary. 1990. *Ethnic Options: Choosing Identities in America.* Berkeley, CA: University of California Press.

Wattel, Harold. 1958. "Levittown: A suburban community." In William M. Dobriner, ed., *The Suburban Community.* New York: Putnam.

Watts, Duncan. 2003. *Six Degrees: The Science of a Connected Age.* New York: Norton.

Wearing, Stephen; and Wearing, Michael. 1999. "Decommodifying ecotourism: Rethinking global-local interactions with host communities." *Loisir et Société/Society and Leisure*, vol. 22, no. 1: 39–70.

Weber, Max. 1930 (orig. 1904). *The Protestant Ethic and the Spirit of Capitalism.* Trans. Talcott Parsons. New York: Scribner's.

———. 1962 (orig. 1913). *Basic Concepts of Sociology.* Westport, CT: Greenwood Publishing.

———. 1946 (orig. 1925). "Science as a vocation." In Hans Gerth and C. Wright Mills, ed. and trans., *From Max Weber: Essays in Sociology.* New York: Oxford University Press.

———. 1968 (orig. 1921). *Economy and Society.* Ed. and trans. Guenther Roth and Claus Wittich. New York: Bedminster Press.

Weedon, Joey R. 2004. "Voting rights restored." *Corrections Today*, vol. 66, iss. 6: 16.

Weinberg, Adam; Bellows, Story; and Ekster, Dara. 2002. "Sustaining ecotourism: Insights and implications from two successful case studies." *Society and Natural Resources*, vol. 15, no. 4: 371–380.

Weinberg, George. 1972. *Society and the Healthy Homosexual.* New York: St. Martin's Press.

Weinstein, Deena. 1991. *Heavy Metal: A Cultural Sociology.* New York: Macmillan/Lexington.

———. 2000. *Heavy Metal: The Music and Its Culture.* New York: DaCapo.

Weinstein, Harvey. 2003. "Controversial ruling on pledge reaffirmed." *Los Angeles Times*, Metro Desk, March 1, 1:1.

Weise, D.; and Daro, D. 1995. *Current Trends in Child Abuse Reporting and Fatalities.* Chicago: National Committee to Prevent Child Abuse.

Weiss, Kenneth R. 2001. "Minority applications to UC rise." *Los Angeles Times*, January 31.

Weissbourd, Richard. 1994. "Divided families, whole children." *American Prospect*, vol. 18 (summer): 66–72.

Wellman, Barry. 2004. "Connecting community: On- and off-line." *Contexts* vol. 3, no. 4 (fall): 22–28.

West, Heather C. 2010. "Prison Inmates at Midyear 2009—Statistical Tables." Bureau of Justice Statistics. http://bjs.ojp.usdoj.gov/content/pub/pdf/pim09st.pdf

Weston, Kath. 1991. *Families We Choose.* New York: Columbia University Press.

Whalen, J.; Zimmerman, D.; and Whalen, M. 1988. "When words fail: a single case analysis." *Social Problems*, vol. 35, no. 4: 335–362.

Wharton, Amy S.; and Blair-Loy, Mary. 2002. "Employees' use of work–family policies and the workplace social context." *Social Forces*, vol. 80, no. 3: 813–845.

Whatley, Marianne H.; and Henken, Elissa R. 2000. *Did You Hear About the Girl Who . . . ? Contemporary Legends, Folklore, and Human Sexuality.* New York: New York University Press.

Whitacre, Paula Tarnapol; Tsai, Peggy, and Mulligan, Janet (Rapporteurs); National Research Council. 2009. *The Public Health Effects of Food Deserts: Workshop Summary.* Washington, D.C: The National Academies Press.

White, Glen. 1989. "Groupthink reconsidered." *Academy of Management Review*, vol. 14.

The White House. 2011. Health Care Reform. www.whitehouse.gov/healthreform

Whitehead, Jay. 2005. "Outsourcing pioneers another niche." *Human Resources Outsourcing Today Magazine*, June.

Whorf, Benjamin. 1956. *Language, Thought and Reality: Selected Writings of Benjamin Lee Whorf.* Ed. John B. Carroll. Cambridge, MA: MIT Press.

Whyte, W. H. 1956. *The Organization Man.* New York: Simon & Schuster.

Wicks-Lim, Jeannette; Thompson, Jeffrey. 2010. "Combining Minimum Wage and Earned Income Tax Credit Policies to Guarantee a Decent Living Standard to All U.S. Workers." Amherst, MA:

Political Economy Research Institute. October 18. www.peri.umass.edu/236/hash/9b8a787cfa16226190e4f96e582348cd/publication/428/

Wilkinson, Richard G. 2005. *The Impact of Inequality*. New York: The New Press.

Williams, Christine L. 1995. *Still a Man's World: Men Who Do Women's Work*. Berkeley, CA: University of California Press.

Williams, David E. 2006. "Boutique medicine: When wealth buys health." CNN, October 20. www.cnn.com/2006/US/10/19/bil.healthy.wealthy/index.html?iref=allsearch

Williams, Patricia J. 1997. "Of race and risk." *The Nation*, December 29:10.

Williams, Robin. 1965. *American Society: A Sociological Interpretation*. 2nd ed. New York: Knopf.

Wilson, William Julius. 1980. *The Declining Significance of Race*. Chicago: University of Chicago Press.

———. 1996. *When Work Disappears: The World of the New Urban Poor*. New York: Knopf.

———. 2009. *More Than Just Race: Being Black and Poor in the Inner City*. New York: Norton.

Wirth, Louis. 1938. "Urbanism as a way of life." *American Journal of Sociology*, vol. 44: 3–24.

———. 1945. "The problem of minority groups." In Ralph Litton, ed., *The Science of Man in the World Crisis*. New York: Columbia University Press.

Wiseman, Rosalind. 2002. *Queen Bees and Wannabes*. New York: Three Rivers Press.

Wolf, Rosalie S. 2000. "The nature and scope of elder abuse." *Generations*, vol. 24 (summer): 6–12.

Wolff, Edward. 2002. *Top Heavy: The Increasing Inequality of Wealth in America and What Can Be Done About It*. New York: New Press.

———. 2004. "Changes in household wealth in the 1980s and 1990s in the U.S." Working paper no. 407. Levy Economics Institute of Bard College. April.

Wolfinger, Nicholas H. 1999. "Trends in the intergenerational transmission of divorce." *Demography*, vol. 36, no. 3: 415–420.

———. 2000. "Beyond the intergenerational transmission of divorce: Do people replicate the patterns of marital instability they grew up with?" *Journal of Family Issues*, vol. 21: 1061–1086.

———. 2003. "Parental divorce and offspring marriage: Early or late?" *Social Forces*, vol. 82, no. 1: 337–353.

Wolfson, Andrew. 2005. "A hoax most cruel." *Courier-Journal*. Louisville, KY. October 9. www.courier-journal.com/apps/pbcs.dll/article?AID=/20051009/NEWS01/510090392

WomensHealth.gov. 2010. The National Women's Health Information Center. U.S. Department of Health and Human Services. www.womenshealth.gov/faq/alpha-index.cfm

Wood, Megan Epler. 2002. *Ecotourism: Principles, Practices and Policies for Sustainability*. Burlington, VT: International Ecotourism Society.

World at Work. 2009. "Telework Trend Lines." www.workingfromanywhere.org/news/Trendlines_2009.pdf

World Bank. 2008a. GDP (current US$). Economic Policy and External Debt Indicators, 2008. http://data.worldbank.org/indicator/NY.GDP.MKTP.CD/countries?order=wbapi_data_value_2009%20wbapi_data_value%20wbapi_data_value-last&sort=desc&display=default

———. 2009. GDP (current US$). Economic Policy and External Debt Indicators, 2009. http://data.worldbank.org/indicator/NY.GDP.MKTP.CD/countries?order=wbapi_data_value_2009%20wbapi_data_value%20wbapi_data_value-last&sort=desc&display=default

World Health Organization (WHO). 1946. "Constitution of the World Health Organization." World Health Organization, July 26. www.who.int/governance/eb/constitution/en/

———. 2008. "The 10 leading causes of death by broad income group (2004)." Fact sheet no. 310, October. www.who.int/mediacentre/factsheets/fs310/en/index.html

World Medical Association. 1964. "Laws related to the protection of human subjects: World Medical Association declaration of Helsinki." Adopted by the 18th World Medical Assembly, Helsinki, Finland, June 1964 (latest amendment by 41st Assembly, Hong Kong, September 1989). Office of History, National Institutes of Health. http://history.nih.gov/about/timelines/helsinki.html

Worobey, Michael, et al. 2010. "Island biogeography reveals the deep history of SIV." *Science*, vol. 329, no. 5998: 1487.

Wray, M.; Miller, M.; Gurvey, J.; Carroll, J.; and Kawachi, I. 2008. "Leaving Las Vegas: Exposure to Las Vegas and risk of suicide." *Social Science and Medicine*, vol. 67, no. 11: 1882–1888.

Wright, Erik Olin. 1997. *Class Counts: Comparative Studies in Class Analysis*. Cambridge, UK: Cambridge University Press.

Wright, Erik Olin; Costello, Cynthia; Hachen, David; and Spragues, Joey. 1982. "The American class structure." *American Sociological Review*, vol. 47, no. 6: 709–726.

Yen, Hope. 2011. "Rural US Disappearing? Population Share Hits Low." Associated Press. July 27.

Yin, Sandra. 2003. "The art of staying at home." *American Demographics*, vol. 25, no. 9 (November 1).

Yuan, Jada. 2007. "The White-Castle Ceiling." *New York Magazine*, March 4.

Zellner, William W. 1995. *Countercultures: A Sociological Analysis*. New York: St. Martin's Press.

Zemke, Ron; and Schaaf, Dick. 1990. *The Service Edge: 101 Companies That Profit from Customer Care*. New York: Plume.

Zerubavel, Eviatar. 2003. *Time Maps: Collective Memory and the Social Shape of the Past*. Chicago: University of Chicago Press.

Zimbardo, Philip G. 1971. "The power and pathology of imprisonment." *Congressional Record*. (Serial No. 15, October 25, 1971). Hearings before Subcommittee No. 3, of the Committee on the Judiciary, House of Representatives, 92nd Congress, *First Session on Corrections, Part II, Prisons, Prison Reform and Prisoner's Rights: California*. Washington, DC: U.S. Government Printing Office.

Zirakzadeh, C. 1997. *Social Movements in Politics: A Comparative Study*. London: Longman.

Zuger, Abigail. 2005. "For a retainer, lavish care by 'boutique doctors.'" *New York Times*, October 30. www.nytimes.com/2005/10/30/health/30patient.html

Zukin, S. 1987. "Gentrification: Culture and capital in the urban core." *American Review of Sociology*, vol. 13: 139–147.

———. 1989. *Loft Living: Culture and Capital in Urban Change*. New Brunswick, NJ: Rutgers University Press.

———. 2004. *Point of Purchase: How Shopping Changed American Culture*. London: Routledge.

Zurcher, Louis. 1977. *The Mutable Self*. Beverly Hills, CA: Sage.

Zwingle, Erla. 2002. "Map of megacities." In "Cites: Challenges for humanity," *National Geographic*, November. Ng Maps/National Geographic Image Collection.

CREDITS

Text

Box 3.3: "Moore Thoughts and Girl Interrupted" by James Sosnicky, copyright © 2006 by James Sosnicky, "Introduction and Headnotes" by Andrew Carroll, copyright © 2006 by Andrew Carroll, "One Small Village" by Jared Jones, copyright © 2006 by Jared Jones, from *Operation Homecoming*, edited by Andrew Carroll. Used by permission of Random House, Inc.

Box 12.4: "Busy Schedule has This Family Bushed" by Ross Werland, from *The Chicago Tribune*, Dec. 10, 2000. Reprinted with permission of the Chicago Tribune; copyright Chicago Tribune, all rights reserved.

Figure 12.1: Figure 12.1, "Annual Divorce Rate, United States, 1860–2002," *Public and Private Families*: An Introduction, 5th Edition by Andrew J. Cherlin, p. 406. © 2008. Reprinted by permission of The McGraw-Hill Companies, Inc.

Photo

Part Opener I: p. 2 top Reprinted through the courtesy of the Editors of TIME Magazine © 2009 Time Inc.; **p. 2 bottom** AP Photos; **p. 3** Courtesy Pepper Schwartz

Chapter 1: p. 4 The Kobal Collection/MTV; **p. 5** The Kobal Collection/MTV; **p. 9** AP/Wide World Photos; **p. 11 center** Olivier Douliery/UPI/Landov; **p. 11 left** Bettmann/Corbis; **p. 11 right** © New Line/courtesy Everett Collection; **p. 12** James Leynse/Corbis; **p. 13** Time & Life Pictures/Getty Images; **p. 14 left** AP Photo/Demitrius Balevski; **p. 14 right** AP Photo/Demitrius Balevski; **p. 15** Mark Scheuern/Alamy; **p. 17 left** Bettmann/Corbis; **p. 17 right** Hulton-Deutsch Collection/Corbis; **p. 18 bottom** Bettmann/Corbis; **p. 18 top** Bridgeman Art Library; **p. 21 left** American Sociological Association; **p. 21 right** American Sociological Association; **p. 22** Bettmann/Corbis; **p. 24 bottom** Librado Romero/The New York Times/Redux; **p. 24 top** AP/Wide World Photos; **p. 25** Getty Images; **p. 26** Library of Congress; **p. 27** Library of Congress; **p. 28** Trip/Alamy; **p. 29** Granger Collection, NY; **p. 30** Courtesy of University Archives, University of Missouri at Columbia; **p. 31** University of Pennsylvania Archives; **p. 32 bottom** Rob Kim/Landov; **p. 32 top** Shirlaine Forrest/Getty Images; **p. 33 center** STF/AFP/Getty Images; **p. 33 left** Steve Pyke/Getty Images; **p. 33 right** Steve Pyke/Getty Images; **p. 37 left** © Think Film/courtesy Everett; **p. 37 right** © Dosfotos/Lebrecht Music & Arts

Chapter 2: p. 29 Photograph by for the U.S. Census Bureau, Public Information Office (PIO); **p. 30** Photograph by for the U.S. Census Bureau, Public Information Office (PIO); **p. 40** © Ovie Carter; **p. 41** Bandura, Ross and Ross, from "Social Learning of Aggression through Imitation of Film-Mediated Aggressive Models," *Journal of Abnormal and Social Psychology* 66 (1963), 3–11; **p. 42** Photofest; **p. 45** AP Photo; **p. 46** © Kathryn Edin and Maria Kefalas. University of California Press; 2 edition (March 21,

2007); **p. 47** AP Photos; **p. 50** Brooke Fasini/Corbis; **p. 54** Bettmann/Corbis; **p. 55** Rick Friedman/The New York Times/Redux; **p. 57** Michael Dunning/Getty Images; **p. 60** Bettmann/Corbis; **p. 62** Corbis; **p. 65 bottom** First Run Pictures; **p. 65 top** © Kai T. Erikson. Allyn & Bacon; Revised edition (October 1, 2004).

Part Opener II: p. 68 Courtesy Verta Taylor and Leila Rupp; **p. 69 top** Courtesy Verta Taylor and Leila Rupp; **p. 69 bottom** Courtesy Verta Taylor and Leila Rupp

Chapter 3: p. 70 Chris Hondros/Getty Images; **p. 71** Chris Hondros/Getty Images; **p. 73** Getty Images; **p. 75 bottom** AP Photo; **p. 75 center** AP Photo; **p. 75 top** Robert Nickelsberg/Getty Images; **p. 76** Carl & Ann Purcell/Corbis; **p. 77 bottom center** AP/Wide World Photos; **p. 77 bottom left** AP/Wide World Photos; **p. 77 bottom right** CARL DE SOUZA/AFP/Getty Images; **p. 77 top center** Alessandro Digaetano/Polaris **p. 77 top left** Peter A. Smith/Boston Herald/Polaris; **p. 77 top right** Getty Images; **p. 79 left** Everett Collection; **p. 79 right** Mean Girls, 2004. Paramount Pictures; **p. 80 left** AP Photo/Alex Brandon; **p. 80 right** Eric Grigorian/Polaris; **p. 82 left** Tom Strickland/ABC/American Broadcasting Companies, Inc.; **p. 82 right** AP/Wide World Photos; **p. 83 left** Bettmann/Corbis; **p. 83 right** AFP/Getty Images; **p. 84 bottom** George A. Hirliman Productions Inc./Photofest; **p. 84 top** Everett Collection; **p. 85 left** AP Photo/Jan Bauer; **p. 85 right** AP Photo/Orlin Wagner; **p. 87** Robert W. Ginn/Photo Edit; **p. 88** AP Photo/Hiroshi Otabe; **p. 91** Howard Davies/Corbis; **p. 95** Cover of REEFER MADNESS by Eric Schlosser. © 2003 by Eric Schlosser. Reprinted by permission of Houghton Mifflin Harcourt Publishing Company. All rights reserved.

Chapter 4: p. 97 AP Photos; **p. 97** AP Photos; **p. 99** © Walt Disney Pictures/Courtesy: Everett Collection; **p. 100** Smithsonian American Art Museum, Washington, DC/Art Resource, NY. © 2009 The Jacob and Gwendolyn Lawrence Foundation, Seattle/Artists Rights Society (ARS), New York; **p. 102 left** Jupiter Images; **p. 102 right** Getty Images; **p. 104** FRANCIS SPECKER/epa/Corbis; **p. 108** Photofest; **p. 109** The Kobal Collection/Company Pictures; **p. 111 left** AP Photos; **p. 111 right** AP Photos; **p. 113 left** Courtesy Sister Pauline Quinn; **p. 113 right** Courtesy Sister Pauline Quinn; **p. 115** Ohio State Athletics; **p. 116** AP/Wide World Photos; **p. 117 bottom** AP Images; **p. 117 center** Alan Chin/Corbis Sygma; **p. 117 top** AP Images; **p. 119 left** AP Images; **p. 119 right** AP Photos; **p. 121 bottom right** © Universal/courtesy Everett Collection; **p. 121 left** © Arlie Russell Hochschil. University of California Press; 2nd edition (May 5, 2003); **p. 121 top right** © MGM/courtesy Everett Collection

Chapter 5: p. 122 AFP/Getty Images; **p. 123** AFP/Getty Images; **p. 125** AP Photos; **p. 128 left** Bettmann/Corbis; **p. 128 right** Getty Images; **p. 130** Alamy; **135** Mary Armstrong Republic, Ohio. www.lincoln-presenters.org; **p. 137** AP Images; **p. 139** Courtesy of Alexandra Milgram; **p. 140** PGZimbardo Inc.; **p. 141** PETER MCKENZIE/Maxppp/Landov; **p. 143 left** Jeff Mitchell/Reuters/Corbis; **p. 143 right** Tim de Waele/Corbis; **p. 144** © 2006 Scott Adams, Inc. Dist. By UFS, Inc.; **p. 145 bottom** Reuters/CORBIS; **p. 145 center** Andy Rain/epa/Corbis; **p. 145 top** Kapoor Baldev/Sygma/

Contrasto/Redux; **p. 414 right** Riccardo Venturi/Contrasto/Redux; **p. 415** Jeff Greenberg/The Image Works; **p. 416** Christine Cotter/The New York Times/Redux; **p. 417** TIMOTHY A. CLARY/AFP/Getty Images; **p. 419** BRIAN SNYDER/Reuters/Landov; **p. 422** © USA Networks/Courtesy Everett Collection; **p. 424** Carlos Javier Ortiz/Redux; **p. 425** Erik S. Lesser/The New York Times/Redux; **p. 426** Chris Hondros/Getty Images; **p. 428** AGStockUSA/Alamy; **p. 429 left** Phil Caruso/©Showtime Networks Inc./Courtesy Everett Collection; **p. 429 right** Fox Broadcasting Co./Photofest; **p. 431** AP Photo/J. Scott Applewhite; **p. 433** © Anne Fadiman. Farrar, Straus and Giroux; 1 edition (September 28, 1998); **p. 434** Tek Image/Photo Researchers, Inc.; **p. 437 bottom right** © Lions Gate/Courtesy Everett Collection; **p. 437 top right** © 2007 by Barbara Kingsolver, Stephen L. Hopp, and Camille Kingsolver; **p. 437 left** © HBO/courtesy Everett Collection

Part Opener V: p. 282 top Maury Tannen/Polaris Images; **p. 282 bottom** Getty Images; **p. 283** AP Photo

Chapter 15: p. 442 Galen Rowell/Corbis; **p. 443** Galen Rowell/Corbis; **p. 453** NASA/Goddard Space Flight Center, The SeaWiFS Project and GeoEye, Scientific Visualization Studio; **p. 455 left** Mark Peterson/Redux; **p. 455 right** Joshua Lutz/Redux; **p. 456** AP Photo; **p. 457 left** Richard Levine/Alamy; **p. 457 right** Larry Brownstein/Ambient Images; **p. 458** AP Photo; **p. 459** © Columbia/Tristar Pictures/Courtesy Everett Collection; **p. 461** PhotoAlto/Alamy; **p. 462** New York Daily News; **p. 464** Joe Raedle/Getty Images; **p. 465 left** Galen Rowell/Corbis; **p. 465 right** NASA/Getty Images; **p. 466 left** Julio Etchart/Alamy; **p. 466 right** Rickey Rogers/Reuters/Corbis; **p. 468** AP Photo/Mohammed Seeneen; **p. 469** Stephen Shaver/UPI/Landov; **p. 473** Library of Congress; **p. 475** AP Photo; **p. 476** Bettmann/Corbis; **p. 477** AP Photo; **p. 481 bottom right** INTO THE WILD, Emile Hirsch, 2007. © Paramount. Courtesy Everett Collection; **p. 481 left** © Mike Davis. Vintage; 1st Vintage Books ed edition (September 7, 1999); **p. 481 top right** AN INCONVENIENT TRUTH, Al Gore, 2006, © Paramount Classics. Courtesy Everett Collection

Chapter 16: p. 482 Kacper Pemple/Reuters/Landov; **p. 483** Kacper Pemple/Reuters/Landov; **p. 485** Ian Waldie/Getty Images; **p. 486** David Butow/Corbis Saba; **p. 488** © AMC/courtesy Everett Collection; **p. 489** AP Photos; **p. 490** Phil Schermeister/Corbis; **p. 491** AP Photos; **p. 493** Image courtesy of adbusters.org; **p. 496 left** Spencer Grant/Photo Edit; **p. 496 right** Mario Villafuerte/Getty Images; **p. 497** The Yomiuri Shimbun via AP Images; **p. 499** Reuters/STAFF/LANDOV; **p. 501** Ana Cecila Gonzalez-Vigil/The New York Times/Redux; **p. 502** The Kobal Collection/CBS-TV/Flemming, Sonja; **p. 505** Alamy; **p. 507 bottom left** © Charles Mackay. Broadway (July 25, 1995); **p. 507 bottom right** © Magnolia Pictures/Courtesy Everett Collection; **p. 507 top** © Ross Haenfler. Rutgers University Press (June 25, 2006)

INDEX

Note: Page numbers in **boldface** refer to definitions of key words.

microsociology, 14–15, **14**, 34
Microsoft, 194, 327, 334, 335, 352
MidAmerica Bank, 211
middle class, 189–91, **191**
Middletown studies, 61
midrange theory, 34–35, **34**
Mi Familia, 373
migrant farm workers, 497
migration, **446**
Milgram, Stanley, 138–39
Milgram experiment, 138–39
military, U.S.:
    cultural connections and, 93, 96
    gender harassment in, 262–64
    gender inequality and, 262–64
militia movement, 83
Miller, Alice, 54
Miller, Donald and Lorna, 240
Miller, Laura, 263
Mills, C. Wright, 13, 28, 292, 484
Milošević, Slobodan, 240
Miner, Horace, 73–74
minimal effects theories, 397
minority group, **228**
Minutemen of the American
    Revolution, 83
miscegenation, 232, 359, 360
missionaries and their families, 500–501
Mitchell, Richard, 47
Miyazaki, Hayao, 92
modern environmental movement, **473**
modernism, **33**
modernity, **503**
monarchies, **288**
monogamy, **359**
monopoly, **390**
monotheistic religions, **312**
Montel Williams, 393
Moore, Michael, 214–15
Moore, Wilbert, 200
Moore's Law, 327
moral reasoning, 98
mores, **80**
Mormons, 74, 240, 312
Morris, Marilyn, 423
mortality rates, 444–45, **444**
Moseley, Winston, 460
mosquitoes, 419
motherhood, 34
Mothers of East Los Angeles, 211
Motion Picture Association of America
    movie ratings, 393
Motor-Voter Act of 2000, 291
Mott, Lucretia, 267
MoveOn.org, 294, 493
Muir, John, 473
multiculturalism (pluralism), 82, **82**,
    242–43, **242**

multiracial background, 221
murders, 172
    race and, 239
Museum of Contemporary Art (MOCA),
    290–91
music industry:
    musicians, stereotypes of, 389
    non-mainstream musicians and, 75
    warning labels, 393
Muslims, 153, 311–12, 316–18
Myanmar, 91
My Lai massacre, 177
MySpace, 55, 118, 130–31, 169

NAAFA (National Association to
    Advance Fat Acceptance), 165
Nacirema culture, 73–74
Nader, Ralph, 214, 476
NAFTA, 341
National Association for the Advancement
    of Colored People (NAACP),
    26, 27, 291–92
National Center for Health Statistics, 200
National Commission on Excellence in
    Education, 305
National Endowment of the Arts, 384
National Marriage Project, 51–52
National Marriage Project at Rutgers
    University, 51–52
National Organization for Women
    (NOW), 267
national parks, 473
National Park Service, 472
National Public Radio, 462
National School Climate Survey, 275
National Volunteer Week, 350
Nation at Risk, A, 305
Native Americans:
    assimilation of, 242
    berdaches among, 250–51
    genocide and, 239
    "Trail of Tears" and, 239
    voting rights of, 288
natural disasters, social change and, 485
natural increase (in population), **449**
natural selection, 29
nature vs. nurture debate, **98**
    gender and, 249
Nazis, Nazi Germany, 62, 138, 222, 239,
    240
NBC, 390
negative questions, **51**
negative sanctions, 80
neglect, **372**
Nelson, Gaylord, 474
neo-functionalism, 21
neo-Marxism (Frankfurt School), 24
Neo-or New Malthusians, **447**

"netiquette," 129
net migration, **446**
networks, social, *see* social networks
neutralization of commitment, 166
New Deal, 207–8
Newdow, Michael, 285
new ecological paradigm, **472**
New England Journal of Medicine, 419,
    429
New Orleans, La., 146–47
    Hurricane Katrina and, 125
New Republic, The, 394
Newsom, Gavin, 360
Newsweek, 54
New York, N.Y.:
    alienation and altruism in, 460–63
    homelessness in, 211–12
    immigrants and, 223
New York Times, 44, 349, 462
New York Yankees, 434
*Nickel and Dimed:On (Not) Getting By in
    America* (Ehrenreich), 333
Nike, 344
NIMBY ("not in my back yard"), 476, **476**
Nixon, Richard, 292, 296–97, 430
Nobel Peace Prize, 27, 91
No Child Left Behind Act, 305–6, 308
nonrenewable resources, **466**
nonverbal communication, *see* gestures
Nordstrom, 118–19
norms, 79–80, **80**
    changing, 84–85
    internalizing of, 105
    state of normlessness, *see* anomie
North American Free Trade Agreement
    (NAFTA), 341
Norton, Eleanor Holmes, 310
nuclear family, **358**, 360, 366, 369, 379
nuclear weapons, 91
Nuremberg Code, 62
Nuremberg Military Tribunals, 62
Nurse Jackie, 429
nurture vs. nature debate, **98**
nutrition, 414
NYPD Blue, 276

Obama, Barack, 274, 299
    election of, 289
    presidential campaign funding and, 293
    racial identity and, 234
    religion and, 318
Obama, Michelle Robinson, 10–11
obesity, 416, 423–24
objectivity, 58–60, **59**
occupations:
    gendered, 258–62
    helping professions, 496
    on prime time television, 328–30

INDEX OF INFOGRAPHICS

Sociology's Family Tree
Chapter 1, p. 19

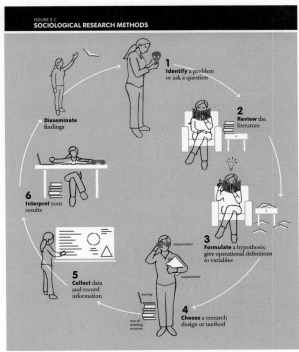

Sociological Research Methods
Chapter 2, p. 43

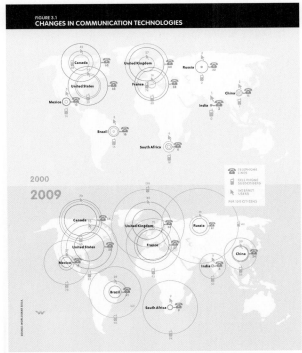

Changes in Communication Technologies
Chapter 3, p. 89

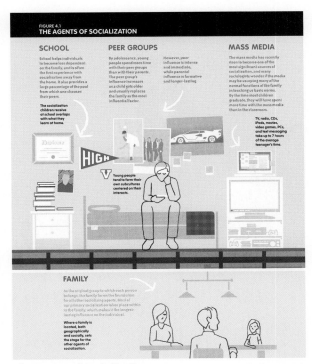

The Agents of Socialization
Chapter 4, p. 107

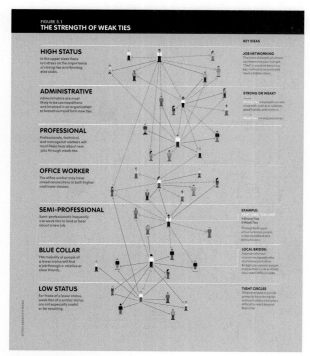

The Strength of Weak Ties
Chapter 5, p. 127

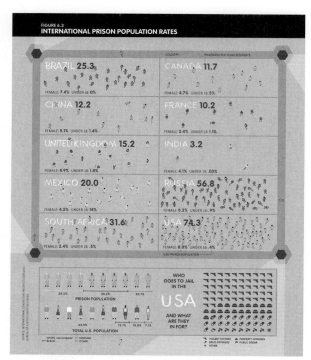

International Prison Population Rates
Chapter 6, p. 175

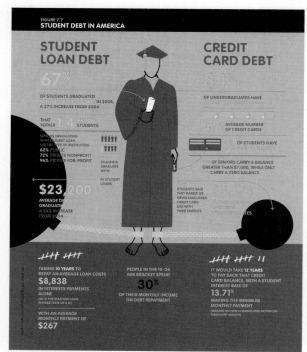

Student Debt in America
Chapter 7, p. 217

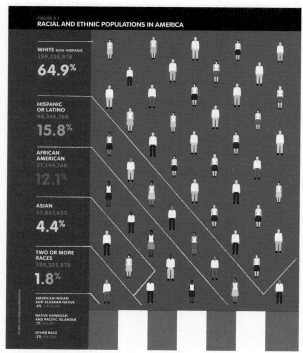

Racial and Ethnic Populations in America
Chapter 8, p. 227

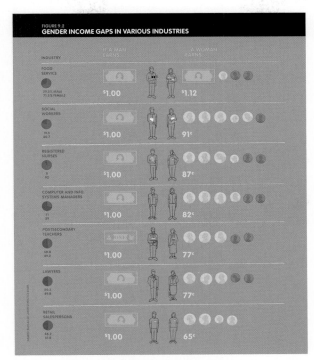

Gender Income Gaps in Various Industries
Chapter 9, p. 261

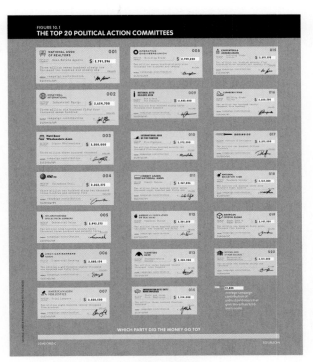

The Top 10 Political Action Committees
Chapter 10, p. 295

Ranking the World Economies
Chapter 11, p. 343

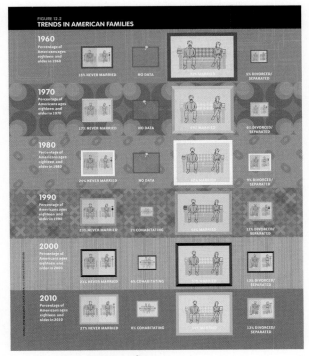

Trends in American Families
Chapter 12, p. 377

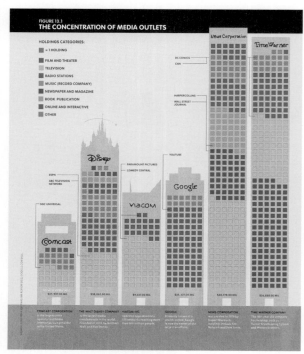

The Concentration of Media Outlets
Chapter 13, p. 391

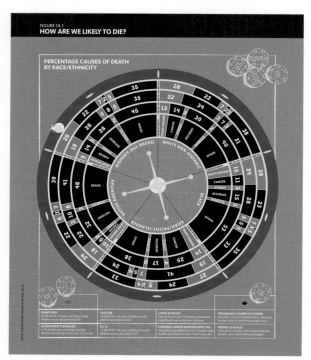

How Are We Likely to Die?
Chapter 14, p. 421

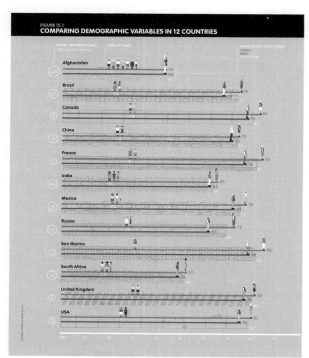

Comparing Demographic Variables in 12 Countries
Chapter 15, p. 445

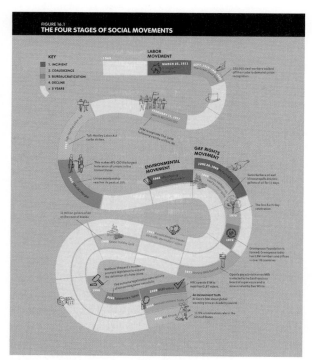

The Four Stages of Social Movements
Chapter 16, p. 495